The World of Business

The Information Economy

SEND IN NOW!

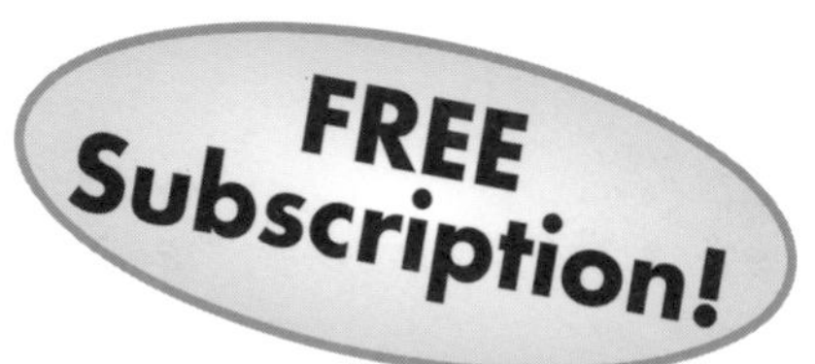

Dear Student

Your purchase of this new copy of **McEachern's** ***Economics: A Contemporary Introduction,*** **5e** entitles you to

THE WALL STREET JOURNAL.

To start your subscription, simply fill out the card below. After you fill out the card, drop it in a mailbox and your subscription will begin right away.

Thank you for purchasing this Wall Street Journal Special Edition of McEachern's textbook, and enjoy your subscription.

ECONOMICS

A Contemporary Introduction

FIFTH EDITION

William A. McEachern

Professor of Economics

University of Connecticut

South-Western College Publishing
Thomson Learning™

Australia • Canada • Denmark • Japan • Mexico • New Zealand • Philippines
Puerto Rico • Singapore • South Africa • Spain • United Kingdom • United States

Acquisitions Editor:	Keri L. Witman
Developmental Editor:	Dennis Hanseman
Marketing Manager:	Lisa L. Lysne
Sr. Production Editor:	Sharon L. Smith
Manufacturing Coordinator:	Georgina Calderon
Internal Design:	A Small Design Studio/Ann Small
Cover Design:	Tin Box Studio
Cover Illustrator:	John Mattos
Photo Researcher:	Feldman & Associates, Inc.
Production House:	Pre-Press Company, Inc.
Printer:	Von Hoffmann Press, Inc.

Printed in the United States of America
2 3 4 02 01 00 99

For more information contact South-Western College Publishing, 5101 Madison Road, Cincinnati, Ohio, 45227. Or you can visit our Internet site at http://www.swcollege.com

Library of Congress Cataloging-in-Publication Data
McEachern, William A.
Economics: a contemporary introduction/William A. McEachern.—5th ed.
p. cm.
Includes bibliographical references and index.
1. Economics. I. Title.
HB171.M475 1999 99-11640
330—dc21

ISBN: 0-538-88849-0

This book is printed on acid-free paper.

About the Author

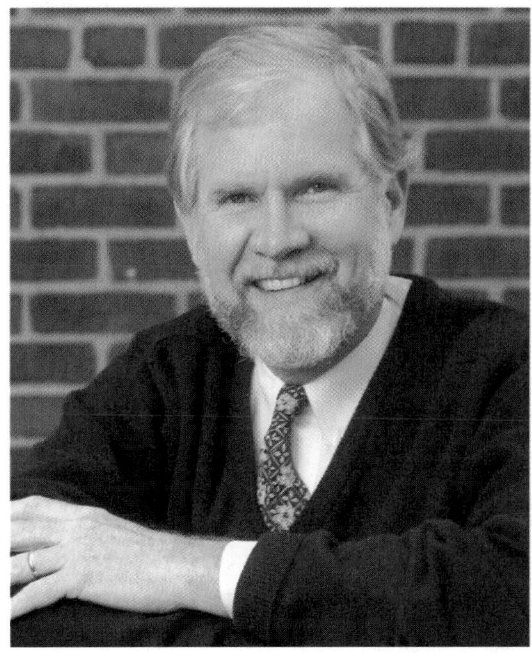

William A. McEachern, Professor of Economics at the University of Connecticut, has taught principles of economics since 1973 and has offered teaching workshops since 1980. His research has appeared in a variety of journals, including *Economic Inquiry, National Tax Journal, Journal of Industrial Economics,* and *Public Choice.* He is Founding Editor of *The Teaching Economist,* a newsletter that focuses on teaching economics at the college level, and is Editor in Chief of *The Connecticut Economy: A University of Connecticut Quarterly Review.* Professor McEachern has advised federal, state, and local governments on policy matters and directed a bipartisan commission examining Connecticut's finances. Publications in which he has been quoted include the *New York Times, London Times, Wall Street Journal, Christian Science Monitor, USA Today,* and *Reader's Digest.* The University of Connecticut Alumni Association conferred on him its Faculty Award for Distinguished Public Service, and the Connecticut Academy of Arts and Sciences elected him to membership. He was born in Portsmouth, N.H., earned an undergraduate degree with honors from Holy Cross College and an M.A. and Ph.D. from the University of Virginia.

To Pat

Brief Contents

PART 4

INTRODUCTION TO THE MARKET SYSTEM

PART 5

MARKET STRUCTURE AND PRICING

PART 6

RESOURCE MARKETS

PART 7

MARKET FAILURE AND PUBLIC POLICY

PART 8

THE INTERNATIONAL SETTING

Contents

PART 1

INTRODUCTION TO ECONOMICS

CHAPTER 22
Monopoly 492

CHAPTER 23
Monopolistic Competition and Oligopoly 514

PART 6
RESOURCE MARKETS

CHAPTER 24
Resource Markets 538

CHAPTER 25
Labor Markets and Labor Unions 561

Preface

Economics has a short history but a long past. As a distinct discipline, economics has been studied for only a few hundred years, yet civilizations have confronted the economic problem of scarce resources but unlimited wants for millennia. Economics, the discipline, may be centuries old, but it is new every day as fresh evidence supports or reshapes economic theory. In *Economics: A Contemporary Introduction*, I draw upon more than a quarter century of teaching experience to convey the vitality, timeliness, and evolving nature of economics.

LEADING BY EXAMPLE

Remember the last time you were in unknown parts and had to ask for directions? Along with the directions came the standard comment "You can't miss it!" So how come you missed it? Because the "landmark" that was obvious to the neighborhood resident who gave the directions might as well have been invisible to you, a stranger. Writing a principles text is much like giving directions. The author must be familiar with the material, but familiarity can also dull one's perceptions, making it difficult to see things through the fresh eyes of new students. Some authors try to compensate by telling all they know, in the process overwhelming students with so much detail that the central point gets lost. Other authors take a minimalist approach by offering little of what students may already know intuitively, and instead talking abstractly about good *x* and good *y*, units of labor and units of capital, or the proverbial widget. This turns economics into a foreign language.

Good directions rely on landmarks familiar to us all—a stoplight, a fork in the road, a white picket fence. Likewise, a good textbook builds bridges from the familiar to the new. How? In essence, I try to *lead by example*. I provide examples that draw on the students' common experience. I try to create graphic images that need little explanation, thereby eliciting from the reader that light of recognition, that "Aha!" Examples should be self-explanatory; they should convey the point quickly and directly. Having to explain an example is like having to explain a joke—the point gets lost. Throughout, I provide just enough intuitive information and institutional detail to get the point across without overwhelming the student. My emphasis is on economic ideas, not economic jargon.

Students arrive the first day of class with eighteen or more years of experience with economic choices, economic institutions, and economic events. Each student grew up in a household—the central economic institution. As consumers, students are familiar with fast-food restaurants, movie theaters, car dealerships, and dozens of stores at the mall. Most students have been resource suppliers—more than half held jobs while in high school. Students also have experience with government—they know about taxes, drivers' licenses, speed limits, and public education. And, from imported cars to the World Wide Web, students are becoming more familiar with the rest of the world.

Thus, students have abundant experience with the stuff of economics. They may not recognize the economic content of that experience, but they possess it nonetheless. Yet many principles authors neglect this rich lode of experience and, instead, try to create for the student a new world of economics. Such an approach fails to make the connection between economics and what Alfred Marshall called "the ordinary business of life."

Since instructors can cover only a fraction of the textbook material in class, principles texts should, to the extent possible, be self-explanatory, thereby providing instructors with greater flexibility to emphasize topics of special interest. My approach is to start where students are, not where we would like them to be. For example, to explain the division of labor, rather than refer to Adam Smith's pin factory, I call attention to the division of labor at McDonald's. To explain resource substitution, rather than referring to abstract units of labor and capital, I discuss a specific example, such as labor-capital combinations for washing a car—ranging from a drive-through car wash (much capital and little labor) to a Saturday-morning-send-the-band-to-Disney-World charity car wash (little capital and much labor). This edition is loaded with similar down-to-earth examples.

CLARITY BY DESIGN

In many principles textbooks, chapters are interrupted by boxed material, parenthetical explanations, qualifying footnotes, and other distractions that disrupt the flow of the material. Students remain uncertain about when or if such segregated elements should be read. In contrast, this book has a natural flow. Each chapter opens with a few questions aimed at stimulating interest, then tells a compelling story, using logical sections and subsections. Qualifying footnotes are used sparingly, and parenthetical explanations are used hardly at all. Moreover, case studies are not boxed off but appear in the natural sequence of the chapter. Students can thus read each chapter smoothly from the opening questions to the conclusion and summary. I also employ a "just-in-time" approach to introduce material just as it is needed to develop an argument. Overall, the Fifth Edition is a bit leaner, economic jargon has been reduced, and many tables have been converted to charts and graphs.

In most textbooks, the page design—the layout of the page and the use of color—is an afterthought, conceived without regard to how students learn. No element in the design of this book is wasted, and all elements work together for the maximum pedagogical value.

Page Design. By design, all elements of each chapter have been carefully integrated. Every effort has been made to present students with an open, readable page design. The size of the typeface, the length of the text line, and the amount of "white space" were all chosen to make learning easier. Graphs are uncluttered and accompanied by captions explaining the key features. These features are all optimal for students encountering college textbooks for the first time.

Use of Color. Color is used systematically within graphs, charts, and tables to ensure that students quickly and easily see what's going on. Throughout the book, demand curves are blue and supply curves are red. In comparative statics examples, the curves determining the final equilibrium point are lighter than the initial curves. Color shading distinguishes key features of many graphs, such as measures of economic profit or loss, tax incidence, consumer and producer surplus, and the welfare effects of tariffs and quotas. In short, color is more than mere face entertainment—it is employed consistently and with forethought to help students learn.

THE FIFTH EDITION

I build on the success of earlier editions to make the material even more student-friendly through concrete examples, more questions along the way, and additional summaries as each chapter unfolds. And by making the material both more personal and more natural, I try to draw students into a collaborative discussion. I have also built on the success of the Fourth Edition's Internet support to make the use of technology even more innovative and helpful. This edition features an even tighter integration of text and technology.

Introductory Chapters Topics common to both macroeconomics and microeconomics are covered in the first four chapters. Limiting the introductory material to four chapters saves precious class time, particularly at institutions where students may take macro and micro courses in either order (and hence where introductory material must be repeated).

Macroeconomics Chapters Rather than focus on the differences among competing schools of thought, I use the aggregate demand and aggregate supply model to underscore the fundamental distinction between the active approach, which views the economy as unstable and in need of government intervention when it gets off track, and the passive approach, which views the economy as essentially stable and self-correcting. In developing aggregate supply, I have taken more care in laying out the logic of the model to help students see what's going on. I also provide more review along the way.

Wherever possible, I rely on student experience and intuition to explain the theory behind macroeconomic abstractions such as aggregate demand and aggregate supply. For example, to explain how employment can temporarily exceed its natural rate, I note how students, as the term draws to a close, can temporarily shift into high gear, studying for final exams and finishing term papers.

I have made the graphs more readable and more intuitively obvious by using numbers, such as $8.0 trillion, rather than letters, such as *Y*. And to convey a feel for the size of the U.S. economy, I usually talk in terms of trillions of dollars rather than billions of dollars. New material in this edition includes discussions of banking consolidation around the globe, banking troubles in Japan, the Fed's targeting of the federal funds rate, balancing the federal budget, and trouble ahead for the Social Security system.

Microeconomics Chapters My approach to microeconomics underscores the role of time and information in production and consumption. For example, both time and information are scarce resources and, as such, are valued by consumers and producers. The microeconomic presentation also reflects the growing interest in the economic institutions that underpin impersonal market activity. More generally, I try to convey the intuition that most microeconomic principles operate like gravity: Market forces work whether or not individual economic actors understand them.

At every opportunity, I turn the abstract into the concrete. For example, rather than talking in terms of an abstract monopolist, the monopoly chapter focuses throughout on the De Beers diamond monopoly. New material in this edition includes discussions of antitrust moves against Microsoft, the economics of tobacco legislation, winner-take-all labor markets, intellectual property, and welfare reform. To streamline the presentation of resource markets, I combine material on labor markets and on labor unions into a single chapter. And the chapter that had covered public choice now includes much more on public goods.

International Chapters This edition reflects the growing impact of the world economy on U.S. economic welfare. International issues are introduced early and discussed often. For example, the rest of the world is introduced in Chapter 1 and comparative advantage and the production possibilities frontier are each discussed from a global perspective in Chapter 2. International coverage is woven into the text. For example, students gain a better perspective about such topics as economic growth, productivity, unemployment, inflation, central bank independence, unionization trends, antitrust laws, pollution, environmental laws, tax rates, and the distribution of income if the U.S. experience is compared with that of other countries around the world.

New international material includes discussions of the euro, economic troubles in Asia, "crony capitalism," declining fertility rates around the world, and the painful progress of transitional economies. Although international references are scattered throughout the book, including a number of case studies, the final three chapters focus exclusively on international trade, international finance, and developing and transitional economies, respectively.

Case Studies Some books use case studies as boxed-off asides to cover material that otherwise doesn't quite fit. I use case studies as real-world applications that reinforce ideas in the chapter and demonstrate the relevance of economic theory. My case studies are different enough to offer variety in the presentation yet are integrated enough into the flow of the chapter to let students know they should be read. This edition distinguishes among four categories of case studies: (1) "The World of Business" offers students a feel for the range of choices confronted by business decision makers today; (2) "The Information Economy" underscores the critical role of information in the new economy, from the computer revolution to the value of intellectual property; (3) "Other Times, Other Places" involves applications either from economic history or from other economies around the world; and (4) "Public Policy" cases highlight the tradeoffs in the public sector. All case studies are supported by references and relevant Web addresses and are tied to further analysis on the Web with questions, navigation tips, and other information that can be accessed through the McEachern Interactive Study Center at http://mceachern.swcollege.com.

Net Bookmarks Each chapter includes a Net Bookmark. These margin notes identify interesting Web sites that illustrate real-world examples of chapter topics, giving students the opportunity to explore some of those sites and build their economic research skills. And they are extended at our Web site with additional information on resources as well as step-by-step navigation hints. They can be accessed through the McEachern Interactive Study Center at http://mceachern.swcollege.com.

The *Wall Street Journal* Edition The Fifth Edition makes it easy to bring the real world into the classroom. This *Wall Street Journal* Edition provides numerous opportunities to relate economic concepts to late-breaking news stories. A special Preface guides students in their use of the *Wall Street Journal.* And there is a question at the end of each chapter that asks students to read and analyze information from the *Wall Street Journal.*

Experiential Exercises New to this edition are end-of-chapter questions that encourage students to develop their research and critical thinking skills. These Experiential Exercises ask students to apply what they have learned to real-world, hands-on economic analysis. Most of these exercises involve the Internet, the *Wall Street Journal*, or other media resources.

The Internet

As mentioned already, we devoted careful attention to capitalizing on the vast array of economic resources and alternative learning technologies the Internet can deliver. I gave much thought to two basic questions: What can this technology do that a textbook cannot do? And how can Web-based enhancements be employed to bring the greatest value to teaching and learning?

It's clear that students learn more when they are involved and engaged. The Internet provides a way to heighten student involvement while keeping the introductory economics course as current as today's news. With these ideas in mind, we have undertaken a major upgrading of the text's Web site to more tightly integrate the book and the Internet. We have done this in a way that exploits the comparative advantage of each medium, and in a structure that optimizes both teaching and learning experiences.

The McEachern Interactive Study Center (http://mceachern.swcollege.com) Through McEachern Interactive, students benefit from the best textual presentation as well as the most innovative on-line experience. This edition offers a structured approach to the Internet, providing a comprehensive chapter-by-chapter on-line study guide that includes graphical support, interactive quizzes, a glossary, updated and extended applications from the text, and numerous other features. Some highlights include:

Over 170 Examples and Exercises The Internet-enhanced text features such as Net Bookmarks, Case Studies, and end-of-chapter Experiential Exercises are tied to the Study Center, where students will find clear links to relevant Web sites. These applications are interesting and easy-to-use. All of the in-text features that are extended on the Web are indicated by a special McEachern Interactive icon (Shown at right).

On-Line Graphing Tutorials Key graphs from the text—also indicated by the McEachern Interactive icon—are brought to life as students explore interactive graphing tutorials that feature helpful audio explanations.

Interactive Quizzes These multiple-choice on-line quizzes provide a perfect review resource and solid exam preparation. They feature detailed feedback for right and wrong answers as well as the option of e-mailing quiz results to the instructor.

It is important to note that none of these features requires detailed knowledge of the Internet. Nor are they required for a successful classroom experience if an instructor wants to assign only the materials contained within the text. The on-line enhancements simply offer optional paths for further study and exploration—new ways for students to employ their individual learning styles and new ways for instructors to experiment with technology and a wider range of assignment materials.

THE SUPPORT PACKAGE

The teaching and learning support package that accompanies *Economics: A Contemporary Introduction* provides instructors and students with focused, accurate, and innovative supplements to the textbook.

Student Supplements

Study Guide *Study Guides*, written by John Lunn of Hope College, are available for the full textbook, as well as for the Macro and Micro "split" versions. Each chapter of the *Study Guide* corresponds to a chapter in the text and offers: (1) an introduction; (2) a chapter outline, with definitions of all terms; (3) a discussion of the chapter's main points; (4) a *lagniappe*, or bonus, which supplements material in the chapter and includes a "Question to Think About"; (5) a list of key terms; (6) a variety of true-false, multiple-choice, and discussion questions; and (7) answers to all these questions. Visit the McEachern Interactive Study Center at http://mceachern.swcollege.com for more details.

Graphing Primer One of the most difficult challenges for many introductory economics students is working with graphs. The *Graphing Primer* is a print supplement that helps students create, interpret, and understand graphs.

McEachern Interactive CD-ROM This CD-ROM provides a powerful collection of electronic study tools:

PowerPoint Lecture Review Slides Students can visually review key concepts and exhibits from each chapter, and print the slides to use as note-taking guides during class lectures.

South-Western Economics Tutorial Software James T. Doak has developed tutorial software compatible with Microsoft Windows. It is organized around major macroeconomic and microeconomic topics, and correlated to relevant text chapters. Each topic provides a series of interactive graphing exercises that help students test their understanding of key concepts. Students can also track and record their progress.

McEachern Interactive Graphing Tutorials The 37 graphing tutorials found at the McEachern Study Center are also included on this CD-ROM.

***Economics Guide* Tutorial Software** Robert Brooker, of Gannon University, has developed this economics tutorial software, compatible with Microsoft Windows. Through the use of a sophisticated testing engine, it presents students with an unlimited supply of quizzes over the topics covered in each chapter. Students are able to track and record their progress throughout the course. *Economics Guide* software is perfect for review or for test preparation

Economics Alive! CD-ROMs—Interactive Study Guides The *Economics Alive!* CD-ROMs, created by Willie Belton, Richard Cebula, and John McLeod, Jr. of the Georgia Institute of Technology, are compatible with Microsoft Windows and with the Apple Macintosh. These multimedia CD-ROMs combine interactive lessons, graphing tools, and simulations to bring microeconomic and macroeconomic concepts to life. To learn more about these CDs, visit the *Economics Alive!* Web site at http://econalive.swcollege.com.

The McEachern Web Site The McEachern Web site at http://mceachern.swcollege.com. offers a variety of learning tools. In addition to the helpful tools available at the McEachern Interactive Study Center, students can also find summaries of current news stories, review current and historical economic data, keep up-to-date through current examples and policy applications, access information about saleable supplements, correspond with me, and take advantage of other benefits.

Instructor Supplements

Instructor's Manual The *Instructor's Manual*, revised by Dorothy Siden of Salem State College, is keyed to the text. For each text chapter, it includes (1) a detailed lecture outline and brief overview; (2) a summary of main points; (3) pedagogical tips that expand on points raised in the chapter; and (4) suggested answers to all end-of-chapter questions and problems. New to this edition is a set of classroom economic experiments developed by Michael Haupert of the University of Wisconsin, La Crosse and Noelwah Netusil of Reed College. Each experiment comes with an abstract, an overview, a clear set of instructions for running the experiment, and forms for recording the results.

Teaching Assistance Manual I have revised my *Teaching Assistance Manual* to provide additional support beyond the Instructor's Manual. It is especially useful to new instructors, graduate assistants, and teachers interested in generating more class discussion. This manual offers: (1) overviews and outlines of each chapter; (2) chapter objectives and quiz material; (3) material for class discussion; (4) topics warranting special attention; (5) supplementary examples; and (6) "What if?" discussion questions. Appendices provide guidance on (a) presenting material; (b) generating and sustaining class discussion; (c) preparing, administering, and grading quizzes; and (d) coping with the special problems confronting foreign graduate assistants.

Test Banks Thoroughly revised for currency and accuracy, the *Macroeconomics* and *Microeconomics Test Banks* contain over 6,600 questions in multiple-choice and true-false formats. All multiple choice questions have five possible responses, and each is rated by degree of difficulty. For this edition, Nathan Eric

Hampton of St. Cloud State University has thoroughly reworked the *Test Banks* and has grouped all questions according to chapter subheadings. This makes it easy to find just the questions you want and to make sure your questions are representative of material you teach in class.

Testing Tools—Computerized Testing Software *Testing Tools* is an easy-to-use test creation software package that is available in versions compatible with Microsoft Windows and with the Apple Macintosh. It contains all of the questions in the printed Test Banks. Instructors can add or edit questions, instructions, and answers, and select questions by previewing them on the screen and then choosing them by number, or at random. Instructors can also create and administer quizzes on-line, either over the Internet, through a local area network (LAN), or through a wide area network (WAN).

Microsoft PowerPoint Lecture Slides Tables and graphs from the text, as well as additional instructional materials, are available as PowerPoint slides to enhance lectures and help integrate technology into the classroom.

Transparency Acetates Most of the tables and graphs from this text are reproduced as full-color transparency acetates.

CNN Economics Video The CNN Economics Video provides a variety of brief video clips, taken from Cable News Network (CNN) programs, that illustrate various aspects of economics.

On-line Course Creation and Delivery Systems South-Western College Publishing now makes taking your course to the Web as easy as typing. Visit ITP Electronic Learning at http://www.itped.com to learn about simple-to-use options for creating an on-line course or a Web site for your traditional course.

The Teaching Economist For nearly a decade, I have edited *The Teaching Economist*, a newsletter aimed at making teaching more interesting and more fun. The newsletter discusses imaginative ways to present topics—for example, how to "sensationalize" economic concepts, useful resources on the Internet, economic applications from science fiction, and more generally, ways to teach just for the fun of it. A regular feature of *The Teaching Economist*, "The Grapevine," offers teaching ideas suggested by colleagues from across the country.

The latest issue—and back issues—of *The Teaching Economist* are available on-line at http://economics.swcollege.com.

ACKNOWLEDGEMENTS

Many people contributed to this book's development. I gratefully acknowledge the insightful comments of those who have reviewed chapters for the Fifth Edition. Their suggestions made me think more and made the book better.

Donna Anderson	University of Wisconsin, LaCrosse
Mohsen Bahmani	University of Wisconsin, Milwaukee
Jay Bhattacharya	Okaloosa Walton Community College
Doug Conway	Mesa Community College

Thomas Creahan	Morehead State University
Ron Elkins	Central Washington University
Roger Frantz	San Diego State University
J.P. Gilbert	MiraCosta College
Robert Gordon	San Diego State University
Fred Graham	American University
Nathan Eric Hampton	St. Cloud State University
Mehdi Haririan	Bloomsburg University
Julia Heath	University of Memphis
James Henderson	Baylor University
Bryce Kanago	Miami University
Robert Kleinhenz	California State University, Fullerton
Faik Koray	Louisiana State University
Marie Kratochvil	Nassau Community College
Jim Lee	Ft. Hays State University
Ken Long	New River Community College
Michael Magura	University of Toledo
Richard Martin	Agnes Scott College
KimMarie McGoldrick	University of Richmond
Mark McNeil	Irvine Valley College
Art Meyer	Lincoln Land Community College
Carrie Meyer	George Mason University
Bruce Mills	Troy State University
Shannon Mitchell	Virginia Commonwealth University
Maureen O'Brien	University of Minnesota, Duluth
Jaishankar Raman	Valparaiso University
Mitch Redlo	Monroe Community College
Simran Sahi	University of Minnesota, Twin Cities
George Santopietro	Radford University
Carol Scotese	Virginia Commonwealth University
Alden Shiers	California Polytechnic State University
Frederica Shockley	California State University, Chico
Gerald Simons	Grand Valley State University
Mark Stegeman	Virginia Polytechnic Institute
John Tribble	Russell Sage College
Robert Whaples	Wake Forest University
Mark Wheeler	Western Michigan University
Michael White	St. Cloud State University
Patricia Wyatt	Bossier Parish Community College

To practice what I preach, I relied on the division of labor based on comparative advantage to help put together the most complete teaching package on the market today. John Lunn of Hope College authored the *Study Guide*, which has been quite popular. Dorothy Siden of Salem State College authored the *Instructor's Manual*. And Nathan Eric Hampton of St. Cloud State University undertook a major reworking of the *Test Bank*. I thank them for their imagination and discipline.

The talented staff at South-Western College Publishing provided invaluable editorial, administrative, and sales support. I would especially like to single out the guidance of Dennis Hanseman, Development Editor and Ph.D. in economics, who helped me every step of the way, from the reviews of the previous edition to final proof pages. I also appreciate very much the excellent design work of Joe Devine, the superlative project coordination by Senior Production Editor Sharon Smith, the photography management of Cary Benbow, and the production assistance of Mary Ansaldo of Pre-Press Company, the production house for this edition. Kurt Gerdenich and Vicky True have been particularly helpful in developing the McEachern Interactive Study Center.

In addition, I am most grateful to Bob Lynch, President of South-Western, Jack Calhoun, Publishing Team Director, Keri Witman, Acquisitions Editor, and especially Lisa Lysne, the Marketing Manager who knows the book inside and out. As good as the book is, all our efforts would be wasted unless students use it. To that end, I greatly appreciate South-Western's dedicated service and sales force, who have contributed in a substantial way to the success of previous editions.

Finally, I owe an abiding debt to my wife, Pat, who provided abundant encouragement and support along the way.

William A. McEachern

PREVIOUS EDITION REVIEWERS

Polly Reynolds Allen	University of Connecticut
Ted Amato	University of North Carolina, Charlotte
Richard Anderson	Texas A&M University
James Aylesworth	Lakeland Community College
Dale Bails	Christian Brothers College
Andy Barnett	Auburn University
Klaus Becker	Texas Tech University
David Brasfield	Murray State University
Jurgen Brauer	Augusta College
Gardner Brown, Jr.	University of Washington
Judy Butler	Baylor University
Charles Callahan III	SUNY College at Brockport
Giorgio Canarella	California State University, Los Angeles
Larry Clarke	Brookhaven College

Rebecca Cline	Middle Georgia College
Stephen Cobb	Xavier University
James P. Cover	University of Alabama
James Cox	DeKalb College
Jerry Crawford	Arkansas State University
Joseph Daniels	Marquette University
Elynor Davis	Georgia Southern University
Susan Davis	SUNY College at Buffalo
A. Edward Day	University of Central Florida
David Dean	University of Richmond
Janet Deans	Chestnut Hill College
David Denslow	University of Florida
John Edgren	Eastern Michigan University
Donald Elliott, Jr.	Southern Illinois University
G. Rod Erfani	Transylvania University
Gisela Meyer Escoe	University of Cincinnati
Mark Evans	California State University, Bakersfield
Eleanor Fapohunda	SUNY College at Farmingdale
Mohsen Fardmanesh	Temple University
Paul Farnham	Georgia State University
Rudy Fichtenbaum	Wright State University
T. Windsor Fields	James Madison University
Rodney Fort	Washington State University
Gary Galles	Pepperdine University
Edward Gamber	Lafayette College
Adam Gifford	California State University, Northridge
Robert Gillette	University of Kentucky
Art Goldsmith	Washington and Lee University
Philip Graves	University of Colorado, Boulder
Daniel Gropper	Auburn University
Simon Hakim	Temple University
Robert Halvorsen	University of Washington
William Hart	Miami University
Baban Hasnat	SUNY College at Brockport
James Hill	Central Michigan University
Jane Smith Himarios	University of Texas, Arlington
Dennis Hoffman	Arizona State University
Bruce Horning	Fordham University
Calvin Hoy	County College of Morris

Beth Ingram	University of Iowa
Joyce Jacobsen	Wesleyan University
Nancy Jianakoplos	Colorado State University
Nake Kamrany	University of Southern California
John Kane	SUNY College at Oswego
David Kennett	Vassar College
Joseph Kotaska	Monroe Community College
Joseph Lammert	Raymond Walters College
Dennis Leyden	University of North Carolina, Greensboro
C. Richard Long	Georgia State University
Thomas Maloy	Muskegon Community College
Gabriel Manrique	Winona State University
Robert Margo	Vanderbilt University
Wolfgang Mayer	University of Cincinnati
John McDowell	Arizona State University
James McLain	University of New Orleans
Martin Milkman	Murray State University
Milton Mitchell	University of Wisconsin, Oshkosh
Kathryn Nantz	Fairfield University
Reza Ramazani	St. Michael's University
Carol Rankin	Xavier University
Robert Rossana	Wayne State University
Mark Rush	University of Florida
Richard Saba	Auburn University
Rexford Santerre	Bentley College
Ted Scheinman	Mt. Hood Community College
Peter Schwartz	University of North Carolina, Charlotte
Roger Sherman	University of Virginia
William Shughart II	University of Mississippi
Calvin Siebert	University of Iowa
Phillip Smith	DeKalb College
V. Kerry Smith	Duke University
David Spencer	Brigham Young University
Jane Speyrer	University of New Orleans
Houston Stokes	University of Illinois, Chicago
Robert Stonebreaker	Indiana University of Pennsylvania
William Swift	Pace University
Lee J. Van Scyoc	University of Wisconsin, Oshkosh
Percy Vera	Sinclair Community College

Jin Wang	University of Wisconsin, Stevens Point
Gregory Wassall	Northeastern University
William Weber	Eastern Illinois University
David Weinberg	Xavier University
Donald Wells	University of Arizona
Richard Winkelman	Arizona State University
Kenneth Woodward	Saddleback College
Peter Wyman	Spokane Falls Community College
Mesghena Yasin	Morehead State University
Edward Young	University of Wisconsin, Eau Claire
William Zeis	Bucks Community College

THE WALL STREET JOURNAL.

DOWJONES

Educational Edition

How to Read Between the Lines

An Introduction to The Wall Street Journal

An invitation to learn more

about the world's business daily.

An opportunity to go behind

the scenes at America's most

important business publication.

THE WALL STREET JOURNAL.

DOW JONES

Educational Edition

The First Section

Caveat Lender

Southeast Asian Banks Contribute to a Bust In the Economic Boom

Financial-Sector Weaknesses Are Roiling Currencies; Regulation Has Been Lax

Columns 1 and 6: The Lead Stories

Column Six always provides the day's top business story about a company, industry or event, while Column One ranges further afield: It may take on politics, international affairs or social issues as well as business and finance.

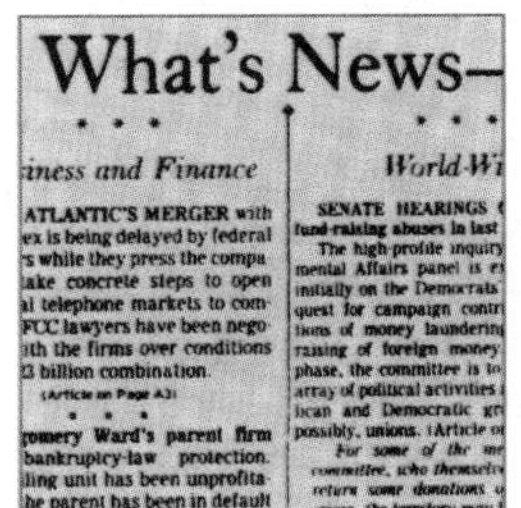

What's News–

Business and Finance

World-Wide

Columns 2 and 3: What's News

"World-Wide" is a concise digest of the latest news developments from around the globe, while "Business and Finance" summarizes the top stories from those spheres.

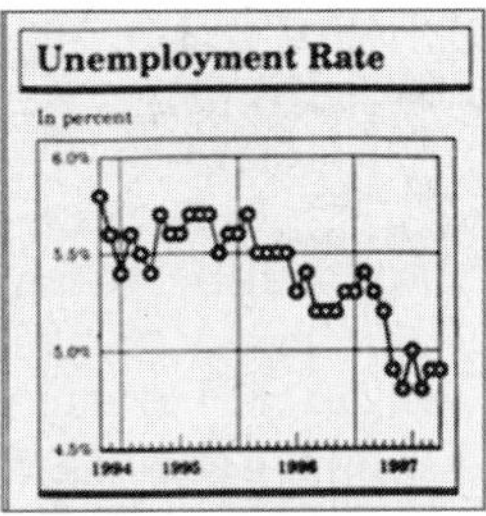

Column 4: Performance Graph

Each issue contains a different graph of a major economic indicator to help make the complex more easy to understand.

Column 4: The A-Hed

Ranging from silly to serious, quirky to downright bizarre, the A-Hed gives free rein to our reporters' imagination.

The Outlook

Why an Acquisition? Often, It's the People

WASHINGTON

WorldCom Inc.'s audacious $30 billion bid to acquire MCI Communications Corp. is the latest vivid example of how big companies try to become gigantic companies to gain clout and dominance over an industry. But while the power

MONDAY:

The Outlook

Emphasizing markets and investing, reporters from every bureau contribute perspective and points of view on policy, trends and developments around the world.

Work Week

A Special News Report About Life On the Job—and Trends Taking Shape There

WORKPLACE ACCIDENTS can mean criminal charges for executives.

Prosecutors blame corporate managers for poor workplace safety. In Boston Thomas E. Bowley, chief executive of Tewksbury Industries Inc., is indicted on manslaughter charges after two company workers were killed in separate accidents

TUESDAY:

Work Week

Taking the broadest definition of work as its beat, this column charts the changing world of the office, factory and service sector.

ECONOMY

s No Ra

milar degree of strength

rket indicators," such a

Economy

The Journal's economic news, on page A2, provides clear, straightforward stories about the latest news of inflation, unemployment, government announcements, Federal Reserve policy, economic forecasts, durable-goods prices and more. These complicated matters become understandable and meaningful as you realize how this news affects your life and your livelihood.

POLITICS & POLICY

ed Choice for Civ

onservatives Des

Some past chiefs of some rejected nomi

Politics & Policy

The back page of our first section is home to a collection of wide-ranging articles on politics at every level, from local to state to federal. On any day, you might find exclusive Journal polls, in-depth personal profiles, innovative examples of municipal governance and informed commentary on administration initiatives.

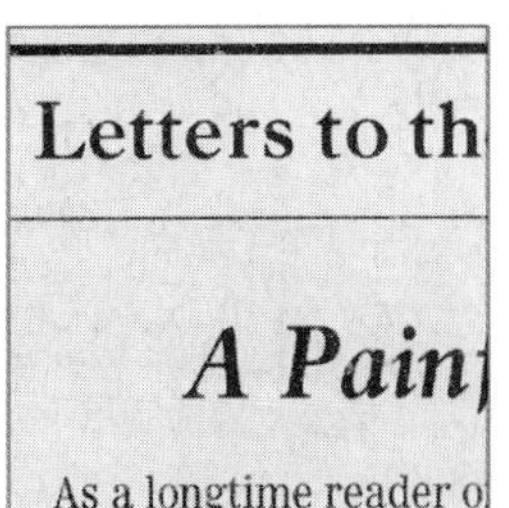

Letters to th

A Pain

As a longtime reader o

The Editorial Pages

Daily, we publish the best of over 2,000 letters received weekly from prominent leaders in every field. Whether amplifying a comment, challenging an opinion, or debating with influencial readers, they provide some lively writing. This creates the single most influential editorial page in the nation. Love it or hate it – but disregard it only at your peril.

The Marketplace

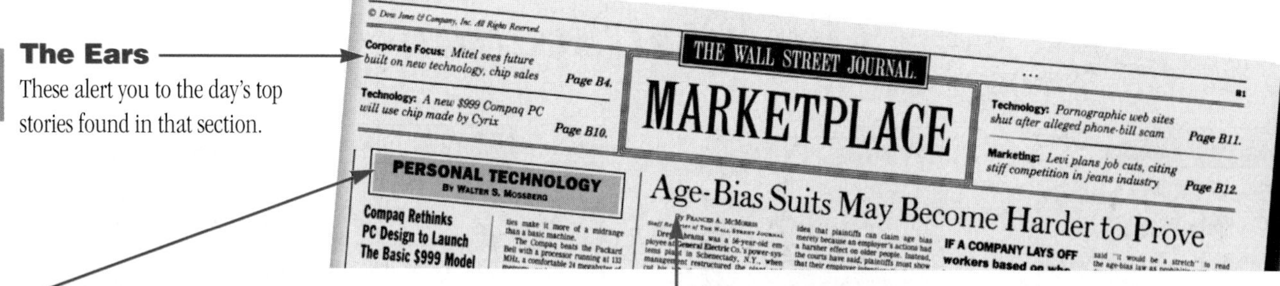

© Dow Jones & Company, Inc. All Rights Reserved

Corporate Focus: Mitel sees future built on new technology, chip sales Page B4.

Technology: A new $999 Compaq PC will use chip made by Cyrix Page B10.

THE WALL STREET JOURNAL.

MARKETPLACE

Technology: Pornographic web sites shut after alleged phone-bill scam Page B11.

Marketing: Levi plans job cuts, citing stiff competition in jeans industry Page B12.

PERSONAL TECHNOLOGY
By Walter S. Mossberg

Compaq Rethinks PC Design to Launch The Basic $999 Model

Age-Bias Suits May Become Harder to Prove

IF A COMPANY LAYS OFF workers based on who...

The Ears

These alert you to the day's top stories found in that section.

The Rotating Column

Here seasoned Journal writers, who are experts in their fields, inject personal opinion and informed judgements into their news stories.

MONDAY: **Health Journal**
TUESDAY: **Managing Your Career**
WEDNESDAY: **Work & Family, Business & Race**
THURSDAY: **Personal Technology**
FRIDAY: **The Front Lines**

The Top News

News with an individual perspective, you might find front-page articles about autos, travel, advertising, healthcare, pharmaceuticals, technology, law, marketing and the media.

Inside The Marketplace

MARKETING & MEDIA

ADVERTISING / By Sally Goll Beatty

FTC Pressures Cable Networks To Scrutinize Dubious Ad Claims

Disney Soap Operas Are Coming Soon To Comcast's Q2

Cable Channel to Carry Shows Prime Time on Same Day

Novell Satellite Feed Gives CNN Anchor More Exposure Than She Was Expecting

By Anita Sharpe

B6 THE WALL STREET JOURNAL

NET INTEREST

WATCHING THE WEB

BY THOMAS E. WEBER

New Software Le... Move Out of the...

ENTERPRISE

Knives: The Cutting Edge of Collectibles

By Roger Ricklefs

INDEX TO BUSINESSES

This index of businesses mentioned in today's issue of The Wall Street Journal is intended to include all significant references to parent companies. First references to these companies appear in boldface type in all articles except those on page one, the editorial pages and the Leisure & Arts page. The index doesn't cite companies listed solely in the Digest of Earnings, which appears today on page C16. Page numbers listed here refer to the pages where the articles begin.

Marketing & Media

Fifteen reporters and editors, focusing on the big stories first, cover all the news from the media, advertising and entertainment industries.

Net Interest/ Watching the Web

"Net Interest", a monthly column, takes a consumer's perspective to the Internet's promises, failures and personalities. "Watching the Web" is a directory of reviews that focus on must-visit or must-avoid sites.

Enterprise

Here you'll find news on trends, issues and legislation that affects small business, and illuminating news stories on why some small companies succeed while others fail.

Index to Business

Is there a company in which you're particularly interested? The Index, on page B2, lets you know at a glance if we've covered it in today's paper.

Inside The Marketplace (Continued)

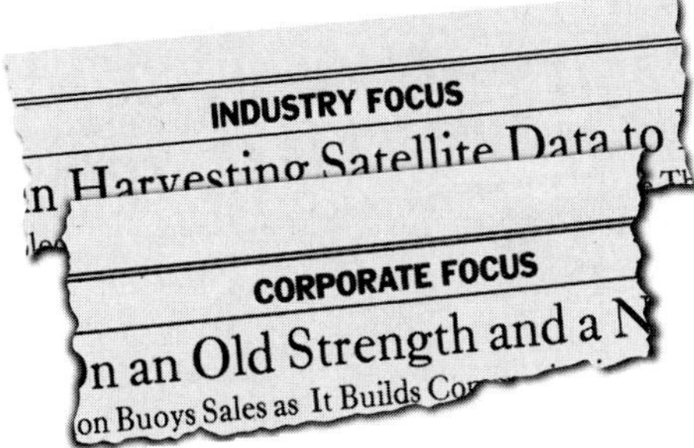

Industry/Corporate Focus

Every day, we take a detailed look at a specific corporation – its competitive situation, corporate strategy, problems and successes – or an entire industry. In the latter case, our reporters covering the beat put together an insightful overview of an industry's current situation and future prospects.

Law

Here's legal news from a unique perspective: In our daily "Legal Beat" column and feature articles, we write about the law as a service that most people need, sooner or later. And we do so with uncommon expertise, as four of our seven reporters on the beat are lawyers themselves.

Technology

Our technology coverage may be anchored on a Marketplace page – in columns such as "In the Lab", "Technology & Medicine" and "Technology & Environment" – but it is also found all throughout the publication, from the front page to the last.

Who's News

Make it big in business, and you might find your name and picture in this column, where we chart the comings and goings of the upper reaches of corporate management. If you're thinking of working for a company, or investing in it, you might do well to keep your eye here, to find out who's running it.

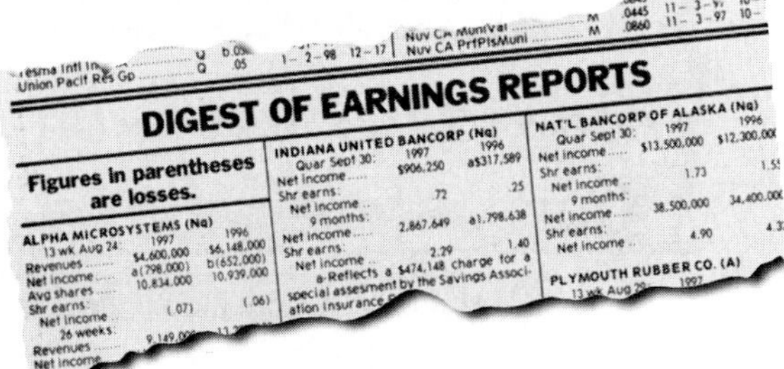

Digest of Earnings Report

Public corporations can satisfy their legal obligation to announce quarterly and annual figures by publishing them in the Journal. (Of course, we have to be satisfied of their veracity before we'll print them.) This extensive compilation, which can feature over 200 companies in a single issue, is a must for investors.

Money & Investing: All the Numbers

Expert analysis, straight-forward explanations and comprehensive statistics create an easy-to-navigate guide to the stock market and other markets that affect both America's business and your finances.

THE WALL STREET JOURNAL.

MONEY & INVESTING

MARKETS DIARY

STOCKS

BONDS

INTEREST

Investors Yank the Welcome Mat for 'Global Citizens'

Global Doubts

Fund Manager Gets Lesson in Pitfalls For Contrarians

HEARD ON THE STREET

Taking a Fall

Small Stocks Set Record; Blue Chips Hurt by IBM

TUESDAY'S MARKETS

Markets Diary

A prominent display of Yesterday's results in the stock, bond and commodities markets as well as the previous week's activity, interest rates, and the performance of the U.S. dollar relative to other major currencies.

The Top News

Here you'll find feature stories that carry the hottest news from the world of finance.

Pan Markets

Here's where you'll find all of yesterday's activity from the stock, bond and dollar markets are brought together in a concise and comprehensive overview of what happened and what it means.

Money & Investing Columns

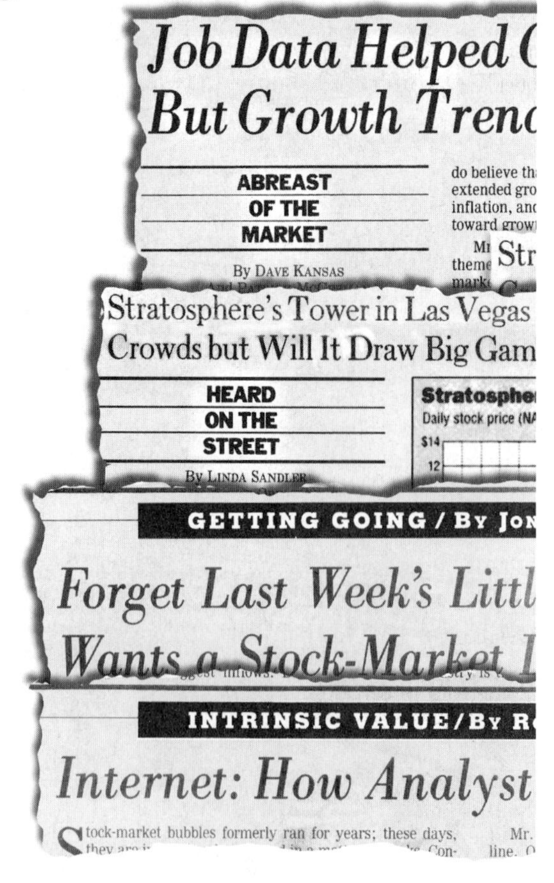

Job Data Helped

But Growth Tren

ABREAST OF THE MARKET

By Dave Kansas

Stratosphere's Tower in Las Vegas

Crowds but Will It Draw Big Gam

HEARD ON THE STREET

By Linda Sandler

GETTING GOING / BY JO

Forget Last Week's Littl

Wants a Stock-Market

INTRINSIC VALUE/BY R

Internet: How Analyst

Stock-market bubbles formerly ran for years; these days,

Abreast of the Market/Small Stock Focus

Look to these columns first, for the authoritative word that explains market activity. While "Abreast" trains its sights on large-capitalization stocks, "Small Stock" does the same for small and medium-cap issues. Together, they constitute the most respected daily analysis of the stock market in print.

Heard on the Street

Every day, "Heard" brings our readers the first word on subjects and stocks that Wall Street denizens are talking about among themselves.

Getting Going

Whether you've got $3,000 to invest or $3 million, "Getting Going" gets you started in the right direction. Because Jonathon Clements has a rare ability to explain the first principles of investing in simple terms. His column every Tuesday will help you learn the most important criteria by which to evaluate what kind of fund is right for you.

Intrinsic Value

Once you've got some trades under your belt, take a look at Roger Lowenstein's "Intrinsic Value", which appears on Fridays. It's a sophisticated analysis of the fundamentals underlying the numbers, written with obvious expertise and marked by a strong ethical underpinning.

Money & Investing Columns (Continued)

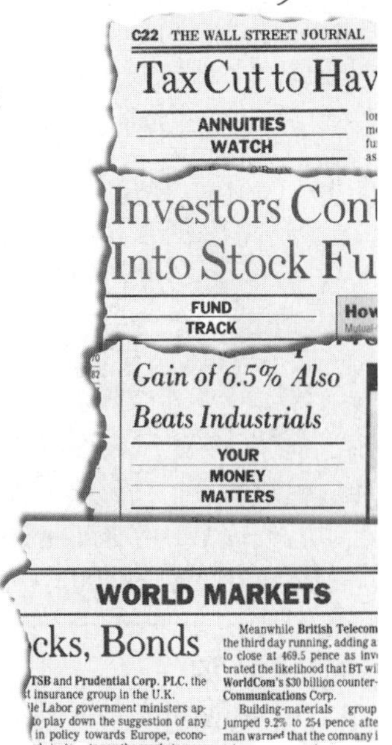
C22 THE WALL STREET JOURNAL

Tax Cut to Hav

ANNUITIES WATCH

Investors Con

Into Stock Fu

FUND TRACK

Gain of 6.5% Also Beats Industrials

YOUR MONEY MATTERS

WORLD MARKETS

cks, Bonds

Annuities Watch

As more people take responsibility for their own retirement planning, annuities have rapidly grown in popularity. In response, the Journal introduced this column and an accompanying page of variable-annuity statistics.

Fund Track

The mutual fund, an essential financial instrument, is the centerpiece of our news coverage and analysis in "Fund Track." This major daily column's primary purpose is to break news on the industry, but it also takes an advisory tone on matters of personal finance.

Your Money Matters

"Your Money Matters" sticks to the basics of money management and, through the course of a year, covers virtually everything of importance to the individual, from buying a home to financing an education, from evaluating stocks to planning an estate.

World Markets

Sara Webb gained years of expertise covering global equities markets for The Asian Wall Street Journal and the Wall Street Journal/Europe. Now, American readers get the benefit of her insight.

Money & Investing Statistics

The Journal's financial statistics are so comprehensive and extensive, it would take pages to introduce you to them in detail. Suffice it to say this: Whatever you need to know about the markets, either as an investment professional or individual investor, you'll find here. In most cases, you'll also find accompanying news columns that provide daily context and informed perspective on the movements of the particular market. Here's a brief look at some of the broad categories of data you'll find in "Money & Investing" every business day.

Stock Prices & the Stock Market

The Stock Market

The New York Stock Exchange, American Stock Exchange and Nasdaq National Market Issues lead the stock tables, but the Journal also includes regional and foreign stock exchange listings.

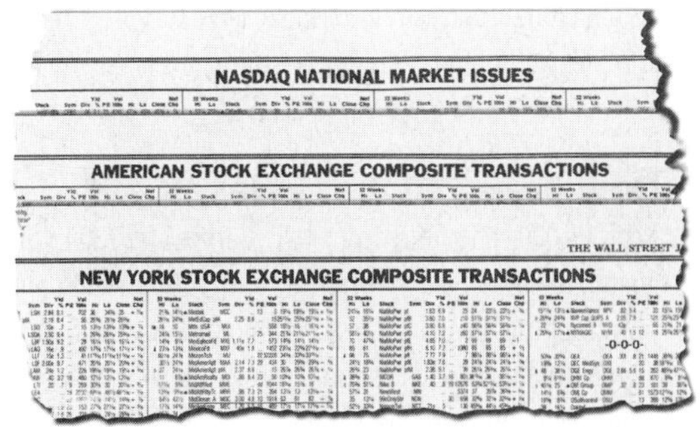
NASDAQ NATIONAL MARKET ISSUES

AMERICAN STOCK EXCHANGE COMPOSITE TRANSACTIONS

NEW YORK STOCK EXCHANGE COMPOSITE TRANSACTIONS

Stock Market Data Bank

Many analysts look at several indexes, not just the DJIA, and a variety of them are published at the top of the Stock Market Data Bank, which appears daily on page C2. Besides the Dow Jones Averages, there are the New York Stock Exchange indexes of all stocks traded on the exchange, and the NYSE indexes of major sectors. Indexes compiled by Standard & Poor's Corp. are market-weighted; the 500-stock index is often used as a benchmark of overall New York Stock Exchange performance. It is made up of 400 industrial, 20 transportation, 40 utility and 40 financial stocks. For each index, the Data Bank shows the latest day's closing level and changes from the previous day, a year earlier and the end of the previous year, both in absolute terms and as a percentage of the previous figure. The high and low for the latest 12 months also are shown. You can also find Nasdaq, American Stock Exchange, the 1,700 -stock Value Line and the 5,000-stock Wilshire indexes.

STOCK MARKET DATA BANK

MAJOR INDEXES

†12-MO HIGH	†12-MO LOW		DAILY HIGH	DAILY LOW	CLOSE	NET CHG	% CHG	†12-MO CHG	% CHG	FROM 12/31	% CHG
		DOW JONES AVERAGES									
8259.31	5921.67	30 Industrials	8144.42	7956.07	8038.56	+ 11.05	+ 0.14	+ 2045.72	+ 34.14	+ 1590.31	+ 24.66
3227.78	2049.63	20 Transportation	3258.86	3191.67	3207.79	− 19.99	− 0.62	+ 1105.65	+ 52.60	+ 952.12	+ 42.21
243.74	209.47	15 Utilities	246.70	241.22	242.81	− 0.93	− 0.38	+ 20.90	+ 9.42	+ 10.28	+ 4.42
2574.12	1863.88	65 Composite	2605.87	2549.31	2569.54	− 4.58	− 0.18	+ 679.47	+ 35.95	+ 543.71	+ 26.84
913.35	657.44	DJ Global-US	922.59	904.67	913.35	+ 4.32	+ 0.48	+ 249.06	+ 37.49	+ 212.79	+ 30.37
		NEW YORK STOCK EXCHANGE									
505.69	370.35	Composite	510.31	501.42	505.69	+					
633.67	469.02	Industrials									

Understanding the Stock Market Tables

52 Week Hi and Lo:
Highest and lowest prices paid for the stock over the past 52 weeks, excluding the latest day's trading

Stock Symbol:
Used when looking up the stock on online systems

Dividend:
Stock's annual cash dividend, if any, based on the rate of the last quarterly payout to shareholders

Vol 100s:
Number of shares traded in each stock in the previous day, expressed in hundreds. Thus 57 means 5,700 shares were traded. Transactions generally take place in units of 100 shares. A "z" footnote before the volume figure means it represents the total shares traded; z57 means 57 shares were traded, not 5,700. Stocks with unusually high volume compared with that stock's average trading volume are underlined.

Stock Name

	52 Weeks Hi	Lo	Stock	Sym	Div	Yld %	PE	Vol 100s	Hi	Lo	Close	Net Chg
	42¾	28⅜	ColesMyer	CM	1.39e	3.6	...	38	39⅛	39 1/16	39⅛	...
s	78 11/16	40 13/16	ColgatePalm	CL	1.10	1.7	29	9547	65 11/16	64 9/16	64¾	– ⅜
	12⅜	5½	CollinsAikman	CKC		...	5	340	11 5/16	11	11 5/16	+ 5/16
s	28 9/16	16 15/16	ColBgp	CNB	.60	2.1	17	358	28	27½	27 15/16	...

Latest day's price data –
high, low, close and change from the previous day's closing. If one of these is a record for the previous 52 weeks, a small up or down arrow will appear to the far left of that stock's listing that day. The new extreme will be reflected in the 52-week high or low for the next day. A special table lists new highs and lows of NYSE listed stocks established that day. The length of this list can be an indicator of the market's performance. When a lot of issues reach new highs, there probably is a lot of buying pressure in the market. A large number of new lows indicates a bearish tone. Stocks that close up or down more than 5% from the previous day's closing price are printed in boldface.

Yld %:
Yield Percentage is obtained by dividing the cash dividend by the closing price of the stock. This enables dividend yields to be compared with other stocks and with the interest paid on debt instruments.

PE:
The P-E ratio is used as an indicator of relative stock performance. High P-Es indicate a stock price that's a high multiple of a company's earnings – suggesting optimism about the stock. Low P-E stocks often represent lower investor favor, but there isn't any "best" ratio. Reasons for high and low P-Es include the company's growth outlook, the company's industry, accounting policies, riskiness or the stability of the earnings. P-E ratio is the result of dividing the latest closing price by the latest available earnings per share, based on primary per-share earnings for the most recent four quarters.

Footnote:
An explanation of the footnotes appears daily underneath the graphs of the Dow Jones Averages. This box also recaps the meaning of the numbers in each of the stock-listing columns. For example, an "n" indicates a new issue of stock.

Dow Jones Global Indexes

Nearly 3,000 companies from 16 countries and 120 industry groups go into the most extensive foreign listings in any U.S. publication. The groupings divide these stocks into nine sectors that reflect large segments of the world economy; these nine sectors are then further subdivided into more specific industries. Countries are being added to the index as the global economy evolves. Over time, it will include every country whose stocks are available to foreign investors. As investor interest in global markets continues to grow, the Dow Jones World Stock Index has become an increasingly crucial measurement of world-wide stock performance.

financials generally" says HSBC James ... ing companies, as well as financial stocks

DOW JONES GLOBAL INDEXES

5:30 p.m., Friday, October 3, 1997

REGION/ COUNTRY	DJ GLOBAL INDEXES, LOCAL CURRENCY	PCT. CHG.	5:30 P.M. INDEX (IN U.S. DOLLARS)	CHG.	PCT. CHG.	12-MO HIGH	12-MO LOW	12-MO CHG.	PCT. CHG.	FROM 12/31	PCT. CHG.
Americas			225.88	+ 1.05	+ 0.47	225.88	162.78	+ 61.52	+ 37.43	+ 52.50	+ 30.28
Canada	196.41	+ 0.52	165.38	+ 1.05	+ 0.64	165.38	125.00	+ 40.39	+ 32.31	+ 29.86	+ 22.03
Mexico	378.41	– 0.20	149.12	[illegible]	[illegible]	[illegible]	[illegible]	[illegible]	[illegible]	[illegible]	[illegible]
Thailand	[illegible]	+ 0.23	60.54	– 0.03	– 0.05	153.18	55.31	– 89.20	– 59.57	– 64.57	– 51.61
Asia/Pacific (ex. Japan)			181.87	– 1.27	– 0.69	213.96	176.35	– 14.56	– 7.41	– 27.11	– 12.97
World (ex. U.S.)			140.12	+ 1.22	+ 0.88	145.41	120.96	+ 11.98	+ 9.35	+ 10.73	+ 8.30
DJ WORLD STOCK INDEX			175.17	+ 1.19	+ 0.68	176.23	143.10	+ 31.03	+ 21.53	+ 26.82	+ 18.08

The Index offers superior measures of stock-market performance by providing investors with two comparative views: geographic and industrial. Investors can assess the political, economic and financial forces affecting the global market and measure how an individual issue has performed against its peers globally, regionally or nationally.

Dow Jones Averages

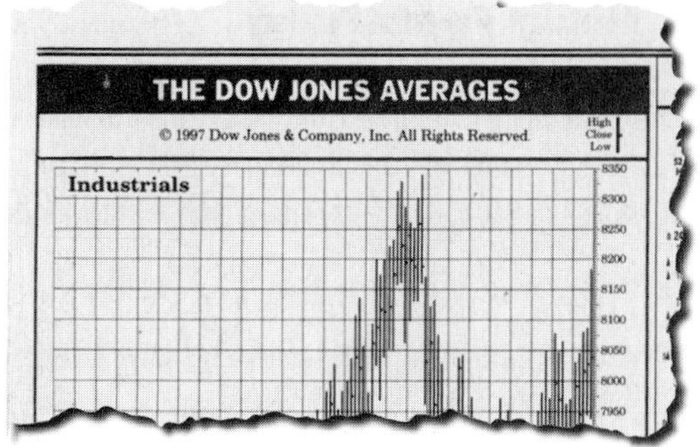

The universal standard barometer that charts the health of the market comes from Dow Jones & Company, the publisher of the Journal. When people ask "How's the market doing?" they usually mean the first of these indicators, the 30 stock Dow Jones Industrial Average. But there are indexes covering 20 transportation company stocks and 15 utility-company stocks, along with a composite index of the 65 stocks in the three indexes. The names of the stocks in each index appear daily next to the respective graph.

The daily graphs of the Dow Jones Averages are fairly self-explanatory. A vertical line, or bar, is drawn for each day. The top of the line represents the high of the day, the bottom the low. The small horizontal cross-bar represents the closing level of the day. Another bar chart below the three Averages' graphs depicts New York Stock Exchange volume for the days corresponding to the ones in the index charts.

The Dow Jones stock averages are price-weighted. This means a high-priced stock has a greater effect on the index than a low-priced one. There are other market indicators that attach weights to prices to give greater significance to stocks with greater market value. Market value is the price of a stock multiplied by the number of its shares outstanding. This system gives greater significance to larger companies. These are called market-weighted indexes.

You'll find the previous day's Dows detailed on page C3, along with other indexes of interest primarily to financial professionals.

Dow Jones Global Industry Groups

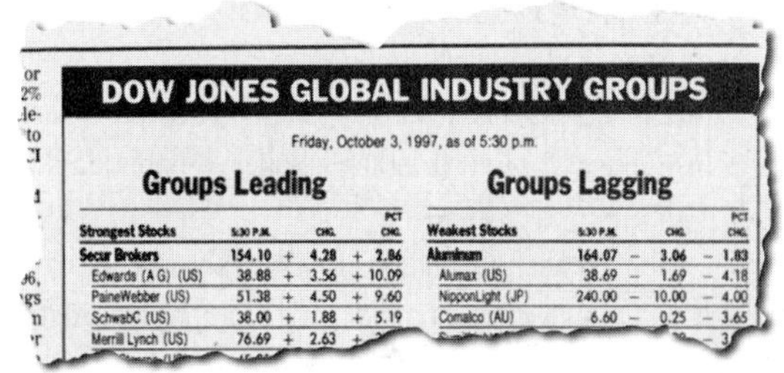

DOW JONES GLOBAL INDUSTRY GROUPS

Friday, October 3, 1997, as of 5:30 p.m.

Groups Leading

Strongest Stocks	5:30 P.M.	CHG.	PCT CHG.
Secur Brokers	154.10	+ 4.28	+ 2.86
Edwards (A G) (US)	38.88	+ 3.56	+ 10.09
PaineWebber (US)	51.38	+ 4.50	+ 9.60
SchwabC (US)	38.00	+ 1.88	+ 5.19
Merrill Lynch (US)	76.69	+ 2.63	+ [illegible]

Groups Lagging

Weakest Stocks	5:30 P.M.	CHG.	PCT CHG.
Aluminum	164.07	− 3.06	− 1.83
Alumax (US)	38.69	− 1.69	− 4.18
NipponLight (JP)	240.00	− 10.00	− 4.00
Comalco (AU)	6.60	− 0.25	− 3.65

The Dow Jones Global Industry Group Table shows at a glance the relative performance of broad economic sectors both day-to-day and over the long term.

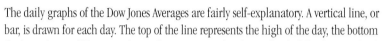

Unlike the Dow Jones Industrial Average, the World Stock Index World Industry Group Performance Table is market-weighted, not price-weighted – companies with large total-market values have the most effect on the movement of the indexes. They are all calculated based on a common value of 100 on June 30, 1982, so that their relative performance can be determined at a glance. Every day, the Journal reports on how each industry group fared compared with its close on the previous day, and the groups with the best and worst performance are displayed at the top of the Industry Group box along with the strongest and weakest stocks in each group.

Investment Funds

In many ways and for many reasons, the 1990s have seen America's first experiment with popular capitalism. In other words, investing is no longer just for the wealthy – it's become part of all our lives. One reason and result of this development is the explosive growth of investment funds, in which large and small investors pool their money and place it in the care of professional money managers. There are now thousands of funds with scores of investment objectives: growth funds, income funds, foreign-stock funds, bond funds...you get the picture. And you get all the data about all of them in the Journal. The best-known and most widely held, open-ended mutual and money-market funds are tracked daily. These funds continuously issue new shares if people wish to buy them back at prices based on the net asset value (NAV), or the value of the fund's portfolio less liabilities, divided by the number of shares outstanding. Unlike open-ended funds, closed-end funds offer a fixed number of shares–influenced by supply and demand but usually at prices that are very close to the net asset value. They trade on exchanges or over the counter; a table of closed-end funds is published on Mondays in the Journal. Each listing includes the closing NAV and exchange or over-the-counter price, the percentage difference and the market return for the latest 52-week period.

Mutual Funds

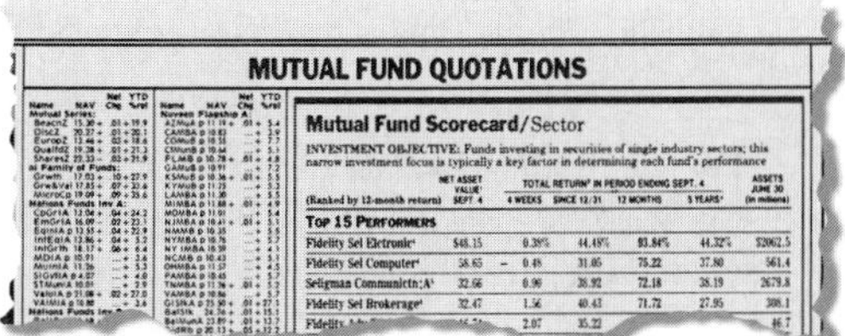

MUTUAL FUND QUOTATIONS

Mutual Fund Scorecard/Sector

INVESTMENT OBJECTIVE: Funds investing in securities of single industry sectors; this narrow investment focus is typically a key factor in determining each fund's performance

(Ranked by 12-month return)	NET ASSET VALUE SEPT. 4	TOTAL RETURN IN PERIOD ENDING SEPT. 4: 4 WEEKS	SINCE 12/31	12 MONTHS	5 YEARS	ASSETS JUNE 30 (in millions)
TOP 15 PERFORMERS						
Fidelity Sel Elctronic	$48.15	0.39%	44.45%	93.84%	44.32%	$2062.5
Fidelity Sel Computer	58.65	− 0.48	31.05	75.22	37.80	561.4
Seligman Communictn;A	32.66	0.96	38.92	72.18	38.19	2679.8
Fidelity Sel Brokerage	32.47	1.56	40.43	71.72	27.95	308.1
Fidelity [illegible]	[illegible]	2.07	35.22	[illegible]	[illegible]	46.7

On Mondays through Thursdays, you'll find the fund's net asset value (NAV, or value per share); change from the previous day; and change for the year to date for every fund with assets of $25 million or more, or 1,000+ shareholders.

Mutual Funds–Friday

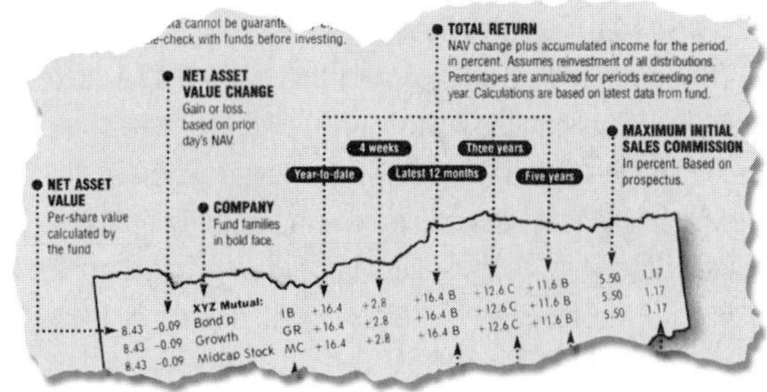

On Fridays, the listings expand to include the fund's investment objectives; total return over a month, year, three years and five years; its maximum load, or initial commission; and its annual expenses. In addition, each fund is ranked from A to E to compare its performance to other funds with the same objectives.

A charge, or sales commission of up to 8.5%, may apply to the mutual fund purchase price. Also, some funds may charge an exit fee when an investor redeems the shares. Other funds are sold on a no-load (NL) basis, i.e., without any sales commission. No-load shares usually are purchased directly from the fund, not through a broker. But these funds, like all others, usually charge an asset-management fee for investment advice or pay a fee to the outside firm that makes investment decisions for the fund. This annual fee is based on the average assets of the fund and typically averages less than 1% but can be higher.

Money Market Mutual Funds

Another type of open-ended fund is the money-market fund, which is limited to short-term instruments, such as CDs in large banks, commercial paper issued by major corporations and Treasury bills.

These money-market instruments often require a minimum investment of $100,000, but money-market funds allow smaller investors to participate in the higher interest rates offered by these instruments for a considerably smaller sum. But unlike bank deposits, money-market funds usually aren't guaranteed by the federal government.

Money-market fund quotes appear weekly on Thursdays. Each listing shows the average maturity for the portfolio in days, the average annual yield as a percentage based on the market for the past seven days, and total assets in millions of dollars.

Foreign Currency

Whether you're working at a company that does business overseas, or traveling to foreign shores, the foreign currency tables are the place to look for exchange rates, foreign currency futures prices and currency cross-rate tables that make it easy to convert one foreign currency into another.

Currency Trading Table

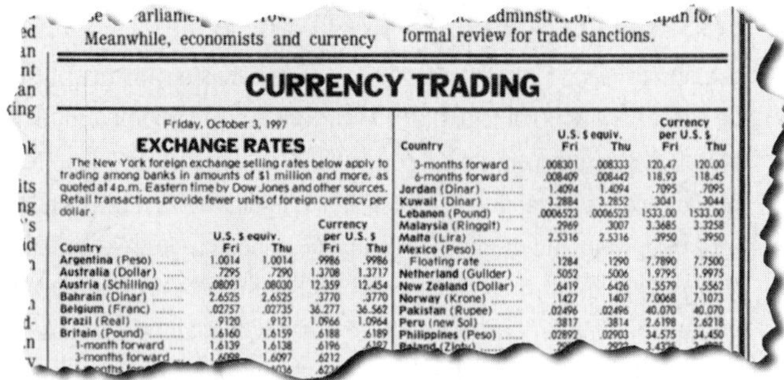

Meanwhile, economists and currency

formal review for trade sanctions.

CURRENCY TRADING

Friday, October 3, 1997

EXCHANGE RATES

The New York foreign exchange selling rates below apply to trading among banks in amounts of $1 million and more, as quoted at 4 p.m. Eastern time by Dow Jones and other sources. Retail transactions provide fewer units of foreign currency per dollar.

Country	U.S. $ equiv. Fri	U.S. $ equiv. Thu	Currency per U.S. $ Fri	Currency per U.S. $ Thu
Argentina (Peso)	1.0014	1.0014	.9986	.9986
Australia (Dollar)	.7295	.7290	1.3708	1.3717
Austria (Schilling)	.08091	.08030	12.359	12.454
Bahrain (Dinar)	2.6525	2.6525	.3770	.3770
Belgium (Franc)	.02757	.02735	36.277	36.562
Brazil (Real)	.9120	.9121	1.0966	1.0964
Britain (Pound)	1.6160	1.6159	.6188	.6189
1-month forward	1.6139	1.6138	.6196	[illegible]
3-months forward	[illegible]	1.6097	.6212	[illegible]
3-months forward	.008301	.008333	120.47	120.00
6-months forward	.008409	.008442	118.93	118.45
Jordan (Dinar)	1.4094	1.4094	.7095	.7095
Kuwait (Dinar)	3.2884	3.2852	.3041	.3044
Lebanon (Pound)	.0006523	.0006523	1533.00	1533.00
Malaysia (Ringgit)	.2969	.3007	3.3685	3.3258
Malta (Lira)	2.5316	2.5316	.3950	.3950
Mexico (Peso)				
Floating rate	.1284	.1290	7.7890	7.7500
Netherland (Guilder)	.5052	.5006	1.9795	1.9975
New Zealand (Dollar)	.6419	.6426	1.5579	1.5562
Norway (Krone)	.1427	.1407	7.0068	7.1073
Pakistan (Rupee)	.02496	.02496	40.070	40.070
Peru (new Sol)	.3817	.3814	2.6198	2.6218
Philippines (Peso)	.02892	.02903	34.575	34.450

Gives the exchange rates prevailing at 3 p.m. Eastern time, expressed both as dollars per unit of foreign currency and as units of foreign currency per dollar. The former is the U.S. way of looking at things, the latter is the foreign way. Readers may encounter both ways. These rates apply to transactions among banks in amounts of $1 million or more. Rates for smaller transactions will be less favorable. Banks usually offer individuals better rates than commercial establishments do. Some currencies, such as the Belgian franc, have different rates for financial or commercial transactions. For some major currencies, such as the British pound and the German mark, rates also are given for future delivery.

At the bottom of the table is the conversion rate for the SDR, or Special Drawing Right, which is a reserve asset created by the International Monetary Fund for settlements among central banks. It also is used as a unit of account in international bond markets and by commercial banks. Based 42% on the U.S. dollar, 19% on the German mark and 13% each on the British pound, French franc and Japanese yen, the SDR's value fluctuates less than any single component currency. Also in the Journal every day is a currency cross-rates table that makes it more convenient to translate one foreign currency directly into another.

Exchange rates between important currencies used to be fixed, with sudden large changes forced only by the pressures of crises. Eventually the pressures became too great and too persistent, so rates now vary daily among major currencies. The system is known as floating exchange rates.

Since most international trade involves a delay between setting the price of a transaction and getting paid, this means at least one of the parties to such a transaction has a risk of losing money because the exchange rate may vary before payment is made.

This risk can be minimized by purchasing or selling foreign currency for future delivery at a specified exchange rate. For large amounts, this can be accomplished through banks in what is called the forward market; the 30-, 60-, 90- and 180-day rates in the Foreign Exchange table reflect this. Some foreign currencies also can be traded in futures markets, in smaller amounts; these are quoted daily (see "Futures above). There are also foreign currency options and futures options. The futures exchanges are increasingly providing a kind of secondary market in foreign exchange.

Money and Credit Markets *In other words (& very broadly): bonds, interest rates and the money supply.*

This can be a complicated world of secondary markets and over-the-counter trading among securities dealers, so let's just say this: This is the safest realm of investing, where the returns are lower but the security lets you sleep at night. Bonds and other instruments issued or backed by federal, state or local governments are considered virtually risk-free.

All types are covered thoroughly in our tables, with data that includes issue date, maturity, yield and asked/bid prices. We also include complete information on corporate bonds traded on the New York Stock Exchange and four major foreign-government bond markets.

Allied to these data is our information on the supply of and demand for money. The Federal Reserve Report, which we publish every Friday, gives important indicators for both, as do our daily Money Rates box (which lists the current prime lending rate) and the weekly Key Interest Rates table and Consumer Savings Rates List, which shows the rates paid by 100 banks in 10 large cities.

Treasury Issues

The Treasury issues instruments, due after various lengths of time, known as maturities. The shortest regularly issued maturities, three or six months, take the form of Treasury bills. These are issued every Monday in minimum denominations of $10,000 and in increments of $5,000 above the minimum. Investors bid for them at a discount, by offering, say $97.50 for every $100 of bills. At maturity, the investors will receive $100 for every $97.50 they paid. Yields are expressed on an annual basis.

Similar bills due in one year are sold monthly. The Treasury also issues cash-management bills on an irregular basis, generally for short periods, such as a few days. Treasury issues maturing in between one and 10 years are called notes. Those maturing in more than 10 years are called bonds. The process of selling these to the public takes place in the primary market, with the proceeds going to the issuer.

Secondary markets are made by securities dealers in all maturities of Treasury issues. In the secondary market, the prices of bills, notes and bonds fluctuate according to changes in interest rates. But, in one of the more confusing aspects of financial markets, the prices fluctuate inversely to the interest rates. Thus, when interest rates rise, bond prices go down, and when they fall, bond prices go up.

The rationale for this is as follows. Say the Treasury issues some 30-year bonds with an interest rate of 10%, or $10 of every $100. In time, interest rates may rise to 12%. Then, no one in the secondary market will want to pay full price for bonds paying 10% interest when they can buy new ones at 12%. However, they might be willing to pay less than $100 for every $100 of the old bonds. Tables and calculators exist which show the exact price to pay so the yield to maturity on a 10% bond is 12%, taking into account the time left to maturity when the purchase is made.

Similarly, when interest rates fall, bond prices will rise because sellers will hold out for a higher price to compensate for the higher-than-market interest paid on their holdings.

These changing prices are the basis of the Journal's tables for bonds and other debt securities. These issues are traded over the counter by securities dealers.

For bonds and notes, the price quotations are given per hundred dollars of face value.

Bonds issued some time ago may mature sooner than recently issued notes; this list is chronological. Some newer issues, designated "p", are exempt from withholding tax if held by nonresident aliens.

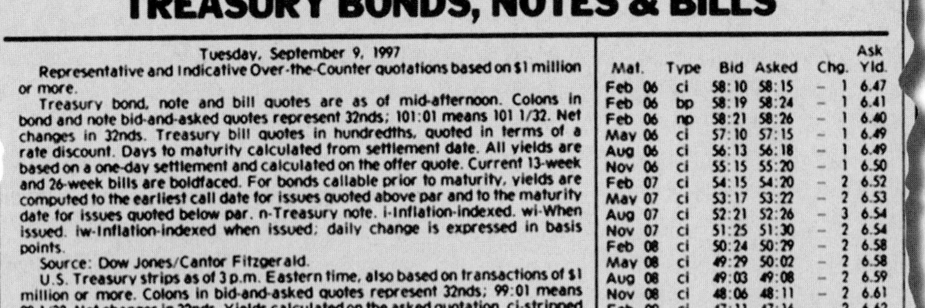

TREASURY BONDS, NOTES & BILLS

Tuesday, September 9, 1997

Representative and Indicative Over-the-Counter quotations based on $1 million or more.

Treasury bond, note and bill quotes are as of mid-afternoon. Colons in bond and note bid-and-asked quotes represent 32nds; 101:01 means 101 1/32. Net changes in 32nds. Treasury bill quotes in hundredths, quoted in terms of a rate discount. Days to maturity calculated from settlement date. All yields are based on a one-day settlement and calculated on the offer quote. Current 13-week and 26-week bills are boldfaced. For bonds callable prior to maturity, yields are computed to the earliest call date for issues quoted above par and to the maturity date for issues quoted below par. n-Treasury note. i-Inflation-indexed. wi-When issued. iw-Inflation-indexed when issued; daily change is expressed in basis points.

Source: Dow Jones/Cantor Fitzgerald.

U.S. Treasury strips as of 3 p.m. Eastern time, also based on transactions of $1 million or more. Colons in bid-and-asked quotes represent 32nds; 99:01 means 99 1/32. Net changes in 32nds. Yields calculated on the asked quotation. ci-stripped coupon interest. bp-Treasury bond, stripped principal. np-Treasury note, stripped principal. For bonds callable prior to maturity, yields are computed to the earliest call date for issues quoted above par and to the maturity date for issues below par.

Source: Bear, Stearns & Co. via Street Software Technology Inc.

GOVT. BONDS & NOTES

Rate	Maturity Mo/Yr	Bid	Asked	Chg.	Ask Yld.
5½	Sep 97n	99:31	100:01	....	4.81
5¾	Sep 97n	99:31	100:01	....	5.05
8¾	Oct 97n	100:09	100:11	....	4.96
5⅝	Oct 97n	100:00	100:02	....	5.07
5¾	Oct 97n	100:00	100:02	....	5.19
[illegible]	Nov 97n	100:09	[illegible]	....	5.31

Rate	Maturity Mo./Yr.	Bid	Asked	Chg.	Ask Yld.
5⅝	Feb 04n	97:27	97:29	+ 1	6.27
7¼	May 04n	105:02	105:04	+ 1	6.30
12⅜	May 04	132:16	132:22	+ 2	6.30
7¼	Aug 04n	105:04	105:06	+ 2	6.31
13¾	Aug 04	140:31	141:05	+ 2	6.32
7⅞	Nov 04n	108:23	108:25	[illegible]	[illegible]
11⅝	Nov 04	129:30	[illegible]	[illegible]	[illegible]

Mat.	Type	Bid	Asked	Chg.	Ask Yld.
Feb 06	ci	58:10	58:15	– 1	6.47
Feb 06	bp	58:19	58:24	– 1	6.41
Feb 06	np	58:21	58:26	– 1	6.40
May 06	ci	57:10	57:15	– 1	6.49
Aug 06	ci	56:13	56:18	– 1	6.49
Nov 06	ci	55:15	55:20	– 1	6.50
Feb 07	ci	54:15	54:20	– 2	6.52
May 07	ci	53:17	53:22	– 2	6.53
Aug 07	ci	52:21	52:26	– 3	6.54
Nov 07	ci	51:25	51:30	– 2	6.54
Feb 08	ci	50:24	50:29	– 2	6.58
May 08	ci	49:29	50:02	– 2	6.58
Aug 08	ci	49:03	49:08	– 2	6.59
Nov 08	ci	48:06	48:11	– 2	6.61
Feb 09	ci	47:11	47:16	– 2	6.62
May 09	ci	46:17	46:22	– 2	6.63
Aug 09	ci	45:24	45:29	– 2	6.63
Nov 09	ci	44:30	45:03	– 2	6.65
Nov 09	bp	44:17	44:22	– 1	6.72
Feb 10	ci	44:05	44:10	– 2	6.66
May 10	ci	43:12	43:17	– 2	6.67
Aug 10	ci	42:20	42:25	– 2	6.68
Nov 10	ci	41:28	42:01	– 2	6.69
Feb 11	ci	41:06	41:11	....	6.69
May 11	ci	40:14	40:19	– 2	6.70
Aug 11	ci	39:23	39:29	– 2	6.71
Nov 11	ci	39:01	39:06	– 2	6.72
[illegible]	[illegible]	[illegible]	38:17	– 2	6.72

Month and Year of the security "n" designates notes; the rest are bonds.

The original interest rate.

Mid-afternoon bid price at which dealers were willing to buy the issue that day

Asked, or dealer, selling price

Changes in the bid price from the day before

Yield, or effective return on the investment. This is a calculation that takes into account the original interest rate, the current asked price and the amount of time left to maturity.

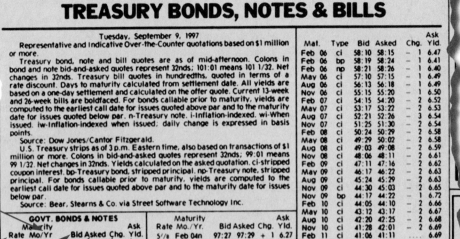

In the bond market, a price of 100 is called par and each one-hundredth of par is called a point. Normally, the minimum price fluctuation is 1/32nd of a point. To avoid repeating the figure 32 all the time, and to save space, there is a convention in the bond market that figures after a decimal point in a price represent 32nds. Thus, a quotation of 90.16 means 90 and 16/32nds or 90½.

In the Treasury bill section of this table, however, the decimal takes on its customary meaning: 16.50 means 16µ. Maturities are given as months and dates; 5-28 means May 28. The quotations are for discounts, as explained above. The yield, as for longer-term issues, represents the effective total return and is used for comparison with other investments.

Corporate Bonds, There are three main types:

- Mortgage bonds: secured by real property, such as buildings
- Debentures: backed by a company's earning power rather than by specific hard assets
- Convertible bonds:can be exchanged for shares of the issue's stock.

Prices of a large number of corporate bonds are given in a table called New York Exchange Bonds. This covers bonds traded on the New York Stock Exchange, where only a small proportion of trading in these bonds takes place. Most bond trading is over the counter among securities dealers.

At the top of this table, there are data on the year's volume to date and a market diary. There is also a set of Dow Jones Averages for bond prices. The main index covers 20 bonds. There are component indexes for the 10 industrials and the 10 utilities. The New York table is followed by a short listing of bonds traded on the American Stock Exchange.

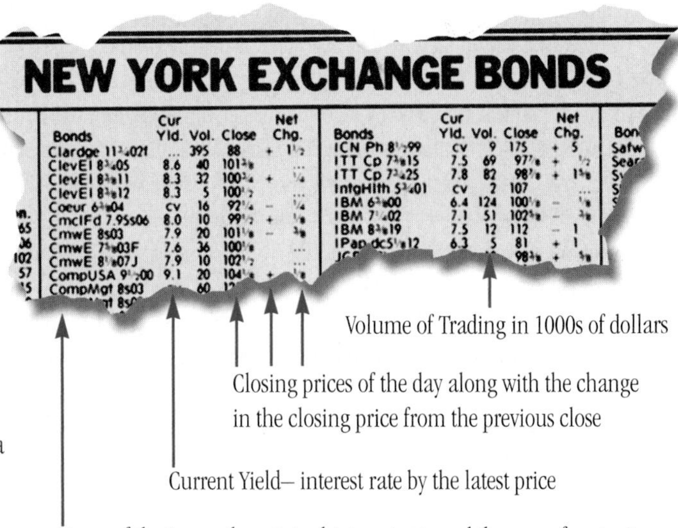

NEW YORK EXCHANGE BONDS

Bonds	Cur Yld.	Vol.	Close	Net Chg.
Clardge 11¾021	...	395	88	+ 1½
ClevEl 8¾05	8.6	40	101⅜	...
ClevEl 8¾s11	8.3	32	100¾	+ ¼
ClevEl 8¾s12	8.3	5	100½	...
Coeur 6⅜s04	cv	16	92¼	– ¼
CmclFd 7.95s06	8.0	10	99½	+ ⅛
CmwE 8s03	7.9	20	101⅛	– ⅜
CmwE 7⅝s03F	7.6	36	100⅛	...
CmwE 8⅛s07J	7.9	10	102½	...
CompUSA 9½00	9.1	20	104⅛	+ ⅛
CompMgt 8s03	[illegible]	60	[illegible]	[illegible]

Bonds	Cur Yld.	Vol.	Close	Net Chg.
ICN Ph 8½99	cv	9	175	+ 5
ITT Cp 7⅜s15	7.5	69	97⅞	+ ½
ITT Cp 7¾25	7.8	82	98⅞	+ 1⅜
IntgHlth 5¾01	cv	2	107	...
IBM 6⅜s00	6.4	124	100⅛	– ⅛
IBM 7¼02	7.1	51	102⅜	– ⅜
IBM 8⅜s19	7.5	12	112	– 1
IPap dc5⅛s12	6.3	5	81	+ 1
[illegible]	[illegible]	[illegible]	98⅜	+ ⅛

Volume of Trading in 1000s of dollars

Closing prices of the day along with the change in the closing price from the previous close

Current Yield– interest rate by the latest price

Name of the issuer, the original interest rate and the year of maturity, with an "s" where needed for ease of pronunciation.
Thus, 9s04 means "nines of oh-four," or 9% bonds due in 2004.

Other Government Bonds

Quotations for a selection of Government, Agency and miscellaneous securities are given in a separate table (at right), which is displayed much like Treasury bonds. Indexes measuring the performance of GNMA and FNMA issues are also included daily in the Bond Market Data Bank, as are prices and yields on representative individual mortgage-backed securities. Next to the Mortgage-Backed Securities list in the Data Bank, a small table lists the differential in yield between mortgage-backed securities and Treasury issues of comparable maturity.

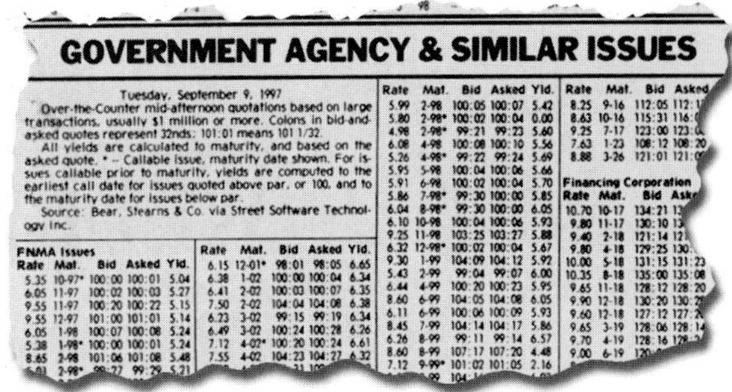

GOVERNMENT AGENCY & SIMILAR ISSUES

Tuesday, September 9, 1997

Over-the-Counter mid-afternoon quotations based on large transactions, usually $1 million or more. Colons in bid-and-asked quotes represent 32nds; 101:01 means 101 1/32.

All yields are calculated to maturity, and based on the asked quote. * – Callable issue, maturity date shown. For issues callable prior to maturity, yields are computed to the earliest call date for issues quoted above par, or 100, and to the maturity date for issues below par.

Source: Bear, Stearns & Co. via Street Software Technology Inc.

FNMA Issues

Rate	Mat.	Bid	Asked	Yld.
5.35	10-97*	100:00	100:01	5.04
6.05	11-97	100:02	100:03	5.27
9.55	11-97	100:20	100:22	5.15
9.55	12-97	101:00	101:01	5.14
6.05	1-98	100:07	100:08	5.24
5.38	1-98*	100:00	100:01	5.24
8.65	2-98	101:06	101:08	5.48
6.01	2-98*	99:27	99:29	5.21

Rate	Mat.	Bid	Asked	Yld.
6.15	12-01*	98:01	98:05	6.65
6.38	1-02	100:00	100:04	6.34
6.41	2-02	100:03	100:07	6.35
7.50	2-02	104:04	104:08	6.38
6.23	3-02	99:15	99:19	6.34
6.49	3-02	100:24	100:28	6.26
7.12	4-02*	100:20	100:24	6.61
7.55	4-02	104:23	104:27	6.32

Rate	Mat.	Bid	Asked	Yld.
5.99	2-98	100:05	100:07	5.42
5.80	2-98*	100:02	100:04	0.00
4.98	2-98*	99:21	99:23	5.60
6.08	4-98	100:08	100:10	5.56
5.26	4-98*	99:22	99:24	5.69
5.95	5-98	100:04	100:06	5.66
5.91	6-98	100:02	100:04	5.70
5.86	7-98*	99:30	100:00	5.85
6.04	8-98*	99:30	100:00	6.05
6.10	10-98	100:04	100:06	5.93
9.25	11-98	103:25	103:27	5.88
6.32	12-98*	100:02	100:04	5.67
9.30	1-99	104:09	104:12	5.92
5.43	2-99	99:04	99:07	6.00
6.44	4-99	100:20	100:23	5.95
8.60	6-99	104:05	104:08	6.05
6.11	6-99	100:06	100:09	5.93
8.45	7-99	104:14	104:17	5.86
6.26	8-99	99:11	99:14	6.57
8.60	8-99	107:17	107:20	4.48
7.12	9-99*	101:02	101:05	2.16

Rate	Mat.	Bid	Asked
8.25	9-16	112:05	[illegible]
8.63	10-16	115:31	[illegible]
9.25	7-17	123:00	[illegible]
7.63	1-23	108:12	108:20
8.88	3-26	121:01	[illegible]

Financing Corporation

Rate	Mat.	Bid	Asked
10.70	10-17	134:21	[illegible]
9.80	11-17	130:10	[illegible]
9.40	2-18	121:14	[illegible]
9.80	4-18	129:25	[illegible]
10.00	5-18	131:15	131:23
10.35	8-18	135:00	135:08
9.65	11-18	128:12	128:20
9.90	12-18	130:20	[illegible]
9.60	12-18	127:12	[illegible]
9.65	3-19	128:06	128:14
9.70	4-19	128:16	[illegible]
9.00	6-19	[illegible]	[illegible]

Municipal Bonds

Besides the U.S. government and its agencies, bonds may be issued by a variety of other government bodies that are lumped together under the heading "municipal," even though they include states, highway authorities and other noncity entities, as well as cities and their agencies. Usually, interest on these issues is exempt from income tax by the Federal government and by the state (and sometimes the city) in which the borrower is located. Because of this privilege, the issuer can apply a lower rate of interest, and investors have to consider the after-tax yield, based on their own income-tax situation, when comparing yields on these with those of other bonds. These bonds are also known as tax-exempts. The Journal prints a list of some of the most actively traded tax-exempts each day in the Bond Market Data Bank. The list is supplied by "The Bond Buyer," a New York trade publication.

Bond Market Data Bank

In addition to these market listings of individual bond prices, a further listing of the prices of 20 representative, actively traded corporate bonds is compiled by First Boston Corp. and appears daily in the Bond Market Data Bank. The Data Bank also lists the performance of several other indexes made up of various categories of corporate and convertible bond issues. The Merrill Lynch Corporate Master index, for example, represents a portfolio of about 4,400 nonconvertible bonds with remaining maturities of at least one year, a minimum of $1 million outstanding, and an average credit rating of A-1.

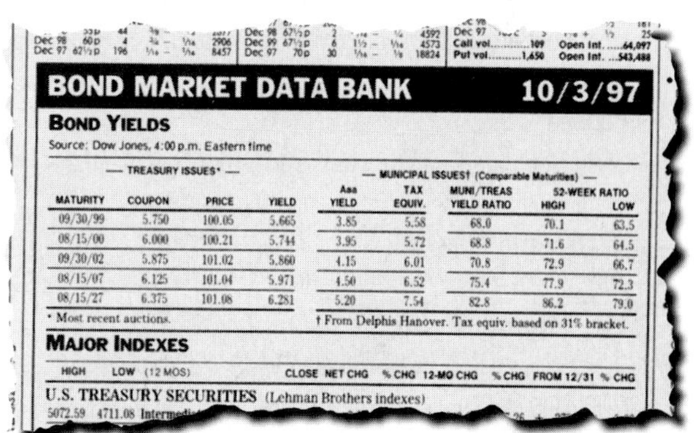

BOND MARKET DATA BANK 10/3/97

BOND YIELDS

Source: Dow Jones, 4:00 p.m. Eastern time

— TREASURY ISSUES* —				— MUNICIPAL ISSUES† (Comparable Maturities) —				
MATURITY	COUPON	PRICE	YIELD	Aaa YIELD	TAX EQUIV.	MUNI/TREAS YIELD RATIO	52-WEEK RATIO HIGH	LOW
09/30/99	5.750	100.05	5.665	3.85	5.58	68.0	70.1	63.5
08/15/00	6.000	100.21	5.744	3.95	5.72	68.8	71.6	64.5
09/30/02	5.875	101.02	5.860	4.15	6.01	70.8	72.9	66.7
08/15/07	6.125	101.04	5.971	4.50	6.52	75.4	77.9	72.3
08/15/27	6.375	101.08	6.281	5.20	7.54	82.8	86.2	79.0

* Most recent auctions.

† From Delphis Hanover. Tax equiv. based on 31% bracket.

MAJOR INDEXES

HIGH	LOW (12 MOS)		CLOSE	NET CHG	% CHG	12-MO CHG	% CHG	FROM 12/31	% CHG

U.S. TREASURY SECURITIES (Lehman Brothers indexes)

5072.59 4711.08 Interm...

The Data Bank also lists bond prices and yields from four major foreign-government bond markets. All yields are semiannual, and compounded to maturity, to allow investors to make comparisons with domestic bonds. The Total Rates of Return box in the Data Bank provides an overall performance measure of the world's major bond markets.

Federal Reserve Report

One of the main influences on interest rates and the money markets is the supply of and demand for money. The Federal Reserve Report, published every Friday, gives important indicators of both. The level of commercial and industrial loans, for example, is an indicator of the demand for credit. In addition to the weekly report, a monthly chart shows the recent performance of the money supply indicators, compared with the Federal Reserve's targets. If one or more of the indicators is persistently outside the target range, the Fed may adjust its monetary policy and bring about a different level of interest rates.

Interest Rates

The Journal prints several features that track the levels of key interest rates affecting business and consumers. The daily Money Rates box lists the current prime lending rate as well as current yields and rates on a variety of short-term investments and loans. The weekly Key Interest Rates table is put together by the Federal Reserve Board and concentrates on returns for treasury issues. A weekly Consumer Savings Rates List shows the rates paid by 100 banks in 10 large metropolitan areas. Finally, on Wednesdays, the Banxquote Online deposits listings summarize rates paid on bank certificates of deposit.

THE WALL STREET JOURNAL.

WEEKEND JOURNAL.

All the Reasons You Work So Hard

It's Friday. The Wall Street Journal kicks off its shoes, and turns its attention to the world beyond Mondays-to-Fridays, 9-to-5. Every Friday, Journal subscribers smooth the transition from fast-paced to set-your-own speed with Weekend Journal, a regular section that celebrates the proposition that men and women do not thrive on work alone. Look inside, and you'll find great ideas on how to spend your well-earned time and money. If it's in your weekend, it's in Weekend Journal.

Inside Weekend Journal

Futures & Options

Diversions and Excursions. Weekly alerts on upcoming festivals, concerts, performances and gatherings. Previews of exceptional events throughout the U.S.

Travel

Weekend Journal's Travel page alerts you to the trends in airfares, critically examines vacation resorts and accommodations, from off-beat to the lap of luxury.

The Home Front

The Home Front page extols virtues (and vices) in personal real estate, offering one-of-a kind properties, valuable insight on the recoverable costs of improvements – and weekly data that reveals where prices are headed in communities across the country, courtesy of The Dow Jones Real Estate Index.

Sports

Sports page offers unique perspectives and postscripts on teams, individuals, tournaments, finals. You'll find surprising data and indices to change the way you think about, watch and participate in sporting events.

Entertainment

Weekend Journal looks behind the scenes and at the catalysts driving the entertainment business: performers, moguls, impresarios, marketing tie-ins. Reviews, alerts, cautions and catcalls for the performing arts on the road and in major cities.

Tastings

Tough-but-fair critics will get you to the bottom line: Is it worth $45 a bottle? Is it a find at $11? Are the entrees genuinely superb? Are you better served at home? Savory reports every week.

FUTURES & OPTIONS / Diversions & Excursions: March
The Dow Jones Travel Index
Lowest Round-Trip Airfare Next Week
D20 THE WALL STREET JOURNAL
THE HOME FRONT
PRIVATE PROPERTIES
When Renovations
W8 THE WALL STREET JOURNAL
SPORTS
On Sports / By Frederick C. Klein
ENTERTAINMENT
SHOW BUSINESS
By A. Journal Writer
TASTINGS / By Dorothy J. Gaiter
Cheap Thrills W
A Casual Bottle of Wine
Doesn't Have to Taste
Like a Lab Experiment

ECONOMICS

A Contemporary Introduction

CHAPTER

1 The Art and Science of Economic Analysis

Why are most comic strip characters, such as those in Hagar the Horrible, B.C., Cathy, and Peanuts, missing a finger? And how come Dilbert has no mouth? Why does Japan have twice as many vending machines per capita as does the United States and ten times as many as Europe? In what way are people who pound on vending machines relying on a theory? What's the big idea with economics? These and other questions are answered in this chapter, which introduces the art and science of economic analysis.

You have been reading and hearing about economic issues for years—unemployment, inflation, poverty, the federal budget, tuition, air fares, the stock market, computer prices, gas prices. When the explanations of these issues go into any depth, your eyes may glaze over and you may tune out the same way you do

Visit the McEachern
nteractive Study Center
for this chapter at
p://mcisc.swcollege.com

when a weather forecaster tries to provide an in-depth analysis of high-pressure fronts colliding with moisture carried in from the coast.

What many people fail to realize is that economics is much more lively than the dry accounts offered by the news media. Economics is about making choices, and you make economic choices every day—choices about whether to get a part-time job or focus on your studies, to live in a dorm or off-campus, to take a course in accounting or one in history, to pack a lunch or buy a Big Mac. You already know much more about economics than you realize. You bring to the subject a rich personal experience, an experience that we will tap throughout the book, to reinforce your understanding of the basic ideas. Topics discussed in this chapter include:

- The economic problem
- Marginal analysis
- Rational self-interest
- Scientific method
- Normative versus positive analysis
- Pitfalls of economic thinking

THE ECONOMIC PROBLEM: SCARCE RESOURCES BUT UNLIMITED WANTS

Would you like a new car, a nicer home, better meals, more free time, a more interesting social life, more spending money, more sleep? Who wouldn't? But even if you can satisfy some of these desires, others will pop up. *The problem is that, although your wants, or desires, are virtually unlimited, the resources available to satisfy these wants are scarce.* A resource is *scarce* when it is not freely available—that is, when its price exceeds zero. Because resources are scarce, you must choose from among your many wants and, whenever you choose, you must forgo satisfying some other wants. The problem of scarce resources but unlimited wants exists to a greater or lesser extent for each of the six billion people around the world. Everybody—taxicab drivers, farmers, brain surgeons, shepherds, students, politicians—faces the problem.

Economics The study of how people use their scarce resources to satisfy their unlimited wants

Economics examines how people use their scarce resources in an attempt to satisfy their unlimited wants. The taxicab driver uses the cab and other scarce resources, such as knowledge of the city, driving skills, and time, to earn income. The income, in turn, can be exchanged for housing, groceries, clothing, trips to Disney World, and thousands of other goods and services that help satisfy some of the driver's unlimited wants.

Let's pick apart the definition of economics, beginning with resources, next examining goods and services, and finally focusing on the heart of the matter: economic choice, which arises from scarcity.

Resources

Resources The inputs, or factors of production, used to produce the goods and services that humans want; they consist of labor, capital, land, and entrepreneurial ability

Labor The physical and mental effort of humans used to produce goods and services

Resources are the inputs, or factors of production, used to produce the goods and services that humans want. *Goods and services are scarce because resources are scarce.* We can divide resources into four general categories: labor, capital, land, and entrepreneurial ability. **Labor** is the broad category of human effort, both physical and mental. It includes the effort of the cab driver and the brain surgeon. Labor itself comes from a more fundamental resource: *time.* Without time we can accomplish nothing. We allocate our time to alternative uses: we can *sell* our time as labor, or we can *spend* our time doing other things such as sleeping, reading, or watching TV.

Capital includes human creations used to produce goods and services. We often distinguish between physical capital and human capital. *Physical capital* consists of factories, machines, tools, buildings, airports, highways, and other manufactured items employed to produce goods and services. Physical capital includes the driver's cab, the surgeon's scalpel, the farmer's tractor, the interstate highway system, and the building where your economics class meets. *Human capital* consists of the knowledge and skill people acquire to enhance their labor productivity, such as the taxi driver's knowledge of the city's streets and the surgeon's knowledge of human biology.

Capital The buildings, equipment, and human skill used to produce goods and services

Land includes not only land in the conventional sense of plots of ground, but all other natural resources—all so-called *gifts of nature,* including bodies of water, trees, oil reserves, minerals, even animals.

Land Plots of ground as well as other natural resources used to produce goods and services

A special kind of human skill called **entrepreneurial ability** is the talent required to dream up a new product or find a better way to produce an existing one. The entrepreneur tries to discover and act on profitable opportunities by hiring resources and assuming the risk of business success or failure. The largest firms in the world today, such as Ford, IBM, and Microsoft, each began as an idea in the mind of an individual entrepreneur.

Entrepreneurial ability Managerial and organizational skills, combined with the willingness to take risks

Resource owners are paid **wages** for their labor, **interest** for the use of their capital, and **rent** for the use of their land. The entrepreneur's effort is rewarded by **profit,** which is the difference between *total revenue* from sales and the *total cost* of the resources employed. The entrepreneur claims what is left over after paying other resource suppliers. Sometimes the entrepreneur suffers a loss. Resource owners are usually paid for the *time* their resources are employed by entrepreneurs. Resource payments therefore have a time dimension, as in a wage of $10 *per hour,* interest of 6 percent *per year,* rent of $600 *per month,* or profit of $10,000 *per year.*

Wages The payment that resource owners receive for their labor

Interest The payment that resource owners receive for the use of their capital

Rent The payment that resource owners receive for the use of their land

Profit The payment resource owners receive for their entrepreneurial ability; the total revenue from sales minus the total cost of resources employed by the entrepreneur

Goods and Services

Resources are combined in a variety of ways to produce goods and services. A farmer, a tractor, fifty acres of land, seeds, and fertilizer produce a good: corn. One hundred musicians, musical instruments, some chairs, a conductor, a musical score, and a music hall combine to produce a service: Beethoven's Fifth Symphony. Corn is a **good** because it is something we can see, feel, and touch; it requires scarce resources to produce; and it is used to satisfy human wants. The book you are now holding, the chair you are sitting in, the clothes you are wearing, and your next meal are all goods. The performance of the Fifth Symphony is a **service** because it is intangible, yet it uses scarce resources to satisfy human wants. Lectures, movies, concerts, phone calls, on-line computer services, piano lessons, dry cleaning, and haircuts are all services.

Good A tangible item that is used to satisfy human wants

Service An activity that is used to satisfy human wants

Because goods and services are produced using scarce resources, they are themselves scarce. A good or service is scarce if the amount people desire exceeds the amount that is available at a zero price. Since we cannot have all the goods and services we would like, we must continually choose among them. We must choose among more pleasant living quarters, better meals, nicer clothes, more reliable transportation, faster computers, and so on. Making choices in a world of **scarcity** means we must pass up some goods and services.

Scarcity When the amount people desire exceeds the amount available at a zero price

A few goods and services seem *free* because the amount freely available (that is, available at a zero price) exceeds the amount people desire. For example, air and seawater often seem free because we can breathe all the air we want and have all the seawater we can haul away. Yet, despite the old saying that "The best things in life are free," most goods and services are scarce, not free, and even those that appear to be free come with strings attached. For example, *clean* air and *clean* seawater have become scarce. *Goods and services that are truly free are not the subject matter of economics. Without scarcity, there would be no economic problem and no need for prices.*

Sometimes we mistakenly think of certain goods as free because they involve no apparent cost to us. Those subscription cards that fall out of magazines appear to be free. At least it seems we would have little difficulty rounding up about three thousand of them if necessary! Producing the cards, however, absorbs scarce resources, resources drawn away from competing uses, such as producing higher-quality magazines. You may have heard the expression "There is no such thing as a free lunch." There is no free lunch because all goods and services involve a cost to someone. The lunch may seem free to us, but it draws scarce resources away from the production of other goods and services, and whoever provides a free lunch likely expects something in return. A Russian proverb makes a similar point, but with a bit more bite: "The only place you find free cheese is in a mousetrap." Albert Einstein said, "Sometimes one pays the most for things one gets for nothing."

Economic Decision Makers

There are four types of decision makers, or participants, in the economy: households, firms, governments, and the rest of the world. The interaction between these decision makers determines how an economy's resources are allocated. *Households* play the leading role. As consumers, households demand the goods and services produced. As resource owners, households supply labor, capital, land, and entrepreneurial ability to firms, to governments, and to the rest of the world. *Firms, governments,* and *the rest of the world* demand the resources that households supply and use them to produce and supply the goods and services that households demand. The rest of the world includes foreign households, firms, and governments, which supply resources and products to U.S. markets and demand resources and products from U.S. markets.

Market A set of arrangements through which buyers and sellers carry out exchange at mutually agreeable terms

Markets are the means by which buyers and sellers carry out exchange; markets bring together the two sides of exchange—supply and demand—to determine price and quantity. Markets are often physical places, such as a supermarket, department store, shopping mall, or flea market. But markets also include the mechanisms by which buyers and sellers communicate, such as classified ads, radio and television ads, telephones, bulletin boards, the Internet, and face-to-face bargaining. These market mechanisms provide information about the quantity, quality, and price of products offered for sale. Goods and services are bought and sold in **product markets;** resources are bought and sold in **resource markets.** The most important resource market is the labor, or job, market. Think of your own experience looking for a job, and you get some idea of this market.

Product market A market in which a good or service is bought and sold

Resource market A market in which resources are bought and sold

Microeconomics and Macroeconomics

Although you have made thousands of economic choices, you probably have seldom thought about your own economic behavior. For example, why did you choose to spend your scarce resource—*time*—reading this book right now rather than doing something else?

Microeconomics The study of the economic behavior in particular markets, such as that for computers or for unskilled labor

Microeconomics is the study of your economic behavior and the economic behavior of others who make choices about such matters as what to buy and what to sell, how much to work and how much to play, how much to borrow and how much to save. Microeconomics examines the factors that influence individual economic choices and how the choices of various decision makers are coordinated by markets. For example, microeconomics explains how price and output are determined in individual markets, such as that for breakfast cereal, for sports equipment, or for Beanie Babies.

You have probably given little thought to the factors that influence your own economic choices. You have likely given even less thought to how your choices link up with those made by hundreds of millions of others in the U.S. economy to determine economy-wide sums such as total production, employment, and economic growth. **Macroeconomics** studies the performance of the economy as a whole. Whereas microeconomics studies the individual pieces of the economic puzzle, as reflected in particular markets, macroeconomics puts all the pieces together to focus on the big picture.

Macroeconomics The study of the economic behavior of entire economies

THE ART OF ECONOMIC ANALYSIS

An economy results from the choices that millions of individuals make in attempting to satisfy their unlimited wants. Because these choices lie at the very heart of the economic problem—coping with scarce resources but unlimited wants—they deserve a closer look. Developing an understanding of the forces that shape economic choice is the first step toward mastering the art of economic analysis.

Rational Self-Interest

A key economic assumption is that individuals, in making choices, rationally select alternatives they perceive to be in their best interests. By *rational,* economists mean simply that people try to make the best choices they can, given the available information. People may not know with certainty which alternative will turn out to be the best. They simply select the alternatives they *expect* will yield them the most satisfaction and happiness. *In general, rational self-interest means that individuals try to minimize the expected cost of achieving a given benefit or maximize the expected benefit achieved with a given cost.*

Rational self-interest should not be viewed as blind materialism, pure selfishness, or greed. We all know people who are tuned in to radio station WIIFM (What's In It For Me?). For most of us, however, self-interest often includes the welfare of our family, our friends, and perhaps the poor of the world. Even so, our concern for others is influenced by economic considerations. We may readily volunteer to drive a friend to the airport on Saturday afternoon, but we are less likely to offer a ride if the plane leaves at 6:00 A.M. We are more likely to donate old clothes rather than new ones to organizations such as Goodwill Industries. We tend to give more to our favorite charities if our contributions are tax deductible. TV stations are more likely to donate air time for public-service announcements during the dead of night than during prime time (in fact, 80 percent of such announcements air between 11:00 P.M. and 7:00 A.M.[1]). *The notion of self-interest does not rule out concern for others; it simply means that concern for others is to*

***Net*Bookmark**

To make good use of the Internet, you will need the Adobe Acrobat Reader. It can be downloaded from http://www.adobe.com/prodindex/acrobat/readstep.html. An economic question is: Why does Adobe give the Reader away free?

1 As reported in Sally Goll Beatty, "Media and Agencies Brawl Over Do-Good Advertising," *Wall Street Journal,* 29 September 1997.

some extent influenced by the same economic forces that affect other economic choices. The lower the personal cost of helping others, the more help we offer.

Economic Analysis Is Marginal Analysis

Economic choice usually involves some adjustment to the existing situation, or status quo. The software producer must decide whether to revise a word processing program. The town manager must decide whether to hire another worker for street maintenance. Your favorite jeans are on sale, and you must decide whether to buy another pair. You are wondering whether you should carry an extra course next term. You have just finished dinner and are deciding whether to have dessert.

Marginal Incremental, additional, or extra; used to describe the result of a change in an economic variable

Economic choice is based on a comparison of the *expected marginal cost* and the *expected marginal benefit* of the action under consideration. **Marginal** means incremental, additional, or extra. Marginal refers to a change in an economic variable, a change in the status quo. *You, as a rational decision maker, will change the status quo as long as your expected marginal benefit from the change exceeds your expected marginal cost.* For example, you compare the marginal benefit you expect from eating dessert (the added pleasure and satisfaction) with its marginal cost (the added money, time, and calories). Likewise, the software producer compares the marginal benefit expected from revising a software program (the added sales revenue) with the marginal cost (the added cost of the resources required).

Typically the change under consideration is small, but a marginal choice can involve a major economic adjustment, as in the decision to quit school and get a job. For a firm, a marginal choice might mean introducing a new product, building a plant in Mexico, or even filing for bankruptcy. By focusing on the effect of a marginal adjustment to the status quo, the economist is able to cut the analysis of economic choice down to manageable size. Rather than confront a bewildering economic reality head-on, the economist can begin with a marginal choice and then see how this choice affects a particular market and shapes the economic system as a whole. Incidentally, to the noneconomist, "marginal" usually means relatively inferior, as in "restaurant meals of marginal quality." Forget that meaning for this course and instead think of marginal as meaning incremental, additional, or extra.

Choice Requires Time and Information

Rational choice takes time and requires information, but time and information are scarce and valuable. If you have any doubts about the time and information required to make choices, talk to someone who recently purchased a home, a car, or a personal computer. Talk to a corporate official deciding whether to introduce a new product, build a new factory, or acquire another firm. Or think back to your own experience in selecting a college. You probably talked to friends, relatives, teachers, and guidance counselors. You likely looked at school catalogs and college guides. You may have visited campuses to meet with the admissions staff and anyone else willing to talk. The decision took time and money, and it probably involved aggravation and anxiety.

Because information is costly to acquire, we are often willing to pay others to gather and digest it for us. The existence of markets for college guidebooks, stock analysts, travel agents, real-estate brokers, career counselors, restaurant guidebooks, and *Consumer Reports* magazine indicates our willingness to pay for information that will improve our economic choices. *Rational decision makers will continue to acquire information as long as the expected marginal benefit from the information exceeds its expected marginal cost.*

Normative Versus Positive

Economists usually try to explain how the economy works. Sometimes they concern themselves not with how the economy *does* work but how it *should* work. Compare these two statements: "The U.S. unemployment rate is 5.1 percent" and "The U.S. unemployment rate should be lower." The first is called a **positive economic statement** because it is an assertion about economic reality that can be supported or rejected by reference to the facts. The second is called a **normative economic statement** because it reflects an opinion. And an opinion is merely that—it cannot be shown to be true or false by reference to the facts. Positive statements concern what *is;* normative statements concern what, in someone's opinion, *should be.* Positive statements need not necessarily be true, but they must be subject to verification or refutation by reference to the facts.

Positive economic statement A statement that can be proved or disproved by reference to facts

Normative economic statement A statement that represents an opinion, which cannot be proved or disproved

Theories are expressed as positive statements such as "If the price increases, then the quantity demanded will decrease." Most of the disagreement among economists involves normative debates—for example, the appropriate role of government—rather than statements of positive analysis. To be sure, many theoretical issues remain unresolved, but economists largely agree on most fundamental theoretical principles—that is, about positive economic analysis. For example, in a survey of 464 U.S. economists, only 6.5 percent disagreed with the statement "A ceiling on rents reduces the quantity and quality of housing available." This is a positive statement because it can be shown to be consistent or inconsistent with the evidence. In contrast, there was much less agreement on normative statements such as "The distribution of income in the United States should be more equal." Half the economists surveyed "generally agreed," a quarter "generally disagreed," and a quarter "agreed with provisos."[2]

Normative statements, or value judgments, have a place in policy debates about the proper role of government, provided that statements of fact are distinguished from statements of opinion. It's been said that "You are entitled to your own opinion, but you are not entitled to your own facts."

To review: The art of economic analysis focuses on how individuals use their scarce resources in an attempt to satisfy their unlimited wants. Rational self-interest guides individual choice. Choice involves a comparison of the marginal cost and marginal benefit of alternative actions, a comparison that requires time and information. Care must be taken to distinguish between positive statements, which focus on how the economy works, and normative statements, which represent people's opinions about how the economy should work.

THE SCIENCE OF ECONOMIC ANALYSIS

Economists use scientific analysis to develop theories, or models, that help explain how economic choices are made and how the economy works. An **economic theory,** or **economic model,** is a simplification of economic reality that *is used to make predictions about the real world.* A theory, or model, captures

Economic theory, economic model A simplification of reality used to make predictions about the real world

2 Richard M. Alston, et al., "Is There a Consensus Among Economists in the 1990s?," *American Economic Review* 82 (May 1992): pp. 203–209, Table 1.

the important elements of the problem under study; it need not spell out every detail and interrelation. In fact, the more details a theory contains, the more unwieldy it becomes and the less useful it may be. The world we live in is so complex that we must simplify if we want to make any sense of things. Similarly, comic strips simplify characters; most are missing fingers, and some lack other features (Dilbert has no mouth). You might think of economic theory as a stripped-down version of economic reality.

The Role of Theory

People often don't understand the role of theory. Perhaps you have heard "Oh, that's fine in theory, but in practice it's another matter." The implication is that the theory provides little aid in practical matters. People who say this fail to realize that they are merely substituting their own theory for a theory they either do not believe or do not understand. They are really saying "I have my own theory, which works better."

All of us employ theories, however poorly defined or understood. Someone who pounds on the Pepsi machine that just ate a quarter has a crude theory about how that machine works and what went wrong. One version of that theory might be "The quarter drops through a series of whatchamacallits, but sometimes the quarter gets stuck. *If* I pound on the machine, *then* I can free up the quarter and send it on its way." Evidently this theory is so prevalent that many people continue to pound on machines that fail to perform (a real problem for the vending machine industry and a reason why newer machines are fronted with glass). Yet, if you asked this mad pounder to explain the "theory" about how the machine operates, he or she would look at you as if you were crazy.

The Scientific Method

To study economic problems, economists employ a process of theoretical investigation called the *scientific method,* which consists of four steps.

Step One: Identify the Question and Define Relevant Variables. The first step is to identify the economic question and define the variables that are relevant to the solution. For example, the question might be "What is the relationship between the *price* of Pepsi and the *quantity* of Pepsi purchased." In this case the relevant variables are price and quantity. A **variable** is a measure that can take on different values. The variables of concern become the elements of the theory, so they must be selected with care.

Variable A measure, such as price or quantity, that can take on different possible values

Step Two: Specify Assumptions. The second step is to specify the assumptions under which the theory is to apply. One major category of assumptions is the **other-things-constant assumption**—in Latin, the *ceteris paribus* assumption. The idea is to identify the variables of interest, then to focus exclusively on the relations among them, assuming that nothing else of importance will change—that other things will remain constant. Again, suppose we are interested in how the price of Pepsi influences the amount purchased. To isolate the relation between the price of Pepsi and the quantity purchased, we assume that there are no changes in other relevant variables such as consumer income, the price of Coke, and the average temperature.

Other-things-constant assumption The assumption, when focusing on key economic variables, that other variables remain unchanged

We also make assumptions about how people will behave; these are called **behavioral assumptions.** Perhaps the most fundamental behavioral assumption

Behavioral assumption An assumption that describes the expected behavior of economic decision makers

is rational self-interest. Earlier we assumed that individual decision makers pursue their self-interest rationally and make choices accordingly. Rationality implies that each consumer buys the products expected to maximize his or her level of satisfaction. Rationality also implies that each firm supplies the products expected to maximize that firm's profit. These kinds of assumptions are called behavioral assumptions because they specify how we expect economic decision makers to behave—what makes them tick, so to speak.

Step Three. The third step is to formulate a **hypothesis,** a theory about how key variables relate to each other. For example, one hypothesis holds that *if* the price of Pepsi goes up, other things constant, *then* the quantity purchased will decline. The hypothesis becomes a prediction of what will happen to the quantity purchased if the price goes up. The purpose of this hypothesis, like that of any theory, is to help make predictions about the real world.

Hypothesis A statement about relationships among key variables

Step Four. The validity of a theory is tested by comparing its predictions with evidence. To test a hypothesis, we must focus attention on the variables in question, while at the same time carefully controlling for other effects, which are assumed not to change. The test will lead us either to reject the theory as inconsistent with the evidence or to continue using the theory until a better one comes along. Even though a particular theory may not predict well at all times, it may still predict better than competing theories.

Economists Tell Stories

Despite economists' reliance on the scientific method for developing and evaluating theories, economic analysis is perhaps as much art as science. Formulating a question, isolating the key variables, specifying the assumptions, proposing a theory to answer the question, and devising a way to test the predictions all involve more than simply an understanding of economics and the scientific method.

Carrying out these steps requires good intuition and the imagination of a storyteller. Economists explain their theories by telling stories about how they think the economy works. To tell a compelling story, an economist relies on case studies, anecdotes, parables, and the personal experience of the listener. Throughout this book you will hear stories that bring you closer to the ideas under consideration. The story about the Pepsi machine mentioned earlier is one of those stories that help breathe life into economic theory and help you personalize abstract ideas. As an example, here is a case study about the popularity of vending machines in Japan.

CaseStudy McEachern Interactive

Other Times, Other Places

A Yen for Vending Machines

In recent decades, the rate of unemployment has usually been lower in Japan than in other countries. Because of a declining birth rate, negligible immigration, and an aging population, Japan faces a steady drop in the number of people of working age. Because labor is relatively scarce in Japan, it is relatively costly. To sell products, Japanese retailers rely more on capital, particularly vending machines. Vending machines eliminate the need for a sales clerk.

Speaking of storytelling, could an economist explain the arrangement of letters on your computer's keyboard? One story is told by David Tenenbaum in "Dvorak Keyboards" in *Technology Review* at http://www.techreview.com/articles/july96/trends.html.

Japan has more vending machines per capita than any other country in the world—more than twice as many as the United States and nearly ten times as many as Europe. Also vending machines in Japan are more sophisticated. For example, through a phone link, some vending machines tell vendors when more product or more change is needed, thereby eliminating unnecessary trips to restock the machines. Vending machines that sell cigarettes or alcohol now have a device that can verify a driver's license to check whether the customer is old enough to purchase these products legally. Robo Shop Super 24, a convenience store in Tokyo, is completely automated. After browsing long display cases, customers can make selections by punching product numbers on a keyboard. A bucket whirs around the store, rounding up the selections. Robo Shop is a giant vending machine.

A relatively low unemployment rate is not the only reason that vending machines are so popular in Japan. We already discussed how it is common practice in the United States to shake down vending machines that perform poorly. Such abuse increases the probability that the machines will malfunction in the future, leading to yet more abuse. In Japan, however, vending machines get more respect, in part because they are more sophisticated and more reliable and in part because of Japan's lower crime rate and greater respect for property. (For example, the automobile theft rate in Japan is only one-twentieth the U.S. rate.)

Japanese consumers use vending machines with great frequency. Sales per machine in Japan are double the U.S. level. Vending machines in Japan also sell a wider range of products, including videos, boxer shorts, stuffed animals, whisky, hot pizza, and even dating services. Some vending machines look like robots, which may seem natural in gadget-crazy Japan, where many childhood heroes are robotic characters. Despite the relative abundance of vending machines in Japan, their use is expected to grow even more, spurred on in part by technological innovations and a shrinking labor pool.

Sources: Nicholas Kristof, "In Japan, Chicken Little Lays the Golden Egg," *New York Times*, 30 July 1995; "The Coke Machine is Calling Again On Line 1," *The Nikkei Weekly*, 1 September 1997; "Economic Indicators," *The Economist*, 3 October 1997; and Serv-o-matic International, a worldwide seller of vending machines at http://www.ecity.net/~servom/.

This case study makes two points. First, producers combine resources in a way that conserves, or economizes on, the resource that is more costly, in this case labor. Second, the customs and conventions of the marketplace may differ across countries, and this may result in different types of economic arrangements, such as the more extensive use of vending machines in Japan.

Predicting Average Behavior

The task of an economic theory is to predict the impact of an economic event on economic choices and, in turn, the effect of these choices on particular markets or on the economy as a whole. Does this mean that economists try to predict the behavior of particular consumers or producers? Not necessarily, because any particular individual may behave in an unpredictable way. But the unpredictable actions of numerous individuals tend to cancel one another out, so the *average behavior* of groups can be predicted more accurately. For example, if the federal government cuts personal income taxes, certain households may decide to save the entire tax cut. On average, however, household spending in the economy will increase. Likewise, if Burger King cuts the price of Whoppers, the manager can better predict how much Whopper sales will increase than how a given customer will respond. *The random actions of individuals tend to offset one another, so the average behavior of a large group can be predicted more accurately than the behavior of a particular individual.* Consequently, economists tend to focus on the average, or typical, behavior of people in groups—for example, as average taxpayers or Whopper consumers—rather than on the specific behavior of a particular individual.

Some Pitfalls of Faulty Economic Analysis

Economic analysis, like other forms of scientific inquiry, is subject to common mistakes in reasoning that can lead to faulty conclusions. We will discuss three possible sources of confusion.

The Fallacy That Association Is Causation. Does something like this sound familiar: "The stock market was up today as traders reacted favorably to higher profits reported by Intel"? Although stock market analysts typically claim that millions of stock market transactions spring from a single event, such simplifications are often misleading and even wrong. To assume that event *A* caused event *B* simply because *B* followed *A* in time is to commit the **association-is-causation fallacy,** a common error. The fact that one event precedes another or that the two occur simultaneously does not necessarily mean that one causes the other. Remember: *Association is not necessarily causation.*

Association-is-causation fallacy The incorrect idea that if two variables are associated in time, one must necessarily cause the other

The Fallacy of Composition. Standing up at a football game to get a better view does not work if others stand as well. Arriving early to get in line for concert tickets does not work if many others have the same idea. Selling shares of stock before the price drops will not work if many others also try to sell. These are examples of the **fallacy of composition,** which is an erroneous belief that what is true for the individual or the part is also true for the group or the whole.

Fallacy of composition The incorrect belief that what is true for the individual or part must necessarily be true for the group or whole

The Mistake of Ignoring the Secondary Effects. In many cities, public officials, out of concern about rising rents, have imposed rent controls on apartments. The *primary effect* of this policy, the effect on which policy makers focus, is to keep rents from rising. Over time, however, fewer new apartments get built because the rental business becomes less profitable. Moreover, existing rental units deteriorate because owners have no incentive to pay for maintenance. Thus, the quantity and quality of housing may well decline as a result of what appears to be a reasonable measure to control rents. The policy makers' mistake was to ignore the **secondary effects,** or the *unintended consequences,* of their policy. Economic actions have secondary effects that often turn out to be more important than the primary effects. Secondary effects may develop more slowly and may not be obvious, but good economic analysis takes them into account.

Secondary effects Unintended consequences of economic actions that may develop slowly over time as people react to events

If Economists Are So Smart, Why Aren't They Rich?

Why aren't economists rich? Well, some of them are. Until his death, Taikichiro Mori, of Japan, a former economics professor, was reportedly the richest person in the world. Some economists earn as much as $25,000 per appearance on the lecture circuit. Others earn thousands of dollars a day as consultants. Economists have been appointed to the cabinet positions of Secretaries of Commerce, Defense, Labor, State, and Treasury. Economics is the only social science and the only business discipline for which the prestigious Nobel Prize is awarded, and pronouncements by economists are reported in the media daily.

A columnist for the *New York Times* wrote that business owners "employ economists in large numbers or consult them at high fees, believing that their cracked crystal balls are better than none at all. The press pursues the best-known seers. While many laymen may be annoyed by economists, other social scientists *hate* them—for their fame, Nobel Prizes, and ready access to political power."[3] A recent article in *The Economist,* a widely respected news weekly from London, argues that economic ideas have influenced policy "to a degree that would make other social scientists drool."[4]

Despite its critics, the economics profession thrives because its models usually do a better job of making economic sense out of a confusing world than do alternative approaches. But not all economists are wealthy, nor is personal wealth the objective of the discipline. In a similar vein, not all doctors are healthy; not all carpenters live in perfectly built homes; not all marriage counselors are happily married; and not all child psychologists have well-adjusted children. Still, those who study economics do reap rewards, as discussed in this closing case study, which looks at the link between earnings and the choice of a college major.

The Federal Reserve Bank of Minneapolis asked some Nobel Prize winners how they became interested in economics. Their stories can be found at http://woodrow.mpls.frb.fed.us/pubs/region/98-12/quotes.html.

College Major and Career Earnings

Earlier in the chapter, you learned that economic choice is based on a comparison of expected marginal cost and expected marginal benefit. Surveys show that students go to college because they believe a college diploma is the ticket to better jobs and higher pay. Put another way, for about two-thirds of high school graduates, college's expected marginal benefit seems to exceed its expected marginal cost. We'll discuss the cost of college in the next chapter; here let us focus on the benefits of college, particularly expected earnings.

Among college graduates, all kinds of factors affect earnings, such as general ability, choice of occupation, personal characteristics, college attended, college major, and highest degree earned. Until recently there had been little systematic evidence linking earnings to the college major, but then the National Science Foundation sponsored a huge survey of college graduates to examine that relationship. To isolate the effects of college major on earnings, the survey focused on people in specific age groups who worked full time in 1993 and who had earned a bachelor's degree as their highest degree.

Exhibit 1 shows the average earnings by major in 1993 for men and women aged 35 to 44. As a point of reference, the *median* annual earnings for men was $43,199. (Half earned more than $43,199 and half earned less.) The median earnings for women was $32,155, only 75 percent of the median for men. Among men, the top median pay was the $53,286 earned by engineering majors; that pay was 23 percent above the median for all men aged 35 to 44. Among women, the

3 Leonard Silk, *Economics in Plain English* (New York: Simon and Schuster, 1978), p. 17 (emphasis in original).
4 "The Puzzling Failure of Economics," *The Economist* 23 August 1997, p. 11.

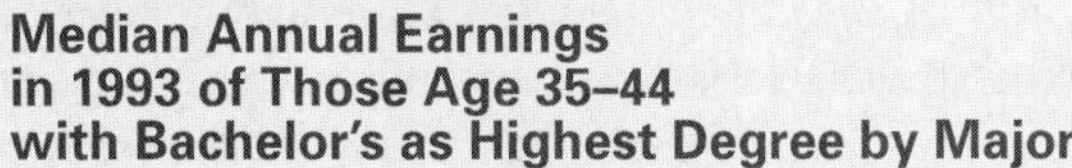

Median Annual Earnings in 1993 of Those Age 35–44 with Bachelor's as Highest Degree by Major

Engineering
Mathematics
Computers
Pharmacy
Physics
Accounting
Economics
Chemistry
Business
Nursing
All Majors
Architecture
Biology
PoliSci./Gov.
Psychology
Criminal Justice
Communications
English
History
Sociology
Agriculture
Health
Education
Linguistics/For. Lang.
Visual & Perf. Arts
Social Work
Home Economics
Philosophy/Religion

Men Women

0 $10,000 $20,000 $30,000 $40,000 $50,000

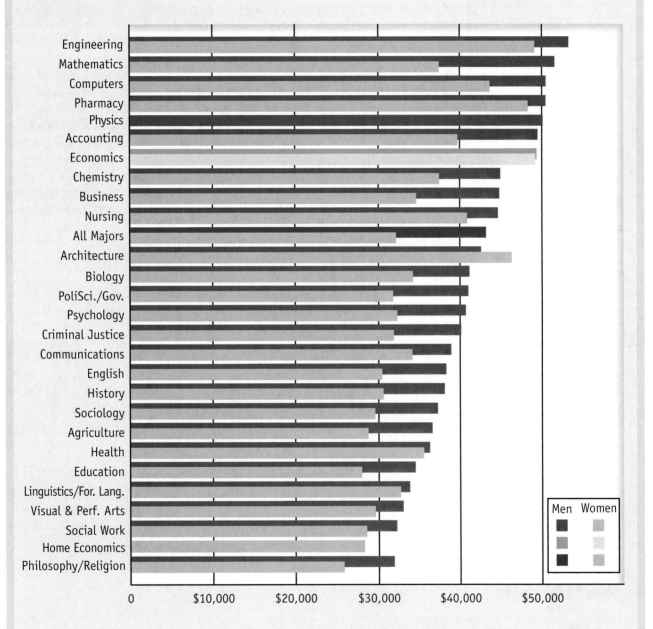

Source: Earnings based on figures reported by Daniel Hacker in "Earnings of College Graduates, 1993," *Monthly Labor Review*, December 1995, pp. 3–17.

top median pay was the $49,170 earned by economics majors; that pay was 53 percent above the median for all surveyed women aged 35 to 44.

Incidentally, men who majored in economics earned a median of $49,377, ranking them seventh among 27 majors and 14.3 percent above the median for all men aged 35 to 44 in the survey. Thus, even though the median pay for women was only 75 percent of the median pay for men, among those who majored in economics, women earned 99.6 percent of the men's salary. We can say that economics majors earned more than most, and they experienced little pay difference based on gender.

Notice that among both men and women, the majors ranked toward the top of the list tend to be those that are more quantitative and analytical. According to the study's author, "Employers may view certain majors as more difficult and may assume that graduates in these fields are more able and hard working, whereupon they offer them higher salaries." The selection of a relatively more challenging major such as economics sends a favorable signal to future employers.

The study also examined the kinds of jobs different majors actually found. Those who majored in economics became top and mid-level managers, executives, and administrators. They also found jobs in sales, computer analysis, financial analysis, and economic analysis. Remember, the survey was limited to those whose highest degree was the baccalaureate, so it excluded the many economics majors who went on to pursue graduate studies in law, business, economics, journalism, and other fields.

A number of world leaders majored in economics, including former Presidents Ford, Reagan, and Bush and Supreme Court Justice Sandra Day O'Connor. Other well-known economics majors include actor Arnold Schwarzenegger, rocker Mick Jagger, high-tech guru Esther Dyson, and "Dilbert" creator Scott Adams. Schwarzenegger, who reportedly earned $74 million in 1996 and 1997, has built an empire around his celebrity, including extensive real-estate holdings. Jagger, who attended the London School of Economics, heads what's been called "rock's most efficient corporation" (the Rolling Stones earned $68 million in 1996 and 1997). Both Schwarzenegger and Jagger rank among the dozen highest-paid entertainers in the world. Dyson, called by *The New York Times* "the most influential woman in all the computer world," authored *Release 2.0: A Design for Living in the Digital Age*, a book that helps people understand the wired world. She also publishes an influential high-tech newsletter and runs computer forums around the world. Adams has turned his "Dilbert" comic strip into a thriving industry including syndication in more than 1600 newspapers (in seventeen languages and thirty-nine countries), a TV program, best-selling books, plus dozens of tie-in products.

Sources: Scott Adams, *The Dilbert Principle* (New York, NY: HarperCollins, 1996); Daniel E. Hacker, "Earnings of College Graduates," *Monthly Labor Review*, December 1995; Robert La Franco, "The *Forbes* Top 40," *Forbes*, 22 September 1997; "The Accidental 'Techie'," *Newsweek*, 13 October 1997; Derek Bickerton, "Digital Dreams," *New York Times*, 30 November 1997.

CONCLUSION

This textbook describes how economic factors affect individual choices and how all these choices come together to shape the economic system. Economics is not the whole story, and economic factors are not always the most important. But economic considerations have important and predictable effects on individual choices, and these choices affect the way we live.

Sure, economics is a challenging discipline, but it is also an exciting and rewarding one. The good news is that you already know a great deal about economics. To use this knowledge, however, you must cultivate the art and science of economic analysis. You must be able to simplify the real world to formulate questions, isolate the relevant variables, and then tell a persuasive story about how these variables relate.

An economic relation can be expressed in words, represented as a table of quantities, described by a mathematical equation, or illustrated as a graph. The Appendix to this chapter provides an introduction to the use of graphs. You may find the Appendix unnecessary. If you are already familiar with graphs—such as relations among variables, slopes, tangents, and the like—you can probably just browse. If you have little recent experience with graphs, you may benefit from a more careful reading with pencil and paper in hand.

In the next chapter we will introduce some key ideas of economic analysis. Subsequent chapters will use these ideas to explore economic problems and to explain economic behavior that may otherwise appear puzzling. You must walk before you can run, however, and in the next chapter you will take those first wobbly steps.

SUMMARY

1. Economics is the study of how people choose to use their scarce and limited resources to produce, exchange, and consume goods and services in an attempt to satisfy their unlimited wants. The economic problem arises from the conflict between scarce resources and unlimited wants. If wants were limited or if resources were not scarce, there would be no need to study economics.

2. Economic resources are combined in a variety of ways to produce goods and services. Major categories of resources include labor, capital, land (representing all natural resources), and entrepreneurial ability. Because economic resources are scarce, only a limited number of goods and services can be produced with them; therefore, choices must be made.

3. Microeconomics focuses on choices made in households, firms, and governments and how these choices affect particular markets, such as the market for used cars. Each choice is assumed to be guided by rational self-interest. Choice typically requires time and information, both of which are scarce and valuable. Whereas microeconomics examines the individual pieces of the puzzle, macroeconomics steps back to look at the big picture—the performance of the economy as a whole as reflected by such measures as total production, employment, the price level, and economic growth.

4. Economists use theories, or models, to help understand the effects of economic changes, such as a change in price or income, on individual choices and, in turn, how these choices affect particular markets and the economy as a whole. Economists employ the scientific method to study an economic problem by (1) formulating the question and isolating relevant variables, (2) specifying the assumptions under which the theory operates, (3) developing a theory, or hypothesis, about how the variables relate, and (4) testing that theory by comparing its predictions with the evidence. A theory may not work perfectly, but it will be useful as long as it predicts better than competing theories do.

5. Positive economics aims to discover how the economy works. Normative economics is concerned more with how, in someone's opinion, the economy should work. Those who are not careful can fall victim to the fallacy that association is causation, the fallacy of composition, and ignorance of the secondary effects.

QUESTIONS FOR REVIEW

1. *(Definition of Economics)* What determines whether or not a resource is scarce? Why is the concept of scarcity important to the definition of economics?

2. *(Resources)* To which category of resources does each of the following belong?
   a. A taxicab
   b. Computer software
   c. One hour of legal counsel
   d. A parking lot
   e. A forest
   f. The Mississippi River
   g. An individual introducing a new way to market products on the Internet

3. *(Goods and Services)* Explain why each of the following would *not* be considered "free" for the economy as a whole:
   a. Food stamps
   b. U.S. aid to developing countries
   c. Corporate charitable contributions
   d. Noncable television programs
   e. Public high school education

4. *(Economic Decision Makers)* Which group of economic decision makers plays the leading role in the economic system? Which groups play supporting roles? In what sense are they supporting actors?

5. *(Micro versus Macro)* Determine whether each of the following is primarily a microeconomic or a macroeconomic issue:
   a. Determining the price to charge for an automobile
   b. Measuring the impact of tax policies on total consumption spending in the economy
   c. A household's decisions about how to allocate its disposable income among various goods and services
   d. A worker's decision regarding how many hours to work each week
   e. Designing a government policy to affect the level of employment

6. *(Micro versus Macro)* Some economists believe that in order to really understand macroeconomics, you must fully understand microeconomics. How does microeconomics relate to macroeconomics?

7. *(Normative versus Positive Analysis)* Determine whether each of the following statements is normative or positive:
   a. The U.S. unemployment rate was below 5 percent in 1998.
   b. The inflation rate in the United States is too high.
   c. The U.S. government should increase the minimum wage.
   d. U.S. trade restrictions cost consumers $19 billion annually.

8. *(Role of Theory)* What good is economic theory if it cannot predict an individual's behavior?

PROBLEMS AND EXERCISES

9. *(Rational Self-Interest)* Discuss the impact of rational self-interest on each of the following decisions:
   a. Whether to attend college full time or enter the full-time workforce
   b. Whether to buy a new or a used textbook
   c. Whether to attend a local college or an out-of-town college

10. *(Rational Self-Interest)* If behavior is governed by rational self-interest, why do people make contributions to charity?

11. *(Marginal Analysis)* The owner of a small pizzeria is deciding whether to increase the radius of its delivery area by one mile. What considerations must be taken into account if such a decision is to contribute to profitability?

12. *(Time and Information)* It is often costly to obtain information necessary to make good decisions. Yet your own interests can be best served by rationally weighing all options available to you. This requires completely informed decision making. Does this mean that making uninformed decisions is irrational? How do you determine what amount of information is the right amount?

13. *(**CaseStudy:** A Yen for Vending Machines)* Do vending machines conserve on any resources other than labor? Does your answer offer any additional insight into the widespread use of vending machines in Japan?

14. *(**CaseStudy:** A Yen for Vending Machines)* Suppose you had the choice of purchasing identically priced lunches

from a vending machine or at a cafeteria. Which would you choose? Why?

15. *(Pitfalls of Economic Analysis)* Review the discussion of pitfalls in economic thinking in this chapter. Then identify the fallacy or mistake in thinking in each of the following statements:
    a. Raising taxes will always increase government revenues.
    b. Whenever there is a recession, imports decrease. Therefore, to stop a recession, we should increase imports.
    c. Raising the tariff on imported steel will help the U.S. steel industry. Therefore, the entire economy will be helped.
    d. Gold sells for about $300 per ounce. Therefore, the U.S. government could sell all of the gold in Fort Knox at $300 per ounce and eliminate the national debt.

16. *(Association versus Causation)* Suppose I observe that communities with lots of doctors tend to have relatively high rates of illness. I conclude that doctors cause illness. What's wrong with this reasoning?

EXPERIENTIAL EXERCISES

17. *(Microeconomics and Macroeconomics)* Go to the Bank of Sweden's page on the Nobel Prize in economic science at http://www.ee.nobel.se/prize/memorial.html. Review the descriptions of some recent awards and try to determine whether those particular awards were primarily for work in macroeconomics or in microeconomics.

18. *(**CaseStudy:** College Major and Career Earnings)* The Bureau of Labor Statistics maintains online copies of articles from their *Monthly Labor Review*. Go to the site http://stats.bls.gov/opub/mlr/mlrhome.htm, click on "Archives" and find the article by Daniel Hecker entitled "Earnings of College Graduates: Women versus Men" (March, 1998). What can you learn about the payoff to college education for both women and men? (Note: You will need an Adobe Acrobat reader to get the full text of this article. You can download a copy of the reader at http://www.adobe.com/prodindex/acrobat/.

19. *(Wall Street Journal)* Detecting economic fallacies is a key skill. Review the section titled "Some Pitfalls of Economic Analysis" in this chapter. Then use the *Wall Street Journal* to find at least one example of faulty reasoning. (Hint: Begin with the "Markets Diary" column in the "Money & Investing" section.)

Appendix

UNDERSTANDING GRAPHS

Take out a pencil, a ruler, and a blank piece of paper. Go ahead, do it. Put a point in the middle of the paper. This is our point of departure, called the **origin.** With your pencil at the origin, draw a three-inch straight line off to the right. This line is called the **horizontal axis.** The value of the variable *x* measured along the horizontal axis increases as you move to the right of the origin. Now mark off this line into increments of 5 units each, from 0 to 20. Returning to the origin, draw another three-inch line straight up. This line is called the **vertical axis.** The value of the variable *y* measured along the vertical axis increases as you move upward. Now mark off this line into increments of 5 units each, from 0 to 20.

Within the space framed by the axes, you can plot possible combinations of the variables measured along each axis. Each point identifies a value measured along the horizontal, or *x,* axis *and* a value measured along the vertical, or *y,* axis. For example, place point *a* in your graph to reflect the combination where *x* equals 5 units and *y* equals 15 units. Likewise, place point *b* in your graph to reflect 10 units of *x* and 5 units of *y*. Now compare your results with those shown in Exhibit 2.

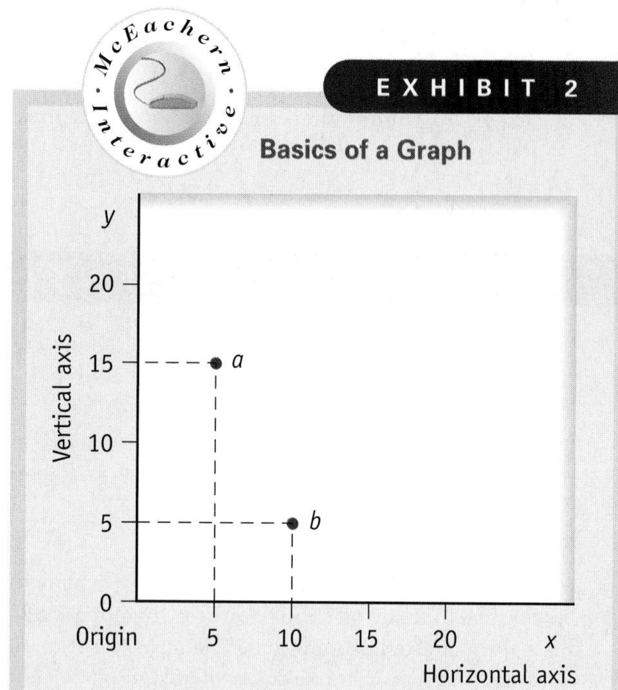

Any point on a graph represents a combination of particular values of two variables. Here point *a* represents the combination of 5 units of variable *x* (measured on the horizontal axis) and 15 units of variable *y* (measured on the vertical axis). Point *b* represents 10 units of *x* and 5 units of *y*.

A **graph** is a picture showing how variables relate, and a picture can be worth a thousand words. Take a look at Exhibit 3, which shows the U.S. annual unemployment rate since 1900. The year is measured along the horizontal axis and the unemployment rate along the vertical axis. Exhibit 3 is a **time-series graph** because it shows the value of a variable, in this case the unemployment rate, over time. If you had to describe the information presented in Exhibit 3 in words, the explanation could take pages and would be mind-numbing. The picture shows not only how one year compares to the next, but also how one decade compares to another and how the rate has trended over time. Your eyes can wander over the hills and valleys to observe patterns that would be hard to convey in words. The sharply higher unemployment rate during the Great Depression of the 1930s is unmistakable. *Graphs convey information in a compact and efficient way.*

This appendix shows how graphs express a variety of possible relations among variables. Most of the graphs of interest in this book reflect the relationship between two economic variables, such as the year and the unemployment rate, the price of a product and the quantity demanded, or the cost of production and the quantity supplied. Because we focus on just two variables at a time, we usually assume that other relevant variables remain constant.

We often observe that one variable appears to depend on another. The time it takes you to drive home depends on your average speed. Your weight depends on how much you eat. The amount of Pepsi purchased depends on its price. A *functional relation* exists between two variables when the value of one variable *depends* on the value of another variable. The value of the **independent variable** determines the value of the **dependent variable**.

The task of the economist is to isolate economic relations and determine the direction of causality, if any. Recall that one of the pitfalls of economic thinking is the erroneous belief that association is causation. We cannot conclude, simply because two events are related in time, that the first event causes the second. There may be no relation between the two events.

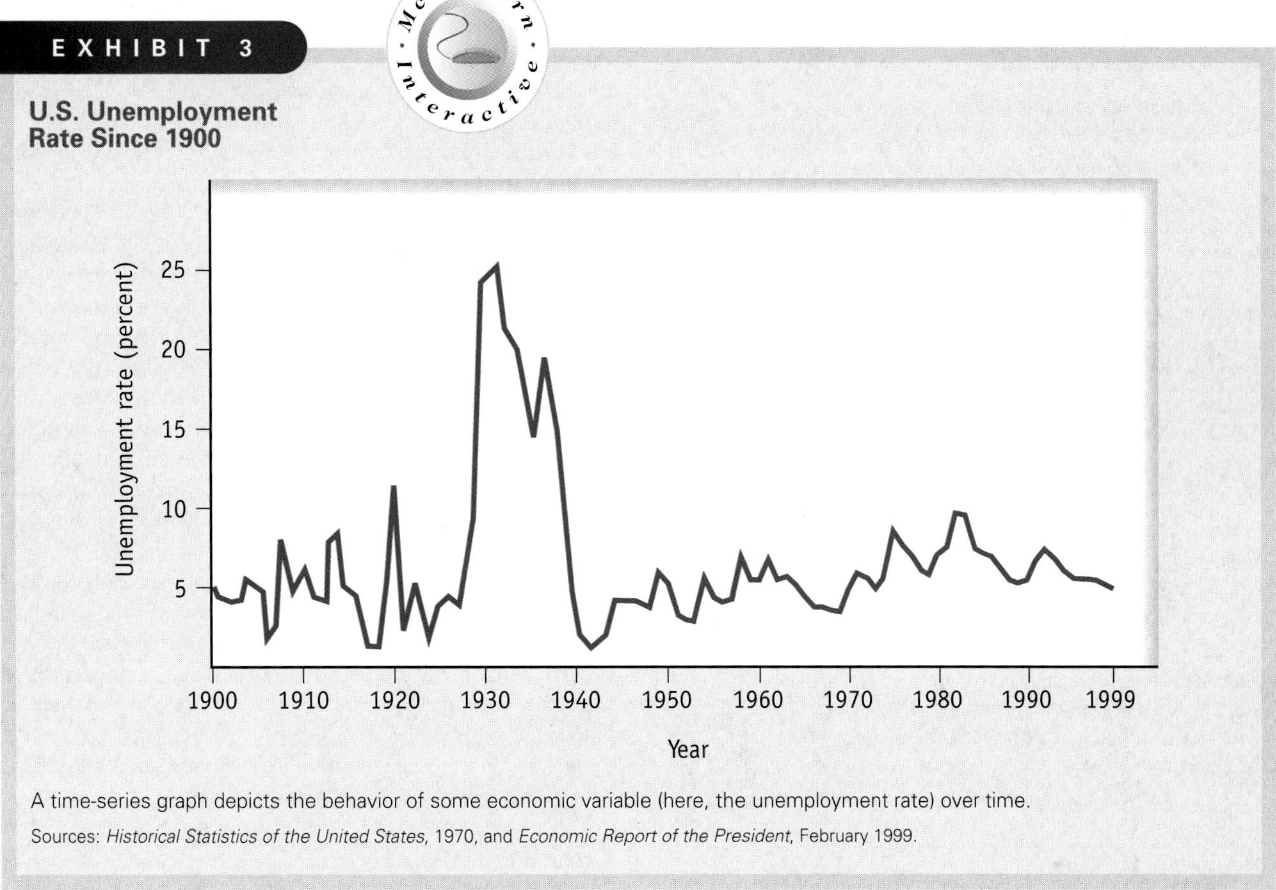

A time-series graph depicts the behavior of some economic variable (here, the unemployment rate) over time.

Sources: *Historical Statistics of the United States*, 1970, and *Economic Report of the President*, February 1999.

DRAWING GRAPHS

Let's begin with a simple relation. Suppose you are planning to drive across country and want to determine how far you will travel each day. You estimate that your speed will average 50 miles per hour. Possible combinations of driving time and distance traveled appear in Exhibit 4. One column lists the hours driven per day, and the next column gives the number of miles traveled per day, assuming an average speed of 50 miles per hour. The distance traveled, the dependent variable, depends on the number of hours driven, the independent variable. We identify combinations of hours driven and distance traveled as *a, b, c,* and so on. We can plot these combinations as a graph in Exhibit 5, with hours driven per day measured along the horizontal axis and total distance traveled along the vertical axis. Each combination of hours driven and distance traveled is represented by a point in Exhibit 5. For example, point *a* shows that when you drive for only 1 hour, you travel only 50 miles. Point *b* indicates that when you drive for 2 hours, you travel 100 miles. By connecting the points, or combinations, we create a line running upward and to the right. This makes sense because the longer you drive, the farther you travel. Held constant along this line is the average speed of 50 miles per hour.

EXHIBIT 4

Schedule Relating Distance Traveled to Hours Driven

	Hours Driven per Day	Distance Traveled per Day (miles)
a	1	50
b	2	100
c	3	150
d	4	200
e	5	250

EXHIBIT 5

Graph Relating Distance Traveled to Hours Driven

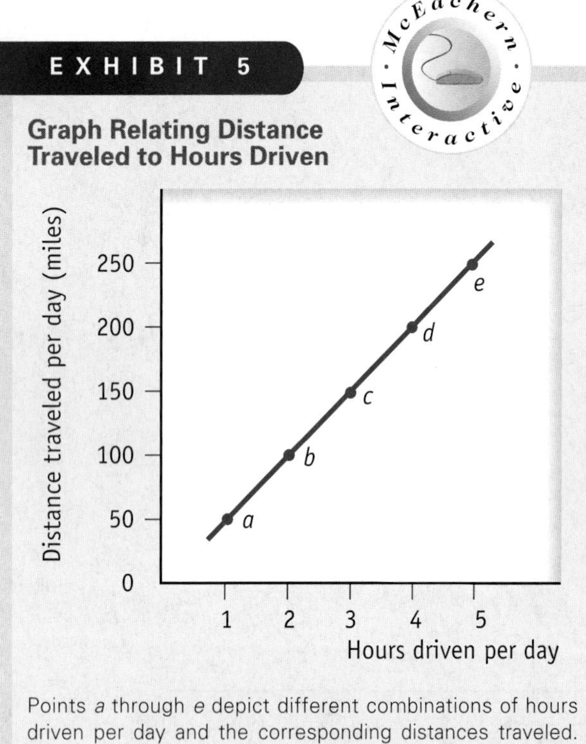

Points *a* through *e* depict different combinations of hours driven per day and the corresponding distances traveled. Connecting these points creates a graph.

Types of relations between variables include the following: (1) As one variable increases, the other increases, too—as in Exhibit 5; in this case there is a **positive,** or **direct, relation** between the variables; (2) as one variable increases, the other decreases; in this case there is a **negative,** or **inverse, relation;** and (3) as one variable increases, the other remains unchanged; in this case the two variables are said to be *independent,* or *unrelated.* One of the advantages of graphs is that they easily convey the relation between variables. We do not need to examine the particular combinations of numbers; we need only focus on the shape of the curve.

THE SLOPES OF STRAIGHT LINES

A more precise way to describe the shape of a curve is to measure its slope. The **slope** of a line indicates how much the vertical variable changes for a given increase in the horizontal variable. Specifically, the slope between any two points along any straight line is the vertical change between these two points divided by the horizontal increase, or

$$\text{Slope} = \frac{\text{Change in the vertical distance}}{\text{Increase in the horizontal distance}}$$

Each of the four panels in Exhibit 6 indicates a vertical change, given a 10-unit increase in the horizontal variable. In panel (a), the vertical distance increases by 5 units when the horizontal distance increases by 10 units. The slope of the line in panel (a) is therefore 5/10, or 0.5. Notice that the slope in this case is a positive number because the relation between the two variables is positive, or direct. This slope indicates that for every 1-unit increase in the horizontal variable, the vertical variable increases by 0.5 units. The slope, incidentally, does not imply causality; the increase in the horizontal variable does not necessarily *cause* the increase in the vertical variable. The slope simply indicates in a uniform way the relation between an increase in the horizontal variable and the associated change in the vertical variable.

In panel (b), the vertical distance declines by 7 units when the horizontal distance increases by 10 units, so the slope equals –7/10, or –0.7. The slope in this case is a negative number because the two variables have a negative, or inverse, relation. In panel (c), the vertical variable remains unchanged as the horizontal variable increases by 10, so the slope equals 0/10, or 0. These two variables are unrelated. Finally, in panel (d), the vertical variable can take on any value, although the horizontal variable remains unchanged. In this case any change in the vertical measure, for example a 10-unit change, is divided by 0, since the horizontal value does not change. Any change divided by 0 is infinitely large, so we say that the slope of a vertical line is infinite. Again, the two variables are unrelated.

THE SLOPE, UNITS OF MEASUREMENT, AND MARGINAL ANALYSIS

The mathematical value of the slope depends on the units of measurement on the graph. For example, suppose copper tubing costs $1 a foot to produce. Graphs depicting the relation between output and total cost are shown in Exhibit 7. In panel (a), total cost of production increases by $1 for each 1-foot increase in the amount of tubing produced. Thus, the slope in panel (a) equals 1/1, or 1. If the cost remains the same but the unit of measurement is not *feet* but *yards,* the relation between output and total cost is as depicted in panel (b). Now, total cost increases by $3 for each 1-yard increase in output, so the slope equals 3/1, or 3. Because of differences in the units used to measure copper tubing, the two panels reflect different slopes, even though the cost of tubing is $1 per foot in each panel. Keep in mind that *the slope will depend in part on the units of measurement.*

Economic analysis usually involves *marginal analysis,* such as the marginal cost of producing one more unit of output. The slope is a convenient device for measuring marginal effects because it reflects the change in total cost along the vertical axis for each 1-unit change along the horizontal axis. For example, in panel (a) of Exhibit 7, the marginal cost of

EXHIBIT 6

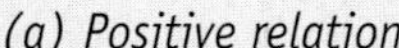

Alternative Slopes for Straight Lines

(a) Positive relation

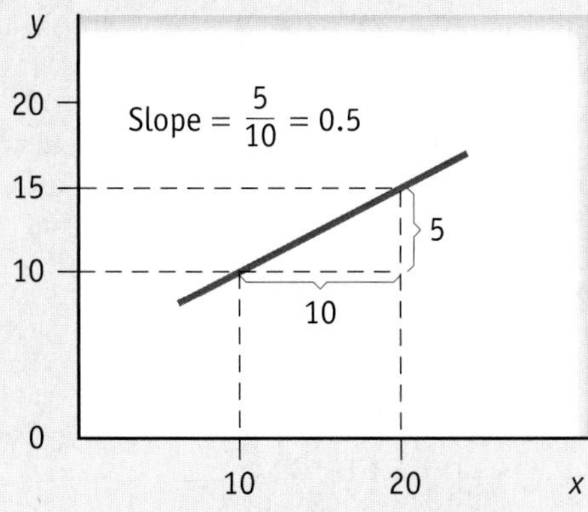

(b) Negative relation

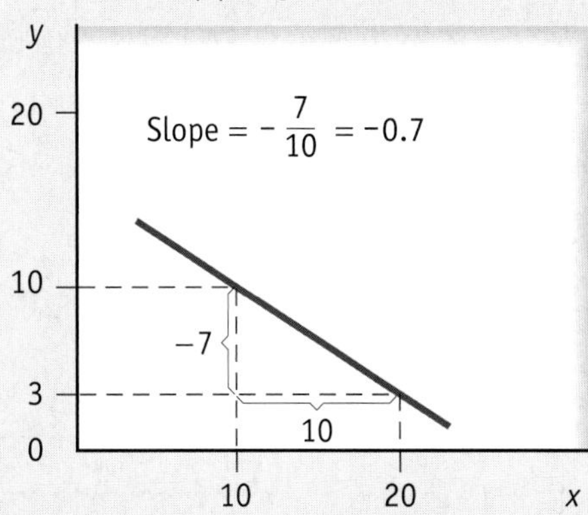

(c) No relation: zero slope

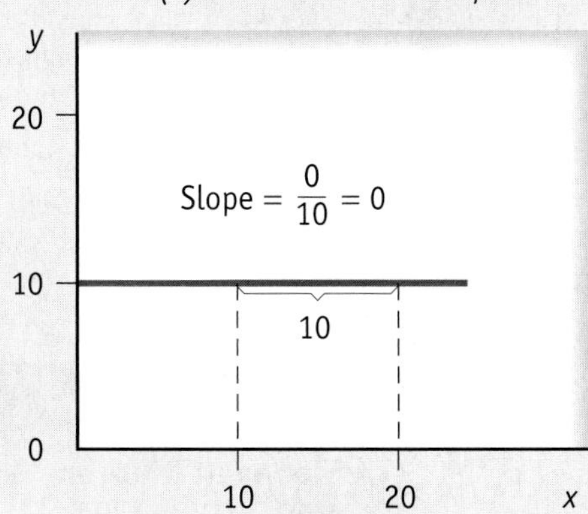

(d) No relation: infinite slope

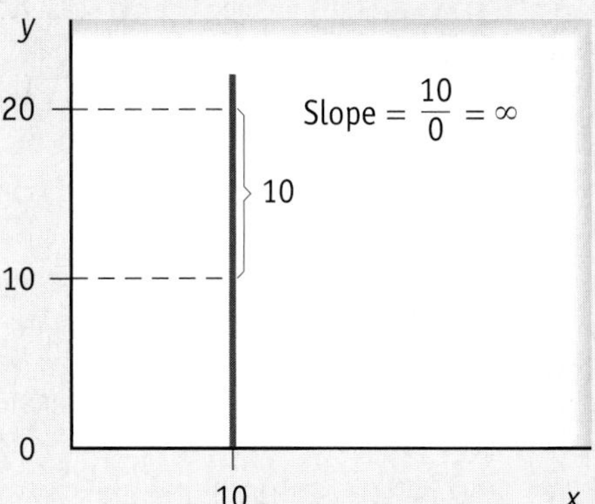

The slope of a line indicates how much the vertically measured variable changes for a given increase in the variable measured on the horizontal axis. Panel (a) shows a positive relation between two variables; the slope is 0.5, a positive number. Panel (b) depicts a negative, or inverse, relation. When the *x* variable increases, the *y* variable decreases; the slope is –0.7, a negative number. Panels (c) and (d) represent situations in which two variables are unrelated. In panel (c), the *y* variable always takes on the same value; the slope is 0. In panel (d), the *x* variable always takes on the same value; the slope is infinite.

another *foot* of copper tubing is $1, which also equals the slope of the line. In panel (b), the marginal cost of another *yard* of tubing is $3, which again is the slope of that line. Because of its applicability to marginal analysis, the slope has special significance in economics.

THE SLOPES OF CURVED LINES

The slope of a straight line is the same everywhere along that line, but the slope of a curved line varies at different points along the curve, as in Exhibit 8. To find the slope of that curved line at a particular point, draw a straight line that just touches the curve at that point but does not cut or cross the curve. Such a line is called a **tangent** to the curve at that point. The slope of the tangent is the slope of the curve at that point. Look at the line *AA*, which is tangent to the curve at point *a*. As the horizontal value increases from 0 to 10, the vertical value drops along *AA* from 40 to 0. Thus, the vertical change divided by the horizontal change equals –40/10, or –4, which is the slope of the curve at point *a*. This slope is negative because the curve slopes downward at that point. Along *BB*, a line drawn tangent to the curve at point *b*, the

EXHIBIT 7

Slope Depends on the Unit of Measure

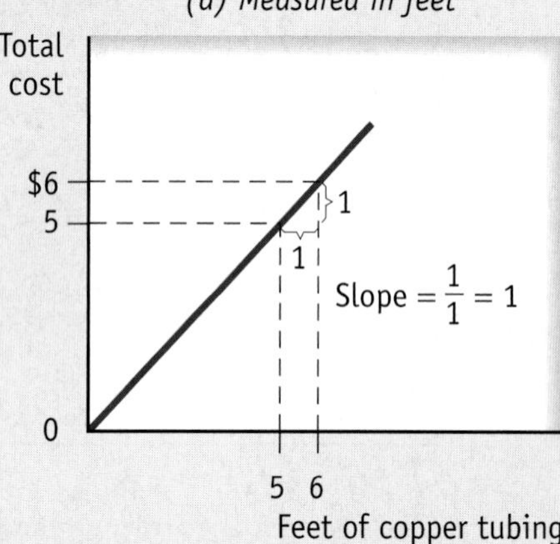

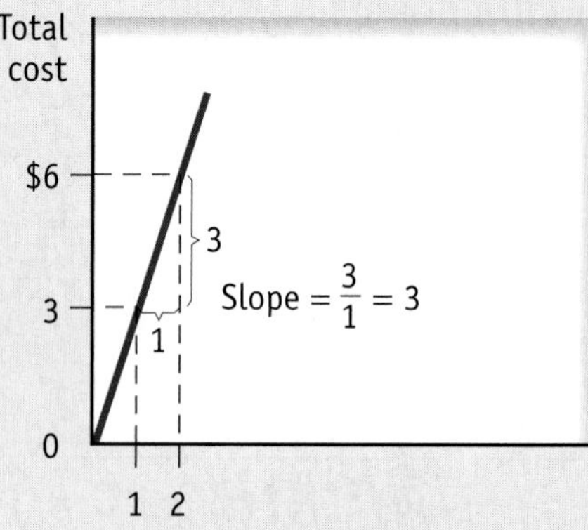

The value of the slope depends on the units of measure. In panel (a), output is measured in feet of copper tubing; in panel (b), output is measured in yards. Although the cost of production is $1 per foot in each panel, the slope is different in the two panels because copper tubing is measured using different units.

slope again is the change in the vertical divided by the change in the horizontal, or –10/30, which equals –0.33. As you can see, the curve depicted in Exhibit 8 gets flatter as the horizontal variable increases, so the value of its slope approaches zero.

Other curves, of course, will reflect different slopes as well as different changes in the slope along the curve. Downward-sloping curves have a negative slope, and upward-sloping curves, a positive slope. Sometimes curves are more complex, having both positive and negative ranges, such as in the hill-shaped curve in Exhibit 9. For relatively small values of x, there is a positive relation between x and y, so the slope is positive. As the value of x increases, however, the slope declines and eventually becomes negative. We can divide the curve into two segments: (1) the segment between the origin and point a, where the slope is positive, and (2) the segment of the curve to the right of point a, where the slope is negative. The slope of the curve at point a is 0. The U-shaped curve in Exhibit 9 represents the opposite relation: x and y are negatively related until point b is reached; thereafter they are positively related. The slope equals 0 at point b.

CURVE SHIFTS

Let's go back to your cross country trip, where we were trying to determine how many miles you traveled per day. Re-

EXHIBIT 8

Slopes at Different Points on a Curved Line

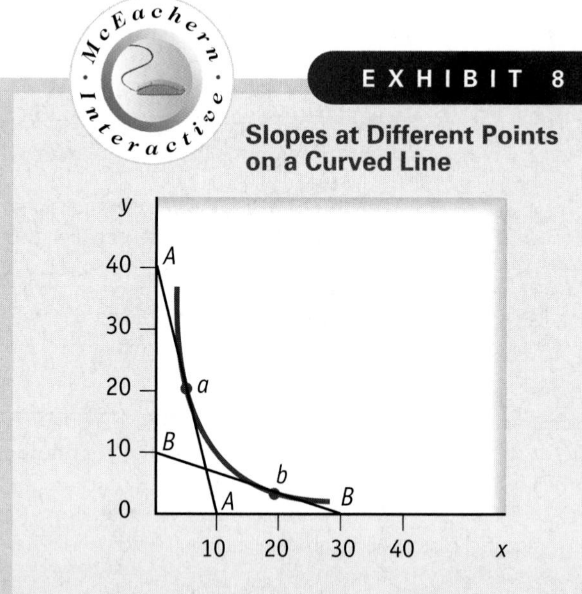

The slope of a curved line varies from point to point. At a given point, such as a or b, the slope of the curve is equal to the slope of the straight line that is tangent to the curve at that point.

EXHIBIT 9

McEachern Interactive

Curves with Both Positive and Negative Ranges

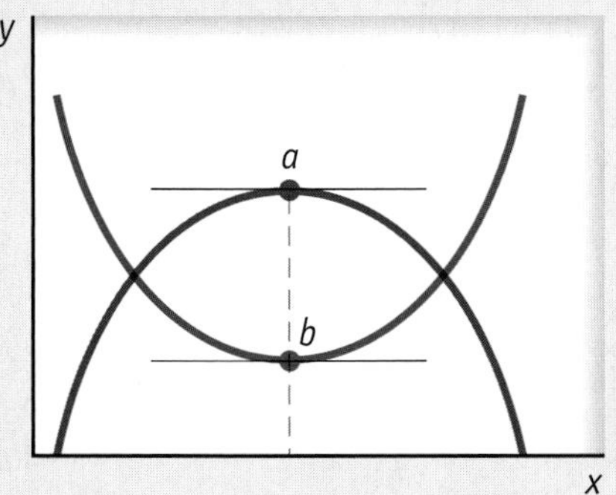

Some curves have both positive and negative slopes. The hill-shaped curve has a positive slope to the left of point *a*, a slope of 0 at point *a*, and a negative slope to the right of that point. The U-shaped curve starts off with a negative slope, has a slope of 0 at point *b*, and has a positive slope to the right of that point.

EXHIBIT 10

McEachern Interactive

Shift in Curve Relating Distance Traveled to Hours Driven

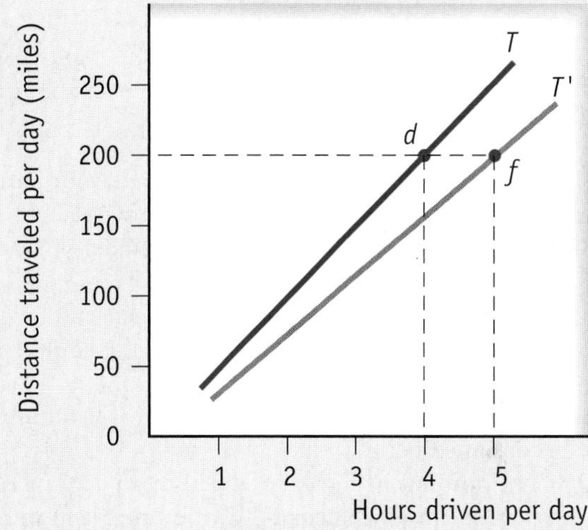

Curve *T* appeared originally in Exhibit 5 to show the relation between hours driven per day and distance traveled per day, assuming an average speed of 50 miles per hour. If the average speed is only 40 miles per hour, the entire relation shifts to the right to *T*', indicating that each distance traveled requires more driving time. For example, 200 miles traveled takes 4 hours of driving at 50 miles per hour, but that distance takes 5 hours at 40 miles per hour.

call that we measured hours driven per day on the horizontal axis and distance traveled per day on the vertical axis, assuming an average speed of 50 miles per hour. That same relation is shown as curve *T* in Exhibit 10. What if the average speed is not 50 miles per hour, but instead is 40 miles per hour? The entire relation between hours driven and distance traveled would change, as shown by the shift to the right in the curve to *T*'. With a slower average speed, any distance traveled per day now requires more driving time. For example, 4 hours of driving result in 200 miles traveled when the average speed is 50 miles per hour (as shown by point *d* on curve *T*), but that distance takes five hours when the speed averages 40 miles per hour (as shown by point *f* on curve *T*'). Thus, *a change in the assumption about average speed changes the relationship between the two variables observed.* This changed relationship is expressed by a shift in the curve that shows how the two variables relate.

With this we close our once-over of graphs. Return to this appendix when you feel you need to review.

APPENDIX QUESTIONS

1. *(Understanding Graphs)* Look at Exhibit 3 and answer the following questions:
   a. In what year (approximately) was the unemployment rate the highest? In what year was it the lowest?
   b. In what decade, on average, was the unemployment rate highest? In what decade was it lowest?
   c. Between 1950 and 1980, did the unemployment rate *generally* increase, decrease, or remain about the same?

2. *(Drawing Graphs)* Sketch a graph to illustrate your idea of each of the following relationships. Be sure to label both axes appropriately. In each case, explain under what circumstances, if any, the curve could shift:
   a. The relationship between a person's age and height
   b. Average monthly temperature over the course of a year
   c. A person's income and the number of hamburgers consumed per month
   d. The amount of fertilizer added to an acre of land and the amount of corn grown on that land in one growing season
   e. An automobile's horsepower and its gasoline mileage (in miles per gallon)

3. *(Slope)* Suppose you are given the following data on wage rates and number of hours worked:

Point	Hourly Wage	Hours Worked Per Week
A	$ 0	0
B	5	0
C	10	30
D	15	35
E	20	45
F	25	50

   a. Construct and label a set of axes and plot these six points. Label each point. What variable do you think should be measured on the vertical axis, and which variable should be measured on the horizontal axis?
   b. Connect the points. Describe the curve you find. Does it make sense to you?
   c. Compute the slope of the curve between points A and B. Between points B and C. Between points C and D. Between points D and E. Between points E and F. What happens to the slope as you move from point A to point F?

CHAPTER

2 Some Tools of Economic Analysis

Why are you reading this book right now rather than doing something else? What does college attendance cost you? Why will you eventually major in one discipline rather than take courses in many different disciplines? Why is fast food so fast? Why is there no sense crying over spilt milk? These and other questions are addressed in this chapter, which introduces some tools of economics—some tools of the trade.

The first chapter introduced the idea that scarcity forces us to make economic choices, but the chapter said little about how to make good choices. In this chapter we develop a framework for evaluating economic alternatives. First, we think about the cost involved in selecting one alternative over others. Next, we develop tools to explore the production choices available to

Visit the McEachern
teractive Study Center
for this chapter at
://mcisc.swcollege.com

individuals and to the economy as a whole. Finally, we examine the questions that different economies must answer—questions about what goods and services to produce, how to produce them and for whom. Topics discussed in this chapter include:

- Opportunity cost
- Division of labor
- Comparative advantage
- Specialization
- Production possibilities frontier
- Three economic questions
- Economic systems

CHOICE AND OPPORTUNITY COST

Think about a decision you just made: the decision to read this chapter right now rather than use the time to study for another course, play sports, watch TV, get some sleep, or do something else. Suppose your best alternative to reading right now is getting some sleep. The cost of reading is passing up the opportunity to sleep. Because of scarcity, whenever you make a choice, you must pass up another opportunity; you must incur an *opportunity cost.*

Opportunity Cost

Opportunity cost The value of the best alternative forgone when an item or activity is chosen

What do we mean when we talk about the cost of something? Isn't it what we have to give up—to sacrifice—to get that thing? The **opportunity cost** of the chosen item or activity is *the value of the best alternative that is forgone.* You might think of opportunity cost as the *opportunity lost.* Sometimes opportunity cost can be measured in terms of money, although, as we shall see, money is usually only part of the opportunity cost.

How many times have you heard people say they did something because they "had nothing better to do"? They actually mean they had no alternatives as attractive as the choice they selected. Yet, according to the idea of opportunity cost, people *always* do what they do because they have nothing better to do. The choice selected seems, at the time, preferable to any other possible choice. You are reading this chapter right now because you have nothing better to do. In fact, you are attending college for the same reason: College appears more attractive than your best alternative. In the following case study, consider the opportunity cost of attending college.

CaseStudy

The World of Business

Is college a sensible investment for you? Find out by trying Professor Jane Leuthold's COLLEGE CHOICE program at http://www.cba.uiuc.edu/college/econ/choice/choice.html.

The Opportunity Cost of College

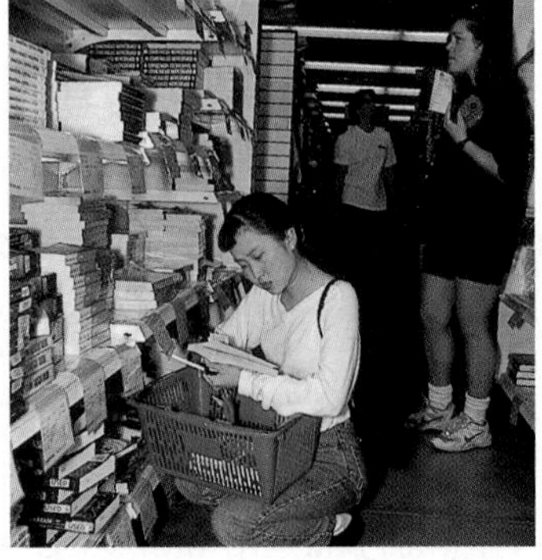

What is your opportunity cost of attending college full time this year? What was the most valued alternative you gave up to attend college? If you had a job, you have a good idea of the income you gave up to attend college. Suppose you expected to earn $16,000 a year, after taxes, from a full-time job. As a college student, you can work part time during the school year and full time during the summer. Suppose you can earn a total of $7,000 throughout the year after taxes. Thus, by attending college this year you are giving up net earnings of $9,000 (= $16,000 – $7,000).

There is also the direct cost of college itself. Suppose you are paying $5,000 this year for tuition, fees, and books at a public college. This money is unavailable to you (or your family) to spend elsewhere. So the opportunity cost of paying for tuition, fees, and books is the value of the goods and services that money could have purchased. Tuition, fees, and books would be much higher at a private college—more like $15,000 to $20,000.

Expenses for room and board are not necessarily opportunity costs because, even if you were not attending college, you would still need to live somewhere and eat something (though these costs could be higher at college). Likewise, whether or not you attended college, you would still incur outlays for items such as entertainment, clothes, toiletries, and laundry. Such expenses do not represent an opportunity cost of attending college. They are personal upkeep costs that arise regardless of what you are doing. For simplicity, let's assume that room, board, and personal expenses are the same whether or not you attend college; so they are not an opportunity cost of college. Thus, the forgone earnings of $9,000 plus the $5,000 for tuition, fees, and books yield an opportunity cost of $14,000 for attending college this year at a public college (at a private college, your opportunity cost could be double that amount).

This analysis assumes that other things are constant. If, in your view, attending college is more of a pain than you expected the most valued alternative to be, the opportunity cost of attending college is even higher. In other words, if you are one of those people who find college difficult, often boring, and in most ways more unpleasant than a full-time job, then the cost in money terms understates your true opportunity cost. Not only are you incurring the expense of college, but you are forgoing a more pleasant quality of life. If, on the contrary, you think the wild and crazy life of a college student is more enjoyable than a full-time job, then $14,000 overstates your true opportunity cost, because the best alternative involves a less satisfying quality of life.

Evidently, you view college as a wise investment in your future, even though it is costly and perhaps even painful. In fact, a growing fraction of college students are willing to go into debt to finance their education. Some students, even those who attend public universities, graduate with debts exceeding $20,000.

Still, college is not for everyone. Some people find college less attractive than alternatives. Tiger Woods, once an economics major at Stanford, dropped out after two years to earn millions in professional golf. Some high school seniors who believe they are ready for professional basketball skip college altogether, as do most pro tennis players and many actors. (Tom Cruise even dropped out of high school.)

Sources: "Debt Load—Class of '96," *America's Best Colleges: 1998, U.S. News & World Report,* pp. 63–64; Ellen Graham, "Study Now, Pay Later: Students Pile on Debt," *Wall Street Journal,* 11 August 1995; and CollegeNET, the "Internet Guide to Colleges and Universities" at http://www.collegenet.com.

Opportunity Cost Is Subjective

Opportunity cost is subjective. Only the individual chooser can select the most attractive alternative. And the chooser seldom knows the actual value of the best alternative forgone, since that alternative is "the road not taken." (Incidentally, focusing on only the best alternative forgone makes all other alternatives irrelevant.) Thus, if you give up an evening of pizza and conversation with friends to work on a term paper, you will never know the exact value of what you gave up. You know only what you *expected*. Evidently you expected the value of working on that paper to exceed the value of the best alternative.

Calculating Opportunity Cost Requires Time and Information. We have assumed that people rationally choose the most valued alternative. This does not mean they exhaustively calculate the value of all possible alternatives. Since acquiring information about alternatives is costly and time consuming, people usually make choices based on limited or even incorrect information. Indeed, some choices may turn out to be poor ones (as examples, you went on a picnic and it rained; the movie you rented was boring; the shoes you bought gave you blisters). At the time you made the choice, however, you thought you were making the best use of all your scarce resources, including the time required to gather and evaluate information about your alternatives.

Time Is the Ultimate Constraint. The Sultan of Brunei is among the world's richest people, based on the huge oil revenues that flow into his tiny country. His palace has 2,000 rooms, with walls of fine Italian marble. His throne room is the size of a football field. He owns 150 Rolls Royces.[1] Supported by such wealth, he appears to have overcome the economic problem caused by scarce resources but unlimited wants. But even though the Sultan can buy whatever he wants, the *time* he has to enjoy his acquisitions is limited. If he pursues one activity, he cannot at the same time do something else, so each activity he undertakes has an opportunity cost. Consequently, the Sultan must choose from among the competing uses of his scarcest resource, time. Though your alternatives are not as exotic as the Sultan's, you, too, face a time constraint, especially toward the end of the college term.

Opportunity Cost May Vary with Circumstance. Opportunity cost depends on the value of your alternatives. This is why you are more likely to study on a Tuesday night than on a Saturday night. On a Tuesday night, the opportunity cost of studying is lower because you have fewer attractive alternatives than on a Saturday night, when more is happening. Suppose you choose a movie for Saturday night. The opportunity cost of the movie is the value forgone from your best alternative, which might be attending a sporting event. For some of you, studying on Saturday night may be well down the list of alternatives—perhaps ahead of reorganizing your closet, but certainly behind watching trucks being unloaded at the supermarket.

Opportunity cost is subjective, but in some circumstances money paid for goods and services is a good approximation of their opportunity cost. For example, the opportunity cost of the new CD player you bought is the value of spending that $300 on the best forgone alternative. However, sometimes the monetary-cost definition may leave out some important elements, particularly the time involved. For example, watching a video costs you not only the rental fee but also the time and travel expense to get it, watch it, and return it.

1 These figures are reported by Kieran Cooke in "Sultan's Swing to Reform," *London Financial Times,* 4 August 1995.

Sunk Cost and Choice

Suppose you have just finished shopping for groceries and are wheeling your grocery cart toward the row of checkout counters. How do you decide which line to join? You pick the line you think will involve the least time. Suppose, after waiting for 10 minutes in a line that barely moves, you notice that a cashier has opened another register and invites you to check out. Do you switch to the new line, or do you think, "Since I have already spent 10 minutes in this line, I'm going to stay here"? The 10 minutes you already waited represents a *sunk cost*, which is a cost that you cannot recover regardless of what you do. **Sunk costs** are costs that cannot be avoided, regardless of what you do in the future, because they have already been incurred. You should ignore sunk costs in making economic choices, because your choice has no impact on something that has already happened. Therefore, you should switch to the newly opened line.

Sunk cost A cost that has already been incurred in the past and, hence, a cost that is irrelevant to present and future economic decisions

Economic decision makers should consider only those costs that are affected by the choice. Sunk costs have already been incurred and thus are not affected by the choice, so they are irrelevant. Likewise, you should walk out on a boring movie even if the admission cost you $8. The irrelevance of sunk costs is underscored by the proverb is "There is no sense crying over spilt milk." Remember, you should ignore sunk costs because they have already been incurred; the milk has already spilled, so whatever you do now has no impact on those costs.

SPECIALIZATION, COMPARATIVE ADVANTAGE, AND EXCHANGE

Suppose you live in a dormitory. You and your roommate have such busy schedules that you each can spare only about an hour per week for such mundane tasks as typing and ironing. Each of you must turn in a three-page typed paper every week, and you each prefer to have your shirts ironed if you have the time. Suppose it takes you a half hour to type the three-page paper. Your roommate is from the hunt-and-peck school and takes about an hour to type the paper. But your roommate is talented at ironing and can iron a shirt in 5 minutes flat (or should that be, iron it flat in 5 minutes). You take about twice as long, or 10 minutes, to iron a shirt.

During the hour available each week for typing and ironing, the typing takes priority. If you each do your own typing and ironing, your roommate takes the entire hour to type the paper and so has no time left for ironing. You type your paper in a half hour and iron three shirts in the remaining half hour. Thus, with each of you performing your own tasks, the combined output is two typed papers and three ironed shirts.

The Law of Comparative Advantage

Before long, you each realize that total output would increase if you did all the typing and your roommate did all the ironing. In the hour available for these tasks, you type both papers and your roommate irons twelve shirts. As a result of specialization, total output increases by nine shirts! You strike a deal to exchange your typing for your roommate's ironing, so you each end up with a typed paper and six ironed shirts. Thus, *each of you is better off as a result of specialization and exchange.* By specializing in the task that you each do best, you both employ the **law of comparative advantage,** which states that the individual with the lower opportunity cost of producing a particular output should specialize in producing that output.

Law of comparative advantage The individual, firm, region, or country with the lowest opportunity cost of producing a particular good should specialize in producing that good.

Absolute and Comparative Advantage

The gains from specialization and exchange in the previous example seem obvious. A more interesting case arises if you are not only a faster typist but also a faster ironer. Suppose we change the example so that your roommate takes 12 minutes to iron a shirt, compared to your 10 minutes. You now have an *absolute advantage* in both tasks, meaning each task takes you less time than it does your roommate. More generally, having an **absolute advantage** means being able to produce a product using fewer resources than other producers require.

Absolute advantage The ability to produce something using fewer resources than other producers use

Does your absolute advantage in both activities mean specialization is no longer a good idea? Recall that the law of comparative advantage states that the individual with *the lower opportunity cost* of producing a particular good should specialize in producing that good. You still take 30 minutes to type a paper and 10 minutes to iron a shirt, so your opportunity cost of typing a paper is ironing 3 shirts. Your roommate takes an hour to type a paper and 12 minutes to iron a shirt, so your roommate could iron 5 shirts in the time taken to type a paper. Hence your opportunity cost of typing a paper is ironing 3 shirts, and your roommate's opportunity cost is ironing 5 shirts. *Because your opportunity cost of typing is lower than your roommate's, you have a comparative advantage in typing.* Since you have a comparative advantage in typing, your roommate must have a comparative advantage in ironing (try working this out to your satisfaction). Hence you should do all the typing and your roommate, all the ironing. Although you have an absolute advantage in both tasks, your **comparative advantage** calls for specializing in the task for which you have the lower opportunity cost—in this case, typing.

Comparative advantage The ability to produce something at a lower opportunity cost than other producers face

If neither of you specialized, you could type one paper and iron three shirts; your roommate could still type just the one paper. Your combined output would be two papers and three shirts. If you each specialized according to comparative advantage, in an hour you could type both papers and your roommate could iron five shirts. Thus, specialization increases total output by two ironed shirts. Exhibit 1 summarizes this example. Even though you are better at both tasks than your roommate, you are comparatively better at typing. Put another way, your roommate, although worse at both tasks, is not quite as poor at ironing as at typing.

Don't think this is simply common sense. Common sense would lead you to do your own ironing and typing, since you are more skilled at both. *Absolute advantage focuses on who uses the fewest resources, but comparative advantage focuses on what else those resources could have been used to produce—that is, on the opportunity cost of those resources.* Comparative advantage is the better guide to who should do what.

The law of comparative advantage applies not only to individuals but also to firms, regions of a country, and entire nations. Those individuals, firms, regions, or countries with the lowest opportunity cost of producing a particular good should specialize in producing that good. Because of such factors as climate, the skills of the workforce, plus the capital and natural resources available,

EXHIBIT 1

CASE 1: *You are a faster typist and your roommate is a faster ironer.*

	Output per Hour			
	Each Does Own		Each Specializes	
	Typed Papers	Ironed Shirts	Typed Papers	Ironed Shirts
You	1	3	2	0
Roommate	1	0	0	12
Total	2	3	2	12

CASE 2: *You are a faster typist and a faster ironer, but you are a comparatively faster typist.*

	Output per Hour			
	Each Does Own		Each Specializes	
	Typed Papers	Ironed Shirts	Typed Papers	Ironed Shirts
You	1	3	2	0
Roommate	1	0	0	5
Total	2	3	2	5

Comparative Advantage: Maximizing Output

Cases 1 and 2 both show gains from specialization and exchange for you and your roommate. In both cases it takes you half an hour to type the paper and 10 minutes to iron one shirt. In both cases your roommate takes 1 hour to type the paper. But, whereas in Case 1 it takes your roommate only 5 minutes to iron a shirt, in Case 2 it takes 12 minutes to iron a shirt. In Case 1 you have an absolute advantage and a comparative advantage in typing, so total output is greater if you do all the typing and your roommate does all the ironing. In Case 2 you have an absolute advantage in both typing and ironing. But you have a comparative advantage only in typing because you have a lower opportunity cost of typing than does your roommate. So in Case 2 output is maximized if you do all the typing and your roommate does all the ironing.

certain parts of the country and certain parts of the world have a comparative advantage in producing particular goods. From Apple computers in California's Silicon Valley to oranges in sunny Florida, from VCRs in Korea to bananas in Honduras—*resources are allocated most efficiently across the country and around the world when production and trade conform to the law of comparative advantage.*

Specialization and Exchange

In the previous example, you and your roommate specialized and then exchanged your output. No money was involved. In other words, you engaged in barter. **Barter** is a system of exchange in which products are traded directly for other products. Barter works satisfactorily in very simple economies where there is little specialization and few different goods to trade. But for economies with greater specialization, *money* plays an important role in facilitating exchange. Money—coins, bills, and checks—serves as a *medium of exchange* because it is the one thing that everyone is willing to accept in return for all goods and services.

Barter The direct exchange of one good for another without the use of money

Because of specialization and comparative advantage, most people consume little of what they produce and produce little of what they consume. People specialize in particular activities, such as plumbing or carpentry, and they exchange their products for money, which in turn is exchanged for goods and services produced by others. Did you make any article of the clothing you are wearing? Probably not. Think about the degree of specialization that goes into your cotton shirt. Some farmer in a warm climate grew the cotton and sold it to someone who spun it into thread, who sold it to someone who wove it into fabric, who sold it to someone who sewed the shirt, who sold it to a wholesaler, who sold it to a retailer, who sold it to you. Your shirt was produced by many specialists.

Division of Labor and Gains from Specialization

Picture a visit to McDonald's: "Let's see, I'll have a Big Mac, an order of fries, and a chocolate shake." About a minute later your order is ready. It would take you about an hour to make a homemade version of this meal. Why is the McDonald's meal faster, cheaper, and—for some people—better tasting than one you could make yourself? Why is fast food so fast?

Division of labor Organizing production of a good into its separate tasks

McDonald's is taking advantage of the gains resulting from the **division of labor.** Rather than have each worker prepare an entire individual meal, McDonald's breaks down meal preparation into various tasks and has individuals specialize in these separate tasks. This division of labor allows the group to produce much more than it could if each person tried to prepare an entire meal. Instead of each of 10 workers doing it all and making a total of, say, 50 complete meals in an hour, workers specialize and produce more like 500 meals per hour.

How is this increase in productivity possible? First, the manager can assign tasks according to *individual preferences and abilities*—according to comparative advantage. The employee with the toothy smile and pleasant personality can handle the customers up front; the employee with the strong back but few social graces can do the heavy lifting out back. Second, a worker who performs the same task again and again gets better at it. Experience is a good teacher. The employee filling orders at the drive-through window, for example, becomes better at handling the special problems that arise in dealing with customers. Third, there is no time lost in moving from one task to another. Finally, and perhaps most important, the **specialization of labor** allows for the introduction of more sophisticated production techniques, techniques that would not make economic sense on a smaller scale. For example, McDonald's large shake machine would be impractical in the home. The specialization of labor allows for the introduction of specialized machines, and these machines make each worker more productive.

Specialization of labor Focusing an individual's efforts on a particular product or a single task

To review: The specialization of labor takes advantage of individual preferences and natural abilities, allows workers to develop more experience at a particular task, reduces the time required to shift between different tasks, and permits the introduction of labor-saving machinery. Specialization and the division of labor occur not only among individuals but also among firms, regions, and indeed entire countries. The clothing production mentioned earlier might involve growing cotton in one country, turning the cotton into cloth in another, sewing the clothing in a third country, and marketing that clothing in a fourth country.

We should also note that specialization can create problems, since doing the same thing all day often becomes tedious. Consider, for example, the assembly line worker whose task is to tighten a particular bolt. Such a job could drive that worker nuts. Repetitive motion can also lead to injury. Thus, the gains from breaking production down into individual tasks must be weighed against the problems caused by assigning workers to repetitive and tedious jobs. Specialization is discussed in the following case study.

CaseStudy

The World of Business

Economics is a subject that has benefited from specialization and the division of labor. To get a feel for the many different subjects that economists investigate, take a look at the *Journal of Economic Literature*'s classification system at http://www.econlit.org/elclasbk.htm.

Evidence of Specialization

Evidence of specialization is all around us. Dozens of "specialty stores" at the mall focus on products ranging from luggage to party supplies to pet products. Restaurants specialize in cuisine from soup to sushi. Let your fingers do the walking through the Yellow Pages, and you will find thousands of separate specializations. Listings under "Physicians" alone offer dozens of medical specialties. Without moving a muscle, you can witness the division of labor within a single industry; watch the credits roll at the end of a movie, and you will see dozens and sometimes hundreds of specialists are listed—everyone from the gaffer (lighting electrician) to the assistant location scout.

Perhaps the easiest way to explore specialization and the division of labor is on the Internet, where millions of individual sites offer specialized products or activities. For example, Cyberian Outpost sells computers around the world; its Web site takes orders in more than a dozen languages. BigBook, a huge online phone directly offering over 16 million business listings allows you to look up any specialty listing for any U.S. state or city. For example, South Carolina has only one tattoo parlor, whereas Oregon, a state with a smaller population, has 43.

With a search engine such as Lycos, you can identify the number of Web sites that reference any specialty. For example, at last count, "economist" yielded about 13,000 sites, compared to 11,000 for "accountant," 7,000 for "physicist," and 2,000 for "sociologist." "Economics" turns up about 100,000 sites. "Entrepreneurs" are found at over 12,000 sites. From "aardvark" to "zucchini," the Internet identifies more specialties than any other reference source in the world.

Sources: Lycos technology is developed and marketed by Lycos, Inc., an independent operating company of CMG Information Services; BigBook's address is http://www.bigbook.com.

THE ECONOMY'S PRODUCTION POSSIBILITIES

The focus to this point has been on how individuals choose to use their scarce resources to satisfy their unlimited wants or, more specifically, how they specialize based on comparative advantage. This emphasis on the individual has been appropriate because the economy is shaped by the choices of individual decision makers, whether they are consumers, producers, or public officials. Just as resources are scarce for the individual, they are also scarce for the economy as a whole (no fallacy of composition here). An economy has millions of different resources that can be combined in all kinds of ways to produce millions of possible goods and services. In this section, we step back from the immense complexity of the real economy to develop our first model, which presents the economy's production options.

Efficiency and the Production Possibilities Frontier

Let's develop a model to get some idea how much can be produced in the economy with the resources available. What is the economy's production capabilities? Here are the model's simplifying assumptions:

1. To reduce the analysis to manageable proportions, we limit the output to just two broad classes of products. In our example they are consumer goods, such as pizzas and haircuts, and capital goods, which includes physical capital such as tractors, and human capital, such as college education.
2. The focus is on production during a given time period—in this case, a year.
3. The resources available in the economy are fixed in both quantity and quality during the time period.
4. Society's knowledge about how these resources can be combined to produce output—that is, the available *technology*—does not change during the year.

The point of these assumptions is to freeze the economy in time and to focus on the economy's production alternatives based on the resources and technology available during that time.

Production possibilities frontier (PPF) A curve showing alternative combinations of goods that can be produced when available resources are used efficiently

Efficiency The condition that exists when there is no way resources can be reallocated to increase the production of one good without decreasing the production of another

Given the resources and the technology available in the economy, the **production possibilities frontier,** or **PPF,** identifies the various possible combinations of the two types of goods that can be produced when all available resources are employed efficiently. *Resources are said to be employed efficiently when there is no change in the way the resources are combined that could increase the production of one type of good without decreasing the production of the other type of good.* **Efficiency** involves getting the maximum possible output from available resources.

The economy's PPF for consumer goods and capital goods is shown by the curve *AF* in Exhibit 2. Point *A* identifies the amount of consumer goods produced per year if all the economy's resources are used efficiently to produce consumer goods, and *F* identifies the amount of capital goods produced per year if all the economy's resources are used efficiently to produce capital goods. Points along the curve between *A* and *F* identify possible combinations of the two types of goods that can be produced when all the economy's resources are used *efficiently*.

Inefficient and Unattainable Production

Points inside the PPF, including *G* in Exhibit 2, represent combinations that either do not employ resources fully or employ them inefficiently. Note that point *C* yields more consumer goods and no fewer capital goods than *G*. And point *E* yields more capital goods and no fewer consumer goods than *G*.

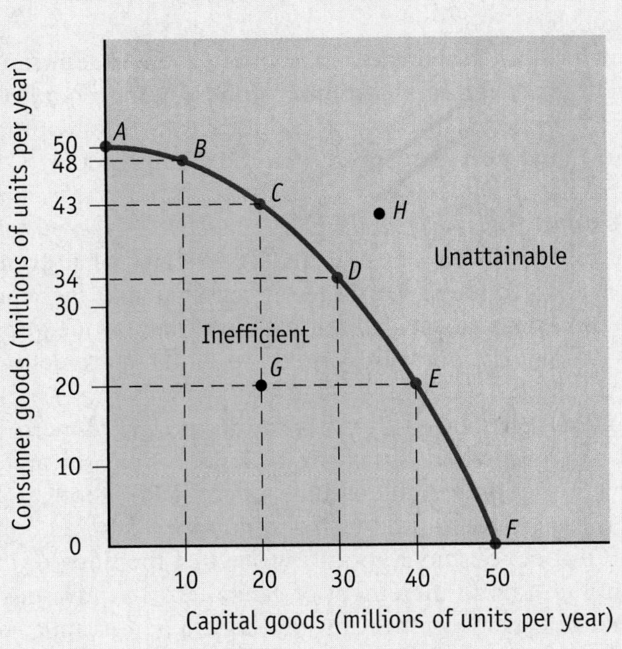

EXHIBIT 2

The Economy's Production Possibilities Frontier

If the economy uses its available resources and technology fully and efficiently in producing consumer goods and capital goods, it will be on its production possibilities frontier curve *AF*. The PPF is bowed out to illustrate the law of increasing opportunity cost: additional units of capital goods require the economy to sacrifice more and more units of consumer goods. Note that more consumer goods must be given up in moving from *D* to *E* than in moving from *A* to *B*, although in each case the gain in capital goods is 10 million units. Points inside the PPF, such as *G*, represent inefficient use of resources. Points outside the PPF, such as *H*, represent unattainable combinations.

Indeed, any point along the PPF between *C* and *E*, such as point *D*, yields both more consumer goods and more capital goods than *G*. Hence, point *G* is *inefficient*; by using resources more efficiently or by using previously idle resources, the economy can produce more of at least one good without reducing the production of the other good.

Points outside the PPF, such as *H* in Exhibit 2, represent *unattainable* combinations, given the resources and the technology available. Thus *the PPF not only reflects efficient combinations of production but also identifies the border between inefficient combinations inside the frontier and unattainable combinations outside the frontier.*

Shape of the Production Possibilities Frontier

Focus again on point *A* in Exhibit 2. Any movement along the PPF involves giving up some of one good to get more of the other. Movements down along the curve indicate that the opportunity cost of more capital goods is fewer consumer goods. For example, moving from point *A* to point *B increases* the amount of capital goods produced from none to 10 million units and *reduces* production of consumer goods from 50 million to 48 million units, a decline of only 2 million units. Increasing production of capital goods to 10 million units causes the production of consumer goods to fall just a little, because capital production initially draws upon resources (such as heavy machinery used to build factories) that add little to production of consumer goods but are quite productive in making capital goods.

As shown by the dashed lines in Exhibit 2, each additional 10 million units of capital goods reduces consumer goods by more and more. As more capital goods are produced, the resources drawn away from consumer goods are those that are better suited to producing consumer goods. *Opportunity cost increases as the economy produces more capital goods, because the resources in the economy are not all perfectly adaptable to the production of both types of goods.* The shape of the production possibilities frontier reflects the **law of increasing opportunity cost.** If the economy uses all resources efficiently, the law of increasing opportunity cost states that each additional increment of one good requires the economy to sacrifice successively larger and larger increments of the other good.

Law of increasing opportunity cost To produce each additional increment of a particular good, a successively larger increment of an alternative good must be sacrificed if the economy's resources are already being used efficiently

The PPF derives its bowed-out shape from the law of increasing opportunity cost. For example, whereas the first 10 million units of capital goods have an opportunity cost of only 2 million units of consumer goods, the final 10 million—that is, the increase from point *E* and point *F*—have an opportunity cost of 20 million units of consumer goods. Notice that the slope of the PPF shows the opportunity cost of an increment of capital. As we move down the curve, the curve becomes steeper, reflecting the higher opportunity cost of capital goods in terms of forgone consumer goods. The law of increasing opportunity cost also applies when moving from the production of capital goods to the production of consumer goods. Incidentally, if resources were perfectly adaptable to alternative uses, the PPF would be a straight line, reflecting a constant opportunity cost along the PPF.

What Can Shift the Production Possibilities Frontier?

When we construct the production possibilities frontier, we assume that resources available in the economy and the level of technology are fixed. Over time, however, the PPF may shift as a result of changes in resource availability or in technology. A shift outward in the PPF reflects **economic growth,** which shows an expansion in the economy's ability to produce goods and services.

Economic growth A shift outward in the production possibilities frontier; an increase in the economy's ability to produce goods and services

Changes in Resource Availability. If people decide to work longer hours, the PPF will shift outward, as shown in panel (a) of Exhibit 3. An increase in the size or the health of the labor force, an increase in the skills of the labor force, or an increase in the availability of other resources, such as new oil discoveries, will also shift the PPF outward. In contrast, a decrease in the availability or the quality of resources will shift the PPF inward, as depicted in panel (b). For example, in 1990 Iraq invaded Kuwait, setting oil fields ablaze and destroying much of Kuwait's physical capital, thereby shifting Kuwait's PPF inward. In West Africa the encroaching sands of the Sahara cover and destroy thousands of square miles of productive farmland each year, shifting the PPF of that economy inward.

EXHIBIT 3

Shifts in the Economy's Production Possibilities Frontier

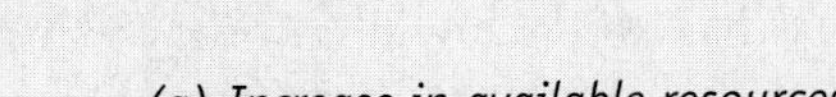

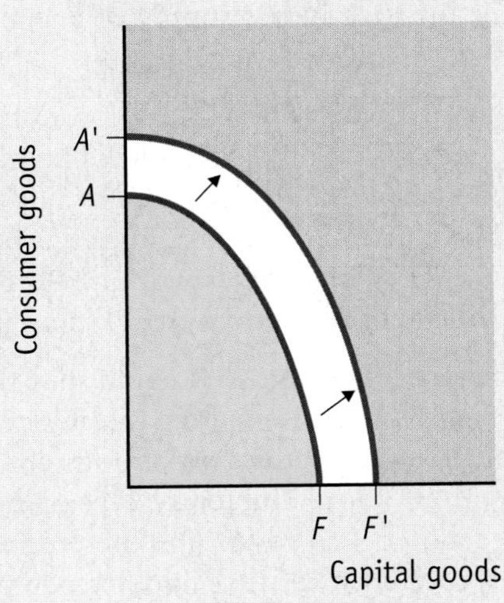

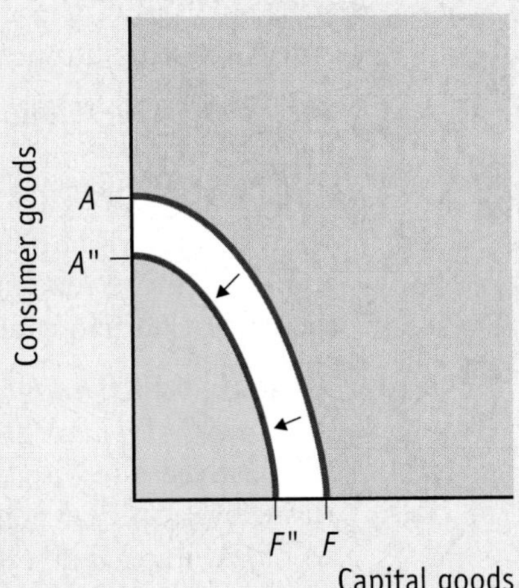

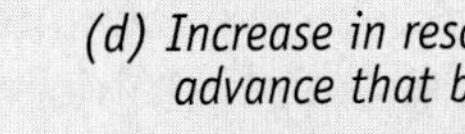

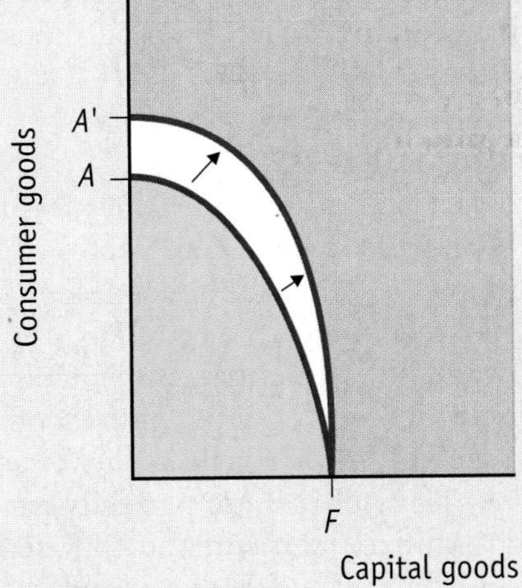

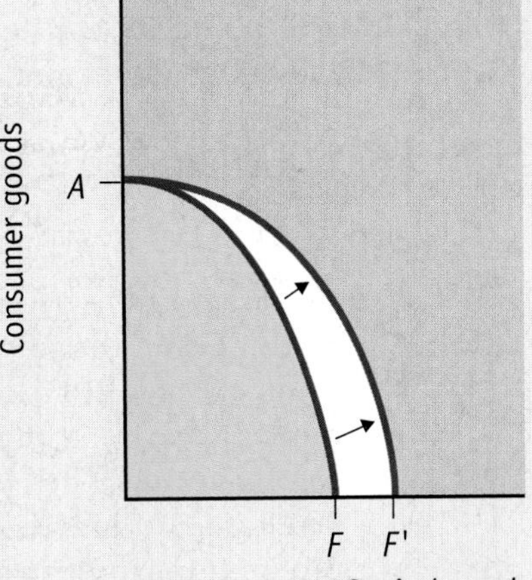

When the resources available to an economy change, the PPF shifts. If more resources become available, the PPF shifts outward, as in panel (a), indicating that more output can be produced. A decrease in available resources causes the PPF to shift inward, as in panel (b). Panel (c) shows a change affecting consumer goods production. More consumer goods can now be produced at any given level of capital goods. Panel (d) shows a change affecting capital goods production.

The new PPFs in both panels (a) and (b) appear to be parallel to the original PPF, indicating that the resource that changed could produce either good. For example, an increased supply of electrical power can be used in the production of both consumer goods and capital goods. If, however, a resource (such as farmland, for example) is suited only to the production of consumer goods, then an increase in the supply of that resource will shift the PPF more along the consumer goods axis than along the capital goods axis, as shown in panel (c). Panel (d) shows the effect of an increase in the supply of a resource (such as construction equipment) that is suited only to capital goods.

Increases in the Capital Stock. An economy's production possibilities frontier depends in part on the stock of human and physical capital. The more capital an economy accumulates during one period, the more output can be produced in the next period. Thus, increased production of capital goods this period (for example, by more machines in the case of physical capital or better education in the case of human capital) will shift out the economy's PPF next period.

Technological Change. Another type of change that could shift the economy's PPF outward is a technological discovery that employs available resources more efficiently. Some discoveries enhance the production of both products, such as an innovation that manages resources more efficiently. This is shown in panel (a) of Exhibit 3. The effect of a technological advance in the production of consumer goods, such as genetically altered seeds that double crop production, is reflected by a shift outward of the PPF along the consumer goods axis, as shown in panel (c) of Exhibit 3 (note that point *F* remains unchanged since the technological breakthrough does not affect the production of capital goods). Panel (d) shows the result of a technological advance in the production of capital goods, such as the development of improved software that reduces the cost of designing and manufacturing heavy machinery.

What We Can Learn from the PPF

The production possibilities frontier demonstrates several ideas introduced so far. The first is *efficiency*: The PPF describes the efficient combinations of output that are possible, given the economy's resources and technology. The second is *scarcity*: Given the resources and the technology, the economy can produce only so much. The PPF slopes downward, indicating that, as the economy produces more of one good, it produces less of the other good. This tradeoff demonstrates *opportunity cost*. The bowed-out shape of the PPF reflects the *law of increasing opportunity cost;* it arises because not all resources are perfectly adaptable to the production of each good. And a shift outward in the PPF reflects *economic growth*. Finally, because society must somehow choose a specific combination of output—a single point—along the PPF, the PPF also underscores the need for *choice*. That choice will determine not only current consumption but also the capital stock available next period. One thing the PPF does not tell us is which combination to choose; the PPF tells us only about the costs, not the benefits, of the two goods. To make a selection, we need information on both costs *and* benefits. How society goes about choosing a particular combination will depend upon the nature of the economic system, as we will see in the next section.

Three Questions Every Economic System Must Answer

Each point along the economy's production possibilities frontier is an efficient combination of output. Whether the economy produces efficiently and how the economy selects the most preferred combination will depend on the decision-making rules employed. Regardless of how decisions are made, each economy must answer three fundamental questions: What goods and services will be produced? How will they be produced? For whom will they be produced? An **economic system** is the set of mechanisms and institutions that resolve the *what, how,* and *for whom* questions. Some criteria used to distinguish among economic systems are (1) who owns the resources, (2) what decision-making process is used to allocate resources and products, and (3) what types of incentives guide the economic decision makers.

Economic system The set of mechanisms and institutions that resolve the what, how, and for whom questions

What Goods and Services Will Be Produced? Most of us take for granted the incredible number of choices that go into deciding what gets produced—everything from which new kitchen appliances are introduced and which aspiring novelists get published to which roads get built. Although different economies resolve these and millions of other questions using different decision-making rules and mechanisms, all economies must somehow make such choices.

How Will Goods and Services Be Produced? The economic system must determine how output is to be produced. Which resources should be used, and how should they be combined to produce each product? How much labor should be used, and at what skill levels? What kinds of machines should be used? What type of fertilizer should be applied to grow the best strawberries? Should the factory be built in the city or closer to the interstate highway? Millions of individual decisions determine which resources are employed and how these resources are combined.

For Whom Will Goods and Services Be Produced? Who will actually consume the goods and services produced? The economic system must determine how to allocate the fruits of production among the population. Should equal amounts be provided to everyone? Should the weak and the sick get more? Should those willing to wait in line the longest receive more? Should goods be allocated according to height? Weight? Religion? Age? Gender? Race? Looks? Strength? Political connections? The value of resources supplied? The question "For whom will goods and services be produced?" is often referred to as the *distribution question.*

ECONOMIC SYSTEMS

Although we discussed the three economic questions separately, they are closely interwoven. The answer to one depends very much on the answers to the others. For example, an economy that distributes goods and services in uniform amounts to all will, no doubt, answer the what-is-to-be-produced question differently than an economy that somehow allows each person to choose a unique mix of goods and services. Laws about resource ownership and the extent to which the government attempts to coordinate economic activity determine the "rules of the game"—the set of conditions that shape individual incentives and constraints. Along a spectrum ranging from the most free to the most regimented type of economic system, the *market system* would be at one end and the *command system* would be at the other end.

Pure Market System

Pure market system An economic system characterized by private ownership of resources and the use of prices to coordinate economic activity in unregulated markets

Under the **pure market system,** the rules of the game include the private ownership of all resources and the coordination of economic activity based on the price signals generated in free, unrestricted markets. Any income derived from supplying labor, capital, land, or entrepreneurial ability goes exclusively to the individual owners of those resources. Owners have *property rights* to the use of their resources and are therefore free to supply those resources to the highest bidder. Producers are free to make and sell whatever they think will be profitable. Consumers are free to buy whatever goods they can afford. All this voluntary buying and selling is coordinated by unrestricted markets, where buyers and sellers make their wishes known. Market prices guide resources to their highest-valued use and channel goods and services to consumers who value them the most.

Under the market system, markets answer the what, how, and for whom questions. Markets transmit information about relative scarcity, provide individual incentives, and distribute income among resource suppliers. No single individual or small group coordinates these activities. Rather, it is the voluntary choices of many buyers and sellers responding only to their individual incentives and constraints that direct resources and products to those who value them the most. According to Adam Smith (1723–1790), one of the first to explain the allocative role of markets, market forces coordinate as if by an "invisible hand"—an unseen force that harnesses the pursuit of self-interest to direct resources where they earn the greatest payoff. According to Smith, *although each individual pursues his or her self-interest, the "invisible hand" of markets promotes the general welfare.* The market system is sometimes called laissez-faire; translated from the French, this phrase means "to let do," or to let people do as they choose without government intervention. Thus, under the market system, voluntary choices based on rational self-interest are made in unrestricted markets to answer the questions what, how, and for whom.

***Net*Bookmark**

The Center for International Comparisons at the University of Pennsylvania at http://pwt.econ.upenn.edu/ is a good source of information on the performance of economies around the world.

As we shall see in later chapters, a pure market system has its flaws. The most notable market failures are the following:

1. There is no central authority that can protect property rights, enforce contracts, and otherwise ensure that the rules of the game are followed.
2. People with no resources to sell may starve.
3. Some producers may try to monopolize markets by eliminating the competition.
4. The production or consumption of some goods generates byproducts, such as pollution, that affect those not involved in the market transaction.
5. So-called *public goods*, such as national defense, will not be produced by private firms because private firms cannot prevent nonpayers from enjoying the benefits of public goods.

Because of these limitations, countries have modified the pure market system to allow a role for government. Even Adam Smith believed government should play a role. Hong Kong is perhaps the most market-oriented economy in the world today.

Pure Command System

In a **pure command system,** resources are directed and production is coordinated based on the "command," or central plan, of government rather than by markets. At least in theory, there is public—communal—ownership of property. Government planners, as representatives of all the people, answer such questions as how much steel, how many cars, how many homes, and how many loaves of bread to produce. They also decide how to produce these goods and how to allocate them.

Pure command system An economic system characterized by public ownership of resources and centralized economic planning

In theory, the pure command system incorporates individual choices into collective choices, which, in turn, are reflected in central planning decisions. In practice, the pure command system also has flaws. Most notably:

1. Running an economy is so complicated that some resources are used inefficiently.
2. Since nobody in particular owns resources, people have less incentive to employ them in their highest-valued use; so some resources are wasted.
3. Central plans may reflect more the preferences of central planners than those of society.
4. Since the central government is responsible for all production, the variety of products is much more limited than what is available in a competitive economy.
5. Each individual has less personal freedom in making economic choices.

Because of these limitations, countries have modified the pure command system to allow a role for markets. North Korea is perhaps the most centrally planned economy in the world today.

Mixed and Transitional Economies

No country on earth exemplifies either type of economic system in its pure form. Economic systems have grown more alike over time, with the role of government increasing in market economies and the role of markets increasing in command economies. The United States represents a **mixed system,** with government directly accounting for about one-third of all economic activity. What's more, government regulates the private sector in a variety of ways. For example, local zoning boards determine lot sizes, home sizes, and the types of industries allowed. Federal bodies regulate workplace safety, environmental quality, competitive fairness, and many other activities.

Mixed system An economic system characterized by private ownership of some resources and public ownership of other resources; some markets are unregulated and others are regulated.

Nearly all countries around the world have mixed economies. Countries with command systems are currently introducing more market incentives. For example, about 20 percent of the world's population live in the People's Republic of China, which grows more market oriented each day. The former Soviet Union dissolved into 15 independent republics; most are trying to privatize what had been state-owned enterprises. From Hungary to Mongolia, the transition to mixed economies now under way in former command economies will shape the 21st century.

Economies Based on Custom or Religion

Finally, some economic systems are molded largely by custom or religion. For example, caste systems in India and elsewhere restrict occupational choice.

Family relations also play important roles in organizing and coordinating economic activity. Your own pattern of consumption and choice of occupation may be influenced by some of these factors.

CONCLUSION

Although economies can answer the three economic questions in a variety of ways, this book will focus primarily on the mixed market system found in the United States. This type of economy blends *private choice*, guided by the price system in competitive markets, with *public choice*, guided by democracy in political markets. The study of mixed market systems grows more relevant as former command economies try to develop market economies.

If you were to stop reading right now, you would already know more economics than most people. But to understand market economies, you must learn how markets work. You will do so in the next chapter, which introduces the market interaction of demand and supply.

SUMMARY

1. Resources are scarce, but human wants are unlimited. Since we cannot satisfy all wants, we must choose, and choice always involves an opportunity cost. The opportunity cost of the selected option is the value of the best alternative forgone.
2. The law of comparative advantage states that the individual, firm, region, or country with the lowest opportunity cost of producing a particular good should specialize in the production of that good. Specialization according to the law of comparative advantage promotes the most efficient use of resources.
3. The specialization of labor increases efficiency by (1) taking advantage of individual preferences and natural abilities, (2) allowing each worker to develop more experience at a particular task, (3) reducing the time required to move between different tasks, and (4) allowing for the introduction of more specialized capital and production techniques.
4. The production possibilities frontier shows the productive capabilities of an economy when all resources are used efficiently. The frontier's bowed-out shape reflects the law of increasing opportunity cost, which arises because some resources are not perfectly adaptable to the production of different goods. Over time, the frontier can shift in or out as a result of changes in the availability of resources or in technology. The frontier demonstrates several economic concepts, including efficiency, scarcity, opportunity cost, the law of increasing opportunity cost, economic growth, and the need for choice.
5. All economic systems, regardless of their decision-making processes, must answer three fundamental questions: What is to be produced? How is it to be produced? For whom is it to be produced? Economies answer the questions differently, depending on who owns their resources and how economic activity is coordinated.

QUESTIONS FOR REVIEW

1. *(Opportunity Costs)* Discuss the ways in which the following conditions might affect the opportunity cost of going to a movie tonight:
   a. You have a final exam tomorrow.
   b. School will be out for one month starting tomorrow.
   c. The same movie will be shown on TV next week.
2. *(Opportunity Costs)* Determine whether each of the following statements is true, false, or uncertain. Explain your answers:
   a. The opportunity cost of an activity is the total value of all the alternatives passed up.
   b. Opportunity cost is an objective measure of cost.

c. When making choices, people gather all available information about the costs and benefits of alternative choices.
d. A decision maker seldom knows the actual value of a forgone alternative and must base decisions on expected values.

3. *(Law of Comparative Advantage)* "You should never buy precooked frozen foods because you are paying for the labor costs of preparing food." Is this conclusion always valid, or can it be invalidated by the principle of comparative advantage?

4. *(Specialization and Exchange)* Explain how the specialization of labor can lead to increased productivity.

5. *(Production Possibilities)* Under what conditions is it possible to increase production of one good without decreasing production of another good?

6. *(Production Possibilities)* Under what conditions would an economy be operating inside its PPF? Outside its PPF?

7. *(Shifting Production Possibilities)* In response to an influx of illegal aliens, Congress made it a federal offense to hire them. How do you think this measure affected the U.S. production possibilities frontier? Do you think all industries were affected equally?

8. *(Production Possibilities)* "If society decides to use its resources fully (that is, to produce *on* its production possibilities frontier), then future generations will be worse off because they will not be able to use these resources." If this assertion is true, full employment of resources may not be a good thing. Comment on the validity of this assertion.

9. *(Economic Questions)* What basic economic questions must be answered in a barter economy? In a primitive economy? In a pure capitalist economy? In a command economy?

10. *(Economic Systems)* What are the major differences between a pure market system and a pure command system? Is the United States more like a pure market system or more like a pure command system?

PROBLEMS AND EXERCISES

11. ***CaseStudy:*** *The Opportunity Cost of College)* During the Vietnam War, colleges and universities were overflowing with students. Was this bumper crop of students caused by a greater expected return on a college education or by a change in the opportunity cost of attending college? Explain.

12. *(Sunk Cost and Choice)* You go to a restaurant and buy an expensive meal. Halfway through, in spite of feeling full, you decide to clean your plate. After all, you think, you paid for the meal, so you are going to eat all of it. What's wrong with this thinking?

13. *(Comparative and Absolute Advantage)* You have the following information concerning the production of wheat and cloth in the United States and England:

Labor Hours Required to Produce One Unit

	England	United States
Wheat	2	1
Cloth	6	5

a. What is the opportunity cost of producing a unit of wheat in England? In the United States?
b. Which country has an absolute advantage in producing wheat? In producing cloth?
c. Which country has a comparative advantage in producing wheat? In producing cloth?
d. Which country should specialize in producing wheat? In producing cloth?

14. ***CaseStudy:*** *Evidence of Specialization)* Provide some examples of specialized markets or retail outlets. What makes a medium like the World Wide Web conducive to specialization?

15. *(Shape of the PPF)* Suppose a production possibilities frontier includes the following data points:

Cars	Washing Machines
0	1,000
100	600
200	0

a. Graph the production possibilities frontier, assuming that it has no curved segments.
b. What is the cost of producing an additional car when 50 cars are being produced?
c. What is the cost of producing an additional car when 150 cars are being produced?
d. What is the cost of producing an additional washing machine when 50 cars are being produced? When 150 cars are being produced?
e. What do your answers tell you about opportunity costs?

16. *(Production Possibilities)* Suppose that there are two resources in the economy (labor and capital) that are used to produce two goods (wheat and cloth). Capital is relatively more useful in producing cloth, and labor is relatively more useful in producing wheat. If the supply of capital falls by 10 percent and the supply of labor increases by 10 percent, how will the PPF for wheat and cloth change?

17. *(Production Possibilities)* There's no reason why a production possibilities frontier could not be used to represent the situation facing an individual. Imagine your own PPF. Right now—today—you have certain resources—your time, your skills, perhaps some capital. And you can produce various outputs. Suppose you can produce combinations of two outputs, call them studying and partying.
    a. Draw your PPF for studying and partying. Be sure to label the axes of the diagram appropriately. Label the points where the PPF intersects the axes, as well as several other points along the frontier.
    b. Explain what it would mean for you to move upward and to the left along your personal PPF. What kinds of adjustments would you have to make in your life to make such a movement along the frontier?
    c. Under what circumstances would your personal PPF shift outward? Do you think the shift would be a "parallel" one? Why, or why not?

18. *(Shifting Production Possibilities)* Determine whether each of the following would cause the economy's PPF to shift inward, outward, or not at all:
    a. An increase in average length of annual vacations.
    b. An increase in immigration.
    c. A decrease in the average retirement age.
    d. The migration of skilled workers to other countries.

19. *(Economic Systems)* The United States is best described as having a "mixed" economic system. What are some elements of command in the U.S. economy? What are some elements of tradition?

EXPERIENTIAL EXERCISES

20. *(Production Possibilities Frontier)* Here are some data on the U.S. economy taken from the *Economic Report of the President* at http://www.access.gpo.gov/eop/.

Year	Unemployment Rate	Real Government Spending (billions)	Real Civilian Spending (billions)
1982	9.7%	$ 947.7	$3,672.6
1983	9.6	960.1	3,843.6
1996	5.4	1,257.9	5,670.5
1997	4.9	1,270.6	5,920.8

    a. Sketch a production possibilities frontier for the years 1982 and 1983, showing the tradeoff between public-sector (government) and private-sector (civilian) spending. Assume that resource availability and technology were the same in both years, but notice that the unemployment rate was relatively high.
    b. Sketch a PPF for the years 1996 and 1997. Assume that resource availability and technology were the same in both years, but higher than in 1982 and 1983. Note that the unemployment rate in the late 1990s was much lower than in the early 1980s.
    c. What lessons did you learn about the U.S. economy during the past 20 years?

21. *(Economic Systems)* The transitional economies of Eastern Europe are frequently in the news since they provide testing grounds for the transition from socialist central planning to freer, more market-oriented economies. Take a look at the World Bank's *Transition Newsletter* at http://www.worldbank.org/html/prddr/trans/WEB/trans.htm. Choose a particular economy and try to determine how smoothly the transition is proceeding. What problems is that nation encountering?

22. *(Wall Street Journal)* The ability to measure the true (opportunity) cost of a choice is a skill that will pay you great dividends. Use any issue of the *Wall Street Journal*, and find an article that discusses a decision some firm has made. (Try the "Business Bulletin" column on the front page of Thursday's issue.) Then review this chapter's section titled "Choice and Opportunity Cost." Finally, make a list of the kinds of opportunity costs involved in the firm's decision.

CHAPTER

3 The Market System

Why do roses cost more on Valentine's Day than during the rest of the year? Why does TV advertising time cost more during the Super Bowl ($1.2 million for 30 seconds) than during *Nick-at-Nite* reruns. Why do hotel rooms in Phoenix cost more in February than in August? Why do surgeons earn more than butchers? Why do pro basketball players earn more than pro hockey players? Why do economics majors earn more than most other majors? Answers to these and most economic questions boil down to the workings of demand and supply, which will be examined in this chapter.

This chapter will introduce you to the underpinnings of demand and supply and show you how they interact in competitive markets. *Demand and supply are the most fundamental and the most powerful of all economic tools—important enough*

Visit the McEachern Interactive Study Center for this chapter at http://mcisc.swcollege.com

to warrant their own chapter. Indeed, some believe that if you programmed a computer to respond "demand and supply" to every economic question, you could put many economists out of work. An understanding of the two concepts will take you far in mastering the art and science of economic analysis. As you will see, the correct analysis of demand and supply takes skill and care. This chapter uses graphs extensively, so you may want to refer to the Appendix of Chapter 1 for a refresher. Topics discussed in this chapter include:

- Demand and quantity demanded
- Supply and quantity supplied
- Markets
- Equilibrium price and quantity
- Changes in demand and in supply
- Disequilibrium

DEMAND

Demand A relation showing the quantities of a good that consumers are willing and able to buy at various prices during a given period of time, other things constant

How much Pepsi will consumers buy each week if the price is $3 per six-pack? If the price is $2? If it's $4? The answers reveal the relationship between the price of Pepsi and the quantity purchased. Such a relationship is called the *demand* for Pepsi. **Demand** indicates the quantity of a product that consumers are both *willing* and *able* to buy at each possible price during a given period of time, other things constant. Because demand pertains to a specific period of time, such as a day, a week, or a month, think of demand as the desired *rate of purchase* per time period at each possible price. Also, note the emphasis on *willing* and *able*. You may be *able* to buy a motorcycle at a price of $4,000 because you can afford one, but you may not be *willing* to buy one if motorcycles don't interest you.

The Law of Demand

In a remote region of western Pennsylvania is a poorly lit, run-down yellow building known as Pechin's Mart. The aisles are unmarked and strewn with half-empty boxes arranged in no apparent design. The sagging roof leaks when it rains. Why do shoppers come from as far away as Maryland and put up with the chaos and the grubbiness of Pechin's Mart to buy as many groceries as they can haul away? The store has violated nearly all the traditional rules of retailing, yet it thrives, with annual sales more than four times the national average. The store thrives because it reflects a rule merchants have known for thousands of years: Its prices are the lowest around.

Law of demand The quantity of a good demanded in a given time period is inversely related to its price, other things constant

As a consumer, you have little trouble understanding that people will buy more of a product at a lower price than at a higher price. Sell the product for less, and the world will beat a path to your door. This relation between the price of a product and the quantity demanded is an economic law. The **law of demand** states that the quantity of a product demanded during a given time period varies inversely with its price, other things constant. Thus, the higher the price, the smaller the quantity demanded; the lower the price, the greater the quantity demanded.

Demand, Wants, and Needs. Consumer *demand* and consumer *wants* are not the same thing. As we have seen, wants are unlimited. You may *want* a Mercedes-Benz 500-SL, but the $130,000 price is likely beyond your budget (that is, the quantity you demand at that price is zero). Nor is *demand* the same as *need*. You may *need* a new muffler for your car, but if the price is $200, you may decide

"I am not going to pay a lot for this muffler." Apparently, you have better ways to spend your money. If, however, the price of mufflers drops enough—say, to $90—then you become both willing and able to buy one.

The Substitution Effect of a Price Change. What explains the law of demand? Why, for example, is more demanded when the price is lower? The explanation begins with unlimited wants confronting scarce resources. Many goods and services are capable of satisfying particular wants. For example, you can satisfy your hunger with pizza, tacos, burgers, chicken, or dozens of other dishes. Similarly, you can satisfy your desire for warmth in the winter with warm clothing, a home-heating system, a trip to Hawaii, or many other ways. Clearly, some ways of satisfying your wants will be more appealing than others (a trip to Hawaii is more fun than warmer clothing). In a world without scarcity, everything would be free, so you would always choose the most attractive alternative. Scarcity, however, is a reality, and the degree of scarcity of one good relative to another helps determine each good's *relative* price.

NetBookmark

The Inomics search engine is devoted solely to economics http://www.inomics.com/query/show?what=welcome. Use it to investigate topics related to supply and demand and to other economic models.

Notice that the definition of demand includes the "other-things-constant" assumption. Among "other things" assumed to remain constant are the prices of other goods. When the price of pizza declines and other prices remain constant, pizza becomes relatively cheaper. Consumers are then more *willing* to purchase pizza when its relative price falls; they tend to substitute pizza for other goods. This is called the **substitution effect** of a price change. On the other hand, an increase in the price of pizza, other things constant, causes consumers to substitute other goods for the now higher-priced pizza. Remember, *it is the change in the relative price—the price of one good relative to the prices of other goods—that causes the substitution effect*. If all prices changed by the same percentage, there would be no change in relative prices and no substitution effect.

Substitution effect When the price of a good falls, consumers will substitute that good for other goods, which are now relatively more expensive

The Income Effect of a Price Change. A fall in the price of a product increases the quantity demanded for a second reason. Suppose you earn $30 a week from a part-time job and spend all your income on pizza, buying three a week at $10 per pizza. What if the price drops to $6? At that price you can now afford five pizzas a week with your income. The decrease in the price of pizza has increased your **real income**—that is, your income measured in terms of what it can buy. The price reduction, other things constant, increases the *purchasing power* of your income, thereby increasing your *ability* to purchase pizza. The quantity of pizza you demand will likely increase because of this **income effect** of a price decrease. You may not increase your quantity demanded to five pizzas, but you could. If you purchase four pizzas per week when the price drops to $6, you would have $6 left over to buy other goods. Thus, the income effect of a lower price increases your real income and thereby increases your ability to purchase all goods.

Real income Income measured in terms of the goods and services it can buy

Income effect A fall in the price of a good increases consumers' real income, making the consumers more able to purchase all goods; for normal goods, the quantity demanded increases

More generally, because of the income effect of a price decrease, other things constant, consumers typically increase their quantity demanded. Conversely, an increase in the price of a good, other things constant, reduces real income, thereby reducing the *ability* to purchase all goods. Because of the income effect of a price increase, consumers typically reduce their quantity demanded.

The Demand Schedule and Demand Curve

Demand can be expressed as a *demand schedule* or as a *demand curve*. Panel (a) of Exhibit 1 shows a hypothetical demand schedule for milk. When we describe

EXHIBIT 1

The Demand Schedule and Demand Curve for Milk

(a) Demand schedule

	Price per Quart	Quantity Demanded per Month (millions of quarts)
a	$1.25	8
b	1.00	14
c	0.75	20
d	0.50	26
e	0.25	32

(b) Demand curve

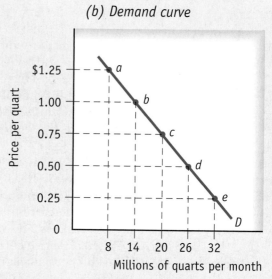

The market demand curve, *D*, shows the quantity of milk demanded, at various prices, by all consumers.

demand, we must specify the units being measured and the time period considered. In our example, the price is for a quart of milk, and the time period is a month. The milk is of uniform quality, in this case grade A homogenized whole milk. The schedule lists possible prices, along with the quantity demanded at each price. At a price of $1.25 per quart, for example, consumers demand 8 million quarts per month. As you can see, the lower the price, other things constant, the greater the quantity demanded. If the price drops as low as $0.25 per quart, consumers demand 32 million quarts per month. As the price of milk falls, consumers substitute milk for other goods. And as the price falls, the real income of consumers increases, causing them to increase the quantity of milk demanded.

Demand curve A curve showing the quantities of a particular good demanded at various possible prices during a given time period, other things constant

The demand schedule in panel (a) appears as a **demand curve** in panel (b), with price on the vertical axis and the quantity demanded per month on the horizontal axis. Each combination of price and quantity demanded listed in the demand schedule in panel (a) becomes a point in panel (b). Point *a*, for example, indicates that if the price is $1.25, consumers demand 8 million quarts per month. These points connect to form the demand curve for milk, labeled *D*. Note that the demand curve slopes downward, reflecting the *law of demand*: Price and quantity demanded are inversely related, other things constant. Assumed to be constant along the demand curve are the prices of other goods. Thus, along the demand curve for milk, the price of milk changes *relative to the prices of other goods*. The demand curve shows the effect of a change in the *relative price* of milk—that is, relative to other prices, which do not change.

Take care to distinguish between the *demand* for milk and the *quantity demanded*. The *demand* for milk is not a specific quantity, but rather the *entire relation* between price and quantity demanded—represented by the demand schedule or demand curve. An individual point on the demand curve shows the *quantity demanded* at a particular price. For example, at a price of $0.75 per quart, the quantity demanded is 20 million quarts per month. When the price of milk changes from, say, $0.75 to $1.00, this change is shown in Exhibit 1 by a movement along the demand curve—in this case from point *c* to point *b*. Any movement along a demand curve reflects a *change in quantity demanded*, not a change in demand.

The law of demand applies to the millions of products sold in grocery stores, department stores, clothing stores, drug stores, music stores, book stores, travel agencies, and restaurants, as well as through mail-order catalogues, the Yellow Pages, classified ads, the Internet, stock markets, real estate markets, job markets, flea markets, and all other markets. The law of demand applies even to choices that seem more personal than economic, such as whether or not to own a pet. For example, after New York City passed an anti-dog-litter law, owners had to follow their dogs around the city's sidewalks with scoopers, plastic bags, or whatever else would do the job. Because the law raised the cost, or price, of owning a dog, the quantity demanded decreased. The number of dogs left at animal shelters doubled. Many owners simply abandoned their dogs, raising the number of strays in the city. The law of demand predicts such behavior.

It is useful to distinguish between *individual demand*, which is the demand of an individual consumer, and *market demand*, which is the sum of the individual demands of all consumers in the market. In most markets, there are many consumers, sometimes millions. Unless otherwise noted, when we talk about demand, we will be referring to market demand, as in Exhibit 1.

CHANGES IN DEMAND

A demand curve isolates the relation between the price of a good and the quantity demanded, when other factors that could affect demand remain unchanged. What are these other factors, and how do changes in them affect demand? Variables that can affect market demand are (1) consumer income, (2) the prices of related goods, (3) consumer expectations, (4) the number and composition of consumers in the market, and (5) consumer tastes. Let's see how a change in each variable influences demand.

Changes in Consumer Income

Exhibit 2 shows the market demand curve for milk, *D*. This demand curve assumes a given level of consumer incomes. Suppose consumer incomes increase. Consumers will then be willing and able to purchase more milk at each price, so the demand for milk will increase; the demand curve shifts to the right from *D* to *D'*. For example, at a price of $1.00, the quantity demanded increases from 14 million to 20 million quarts per month, as indicated by the movement from point *b* on *D* to point *g* on *D'*.

An increase in the demand for milk also means that consumers are willing and able to pay a higher price for each *quantity* of milk. For example, consumers were initially willing and able to pay $1.00 per quart for 14 million quarts, as

EXHIBIT 2

An Increase in the Market Demand for Milk

An increase in the demand for milk is reflected by an outward shift in the demand curve. After the increase in demand, the quantity of milk demanded at a price of $1 per quart increases from 14 million quarts (point *b*) to 20 million quarts (point *g*). Another way to interpret the shift is to say that the maximum price consumers are willing to pay for 14 million quarts has increased from $1 per unit (at point *b*) to $1.25 per unit (at point *f*).

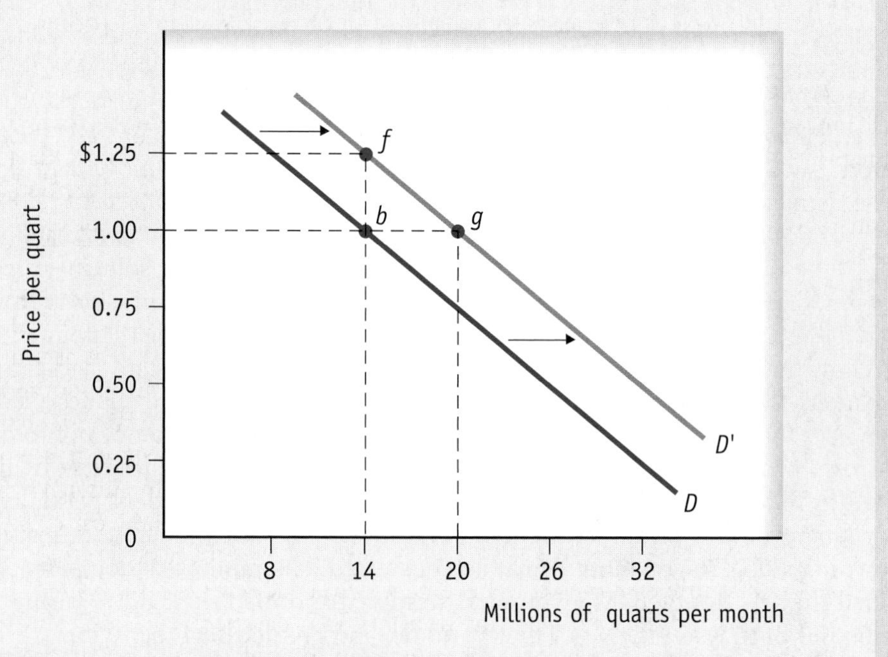

reflected by point *b*. After the increase in income, consumers are willing and able to pay $1.25 per quart for 14 million quarts, as reflected by point *f* on the new demand curve, which is directly above point *b* on the original demand curve. In short, *an increase in demand—that is, a shift to the right, or a shift upward, in the demand curve—means that consumers are willing and able to buy more units at each price and to pay more per unit at each quantity.*

Normal good A good for which demand increases as consumer incomes rise

Inferior good A good for which demand decreases as consumer incomes rise

We classify goods into two broad groupings, depending on how demand for the good responds to changes in income. The demand for **normal goods** increases as income increases. Because milk is a normal good, the demand for milk increases when consumer income increases. Most goods are normal goods. In contrast, the demand for **inferior goods** actually declines as income increases. Examples of inferior goods include ground chuck, trips to the laundromat, and bus rides. As income increases, consumers tend to switch from consuming these inferior goods to consuming normal goods (steak, their own washers and dryers, and automobile or plane rides), so the demand curves for inferior goods shift to the left.

Changes in the Prices of Related Goods

As we've seen, the prices of other goods are assumed to be constant along a given demand curve. Now let's bring these other prices into play. There are various ways of trying to satisfy any particular want. Consumers choose among substitutes partly on the basis of their relative prices. For example, milk and juice are substitutes. Obviously they are not perfect substitutes (you wouldn't pour juice on cereal or use it to make hot chocolate). Yet an increase in the price of juice, other things constant, will prompt some consumers to buy less juice and more milk. Two goods are **substitutes** if an increase in the price of one leads to an increase in the demand for the other and, conversely, if a decrease in the price of one leads to a decrease in the demand for the other.

Substitutes Goods that are related in such a way that an increase in the price of one leads to an increase in the demand for the other

Certain goods are used in combination to satisfy a want. Milk and chocolate chip cookies, computer hardware and software, popcorn and movies, and airline tickets and rental cars are complements. Two goods are **complements** if a decrease in the price of one leads to an increase in the demand for the other. For example, a decrease in the price of computers leads to an increase in the demand for software. Most pairs of goods selected at random are *unrelated*—for example, milk and housing, pizza and socks, dental floss and trail bikes.

Complements Goods that are related in such a way that an increase in the price of one leads to a decrease in the demand for the other

Changes in Consumer Expectations

Another factor assumed to be constant along a given demand curve is consumer expectations about factors that influence demand, such as future income and the future price of the good. A change in consumer expectations can change demand. For example, a consumer who learns about a future pay increase may increase current demand well before that pay increase occurs. In anticipation of a steady paycheck, a college senior who lands a job may buy a new car even before graduation. Changes in price expectations can also affect demand. For example, if consumers come to believe that home prices will jump next year, some will increase their demand for housing this year, before prices go up. On the other hand, expectations of a lower price in the future will encourage some consumers to postpone current purchases, thereby reducing current demand.

Changes in the Number or Composition of Consumers

As mentioned earlier, market demand is the sum of the individual demands of all consumers in the market. If the number of consumers in the market changes, demand will change. For example, if the population grows, the demand for food will increase. Even if the total population remains the same, demand could change as a result of a change in composition of the population. For example, if the number of retired persons increases, the demand for recreational vehicles will probably increase. If the infant population booms, the demand for baby food, baby clothes, and playpens will jump.

Changes in Consumer Tastes

Do you like anchovies on your pizza or sauerkraut on your hot dog? How about tattoos and body piercing? Is music to your ears more likely to be rock, country, heavy metal, rap, reggae, jazz, or classical? Choices in food, body art, music, clothing, reading, movies, TV shows—indeed, all consumer choices—are influenced by consumer tastes. **Tastes** are nothing more than your likes and dislikes as a consumer. Tastes are assumed to be constant along a demand curve. What determines tastes? Who knows? Economists certainly don't, nor do they spend much time worrying about it. They recognize, however, that tastes are important in shaping demand.

Tastes Consumer preferences; likes and dislikes in consumption

Economists assume that tastes are relatively stable. Because a change in tastes is so difficult to isolate from other economic changes, we should be reluctant to attribute a change in demand to a change in tastes. In our analysis of consumer demand, *we will assume that tastes are given and are relatively stable over time.* We know, for example, that younger people usually prefer rock music, whereas older people tend to prefer other kinds of music. The music piped into shopping malls tends to be so-called easy-listening music, intended to encourage older, higher-income customers to stay longer, be at ease, and spend more, while discouraging younger people from hanging out any longer than needed to do their shopping.

Change in quantity demanded A movement along the demand curve in response to a change in the price, other things constant

Change in demand A shift in a given demand curve caused by a change in any of the determinants of demand for the good other than its price

Remember, a movement along a given demand curve is called a **change in quantity demanded.** A change in quantity demanded results from a change in *price*, other things constant. A shift in the demand curve is called a **change in demand.** A change in demand results from a change in determinants of demand other than the price of the good—such as a change in income, a change in the price of related goods, a change in consumer expectations, a change in the number or composition of consumers, or a change in consumer tastes.

SUPPLY

Supply A relation showing the quantities of a good producers are willing and able to sell at various prices during a given time period, other things constant

Law of supply The quantity of a product supplied in a given time period is usually directly related to its price, other things constant

Supply curve A curve showing the quantities of a good supplied at various prices, other things constant

Just as demand is a relation between price and quantity demanded, supply is a relation between price and quantity supplied. Specifically, **supply** indicates how much of a good producers are *willing* and *able* to offer for sale per period at each possible price, other things constant. The **law of supply** states that the quantity supplied is usually directly related to its price, other things constant. Thus, the lower the price, the smaller the quantity supplied; the higher the price, the greater the quantity supplied.

The Supply Schedule and Supply Curve

Exhibit 3 presents the market *supply schedule* and market **supply curve,** *S*, for milk. It shows the quantities of milk supplied per month at various possible prices by thousands of dairy farmers. As you can see, price and quantity supplied are directly, or positively, related. Producers offer more for sale at a higher price than at a lower price, so the supply curve slopes upward.

There are two reasons producers tend to offer more goods for sale when the price rises. First, as the price of a good increases, other things constant, a producer becomes more *willing* to supply the good. Prices act as signals to existing and potential suppliers about the rewards for producing various goods. An increase in the price of milk provides farmers with a profit incentive to shift some resources out of the production of other goods such as corn, for which the price is now relatively lower, and into milk, for which the price is now relatively higher. *A higher milk price attracts resources from lower-valued uses to the higher-valued use.*

A second reason the supply curve tends to slope upward is that higher prices increase the producer's *ability* to supply the good. The law of increasing opportunity cost, as noted in Chapter 2, states that the opportunity cost of producing more of a particular good rises as output increases—that is, the *marginal cost* of production increases as output increases. Since producers face a higher marginal cost for additional output, they must receive a higher price for that output in order to be *able* to increase the quantity supplied. For example, when milk production is low, farmers are able to employ resources that are well suited to the task. As output increases, however, producing the additional increments of milk draws on resources that may be better suited to producing other goods. To feed additional cows, for example, a farmer may have to convert a corn field

EXHIBIT 3

The Supply Schedule and Supply Curve for Milk

(a) Supply schedule

Price per Quart	Quantity Supplied per Month (millions of quarts)
$1.25	28
1.00	24
0.75	20
0.50	16
0.25	12

(b) Supply curve

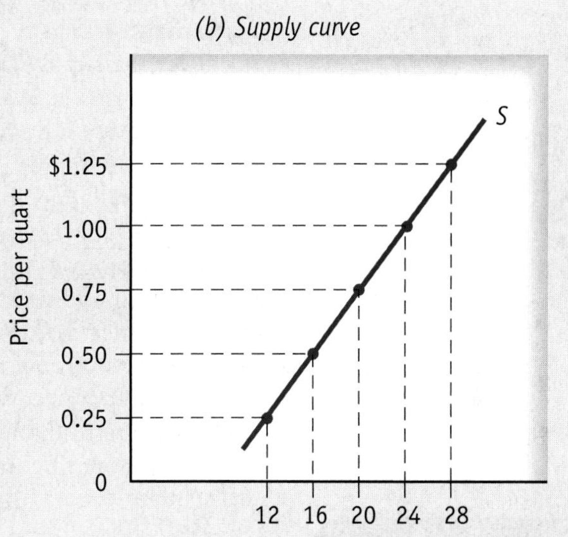

The market supply curve, *S*, shows the quantity of milk supplied, at various prices, by all farmers.

into a pasture. Therefore, additional output has a higher opportunity cost. *Higher milk prices make farmers better able to draw resources away from alternative uses.* Similarly, a higher price for gasoline increased oil companies' ability to explore in less accessible locations, such as the remote jungles of the Amazon, the stormy waters of the North Sea, and the frozen tundra of Alaska and Siberia. On the other hand, a decade-long slide in the price of gold has shut down some gold mines that could no longer operate profitably.

Thus, a higher price makes producers more *willing* and more *able* to increase the quantity of goods offered for sale. Producers are more *willing* because production of the higher-priced good is now relatively more attractive than the alternative uses of the resources involved. Producers are more *able* because the higher price allows them to cover the higher marginal cost that typically results from a higher rate of production.

As with demand, we distinguish between *individual* supply and *market* supply. Market supply is the sum of the amounts supplied at each price by all the individual suppliers. Unless otherwise noted, when we talk about supply, we will be referring to market supply. We also distinguish between *supply* and *quantity supplied*. Supply is the relation between the price and quantity supplied, as reflected by the entire supply schedule or supply curve. Quantity supplied refers to a particular amount offered for sale at a particular price, as reflected by a point on a given supply curve.

CHANGES IN SUPPLY

The supply curve expresses the relation between the price of a good and the quantity supplied, other things constant. Assumed constant along a supply curve are the determinants of supply other than the price of the good, including (1) the state of technology, (2) the prices of relevant resources, (3) the prices of alternative goods, (4) producer expectations, and (5) the number of producers in the market. Let's see how a change in each of these determinants of supply will affect the supply curve.

Changes in Technology

Recall from Chapter 2 that the state of technology represents the economy's stock of knowledge about how to combine resources most efficiently. Along a given supply curve, technology is assumed to remain unchanged. If a more efficient technology is discovered, production costs will fall; so suppliers will be more willing and more able to supply the good at each price. Consequently, supply will increase, as reflected by a rightward shift of the supply curve. For example, suppose a new milking machine called The Invisible Hand has a soothing effect on cows; cows find the new machine so "udderly" delightful that they produce more milk. Such a technological advance increases the market supply of milk, as shown by the shift from *S* to *S*' in Exhibit 4.

EXHIBIT 4

An Increase in the Supply of Milk

An increase in the supply of milk is reflected by a shift to the right in the supply curve, from *S* to *S*'. After the increase in supply, the quantity of milk supplied at a price of $1 per quart increases from 24 million quarts (point *h*) to 28 million quarts (point *i*). Another way to interpret the shift is to say that it shows a reduction in the minimum price suppliers require in order to produce 24 million quarts. Previously, a price of $1 per quart was required (point *h*); after the increase in supply, suppliers require a price of only $0.75 per quart (point *j*).

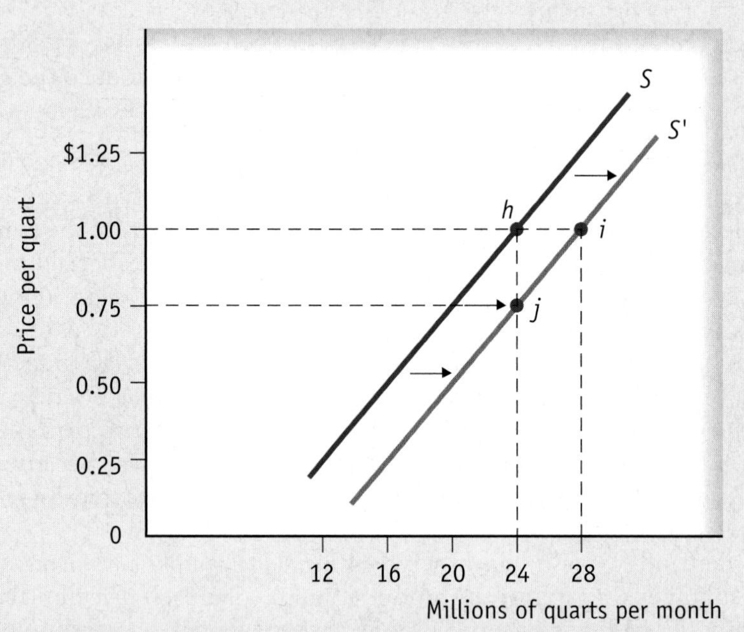

Notice that, just as a change in demand can be interpreted in two different ways, so can a change in supply. First, an increase in supply means that dairy farmers supply more milk at each possible price. For example, when the price is $1.00 per quart, the amount of milk supplied increases from 24 million to 28 million quarts per month, as shown in Exhibit 4 by the movement from point *h* to point *i*. Second, an increase in supply means that farmers are willing and able to supply the same quantity at a lower price. For example, farmers originally supplied 24 million quarts when the price was $1.00 per quart; on the new supply curve, that same quantity is supplied for only $0.75 per quart, as shown by the movement from point *h* down to point *j*.

Changes in the Prices of Relevant Resources

Relevant resources are those employed in the production of the good in question. For example, suppose the price of cow fodder falls. This lower resource price reduces the cost of milk production. Dairy farmers are therefore more willing and better able to supply milk. The supply curve for milk shifts to the right or shifts down, as shown in Exhibit 4. On the other hand, an increase in the price of a relevant resource reduces supply. For example, higher electricity rates increase the cost of lighting the barn and operating the milking machines. These higher production costs decrease supply, meaning that supply shifts to the left, or shifts up.

Relevant resources Resources used to produce the good in question

Changes in the Prices of Alternative Goods

Nearly all resources have alternative uses. The farmer's labor, tractor, barn, field, and planning skills could produce a variety of crops. **Alternative goods** are those that use some of the same resources as are employed to produce the good under consideration. For example, as crop prices increase, so does the opportunity cost of dairy farming. Some farmers will shift out of dairy farming and into crop farming, so the supply of milk will decrease, or shift to the left. On the other hand, a fall in the price of an alternative good, such as crops, makes milk production relatively more attractive. As resources shift into milk production, the supply curve for milk will increase, or shift to the right.

Alternative goods Other goods that use some of the same resources as used to produce the good in question

Changes in Producer Expectations

Changes in producer expectations about market factors can change current supply. For example, a farmer expecting higher prices for milk in the future may begin to expand her dairy today, thereby increasing the current supply of milk and shifting the supply of milk to the right. When a good can be stored easily (crude oil, for example, can be left in the ground), expecting higher prices in the future prompts producers to *reduce* their current supply and await the higher price. Their decrease in supply is reflected by a shift to the left in the supply curve. Thus, an expectation of higher prices in the future could either increase or decrease the current supply, depending on the nature of the good under consideration. More generally, any change expected to affect future profitability, such as a change in business taxes, could change current supply.

Changes in the Number of Producers

Since market supply is the sum of the amounts supplied by all producers, market supply depends on the number of producers in the market. If the number of producers increases, supply will increase, or shift to the right; if the number decreases, supply will decrease, or shift to the left. For example, the number of coffee bars has more than quadrupled in the United States during the last decade, shifting the supply curve of coffee to the right.

Change in quantity supplied A movement along the supply curve in response to a change in the price, other things constant

Change in supply A shift in a given supply curve caused by a change in one of the determinants of the supply of the good other than its price

Finally, note the distinction between (1) a **change in quantity supplied,** which is the producer response to a change in the *price* of the good, other things constant, and is represented as a movement along a given supply curve, and (2) a **change in supply,** which is the response to a change in one of the determinants of supply other than the price of good and is represented as a shift in the entire supply curve.

We are now ready to bring demand and supply together.

DEMAND AND SUPPLY CREATE A MARKET

Suppliers and demanders have different views of price, because demanders pay the price and suppliers receive it. Thus, a higher price is bad news for consumers but good news for producers. As the price rises, consumers reduce their quantity demanded and producers increase their quantity supplied. How is this conflict between producers and consumers resolved?

Markets

A product's market sorts out the conflicting price perspectives of individual participants—suppliers and demanders. A *market*, as we know from Chapter 1, is the means by which individuals interact to buy or to sell; it is a mechanism that coordinates the independent intentions of buyers and sellers. A market represents all the arrangements used to buy and sell a particular good or service. Markets reduce the **transaction costs** of exchange—the costs of time and information required for exchange. For example, suppose you are looking for a summer job. One approach would be to go from employer to employer looking for openings. This approach would be time consuming and could involve extensive travel. A better strategy would be to pick up a copy of the local newspaper and read through the help-wanted ads. These ads, which are one element of the job market, reduce the transaction costs required to bring workers and employers together. .

Transaction costs The costs of time and information required to carry out market exchange

The coordination that occurs through markets takes place not because of some central plan but because of Adam Smith's "invisible hand." For example, most of the auto dealers in your community tend to locate together, usually on the outskirts of town where land is cheaper. The dealers congregate, not because someone told them to or because they like one another's company, but because each wants to be where customers shop for cars—that is, near other dealers. Similarly, stores group together downtown and in shopping malls to be where shoppers shop. Disney World, Sea World, Universal Studios, and Universal City located together in Orlando to be where tourists tour. Theme parks cluster in the Los Angeles area for the same reason.

Market Equilibrium

To see how a market works, let's bring together market demand and market supply. Exhibit 5 shows the demand for and supply of milk, using schedules in panel (a) and curves in panel (b). To start, suppose the price initially is $1.00 per quart.

At that price, producers supply 24 million quarts per month, but consumers demand only 14 million quarts per month. The quantity supplied exceeds the quantity demanded, resulting in an *excess quantity supplied*, or a **surplus,** of 10 million quarts per month/This unsold milk tells producers that the price is too high. Unless the price falls, the surplus will continue and milk will sour on store shelves. The suppliers' desire to eliminate the surplus puts downward pressure on the price, as reflected by the arrow pointing downward in panel (b). As the price falls, producers reduce their quantity supplied and consumers increase their quantity demanded. As long as quantity supplied exceeds quantity demanded, the surplus will force the price lower.

Surplus An excess of quantity supplied compared to quantity demanded at a given price; a surplus puts downward pressure on the price

Alternatively, suppose the price is initially $0.50 per quart. You can see from Exhibit 5 that at this price consumers demand 26 million quarts per month but producers supply only 16 million quarts per month, resulting in an *excess*

EXHIBIT 5

Equilibrium in the Milk Market

Market equilibrium occurs at a price at which the quantity demanded by consumers is equal to the quantity supplied by producers. This is shown at point *c*. At prices above the equilibrium price, the quantity supplied exceeds the quantity demanded; at these prices there is a surplus, and there is a downward pressure on the price. At prices below equilibrium, quantity demanded exceeds quantity supplied; the resulting shortage puts upward pressure on the price.

(a) Market schedules

	Millions of Quarts per Month			
Price per Quart	**Quantity Demanded**	**Quantity Supplied**	**Surplus or Shortage**	**Price Will**
$1.25	8	28	Surplus of 20	Fall
1.00	14	24	Surplus of 10	Fall
0.75	20	20	Equilibrium	Remain the same
0.50	26	16	Shortage of 10	Rise
0.25	32	12	Shortage of 20	Rise

(b) Market curves

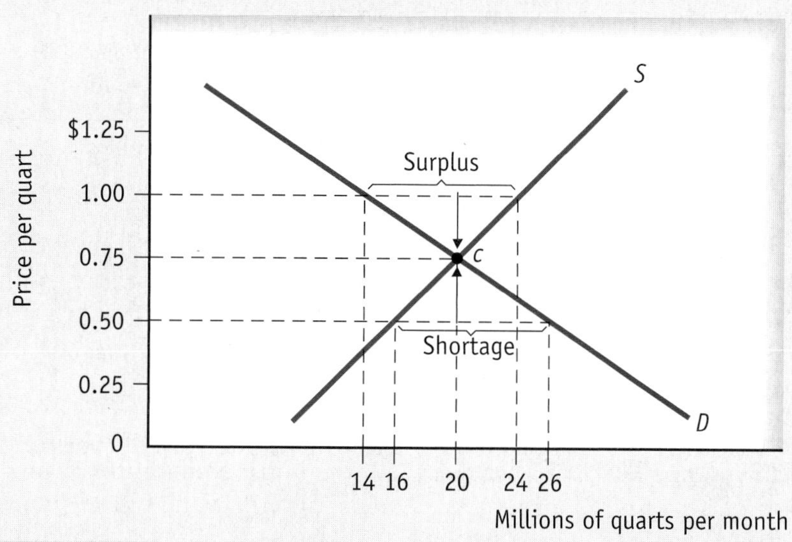

Shortage An excess of quantity demanded compared to quantity supplied at a given price; a shortage puts upward pressure on price

quantity demanded, or a **shortage,** of 10 million quarts per month. Producers quickly notice that the quantity supplied has sold out and customers are grumbling because milk is no longer available. Empty store shelves, frustrated consumers, and the profit incentives of producers create market pressure for a higher price, as reflected by the arrow pointing upward in panel (b). As the price rises, producers increase their quantity supplied and consumers reduce their quantity demanded. The price will continue to rise as long as quantity demanded exceeds quantity supplied.

Thus, a surplus creates downward pressure on the price, and a shortage creates upward pressure on the price. So long as quantity demanded and quantity supplied differ, this difference will force a price change, which will change both quantity demanded and quantity supplied. Note that a shortage or a surplus must always be defined at a particular price. There is no such thing as a general shortage or a general surplus.

Equilibrium The condition that exists in a market when the plans of the buyers match the plans of the sellers; the market clears

When the quantity that consumers are willing and able to buy equals the quantity that producers are willing and able to sell, the market is in equilibrium. In **equilibrium,** the independent plans of both buyers and sellers exactly match, so market forces will exert no pressure to change price and quantity. In panel (b) of Exhibit 5, the demand and supply curves intersect at the *equilibrium point*, identified as point *c*. The *equilibrium price* is $0.75 per quart, and the *equilibrium quantity* is 20 million quarts per month. At that price and quantity, the market *clears*. There is no shortage and no surplus, so there is no pressure for change.

A market finds equilibrium through the independent actions of thousands, or even millions, of buyers and sellers. In one sense, the market is personal because each consumer and each producer makes a personal decision regarding how much to buy or sell at a given price. In another sense, the market is impersonal because it requires no conscious coordination among consumers or producers. *Impersonal market forces synchronize the personal and independent decisions of many individual buyers and sellers to determine equilibrium price and quantity.*

CHANGES IN EQUILIBRIUM PRICE AND QUANTITY

Recall that equilibrium is the combination of price and quantity at which the intentions of demanders and suppliers exactly match. Once a market reaches equilibrium, that price and quantity will continue to prevail until one of the determinants of demand or supply changes. A change in any one of these determinants will usually change equilibrium price and quantity in a predictable way, as we shall see.

Impact of Changes in Demand

In Exhibit 6, demand curve *D* and supply curve *S* intersect to yield the initial equilibrium price of $0.75 per quart and the initial equilibrium quantity of 20 million quarts of milk per month. Now suppose that one of the determinants of demand changes in a way that increases demand, shifting the demand curve to the right from *D* to *D'*. Any of the following changes could increase the demand for milk: (1) an increase in consumer income (since milk is a normal good); (2) an increase in the price of a substitute, such as juice, or a decrease in

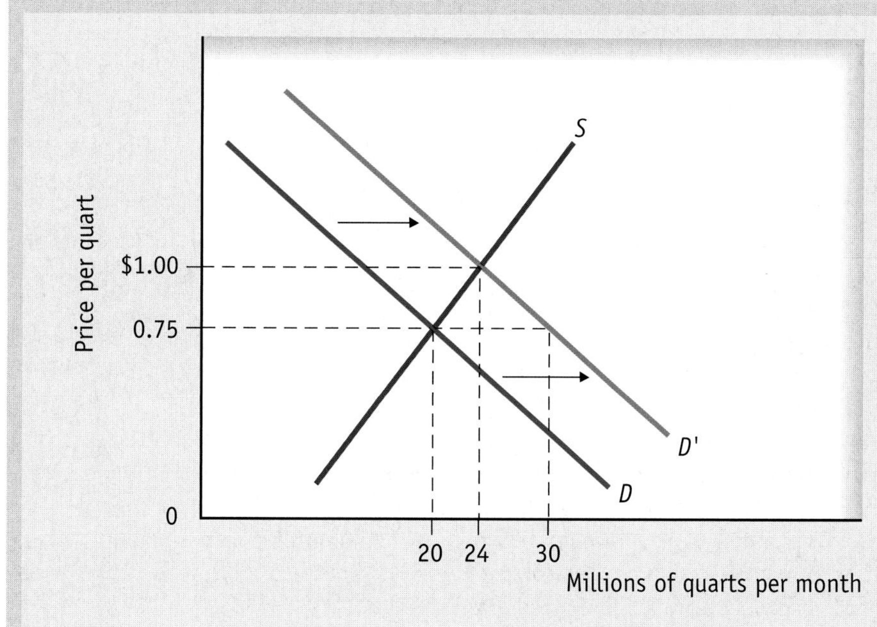

EXHIBIT 6

Effects of an Increase in Demand

After an increase in demand shifts the demand curve from *D* to *D'*, quantity demanded exceeds quantity supplied at the old price of $0.75 per quart. As the price rises, quantity supplied increases along supply curve *S*, and quantity demanded falls along demand curve *D'*. When the new equilibrium price of $1.00 per quart is reached, the quantity demanded will once again equal the quantity supplied. Both price and quantity are higher following the increase in demand.

the price of a complement, such as cereal; (3) a change in consumers' expectations that encourages them to buy more milk now; (4) an increase in the number of consumers; or (5) a change in consumer tastes—based, for example, on a discovery that milk consumption improves mental health.

After the increase in demand to *D'*, as reflected in Exhibit 6, the quantity demanded at the initial price of $0.75 is 30 million quarts, which exceeds the quantity supplied of 20 million quarts by 10 million quarts. This shortage puts upward pressure on the price. As the price increases, the quantity demanded decreases along the new demand curve, *D'*; and the quantity supplied increases along the existing supply curve *S* until the two quantities are equal in equilibrium once again. The new equilibrium price is $1.00 per quart, and the new equilibrium quantity is 24 million quarts per month. Thus, given an upward-sloping supply curve, an increase in demand increases both equilibrium price and quantity. A decrease in demand would lower both equilibrium price and quantity. We can summarize these results as follows: *Given an upward-sloping supply curve, any change in demand will change both equilibrium price and quantity in the same direction as the change in demand.*

Impact of Changes in Supply

Let's look now at the impact of a change in supply. In Exhibit 7, as before, we begin with demand curve *D* and supply curve *S* to yield the initial equilibrium price of $0.75 per quart and the initial equilibrium quantity of 20 million quarts per month. Suppose one of the determinants of supply changes, resulting in a supply increase from *S* to *S'*. Changes that could increase the supply of milk include: (1) a

EXHIBIT 7

Effects of an Increase in Supply

An increase in supply is depicted as a shift to the right in the supply curve, from *S* to *S*'. At the new equilibrium, quantity is greater and price is lower than before the increase in supply.

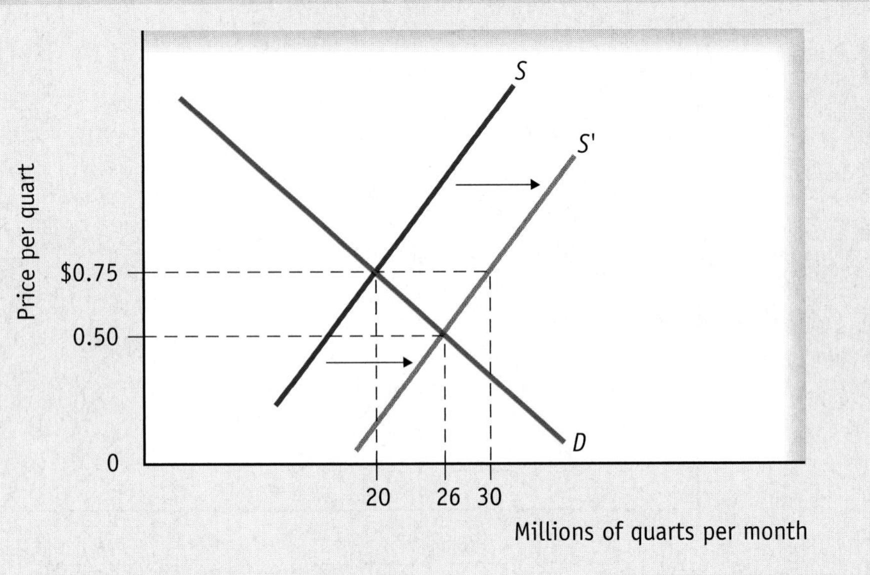

technological advance in milk production, such as development of milk-enhancing hormones; (2) a reduction in the price of a relevant resource, such as cow feed; (3) a decline in the price of an alternative good, such as corn; (4) a change in expectations that encourages farmers to supply more milk now, such as expectations of higher prices in the future; or (5) an increase in the number of dairy farmers.

After the increase in supply in Exhibit 7, the amount supplied at the initial equilibrium price of $0.75 increases from 20 million to 30 million quarts, resulting in a 10 million quart surplus. This surplus forces the price down. As the price falls, the quantity supplied declines along the new supply curve and the quantity demanded increases until a new equilibrium point is established. The new equilibrium price is $0.50 per quart, and the new equilibrium quantity is 26 million quarts. The increase in supply reduces the equilibrium price but increases the equilibrium quantity.

Alternatively, a reduction in supply—that is, a shift to the left in the supply curve—increases equilibrium price but reduces equilibrium quantity. Thus, *given a downward-sloping demand curve, a shift in the supply curve changes equilibrium quantity in the same direction as the change in supply but changes equilibrium price in the opposite direction.* An easy way to remember this is to picture the supply curve shifting along a given downward-sloping demand curve. If the supply curve shifts to the right, price decreases but quantity increases; if the supply curve shifts to the left, price increases but quantity decreases.

Simultaneous Changes in Demand and Supply

As long as only one curve shifts, we can say for sure what will happen to equilibrium price and quantity. If both curves shift, however, the outcome is less obvious. For example, suppose both demand and supply increase, as in Exhibit 8. Note that in panel (a) demand increases more than supply, and in panel (b) supply increases more than demand. In both panels, equilibrium quantity increases. The

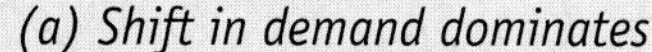

Indeterminate Effect of an Increase in Both Supply and Demand

(a) Shift in demand dominates

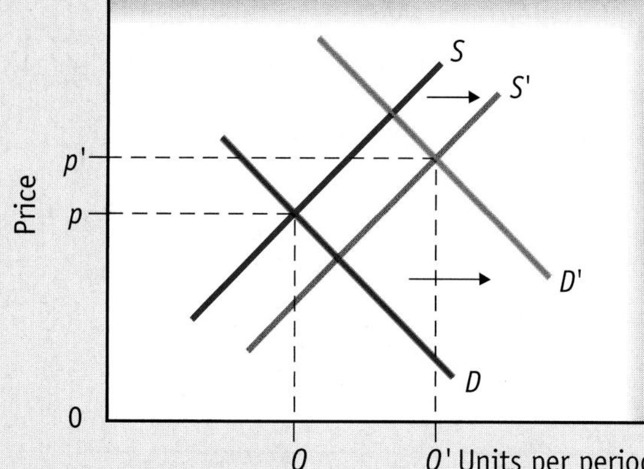

(b) Shift in supply dominates

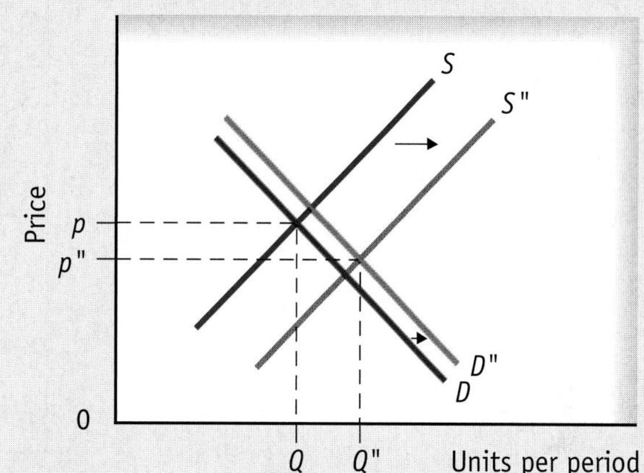

When both supply and demand increase, the quantity exchanged—the equilibrium quantity—also increases. The effect on price depends on which curve shifts farther. In panel (a), the shift in demand is greater than the shift in supply; as a result, the price rises. In panel (b), the shift in supply is greater, so the price falls.

change in equilibrium price, however, depends on the size of the increase in demand relative to the increase in supply. If the increase in demand is greater, as in panel (a), equilibrium price increases from p to p'. If the increase in supply is greater, as in panel (b), equilibrium price decreases from p to p''.

Conversely, if both demand and supply decrease, the equilibrium quantity decreases; but again we cannot say what will happen to the equilibrium price unless we examine the relative shifts. (You can use Exhibit 8 to examine decreases in demand and supply by viewing D' and S' as the initial curves.) If the decrease in demand exceeds the decrease in supply, the price will fall. If the decrease in supply exceeds the decrease in demand, the price will rise.

If demand and supply move in opposite directions, we can say what will happen to the equilibrium price. *The equilibrium price will increase if demand increases and supply decreases; the equilibrium price will decrease if demand decreases and supply increases.* Without reference to particular shifts, however, we cannot say what will happen to the equilibrium quantity.

These results are no doubt confusing, but Exhibit 9 summarizes the four possible combinations of changes. For example, the upper left-hand corner of Exhibit 9 shows the results just depicted with graphs in Exhibit 8. Using Exhibit 9 as a reference, work through some hypothetical shifts in demand and supply to develop an understanding of the results. Then evaluate the effect of an increase in demand for professional basketball in the following case study.

EXHIBIT 9

Effects of Changes in Both Supply and Demand

When the supply and demand curves shift in the same direction, equilibrium quantity also shifts in that direction; the effect on equilibrium price depends on which curve shifts more. If the curves shift in opposite directions, equilibrium price will move in the same direction as demand; the effect on equilibrium quantity depends on which curve shifts more.

Change in Supply	Change in Demand: Demand increases	Change in Demand: Demand decreases
Supply increases	Equilibrium price change is indeterminate. Equilibrium quantity increases.	Equilibrium price falls. Equilibrium quantity change is indeterminate.
Supply decreases	Equilibrium price rises. Equilibrium quantity change is indeterminate.	Equilibrium price change is indeterminate. Equilibrium quantity decreases.

CaseStudy

The World of Business

The Busine$$ of Sport$ is a Web page devoted to economic issues surrounding (mainly) professional sports at http://www.bizsports.com/index.html. What is the latest on the market for pro basketball?

The Market for Professional Basketball

Toward the end of the 1970s, the National Basketball Association (NBA) seemed on the verge of collapse. Game attendance had sunk to only 58 percent of capacity. One-fifth of the teams were nearly bankrupt. The NBA championship game did not even merit prime-time television coverage.

During the 1980s, however, three superstars turned the league around. Michael Jordan, Larry Bird, and Magic Johnson brought new life to the sagging game and attracted millions of new fans. Since 1980, total attendance has doubled, the number of NBA teams has increased from 22 to 29 (with new franchises selling for record amounts), and the value of television broadcast rights has jumped *35*-fold from $76 million in 1978–1982 to $2.64 billion in 1998–2002.

The NBA is more popular than ever, though a labor dispute during what would have been the 1998–99 season took some luster off that popularity. Celebrities such as Jack Nicholson and Spike Lee have become fixtures in court-side seats (seats that sell for as much as $500 per game). Basketball's popularity has also increased around the world. The NBA formed global marketing alliances with Coca-Cola, McDonald's, and IBM; and the 1998 NBA finals were televised in more than 165 countries.

The players are the key resource in the production of NBA games. The growth in demand for pro basketball, coupled with a collective bargaining agreement that gave players more than half of total revenue (in 1997–98 players were paid 57 percent of total league revenues), jacked up average player salaries from $170 thousand in 1980 to $2.5 million in 1997–98. Basketball players are now the highest-paid team professionals in the world; their average pay is more than double that in pro football and pro hockey.

The primary source of talent for the NBA is college basketball. College games, especially the NCAA tournament nicknamed "March Madness," serve to heighten interest in the NBA, because fans can follow top collegiate players into the professional ranks. Top college prospects sign multimillion-dollar contracts. Such numbers attract talented players earlier and earlier in their academic years, since top players who remain in school risk a costly injury. In 1997, Kevin Garnett, who entered the NBA right out of high school in 1995, signed a seven-year contract worth $121 million. Because of basketball's worldwide popularity, talented players who fail to make the NBA often can sign attractive contracts overseas.

The high pay earned by the top players stems from the limited supply of those with such talent, combined with a large and growing demand for that talent. But rare talent alone is not enough. For example, top rodeo riders, top bowlers, and top women basketball players also possess rare talent, but the demand for their talent is not great enough to support pay anywhere close to NBA levels. Both supply *and* demand determine the average pay level.

Sources: "Garnett Accepts $121 Million," *Hartford Courant*, 2 Oct. 1997; Anthony Bianco, "David Stern: This Time It's Personal," *Business Week*, 13 July 1998, pp. 114–118; *The American Almanac: Statistical Abstract of the United States: 1996–1997*, Bureau of the Census (Austin, Texas: Hoover's Business Press, 1996).

DISEQUILIBRIUM PRICES

A surplus exerts downward pressure on the price; a shortage exerts upward pressure on the price. Markets, however, do not always attain equilibrium quickly. During the time required for adjustment, the market is said to be in disequilibrium. **Disequilibrium** is usually a temporary phase when the market gropes for equilibrium. For example, popular toys, best-selling books, and chart-busting compact discs often sell out and are temporarily unavailable. On the other hand, some new products attract few customers and pile up unsold on store shelves, awaiting a "clearance sale." Sometimes, however, often as a result of government intervention in markets, disequilibrium can last a long time, as we will see next.

Disequilibrium A mismatch between quantity supplied and quantity demanded as the market seeks equilibrium

Price Floors

Sometimes public officials set prices above their equilibrium values. For example, the federal government often regulates the prices of some agricultural commodities in an attempt to ensure farmers a higher and more stable income than they would otherwise earn. To achieve higher prices, the federal government sets a **price floor,** or a *minimum* selling price above the equilibrium price. Panel (a) of Exhibit 10 shows the effect of a $1.00 per quart price floor for milk. At that price, farmers supply 24 million quarts of milk per month, but

Price floor A minimum legal price below which a good or service cannot be sold; to be effective, a price floor must be set above the equilibrium price

Effects of a Price Floor and a Price Ceiling

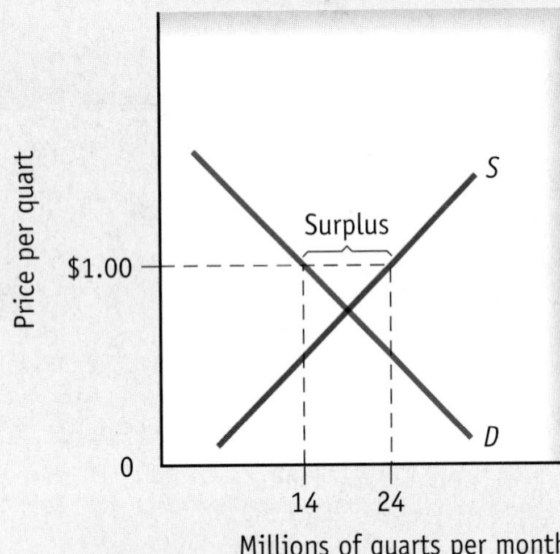

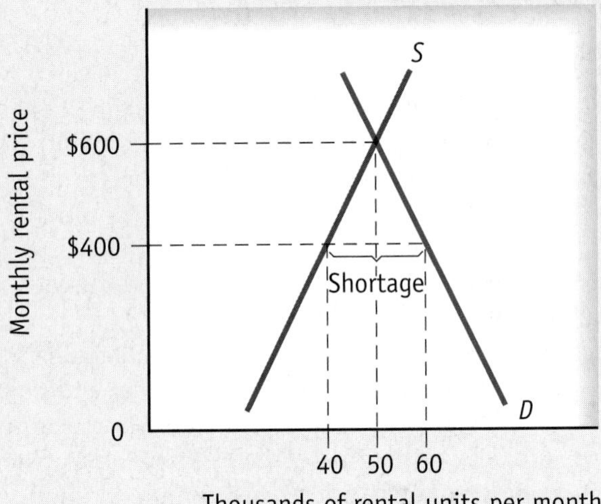

If a price floor is established above the equilibrium price, a permanent surplus will result. A price floor established at or below the equilibrium price will have no effect. If a price ceiling is established below the equilibrium price, a permanent shortage will result. A price ceiling established at or above the equilibrium price will have no effect.

consumers demand only 14 million quarts. Thus the price floor results in a surplus of 10 million quarts. This surplus, unless somehow eliminated, will force the price down. So, as part of the price support program, the government usually agrees to buy the surplus milk to take it off the market. The federal government, in fact, has spent billions buying and storing surplus agricultural products.

Price Ceilings

Sometimes public officials try to keep prices below their equilibrium values by establishing a **price ceiling,** or a *maximum* selling price. For example, concern about the rising cost of rental housing in some cities prompted legislation to impose rent ceilings. Panel (b) depicts the demand and supply for rental housing in a hypothetical city; the vertical axis shows the monthly rent, and the horizontal axis shows the quantity of rental units. The equilibrium, or market-clearing, rent is $600 per month, and the equilibrium quantity is 50,000 housing units.

Price ceiling A maximum legal price above which a good or service cannot be sold; to be effective, a price ceiling must be set below the equilibrium price

Suppose the government sets a maximum rent of $400 per month. At that ceiling price, 60,000 rental units are demanded, but only 40,000 are supplied, resulting in a housing shortage of 20,000 units. Because of such excess demand, the rental price no longer rations housing to those who value it the most. Other devices emerge to ration housing, such as waiting lists, political connections, and the willingness to pay under-the-table charges, such as "key fees," "finder's fees," higher security deposits, and the like.

To have an impact, a price floor must be set above the equilibrium price. A price ceiling, to have an impact, must be set below the equilibrium price.[1] Effective price floors and ceilings distort market forces. Price floors above the equilibrium price create surpluses, and price ceilings below the equilibrium price create shortages. Various nonprice allocation devices emerge to cope with the disequilibrium resulting from the market interference.

Government intervention in the market is not the only source of disequilibrium, as shown in the following case study.

Toys Are Serious Business

CaseStudy

The World of Business

If you are interested in learning more about the serious business of toys, you can find a wealth of information at ToySource http://www.toysource.com/faq1.htm.

U.S. toy sales exceed $25 billion a year, but the business is not much fun for toy makers. Most toys don't make it from one season to the next, turning out to be costly duds. A few have staying power; for example, G.I. Joe could retire after more than 30 years of military service, Barbie is over 35 years old, and the Wiffle Ball is still a hit after 40 years.

Store buyers must order in February for Christmas delivery. Can you imagine the uncertainty of this market? Who, for example, could have anticipated the phenomenal success of Tickle-Me-Elmo, Beanie Babies, Teletubbies, or Furbies? How about the Cabbage Patch Kids frenzy that some of you experienced as toddlers? Over 20 million Kids were sold for about $30 each, and there was still a shortage at that price. The shortage attracted boatloads of counterfeit dolls from overseas. Some of these illegal aliens were detained at the border, but many more made it through.

A few years ago, the Mighty Morphin Power Rangers were the hot toy. Between 1993 and 1994, the manufacturer expanded production tenfold, with 11 new factories churning out nearly $1 billion worth of Rangers. Still, at a selling price of $13, the quantity demanded exceeded quantity supplied. A more recent hit toy was Tomagotchi, a virtual pet. The manufacturer had nine plants around the world turning them out.

Why didn't toy manufacturers simply allow the price to seek its market-clearing level? Suppose, for example, that the market-clearing price of Cabbage Patch Kids was $60, twice the actual price. Consumers may have resented paying such a high price for a doll, and Coleco, a producer of a variety of toys, may not have wanted to risk criticism for being opportunist, a "price gouger." After all, a firm's reputation is important. Suppliers who hope to retain customers over the long haul will often avoid appearing greedy. That's why the local hardware store doesn't raise the price of snow shovels after the first winter storm, why Wal-Mart doesn't jack up prices of air conditioners during the dog days of summer, and why Mercedes-Benz prefers long waiting lists to raising prices still higher for its new utility vehicle.

Eventually, market equilibrium is achieved. But in the meantime, disequilibrium prevails. Uncertainty abounds in the market for new products such as

1 Note that the terms "price floor" and "price ceiling" are used to describe situations in a way that is opposite from the way we usually think of the floor and ceiling of a room. A price floor is up high, where we find a room's ceiling, and a price ceiling is down low, where we find a room's floor.

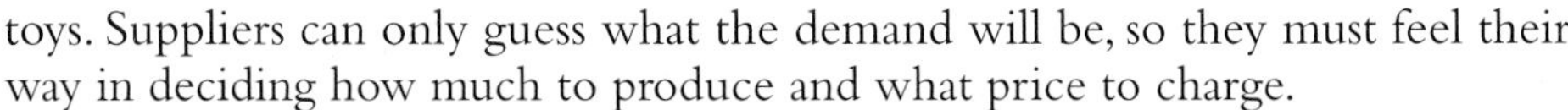

toys. Suppliers can only guess what the demand will be, so they must feel their way in deciding how much to produce and what price to charge.

Sources: Patrice Apodaca, "Chicken Boom: Bandai Basks in Digital Pet Success," *Los Angeles Times*, 22 August 1997; Gretchen Morgenson, "Saturation Barbie?" *Forbes*, 20 Oct. 1997; and "Cabbage Patch Comeback Kids," *Business Week*, 14 August 1995;. Visit the Virtual Toy Store Directory at http://www.halcyon.com/uncomyn/home.html; or visit FAO Schwarz at http://www.faoschwarz.com/.

CONCLUSION

Although a market usually involves the interaction of many buyers and sellers, few markets are consciously designed. Just as the law of gravity works whether or not we understand Newton's principles, market forces operate whether or not market participants understand demand and supply. These forces arise naturally, much the way car dealers cluster on the outskirts of town. Demand and supply are the foundation of a market economy.

Markets have their critics. Some observers are troubled, for example, that U.S. consumers spend billions each year on pet food, when some people do not have enough to eat. On your next trip to the supermarket, notice how much shelf space is devoted to pet products—often an entire aisle. Petsmart, a chain store for pet products, sells over 12,000 different items. Veterinarians charge up to $10,000 for cancer treatment, cataract removal, and other high-tech medical care for pets. Pet owners can even buy pet health insurance.[2] In the next chapter we'll discuss some limitations of market economies and introduce the role of government.

2 See Pamela Sebastian, "Canine Oncology and Other Advances Propel Costs and Insurance," *Wall Street Journal*, 23 October 1997.

SUMMARY

1. Demand is a relationship between the price of a good and the quantity consumers are willing and able to buy per time period, other things constant. According to the law of demand, the price of a good varies inversely with the quantity demanded, so the demand curve slopes downward.

2. A demand curve slopes downward for two reasons. A decrease in the price of a good (1) makes consumers more willing to substitute this good for other goods and (2) increases the real income of consumers, making them more able to buy the good.

3. Assumed to be constant along a demand curve are (1) consumer incomes, (2) the prices of related goods, (3) consumer expectations, (4) the number and composition of consumers in the market, and (5) consumer tastes. A change in any one of these could shift the demand curve.

4. Supply is a relationship between the price of a good and the quantity producers are willing and able to sell per period, other things constant. According to the law of supply, price and quantity supplied are usually directly related, so the supply curve typically slopes upward. The supply curve slopes upward because higher prices (1) make producers more willing to supply this good rather than alternative goods and (2) make producers better able to cover the higher marginal cost associated with greater output rates.

5. Assumed to be constant along a supply curve are (1) the state of technology, (2) the prices of relevant resources, (3) the prices of alternative goods, (4) producer expectations, and (5) the number of producers. A change in any one of these could shift the supply curve.

6. Demand and supply come together in the market for a given product. Markets provide information about the price, quantity, and quality of the product for sale. They also reduce the transaction costs of exchange—the costs of time and information required to undertake exchange. The interaction of demand and supply guides resources and products to their highest-valued use.

7. Impersonal market forces reconcile the personal and independent intentions of buyers and sellers. Market equilibrium, once established, will continue unless there is a change in one of the determinants of demand or supply. Disequilibrium is usually a temporary phase while markets seek equilibrium, but sometimes it lasts a while.

QUESTIONS FOR REVIEW

1. *(Law of Demand)* What is the law of demand? Give two examples of how you have observed the law of demand at work in the "real world." How is the law of demand related to the demand curve?
2. *(Changes in Demand)* What variables influence the demand for a normal good? Explain why a reduction in the price of a normal good does not increase the demand for that good.
3. *(Substitution and Income Effects)* Distinguish between the substitution and income effects of a price change. If a good's price increases, does each effect have a positive or a negative impact on the quantity demanded?
4. *(Demand)* Explain the effect of an increase in consumer income on demand for a good.
5. *(Income Effects)* When moving along the demand curve, income must be assumed constant. Yet one factor that can cause a change in the quantity demanded is the "income effect." Reconcile these seemingly contradictory facts.
6. *(Supply)* What is the law of supply? Give an example of how you have observed the law of supply at work. What is the relationship between the law of supply and the supply curve?
7. *(Changes in Supply)* What kinds of changes in underlying conditions can cause the supply curve to shift? Give some examples and explain the direction in which the curve shifts.
8. *(Markets)* How do markets coordinate the independent decisions of buyers and sellers
9. **(CaseStudy:** *The Market for Professional Basketball)* In what sense can we speak of a market for professional basketball? Who are the demanders and who are the suppliers? What are some examples of how changes in supply or demand conditions have affected this market? (If you are interested in learning more about the economics of sports, visit the Busine$$ of Sport$ page at http://www.bizsports.com/index.html.

PROBLEMS AND EXERCISES

10. *(Shifting Demand)* Using supply and demand curves, show the effect of each of the following events on the market for cigarettes:
    a. A cure for lung cancer is found.
    b. The price of cigars increases.
    c. Wages increase substantially in states that grow tobacco.
    d. A fertilizer that increases the yield per acre of tobacco is discovered.
    e. There is a substantial increase in the price of matches and lighter fluid.
    f. More states pass laws restricting smoking in public places.
11. *(Substitutes and Complements)* For each of the following pairs, determine whether the goods are substitutes, complements, or unrelated:
    a. Peanut butter and jelly
    b. Private and public transportation
    c. Coke and Pepsi
    d. Alarm clocks and automobiles
    e. Golf clubs and golf balls
12. *(Equilibrium)* "If a price is not an equilibrium price, there is a tendency for it to move to its equilibrium value. Regardless of whether the price is too high or too low to begin with, the adjustment process will increase the quantity of the good purchased." Explain, using a supply and demand diagram.
13. *(Market Equilibrium)* Determine whether each of the following statements is true, false, or uncertain. Then provide a short explanation for your answer.
    a. In equilibrium, all sellers can find buyers.
    b. In equilibrium, there is no pressure on the market to produce or consume more than is being sold.
    c. At prices above equilibrium, the quantity exchanged exceeds the quantity demanded.
    d. At prices below equilibrium, the quantity exchanged is equal to the quantity supplied.
14. *(Supply and Demand)* How do you think each of the following affected the world price of oil? (Use basic supply and demand analysis.)

a. Tax credits were offered for expenditures on home insulation.
b. The Alaskan oil pipeline was completed.
c. The ceiling on the price of oil was removed.
d. Oil was discovered in Mexico and the North Sea.
e. Sport utility vehicles and minivans became popular.
f. The use of nuclear power decreased.

15. *(Equilibrium)* Consider the following graph in which demand and supply are initially *D* and *S*, respectively. What are the equilibrium price and quantity? If demand increases to *D'*, what are the new equilibrium price and quantity? What happens if the government does not allow the price to change when demand increases?

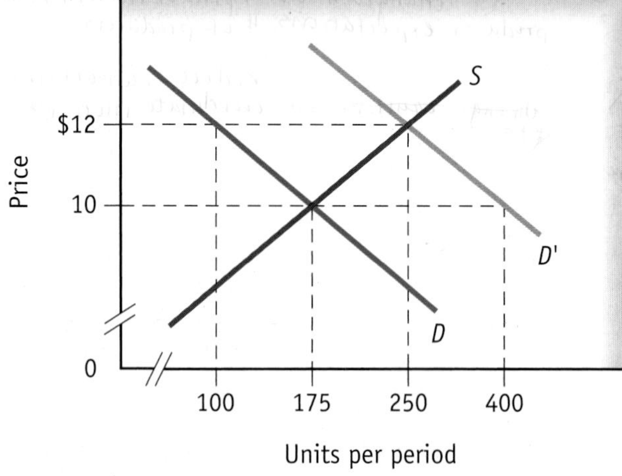

16. *(Demand and Supply)* What happens to the equilibrium price and quantity of ice cream in response to each of the following? Explain your answers.
   a. The price of dairy cow fodder increases.
   b. The price of beef decreases.
   c. Concerns arise about the fat content of ice cream. Simultaneously, the price of sugar (used to produce ice cream) increases.

17. *(Changes in Equilibrium)* What are the effects on the equilibrium price and quantity of steel if the wages of steelworkers rise and, simultaneously, the price of aluminum rises?

18. *(Price Floor)* There is considerable interest in whether the minimum wage rate contributes to teenage unemployment. Draw a supply and demand diagram for the unskilled labor market, and discuss the effects of a minimum wage. Who is helped and who is hurt by the minimum wage?

19. *(Price Ceilings)* Suppose the supply and demand curves for rental housing units have the typical shapes and that the rental housing market is in equilibrium. Then, government establishes a rent ceiling below the equilibrium level.
   a. What happens to the quantity of housing consumed?
   b. Who gains from rent control?
   c. Who loses from rent control?

20. *(Case**Study**: Toys Are Serious Business)* Use a supply and demand graph to describe developments in the market for Mighty Morphin Power Rangers toys. Keep in mind the shortage at the $13 selling price, the development of new factories, and the continued shortage.

EXPERIENTIAL EXERCISES

21. *(Market Demand)* Together with some other students in your class, determine your market demand for gasoline. Make up a chart listing a variety of prices per gallon of gasoline—$1.00, $1.25, $1.50, $1.75, $2.00, $2.25. Ask each student—and yourself—how many gallons *per week* they would purchase at each possible price. Then
   a. Plot each student's demand curve. Check to see whether each student's responses are consistent with the law of demand.
   b. Derive the "market" demand curve by adding up the quantities demanded by *all* students at each possible price.
   c. What do you think will happen to that market demand curve after your class graduates and your incomes rise?

22. *(Price Floors)* The minimum wage is a price floor in a market for labor. The government sets a minimum price per hour of labor in certain markets and no employer is permitted to pay a wage lower than that. Go to the Department of Labor's minimum wage page to learn more about the mechanics of the program http://www.dol.gov/dol/esa/public/minwage/main.htm. Then use a supply and demand diagram to illustrate the effect of imposing an above-equilibrium minimum wage on a particular labor market. What happens to quantity demanded and quantity supplied as a result of the minimum wage?

23. *(Wall Street Journal)* After reading this chapter, you have a basic understanding of how supply and demand determine market price and quantity. Find an article in the "first section" of today's *Wall Street Journal* and interpret the article, using a supply and demand diagram. Explain at least one case in which a curve shifts. What caused the shift, and how did it affect price and quantity?

CHAPTER

4 Economic Decision Makers: Households, Firms, Governments, and the Rest of the World

If we live in the age of specialization, then why haven't specialists taken over all production—that is, why do most of you still do your own laundry and perform dozens of other tasks for yourself? If the "invisible hand" of competitive markets is such an efficient allocator of resources, why did government get into the act? Finally, how can it be said in economics that "what goes around comes around"? Answers to these and other questions are addressed in this chapter, which examines the four economic decision makers: households, firms, governments, and the rest of the world.

To develop a better understanding of how the economy works, you must become more acquainted with these key players in the economy. You already know more about them than you realize. You grew up in a household. You

Visit the McEachern
teractive Study Center
for this chapter at
://mcisc.swcollege.com

have dealt with firms all your life, from Wal-Mart to Subway. You know a lot about governments, from taxes to public education. And you have a growing awareness of the rest of the world, from foreign travel to the World Wide Web.

In this chapter you will draw on your abundant personal experience with economic decision makers to consider their structure, organization, and objectives. After considering all four groups, we will summarize how they interact. Topics discussed in this chapter include:

- Evolution of the household
- Evolution of the firm
- Household production versus firm production
- Role of government
- Government spending and taxation
- International trade and finance
- Trade restrictions
- Circular flow model

THE HOUSEHOLD

Households play the starring role in the economy. First, they demand goods and services from product markets and thereby help determine what gets produced. Second, households supply labor, capital, land, and entrepreneurial ability to resource markets and thereby make what gets produced. As demanders of goods and services and suppliers of resources, households make all kinds of choices, such as what to buy, how much to save, where to live, and where to work. Although a household usually consists of several individuals, we will think of each household as acting like a single decision maker; we will refer to that decision maker as the **householder.**

Householder The key decision maker in the household

The Evolution of the Household

In earlier times, when the economy was primarily agricultural, a farm household was largely self-sufficient. Individual family members specialized in specific farm tasks, such as making furniture, sewing clothes, tending livestock, and so on. These early households produced what they consumed and consumed what they produced. With the introduction of new seed varieties, fertilizers, and labor-saving machinery, farm productivity increased sharply. Fewer farmers were needed to grow enough food to feed a nation. Simultaneously, the growth of urban factories increased the demand for factory labor. As a result, many people moved from farms to cities, where they were far less self-sufficient.

Households have evolved in other ways. For example, in 1950 only about 15 percent of married women with children under 18 years of age were in the labor force. Since then, higher levels of education among married women and a growing demand for labor increased women's earnings, which raised their opportunity cost of working in the home. This rising opportunity cost likely contributed to growing labor participation.[1] Today more than half of married women with young children are in the labor force.

1 Professor Claudia Goldin, an economic historian from Harvard, argues that the increase in the wages, the growth of white-collar jobs, and the decline in the average work week increased the labor participation rate among women. See Goldin's *Understanding the Gender Gap: An Economic History of American Women* (New York: Oxford University Press, 1990).

The rise of two-earner households has affected the family as an economic unit. Less production occurs in the home, and more goods and services are demanded from the market. For example, child-care services and fast-food restaurants have displaced some household production. Most people eat at least one meal a day away from home. The rise in two-worker families has reduced the advantages of specialization within the household—a central feature of the farm family, where each family member specialized in particular tasks. Nonetheless, some production still occurs in the home, as we will explore in a later section.

Households Maximize Utility

There are more than 100 million households in the United States. All those who live under one roof are considered part of the same household. What exactly do householders attempt to accomplish in making decisions? Economists assume that people attempt to maximize their level of satisfaction, sense of well-being, or overall welfare. For the sake of brevity, we can say that householders attempt to maximize the household's **utility.** Householders, like other economic decision makers, are viewed as rational, meaning that they try to act in the household's best interests and would not deliberately make choices that are likely to make them worse off. Utility maximization depends on each household's subjective goals, not on some objective standard. For example, some households maintain a neat home with a well-groomed lawn; others pay no attention to their home and use the lawn as a junkyard.

Utility The satisfaction received from consumption; sense of well-being

Households as Resource Suppliers

Householders use their limited resources—labor, capital, land, and entrepreneurial ability—in an attempt to satisfy their unlimited wants. They can use these resources to produce goods and services in their homes. For example, they can prepare their own meals, mow the lawn, and fix that leaky roof. They can also sell these resources in the resource market and use the income to buy goods and services in the product market. The most valuable resource sold by most households is labor.

Exhibit 1 shows the sources of personal income received by U.S. households in 1998, when personal income totaled $7.3 trillion. As you can see, 63 percent, or nearly two-thirds, of personal income is from wages, salaries, and other labor income. Tied for second place at 11 percent each are interest earnings and transfer payments (to be discussed shortly), followed by proprietors' income at 8 percent. *Proprietors* are people who work for themselves rather than for employers; farmers, plumbers, and doctors are often self-employed. Only 5 percent of personal income comes from dividends and only 2 percent comes from rental income. *The majority of personal income in the United States is from labor earnings, rather than from the ownership of other resources such as capital or land.*

Because of a poor education, disability, discrimination, time demands of caring for small children, or bad luck, some households have few resources that are valued in the market. Society has made the political decision that individuals in such circumstances should receive short-term public assistance. Consequently, the government gives some households **transfer payments,** which are outright grants to certain households. *Cash transfers* are monetary payments, such as welfare benefits, unemployment compensation, and disability benefits. *In-kind* transfers, such as food stamps, Medicare, and Medicaid, provide specific goods and services.

Transfer payments Cash or in-kind benefits given to individuals as outright grants from the government

EXHIBIT 1

Sources of U.S. Personal Income in 1998

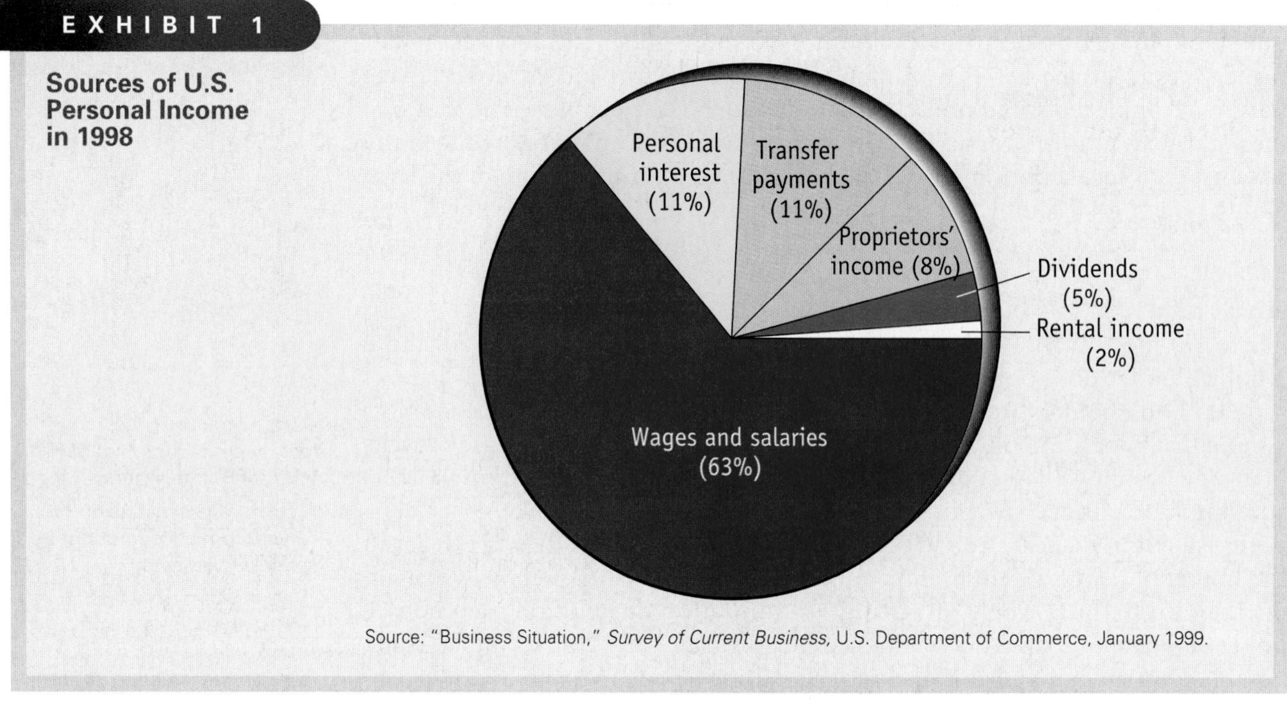

Source: "Business Situation," *Survey of Current Business,* U.S. Department of Commerce, January 1999.

Households as Demanders of Goods and Services

What happens to personal income, once it comes into the household? Personal income is allocated among personal consumption, saving, and taxes. On average, about 80 percent of U.S. personal income goes to personal consumption, about 5 percent is saved, and about 15 percent goes to taxes. Personal consumption sorts into three broad spending categories: (1) *durable goods*, such as automobiles and refrigerators, which are designed to last three years or more; (2) *nondurable goods*, such as food, clothing, and gasoline; and (3) *services*, such as haircuts, plane trips, and medical care. Durable goods make up 13 percent of U.S. personal consumption, nondurables make up 30 percent, and services make up 57 percent. The service sector is the fastest growing, because many activities—such as meal preparation and child care—that formerly were produced in the household are now often purchased in the market.

THE FIRM

Members of households once built their own homes, made their own clothes and furniture, grew their own food, and amused themselves. Over time, however, the efficiency arising from comparative advantage resulted in a greater specialization among resource suppliers. In this section, we take a look at firms, beginning with their evolution.

The Evolution of the Firm

For about 200 years, profit-seeking entrepreneurs relied on "putting out" raw material, such as wool and cotton, to rural households that turned this raw material into finished goods, such as woolen goods made from yarn. The system developed in the British Isles, where workers' cottages served as tiny factories. This approach to production, which came to be known as the *cottage industry system*, still exists in some parts of the world.

As the British economy expanded in the 18th century, entrepreneurs began to organize the various stages of production under one roof. Technological developments increased the productivity of each worker and contributed to the shift of employment from rural areas to urban factories. *Work, therefore, became organized in large, centrally powered factories that (1) promoted a more efficient division of labor, (2) allowed for the direct supervision of production, (3) reduced transportation costs, and (4) facilitated the use of machines far bigger than anything that had been used in the home.* The development of large-scale factory production, known as the **Industrial Revolution,** began in Great Britain around 1750 and spread to the rest of Europe, North America, and Australia.

Industrial Revolution Development of large-scale factory production that began in Great Britain around 1750 and spread to the rest of Europe, North America, and Australia

Production, then, evolved from self-sufficient rural households, through the cottage industry system, where specialized production occurred in the household, to the current system of handling much production under one roof. Today, entrepreneurs combine resources in firms such as factories, mills, offices, stores, and restaurants. **Firms** are economic units formed by profit-seeking entrepreneurs who combine labor, capital, and land to produce goods and services. Just as we assume that householders attempt to maximize utility, we assume that firms attempt to *maximize profit*. Profit, the entrepreneur's reward, is total revenue minus the total cost of production.

Firms Economic units, formed by profit-seeking entrepreneurs who employ resources to produce goods and services for sale

Why Does Household Production Still Exist?

Why are such activities as house cleaning and meal preparation still undertaken primarily by households, not by firms? Some people fix their own cars, paint their own homes, and perform many other tasks that are also performed by firms. Why hasn't all production shifted to firms?

If a householder's opportunity cost of performing a task is below the market price of the task, then the householder usually performs that task. Thus, householders with a lower opportunity cost of time will tend to do more for themselves. For example, janitors typically mow their own lawns; physicians do not. Let's look at some reasons for household production.

No Skills or Specialized Resources Are Required. Some activities require so few skills or specialized resources that households find it cheaper to do these jobs themselves. Sweeping the floor requires only a broom and time, and so this job is usually performed by household members. Sanding the floor, however, involves costly machinery and special skills, so this service is usually purchased in the market. Similarly, although you wouldn't hire someone to brush your teeth each morning and evening, dental work is another matter. *Households usually perform tasks that demand neither particular skills nor specialized machinery.*

Household Production Avoids Taxes. Governments tax income, sales, and other market transactions. Suppose you are trying to decide whether to paint your home or hire a painter. If the income tax rate is one-third, a painter who requires $2,000 net of taxes to do the job must charge you $3,000 to net $2,000 after paying $1,000 in taxes. You must earn $4,500 before taxes in order to have $3,000 after taxes to pay the painter. Thus, you must earn $4,500 so that the painter can net

$2,000 after taxes. If you paint the house yourself, no taxes are imposed. *The tax-free nature of do-it-yourself activity favors household production over market purchases.*

Household Production Reduces Transaction Costs. Lining up bids from painting contractors, hiring a contractor, negotiating terms, and monitoring job performance all take time and require information. Doing the job yourself reduces these *transaction costs*. Household production also allows for more personal control over the final product than is usually available through the market. For example, some people prefer home-cooked meals to restaurant food, in part because home-cooked meals can be prepared according to individual tastes.

Technological Advances Increase Household Productivity. Technological breakthroughs are not confined to market production. Vacuum cleaners, dishwashers, microwave ovens, and other modern appliances reduce the time and often the skill required to perform household tasks. Also, modern technologies such as VCRs, CD players, cable TV, and computer games produce home entertainment. In fact, microchip-based technologies have shifted some production from the firm back to the household, as discussed in the following case study.

*Case***Study**

The Information Economy

Economists have begun to study the economic implications of the virtual office and other virtual phenomena. Visit Yahoo! (http://www.yahoo.com/) and Excite (http://www.excite.com/) and search for the words "virtual" and "economics." Try it, and see what you find.

The Electronic Cottage

The Industrial Revolution shifted production from rural cottages to large urban factories. But the *Information Revolution* spawned by the invention of the microchip is decentralizing the acquisition, analysis, and transmission of information. These days people who say they work at a home office are often referring not to corporate headquarters, but to the room just off their kitchen. There are an estimated 8 to 11 million telecommuters in the United States, including nearly half the white-collar work force at AT&T. Merrill Lynch's Telecommuting Simulation Lab helps people learn how to work at home.

People with a personal computer, a modem, a fax machine, a cellular phone, and Internet access are ready for business. They can send a memo via fax or e-mail to colleagues around the corner, around the country, or around the globe. With the right software, they can write a document with coworkers scattered throughout the world. They can also buy or sell thousands of products from securities to hot sauce. And they can do all this without leaving home. An entire industry has sprung up to serve those who work at home, including magazines, newsletters, Web pages, even national conferences, such as the Telecommuting & Home Office Conference in San Francisco.

In fact, an office need not even be in a specific place. With chip-based technology, some people now work in a *virtual office*, which has no permanent location—"deals on wheels," so to speak. For example, accountants at Ernst & Young spend most of their time in the field. When workers need to return to company headquarters, they call a few hours ahead to reserve an office.

Newly developed software such as Netscape Virtual Office®, Virtual File Cabinet®, or Netopia Virtual Office® allows thousands of employees to share electronic files. When Anderson Consulting moved its headquarters from Boston to a suburb, the company got rid of 120 tons of paper, replacing it with a huge on-line data base accessible any time of the day or night from anywhere in the world. Computers have changed the world of work.

Sources: Gene Marcial, "Netopia: An Internet Sleeper," *Business Week*, 27 July 1998; "A Connected World," *The Economist*, 13 September 1997; Mark Davis, "Consulting Firm Puts Office Space Up for Grabs as Day-by-Day Commodity," *Kansas City Star*, 26 September 1997; Godfrey Nolan, "A Good Day at the Virtual Office," *The Irish Times*, 27 July 1997; and as an example of sales over the Internet, visit Hot Hot Hot, "the Net's coolest hot sauce shop" http://www.hot.presence.com/g/p/H3/.

Kinds of Firms

There are about 22 million for-profit businesses in the United States. Two-thirds of these are small retail businesses, small service operations, part-time home-based businesses, and small farms. Each year more than a million new businesses are started, many of which fail. Entrepreneurs organize firms in one of three ways: as a sole proprietorship, as a partnership, or as a corporation. Let's examine the advantages and disadvantages of each.

Sole Proprietorships. The simplest form of business organization is the **sole proprietorship,** a single-owner firm. Examples are a self-employed plumber, electrician, farmer, or family physician. To organize a sole proprietorship, the proprietor simply opens for business by, for example, taking out a classified ad announcing availability for carpentry, snow plowing, or lawn mowing. The owner is in complete control. But he or she faces *unlimited liability* for any business debts and could lose everything, including a home and other assets, as a result of a debt or claim against the business. Also, since the sole proprietor has no partners or other financial backers, raising enough money to get the business up and running can be difficult. One final disadvantage is that sole proprietorships usually go out of business upon the death of the proprietor. Still, they are the most common form of business organization, accounting most recently for 73 percent of all U.S. businesses. Because this type of firm is typically small, proprietorships generate a small portion of all U.S. business sales—only 6 percent.

Sole proprietorship A firm with a single owner who has the right to all profits and who bears unlimited liability for the firm's debts

Partnerships. A more complicated form of business organization is the **partnership,** which involves two or more individuals who agree to contribute resources to the business in return for a share of the profit or loss. Law, accounting, and medical partnerships typify this business form. Partners have strength in numbers and often find it easier than the sole proprietor to raise sufficient funds to get the business going. But the partners may not always agree. Also, each partner usually faces unlimited liability for all the debts and claims against the partnership, so one partner could lose everything because of another's foolish mistake. Finally, the death or departure of one partner may disrupt the firm's continuity and could require a complete reorganization. The partnership is the least common form of U.S. business organization, making up only 7 percent of all firms and accounting for just 5 percent of all business sales.

Partnership A firm with multiple owners who share the firm's profits and each of whom bears unlimited liability for the firm's debts

Corporations. By far the most important form of business organization is the corporation. The **corporation** is a legal entity established through articles of incorporation. The owners of a corporation are issued shares of stock entitling them to corporate profits in proportion to their stock ownership. A major advantage of the corporate form is that many individuals—hundreds, thousands,

Corporation A legal entity owned by stockholders whose liability is limited to the value of their stock

even millions—can pool their money, so incorporating represents the easiest way to amass large sums of money to finance the firm. Also, stockholders have *limited liability*, meaning their liability for any losses is limited to the value of their stock. A final advantage of this form of organization is that the corporation has a life apart from those of the owners. The corporation continues to exist even if ownership changes hands, and it can be taxed and sued as if it were a person.

The corporate form has some disadvantages as well. A stockholder's ability to influence corporate policy is limited to voting for a board of directors, which oversees the operation of the firm. Each share of stock usually carries with it one vote; the typical stockholder of a large corporation owns only a tiny fraction of the shares and thus has little say. Whereas the income from sole proprietorships and partnerships is taxed only once, corporate income is taxed twice: first as corporate profits and second as stockholder income, either as corporate dividends or as realized capital gains. A *realized capital gain* is any increase in the market value of a share that occurs between the time the share is purchased and the time it is sold.

A hybrid type of corporation has evolved to take advantage of the limited liability feature of the corporate structure, while reducing the impact of double taxation. The *S corporation* provides owners with limited liability, but profits are taxed only once—as income on each shareholder's personal income tax return. To qualify as an S corporation, a firm must have no more than 35 stockholders and must have no foreign or corporate stockholders.

Corporations make up only 20 percent of all U.S. businesses, but because they tend to be much larger than the other two forms of business, corporate sales represent 89 percent of all business sales. Exhibit 2 shows, by type of U.S. firm, the percentage of firms and the percentage of total sales. *The sole proprietorship is the most important form in terms of total numbers, but the corporation is the most important in terms of total sales.*

Nonprofit Institutions

To this point we have considered firms that maximize profit. Some institutions, such as museums, ballet companies, nonprofit hospitals, the Red Cross, the Salvation Army, churches, synagogues, mosques, and perhaps the college you attend, are private organizations that do not have profit as an explicit objective. Yet even nonprofit institutions must somehow pay for the resources they employ. Revenue sources typically include some combination of voluntary contributions and service charges, such as college tuition and hospital bills. Although there are millions of nonprofit institutions, when we talk about firms in this book, we will be referring to for-profit firms.

THE GOVERNMENT

You might think that production by firms and by households could satisfy all consumer demands. Why must yet another economic decision maker get into the act?

The Role of Government

Market failure A condition that arises when unrestrained operation of markets yields socially undesirable results

Sometimes the unrestrained operation of markets has undesirable results. Too many of some goods and too few of other goods may be produced. In this section we discuss the sources of **market failure** and how society's overall welfare could at times be improved through government intervention.

EXHIBIT 2

Number and Sales of Each Type of Firm

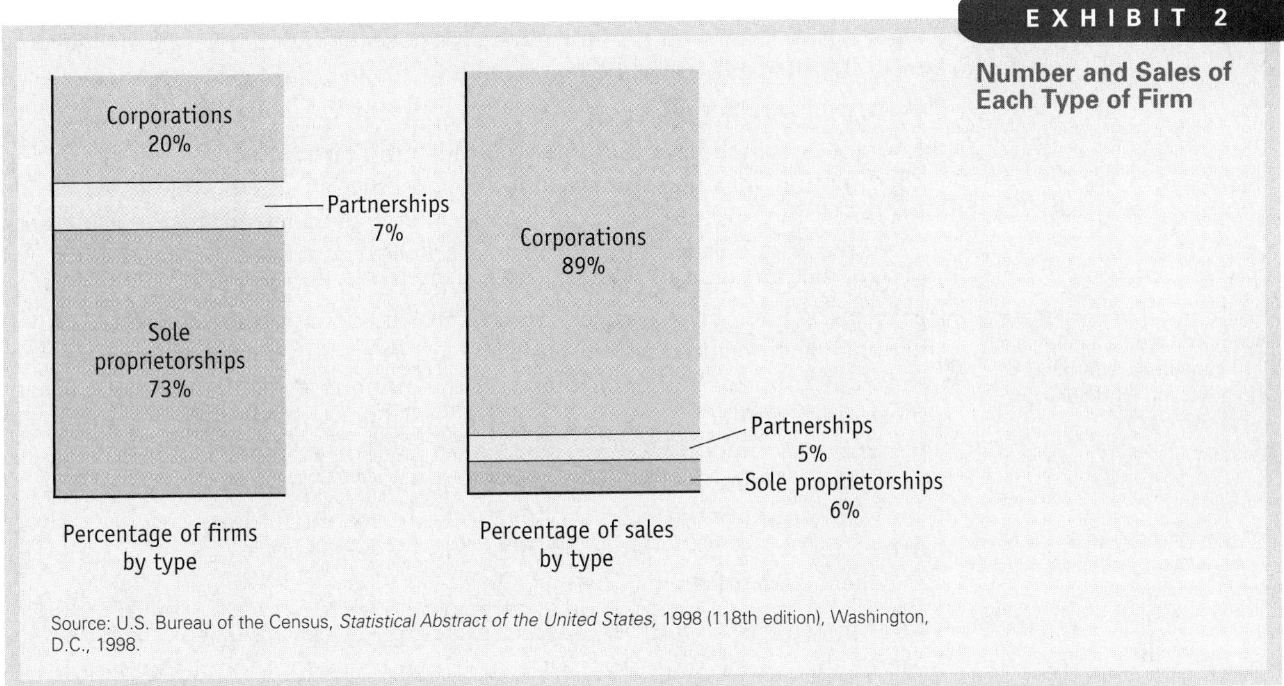

Source: U.S. Bureau of the Census, *Statistical Abstract of the United States,* 1998 (118th edition), Washington, D.C., 1998.

Establishing and Enforcing the Rules of the Game. Market efficiency depends on people like you using your resources to maximize your utility. But what if you were repeatedly robbed of your paycheck on your way home from work? Or what if, after you worked a month, your employer said you would not get paid? Why bother working? The system of private markets would break down if you could not safeguard your private property or if you could not enforce contracts. Governments play a role in *safeguarding private property* through police protection and in *enforcing contracts* through a judicial system. More generally, governments try to make sure that market participants play fair and abide by the "rules of the game." These rules are established through laws and through the customs and conventions of the market.

Promoting Competition. Although the "invisible hand" of competition usually promotes an efficient allocation of resources, some firms try to avoid competition through *collusion,* which is an agreement among firms to divide the market or to fix the market price. An individual firm may try to eliminate the competition by using unfair business practices. For example, to drive out local competitors, a large firm may temporarily sell at a price below its cost. *Government antitrust laws try to promote competition by prohibiting collusion and other anticompetitive practices.*

Regulating Natural Monopolies. Competition usually keeps the product price lower than it is when the product is sold by a **monopoly,** a sole supplier to the market. In rare instances, however, a monopoly can produce and sell the product for less than could several competing firms. For example, electricity is delivered more efficiently by a single firm that wires the community than by competing firms stringing their own wires. When it is cheaper for one firm to serve the market than for two or more firms to do so, that firm is called a **natural monopoly.**

Monopoly A sole producer of a product for which there are no close substitutes

Natural monopoly One firm that can serve the entire market at a lower per-unit cost than can two or more firms

Since a natural monopoly faces no competition, it maximizes profit by charging a higher price than is optimal from society's point of view. Therefore, the government usually regulates the natural monopoly, forcing it to lower the price.

Providing Public Goods. So far in this book, we have been talking about private goods, which have two important features. First, private goods are *rival* in consumption, meaning that the amount consumed by one person is unavailable for others to consume. For example, when you and a friend share a pizza, each slice your friend eats is one less slice available to you. Second, the supplier of a private good can easily exclude those who fail to pay. Only paying customers get a pizza. Thus, private goods are *exclusive*. In contrast, **public goods,** such as national defense and a system of justice, are *nonrival* in consumption. One person's consumption does not diminish the amount available to others. What's more, once produced, public goods are available to all. Suppliers cannot easily prevent consumption by those who fail to pay. For example, national defense is *nonexclusive*. It is available to all in the community, regardless of who pays for it and who does not. Because public goods are *nonrival* and *nonexclusive*, private firms cannot sell them profitably. The government, however, has the authority to collect taxes for public goods.

Public good A good that, once produced, is available for all to consume, regardless of who pays and who does not

Dealing with Externalities. Market prices reflect the *private* costs and benefits of producers and consumers. But sometimes production or consumption imposes costs or benefits on third parties—on those who are neither suppliers nor demanders in a market transaction. For example, a paper mill fouls the air breathed by nearby residents, but the price of paper, as determined in the private market, fails to reflect the cost such pollution imposes on society. Since these pollution costs are outside, or *external* to, the market activity, they are called *externalities*. An **externality** is a cost or a benefit that falls on third parties. A *negative externality* imposes on third parties a cost such as factory pollution, jet noise, or auto emissions. A *positive externality* confers on third parties an external benefit, such as getting a flu shot so you will not contract and transmit the disease, observing traffic signs and speed limits so you don't hit other cars, and planting a flower garden in your front yard, where it beautifies the neighborhood.

Externality A cost or a benefit that falls on third parties and is therefore ignored by the two parties to the market transaction

Because market prices do not reflect externalities, governments often employ taxes, subsidies, and regulations to discourage negative externalities and to encourage positive externalities. For example, because education generates positive externalities (educated people are more apt to be able to read road signs and are less likely to resort to violent crime for income), government tries to encourage people to get more education. One approach is to pass laws requiring students to stay in school until they are 16 years old. Another approach is for taxpayers to fund education so the cost to students is minimal, as with free public schools, or to subsidize education, as with public higher education.

NetBookmark

The annual *Economic Report of the President* is an invaluable source of information on current economic policy. It also contains many useful data tables. You can find it on-line at http://www.access.gpo.gov/eop/.

A More Equal Distribution of Income. As mentioned earlier, some people—because of a lack of education, mental or physical disabilities, or perhaps the need to care for small children—may be unable to earn enough to support themselves and their family. Since resource markets do not guarantee each household even a minimum level of income, transfer payments reflect society's attempt to provide a basic standard of living to all households. Nearly all citizens agree that, through government transfer payments, society should alter some of the results of the market by redistributing income to the poor. (Notice the normative nature of this statement.) But differences of opinion arise in deciding just how much redistribution should occur, what form it should take, who should receive the benefits, and how long those benefits should continue.

Full Employment, Price Stability, and Economic Growth. The government, through its ability to tax and spend and its control of the money supply, attempts to promote full employment, price stability, and an adequate rate of growth in the economy. The government's pursuit of these objectives through taxing and spending is called **fiscal policy** and pursuing them by regulating the money supply is called **monetary policy.** The study of macroeconomics examines these policies.

Fiscal policy The use of government purchases, transfer payments, taxes, and borrowing to influence aggregate economic activity

Monetary policy Regulation of the money supply in order to influence aggregate economic activity

Government's Structure and Objectives

The United States has a *federal system* of government, meaning that responsibilities are shared across levels of government. State governments grant some powers to local governments and surrender some powers to the national, or federal, government. As the system has evolved, the federal government has assumed primary responsibility for national security and the stability of the economy. State governments fund public higher education, prisons and, with aid from the federal government, highways and welfare. Local government responsibilities include primary and secondary education, plus police and fire protection.

Difficulty in Defining Government Objectives. We assume that households maximize utility and firms maximize profit, but what about governments—or, more specifically, what about government decision makers? What do they maximize? One problem is that the federal system consists of many governments—more than 80,000 separate jurisdictions in all. What's more, because the federal government relies on offsetting, or countervailing, powers among the *executive*, *legislative*, and *judicial* branches, government does not act as a single, consistent decision maker. Even within the federal executive branch, there are so many agencies and bureaus that at times they seem to work at cross purposes. For example, at the same time as the U.S. Surgeon General requires health warnings on cigarettes, the U.S. Department of Agriculture subsidizes tobacco farmers. Given this thicket of jurisdictions, branches, and bureaus, one useful theory of government behavior is that elected officials try to maximize the number of votes they will get in the next election. Thus, we can assume that elected officials *maximize votes*. In this theory, vote maximization guides the decisions of elected officials who, in turn, control government employees.

Voluntary Exchange Versus Coercion. Market exchange relies on the voluntary behavior of buyers and sellers. If you don't like tofu, no problem—just don't buy any. But in political markets the situation is different. Any voting rule except unanimous consent will involve some government coercion. Public choices are enforced by the police power of the state. Those who fail to pay their taxes could go to jail, even though they may object to programs those taxes support.

Absence of Market Prices. Another distinguishing feature of governments is that the selling price of public output is usually either zero or some amount below its cost. If you are now attending a state college or university, your tuition probably covers less than half of the total cost of providing your education. Since the revenue side of the government budget is usually separate from the expenditure side, there is no necessary link between the cost and benefit of a public program. In the private sector, however, marginal benefits are at least equal to marginal costs; otherwise, market exchange would not occur.

Size and Growth of U.S. Government

One way to track the role of government over time is by measuring government spending relative to the U.S. *gross domestic product*, or *GDP*, which is the total value of all final goods and services produced in the United States. In 1929, the year the Great Depression began, government spending, mostly by state and local governments, totaled just one-tenth the size of GDP. At that time, the federal government played a minor role. In fact, during the country's first 150 years, spending by the federal government, except during times of war, never exceeded 3 percent of the size of GDP.

The Great Depression, World War II, and a change in mainstream macroeconomic thinking expanded the role of the federal government in the economy. By 1998, government spending was 32 percent as large as GDP, with 21 percent by the federal government and 11 percent by state and local governments. In comparison, government spending relative to GDP was 36 percent in Japan, 39 percent in the United Kingdom, 42 percent in Canada, 47 percent in Germany, 50 percent in Italy, and 54 percent in France. The average for 18 other industrial economies was 42 percent.[2]

Thus, government spending in the United States is small, compared to the rest of the industrialized world. Since 1960, defense spending has declined from over half of all federal spending to less than one-fifth today. Spending on Social Security and Medicare, programs aimed primarily at the elderly, has increased from about 10 percent of the federal budget in 1960 to about one-third today.

Sources of Government Revenue

Taxes provide the bulk of revenue at all levels of government. The federal government relies primarily on the individual income tax, state governments rely on income and sales taxes, and local governments rely on the property tax. In addition to taxes, other revenue sources include user charges, such as highway tolls, and borrowing. Some states also sell stuff, such as lottery tickets and liquor, to raise money.

Exhibit 3 focuses on sources of federal revenue since 1940. The individual income tax has accounted for about 45 percent of federal revenues since shortly after World War II. In the early 1950s, payroll taxes accounted for only about 10 percent of federal receipts, compared to 36 percent most recently. *Payroll taxes* are deducted from paychecks to support Social Security, unemployment benefits, and medical care for the elderly. Corporate income taxes and revenue from other sources, such as excise (sales) taxes and user charges, have declined as a share of the total since the 1950s.

Tax Principles and Tax Incidence

Ability-to-pay-tax principle Those with a greater ability to pay should pay more tax

The structure of a tax is often justified on the basis of one of two general principles. First, a tax could relate to the individual's **ability to pay,** so those with a greater ability pay more taxes. Income or property taxes often rely on this ability-to-pay principle. Alternatively, a tax could relate to the **benefits received** from the government activity funded by the tax. For example, the tax on gaso-

2 Figures for foreign countries are from the Organization for Economic Cooperation and Development (OECD).

EXHIBIT 3

Percent Composition of Federal Government Receipts Since 1940 (share of total)

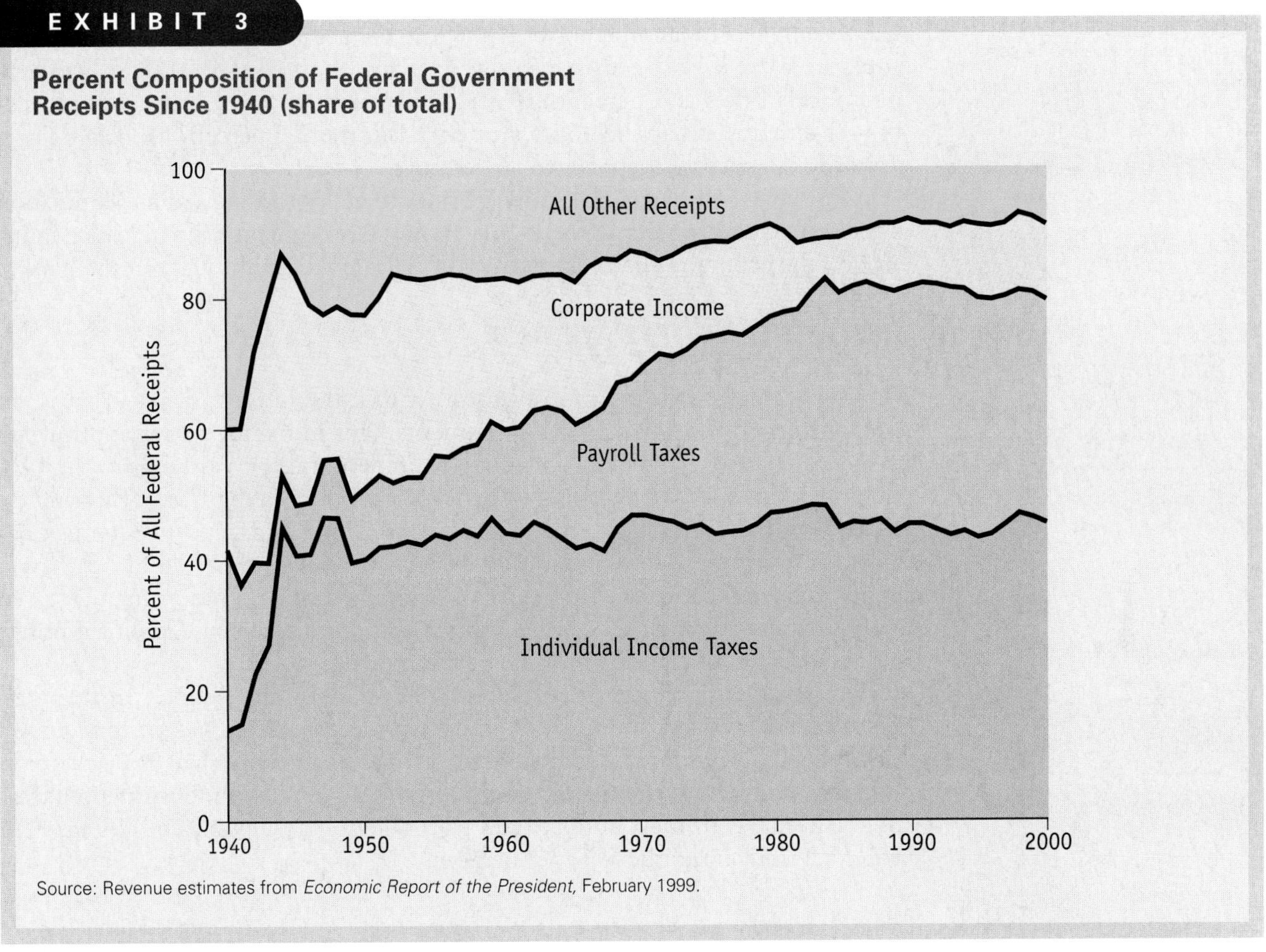

Source: Revenue estimates from *Economic Report of the President,* February 1999.

line funds highway construction and maintenance, thereby linking tax payment to road use, since the more people drive, the more gas tax they pay.

Tax incidence indicates who actually bears the burden of the tax. One way to evaluate tax incidence is by measuring the tax as a percentage of income. Under **proportional taxation,** taxpayers at all income levels pay the same percentage of their income in taxes. A proportional income tax is also called a flat-rate tax, because the tax as a percentage of income remains constant, or flat, as income increases. Under **progressive taxation,** the percentage of income paid in taxes increases as income increases.

The **marginal tax rate** indicates the percentage of each additional dollar of income that goes to taxes. Because high marginal rates reduce the after-tax return from working or investing, they can reduce people's incentives to work and to invest. In 1999, there were 5 marginal rates under the U.S. federal personal income tax—15 percent, 28 percent, 31 percent, 36 percent, and 39.6 percent—so that tax is progressive. By way of comparison, the top marginal tax rate is 65 percent in Japan, 55 percent in England and Canada, and 53 percent in France and Germany.

Finally, under **regressive taxation,** the percentage of income paid in taxes decreases as income increases, so the marginal tax rate declines as income

Benefits-received tax principle Those who receive more benefits from the government program funded by a tax should pay more tax

Tax incidence The distribution of tax burden among taxpayers

Proportional taxation The tax as a percentage of income remains constant as income increases; also called a flat-rate tax

Progressive taxation The tax as a percentage of income increases as income increases

Marginal tax rate The percentage of each additional dollar of income that goes to taxes

Regressive taxation The tax as a percentage of income decreases as income increases

increases. Most U.S. *payroll taxes* are regressive, because they impose a flat rate up to a certain level of income, above which the marginal rate drops to zero. For example, in 1999, Social Security taxes were levied on the first $72,600 of workers' income. Half the 12.4 percent tax is paid by employers and half by employees (the self-employed pay the entire amount). But the 2.9 percent Medicare tax is proportional, because it applies to all earnings.

This discussion of revenue sources brings to a close, for now, our examination of the role of government in the U.S. economy. Government has a pervasive influence on the economy, and discussions of its role are woven throughout the book.

THE REST OF THE WORLD

Thus far we have focused on institutions within the United States—that is, on *domestic* households, firms, and governments. This initial focus was appropriate because our primary objective has been to understand the workings of the U.S. economy, which is by far the largest national economy in the world. But the rest of the world affects what U.S. households consume and what U.S. firms produce. For example, Asian economies such as those of Japan and South Korea supply U.S. markets with autos, electronic equipment, and other manufactured goods, thereby affecting U.S. prices, wages, and profits. Likewise, political unrest in the Persian Gulf can drive up the price of oil.

Foreign decision makers, therefore, have a significant effect on the U.S. economy—on what we consume and what we produce. The *rest of the world* consists of the households, firms, and governments in more than 200 sovereign countries throughout the world, ranging from countries with fewer people than any of the states in the United States to the People's Republic of China, with more than four times the U.S. population.

International Trade

In Chapter 2 you learned about comparative advantage and the gains from specialization. These gains explain why householders stopped trying to do everything for themselves and began to specialize. International trade arises for the same reasons. *International trade occurs because the opportunity cost of producing specific goods differs among countries.* Americans import raw materials such as crude oil, diamonds, and coffee beans and finished goods such as cameras, VCRs, and automobiles. U.S. producers export sophisticated products such as computer hardware and software, aircraft, and movies, as well as agricultural products such as wheat and corn.

International trade between the United States and the rest of the world has increased in recent decades. In 1970 U.S. exports of goods and services amounted to only 6 percent of gross domestic product. That figure has since more than doubled to 14 percent. Our chief U.S. trading partners in order of importance are Canada, Japan, Mexico, Great Britain, Germany, France, South Korea, and Taiwan.

Merchandise trade balance The value of a country's exported goods minus the value of its imported goods during a given time period

The **merchandise trade balance** equals the value of exported goods minus the value of imported goods. Goods in this case are distinguished from services, which show up in another trade account. For the last two decades, the United States has experienced a merchandise trade deficit, meaning that the value of goods imported into the U.S. has exceeded the value of U.S. goods exported. Just as a household must cover its spending, so too must a nation. The deficit in our merchandise trade balance must be offset by a surplus in one or more of the other *balance-of-*

payments accounts. A nation's **balance of payments** is the record of all economic transactions between its residents and the residents of the rest of the world.

Balance of payments A record of all economic transactions between residents of one country and residents of the rest of the world during a given time period

Exchange Rates

The lack of a common currency complicates trade between countries. How many U.S. dollars buys a Porsche? An American buyer cares only about the dollar cost; the German car maker cares only about the *euros* received (the new common currency of 11 European countries). To facilitate trade when two currencies are involved, a market for foreign exchange has developed. **Foreign exchange** is a foreign currency needed to carry out international transactions. The supply and demand for foreign exchange come together in *foreign exchange markets* to determine an equilibrium exchange rate. The *exchange rate* measures the price of one currency in terms of another. For example, the exchange rate between the euro and the dollar might indicate that one euro exchanges for $1.10. At that exchange rate, a Porsche selling for 60,000 euros costs $66,000. The greater the demand for a particular foreign currency or the smaller the supply, the higher its exchange rate—that is, the more dollars it will cost. The exchange rate affects the prices of imports and exports and thus helps shape the flow of foreign trade.

Foreign exchange Foreign currency needed to carry out international transactions

Trade Restrictions

Although there are clear gains from international specialization and exchange, nearly all nations restrict trade to some extent. These restrictions can take the form of (1) **tariffs**, which are taxes on imports; (2) **quotas**, which are legal limits on the quantity of a particular good that can be imported; and (3) other restrictions, such as the voluntary agreement by Japanese automobile manufacturers to limit their exports to the United States.

Tariff A tax on imports or exports

Quota A legal limit on the quantity of a particular product that can be imported or exported

If specialization according to comparative advantage is so beneficial, why do most countries restrict trade? Restrictions benefit certain domestic producers that lobby their governments for these benefits. For example, U.S. textile manufacturers have sought and received from Congress protective legislation restricting textile imports, thereby raising U.S. textile prices. These higher prices harm domestic consumers, but consumers are usually unaware of this harm. Trade restrictions interfere with the free flow of products across borders and tend to harm the overall economy. International trade in the auto industry is discussed in the following case study.

Wheel of Fortune

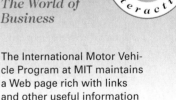

The World of Business

The International Motor Vehicle Program at MIT maintains a Web page rich with links and other useful information about automobile production worldwide. You can find it at http://web.mit.edu/org/c/ctpid/www/imvp/IMVP-links.html.

The U.S. auto industry is huge, with annual sales of more than $250 billion, an amount exceeding the gross domestic product of 90 percent of the world's economies. Imports accounted for only 0.4 percent of U.S. auto sales in the decade following World War II. In 1973, however, the suddenly powerful Organization of Petroleum Exporting Countries (OPEC) more than tripled oil prices. In response, Americans scrambled for more fuel-efficient automobiles, which at the time were sold primarily by foreign manufacturers, especially the Japanese. As a result, imports jumped to 21 percent of U.S. auto sales by 1980.

In the early 1980s, at the urging of the Big Three auto makers (General Motors, Ford, and Chrysler), the Reagan administration persuaded Japanese producers to adopt "voluntary" import quotas limiting the number of Japanese automobiles they exported to the United States. The quotas, or supply restrictions, drove up the price of Japanese imports. U.S. auto producers used this as an opportunity to raise their own prices. Experts estimate that the so-called protection from foreign competition cost U.S. consumers over $15 billion.

The quotas had two effects on Japanese producers. First, faced with a strict limit on the number of cars they could export to the United States, they began shipping more upscale models instead of subcompacts. Second, the quotas encouraged Japanese producers to establish manufacturing plants in the United States. By making autos here, Japanese manufacturers also reduced the problem caused by fluctuations in the value of the yen relative to the dollar. Japanese-owned auto plants in the U.S. now account for more than one-quarter of car production in the United States. Two German auto makers, Mercedes and BMW, have also built plants here.

Imports still make up about one-quarter of U.S. car sales, with Japanese manufacturers accounting for most of that. Imports include cars produced abroad by foreign firms but sold under the names of U.S. firms. The Big Three also produce around the world. In fact, Ford is the largest auto maker in Australia, Great Britain, Mexico, and Argentina.

In China, India, and Latin America, the potential car market is enormous. Here's something to think about: There are more people in China under 26 years of age than the combined population of the United States, Japan, Germany, the United Kingdom, and Canada. Automobile production in China jumped from 23,500 in 1988 to about 2 million in 1998. Only about 100,000 vehicles were imported.

Sources: Rebecca Blumenstein and Gregory White, "In Aftermath of UAW Strikes, GM Seeks to Justify the Costs," *Wall Street Journal*, 30 July 1998; Walter Adams and James Brock, "Automobiles," in *The Structure of American Industry*, 9th ed. (Englewood Cliffs, N.J.: Prentice Hall, 1995): pp. 65–92; Michelle Krebs, "Heavy Traffic to the Third World," *The New York Times*, 3 Oct. 1997; Andrea Pulchalsky, "Camry Whizzes Past Taurus as Best-Selling Car in the U.S.," *Wall Street Journal*," 30 September 1997.

THE CIRCULAR FLOW MODEL

Circular flow model A diagram that outlines the flow of resources, products, income, and revenue among households, firms, governments, and the rest of the world

Now that we have examined each economic decision maker in detail, let's review how they interact. Such a picture is conveyed by the **circular flow model,** which describes the flow of resources, products, income, and revenue among households, firms, governments, and the rest of the world.

Flows Between Households and Firms

We begin with the most fundamental interaction in a market economy—that between households and firms. Exhibit 4 shows households on the left and firms on the right. Households supply labor, capital, land, and entrepreneurial ability to firms through resource markets, shown on the lower portion of the exhibit. In return, households demand goods and services from firms through product markets, shown on the upper portion of the exhibit. Viewed from the business end, firms supply goods and services to households through product markets, and they

EXHIBIT 4

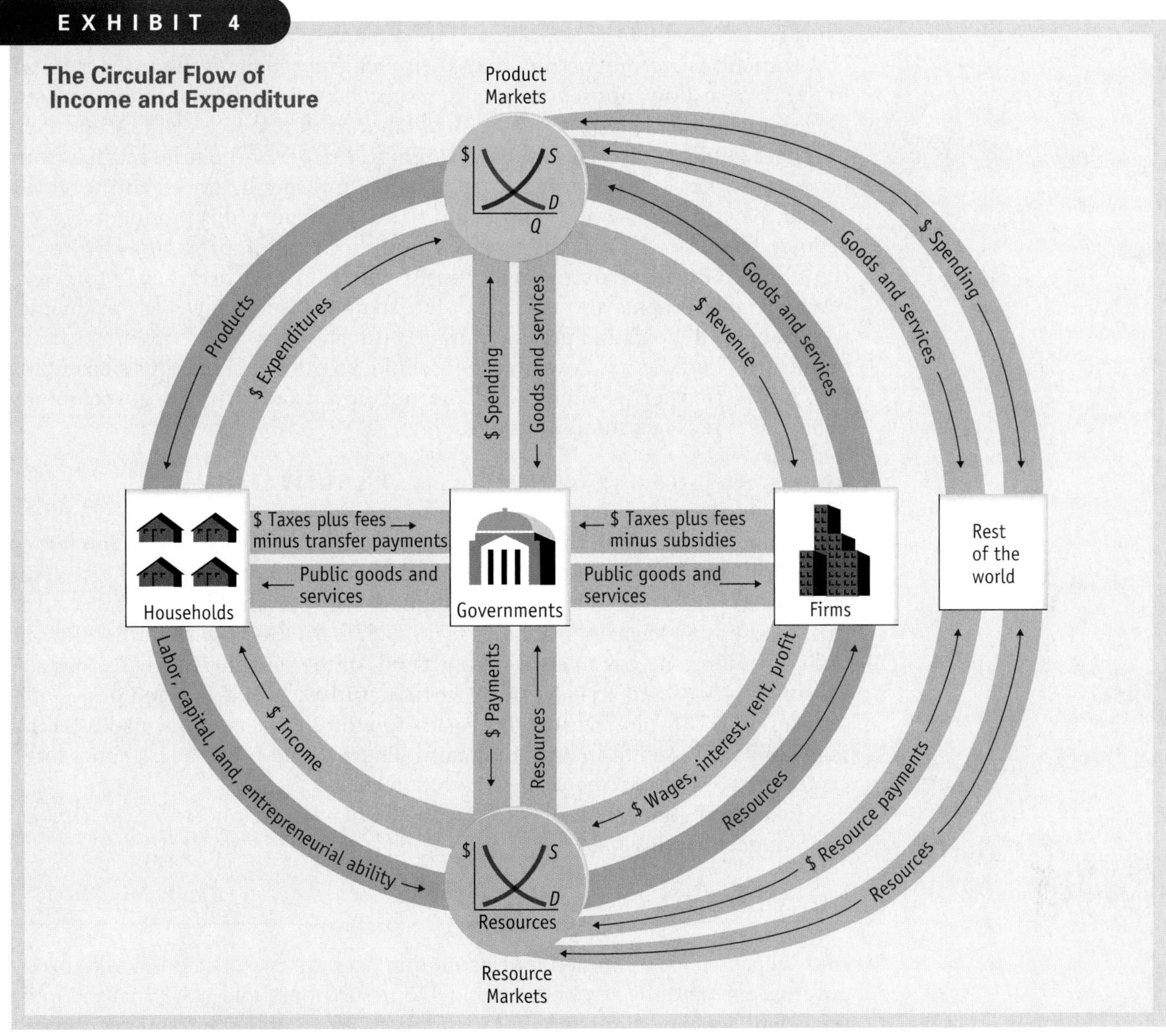

demand labor, capital, land, and entrepreneurial ability from households through resource markets. Resources and products flow in a counterclockwise direction.

In a barter economy, exchange is limited to physical flows of resources and products. But in nearly all economies of the world, the flows of resources and products are supported by flows of income and expenditure—that is, by the flow of money. So let's add money to the picture. Supply and demand in resource markets determine equilibrium wages, interest, rents, and profits, which—when multiplied by the quantity of resources supplied—flow as income to households. Supply and demand in product markets determine equilibrium prices for goods and services, which—when multiplied by the quantities of goods and services demanded—flow as revenue to firms. In the diagram note that resources and products flow in a counterclockwise direction, and that corresponding payments for these products and resources flow in a clockwise direction.

Government-Related Flows

Thus far we have focused on the private sector. But another decision maker is government. Governments are linked with all four elements discussed thus far in the circular flow: households, firms, resource markets, and products markets. Governments purchase resources such as labor from resource markets, and they purchase goods and services such as computer paper and phone service from product markets. Governments convert these into public goods and services, which they provide to households and firms. To finance this production, governments rely on the revenue received from households, firms, and the rest of the world. Government revenue consists of taxes and user fees. From this revenue, governments also make transfer payments (such as welfare payments) to certain households and provide subsidies (such as farm price supports) to certain firms. Thus, the net flow from households to governments equals taxes plus fees minus transfer payments, and the net flow from firms to governments equals taxes plus fees minus subsidies.

Flows To and From the Rest of the World

The discussion so far has been limited to the domestic economy. To complete the picture, we must add the flows to and from the rest of the world. The rest of the world supplies resources to our resource markets and demands resources from those markets. For example, foreigners sell specialized machines to U.S. firms and buy specialized machines from U.S. firms. Because resources flow in both directions, there is an arrow at both ends of the pipeline. Likewise, foreigners supply goods and services to U.S. product markets and demand goods and services from U.S. product markets. Again, to indicate the two-way nature of the flows, the arrows point in both directions. The same goes for the pipelines indicating the resource payments and product revenues.

Take a little time right now to review the big picture offered by the circular flow model in Exhibit 4.

CONCLUSION

In this chapter we examined four economic decision makers: households, firms, governments, and the rest of the world. Domestic households are by far the most important, for they, along with foreign households, supply the resources and demand the goods and services produced. In recent years, the U.S. economy has come to depend more on the rest of the world as a market for U.S. goods and as a source of products.

SUMMARY

1. Most household income arises from the sale of labor, and most household income is spent on personal consumption, which consists of spending on durable goods, nondurable goods, and services—the last being the fastest-growing portion of personal consumption. Income not spent on personal consumption is either saved or paid as taxes.
2. Members of households once built their own homes, made their own clothes and furniture, grew their own food, and amused themselves. Over time, however, the efficiency arising from comparative advantage resulted in a greater specialization among resource suppliers.

3. Firms bring together specialized resources. Firms can be organized in three different ways: as sole proprietorships, partnerships, or corporations. Because corporations are typically large, they account for the bulk of all sales by U.S. firms.

4. When private markets yield socially undesirable results, government may intervene to address these market failures. Government programs are designed to (1) protect private property and enforce contracts; (2) promote competition; (3) regulate natural monopolies; (4) provide public goods; (5) discourage negative externalities and encourage positive externalities; (6) provide for greater equality in the distribution of income; and (7) promote full employment, price stability, and growth.

5. In the United States, the federal government relies primarily on the personal income tax, the states rely on income and sales taxes, and the localities rely on the property tax. A tax is often justified by basing it on (1) the individual's ability to pay or (2) the benefits the taxpayer receives from the activities financed by the tax.

6. The rest of the world is also populated by households, firms, and governments. International trade takes advantage of the gains that arise from comparative. The balance of payments summarizes the transactions between the residents of one country and the residents of the rest of the world. Despite the benefits from comparative advantage, nearly all countries impose trade restrictions to protect specific domestic industries.

7. The circular flow model describes the flow of resources, products, income, and revenue among households, firms, governments, and the rest of the world.

QUESTIONS FOR REVIEW

1. *(Households as Demanders of Goods and Services)* Classify each of the following as a durable good, a nondurable good, or a service:
   a. A gallon of milk
   b. A lawn mower
   c. A videocassette recorder
   d. A manicure
   e. A pair of shoes
   f. An eye exam
   g. A personal computer
   h. A neighborhood teenager mowing a lawn

2. *(**CaseStudy:** The Electronic Cottage)* How has the development of personal computer hardware and software reversed some of the trends brought on by the Industrial Revolution?

3. *(Evolution of the Firm)* Explain how production after the Industrial Revolution differed from production under the cottage industry system.

4. *(Household Production)* What factors does a householder consider when deciding whether to produce a good or service at home or buy it in the marketplace?

5. *(Corporations)* Why did the institution of the firm appear after the advent of the Industrial Revolution? What type of business organization existed before this?

6. *(Sole Proprietorships)* What are the disadvantages of the sole proprietorship form of business?

7. *(Government)* Often it is said that government is necessary when private markets fail to work effectively and fairly. Based on your reading of the text, discuss how private markets might break down.

8. *(Externalities)* Suppose there is an external cost associated with production of a certain good. What's wrong with letting the market determine how much of this good will be produced?

9. *(Government Revenue)* What are the sources of government revenue in the United States? Which types of taxes are most important at each level of government? Which two taxes provide the most revenue to the U.S. federal government?

10. *(Objectives of the Economic Decision Makers)* In economic analysis, what are the assumed objectives of households, firms, and the government?

11. *(International Trade)* Why does international trade occur? What does it mean to run a deficit in the merchandise trade balance?

12. *(International Trade)* Distinguish between a tariff and a quota. Who benefits from and who is harmed by such restrictions on imports?

13. *(**CaseStudy:** Wheel of Fortune)* What factors led Japanese auto producers to build factories in the United States?

14. *(Circular Flow)* Review the illustration of the circular flow of income and expenditure in Exhibit 4. Which flows take the form of money, and which take the form of goods and services? What role does international trade play in this circular flow?

PROBLEMS AND EXERCISES

15. *(Evolution of the Household)* Determine whether each of the following would increase or decrease the opportunity costs for mothers who choose not to accept paid employment outside the home. Explain your answers.
    a. Higher levels of education for women
    b. Higher unemployment rates for women
    c. Higher average pay levels for women
    d. Lower demand for labor in industries that traditionally employ large numbers of women

16. *(Household Production)* Many households supplement their food budget by cultivating small vegetable gardens. Explain how each of the following might influence this kind of household production:
    a. Both husband and wife are professionals who earn high salaries.
    b. The household is located in a city rather than in a rural area.
    c. The household is located in a region where there is a high sales tax on food.
    d. The household is located in a region that has a high property tax rate.

17. *(Government)* Complete each of the following sentences:
    a. When the private operation of a market leads to overproduction or underproduction of some good, this is known as a(n) ________________.
    b. Goods that are nonrival and nonexcludable are known as ________________.
    c. ________________ are cash or in-kind benefits given to individuals as outright grants from the government.
    d. A(n) ________________ confers an external benefit on third parties that are not directly involved in a market transaction.
    e. ________________ refers to the government's pursuit of full employment and price stability through variations in taxes and government spending.

18. *(Tax Rates)* Suppose taxes are related to income level as follows:

Income	Taxes
$1,000	$200
$2,000	$350
$3,000	$450

    a. What percent of income is paid in taxes at each level?
    b. Is the tax rate progressive, proportional, or regressive?
    c. What is the marginal tax rate on the first $1,000 of income? The second $1,000? The third $1,000?

EXPERIENTIAL EXERCISES

19. *(The Evolution of the Firm)* Get a library copy of *The Wealth and Poverty of Nations* by David Landes and read pages 207–210. How would you interpret Landes' story about mechanization using the ideas developed in this chapter?

20. *(The Evolution of the Firm)* The Center for Research on Contracts and the Structure of Enterprise at the University of Pittsburgh http://crcse.business.pitt.edu/ maintains lots of interesting information about the evolution of the firm. Visit that site to familiarize yourself with the kinds of issues economists are studying.

21. *(International Trade)* Visit McEachern Interactive Web Site http://mceachern.swcollege.com and click on EconDebates Online. Review the materials on "Does the U.S. Economy Benefit from Foreign Trade?" What are some of the benefits of international trade—not just to the U.S., but to all nations?

22. *(Wall Street Journal)* The household is the most important decision-making unit in our economy. Look through the rotating columns (e.g., "Work and Family," and "Personal Technology") in the *Wall Street Journal* this week. Find a description of some technological change that might affect household production. Explain how production would be affected.

CHAPTER

5 Introduction to Macroeconomics

What's the big deal with macroeconomics? Why is the focus of macroeconomics typically the national economy? What are the similarities and differences between the economy and the human body? How do we measure the performance of an economy over time? Answers to these and related questions are provided in this chapter, which introduces macroeconomics.

In macroeconomics we think big—not about the demand and supply for apples but the demand and supply for everything produced in the economy; not about the price of computers but the average price of all goods and services produced in the economy; not about consumption by the Jackson household but consumption by all households; not about the investment by Intel but the investment by all firms in the economy.

Visit the McEachern Interactive Study Center for this chapter at http://mcisc.swcollege.com

Macroeconomists develop and test theories about how the economy as a whole works—theories they can use to predict the consequences of economic policies and events. They are concerned not only with what determines such big-picture measures as the level of the economy's prices, employment, and production but also with understanding how these variables fluctuate over time.

Macroeconomists are especially interested in what makes an economy grow over time, because a growing economy usually means more job opportunities and more goods and services—in short, growth means a rising standard of living. What determines the economy's ability to use resources productively, to adapt, to grow? In this chapter, we will begin to explore these questions; then in Chapter 6 we will introduce a major concern of the day—economic growth. Topics discussed in this chapter include:

- The national economy
- Economic fluctuations
- Aggregate demand and aggregate supply
- Short history of the U.S. economy
- Demand-side economics
- Supply-side economics

THE NATIONAL ECONOMY

Economy The structure of economic life or economic activity in a community, a region, a country, a group of countries, or the world

Macroeconomics concerns the overall performance of the *economy*. The term **economy** describes the structure of economic life, or economic activity, in a community, a region, a country, a group of countries, or the world. We could talk about the Chicago economy, the Illinois economy, the Midwest economy, the U.S. economy, the North American economy, or the world economy. We measure an economy's performance in different ways, such as the number of workers employed, their average earnings, the amount produced, or the size and number of firms. The most commonly used measure of an economy's performance is the *gross product,* which measures the market value of final goods and services produced in a particular geographical region during a given time period, usually one year. If the focus is the Illinois economy, we consider the *gross state product.*

Gross domestic product, or GDP The market value of all final goods and services produced by resources located in the United States, regardless of who owns those resources

If the focus is the U.S. economy, we consider the **gross domestic product,** or **GDP,** which measures the market value of all final goods and services produced in the United States during a given time period, usually a year. GDP helps federal statisticians keep track of the economy's incredible variety of goods and services, from trail bikes to pedicures. We can use the gross product to track the same economy over time or to compare different economies at the same time.

What's Special About the National Economy

The national economy deserves special attention. Here's why. If you were to drive west on Interstate 10 in Texas, you would hardly notice crossing the state line into New Mexico. If, however, you took the Juarez exit off I-10 south into Mexico, you would be stopped at the border, asked for identification, and possibly searched. You would be quite aware that you were crossing an international border. Like most countries, the United States and Mexico usually allow freer movement of people and goods *within* their borders than *across* their borders.

The differences between the United States and Mexico are far greater than the differences between Texas and New Mexico. For example, each country has its own culture and language, its own communication and transportation systems, its own system of government, its own currency, and, most importantly, its own "rules of the game"—that is, its own laws, regulations, customs, and conventions for conducting economic activity both within and across its borders.

Macroeconomics typically focuses on the performance of the national economy, including how the national economy interacts with other economies around the world. To get some idea of the complex nature of the U.S. economy, consider this profile of households, firms, governments, and the rest of the world. In the United States, there are more than 100 million households, about 22 million for-profit businesses, and about 80,000 separate units of government. And there are more than 200 sovereign countries throughout the world, ranging from tiny Liechtenstein, with a population of only 30,000, to immense China, with 1.3 billion people. These numbers offer snapshots of economic decision makers, but the economy is a moving picture—too complex to describe in snapshots. This is why we use theoretical models to simplify the key relationships. Let's begin with an analogy.

The Human Body and the Economy

Consider the similarities and differences between the human body and the economy. The body consists of millions of cells, each performing particular functions yet each linked to the operation of the entire body. Similarly, the economy is composed of millions of economic units, each acting with some independence yet each connected with the economy as a whole. The economy, like the body, is continually renewing itself, with new households, new businesses, a changing set of public officials, and new foreign competitors.

Blood circulates throughout the body, facilitating the exchange of vital nutrients among cells. Similarly, **money** circulates throughout the economy, facilitating the exchange of resources and products among individual economic units. In fact, money is called a *medium of exchange*. In Chapter 4 we saw that the movement of money, products, and resources throughout the economy follows a *circular flow,* as does the movement of blood and nutrients throughout the body.

Money Something accepted as a medium of exchange

FLOWS AND STOCKS. Just as the same blood circulates again and again in the body, the same money circulates again and again in the economy to finance transactions. The same dollars you spend on blueberry muffins are spent by the baker on butter, then spent by the dairy farmer on work boots. The dollars *flow* through the economy. To measure a flow, we use a **flow** variable, which is a measure per period of time, such as heartbeats per minute or your earnings per week. We distinguish between a *flow* variable and a *stock* variable. A **stock** variable represents an amount of something at a particular point in time, such as the volume of blood in your body or the number of dollars in your possession right now.

Flow A variable that measures the amount of something over an interval of time, such as the amount of money you spend on food per week

Stock A variable that measures the amount of something at a particular point in time, such as the amount of food in your refrigerator or the amount of money you have with you right now

ROLE OF EXPECTATIONS. In both medicine and macroeconomics, *expectations* play an important role. For example, if the patient expects a medicine to work, it often does work, even if it is only a sugar pill, or placebo. A similar mechanism can operate in the economy. Suppose, for example, that all firms expect greater demand for their products. To expand output, firms buy more capital and hire more workers. As a result, households, as resource suppliers, earn more income and so increase their demand for goods and services. Thus, producers may help bring about the very prosperity they expect. Negative expectations can also be self-fulfilling. If firms expect demand to fall, they invest less and hire fewer workers. As a result, household incomes decline, reducing the demand for goods and services. As we will see later, the role of expectations is especially important in evaluating the appropriate role of government in the macroeconomy.

Differences of Opinion. Both in medicine and in macroeconomics, matters are subject to different interpretations. First, experts within each field may disagree about what ails the patient or the economy. In macroeconomics, experts may differ about the source of the problem. Second, even when experts agree about what's wrong, they may disagree over what to do about it. Medical researchers, however, have two big advantages over macroeconomists: They have collected vastly more information about their subject, and they can test their theories in a laboratory setting.

Testing New Theories

Physicians and other natural scientists can test theories using controlled experiments. Macroeconomists have no laboratory and little ability to run experiments of any kind. Granted, they can study different economies throughout the world, but each economy is unique, so comparisons across countries are tricky. Controlled experiments also provide scientists with something seldom available to macroeconomists—the chance, or serendipitous, discovery (such as penicillin). But with only one patient—the U.S. economy—the macroeconomist cannot introduce particular policies in a variety of ways. Cries of "Eureka!" are seldom heard from macroeconomists.

Knowledge and Performance

Throughout history, little was known about human biology, yet many people enjoyed good health. For example, the fact that blood circulates in our bodies was not discovered until 1638; it took scientists another 150 years to figure out why. Similarly, over the millennia various complex economies developed and flourished, although there was little understanding or even concern about how these economies worked.

The economy is much like the body: As long as it functions smoothly, policy makers need not understand its operation. But if a problem develops—severe unemployment, high inflation, or sluggish growth, for example—we must know how a healthy economy works before we can consider if and how the problem can be corrected. We need not know every detail of the economy, just as we need not know every detail of the body. But we must understand the essential relationships among key economic variables. For example, we would like to know the extent to which the economy is self-adjusting. Does the economy work well enough on its own, or does it often perform poorly? If the economy does perform poorly, what are the policy options and can we be sure that the proposed remedy won't do more harm than good?

When doctors did not understand how the body works, their cures were often worse than the disease. Much of the history of medicine describes misguided attempts to deal with maladies. As recently as the 19th century, for example, medical "remedies" included "bleeding, cupping, violent purging, the raising of blisters by vesicant ointments, the immersion of the body in either ice water or intolerably hot water, endless lists of botanical extracts evoked up and mixed together under nothing more than pure whim."[1] Even today, medical care is based on less scientific evidence than we think. According to one researcher, only one in seven medical interventions is supported by reliable scientific evidence.[2]

Likewise, national policy makers have sometimes implemented the wrong economic prescription because of a flawed theory about how the economy works. At one time, for example, a nation's economic vitality was thought to spring from the stock of precious metals accumulated in the public treasury. This theory spawned a policy called *mercantilism,* which held that, as a way of accumulating gold and silver, a nation should sell more output to foreigners than it bought from them. To achieve this, nations restricted imports by such devices as tariffs and quotas. But these restrictions reduced international trade, thereby reducing the gains from specialization that arise from trade. Another flawed economic theory prompted President Herbert Hoover to introduce a major tax *increase* while the nation was suffering through the Great Depression. We have since learned that such a policy does more harm than good.

Let's turn now to the performance of the U.S. economy over time.

ECONOMIC FLUCTUATIONS AND GROWTH

The U.S. economy and other industrial market economies historically have experienced alternating periods of expansion and contraction in the level of economic activity. **Economic fluctuations** are the rise and fall of economic activity relative to the long-term growth trend of the economy. These fluctuations, or *business cycles,* vary in length and intensity, yet some features appear common to all. The ups and downs usually involve the entire nation and often the world, and they affect nearly all dimensions of economic activity, not simply employment and production levels.

NetBookmark

How long do economic expansions last? Why do they end? Find out by reading Joseph Haimowitz's "The Longevity of Expansions," which can be downloaded from http://www.kc.frb.org/publicat/econrev/er98q4.htm#expansions.

Economic Fluctuation Analysis

Perhaps the easiest way to understand economic fluctuations is to examine their components. During the 1920s and 1930s, Wesley C. Mitchell, director of the National Bureau of Economic Research (NBER), analyzed economic fluctuations. The economy, according to Mitchell, has two phases: periods of expansion and periods of contraction. Before World War II, some contractions were so severe that they were called *depressions.* Although there is no official definition, a **depression** is a sharp reduction in the nation's total production, accompanied by high unemployment that lasts more than a year. A milder contraction is called a **recession,** which the NBER identifies as a period of decline in total output and employment, usually lasting at least two consecutive quarters, or six months. Prior to World War II, the economy experienced both recessions and depressions. Since World War II, there have been recessions but no depressions.

Economic fluctuations The rise and fall of economic activity relative to the long-term growth trend of the economy; also called business cycles

Depression A severe reduction in an economy's total production accompanied by high unemployment lasting more than a year

Recession A period of decline in total output usually lasting at least six months and marked by contractions in many sectors of the economy

Despite these ups and downs, the U.S. economy has grown dramatically over the long run. Measured by the amount of goods and services produced, the economy today is eight times larger than it was in 1940, reflecting an average

1 As described by Lewis Thomas in *The Youngest Science: Notes of a Medicine Watcher* (New York: Viking Press, 1983), p. 19.

2 See Sherwin Nuland, "Medical Fads: Bran, Midwives and Leeches," *New York Times*, 25 January 1995.

EXHIBIT 1

Hypothetical Business Fluctuations

Business fluctuations reflect movements of economic activity around a trend line that shows long-term growth. A recession (shown in pink) begins after a previous expansion (shown in gold) has reached its peak and continues until the economy reaches a trough. An expansion begins when economic activity starts to increase and continues until the economy reaches a peak.

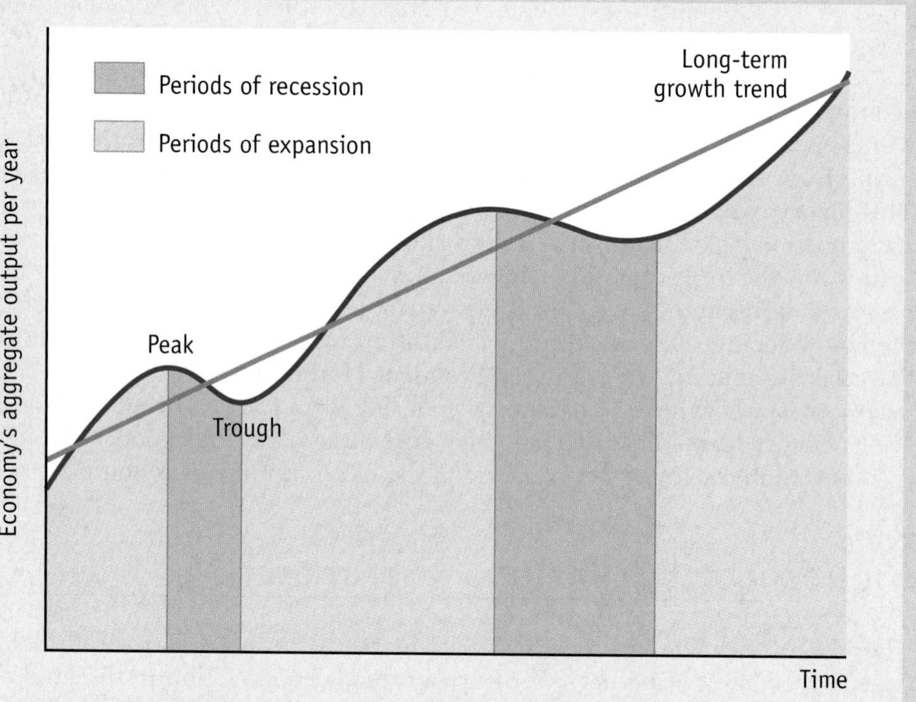

EXHIBIT 2

Historical Business Fluctuations in the United States

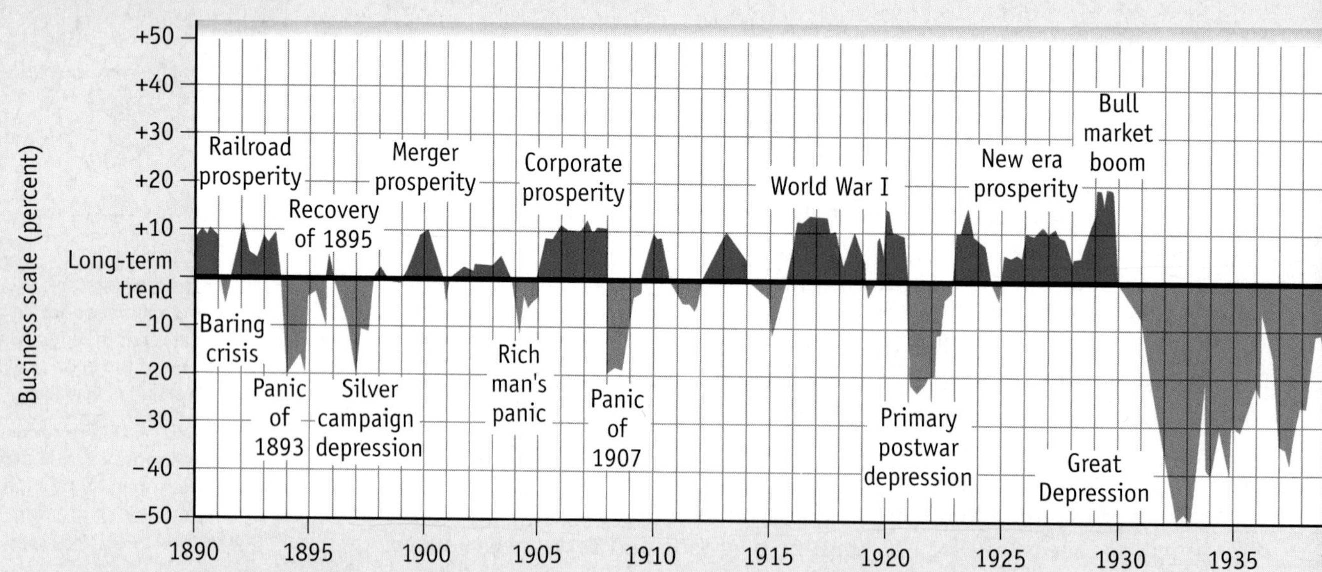

This historical chart shows the phases of business fluctuations since 1890. The vertical scale indicates the percentage by which the level of business activity exceeded or fell short of the long-term trend.

Source: "American Business Activity from 1790 to Today," Ameritrust Corporation, January 1988. Updated by author.

annual growth in production of 3.6 percent per year. Production tends to increase over the long run because of (1) increases in the amount and quality of resources, (2) better technology, and (3) improvements in the "rules of the game" that facilitate production and exchange, such as property rights, patent laws, the legal system, and customs of the market. Exhibit 1 shows such a long-term growth trend as an upward-sloping straight line. Economic fluctuations reflect movements around this growth trend. A recession begins after the previous expansion has reached its *peak* and continues until the economy reaches a *trough*. The period between the peak and the trough is a *recession,* and the period between the trough and the subsequent peak is an **expansion.** Note that expansions tend to last longer than recessions, and the length of the full cycle varies.

Expansion A phase of economic activity during which there is an increase in the economy's total production

The U.S. economic record appears in Exhibit 2, which shows the annual percentage change in economic activity relative to the long-term trend during the last hundred years. As you can see, the fluctuations vary widely in duration and in rate of change. The big declines during the Great Depression of the 1930s and the sharp gains during World War II stand in stark contrast to one another. Analysts at NBER have been able to track the U.S. economy back to 1854. Since then, the country has experienced 31 full peak-to-trough fluctuations. No two have been exactly alike. The longest *peacetime* expansion began in the spring of 1991 and was eight years old by the spring of 1999. The longest contraction lasted five and a half years, from 1873 to 1879.

Since 1933, the U.S. economy has completed 11 cycles of peaks and troughs. During this period, peacetime expansions averaged about 5 years and

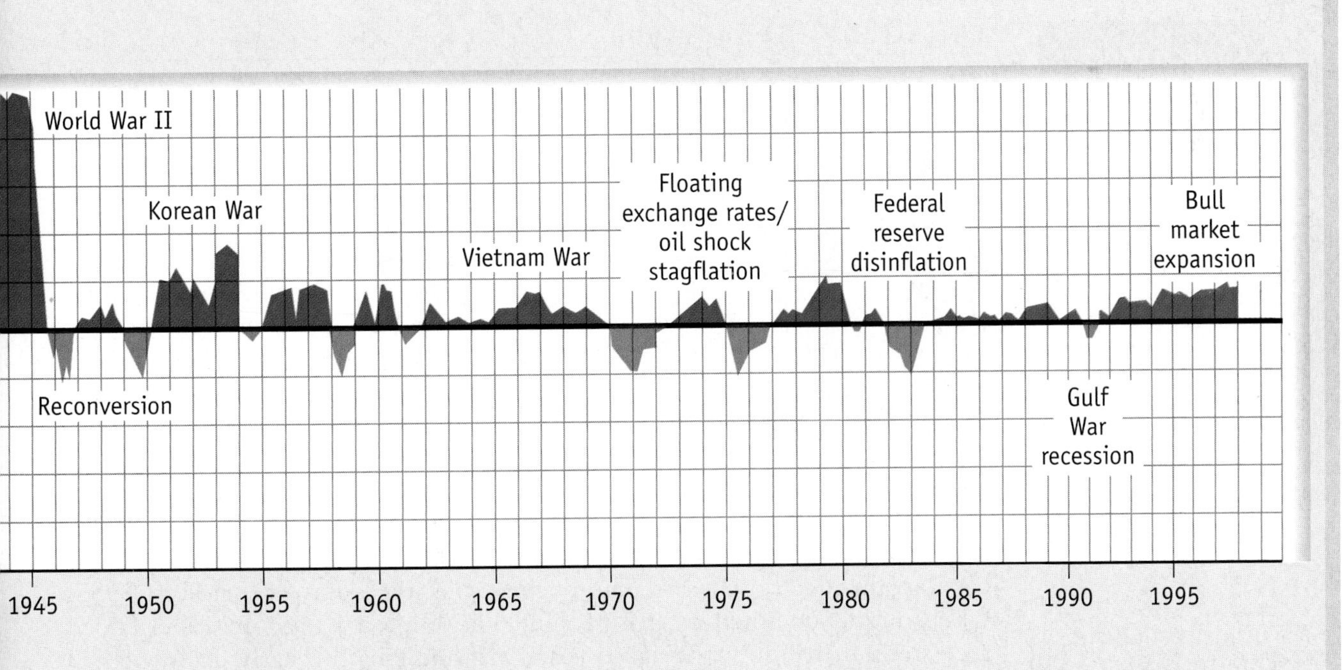

peacetime recessions about 1 year; wartime expansions were longer. The entire cycle lasts about 6 years on average. Again, despite the ups and downs, the economy has grown substantially over the long term, so the growth during expansions more than offsets the decline during recessions. As we will see in the next chapter, growth has not been uniform, but it has been nonetheless impressive: Since 1940 the U.S. economy has doubled its size every 20 years on average.

The intensity of the economic fluctuations varies from region to region across the United States. For example, a recession hits hardest those regions that produce durable goods, such as appliances, furniture, and automobiles; with the onset of a recession, the demand for these items falls more than the demand for nondurable goods, such as groceries, clothing, and gasoline.

Because of seasonal fluctuations and random disturbances, the economy does not move smoothly through phases of economic fluctuations. We cannot always distinguish between temporary setbacks in economic activity and the beginning of a downturn. The drop in production in a particular month may be the result of a snowstorm or a poor harvest rather than the onset of a recession. Turning points—peaks and troughs—are thus identified by the NBER only after the fact. Since a recession usually involves declining output for two consecutive quarters, a recession is not so designated until at least six months after it begins.

As noted earlier, the U.S. economy's ups and downs usually involve the entire nation; indeed, business fluctuations seem to be linked across economies around the world. The following case study compares the year-to-year change in production in the United States with another leading economy, the United Kingdom.

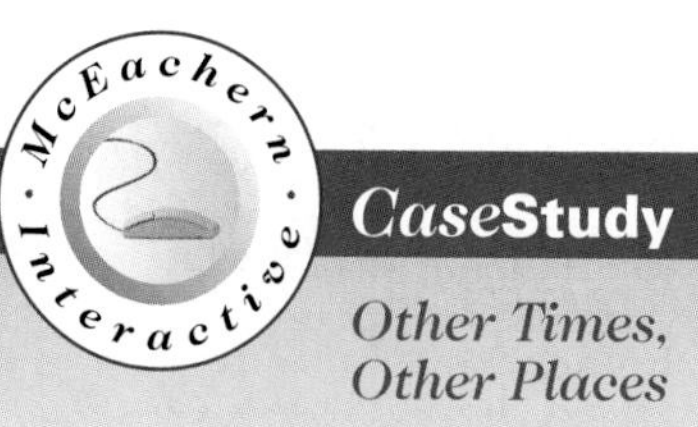

CaseStudy

Other Times, Other Places

The Foundation for International Business and Economic Research maintains a rich set of information regarding the international transmission of economic fluctuations. You can find their Web Site at http://www.global-trends.com/fiber2.htm.

The Global Economy

Though economic fluctuations are not perfectly synchronized across countries, a link is often apparent. Consider the recent experience in two leading economies—the United States and the United Kingdom, nations separated by the Atlantic Ocean. Exhibit 3 shows the year-to-year percentage change in their total output—their *real gross domestic product*, or *real GDP*. "Real" in this context means that the effects of inflation have been eliminated, so remaining changes are "real" changes (more on this later in this chapter).

If you spend a little time following the year-to-year changes in each country, you will begin to see similarities. For example, U.S. real GDP declined, or had a negative growth rate, in 1980, 1982, and 1991, reflecting recessions during those years. The deepest U.S. recession occurred in 1982, when output declined by 2.2 percent. The United Kingdom experienced recessions in roughly the same years, although in the early 1980s it had one long recession rather than the two shorter ones experienced in the United States.

EXHIBIT 3

U.S. and U.K. Annual Growth Rates in Real GDP

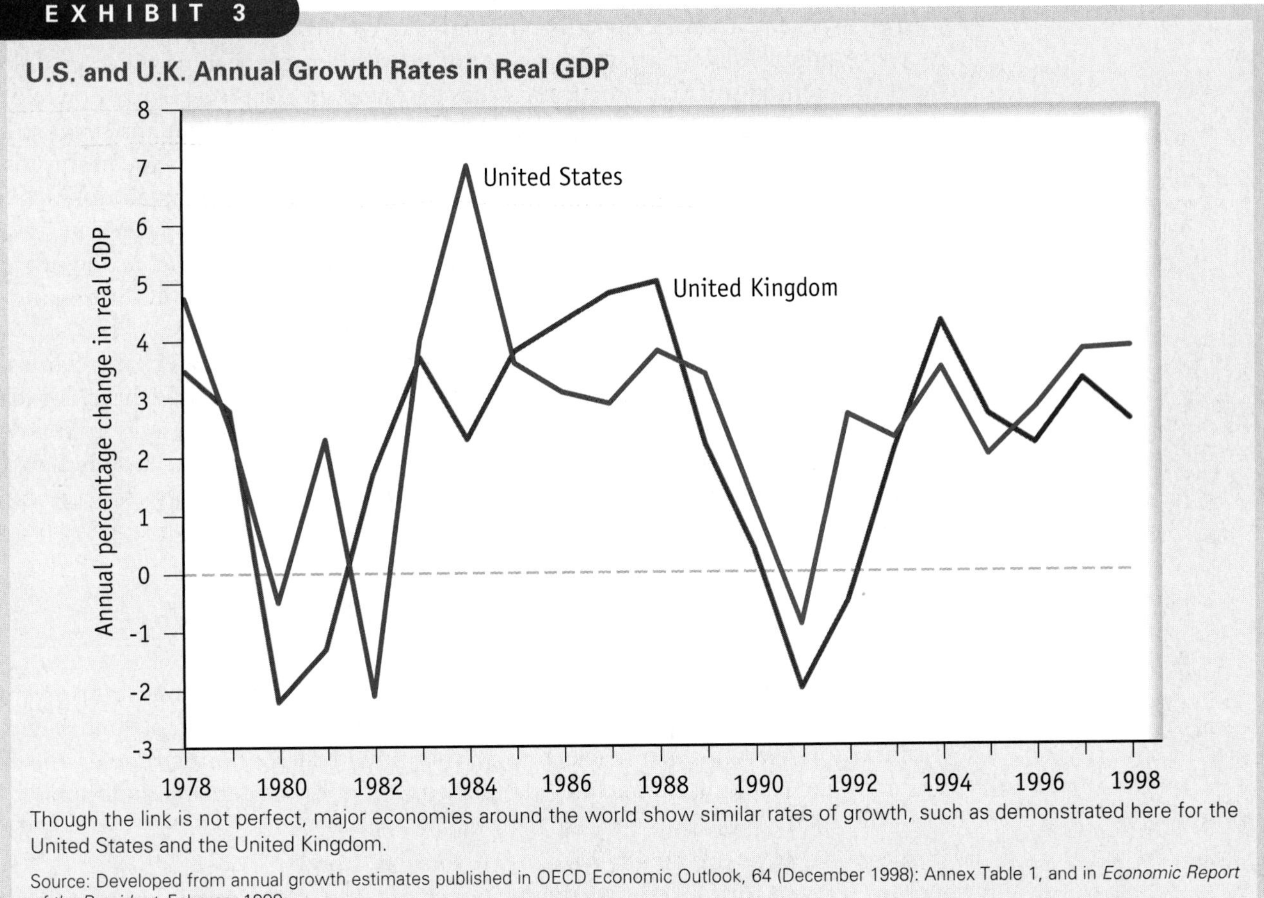

Though the link is not perfect, major economies around the world show similar rates of growth, such as demonstrated here for the United States and the United Kingdom.

Source: Developed from annual growth estimates published in OECD Economic Outlook, 64 (December 1998): Annex Table 1, and in *Economic Report of the President*, February 1999.

One problem with this linkage of business activity across economies is that the swings tend to reinforce one another. For example, a slump of economies abroad could cause a recession in the United States, and vice-versa. Evidence of such ties can be found in the relationship between stock markets around the world. Recent troubles in Asia and Russia, for example, resounded in stock markets in Europe and the Americas.

Although year-to-year fluctuations in output are of interest, even more important is an economy's long-term growth trend in output. Between 1978 and 1998, for example, U.S. real GDP grew on average by 2.6 percent per year, compared to 2.3 percent in the United Kingdom. These growth rates may seem similar, but tiny differences compound over the years to make a big difference. For example, if U.S. real GDP had averaged only 2.3 percent growth, output in 1998 would have been $450 billion below that achieved by 2.6 percent growth. In per capita terms, the lower rate would have reduced U.S. production per capita in 1998 by about $1,700. That's enough to provide everyone in the nation a powerful computer plus Internet service for a year.

Sources: Annual growth data from *Economic Report of the President*, February 1998; "Farewell, Golden Goose, *The Economist*, 13–19 December 1997; and *OECD Economic Outlook*, 63 (June 1998).

Leading Economic Indicators

Certain events foreshadow a turning point in economic activity. Months before a recession is fully under way, changes in the leading economic indicators point to the coming storm. In the early stages of a recession, business slows down, orders for machinery and equipment slip, and the stock market, in anticipation of lower profits, turns down. The confidence consumers have in the economy also begins to sag, and households reduce their spending on big-ticket items, such as automobiles and new homes. All these activities are called *leading economic indicators* because they are the first variables to predict, or *lead to,* a downturn. Upturns in leading indicators point to an economic recovery. But leading indicators cannot predict precisely *when* turning points will occur.

Our introduction to economic fluctuations has been largely mechanical, focusing on the history and measurement of these fluctuations. We have not discussed the reasons behind the fluctuations, in part because such a discussion requires a firmer footing in macroeconomic theory and in part because the causes remain in dispute. In the next section we begin to build a macroeconomic framework by introducing a key model of analysis.

AGGREGATE DEMAND AND AGGREGATE SUPPLY

The economy is so complex that we need to simplify, or to abstract from the millions of relationships, in order to isolate the important elements under consideration. We must step back from all the individual economic transactions to survey the resulting mosaic. Let's begin with the tools of demand and supply.

Aggregate Output and the Price Level

The demand for food shows the relationship between the relative price of food and the quantity of food demanded. When we consider the demand for food, we must take into account a diverse array of products—milk, bread, fruit, seafood, vegetables, meat, and so on. Moving from the demand for a specific product, milk, to the demand for a general product, food, is not conceptually difficult. Likewise, we can make the transition from the demand for food, housing, clothing, entertainment, transportation, or medical care to the demand for all output produced in the economy—the demand for aggregate output. **Aggregate output** is the total quantity of goods and services produced in the economy during a given time period. A unit of aggregate output is a composite measure of all output in the same sense that a unit of food is a composite measure of all food.

Aggregate output A composite measure of all final goods and services produced in an economy during a given time period; real GDP

Aggregate demand The relationship between the price level in the economy and the quantity of aggregate output demanded, other things held constant

Price level A composite measure reflecting the prices of all goods and services in the economy relative to prices in a base year

Aggregate demand is the relationship between the average price level of *all* goods and services in the economy and the quantity of *all* goods and services demanded. The **price level** in the economy is a composite measure reflecting the average price of food, housing, clothing, entertainment, transportation, medical care, and all other production.

You are more familiar than you may think with these aggregate measures. Media reports of economic growth or an economic slowdown refer to changes in the *gross domestic product,* or *GDP,* the most common measure of aggregate output. As noted earlier, the gross domestic product measures the market value of all final goods and services produced in the United States during a given time period, usually a year. And the economy's price level relates to the "cost of living" so often mentioned in news reports. Two common measures of the price level are (1) the *consumer price index,* which tracks the average price of a "basket" of goods and services consumed by the typical family, and (2) the *GDP price index,* which tracks the average price of all items in the gross domestic product.

In Chapter 8, you will learn how the economy's price level is computed. All you need to know now is that the economy's price level reflects the average price level in a particular year relative to the average level in some base, or reference, year. If we say that the price level is relatively high or low, we mean compared to the price level of some base year. In earlier chapters, we talked about the price of a particular product, such as milk, *relative to the prices of other products.* Here we talk about the *average price* of all goods and services produced in the economy compared to the price level in some base year.

The price level in the *base year* is set at a benchmark value of 100, and the price levels in other years are expressed relative to the base-year price level. For example, in 1998 the U.S. GDP price index averaged 113, indicating that the price level that year averaged 13 percent higher than its value of 100 in the base year of 1992.

Economists use the GDP *price index* to "deflate" the gross domestic product—that is, to eliminate any year-to-year changes in GDP due solely to changes in the average price level. After deflation, remaining changes are thus changes in real output—the amount of goods and services produced. After deflating GDP for price changes, we end up with what is called the *real* gross domestic product.

Aggregate Demand Curve

In Chapter 3 we learned about the demand for a particular product. Now let's talk about the demand for our composite measure of output—aggregate output. The **aggregate demand curve** shows the relationship between the price level in the economy and the amount of aggregate output demanded, other things constant. Exhibit 4 pictures a hypothetical aggregate demand curve, *AD.* The vertical axis measures an index of the economy's price level (relative to a 1992 base-year price level of 100). The horizontal axis measures aggregate output as real GDP, or real gross domestic product. Real GDP is measured by the dollar value of output, in this case using prices that prevailed in 1992.

Aggregate demand curve
A curve representing the relationship between the economy's price level and the amount of aggregate output demanded per period, other things held constant

The aggregate demand curve in Exhibit 4 reflects an inverse relationship between the price level in the economy and real GDP demanded. Aggregate demand reflects demand by households, firms, governments, and the rest of the world. As the price level falls, other things constant, households demand more Snapple and sneakers, firms demand more trucks and tools, governments demand more computer software and military hardware, and the rest of the world demands more U.S. grain and U.S. aircraft.

The reasons behind this inverse relationship will be examined more closely in later chapters. Here's a quick summary. The quantity of aggregate output demanded depends in part on household *wealth.* Some wealth is usually held in bank accounts and currency. An increase in the price level, other things constant, decreases the purchasing power of bank accounts and currency. Therefore, households are poorer when the price level increases, so the quantity of

EXHIBIT 4

Aggregate Demand Curve

The quantity of output demanded is inversely related to the price level, other things equal. This inverse relationship is reflected by the aggregate demand curve *AD*.

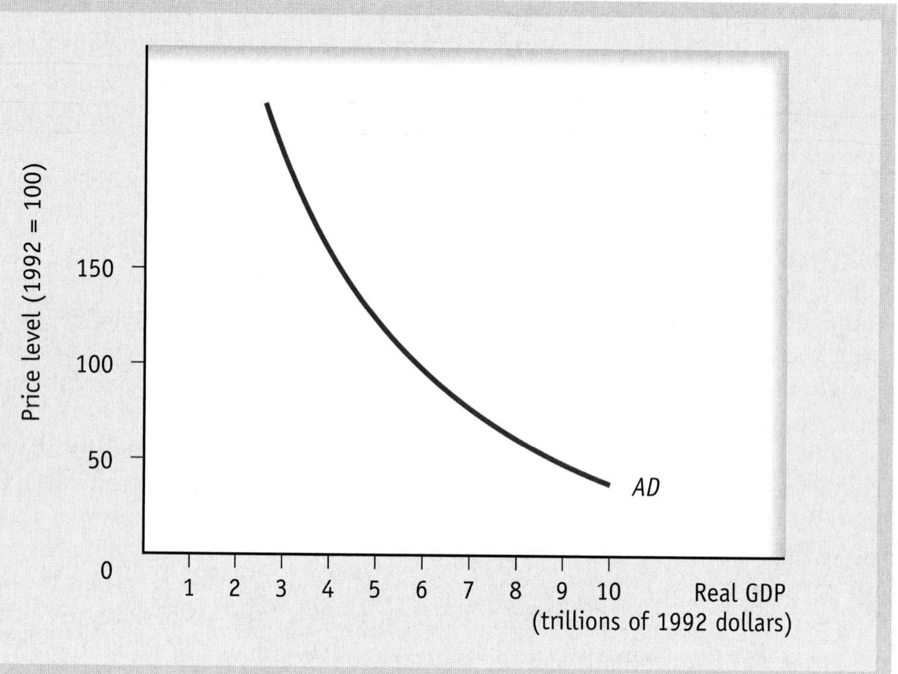

aggregate output they demand decreases. Conversely, a reduction in the price level increases the purchasing power of bank accounts and currency. Because households are richer as the price level decreases, the quantity of aggregate output they demand increases.

Among the factors held constant along a given aggregate demand curve are the price levels in other countries as well as the exchange rates between the U.S. dollar and foreign currencies. When the U.S. price level falls, U.S. products become cheaper relative to foreign products. Consequently, households, firms, and governments both here and abroad increase the quantity of U.S. output they demand. On the other hand, a higher U.S. price level makes U.S. goods relatively more costly compared to foreign goods, so the quantity of U.S. output demanded decreases.

Aggregate Supply Curve

Aggregate supply curve
A curve representing the relationship between the economy's price level and the amount of aggregate output supplied per period, other things held constant

The **aggregate supply curve** shows how much output U.S. producers are willing and able to supply at each price level, other things constant. How does the quantity supplied respond to changes in the price level? The shape of the aggregate supply curve and the reasons for that shape remain controversial issues among macroeconomists. This section bypasses the controversy to present a relatively simple approach.

The upward-sloping aggregate supply curve, *AS,* in Exhibit 5 depicts a positive relationship between the price level and the quantity of aggregate output that producers supply, other factors held constant. Held constant along an aggregate supply curve are (1) resource owners' willingness and ability to supply

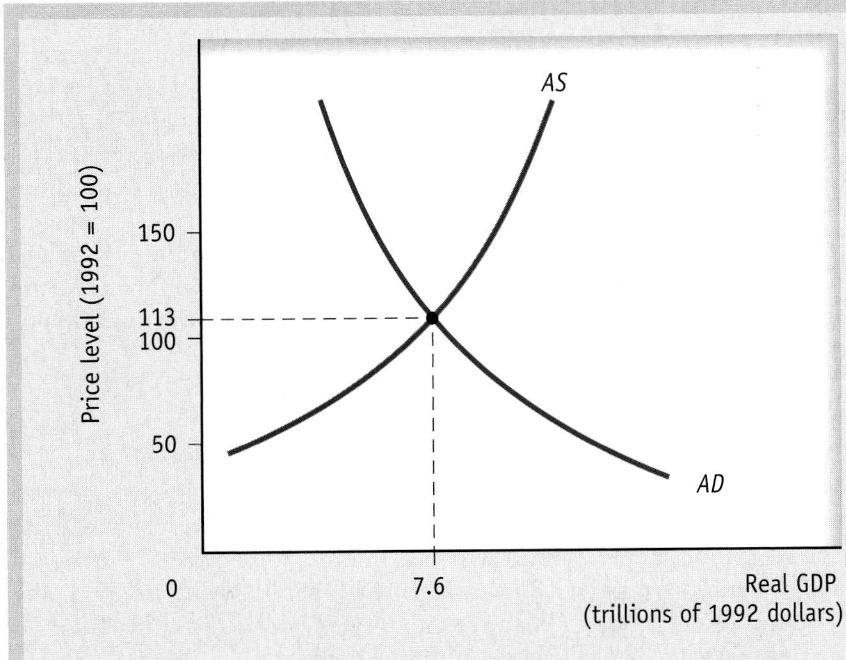

EXHIBIT 5

Aggregate Demand and Supply

The total output of the economy and its price level are determined at the intersection of the aggregate demand and aggregate supply curves. The equilibrium reflects real GDP and the price level for 1998, using 1992 as the base year.

resources, (2) the state of technology, and (3) the "rules of the game" that provide production incentives, such as patent and copyright laws. Wage rates are typically assumed to be constant along the aggregate supply curve. With wages constant, firms find a higher price level more profitable so they increase the quantity of output supplied. *Whenever the prices firms receive rise by more than the cost of production, firms find it profitable to expand output, so the aggregate output supplied varies directly with the economy's price level.*

Equilibrium

The intersection of the aggregate demand curve and aggregate supply curve determines the equilibrium levels of price and aggregate output in the economy. Exhibit 5 is a rough depiction of aggregate demand and supply in 1998; the equilibrium price level in 1998 was 113 (compared to a price level of 100 in the base year of 1992). The equilibrium real GDP in 1998 was $7.6 trillion (measured in dollars of 1992 purchasing power).

Incidentally, although employment is not measured directly along the horizontal axis, firms usually must hire more workers to produce more output. So higher levels of real GDP are beneficial because (1) more people in the economy are employed and fewer are unemployed, and (2) more goods and services are available in the economy.

Perhaps the best way to understand aggregate demand and aggregate supply is to apply these tools to the U.S. economy. In the following section we simplify U.S. economic history to review changes in the price and output levels over time.

A SHORT HISTORY OF THE U.S. ECONOMY

The history of the U.S. economy can be crudely divided into four economic eras: (1) prior to and including the Great Depression, (2) after the Great Depression to the early 1970s, (3) from the early 1970s to the early 1980s, and (4) since the early 1980s. The first era was marked by a series of recessions and depressions, culminating in the Great Depression of the 1930s. These depressions were often accompanied by a falling price level. The second era was one of generally strong economic growth, with only moderate increases in the price level. The third era was characterized by episodes of both high unemployment and high inflation. And the fourth era was more like the second, with good economic growth and moderate increases in the price level.

The Great Depression and Before

Prior to World War II, the U.S. economy alternated between periods of prosperity and sharp economic declines. As noted earlier, the longest contraction on record occurred between 1873 and 1879, when 80 railroads went bankrupt and most of the steel industry was shut down. During the depression of the 1890s, the unemployment rate topped 18 percent. In October 1929 the stock market crashed, beginning what was to become the deepest economic contraction in our nation's history, the Great Depression of the 1930s.

In terms of aggregate demand and aggregate supply, the Great Depression can be viewed as a shift to the left in the aggregate demand curve, as shown in Exhibit 6. AD_{1929} is the aggregate demand curve in 1929, before the onset of the depression. Real GDP in 1929 was $791 billion (measured in dollars of 1992 purchasing power) and the price level was 13.1, relative to a base-year (1992) price level of 100. By 1933, aggregate demand had decreased to AD_{1933}.[3] Why did aggregate demand fall so sharply? Though the causes are still debated, grim business expectations, a drop in consumer spending, a sharp decline in the nation's money supply, and restrictions on world trade each contributed to the drop in aggregate demand.

Because of this decline in aggregate demand, both the price level and real GDP declined. Between 1929 and 1933, the price level decreased by 25 percent, from 13.1 to 9.8, and real GDP fell by 27 percent, from $791 billion to $577 billion. As aggregate output declined, the unemployment rate jumped, climbing from about 3 percent in 1929 to 25 percent in 1933, the highest U.S. rate ever recorded.

Prior to the Great Depression, macroeconomic policy was based primarily on the *laissez-faire* philosophy of Adam Smith. Smith, you may recall, argued in his book *The Wealth of Nations* that if people were allowed to pursue their self-interest in free markets, resources would be guided as if by an "invisible hand" to produce the greatest, most efficient level of aggregate output. Although the U.S. economy had suffered several sharp contractions since the beginning of the 19th century, most economists of the day viewed these as a natural phase of the economy—unfortunate but therapeutic and essentially *self-correcting.*

3 The aggregate supply curve probably also shifted somewhat during this period, but for simplicity we assume it was unchanged. Most economists agree that the shift in the aggregate demand curve was the dominant factor.

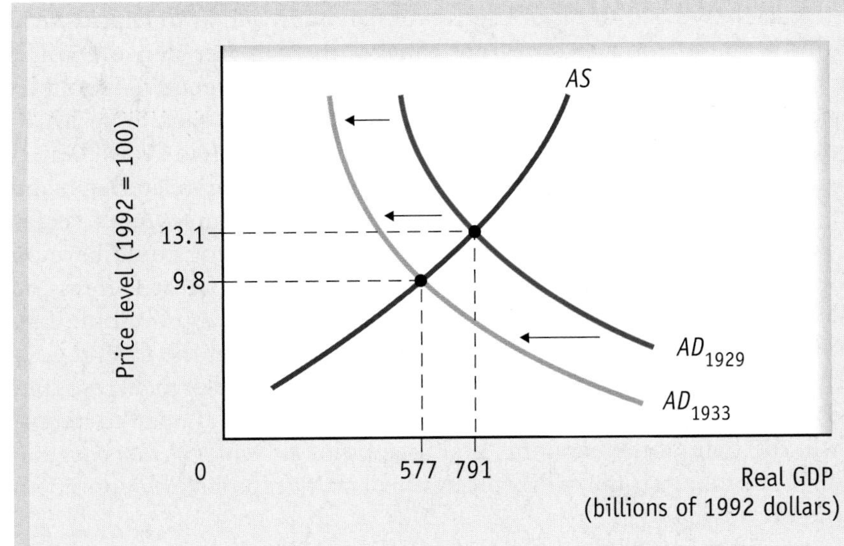

EXHIBIT 6

The Decrease in Aggregate Demand Between 1929 and 1933

The Great Depression of the 1930s can be represented by a shift to the left of the aggregate demand curve, from AD_{1929} to AD_{1933}. In the resulting depression, real GDP fell from $791 billion to $577 billion, and the price level dropped from 13.1 to 9.8.

The Age of Keynes: After the Great Depression to the Early 1970s

The Great Depression was so severe that it stimulated new thinking about how the economy worked (or didn't work). In 1936, John Maynard Keynes (1883–1946) published *The General Theory of Employment, Interest, and Money,* perhaps the most famous economics book of the 20th century. In it, Keynes argued that aggregate demand was inherently unstable, in part because investment decisions were often guided by the unpredictable "animal spirits" of business expectations. Thus, if businesses grew pessimistic about the economy, they would cut back on their demand for investment, which would reduce aggregate demand, output, and employment. Keynes saw no natural forces operating to ensure that the economy, even if allowed a reasonable time to adjust, would return to a higher level of output and employment.

Keynes proposed that the government jolt the economy out of its depression by increasing aggregate demand. He recommended an *expansionary fiscal policy* to deal with contractions. The government could achieve this directly by increasing its spending, or indirectly by cutting taxes to stimulate the primary components of private-sector demand, consumption and investment. Either action would likely result in a government budget deficit. A **government budget deficit** is a flow variable that measures, for a particular period, the amount by which total government outlays exceed total government revenues.

Government budget deficit A flow variable that measures the amount by which total government outlays exceed total government revenues in a particular period

To understand what Keynes had in mind, imagine federal budget policies that increase aggregate demand in Exhibit 6, shifting the aggregate demand curve to the right, back to its original position. Such a shift would raise the equilibrium level of aggregate output and employment. According to the Keynesian prescription, the miracle drug of government fiscal policy—changes in government spending and taxes—was needed to compensate for what he viewed as the inherent instability of private spending, especially investment. If

Demand-side economics Macroeconomic policy that focuses on changing aggregate demand as a way of promoting full employment and price stability

demand in the private sector declined, Keynes said the government should pick up the slack. We can think of the Keynesian approach as **demand-side economics** because it focused on how changes in aggregate demand could promote full employment. Keynes argued that government spending could be just the tonic to shock the economy out of its depression and back to health.

The U.S. economy languished during the 1930s, but when World War II broke out, huge federal budget deficits financed the war. War-related demand for tanks, ships, aircraft, and the like stimulated output and employment, seeming to confirm the powerful impact that government spending could have on the economy. Immediately after the war, memories of the Great Depression were still vivid. Trying to avoid another depression, Congress approved the *Employment Act of 1946,* which imposed a clear responsibility on the federal government to foster, in the language of the act, "maximum employment, production, and purchasing power." The act also required the president to report annually on the state of the economy and to appoint a *Council of Economic Advisers,* a three-member group with a professional staff, to provide the president with economic advice.

The economy seemed to prosper during the 1950s largely without the added stimulus of fiscal policy. The 1960s, however, proved to be the *golden age of Keynesian economics,* a period when fiscal policy makers thought they could "fine-tune" the economy to avoid recessions—just as a mechanic fine-tunes a race car to achieve high performance.

Inflation A sustained increase in the economy's average price level

During the 1960s, nearly all developed economies of the world enjoyed low unemployment and healthy growth in output with only modest **inflation,** which is a sustained increase in the price level. In short, the world economy was booming, and the U.S. economy was on top of the world.

The economy was on such a roll that toward the end of the 1960s some economists began to think economic fluctuations were a thing of the past. As a sign of the times, the federal government changed the name of their publication *Business Cycle Developments* to *Business Conditions Digest.* In the early 1970s, however, fluctuations returned with a fury. Worse yet, the problem of recession was compounded by inflation, which increased during the recessions of 1974–1975 and 1979–1980. Until then, inflation was limited primarily to periods of expansion. Confidence in demand-side policies was shaken, and the expression "fine-tuning" passed from economists' vocabularies. What ended the golden age of Keynesian economics?

The Great Stagflation: 1973–1980

During the late 1960s, the federal government escalated the war in Vietnam and increased spending on social programs at home. These efforts stimulated aggregate demand enough that in 1968 the *inflation rate,* the annual percentage increase in the price level, jumped to 4.4 percent, after averaging only 2.0 percent during the previous decade. Inflation climbed to 4.7 percent in 1969 and to 5.3 percent in 1970. These rates were so alarming that in 1971 President Richard Nixon introduced measures to freeze prices and wages.

The freeze was eliminated in 1973, about the time that crop failures around the world caused grain prices to soar. To compound these problems, the Organization of Petroleum Exporting Countries (OPEC) pushed up the world price of oil. The resulting reduction in aggregate supply, shown in Exhibit 7 by the shift to the left in the aggregate supply curve from AS_{1973} to AS_{1975}, created the **stagflation** of the 1970s, meaning a ***stag***nation, or contraction, in the economy's aggregate output combined with in***flation***, or a rise, in the economy's price level. Between 1973 and 1975, real GDP declined by about $50 billion, while the price level jumped nearly 20 percent. The percent of the labor force unemployed jumped from 4.9 percent in 1973 to 8.5 percent in 1975.

Stagflation A contraction, or *stag*nation, of a nation's output accompanied by in*flation* in the price level

Stagflation appeared again at the end of the 1970s, partly as a result of another boost in oil prices. Between 1979 and 1980, real GDP declined; at the same time, the price level increased by 9.2 percent. Macroeconomics has not been the same since. Because the problem of stagflation was primarily on the supply side, not on the demand side, the demand-management prescriptions of Keynes seemed ineffective. If government stimulated aggregate demand, this might reduce unemployment but would worsen inflation.

Experience Since 1980

Increasing aggregate supply seemed an appropriate way to combat stagflation, for such a move would both lower inflation and increase output and employment. Attention therefore turned from aggregate demand to aggregate supply. A key idea behind **supply-side economics** was that the federal government, by lowering tax rates, would increase after-tax earnings and thereby provide resource owners with incentives to increase their supply of labor and other resources. This greater resource supply would increase aggregate supply. According to advocates of the supply-side approach, the increase in aggregate supply would achieve the happy result of increasing real GDP and reducing the price level. But this was easier said than done.

Supply-side economics Macroeconomic policy that focuses on increasing aggregate supply through tax cuts or other changes to increase production incentives

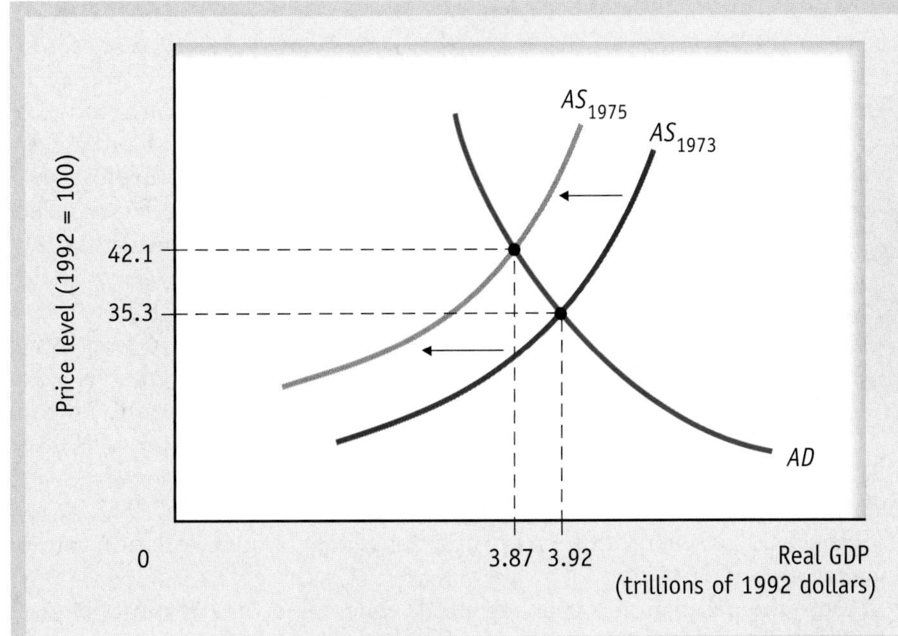

EXHIBIT 7

Stagflation Between 1973 and 1975

The stagflation of the mid-1970s can be represented as a reduction in aggregate supply from AS_{1973} to AS_{1975}. Aggregate output fell from $3.92 trillion to $3.87 trillion (stagnation), and the price level rose from 35.3 to 42.1 (inflation).

In 1981, to provide economic incentives and thereby increase aggregate supply, President Ronald Reagan and Congress cut personal income tax rates by an average of 23 percent. Their hope was that aggregate output would increase enough so that the lower tax rate would actually result in more tax revenue. Put another way, the tax cuts would stimulate enough of an expansion that the government's smaller share of a bigger pie would exceed what had been its larger share of a smaller pie.

But before the tax cut became fully implemented, recession hit in 1982 and the unemployment rate soared to nearly 10 percent of the labor force. After the recession, the economy began what at the time was the longest peacetime expansion on record. During the rest of the 1980s, output grew, unemployment declined, and inflation remained relatively low. During this period, however, the growth in federal spending exceeded the growth in federal tax revenues, so the federal budget deficit swelled.

The deficit worsened with the onset of the recession in 1990. Even though that recession officially ended in March of 1991, the deficit continued to grow. By 1992 it topped $290 billion. Annual deficits accumulated as a huge federal debt. **Government debt** is a stock variable that measures the net accumulation of prior deficits. Measured relative to GDP, the federal debt climbed from 34 percent in 1980 to about 80 percent in 1992.

Government debt A stock variable that measures the net accumulation of prior budget deficits

In early 1993, President Bill Clinton pushed through tax increases and cuts in the rate of growth of government spending aimed at reducing budget deficits. By 1994 these measures, combined with an improving economy, began reducing the deficits, and by 1998 the federal budget was in surplus. The period between 1992 and 1998 was one of growing prosperity, with the unemployment rate falling from 7.5 percent to 4.5 percent and inflation remaining low.

We close with a case study that summarizes the price and output movements in the U.S. economy during the last half century.

Other Times, Other Places

Are you interested in learning more about the economic history of the past century? J. Bradford De Long's brief article, "Slouching Toward Utopia," provides one economist's evaluation of key developments. You can download it at http://www.bos.frb.org/economic/nerr/delo98_3.htm.

A Half Century of Price Levels and Real GDP

Exhibit 8 traces the price level and real GDP since 1947. Aggregate demand and aggregate supply curves are shown only for 1947 and 1998, but all the points in the series reflect such intersections. Years of growing real GDP are indicated as blue points and years of declining real GDP as red points. Despite eight recessions since 1947, the upward long-term trend in the economy is unmistakable. Real GDP, measured in 1992 dollars, climbed from $1.4 trillion in 1947 to $7.6 trillion in 1998—a fivefold increase in production and an average annual growth rate of 3.3 percent. The price level rose faster, climbing from only 17.1 in 1947 to 113 in 1998—nearly a sevenfold increase and an average annual inflation rate of 3.8 percent.

Because the population is growing all the time, the economy must generate new jobs each year just to employ the additional people entering the labor

EXHIBIT 8

Tracking U.S. Real GDP and Price Level Since 1947

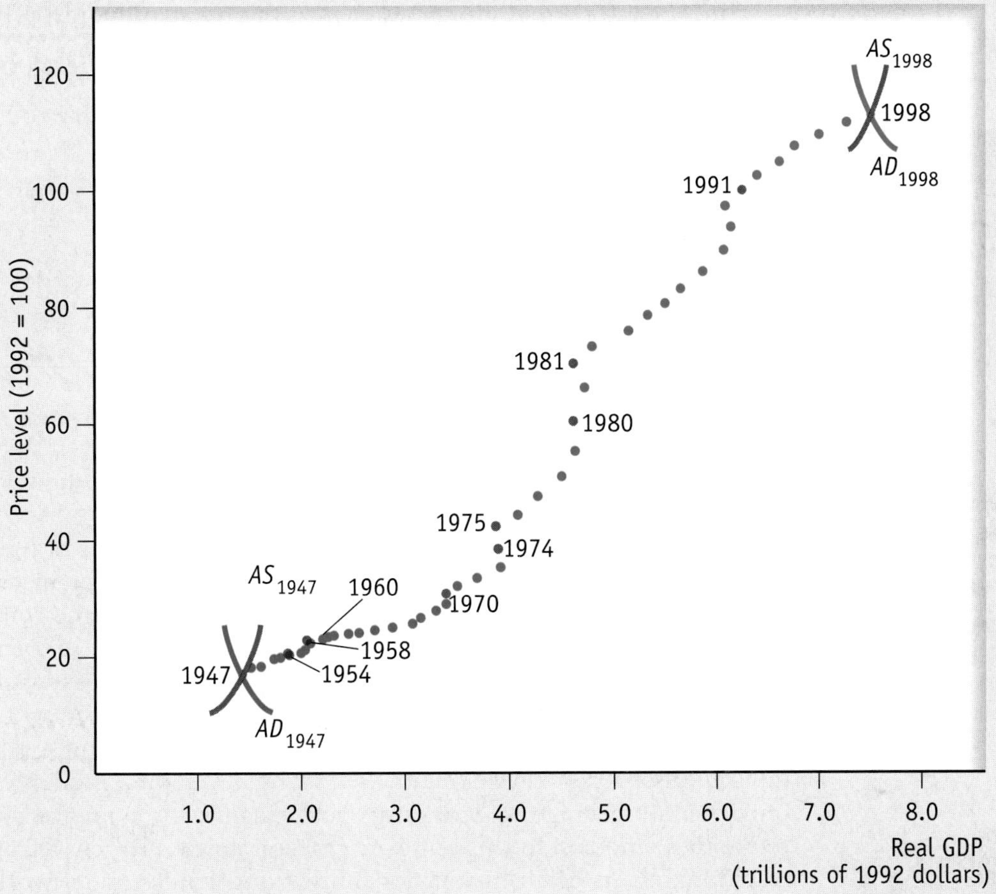

As you can see, both the price level and real GDP have increased sharply since 1947. The blue points indicate years of growing real GDP and the red points are years of declining real GDP. Real GDP was more than six times higher in 1998 than in 1947, and the price level was nearly seven times higher.

Source: Developed from estimates found in *Survey of Current Business* 77 (August 1997), 78 (August 1998), and in *Economic Report of the President*, February 1999.

force. For example, the U.S. population nearly doubled, from 144 million in 1947 to about 269 million in 1998. During that same period, the number of people employed in the economy more than doubled, from 57 million in 1947 to 132 million in 1998. So during the last half century, the labor force has grown faster than the population. During that time, the U.S. economy has been an impressive job machine.

Not only has the number of people working more than doubled, but the average level of education has increased. Employment of other resources in the economy, especially capital, has also increased sharply. What's more, the level of technology has improved steadily, thanks to breakthroughs such as the computer chip, so that machines have become much more sophisticated. The availability of more and higher-quality human capital and physical capital has increased the productivity of each worker, contributing to the fivefold increase in real GDP since 1947.

Since real GDP has grown faster than the population, real GDP *per capita* has climbed as well, nearly tripling from $9,935 in 1947 to $28,253 in 1998. The United States is the largest economy in the world and is also among the world leaders in real GDP per capita. We will examine U.S. productivity and growth more closely in the next chapter.

Source: *Survey of Current Business*, 79 (February 1999); *Economic Report of the President*, February 1999; and *OECD Economic Outlook*, 64 (December 1998).

CONCLUSION

During the 1960s, Keynesian demand-side policies dominated. When stagflation limited the relevance of demand-side economics, interest shifted to other approaches, including supply-side economics. As we shall see, however, there are more than two sides to this story.

Different economists may have different interpretations of the events discussed in this chapter. At this point there is no dominant macroeconomic theory about how the economy works. Some books lay out the competing theories, leaving it to the reader to choose sides. Rather than describe each theory of the economy in detail, we will attempt to integrate theories whenever possible to find common ground.

Because macroeconomists have no test subjects and cannot rely on serendipitous discoveries, they hone their craft by developing models of the economy, then observing the economy's performance for evidence to support or refute these models. In this sense, macroeconomics is largely retrospective, always looking at recent history for hints about which model works best. The macroeconomist is like a traveler with a view only of the road behind, who must find the way using a collection of poorly drawn maps. The traveler must continually check each map (or model) against the landmarks passed to see whether one map appears more consistent with the terrain than the others. Each new batch of information about the economy's performance causes macroeconomists to shuffle through their "maps" to reevaluate their models.

Macroeconomics often emphasizes what can go wrong with the economy. Problems associated with faltering economic growth, high unemployment, and rising inflation capture much of the attention in macroeconomic theory and policy. In Chapter 6 we consider in greater detail the record of economic growth in the United States. In Chapter 7 we discuss two potential problems confronting the economy: unemployment and inflation. Our approach to growth, unemployment, and inflation at this stage will be more descriptive than prescriptive. We must understand how a healthy economy operates before we can consider remedial policies when the economy fails in some important way.

SUMMARY

1. The focus of macroeconomics is the national economy. A standard way of gauging an economy's performance is by measuring the gross domestic product (GDP), the value of final goods and services produced in the nation during the year.

2. Economic fluctuations are the rise and fall of economic activity relative to the economy's long-term growth trend. The economy has two phases: periods of expansion and periods of contraction. Although no two economic cycles are the same, since 1933 peacetime expansions averaged about 5 years and contractions averaged about 1 year.

3. The aggregate demand curve slopes downward, reflecting a negative, or inverse, relationship between the price level and the quantity of aggregate output demanded. The aggregate supply curve slopes upward, reflecting a positive, or direct, relationship between the quantity of aggregate output supplied and the price level. The intersection of the two curves determines the economy's equilibrium price and output levels.

4. The Great Depression prompted Keynes to argue that the economy is inherently unstable, largely because the components of private spending, particularly business investment, are erratic. Keynes did not believe that depressions were self-correcting. He argued that whenever aggregate demand declined, the federal government should stimulate aggregate demand by spending more or taxing less. His demand-side policies dominated macroeconomics between World War II and the late 1960s.

5. During the 1970s, higher energy prices and global crop failures reduced aggregate supply. The result was stagflation, the troublesome combination of declining production and rising inflation. Demand-side policies appeared less effective in an economy suffering from a reduction in aggregate supply, since stimulating aggregate demand would result in still higher inflation.

6. Supply-side tax cuts in the early 1980s were supposed to increase aggregate supply, thereby increasing output while dampening inflation. But federal spending increased faster than federal revenues, resulting in huge budget deficits, which continued through the 1980s and into the early 1990s. Tax increases in 1993 and a growing economy eliminated the federal budget deficit by 1998.

QUESTIONS FOR REVIEW

1. *(The National Economy)* Why do economists pay more attention to national economies (for example, the U.S. or Canadian economies) than to state or provincial economies (such as California or Ontario)?

2. *(The Human Body and the Economy)* Based on your own experiences, extend the list of analogies between the human body and the economy as outlined in this chapter. Then determine which variables in your list are stocks and which are flows.

3. *(Stocks and Flows)* Wages and profits are flow variables, while the money supply and the national debt are stock variables. Explain why this is the case. What is the relationship between the federal budget deficit and the national debt? What is the relationship between annual investment spending and the capital stock?

4. *(Economic Fluctuations)* Describe the various components of fluctuations in economy activity over time. Since the economic activity fluctuates, how is long-term growth possible?

5. *(Economic Fluctuations)* Why does the National Bureau of Economic Research not identify the turning points in economic activity until months after they occur?

6. ***(CaseStudy:** A Half Century of Price Levels and Real GDP)* Real GDP increased fivefold between 1947 and 1998. The price level, however, increased nearly sevenfold during the same period. Does this mean that the rising price level masked an actual decline in output? Why or why not?

7. *(Leading Economic Indicators)* Define *leading economic indicators* and give some examples. You may wish to take a look at The Conference Board's index of leading economic indictors at http://www.conference-board.org/products/frames.cfm?main=lei1.cfm.

8. *(Aggregate Demand Curve)* Describe the relationship illustrated by the aggregate demand curve. Why does this relationship exist?

9. *(Aggregate Demand and Supply)* Why does a decrease in aggregate demand result in a lower level of employment, given a fixed aggregate supply curve?

10. *(Aggregate Demand and Supply)* Is it possible for the price level to fall while production and employment both rise? If it is possible, how could this happen? If it is not possible, explain why not.

11. *(Demand-Side Economics)* What is the relationship between demand-side economics and the federal budget deficit?

12. *(Stagflation)* What were some of the causes of the stagflations of 1973 and 1979? In what ways were these episodes of stagflation different from the Great Depression of the 1930s?

13. ***(CaseStudy:** The Global Economy)* How are economic fluctuations linked among national economies? Could a recession in the United States trigger a recession abroad?

PROBLEMS AND EXERCISES

14. *(Aggregate Demand and Supply)* Review the information on demand and supply curves in Chapter 3. How do the aggregate demand and supply curves presented in this chapter differ from the microeconomics curves of Chapter 3?

15. *(Aggregate Demand and Supply)* Determine whether each of the following would cause a shift in the aggregate demand curve, the aggregate supply curve, neither, or both. Which curve shifts, and in which direction? What happens to aggregate output and the price level in each case?
    a. The price level changes
    b. Consumer confidence declines
    c. The supply of resources increases
    d. The wage rate increases

16. *(Supply-Side Economics)* One supply-side measure advocated by the Reagan administration was a cut in income tax rates. Use an aggregate demand-supply diagram to show what the effect was intended to be. What might happen if such a tax cut also generated a change in aggregate demand?

EXPERIENTIAL EXERCISES

17. *(Economic Fluctuation Analysis)* The National Bureau of Economic Research maintains a Web page devoted to business cycle expansions and contractions at http://www.nber.org/cycles.html. Take a look at this page and see if you can determine how the business cycle has been changing in recent decades. Has the overall length of the cycles been changing? Have recessions been getting longer, or shorter?

18. *(Experience Since 1980)* Review the *Summary of Commentary on Current Economic Conditions by Federal Reserve District* (Beige Book), available through the Federal Reserve System at http://www.bog.frb.fed.us/FOMC/BeigeBook/default.cfm.
    a. Summarize the national economic conditions for the most recent period covered in the report. Overall, is the economy healthy? If not, what problems is it experiencing?
    b. Go to the district report applicable to your local area. Summarize the economic conditions for the last reporting period. Is the economy in your district healthy? If not, what problems is it experiencing?

19. *(Wall Street Journal)* This chapter introduced the tools of aggregate demand and supply. Can you use them? Test your understanding by finding an article in today's *Wall Street Journal* describing an event that may affect the U.S. price level and real GDP. Look under "Economy" or "International" in the First Section of the newspaper. Draw an initial set of *AD* and *AS* curves, then determine which curve will be affected, and in which direction it will shift. What do you predict will happen to the price level and real GDP?

CHAPTER

6 U.S. Productivity and Growth

Why is the standard of living so much higher in some countries than in others? What is key to a rising standard of living? Why is the long-term growth rate of the economy more important than short-term fluctuations in economic activity? Why has the growth in output per hour of work slowed in the United States in the last quarter century? What effect does this slowdown have on your standard of living? Answers to these and other questions are addressed in this chapter, which focuses on arguably the most important criterion for judging an economy's performance—economic growth.

The single most important factor determining a nation's standard of living in the long run is the productivity of its resources. A nation prospers by getting more from its resources. Even relatively small increases in the growth of productivity can, if

Visit the McEachern
teractive Study Center
for this chapter at
://mcisc.swcollege.com

maintained for years, have profound effects on living standards. Growing productivity is therefore key to a rising standard of living. This growth has kept the U.S. standard of living ahead of every other nation on Earth.

Over the last quarter century, however, U.S. productivity *growth* has slowed down. This slowdown could well affect the standard of living you experience during your lifetime. In this chapter we will consider the sources of economic growth and examine some possible causes of the recent slowdown in productivity growth. We will also examine the government's role in fostering economic growth and productivity.

Although the *growth* in U.S. productivity has recently lagged behind the historical trend and behind the growth in most other industrial countries, our *level* of productivity still ranks U.S. workers first in the world. So this chapter is more about the growth in productivity than about the level of productivity. The chapter is more about the future economic leadership of the United States than about our current top ranking. Topics discussed in this chapter include:

- Labor productivity
- Slowdown in productivity growth
- Research and development
- Growth policies
- Technological change

U.S. PRODUCTIVITY

Two centuries ago, most Americans worked in agriculture, where the hours were long and rewards unpredictable. Other workers had it no better, toiling from sunrise to sunset for a wage that bought only the bare necessities. They had little intellectual stimulation and little contact with the outside world. A typical worker's home in the year 1790 was described as follows: "Sand sprinkled on the floor did duty as a carpet. . . . What a stove was he did not know. Coal he had never seen. Matches he had never heard of. . . . He rarely tasted fresh meat. . . . If the food of an artisan would now be thought coarse, his clothes would be thought abominable."[1] In the last two centuries, there has been an incredible increase in U.S. standard of living.

Economic growth is a complicated process, one that economists do not yet fully understand. Since before Adam Smith inquired into the *Wealth of Nations,* economists have been trying to discover what makes some economies prosper while others founder. Because the market economy is not the product of conscious design, it does not divulge its secrets readily, nor can it easily be manipulated in pursuit of growth objectives. We cannot simply push here and pull there to achieve the desired result. Changing the economy is not like remodeling a home by moving a wall out to expand the kitchen. Because we have no clear blueprint of the economy, we cannot make changes to specifications.

Growth and the Production Possibilities Frontier

Perhaps the easiest way to introduce the idea of growth is by beginning with something you already know. The *production possibilities frontier,* first introduced in Chapter 2, shows alternative combinations of goods that can be produced if

1 E. L. Bogart, *The Economic History of the United States* (New York: Longmans, Green, and Co., 1912), pp. 157–158.

available resources are used efficiently. Let's briefly review the assumptions employed in developing the frontier shown in Exhibit 1. During the period under consideration, usually a year, resources in the economy and technology are assumed to be fixed. We classify all production into two broad categories—in this case, consumption goods and capital goods, which are used to produce other goods. Thus, the economy can make pizzas or can make pizza ovens. Pizzas are consumption goods and ovens are capital goods.

When resources are employed efficiently, the production possibilities frontier *CI* in each of the panels of Exhibit 1 shows the possible combinations of consumption goods and capital goods that can be produced by the economy in a given year. Point *C* depicts the amount of consumer goods that can be produced if all the economy's resources are used efficiently to produce consumer goods. Point *I* depicts the same for capital goods. Points inside the frontier show inefficient combinations, and points outside the frontier are unattainable, given the resources and technology available. The production possibilities frontier is bowed out because resources are not perfectly adaptable to the production of both goods; some resources are specialized.

Economic growth is reflected by an outward shift of the production possibilities frontier, as shown in the two panels of Exhibit 1. What will cause such a shift? Let's review what determines the position of the frontier. Most important are resource availability and technology. Any increase in the availability of resources, such as an increase in the labor supply or the capital stock, will shift the frontier outward.

EXHIBIT 1

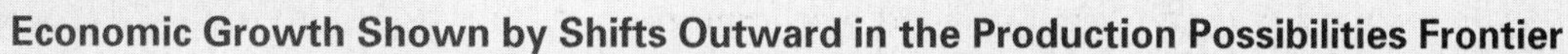

Economic Growth Shown by Shifts Outward in the Production Possibilities Frontier

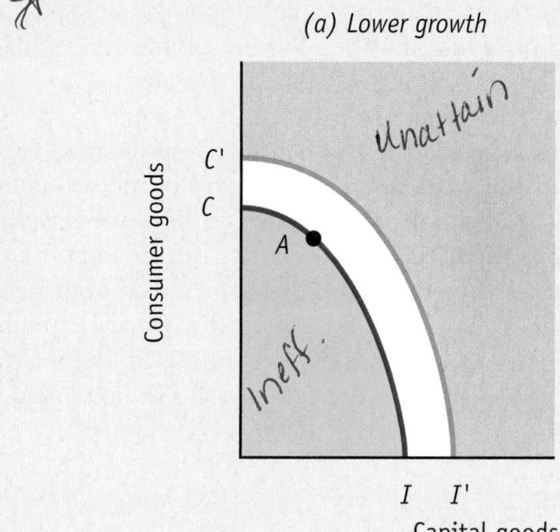

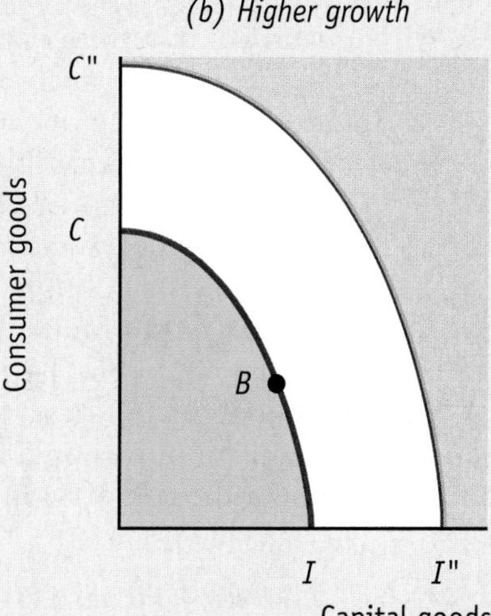

An economy that produces more capital goods will grow more, as reflected by a shifting outward in the production possibilities frontier. More capital goods and fewer consumer goods are produced in panel (b) than in panel (a), so the PPF shifts outward more in panel (b).

Labor can increase either because the population increases or because the existing population is more willing to supply their labor. The capital stock will expand if the economy produces more capital goods. The more capital goods produced, the more the economy will grow, as reflected by a shift outward in the production frontier.

Any improvement in technology also expands the frontier by making more efficient use of existing resources. Technological change often improves the quality of capital, but it can enhance the productivity of any resource. Thus, *the economy can grow because of a greater availability of resources, an improvement in the quality of resources, or technological improvements that make better use of resources.*

The amount of capital the economy produces this year will affect the location of the PPF next year. For example, in Exhibit 1 (panel a), the economy has chosen point *A* from possible points along *CI*. The capital produced this year shifts the PPF from *CI* out to *C'I'*. But if more capital goods are produced this year, as reflected by point *B* in panel (b), the PPF will shift outward farther, to *C"I"*.

What Is Productivity?

Production can be viewed as a process that transforms resources into products. Resources coupled with technology produce output. Productivity measures how efficiently resources are employed. In the simplest terms, the greater the productivity, the more goods and services can be produced from a given amount of resources. **Productivity** is defined as the ratio of a specific measure of output to a specific measure of input. Productivity usually reflects an average, expressing total output divided by the total input of a specific kind of resource. For example, **labor productivity** is the output per unit of labor and is measured as total output divided by the number of units of labor employed to produce that output.

Productivity The ratio of a specific measure of output to a specific measure of input, such as output per hour of labor

Labor productivity Output per unit of labor; measured as total output divided by the number of units of labor employed to produce that output

We can talk about the productivity of any resource, such as labor, capital, or land. All resources contribute to production. When agricultural products made up the bulk of total output, land productivity, or bushels of grain per acre, was the key measure of economic welfare. Where soil was rocky and barren, people were less prosperous than where soil was fertile and fruitful. Even today, in many developing countries throughout the world, the productivity of the soil determines the local standard of living. Industrialization and trade, however, have liberated many economies from dependence on soil quality. Today some of the world's most productive economies have little land or have land of poor fertility. For example, Japan, the second-largest economy in the world (after the United States), has a population about half that of the United States. Yet that population lives on a land area only 4 percent the size of the U.S. land area, or about the size of Montana.

Labor Productivity

Labor is the resource most commonly used to measure productivity. Why labor? First, it accounts for a relatively large share of the cost of production—about 70 percent on average. Second, the quantity of labor is more easily measured than other inputs, whether we speak of hours per week or full-time workers per year. Statistics about employment and hours worked are more readily available and more reliable than those about other resources used.

But the resource most responsible for increasing labor productivity is capital. For example, consider the difference between digging a ditch with your bare hands and digging it with a shovel. Now compare that shovel to a backhoe. The addition of capital obviously makes the digger more productive. As introduced in Chapter 1, the two broad categories of capital are human capital and physical capital. *Human capital* is the accumulated knowledge, skill, and experience of the labor force. As individual workers acquire more human capital, their productivity and, hence, their income grow, which is why surgeons earn more than butchers and accountants earn more than file clerks. You are reading this book right now to enhance your human capital. *Physical capital* includes the machines, buildings, roads, airports, communication networks, and other manufactured creations used to produce goods and services. As an economy accumulates more capital per worker, labor productivity tends to increase and the standard of living grows.

The Per-Worker Production Function

We can express the relationship between the amount of capital per worker and the output per worker as an economy's **per-worker production function.** Exhibit 2 shows the relationship between the amount of capital per worker, measured along the horizontal axis, and output per worker, or labor productivity, measured along the vertical axis, other things held constant—including the level of technology. The production function, *PF*, slopes upward from left to right because an increase in the amount of capital per worker helps each worker produce more output. For example, a bigger truck makes the truck driver more productive. Any point on the curve shows the relationship in the economy between the amount of capital per worker and the output per worker. For example, when there are *k* units of capital per worker, the output per worker in the economy is *y*.

Per-worker production function The relationship between the amount of capital per worker in the economy and the output per worker

EXHIBIT 2

Per-Worker Production Function

The per-worker production function, *PF*, shows a direct relationship between the amount of capital per worker, *k*, and the output per worker, *y*. The bowed shape of *PF* reflects the law of diminishing marginal returns.

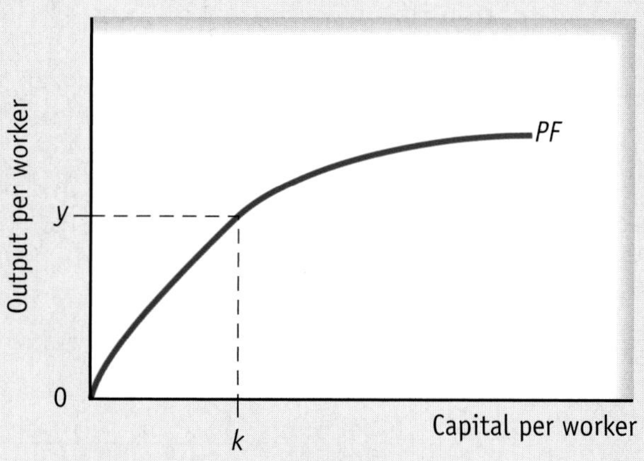

As the quantity of capital per worker increases, the output per worker increases as well but at a diminishing rate, as reflected by the shape of the per-worker production function. The diminishing slope of this curve reflects the *law of diminishing marginal returns,* which when applied to capital says that the larger the capital stock per worker already is, the less additional output can be gained by increasing the capital stock per worker still more. For example, adding more trucks to a shipping company initially increases the productivity of drivers. Once all drivers have trucks, however, additional trucks add little or nothing. Thus, given the level of technology and the supply of other resources, the additional gains from more capital accumulation eventually diminish.

Held constant along a per-worker production function is the level of technology prevailing in the economy. Technological change usually improves the *quality* of capital and represents a major source of increased productivity. For example, a tractor is more efficient than a horse-drawn plow, a word processor is more efficient than a typewriter, an Excel spreadsheet is more efficient than a pencil and paper, and a fiber-optic telephone line is more efficient than copper wire. Improving technology is reflected in Exhibit 3 by an upward rotation in the per-worker production function from *PF* to *PF*′. As a result of a technological breakthrough, more output is produced at each level of capital per worker. For example, when there are *k* units of capital per worker, the improvement in technology increases the output per worker in the economy from *y* to *y*′.

Thus, two kinds of changes in capital improve worker productivity: (1) an increase in the *quantity* of capital relative to labor, as reflected by a movement along the curve, and (2) an improvement in the *quality* of capital, as reflected by technological change that rotates the curve upward. Over time, improvements in per-capita output, otherwise known as the standard of living, result from both more capital per worker and better capital per worker.

EXHIBIT 3

Impact of a Technological Breakthrough on the Per-Worker Production Function

A technological breakthrough increases output per worker at each level of capital per worker. Better technology makes workers more productive.

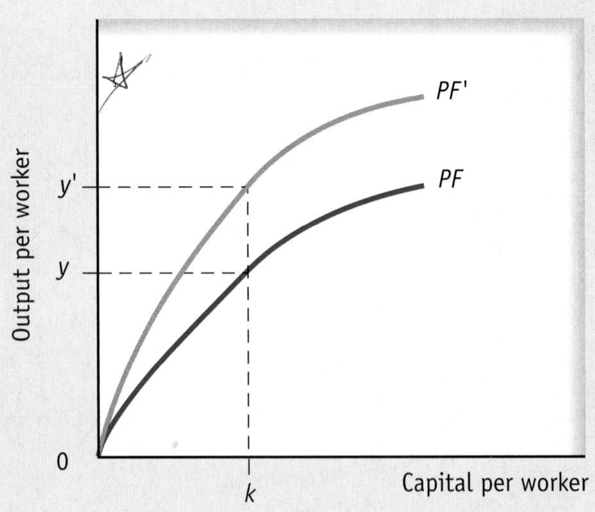

Long-Term Productivity Growth

What has been the growth of labor productivity in the United States? Exhibit 4 offers a long-run perspective, showing productivity growth since 1870 as measured by real output per work hour. Annual productivity growth is averaged by decade, beginning with the 1870s and ending with 1990s. The huge dip in productivity growth during the 1930s due to the Great Depression and the rebound during the 1940s due to World War II are unmistakable. During the entire period since 1870, labor productivity growth averaged 2.1 percent per year. This may not seem like much, but because of the power of compounding, output per work hour has grown about 1,390 percent since 1870. To put this in perspective, suppose that in 1870 a roofer could shingle a roof in one day. If roofers experienced a 1,390 percent increase in labor productivity, today's roofer could shingle about 15 roofs in a day.

Over long periods, small differences in productivity growth rates have significant impacts on the economy's ability to produce and, therefore, on the standard of living. For example, if productivity growth had averaged only 1.1 percent instead of

EXHIBIT 4

Long-Term Trends in Labor Productivity: Annual Averages by Decade

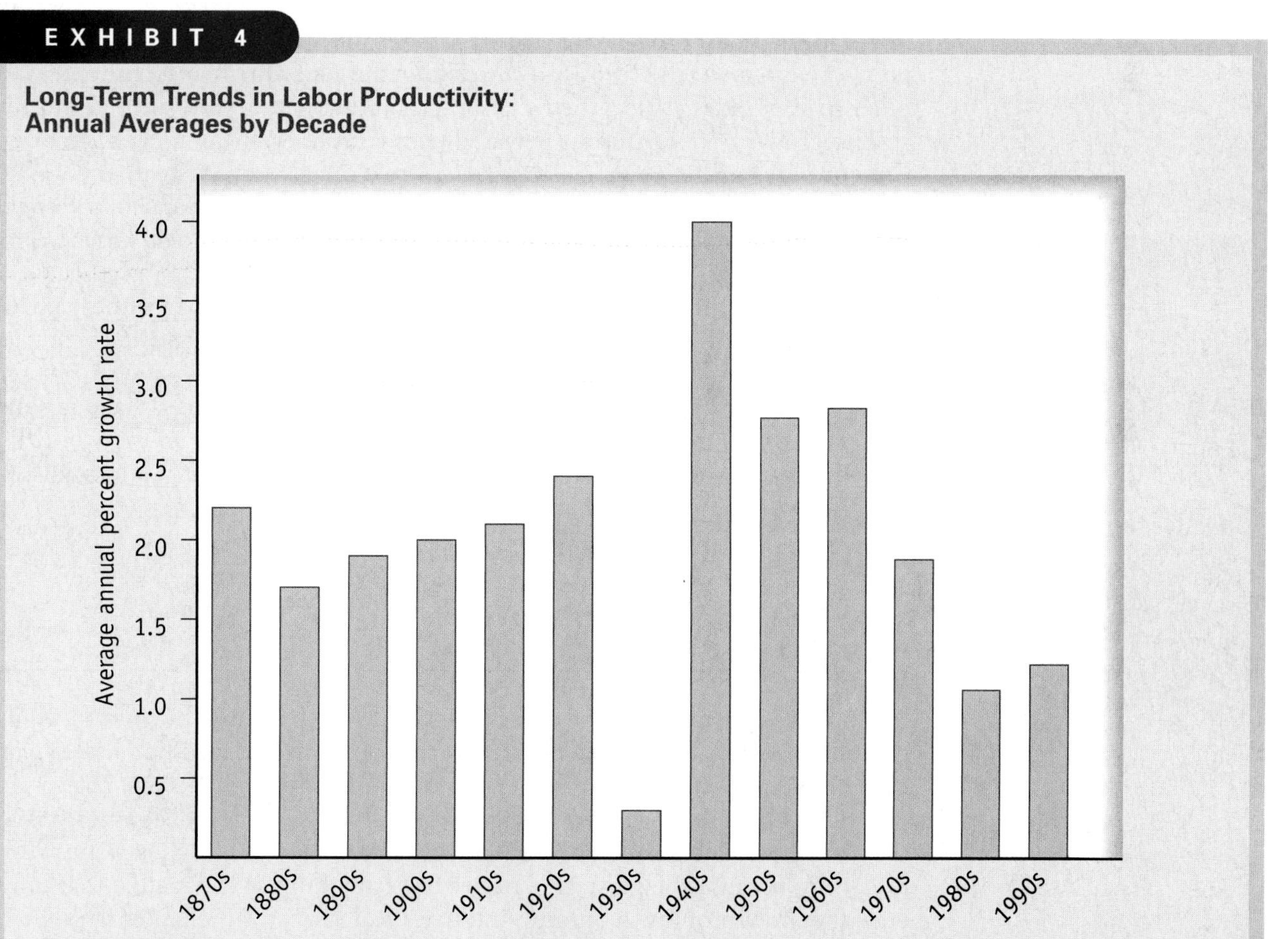

Sources: Angus Maddison, *Phases of Capitalist Development* (New York: Oxford University Press, 1982). Figures since 1948 are from the Bureau of Labor Statistics.

2.1 percent, output per work hour since 1870 would have increased by only 315 percent, not 1,390 percent. On the other hand, if productivity had increased an average of 3.1 percent per year, output per work hour since 1870 would have increased by 5,190 percent! The wheels of progress seem to grind slowly but they grind very fine, and the cumulative effect can be awesome. Productivity has grown more in some industries than in others. In ocean shipping, for example, cargo carried per worker on state-of-the art ships is 65 times greater today than it was in 1900. On the other hand, output per work hour in wooden office furniture is only about three times greater today than it was in 1900.

Higher productivity can easily make up for output lost during recessions. For example, if the U.S. economy averages annual growth in productivity of 2.0 percent instead of 1.5 percent, in a decade that higher growth would yield about $400 billion in additional total output, which would more than make up for the output lost during three typical recessions. *This cumulative power of productivity growth is why economists now focus less on short-term fluctuations in output and more on long-term growth.*

The Recent Slowdown in Productivity Growth

You can see in Exhibit 4 the decade-by-decade slowdown in the growth of productivity since the 1940s. By breaking the data down into time periods other than decades, we can better examine productivity trends since World War II. The growth rate of output per labor hour declined from an average of 2.8 percent per year between 1948 and 1973 to 1.2 percent per year since 1974. *Thus, the rate of growth in labor productivity since 1974 has been less than half what it was during the quarter century following World War II and, except for the Great Depression, less than it was in any decade during the previous century.*

Such a slowdown in labor productivity growth usually means the standard of living also grows more slowly. For example, between 1948 and 1973, median family income adjusted for inflation more than doubled. But since 1974, real median family income has increased by only about 25 percent.[2] Make no mistake, workers in the United States are still the most productive in the world, but the slowdown in recent productivity growth has narrowed our world lead. Let's examine why the growth in labor productivity has slowed.

WHY THE SLOWDOWN IN LABOR PRODUCTIVITY GROWTH?

A thorough explanation of the recent slowdown in productivity growth should not only account for the overall trend from period to period but also explain differences in productivity growth across economic sectors. No one has yet developed such a comprehensive explanation. All we have are possible reasons for the slowdown. Nonetheless, possible contributors to the slowdown are worth discussing because they give us a better understanding of the factors that influence the growth of the economy. And that's really what this chapter is about.

2 Officially, the real median family income increased by only about 5 percent since 1974. The 25 percent increase is based on a consumer price index that has been revised downward to adjust for biases in its calculation. This will be explained in Chapter 8.

Factors that economists believe may have contributed to the slowdown in labor productivity growth include (1) slower growth in capital formation, (2) a change in the composition of the labor force, (3) a change in the composition of output, (4) large federal budget deficits between 1975 and 1996, and (5) reduced spending on research and development. This last possibility is potentially so important that it warrants extensive discussion. But let's begin by examining the first four factors.

Rate of Capital Formation

We've seen that labor productivity depends in part on the amount of capital supporting each worker. Every year, a certain amount of plant and equipment depreciates, wears out, or becomes obsolete. On average, about 60 percent of investment spending each year goes toward replacing and maintaining existing plant and equipment. About 20 percent of investment spending goes toward providing sufficient capital to maintain existing capital-to-labor ratios for a growing labor force. And the remaining 20 percent of investment goes toward increasing capital per worker, the key to rising productivity.

Increases in the ratio of capital to labor, called *capital deepening*, added about 0.8 percentage points per year to the growth in productivity since 1974. Prior to 1974, capital deepening contributed a tiny bit more to productivity growth. So *a reduction in the contribution of capital deepening explains a tiny part of the post-1974 slowdown in productivity growth*. Investment spending as a percentage of GDP began increasing in 1993, and this trend should pay off with more capital deepening in the new century.

Changes in the Labor Force

An important component in the production function is the quality of labor—the skill, experience, and education of workers. Some economists argue that changes in the composition of the labor force have slowed productivity growth. Individuals just entering the labor force are typically less productive because they have fewer skills and less work experience than those already in the labor force. As long as the proportion of new workers remains constant over time, however, their presence should not affect productivity measures on average. But if new workers' share of employment increases, as it has since 1966, when post–World War II baby boomers started showing up in the workforce, then productivity growth may suffer. The average job experience of workers has declined slightly in the last three decades, slightly reducing average productivity growth. In addition, the skill level of immigrants coming to this country since 1970 has, on average, been lower than it was prior to 1970.

But the increase in the number of less experienced workers has been offset by the increase in the years of education of the workforce as a whole. In the last three decades, the average educational attainment of the workforce has increased by about two years. The fraction of high school graduates enrolling in college after graduation climbed from about half in 1980 to about two-thirds today. In short, new entrants to the labor force are more educated than workers retiring from the labor force.

So workforce quality has declined because of an increase in the proportion of workers with less experience. But workforce quality has increased because of the increased level of workers' education. On net, *changes in workforce quality appear to bear little or no responsibility for the post-1974 slowdown in productivity growth.*

Changing Composition of Output

Average productivity will decline if workers shift from sectors that experience substantial capital formation and technological change to sectors where capital formation and technological change are less important. Labor productivity grows faster in the goods-producing sector (manufacturing, construction, mining, and farming), where machines can be readily introduced, than in the service sector (government, education, transportation, finance, health care, retailing, and personal services), where machinery is less important. For example, there are more opportunities for technological change in producing automobiles than in producing haircuts.

Since 1948, productivity has grown by an average of 2.8 percent yearly in the goods-producing sector but by only 1.4 percent in the service sector. The goods-producing sector's share of total employment, however, has declined from about 40 percent in 1948 to about 20 percent today. *The service sector's growing share of the labor force has lowered the growth rate of productivity in the economy as a whole, perhaps accounting for half or more of the slowdown. Most economists who have explored the issue agree that the shift from high-productivity to low-productivity sectors accounts for at least some of the slowdown.*

Budget Deficits

In his first State of the Union address, President Clinton argued that large federal deficits were responsible for the slow growth in labor productivity. He said that to finance the deficits, the federal government must borrow huge amounts, muscling aside private borrowers who wanted to invest in physical capital, human capital, and research and development. By raising tax rates and reducing the growth rate in government spending, Clinton proposed reducing the federal deficit as a way of increasing productivity and growth.

Despite Clinton's assertion, the link between federal deficits and labor productivity growth remains unclear. For example, between 1973 and 1981, federal deficits averaged less than $50 billion per year; between 1982 and 1995, they averaged $200 billion per year. But during both periods, the growth in labor productivity averaged about the same. Thus, we cannot simply attribute the recent slowdown in productivity growth to higher federal deficits per se.

But one piece of evidence lends support to the view that high deficits slowed productivity. When the deficit dropped sharply between 1996 and 1998, labor productivity increased to an annual average of 1.9 percent, after averaging only 1.1 percent during the era of big deficits. Granted, association is not causation, and three years is not long enough to measure a trend in productivity, but falling deficits could have contributed to the higher productivity.

Ironically, despite high federal deficits between 1981 and 1995, government investments in roads, bridges, and airports—called *public capital*—declined in relative terms. In 1970, the value of the nation's public capital stock was about half as large as GDP; this figure declined to about 40 percent by 1995. Some argue that declining investment in public infrastructure serves as a drag on productivity growth. For example, the failure to invest sufficiently in airports and in the air traffic control system has resulted in congested airports and flight delays. Government spending on public infrastructure can have a powerful effect on productivity. For example, the Internet was originally created by the U.S. government and most of the early operating costs were borne by the government.

The single most important source of productivity growth is technological change. In the next section we examine research and development, the fuel for technological change.

RESEARCH AND DEVELOPMENT

Simon Kuznets, who won a Nobel prize in part for his analysis of economic growth, claimed that technological change and the ability to apply such breakthroughs to all aspects of production were the driving forces behind modern economic growth in developed market economies. Kuznets argued that changes in the *quantities* of labor and capital account for only one-tenth of the increase in economic growth. Nine-tenths of the increase results from improvements in the *quality* of inputs.

Basic and Applied Research

A major contributor to productivity growth has been an improvement in the quality of human and physical capital. In terms of human capital, this quality improvement results from more education and more job training. In terms of physical capital, quality improvement springs from better technology embodied in this capital. For example, because of extensive investments in cellular transmission, new satellites, and fiber optics technology, labor productivity in the telecommunications industry increased by an average of 5.5 percent per year in the last three decades.

Improvements in technology arise from scientific discovery, which is the fruit of research. We distinguish between basic research and applied research. **Basic research,** the search for knowledge without regard to how that knowledge will be used, is a first step toward technological advancement. In terms of economic growth, however, scientific discoveries are meaningless until they are implemented, which requires applied research. **Applied research** seeks to answer particular questions or to apply scientific discoveries to the development of specific products. Since technological breakthroughs may or may not have commercial possibilities, the payoff is less immediate with basic research than with applied research. Yet basic research likely yields a higher rate of return to society as a whole than does applied research.

Basic research The search for knowledge without regard to how that knowledge will be used

Applied research Research that seeks to answer particular questions or to apply scientific discoveries to the development of specific products

A technological breakthrough that has market value becomes *embodied* in new capital. Such technological innovation increases the productivity of other resources by permitting them to be combined in more efficient ways, so total output increases. *From the wheel to assembly-line robots, capital embodies the fruits of scientific inquiry and serves as the primary engine for economic growth.*

Expenditures for Research and Development

Since technological advances spring from the process of research and development (R&D), expenditures on R&D represent one measure of the economy's efforts to improve productivity through technological discovery. One way to track R&D activity is to measure these expenditures relative to gross domestic product, or GDP. Federally supported R&D should be distinguished from private R&D, which consists primarily of industry outlays plus a small amount by the private nonprofit sector. Federally supported R&D fell from a high of nearly 2 percent of GDP in 1964 to about 1 percent recently. Private R&D has grown slightly from about 1 percent of GDP in 1964 to about 1.5 percent recently.

Research suggests that a dollar of federally supported R&D contributes less to economic growth than does a dollar of company-supported R&D,[3] perhaps because most federally supported R&D has military objectives. Thus, although the decline in federal R&D may have contributed to the slowdown in productivity growth during the 1970s, the impact would have been greater had the decline in R&D occurred primarily in the private sector.

In dollar terms, U.S. investment in R&D was recently greater than that in Japan, Germany, and France combined. Relative to GDP, the United States and Japan were tied for first place among major industrialized countries. According to the U.S. Labor Department, *investment in R&D contributed about 0.2 percentage points to the annual growth in labor productivity since 1974, which was about what it contributed annually in the decade prior to 1974.*

Let's summarize the conclusions regarding the role of different contributions to the slower growth in U.S. labor productivity since 1974. First, increases in the ratio of capital to labor—*capital deepening*—added a tiny bit less to the growth in labor productivity since 1974 than it had added prior to 1974. Second, changes in workforce quality appear to bear little or no responsibility for the post-1974 slowdown in labor productivity growth. Third, the service sector's growing share of the labor force accounts for some of the slowdown, perhaps half or more. Fourth, high federal deficits may have contributed to the slowdown, though the evidence remains tentative. And, fifth, R&D spending has not been a deciding factor because it contributed about the same amount to productivity growth in the last quarter century as it had during the decade prior to 1974.

The most dramatic technological development in recent years has been the information revolution powered by the computer chip. The following case study looks at the impact of computers on economic growth.

CaseStudy

The Information Economy

If you would like to learn more about the productivity effect of computers, read Adam Zaretsky's "Have Computers Made Us More Productive? A Puzzle." It's available from the Federal Reserve Bank of St. Louis at http://www.stls.frb.org/publications/re/1998/d/re1998d3.html.

Computers and Productivity Growth

The first microprocessor, the Intel 4004, could execute about 400 instructions per second when it hit the market in 1971. IBM's first PC, introduced a decade later, could execute 330,000 instructions per second. Today a $1,000 computer can handle 200 million instructions per second, and more upscale models can crunch one billion instructions per second, or *2.5 million* times the number the 1971 Intel 4004 could handle.

3 See, for example, Zvi Griliches, "Productivity, R&D, and Basic Research at the Firm Level in the 1970s," *American Economic Review* 76 (March 1986): pp. 141–154.

Such advances in computing power have fueled a boom in computer use. There are now about as many computers as automobiles in the United States. From 1982 to 1996, growth of the computer sector averaged 26 percent annually. U.S. companies and universities are way ahead of other countries in high-technology applications, ranging from software to biotechnology. In 1997 there were about 40 personal computers per 100 persons in the United States, making us the world leader.

Personal computers are moving beyond word processing and spreadsheet analysis to help people work together. For example, design engineers in California can use the Internet to try out new ideas with marketers in New York, cutting development time in half. Sales representatives on the road can use laptops to log orders and provide customer service. U.S. insurance companies can coordinate data entry done as far away as Europe to handle claims more efficiently.

Computers not only improve the quality and safety in the automobile and airline industries but also increase the versatility of machines, which can be reprogrammed for different tasks. A new generation of machines monitor themselves with a computer chip and send messages through the phone lines to a service center, detailing problems when they arise. For example, General Electric uses the Internet to keep tabs on factory equipment thousands of miles away. Many home appliances will soon be Internet compatible. Sharp Electronics, for example, has developed a stereo that downloads music from the Web.

It's been said that we can see computers everywhere except in the productivity statistics. Why hasn't U.S. productivity jumped in response to the growing use of computers? If all the direct and related contributions of computers are included, about one-half of a percentage point of the 2.9 percent average growth in real GDP between 1972 and 1996 came from computers. To be sure, this represents a substantial addition to growth, increasing the rate by one-fifth, but it's disappointingly small for a technology that seems to hold so much promise.

One problem is that despite all we hear about the computer revolution, computers are *not yet* everywhere. For example, though spending on computers represents a growing fraction of all investment, only about 3 percent of the U.S. capital stock consists of computers and peripheral equipment. In contrast, previous technological revolutions captured a much larger share of investment. In 1890, for example, railroads accounted for about one-fifth of the U.S. capital stock. Another problem is that many benefits of computers affect unmeasured attributes of output. For example, computers improve communications among workers with links such as e-mail; and enhance consumer convenience with devices such as automatic teller machines. Thus, some of the productivity gains of computers go unmeasured. A third problem is that we have not yet learned how to measure productivity in some sectors that have benefited most from computers, such as banking and medicine. Finally, some computer uses on the job are counterproductive, such as joyriding on the Internet, gossiping over e-mail, or playing computer games.

An optimistic view is that the big productivity gains from information technology are still to come, as people learn to use computers more effectively and as fresh applications are developed. When new technologies are introduced, productivity often falls initially as workers try to master new and unfamiliar skills.

But over time, experience starts paying off. What's more, the technology itself improves and becomes more user friendly.

Nearly half the Americans who today use computers at home, school, or work are 20 years of age or younger. As these computer-literate people enter the workforce, the rates of return to computer applications should improve. (As a sign of the times, Taco Bell models its cash registers after Nintendo games.) According to this view, change takes time. For example, Thomas Edison designed the first electrical power plant in 1882, but it took another four decades for U.S. companies to convert from water or steam power to electricity. If the optimists are correct, computers could add as much as one percentage point to the annual growth rate of U.S. real GDP by the year 2006. That would be an impressive amount.

Sources: Joseph Haimowitz, "Has the Surge in Computer Spending Fundamentally Changed the Economy?" *Federal Reserve Bank of Kansas City Economic Review*, Second Quarter 1998: pp. 27–42; "Personal Computers," *The Economist*, 8 August 1998, p. 84; Leonard Nakamura, "Is the U.S. Economy Really Growing Too Slowly? Maybe We're Measuring Growth Wrong," *Business Review: Federal Reserve Bank of Philadelphia*, March–April 1997, pp. 1–12; and Thomas Weber, "Companies Gear Up for a Boom in Appliances That Use the Internet," *Wall Street Journal*, 27 August 1998.

International Productivity Comparisons

How does U.S. productivity growth compare with that in other industrial countries? Exhibit 5 shows that average growth in labor productivity between 1960 and 1997 for the United States and the six other leading industrial countries (called the Group of Seven, or G-7, countries). In keeping with what we have learned about productivity growth, the period is divided into two intervals: 1960 to 1973 and 1974 to 1997.

As you can see, during the first interval, the U.S. growth rate trailed all the others except Canada. The 2.9 percent U.S. average growth rate between 1960 and 1973 was a little more than half the 5.2 percent average for the six other G-7 countries. Why was the U.S. rate so low? With the exception of Canada, the other countries were starting from a lower level because of destruction during World War II. Because the level of productivity was relatively low in these other countries, it was easier to show improvement. During the more recent period, U.S. productivity growth was still below the average for the six other countries, but their lead declined from an average of 2.3 percentage points in 1960–1973 to 0.6 percentage points in 1974–1997.

Some final thoughts before turning to other matters. U.S. productivity growth since 1974 appears slow compared to the high growth rates immediately following World War II. But many economists believe the rapid growth prior to 1973 occurred because the economy was making up for opportunities lost during the crushing depression. Such growth, they say, should not be used as the benchmark against which to judge current growth rates. U.S. productivity growth since 1974, though still below the historical average, is not that far below the average of other industrial economies. What's more, U.S. productivity growth has improved recently, averaging 1.9 percent between 1996 and 1998. Let's not forget, the U.S. economy is still considered the world's most competitive, and Americans continue to enjoy the world's highest standard of living.

EXHIBIT 5

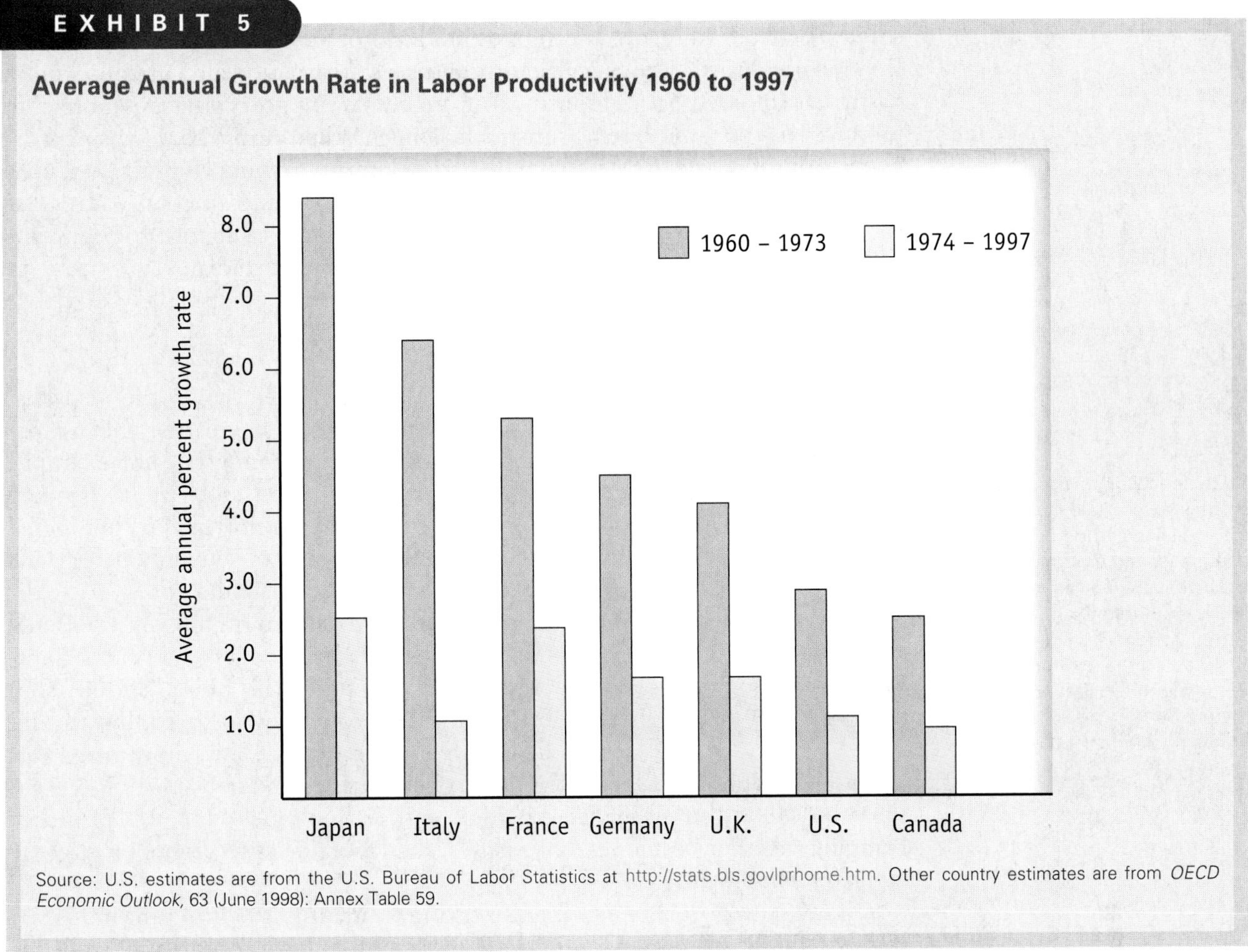

Source: U.S. estimates are from the U.S. Bureau of Labor Statistics at http://stats.bls.govlprhome.htm. Other country estimates are from *OECD Economic Outlook*, 63 (June 1998): Annex Table 59.

OTHER ISSUES OF TECHNOLOGY AND GROWTH

In this section we consider some other issues of technology and growth, beginning with the government's ability to identify and nurture technologies of the future.

Industrial Policy

Policy makers have debated whether the federal government should become more involved in shaping the nation's technological future. One concern is that technologies of the future will require huge sums to develop and implement, sums that individual firms cannot always raise. Another concern is that some technological breakthroughs benefit other firms and other industries, but the firm that develops the breakthrough may not be in a position to reap benefits from these spillover effects, so individual firms may under-invest in such research. One possible solution is more government involvement.

Industrial policy is the idea that government, using taxes, subsidies, regulations, and coordination should help nurture the industries and technologies of

Industrial policy The view that government—using taxes, subsidies, regulations, and coordination—should nurture the industries and technologies of the future, to give domestic industries an advantage over foreign competition

the future to give domestic industries an advantage over foreign competition. The objective is to secure a leading role for domestic industry. One example of European industrial policy is Airbus Industrie, a four-nation aircraft consortium. With an estimated $20 billion in aid from European governments, the aircraft producer has become Boeing's main challenger. When Airbus seeks business orders around the world, it can draw on government backing to promise special terms, such as landing rights at key European airports and an easing of regulatory constraints. U.S. producers do not get such extensive support from government. Industrial policy is discussed in the following case study.

State and local governments sometimes engage in industrial policies of their own. For examples, and arguments against such policies, read Melvin L. Burstein and Arthur J. Rolnick's "Congress Should End the Economic War Among the States" at http://woodrow.mpls.frb.fed.us/pubs/ar/ar1994.html.

Picking Technological Winners

U.S. industrial policy over the years has been aimed at creating the world's most advanced military industry. For example, the Defense Advanced Research Projects Agency tried to help develop new technologies, such as computer graphics, semiconductors, and computer-controlled machine tools. With the demise of the Soviet Union, however, defense technologies have become less important. Some argue that U.S. industrial policy should shift from a military to a civilian focus. During his first campaign President Clinton promised that he would establish a powerful agency to help finance and coordinate R&D for what he called "cutting-edge products and technologies." He also proposed bringing together businesses, universities, and laboratories to carry out R&D in civilian technologies.

Many state governments are also trying to identify the group of industries that should be promoted in the state. Economists have long recognized that firms in some industries gain a performance advantage by *clustering*—that is, by locating in a region already thick with firms in that particular industry or in related industries. Clusters such as Hollywood's show business, Madison Avenue's advertising business, Wall Street's financial business, and Silicon Valley's computer business facilitate communication and promote healthy competition among cluster members. The flow of information and cooperation between firms, as well as the competition among firms in close proximity, stimulates regional innovation and propels growth.

But skeptics wonder whether the government should be trusted to identify emerging technologies and to pick the industry clusters that will lead the way. Critics of industrial policy believe that the market better allocates scarce resources than the government. For example, the costly attempt of European governments to develop the supersonic transport, Concorde, did not work. As another example, in the early 1980s the U.S. government spent $1 billion to help military contractors develop a high-speed computer circuit. But Intel, a company receiving no federal support, was the first to develop the circuit.

There is concern that an industrial policy would evolve into another government giveaway program. Rather than going to the most promising technologies, the money and the competitive advantages would be awarded based on political connections. Critics also wonder how wise it is to sponsor corporate research when beneficiaries may share their expertise with foreign companies and may even build factories abroad. Sematech, for example, was a U.S. government–backed alliance of companies in the semiconductor industry. One of its members, Advanced Micro Devices, teamed up with a Japanese company to make semiconductors in Japan. Most economists would prefer to let Microsoft, Cisco Systems, or some Yahoo! upstart gamble on the important technologies of the future.

Sources: "Reshaping Defense," *The Economist*, 15 November 1997; "The President Bets on Technology," *New York Times*, 23 October 1997; Gene Grossman, "Promoting Industrial Activities: A Survey of Recent Arguments and Evidence," *OECD Economic Studies* (Spring 1990): pp. 87–125; and Richard Rapaport, "The Playground of Big Science," *Wired*, October 1995, pp. 152–159, 215.

Does Technological Change Lead to Unemployment?

Technological change can sometimes free resources for new uses. For example, now that fiber optics technology has become the most efficient means of communicating, the copper from existing telephone lines becomes available for other uses. In fact, AT&T controls most of the world's known stock of copper in the form of existing wires and cables that will gradually be replaced by fiber-optic cables and cellular technology.

Technological change often reduces the number of workers needed to produce a given amount of output. Consequently, some observers fear that new technology will throw people out of work and lead to higher unemployment. True, technological change can lead to unemployment in some industries and can thus create dislocations as workers must find new jobs (e.g., ATMs replaced many bank tellers). But technology can also increase production and employment by making products more affordable. For example, the introduction of the assembly line made automobiles affordable to the average household, stimulating production and employment in that industry. Even in industries where some workers are displaced by machines, those who keep their jobs are more productive. *As long as human wants are unlimited, displaced workers will usually find jobs producing other goods and services demanded in a growing economy.* More generally, as labor productivity rises, so do wages and consumption.

Although data from the 19th century are sketchy, there is no evidence that the unemployment rate is any higher today than it was in 1870. Since then, worker productivity has increased about 1,400 percent and the length of the average work week has dropped more than one-third. Although technological change may displace some workers in the short run, the long-run benefits include higher real incomes on average and more leisure—in short, a higher standard of living.

If technological change caused unemployment, then the slowdown in productivity growth that has occurred since 1974 should have resulted in lower unemployment. But, as we will see in the next chapter, the unemployment rate since 1974 has averaged above the 1948–1973 level. And if technological change causes unemployment, then unemployment rates should be lower where modern technology has not yet been introduced, such as in developing countries. But unemployment rates are typically much higher in such countries, and those who are employed there earn relatively little because they are not very productive.

Again, there is no question that technological change often creates job dislocations and hardships in the short run, as workers scramble to adjust to a changing world. Some workers with specialized skills made obsolete by technology may be unable to find jobs that pay as well as the ones they lost. These temporary dislocations are one price of progress. Over time, however, most displaced workers find other jobs, often in new industries created by technological change.

Output Per Capita

Output per capita Total output in the economy divided by the population

So far we have focused on growth resulting from increased labor productivity—that is, growth achieved by getting more output from each hour worked. Growth in the economy depends on labor productivity and the number of people employed. The economy may grow by increasing labor productivity, by increasing employment, or both. **Output per capita**, which is simply total output divided by the population, captures the combined effects of growing productivity and a growing workforce. *If employment grows faster than the population as a whole, output per capita can increase faster than productivity per worker.* Take a minute to think that one through.

Exhibit 6 presents real GDP per capita since 1959 for the United States. Note the general upward trend, interrupted by six recessions, indicated by the shading. Real GDP per capita during the period more than doubled, from about $12,500 in 1959 to more than $28,000 in 1998, for an average annual growth rate of 2.1 percent.

Let's now take a longer view looking across nations. Exhibit 7 on page 130 shows average annual growth in *real GDP per capita* since 1948 for the United States and the six other leading industrial countries. Again, the period is divided into two intervals: 1948 to 1973 and 1974 to 1997. As you can see, during the first interval, the U.S. growth rate trailed all the others. The 2.4 percent U.S. annual growth rate between 1948 and 1973 was only about half the 4.7 percent average for the six other countries listed. As explained earlier, with the exception of Canada, the six other developed countries were starting from low levels of output and productivity after being ravaged by World War II, so it was easier for these countries to show an improvement.

During the more recent period, the U.S. growth rate was still lower than that of most other countries listed, but the average difference declined. Between the periods 1948–1973 and 1974–1997, the U.S. annual growth rate declined from 2.4 percent to 1.4 percent, or by 1.0 percentage point, but growth rates for the six other countries declined on average from 4.7 percent to 1.8 percent, or by 2.9 percent. Japan's growth rate fell by two-thirds, from 7.8 percent to 2.4 percent, between those two periods.

Note that since 1974 the growth rate of U.S. GDP per capita averaged about 1.4 percent per year, while the growth rate in output per labor hour averaged only 1.2 percent per year. Why the difference? *During that period, the growth in employment exceeded the growth in population. With a higher percentage of the population working, output per capita grew faster than output per labor hour.*

EXHIBIT 6

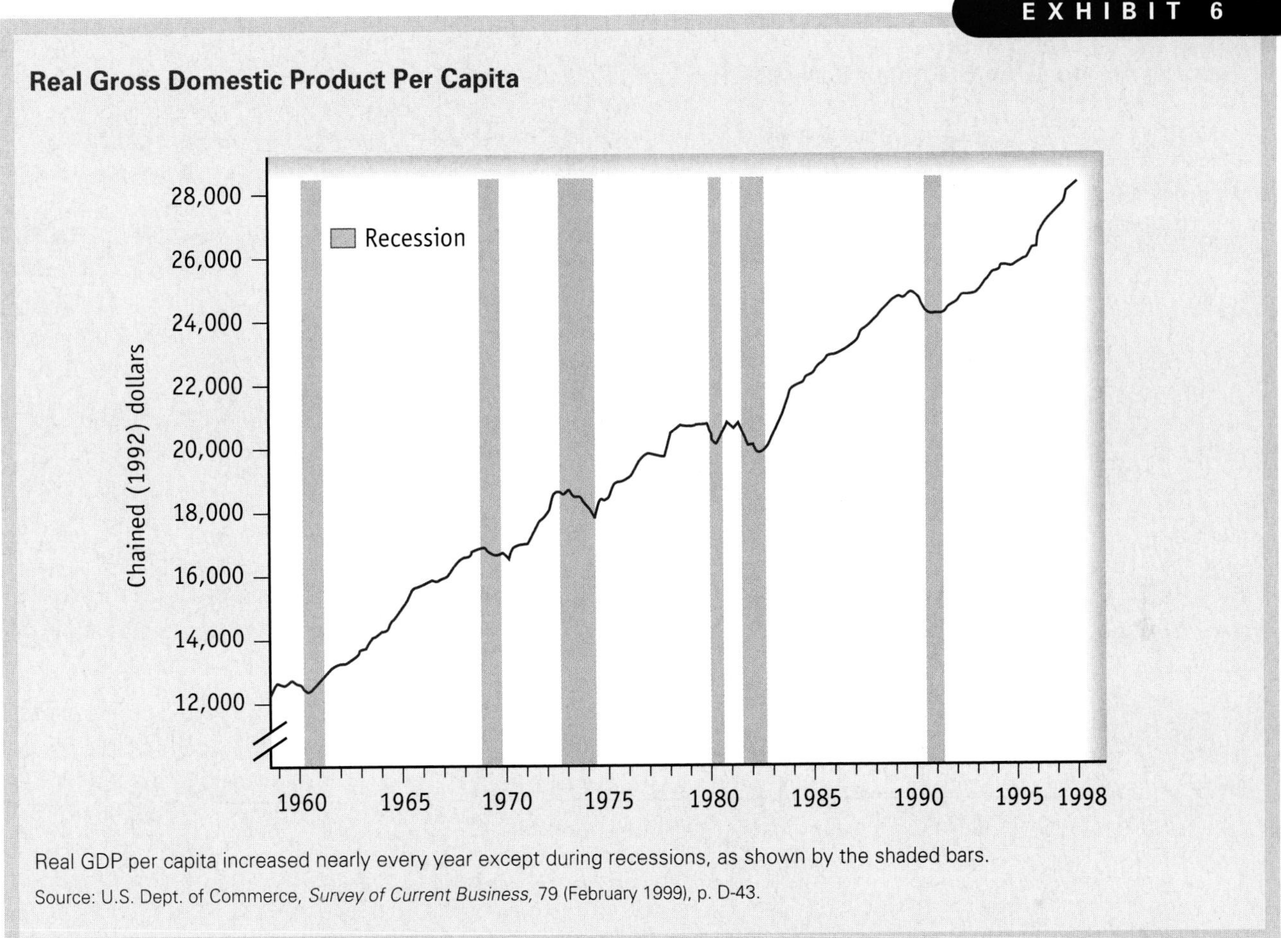

Real GDP per capita increased nearly every year except during recessions, as shown by the shaded bars.

Source: U.S. Dept. of Commerce, *Survey of Current Business,* 79 (February 1999), p. D-43.

Do Economies Converge?

How could it be that the United States, with one of the highest levels of productivity in the world, is also among the countries where productivity growth is slowest? Some observers suggest that this is to be expected. It is easier to copy new technology once it is developed than to develop that technology in the first place. Countries that start out far behind have the advantage of being able to increase their productivity by copying existing technology. But economies that are already using the latest technology can boost productivity only with a steady stream of technological breakthroughs.

The slow-growing-leader, fast-growing-follower pattern may simply reflect the dynamics of technological catch-up. Leader countries such as the United States will find their productivity growth limited by the rate of creation of new knowledge and improved technology. But follower countries can grow more quickly by closing the technological gap—by, for example, adding computers where they previously had none. Until 1995, the United States, which makes up just 5 percent of the world's population, accounted for the majority of home purchases of personal computers. Now more than 60 percent of PC sales are to the rest of the world.

EXHIBIT 7

Average Annual Growth Rate in Real GDP Per Capita, 1948–1997

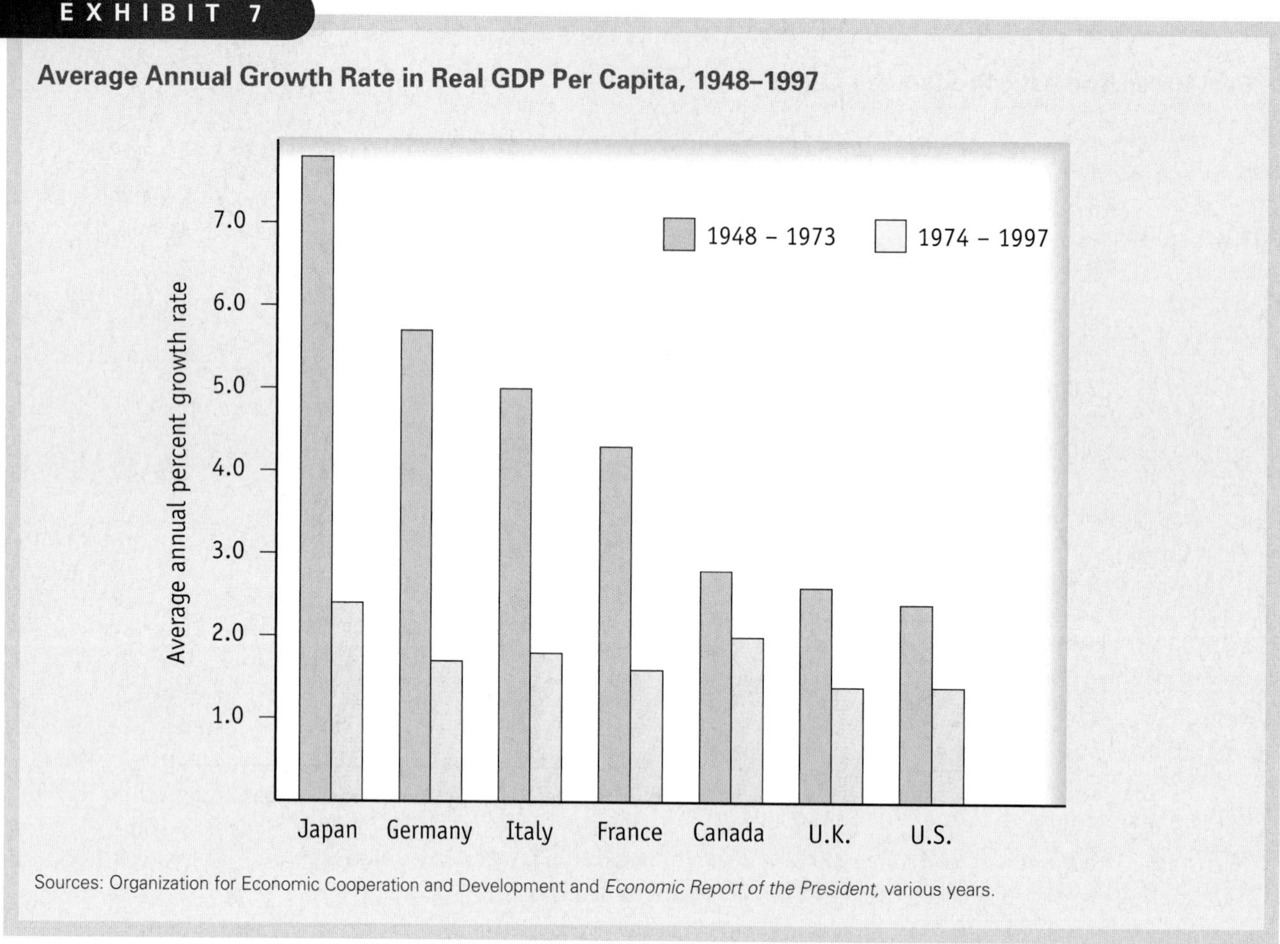

Sources: Organization for Economic Cooperation and Development and *Economic Report of the President*, various years.

Convergence A theory that the standard of living in economies around the world will grow more similar over time, with poorer countries catching up with richer countries

The **convergence** theory argues that economies around the world will become more similar as less-developed countries grow faster than more-developed countries. The evidence for this theory is mixed. On the one hand, among the most developed countries of the world, there has been convergence since 1950. Productivity levels in countries such as Japan, Germany, and France have grown closer to the U.S. level.[4] Newly industrialized East Asian countries have invested heavily in technology acquisition and human resources and began closing the gap with the world leaders until recent economic troubles in Asia slowed progress. On the other hand, since 1950, some of the very poorest countries of Latin America, Africa, Asia, and Eastern Europe have failed to close the gap with more-developed countries.

One reason why convergence may not occur is the vast differences in the quality of human capital across countries. Whereas technology is indeed portable, the knowledge, skill, and training often required to take advantage of that technology are not. Countries with a high level of human capital can make up for other shortcomings. For example, much of the physical capital stock in

4 See the discussion by Howard Pack, "Endogenous Growth Theory: Intellectual Appeal and Empirical Shortcomings," *Journal of Economic Perspectives* 8 (Winter 1994): pp. 55–72.

Japan and Germany was destroyed during World War II. But the two countries retained enough of their well-educated and highly skilled labor force to become industrial leaders again in little more than a generation.[5] But some countries simply do not have the human capital needed to identify and absorb new technology. With a few exceptions, less-developed economies tend to have low education levels and low literacy rates. And some countries lack the stable macroeconomic environment and the established institutions needed to help nurture economic growth.

*Net***Bookmark**

Is economic growth an unmixed blessing? For one perspective, read Mary C. Daly's "Assessing the Benefits of Economic Growth," available from the Federal Reserve Bank of San Francisco at http://www.frbsf.org/econrsrch/wklyltr/el97-30.html.

CONCLUSION

The disappointing U.S. growth rate in labor productivity since 1974 places the spotlight on efforts to increase the economy's growth and productivity. The productivity of an economy depends on the availability and quality of various resources, the level of technology, methods for organizing production, the energy and enterprise of entrepreneurs and workers, and a variety of institutional and social factors that affect the incentives and behavior of various resource suppliers. These factors interact to determine the level and growth of productivity.

The factors that contribute to productivity are strongly correlated with one another. A country with low productivity will probably be deficient in the quality of its workforce, in the quantity or quality of its physical capital, and in the level of its technology. Similarly, a country with high productivity is likely to excel in all measures.

If U.S. productivity grows at a rate of 2.1 percent per year, which has been the long-term trend, output per worker will double every 33 years. But if our productivity growth averages 1.2 percent per year, as it has since 1974, output per worker will take 58 years to double. *In the long run, small differences in productivity growth may determine whether the United States remains an economic leader.*

One final point bears repeating. Though the *growth* in U.S. productivity has in recent decades lagged behind the growth in other industrial countries, our *level* of productivity is still the highest in the world. U.S. workers are still the most productive on Earth, and the U.S. standard of living is unsurpassed. Real per-capita income in the United States is one-third higher than it is in Japan and in other developed economies. In fact, real per-capita income in the United States is about 20 times greater than it is for over half the human race. So don't confuse our *level* of productivity, which remains tops, with our *growth* in productivity, which slowed during the last quarter century.

SUMMARY

1. Because the population is continually increasing, an economy must produce more goods and services simply to maintain its standard of living, as measured by the output per capita. If output grows faster than the population, the standard of living will rise.

2. Over the last 130 years, labor productivity has grown an average of 2.1 percent per year. Output per hour of work is about 15 times greater today than in 1870. Research suggests that the *quality* of labor and capital is much more important than the *quantity* of these

5 Further issues of economic development are discussed in the final chapter, entitled "Developing and Transitional Economies."

resources. Productivity growth has slowed somewhat since 1974, especially in comparison to the robust growth between the end of World War II and 1973, although it picked up a bit in 1996, 1997, and 1998.

3. A variety of factors could explain the recent decline in productivity growth, including (1) a slower rate of growth in physical capital formation, (2) an increase in the share of less-experienced workers in the labor force, (3) the changing composition of output from goods to services, (4) higher federal deficits, and (5) a decline in research and development expenditures. Of these, the most likely candidate is the changing composition of output from goods to services.

4. Some governments use industrial policy to nurture the industries and technologies of the future to give domestic industries an advantage over foreign competitors.

5. Convergence is a theory that economies around the world will grow more alike, as poorer countries catch up with richer countries. The advanced industrial economies now look more similar than they did in 1950, but many poor countries have failed to close the gap with the advanced industrial economies.

QUESTIONS FOR REVIEW

1. *(Productivity)* As discussed in the text, per capita GDP in many developing countries depends on the productivity of land there. However, many richer economies have little land or land of poor quality. How can a country become rich despite these detriments?

2. *(Labor Productivity)* What two kinds of changes in the capital stock can improve labor productivity? How can each type be illustrated with a per-worker production function? What determines the slope of the per-worker production function?

3. *(Output Per Capita)* Explain how output per capita can grow faster than labor productivity. Is it possible for labor productivity to grow faster than output per capita?

4. *(Slowdown in Labor Productivity Growth)* What is the relationship between labor productivity and: (a) the rate of capital formation, (b) skill and education levels, and (c) the composition of output? How has each of these factors contributed to the slowdown in U.S. labor productivity growth since 1974?

5. *(Technology and Productivity)* What measures can government take to promote the development of practical technologies?

6. *(Basic and Applied Research)* What is the difference between basic and applied research? Relate this to the human genome project—research aimed at developing a complete map of human chromosomes, showing the location of every gene.

7. *(**CaseStudy:** Computers and Productivity Growth)* How has the increased use of computers affected U.S. productivity in the last few years? Is the contribution of computers expected to increase or decrease in the near future? Explain.

8. *(International Productivity Comparisons)* How does output per capita in the United States compare with output per capita in other industrial economies? How has this comparison changed over time?

9. *(Industrial Policy)* Define industrial policy. What are some arguments in favor of industrial policy?

10. *(**CaseStudy:** Picking Technological Winners)* What was the central focus of U.S. industrial policy in the past? Is the same focus appropriate today? What are the arguments against an active U.S. industrial policy?

11. *(Technological Change and Unemployment)* Explain how technological change can lead to unemployment in certain industries. How can it lead to increased employment?

12. *(Convergence)* Explain the convergence theory. Under what circumstances is convergence unlikely to occur?

13. *(Productivity)* What factors might contribute to a low *level* of productivity in an economy? Regardless of the level of labor productivity, what impact does slow *growth* in labor productivity have on the economy's standard of living?

PROBLEMS AND EXERCISES

14. *(Growth and the PPF)* Use the production possibilities frontier (PPF) to demonstrate economic growth.
    a. With consumption goods on one axis and capital goods on the other, show how the combination of goods selected this period affects the PPF in the next period.
    b. Extend this comparison by choosing a different point on this period's PPF and determining whether that combination leads to more or less growth over the next period.

15. *(Long-Term Productivity Growth)* Suppose that two nations start out in 1999 with identical levels of output per work hour—say, $100 per hour. In the first nation, labor productivity grows by 1 percent per year. In the second, it grows by 2 percent per year. Use a calculator or a spreadsheet to determine how much output per hour each nation will be producing 20 years later, assuming that the growth rates do not change. Then, determine how much each will be producing per hour 100 years later. What do your results tell you about the effects of small differences in growth rates?

16. *(Technological Change and Unemployment)* What are some examples, other than those given in the chapter, of technological change that has caused unemployment? And what are some examples of new technologies that have created jobs? How do you think you might measure the net impact of technological change on overall employment and GDP in the United States?

EXPERIENTIAL EXERCISES

17. *(Labor Productivity)* Go to the Bureau of Labor Statistics (BLS) page on Quarterly Labor Productivity at http://stats.bls.gov/lprhome.htm and get the latest news release on productivity and costs. Rank the various sectors of the U.S. economy from highest to lowest according to their most recent productivity growth rates. Does what you found make sense to you?

18. *(International Productivity Comparisons)* The BLS also compiles international data on productivity in manufacturing at http://stats.bls.gov/news.release/prod4.toc.htm. For the most recent period, which nations have enjoyed the most rapid growth in manufacturing productivity? Which nations have experienced the slowest growth? Has productivity actually declined anywhere? How could this be related to the convergence theory explained in this chapter?

19. *(Wall Street Journal)* Technological change is an important driver of economic growth. Refer to the "Technology" column in the Marketplace section of a recent *Wall Street Journal*. Find a story about some technological innovation that seems interesting to you. How will this innovation affect the U.S. production possibilities frontier? Does it seem likely to affect employment as well? If so, which types of workers will be harmed, and which types will benefit?

CHAPTER

7 Unemployment and Inflation

Who among the following would be counted as unemployed: a college student who is not working, a bank teller displaced by an automatic teller machine, Julia Roberts between movies, or baseball slugger Mark McGwire in the off-season? What type of unemployment might be healthy for the economy? What's so bad about inflation? Why is anticipated inflation better than unanticipated inflation? These and other questions are answered in this chapter, where we explore two macroeconomic problems: unemployment and inflation.

To be sure, unemployment and inflation are not the only problems an economy could face. Sluggish growth, rising poverty, and a huge federal debt are some others. But low unemployment and low inflation go a long way toward helping diminish the effects of other economic problems. Although unemployment

Visit the McEachern Interactive Study Center for this chapter at *http://mcisc.swcollege.com*

and inflation are often related, we will initially describe each separately. Our focus will be more on the extent and consequences of these problems than on their causes. The causes of each and the relationship between the two will become clearer in later chapters, as you learn more about how the economy works.

As this chapter will show, not all unemployment nor all inflation harms the economy. Even in a healthy economy, a certain amount of unemployment reflects the voluntary choices of workers and employers seeking their best opportunities. And inflation that is fully anticipated creates fewer distortions than does unanticipated inflation. Topics discussed in this chapter include:

- Measuring unemployment
- Frictional, structural, seasonal, and cyclical unemployment
- Meaning of full employment
- Sources and consequences of inflation
- Relative price changes
- Nominal and real interest rates

UNEMPLOYMENT

"They scampered about looking for work . . . . They swarmed on the highways. The movement changed them; the highways, the camps along the road, the fear of hunger and the hunger itself, changed them. The children without dinner changed them, the endless moving changed them."[1] There is no question, as John Steinbeck wrote in *The Grapes of Wrath*, that a long stretch of unemployment can have a profound effect on the individual and the family. The most obvious loss is a steady paycheck, but those who are unemployed often suffer a loss of self-esteem, as well. Moreover, unemployment appears to be linked to a greater incidence of crime and to a variety of afflictions including heart disease, suicide, and mental illness. However much people complain about their jobs, they rely on those same jobs not only for income but also for part of their personal identity. When strangers meet, the "What-do-you-do" question is usually one of the first to come up. The loss of a long-held job usually involves some loss of that identity.

In addition to these personal costs, unemployment imposes a cost on the economy as a whole, because fewer goods and services are produced. When the economy does not generate enough jobs to employ all those who are willing and able to work, that unemployed labor service is lost forever. *This lost output coupled with the economic and psychological damage to unemployed workers and their families represents the true cost of unemployment.* As we begin our analysis, keep in mind that unemployment statistics reflect millions of individuals with their own stories. As President Harry Truman said, "It's a recession when your neighbor loses his job; it's a depression when you lose your own." For some people, unemployment is a brief break between jobs. For others, a long stretch of unemployment can have a lasting effect on self-esteem, on family stability, and on economic welfare.

Measuring Unemployment

The unemployment rate is perhaps the most widely reported measure of the nation's economic health. What does the unemployment rate measure, what are the sources of unemployment, and how does unemployment change over time?

1 John Steinbeck, *The Grapes of Wrath* (New York: Viking Press, 1939), p. 392.

These are some of the questions explored in this section. Let's start by considering how unemployment is measured.

We begin with the U.S. *civilian noninstitutional adult population*, which consists of all civilians 16 years of age and older, except those who are institutionalized in prisons or mental hospitals. The adjective *civilian* means that the definition excludes those in the military. In this chapter, when we refer to the *adult population,* we will mean the civilian noninstitutional adult population. The **labor force** consists of those in the adult population who are either working or looking for work. *Those looking for work are considered unemployed.* More specifically, the Bureau of Labor Statistics surveys 50,000 households monthly and counts people as unemployed if they have no job but have looked for work at least once during the preceding four weeks. Thus, the college student, displaced bank teller, Julia Roberts, and Mark McGwire would all be counted as unemployed if they looked for work in the previous month but could not find a suitable job. The unemployment rate measures the percentage of those in the labor force who are unemployed. Hence, the **unemployment rate,** which is reported monthly, equals the number unemployed—that is, those without jobs who are looking for work—divided by the number in the labor force.

Labor force Individuals 16 years of age and older who are either working or actively looking for work

Unemployment rate The number of unemployed individuals expressed as a percentage of the labor force

Only a fraction of adults who are not working are considered unemployed. The others may have retired, may have chosen to remain at home to care for small children, may be full-time students, or may simply not want to work. Others may be unable to work because of long-term illness or disability. Some people may have become so discouraged by a long, unfruitful job search that they have given up their search in frustration. These **discouraged workers** have, in effect, dropped out of the labor force, so they are not counted as unemployed. Finally, about one-third of those who are working part time would prefer to work full time, yet all part-time workers are counted as employed. Because the official unemployment rate does not include discouraged workers and counts all part-time workers as employed, it may underestimate the true extent of unemployment in the economy. Later we will consider some factors that could cause the official rate to exceed the true rate.

Discouraged worker A person who has dropped out of the labor force because of lack of success in finding a job

These definitions are illustrated in Exhibit 1, where circles represent the various groups and subgroups, and the number (in millions) of individuals in each category and subcategory is listed in parentheses. The circle on the left depicts the entire U.S. labor force, including both those who are employed and those who are unemployed. The circle on the right represents those in the adult population who, for whatever reason, are not working. These two circles reflect the entire adult population. The overlapping area identifies the number of *unemployed* workers—that is, the number in the labor force who aren't working.

The unemployment rate is found by dividing the number unemployed by the number in the labor force; in 1998, the unemployment rate averaged 4.5 percent.

The productive capability of any economy depends in part on the proportion of adults who are in the labor force, called the *labor force participation rate.* Let's step back from the unemployment rate to bring into the picture this more fundamental measure. In Exhibit 1, the U.S. adult population equals those in the labor force (137.7 million) plus those not in the labor force (67.5 million)—a total of 205.2 million. The **labor force participation rate** therefore equals the number in the labor force divided by the adult population, or

Labor force participation rate The ratio of the number in the labor force to the adult population

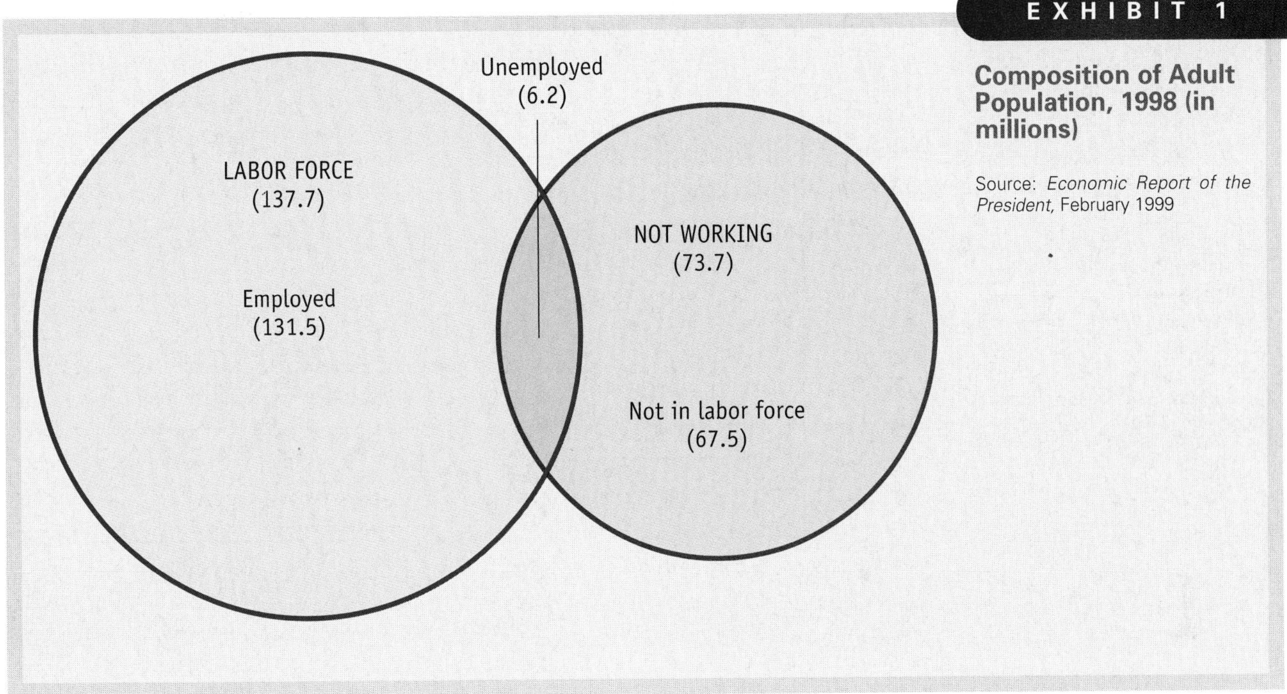

EXHIBIT 1

Composition of Adult Population, 1998 (in millions)

Source: *Economic Report of the President,* February 1999

67.1 percent (137.7/205.2). So, on average, about two out of three adults are in the labor force. The labor force participation rate increased from about 60 percent in 1970 to about 67 percent in 1990, and it has remained relatively constant since then.

Changes over Time in Unemployment Statistics

The noninstitutional adult population changes slowly over time. The only way to join that group is to become 16 years of age, get released from prison or a mental hospital, or immigrate to the United States. The only way to leave the adult population is to die, become institutionalized, or emigrate from the United States to another country. Since 1950, the adult population in the United States has grown by an average of 1.4 percent per year.

The labor force participation rate can change more quickly than the adult population, because moving in and out of the labor force is easier than moving in and out of the adult population. One striking development since World War II has been the convergence in the labor force participation rates of men and women. In 1950, only 34 percent of adult women were in the labor force; today that rate is 60 percent, with the largest increase among younger women. The labor force participation rate among men has declined from 86 percent in 1950 to about 75 percent today, primarily because of earlier retirement. The participation rate is slightly higher among white males than black males, but higher among black females than white females.

But, over time, what changes even more quickly than the labor force participation rate or the adult population is the unemployment rate. Exhibit 2 depicts the U.S. unemployment rate since 1900, with shading to indicate years of recession or depression. As you can see, the rate rises during recessions and falls

NetBookmark

The Bureau of Labor Statistics provides abundant data on labor market conditions, including unemployment rates, labor force estimates, and earnings data. Visit their Web site at http://stats.bls.gov:80/blshome.html. Click on "Economy at a Glance" for easy access to the latest data.

EXHIBIT 2

The U.S. Unemployment Rate Since 1900

Since 1900 the unemployment rate has fluctuated widely, rising during recessions and falling during expansions. During the Great Depression of the 1930s, the rate rose as high as 25.2 percent.

Sources: *Historical Statistics of the United States*, 1970; and *Economic Report of the President*, February 1996.

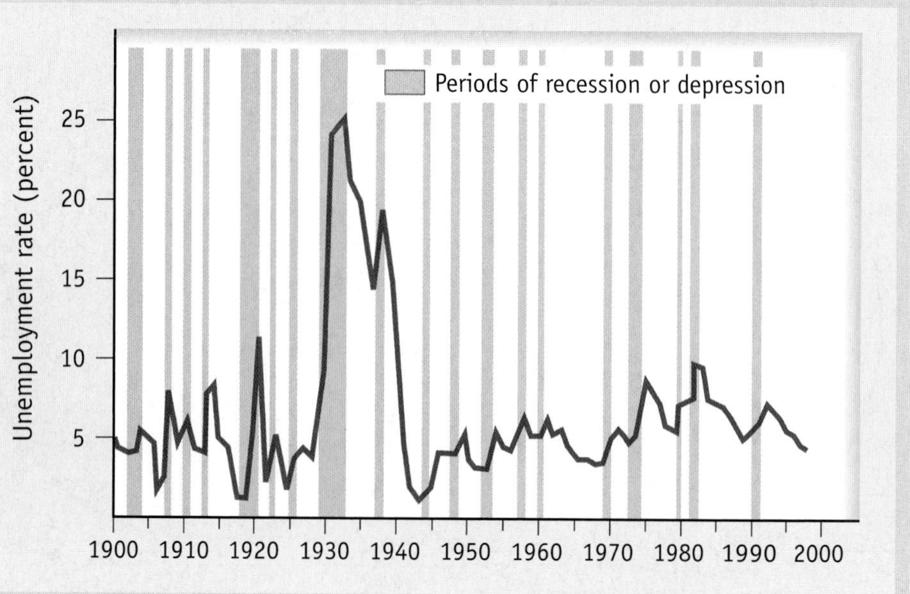

during expansions. Perhaps the most striking feature of the graph is the dramatic jump that occurred during the Great Depression, when the unemployment rate peaked at 25 percent. Note that since the end of World War II the unemployment rate trended upward until the early 1980s, and then came back down.

Since 1970, the entry of baby boomers—coupled with a rising female labor force participation rate—boosted U.S. employment by well over 50 million workers. In fact, since 1970 the United States has been called an incredible job machine and is the envy of the world. At the same time that the U.S. economy was creating over 50 million jobs, the industrialized countries of Western Europe experienced only modest employment growth.

Unemployment in Various Groups

The overall unemployment rate says nothing about who is unemployed or for how long. Even a low overall rate often hides wide differences in unemployment rates across age, race, gender, and geographical area. Unemployment rates since 1972 for different groups appear in Exhibit 3. Each panel presents the unemployment rate by race and by gender. Panel (a) considers those 20 years of age and older, and panel (b) those 16 to 19 years old. Years of recession are shaded. As you can see, rates are higher among blacks than among whites, and rates are higher among teenagers than among those aged 20 and older. During recessions, the rates of all groups climbed. For all groups, rates peaked during the recession of 1982. The unemployment rate among blacks aged 20 and older fell below double digits in 1995 for the first time in two decades.

Why are unemployment rates among teenagers about twice as high as among older workers? Young workers enter the job market with little training and so are usually employed in relatively unskilled positions, where they are

EXHIBIT 3

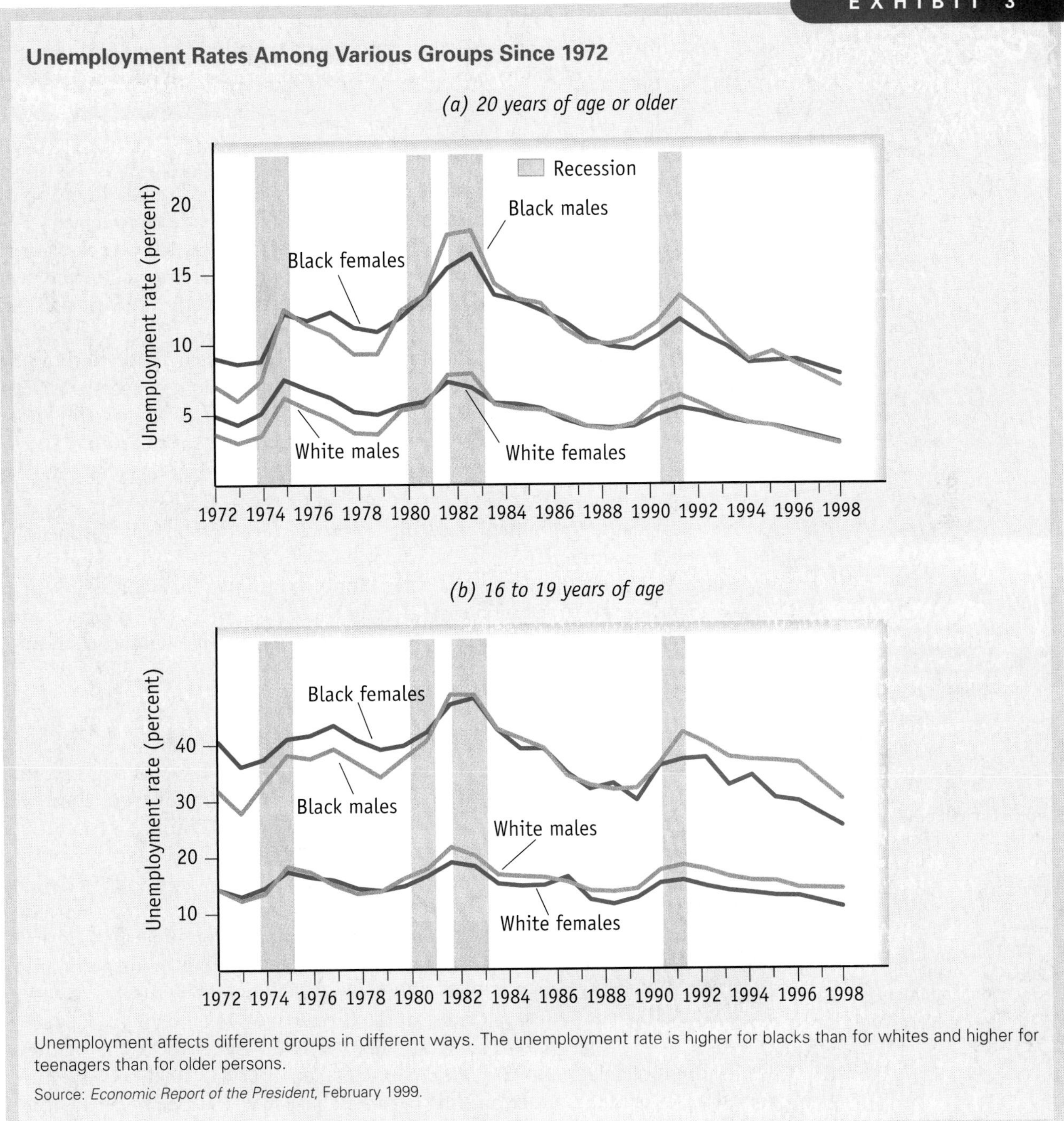

Unemployment affects different groups in different ways. The unemployment rate is higher for blacks than for whites and higher for teenagers than for older persons.

Source: *Economic Report of the President*, February 1999.

among the first dismissed if the economy stalls. Young workers also move in and out of the job market frequently during the year as they juggle school demands. Even those who have left school often shop around more than older workers, quitting one job and searching for another that suits them better.

Unemployment also varies by occupational group. Professional and technical workers experience lower unemployment rates than blue-collar workers. Construction workers experience the highest average unemployment rate because that business is seasonal and is subject to swings over the business cycle.

Duration of Unemployment

Any given unemployment rate says little about how long people have been unemployed—that is, the *average duration of unemployment*. The average duration of unemployment rises during recessions and starts to fall soon after a recovery begins. The average duration of unemployment in 1998 was 14.5 weeks. Some were unemployed longer than others: 42 percent were unemployed fewer than 5 weeks; 31 percent from 5 to 14 weeks; 13 percent from 15 to 26 weeks; and 14 percent 27 weeks or longer. Typically, a rise in the unemployment rate reflects both a larger number of unemployed and a longer average duration of unemployment. The duration of unemployment varies across countries. For example, only 6 percent of the U.S. jobless in 1997 were out of work for more than a year, compared to 37 percent in France and 51 percent in Spain.

Unemployment Differences Across the Country

The national unemployment rate masks much variation in rates across the country. For example, in 1998, the unemployment rates in Alaska, New Mexico, and West Virginia were more than double the rates in Nebraska, North Dakota, and South Dakota. To look behind the numbers, let's consider the experience of one troubled county in West Virginia, in the following case study.

Carolyn Sherwood-Call of the Federal Reserve Bank of San Francisco has written "The 1980s divergence in state personal incomes: What does it tell us?" Download her article at http://www.frbsf.org/econrsrch/econrev/96-1/14-25.pdf to learn more about the shifting fortunes of various U.S. regions—your own included.

Poor King Coal

For decades, McDowell County, West Virginia, prospered by supplying the coal that fired the nation's steel mills. Mining jobs were abundant and wages attractive. Many miners earned over $40,000 a year in 1980, which would exceed the purchasing power of $75,000 in today's dollars. Most young people, rather than finish their education, became miners (more than half of those over age 25 are high school dropouts). The mining companies dominated the county, owning most of the property.

But between 1980 and 1985, the value of the dollar rose relative to foreign currencies, so American steel became more expensive overseas and foreign steel became cheaper in the United States. Steel imports increased by 56 percent between 1980 and 1985. As the world's demand for U.S. steel fell, so did the demand for the coal needed to produce that steel. Coal mines in McDowell County shut down, and by the end of the decade, the official unemployment rate for the county was more than double the national average. Local officials claimed the actual rate was much higher because of discouraged workers. According to the 1990 census, half those under 18 lived in poverty, as did 36 percent of those 18 to 64 years of age.

The county tried to attract new industry—even a nuclear-waste dump—but met with little success. The county's poor roads and bridges and a labor force trained only for mining scared off potential employers. By 1995, transfer payments exceeded all earnings as a source of income; the largest employer in the county was state and local government. In short, the county had all its eggs in one basket—mining—but that basket fell.

Sources: Walter Adams, "Steel," *The Structure of American Industry*, Walter Adams and James Brock, eds. (Englewood Cliffs, N.J.: Prentice Hall, 1995), pp. 93–118. Recent employment and income figures for McDowell County can be found at Internet site http://musom.mu.wvnet.edu/0u:/wvvhs/root.html.

Types of Unemployment

Pick up any metropolitan newspaper and thumb through the classified pages. The "Help Wanted" section may run more than 40 pages and include thousands of jobs, from accountants to x-ray technicians. Why, when millions are unemployed, are so many jobs unfilled? To understand this paradox, we must take a closer look at the reasons behind unemployment.

Think about all the ways people can become unemployed. They may quit or get fired from their jobs. They may be looking for a first job, or they may be reentering the labor force after an absence. An examination of the reasons behind unemployment during 1998 indicates that 45 percent of the unemployed lost their previous jobs, 12 percent quit their previous jobs, 9 percent were entering the labor market for the first time, and 34 percent were reentering the market. *Thus, 55 percent were unemployed either because they quit their jobs or because they were just joining or rejoining the labor force.*

We distinguish four types of unemployment, based on the source: frictional, structural, seasonal, and cyclical.

Frictional Unemployment. Just as employers do not always hire the first applicant who comes through the door, workers do not always accept their first job offer. Both employers and job applicants need time to explore the job market. Employers need time to learn about the talent available, and job seekers need time to learn about employment opportunities. The time required to bring together labor suppliers and labor demanders results in **frictional unemployment.** Although unemployment often creates economic and psychological hardships, not all unemployment is necessarily bad. Frictional unemployment does not usually last long and results in a better match-up between workers and jobs, so the entire economy becomes more efficient.

Frictional unemployment
Unemployment that arises because of the time needed to match qualified job seekers with available job openings

Structural Unemployment. A second reason job vacancies and unemployment coexist is that unemployed workers often do not have the skills demanded by employers or do not live in the area where their skills are in demand. For example, the Lincoln Electric Company in Euclid, Ohio, could not fill 200 job openings because few of the thousands who applied could operate computer-controlled machines. Unemployment arising from a mismatch of skills or geographic location is called **structural unemployment.** *Structural unemployment occurs because changes in tastes, technology, taxes, or competition reduce the demand for certain skills and increase the demand for other skills.* In our dynamic economy, some

Structural unemployment
Unemployment that arises because (1) the skills demanded by employers do not match the skills of the unemployed, or (2) the unemployed do not live where the jobs are located

workers, such as the coal miners in West Virginia, are stuck with skills that are no longer demanded. Likewise, golf carts replaced caddies and ATMs put many bank tellers out of work.

Whereas most frictional unemployment is short-term and voluntary, structural unemployment poses more of a problem because workers must seek jobs elsewhere or must develop the skills that are in demand. For example, unemployed coal miners and bank tellers must seek work in other industries or in other regions. But moving to where the jobs are is easier said than done. People prefer to remain near friends and relatives. Those laid off from high-wage jobs may be reluctant to leave an area because they hope to be rehired. Families in which one spouse is still employed may not want to give up one job to seek two jobs elsewhere. Finally, available jobs may be in areas where the cost of living is much higher. So the unemployed often stay put, remaining structurally unemployed.

Seasonal unemployment Unemployment caused by seasonal shifts in labor supply and demand

Seasonal Unemployment. Unemployment caused by seasonal changes in labor supply and demand during the year is called **seasonal unemployment.** During cold winter months, demand for farm hands, lifeguards, golf instructors, and lawn-care specialists shrinks, as it does for dozens of other seasonal occupations. Likewise, the tourist trade in places such as Miami and Phoenix melts in the summer heat. The Christmas season increases the demand for sales clerks, postal workers, and Santa Clauses. Those with seasonal jobs know they will probably be unemployed in the off-season. Some may even have chosen a seasonal occupation to complement their lifestyle or academic schedule. To eliminate seasonal unemployment, we might have to outlaw winter and abolish Christmas. Monthly employment statistics are usually "seasonally adjusted" to smooth out the bulges that result from seasonal factors.

Cyclical unemployment Unemployment that fluctuates with the business cycle, increasing during recessions and decreasing during expansions

Cyclical Unemployment. As production declines during recessions, many firms reduce their demand for inputs, including labor. **Cyclical unemployment** is the fluctuation in unemployment that is caused by the business cycle. Cyclical unemployment increases during recessions and decreases during expansions. Between 1932 and 1934, when unemployment averaged about 24 percent, there was clearly much cyclical unemployment. Between 1942 and 1945, when the unemployment rate averaged only 1.6 percent, there was no cyclical unemployment. Government policies that stimulate aggregate demand during recessions are aimed at reducing cyclical unemployment.

The Meaning of Full Employment

In an ever-changing economy such as ours, changes in product demand and changes in technology continually alter the supply and demand for particular types of labor. Thus, even in a healthy economy, there will be some frictional, structural, and seasonal unemployment. The economy is viewed as operating at *full employment* if there is no cyclical unemployment. When economists talk about "full employment," they do not mean zero unemployment, but relatively low unemployment, with estimates ranging from 4 to 6 percent. Even when the economy is at **full employment,** there will be some frictional, structural, and seasonal unemployment. After all, more than half of those unemployed have quit their last job or are new entrants or reentrants into the labor force. A large proportion of this group could be counted among the frictionally unemployed.

Full employment The level of employment when there is no cyclical unemployment

Unemployment Compensation

We know that unemployment often imposes an economic and psychological hardship on those unemployed. For a variety of reasons, however, the burden of unemployment on the individual and the family may not be as severe today as it was during the Great Depression. Today, a large proportion of households have two workers in the labor force, so if one becomes unemployed, another is likely to have a job, a job that often provides health insurance and other benefits. When a household has more than one person in the labor force, the economic shock of unemployment is cushioned to some extent.

Moreover, workers who lose their jobs now often receive unemployment benefits. In response to the massive unemployment of the Great Depression, Congress passed the Social Security Act of 1935, which provided unemployment insurance financed by a tax on employers. Unemployed workers who meet certain qualifications can receive **unemployment benefits** for up to six months, provided they actively seek work. During recessions, benefits are often extended beyond six months in states with especially high unemployment rates. The insurance is aimed primarily at those who have lost jobs. Not covered are those just entering or reentering the labor force, those who quit their last job, or those fired for just cause such as excessive absenteeism or theft. Because of these restrictions, only about half of all unemployed workers receive unemployment benefits.

Unemployment benefits Cash transfers provided to unemployed workers who actively seek employment and who meet other qualifications

Unemployment insurance usually replaces more than half of a person's take-home pay. In 1998, for example, an average of $200 per week was paid to the unemployed who received benefits. Because unemployment benefits reduce the opportunity cost of remaining unemployed, they may reduce incentives to find work. For example, if you faced the choice of washing dishes for a take-home pay of $200 per week or collecting $150 per week in unemployment benefits, which would you choose? Evidence suggests that unemployed workers who receive insurance benefits tend to search less actively than those without such benefits. Therefore, although unemployment insurance provides a safety net for the unemployed, it may also reduce the urgency of finding work, thereby increasing the average duration of unemployment and the unemployment rate. On the plus side, unemployment insurance may allow for a higher-quality search, since the insured job seeker has walking-around money and need not take the first job that comes along. As a result of a better search, there is a better match between job skills and job requirements; and this promotes economic efficiency in the economy.

International Comparisons of Unemployment

How do U.S. unemployment rates compare with those around the world? In January 1999, when the civilian unemployment rate was 4.3 percent in the U.S., it was 7.8 percent in Canada, 10.6 percent in Germany, 11.4 percent in France, 6.2 percent in the United Kingdom, 12.3 percent in Italy, and 4.4 percent in Japan. Unemployment rates in Europe tend to be higher than in the United States. The ratio of unemployment benefits to average pay tends to be higher in Europe, and unemployment insurance tends to last longer, sometimes for years.

We should view international comparisons carefully, however, because the definitions of unemployment differ across countries with respect to age limits, the criteria used to determine whether a person is looking for work, the way layoffs are treated, how those in the military are counted, and in other subtle ways.

These differences can affect estimates of unemployment. For example, most countries in North and South America and some European countries base their unemployment estimates on periodic surveys of the labor force. Each month the U.S. Bureau of Labor Statistics surveys 50,000 households around the nation. Experts believe that such extensive surveys yield the most reliable results.

But most other countries, including Germany, the United Kingdom, and a majority of less-developed countries, base official estimates on registrations with government employment offices. Reliance on such self-reporting tends to underestimate the actual level of unemployment, particularly in less-developed countries where there are few jobs, no unemployment benefits, and hence no real reason to bother registering with the government as unemployed. Command economies, such as North Korea and Cuba, usually do not publish unemployment rates.

Employment practices differ across countries. For example, Germany imposes penalties on firms for "socially unjustified" layoffs, and Swedish law makes it harder to lay off Swedish citizens than foreign workers. In Japan, many firms have offered job security for life. As a result, some employees there who do little or no work are still carried on the company's payroll. Layoffs in Japan are limited by both labor laws and social norms. Unemployment has increased there lately only because many firms are going bankrupt and have no alternative but to lay off workers.

Problems with Official Unemployment Figures

Official unemployment statistics are not without their problems. As we saw earlier, not counting discouraged workers in the official labor force understates unemployment. Official employment data also ignore the problem of **underemployment**, which arises because people are counted as employed even if they can find only part-time jobs or are vastly overqualified for their job, as when someone with a Ph.D. in English can find employment only as a bookstore clerk. Counting overqualified and part-time workers as employed tends to understate the actual amount of unemployment.

Underemployment A situation in which workers are overqualified for their jobs or work fewer hours than they would prefer

On the other hand, because unemployment insurance and most welfare programs require recipients to seek employment, some people may act as if they are looking for work just to qualify for such programs. If these people do not in fact want to find a job, their inclusion among the unemployed tends to overstate the official unemployment figures. Also, people working in the underground economy may not readily acknowledge employment on a government survey since their intent is to evade taxes or skirt the law. *On net, however, most experts believe that official U.S. unemployment figures tend to underestimate unemployment because of the exclusion of discouraged workers and because underemployed workers are counted as employed.* Despite several qualifications and limitations, the unemployment rate is a useful measure of unemployment trends over time.

We turn next to the second major concern in today's economy: inflation.

INFLATION

Let's begin our discussion of inflation with a case study that highlights the cost of high inflation by focusing on the recent experience of Brazil.

Hyperinflation in Brazil

CaseStudy

Other Times, Other Places

What's happening in Brazil? The Brazilian Ministry of Finance maintains a comprehensive Web page devoted to economic developments there. You can find it at http://www.brasil.emb.nw.dc.us/econmenu.htm.

Between 1988 and 1994, year-to-year inflation rates in Brazil were 1,300 percent, 2,900 percent, 440 percent, 1,000 percent, 1,260 percent, and 1,740 percent. Six years of such inflation meant that prices on average were about *4 million* times higher in 1994 than in 1988! To put this in perspective, if that inflation rate had prevailed in the United States, the price of a gallon of gasoline would have climbed from $1.25 in 1988 to $5 million in 1994. A pair of jeans that sold for $35 in 1988 would have cost $140 million in 1994!

With the value of the Brazilian cruzeiro cheapening by the hour, people understandably did not want to hold cruzeiros. As soon as workers got paid, they tried either to buy goods and services before prices increased or to exchange cruzeiros for a more stable currency, such as the U.S. dollar. With such wild inflation, everyone, including merchants, had difficulty keeping track of prices. Price differences among sellers of the same product increased, prompting shoppers to incur the "shoe-leather cost" of looking for the lowest price.

The huge increase in the average price level meant that wads of money were needed to carry out even the simplest transactions. Think again in terms of dollars. To carry in 1994 the equivalent of $20 in preinflated spending power for pizza and a movie, you would have to load yourself down with $80 million. Even in $100 bills, this amount of currency would weigh nearly a ton. That's one fat wallet! Because carrying even small amounts of purchasing power became physically impossible, Brazilian officials issued currencies in larger and larger denominations. Between the mid-1980s and 1994, new currency denominations were issued on five separate occasions. Each new currency was worth a large multiple of the previous one. For example, the 1994 issue of the new *cruzeiro real* (now called simply the *real*) exchanged for 2,750 of the cruzeiro it replaced. New currency issues made transactions easier.

Lugging money around, shopping for the lowest price, and constant preoccupation with money matters all take time and energy away from production. Thus, high and unpredictable inflation leads to wasteful activity, such as immediately converting each day's pay into another currency or into goods and services. Such activity is rational for each individual but unproductive for the economy as a whole. Inflation in Brazil dropped from the runaway levels of the early 1990s to only 5 percent in 1997, though inflation was starting to heat up again in 1998.

Sources: "Latin America Seeks Shelter," *The Economist*, 29 August 1998, pp. 63–65; Thomas Vogel and Pamela Druckerman, "Brazil Appears to Thwart Speculative Attack on Real," *Wall Street Journal*, 30 Oct. 1997; "Brazil: Another Try," *The Economist* 9 July 1994, p. 44; and "Brazil," *Britannica Book of the Year* (Encyclopaedia Britannica: Chicago, 1994), pp. 570–571.

We have already discussed inflation in different contexts. *Inflation* is a sustained increase in the average level of prices. If the price level bounces around—moving up one month, falling back another—any particular increase in the price

Hyperinflation A very high rate of inflation

Deflation A sustained decrease in the price level

Disinflation A reduction in the rate of inflation

level would not necessarily be called inflation. Extremely high inflation, as in Brazil, is called **hyperinflation.** A sustained *decrease* in the average level of prices is called **deflation,** as occurred during the Great Depression. And a reduction in the rate of inflation is called **disinflation.** For example, during the disinflation of 1982 to 1984, U.S. inflation fell to less than one-third its 1978 to 1980 rate.

We typically measure inflation on an annual basis. The annual *inflation rate* is the percentage increase in the average price level from one year to the next. For example, between 1997 and 1998, the U.S. consumer price index increased by 1.6 percent. In this section, we first consider two sources of inflation. We then examine the extent and consequences of inflation in the United States and around the world.

Two Sources of Inflation

Demand-pull inflation A sustained rise in the price level caused by increases in aggregate demand

Inflation can be depicted as a sustained increase in the economy's price level resulting from increases in aggregate demand or decreases in aggregate supply. Panel (a) of Exhibit 4 shows that an increase in aggregate demand raises the price level from *P* to *P*'. Inflation resulting from increases in aggregate demand is often called **demand-pull inflation.** In such cases, a rising aggregate demand curve *pulls up* the price level. To generate continuous demand-pull inflation, the aggregate demand curve would have to keep shifting out along a given aggregate supply curve. Rising U.S. inflation rates during the late 1960s resulted from demand-pull inflation, when the federal spending growth both for the Vietnam War and for expanded social programs increased aggregate demand.

EXHIBIT 4

Inflation Caused by Shifts in the Aggregate Demand and Aggregate Supply Curves

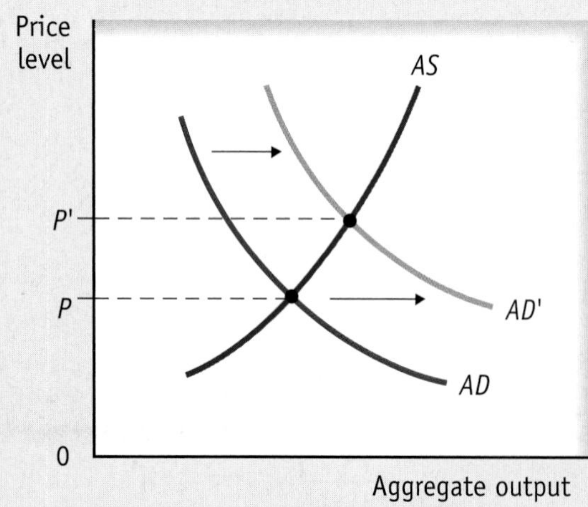

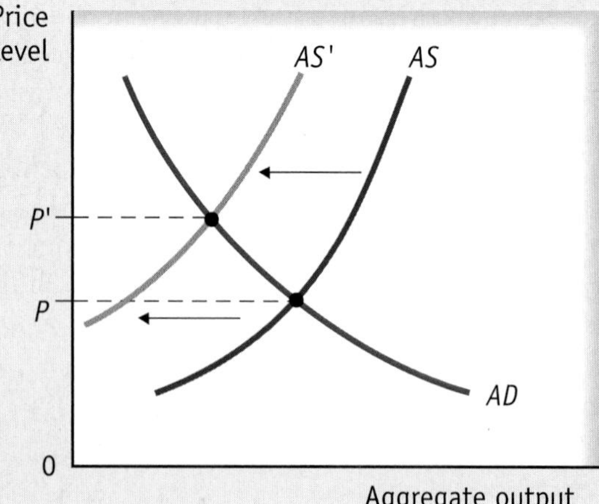

Panel (a) illustrates demand-pull inflation. An outward shift of the aggregate demand to *AD*' "pulls" the price level up from *P* to *P*'. Panel (b) shows cost-push inflation, in which a decrease in aggregate supply to *AS*' "pushes" the price level up from *P* to *P*'.

Alternatively, inflation can arise from reductions in aggregate supply, as shown in panel (b) of Exhibit 4, where a shift to the left in the aggregate supply curve raises the price level. For example, crop failures and decreases in the supply of oil reduced aggregate supply during 1974 and 1975, thereby raising the price level. Inflation stemming from decreases in aggregate supply is often called **cost-push inflation,** suggesting that increases in the cost of production *push up* the price level. Decreases in aggregate supply usually lead not only to a higher price level but also to a falling level of output, a combination that was identified in Chapter 5 as *stagflation*. Again, to generate sustained and continuous cost-push inflation, the aggregate supply curve would have to keep shifting to the left along a given aggregate demand curve.

Cost-push inflation A sustained rise in the price level caused by reductions in aggregate supply

A Historical Look at Inflation and the Price Level

The consumer price index is the measure of the price level you most often encounter, so we accord it more attention here. As you will learn in the next chapter, the **consumer price index,** or **CPI,** measures the cost of a fixed "market basket" of consumer goods and services over time. Exhibit 5 indicates the movement of the price level in the United States since 1900, as measured by the consumer price index. Panel (a) shows the *level* of prices in each year, which is measured by an index relative to the base period of 1982 to 1984. As you can see, the price level was not much higher in 1940 than in 1900. Since 1940, however, it has risen steadily, especially during the 1970s.

Consumer price index (CPI) A measure of the cost of a fixed "market basket" of consumer goods and services

Most people are concerned less about the level of prices than about the year-to-year changes in that level. Panel (b) shows the annual *rate of change* in the CPI, or the annual rate of *inflation* or *deflation,* since 1900. The decade of the 1970s was not the only period of high inflation during this century. Inflation also exceeded 10 percent from 1917 to 1920, in 1942, and in 1947—periods associated with world wars. Prior to the 1950s, inflation was primarily a war-related phenomenon and was usually followed by deflation. Such an inflation-deflation cycle has characterized war and peace stretching back over the last two centuries. In fact, between the Revolutionary War and World War II, the price level declined in about as many years as it increased. At the end of World War II, the price level was about where it had been at the end of the Civil War.

So changes in the price level are nothing new. The price level has varied for as far back as we have records. But prior to World War II, periods of inflation and deflation balanced out over the long run. Therefore, people had good reason to believe the dollar would retain its purchasing power when averaged over the long term. Since the end of World War II, however, the price level has increased by an average of 3.9 percent per year. That may not sound like much, but it translates into a *sevenfold* increase in the consumer price index since 1946. Put another way, today's dollar can purchase one-seventh the real goods and services that a 1946 dollar could purchase. *Inflation has reduced confidence in the value of the dollar over the long term.*

Anticipated Versus Unanticipated Inflation

What is the effect of inflation on the economy's performance? *Unanticipated inflation* creates more problems for the economy than does *anticipated inflation*. To the extent that inflation is higher or lower than anticipated, it arbitrarily creates

EXHIBIT 5

Consumer Price Index Since 1900

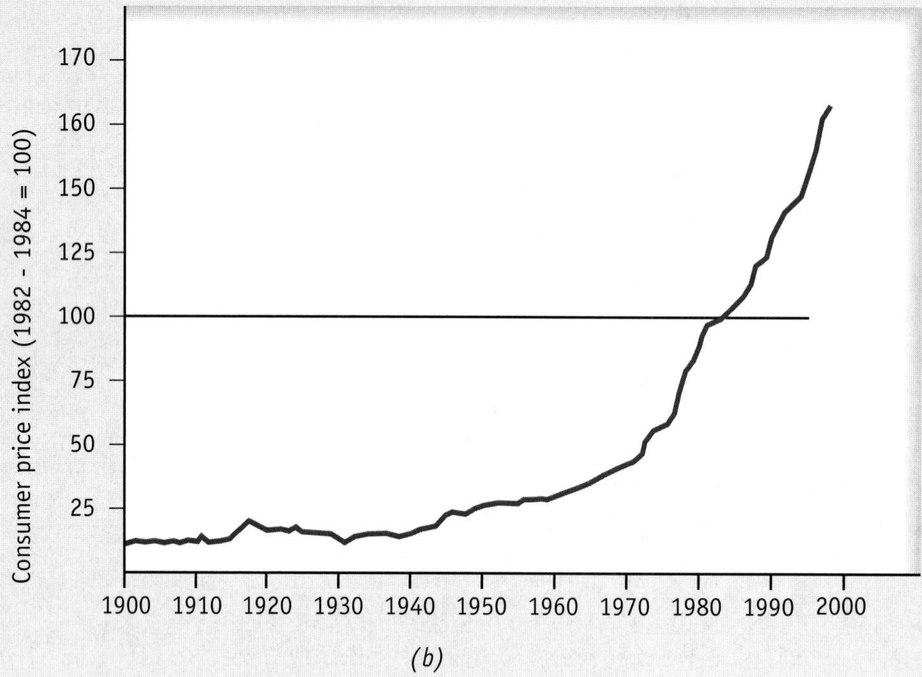

(b)

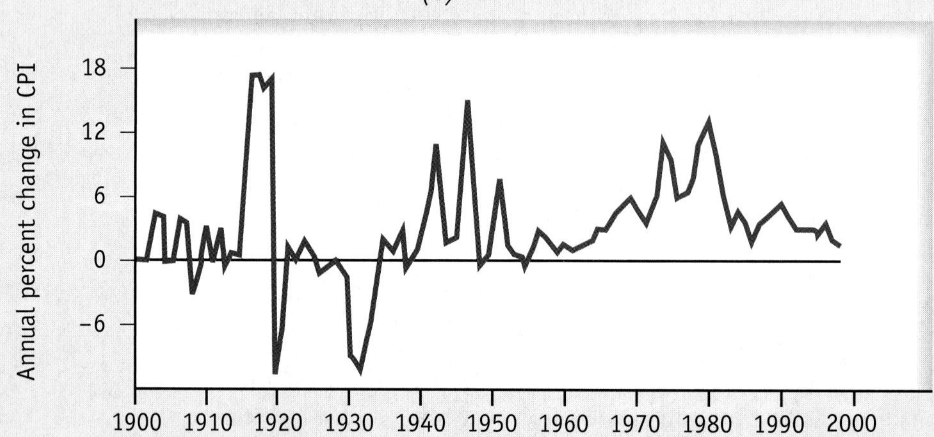

Panel (a) shows that, despite some fluctuations, the price level, as measured by the consumer price index, was not much higher in 1940 than it had been in 1900. Since 1940, the price level has risen almost every year. Panel (b) shows the annual rate of change in the price level. Between 1900 and 1946, the average annual inflation rate was 1.3 percent. Since 1946, the inflation rate has averaged 3.9 percent annually.

Sources: *Historical Statistics of the United States*, 1970; *Economic Report of the President*, February 1999; and the CPI home page of the U.S. Bureau of Labor Statistics at ftp://ftp.bls.gov/pub/specialrequests/cpi/cpiai.txt.

economic winners and losers. If inflation is higher than expected, the winners are all those who had contracted to buy for a price that does not reflect the higher inflation. For example, winners include firms that arranged to hire resources based on a lower expected inflation level. The losers are all those who agreed to sell at that price, including resource owners who agreed to sell based on a lower expected price level. If inflation is lower than expected, the situation is reversed: The winners are all those who contracted to sell at a price that anticipates higher inflation, and the losers are all those who contracted to buy at that price.

Suppose inflation next year is expected to be 3 percent, and you agree to work for a *nominal,* or money, wage that is 3 percent higher than your nominal wage this year. In this case you expect your *real* wage—that is, your wage measured in dollars of constant purchasing power—to remain unchanged. If inflation turns out to be 3 percent, you and your employer will both be satisfied with your nominal wage increase of 3 percent. If inflation turns out to be 5 percent, your real wage will fall, so you will be a loser and your employer will be a winner. If inflation turns out to be only 1 percent, your real wage will increase, so you will be a winner and your employer, a loser. *The arbitrary gains and losses arising from unanticipated changes in inflation are one reason that inflation is so unpopular.*

The Transaction Costs of Variable Inflation

During long periods of price stability, people correctly believe that they can predict future prices and can therefore plan accordingly. But when inflation accelerates unexpectedly, the purchasing power of the dollar declines and the future value of the dollar becomes more uncertain. Since the future is more cloudy, planning becomes more difficult. Uncertainty about inflation undermines the ability of money to serve as a link between the present and the future.

Firms that deal with the rest of the world face added complications, for they must not only plan for U.S. inflation, they must also anticipate how the value of the dollar might change relative to foreign currencies. Inflation uncertainty and the resulting exchange-rate uncertainty increase the difficulty of making international business decisions. In this more uncertain environment, managers must shift their attention from production to anticipating the effects of inflation and exchange-rate variations on the firm's finances. The *transaction costs* of drawing up contracts, particularly long-term contracts, increase as inflation becomes more unpredictable. Some economists suspect that the high and variable inflation rates in the United States during the 1970s and early 1980s contributed to the slower growth rate of the economy during that period.

Inflation Obscures Relative Price Changes

Even with no inflation, some prices would go up and some would go down, reflecting the healthy workings of supply and demand for different products. For example, during the last two decades, the price level in the United States more than doubled, yet the prices of color televisions, VCRs, pocket calculators, computers, and many other items declined steadily. Because the prices of various goods change by different amounts, *relative prices* change. Whereas the price level describes the terms at which some representative bundle of goods is exchanged for *money,* relative prices describe the terms at which individual goods are exchanged for *one another.*

Inflation does not necessarily cause the change in relative prices, but inflation can obscure these changes. During periods of volatile inflation, there is greater uncertainty about the price of one good relative to another—that is, about relative prices. In his Nobel prize address, Milton Friedman noted, "The more volatile the rate of general inflation, the harder it becomes to extract the signal about relative prices from the absolute prices; the broadcast about relative prices is, as it were, being jammed by the noise coming from the inflation broadcast."[2] But relative price changes are important for allocating the economy's resources efficiently.

If all prices moved together, producers could simply link the selling prices of their goods to the overall inflation rate. Since prices usually do not move in unison, however, tying a particular product's price to the overall inflation rate may result in a price that is too high or too low based on market conditions. The same is true of agreements by employers to raise wages in accord with inflation. If the price of an employer's product grows more slowly than the rate of inflation in the economy, the employer will be hard-pressed to increase wages by the rate of inflation. Consider the problem confronting oil producers who signed labor contracts agreeing to pay their workers cost-of-living wage increases. In certain years, such as 1998, those employers had to provide pay increases at a time when the price of oil was falling like a rock.

International Comparisons of Inflation

In 1998, the U.S. inflation rate as measured by consumer prices was 1.6 percent, compared to 0.2 percent in Japan, 0.2 percent in Germany, 0.2 percent in France, 2.4 percent in the United Kingdom, 1.5 percent in Italy, and 0.6 percent in Canada. Exhibit 6 presents the annual rates of change in consumer prices since 1967 in these seven industrialized countries (G-7) . Periods of U.S. recession are shaded. Note that all countries except Germany experienced a spike in inflation during the oil crisis of 1974. Since 1985, inflation has been relatively low, except in the United Kingdom, where the rate climbed above 10 percent during the first half of 1990. Inflation during the 1990s has been much higher in Argentina, Bolivia, Brazil, and Turkey, and in the emerging transitional economies of Eastern Europe and the former Soviet Union, especially Russia.

As with unemployment statistics, the quantity and quality of data collected to track movements in the price level vary across countries. Governments in less-developed countries sample fewer products and measure prices only in the capital city. Whereas some 400 items are sampled in the United States, as few as 30 might be sampled in some less-developed countries.

Inflation and Interest Rates

Interest The dollar amount paid by borrowers to lenders to forgo present consumption

Interest rate Interest per year as a percentage of the amount loaned

No discussion of inflation would be complete without some mention of the role of interest. **Interest** is the dollar amount paid by borrowers to lenders; lenders must be rewarded for forgoing present consumption. The **interest rate** is the interest per year as a percentage of the amount loaned. For example, if the interest rate is 5 percent, the interest is $5 per year for a $100 loan. The greater the interest rate, other things constant, the greater the reward for lending money. Thus the quantity of money people are willing to lend increases as the interest rate rises,

2 Milton Friedman, "Nobel Lecture: Inflation and Unemployment," *Journal of Political Economy* 85 (June 1977): p. 467.

EXHIBIT 6

International Consumer Prices

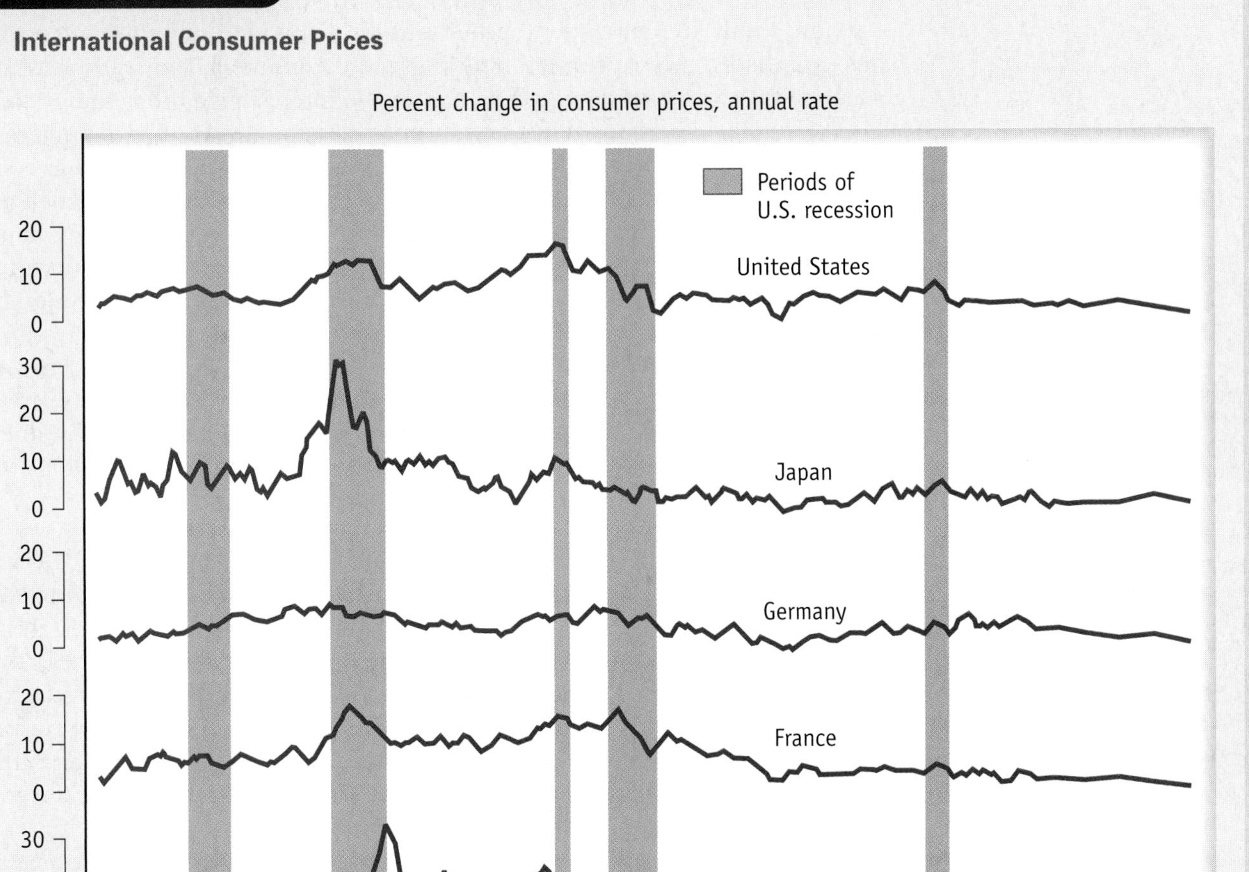

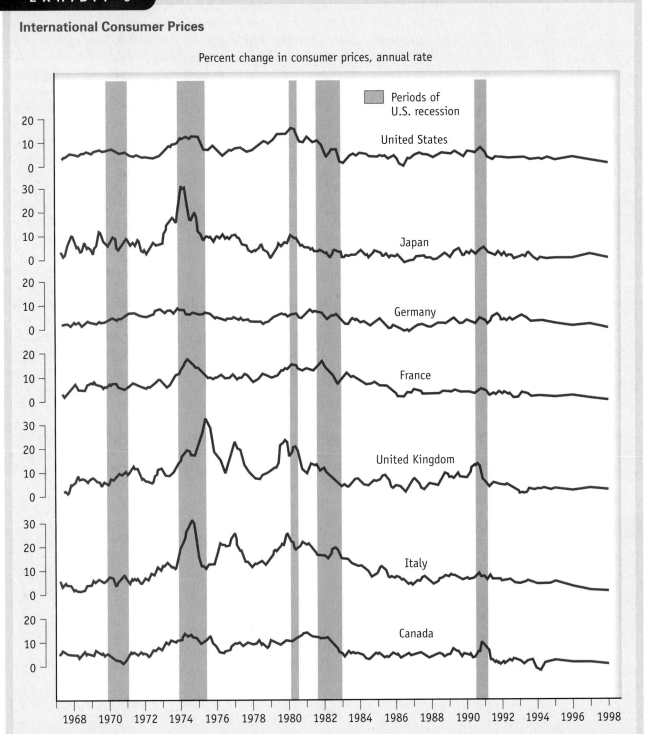

Source: For data through 1995, U.S. Department of Commerce, *Survey of Current Business* 75 (Nov./Dec. 1995): p. C-25. For data since 1995, *OECD Economic Outlook*, 63 (December 1998), Annex Table 16.

other things constant. The supply curve for the amount people are willing to lend, *loanable funds*, therefore slopes upward, as indicated by line S in Exhibit 7.

These funds are demanded by households, firms, and governments to finance purchases, such as homes, buildings, and machinery, and in the case of governments, to finance deficits. The higher the interest rate, other things constant, the higher the opportunity cost of borrowing funds. Hence, the quantity of loanable funds demanded decreases as the interest rate rises, other things constant. That is, the interest rate and the quantity of loanable funds demanded are inversely related. The demand curve for loans therefore slopes downward, as indicated by curve D in Exhibit 7. The downward-sloping demand curve for loanable funds and the upward-sloping supply curve intersect at the equilibrium point to yield the equilibrium nominal rate of interest, i.

Nominal rate of interest The interest rate expressed in current dollars as a percentage of the amount loaned; the interest rate on the loan agreement

Real rate of interest The interest rate expressed in dollars of constant purchasing power as a percentage of the amount loaned; the nominal rate of interest minus the inflation rate

The **nominal rate of interest** measures interest in terms of the current dollars paid. The nominal rate of interest is the rate that appears on the borrowing agreement; it is the rate discussed in the news media and is often of political significance. The **real rate of interest** is the nominal rate of interest minus the inflation rate:

$$\text{Real interest rate} = \text{nominal interest rate} - \text{inflation rate}$$

For example, if the nominal interest rate is 5 percent and the annual rate of inflation is 3 percent, the real interest rate is 2 percent. If there were no inflation, the nominal interest rate and the real interest rate would be identical. But with inflation, the real interest rate will be less than the nominal interest rate. Lenders and borrowers are concerned more about the real interest rate than the nominal interest rate. The real rate of interest, however, is known only after the fact—that is, only after inflation actually occurs. The nominal rate of interest is always positive; the real rate could turn out to be negative.

Because the future is uncertain, lenders and borrowers must form expectations about inflation, and base their willingness to lend and to borrow on these expectations. Other things constant, the higher the *expected* rate of inflation, the higher the nominal rate of interest that lenders require and that borrowers are

EXHIBIT 7

The Market for Loanable Funds

The upward-sloping supply curve, S, shows that more funds are supplied to financial markets at higher interest rates. The downward-sloping demand curve, D, shows that the quantity of loanable funds demanded is greater at lower interest rates. The two curves intersect to determine the equilibrium interest rate, i.

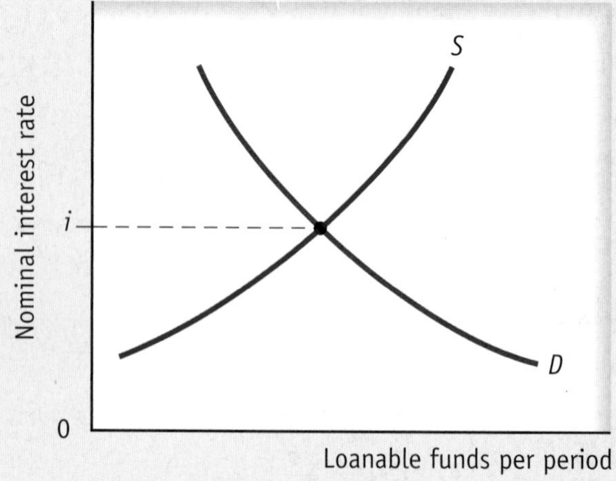

willing to pay. Lenders and borrowers base their decisions on the *expected* real interest rate, which equals the nominal rate of interest minus the expected inflation rate.[3]

Why Is Inflation So Unpopular?

Whenever the price level increases, more money must be spent to buy the same goods and services. If you think of inflation only in terms of spending, you consider only the problem of paying those higher prices. But if you think of inflation in terms of the higher money incomes that result, you see that higher prices mean higher receipts for resource suppliers. When viewed from the income side, inflation is not so bad.

If every higher price is received by some resource supplier, why are people so troubled by inflation? Whereas people view their higher incomes as well-deserved rewards for their labor, they see inflation as a penalty that unjustly robs them of purchasing power. Most people do not stop to realize that, unless their labor productivity increases, higher wages *must* result in higher prices. Prices and wages are simply two sides of the same coin. To the extent that nominal wages on average keep up with inflation, most workers do not suffer a loss of real income as a result of inflation. In a recent survey of 1,000 adults, more than two-thirds believed that price increases are due to companies trying to manipulate their prices to increase profits.[4] Fewer than one-third attributed price increases to the workings of supply and demand.

Presidents Ford and Carter could not control inflation and were turned out of office. Inflation slowed significantly during the Reagan administration, and President Reagan was reelected in a landslide, even though the level of unemployment was higher during his first term than during President Carter's tenure. During the 1988 presidential election, George Bush won in part by reminding voters what the rate of inflation was in 1980, the last time a Democrat had been president. Since then, inflation has been so low that it has not been a campaign issue.

Although inflation affects everyone, it hits hardest those whose incomes are fixed in nominal terms. For example, pensions are often fixed and are eroded by inflation, although the benefits paid by the largest pension program, Social Security, are adjusted annually for changes in the CPI. Retirees who rely on fixed nominal interest income also see their incomes eroded by inflation.

In summary, to the extent that the level and composition of inflation are fully anticipated by all market participants, inflation is of less concern in macroeconomic analysis than unanticipated inflation. *Unanticipated inflation arbitrarily redistributes income and wealth from one group to another, reduces the ability to make long-term plans, and forces buyers and sellers to pay more attention to prices.* The more variable and unpredictable inflation is, the greater the difficulty of negotiating long-term contracts. The overall productivity of the economy falls, because people must spend more time coping with the uncertainty created by inflation, leaving less time for production or consumption.

---

3 Although the discussion has implied that there is only one rate of interest, there are actually many rates. Rates differ depending on such factors as the risk, the maturity of different loans, and tax treatment of the interest.

4 As reported in Robert J. Blendon, et al., "Bridging the Gap Between the Public's and Economists' Views of the Economy," *Journal of Economic Perspectives,* Vol. 11 (Summer 1997), p. 116.

CONCLUSION

This chapter has focused on two macroeconomic problems: unemployment and inflation. Although we have discussed them separately, they are related in a variety of ways, as we will see in later chapters. Politicians sometimes add the unemployment rate to the rate of inflation to come up with what they refer to as the "misery index." In 1980, for example, an unemployment rate of 7.1 percent combined with a CPI increase of 13.6 percent to yield a misery index of 20.6—a number that explains why President Carter was not reelected that year. By 1984 the misery index had dropped to 11.8, and by 1988 to 9.6; Republicans retained the White House in both elections. In 1992, the index climbed slightly to 10.4 percent, an increase that spelled trouble for President Bush. And in 1996, the index fell back to 8.4 percent, assuring President Clinton's reelection.

In Chapter 8, we will address how to measure economic activity and how to adjust data for inflation. In later chapters, we will develop aggregate demand and aggregate supply curves to build a model of the economy. Once we have some idea how a healthy economy works, we can consider the policy options in the face of high unemployment, high inflation, or both.

SUMMARY

1. The unemployment rate equals the number of people looking for work divided by the number in the labor force. The overall unemployment rate masks differences in rates among particular groups. The lowest rate is among white adults; the highest rate is among black teenagers.

2. There are four types of unemployment. Frictional unemployment arises because employers and qualified job seekers need time to find one another. Structural unemployment arises because changes in taste, technology, taxes, and competition reduce the demand for certain skills. Seasonal unemployment stems from the effects of the weather and the calendar on certain industries, such as construction and agriculture. Cyclical unemployment results from the fluctuations in employment over the business cycle. Full employment occurs when cyclical unemployment is zero.

3. Unemployment imposes both an economic and a psychological burden on the unemployed. For some people, this burden is reduced by an employed spouse and by unemployment insurance, which typically replaces more than half of their take-home pay. Unemployment insurance provides a safety net for some people who are unemployed, but it also may reduce their incentive to find work.

4. Inflation is a sustained rise in the average level of prices. Demand-pull inflation results from an increase in aggregate demand. Cost-push inflation results from a decrease in aggregate supply. Until World War II, both increases and decreases in the price level were common; but since then the price level has steadily increased.

5. Anticipated inflation causes fewer distortions in the economy than does unanticipated inflation. Unanticipated inflation arbitrarily creates winners and losers, and forces people to spend more time and energy coping with the effects of inflation. The negative effects of high and variable inflation on an economy's productivity can be observed in countries that have experienced hyperinflation, such as Brazil.

6. Because not all prices change by the same amount during inflationary periods, people have difficulty keeping track of relative prices. Inflation fuels uncertainty about relative prices, making long-term planning more costly and more risky.

7. The intersection of the supply curve and demand curve for loanable funds indicates the equilibrium interest rate. The nominal rate of interest equals the real rate of interest plus the rate of inflation. The higher the expected inflation rate, the higher the nominal rate of interest. Borrowers and lenders base decisions on the expected real rate of interest.

QUESTIONS FOR REVIEW

1. *(Labor Force)* Refer to Exhibit 1 in the chapter to determine whether the following statements are true or false.
   a. Some people who are officially unemployed are not in the labor force.
   b. Some people in the labor force are not working.
   c. Everyone who is not unemployed is in the labor force.
   d. Some people who are not working are not unemployed.
2. *(Unemployment in Various Groups)* Does the overall unemployment rate provide an accurate picture of the impact of unemployment on all U.S. population groups?
3. *(Case**Study**: Poor King Coal)* Is the unemployment in McDowell County primarily frictional, seasonal, structural, or cyclical? Explain your answer, using the text definitions for these categories of unemployment.
4. *(The Meaning of Full Employment)* When the economy is at full employment, is the unemployment rate at 0 percent? Why or why not? How would a more generous unemployment insurance system affect the full employment figure?
5. *(International Comparisons of Unemployment)* In recent years how has the U.S. unemployment rate compared with unemployment rates in other industrial economies? Why should we be careful in comparing unemployment across countries? (If you wish to look at the latest data, refer to the Bureau of Labor Statistics' Web page on International Comparisons of Foreign Labor Statistics at http://stats.bls.gov/flsdata.htm.
6. *(Official Unemployment Figures)* Explain why most experts believe that official U.S. data underestimate the actual rate of unemployment. What factors could make the official rate overstate the actual unemployment rate?
7. ***(CaseStudy:** Wild Inflation in Brazil)* In countries such as Brazil and Russia, which have had problems with high inflation, the increased use of another country's currency (such as the U.S. dollar) is common. Why do you suppose this occurs?
8. *(Source of Inflation)* What are the two sources of inflation? How would you illustrate them graphically?
9. *(Anticipated versus Unanticipated Inflation)* If actual inflation exceeds anticipated inflation, who will lose purchasing power and who will gain?
10. *(Inflation and Relative Price Changes)* What does the consumer price index measure? Does the index measure changes in relative prices? Why, or why not?
11. *(Inflation and Interest Rates)* For much of 1998, the spread between short- and long-term interest rates on U.S. government debt was at a record low. What does this say about expectations of inflation in the near term versus expectations for the distant future?
12. *(Inflation and Interest Rates)* Explain as carefully as you can why borrowers would be willing to pay a higher rate of interest if they expected the inflation rate to increase in the future.
13. *(Inflation)* Why is a relatively constant inflation rate less harmful to an economy than a rate that fluctuates a lot?

PROBLEMS AND EXERCISES

14. *(Measuring Unemployment)* Determine the impact on each of the following if 2 million formerly unemployed workers decide to return to school full time and stop looking for work:
    a. The labor force participation rate
    b. The size of the labor force
    c. The unemployment rate
15. *(Measuring Unemployment)* Suppose that the U.S. noninstitutional adult population is 206 million and the labor force participation rate is 67 percent.
    a. What is the size of the U.S. labor force?
    b. If 74 million adults are not working, what is the unemployment rate?
16. *(Types of Unemployment)* Determine whether each of the following would be considered frictional, structural, seasonal, or cyclical unemployment:
    a. A UPS employee who was hired for the Christmas season is laid off after Christmas.
    b. A worker is laid off due to reduced aggregate demand in the economy.

c. A worker in the audiocassette manufacturing industry becomes unemployed as compact disks replace cassettes.

d. A new college graduate is looking for employment during the summer after graduation.

17. *(Inflation)* Here are some recent data on the U.S. consumer price index:

Year	CPI	Year	CPI	Year	CPI
1985	107.6	1990	130.7	1995	152.4
1986	109.6	1991	136.2	1996	156.9
1987	113.6	1992	140.3	1997	160.5
1988	118.3	1993	144.5	1998	163.0
1989	124.0	1994	148.2		

Compute the inflation rate for each year 1986–1998 and determine which years were years of inflation. In which years did deflation occur? In which years did disinflation occur? Was there hyperinflation in any year?

18. *(Sources of Inflation)* Using the concepts of aggregate supply and aggregate demand, explain why inflation usually accelerates during wartime.

19. *(Inflation and Interest Rates)* Using a supply-demand diagram for loanable funds (like Exhibit 7), show what happens to the nominal interest rate and the equilibrium quantity of loans when both borrowers and lenders increase their estimates of the expected inflation rate from 5 percent to 10 percent.

EXPERIENTIAL EXERCISES

20. *(Measuring Unemployment)* The chapter explains the definitions the government employs in measuring unemployment. Interview 10 members of your class to determine their labor market status—employed, unemployed, or not in the labor force. Include yourself, and then compute the unemployment rate and the labor force participation rate for these 11 people.

21. *(International Comparisons of Inflation)* In recent years how has the U.S. inflation rate compared with rates in other industrial economies? Why should we be careful in comparing inflation rates across countries? The Federal Reserve Bank of St. Louis maintains a page devoted to international economic trends: http://www.stls.frb.org/publications/iet/. Choose two countries and compare their recent inflation experiences. (If you have an Adobe Acrobat reader, you can look at bar charts of the data.)

22. *(Wall Street Journal)* Scan the "Economy" page in the First Section of today's *Wall Street Journal*. You are almost sure to find a discussion of a policy proposal that will affect unemployment, inflation, or both. Use the aggregate demand and supply model to describe the effect of the proposal—if enacted—on the U.S. unemployment and inflation rates.

CHAPTER

8

Measuring Economic Aggregates and the Circular Flow of Income

How do we keep score of the most complex economy in the history of the world? What's gross about the gross domestic product? What's domestic about it? If you make yourself a tuna sandwich, how much does your effort add to the gross domestic product? Since prices change over time, how can we compare the economy's production in one year with that in other years? Answers to these and other questions are addressed in this chapter, which introduces an economic scorecard for tracking an $8 trillion economy.

Although Americans account for only 5 percent of the world's population, they produce 20 percent of the world's output. In this chapter you will learn how economists keep track of the billions of economic transactions that constitute the U.S. economy. The scorecard is the national income accounting system,

Visit the McEachern Interactive Study Center for this chapter at ://mcisc.swcollege.com

which reflects the performance of the economy as a whole by reducing a huge network of economic activity to a few aggregate measures. This chapter focuses on the most important measure of economic activity: gross domestic product, or GDP, a term already introduced.

As you shall see, the value of total output can be measured either from the total spending on aggregate output or from the total income derived from producing that output. We will examine both approaches, see why they are equivalent, and learn how to adjust for the effects of inflation over time. The major components and important equalities built into the national income accounts are offered here as another way of understanding how the economy works—not as a foreign language to be mastered before the next exam. The emphasis is more on economic intuition than on accounting precision. The main part of this chapter provides the background sufficient for later chapters. More details about the national income accounts are offered in the appendix to this chapter. Topics discussed in this chapter include:

- Gross domestic product
- National income accounts
- Expenditure and income approaches
- Circular flow of income and expenditure
- Leakages and injections
- Limitations of national income accounting
- Consumer price index
- GDP price index

THE PRODUCT OF A NATION

How do we measure the economy's performance? During much of the 17th and 18th centuries, when the dominant economic policy was mercantilism, many thought that economic prosperity was best measured by the *stock* of precious metals a nation accumulated. This policy of mercantilism led to tariffs and quotas aimed at restricting imports, which had the unintended consequence of limiting the gains from comparative advantage and trade.

In the latter half of the 18th century, Francois Quesnay became the first to measure economic activity as a *flow*. In 1758 he published his *Tableau Économique*, which described the *circular flow* of output and income among different sectors of the economy. His insight was probably inspired by his knowledge of the circular flow of blood in the body—Quesnay was the court physician to King Louis XV of France.

Rough measures of national income were developed in England some two centuries ago, but detailed calculations built up from microeconomic data were refined in the United States during the Great Depression. The resulting *national income accounting system* organizes huge quantities of data collected from a variety of sources around the country. These data are summarized, assembled into a coherent framework, and reported periodically by the federal government. The U.S. national income accounts are the most widely reported and among the most highly regarded in the world and have earned their developer, Simon Kuznets, a Nobel prize.

National Income Accounts

How do the national income accounts keep track of the economy's incredible variety of goods and services, from hiking boots to guitar lessons? As you learned earlier, the *gross domestic product*, or GDP, measures the market value of all final goods and services produced during a year by resources located in the United States, regardless of who owns those resources. For example, GDP includes U.S. production by foreign firms, but excludes foreign production by U.S. firms.[1]

The national income accounts are based on the idea that *one person's spending is another person's receipts.* This idea that spending equals receipts is expressed in a double-entry bookkeeping system in which spending on aggregate output is recorded on one side of the ledger and resource income is recorded on the other side. GDP can be measured either by total spending on U.S. production or by total income received from that production. The **expenditure approach** involves adding up the aggregate expenditure on all final goods and services produced during the year. The **income approach** involves adding up the aggregate income earned during the year by those who produce that output.

Expenditure approach to GDP A method of calculating GDP by adding up spending on all final goods and services produced during the year

Income approach to GDP A method of calculating GDP by adding up all payments to owners of resources used to produce output during the year

Gross domestic product includes only **final goods and services,** which are goods and services sold to the final, or ultimate, user. A toothbrush, a pair of contact lenses, and a bus ride are examples of final goods and services. Whether a sale is to the final user often depends on who buys the product. Your purchase of chicken from a grocer is reflected in GDP. When a KFC franchise purchases chicken, however, this transaction is not directly recorded in GDP because the franchise is not the final consumer. Only after the chicken is prepared, deep fried, and sold to consumers is a sale recorded as part of GDP.

Final goods and services Goods and services sold to final, or ultimate, users

Intermediate goods and services are those purchased for additional processing and resale, such as the chicken purchased by KFC. This additional processing may be imperceptible, as when a grocer buys canned goods to stock the shelves. Or the intermediate goods can be dramatically altered, as when an artist transforms paint and canvas into a work of beauty.

Intermediate goods and services Goods and services purchased for further reprocessing and resale

Sales of intermediate goods and services are excluded from GDP to avoid the problem of **double counting,** which is counting an item's value more than once. For example, suppose the grocer buys a can of tuna for \$0.60 and sells it for \$1.00. If GDP included both the intermediate transaction of \$0.60 and the final transaction of \$1.00, that can of tuna would be counted twice in GDP, and its recorded value of \$1.60 would exceed its final value by \$0.60. Hence, the gross domestic product counts only the final value of the product. GDP also ignores the secondhand value of used cars, existing homes, and used textbooks. These goods were counted in GDP the year they were produced. (But just as the value of services provided by the grocer is included in GDP, so is the value of services provided by used-car dealers, realtors, and booksellers.)

Double counting The mistake of including the value of intermediate goods plus the value of final goods in gross domestic product; counting the value of the same good more than once

GDP Based on the Expenditure Approach

As noted already, one way to measure the value of GDP is to add up all spending on final goods and services produced in the economy during the year. The easiest way to understand the spending approach to GDP is to divide aggregate expenditure into its four components: consumption, investment, government purchases, and net exports. We will discuss each in turn.

Consumption, or more specifically, *personal consumption expenditures*, consists of purchases of final goods and services by households during the year.

Consumption All household purchases of final goods and services

1 Prior to 1992, the federal government's measure of output was gross national product, or GNP, which measures the market value of all goods and services produced by resources supplied by U.S. residents and firms, regardless of the location of the resources.

Consumption is the easiest to understand and the largest spending category, accounting during the 1990s for about two-thirds of U.S. GDP. Along with services such as dry cleaning, haircuts, and air travel, consumption includes purchases of nondurable goods, such as soap and soup, and durable goods, such as televisions and furniture. Durable goods are those expected to last at least three years.

Investment The purchase of new plants, new equipment, new buildings, new residences, and net additions to inventories

Physical capital Manufactured items used to produce goods and services

Residential construction Building new permanent homes or dwelling places

Inventories Producers' stocks of finished or in-process goods

Investment, or more specifically, *gross private domestic investment*, consists of spending on new capital goods and additions to inventories. More generally, investment consists of spending on current production that is not used for current consumption. The most important category of investment is new **physical capital,** such as new buildings and new machinery purchased by firms and used to produce goods and services. Investment also includes purchases of new **residential construction.** Although investment fluctuates from year to year, on average it accounted for about one-seventh of U.S. GDP during the 1990s.

Changes in firms' inventories are another category of investment. **Inventories** are stocks of goods in process, such as computer parts, and stocks of finished goods, such as new computers awaiting sale. Inventories help manufacturers deal with unexpected changes in the supply of their resources or in the demand for their products. A *net* increase in inventories during the year counts as investment, since inventories are not used for current consumption. Conversely, a net decrease in inventories during the year counts as negative investment, or *disinvestment*, since net inventory reductions represent the sale of output already credited to a prior year's GDP. Disinvestment reduces investment.

Investment excludes household purchases of durable goods, such as furniture and major appliances (which are counted as consumption). Investment also excludes purchases of *existing* buildings, machines, and financial assets, such as stocks and bonds. Existing buildings and machines were counted in GDP when they were built. Purchases of stocks and bonds sometimes provide firms the funds to invest, but stocks and bonds are not themselves investments.

Government purchases Spending for goods and services by all levels of government; government outlays minus transfer payments

Government purchases, or more specifically, *government consumption and gross investment*, include spending by all levels of government for goods and services—from clearing snowy roads to clearing court dockets, from library books to the librarian's pay. Government purchases accounted for a little less than one-fifth of U.S. GDP during the 1990s. Government purchases, and therefore GDP, do not include transfer payments, such as Social Security, welfare benefits, and unemployment insurance. Such payments reflect an outright grant from the government to recipients and are not true purchases by the government or true earnings by the recipients.

Net exports The value of a country's exports minus the value of its imports

The final component of aggregate expenditure results from the interaction between the U.S. economy and the rest of the world. **Net exports** equal the value of U.S. exports of goods and services minus the value of U.S. imports of goods and services. Net exports include the value of not only *merchandise* trade—that is, goods, or stuff you can drop on your feet—but also services, or so-called *invisibles*, such as tourism, insurance, accounting, and consulting. Since spending on consumption, investment, and government purchases includes purchases of foreign goods and services, that spending does not count as part of U.S. GDP, so we subtract imports from exports to get the net effect of the rest of the world on GDP. The value of U.S. imports has exceeded the value of our exports nearly every year for the last several decades, meaning U.S. net exports have been negative.

With the expenditure approach, the nation's **aggregate expenditure** equals the sum of consumption, C, investment, I, government purchases, G, and net exports, which is the value of exports, X, minus the value of imports, M, or $(X - M)$. Summing these spending components yields aggregate expenditure, or GDP:

Aggregate expenditure Total spending on final goods and services during a given time period, usually a year

$$C + I + G + (X - M) = \text{Aggregate expenditure} = \text{GDP}$$

GDP Based on the Income Approach

The expenditure approach sums, or aggregates, spending on production. The income approach sums, or aggregates, income arising from that production. Again, double-entry bookkeeping ensures that the value of aggregate output equals the aggregate income paid for resources used to produce that output: the wages, interest, rent, and profit arising from production. The price of a Hershey Bar® reflects income earned by all resource suppliers who bring the candy bar to the grocer's shelf. **Aggregate income** equals the sum of all the income earned by resource suppliers in the economy. Thus, we can say that

Aggregate income The sum of all income earned by resource suppliers in an economy during a given time period

$$\text{Aggregate expenditure} = \text{GDP} = \text{Aggregate income}$$

A finished product is usually processed by several firms on its way to the consumer. A wooden desk, for example, starts as raw timber, which is usually cut by one firm, milled by another, made into a desk by a third, and retailed by a fourth. Double counting is avoided either by including only the market value of the desk when it is sold to the final user or by *calculating the value added at each stage of production*. The **value added** by each firm equals that firm's selling price minus the amount paid for inputs from other firms. The value added at each stage represents income to resource suppliers at that stage. *The sum of the value added at all stages equals the market value of the final good, and the sum of the value added for all final goods and services equals the GDP based on the income approach.* For example, suppose you buy a wooden desk for $200, which is the final market value added directly into GDP. Consider the history of that desk. Suppose the tree that gave its life for your studies was cut into a log that was sold to a miller for $20. That log was milled into lumber and sold for $50 to a manufacturer, who assembled your desk and sold it for $120 to a retailer, who sold it to you for $200.

Value added The difference at each stage of production between the value of a product and cost of intermediate goods bought from other firms

Column (1) of Exhibit 1 lists the selling price at each stage of production. If all of these transactions were added together, the desk would add a total of $390 to GDP. To avoid double counting, we include only the value added at each stage of production, listed in column (3) as the difference between the purchase price and the selling price. Again, *the value added at each stage equals the income to all who supplied resources at that stage.* For example, the $80 in value added by the retailer represents income to all who contribute resources at that final stage, from the newspaper that carries the retailer's advertising and the electric utility that lights the store showroom to the trucker who provides "free delivery" of your desk. The value added at all stages totals $200, which is both the final market value of the desk and the total income earned by all resource suppliers along the way.

EXHIBIT 1

Computation of Value Added for a New Desk

Stage of Production	Sale Value (1)	Cost of Intermediate Goods (2)	Value Added (3)
Logger	$ 20	—	$ 20
Miller	50	$ 20	30
Manufacturer	120	50	70
Retailer	200	120	80
			$200

To reinforce your understanding of the equality of income and spending, let's return to a familiar tool, the circular flow model.

THE CIRCULAR FLOW OF INCOME AND EXPENDITURE

Chapter 4 introduced the circular flow of money and products among the four economic decision makers in the economy. In this section we utilize the same idea but focus on the accounting equality of aggregate income and aggregate expenditure. The circular flow model shown in Exhibit 2 details the flow of income and spending in the economy. The main stream flows clockwise around the circle, first as income from firms to households (in the lower half of the circle), then as spending from households back to firms (in the upper half of the circle). For each flow of money there is an equal and opposite flow of goods or resources.

The Income Half of the Circular Flow

In the process of developing a circular flow model of income and expenditure we must make some simplifying assumptions that allow us to depict the flows without complicating the model so much that we lose sight of the big picture. Specifically, by assuming that capital does not wear out (no depreciation) and that firms pay out all profits to firms' owners (firms retain no earnings), we can say that *GDP equals aggregate income*.

The circular flow is a continuous process, but the logic of the model is clearest if we begin at juncture (1) in Exhibit 2, where firms in the United States make production decisions. After all, production must occur before output is sold and income is earned. As Henry Ford said, "It is not the employer who pays the wages—the employer only handles the money. It is the product that pays wages." Production of aggregate output, or GDP, gives rise to an equal amount of aggregate income. Households supply their labor, capital, land, and entrepreneurial ability to firms and get paid wages, interest, rent, and profit.

Thus, at juncture (1), aggregate output equals aggregate income. But not all that income is available to households. At juncture (2) governments collect taxes. Some of these tax dollars are returned to the income stream as transfer payments at juncture (3). By subtracting taxes and adding transfers, we transform aggregate

EXHIBIT 2

The Circular Flow of Income and Expenditure

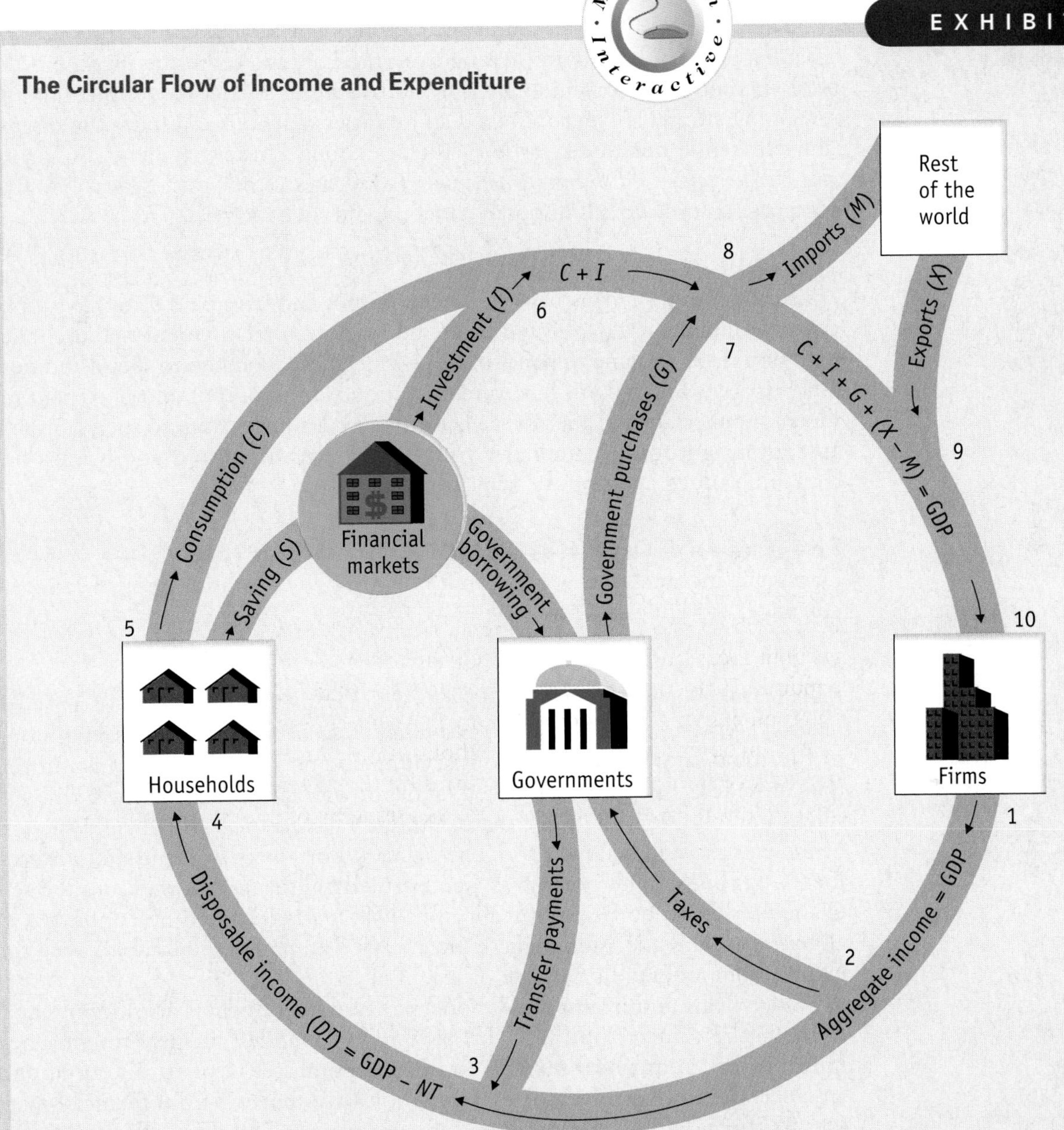

The circular flow diagram captures important relationships in the economy. The bottom half of the diagram depicts the income flow arising from production. At juncture (1) GDP equals aggregate income. Taxes leak out of the flow at point (2), but transfer payments augment the flow at point (3). Taxes minus transfer payments equals net taxes, *NT*. Aggregate income minus taxes plus transfer payments equals disposable income, which flows to households at juncture (4).

The top half of the diagram shows the flow of expenditures on GDP. At juncture (5) households split their disposable income between consumption and saving. The saving stream flows into financial markets, where it is channeled to government borrowing and to business investment. At point (6) the injection of investment augments the spending stream. At juncture (7) government purchases represent another injection into the circular flow. At point (8) imports are a leakage of spending, and at point (9) exports are an injection of spending into the circular flow. Consumption plus investment plus government purchases plus exports minus imports, or net exports, equals the aggregate expenditure of GDP received by firms at point (10).

Disposable income (DI) The income households have available to spend or save after paying taxes and receiving transfer payments

income into **disposable income,** or **DI,** which flows to households at juncture (4). Disposable income is take-home pay, which households can spend or save.

The bottom half of this circular flow is the *income half* because it focuses on what happens to the income arising from production. Aggregate income is the total income from producing GDP, and disposable income is the income remaining after taxes are subtracted and transfers added. To simplify the discussion, we define **net taxes,** or ***NT,*** as taxes minus transfer payments. So *disposable income equals GDP minus net taxes.* To put it another way, we can say that aggregate income equals disposable income plus net taxes:

Net taxes (NT) Taxes minus transfer payments

$$\text{GDP} = \text{Aggregate income} = DI + NT$$

At juncture (4), firms have produced output and have paid resource suppliers; governments have collected taxes and made transfer payments. Households, with disposable income in hand, must now decide how much to spend and how much to save. Since firms have already produced the output and have paid resource suppliers, firms await to see how much consumers want to spend. Should any output go unsold, suppliers will be stuck with it; unsold goods must become unplanned additions to firm inventories.

The Expenditure Half of the Circular Flow

Disposable income splits at juncture (5). Part flows to consumption, C, and the remainder to saving, S. Thus,

$$DI = C + S$$

Spending on consumption remains in the circular flow and represents the most important source of aggregate expenditure, about two-thirds of the total. Household saving flows to **financial markets,** which consist of banks and other financial institutions that provide a link between savers and borrowers. For simplicity, Exhibit 2 shows households as the only savers, although governments, firms, and the rest of the world could be savers too. The primary borrowers are firms and governments, but households borrow as well, particularly for new homes, and the rest of the world also borrows. In reality, financial markets should be connected to all four economic decision makers, but we have simplified the flows to keep the exhibit from looking like a plate of spaghetti.

Financial markets Banks and other institutions that facilitate the flow of loanable funds from savers to borrowers

Since firms in our simplified model pay resource suppliers an amount equal to the entire value of output, firms have no revenue left for investment. They must borrow in financial markets to finance purchases of physical capital plus any increases in their inventories. Households also borrow from financial markets to purchase new homes. Therefore, investment, I, consists of spending on new capital by firms, including inventory changes, plus spending on residential construction. Investment spending enters the circular flow at juncture (6), so aggregate spending at that point totals $C + I$.

Governments must also borrow whenever they incur deficits, that is, whenever their total outlays—transfer payments plus purchases of goods and services—exceed their revenues. Government purchases of goods and services, represented by G, enter the spending stream in the upper half of the circular flow at juncture (7). Remember that G *excludes* transfer payments, which already entered the income stream at juncture (3).

Some spending by households, firms, and governments goes for imports. Since spending on imports, M, flows to foreign producers, not U.S. producers, import spending leaks from the circular flow at juncture (8). But the rest of the world also buys U.S. products, so foreign spending on U.S. exports, X, enters the circular flow at juncture (9). The net impact of the *rest of the world* on aggregate expenditure equals exports minus imports, or net exports, $X - M$, which can be positive, negative, or zero.

The upper half of the circular flow can be viewed as the *expenditure half* because it focuses on the components that make up aggregate expenditure: consumption, C, investment, I, government purchases, G, and net exports, $X - M$. Aggregate expenditure flows into firms at juncture (10). Total spending on U.S. output equals the market value of aggregate output in the economy, or GDP. In other words,

$$C + I + G + (X - M) = \text{Aggregate expenditure} = \text{GDP}$$

Leakages Equal Injections

Let's step back now to grasp the big picture. In the lower half of the circular flow, aggregate income equals disposable income plus net taxes. In the upper half, aggregate expenditure equals the total spending on U.S. output. *The aggregate income arising from production equals the aggregate expenditure on that production.* This is the first accounting identity. Thus, aggregate income (disposable income plus net taxes) equals aggregate expenditure (spending by each sector), or

$$DI + NT = C + I + G + (X - M)$$
$$\text{Aggregate income} = \text{Aggregate expenditure}$$

Since disposable income equals consumption plus saving, we can substitute $C + S$ for DI in the above equation to yield

$$C + S + NT = C + I + G + (X - M)$$

After subtracting C from both sides and adding M to both sides, the equation reduces to

$$S + NT + M = I + G + X$$

Note that at various points around the circular flow, some of the flow leaks from the main stream. Saving, S, net taxes, NT, and imports, M, are **leakages** from the circular flow. **Injections** into the main stream also occur at various points around the circular flow. Investment, I, government purchases, G, and exports, X, are *injections* of spending into the circular flow. As you can see from the preceding equation, *leakages from the circular flow equal injections into that flow.* This leakages-injections equation demonstrates a second accounting identity based on the principles of double-entry bookkeeping.

Leakage Any diversion of income from the domestic spending stream; includes saving, taxes, and imports

Injection Any payment of income other than by firms or any spending other than by domestic households; includes investment, government purchases, transfer payments, and exports

Planned Investment Versus Actual Investment

As we have learned already, at juncture (1) in the circular flow, firms produce the aggregate output expected to meet the demand. But aggregate expenditure may not match production. Suppose, for example, that firms produce \$8.0 trillion in output, but the spending components add up to only \$7.8 trillion. Firms will end up with $0.2 trillion in unsold products, which must be added to their inventories. Since increases in inventories are counted as investment, *actual* investment turns out to be $0.2 trillion greater than firms had *planned*.

Planned investment The amount of investment firms plan to undertake during a year

Actual investment The amount of investment actually undertaken during a year; equals planned investment plus unplanned changes in inventories

Note the distinction here between **planned investment,** the amount firms plan to invest before they know how much output will be sold, and **actual investment,** which includes both planned investment and any unplanned changes in inventories. Unplanned increases in inventories will cause firms to smarten up and decrease their production next time around so as not to get stuck with more unsold goods. Only when there are no unplanned changes in inventories will the level of GDP be at what we will call an *equilibrium level*—that is, *a level that can be sustained period after period*. Only in equilibrium will planned investment equal actual investment.

The relationship between actual and planned investment will be examined more closely in Chapter 10. For now, you need only understand that the national income accounting system reflects *actual* investment, not necessarily *planned* investment. *The national income accounts always look at economic activity after transactions have occurred—after the dust has settled.* Although planned leakages may differ from planned injections, actual leakages must always equal actual injections.

LIMITATIONS OF NATIONAL INCOME ACCOUNTING

Imagine the difficulty of developing an accounting system that must capture the subtleties of a complex and dynamic economy, such as the United States'. In the interest of clarity and simplicity, some features of the economy are neglected; others receive perhaps too much weight. In this section, we examine some limitations of the national income accounting system, beginning with productive activity that is not captured by GDP.

Some Production Is Not Included in GDP

With some minor exceptions, GDP includes only those products that are sold in markets, thereby neglecting all "do-it-yourself" household production. Household services not purchased in the market are excluded from GDP—child care, meal preparation, house cleaning, and do-it-yourself home repair. Thus an economy in which householders are largely self-sufficient will have a lower GDP than will an otherwise similar economy in which households specialize and sell goods and services to one another.

During the 1950s, more than 80 percent of mothers with small children stayed at home caring for the family, but all this care added not one whit to GDP. Today more than half of mothers with small children are in the work force, where their market labor is captured in GDP. What's more, GDP has increased because household services, such as meals and child care, are now more frequently purchased in markets rather than provided by householders. In less developed economies, more economic activity is do-it-yourself or provided by the extended family. *Because official GDP figures ignore most home production, these figures understate the household goods and services produced in less-developed countries.*

Underground economy An expression used to describe all market exchange that goes unreported either because it is illegal or because those involved want to evade taxes

GDP also ignores production for which no official records are kept. The **underground economy** is an expression used to describe all market exchange that goes unreported either because the activity itself is illegal or because those involved want to evade taxes on otherwise legal activity. Although there are no official estimates on the extent of the underground economy, most economists agree that it is substantial. Recent estimates range from 5 percent to 15 percent of GDP.[2] A Census Bureau study suggests that the nation's underground economy amounts to about 7.5 percent of GDP, or about $625 billion in 1999.

Even though some production is not reflected in GDP, the *imputed income* from certain activities that do not pass across recorded markets is included. Income must be imputed, or estimated, because market exchange does not occur. For example, included in GDP is an *imputed rental income* that homeowners receive from home ownership, even though no rent is actually paid or received. (This imputed income is discussed in the appendix to this chapter.) Also included in GDP is an imputed dollar amount for (1) wages paid *in kind*, such as employers' payments for employees' medical insurance, and (2) food produced on the farm for that farm family's own consumption. The national income accounts therefore reflect some economic production that does not involve market exchange.

Leisure, Quality, and Variety

The average U.S. work week is much shorter now than it was at the turn of the century, so people work less to produce today's output. People also retire now at a much earlier age. The increase over the years in the amount of leisure available has resulted in a higher quality of life. But leisure time is not reflected in GDP because leisure is not explicitly bought and sold in a market. The quality and variety of products available have on average also improved over the years, as a result of technological advances and competition, yet most of these improvements are not reflected in GDP. For example, improvements have occurred in recording systems, computers, tires, running shoes, and hundreds of other products. Also, new products are getting introduced all the time, such as digital videodisks and high-definition television. *The gross domestic product fails to reflect changes in the availability of leisure time and sometimes fails to reflect changes in the quality of existing products as well as changes in the availability of new products.* The special problem of measuring production in an economy shaped by changing technology is discussed in the following case study.

CaseStudy

The Information Economy

The Bureau of Economic Analysis is charged with estimating GDP and its components. At http://www.bea.doc.gov/bea/dn/niptbl-d.htm you can find recent data on real GDP (in Table 1) and the sources of change in GDP (in Table 2). Review Table 2 and find the components of spending that have been most important in the GDP growth of the mid to late 1990s. You can compare current real GDP to previous years from 1929 on at http://www.bea.doc.gov/bea/dn/0898nip3/tab2a.htm. What was real GDP during the year you were born? How many times larger is it today?

Tracking an $8 Trillion Economy

How does the government keep track of this, the most sophisticated economy in the history of the world? Ever since Article I of the U.S. Constitution required a decennial population census, the federal government has been gathering data. The three main data-gathering agencies are the Bureau of the Census, the Bureau of Economic Analysis, and the Bureau of Labor Statistics. Since 1980, real GDP has increased by more than two-thirds, employment has increased by more than 30 million, and real foreign trade has tripled. Yet the federal budget

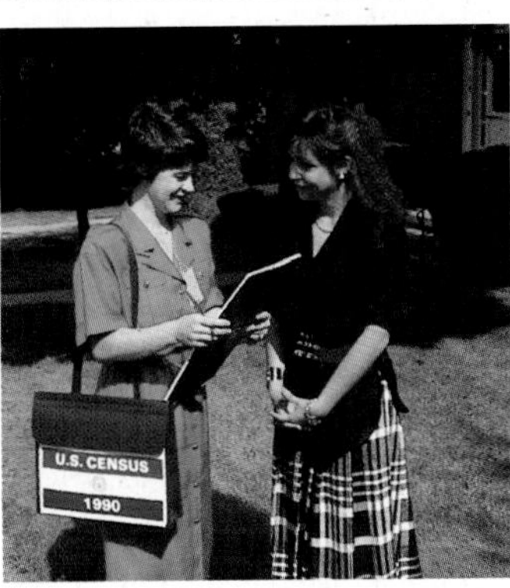

2 See Joel F. Houston, "The Underground Economy: A Troubling Issue for Policymakers," *Federal Reserve Bank of Philadelphia Business Review* (September–October 1987): 3–12.

for data-gathering agencies has declined in real terms. Only 0.2 percent of the federal budget goes toward keeping track of the economy.

Federal budget cuts have eliminated some data-collection efforts and have slowed down others. For example, computations of monthly international trade statistics have become so overwhelming that as many as half of the imports counted for a particular month reflect a "carryover" from previous months. And the monthly household sample used to track unemployment has been cut from 60,000 to 50,000. Some agencies must do more with the same staff. For example, in 1980 the Bureau of Labor Statistics had 18 analysts to monitor productivity in 95 different industries. The number of industries they track now has quadrupled, but the number of analysts has hardly changed.

The traditional ways of monitoring economic activity were originally developed in the 1930s and 1940s, when manufacturing dominated. Manufacturing output is relatively easy to measure because the output is tangible, such as automobiles, toasters, or in-line skates. But service output, such as financial advice, physical therapy, or on-line services, is intangible, and is therefore more difficult to measure.

Because services are intangible, measures for the service sector tend to be less reliable than those for the manufacturing sector. Measures of service output often fail to reflect improvements in the speed or quality of services. For example, computerized checkout systems not only save time and provide customers with detailed receipts but also allow retailers to track inventory and order new supplies. Likewise, speedier modems cut the time of using on-line services. Or consider the Wisconsin trucking firm that uses onboard computers in its vehicles to map the most efficient routes and remap the routes should priorities change. The firm has become so efficient that the number of ton-miles (tonnage times miles) carried per month has declined. Yet, according to Government statisticians, these truck drivers are less productive because ton-miles is how output is measured.

Government statisticians have no way of measuring output in a wide range of industries, including banking, medicine, software, legal services, wholesale trade, and communications. For example, productivity measures do not reflect the benefits of new surgical procedures that are safer and require less recuperation time, such as microsurgical techniques that remove cataracts and arthroscopic surgery that repairs torn knee ligaments.

There are indications that output and productivity in the service sector may be rising faster than official estimates show. For example, capital investment in the service sector has grown more in recent years than has investment in the manufacturing sector. And the United States has experienced a growing trade surplus in services, suggesting that the U.S. service sector is competitive and relatively productive, at least when compared to services produced abroad. In contrast, the trade balance on goods has been in deficit, and this deficit has been growing.

Sources: Robert D. Hersey, "Concern Is Voiced Over Quality of Economic Data," *New York Times*, 24 November 1996; "The Real Truth about the Economy," *Business Week* (7 November 1994): 110–118; and Leonard Nakamura, "Is the U.S. Economy Really Growing Too Slowly? Maybe We're Measuring Growth Wrong," *Federal Reserve Bank of Philadelphia Business Review* (March–April 1997): 1–12.

Gross Domestic Product Ignores Depreciation

In the course of producing GDP, some capital wears out, such as the delivery truck that finally dies, and some capital becomes obsolete, such as an aging computer that can't keep up with the latest software. A new truck that logs

100,000 miles its first year has been subject to wear and tear, and therefore has a diminished value as a resource. A truer picture of the *net* production that actually occurs during a year is found by subtracting this *depreciation* from GDP. **Depreciation** measures the value of the capital stock that is used up or grows obsolete in the production process. The gross domestic product is called "gross" because it fails to take into account this depreciation. **Net domestic product** equals gross domestic product minus depreciation—the value of the capital stock used up in the production process.

Depreciation The value of capital stock used up during a year in producing GDP

Net domestic product Gross domestic product minus depreciation

We can now distinguish between two definitions of investment. *Gross investment* measures the value of all investment during a year. Gross investment is used in computing GDP. *Net investment* equals gross investment minus depreciation. The economy's production possibilities depend on what happens to net investment. If net investment is negative—that is, if depreciation exceeds gross investment—the capital stock declines, so its contribution to output will decline as well. If net investment is zero, the capital stock remains constant, as does its contribution to output. And if net investment is positive, the capital stock grows, as does its contribution to output.

As the names imply, *gross* domestic product (GDP) reflects gross investment and the *net* domestic product (NDP) reflects net investment. But developing a figure for depreciation involves much guesswork. For example, what is the appropriate measure of depreciation for the roller coasters at Busch Gardens, the metal display shelves at Wal-Mart, the 5,000-gallon casks used to age wine in the Napa Valley, the parking lots at Disney World, or the Library of Congress building in Washington, D.C.?

GDP Does Not Reflect All Costs

Some production and consumption degrades the quality of our environment. Trucks and automobiles pump carbon monoxide into the atmosphere. Housing developments displace forests. Most paper mills foul the lungs and burn the eyes. These negative externalities—costs that fall on those not directly involved in the transactions—are largely ignored in GDP accounting, even though they diminish the quality of life and may limit future production. To the extent that growth in GDP also involves growth in such negative externalities, a rising GDP may not be as attractive as it would first appear.

Although the national income accounts reflect the depreciation of buildings, machinery, vehicles, and other manufactured capital, this accounting ignores the depletion of natural resources, such as standing timber, fish stocks, and soil fertility. So national income accounts reflect depreciation of the manufactured capital stock but not the natural capital stock. For example, suppose intensive farming raises farm productivity temporarily but depletes the fertility of the soil. The additional farm production adds to GDP but subtracts from the soil's fertility. And some economic development may cause the extinction of certain plants and animals. The U.S. Commerce Department is now in the process of developing so-called "green" accounting to reflect the impact of production on air pollution, water pollution, lost trees, soil depletion, and the loss of other natural resources.

GDP and Economic Welfare

In computing GDP, the market price of output is the measure of its value. Therefore, each dollar spent on handguns or cigarettes is counted in GDP the same as each dollar spent on baby formula or bibles. Positive economic analysis tries to avoid making value judgments about how people choose to spend their money. Because the level of GDP provides no information about its composition, many economists question whether GDP is a good measure of the nation's economic welfare. For example, at a time when some people in the nation are hungry and homeless, Americans spend billions on tobacco products, even though these products are linked to illness and death.

Despite the limitations and potential distortions associated with official GDP estimates, the trend of GDP over time provides a fairly accurate picture of the overall movement of the U.S. economy. Inflation, however, distorts the direct comparability of dollar amounts from one year to the next. In the next section we discuss how to adjust GDP for changes in the economy's price level.

ACCOUNTING FOR PRICE CHANGES

As noted earlier, the national income accounts are based on the market values of final goods and services produced in a particular year. Gross domestic product measures the value of output in *current dollars*—that is, in the dollar values at the time the output is produced. When GDP is based on current dollars, the national income accounts measure the *nominal value* of national output. Hence, the current-dollar GDP, or **nominal GDP,** is based on the prices prevailing when the output is produced.

Nominal GDP GDP based on prices prevailing at the time of the transaction; current-dollar GDP

The system of national income accounting based on current, or nominal, dollars allows us to make comparisons among income or expenditure components in a particular year. Since the economy's average price level changes over time, however, current-dollar comparisons across years can be misleading. For example, between 1979 and 1980, nominal GDP increased by about 9 percent. That sounds impressive, but the economy's average price level rose more than 9 percent. Hence, the growth in nominal GDP resulted entirely from inflation. **Real GDP**—that is, GDP measured in terms of the goods and services produced—in fact declined.

Real GDP GDP adjusted for changes in the price level

If nominal GDP increases in a given year, part of this increase may simply result from inflation—pure hot air. To make meaningful comparisons of GDP across years, we must take out the hot air, or *deflate* nominal GDP. We focus on *real* changes in production by eliminating changes due solely to inflation. To account for inflation, we need to compare the price level in one year with the price level in another year.

Price Indexes

To compare the price level over time, let's first establish a point of reference, a base year to which prices in other years can be compared. An *index number* compares the value of some variable in a particular year to its value in a base year, or reference year. Consider the simplest index number imaginable. Suppose bread is the only good produced in an economy. As a reference point, let's look at the price in some specific year. The year selected is called the **base year;** prices in other years are expressed in terms of the base-year price.

Base year The year with which other years are compared when constructing an index; the index equals 100 in the base year

Price index A number that shows the average price of a market basket of goods; changes in a price index over time show changes in the average price level

Suppose the base year is 1997, when a loaf of bread in our simple economy sold for $1.25. Let's say the price of bread increased to $1.30 in 1998, and to $1.40 in 1999. We construct a **price index** by dividing each year's price by the price in

EXHIBIT 3

Hypothetical Example of a Price Index (base year = 1997)

Year	Price of Bread in Current Year (1)	Price of Bread in Base Year (2)	Price Index (3) = (1)/(2) × 100
1997	$1.25	$1.25	100
1998	1.30	1.25	104
1999	1.40	1.25	112

the base year and then multiplying by 100, as shown in Exhibit 3. For 1997, the base year, we divide the base price of bread by itself, $1.25/$1.25, which equals 1, so the price index in 1997 equals 1 × 100 = 100. *The price index in the base year is always 100.* The price index in 1998 is $1.30/$1.25, which equals 1.04, which when multiplied by 100 equals 104. In 1999, the index is $1.40/$1.25, or 1.12, which when multiplied by 100 equals 112. Thus, the index in 1998 is 4 percent higher than in the base year; in 1999 it is 12 percent higher than in the base year.

The price index permits comparisons between any two years. For example, what if you were presented with the indexes for 1998 and 1999 and asked what happened to the price level between the two years? By dividing the 1999 price index by the 1998 price index, 112/104, you would find that the price level rose by 7.7 percent.

This section has shown how to develop a price index assuming we already know the price level each year. Determining the price level is a bit more involved, as we now see.

Consumer Price Index

The price index most familiar to you is the consumer price index, or CPI, which measures changes over time in the cost of buying a "market basket" of goods and services purchased by a typical family. Changes in the cost of this basket are often referred to as changes in the "cost of living." For simplicity, suppose a typical family's market basket for the year includes 365 packages of Twinkies, 500 gallons of fuel oil, and 12 months of cable TV service. Prices in the base year are listed in column (2) of Exhibit 4. The total cost of each product in the base year is found by multiplying price by quantity, as shown in column (3). The cost of the market basket in the base year is shown at the bottom of column (3) to be $1,184.85.

Current-year prices are listed in column (4). Notice that not all prices changed by the same amount since the base year. The price of fuel oil increased by 50 percent, but the price of Twinkies declined. The cost of purchasing that same basket in the current year is $1,398.35, shown as the total of column (5). To compute the consumer price index for the current year, we simply divide the total cost in the current year by the total cost of that same basket in the base year, $1,398.35/$1,184.85, then multiply by 100. This yields a price index of 118.0. We could say that between the base period and the current year, the "cost of living" increased by 18.0 percent, although not all prices increased by the same percentage.

EXHIBIT 4

Hypothetical Market Basket Used to Develop the Consumer Price Index

Good or Service	Quantity in Market Basket (1)	Prices in Base Year (2)	Cost of Basket in Base Year (3) = (1) × (2)	Prices in Current Year (4)	Cost of Basket in Current Year (5) = (1) × (4)
Twinkies	365 packages	$ 0.84/package	$ 324.85	$ 0.79	$ 288.35
Fuel Oil	500 gallons	1.00/gallon	500.00	1.50	750.00
Cable TV	12 months	30.00/month	360.00	30.00	360.00
			$1,184.85		$1,398.35

The federal government uses the years 1982 to 1984 as the base period for calculating the CPI for a market basket of 400 goods and services in eight major categories. The CPI is reported monthly based on price data collected from about 15,000 sellers in 87 urban localities across the country. In reality each household consumes a unique market basket, so we could theoretically develop about 100 million CPIs—one for each U.S. household.

NetBookmark

Possible biases in the CPI are discussed in detail by Brian Motley in his "Bias in the CPI: Roughly right or precisely wrong?" available from Federal Reserve Bank of San Francisco at http://www.frbsf.org/econrsrch/wklyltr/el97-16.html.

Problems with the CPI

There is no perfect way to measure changes in the price level. As we have already seen, the quality and variety of some products are improving all the time, so some price increases may be as much a reflection of quality improvements as of inflation. Thus, there is a *quality bias* in the CPI, since it assumes that the quality of the market basket remains relatively constant over time. *As a result of ignoring quality improvements, the CPI overstates the true extent of inflation.*

The CPI tends to overstate inflation for another reason. Recall that the CPI holds constant over time the kind and amount of goods and services in the typical market basket. Since not all items in the market basket experience the same rates of price change, relative prices change over time. A family would respond to changes in relative prices by purchasing less of the relatively more expensive products and more of the relatively cheaper products. But, because the CPI holds the composition of the market basket constant for long periods (the basket gets updated about every 10 years, most recently in 1998),[3] the CPI is slow to incorporate consumer responses to changes in relative prices. *The CPI calculations, by underestimating the possibility of substitution in consumption, thus assume uneconomical consumer behavior, thereby overstating the true extent of inflation experienced by the typical family.*

The CPI has also failed to keep up with the consumer shift toward discount stores such as Wal-Mart and Home Depot. Government statisticians consider goods sold at discount retailers as distinct from similar or identical goods sold by traditional retailers. The discounter is assumed to be offering a different good, one with lower services and fewer consumer amenities. Hence the discounter's lower price does not translate into a reduction in the cost of living.

3 The Bureau of Labor Statistics had planned to rebase the CPI series to 1993–1995 but decided at the last minute to keep prices based on the old series of 1982–1984, although the goods in the basket were revised to reflect 1993–1995 consumption patterns instead of 1982–1984 consumption patterns.

A panel of five prominent economists headed by Michael Boskin of Stanford University evaluated the CPI for Congress. The panel concluded that the CPI overstates increases in the cost of living by 1.1 percent per year. This breaks down as follows: (1) Failure to reflect new products and improving quality adds 0.6 percent, (2) failure to reflect consumer adjustments to relative price changes adds 0.4 percent; and (3) failure to include the shift toward discount outlets adds 0.1 percent.

The CPI is of more than academic concern since the index determines changes in tax brackets and in an array of payments, including union wages, Social Security benefits, and welfare payments. In fact, about 30 percent of federal outlays are tied to changes in the CPI. A 1 percent correction in the upward bias of the CPI would save the federal budget $180 billion annually by the year 2008.

Overstating the CPI also distorts other measures of the economy that use the CPI to adjust for inflation, such as the real wage. For example, based on the official CPI, the average real wage fell by a total of about 2 percent between 1980 and 1998. But if the CPI overstates inflation by 1.1 percent per year, as researchers conclude, then the real wage, instead of dropping, actually increased by more than 20 percent during that period.

The Bureau of Labor Statistics in 1997 introduced an experimental version of the CPI that would reduce measured inflation and thus save the government billions of dollars a year in payments to Social Security recipients and beneficiaries of other programs. The new version was initially reported in 1997, alongside the CPI using the standard methodology. Part of the experiment uses scanner data at supermarkets to find out how consumers respond, for example, to a rise in the price of romaine lettuce relative to iceberg lettuce, two products assumed to be reasonable substitutes. The experiment does not include higher-level substitution, such as switching to chicken if the price of beef increases. This approach, if ultimately accepted, is expected to trim growth in the price index by about one-quarter of a percentage point per year. Other experiments aimed at making the CPI more accurate are also in the works.

The GDP Price Index

Price indexes are weighted sums of various prices. Whereas the CPI focuses on just a sample of consumer purchases, a more complex and more comprehensive price index, the **GDP price index,** measures the average level of prices of all goods and services that are included in GDP. To calculate the GDP price index, we use the formula

GDP price index A comprehensive price index of all goods and services included in the gross domestic product

$$\text{GDP price index} = \frac{\text{nominal GDP}}{\text{real GDP}} \times 100$$

where nominal GDP is the dollar value of this year's GDP measured in current year's prices and real GDP is the dollar value of this year's GDP measured in base-year prices. A change in the price of some products in the economy without any change in the quantity produced will affect nominal GDP but not real GDP. Price changes alone will be reflected in the GDP price index. For example, if prices on average are 10 percent higher in the current year than in the base year, the change in the GDP price index equals 10 percent (since quantities remain unchanged from the base year).

If we know both nominal GDP and real GDP, then finding the GDP price index is easy. Nominal GDP is simply current-dollar GDP. The challenge is finding real GDP. Any measure of real GDP is constructed as the weighted sum of thousands of different goods and services produced in the economy. The question is what weights, or prices, to use. Between World War II and 1995, the Bureau of Economic Analysis (BEA) used prices of a particular year (most recently, 1987) to estimate real GDP. In this case, the quantity of each output in a particular year was valued by using the 1987 price of each output. So real GDP in, say, 1994 was the sum of 1994 outputs valued at 1987 prices.

Moving from Fixed Weights to Chain Weights

Estimating real GDP by using prices from a base period yields an accurate measure of real GDP as long as the year in question is close to the base year. But prices that prevailed in 1987 were used by BEA to value production in years from 1929 to 1995. In early 1996 BEA switched from a fixed-price weighting system to a *chain-weighted system*, using a complicated process that changes price weights from year to year. All you need to know is that the chain-weighted real GDP adjusts the weights more or less continuously from year to year, getting rid of much of the bias caused by a fixed-price weighting system.

Even though the chain-type index adjusts the weights from year to year, any index, by definition, must still use some year as an anchor, a reference point—that is, any index must answer the question "compared to what?" To provide such a reference point, BEA measures real GDP and its components in *chained (1992) dollars*. Exhibit 5 presents current-dollar estimates of GDP as

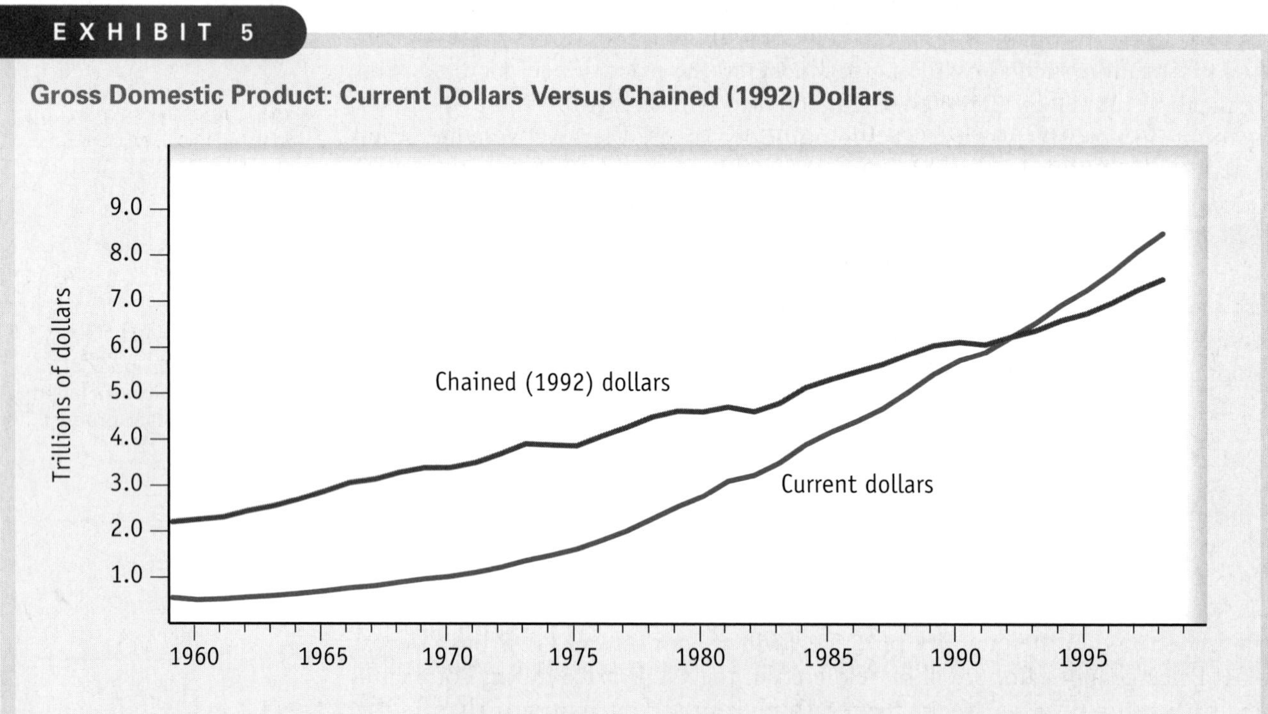

Gross Domestic Product: Current Dollars Versus Chained (1992) Dollars

Source: Developed from estimates by the U.S. Department of Commerce in *Survey of Current Business*, 77 (August 1997) and 79 (January 1999).

well as chained (1992) dollar estimates of real GDP. The blue line indicates current-dollar GDP, or nominal GDP, since 1959. The red line indicates real GDP since 1959, or GDP measured in chained (1992) dollars. The two lines intersect in 1992, when real GDP equaled nominal GDP. Nominal, or current-dollar, GDP is below real GDP in years prior to 1992 because real GDP is based on chained (1992) prices, which are above current prices during years prior to 1992. Nominal, or current-dollar, GDP grows faster than real GDP because the growth in current-dollar GDP reflects growth in both real GDP and the price level.

An example of the bias resulting from a fixed-price weighting system involves computers, as discussed in this closing case study.

Computer Prices and GDP Estimation

McEachern Interactive

CaseStudy

The Information Economy

How does the Bureau of Economic Analysis go about incorporating changes in the quality of computers in national income statistics? For the entire story, you can read "Price Indexes for Selected Semiconductors, 1974–96" by Bruce T. Grimm at http://www.bea.doc.gov/bea/an/0298od/maintext.htm. You may prefer the shorter, and less technical, explanation he provides in Box 1 at http://www.bea.doc.gov/bea/an/0298od/box1.htm. What do economists mean by a "hedonic index," according to Grimm? To see how dramatic the price changes have been for memory and chips, look at Charts 1 and 2, available through links in the main text.

As noted already, until 1996 federal statisticians based their real GDP estimates on 1987 prices. Relying on such estimates, most observers believed that the economic recovery that began in the spring of 1991 was spurred primarily by investment spending, especially spending on new computers. In this case study, we reconsider the role of computer production as an economic stimulus to that recovery.

Computer prices have fallen by an average of about 13 percent per year since 1982. Based on this rate of decline, a computer that cost, say, $10,000 in 1982 cost about $5,000 in 1987 and only about $1,000 in 1998. According to these prices, that computer cost about the same in 1982 as a Chrysler minivan; in 1998, you could buy more than twenty computers for the cost of a minivan. So computers became much less expensive between 1982 and 1998.

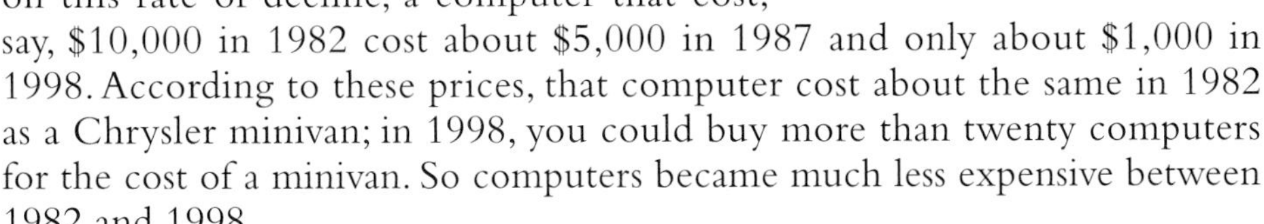

The sharp decline in computer prices spurred purchases for the office and the home. Suppose the number of computers purchased jumped from 1 million in 1982 to 5 million in 1998. If computers are valued at the 1987 price of $5,000, computer production would increase from $5 billion in 1982 to $25 billion in 1997, a fivefold jump. But if priced in current, or nominal, dollars, spending on these computers would decline from $10 billion in 1982 to $5 billion in 1998, a drop of 50 percent. Using the 1987 price understates the value of computer production in 1982, overstates it in 1998, and thus exaggerates the growth between 1982 and 1998. It was this exaggeration in the value of computer production in 1991 that led to the incorrect belief that the recovery resulted primarily from investment spending.

The chain-weighted measure adjusts for some of the distortion that comes from using 1987 fixed prices. Under the chain-weighted measure, investment grew less rapidly during the recovery that began in 1991 than during the four previous recoveries, so investment turned out to be less of a factor in stimulating economic expansion than it had been in the previous two decades. The chain-weighting system, although it is more complicated

than the fixed-price weighting system, provides a more reliable picture of year-to-year changes in real output.

Sources: "Improved Estimates of the National Income and Product Accounts for 1959–95: Results of the Comprehensive Revision," *Survey of Current Business*, Vol. 76 (January/February 1996): 1–31; "Current and Historical Data," *Survey of Current Business*, Vol. 77 (December 1997); and Joseph Haimowitz, "Has the Surge in Computer Spending Fundamentally Changed the Economy?" *Federal Reserve Bank of Kansas City Economic Review* (Second Quarter 1998): 27–47.

CONCLUSION

This chapter examined how GDP is measured and how it is adjusted for changes in the economy's price level. In subsequent chapters we will refer to distinctions between real and nominal values. Although no price index is perfect, the price indexes now in use provide reasonably good measures of the trend in price levels over time. The national income accounts have limitations, but they do offer a reasonably accurate measure of year-to-year movements in the economy. The national income accounts are published in much greater detail than the preceding discussion suggests. The appendix to this chapter provides some additional detail.

SUMMARY

1. The gross domestic product, or GDP, measures the market value of all final goods and services produced during the year by resources located in the United States, regardless of who owns those resources.
2. The expenditure approach to GDP adds up the market value of all final goods and services produced in the economy during the year. The income approach to GDP adds up all the income generated as a result of that production during the year.
3. The circular flow model summarizes the flow of income and spending through the economy. Saving, net taxes, and imports are leakages from the circular flow. These leakages equal the injections into the circular flow: investment, government purchases, and exports.
4. GDP reflects market production. Most household production and the underground economy are excluded from GDP. Improvements in the quality and variety of goods are often not reflected in GDP, either. In other ways GDP may overstate the true amount of production that occurs. GDP fails to subtract for depreciation of the capital stock and fails to account for negative externalities arising from production or for the depletion of natural resources.
5. Nominal GDP in a particular year values output based on market prices prevailing that year. To determine real GDP, nominal GDP must be adjusted for the effects of changes in the price level. Two indexes used to track the price level are the consumer price index, or CPI, which tracks prices for a basket of goods over time, and the GDP price index, which measures price changes for all output. No adjustment for changes in the price level is perfect.

QUESTIONS FOR REVIEW

1. *(National Income Accounting)* Identify the component of aggregate expenditure to which each of the following belongs:
   a. A U.S. resident's purchase of a new automobile manufactured in Japan
   b. A household's purchase of one hour of legal advice
   c. Construction of a new house
   d. An increase in semiconductor inventories over last year's level
   e. A city government's acquisition of 10 new police cars
2. *(National Income Accounting)* Define *gross domestic product*. Determine whether each of the following would be included in the 1999 U.S. gross domestic product:

a. Profits earned by Ford Motor Company in 1999 on automobile production in Ireland
b. Automobile parts manufactured in the United States in 1999 but not used until 2000
c. Social Security benefits paid by the U.S. government in 1999
d. Ground beef purchased and used by McDonald's in 1999
e. Ground beef purchased and consumed by a private U.S. household in 1999
f. Goods and services purchased in the United States in 1999 by a Canadian tourist

3. *(National Income Accounting)* Explain why intermediate goods and services generally are not included directly in GDP. Are there any circumstances under which they would be included directly?

4. *(Leakages and Injections)* What are the leakages from and injections into the circular flow? How are leakages and injections related to the circular flow?

5. *(Planned Versus Actual Investment)* Explain the distinction between planned investment and actual investment. Which is included in the circular flow?

6. *(Investment)* In national income accounting, one component of measured investment is net changes in inventories. Last year's inventories are subtracted from this year's inventories to obtain a net change. Explain why net inventory changes are considered part of GDP. Also, discuss why it is not sufficient to measure the level of inventories only for the current year. (Remember the difference between stocks and flows.)

7. *(Limitations of National Income Accounting)* Explain why each of the following should be taken into account when GDP data are used to compare the "level of well-being" in different countries.
   a. Population levels
   b. The distribution of income
   c. The amount of production that takes place outside of markets
   d. The length of the average work week
   e. The level of environmental pollution

8. *(**CaseStudy:** Tracking an $8 Trillion Economy)* Why has it become increasingly difficult for the federal government to monitor economic activity in the United States?

9. *(Nominal GDP)* Which of the following is a necessary condition—something that must occur—in order for nominal GDP to rise? Explain your answers.
   a. Actual production must increase.
   b. The price level must increase.
   c. Real GDP must increase.
   d. Both the price level and actual production must increase.
   e. Either the price level or real GDP must increase.

10. *(Price Indexes)* Home computers and videocassette recorders have not been part of the U.S. economy for very long. Both goods have been decreasing in price and improving in quality. What problems does this situation pose for people who are responsible for computing a price index?

11. *(GDP and Depreciation)* What is gross about gross domestic product? Could an economy enjoy a constant—or growing—GDP while not replacing worn-out capital?

12. *(Consumer Price Index)* One form of the CPI that has been advocated by lobbying groups is a "CPI for the elderly." The Bureau of Labor Statistics currently produces only indexes for "all urban households" and "urban wage earners and clerical workers." Should the BLS produce such an index for the elderly?

13. *(GDP Price Index)* The health expenditure component of the GDP price index has been rising steadily. How might this index be biased by quality and substitution effects? Are there any substitutes for health care?

14. *(**CaseStudy:** Computer Prices and GDP Estimation)* Compared to the fixed-price weighting system, how does the chain-weighted system better account for the economic incentives provided by price changes?

PROBLEMS AND EXERCISES

15. *(Income Approach to GDP)* How does the income approach to measuring GDP differ from the expenditure approach? Explain the meaning of value added and its importance in the income approach. Consider the following data for the selling price at each stage in the production of a five-pound bag of flour sold by your local grocery. Calculate the final market value of the flour.

Stage of Production	Sale Price
Farmer	$0.30
Miller	0.50
Wholesaler	1.00
Grocer	1.50

16. *(Expenditure Approach to GDP)* You have the following annual information about a hypothetical country:

	Billions of Dollars
Personal consumption expenditures	$200
Personal taxes	50
Exports	30
Depreciation	10
Government purchases	50
Gross private domestic investment	40
Imports	40
Government transfer payments	20

a. What is the value of GDP?
b. What is the value of net domestic product?
c. What is the value of net investment?
d. What is the value of net exports?

17. *(Investment)* Answer these questions using these data:

	Billions of Dollars
New residential construction	$500
Purchases of existing homes	250
Sales value of newly issued stocks and bonds	600
New physical capital	800
Depreciation	200
Household purchases of new furniture	50
Net change in firms' inventories	100
Production of new intermediate goods	700

a. What is the value of gross private domestic investment?
b. What is the value of net investment?
c. Are any intermediate goods counted in gross investment?

18. *(Consumer Price Index)* Calculate a new consumer price index for the data in Exhibit 4 in this chapter. Assume that current-year prices of Twinkies, fuel oil, and cable TV are $0.89/package, $1.25/gallon, and $15.00/month, respectively. Calculate the current year's cost of the market basket and the value of the current year's price index. What is this year's percent change in the price level compared to the base year?

19. *(Consumer Price Index)* Given the following data, what was the value of the consumer price index in the base year? Calculate the annual rate of consumer price inflation in 2000 in each of the following situations:
a. The CPI equals 200 in 1999 and 240 in 2000.
b. The CPI equals 150 in 1999 and 175 in 2000.
c. The CPI equals 325 in 1999 and 340 in 2000.
d. The CPI equals 325 in 1999 and 315 in 2000.

EXPERIENTIAL EXERCISES

20. *(Limitations of National Income Accounting)* One often-heard criticism of the U.S. national income accounts is that they ignore the effect of environmental pollution. The World Bank's group on Environmental Economics and Indicators has been investigating ways of assessing environmental degradation. Take a look at their work on "green accounting" at http://www-esd.worldbank.org/eei/text/greenacc.html. What kinds of problems have they identified, and what proposals have they made to deal with those problems?

21. *(Problems with the CPI)* A Web site devoted to issues of bias in the Consumer Price Index can be found at http://www.geocities.com/CapitolHill/2394/. Take a look, and determine what are some of the criticisms of the CPI as presently calculated.

22. *(Wall Street Journal)* Data on the Consumer Price Index are released near the middle of each month. (You can find the exact date by consulting the on-line calendar at http://www.leggmason.com/CAL/calendar.html. Data on GDP are released on the last Friday of each month (in preliminary, revised, and then final form). Analysis of these data releases appears in the first section of the following weekday's *Wall Street Journal*. Look in the "Economy" section to find the story. What do the latest available data tell you about the current rate of inflation and the current rate of GDP growth? Is the economy in a recession or an expansion?

Appendix

NATIONAL INCOME ACCOUNTS

This chapter has focused on gross domestic product, or GDP, the measure of output that will be of most interest in subsequent chapters. Other economic aggregates also convey useful information and receive media attention. One of these, *net domestic product*, has already been introduced. Exhibit 6 shows that net domestic product equals gross domestic product minus depreciation. In this appendix we examine other aggregate measures.

NATIONAL INCOME

Thus far we have been talking about the value of production from resources located in the United States, regardless of who owns the resources. Sometimes we want to know how much American resource suppliers earn for their labor, capital, land, and entrepreneurial ability. **National income** captures all income earned by American-owned resources, whether those resources are located in the United States or abroad. *National income* results from several adjustments to net domestic product. First, the net value of production from American-owned resources abroad, and hence the net income earned from that production, must be added to net domestic product. To get the net value of production, we add income earned by American resources abroad and subtract income earned by foreign-owned resources in the United States.

Second, the value of final goods and services is computed at market prices, but, because of **government subsidies,** such as payments to suppliers of low-income housing, some products sell for less than resource suppliers receive. Since subsidies are received as income, they should be included in national income, even though they are not part of the selling price.

Third, because of **indirect business taxes,** such as sales, excise, and property taxes, some products sell for more than resource suppliers receive. For example, a gallon of gasoline may sell for $1.25, but about $0.25 in taxes must be paid to the government before any resource supplier earns a penny. Since indirect business taxes are not received as income by any individual, they should not be included in national income, even though they are part of the selling price. Since indirect business taxes are about 20 times greater than government subsidies, we simplify the reporting by computing *indirect business taxes net of subsidies*.

National income therefore equals net domestic product plus net earnings from American resources abroad minus indirect business taxes (net of subsidies). Exhibit 6 shows how to go from net domestic product to national income. We have now moved from gross domestic product to net domestic product to national income. Next we peel back another layer to arrive at personal income, the income people actually receive.

EXHIBIT 6

Deriving Net Domestic Product and National Income Using 1998 Data (in trillions of dollars)

Gross domestic product (GDP)	$8.51
Minus depreciation	–0.91
Net domestic product	7.60
Plus net earnings of American resources abroad minus indirect business taxes (net of subsidies)	–0.60
National income	$7.00

Source: *Economic Report of the President*, February 1999, and *Survey of Current Business* 79 (February 1999).

PERSONAL INCOME

Some of the income received this year was not earned this year, and some of the income earned this year was not actually received this year by those who earned it. By adding to national income the income received but not earned and subtracting the income earned but not received, we convert national income into all income *received* by individuals, which is termed **personal income.** Personal income, a widely reported measure of economic welfare, is computed by the federal government monthly.

The adjustment from national income to personal income is shown in Exhibit 7. Income *earned but not received* includes the employer's share of Social Security taxes, corporate income taxes, and undistributed corporate profits, which are profits the firm retains rather than pays as dividends. Income *received but not earned* in the current period includes government transfer payments, receipts from private pension plans, and interest paid by government and by consumers.

DISPOSABLE INCOME

Although several taxes have been considered so far, we have not yet discussed personal taxes. Personal taxes consist primarily of federal, state, and local personal income taxes and the employee's share of the Social Security tax. Subtracting

EXHIBIT 7

Deriving Personal Income and Disposable Income Using 1998 Data (in trillions of dollars)

National income	$7.00
Minus income earned but not received (Social Security taxes, corporate income taxes, undistributed corporate profits)	–2.06
Plus income received but not earned (government and business transfers, net personal interest income)	2.18
Personal income	7.12
Minus personal tax and nontax charges	–1.10
Disposable income	$6.02

Source: *Economic Report of the President*, February 1999, and *Survey of Current Business* 79 (February 1999).

personal taxes and other government charges from personal income yields *disposable income*, which is the amount available for spending or saving—the amount that can be "disposed of" by the household. Think of disposable income as take-home pay. Exhibit 7 shows that personal income minus personal taxes and other government charges yields disposable income.

SUMMARY OF NATIONAL INCOME ACCOUNTS

The income side of national income accounts can be summarized as follows. We begin with *gross domestic product*, or *GDP*, the market value of final goods and services produced during the year by resources located in the United States. We subtract depreciation from GDP to yield the *net domestic product*. To net domestic product we add net earnings from American resources abroad and subtract indirect business taxes (net of subsidies) to yield *national income*. We obtain *personal income* by subtracting from national income all income earned but not received (e.g., undistributed corporate profits) and by adding all income received but not earned (e.g., transfer payments). By subtracting personal taxes and other government charges from personal income, we arrive at the bottom line: *disposable income*, the amount people are actually free either to save or to spend.

SUMMARY INCOME STATEMENT OF THE ECONOMY

Exhibit 8 presents an annual income statement for the entire economy. The upper portion lists aggregate expenditure, which consists of consumption, gross investment, government purchases, and net exports. Because imports exceeded exports, net exports are negative. You might think of aggregate expenditure as the revenue of a giant firm. The income from this expenditure is broken down in the lower portion of Exhibit 8. After subtracting both depreciation and net indirect business taxes, and adding net earnings from American resources abroad to the remaining forms of income, we get national income. National income, which is the sum of all earnings from resources supplied by U.S. residents and firms, can be divided into its five components: employee compensation, proprietors' income, corporate profits, net interest, and rental income of persons.

Employee compensation, which is by far the largest source of income, includes both money wages and employer contributions to cover Social Security taxes, medical insurance, and other fringe benefits. **Proprietors' income** includes the earnings of unincorporated businesses. **Corporate profits** are the net revenues received by incorporated businesses before subtracting corporate income taxes.

EXHIBIT 8

Expenditure and Income Statement for the U.S. Economy Using 1998 Data (in trillions of dollars)

Aggregate Expenditure	
Consumption (*C*)	$5.81
Gross investment (*I*)	1.37
Government purchases (*G*)	1.49
Net exports (*X* – *M*)	–0.16
GDP	$8.51
Allocation of Income	
Depreciation	$0.91
Net earnings of American resources abroad	–0.02
Net indirect business taxes	0.62
Compensation of employees	4.98
Proprietors' income	0.58
Corporate profits	0.83
Net interest	0.45
Rental income of persons	0.16
GDP	$8.51

Source: *Economic Report of the President*, February 1999, and *Survey of Current Business* 79 (February 1999).

Net interest is the interest received by individuals, excluding interest paid by consumers to businesses and interest paid by government.

Each family that owns its own home is viewed as a tiny firm that rents its home to itself. Since homeowners do not, in fact, rent homes to themselves, an imputed rental value is estimated based on what the market rent would be. **Rental income of persons** consists primarily of the imputed rental value of owner-occupied housing minus the cost of owning that property (such as property taxes, insurance, depreciation, and interest paid on the mortgage). From the totals in Exhibit 8, you can see that aggregate spending in the economy equals the income generated by that spending.

APPENDIX QUESTIONS

1. *(National Income Accounting)* Use the following data to answer the questions below:

	Billions of Dollars
Net investment	$110
Depreciation	30
Exports	50
Imports	30
Government purchases	150
Consumption	400
Indirect business taxes (net of subsidies)	35
Income earned but not received	60
Income received but not earned	70
Personal income taxes	50
Employee compensation	455
Corporate profits	60
Rental income	20
Net interest	30
Proprietor's income	40
Net earnings of U.S. resources abroad	40

   a. Calculate GDP using the income and the expenditure methods.
   b. Calculate gross investment.
   c. Calculate net domestic product, national income, personal income, and disposable income.

2. *(National Income Accounting)* According to Exhibit 8 in this chapter, GDP can be calculated either by adding up expenditures on final goods or by adding up the allocations of these expenditures to the resources used to produce these goods. Why do you suppose the portion of final goods expenditures that goes to pay for intermediate goods or raw materials is excluded from the income method of calculation?

CHAPTER

9

Aggregate Expenditure: Consumption, Investment, Government Purchases, and Net Exports

When driving through a neighborhood new to you, how can you figure out the income status of residents? What's the most predictable and useful relationship in macroeconomics? Why is so much attention paid to consumer confidence and business confidence? Answers to these and other questions are addressed in this chapter, which focuses on the components of aggregate expenditure. Consumption is the most important spending component, accounting for about two-thirds of all spending, but in this relatively short chapter we also discuss investment, government purchases, and net exports. You will learn whether and how each component relates to the level of income in the economy.

Let's preview where this leads. In Chapter 10, we will combine these spending components to show the link between aggregate spending and income, then

Visit the McEachern Interactive Study Center for this chapter at http://mcisc.swcollege.com

derive the aggregate demand curve. In Chapter 11 we will develop the aggregate supply curve and see how it interacts with the aggregate demand curve to determine the economy's equilibrium levels of price and output. The role of government will be examined in Chapter 12. Topics discussed in this chapter include:

- Consumption and income
- Marginal propensities to consume and to save
- Changes in consumption and saving
- Investment
- Government purchases
- Net exports
- Composition of spending

CONSUMPTION

Suppose a new college friend invited you home for the weekend. One thing you would learn from your visit is how well off the family is—you would get an impression of their standard of living. Is their home something you might see on *Lifestyles of the Rich and Famous*, or is it more modest? Do they drive a new BMW or take the bus? What do they eat? What do they wear? The simple fact is that consumption tends to reflect income.

You can usually tell much about a family's economic status by observing their consumption pattern. Although you sometimes come across people who live well beyond their means and others who still have the first nickel they ever earned, by and large consumption and income tend to be highly correlated. *The positive and stable relationship between consumption and income, both for the household and for the economy as a whole, is the main point of this chapter.* Got it?

A key decision in the circular flow model developed in the previous chapter is how much households spend on consumption. Consumption depends primarily on income and income depends on how much is produced. Although this seems obvious, the link between income and consumption is fundamental to an understanding of how the economy works. Let's look at this income-consumption link over time in the U.S. economy.

An Initial Look at Income and Consumption

The red line in Exhibit 1 depicts disposable income in the United States for the last four decades, and the blue line depicts consumer spending. (Data have been adjusted for inflation so that dollars are of constant purchasing power, in this case 1992 dollars.) *Disposable income*, remember, is the income actually available for spending and saving.

Note in Exhibit 1 that consumer spending and disposable income tend to move together over time. Both are measured along the vertical axis in 1992 dollars. Consumer saving is the difference between disposable income and consumer spending; saving is indicated in Exhibit 1 by the vertical distance between the two lines. Both consumer spending and disposable income increased nearly every year, and the relationship between consumption and income has been relatively stable. Specifically, consumer spending averaged 90 percent of disposable income during the 1960s, 89 percent during the 1970s, 90 percent during the 1980s, and 92 percent during the 1990s. Put another way, saving averaged 10 percent of disposable income during the 1960s, 11 percent during the 1970s, 10 percent during the 1980s, and 8 percent during the 1990s.

EXHIBIT 1

Consumer Spending and Disposable Income in the United States

Income and consumer spending move together over time. Saving is the difference between disposable income and consumer spending.

Source: *Economic Report of the President*, February 1999.

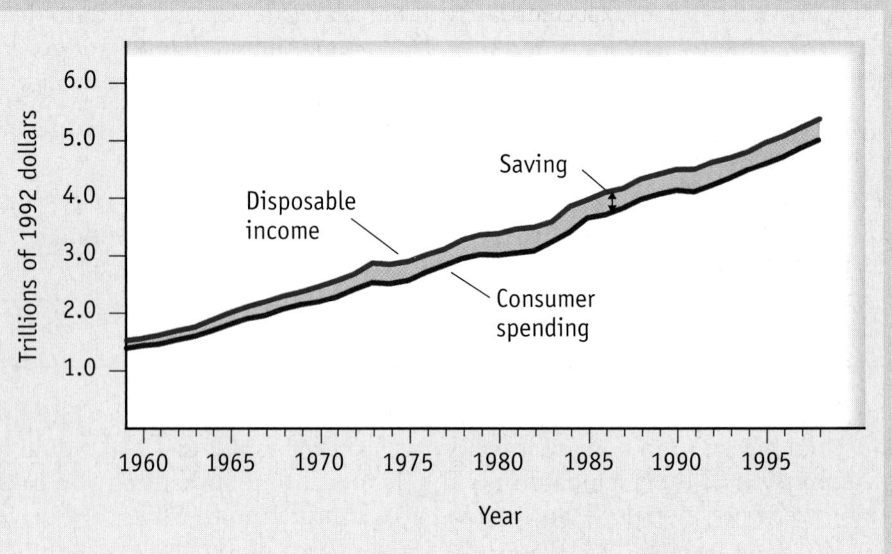

Another way to graph the relationship between income and consumption over time is shown in Exhibit 2, where U.S. disposable income is measured along the horizontal axis and U.S. consumption along the vertical axis. Notice that each axis measures the same units: trillions of dollars of 1992 purchasing power. Each year is depicted by a point that reflects two values: disposable income and consumption. In 1976, for example, disposable income (read from the horizontal axis) was $3.0 trillion, and consumption (read from the vertical axis) was $2.7 trillion.

As you can see, there is a clear and direct relationship between consumption and disposable income, a relationship that should come as no surprise after Exhibit 1. You need little imagination to see that by connecting the points on the graph in Exhibit 2, you could trace a line relating consumption to income. That relationship has special significance in macroeconomics.

The Consumption Function

So far we have examined the link between consumption and income and have found it to be quite stable. Given their level of disposable income, households decide how much to consume and how much to save. So consumption depends on disposable income. *Disposable income is the independent variable, and consumption the dependent variable.*

Consumption function The relationship between the level of income in an economy and the amount households plan to spend on consumption, other things constant

Because consumption depends on income, we say that consumption is a *function* of income. Exhibit 3 presents a hypothetical **consumption function,** which shows a positive relationship between the level of disposable income in the economy and the amount spent on consumption, with other determinants of consumption held constant. Again, both disposable income and consumption are measured in real terms, or in inflation-adjusted dollars. Notice that our hypothetical consumption function in Exhibit 3 looks similar to the actual historical relationship between consumption and disposable income, shown in Exhibit 2.

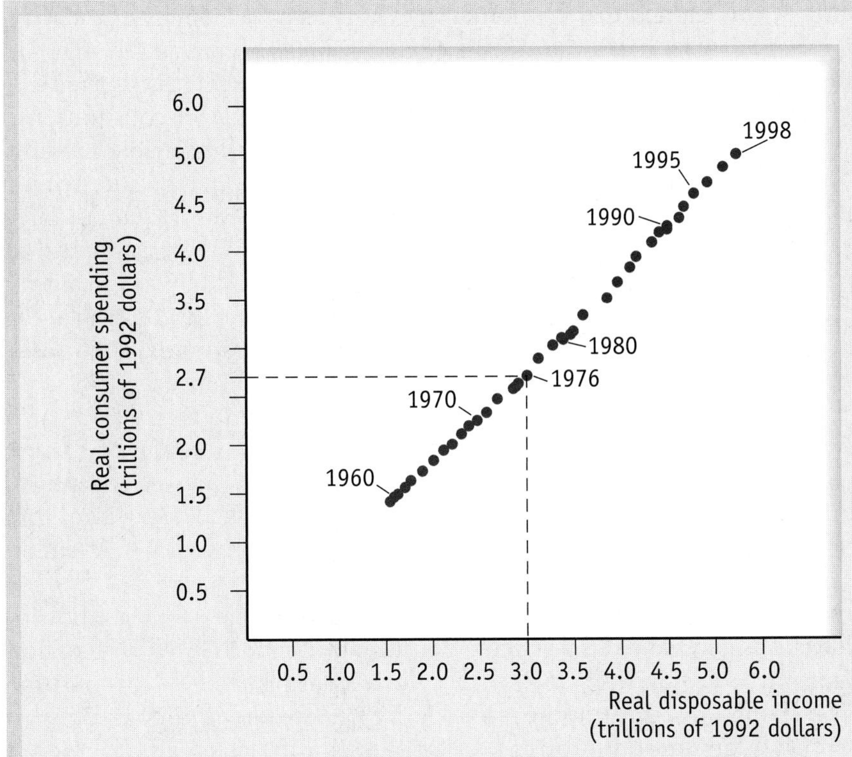

EXHIBIT 2

Dependence of Consumer Spending on Disposable Income

Source: Developed based on estimates found in *Economic Report of the President*, February 1999.

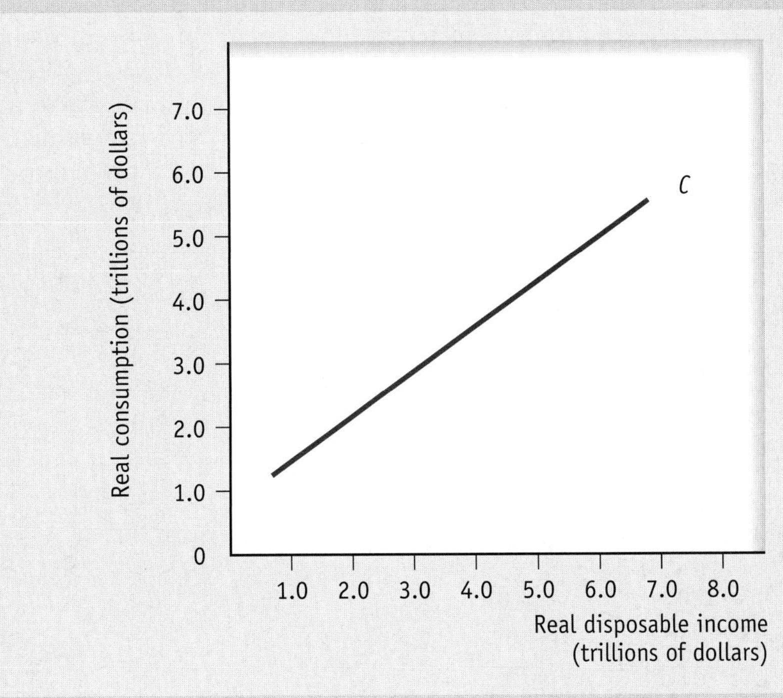

EXHIBIT 3

The Consumption Function

The consumption function, *C*, shows the relationship between consumption expenditure and disposable income, other things constant.

Marginal Propensities to Consume and to Save

In Chapter 1, you learned that economic analysis focuses on activity at the margin. For example, what happens to consumption if income changes by a certain amount? To study such changes, we must apply marginal analysis to the relationship between changes in disposable income and changes in consumption. Suppose U.S. households receive another billion dollars in disposable income. Some of this additional income will be spent on consumption and some will be saved. The fraction of the additional income that is consumed is called the marginal propensity to consume. More precisely, the **marginal propensity to consume,** or **MPC,** equals the change in consumption divided by the change in income. Likewise, the fraction of that additional income that is saved is called the marginal propensity to save. More precisely, the **marginal propensity to save,** or **MPS,** equals the change in saving divided by the change in income.

Marginal propensity to consume (MPC) The fraction of a change in income that is spent on consumption; the change in consumption spending divided by the change in income that caused it

Marginal propensity to save (MPS) The fraction of a change in income that is saved; the change in saving divided by the change in income that caused it

These propensities can be best understood by reference to Exhibit 4, which presents the hypothetical data underlying the consumption function of Exhibit 3. The table shows, for a range of possible incomes, how much consumers would like to spend and how much they would like to save. The first column presents alternative levels of disposable income, *DI,* beginning with $6.0 trillion and ranging up to $8.0 trillion in increments of $0.5 trillion.

As you can see from the table, if income increases from $6.0 trillion to $6.5 trillion, an increase of $0.5 trillion, consumption increases by $0.4 trillion and saving increases by $0.1 trillion. The marginal propensity to consume equals the change in consumption divided by the change in income. In this case, the change in consumption is $0.4 trillion and the change in income is $0.5 trillion, so the marginal propensity to consume is 0.4/0.5, or 4/5. Notice that each time income increases by $0.5 trillion, as indicated in column (2), consumption increases by $0.4 trillion, as indicated in column (4). Therefore the MPC, listed in column (7), is 4/5 at all levels of income shown.

At each income level, disposable income not spent on consumption is saved. Notice from column (6) that saving increases by $0.1 trillion with each $0.5 trillion increase in disposable income, so the marginal propensity to save equals 0.1/0.5, or 1/5, at all levels of income. The MPS is listed in column (8). Since disposable income is either spent or saved, the marginal propensity to

EXHIBIT 4

Marginal Propensity to Consume and Marginal Propensity to Save (trillions of dollars)

Income (Real *DI*) (1)	Change in Income (ΔDI) (2)	Consumption (*C*) (3)	Change in *C* (ΔC) (4)	Saving (*S*) (5)	Change in Saving (ΔS) (6)	MPC = (4) ÷ (2) ($\Delta C/\Delta DI$) (7)	MPS = (6) ÷ (2) ($\Delta S/\Delta DI$) (8)
6.0		5.7		0.3			
	0.5		0.4		0.1	0.4/0.5 = 4/5	0.1/0.5 = 1/5
6.5		6.1		0.4			
	0.5		0.4		0.1	4/5	1/5
7.0		6.5		0.5			
	0.5		0.4		0.1	4/5	1/5
7.5		6.9		0.6			
	0.5		0.4		0.1	4/5	1/5
8.0		7.3		0.7			

consume plus the marginal propensity to save must add up to 1. In our example, 4/5 + 1/5 = 1. We can say more generally that MPC + MPS = 1.

MPC, MPS, and the Slope of the Consumption and Saving Functions

You may recall from the appendix to Chapter 1 that the slope of a straight line is equal to the vertical distance between any two points divided by the horizontal distance between those points. Consider, for example, the slope between points *a* and *b* on the consumption function in panel (a) of Exhibit 5. The horizontal distance between these points shows the change in disposable income (denoted ΔDI)—in this case, \$0.5 trillion. The vertical distance shows the change in consumption (denoted ΔC)—in this case, \$0.4 trillion. The slope equals the vertical distance divided by the horizontal distance, or 0.4/0.5, which equals the marginal propensity to consume of 4/5.

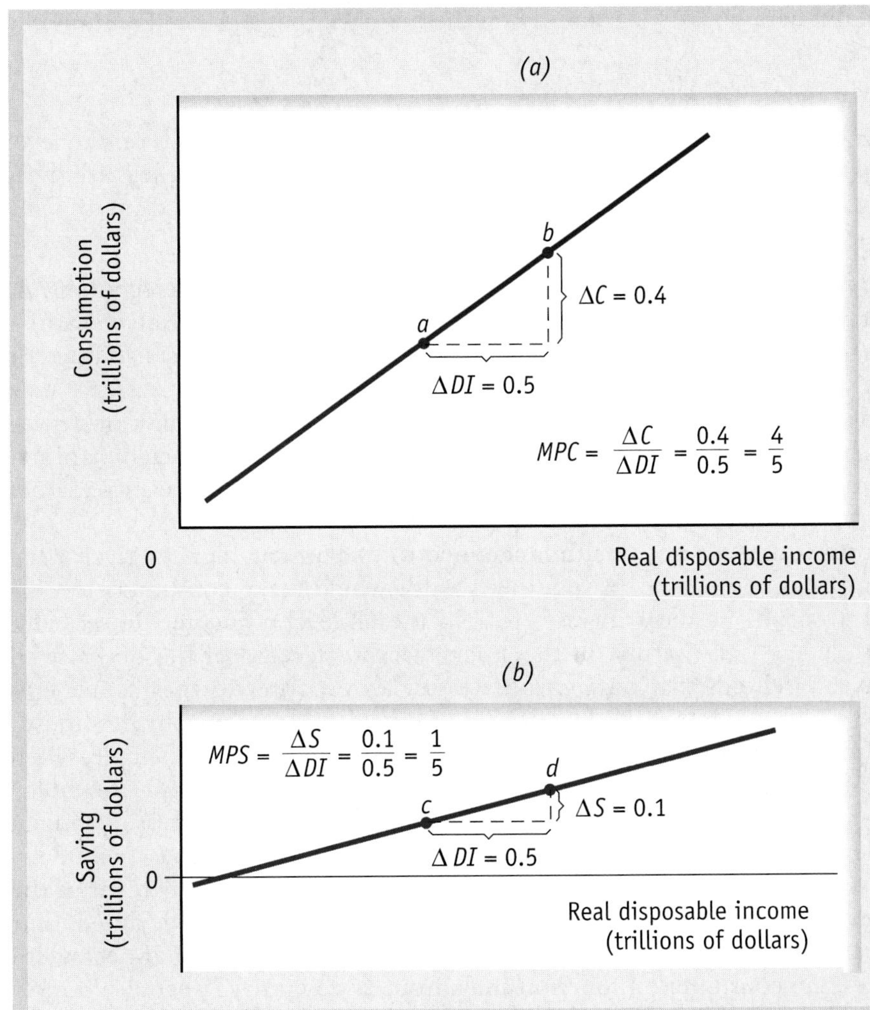

EXHIBIT 5

Marginal Propensities to Consume and to Save

The slope of the consumption function equals the marginal propensity to consume. For the straight-line consumption function of panel (a), the slope is the same at all levels of income and is given by the change in consumption divided by the change in disposable income that causes it. Hence, the marginal propensity to consume equals $\Delta C/\Delta DI$, or 0.4/0.5 = 4/5. The slope of the saving function equals the marginal propensity to save, $\Delta S/\Delta DI$, or 0.1/0.5 = 1/5.

Thus, *the marginal propensity to consume is measured graphically by the slope of the consumption function.* After all, the slope is nothing more than the increase in consumption divided by the increase in income. *Because the slope of any straight line is constant everywhere along the line, the MPC for any linear, or straight-line, consumption function will be constant at all levels of income.* We are assuming for convenience that the consumption function is a straight line, though it need not be.

Saving function The relationship between saving and the level of income in the economy, other things constant

Panel (b) of Exhibit 5 presents the **saving function,** *S,* which relates saving to the level of income, reflecting the hypothetical data presented in Exhibit 4. The saving function can be subjected to the same sort of graphical analysis as the consumption function. The slope between any two points on the saving function measures the change in saving divided by the change in income. For example, between points *c* and *d* in panel (b) of Exhibit 5, the change in income is $0.5 trillion and the resulting change in saving is $0.1 trillion. The slope between these two points therefore equals 0.1/0.5, or 1/5, which by definition equals the marginal propensity to save. Since the marginal propensity to consume and the marginal propensity to save are simply different sides of the same coin, from here on we focus mostly on the marginal propensity to consume.

Nonincome Determinants of Consumption

Along a given consumption function, consumer spending depends on the level of disposable income in the economy, other things constant. Now let's see what factors are held constant and how changes in these factors could cause the entire consumption function to shift.

Net wealth The value of a household's assets minus its liabilities

Net Wealth and Consumption. Given the level of income in the economy, an important factor influencing consumption is each household's **net wealth**—that is, the value of all assets that each household owns minus any liabilities, or debts owed. Consider your own family. Your family's assets may include a home, cars, furniture, bank accounts, cash, and the value of stocks, bonds, and pension funds. Your family's liabilities, or debt, may include a mortgage, car loans, student loans, credit card balances, and the like. To increase net wealth, your family can save or can pay off debts.

Total household net wealth is assumed to be constant along a given consumption function. A decrease in net wealth would make consumers less inclined to spend and more inclined to save at each level of income. To see why, suppose prices fall sharply on the stock market. Because of the decrease in wealth, households that own corporate stock are poorer so they spend less. Hence, a decrease in net wealth, other things held constant, encourages households to save more and spend less at each level of income. For example, when stock market prices fell sharply in October of 1987, the decrease in stockholders' net wealth prompted them to reduce consumption and increase saving at each level of income. Household saving as a percent of disposable income increased from 3.9 percent in the quarter before the crash to 5.7 percent in the quarter following the crash. Spending on new homes and cars declined. Our original consumption function is depicted as line *C* in Exhibit 6. If net wealth declines, the consumption function shifts from *C* down to *C'*, because households now want to spend less and save more at every level of income.

Conversely, suppose stock prices on average increase sharply. This increase in net wealth increases the desire to spend. For example, stock prices surged in

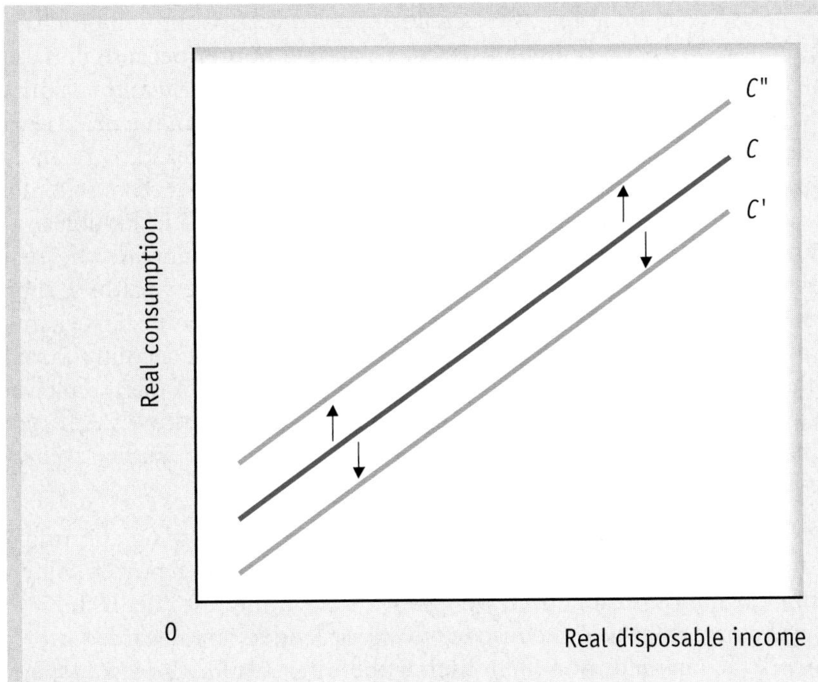

EXHIBIT 6

Shifts in the Consumption Function

A downward shift in the consumption function, such as from *C* to *C'*, can be caused by a decrease in wealth, an increase in the price level, an unfavorable change in consumer expectations, or an increase in the interest rate. An upward shift, such as that from *C* to *C"*, can be caused by an increase in wealth, a decrease in the price level, a favorable change in expectations, or a decrease in the interest rate.

1995, 1996, and 1997, and in the first half of 1998, increasing stockholders' net wealth. Consumption averaged 93 percent of disposable income during these three years, compared to an average of about 90 percent between 1960 and 1990. Sales of homes and cars took off. According to the *Economist,* a highly regarded publication, the strong stock market "made consumers feel richer, and as a result, they saved less and consumed more. In the second quarter [of 1998] America's personal saving rate fell to a historic low."[1]

As a result of an increase in net wealth, the consumption function shifts from *C* up to *C"*, reflecting households' desire to spend more at every level of income. Again, *it is a change in net wealth, not a change in disposable income, that shifts the consumption function. A change in disposable income, other things held constant, is reflected by a movement along a given consumption function, not a shift in that function.* Be mindful of the difference between a *movement along* the consumption function, which results from a change in income, and a *shift in* the consumption function, which results from a change in one of the nonincome determinants of consumption, such as net wealth.

The Price Level. Another variable that can affect the consumption function is the price level prevailing in the economy. As we have seen, households' net wealth is an important determinant of consumption. The greater the net wealth, other things constant, the greater consumption will be at each level of income. Some household wealth is held in dollar-denominated assets, such as bank accounts and cash. When the price level changes, so does the real value of bank accounts, cash, and other dollar-denominated financial assets.

1 "On the Edge," *Economist* (5 September 1998): 20.

For example, suppose your stock of wealth consists of $20,000 in a bank account. If the price level increases by 5 percent, your bank account will purchase about 5 percent fewer real goods and services. You feel poorer because you are poorer. The real value of your wealth has declined. To rebuild your wealth to some desired level, you decide to spend less and save more. An increase in the price level reduces the purchasing power of wealth held in fixed-dollar assets and, as a consequence, causes households to consume less and save more at each level of income. So the consumption function shifts down from C to C', as shown in Exhibit 6.

Conversely, should the price level ever fall, that would increase the real value of dollar-denominated assets. Since households would be wealthier, they would be willing and able to consume more at each level of income. For example, if the price level declined by 5 percent, your $20,000 bank account would then buy about 5 percent more real goods and services. A drop in the price level is reflected by a shift in the consumption function from C up to C''. *At each level of income, a change in the price level influences consumption by affecting the real value of net wealth.*

The Interest Rate. Interest is the reward paid to savers for deferring consumption and the amount paid by borrowers for current spending power. When graphing the consumption function, we assume a given interest rate. If the rate of interest increases, other things constant, savers, or lenders, are rewarded more, and borrowers are charged more. The higher the interest rate, the less is spent on those items typically purchased on credit, such as homes and cars. Thus at a higher rate of interest, households will save more, borrow less, and spend less. Greater saving at each level of income means less consumption. Simply put, *a rise in the interest rate, other things constant, will shift the consumption function downward.* Conversely, *a drop in the interest rate, other things constant, will shift the consumption function upward.*

Expectations. As we've seen, expectations influence economic behavior in a variety of ways. For example, suppose you are a senior in college and you land a high-paying job that starts upon graduation. Your consumption will probably jump long before the job actually begins. Conversely, a worker who receives a layoff notice to take effect at the end of the year will likely reduce consumption immediately, well before the actual date of the layoff. More generally, if people grow concerned about job security, they will reduce the amount consumed at each level of income.

Changing expectations about price levels and interest rates also affect consumption. For example, a change that leads householders to expect higher car prices or higher interest rates in the future will prompt some to purchase new cars now. On the other hand, a change leading householders to expect lower prices or lower interest rates in the future will cause some to defer car purchases. Thus expectations affect spending at each level of income, and a change in expectations can shift the consumption function. This is why consumer confidence is monitored so closely by economic forecasters.

Again, keep in mind the distinction between *movements along a given consumption function* as a result of a change in income and *shifts in the consumption function* as a result of a change in another variable. We conclude our introduction to consumption with the following case study, which discusses consumption and saving patterns over people's lifetimes.

The Life-Cycle Hypothesis

Do people who earn a high income save a larger fraction of their incomes than do those with low income? Both theory and evidence suggest that they do. The easier it is to make ends meet, the more likely it is that income will be left over for saving. Does it follow from this that richer economies save more than poorer ones—that economies save a larger fraction of total disposable income as they grow? In his famous book, *The General Theory*, published in 1936, John Maynard Keynes drew that conclusion. But as later economists studied the data—such as that presented in Exhibit 2—it became clear that Keynes was wrong. *For societies, the fraction of total disposable income saved seems to stay constant as the economy grows.*

So how can it be that richer individuals save more than poorer individuals, yet richer countries do not necessarily save more than poorer countries? By the early 1950s, several answers had been proposed. One of the most important of these was the *life-cycle model of consumption.* According to this model, people tend to borrow when they are young to finance education and home purchases; in middle age, they pay off their debts and save more; in old age, they draw down their savings, or dissave. Some people still have substantial wealth at death, because they are not sure when death will occur and because some parents want to pass wealth to their children. But net savings over a person's entire lifetime tend to be relatively small.

The life-cycle hypothesis suggests that the saving rate for an economy as a whole depends on, among other things, the relative number of savers and dissavers in the population. Other factors that influence the saving rate across countries include the manner in which saving is taxed, the convenience and reliability of saving institutions, and the relative cost of each household's major purchase—housing. In Japan, for example, about 25,000 post offices nationwide offer convenient savings accounts, and more than half the country's population hold accounts. In fact, Japan's postal savings system, with over $2 trillion in savings deposits, is the world's largest financial institution. Also, a home buyer in Japan must come up with a substantial down payment that represents a relatively large fraction of the home's purchase price, and housing there is more expensive than in the United States. All this calls for substantial savings. Since saving in Japan is both necessary and convenient, the country has one of the highest saving rates in the world. In 1998, the Japanese saved a much higher percentage of their disposable income than did Americans.

Sources: Stephanie Strom, "Minister Hopes to Privatize Japan's Postal System, but Faces Uphill Battle," *New York Times* (18 November 1997); Malcolm Fisher, "Life Cycle Hypothesis," *The New Palgrave: A Dictionary of Economics* 3 (London: Macmillan Press, 1987), pp. 177–179; and *OECD Economic Outlook* 63 (June 1998), Annex Table 26.

CaseStudy

Public Policy

The Japanese government has been trying various changes in government spending and tax policies to encourage more consumer spending. However, the Japanese public often just puts any extra income into savings. How can they be persuaded to spend more? A new, innovative policy is to issue purchase vouchers. The Japanese Information Agency reports on these at http://jin.jcic.or.jp/trends/honbun/ntj981201.html. To whom does the government intend to distribute these coupons? Why? Would receiving 20,000 yen in vouchers ensure that spending would increase by that amount?

We next consider the second component of aggregate expenditure: investment. Our ultimate objective is to understand the relationship between the total spending in the economy and the level of income.

INVESTMENT

The second component of aggregate expenditure is investment, or, more precisely, *gross private domestic investment.* By investment, we do not mean buying stocks, bonds, or other financial assets. Investment consists of spending on (1) new factories and new equipment such as computers, (2) new housing, and (3) net increases in inventories.

Business investment involves buying capital goods now in the expectation of a future return. Since the return is in the future, a would-be investor must estimate how much a particular investment will yield this year, next year, the year after, and in all future years covered by the productive life of the investment. *Firms buy new capital goods only if they expect this investment to yield a greater return than other possible uses of their funds.*

The Demand for Investment

To understand the investment decision, let's study a simple example. The operators of the Hacker Haven Golf Club are contemplating buying solar-powered golf carts to rent to golfers. The model under consideration, called the Weekend Warrior, sells for $2,000, requires no maintenance or operating expenses, and is expected to last indefinitely. *The expected rate of return equals the annual dollar earnings expected from the investment divided by the purchase price.* The first cart purchased is expected to earn a rental income of $400 per year. This income, divided by the cost of the cart, yields an expected rate of return on the investment of 400/2,000, or 20 percent per year. Additional carts will be used less. A second cart is expected to generate $300 per year in rental income, yielding a rate of return of 300/2,000, or 15 percent; a third cart, $200 per year, or 10 percent; and a fourth cart, $100 per year, or 5 percent. A fifth cart would not be used at all, so it has a zero expected rate of return.

Should the operators of Hacker Haven purchase any carts, and if so, how many? Suppose they plan to borrow the money to buy the carts. The number of carts they purchase will depend on the rate of interest they must pay to borrow money. If the market rate of interest exceeds 20 percent, their cost of borrowing exceeds the expected rate of return for even the first cart, so no carts will be purchased. What if the operators have enough money on hand to buy the carts? The market rate of interest also reflects what the club owners could earn on savings. If the interest rate paid on savings exceeds 20 percent, they could earn a higher rate of return by saving any funds on hand than by investing these funds in golf carts, so no carts would be purchased. *The market rate of interest represents the opportunity cost of investing in capital.*

Suppose the market rate of interest is 8 percent per year. At that rate, the first three carts, with expected rates of return exceeding 8 percent, would more than pay for themselves. A fourth cart would lose money, since its expected rate of return is only 5 percent. Exhibit 7 measures the nominal interest rate along the vertical axis and the amount invested in golf carts along the horizontal axis. The step-like relationship shows the expected rate of return earned on additional dollars invested in golf carts. This relationship also indicates the amount invested in golf carts at each interest rate, so you can view this step-like relationship as Hacker Haven's demand curve for this type of investment. For example, the first cart costs $2,000 and earns a rate of return of 20 percent. A firm

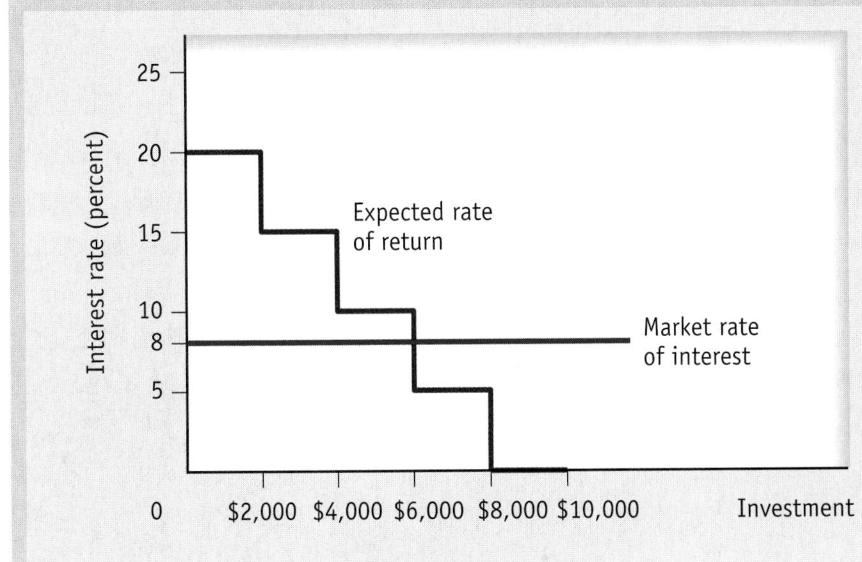

EXHIBIT 7

Rate of Return on Golf Carts and the Opportunity Cost of Funds

An individual firm will invest in any project whose rate of return exceeds the market interest rate. At an interest rate of 8 percent, Hacker Haven would purchase three golf carts, which represents investment spending of $6,000.

should reject any investment opportunity for which the expected rate of return falls below the market rate of interest.

The horizontal line at 8 percent indicates the market rate of interest, which represents Hacker Haven's opportunity cost of investing. Recall that the course operators' objective is to choose an investment strategy that maximizes profit. Profit is maximized when $6,000 is invested in the carts—that is, when three carts are purchased. The expected return from a fourth cart is 5 percent, which is below the opportunity cost of funds. Therefore, investing in four or more carts would lower total profit.

From Micro to Macro

So far we have examined the investment decision for a single golf course, but there are about 13,000 golf courses in the United States. The industry demand for golf carts shows the relationship between the amount all course operators invest and the expected rate of return. Like the step-like relationship in Exhibit 7, the investment demand curve for the golf industry slopes downward.

Let's move beyond golf carts and consider the investment decisions in all industries: publishing, hog farming, fast foods, apparel, and hundreds more. Individual industries generally have downward-sloping demand curves for investment. More is invested when the opportunity cost of borrowing is lower, other things equal. A downward-sloping investment demand curve for the entire economy can be derived, with some qualifications, from a horizontal summation of all industries' downward-sloping investment demand curves. The economy's *investment demand curve* is represented as *D* in Exhibit 8, which shows the inverse relationship between the quantity of investment demanded and the market rate of interest, other things—including business expectations—held constant. For example, in Exhibit 8, when the market rate of interest is 8 percent, the

EXHIBIT 8

Investment Demand Curve for the Economy

The investment demand curve for the economy is obtained by summing the amount of investment undertaken by each firm at each interest rate. At lower interest rates, more investment projects become profitable for individual firms, so the total investment spending in the economy increases.

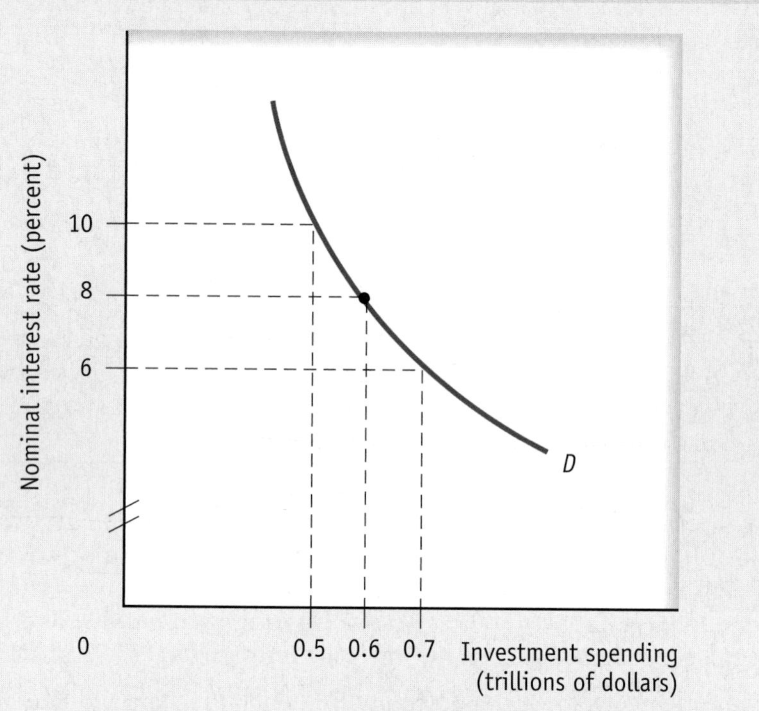

quantity of investment demanded is \$0.6 trillion. If the interest rate rises to 10 percent, investment spending declines to \$0.5 trillion, and if the interest rate falls to 6 percent, investment increases to \$0.7 trillion. Held constant along the investment demand curve are business expectations about the economy. If firms grow more optimistic about profit prospects, the demand for investment increases, and the entire curve shifts to the right.

Planned Investment and the Economy's Level of Income

To integrate the discussion of investment with our earlier analysis of consumption, we need to know if and how investment varies with the level of income in the economy. Whereas we were able to present empirical evidence relating consumption to disposable income over time, the link between investment and disposable income is much weaker. Over the last dozen years, for example, investment shows little relation to the level of income. *Investment depends more on interest rates and on business expectations than on the prevailing level of income.* One reason investment is less related to the current level of income is that some investments, such as a new electric power plant, take years to complete. And once investment is in place, it is expected to last for years, even decades. The investment decision is thus said to be "forward looking," based more on expected profit than on current levels of income and output.

Investment function The relationship between the amount businesses plan to invest and the level of income in the economy, other things constant

So how does planned investment relate to disposable income? The simplest **investment function** assumes that planned investment is unrelated to the current level of disposable income; investment is assumed to be **autonomous** with respect to income. For example, suppose that, given current business expectations and an interest rate of 8 percent, firms plan to invest \$0.6 trillion, regardless of the economy's income level. Exhibit 9 measures disposable income on the horizontal axis and planned investment on the vertical axis. Investment of \$0.6 trillion is shown by the flat investment function, *I*. As you can see, along investment function *I*, planned investment does not vary even though real disposable income does.

Autonomous A term that means "independent"; autonomous investment is independent of the level of income

Nonincome Determinants of Investment

The investment function isolates the relationship between the level of income in the economy and *planned investment*—the amount firms would like to invest, other things constant. We have already mentioned two important determinants that are held constant: the interest rate and business expectations. Now let's look at the effect of changes in these factors on investment.

Market Interest Rate. Exhibit 8 showed that if the interest rate were 8 percent, desired, or planned, investment would be \$0.6 trillion. This level of investment is shown as *I* in Exhibit 9. If the interest rate increases because of, say, a change in the nation's monetary policy that reduces the supply of loanable funds in the economy (as happened in 1994), the cost of borrowing increases and this increases the opportunity cost of investment. For example, if the interest rate increases from 8 percent to 10 percent, planned investment drops from \$0.6 trillion to \$0.5 trillion; this decrease is reflected in Exhibit 9 by a downward shift of the investment function from *I* to *I'*. Conversely, a drop in the rate of interest from 8 percent to 6 percent, other things held constant, will reduce the cost of borrowing and increase planned investment from \$0.6 trillion to

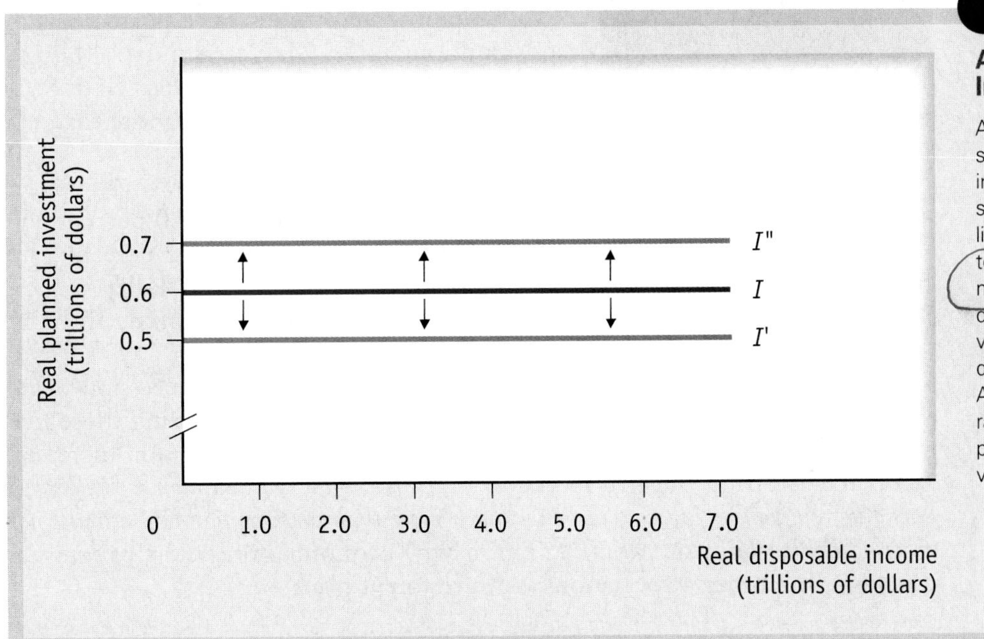

EXHIBIT 9

Autonomous Investment Function

Autonomous investment spending is assumed to be independent of income, as shown by the horizontal lines. An increase in the interest rate or declining business expectations can decrease autonomous investment, as shown by the downward shift from *I* to *I'*. A decrease in the interest rate or upbeat business expectations can shift the investment function up to *I"*.

NetBookmark

For a personal view on J.M. Keynes and his work, read "Cairncross on Keynes," an obituary written by one of his students, Sir Alec Cairncross. It originally appeared in the *Economist* and is now available on line at a site maintained by Prof. Brad De Long at http://econ161.berkeley.edu/Economists/cairncrossonkeynes.html.

$0.7 trillion, as reflected by the upward shift of the investment function from I to I''. Notice that the shifts in Exhibit 9 mirror interest-rate movements along the investment demand curve in Exhibit 8.

Business Expectations. As we saw in Chapter 5, investment depends primarily on business expectations, or on what Keynes called the "animal spirits" of business. Suppose planned investment initially is $0.6 trillion, as depicted by I in Exhibit 9. If most firms now become more pessimistic about profit prospects, perhaps expecting a recession, their planned investment will decrease at every level of income, as reflected in Exhibit 9 by a shift of the investment function from I down to I'. On the other hand, if profit expectations become rosier, firms will be more willing to invest, thereby increasing the investment function from I up to I''. *Examples of factors that could affect business expectations, and hence investment plans, include wars, technological change, changes in the tax structure, and financial crises around the world, such as occurred in Asia and Russia in 1998.* Changes in business expectations also shift the investment demand curve in Exhibit 8.

Now that we have examined consumption and investment individually, let's take a look at their year-to-year variability in the following case study.

Visit the Web site for the Research Seminar in Quantitative Economics at the University of Michigan at http://rsqe.econ.lsa.umich.edu/index.html. RSQE is "an economic modeling and forecasting unit which has been in operation at the University of Michigan since 1952. RSQE provides forecasts of the economic outlook for the U.S. and Michigan economies, based on quarterly econometric models." Read the latest Executive Summary for their U.S. forecast. What are the "seeds" or sources of the predicted trend? How, specifically, do the forecasters believe that the types of consumption and investment spending cited in the text will change and affect real GDP?

Variability of Consumption and Investment

We already know that consumption makes up about two-thirds of GDP and that investment spending varies from year to year, averaging about one-seventh of GDP in the last decade. Now let's compare the year-to-year variability in consumption, investment, and GDP. Exhibit 10 shows the annual percentage changes since 1960 in consumption, investment, and GDP, all measured in real terms.

Two points are obvious. First, fluctuations in consumption and in GDP are similar, although consumption varies slightly less than GDP. Second, investment fluctuates much more than either consumption or GDP. For example, in the recession year of 1982, GDP declined by 2.1 percent but investment declined by 14.4 percent; consumption actually increased by 1.2 percent. In 1984, GDP increased by 7.0 percent, investment increased 29.8 percent, and consumption increased 5.2 percent. The recession that stretched into the first quarter of 1991 reduced GDP that year by 0.9 percent; investment declined by 9.4 percent, and consumption declined by 0.6 percent

During the 38 years since 1960, GDP declined during five recession years, with the decline averaging 0.9 percent annually. Investment during those five years declined an average of 12.2 percent. On average, consumption increased 0.3 percent during the five recession years. So *while consumption is the largest spending component, investment varies much more than consumption and accounts for most of the variability in real GDP.* This is why economic forecasters pay special attention to business expectations and investment plans.

Sources: *Economic Report of the President,* February 1999; U.S. Department of Commerce, *Survey of Current Business* 78 (December 1998); and *OECD Economic Outlook* 64 (December 1998).

EXHIBIT 10

Annual Percentage Changes in U.S. Real GDP, Real Consumption, and Real Investment

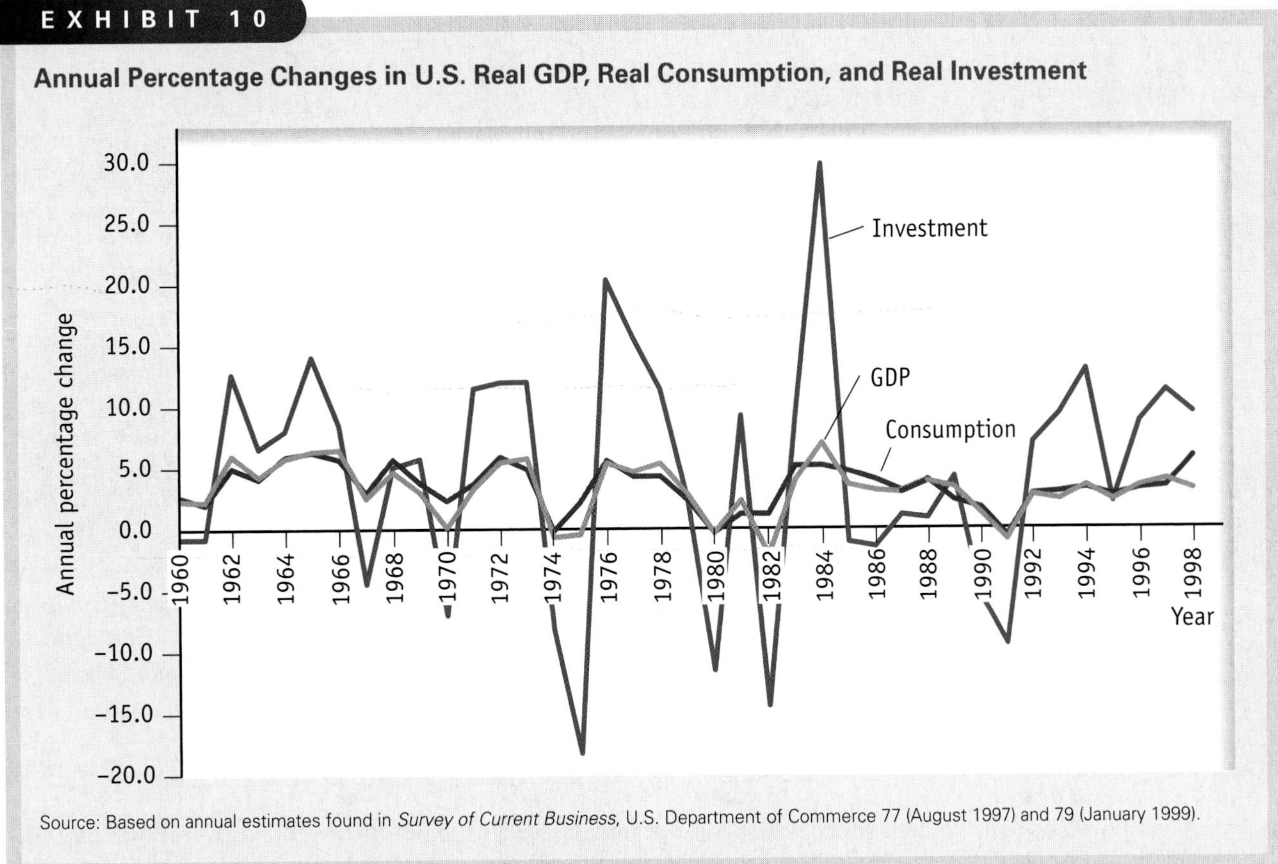

Source: Based on annual estimates found in *Survey of Current Business,* U.S. Department of Commerce 77 (August 1997) and 79 (January 1999).

GOVERNMENT

The third component of aggregate expenditure is government purchases of goods and services. Federal, state, and local governments purchase thousands of goods and services, ranging from weapon systems to road signs. In the United States, government purchases in 1998 accounted for about 17 percent of GDP—about one-third of which was by the federal government and about two-thirds by state and local governments.

Government Purchase Function

The **government purchase function** relates government purchases to the level of income in the economy, other things constant. Since decisions about government purchases are largely under the control of public officials, such as the decision to build an interstate highway system or to reduce military spending, these purchases do not depend directly on the level of income in the economy. We therefore assume that *government purchases, G,* are autonomous, or independent of the level of income. Such a function would relate to income as a flat line similar to the investment function shown in Exhibit 9. An increase in government purchases would result in a shift up in the government purchase

Government purchase function The relationship between government purchases and the level of income in the economy, other things constant

function. And a decrease in government purchases would result in a shift down in the government purchase function.

Net Taxes

As noted earlier, government purchases represent only one of the two components of government outlays; the other is *transfer payments,* such as Social Security, welfare benefits, and unemployment benefits. Transfer payments, which are outright grants from governments to households, make up about one-third of government outlays. Transfer payments vary inversely with income; as income increases, transfer payments decline.

To fund government outlays, governments impose taxes. Taxes vary directly with income; as income increases, so do taxes. *Net taxes* equal taxes minus transfers. Since taxes tend to increase with income but transfers tend to decrease with income, for simplicity, let's assume that net taxes do not vary with income. Thus, we say that *net taxes*, or *NT,* are *autonomous,* or independent of the level of income.

Net taxes affect aggregate spending indirectly by changing disposable income, which changes consumption. We saw from the discussion of the circular flow that by subtracting net taxes, we transform real GDP into *disposable income.* Disposable income is take-home pay—the income households can spend or save. We will examine the impact of net taxes in the next few chapters.

NET EXPORTS

The rest of the world affects aggregate expenditure through imports and exports and has a growing influence on the U.S. economy. The United States, with only one-twentieth of the world's population, accounts for about one-sixth of the world's imports and one-eighth of the world's exports.

Net Exports and Income

How do imports and exports relate to the level of income in the economy? When their incomes rise, Americans spend more, and some of this increased spending goes for imported goods. Higher incomes lead to more spending on Persian rugs, French wine, Korean VCRs, trips to Europe, and thousands of other foreign goods and services.

How does the value of U.S. exports relate to the economy's level of income? The amount of U.S. exports purchased by the rest of the world depends on the income of foreigners, not on the U.S. level of income. The desire of the French to purchase U.S. computers or the desire of Saudi Arabians to purchase U.S. military hardware is not influenced by the level of disposable income in the United States.

Net export function The relationship between net exports and the level of income in the economy, other things constant

The **net export function** shows the relationship between net exports and the level of income in the economy, other things constant. Since our exports are relatively insensitive to the level of U.S. income but our imports tend to increase with income, *net exports,* which equal the value of exports minus the value of imports, tend to decline as income increases. Such an inverse relationship is developed graphically in the appendix to this chapter. For now, we simplify the analysis by assuming that net exports are *autonomous,* or independent of the level of disposable income.

If exports exceed imports, net exports are positive; if imports exceed exports, net exports are negative; and if exports equal imports, net exports equal zero. U.S. net exports have been negative in nearly every year during the last three decades, so let's suppose net exports are autonomous and equal to –$0.1 trillion, or –$100 billion, as shown by the net export function $X - M$ in Exhibit 11.

Nonincome Determinants of Net Exports

Factors held constant along the net export function include the U.S. price level, the price levels in other countries, interest rates here and abroad, foreign income levels, and the exchange rate between the dollar and foreign currencies. Consider the effects of a change in one of these factors. Suppose the value of the dollar increases relative to foreign currencies such as those of Asia, as happened in 1998. With the dollar worth more on world markets, foreign products become cheaper for Americans and U.S. products become more costly for foreigners. A rise in the dollar's exchange value will increase imports and decrease exports, resulting in a decrease in net exports, shown in Exhibit 11 by a parallel drop in the net export line from $X - M$ down to $X' - M'$, a drop from –$100 billion to –$120 billion.

A decline in the value of the dollar, as occurred in 1994, will have the opposite effect, increasing exports and decreasing imports. An increase in autonomous net exports is shown in our example by a parallel increase in the net export function, from $X - M$ up to $X'' - M''$, reflecting an increase in autonomous net exports from –$100 billion to –$80 billion. Countries often devalue their currency in an attempt to increase their net exports and increase employment. The effect of changes in net exports on aggregate spending will be taken up in the next chapter.

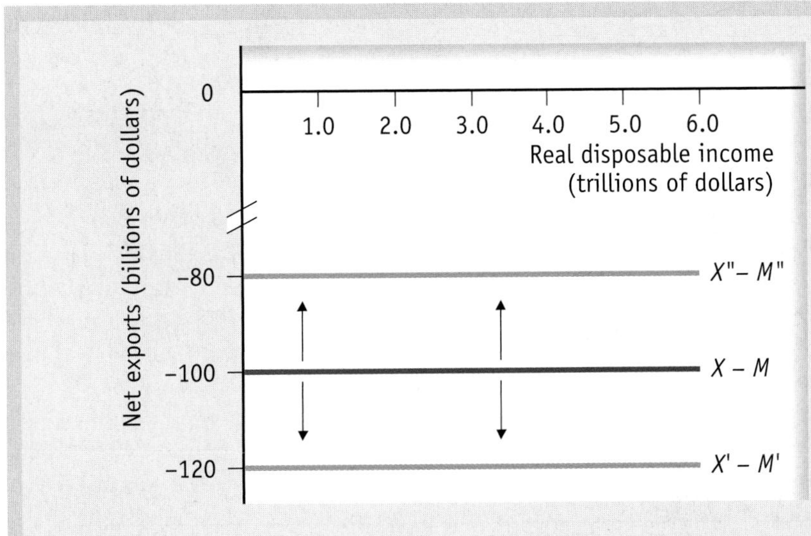

EXHIBIT 11

Autonomous Net Export Function

Autonomous net exports are assumed to be independent of disposable income, as shown by the horizontal lines. $X - M$ is the net export function if net exports equal –$100 billion. An increase in the value of the dollar relative to other currencies would cause net exports to decrease, as shown by the shift down to $X' - M'$. A decrease in the value of the dollar would cause net exports to increase, as shown by the shift up to $X'' - M''$.

COMPOSITION OF AGGREGATE EXPENDITURE

Now that we have examined each component of aggregate spending, let's get some idea of the breakdown of GDP among the spending components over time. Exhibit 12 shows the percentage composition of spending in the United States for the last four decades. As you can see, consumption's share of GDP was relatively stable from year to year, but the long-term trend showed an increase from an average of 61.9 percent during the 1960s to 67.8 during the 1990s. Investment bounced around the most from year to year, with a modest trend upward during that period. Investment spending as a percent of GDP increased from an average of 12.7 percent during the 1960s to 14.5 percent during the 1990s.

Government purchases declined from an average of 26.6 percent of GDP during the 1960s to 19 percent during the 1990s. Declines in defense spending accounted for most of this drop. By 1998, government purchases made up only 17.2 percent of GDP, the smallest share since 1930. Incidentally, in Chapter 4 you learned that all government *outlays,* which include both purchases and transfers, have increased relative to GDP. The sharp growth in transfer payments, especially Social Security, accounts for all the growth in government outlays relative to GDP (recall that government purchases do not include transfer payments).

EXHIBIT 12

U.S. Spending Components as a Percentage of GDP

Source: Based on estimates from U.S. Department of Commerce, *Survey of Current Business* 77 (August 1997) and 79 (January 1999); and *Economic Report of the President*, February 1999.

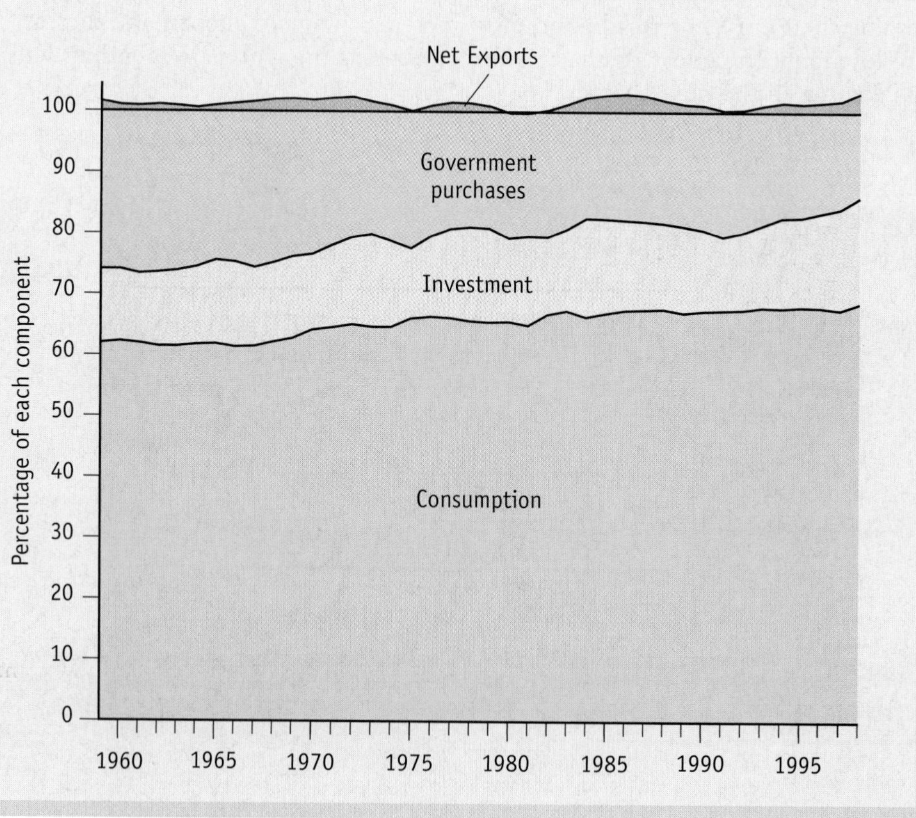

Net exports have been negative nearly every year shown. Negative net exports mean that the sum of consumption, investment, and government purchases exceeds GDP, the amount produced in the U.S. economy. Americans can spend more than they make by borrowing from abroad. So U.S. spending exceeds U.S. GDP by the amount shown as negative net exports. Since the spending components must sum to GDP, *negative* net exports are expressed in Exhibit 12 by that portion of spending that exceeds 100 percent of GDP.

In summary, during the last four decades, consumption's share of aggregate spending has increased and the share of spending going to government purchases has decreased, primarily because of declines in defense spending. Investment spending has bounced around, with a modest upward trend, and net exports have been negative.

CONCLUSION

This chapter has focused on the relationship between spending and income. We studied the four components of aggregate expenditure: consumption, investment, government purchases, and net exports. Consumption is related positively to the level of income in the economy. Investment relates more to such factors as interest rates and business expectations than to income. Government purchases are also assumed to be autonomous, or independent of income. And net exports are assumed, for now, to be affected more by such factors as the exchange rate than by the level of domestic income. (The appendix to this chapter develops a more realistic but also more complicated picture by showing how net exports decline as the level of income increases.) In the next chapter we will see how aggregate spending depends on income and how this relationship helps determine the aggregate output demanded.

SUMMARY

1. One of the most predictable and useful relationships in macroeconomics is that between consumption and disposable income. The consumption function indicates that the more income people have, the more they spend on consumption, other things constant.

2. The consumption function shows the link between desired consumption and income in the economy. The slope of the consumption function reflects the marginal propensity to consume, which equals the change in consumption divided by the change in income. The slope of the saving function reflects the marginal propensity to save, which equals the change in saving divided by the change in income.

3. Certain factors can cause consumers to change the amount they want to spend at each level of income. An increase in net wealth reduces households' need to save and hence increases consumption at every level of income. A higher price level reduces the value of dollar-denominated assets such as currency and bank deposits, thereby reducing net wealth, which reduces consumption. An increase in the interest rate makes saving more rewarding and borrowing more costly and hence decreases consumption. Expectations about future income and price levels also influence consumption.

4. Planned investment depends on the market rate of interest and on business expectations. Investment, which averaged about one-seventh of GDP during the 1990s, tends to be unrelated to the level of income in the economy.

5. Government purchases of goods and services made up about 19 percent of GDP during the 1990s, with about one-third of that spending by the federal governments.

Government purchases are based on the public choices of elected officials and are assumed to be autonomous, or independent of the level of income in the economy. Net taxes, or taxes minus transfers, are also assumed for now to be unrelated to income.

6. Net exports equal the value of exports minus the value of imports. Exports are unrelated to the level of income in this country. Imports tend to be positively related to income. Thus, net exports tend to decline as income increases. For simplicity, we initially assume that net exports are autonomous, or unrelated to domestic income. The appendix to this chapter deals with net exports that decline with income.

QUESTIONS FOR REVIEW

1. *(Consumption Function)* How would an increase in each of the following variables affect the consumption function? How would it affect the saving function?
   a. Autonomous net taxes
   b. The interest rate
   c. Consumer optimism, or confidence
   d. The price level
   e. Real wealth
   f. Disposable income
2. *(Consumption Function)* A number of factors can cause the consumption function to shift. What, if anything, happens to the saving function when the consumption function shifts? Explain.
3. *(**CaseStudy:** Life-Cycle Hypothesis)* According to the life-cycle hypothesis, what is the typical pattern of saving for an individual over his or her lifetime? What impact does this behavior have on an individual's lifetime consumption pattern? What impact does the behavior have on the saving rate in the overall economy?
4. *(Investment Spending)* What are the components of gross private domestic investment? What is the difference between the investment curve shown in Exhibit 7 and the one shown in Exhibit 8? Do these curves refer to actual or planned investment?
5. *(Investment)* Why would the following investment expenditures increase as the interest rate declines?
   a. Purchases of a new plant and equipment
   b. Construction of new housing
   c. Accumulation of planned inventories
6. *(Nonincome Determinants of Investment)* What are some factors that can cause the autonomous investment function to shift? What kinds of changes could cause investment spending to increase at each level of real disposable income?
7. *(**CaseStudy:** Variability of Consumption and Investment)* Why do economic forecasters pay special attention to investment plans? Take a look at the Conference Board's index of leading economic indictors at http://www.conferenceboard.org. Which of those indicators might affect investment plans?
8. *(Government Spending)* How do changes in disposable income affect government purchases and the government purchase function? How do changes in net taxes affect the consumption function?
9. *(Net Exports)* What factors are assumed constant along the net export function? What would be the impact on net exports of a change in real disposable income?

PROBLEMS AND EXERCISES

10. *(Consumption)* Use the following data to answer the questions below.

Real Disposable Income	Consumption Expenditures
$100	$150
200	200
300	250
400	300

   a. Graph the consumption function with consumption spending on the vertical axis and disposable income on the horizontal axis.
   b. If the consumption function is a straight line, what is its slope?
   c. If investment is equal to $100, at what level of disposable income does saving equal investment?

11. *(MPC and MPS)* If consumption increases by $12 billion when real disposable income increases by $15 billion, what is the value of the MPC? What is the relationship between the MPC and the MPS? If the MPC rises, what must happen to the MPS? How is the MPC related to the consumption function? How is the MPS related to the saving function?

12. *(Consumption and Saving)* Suppose that consumption equals $500 billion when disposable income is $0 and that each increase of $100 billion in disposable income causes consumption to increase by $70 billion. Draw a graph of the saving function using this information.

13. *(Investment Spending)* Review Exhibit 7 in this chapter. If the owners of the golf course revised their revenue estimates so that each cart is expected to earn $100 less, how many carts would they buy at an interest rate of 8 percent? How many would they buy if the interest rate is 3 percent?

EXPERIENTIAL EXERCISES

14. *(Marginal Propensity to Consume)* Find some recent data on U.S. real disposable income and real consumption spending. (One possible source is the *Economic Report of the President* at http://www.access.gpo.gov/eop/, but there are many others.) Use the data to compute the marginal propensity to consume for each year, 1991 to 1998. Has the MPC been relatively constant?

15. *(Variability of Consumption and Investment)* Expectations and consumer confidence are important in determining fluctuations in aggregate spending. What is the present status of consumer confidence as measured by the Conference Board's index? You can find the data, with interpretation, at The Dismal Scientist at http://www.dismal.com/economy/releases/consumer.asp.

16. *(Wall Street Journal)* Business investment spending is an important component of aggregate expenditure. Review the "Business Bulletin" column on the front page of Thursday's *Wall Street Journal*. What are some recent trends in investment spending? Are they likely to increase or decrease aggregate expenditure? (Remember that purchases of stocks and bonds are *not* investment, in the sense described in this chapter!)

Appendix

VARIABLE NET EXPORTS

In this appendix, we examine more closely the relationship between net exports and the U.S. level of income. We first look at exports and imports separately and then consider exports minus imports, or net exports.

NET EXPORTS AND INCOME

As noted in the chapter, the amount of U.S. output purchased by foreigners depends not on the U.S. level of income but on income levels in their own countries. We therefore assume that U.S. exports do not vary with respect to the U.S. income level. Specifically, suppose the rest of the world spends \$0.6 trillion per year on U.S. exports of goods and services; the export function, X, is as shown in panel (a) of Exhibit 13. On the other hand, when disposable income increases, U.S. consumers spend more on all goods and services, including imported goods and services. Thus, the relationship between imports and income is positive, as expressed by the upward-sloping import function, M, in panel (b) of Exhibit 13. Imports are assumed to be 10 percent of disposable income, so when disposable income is \$6.0 trillion, imports are \$0.6 trillion.

So far we have considered imports and exports as separate functions of income. What matters in terms of total spending on U.S. products are exports, X, minus imports, M, or net exports, $X - M$. Since money spent on imports goes to foreign producers, not U.S. producers, imports are subtracted from the circular flow of spending. By subtracting the import function depicted in panel (b) from the export function in panel (a), we derive the *net export function*, depicted as $X - M$ in panel (c) of Exhibit 13. Note that when income is \$6.0 trillion, *imports* in panel (b) equal \$0.6 trillion.

Since *exports* in panel (a) equal \$0.6 trillion at all levels of income, net exports equal zero when U.S. disposable income equals \$6.0 trillion. At levels of income below \$6.0 trillion, net exports are positive because exports exceed imports. At levels of income greater than \$6.0 trillion, net exports are negative because imports exceed exports. The United States has experienced negative net exports during most of the last four decades. Our high trade deficit in recent years traces in part to the economic expansion in the United States. The trade deficit shrank during the recession of the early 1990s, but then increased again as the U.S. economy recovered.

EXHIBIT 13

Imports, Exports, and Net Exports

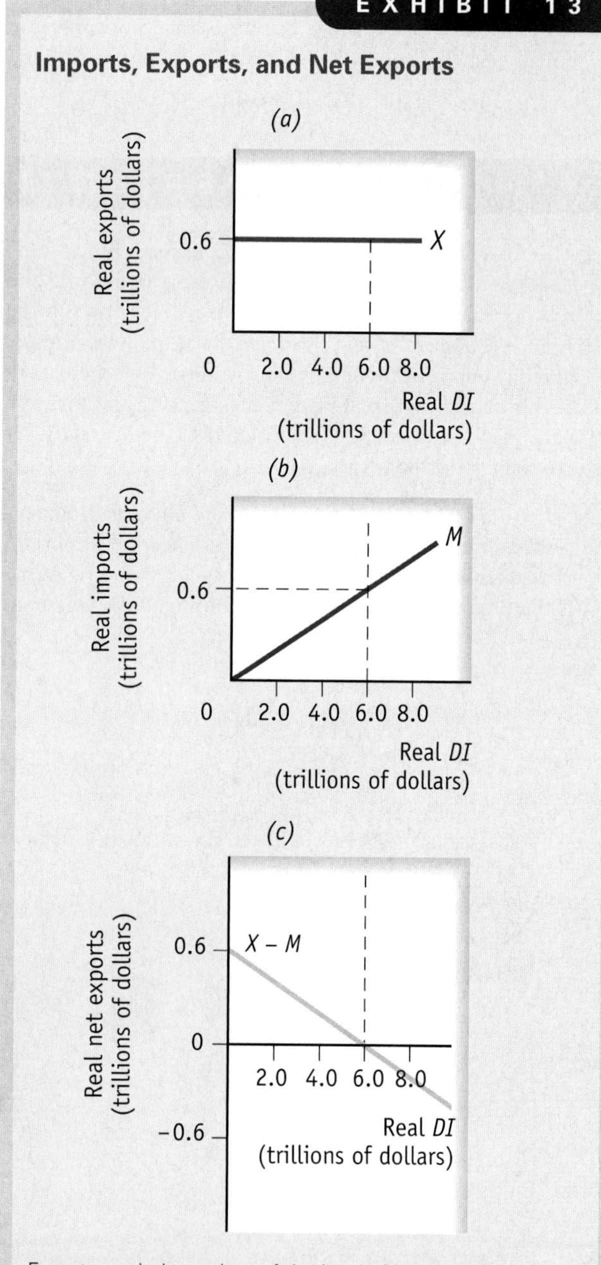

Exports are independent of the level of income, as shown in panel (a). Imports are positively related to income, as shown in panel (b). Net exports equal exports minus imports; net exports are negatively related to income, as shown in panel (c).

SHIFTS IN NET EXPORTS

The net export function, $X - M$, shows the relationship between net exports and disposable income, other things constant. Suppose the value of the dollar increases relative to foreign currencies, as it did in 1998. With the dollar worth more on world markets, foreign products become cheaper for Americans and U.S. products become more expensive for foreigners. The impact of a rising dollar is to decrease exports but increase imports at each level of income. This decreases net exports, as shown in Exhibit 14 by the shift from $X - M$ down to $X' - M'$. A decline in the dollar's value will have the opposite effect, increasing exports and decreasing imports, as reflected in Exhibit 14 by an upward shift in the net export function from $X - M$ to $X'' - M''$.

In summary, in this appendix we assumed that *imports relate positively to the level of income, whereas exports are independent of the domestic level of income. Net exports, which equal exports minus imports, therefore vary inversely with the level of income.* The net export function shifts upward if the value of the dollar falls and shifts downward if the value of the dollar rises.

EXHIBIT 14

Shifts in Net Exports

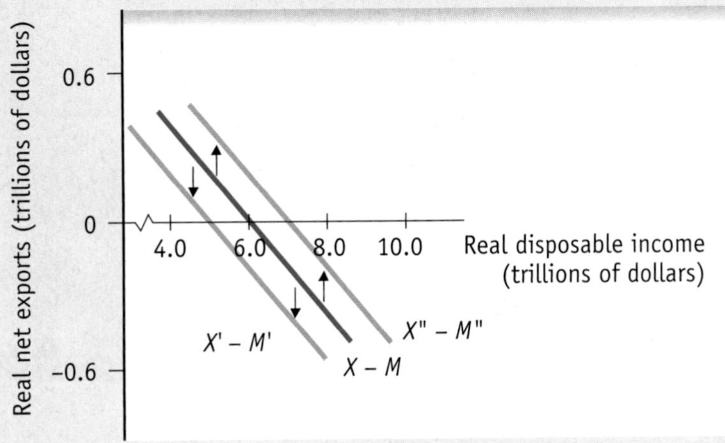

A rise in the value of the dollar, other things held constant, will decrease exports and increase imports, thereby contributing to a decrease in net exports, as shown by the shift from $X - M$ down to $X' - M'$. A decrease in the value of the dollar will increase exports and decrease imports, causing net exports to rise, as shown by the shift from $X - M$ up to $X'' - M''$.

APPENDIX QUESTION

(Rest of the World) Using a graph of net exports ($X - M$) against disposable income, show the effects of the following:

a. An increase in foreign income
b. An increase in U.S. income
c. An increase in the U.S. interest rate
d. An increase in the value of the dollar against foreign currencies

Explain each of your answers.

CHAPTER

10 Aggregate Expenditure and Aggregate Demand

How does aggregate spending in the economy relate to income? What is the effect of a change in the price level on aggregate spending? And what does all this have to do with aggregate demand? More fundamentally, what is the link between the economy's price level and the quantity of GDP demanded? Answers to these and other questions are covered in this chapter, which develops the aggregate demand curve.

Your economic success depends to a large extent on the overall performance of the economy. When the economy expands, jobs grow more abundant, so your chances of finding a good one increase. When the economy contracts, job opportunities shrink, as do job prospects. Thus, you should have a personal interest in the economy's level of output and the year-to-year changes

Visit the McEachern Interactive Study Center for this chapter at http://mcisc.swcollege.com

in output. In this chapter we continue to build a model that will help us determine the economy's equilibrium level of output, or real GDP.

Chapter 9 discussed the components of aggregate spending—consumption, investment, government purchases, and net exports—showing how each relates to the level of income in the economy. In this chapter, these components are added up to show how total spending, or aggregate expenditure, relates to the level of income. We then use this information to derive the aggregate demand curve. Aggregate supply will be developed in Chapter 11; then, a fuller treatment of the effects of government spending and taxing will be examined in Chapter 12.

In Appendix A, you can see what happens when imports increase with income. An algebraic approach to the aggregate expenditure framework is developed in Appendix B. Topics discussed in this chapter include:

- Aggregate expenditure line
- Real GDP demanded
- Effect of changes in aggregate expenditure
- Simple spending multiplier
- Effect of changes in the price level
- Aggregate demand curve

AGGREGATE EXPENDITURE AND INCOME

In the previous chapter, the big idea was the link between income and consumption, a link that is the most stable in all of macroeconomics. In this section, we build on the income-consumption relationship to uncover the tie between total spending and income. If we try to confront the economy head-on, it soon becomes a bewildering maze, which is why we often make progress only by making simplifying assumptions. In this chapter, we continue to assume, as we did in developing the circular flow model, that there is no capital depreciation and no business saving. Hence, we can say that *each dollar spent on production translates directly into a dollar of aggregate income.* Therefore, gross domestic product, or GDP, equals aggregate income. We also continue to assume that net exports are autonomous, or independent of the level of income.

The Components of Aggregate Expenditure

Let's begin developing the aggregate demand curve by asking how much aggregate output would be demanded at a given price level. By finding the quantity demanded at a given price level, we'll identify a single point on the aggregate demand curve. We want to consider the relationship between aggregate spending in the economy and aggregate income, or real GDP. By *real* GDP, we mean GDP measured in terms of real goods and services produced.

To get us started, suppose the price level in the economy is 130, meaning that it is 30 percent higher than in the base year. We want to find out how much will be spent at various levels of real GDP, or real income. Exhibit 1 presents the hypothetical data that will serve as building blocks for constructing the relation between aggregate spending and income. This exhibit simply puts into tabular form relationships that were introduced in the previous chapter—consumption, saving, planned investment, government purchases, net taxes, and net exports. Although the entries are hypothetical, they bear some relation to levels observed in the U.S. economy.

EXHIBIT 1

Table for Real GDP, with Net Taxes and Government Purchases (trillions of dollars)

Real GDP (*Y*) (1)	Net Taxes (*NT*) (2)	Disposable Income (*Y* – *NT*) (3) = (1) – (2)	Consumption (*C*) (4)	Saving (*S*) (5)	Planned Investment (*I*) (6)	Government Purchases (*G*) (7)	Net Exports (*X* – *M*) (8)	Planned Aggregate Expenditure (*AE*) (9)	Unintended Inventory Adjustment (*Y* – *AE*) (10) = (1) – (9)
7.0	1.0	6.0	5.7	0.3	0.6	1.0	–0.1	7.2	–0.2
7.5	1.0	6.5	6.1	0.4	0.6	1.0	–0.1	7.6	–0.1
8.0	**1.0**	**7.0**	**6.5**	**0.5**	**0.6**	**1.0**	**–0.1**	**8.0**	**0.0**
8.5	1.0	7.5	6.9	0.6	0.6	1.0	–0.1	8.4	+0.1
9.0	1.0	8.0	7.3	0.7	0.6	1.0	–0.1	8.8	+0.2

The first column in Exhibit 1 lists a range of possible levels of real GDP in the economy, called *Y*. The second column shows *net taxes,* or *NT,* which are assumed to be $1.0 trillion at each level of real GDP. Subtracting net taxes from real GDP yields *disposable income*, listed in column (3) as *Y* – *NT*. Note that at all levels of real GDP, disposable income equals real GDP minus net taxes of $1.0 trillion. Since net taxes are assumed to be autonomous, each time real GDP increases by $0.5 trillion, disposable income also increases by $0.5 trillion.

Households have only two possible uses for disposable income: consumption and saving. Columns (4) and (5) show that the levels of *consumption, C,* and *saving, S,* increase with disposable income. Each time real GDP and disposable income increase by $0.5 trillion, consumption increases by $0.4 trillion and saving increases by $0.1 trillion. Thus, as in the previous chapter, the marginal propensity to consume is 4/5, or 0.8, and the marginal propensity to save is 1/5, or 0.2.

Columns (6), (7), and (8) list three now-familiar injections of spending into the circular flow: *planned investment* of $0.6 trillion, *government purchases* of $1.0 trillion, and *net exports* of – $0.1 trillion. In the table, government purchases equal net taxes, so the government budget is balanced. We want to see how a balanced budget works before we look at the effects of budget deficits or surpluses, which are discussed in Chapter 12. *The sum of consumption, C, planned investment, I, government purchases, G, and net exports, X – M, is listed in column (9) as planned aggregate expenditure, AE, which indicates the amount that households, firms, governments, and the rest of the world plan to spend on U.S. output at each level of real GDP.* Note that the only spending component that varies with the level of real GDP is consumption. As real GDP increases, so does disposable income, which increases the amount households spend on consumption.

The final column in Exhibit 1 lists any unplanned inventory adjustment, which equals real GDP minus planned aggregate expenditure, or *Y* – *AE*. For example, when real GDP is $7.0 trillion, planned aggregate expenditure is $7.2 trillion. Since planned spending exceeds the amount produced by $0.2 trillion, firms must reduce inventories by $0.2 trillion to make up the shortfall in output. So when real GDP is \$7.0 trillion, the unplanned inventory adjustment in column (10) is –\$0.2 trillion. Because firms cannot reduce inventories indefinitely, they respond to such reductions by increasing production, and they continue to do so until the amount they produce just matches planned spending.

If the amount produced exceeds planned spending, firms get stuck with unsold goods, which become unplanned increases in inventories. For example, if real GDP is \$9.0 trillion, planned aggregate expenditure is only \$8.8 trillion, so \$0.2 trillion in output remains unsold. Hence, inventories increase by \$0.2 trillion. Firms respond by reducing production and will do so until the amount produced just equals the amount people want to buy—that is, until real GDP equals planned aggregate expenditure.

When the amount people plan to spend equals the amount produced, there are no unplanned inventory adjustments. More precisely, *for a given price level, the quantity of real GDP demanded is found where real GDP equals planned aggregate expenditure.* In Exhibit 1, this occurs where planned aggregate expenditure and real GDP equal \$8.0 trillion.

Quantity of Real GDP Demanded

Using a table, we have seen how firms adjust output until production just equals desired spending. You may find graphs easier to understand than tables. Graphs are also more general than tables and can show relationships between variables without focusing on specific numbers. The tabular relationship between real GDP and planned aggregate expenditure in Exhibit 1 can be expressed as an **aggregate expenditure line** in Exhibit 2. Like the aggregate expenditure amounts shown in column (9) of Exhibit 1, the aggregate expenditure line in Exhibit 2 reflects the sum of consumption, investment, government purchases, and net exports, or $C + I + G + (X - M)$. Planned aggregate expenditure is measured on the vertical axis.

Aggregate expenditure line A relationship showing, for a given price level, planned spending at each level of income; the total of $C + I + G + (X - M)$ at each level of income

Real GDP, measured along the horizontal axis in Exhibit 2, can be viewed in two ways—as the value of *aggregate output* and as the *aggregate income* generated by that level of output. Because real GDP, or income, is measured on the horizontal axis and aggregate expenditure is measured on the vertical axis, this graph is often called the **income-expenditure model.**[1]

Income-expenditure model A relationship between aggregate income and aggregate spending that determines, for a given price level, where income equals planned spending

To gain perspective on the relationship between income and expenditure, we use a handy analytical device: the 45-degree ray from the origin. The special feature of this line is that any point along it is exactly the same distance from both axes. Thus, the 45-degree line identifies all points where real GDP and planned expenditure are equal. *The quantity of aggregate output demanded at a given price level occurs where real GDP, measured along the horizontal axis, equals planned aggregate expenditure, measured along the vertical axis.* In Exhibit 2, this occurs at point *e*, where the aggregate expenditure line intersects the 45-degree line. At point *e*, the amount people plan to spend equals the amount produced. Keep in mind that this approach was based on a given price level.

1 Note that in Exhibit 2 the horizontal axis measures real GDP. In the previous chapter, the horizontal axis measured disposable income. There is not much of a difference because real GDP minus net taxes equals disposable income. Since net taxes in our example are \$1.0 trillion, every level of real GDP implies a level of disposable income that is \$1.0 trillion lower. The link between real GDP and each spending component was spelled out in Exhibit 1.

EXHIBIT 2

Deriving the Aggregate Output Demanded for a Given Price Level

The aggregate output demanded, given the price level, is found where aggregate expenditure equals real GDP—that is, where desired spending equals the amount produced.

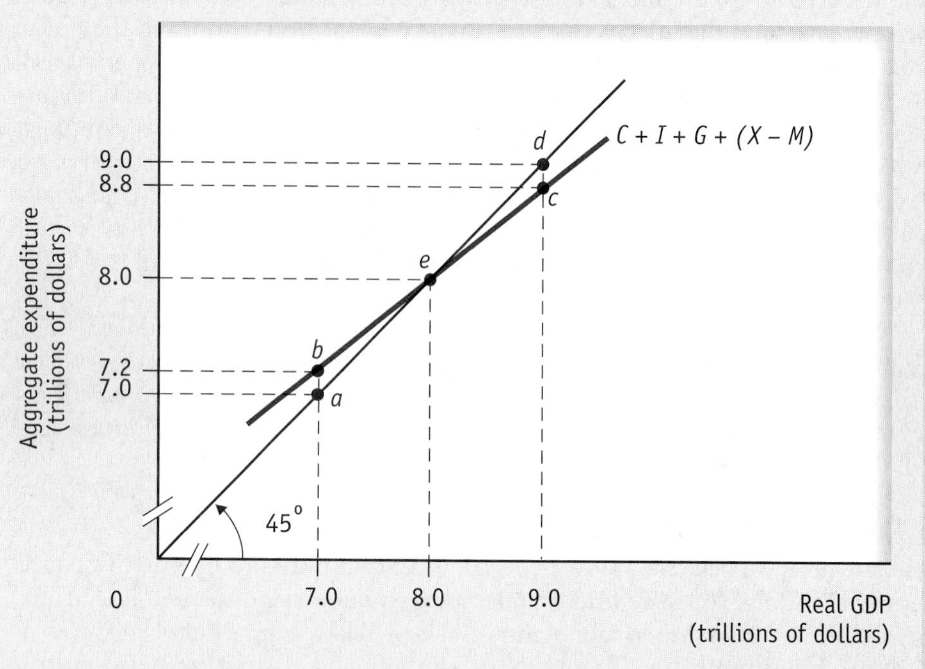

We conclude that, at the given price level, the quantity of real GDP demanded equals \$8.0 trillion.

When Output and Planned Spending Differ

To find the quantity of real GDP demanded at the given price level, consider what happens when real GDP is initially less than \$8.0 trillion. As you can see from Exhibit 2, at levels of real GDP less than \$8.0 trillion, the planned aggregate expenditure line is above the 45-degree line, indicating that planned spending exceeds the amount produced. For example, if real GDP is \$7.0 trillion, planned aggregate expenditure is \$7.2 trillion, as indicated by point *b* on the aggregate expenditure line, so planned spending exceeds output by \$0.2 trillion. When the amount people plan to spend exceeds the amount firms produce, something has to give. Ordinarily what gives is the price level, but remember that we are seeking the quantity of real GDP demanded for a given price level, so the price level is assumed to be constant, at least for now. What gives in this model are firms' *inventories*. Firms are forced to sell from inventories to make up the \$0.2 trillion by which spending exceeds real GDP. Since firms cannot draw from inventories indefinitely, *unplanned inventory reductions* prompt firms to produce more output. That increases real GDP, which increases employment and consumer income, leading to more spending. As long as planned spending exceeds output, firms must increase production to make up the difference. This process of more output, more income, and more spending will continue until planned aggregate expenditure equals real GDP, an equality achieved at point *e*.

When output reaches $8.0 trillion, planned spending exactly matches output, so no unintended inventory adjustments occur. More importantly, when output reaches $8.0 trillion, planned spending equals the amount produced and equals the total income generated by that production. Earlier we assumed a price level of 130. Therefore, $8.0 trillion is the quantity of real GDP demanded at that given price level. In terms of the symbols introduced earlier, we say that *the quantity of real GDP demanded equals aggregate expenditure—the sum of consumption, C, plus planned investment, I, plus government purchases, G, plus net exports, X – M.*

To reinforce the logic of the model, consider what happens when real GDP exceeds $8.0 trillion—that is, when the aggregate expenditure line is below the 45-degree line. Note in Exhibit 2 that, along that portion of the aggregate expenditure line to the right of point *e*, planned spending falls short of production. For example, if the amount produced in the economy is $9.0 trillion, desired spending, as indicated by point *c* on the aggregate expenditure line, is $0.2 trillion less than real GDP, indicated by point *d* on the 45-degree line. Since real GDP exceeds the amount people want to spend, unsold goods accumulate. This swells inventories by $0.2 trillion more than firms wanted. Rather than allow inventories to pile up indefinitely, firms reduce production, which reduces employment and income. *Unplanned inventory buildups* cause firms to cut production until the amount they produce equals aggregate expenditure, which occurs, again, at a level of real GDP of $8.0 trillion.

Given the price level, the quantity of aggregate output demanded is found where the amount people plan to spend equals the amount produced. Hence, *for a given price level, there is only one point along the aggregate expenditure line at which planned spending equals real GDP.*

We have now discussed the forces that determine the quantity of real GDP demanded for a given price level. In the next section, we examine the impact of a shift in the aggregate expenditure line.

THE SIMPLE SPENDING MULTIPLIER

In the previous section, we employed the aggregate expenditure line to determine the quantity of aggregate output demanded for a particular price level. In this section, we continue to assume that the price level remains unchanged, as we trace the effects of changes in planned spending on the quantity of aggregate output demanded. Like a stone thrown into a still pond, the effect of any shift in planned spending ripples through the economy, generating changes in aggregate output that may far exceed the initial shift in planned spending.

Effects of an Increase in Aggregate Expenditure

We begin at point *e* in Exhibit 3, where planned spending equals real GDP at $8.0 trillion. Now let's consider the effect of an increase in one of the components of spending. Suppose that firms become more optimistic about future profit prospects and as a result increase their planned investment. Specifically, suppose planned investment increases from $0.6 trillion to $0.7 trillion per

NetBookmark

As mentioned in Chapter 1, economists are storytellers. One important storyteller is Alan Greenspan, Chair of the Board of Governors of the Federal Reserve. In a January 1998 speech he looked back at the economic events of 1997 and told stories about the forces influencing consumption and investment spending, two key aspects of aggregate demand. You can find the speech at http://www.federalreserve.gov/BoardDocs/Speeches/1998/19980108.htm.

year, as reflected in Exhibit 3 by a change in the aggregate expenditure line, which shifts up by \$0.1 trillion, from $C + I + G + (X - M)$ to $C + I' + G + (X - M)$.

What happens to real GDP demanded? An instinctive response is that real GDP demanded should increase by \$0.1 trillion. In this case, however, instinct is a poor guide. As you can see, the new spending line intersects the 45-degree line at point *e*', where real GDP is \$8.5 trillion. How can a \$0.1 trillion increase in planned spending increase real GDP by \$0.5 trillion? What's going on?

The idea of the circular flow is central to an understanding of the process of adjustment from one level of real GDP to another. As noted earlier, real GDP can be thought of as both the value of production and the income arising from that production. Recall that production yields income, which generates spending. We can think of each trip around the circular flow as a "round" of income and spending.

Round One. An upward shift of the aggregate expenditure line means that, at the initial real GDP level of \$8.0 trillion, planned spending now exceeds output by \$0.1 trillion, or \$100 billion. This is shown in Exhibit 3 by the difference between point *e* and point *a*. Initially this increased spending may be satisfied by

EXHIBIT 3

Effect of an Increase in Autonomous Investment on Real GDP Demanded

The economy is initially at point *e*, where spending and real GDP both equal \$8.0 trillion. A \$0.1 trillion increase in autonomous investment shifts up the aggregate expenditure line vertically by \$0.1 trillion from $C + I + G + (X - M)$ to $C + I' + G + (X - M)$. Real GDP rises until it equals spending at point *e*'. As a result of the \$0.1 trillion increase in autonomous investment, real GDP demanded increases by \$0.5 trillion, to \$8.5 trillion.

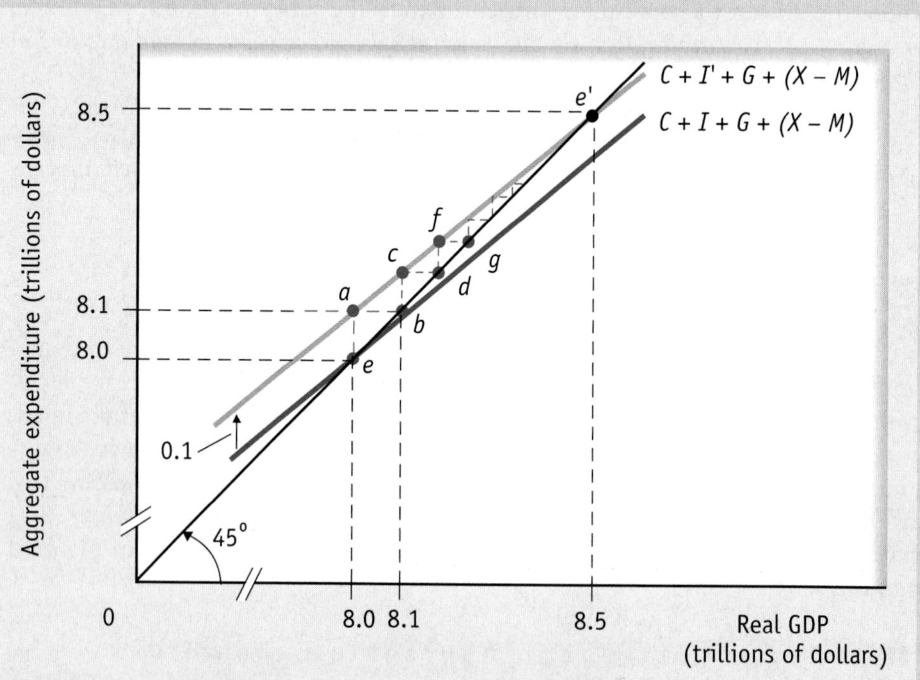

reducing inventories, but shrinking inventories prompt firms to expand production by $100 billion, as shown by the movement from point *a* to point *b*. This increased production generates $100 billion in increased income.

Thus output and income increase by $100 billion in the first round of new spending arising from the increase in planned investment of $100 billion. The movement from *e* to *b* represents the first round in the multiplier process. The income-generating process does not stop there, however, because those who receive this additional income spend some of it and save some of it, laying the basis for round two of spending and income.

Round Two. Given a marginal propensity to consume of 4/5, or 0.8, those who receive the $100 billion as income will spend a total of $80 billion on toasters, movies, backpacks, and thousands of other goods and services. The other $20 billion of that $100 billion will be saved. This $80 billion spending increase is reflected by the move from point *b* to point *c* in Exhibit 3. Firms respond by increasing their output by $80 billion, reflected by the movement from point *c* to point *d*. Thus the initial $100 billion in new income increases real GDP by $80 billion during the second round.

Round Three and Beyond. Focus now on the $80 billion that went toward consumption during round two. Production increases of $80 billion in the second round generate an equal amount of income for resource suppliers. Again, based on the marginal propensity to consume, we know that four-fifths of the additional income will be consumed and one-fifth will be saved. Thus, $64 billion will be spent on still more goods and services, as reflected by the movement from point *d* to point *f* (the remaining $16 billion will be saved). The additional spending causes firms to increase output by $64 billion, as shown by the movement from point *f* to point *g*. This increase in real GDP means that income also increases by $64 billion, laying the basis for subsequent rounds of spending, output, and income. *As long as planned spending exceeds output, production will increase, thereby creating more income, which will generate still more spending.*

Simple Spending Multiplier

When does the income-generating machine run out of fuel? At some point the new rounds of income and spending become so small that they disappear and the process stops. Looked at another way, saving leaks from the circular flow during every round. The more income that leaks as saving, the less that remains to fuel still more spending and income.

The initial increase of $0.1 trillion in autonomous investment has increased real GDP demanded from $8.0 trillion to $8.5 trillion, or by $0.5 trillion. Thus each dollar of increased investment spending has multiplied fivefold. The **simple spending multiplier** is the multiple by which real GDP changes for a given initial change in spending. The simple spending multiplier is computed as the ratio of the change in real GDP demanded to the initial expenditure change that caused it. In our example, the multiplier equals 0.5/0.1, or 5.

Simple spending multiplier The ratio of a change in real GDP demanded to the initial change in expenditure that brought it about; the numerical value of the simple spending multiplier is 1/(1 – MPC); called "simple" because consumption is the only component that varies with income

The quantity of real GDP demanded would have increased by the same amount if consumers had decided to spend $100 billion more at each level of income—that is, if the consumption function, rather than the investment function, had shifted up by $100 billion. Real GDP demanded would likewise have increased if government purchases or net exports had increased by $100 billion. *The change in the quantity of aggregate output demanded depends on how much the aggregate expenditure line shifts, not on which spending component causes the shift.*

Note that, in our example, planned investment increased by $100 billion, or $0.1 trillion, per year. *If this higher level of planned investment is not sustained in the following year, real GDP demanded will fall back.* For example, if planned investment returns to $0.6 trillion, other things constant, real GDP demanded will return to $8.0 trillion.

Numerical Value of the Simple Spending Multiplier

Tracing the rounds of spending is one way to determine the effects of a particular change in spending, but this process is slow and tedious. What we need is a quick way to translate changes in planned spending into changes in the level of real output demanded at a given price level. Recall that the expansion stemming from an increase in autonomous spending depends on the marginal propensity to consume. The spending multiplier and the marginal propensity to consume are related in a way that proves useful in formulating the multiplier. *The larger the fraction of an increase in income that is respent each round, the larger the spending multiplier.* The marginal propensity to consume and the multiplier are directly related; the larger the MPC, the larger the multiplier. Thus, we can define the simple spending multiplier in terms of the MPC as follows:

$$\text{Simple spending multiplier} = \frac{1}{1 - \text{MPC}}$$

Since the MPC is 4/5, the denominator equals 1 – 4/5, or 1/5, and the simple spending multiplier equals the reciprocal of 1/5, which is 5. If the MPC were 3/4, the denominator would equal 1 – 3/4, or 1/4, and the simple spending multiplier would equal the reciprocal of 1/4, which is 4.[2]

Recall from Chapter 9 that the MPC and the MPS add up to 1, so 1 minus the MPC equals the MPS. With this information, we can define the simple spending multiplier in terms of the MPS as follows:

$$\text{Simple spending multiplier} = \frac{1}{1 - \text{MPC}} = \frac{1}{\text{MPS}}$$

The simple spending multiplier is the reciprocal of the MPS. When we express the equation this way, we can see that the smaller the MPS, the larger the fraction of each fresh round of income that is spent and the less leaks out as saving, so the larger the multiplier. This spending multiplier is called *simple* because only consumption varies with the level of real GDP; the other spending components are assumed to be independent of real GDP.

2 A more formal way of deriving the spending multiplier is to total the additions to spending arising from each new round of income and spending. For example, a $1 increase in investment generates $1 in spending in the first round. In the second round, it generates $1 times the MPC. In the third round, the new spending equals the spending that arose in the second round ($1 × MPC) times the MPC. This goes on round after round, with each new round equal to the spending from the previous round times the MPC. Mathematicians have shown that the sum of an infinite series of rounds, each of which is a constant fraction of the previous round, is 1/(1 – MPC) times the initial amount. In our context, 1/(1 – MPC) is the spending multiplier.

The focus of the spending multiplier thus far has been the national economy. But the idea of the multiplier has some relevance for state and regional economies as well, as shown in the following case study.

Hard Times in Connecticut

*Case*Study

Public Policy

Check up on how the employment situation in Connecticut has fared since 1993 at http://www.state.ct.us/ecd/research/digest/articles/nov98art1.html. In this article, "Employment And Wages: Peak To Trough To Present," from the November 1998 online edition of *Connecticut Economic Digest,* Charles Joo reports on employment trends by industry. Which sectors have gained, and which have lost, jobs? How, in particular, has the economic recovery affected the manufacturing sector, which was hurt by the layoffs at UTC and other firms during the hard times in the state in 1992–93?

Because of a cutback in federal defense spending and a fall in worldwide orders for commercial aircraft, the United Technologies Corporation (UTC), a major producer of jet engines, announced in January of 1993 that by the end of 1994 it would eliminate 10,000 manufacturing jobs in Connecticut. UTC also planned to reduce its orders from dozens of Connecticut firms that supplied the company with everything from precision parts to janitorial services, thereby causing several thousand more job losses in the state. The direct layoffs, as well as expected layoffs by subcontractors, reflected an initial payroll loss exceeding $1 billion.

In a state with an expanding economy, job losses in one sector can be made up at least in part by job expansions in other sectors. But such losses proved especially painful in Connecticut, where a long recession had already cut jobs sharply during the previous three years. Consequently, those who lost high-paying jobs making jet engines faced grim alternatives.

This loss in employment and payroll rippled through the Connecticut economy, reducing the demand for housing, clothing, entertainment, restaurant meals, and other goods and services. For example, the unemployed engine makers ate out less frequently, reducing the income of restaurant owners, workers, and suppliers. Those who lost restaurant jobs reduced their own demand for goods and services.

So reductions in jet production had a multiplier effect in Connecticut. But the effect spilled beyond the state's borders. For example, individuals who lost jobs demanded fewer automobiles, cutting the incomes of auto workers living in places such as Detroit and San Diego. Thus, the number of job losses resulting from UTC's job cuts was greater for the nation as a whole than for Connecticut alone. Therefore, the spending multiplier is greater for the nation as a whole than for Connecticut.

Sources: Michael Remez, "State Suppliers to Feel Big Sting from Pratt Cuts," *Hartford Courant* (28 January 1993); and William McEachern, "Picking Up the Pieces After Connecticut's Great Recession," *The Connecticut Economy: A University of Connecticut Quarterly Review* (April 1993).

DERIVING THE AGGREGATE DEMAND CURVE

Thus far in this chapter we have used the aggregate expenditure line to find the quantity of real GDP demanded *for a given price level.* But, as we shall see, for each price level there is a specific aggregate expenditure line, which yields a unique quantity of real GDP demanded. By altering the price level, we can derive the aggregate demand curve.

A Higher Price Level

What is the effect of a higher price level on the economy's aggregate expenditure line and, in turn, on the quantity of real GDP demanded? Recall that consumers hold many assets that are fixed in dollar terms, such as currency and bank accounts. A higher price level decreases the real value of these dollar-denominated assets. Consumers therefore are poorer, so they are less willing to spend at each level of income. For reasons that will be more fully explained in a later chapter, a higher price level also tends to increase the market rate of interest, and a higher interest rate reduces investment. Finally, a higher U.S. price level means that foreign goods become relatively cheaper for U.S. consumers and U.S. goods become relatively more expensive abroad. So imports will rise and exports will fall, decreasing net exports. *A higher price level therefore reduces consumption, planned investment, and net exports, which all reduce aggregate spending.* This decrease in the aggregate expenditure line reduces the quantity of real GDP demanded.

The panels of Exhibit 4 represent different ways of expressing the effects of a change in the price level on the quantity of real GDP demanded. Panel (a) presents the income-expenditure model and panel (b) presents the aggregate demand curve, showing the inverse relationship between the price level and output demanded. The idea is to find, for a given price level, the quantity of aggregate output demanded in panel (a) and express that price-quantity combination as a point on the aggregate demand curve in panel (b).

The two panels are aligned so that levels of real GDP on the horizontal axes correspond. At the initial price level of 130 in panel (a), the aggregate expenditure line, now denoted by *AE*, intersects the 45-degree line at point *e* to yield \$8.0 trillion, the quantity of real GDP demanded. Panel (b) shows more directly the link between the quantity of real GDP demanded and the price level. As you can see, when the price level is 130, the quantity demanded is \$8.0 trillion. This combination of price level and real GDP is identified by point *e* on the aggregate demand curve.

What if the price level increases from 130 to, say, 140? An increase in the price level reduces consumption, investment, and net exports. This reduction in planned spending is reflected in panel (a) by a decrease in the aggregate expenditure line from *AE* down to *AE*'. As a result of this decrease in planned spending, the quantity of real GDP demanded declines from \$8.0 trillion to, say, \$7.5 trillion (we can't say exactly what this new level of real GDP demanded will be unless we know exactly how the component of aggregate expenditure respond to a higher price level). Panel (b) shows that an increase in the price level from 130 to 140 decreases the quantity of real GDP demanded from \$8.0 trillion to \$7.5 trillion, as reflected by point *e*'.

A Lower Price Level

The opposite holds if the price level falls. At a lower price level, the value of bank accounts, currency, and other dollar-denominated assets increases. Consumers on average are richer and are more inclined to spend on consumption at each level of real GDP. A lower price level also tends to decrease the market interest rate, which increases investment. Finally, a lower U.S. price level, other things constant, makes U.S. products relatively cheaper abroad and foreign prod-

EXHIBIT 4

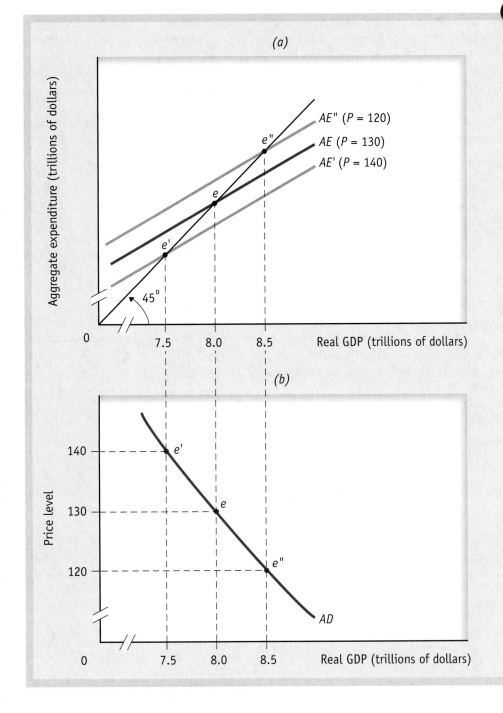

The Income-Expenditure Approach and the Aggregate Demand Curve

At the initial price level of 130, the aggregate expenditure line is *AE*, which identifies real GDP demanded of $8.0 trillion. Hence, this combination of a price level 130 and real GDP demanded of $8.0 trillion determine one point (point *e*) on the aggregate demand curve in panel (b).

At the higher price level of 140, the aggregate expenditure line is lower at *AE'* and real GDP demanded is less at $7.5 trillion. This price-output combination is plotted as point *e'* in panel (b).

At the lower price level of 120, the aggregate expenditure line is higher at *AE"* and so is real GDP demanded. That price-ouput combination is plotted as point *e"* in panel (b).

Connecting points *e*, *e'*, and *e"* gives us the downward-sloping aggregate demand curve that shows how much real GDP is demanded at each price level.

ucts relatively more expensive to Americans, so exports increase and imports decrease. Thus, *because of a decline in the price level, consumption, investment, and net exports increase at each level of real GDP.* A higher aggregate expenditure line leads to a higher quantity of real GDP demanded.

Refer again to Exhibit 4 and consider the effect of a decrease in the price level. Suppose the price level declines from 130 to, say, 120. As explained already, a decline in the price level causes consumption, planned investment, and net exports to increase, as reflected in panel (a) of Exhibit 4 by the shift upward in the aggregate expenditure line from *AE* to *AE*". An increase in planned spending at each level of income increases real GDP demanded from $8.0 trillion to, say, $8.5 trillion, as indicated by the intersection of the top aggregate expenditure line with the 45-degree line at point *e*". This same price decrease can be viewed more directly in panel (b). As you can see, when the price level decreases to 120, the quantity of real GDP demanded increases to $8.5 trillion.

The aggregate expenditure line and the aggregate demand curve portray real output from different perspectives. The aggregate expenditure line shows, for a given price level, how planned spending relates to the level of real GDP in the economy. The quantity of real GDP demanded is found where planned spending equals real GDP.

The aggregate demand curve shows, for various price levels, the quantities of real GDP demanded.

The Multiplier and Shifts in Aggregate Demand

Now that we have some idea how the aggregate expenditure line and the aggregate demand curve relate, we can trace the link between a change in autonomous spending for a given price level and the resulting shift in the aggregate demand curve. Suppose that an increase in business confidence spurs a $0.1 trillion increase in planned investment at each level of real GDP. Each panel of Exhibit 5 represents a different way of expressing the effects of a change in planned spending on the quantity of real GDP demanded, assuming the price level remains unchanged. Panel (a) presents the income-expenditure model and panel (b) the aggregate demand model. Again, the two panels are aligned so that levels of real GDP on the horizontal axes correspond. At a price level of 130 in panel (a), the aggregate expenditure line, $C + I + G + (X - M)$, intersects the 45-degree line at point *e* to yield $8.0 trillion as the quantity of real GDP demanded. Panel (b) shows more directly the link between the quantity of real GDP demanded and the price level. As you can see, when the price level is 130, the quantity demanded is $8.0 trillion. This combination of price level and real GDP is identified by point *e* on the aggregate demand curve *AD*.

Exhibit 5 shows how shifts in the aggregate expenditure line and shifts in the aggregate demand curve are related. In panel (a), a $0.1 trillion increase in investment shifts the aggregate expenditure line up by $0.1 trillion, from $C + I + G + (X - M)$ to $C + I' + G + (X - M)$. As we have seen, because of the multiplier effect, such an increase in spending raises the quantity of real GDP demanded from $8.0 trillion to $8.5 trillion. Panel (b) shows the effect of the increase in spending on the aggregate demand curve, which shifts to the right, from *AD* to *AD*'. At the prevailing price level of 130, real GDP demanded increases from $8.0 trillion to $8.5 trillion as a result of the $0.1 trillion increase in investment.

Our discussion of the simple spending multiplier exaggerates the actual effect we might expect from a given shift in the aggregate expenditure line. For one thing, we assume that the price level remains constant. As we shall see in the next chapter, incorporating aggregate supply into the analysis reduces the impact of a given shift in aggregate expenditure because of resulting price changes.

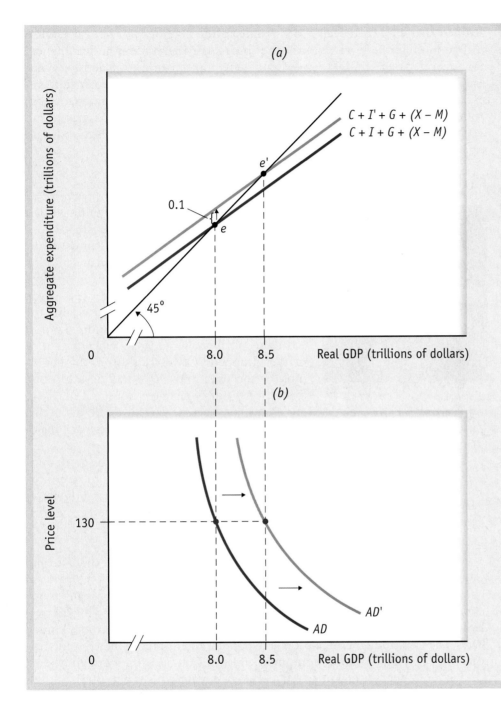

EXHIBIT 5

A Shift in the Aggregate Expenditure Line That Shifts the Aggregate Demand Curve

A shift in the aggregate expenditure line that is not the result of a change in the price level will shift the aggregate demand curve. In panel (a), an increase in investment of \$0.1 trillion, with the price level constant at 130, causes the aggregate expenditure line to increase from $C + I + G + (X - M)$ to $C + I' + G + (X - M)$. As a result, real GDP demanded increases from \$8.0 trillion to \$8.5 trillion. In panel (b), the aggregate demand curve has shifted from *AD* to *AD'*. At the prevailing price level of 130, the amount of output demanded has increased by \$0.5 trillion.

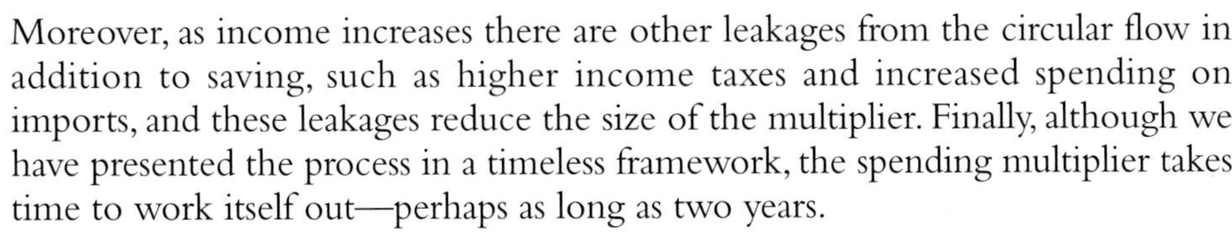
Moreover, as income increases there are other leakages from the circular flow in addition to saving, such as higher income taxes and increased spending on imports, and these leakages reduce the size of the multiplier. Finally, although we have presented the process in a timeless framework, the spending multiplier takes time to work itself out—perhaps as long as two years.

In summary, for a given price level, the aggregate expenditure line relates planned spending to the level of income in the economy, or to real GDP. A change in the price level will shift the aggregate expenditure line, leading to a new quantity of real GDP demanded. These combinations of price levels and real GDP demanded are points along an aggregate demand curve. A shift in a spending component, such as planned investment, consumer spending, or government purchases, will shift the aggregate demand curve.

We close with a case study that considers the problem created when Japanese consumers decided to spend less and save more.

CaseStudy

Other Times, Other Places

Keep track of what is happening in the Japanese economy through a Web page from NikkeiNet at http://www.nni.nikkei.co.jp/AC/FEAT/rec/ sponsored by Nikkei, "the primary source of business information for top executives and decision makers in Japan." What current policies for stimulating consumption can you find among the most current headlines? What are the latest economic indicators reported?

Falling Consumption Triggers Japan's Recession

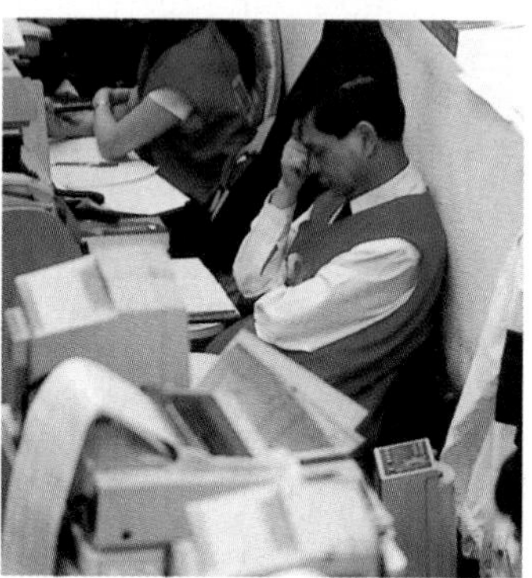

As noted already, consumer spending is the largest component of aggregate expenditure, accounting for about two-thirds of the total. Consumption depends primarily on household income. But at any given income level, the willingness to consume depends on several factors, including household wealth, the interest rate, and consumer expectations. Look at what's been happening in Japan, where the stock market dropped by two-thirds from the beginning of the decade to 1998, taking a big bite from the wealth of Japanese households. What's more, many Japanese banks were in trouble because of real-estate loans that soured as the country's once-booming property market collapsed. Several major financial institutions failed in late 1997 and in 1998.

The sharp reduction in consumer wealth, coupled with an erosion of consumer confidence in the economy, prompted Japanese households to save more and consume less. Thus their consumption function shifted down and their saving function shifted up. Specifically, saving increased from 12.1 percent of disposable income in 1990 to 14.1 percent in 1998. Thus the average saving rate increased by about one-sixth.

Retail sales dropped 3.7 percent in July 1998 from a year earlier, the sixteenth monthly decline in a row. Sales at department and grocery stores fell 3.9 percent. The drop in consumption reduced aggregate demand, triggering Japan's worst economic slide in decades. Incidentally, saving rates in Japan have for the last two decades been much higher—more than three times higher—than in the United States. The case study on the life-cycle hypothesis in Chapter 9 offered some reasons why (e.g., saving is more convenient in Japan, housing is more expensive, and the fraction of the housing price required for a down payment is greater). But this case study calls attention to Japan's increased saving rate during the 1990s.

Japan, the second largest economy in the world (after the United States), is by far the largest economy in Asia. A weakened Japanese economy hurts the already troubled economies across Asia, because Japan is a customer for their exports. And Japanese banks are the world's largest lenders, providing loans around the world. Thus the decline in consumption by Japanese households has global implications.

Sources: *OECD Economic Outlook* 63 (June 1998); "Corporate Japan Goes to Waste," *Economist* (29 August 1998): 55–56; "Japan's Industrial Output Falls," *New York Times* (31 August 1998); and Sara Webb, "Global Markets May Face Further Storms Ahead," *Wall Street Journal* (31 August 1998).

CONCLUSION

The central ideas of this chapter are the forces that determine the amount of real GDP demanded at a given price level, the relationship between the spending multiplier and changes in aggregate output demanded, and how changes in the price level trace out the aggregate demand curve. Then we saw how changes in planned spending shift the aggregate demand curve. The simple multiplier provides a rough idea about the effect of a change in spending on real GDP demanded, but the effect is exaggerated.

This chapter focused on aggregate spending. A simplifying assumption used throughout was that net exports did not vary with the level of income. Appendix A adds realism by considering what happens when imports increase with income. Since imports represent a leakage from the circular flow, this more realistic approach leads to a smaller spending multiplier.

Thus far we have determined the quantity of aggregate output demanded using several approaches, including intuition, tables, and graphs. With the various approaches, we found that for each price level there is a specific quantity of aggregate output demanded, other things constant. Appendix B uses algebra to derive real GDP and the spending multiplier.

SUMMARY

1. The aggregate expenditure line indicates, for a given price level, planned spending at each level of income. At a given price level, the quantity of aggregate output demanded is found where the amount people plan to spend equals the amount produced.
2. The simple spending multiplier indicates the multiple by which a shift in planned spending changes the quantity of aggregate output demanded. The simple spending multiplier developed in this chapter equals $1/(1 - MPC)$. The larger the MPC, the more of each dollar of income will be spent and the less will be saved, so the larger the multiplier.
3. A higher price level causes a downward shift in the aggregate expenditure line, leading to a lower quantity of aggregate output demanded. A lower price level results in an upward shift in the aggregate expenditure line, leading to a greater quantity of aggregate output demanded. By tracing the output demanded at alternative price levels, we can use the income-expenditure model to derive the aggregate demand curve.
4. A shift in the aggregate expenditure line with the price level held constant will cause a shift in the aggregate demand curve.

QUESTIONS FOR REVIEW

1. *(Aggregate Expenditure)* What are the components of aggregate expenditure? In the model developed in this chapter, which components vary with changes in real GDP? What determines the slope of the aggregate expenditure function?
2. *(Quantity of Real GDP Demanded)* In your own words, explain the logic of the income-expenditure model. What determines the amount of real GDP demanded?
3. *(When Output and Spending Differ)* What role do inventories play in determining the level of aggregate output demanded? In answering this question, suppose initially that firms are either overproducing or underproducing.
4. *(Real GDP Demanded)* What equalities hold at the level of real GDP demanded? Answer in terms of both the income-expenditure framework and the leakages-injections framework. When determining real GDP demanded in

these frameworks, what do we assume about the price level? What do we assume about inventories?

5. *(Simple Spending Multiplier)* "A rise in planned investment spending in an economy will lead to a rise in the amount of desired spending." Use the concept of the spending multiplier to verify this statement.

6. *(**CaseStudy:** Hard Times in Connecticut)* How would cutbacks in defense spending, such as those described in the case study "Hard Times in Connecticut," affect the aggregate expenditure function and the aggregate demand curve? Explain fully.

7. *(Deriving the AD Curve)* What is the effect of a lower price level, other things constant, on the aggregate expenditure function and the level of real GDP demanded? How does the multiplier interact with the price change to determine the new level of real GDP demanded?

8. *(**CaseStudy:** Falling Consumption Triggers Japan's Recession)* What happened to consumption in Japan in 1998? Why did this happen? What was the impact on aggregate demand there?

PROBLEMS AND EXERCISES

9. *(Simple Spending Multiplier)* For each of the following values for the MPC, determine the size of the simple spending multiplier and the total change in real GDP demanded following a $10 billion decrease in autonomous spending:
   a. MPC = 0.9
   b. MPC = 0.75
   c. MPC = 0.6

10. *(Simple Spending Multiplier)* Suppose that the MPC is 0.8 and that $8 trillion of real GDP is currently being demanded. The government wants to increase real GDP demanded to $10 trillion. By how much would it have to increase government spending to achieve this goal?

11. *(Simple Spending Multiplier)* Suppose that the MPC is 0.8, while the sum of planned investment, government purchases, and net exports is $500 billion. Suppose also that the government budget is in balance.
    a. What is the sum of saving and net taxes when desired spending equals real GDP? Explain.
    b. What is the value of the multiplier?
    c. Explain why the multiplier is related to the slope of the consumption function.

12. *(Investment and the Multiplier)* This chapter assumes that all investment is autonomous. What would happen to the size of the multiplier if the amount of planned investment increased as real GDP increases? Explain.

13. *(Shifts in Aggregate Demand)* Assume the simple spending multiplier equals 10. Determine the size and direction of any shifts in the aggregate expenditure line, the level of real GDP demanded, and the aggregate demand curve for each of the following changes in autonomous spending:
    a. Autonomous spending rises by $8 billion.
    b. Autonomous spending falls by $5 billion.
    c. Autonomous spending rises by $20 billion.

EXPERIENTIAL EXERCISES

14. *(**CaseStudy:** Hard Times in Connecticut)* The Regional Economic Applications Laboratory at the University of Illinois http://www.uiuc.edu/unit/real/impact.html does economic impact analyses that measure the total impact of local and regional spending. Take a look at some of the examples they provide. Would you expect the multiplier effect of a dollar of spending at the local level to be larger or smaller than the effect at the national level?

15. *(**CaseStudy:** Falling Consumption Triggers Japan's Recession)* Professor Nouriel Roubini of New York University maintains an extensive Web page at http://www.stern.nyu.edu/~nroubini/asia/AsiaHomepage.html devoted to global financial crises. Visit the page and determine what are the latest developments in Japan and around the world.

16. *(Wall Street Journal)* This chapter pointed out that net exports are an important influence on aggregate demand. Find a story in today's *Wall Street Journal* that describes an event that will affect U.S. imports or exports. A good place to look is the "International" page in the first section of the *Journal*. Analyze the story you have chosen, and illustrate the event using both the aggregate expenditure line and the aggregate demand curve.

Appendix A

VARIABLE NET EXPORTS

This chapter has assumed that net exports do not vary with the level of income. A more realistic approach allows net exports to vary inversely with income. Such a model of net exports was developed in the appendix to Chapter 9. The resulting net export function is presented in panel (a) of Exhibit 6. Recall that the higher the income level in the economy, the more is spent on imports, so the lower the net exports. (If necessary, review the appendix to Chapter 9.)

Panel (b) of Exhibit 6 shows what happens when variable net exports are added to consumption, government

EXHIBIT 6

Net Exports and the Aggregate Expenditure Line

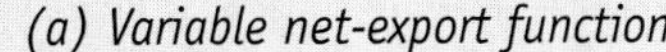

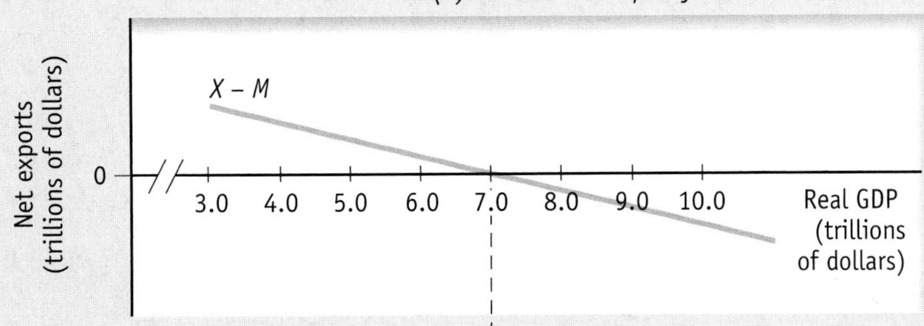

(b) Aggregate expenditure lines

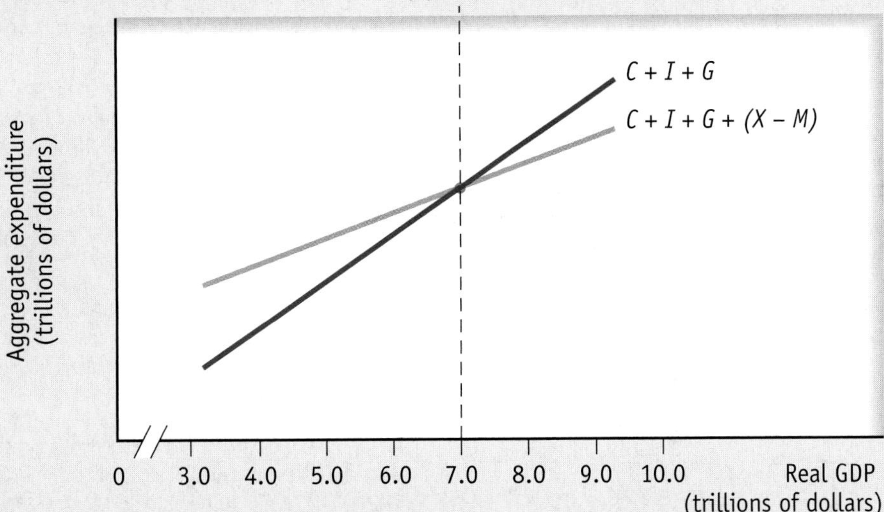

In panel (a), net exports, $X - M$, equal exports minus imports. Net exports are added to consumption, investment, and government purchases in panel (b) to yield $C + I + G + (X - M)$. The addition of net exports has the effect of rotating the spending line about the point where net exports are zero, which occurs where real GDP is $7.0 trillion.

purchases, and investment. We add the variable net export function to the $C + I + G$ spending function to derive the $C + I + G + (X - M)$ spending function. Perhaps the easiest way to see how the addition of net exports affects aggregate expenditure is to begin where real GDP equals $7.0 trillion. Since net exports equal zero when real GDP equals $7.0 trillion (which is also where disposable income equals $6.0 trillion, as shown in the appendix to Chapter 9), the addition of net exports has no effect on the aggregate expenditure line when real GDP is $7.0 trillion. Therefore, the $C + I + G$ and $C + I + G + (X - M)$ lines intersect where real GDP equals $7.0 trillion. At real GDP levels less than $7.0 trillion, net exports are positive, so the $C + I + G + (X - M)$ line is above the $C + I + G$ line. At income levels greater than $7.0 trillion, net exports are negative, so $C + I + G + (X - M)$ is below $C + I + G$. *Because variable net exports and real GDP are inversely related, the addition of variable net exports has the effect of flattening out, or reducing the slope of, the aggregate expenditure line.*

NET EXPORTS AND THE SPENDING MULTIPLIER

The inclusion of variable net exports makes the model more realistic but more complicated, and it requires a reformulation of the spending multiplier. If net exports are autonomous, only the marginal propensity to consume determines how much would be spent and how much would be saved as income increased. The inclusion of variable net exports means that as income increases, U.S. residents spend more on imports. The **marginal propensity to import**, or **MPM,** is the fraction of each additional dollar of disposable income that is spent on imported products. Imports are a leakage from the circular flow. Thus there are now two leakages that grow with income: saving and imports. The introduction of this additional leakage changes the value of the multiplier from 1/MPS to the

$$\text{spending multiplier with variable net exports} = \frac{1}{\text{MPS} + \text{MPM}}$$

The larger the marginal propensity to import, the greater the leakage during each round of spending and the smaller the resulting spending multiplier. Let's assume that the MPM equals about 1/10, or 0.1. If the marginal propensity to save is 0.2 and the marginal propensity to import is 0.1, then only 70 cents of each additional dollar of disposable income gets spent on output produced in the United States. We can compute the new multiplier as follows:

$$\text{spending multiplier with variable net exports} = \frac{1}{\text{MPS} + \text{MPM}} = \frac{1}{0.2 + 0.1} = \frac{1}{0.3} = 3.33$$

Thus the inclusion of net exports reduces the spending multiplier in our hypothetical example from 5 to 3.33. *Because some of each additional dollar of income is spent on imports, less is spent on U.S. products, so any given shift in the aggregate expenditure line has less of an impact on the quantity of output demanded.*

A CHANGE IN AUTONOMOUS SPENDING

What is the level of real GDP demanded, given the net export function described in the previous section, and how does income change when there is a change in autonomous spending? Let's begin in Exhibit 7 with an aggregate expenditure line of $C + I + G + (X - M)$, where net exports vary with income. This aggregate expenditure line intersects the 45-degree line at point *e*, determining real GDP demanded of $8.0 trillion. Suppose now that investment increases by $0.1 trillion at every level of income. This increase in investment will shift the entire aggregate expenditure line up by $0.1 trillion, from $C + I + G + (X - M)$ to $C + I' + G + (X - M)$, as shown in Exhibit 7. As you can see, output demanded increases from $8.0 trillion to $8.333 trillion, representing an increase of $0.333 trillion, or $333 billion, which is $0.1 trillion times the spending multiplier of 3.33. The derivation of the output level and the size of the multiplier are explained in Appendix B.

EXHIBIT 7

Effect of a Shift in Autonomous Spending on Real GDP Demanded

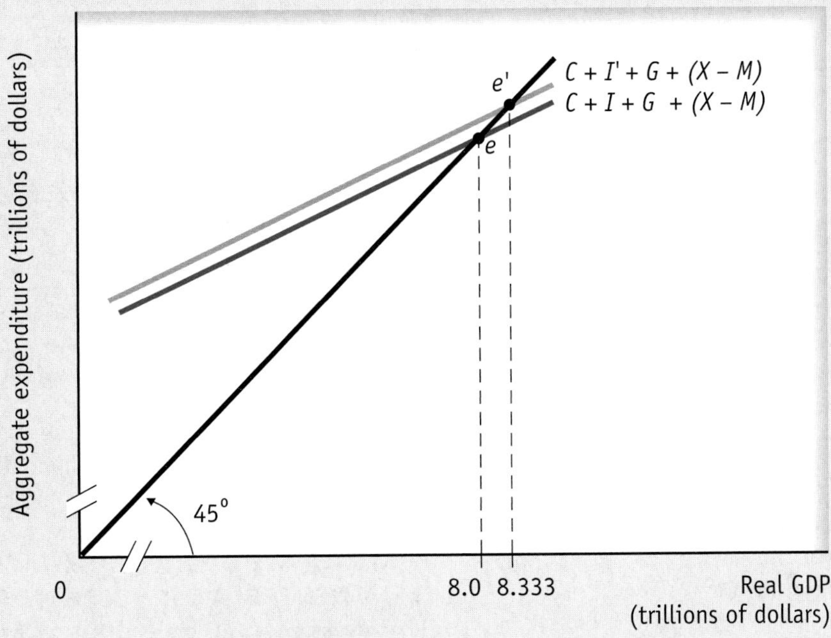

An increase in planned investment, other things constant, shifts the spending line up from $C + I + G + (X - M)$ to $C + I' + G + (X - M)$, increasing the quantity of real GDP demanded.

APPENDIX A QUESTIONS

1. *(Net Exports and the Spending Multiplier)* Suppose that the marginal propensity to consume (MPC) is 0.8 and the marginal propensity to import (MPM) is 0.05.
   a. What is the value of the multiplier?
   b. By how much would the equilibrium level of real GDP demanded change if investment increased by $100 billion?
   c. Using your answer to part (b), calculate the change in net exports caused by the change in aggregate output.

2. *(A Change in Autonomous Spending)* Suppose that when aggregate output equals zero, consumption equals $100 billion, autonomous investment equals $200 billion, government purchases equal $50 billion, and net exports equal $50 billion. Suppose also that MPC is 0.9 and MPM is 0.1.
   a. Construct a table showing the level of aggregate spending, net exports, and saving plus net taxes for aggregate output levels of zero, $500 billion, and $1,000 billion.
   b. Use autonomous spending and the multiplier to calculate the equilibrium level of real GDP demanded.
   c. What would be the new level of real GDP demanded if an increase in the U.S. interest rate caused net exports to change by $50 billion? Explain.

Appendix B

ALGEBRA OF INCOME AND EXPENDITURE

This appendix explains the algebra behind deriving aggregate output demanded. You should see some similarity between the presentation here and the circular-flow explanation of national income accounts.

THE AGGREGATE EXPENDITURE LINE

We first determine where aggregate expenditure equals real GDP and then derive the relevant spending multipliers, assuming a given price level. Initially let's assume net exports are autonomous. Then we'll incorporate variable net exports into the framework.

The quantity of aggregate output demanded occurs where aggregate expenditure equals real GDP. Aggregate expenditure is equal to the sum of consumption, C, investment, I, government purchases, G, and net exports, $X - M$. Algebraically, we can write the equality as

$$Y = C + I + G + (X - M)$$

where Y equals income, or real GDP demanded. To find where real GDP equals planned spending, we begin with the heart of the income-expenditure model: the consumption function. The consumption function used throughout this chapter was a straight line; the equation for this line can be written as

$$C = 0.9 + 0.8(Y - 1.0)$$

The marginal propensity to consume is 0.8, Y is income, or real GDP, and 1.0 is autonomous net taxes in trillions of dollars. Thus, $(Y - 1.0)$ is real GDP minus net taxes, which equals disposable income. The consumption function can be simplified to

$$C = 0.1 + 0.8Y$$

Consumption at each level of real GDP, therefore, equals \$0.1 trillion (which could be called autonomous consumption) *plus* 0.8 times the level of real GDP, which is the marginal propensity to consume times income.

The second component of spending is investment, I, which we have assumed is autonomous and equal to \$0.6 trillion. The third component of spending is autonomous government purchases, G, which we assumed to be \$1.0 trillion. Net exports, $X - M$, the final spending component, we assumed to be –\$0.1 trillion. Substituting the numerical values for each spending component in the aggregate expenditure line, we get

$$Y = 0.1 + 0.8Y + 0.6 + 1.0 - 0.1$$

Notice there is only one variable in this expression: Y. If we rewrite the expression as

$$Y - 0.8Y = 0.1 + 0.6 + 1.0 - 0.1$$
$$0.2Y = 1.6$$

we can solve for the level of real GDP demanded:

$$Y = \frac{1.6}{0.2}$$
$$Y = \$8.0 \text{ trillion}$$

A MORE GENERAL FORM OF INCOME AND EXPENDITURE

The advantage of algebra is that it allows us to derive the equilibrium quantity of real GDP demanded in a more general way. Let's begin with a consumption function of the general form

$$C = a + b(Y - NT)$$

where b is the marginal propensity to consume and NT is net taxes. Consumption can be rearranged to

$$C = a - bNT + bY$$

where $a - bNT$ is *autonomous* consumption—the portion of consumption that is independent of the level of income—and bY is *induced* consumption—that portion of consumption stimulated by the level of income in the economy. The quantity of GDP demanded equals the sum of consumption, C, autonomous investment, I, autonomous government purchases, G, and autonomous net exports, $X - M$, or

$$\text{income} = \text{expenditure}$$
$$Y = a - bNT + bY + I + G + (X - M)$$

Again, by rearranging terms and isolating Y on the lefthand side of the equation, we get

$$Y = \frac{1}{1 - b}(a - bNT + I + G + X - M)$$

The $(a - bNT + I + G + X - M)$ term represents autonomous spending—that is, the amount of spending that is independent of income. And $(1 - b)$ equals 1 minus the MPC. In the chapter we showed that $1/(1 - \text{MPC})$ equals the simple spending multiplier. One way of viewing what's going on is to keep in mind that autonomous spending is *multiplied* through the economy to arrive at the quantity of aggregate output demanded.

The formula that yields the quantity of aggregate output demanded can be used to focus on the origin of the spending multiplier. We can increase autonomous spending by, say, \$1, to see what happens to real GDP demanded.

$$Y' = \frac{1}{1-b}(a - bNT + I + G + X - M + \$1)$$

The difference between this expression and the initial one (that is, between Y' and Y) is $\$1/(1 - b)$. Since b equals the MPC, the simple multiplier equals $1/(1 - b)$. Thus, the change in equilibrium income equals the change in autonomous spending times the multiplier.

INTRODUCING VARIABLE NET EXPORTS

Here we explore the algebra behind variable net exports, first introduced in the appendix to Chapter 9. We begin with the equality

$$Y = C + I + G + (X - M)$$

Exports are assumed to equal \$0.6 trillion at each level of income. Imports increase as disposable income increases, and the marginal propensity to import has been assumed to be 0.1. Therefore, net exports equal

$$X - M = 0.6 - 0.1(Y - 1.0)$$

After incorporating the values for C, I, and G presented earlier, we can express the equality as

$$Y = 0.1 + 0.8Y + 0.6 + 1.0 + 0.6 - 0.1(Y - 1.0)$$

which reduces to $0.3Y = \$2.4$ trillion, or $Y = \$8.0$ trillion. Algebra can be used to generalize these results. If m represents the marginal propensity to import, net exports become $X - m(Y - NT)$. The real GDP demanded can be found by solving for Y in the expression

$$Y = a + b(Y - NT) + I + G + X - m(Y - NT)$$

which yields

$$Y = \frac{1}{1-b+m}(a - bNT + I + G + X + mNT)$$

The expression in parentheses represents autonomous spending. In the denominator, $1 - b$ is the marginal propensity to save and m is the marginal propensity to import. Appendix A demonstrates that $1/(\text{MPS} + \text{MPM})$ equals the spending multiplier when variable net exports are included. Thus aggregate output demanded equals the spending multiplier times autonomous spending. And an increase in autonomous spending times the multiplier gives us the resulting increase in aggregate output demanded.

APPENDIX B QUESTION

Suppose that $C = 100 + 0.75(Y - 100)$, $I = 50$, $G = 30$, and $X - M = -100$. What is the simple spending multiplier? What is the level of real GDP demanded? What would happen to real GDP demanded if government spending increased to 40?

CHAPTER

11 Aggregate Supply

What is your normal capacity for academic work and when do you usually exceed that effort? If the economy is already operating at full employment, how can it produce more? What valuable piece of information do firms and workers lack when they negotiate future wages? Why do workers and employers fail to agree on pay cuts that might save jobs? How might a long stretch of high unemployment reduce the economy's ability to produce in the future? These and other questions are answered in this chapter, which develops the aggregate supply curve in the short run and the long run.

Up to this point we have focused on the quantity of aggregate output demanded at a given price level. We have not yet introduced a theory of aggregate supply. Perhaps no other macroeconomic theory is subject to more debate. The

Visit the McEachern Interactive Study Center for this chapter at http://mcisc.swcollege.com

debate involves the shape of the aggregate supply curve and the reasons for that shape. In this chapter, we will attempt to develop a single, coherent framework for aggregate supply.

Although our focus continues to be on economic aggregates, you should keep in mind that aggregate supply reflects billions of individual production decisions made by millions of individual resource suppliers and firms in the economy. Each firm operates in its own little world, dealing with its own suppliers and customers, and keeping a watchful eye on existing and potential competitors. Yet each firm also recognizes that success in part depends on the performance of the economy as a whole. The theory of aggregate supply we describe here must be consistent with both the microeconomic behavior of individual suppliers and the macroeconomic behavior of the economy. Topics discussed in this chapter include:

- Expected price level and long-term contracts
- Potential output
- Short-run aggregate supply
- Long-run aggregate supply
- Expansionary gaps and contractionary gaps
- Changes in aggregate supply

AGGREGATE SUPPLY IN THE SHORT RUN

As you know, *aggregate supply* is the relationship between the price level in the economy and the quantity of aggregate output firms are willing and able to supply, other things held constant. The other things held constant along a given aggregate supply curve include the supply of resources to firms, the state of technology, and the set of formal and informal institutions that structure production incentives, such as the system of property rights, patent laws, tax systems, and the customs and conventions of the market. The greater the supply of resources, the better the technology, and the more effective the production incentives provided by the economic institutions, the greater the aggregate supply. Let's begin by looking at the key resource: labor.

Labor Supply and Aggregate Supply

Labor is the most important resource, accounting for about 70 percent of production cost. The supply of labor in an economy depends on the size and abilities of the adult population and household preferences for work versus leisure. Along a given labor supply curve—that is, for a given adult population and given preferences for work versus leisure—the quantity of labor supplied depends on the wage rate. The higher the wage, other things constant, the more people are willing and able to work.

So far, so good. Things start getting complicated, however, once we recognize that the purchasing power of any given nominal wage depends on the economy's price level. *The higher the price level, the less any given dollar wage will purchase, so the less attractive that dollar wage is to workers.* Consider wages and the price level over time. Suppose a worker in 1970 was offered a job paying $20,000 per year. That salary may not impress you today, but, at the time, its real purchasing power was the equivalent of more than $75,000 in today's dollars.

Because the price level matters, we must distinguish between the **nominal wage**, which measures the wage in current dollars (the number of dollars on

Nominal wage The wage measured in terms of current dollars; the dollar amount on a paycheck

Real wage The wage measured in terms of dollars of constant purchasing power; hence, the wage measured in terms of the quantity of goods and services it will purchase

your paycheck), and the **real wage**, which measures the wage in constant dollars—that is, dollars in terms of the real goods and services they will buy. A higher real wage means workers can buy more goods and services.

Both workers and employers care more about the real wage than about the nominal wage. The problem is that most labor contracts must be negotiated in terms of nominal wages because nobody knows for sure what price level will prevail during the life of the wage agreement. Some resource prices, such as wages that are set by long-term contracts, remain in force for extended periods, often for two or three years. Workers as well as other resource suppliers must therefore reach agreements with firms based on the *expected* price level.

Even where there are no explicit labor contracts, there is often an implicit agreement that the wage, once negotiated, will not change for a while. For example, in many firms the standard practice is to revise wages annually. So wage agreements may be either *explicit* (based on a labor contract) or *implicit* (based on labor market practices). These explicit and implicit agreements make it difficult to revise contract terms during the life of the agreement, even if the price level in the economy turns out to be higher or lower than expected.

Potential Output and the Natural Rate of Unemployment

Here's how resource owners and firms negotiate resource price agreements for a particular period, say, a year. Firms and resource suppliers expect a certain price level to prevail in the economy during the year. You could think of this as the *consensus* view of inflation for the upcoming year. Based on consensus expectations, firms and resource suppliers reach agreements on resource prices, such as wages. For example, firms and workers may expect the price level to increase 3 percent next year, so they agree on a nominal wage increase of 4 percent, which will increase the real wage by 1 percent. If these price-level expectations are realized, the agreed-upon nominal wage translates into the expected real wage, so everyone is satisfied with the way things work out—after all, that's what they willingly negotiated. When the actual price level turns out as expected, we call the resulting level of output the economy's potential output. *The potential output is the amount produced when there are no surprises associated with the price level.* So, at the given real wage, workers are supplying the quantity of labor they want to and firms are hiring the quantity of labor they want to. Both parties are content with the arrangement.

Potential output The economy's maximum sustainable output level, given the supply of resources, technology, and production incentives; the output level when there are no surprises about the price level

Natural rate of unemployment The unemployment rate that occurs when the economy is producing its potential level of output

We can think of the **potential output** level as the economy's maximum sustainable output level, given the supply of resources, the state of technology, and the formal and informal production incentives. Potential output is also referred to by other terms, including the *natural rate of output* and the *full-employment rate of output*.

The unemployment rate that occurs when the economy is producing its potential GDP is called the **natural rate of unemployment**. The natural rate of unemployment is the rate that prevails when cyclical unemployment is zero. When the economy is producing its potential output, the number of job openings is equal to the number unemployed for frictional, structural, and seasonal reasons. Widely accepted estimates of the natural rate of unemployment range from about 4 percent to about 6 percent of the labor force.

In summary, potential output provides a reference point, an anchor, for the analysis in this chapter. *When the actual price level turns out as anticipated, the expec-*

tations of both workers and firms are fulfilled, and the economy produces its potential output. Complications arise, however, when the actual price level that occurs in the economy differs from the expected price level, as we'll see next.

Actual Price Level Higher Than Expected

As we have already seen, each firm's objective is to maximize profit. Profit equals total revenue minus total cost. Suppose workers and firms, based on their expectations about the price level, have reached a wage agreement. What if the economy's price level turns out to be higher than expected? What happens *in the short run* to the quantity of aggregate output supplied? The **short run** is a period during which many resource prices remain fixed by contract. Does output in the short run exceed the economy's potential, fall short of that potential, or equal that potential?

Short run A period during which at least some resource prices, especially those for labor, are fixed by agreement

Since the prices of many resources have been fixed for the duration of contracts, firms welcome a price level that is higher than expected. After all, the selling prices of their products, on average, are higher than expected, while the costs of at least some of the resources they employ remain constant. *Because a price level that is higher than expected results in higher profits, firms have an incentive in the short run to expand production beyond the economy's potential level.*

At first it might appear contradictory to talk about producing beyond the economy's potential, but remember that potential output means not zero unemployment but the natural rate of unemployment. Even in an economy producing its potential output, there is some unemployed labor and some unused production capacity. If you think of potential GDP as the economy's *normal capacity*, you'll get a better understanding of how the economy can temporarily exceed that capacity. For example, during World War II the United States pulled out all the stops to win the war. Factories operated around the clock. The unemployment rate fell to under 2 percent—well below the natural rate. Overtime was common. People worked longer and harder for the war effort than they normally would have.

Think about your own study habits. During most of the term, you display your normal capacity for academic work. As the end of the term draws near, however, you shift into high gear, finishing term papers, studying late into the night for final exams, and generally running yourself ragged trying to pull things together. During those final frenzied weeks of the term, you study beyond your normal capacity, beyond the schedule you would prefer to follow on a regular or sustained basis. We often observe workers exceeding their normal capacity for short bursts: fireworks displayers around the Fourth of July, accountants during tax-preparation time, farmers during harvest time, and elected officials during the closing days of a campaign or a legislative session. Similarly, firms and their workers are able, *in the short run*, to push output beyond the economy's potential.

Why Costs Rise When Output Exceeds Potential

The economy is flexible enough to expand output above potential GDP, but as output expands, the cost of additional output increases. Even though many workers are bound by contracts, wage agreements may call for overtime pay for extra hours or weekend work. As the economy expands and the unemployment rate declines, additional workers are hard to find. Retirees, homemakers, and students may want extra pay to draw them into the labor force. Some firms may resort to hiring workers who are not properly prepared for the available jobs—those who had been structurally unemployed. If few additional workers are available, if available workers are less qualified, or if workers require additional pay for overtime, the nominal cost of labor will increase as output expands in the short run, even though most workers' nominal wages are fixed by long-term agreements.

As production increases, the demand for non-labor resources increases as well, so the prices of those resources purchased in markets where prices are flexible—such as the market for oil—will increase, reflecting their greater scarcity. Also, as production increases, firms use their machines and trucks more intensively, so this equipment wears out faster and is more subject to breakdown. Thus, the nominal cost per unit of output rises when production is pushed beyond the economy's potential output. But *because the prices of some resources are fixed by contracts, the price level rises faster than the per-unit production cost, so firms increase the quantity supplied.*

In summary, if the price level is higher than expected, firms have a profit incentive to increase the quantity of goods and services supplied. At higher rates of output, however, the per-unit cost of additional output increases. Firms will maximize profits by expanding output as long as the revenue from additional production exceeds the cost of that production.

***Net*Bookmark**

For comprehensive economic data and analysis geared to students and small business people visit The Dismal Scientist at http://www.dismal.com/. It provides access to the latest economic indicators, profiles of regional economies, and numerous articles on current economic issues. It also offers definitions, calculators, and a question and answer message board, all in an easy-to-navigate site.

The Price Level, Real Wages, and Labor Supply

When the actual price level exceeds the expected price level, the real value of an agreed-upon nominal wage declines. We might ask why workers would be willing to increase the quantity of labor they supply when the price level is higher than expected. One answer is that since labor agreements require workers to offer their labor at the agreed-upon nominal wage, workers are simply complying with their contracts. Another possible explanation is that the contracted wage may be higher than needed to attract enough workers. The **efficiency wage theory** argues that by keeping wages above the level required to attract a sufficient number of workers, some firms ensure an abundant worker pool from which to hire. Wages that are higher than necessary also ensure that employees will be less likely to goof off or do anything that might jeopardize what they view as an attractive job. Since wages are higher than necessary, workers willingly increase the quantity of labor supplied when firms expand output.

Efficiency wage theory
The idea that keeping wages above the level required to attract a sufficient pool of workers makes workers compete to get and keep their jobs and results in greater productivity

Actual Price Level Lower Than Expected

We have discovered that if the price level is greater than expected, firms in the short run expand output, but as they do, the per-unit cost of additional production increases. Now let's examine the effects of a price level that is lower than expected. Again, suppose that resource suppliers and firms expect a certain price level. If the price level turns out to be lower than expected, production is less attractive to firms. The prices firms receive for their output are on average lower than they expected, yet many of their production costs, such as the nominal wage, do not fall.

Since production is less profitable when the price level is lower than expected, firms reduce their quantity supplied, so the economy's output is below its potential. As a result, some workers are laid off, those who keep their jobs may work fewer hours, and unemployment exceeds the natural rate. Not only is less labor employed, but machines go unused and delivery trucks sit idle—even entire plants may shut down. For example, auto makers sometimes halt production for weeks.

Just as some costs increase in the short run when output is pushed beyond the economy's potential, some costs decline when output falls below the economy's potential. As output falls below potential, some resources become unemployed, so the prices of resources decline in markets where the price is flexible. Moreover, with an abundance of unemployed resources, firms can become more selective about which resources to retain, laying off the least productive first.

To review: If the price level turns out to be higher than expected, firms maximize profit by increasing the quantity supplied beyond the economy's potential output. As output expands, the per-unit cost of additional production increases, but firms expand production as long as prices rise more than costs. If the price level turns out to be lower than expected, firms reduce output below the economy's potential output because prices fall more than costs. All of this is a long way of saying that *there is a direct relationship in the short run between the actual price level and the quantity of aggregate output supplied.*

The Short-Run Aggregate Supply Curve

Short-run aggregate supply (SRAS) curve A curve that shows the direct relationship between the price level and the quantity of aggregate output supplied in the short run, other things constant

What we have been describing thus far can be used to trace out the **short-run aggregate supply (SRAS) curve**, which shows the relationship between the actual price level and the quantity of aggregate output producers in the economy are willing and able to supply, other things constant. Again, the *short run* in this context is the period during which some resource prices, especially those for labor, are fixed by agreement. For simplicity, we can think of the short run as the duration of labor contracts, which are based on the expected price level.

Suppose the expected price level is 130. The short-run aggregate supply curve in Exhibit 1, $SRAS_{130}$, is based on that expected price level (hence the subscript 130). If the price level turns out to be 130, as expected, producers supply the economy's *potential level of output*, which in Exhibit 1 is \$8.0 trillion. Although not shown in the exhibit, for the price level to turn out as expected, the aggregate demand curve would have to intersect the aggregate supply curve at point *a*. So, given the economy's potential output, the short-run aggregate supply curve depends on the expected price level, which depends on expectations about aggregate demand.

If the economy produces its potential output level, unemployment is at the *natural rate*. Nobody is surprised and all are content with the outcome. There is no tendency to move away from point *a* even if workers and firms have a chance to renegotiate their contract.

In Exhibit 1, levels of output that fall short of the economy's potential are shaded red and levels of output that exceed the economy's potential are shaded blue. The slope of the short-run aggregate supply curve depends on how sharply the cost of additional production rises as aggregate output expands. If, in the short run, increases in production costs per unit are modest as output expands, the supply curve will be relatively flat. If these costs increase sharply as output expands, the supply curve will be relatively steep. Much of the controversy about the short-run aggregate supply curve involves its shape; shapes

EXHIBIT 1

Short-Run Aggregate Supply Curve When the Expected Price Level is 130

The short-run aggregate supply curve is drawn for a given expected price level of 130. Point *a* shows that if the actual price level equals the expected level, producers supply the potential level of output. If the price level exceeds 130, firms increase the quantity supplied. With a price level below 130, firms decrease the quantity supplied. Levels of output that fall short of the economy's potential are shaded red; levels of output that exceed the economy's potential are shaded blue.

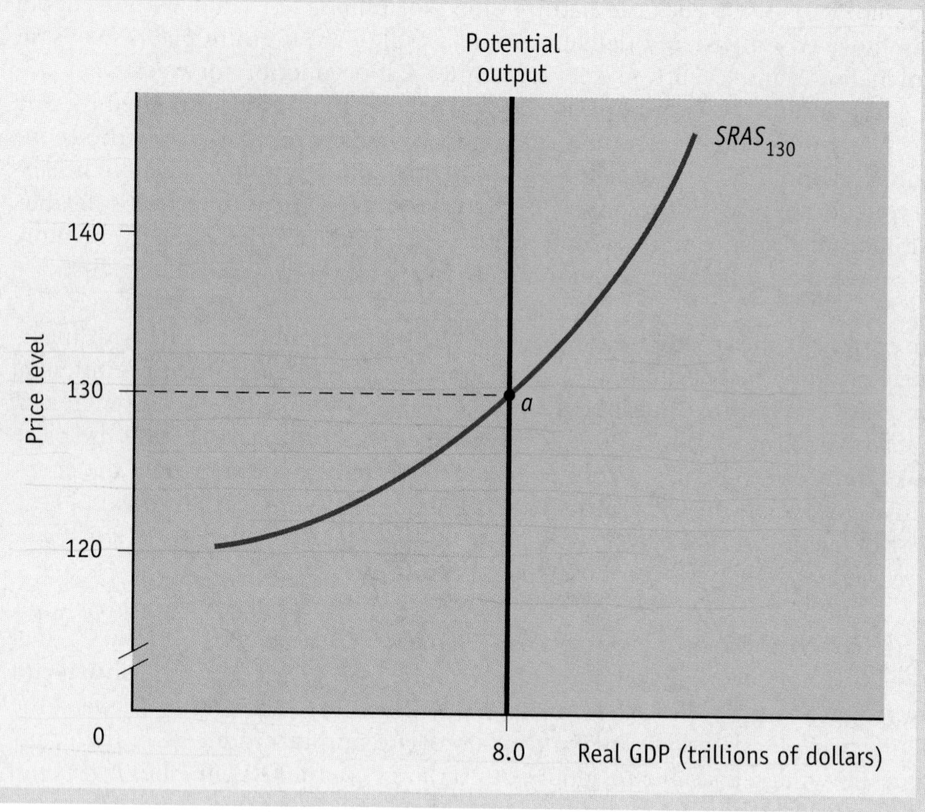

range from relatively flat to relatively steep. Notice that the short-run aggregate supply curve becomes steeper as output increases, because resources become more scarce and hence more costly as output increases.

FROM THE SHORT RUN TO THE LONG RUN

In this section we begin with a short-run equilibrium price level that is higher than the expected price level to see what happens in the long run. The long run is long enough so that firms and resource suppliers are able to renegotiate all agreements based on knowledge of the actual price level. *Hence there are no price surprises in the long run.*

Actual Price Level Higher Than Expected

Let's begin our look at the long-run adjustment in Exhibit 2 with an expected price level of 130. The short-run aggregate supply curve for that expected price level is $SRAS_{130}$. Given this short-run aggregate supply curve, the equilibrium price level and real GDP depend on the aggregate demand curve. The actual price level will equal the expected price level only if the aggregate demand curve intersects the aggregate supply curve at point *a*—that is, where the short-run quantity equals potential output. Point *a* reflects a potential output level of $8.0 trillion and a price level of 130, which is the expected price level.

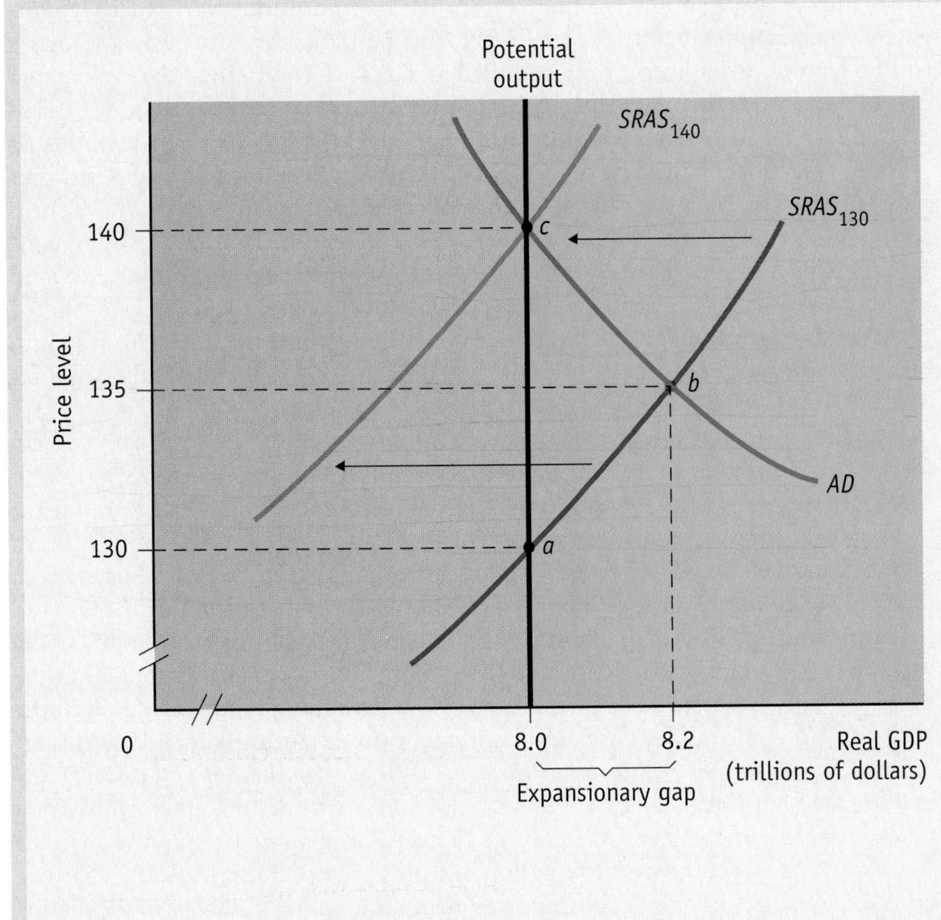

EXHIBIT 2

Short-Run Equilibrium When the Price Level Exceeds Expectations

If the expected price level is 130, the short-run aggregate supply curve is $SRAS_{130}$. If the actual price level turns out as expected, the quantity supplied is the potential output, $8.0 trillion. However, given the aggregate demand curve shown here, the price level ends up being higher than expected, and output exceeds potential as shown by the short-run equilibrium at point *b*. The amount by which output of $8.2 trillion exceeds the economy's potential output is referred to as the expansionary gap. In the long run, price expectations will be revised upward. Costs will rise and the short-run aggregate supply curve will shift upward to $SRAS_{140}$. Eventually, the economy will move to long-run equilibrium at point *c*.

But what if aggregate demand turns out to be greater than expected, as shown by curve *AD*, which intersects the short-run aggregate supply curve $SRAS_{130}$ at point *b*. Point *b* is the **short-run equilibrium**, reflecting a price level of 135 and a real GDP of $8.2 trillion. The actual price level in the short run is higher than expected, and the level of output exceeds the economy's potential of $8.0 trillion.

The amount by which short-run equilibrium output exceeds the economy's potential is often referred to as the **expansionary gap**; in Exhibit 2, that gap is the short-run output of $8.2 trillion minus potential output of $8.0 trillion, or $0.2 trillion. When real GDP exceeds potential output, the actual unemployment rate is less than the natural rate of unemployment. Employees are working overtime, machines are being pushed to the limit, and farmers are sandwiching extra crops between usual plantings. Because the price level prevailing in the short run exceeds the expected price level, the nominal wage based on an expected price level of 130 translates into a lower real wage. As we will see, output exceeding potential GDP creates inflationary pressure in the economy. *The more the short-run output exceeds the economy's potential, the larger the expansionary gap and the greater the upward pressure on the price level.*

Short-run equilibrium Combination of price level and real GDP, where the aggregate demand curve intersects the short-run aggregate supply curve

Expansionary gap The amount by which actual output in the short run exceeds the economy's potential output

Long run A period during which wage contracts and resource price agreements can be renegotiated; the level of output when there are no price surprises

What happens in the long run? The **long run** is a period during which firms and resource suppliers know about market conditions, particularly aggregate demand and the actual price level, and have the time to renegotiate resource payments based on that knowledge. Because the higher-than-expected price level erodes the real value of the nominal wage originally agreed to, workers will try to negotiate a higher nominal wage at their first opportunity. As workers and other resource suppliers negotiate higher nominal payments, this raises production costs for firms, so the short-run aggregate supply curve shifts to the left to reflect the higher expected price level. In Exhibit 2, the expansionary gap in the long run causes the short-run aggregate supply curve to shift to the left to $SRAS_{140}$, which is based on an expected price level of 140. Notice that the short-run aggregate supply curve shifts inward until the equilibrium quantity adjusts to the economy's potential output. *Actual output can exceed the economy's potential in the short run but not in the long run.*

As shown in Exhibit 2, the expansionary gap is closed by long-run market forces that shift the short-run aggregate supply curve from $SRAS_{130}$ left to $SRAS_{140}$. Whereas $SRAS_{130}$ was based on contracts reflecting an expected price level of 130, $SRAS_{140}$ is based on contracts reflecting an expected price level of 140. Because the expected price level and the actual price level are identical at point *c*, the economy at that point is not only in short-run equilibrium but also in **long-run equilibrium**. Consider all the equalities that hold at point *c*: (1) the actual price level equals the expected price level; (2) the quantity supplied in the short run equals potential output, which also equals the quantity supplied in the long run; and (3) the quantity supplied equals the quantity demanded. Put another way, *long-run equilibrium occurs where the aggregate demand curve intersects the vertical line drawn at potential output.* Point *c* will continue to be the equilibrium point unless there is some change in aggregate demand or in aggregate supply.

Long-run equilibrium Combination of price level and real GDP, where (1) actual price level equals expected price level, (2) quantity supplied equals potential output, and (3) quantity supplied equals quantity demanded

Note that *in real terms* the situation at point *c* is no different from what had been expected at point *a*. At both points, firms are willing and able to supply the economy's potential level of output of $8.0 trillion. The same amounts of labor and other resources are employed, and although the price level, the nominal wage rate, and other nominal resource payments are higher at point *c*, the real wage and the real return to other resources are the same as they would have been at point *a*. For example, suppose the nominal wage rate was $13 per hour when the expected price was 130. If the expected price level increased from 130 to 140, an increase of 7.7 percent, the nominal wage rate would also increase by that same percentage to $14 per hour, leaving the real wage unchanged. With no change in the real wage between points *a* and *c*, firms demand enough labor to produce $8.0 trillion of output and workers supply enough labor to produce $8.0 trillion.

Thus if the price level turns out to be higher than expected, the short-run response is to increase the quantity of goods and services supplied. Production exceeding the economy's potential creates inflationary pressure in the economy that in the long run causes the short-run aggregate supply curve to shift to the left, reducing output and increasing the price level.

If an increase in the price level came to be predicted accurately year after year, firms and resource suppliers would build these higher expected price levels into their long-term agreements. The price level would move up each year by the expected amount, but the economy's output would remain at potential GDP, thereby skipping the round-trip beyond the economy's potential and back.

Actual Price Level Lower Than Expected

Let's begin again with an expected price level of 130 as presented in Exhibit 3, where blue shading indicates output levels above potential and red shading indicates output levels below potential. Again, if the price level turned out as expected, the resulting equilibrium combination would occur at *a*, which would be both a short-run and a long-run equilibrium. Suppose this time that the aggregate demand curve intersects the short-run aggregate supply curve to the left of potential output, yielding a price level below that expected. The intersection of the aggregate demand curve, *AD*, with $SRAS_{130}$ establishes the short-run equilibrium point, *d*, where the price level is below expectations and production is less than the economy's potential. The amount by which actual output falls short of potential GDP is called the **contractionary gap**. In this case, the contractionary gap is \$0.2 trillion, and the unemployment rate exceeds its natural rate.

Contractionary gap The amount by which actual output in the short run falls below the economy's potential output

Because the prevailing price level of 125 is below the expected level of 130, the nominal wage, which is based on the expected price level, translates into a higher real wage in the short run. What happens in the long run? Since the price level is lower than expected, employers are no longer willing to pay as high a nominal wage. And with the unemployment rate higher than the natural

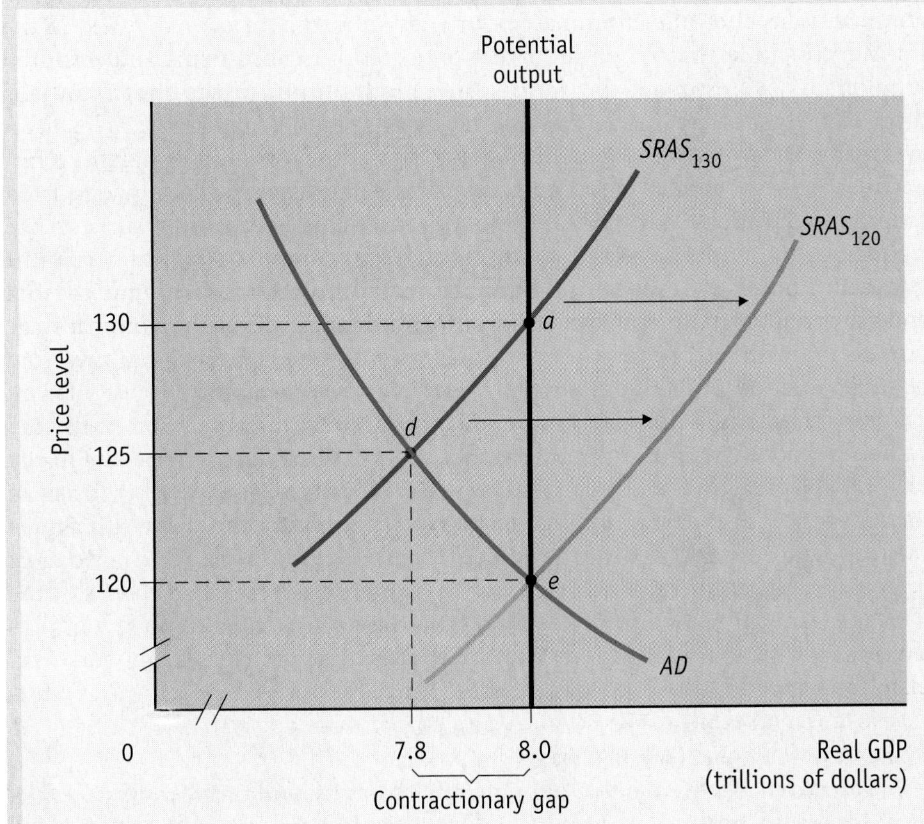

EXHIBIT 3

Short-Run Equilibrium When the Price Level Is Below Expectations

When the price level is below expectations, as indicated by the intersection of the aggregate demand curve *AD* with the short-run aggregate supply curve $SRAS_{130}$ short-run equilibrium occurs at point *d*. Production of \$7.8 trillion is below the economy's potential by the amount of the contractionary gap, \$0.2 trillion. In the long run, resource suppliers and firms will lower their price expectations. As nominal resource costs fall, the short-run aggregate supply curve eventually shifts out to $SRAS_{120}$ and the economy moves to long-run equilibrium at point *e*, with output at the potential level, \$8.0 trillion.

rate, more workers are competing for jobs, putting downward pressure on the nominal wage. If the price level and the nominal wage are flexible enough, the combination of a high real wage and a pool of unemployed workers competing for jobs should make workers more willing to accept a lower nominal wage when wage agreements are negotiated.

If firms and workers negotiate a lower nominal wage, this lowers the cost of production, shifting the short-run aggregate supply curve outward. The short-run supply curve will continue to shift outward until it intersects the aggregate demand curve where the economy produces its potential output. This increase in supply is reflected in Exhibit 3 by a shift to the right in the short-run aggregate supply curve from $SRAS_{130}$ to $SRAS_{120}$. *If the price level and nominal wage are flexible enough, the short-run aggregate supply curve will move outward until the economy produces its potential output.* The new short-run aggregate supply curve is based on an expected price level of 120. Because the expected price level and the actual price level are now identical, the economy is in long-run equilibrium at point *e*.

Although the nominal wage is lower at point *e* than what was originally agreed upon when the expected price level was 130, the real wage is the same at point *e* as it was at point *a*. Since the real wage is the same, the amount of labor that workers supply is the same and real output is the same. All that has changed between points *a* and *e* are nominal measures—the price level, the nominal wage, and other nominal resource payments.

We conclude that when incorrect expectations cause firms and resource suppliers to overestimate the actual price level, output in the short run falls short of the economy's potential. As long as wages and prices are flexible, however, firms and workers, when existing contracts expire, should be able to renegotiate wage agreements based on a lower expected price level. The negotiated drop in the nominal wage will shift the short-run aggregate supply curve to the right until the economy once again produces its potential level of output. If wages and prices are not very flexible, they will not adjust very quickly to a contractionary gap, so shifts in the short-run aggregate supply curve may be slow to move the economy to its potential output. The economy can therefore be stuck at an output and employment level below its potential.

We are now in a position to provide an additional interpretation of the red and blue shaded areas of our exhibits. If a short-run equilibrium occurs in the blue shaded area, that is, to the right of potential output, then market forces in the long run will increase nominal resource costs, shifting the short-run aggregate supply to the left. If a short-run equilibrium occurs in the red shaded area, then market forces in the long run will reduce nominal resource costs, shifting the short-run aggregate supply curve to the right. Only if a short-run equilibrium occurs at potential output will the short-run aggregate supply curve remain unchanged in the long run.

Tracing Potential Output

Long-run aggregate supply (LRAS) curve The vertical line drawn at the economy's potential output; aggregate supply when there are no price surprises

If wages and prices are flexible enough, the economy will produce its potential level of output in the long run, as indicated in Exhibit 4 by the vertical line drawn at the economy's potential GDP, estimated here to be $8.0 trillion. The vertical line drawn at potential GDP is called the economy's **long-run aggregate supply** (LRAS) **curve**. *The long-run aggregate supply curve depends on the*

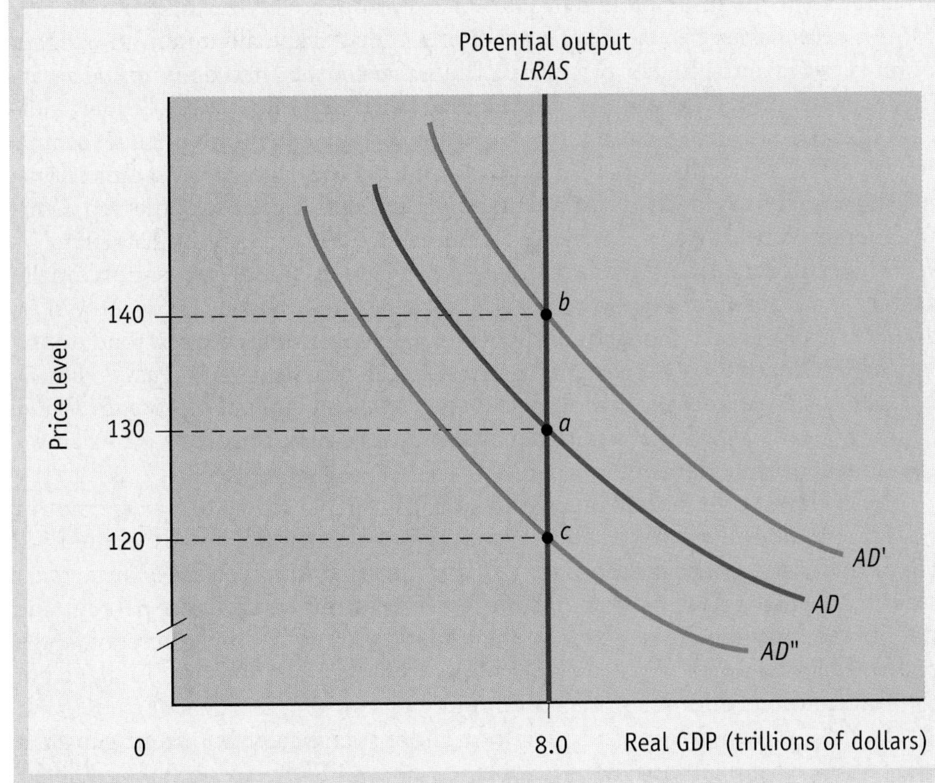

EXHIBIT 4

Long-Run Aggregate Supply Curve

In the long run, when the expected price level equals the actual price level, output will be at the potential level. In the long run, \$8.0 trillion will be supplied regardless of the actual price level. As long as wages and prices are flexible, the economy's potential GDP is consistent with any price level. Thus, changes in aggregate demand will in the long run not affect potential output. The long-run aggregate supply curve, *LRAS*, is a vertical line at potential GDP.

supply of resources in the economy, the level of technology, and the production incentives provided by the formal and informal institutions of the economic system.

Note that as long as wages and prices are flexible, the economy's potential GDP is consistent with any price level. *In the long run, equilibrium real GDP equals potential output, or long-run aggregate supply; the equilibrium price level depends on the aggregate demand curve.* In Exhibit 4, the initial price level of 130 is determined by the intersection of *AD* with the long-run aggregate supply curve. If the aggregate demand curve shifts out to *AD*', then in the long run the equilibrium price level will increase to 140, and equilibrium output will remain at \$8.0 trillion, the economy's potential GDP. Conversely, a decline in aggregate demand from *AD* to *AD*" will, in the long run, lead only to a fall in the price level from 130 to 120, with no change in output. Note that these long-run movements are more like tendencies than smooth and timely adjustments. It may take a long time for resource prices to adjust, particularly when the economy in the short run faces a contractionary gap.

Evidence on Aggregate Supply

What evidence is there that the long-run aggregate supply curve can be depicted by a vertical line drawn at the economy's potential GDP? Except during the Great Depression, unemployment over the last century has varied from year to year, but typically has returned to what would be viewed as a natural rate of unemployment—estimates range from 4 to 6 percent. (See Exhibit 2 in Chapter 7 for the unemployment rate since 1900.)

An *expansionary* gap creates a labor shortage that eventually results in a higher nominal wage and a higher price level. But a *contractionary* gap does not necessarily generate enough downward pressure to lower the nominal wage. Studies indicate that the nominal wage is slow to adjust to high unemployment. Nominal wages have declined in particular industries; during the 1980s, for example, nominal wages fell in airlines, steel, and trucking. But seldom have we observed actual declines in nominal wages across the economy, especially since World War II.

Hence nominal wages do not adjust downward as quickly or as substantially as they adjust upward. The downward response that does occur tends to be slow and relatively weak. Consequently we say that nominal wages tend to be "sticky" in the downward direction. *Since nominal wages fall slowly, if at all, the natural supply-side adjustments needed to return production to potential output may take so long as to seem ineffective.* What, in fact, often closes a contractionary gap is an increase in aggregate demand.

Even though the nominal wage seldom falls, an actual decline in the nominal wage is not necessary to close a contractionary gap. All that is needed is a fall in the real wage. And *the real wage will fall as long as the price level increases more than the nominal wage.* For example, if the price level increases by 4 percent and the nominal wage increases by 2 percent, the real wage falls by 2 percent. If the real wage falls enough, firms will be willing to demand enough additional labor to produce the economy's potential output.

In the following case study, we look more specifically at output gaps and discuss why wages are not more flexible.

Output Gaps and Wage Flexibility

How much more output could we expect if there were no output gap? Is this now different for the new, computerized, information economy? Jason Pontin of the *Red Herring* magazine wrote in the September 1997 issue that "There is no new economy." http://www.redherring.com/mag/issue46/rap.html. How could we estimate the GDP benefits of reducing the output gap? What factors define the limits of economic growth, even when there is no cyclical unemployment? What does Pontin believe is the maximum rate of economic growth?

Let's look at estimates of actual and potential GDP since 1980. Exhibit 5 measures the difference between actual and potential GDP as a percent of potential GDP. For example, actual output was 5.5 percent below potential output in the recession year of 1982; this gap, incidentally, amounted to about $270 billion (in 1992 dollars). The economy need not be in recession for actual output to fall below potential output. During 1992, 1993, 1995, and 1996, actual output remained below potential output, yet real GDP increased. In fact, actual output was below its potential for nine years following 1980, but only in the recession years of 1980, 1982, and 1991 did actual output decline.

So actual output has been below potential output nearly half the years since 1980. Employers and employees clearly would have been better off if these contractionary gaps had been reduced or eliminated. After all, more workers would have been employed and more goods and services would have been available. If workers and employers fail to reach an outcome that seems possible and that all would prefer, then they have failed to coordinate in some way. Contractionary gaps can thus be viewed as resulting from a **coordination failure**.

EXHIBIT 5

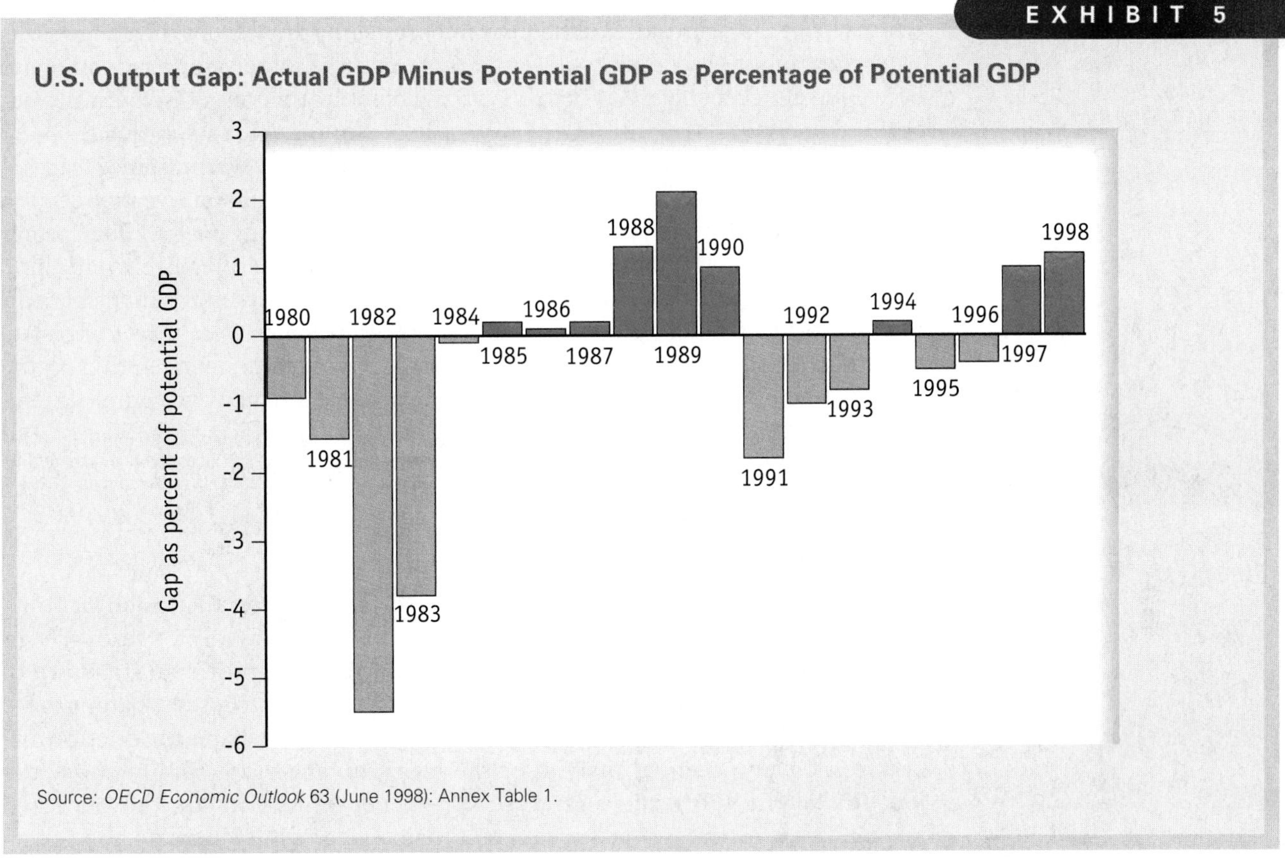

Source: *OECD Economic Outlook* 63 (June 1998): Annex Table 1.

If employers and workers can increase output and employment by agreeing to lower nominal wages, why doesn't such an agreement occur quickly? As we have already seen, many workers are operating under long-term contracts, and wages established by such contracts are not very flexible, particularly in the downward direction. But if long-term contracts reduce the ability to achieve potential output, why not negotiate shorter-term contracts? First, contract negotiations are costly, so longer contracts reduce the frequency, and hence the average annual cost, of negotiations. And second, long-term contracts reduce the frequency of strikes, lockouts, and other settlement disputes that can arise in the course of contract negotiations. Thus both workers and employers gain from longer contracts, even though such contracts make wages more sticky and contractionary gaps more likely.

Coordination failure A situation in which workers and employers fail to achieve an outcome that all would prefer and are unable to jointly choose strategies that would result in a more preferred outcome

When unemployment is high, why do employers appear reluctant to cut nominal wages or to replace existing employees with lower-paid workers from the pool of the unemployed? One possible explanation has already been mentioned. Recall that the *efficiency wage theory* argues that by keeping wages above the level required to attract enough workers, firms make workers compete to keep their jobs. This competition in job performance enhances worker productivity. During recessions, these firms prefer to lay off workers and reduce the hours of remaining workers, rather than cut wages. Wage cuts may save payroll costs, but they can also reduce morale and could harm worker productivity, since workers may have a psychological resistance to wage cuts.

Workers also resist attempts to lower wages, despite the possibility of increased employment, because of the difficulty of coordinating a wage cut on a large scale. A worker might be willing to accept a wage cut if all other workers would also be willing to accept cuts. But because wages are set by millions of individually negotiated contracts, a large-scale wage cut is nearly impossible to coordinate.

Another reason workers may be reluctant to accept lower nominal wages is unemployment benefits. When a worker is laid off, the incentive to accept a lower wage is reduced by the prospect of unemployment benefits. The greater these benefits and the longer their duration, the less the pressure to accept a lower wage. For example, in the latter part of the 1920s, unemployment benefits nearly tripled in Great Britain and eligibility requirements were relaxed. Despite record levels of unemployment, money wages remained unchanged during the period. Unemployment benefits had become a viable alternative to employment.

Sources: Laurence Ball and David Romer, "Sticky Prices and Coordination Failures," *American Economic Review* 81 (June 1991): 539–552; *OECD Economic Outlook* 63 (June 1998): Annex Table 11; and Daniel Benjamin and Levis Kochin, "Searching for an Explanation of Unemployment in Interwar Britain," *Journal of Political Economy* 87 (June 1979): 441–470.

To review: We could sum up our findings so far by saying that potential output, or long-run aggregate supply, depends on (1) the supply of resources in the economy, (2) the state of technology, and (3) the institutional structure of the economic system such as property rights, the tax structure, patent laws, commercial practices, and other laws and customs that shape production incentives. Given potential output, or the long-run aggregate supply curve, the location of the short-run aggregate supply curve depends on the expected price level. An increase in the expected price level would shift up the short-run aggregate supply curve, and a decrease in the expected price level would shift down the short-run aggregate supply curve. When the actual price level differs from the expected price level, output in the short run will depart from the economy's potential. In the long run, however, market forces will shift the short-run aggregate supply curve until the economy once again produces its potential level of output. Thus surprises about the price level will change real GDP in the short run but not in the long run. Shifts in the aggregate demand curve change the price level but do not affect potential output, or long-run aggregate supply.

CHANGES IN AGGREGATE SUPPLY

So far our focus has been on how changes in the expected price level shift the short-run aggregate supply curve. In this section, we consider factors other than changes in the expected price level that may affect aggregate supply. We begin by distinguishing between long-term trends in aggregate supply and **supply shocks**, which are unexpected events that affect aggregate supply, often only temporarily.

Supply shocks Unexpected events that affect aggregate supply, sometimes only temporarily

Increases in Aggregate Supply

The economy's potential output is based on the willingness and ability of households to supply resources to firms, the level of technology, and the institutional underpinnings of the economic system. Any change in these could affect the economy's potential output.[1] The supply of labor may change over time because of a change in the size, composition, or quality of the labor force or a change in household preferences for labor versus leisure. For example, the U.S. labor force has doubled since 1948 as a result of a growth in population and a rising labor force participation rate, especially among women with children. At the same time, job training, education, and on-the-job experience have increased the quality of labor. Increases in both the quantity and the quality of the labor force have increased the economy's potential GDP, or long-run aggregate supply.

The quantity and quality of other resources also change over time. The capital stock—the amount of machines, buildings, and trucks—increases whenever the economy's gross investment exceeds the depreciation of capital. Even the quantity and quality of land can be increased—for example, by claiming land from the sea, as is done in the Netherlands, or by revitalizing soil that has lost its fertility. These increases in the quantity and quality of resources increase the economy's potential output.

Finally, institutional changes that define property rights more clearly or make contracts more enforceable, such as the introduction of clearer patent and copyright laws, will increase the incentives to undertake productive activity and will increase potential output. *Changes in the labor force, in the supply of other key resources, and in the institutional arrangements of the economic system tend to occur gradually over time.* Exhibit 6 depicts a gradual shift in the economy's potential output from $8.0 trillion to $8.5 trillion. The long-run aggregate supply curve shifts from *LRAS* out to *LRAS*'.

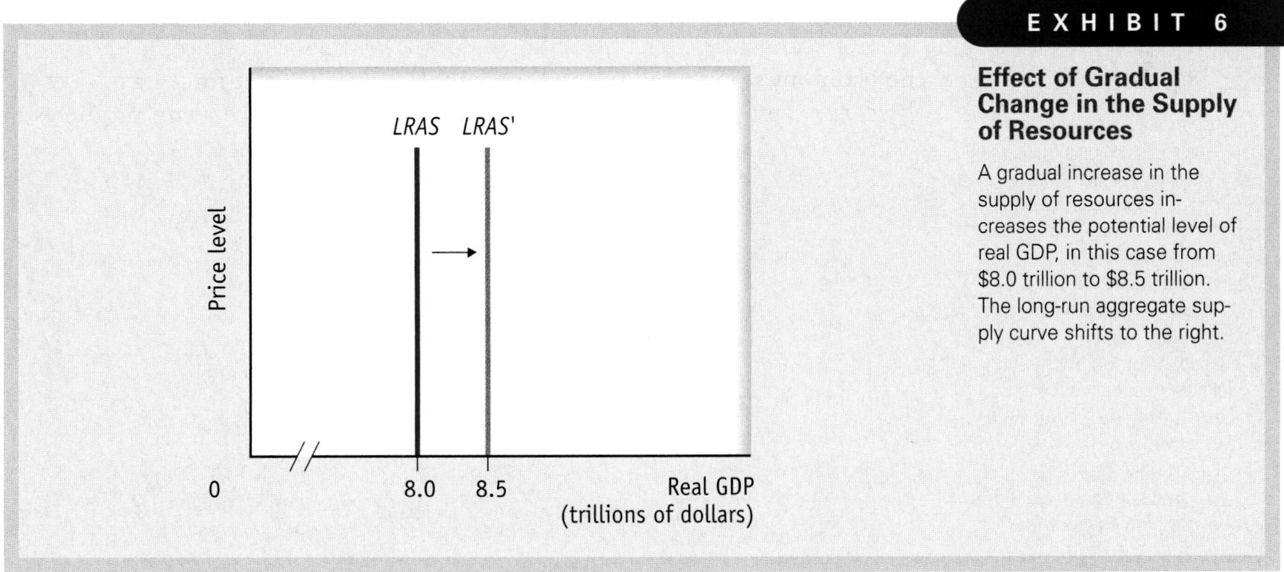

EXHIBIT 6

Effect of Gradual Change in the Supply of Resources

A gradual increase in the supply of resources increases the potential level of real GDP, in this case from $8.0 trillion to $8.5 trillion. The long-run aggregate supply curve shifts to the right.

1 Changes in the economy's potential GDP over time were discussed in greater detail in Chapter 6, which examined U.S. productivity and economic growth.

Beneficial supply shocks Unexpected events that increase aggregate supply, sometimes only temporarily

In contrast to the gradual, or long-term, changes that often occur in the supply of resources, *supply shocks* are unexpected events that change aggregate supply, sometimes only temporarily. **Beneficial supply shocks** increase aggregate supply; examples include (1) abundant harvests that increase the supply of food, (2) discoveries of natural resources, such as oil in Alaska and the North Sea, (3) technological breakthroughs that allow firms to combine resources more efficiently, such as new generations of computer chips, and (4) sudden changes in the economic system that promote more production, such as legislation that reduces the number of frivolous product liability suits.

Exhibit 7 shows the effect of a beneficial supply shock from a technological breakthrough. The beneficial supply shock shown here shifts the short-run and long-run aggregate supply curves. Along the aggregate demand curve, *AD*, the equilibrium combination of price and output moves from point *a* to point *b*. *For a given aggregate demand curve, the happy outcome of a beneficial supply shock is an increase in output and a decrease in the price level.* The new equilibrium at point *b* is a short-run and a long-run equilibrium in the sense that there is no tendency to move from that point as long as whatever caused the beneficial effect continues. New oil discoveries would also have a permanent beneficial effect on the economy. On the other hand, the beneficial supply shock resulting from an unusually favorable growing season is likely to be only temporary and to shift only the short-run aggregate supply curve. If the next growing season returns to nor-

EXHIBIT 7

Effects of a Beneficial Supply Shock on Aggregate Supply

Given the aggregate demand curve, a supply shock expected to have a lasting effect, such as a breakthrough in technology, will shift both the short-run aggregate supply curve and the long-run aggregate supply curve, or potential output. A beneficial supply shock lowers the price level and increases output, as reflected by the change in equilibrium from point *a* to point *b*. A temporary beneficial supply shock, such as would result from an unusually favorable growing season, will shift only the short-run aggregate supply curve. If the next growing season returns to normal, the short-run aggregate supply curves will return to its original equilibrium position at point *a*.

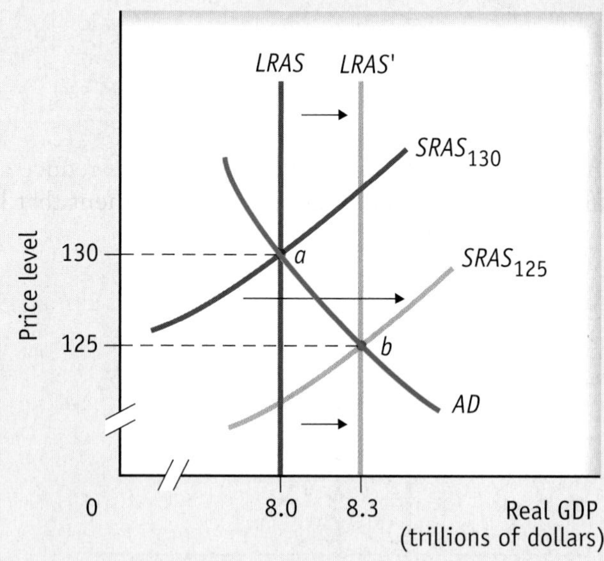

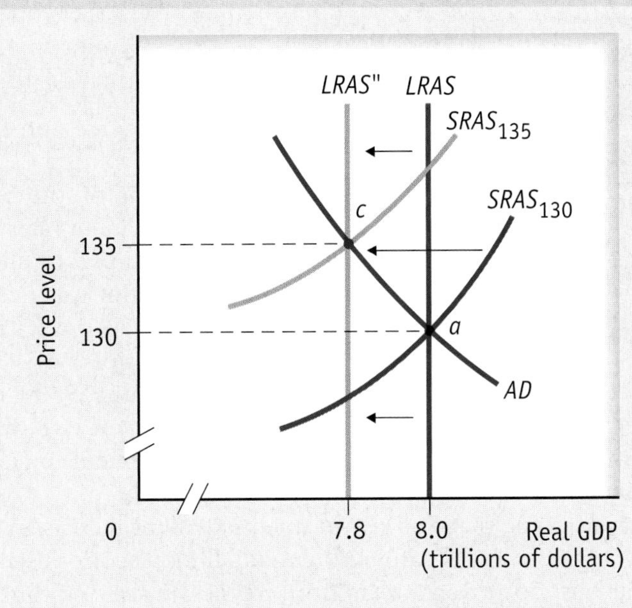

EXHIBIT 8

Effects of an Adverse Supply Shock on Aggregate Supply

Given the aggregate demand curve, an adverse supply shock that is expected to have lasting effects, shifts aggregate supply curves to the left, increasing the price level and reducing aggregate output. This change is shown by the move in equilibrium from point *a* to point *c*. A temporary adverse supply shock, such as would result from a bad growing season, will shift only the short-run aggregate supply curve. If the next growing season returns to normal, the short-run aggregate supply curves will return to its original equilibrium position at point *a*.

mal, the short-run aggregate supply curve will return to its original equilibrium position at point *a* in Exhibit 7.

Decreases in Aggregate Supply

Adverse supply shocks are sudden, unexpected events that reduce aggregate supply, sometimes only temporarily. For example, a government that had been stable could be toppled, destabilizing the economy in the process, as has occurred recently in Russia and Indonesia. Or a drought could reduce the supply of a variety of resources, such as food, building materials, and water-powered electricity. An adverse supply shock expected to have a long-lasting effect is depicted as a shift to the left in the short-run and long-run aggregate supply curves, as shown in Exhibit 8, moving the equilibrium combination from point *a* to point *c* and reducing potential output from $8.0 trillion to $7.8 trillion.

Adverse supply shocks
Unexpected events that reduce aggregate supply, sometimes only temporarily

The combination of reduced output and a higher price level is often referred to as stagflation. The United States encountered stagflation during the 1970s, when the economy was rocked by a series of adverse supply shocks, such as crop failures around the globe and the fourfold increase in oil prices achieved by OPEC in 1974. If the effect of the adverse supply shock is temporary, such as a bad growing season, only the short-run aggregate supply curve shifts, and that curve returns to its original position once things return to normal.

Some economists question an economy's ability to bounce back from recessions, as discussed in the following case study.

CaseStudy

Other Times, Other Places

Learn about current unemployment rates in Europe by finding the most current press release from Eurostat at http://europa.eu.int/en/comm/eurostat/serven/part6/6date99.htm. Then go to the Web site for the Organization for Economic Cooperation and Development, which reports on "Prominent Structural Policy Reforms in the 1990s" undertaken among the industrialized countries. It's available at http://www.oecd.org/eco/freedoc/jobsstra.htm.

What types of changes have been made in taxes, transfers, and employment protection laws in the European countries to deal with their high rates of unemployment? What types of liberalization and other changes have been made in labor and product markets to promote employment?

Why Is Unemployment So High in Europe?

Between World War II and the mid-1970s, unemployment in Western Europe was relatively low. From 1960 to 1974, for example, the unemployment rate in France and the United Kingdom never reached as high as 4 percent. The worldwide recession of the mid-1970s, however, caused unemployment rates to drift up. But unemployment continued to climb in Europe long after the recession was over. The unemployment rates in France and Italy remained above 10 percent for most of the 1980s. After a modest decline in the late 1980s, rates again topped 10 percent in the 1990s. In 1998, the unemployment rate was about 11 percent in Germany, 12 percent in France and Italy, 14 percent in Belgium, and 19 percent in Spain.

Some observers argue that this rise in unemployment reflects an increase in the underlying natural rate of unemployment. Those economists who have studied the issue have borrowed a term from physics, *hysteresis* (pronounced *his-ter-eé-sis*), to explain what they believe happened to the natural rate of unemployment. When applied to the unemployment rate, hysteresis means that the natural rate of unemployment depends in part on the recent history of unemployment. *The longer the actual unemployment rate remains above what had been considered the natural rate, the more the natural rate itself will increase.*

Here are some possible explanations for this phenomenon. First, those who are out of work can lose valuable job skills, thereby reducing their ability to find a job even after the economy recovers. Second, as weeks of unemployment turn into months, the shock and stigma of being unemployed may diminish, so the work ethic weakens, as does the desire to find a job. Reinforcing this second point is that some European countries offer relatively generous unemployment benefits indefinitely, reducing the hardship of unemployment. Some people have collected unemployment benefits for more than a decade.

No consensus exists among economists regarding the validity of hysteresis. The theory seems to be less relevant in the United States, where unemployment rates dropped throughout most of the 1980s and declined again after the recession of 1990–1991 from 7.5 percent in 1992 to 4.5 percent in 1998.

An alternative explanation for high unemployment rates in Europe is that legislation introduced in the 1970s made it more difficult to lay off workers. In most European countries, job dismissals must be approved by work councils, which consider such factors as the marital status, number of dependents, and health of the worker. Severance pay has also become mandatory. With such restrictions on the ability to dismiss workers, hiring became almost an irreversible decision for the employer, so firms have grown reluctant to add workers, particularly untested workers with little job experience. Hence the demand for labor decreased and unemployment increased, particularly among young workers.

Sources: Olivier Blanchard and Lawrence Summers, "Beyond the Natural Rate Hypothesis," *American Economic Review* 78 (May 1988): 182–187; Horst Siebert, "Labor Market Rigidities: At the Root of Unemployment in Europe," *Journal of Economic Perspectives*, 11 (Summer 1997): 37–54; and "Economic Financial Indicators," *Economist* (22 August 1998): 80.

CONCLUSION

This chapter calls attention to the expected price level as a key determinant of the nominal resource prices that shape aggregate supply in the short run. Surprises in the price level can move output in the short run from its potential level. But as firms and resource suppliers fully adjust to price surprises, the economy will return in the long run to its potential output.

SUMMARY

1. Short-run aggregate supply is based on resource supply and demand decisions that reflect the expected price level. If the expected price level actually occurs, the economy produces its potential level of output. If the actual price level exceeds the expected price level, short-run equilibrium output exceeds the economy's potential, opening up an expansionary gap. If the actual price level is below the expected price level, short-run equilibrium output falls short of the economy's potential, opening up a contractionary gap.
2. Output can exceed the economy's potential level in the short run, but in the long run a higher nominal wage will be negotiated at the first opportunity. This higher nominal wage increases the cost of production, shifting the short-run aggregate supply curve inward until equilibrium output equals the economy's potential.
3. If output in the short run falls short of the economy's potential, and if wages and prices in the economy are flexible, then in the long run a lower nominal wage will reduce production costs, shifting the short-run aggregate supply curve outward until equilibrium output equals the economy's potential.
4. Empirical evidence suggests that when output exceeds the economy's potential, wage and price levels increase. But there is less evidence that wage and price levels fall when output is below the economy's potential. Wages appear to be somewhat "sticky" in the downward direction.
5. The long-run aggregate supply curve, or the economy's potential level of output, depends on the amount and quality of resources available in the economy, the state of technology, and formal and informal institutions, such as patent laws and business practices, that structure production incentives. Increases in resource availability, improvements in technology, or institutional changes that provide more attractive production incentives increase aggregate supply and potential output.
6. Supply shocks are unexpected, often temporary changes in aggregate supply. Beneficial supply shocks lead to increased output and a lower price level. Adverse supply shocks result in stagflation—reduced output and a higher price level.

QUESTIONS FOR REVIEW

1. *(Short-Run Aggregate Supply)* In the short run, prices may rise faster than costs do. This chapter discusses why this might happen. Suppose that labor and management agree to adjust wages for any changes in the price level. How would such adjustments affect the slope of the aggregate supply curve?
2. *(Potential Output)* Define the potential output level of an economy. What factors help determine potential output?
3. *(Actual Price Level Higher Than Expected)* Discuss some instances in your life when your actual production for short periods exceeds what you would consider your potential production. Why does this occur only for brief periods?
4. *(Nominal and Real Wages)* Complete each of the following sentences:
   a. The ______ wage measures the wage rate in current dollars, while the ______ wage measures it in constant dollars.
   b. Wage agreements are based on the ______ price level and negotiated in ______ terms. Real wages are then determined by the ______ price level.

c. The higher the actual price level, the ______ is the real wage for a given nominal wage.
d. If nominal wages are growing at 2 percent per year while the annual inflation rate is 3 percent, then real wages change by ______.

5. *(Contractionary Gaps)* After reviewing Exhibit 3 in this chapter, explain why contractionary gaps occur only in the short run and only when the actual price level is below what was expected.

6. *(Short-Run Aggregate Supply)* In interpreting the short-run aggregate supply curve, what does the adjective "short-run" mean? Explain the role of labor contracts along the SRAS curve.

7. *(Output Gaps and Wage Flexibility)* What are some reasons why nominal wages may not fall during a contractionary gap?

8. *(Contractionary Gap)* What does a contractionary gap imply about the actual rate of unemployment relative to the natural rate? What does it imply about the actual price level relative to the expected price level? What must happen to real and nominal wages in order to close a contractionary gap?

9. *(**CaseStudy:** Output Gaps and Wage Flexibility)* Unemployment is costly to employers, employees, and the economy as a whole. What are some explanations for the *coordination failures* that prevent workers and employers from reaching agreements?

10. *(Expansionary Gap)* How does an economy that is experiencing an expansionary gap adjust in the long run?

11. *(Long-Run Adjustment)* In the long run, why does an actual price level that exceeds the expected price level lead to changes in the nominal wage? Why do these changes cause shifts in the short-run aggregate supply curve?

12. *(Long-Run Aggregate Supply)* The long-run aggregate supply curve is vertical at the economy's potential output level. Why is the long-run aggregate supply curve located at this level of output rather than below or above the potential output level?

13. *(Long-Run Aggregate Supply)* Determine whether each of the following, other things held constant, would lead to an increase, a decrease, or no change in long-run aggregate supply.
   a. An improvement in technology
   b. A permanent decrease in the size of the capital stock
   c. An increase in the actual price level
   d. An increase in the expected price level
   e. A permanent increase in the size of the labor force

14. *(Changes in Aggregate Supply)* What are supply shocks? Distinguish between beneficial and adverse supply shocks. Do such shocks affect the short-run supply curve, the long-run supply curve, or both? What is the resulting impact on potential GDP?

PROBLEMS AND EXERCISES

15. *(Real Wages)* In Exhibit 2 in this chapter, how does the real wage rate at point *c* compare with the real wage rate at point *a*? How do nominal wage rates compare at those two points? Explain your answers.

16. *(Natural Rate of Unemployment)* What is the relationship between potential output and the natural rate of unemployment?
   a. If the economy currently has a frictional unemployment rate of 1 percent, structural unemployment of 2 percent, seasonal unemployment of 0.5 percent, and cyclical unemployment of 2 percent, what is the natural rate of unemployment? Where is the economy operating relative to its potential GDP?
   b. What happens to the natural rate of unemployment and potential GDP if cyclical unemployment rises to 3 percent with other types of unemployment unchanged from part (a)?
   c. What happens to the natural rate of unemployment and potential GDP if structural unemployment falls to 1.5 percent with other types of unemployment unchanged from part (a)?

17. *(Expansionary and Contractionary Gaps)* Answer the following questions on the basis of the following graph:
   a. If the actual price level exceeds the expected price level reflected in long-term contracts, real GDP equals ______ and the actual price level equals ______ in the short run.
   b. The situation described in part (a) results in a(n) ______ gap equal to ______.
   c. If the actual price level is lower than the expected price level reflected in long-term contracts, real GDP equals ______ and the actual price level equals ______ in the short run.

d. The situation described in part (c) results in a(n) ________ gap equal to ________.

e. If the actual price level equals the expected price level reflected in long-term contracts, real GDP equals ________ and the actual price level equals ________ in the short run.

f. The situation described in part (e) results in ________ gap equal to ________.

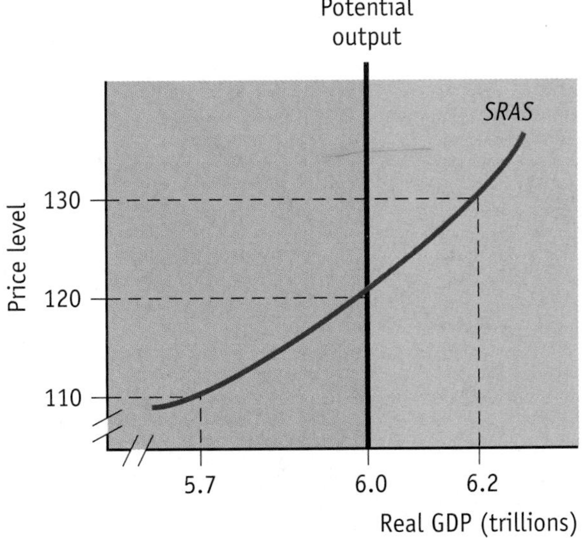

18. *(Long-Run Adjustment)* The ability of the economy to eliminate any imbalances between actual and potential output is sometimes called "self-correction." Using an aggregate supply and aggregate demand diagram, show why this self-correction process involves only temporary periods of inflation or deflation.

19. *(Changes in Aggregate Supply)* List three factors that can change the economy's potential output level. What is the impact of shifts in aggregate demand on potential output? Illustrate your answers with a diagram.

EXPERIENTIAL EXERCISES

20. *(Tracing Potential Output)* Although much of the theory is agreed upon, aggregate supply is still the most controversial topic in modern macroeconomics. To get a sense of some of the issues, read Stuart Weiner's brief article, "Challenges to the Natural Rate Framework," at http://www.kc.frb.org/publicat/econrev/er95q2.htm#Weiner. What are some of the challenges Weiner mentions and what evidence does he provide?

21. ***(CaseStudy:** Why is Unemployment So High in Europe?)* European unemployment is a hot topic. Use any Web browser (for example Alta Vista at http://www.altavist.com) to search for the words "European unemployment". Just by scanning the headlines, see how many possible explanations you can list. How do they compare to the explanations reviewed in the chapter case study?

22. *(Wall Street Journal)* In the short run, some workers' wages are determined by contracts, and some are not. The split between costs that change as production changes and those that do not is a key determinant of the shape of the short-run aggregate supply curve. To get a better feel for wage determination, look at the "Work Week" column in the first section of Tuesday's *Wall Street Journal*. Determine how some of the developments described there are likely to affect aggregate supply. Make sure that you distinguish between the short-run and the long-run effects. Draw a diagram to illustrate your conclusions.

CHAPTER

12 Fiscal Policy

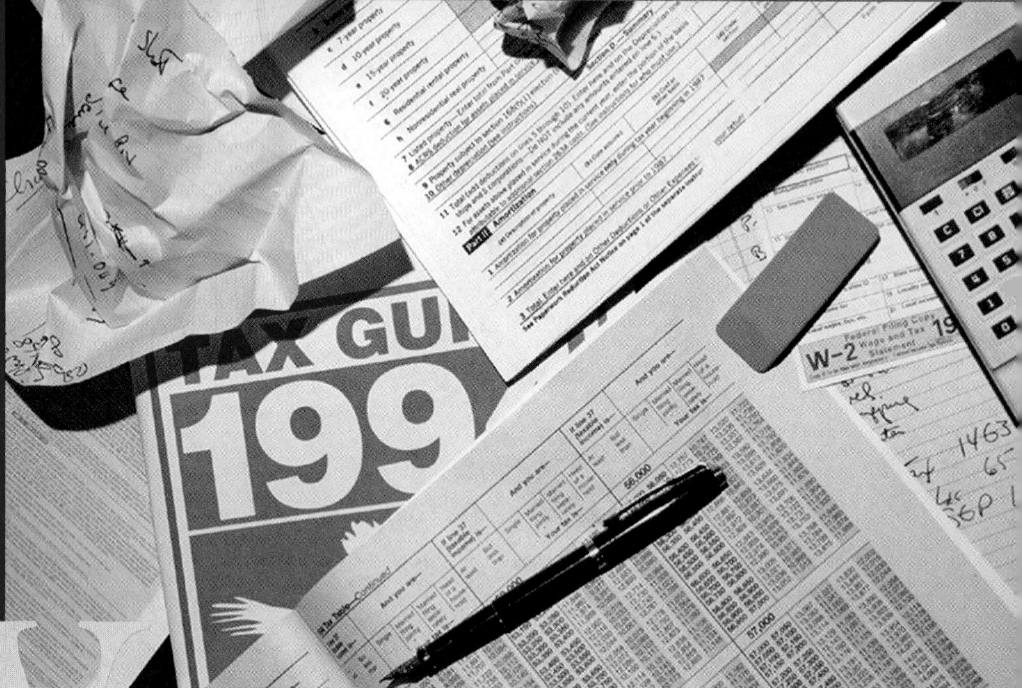

What is the proper role of government taxing and spending in macroeconomic policy? How can fiscal policy curb swings in the business cycle? How might fiscal policy affect aggregate supply? Why has fiscal policy fallen on hard times in the last two decades? Why does introducing aggregate supply reduce the spending and tax multipliers? Under what circumstances are these multipliers zero? Answers to these and other questions are addressed in this chapter, which examines the theory and practice of fiscal policy.

During the 1992 presidential campaign, the candidates argued over the best way to revive the ailing economy, which at the time was barely recovering from the 1990–1991 recession. George Bush proposed tax cuts and a relatively smaller role for government. Bill Clinton proposed increases in government

Visit the McEachern Interactive Study Center for this chapter at http://mcisc.swcollege.com

spending to be financed by tax increases on high-income earners. And Ross Perot wanted to reduce the huge federal budget deficits that had been a part of the fiscal landscape since the early 1980s. All three were talking about *fiscal policy*—the impact of government purchases, transfer payments, taxes, and borrowing on aggregate economic activity. In a more recent example of fiscal policy in practice, the Japanese government adopted a fiscal package in 1998 aimed at cutting taxes and increasing government purchases as a way to stimulate that troubled economy.

In this chapter, we first explore the effects of fiscal policy on aggregate demand. Next, we bring aggregate supply into the picture to consider the impact of taxes and government spending on the level of income and employment in the economy. We then examine the role of fiscal policy in moving the economy to its potential level of output. Finally, we review fiscal policy as it has been practiced since World War II.

Throughout the chapter, we use relatively simple tax and spending programs to explain fiscal policy. A more complex treatment, along with the algebra behind the numbers, appears in the appendix to this chapter. Topics discussed in this chapter include:

- Fiscal policy
- Discretionary fiscal policy
- Automatic stabilizers
- Lags in fiscal policy
- Limits of fiscal policy
- The supply-side experiment

THEORY OF FISCAL POLICY

Thus far, our macroeconomic model has viewed government as relatively passive. But U.S. government purchases and transfer payments at all levels today approach $3 trillion per year, making government an important player in the economy. From welfare reform to balancing the budget, fiscal policy affects the economy in myriad ways. We now move fiscal policy to center stage.

As introduced in Chapter 4, *fiscal policy* uses government purchases, transfer payments, taxes, and borrowing to affect macroeconomic variables such as employment, the price level, and the level of GDP. When economists study fiscal policy, they usually focus on the federal government, although governments at all levels have an impact on the economy.

The tools of fiscal policy can be divided into two categories: automatic stabilizers and discretionary fiscal policy. **Automatic stabilizers** are revenue and spending items in the federal budget that automatically change with the ups and downs of the economy so as to stabilize disposable income and, hence, consumption and real GDP. For example, the federal income tax is an automatic stabilizer because (1) it requires no congressional action to operate year after year and (2) it reduces the drop in income during recessions and reduces the jump in income during expansions. **Discretionary fiscal policy** requires ongoing decisions involving the deliberate manipulation of government purchases, taxation, and transfers to promote macroeconomic goals such as full employment, price stability, and economic growth.

Automatic stabilizers
Structural features of government spending and taxation that smooth fluctuations in disposable income, and hence consumption, over the business cycle

Discretionary fiscal policy
The deliberate manipulation of government purchases, taxation, and transfers in order to promote macroeconomic goals such as full employment, price stability, and economic growth

Using the aggregate expenditure framework developed earlier, we will initially focus on the demand side to consider the effect of changes in government purchases, transfer payments, and taxes on the real quantity of GDP demanded. The short story is that *at any given price level, an increase in government purchases or transfer payments increases the amount of real GDP demanded, and an increase in taxes decreases the amount of real GDP demanded, other things constant.* In this section, we see how and why.

NetBookmark

The Office of Management and Budget prepares a *Citizens' Guide to the Budget* each year, with numerous, easy-to-read charts and graphs indicating sources of revenue and the types of spending. Access to these guides and other budget documents for the current year and previous years is available at http://www.access.gpo.gov/usbudget/index.html.

Changes in Government Purchases

Let's begin by looking at Exhibit 1, with real GDP demanded of \$8.0 trillion, as reflected at point *a,* where the aggregate expenditure line crosses the 45-degree line. This equilibrium was determined in Chapter 10, where government purchases and net taxes each equaled \$1.0 trillion and were assumed to be *autonomous*—that is, they did not vary with income. Since government purchases equal net taxes, the government budget is in balance at point *a.*

Now suppose government purchases increase by \$0.1 trillion, or by \$100 billion, assuming other things, including net taxes, remain constant. This additional spending shifts the aggregate expenditure line up by \$0.1 trillion, to $C + I + G' + (X - M)$. Since, at real GDP of \$8.0 trillion, planned spending now exceeds output, production must increase. This increase in production increases income, which in turn increases planned spending, and so it goes through a series of spending rounds.

The initial increase of \$0.1 trillion in government purchases eventually increases the quantity of real GDP demanded at the given price level from \$8.0 trillion to \$8.5 trillion, shown as point *b* in Exhibit 1. Because output demanded increases by \$0.5 trillion as a result of an increase of \$0.1 trillion in government purchases, the government-purchases multiplier in our example is equal to 5. *As long as consumption is the only source of spending that varies with income, the multiplier for a change in government purchases, other things constant, equals*

EXHIBIT 1

Effect of a \$0.1 Trillion Increase in Government Purchases on Aggregate Expenditure and Real GDP Demanded

As a result of a \$0.1 trillion increase in government purchases, the aggregate expenditure shifts up by \$0.1 trillion, increasing the level of real GDP demanded by \$0.5 trillion.

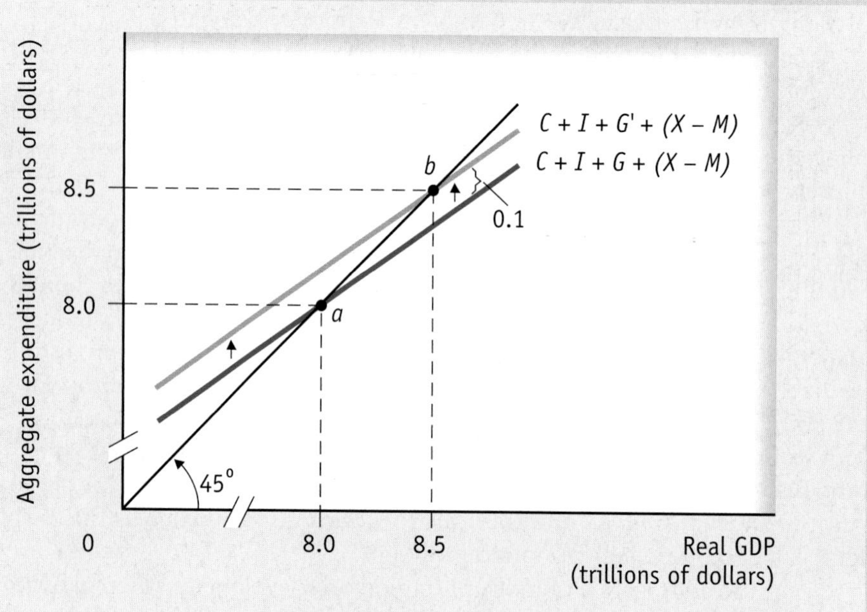

1/(1 – MPC), or 1/(1 – 0.8) in our example. Thus we can say that for a given price level, and assuming that only consumption varies with income,

$$\Delta \text{ real GDP} = \Delta G \times \frac{1}{1 - \text{MPC}}$$

where Δ means "change in". This same multiplier was discussed in Chapter 10, where we focused on shifts in consumption, investment, and net exports.

Changes in Net Taxes

A change in net taxes also affects the quantity of real GDP demanded, but the effect is less direct. A *decrease* in net taxes, other things constant, *increases* disposable income at each level of real GDP, so consumption increases. In Exhibit 2 we begin again at equilibrium point *a,* with real GDP equal to $8.0 trillion. To stimulate aggregate demand, suppose government cuts net taxes by $0.1 trillion, or by $100 billion, other things constant. We continue to assume that net taxes are autonomous—that is, that they do not vary with income. A $100 billion decrease in net taxes could result from a decrease in taxes, an increase in transfer payments, or some combination of the two. The $100 billion decrease in net taxes increases disposable income by $100 billion at each level of real GDP. Because households now have more disposable income, they spend more and save more at each level of real GDP.

But because households save some of the tax cut, consumption increases by less than the full tax cut. Specifically, *consumption spending at each level of real GDP*

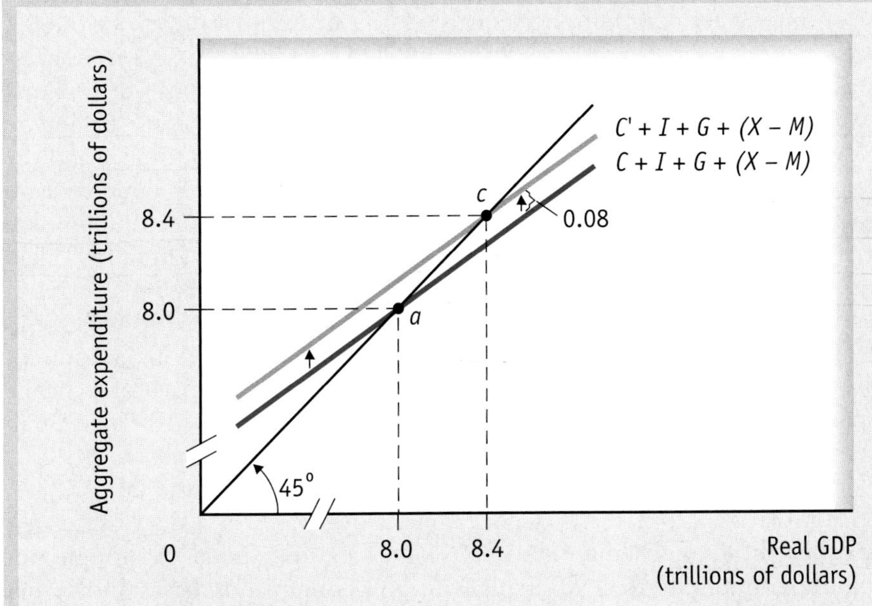

EXHIBIT 2

Effect of a $0.1 Trillion, or $100 Billion, Decrease in Autonomous Net Taxes on Aggregate Expenditure and Real GDP Demanded

As a result of a decrease in autonomous net taxes of $0.1 trillion, or $100 billion, consumers, who are assumed to have a marginal propensity to consume of 0.8, spend $80 billion and save $20 billion. The consumption function shifts up by $80 billion, or $0.08 trillion, as does the aggregate expenditure line. An $80 billion increase in the aggregate expenditure line eventually increases the level of real GDP demanded by $0.4 trillion. Keep in mind that the price level is assumed to be constant.

rises by the decrease in net taxes multiplied by the marginal propensity to consume. In our example, desired consumption spending at each level of real GDP increases by \$100 billion times 0.8, or \$80 billion. Decreasing net taxes by \$100 billion causes the aggregate expenditure line to shift up by \$80 billion at all levels of income, as shown in Exhibit 2. This initial increase in spending triggers subsequent rounds of spending, following a now-familiar pattern in the income-consumption cycle based on the marginal propensities to consume and to save. For example, the \$80 billion increase in consumption increases output and income by \$80 billion, which leads to \$64 billion in consumption and \$16 billion in saving, and so on through successive rounds. As a result, real GDP demanded eventually increases from \$8.0 trillion to \$8.4 trillion per year, or by \$400 billion.

The effect of a change in net taxes on the quantity of real GDP demanded equals the resulting shift in the consumption function times the simple spending multiplier. Thus we can say that the effect of a change in net taxes is

$$\Delta \text{ real GDP} = (-\text{MPC} \times \Delta\, NT) \times \frac{1}{1 - \text{MPC}}$$

Here, the simple spending multiplier is applied to the shift in consumption that results from the change in net taxes. This equation can be rearranged as

$$\Delta \text{ real GDP} = \Delta\, NT \times \frac{-\text{MPC}}{1 - \text{MPC}}$$

Simple tax multiplier The ratio of a change in equilibrium real GDP demanded to the initial change in autonomous net taxes that brought it about; the numerical value of the simple tax multiplier is –MPC/(1 – MPC)

where –MPC/(1 – MPC) is the **simple tax multiplier,** which can be applied directly to the change in net taxes to yield the change in the quantity of real GDP demanded at a given price level (this tax multiplier is called *simple* because, by assumption, net taxes do not vary with income). For example, with an MPC of 0.8, the autonomous net tax multiplier equals –4. In our example, a *decrease* of \$0.1 trillion in net taxes results in an *increase* in real GDP demanded of \$0.4 trillion, assuming a given price level. As another example, an *increase* in net taxes of \$0.2 trillion would, other things constant, *decrease* real GDP demanded by \$0.8 trillion.

Note two differences between the government purchase multiplier and the simple tax multiplier. First, increases in government purchases and in net taxes have opposite effects on the level of real GDP demanded. Second, the absolute value of the multiplier for a given change in government purchases is larger by 1 than the multiplier for an identical change in net taxes. This holds because changes in government purchases affect aggregate spending directly—each \$100 increase in government purchases increases spending in the first round by \$100. In contrast, each \$100 change in net taxes affects consumption indirectly by way of a change in disposable income. Thus, each \$100 decrease in taxes or each \$100 increase in transfer payments increases disposable income by \$100, which, given an MPC of 0.8, increases consumption in the first round by \$80; people save the other \$20.

To summarize, an increase in government purchases or a decrease in net taxes, other things constant, increases real GDP demanded. Although not shown, the combined effect of changes in government purchases and in net taxes is found by adding their individual effects.

Thus far in this chapter, we have focused on the amount of real GDP demanded at a given price level. We are now in a position to bring aggregate supply into the picture.

INCLUDING AGGREGATE SUPPLY

In Chapter 11 we introduced the possibility that natural market forces may take a long time to close a contractionary gap. Let's consider the possible remedial effect of discretionary fiscal policy in such a situation.

Discretionary Fiscal Policy in Response to a Contractionary Gap

Let's begin with a short-run aggregate supply curve, as indicated by $SRAS_{130}$ in Exhibit 3. This supply curve implies that if the price level turns out to be 130, the economy will produce its potential level of output of $8.0 trillion. Suppose instead that the aggregate demand curve, *AD*, intersects aggregate supply at point *e*, yielding the short-run output of $7.5 trillion and price level of 125. Since output falls well short of the economy's potential, this opens a contractionary gap of $0.5 trillion, as Exhibit 3 shows, which increases unemployment to above the natural rate.

If markets adjust naturally to the resulting increase in unemployed resources, the nominal prices of resources would drop enough in the long run that the short-run aggregate supply curve would shift out to achieve an equilibrium at

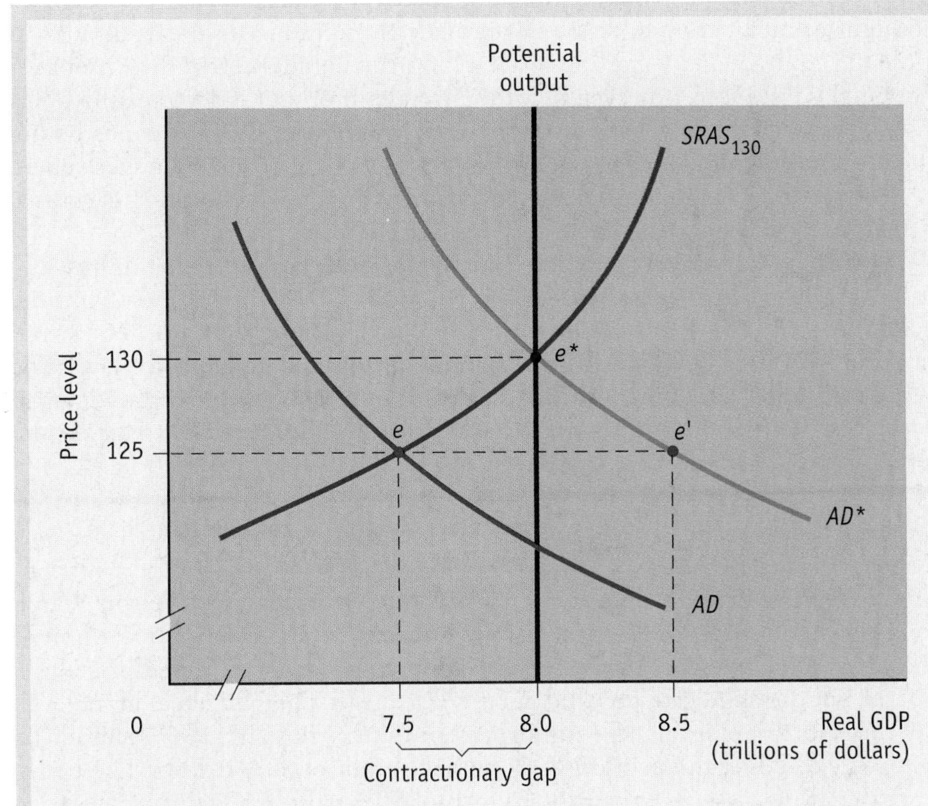

EXHIBIT 3

Discretionary Fiscal Policy to Close a Contractionary Gap

The aggregate demand curve, *AD*, and the short-run aggregate supply curve, $SRAS_{130}$, intersect at point *e*. Because the price level of 125 is below the expected price level of 130, the level of output falls short of the economy's potential. The resulting contractionary gap is $0.5 trillion. This gap could be closed by discretionary fiscal policy that increases aggregate demand by just the right amount. An increase in government purchases, a decrease in net taxes, or some combination of the two could shift aggregate demand to *AD*', moving the economy to its potential level of output at *e**.

the economy's potential output. History suggests, however, that wages and other resource prices may be slow to adjust to a contractionary gap.

Suppose policy makers believe that the move back to potential output will take too long. If they introduce just the right fiscal stimulus through increased government purchases, reduced net taxes, or some combination of the two, they could increase aggregate demand enough to return the economy to its potential level of output. Suppose a $0.2 trillion increase in government purchases provides just enough fiscal stimulus to shift the aggregate demand curve to the right, as shown in Exhibit 3 by the shift from *AD* to *AD**. If the price level remains at 125, this additional spending will increase the quantity demanded from $7.5 to $8.5 trillion. This increase of $1.0 trillion reflects the simple multiplier effect, given a constant price level.

At the original price level of 125, however, there is an excess quantity demanded, which causes the price level to rise. As the price level rises, the quantity of real GDP supplied increases but the quantity of real GDP demanded decreases. The price level will rise until the quantity demanded equals the quantity supplied. In Exhibit 3, the new aggregate demand curve intersects the aggregate supply curve at e^*, where the price level is 130, the one originally expected, and output equals potential GDP of $8.0 trillion.

Since 130 was the price level on which producers originally based their production plans, the intersection at point e^* is not only a short-run equilibrium but also a long-run equilibrium. If fiscal policy makers are accurate enough (or lucky enough), they can provide the appropriate fiscal stimulus to close the contractionary gap and foster a long-run equilibrium at the economy's potential GDP. Note, however, that the increase in output is accompanied by a rise in the price level. What's more, if the federal budget was in balance before the fiscal stimulus, the increase in government spending creates a budget deficit. In fact, until recently, the federal government had been running substantial deficits each year since the early 1980s.

What if policy makers overshoot the mark, and aggregate demand turns out to be greater than needed to achieve potential GDP? In the short run, the economy will produce beyond its potential level of output. In the long run, firms and resource owners will adjust to the unexpectedly high price level. The short-run supply curve will shift back until it intersects the aggregate demand curve at potential output, increasing the price level further but reducing the level of output back to $8.0 trillion.

Discretionary Fiscal Policy in Response to an Expansionary Gap

Suppose the short-run equilibrium price level exceeds the level on which long-term contracts are based, so output exceeds potential GDP. In Exhibit 4, the short-run aggregate supply curve is again based on an expected price level of 130, but the aggregate demand curve, *AD'*, yields a higher actual price level. So the short-run level of equilibrium output is initially $8.5 trillion, an amount exceeding the economy's potential output of $8.0 trillion. The economy therefore faces an expansionary gap of $0.5 trillion. Ordinarily, this gap would be closed by an inward shift in the short-run aggregate supply curve, which would return the economy to the potential level of output but at a higher price level.

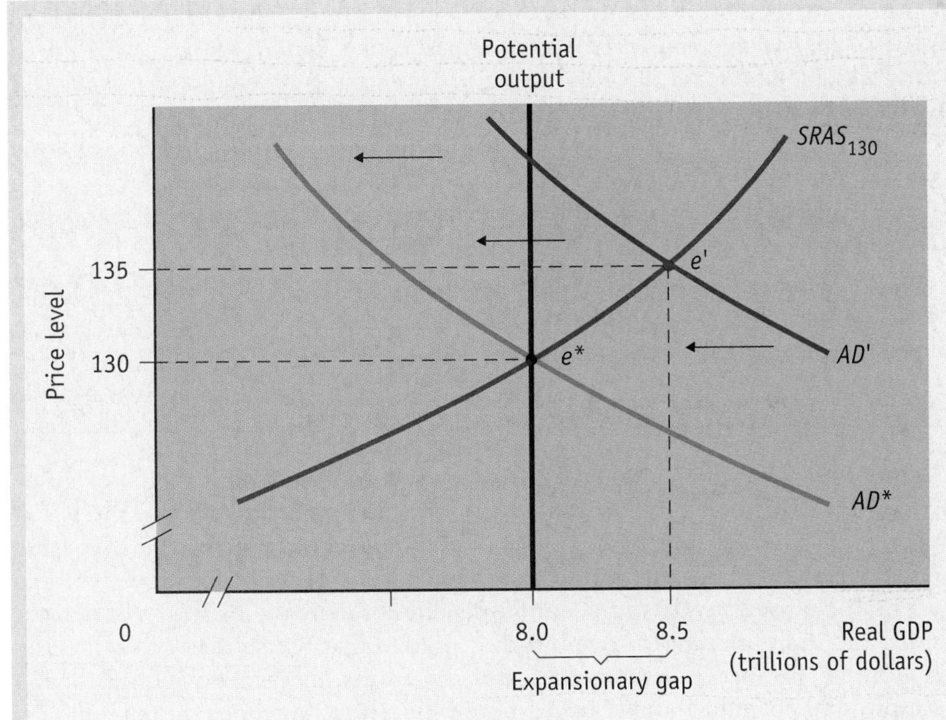

EXHIBIT 4

Discretionary Fiscal Policy to Close an Expansionary Gap

With the price level above the expected level of 130, there is an expansionary gap of $0.5 trillion. The gap could be eliminated by discretionary fiscal policy aimed at reducing aggregate demand by just the right amount. An increase in net taxes, a decrease in government purchases, or some combination of the two could shift the aggregate demand curve back to AD* and move the economy to potential output at point e*.

But the use of discretionary fiscal policy opens the door to another possibility. By reducing government purchases, increasing net taxes, or employing some combination of the two, the government can reduce aggregate demand, moving the economy to its potential level of output while avoiding an increase in the price level. If this policy is successful, the aggregate demand curve in Exhibit 4 will shift to the left from *AD*' to *AD**, and equilibrium will move from point *e*' to point *e**. Again, with just the right reduction in aggregate demand, output will fall to $8.0 trillion, the potential GDP. Closing an expansionary gap through fiscal policy rather than through natural market forces results in a lower price level, not a higher one. Increasing net taxes or reducing government purchases would also reduce a government deficit or increase a surplus.

Such precisely calculated fiscal policies as described here are hard to achieve, for their proper execution assumes that (1) the relevant spending multipliers can be predicted accurately, (2) aggregate demand can be shifted by the appropriate amount, (3) the potential level of output is accurately gauged, (4) various government entities can somehow coordinate their fiscal efforts, and (5) the shape of the short-run aggregate supply curve is known and will remain unaffected by the fiscal policy.

The Multiplier and the Time Horizon

In the short run, the aggregate supply curve slopes upward, so a shift in aggregate demand changes both the price level and the level of output. When aggregate supply gets in the act, the simple multiplier overstates the amount by which output changes. The exact change in equilibrium output in the short run depends on the steepness of the aggregate supply curve, which in turn depends on how sharply production costs increase as output expands. *The steeper the short-run aggregate supply curve, the less impact a given shift in the aggregate demand curve has on output and the more impact it has on the price level, so the smaller the spending multiplier.*

If the economy is already producing its potential output, then, in the long run, any change in fiscal policy aimed at stimulating demand will increase the price level but will not affect the output level. Thus, *if the economy is already producing its potential output, the spending multiplier is zero in the long run.*

You now have some idea of how fiscal policy can work in theory. Let's look at how it has been applied over the years.

THE EVOLUTION OF FISCAL POLICY

Classical economists A group of 18th- and 19th-century economists who believed that recessions were short-run phenomena that corrected themselves through natural market forces; thus they believed the economy was self-correcting

Before the 1930s, discretionary fiscal policy was seldom used explicitly to influence the performance of the macroeconomy. Prior to the Great Depression, public policy was shaped by the views of **classical economists**, who advocated *laissez-faire*, the belief that free markets were the best way to achieve national economic prosperity. Classical economists did not deny the existence of depressions and high unemployment, but they argued that the sources of such crises lay outside the market system, in the effects of wars, tax increases, poor growing seasons, and changing tastes. Such external shocks could reduce output and employment, but classical economists considered these to be short-run phenomena that would be corrected by natural market forces, such as changes in prices, wages, and interest rates.

Simply put, classical economists argued that if the economy's price level was too high to sell all that was produced, prices would fall until the quantity supplied equaled the quantity demanded; if wages were too high to employ all who wanted to work, wages would fall until the quantity of labor supplied equaled the quantity demanded; and if interest rates were too high to channel the amount saved into the amount invested, interest rates would fall until the amount saved equaled the amount invested.

So the classical approach implied that natural market forces, by way of flexible prices, wages, and interest rates, would move the economy toward its potential GDP. There appeared to be no need for government intervention in the economy. Before the onset of the Great Depression, most economists believed that an active fiscal policy would do more harm than good.

The Great Depression and World War II

Although classical economists acknowledged that capitalistic, market-oriented economies could experience temporary unemployment, the prolonged depression of the 1930s strained belief in the economy's ability to correct itself. As we discussed in Chapter 5, the Great Depression was marked by severe unemployment and much unused plant capacity. With abundant yet unemployed resources, output and income fell far short of the economy's potential.

The stark contrast between the natural market adjustments predicted by classical theory and the years of high unemployment during the Great Depression represented a collision of theory and fact. In 1936, John Maynard Keynes, of Cambridge University in England, published *The General Theory*, a book that challenged the classical view of the economy and touched off what has come to be called the Keynesian revolution. *Keynesian theory and policy were developed to address the problem of unemployment arising from the Great Depression.* Keynes's main quarrel with the classical economists was that prices and wages did not appear flexible enough to ensure the full employment of resources. According to Keynes, prices and wages were relatively inflexible—they were "sticky"—so natural market forces would not return the economy to full employment in a timely fashion. Keynes also believed business expectations might at times become so grim that even very low interest rates would not induce firms to invest all that consumers might save.

It is said that geologists learn more about the nature of the Earth's crust from one major upheaval, such as a huge earthquake or major volcanic eruption, than from a dozen more common events. Likewise, economists learned more about the economy from the Great Depression than from many more modest economic fluctuations. Even though this depression began seven decades ago, economists continue to sift through the data from that economic calamity, looking for hints about how the economy really works.

Three developments in the years following the onset of the Great Depression bolstered the use of discretionary fiscal policy in the United States. The first was the influence of Keynes's *General Theory,* in which he argued that natural forces would not necessarily close a contractionary gap. Keynes thought the economy could get stuck at a level of output that was well below its potential, requiring the government to increase aggregate demand so as to stimulate output and employment. The second development was the impact of World War II on output and employment. The demands of war greatly increased production and in the process eliminated cyclical unemployment during the war years, pulling the U.S. economy out of its depression. The third development, largely a consequence of the first two, was the passage of the Employment Act of 1946, which gave the federal government responsibility for promoting full employment and price stability.

Prior to the Great Depression, the dominant fiscal policy was to pursue a balanced budget. Indeed, to head off a modest federal deficit in 1932, a tax increase was approved, an increase that deepened the depression. In the wake of Keynes's *General Theory* and World War II, however, economists and policy makers grew more receptive to the idea that fiscal policy could be used to influence aggregate demand and thereby improve economic stability. No longer was the objective of fiscal policy to balance the budget but to promote full employment with price stability.

Automatic Stabilizers

So far this chapter has focused mostly on discretionary fiscal policy: conscious decisions to change taxes and government spending. Now let's get a clearer picture of automatic stabilizers. *Automatic stabilizers smooth fluctuations in disposable income over the business cycle, thereby boosting aggregate demand during periods of recession and dampening aggregate demand during periods of expansion.*

Let's look at the federal income tax. For simplicity, we earlier assumed net taxes to be independent of the level of income. In fact, the federal income tax system is progressive, meaning that the fraction of income paid in taxes increases as income increases. During an expansion, a growing fraction of income is claimed by taxes, slowing the growth in disposable income and, hence, the growth in consumption. Therefore, the progressive income tax relieves some of the inflationary pressure that might otherwise arise when output increases above its potential during an economic expansion. Conversely, when the economy is in recession, real GDP declines but taxes decline faster, so disposable income does not fall as much as real GDP. Thus the progressive income tax cushions declines in disposable income, in consumption, and in aggregate demand over the business cycle.

Another automatic stabilizer is unemployment insurance. During an economic expansion, the unemployment insurance system automatically increases the flow of unemployment insurance premiums from the income stream into the unemployment insurance fund, thereby moderating aggregate demand. During a recession, unemployment increases and the system reverses itself: Unemployment payments automatically flow from the insurance fund to those who become unemployed, thereby increasing their disposable income and propping up consumption and aggregate demand. Likewise, welfare spending automatically increases as more people become eligible during hard times. *As a result of these automatic stabilizers (1) real GDP fluctuates less than it otherwise would and (2) disposable income varies proportionately less than does real GDP.* And because disposable income varies less than real GDP, consumption also fluctuates less than does real GDP (as we saw in Exhibit 10 of Chapter 9). Because of the greater influence of automatic stabilizers, the economy is more stable today than it was during the Great Depression and before.

Unemployment insurance, welfare benefits, and the progressive income tax were initially designed not so much as automatic stabilizers but as income redistribution programs. Their beneficial roles as automatic stabilizers are secondary effects of the legislation. Automatic stabilizers do not eliminate economic fluctuations, but they do reduce their magnitude. The stronger and more effective the automatic stabilizers are, the less need there is for discretionary fiscal policy.

From the Golden Age to Stagflation

The 1960s were the Golden Age of fiscal policy. John F. Kennedy was the first U.S. president to put into practice the belief that a federal budget deficit could stimulate an economy experiencing a contractionary gap. He expanded the goals of fiscal policy from simply moderating business fluctuations to promoting long-term economic growth, and he set numerical targets of no more than 4 percent unemployment and no less than a 4.5 percent annual growth rate of output. Fiscal policy was also used on occasion to provide an extra kick to an expansion already under way, as in 1964, when Kennedy's successor, President Johnson, cut income tax rates to keep an expansion alive. *This tax cut, introduced to stimulate business investment, consumption, and employment, was perhaps the shining example of the successful use of fiscal policy during the 1960s.* The tax cut seemed to work wonders, increasing disposable income and consumption. The unemployment rate dropped below 5 percent for the first time in seven years, the inflation rate was under 2 percent, and the federal budget deficit in 1964 equaled only about 1 percent of GDP (compared to an average of 4 percent between 1982 and 1996).

Discretionary fiscal policy is a type of demand-management policy because the idea is to increase or decrease aggregate demand to smooth economic fluctuations. Demand-management policies were applied during much of the 1960s. But the 1970s were different. During the 1970s, the problem was stagflation—the double trouble of higher inflation and higher unemployment resulting from a decrease in aggregate supply. Aggregate supply dropped because of crop failures around the world, sharply higher oil prices, and other supply shocks. Demand-management policies were ill-suited to solving the problem of stagflation because an increase in aggregate demand would worsen inflation, whereas a decrease in aggregate demand would worsen unemployment.

Other concerns also caused economists and policy makers to question the effectiveness of discretionary fiscal policy: the difficulty of estimating the natural rate of unemployment, the time lags involved in implementing fiscal policy, the distinction between current and permanent income, and possible feedback effects of fiscal policy on aggregate supply. We will consider each of these concerns in turn.

Fiscal Policy and the Natural Rate of Unemployment

As we have seen, the unemployment rate that occurs when the economy is producing its potential GDP is called the *natural rate of unemployment*. For discretionary policy purposes, public officials must correctly estimate this natural rate. Suppose that the economy is producing its potential output of $8.0 trillion, as in Exhibit 5, and that the natural rate of unemployment is 5.0 percent. Also suppose that government officials believe the natural rate is 4.0 percent and they attempt to increase output and reduce unemployment through discretionary fiscal policy. As a result of the policy, the aggregate demand curve shifts to the

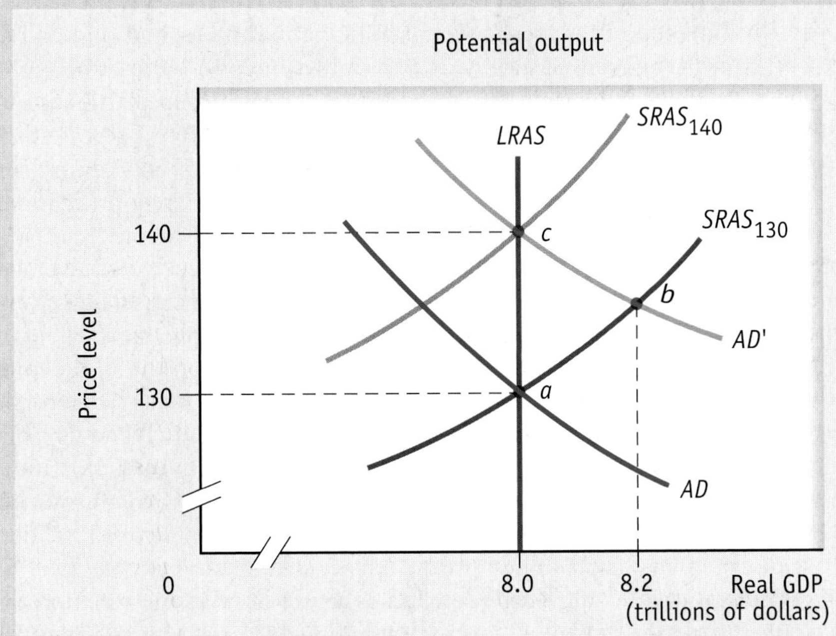

EXHIBIT 5

When Discretionary Fiscal Policy Overshoots

If public officials underestimate the natural rate of unemployment, they may attempt to stimulate aggregate demand even if the economy is producing its potential output, as at point *a*. In the short run, this expansionary policy yields a short-run equilibrium at point *b*, where the price level and output are higher and unemployment is lower, so the policy appears to succeed. But the resulting expansionary gap, will, in the long run, reduce the short-run aggregate supply curve from $SRAS_{130}$ to $SRAS_{140}$, eventually reducing output to its potential level of $8.0 trillion while increasing the price level to 140. Thus, attempts to increase production beyond potential GDP lead only to inflation in the long run.

right, from *AD* to *AD'*. In the short run this stimulation of aggregate demand expands output to \$8.2 billion and reduces unemployment to 4.0 percent, so the policy appears to succeed. But stimulating aggregate demand opens up an expansionary gap, which in the long run pushes up the nominal price of resources, resulting in a leftward shift in the short-run aggregate supply curve from $SRAS_{130}$ to $SRAS_{140}$. This reduction in aggregate supply causes the price level to increase and the output level to fall back to the economy's potential of \$8.0 trillion. Thus increases in output may temporarily persuade policy makers that their plan was a good one, but attempts to increase production beyond potential GDP in the long run lead only to inflation.

Lags in Fiscal Policy

The time required to approve and implement fiscal legislation may hamper its effectiveness and weaken discretionary fiscal policy as a tool of macroeconomic stabilization. Even if a fiscal prescription is appropriate for the economy at the time it is proposed, the months and sometimes years required to approve legislation and to implement the change mean the medicine could do more harm than good. The policy might kick in after the economy has already turned itself around. Since a recession is not usually identified as such until at least six months after it begins, and since the eight recessions since 1949 averaged only 11 months each, this leaves a narrow window in which to execute discretionary fiscal policy. (More will be said about timing problems in Chapter 16.)

Discretionary Policy and Permanent Income

It was once thought that discretionary fiscal policy could be turned on and off like a faucet, stimulating the economy at the right time and by just the right amount. Given the marginal propensity to consume, a relationship that is among the most stable in macroeconomics, tax changes could increase or decrease disposable income to bring about the desired change in consumption. A more recent view is that people base their consumption decisions not merely on changes in their current income but also on changes in their permanent income.

Permanent income Income that individuals expect to receive on average over the long term

Permanent income is the income a person expects to receive on average over the long term. The short-term manipulation of tax rates to influence consumption will not have the desired effects as long as people view the tax changes as only temporary. In 1967, for example, at a time when the U.S. economy was producing its potential level of output, the escalating war in Vietnam increased military spending, pushing real GDP beyond its potential. The combination of a booming domestic economy and increased spending on a widening war produced an expansionary gap by 1968. That year, Congress approved a temporary tax *surcharge,* which raised income tax rates for 18 months. The idea behind this discretionary fiscal policy was to reduce disposable income, thereby reducing consumption and aggregate demand as a way of relieving inflationary pressure in the economy. But the reduction in aggregate demand turned out to be disappointingly small, and inflation was hardly affected. Although several factors help explain why higher taxes failed to reduce consumption, most economists agree that the *temporary* nature of the tax increase meant that consumers faced only a small decrease in their permanent income. Since permanent income changed little, consumption spending changed little. Consumers simply saved less. As another example, in late 1997 Japanese officials announced an income tax cut of about $15 billion, intended to stimulate Japan's flat economy. Economists were skeptical that the plan would work, largely because most people expected the cut to be repealed after a year.[1] In short, *to the extent that consumers base spending decisions on their permanent income, attempts to fine-tune the economy with tax-rate adjustments thought to be temporary will be less effective.*

Feedback Effects of Fiscal Policy on Aggregate Supply

So far we have limited our discussion of fiscal policy to its effect on aggregate demand. Fiscal policy may also affect aggregate supply, although often the effect is unintentional. For example, suppose the government increases unemployment benefits and finances these transfer payments with higher taxes on workers. If the marginal propensity to consume is the same for both groups, the reduction in spending by those whose taxes increase should just offset the increase in spending by transfer recipients. According to a theory of fiscal policy focusing on aggregate demand, there should be no change in aggregate demand and hence no change in equilibrium real GDP.

But consider the possible effects of these changes on labor supply. The unemployed, who benefit from increased transfers, now have less incentive to find work, so they may search at a more leisurely pace. Conversely, workers who find their after-tax wage reduced by the higher tax rates may be less willing to work extra hours or to work a second job since the higher marginal tax rates they face cut their opportunity cost of leisure. In short, the supply of labor could decrease as a result of offsetting changes in taxes and transfers. A decrease in the supply of labor would decrease aggregate supply, reducing the economy's potential GDP.

Both automatic stabilizers, such as unemployment insurance and the progressive income tax, and discretionary fiscal policy, such as changes in tax rates, may affect individual incentives to work, spend, save, and invest, although these effects are usually unintended. We should keep these secondary effects in mind when we evaluate fiscal policies. It was concern about the effects of taxes on the supply of labor that served as a basis for tax cuts introduced in 1981, as we will see next.

U.S. Budget Deficits of the 1980s and 1990s

In 1981, President Reagan and Congress agreed on a 23 percent reduction in average income tax rates and a major buildup in defense programs, with no substantial offsetting reductions in domestic programs. This tax cut reflected a supply-side philosophy that reductions in tax rates would make people more willing to work because they could keep more of what they earned. Lower taxes would increase the supply of labor and other resources in the economy, thereby increasing aggregate supply and the economy's potential GDP. In its strongest form, the supply-side theory held that enough additional real GDP would be generated by the tax cuts that total tax revenue would actually increase—a smaller share of a bigger pie would exceed a larger share of a smaller pie. What happened as a result of the tax cut? Let's examine events during the 1980s in the following case study.

1 See David Hamilton, "Japan's Prime Minister Slashes Taxes in Surprise Move to Boost Nikkei," *Wall Street Journal* (17 December 1997).

The on-line magazine *Intellectual Capital* features a summary and two differing perspectives about supply-side economics in its October 10, 1996 issue at http://www.intellectualcapital.com/issues/96/1010/index.html. Supply-side economics emerged as an issue in the 1996 presidential campaign once Senator Dole chose ardent supply-side advocate Jack Kemp to be his running mate. First read the overview "Issue of the Week" article by Bob Kolasky for context. Then consider the different spins by Robert Shapiro of the Progressive Policy Institute and Stephen Moore of the Cato Institute. What does each side see as the factors that limit economic growth? What changes in public policies does each side advocate for promoting economic growth?

The Supply-Side Experiment

Taking 1981 to 1988 as the time frame for the examination, we can make some tentative observations about the effects of the federal income tax cut of 1981, which was phased in over three years. After the tax cut was approved but before it took effect, a recession hit the economy and the unemployment rate climbed to nearly 10 percent in 1982.

Although it is difficult to untangle the growth generated by the tax cuts from the cyclical upswing following the recession of 1981–1982, we can say that between 1981 and 1988 employment climbed by 15 million and unemployment fell by 2 million. Output per capita increased by about 2.0 percent per year between 1981 and 1988. This rate was higher than the 1.1 percent average annual increase between 1973 and 1981 but lower than the 2.2 percent annual growth rate between 1948 and 1973.

Does the growth in employment and in real GDP mean the supply-side experiment was a success? Part of the growth in employment and output could be explained by the economic stimulus provided by the huge federal deficits during the period. Although policy makers did not make a conscious decision to do so, their tax cuts, in effect, resulted in an expansionary fiscal policy. *The stimulus from the tax cut helped sustain a continued expansion during the 1980s—the longest peacetime expansion to that point in the nation's history.*

Despite the growth in employment, government revenues did not expand enough to offset the combination of tax cuts and increased government spending. Between 1981 and 1988, federal outlays grew at an average rate of 6.8 percent per year, and federal revenue grew at an average rate of 6.3 percent per year. So the tax cut failed to generate the revenue required to fund growing government spending. Prior to 1981, deficits had been relatively small compared to, say, GDP—typically less than 1 percent of GDP. But deficits grew to about $200 billion a year by the middle of the 1980s; relative to GDP, they averaged about 5 percent. These deficits were the largest the nation had ever experienced during peacetime. The recession of the early 1990s pushed the federal deficit up to 6 percent of GDP by 1992. *The national debt, which is the accumulation of annual deficits, more than quadrupled between 1981 and 1996.*

The extensive government borrowing during the 1980s pushed up U.S. interest rates, which attracted investment funds from abroad and increased the value of the dollar on foreign exchange markets. The ready supply of foreign capital meant that investment did not decline during the 1980s. High real U.S. interest rates, a strong dollar during the first half of the decade, and a stable political climate combined to make the United States a "safe haven" where foreigners could put their savings.

Sources: *Economic Report of the President,* February 1999; Herbert Stein, *The Fiscal Revolution in America,* 2nd ed. (Washington, D.C.: The AIE Press, 1996).

During the years of large federal deficits, the sum of U.S. consumption, investment, and government purchases exceeded U.S. income and output. How could this occur? Domestic spending could exceed domestic output because U.S. households, firms, and governments borrowed from abroad to help buy foreign goods. Since early 1976, U.S. imports have exceeded exports, and the resulting trade deficit has been financed in part by borrowing from abroad.

Given the effects of fiscal policy, particularly in the short run, we should not be surprised that elected officials might use discretionary fiscal policy to enhance their reelection prospects. Let's look at how political considerations may shape fiscal policies.

Discretionary Policy and Presidential Elections

CaseStudy

Public Policy

Beginning in 1998, President Clinton and the Republican Congress managed to move the federal budget from deficit to "surpluses as far as the forecasters can see." Could you have balanced the budget? Visit the Web site for the National Budget Simulation at http://garnet.berkeley.edu:3333/budget/budget.html and try your hand at the short game version. Descriptions of each category of spending can be found by clicking on the words to the right. What is the difference between spending and tax expenditure? Which types of spending are, in practical political terms, the least discretionary? Try to change interest payments. Why does the simulation give you only one option for this?

After the recession of 1990–1991, the economy was slow to recover. At the time of the 1992 presidential election, the unemployment rate still languished at 7.5 percent, up two percentage points from where it stood in 1988, when President Bush was elected. The higher unemployment rate was too much of a hurdle to overcome and Bush lost to Clinton.

The link between economic performance and reelection success goes back a long way. Ray Fair of Yale University examined presidential elections dating back to 1916 and found that the state of the economy had a clear impact on the elections' outcomes. Specifically, he found that a declining unemployment rate and strong growth of real GDP per person during an election year increased the chances of election for the candidate of the incumbent party.

Another Yale economist, William Nordhaus, developed a theory of **political business cycles,** arguing that incumbent presidents use expansionary policies to stimulate the economy, often only temporarily, during an election year. They try to increase their chances of reelection by pursuing fiscal policies that reduce unemployment and increase output. For example, observers claim that President Nixon used expansionary policies to increase his chances for reelection in 1972.

Political business cycles Economic fluctuations that result when discretionary policy is manipulated for political gain

The evidence to support the theory of political business cycles is not totally convincing. One problem is that the theory limits presidential motivation to reelection, when in fact presidents may have other policy objectives. For example, President Bush passed up an opportunity to sign a permanent tax cut for the middle class because that measure also called for tax increases on a much smaller group—upper-income taxpayers.

An alternative to the theory of political business cycles is that Democrats care relatively more about unemployment and relatively less about inflation than do Republicans. This view is supported by evidence indicating that during a Democratic administration, unemployment is more likely to fall and inflation is more likely to rise than during a Republican administration. Republican presidents tend to pursue contractionary policies soon after taking office and are more willing to endure a recession in order to reduce inflation. (The country suffered a recession in the second year of each of the last four Republican administrations.) Democratic presidents tend to pursue expansionary policies to reduce unemployment and are willing to put up with higher inflation to do so.

Sources: *Economic Report of the President,* February 1999; Ray Fair, "The Effects of Economic Events on Votes for President," *Review of Economics and Statistics* (May 1978): 159–172; and William Nordhaus, "Alternative Approaches to the Political Business Cycle," *Brookings Papers on Economic Activity* No. 2 (1989): 1–49.

The large federal budget deficits of the 1980s and first half of the 1990s reduced the use of discretionary fiscal policy as a tool for economic stabilization. Because deficits were already large during economic expansions, it was hard to justify increasing deficits still more during a recession. For example, President Clinton proposed a modest stimulus package in early 1993 to boost the recovery that was under way. His opponents blocked the measure, arguing that it would increase the deficit.

Balancing the Federal Budget

Clinton did not get his way with the stimulus package, but he did manage to increase taxes substantially on high-income households in 1993. The Republican Congress elected in 1994 introduced more fiscal discipline on federal spending as part of a plan to balance the budget by the year 2002. Meanwhile the economy experienced a vigorous recovery fueled by growing consumer spending and rising business optimism based on the strongest stock market in history. The confluence of these events—tax increases on the rich, federal spending constraints, and a strengthening economy—changed the dynamic of the federal budget. Tax revenues gushed into Washington, growing an average of 8.0 percent per year between 1993 and 1998; federal spending remained in check, growing only 3.8 percent per year. By 1998 that one-two punch knocked out the federal deficit, a deficit that only six years earlier had topped $290 billion.

Toward the end of the 1990s, the U.S. economy performed extremely well. Whereas inflation and unemployment increased during the stagflation years of the 1970s, they both decreased during 1996, 1997, and 1998. During those three years, the U.S. inflation rate as measured by the CPI declined from 3.0 percent to 2.3 percent then to 1.6 percent; the unemployment rate dropped from 5.4 percent to 4.9 percent then to 4.5 percent. The inflation rate in 1998 was the lowest of any year since 1965, and the unemployment rate in 1998 was the lowest of any year since 1969. The declining unemployment rate boosted output; real GDP increased by 3.4 percent in 1996, and 3.9 percent in 1997 and in 1998. With the economy performing so well, there was no need to even consider using discretionary fiscal policy.

CONCLUSION

In this chapter we reviewed several considerations that reduce the size of the spending multiplier. In the short run, the aggregate supply curve slopes upward, so the impact on equilibrium output of any change in aggregate demand is blunted by a change in the price level. In the long run, the aggregate supply curve is vertical, so if the economy is already producing at its potential, the spending multiplier is zero. To the extent consumers respond primarily to changes in their permanent income, temporary changes in net taxes have less of an impact on consumption, so the net-tax multiplier will be smaller.

Throughout this chapter we assumed constant net taxes and constant net exports. In the real world, income taxes increase with income and net exports decrease with income. In the appendix to this chapter, we develop the spending multiplier that introduces these more realistic assumptions. The resulting spending multipliers and tax multipliers are smaller than those developed to this point.

Because of huge federal deficits between 1982 and 1996, discretionary fiscal policy had fallen out of favor. During this time, discretionary monetary policy took center stage as a tool of economic stabilization. Monetary policy is the regulation of the money supply by the Federal Reserve System. In the next three chapters we will introduce money and financial institutions, examine monetary policy, and discuss the impact of monetary and fiscal policy on economic stability and growth. After we introduce money, we will consider yet another reason why the simple spending multiplier is overstated.

SUMMARY

1. The tools of fiscal policy are automatic stabilizers and discretionary fiscal measures. Automatic stabilizers, such as the federal income tax, once implemented, operate year after year without congressional action. Discretionary fiscal measures require ongoing decisions about government spending and taxation.
2. The effect of a change in government purchases on aggregate demand is the same as that of a change in any other type of spending. The simple multiplier for government purchases equals $1/(1 - MPC)$.
3. A change in net taxes (taxes minus transfer payments) affects consumption by changing disposable income. A given change in net taxes does not affect spending as much as would an identical change in government purchases. The multiplier for a change in autonomous net taxes equals $-MPC/(1 - MPC)$.
4. An expansionary fiscal policy can close a contractionary gap by increasing government purchases or by reducing net taxes. Because the short-run aggregate supply curve slopes upward, an increase in aggregate demand will raise both output and the price level in the short run. Fiscal policy aimed at reducing aggregate demand in order to close an expansionary gap will reduce both output and the price level.
5. Fiscal policy focuses primarily on the demand side, not the supply side. The problems of the 1970s, however, resulted more from a decline in aggregate supply than from a decline in aggregate demand.
6. The tax cuts of the early 1980s were introduced as a way of increasing aggregate supply. But government spending grew faster than tax revenue, resulting in large budget deficits that stimulated aggregate demand, leading to the longest peacetime expansion up to that point in the nation's history. These huge deficits discouraged additional discretionary fiscal policy as a way of stimulating aggregate demand further, but recent success in erasing the deficit could spawn renewed interest in discretionary fiscal policy.

QUESTIONS FOR REVIEW

1. *(Fiscal Policy)* Define fiscal policy. Determine whether each of the following, other factors held constant, would lead to an increase, a decrease, or no change in the level of real GDP demanded:
   a. A decrease in government purchases
   b. An increase in net taxes
   c. A reduction in transfer payments
   d. A decrease in the marginal propensity to consume
2. *(The Multiplier and the Time Horizon)* Explain how the steepness of the short-run aggregate supply curve affects the government's ability to use fiscal policy to change real GDP.
3. *(Evolution of Fiscal Policy)* What did classical economists assume about the flexibility of prices, wages, and interest rates? What did this assumption imply about the self-correcting tendencies in an economy in recession? What disagreements did Keynes have with classical economists?
4. *(Automatic Stabilizers)* Often during recessions there is an increase in the number of young people who volunteer for military service. Could this rise be considered a type of automatic stabilizer? Why or why not?
5. *(Permanent Income)* "If the federal government wants to stimulate consumption by means of a tax cut, it should employ a permanent tax cut. If the government wants to stimulate saving in the short run, it should employ a temporary tax cut." Evaluate this statement.
6. *(Fiscal Policy)* Explain why effective discretionary fiscal policy requires information about each of the following:
   a. The slope of the short-run aggregate supply curve
   b. The natural rate of unemployment
   c. The size of the multiplier
   d. The speed with which self-correcting forces operate
7. *(Automatic Stabilizers)* Distinguish between discretionary fiscal policy and automatic stabilizers. Provide some

examples of automatic stabilizers. What is the impact of automatic stabilizers on disposable income as the economy moves through the business cycle?

8. *(Fiscal Policy Effectiveness)* Determine whether each of the following would make fiscal policy more effective or less effective:
   a. A decrease in the marginal propensity to consume
   b. Shorter lags in the effect of fiscal policy
   c. Consumers suddenly becoming more concerned about permanent income than about current income
   d. More accurate measurement of the natural rate of unemployment

9. **(CaseStudy:** *The Supply-Side Experiment)* Explain why it is difficult to determine whether or not the supply-side experiment was a success.

10. **(CaseStudy:** *Discretionary Policy and Presidential Elections)* Suppose that fiscal policy changes output faster than it changes the price level. How might such timing play a role in the theory of political business cycles?

11. *(Balancing the Federal Budget)* Now that the huge federal budget deficits of the 1980s and first half of the 1990s have been erased, why would policy makers be more inclined to use discretionary fiscal policy?

PROBLEMS AND EXERCISES

12. *(Changes in Government Purchases)* Assume that government purchases decrease by $10 billion, other factors held constant. Calculate the change in the level of real GDP demanded for each of the following values of the MPC. Then calculate the change if the government, instead of reducing its purchases, increased autonomous net taxes by $10 billion.
    a. 0.9 b. 0.8 c. 0.75 d. 0.6

13. *(Fiscal Multipliers)* Explain the difference between the government purchases multiplier and the net tax multiplier. If the MPC falls, what happens to the tax multiplier?

14. *(Changes in Net Taxes)* Using the income-expenditure model, graphically illustrate the impact of a $15 billion drop in government transfer payments on aggregate expenditure if the MPC equals 0.75. Explain why it has this impact. What is the impact on the level of real GDP demanded?

15. *(Fiscal Policy with an Expansionary Gap)* Using the aggregate demand–aggregate supply model, illustrate an economy with an expansionary gap. If the government is to close the gap by changing government purchases, should it increase or decrease those purchases? In the long run, what happens to the level of real GDP as a result of government intervention? What happens to the price level? Illustrate this on an AD–AS diagram, assuming that the government changes its purchases by exactly the amount necessary to close the gap.

16. *(Fiscal Policy)* This chapter shows that increased government purchases, with taxes held constant, can eliminate a contractionary gap. How could a tax cut achieve the same result? Would the tax cut have to be larger than the increase in government purchases? Why or why not?

17. *(Multipliers)* Suppose that investment, in addition to having an autonomous component, also has a component that varies directly with the level of real GDP. How would this affect the size of the government purchase and net tax multipliers?

EXPERIENTIAL EXERCISES

18. *(Fiscal Policy)* The University of Washington's Fiscal Policy Center at http://weber.u.washington.edu/~fpcweb/center/links.htm provides an extensive list of links about U.S. fiscal policy. Visit that site and use the links to determine what tax and spending proposals have been made in Congress during the past six months. Choose one of those proposals and use the AD–AS framework to explain its likely impact.

19. *(The Evolution of Fiscal Policy)* In the United States, fiscal policy is determined jointly by the president and Congress. The Congressional Budget Office at http://www.cbo.gov/index.html provides analysis to Congress, and the Office of Management and Budget at http://www.whitehouse.gov/WH/EOP/OMB/html/ombhome.html does the same for the executive branch. Visit these Web sites to get a sense of the kinds of analysis these groups do and how they might be used in determining fiscal policy.

20. *(Wall Street Journal)* "Washington Wire" is a column that appears on the front page of the *Wall Street Journal* each Friday. Review the latest column to determine what fiscal policy proposals are under consideration. Do the proposals deal more with discretionary fiscal policy, or with automatic stabilizers? Are they designed to affect aggregate demand or aggregate supply?

Appendix

THE ALGEBRA OF DEMAND-SIDE EQUILIBRIUM

In this appendix, we continue to focus on aggregate demand, using algebra. In Appendix B to Chapter 10, we solved for real GDP demanded at a particular price level, then derived the simple spending multiplier for changes in spending, including government purchases. As derived in Appendix B to Chapter 10, the change in GDP demanded, here denoted as ΔY, resulting from a change in government purchases, ΔG, is

$$\Delta Y = \Delta G \times \frac{1}{1 - \text{MPC}}$$

The government spending multiplier is 1/(1 – MPC). In this appendix, we first derive the multiplier for net taxes that do not vary with income. Then we incorporate variable net exports and proportional income taxes into the framework. *Note that multiplier effects assume a given price level, so we limit the analysis to shifts in the aggregate demand curve.*

NET-TAX MULTIPLIER

What is the effect on the quantity of GDP demanded of a $1 increase in net taxes that do not vary with income? We begin with Y, the equilibrium derived in Appendix B to Chapter 10:

$$Y = \frac{1}{1 - b}(a - bNT + I + G + X - M)$$

where b is the marginal propensity to consume and $a - bNT$ is that portion of consumption that is independent of the level of income (review Appendix B to Chapter 10 if you need a refresher).

Now let's increase net taxes by $1 to see what happens to the level of real GDP demanded. Increasing net taxes by $1 yields

$$Y' = \frac{a - b(NT + \$1) + I + G + X - M}{1 - b}$$

The difference between Y' and Y is

$$Y' - Y = \frac{\$1(-b)}{1 - b}$$

Since b is the marginal propensity to consume, this difference can be expressed as $1 times –MPC/(1 – MPC), which is the net-tax multiplier discussed in this chapter. With the MPC equal to 0.8, the net-tax multiplier equals –0.8/0.2, or –4, so the effect of increasing net taxes by $1 is to reduce GDP demanded by $4. For any change larger than $1, we simply scale up the results. For example, the effect of increasing net taxes by $1 billion is to reduce GDP demanded by $4 billion. A different marginal propensity to consume will yield a different multiplier. For example, if the MPC equals 0.75, the net-tax multiplier equals –0.75/0.25, or –3.

THE MULTIPLIER WHEN BOTH *G* AND *NT* CHANGE

Although in the chapter we did not discuss the combined effects of changes in both government purchases and net taxes, we can easily summarize these effects. Suppose that both increase by $1. We can bring together the two changes in the following equation:

$$Y^* = \frac{a - b(NT + \$1) + I + G + \$1 + X - M}{1 - b}$$

The difference between this equilibrium and Y (the income level before introducing any changes in G or NT) is

$$Y^* - Y = \frac{\$1(-b) + \$1}{1 - b}$$

which can be simplified to

$$Y^* - Y = \frac{\$1(1 - b)}{1 - b} = \$1$$

Equilibrium aggregate output demanded increases by $1 as a result of $1 increases in both government purchases and net taxes. This result is referred to as the *balanced budget multiplier*, which is equal to 1.

More generally, we can say that if ΔG represents the change in government purchases and ΔNT represents the change in net taxes, the resulting change in aggregate output demanded, ΔY, can be expressed as

$$\Delta Y = \frac{\Delta G - b\Delta NT}{1 - b}$$

The Multiplier with a Proportional Income Tax

A net tax of a fixed amount is relatively easy to manipulate, but it is not very realistic. Instead, suppose we introduce a **proportional income tax** rate equal to t, where t lies between zero and 1. Incidentally, the proportional income tax is also the so-called *flat tax* that has been discussed in Congress as an alternative to the existing progressive income tax. Tax collections under a proportional income tax equal real GDP, Y, times the tax rate, t. With tax collections of tY, disposable income equals

$$Y - tY = (1 - t)Y$$

We plug this value for disposable income into the consumption function to yield

$$C = a + b(1 - t)Y$$

To consumption, we add the other components of aggregate expenditure, I, G, and $X - M$, to get

$$Y = a - b(1 - t)Y + I + G + (X - M)$$

Moving the Y terms to the left-hand side of the equation yields

$$Y - b(1 - t)Y = a + I + G + (X - M)$$

or

$$Y[1 - b(1 - t)] = a + I + G + (X - M)$$

By isolating Y on the left-hand side of the equation, we get

$$Y = \frac{a + I + G + (X - M)}{1 - b(1 - t)}$$

The numerator on the right-hand side consists of the autonomous spending components. A \$1 change in any of these components would change income by

$$\Delta Y = \frac{\$1}{1 - b(1 - t)}$$

Thus, the spending multiplier with a proportional income tax equals $1/[1 - b(1 - t)]$. Note that as the tax rate increases, the denominator increases, so the multiplier gets smaller. *The higher the proportional tax rate, other things constant, the smaller the multiplier.* Because a higher tax rate means a bigger reduction in disposable income, a higher tax rate reduces spending during each round of spending.

Including Variable Net Exports

The previous section assumed that net exports remained independent of the level of disposable income. If you have been reading the appendixes along with the chapters, you are already acquainted with how variable net exports fit into the picture. *The addition of variable net exports causes the aggregate expenditure line to flatten out, because net exports decrease as real income increases.* Real GDP demanded with variable net exports and a proportional income tax is

$$Y = a - b(1 - t)Y + I + G + X - m(1 - t)Y$$

where $m(1 - t)Y$ shows that imports are an increasing function of disposable income. The above equation reduces to

$$Y = \frac{a + I + G + X}{1 - b + m + t(b - m)}$$

The higher the proportional tax rate, t, or the higher the marginal propensity to import, m, the larger the denominator, so the smaller the spending multiplier. If the marginal propensity to consume is 0.8, the marginal propensity to import is 0.1, and the proportional income tax rate is 0.2, the spending multiplier would be about 2.3, or less than half our simple spending multiplier of 5.

Since we first introduced the simple spending multiplier, we have examined several factors that reduce that simple multiplier: (1) a marginal propensity to consume that responds primarily to permanent changes in income, not transitory changes, (2) a marginal propensity to import, and (3) a proportional income tax. The upward-sloping supply curve also reduces the effect of any given change in aggregate demand on equilibrium real GDP. After we introduce money in the next two chapters, we will consider additional factors that reduce the size of the spending multiplier.

APPENDIX QUESTIONS

1. *(The Algebra of Demand-Side Equilibrium)* Suppose that the autonomous levels of consumption, investment, government purchases, and net exports are \$500 billion, \$300 billion, \$100 billion, and \$100 billion, respectively. Suppose further that the MPC is 0.85, that the marginal propensity to import is 0.05, and that income is taxed at a proportional rate of 0.25.
   a. What is the level of real GDP demanded?
   b. What is the size of the government deficit (or surplus) at this output level?
   c. What is the size of net exports at the level of real GDP demanded?
   d. What is the level of saving at this output?
   e. What change in autonomous spending is required to change equilibrium real GDP demanded by \$500 billion?

2. *(Spending Multiplier)* If the MPC is 0.8, the MPM is 0.1, and the proportional income tax rate is 0.2, what is the value of the spending multiplier? Determine whether each of the following would increase the value of the spending multiplier, decrease it, or leave it unchanged:
   a. An increase in the MPM
   b. An increase in the MPC
   c. An increase in the proportional tax rate
   d. An increase in autonomous net taxes

3. *(The Multiplier with a Proportional Income Tax)* Answer the following questions using the following data. Assume an MPC of 0.8.

Disposable Income	Consumption
$ 0	$ 500
500	900
1,000	1,300
1,500	1,700

a. Assuming that net taxes are equal to $200 regardless of the level of income, graph consumption against income (as opposed to disposable income).
b. How would an increase in net taxes to $300 affect the consumption function?
c. If the level of taxes were related to the level of income (i.e., income taxes were proportional to income), how would this affect the consumption function?

CHAPTER

13 Money and the Financial System

Why are you willing to exchange a piece of paper bearing Alexander Hamilton's portrait and the number 10 in each corner for a pepperoni pizza with extra cheese? If Russia can't pay its bills, what's the problem with simply printing more rubles? Why are so few of the largest banks in the world American? How come someone was able to cash a check written on a pair of underpants? And why is there so much fascination with money, anyway? These and other questions are answered in this chapter, which introduces money and banking.

The word *money* comes from the name of the goddess in whose temple Roman money was coined. Money has come to symbolize all personal and business finance. You can read *Money* magazine and the "Money" section of *USA Today,* and you can watch TV shows such as *Moneyline, Moneyweek,* and

Visit the McEachern Interactive Study Center for this chapter at http://mcisc.swcollege.com

Your Money. You can articulate your preferences with money—after all, money talks. And when money talks, it has a lot to say, as in "put your money where your mouth is" and "show me the money." Money is the oil that lubricates the wheels of commerce. Just as oil makes for an easier fit among interacting gears, money reduces the friction—the transaction costs—of voluntary exchange. But too little oil can leave some parts creaking, and too much oil can gum up the works. Similarly, too little or too much money in circulation creates problems.

This chapter is obviously about money. We begin with the evolution of money, tracing its use from the most primitive economy to our own. Then we turn to monetary developments in the United States.

Topics discussed in this chapter include:

- Barter
- Functions of money
- Commodity and fiat moneys
- The Federal Reserve System
- Depository institutions
- Banking in the 1980s and 1990s

THE EVOLUTION OF MONEY

In the beginning there was no money. The earliest families were largely self-sufficient. Each family produced all it consumed and consumed all it produced, so there was little need for exchange. Without exchange, there was no need for money. When specialization first emerged, as some people went hunting and others took up farming, hunters and farmers had to trade. Thus the specialization of labor resulted in exchange, but the kinds of goods traded were limited enough that people could easily exchange their products directly for other products—a system called *barter.*

Barter and the Double Coincidence of Wants

Barter depends on a **double coincidence of wants,** which occurs only when a trader is willing to exchange his or her product for what another offers. If a hunter is willing to exchange hides for a farmer's corn, that's a coincidence. But if the farmer is also willing to exchange corn for the hunter's hides, that's a double coincidence—hence, the expression *double coincidence of wants.* As long as specialization was limited, say to two or three goods, mutually beneficial trades were relatively easy to discover—that is, trade wasn't much of a coincidence. As the economy developed, however, greater specialization in the division of labor increased the difficulty of finding the particular goods that each trader wanted to exchange. Rather than just two possible types of producers, there were, say, a hundred types of producers.

Double coincidence of wants A situation in which two traders are willing to exchange their products directly

In a barter system, traders must not only discover a double coincidence of wants, they must also agree on a rate of exchange—how many hides should be exchanged for a bushel of corn. If only two goods are produced, only one exchange rate has to be determined, but as the number of goods produced in the economy increases, the number of possible exchange rates grows quickly. Increased specialization raised the transaction costs of the barter system of exchange—exchange became more time-consuming and more cumbersome.

Sometimes differences between values of the units to be exchanged make barter difficult. For example, suppose the hunter wants to buy a home, which exchanges for 2,000 hides. The hunter would be hard-pressed to find a home seller in need of that many hides. These difficulties with barter led people, even in relatively simple economies, to use money.

Earliest Money and Its Functions

Nobody actually recorded the emergence of money. Thus we can only speculate about how it first came into use. Through experience accumulated from barter exchanges, traders may have found that they could easily find a buyer for certain goods. If a trader could not find a good that he or she desired personally, some good with a ready market could be accepted instead. So traders began to accept certain goods not for immediate consumption, but because these goods were readily accepted by others and therefore could be retraded later. For example, corn might become accepted because traders knew that it was always in demand. As one good became generally accepted in return for all other goods, that good began to function as **money.** *Any commodity that acquires a high degree of acceptability throughout an economy thereby becomes money.*

Money Anything that is generally accepted in exchange for goods and services

Money fulfills three important functions. Most importantly, it serves as a *medium of exchange.* Its function as a medium of exchange is what distinguishes money from other assets such as stocks, bonds, or real estate. Money also serves as a *unit of account* and a *store of value.* Let's consider each of these functions in turn.

Medium of Exchange. Separating the sale of one good from the purchase of another requires an item acceptable to all parties involved in the transactions. If a society, by luck or by design, can find one commodity that everyone will accept in exchange for whatever is sold, traders can save time, disappointment, and sheer aggravation. Suppose corn plays this role, a role that clearly goes beyond its usual function as food. We then call corn a medium of exchange because it is accepted in exchange by all buyers and sellers, whether or not they want corn to eat. A **medium of exchange** is anything that is generally accepted in payment for goods and services sold. The person who accepts corn in exchange for some product believes the corn can be used later to purchase whatever is desired.

Medium of exchange Anything that facilitates trade by being generally accepted by all parties in payment for goods or services

Commodity money Anything that serves both as money and as a commodity

In this example, corn both is a *commodity* and serves as *money,* so we call it a **commodity money.** The earliest money was commodity money. Consider some commodities used as money over the centuries. Cattle served as money, first for the Greeks and then for the Romans. In fact, the word "*pecu*niary" ("of or relating to money") derives from the Latin word *pecus,* meaning "cattle." Salt also served as money. Roman soldiers received part of their pay in salt; the salt portion was called the *salarium*—the origin of the word salary. The so-called precious metals—gold and silver—were long popular as commodity moneys. Other commodity moneys used at various times include tobacco and wampum (polished strings of shells) in colonial America, tea pressed into small cakes in Russia, and palm dates in North Africa. Whatever serves as a medium of exchange is called money—no matter what it is, no matter how it first came to serve as a medium of exchange, and no matter why it continues to serve this function.

Unit of Account. As one commodity, such as corn or tobacco, becomes widely accepted, the prices of all other goods come to be quoted in terms of that good. The chosen commodity becomes a common **unit of account,** a standard unit for quoting prices. If the price of shoes or pots is expressed in terms of bushels of corn, corn not only serves as a medium of exchange, it also becomes a com-

Unit of account A common unit for measuring the value of every good or service

mon denominator, a yardstick, for measuring the value of all goods and services. Rather than having to quote the rate of exchange for each good in terms of every other good, as is the case in a barter economy, people can measure the price of everything in terms of a common denominator, such as corn. For example, if a pair of shoes sells for two bushels of corn and a five-gallon pot sells for one bushel of corn, then one pair of shoes has the same value in exchange as two five-gallon pots.

Store of Value. Because people often do not want to make purchases at the time they sell something, the purchasing power acquired through a sale must somehow be preserved. Money serves as a **store of value** when it retains purchasing power over time. The better money is at preserving purchasing power, the better it serves as a store of value.

Store of value Anything that retains its purchasing power over time

At this point it is useful to recall the distinction between a stock and a flow. Recall that a *stock* is an amount measured at a particular point in time, such as the amount of food in your refrigerator, the amount of money you have with you right now, or the amount of gasoline in your car's tank. In contrast, a *flow* is an amount per unit of time, such as the calories you consume per day, the income you earn per week, or the miles you drive per month. *Money* is a stock and *income* is a flow. Money is a medium of exchange and income is a reward for supplying services. Don't confuse money with income. The role of money as a stock is best reflected by money's role as a store of value.

Problems with Commodity Money

There are problems with most commodity moneys. *First,* if a commodity is perishable, such as corn or tobacco, it must be properly stored or its quality deteriorates; even then, it will not maintain its quality for long. *Second,* if a commodity is bulky, exchanges for major purchases are unwieldy. For example, if a new home cost 40,000 bushels of corn, many truckloads of corn would be needed to purchase one. *Third,* commodity money may not be easily divisible into smaller units. For example, when cattle served as money, any price that amounted to a fraction of a cow posed an exchange problem.

Fourth, if all of a particular commodity such as corn or tobacco is valued equally in exchange, regardless of quality, people will tend to keep the best and trade away the rest. As a result, the quality of the commodity in circulation will decline, reducing its acceptability. Sir Thomas Gresham noticed back in the 16th century that "bad money drives out good money," and this has come to be known as **Gresham's Law.** People tend to trade away inferior money and hoard the best; over time the supply of money shrinks and the quality that remains in circulation becomes less acceptable.

Gresham's Law People tend to trade away inferior money and hoard the best

Fifth, commodity money usually ties up otherwise valuable resources as money, so commodity money has a relatively high opportunity cost, compared with, say, paper money. For example, gold that is used for money cannot at the same time be used to make jewelry, dental fillings, and so on.

A final problem of commodity money is that its value depends on its supply and demand, which may vary unpredictably. For example, if a bumper crop increased the supply of corn, corn as a medium of exchange would become less valuable, so more corn would be needed to exchange for any other good. This is what we call *inflation*. Likewise, any change in the demand for corn *as food,* such as occurred with the development of corn chips, would alter the amount available as a medium of exchange, and this, too, would affect the value of corn. Erratic fluctuations in the market for corn limit its usefulness as money, particularly as a unit of account and a store of value.

If people cannot rely on the value of corn over time, they will be reluctant to hold it or to enter contracts in terms of corn for future payment or receipt. More generally, *since the value of money depends on its supply being limited, anything that can be easily gathered or produced does not serve well as a commodity money.* For example, tree leaves or common rocks would not serve well as a commodity money. What all this boils down to is that *the best money is durable, portable, divisible, and of uniform quality, and has a low opportunity cost, and yet its supply can be carefully controlled.*

Coins

The division of commodity money into units was often quite natural, as in bushels of corn or heads of cattle. When rock salt was used as money, it was cut into uniform bricks. Since salt was usually of consistent quality, a trader had only to count the bricks to determine the amount of money. When silver and gold were used as commodity money, both their quantity and quality were open to question. Because precious metals could be *debased* by being alloyed with cheaper metals, the quantity and the quality of the metal had to be ascertained with each exchange.

This quality-control problem was addressed by coining the metal. *Coinage determined both the amount and quality of the metal.* The use of coins allowed payment by count rather than by weight. A table on which this money was counted came to be called the *counter,* a term still used today. Initially, coins were stamped on one side only, but undetectable amounts of the metal could be shaved from the smooth side of the coin. To prevent such shaving, coins were stamped on both sides. But another problem arose: small amounts of the metal could be clipped from the edges. To prevent clipping, coins were bordered with a well-defined rim and were milled around the edges. If you have a dime or a quarter, notice the tiny serrations on the edge and the words along the border. These features, throwbacks from the time when these coins were silver rather than cheaper metals, reduced one's chances of "getting clipped."

The power to coin was vested in the *seignior,* or feudal lord. The power to coin money was considered an act of sovereignty, and counterfeiting was an act of treason. If the face value of the coin exceeded the cost of coinage, the minting of coins became a source of revenue to the seignior. **Seigniorage** (pronounced *seen′-your-edge*) refers to the revenue earned from coinage by the seignior. **Token money** is money whose face value exceeds the value of the material from which it is made. Coins (and paper money) now in circulation in the United States are token money. For example, the 25-cent coin costs the U.S. Mint only about 3 cents to make. The Mint nets about $500 million per year from coin production.

Seigniorage The difference between the face value of money and the cost of supplying it; the "profit" from issuing money

Token money The name given to money whose face value exceeds the cost of producing it

Money and Banking

The word *bank* comes from the Italian word *banca,* meaning "bench," since Italian money changers originally conducted their business on benches. Banking spread from Italy to England, where London goldsmiths offered the community "safekeeping" for money and other valuables. The goldsmiths had to give depositors their money back on request, but since withdrawals by some individuals tended to be offset by deposits by others, the amount of idle cash, or gold, in the vault usually remained relatively constant over time. Goldsmiths found that they could earn interest by making loans from this pool of idle cash.

Keeping money on deposit with a goldsmith was safer than leaving it where it could be easily stolen, but visiting the goldsmith each time money was needed was a nuisance. For example, a farmer might visit the goldsmith to withdraw enough money to buy a horse. The farmer would then pay the horse trader, who would promptly deposit the receipts with the goldsmith. Thus, money took a round trip from goldsmith to farmer to horse trader and back to goldsmith. Depositors grew tired of going to the goldsmith every time they needed to make a purchase, so goldsmiths instituted a practice whereby a purchaser, such as the farmer, could write the goldsmith instructions to pay someone else, such as the horse trader, a given amount from the purchaser's account. The payment amounted to having the goldsmith move gold from one stack (the farmer's) to another (the horse trader's). *These written instructions to the goldsmith were the first checks.* Checks have since become official-looking instruction forms, but they need not be, as evidenced by the actions of a Montana man who paid a speeding fine with a check written on a clean but frayed pair of underpants. The Western Federal Savings and Loan of Missoula honored the check.[1]

NetBookmark

Tour the American Currency Exhibit, an on-line money museum created by the Federal Reserve Bank of San Francisco at http://www.frbsf.org/currency/index.html. You can view pictures of the types of currency used throughout U.S. history. For an informative history of money in America, follow the "Tour Historical Context" link. Who produced money before the Federal Reserve was created? What determined the value(s) of a dollar?

By combining the ideas of cash loans and checks, the goldsmith soon discovered how to make loans by check. Rather than lend idle cash, the goldsmith could create a checking account for the borrower. *The goldsmith could extend a loan by creating an account against which the borrower could write checks. In this way goldsmiths, or banks, were able to create a medium of exchange, or to "create money."* This money, though based only on an entry in the goldsmith's ledger, was accepted because of the public's confidence that these claims would be honored.

The total claims against the goldsmith consisted of claims by people who had deposited their money with the goldsmith plus claims created when the goldsmith extended loans. Because these claims exceeded the value of gold on reserve, this was the beginning of a **fractional reserve banking system,** a system in which the goldsmith's reserves amounted to only a fraction of claims against the goldsmith, or total deposits. The *reserve ratio* measures reserves as a proportion of total claims against the goldsmith, or total deposits. For example, if the goldsmith had gold reserves valued at $5,000 but deposits totaling $10,000, the reserve ratio would be 50 percent.

Fractional reserve banking system A banking system in which only a portion of deposits is backed by reserves

Paper Money

Another way a bank could create money was to issue bank notes. **Bank notes** were pieces of paper promising the bearer specific amounts of gold or silver when the notes were presented to the issuing bank for redemption. In London, goldsmith bankers introduced bank notes about the same time they introduced checks. *Whereas checks could be redeemed only if endorsed by the payee, notes could be redeemed by anyone who presented them.* Paper money was often "as good as gold,"

Bank notes Papers promising a specific amount of gold or silver to bearers who presented them to issuing banks for redemption; an early type of money

1 As reported in "Legal Briefs," *Newsweek* (3 Feburary 1992): 7.

since the bearer could redeem it for gold. In fact, paper money was more convenient than gold because it took up less space and was easier to carry.

The amount of paper money issued by a bank depended on that bank's estimate of the proportion of notes that would be redeemed. The greater the redemption rate, the fewer notes could be issued based on a given amount of reserves. Initially, these promises to pay were issued by private individuals or banks, but over time governments took a larger role in printing and circulating notes.

Fiat money Money not redeemable for any commodity; its status as money is conferred by the government

Legal tender Anything that creditors are required to accept as payment for debts

Once paper money became widely accepted, it was perhaps inevitable that governments would begin issuing **fiat money,** which consists of paper money that derives its status as money from the power of the state, or by *fiat*. Fiat (pronounced *fee'at)* money is money because the government says it is money. The word is from the Latin, meaning "let it be done." Fiat money is not redeemable for anything other than more fiat money; it is not backed by a promise to pay something of intrinsic value. You can think of fiat money as mere paper money. It is acceptable not because it is intrinsically useful or valuable—as corn or gold is—but because the government requires that it be accepted as payment. Fiat money is declared to be **legal tender** by the government, meaning that creditors must accept it as payment for debts. *Gradually, people came to accept fiat money because they believed that others would accept it as well.* The currency issued in the United States today, and indeed paper money throughout most of the world, is fiat money.

In a way, a well-regulated system of fiat money is more efficient for an economy than commodity money. Fiat money uses only paper (the cost of labor and material per bill is about five cents), whereas commodity money requires that valuable commodities be used directly or held in reserve to support the system. As we shall see in the next chapter, paper money makes up only a small fraction of the total money supply. Most modern money consists of checking accounts, which amount to little more than electronic entries in the computers of the nation's banking system.

The Value of Money

Money has grown increasingly more abstract—from a physical commodity, to a piece of paper representing a claim on a physical commodity, to a piece of paper of no intrinsic value, to an electronic entry representing a claim on a piece of paper of no intrinsic value. So why does money have value? The commodity feature of early money bolstered confidence in its acceptability. Commodities such as corn and tobacco had value in use even if for some reason they became less acceptable in exchange. When paper money came into use, its acceptability was initially fostered by the promise to redeem it for gold, silver, or other items of value. But since most paper money throughout the world is now fiat money, there is no promise of redemption. So how come a piece of paper bearing the portrait of Alexander Hamilton and the number 10 in each corner can be exchanged for a large pepperoni pizza or anything else selling for $10? *People accept these pieces of paper because they believe others will do so.*

The value of money reflects in its *purchasing power:* the rate at which money exchanges for goods and services. The higher the price level, the

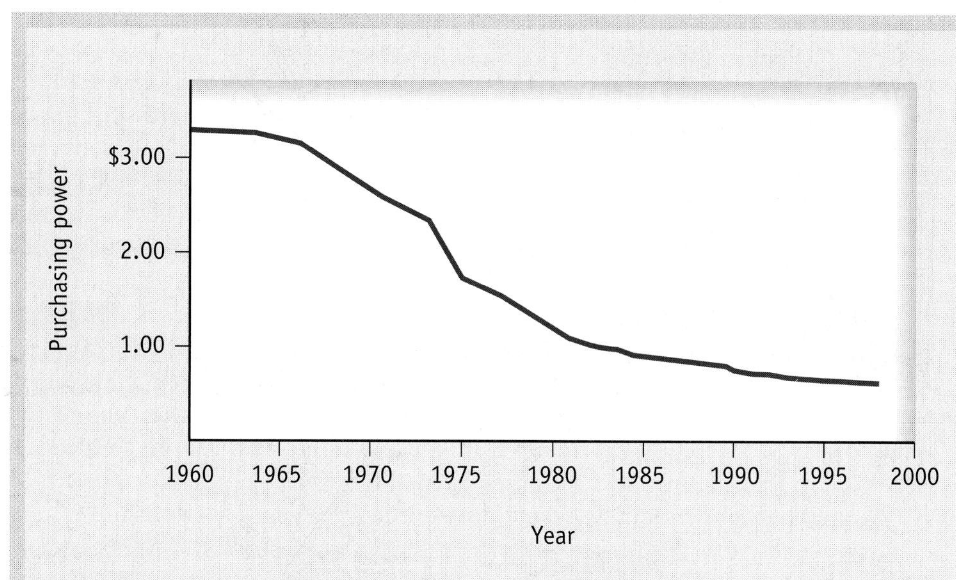

EXHIBIT 1

Purchasing Power of a Dollar Measured in 1982–1984 Constant Dollars

An increase in the price level reduces the amount of goods and services that can be purchased with a dollar. Since 1960, the price level has risen every year, so the purchasing power of the dollar has fallen continually.

Source: *Economic Report of the President,* February 1999.

fewer goods and services that can be purchased with each dollar, so the less each dollar is worth. The purchasing power of each dollar over time varies inversely with changes in the price level. As the price level increases, the purchasing power of money falls. To measure the purchasing power of the dollar in a particular year, first compute the price index for that year, then divide 100 by that price index. For example, relative to the base period of 1982–1984, the consumer price index for January 1999 was 164.3. The purchasing power of a dollar was therefore 100/164.3, or about $0.61, measured in 1982–1984 dollars. Exhibit 1 chronicles the steady decline since 1960 in the value of the dollar.

When Money Performs Poorly

One way to understand the functions of money is to look at situations in which money did not perform these functions well. In Chapter 7, we examined hyperinflation in Brazil. With prices growing by the hour, money no longer represented a stable store of value, so people couldn't wait to exchange rapidly inflating money for goods or for a "harder" currency—that is, one whose value was relatively stable. And with the price level rising rapidly, some merchants were quicker to raise their prices than others, so relative prices became distorted. Thus, money became less useful as a unit of account, or as a way of comparing the price of one good to that of another.

At some point, the inflation rate may become so high that people will no longer accept the nation's money and instead will resort to barter. Likewise, if the supply of money dries up because of hoarding or if the price system is not allowed to function properly, barter may be the only remaining alternative. The following case study discusses instances when money performed poorly.

When the Monetary Systems Break Down

CaseStudy

Other Times, Other Places

Are U.S. dollars still flowing into Russia? Find out from the Bank of Russia's statistics page at http://www.cbr.ru/eng/system/statistics.html. Look under "Foreign Currency Brought into and Taken out of the Russian Federation by Authorised Banks" to see how the flow of dollars has changed over time. For an Internet guide to Russian banks and finance, visit *Russia on the Net* at http://www.ru/.

After Germany lost World War II, money in that country became almost useless because, despite tremendous inflationary pressure in the economy, those who won the war imposed strict price controls. Since prices were set well below what people thought they should be, sellers stopped accepting money, and this forced people to barter. Experts estimate that because of the lack of a viable medium of exchange, the German economy produced only half the output that it would have produced with a smoothly functioning monetary system. The "economic miracle" that occurred in Germany immediately after 1948 can be credited in large part to that country's adoption of a reliable monetary system.

Money became extremely scarce during the 19th century in Brazil because of a copper shortage. Money-financed transactions were difficult because copper coins could no longer be minted, and people hoarded rather than traded the limited supply of coins. In response to this crisis, some merchants and tavern-keepers printed vouchers redeemable for goods and services. These vouchers circulated as money until copper coins reappeared. Similarly, people dealt with the shortage of money in the early American colonies by keeping careful records, showing who owed what to whom.

For a more recent example, consider Panama, a Central American country that relies on the U.S. dollar as a medium of exchange. In 1988, the United States, in response to charges that the leader of Panama was involved in drug dealing, froze Panamanian assets in the United States. This touched off a panic in Panama as bank depositors tried to withdraw their funds; banks were forced to close for nine weeks. Dollars were hoarded, so people resorted to barter. Because barter is much less efficient than a smoothly functioning monetary system, Panama's GDP reportedly fell by 30 percent in 1988.

In Russia, the hyperinflation of the ruble following the breakup of the Soviet Union increased Russian demand for so-called hard currencies, especially the dollar. A Russian central banker estimated that in 1995 the value of Russians' dollar holdings exceeded the value of their ruble holdings. In keeping with Gresham's Law, Russians preferred to trade their rubles and hoard their dollars.

Sources: Peter White, "The Power of Money," *National Geographic* (January 1993): 80–107; Frederic Dannen and Ira Silverman, "The Supernote," *New Yorker* (23 October 1995): 50–55; and "Russia Official Nods to Money Boost," *New York Times* (30 September 1998).

Thus, when the supply of money shrinks as a result of hoarding or when the official money fails to serve as a medium of exchange, some other mechanism often emerges to facilitate exchange. But because more resources must be diverted from production to exchange, this second-best alternative is seldom as efficient as a smoothly functioning monetary system. A poorly functioning monetary system results in higher transaction costs. *It has been said that no machine increases the economy's productivity as much as properly functioning money.* Indeed, it seems hard to overstate the value of a reliable monetary system.

Let's turn now to a discussion of the U.S. monetary system, beginning with the development of money and banking in the United States.

FINANCIAL INSTITUTIONS IN THE UNITED STATES

You have already learned about the origin of modern banks: Goldsmiths lent money from deposits they held for safekeeping. So you already have some idea of how banks operate. Recall from the circular flow model discussed earlier that household saving flows into financial markets, where it is lent to investors. Financial institutions accumulate funds from savers and lend these funds to borrowers, thereby serving as intermediaries between savers and borrowers. Financial institutions, or **financial intermediaries,** earn a profit by "buying low and selling high"—that is, by paying a lower interest rate to savers than they charge borrowers.

Financial intermediaries Institutions that serve as go-betweens, accepting funds from savers and lending them to borrowers

Commercial Banks and Thrifts

A wide variety of financial intermediaries respond to the economy's demand for financial services. **Depository institutions,** such as commercial banks, savings and loan associations, mutual savings banks, and credit unions, obtain funds primarily by accepting *deposits* from the public—hence their name. Our emphasis will be on depository institutions because they play a key role in providing the nation's money supply. Depository institutions can be classified broadly into two types: commercial banks and thrift institutions.

Depository institutions Commercial banks and thrift institutions that accept deposits from the public

Commercial banks are the oldest, largest, and most diversified of depository institutions. They are called **commercial banks** because historically they made loans primarily to *commercial* ventures, or businesses, rather than to households. Commercial banks hold two-thirds of all deposits held by depository institutions. Until recently, commercial banks were the only depository institutions that offered demand deposits, or checking accounts. **Demand deposits** are so named because a depositor with such an account can write a check *demanding* those deposits at any time.

Commercial banks Depository institutions that make short-term loans primarily to businesses

Demand deposits Accounts at financial institutions that pay no interest and on which depositors can write checks to obtain their deposits at any time

Thrift institutions, or **thrifts,** include savings and loan associations, mutual savings banks, and credit unions. Historically, savings and loan associations and mutual savings banks specialized in making mortgage loans, which are loans to finance real estate purchases. Credit unions extend loans only to their "members" to finance homes or other major consumer purchases, such as new cars.

Thrift institutions, or **thrifts** Savings and loan institutions, mutual savings banks, and credit unions; depository institutions that make long-term loans primarily to households

Development of the Dual Banking System

Before 1863, commercial banks in the United States were chartered by the states in which they operated, so they were called *state banks.* These banks, like the English goldsmiths, issued bank notes. More than 10,000 different kinds of notes circulated and nearly all were redeemable for gold. The National Banking Act of 1863 and its later amendments created a new system of federally chartered banks called *national banks.* These national banks were authorized to issue notes and were regulated by the Office of the Comptroller of the Currency, part of the U.S. Treasury. At this time, a tax was introduced on the notes issued by state-chartered banks, the idea being to tax state bank notes out of existence. But state banks survived by substituting checks for notes. Borrowers were issued checking accounts rather than bank notes. State banks held on, and to this day the United States has a *dual banking system* consisting of both state banks and national banks.

Birth of the Federal Reserve System

During the 19th century, the economy experienced a number of panic "runs" on banks by depositors seeking to withdraw their funds. A panic was usually set off by the failure of some prominent financial institution. Following such a failure, other banks were besieged by fearful customers. Borrowers wanted additional loans and extensions of credit, and depositors wanted their money back. Similar bank panics have occurred recently in Russia and parts of Asia. The failure of the Knickerbocker Trust Company in New York triggered the Panic of 1907. This financial calamity underscored the lack of banking stability and so aroused the public that in 1908 Congress established the National Monetary Commission to study the banking system and make recommendations. That group's deliberations led to the Federal Reserve Act, passed in 1913 and implemented in 1914, which established the **Federal Reserve System** as the central bank and monetary authority of the United States.

Federal Reserve System The central bank and monetary authority of the United States; also known as "the Fed"

Nearly all industrialized countries had formed central banks by 1900—the Bundesbank in Germany, the Bank of Japan, the Bank of England. The American public's suspicion of such monopoly power led to the establishment of not one central bank but 12 separate banks in 12 Federal Reserve districts around the country. The new banks were named after the cities in which they were located—the Federal Reserve Bank of Boston, New York, Chicago, San Francisco, and so on. *Throughout most of its history, the United States had what is called a decentralized banking system. The Federal Reserve Act moved the country toward a system that was partly centralized and partly decentralized.* All national banks became members of the Federal Reserve System and were thus subject to new regulations issued by *the Fed,* as it came to be known. For state banks, membership was voluntary; most state banks did not join because their owners did not want to comply with the new regulations.

Powers of the Federal Reserve System

According to the 1913 Act, the Federal Reserve Board was "to exercise general supervision" over the Federal Reserve System to ensure sufficient money and credit in the banking system to support a growing economy. The power to issue bank notes was taken away from national banks and turned over to the Federal Reserve banks. (Take out a dollar bill and notice what it says across the top: FEDERAL RESERVE NOTE. The seal to the left of George Washington's portrait identifies which Reserve bank issued the note.) The Federal Reserve was also given other powers: *to buy and sell government securities, to extend loans to member banks, to clear checks, and to require that member banks hold reserves equal at least to a specified fraction of their deposits.*

Federal Reserve banks typically do not deal with the public directly. Each may be thought of as a bankers' bank. Reserve banks hold deposits of member banks, just as depository institutions hold deposits of the public. Reserve banks extend loans to member banks just as depository institutions extend loans to the public.

Reserves Funds that banks use to satisfy the cash demands of their customers and the reserve requirements of the Fed; reserves consist of deposits at the Fed plus currency physically held by banks

Federal Reserve banks are so named because they hold member bank *reserves* on deposit. **Reserves** are funds that banks have on hand or on deposit with the Fed to promote banking safety, to facilitate interbank transfers of funds, to satisfy the cash demands of their customers, and to comply with Federal Reserve regulations. These reserves allow Reserve banks to clear checks written by a depositor at one commercial bank and deposited in another commercial bank. This check clearance process is, on a larger scale, much like the goldsmith's moving of gold reserves from the farmer's account to the horse trader's account. Reserve banks also make loans to banks. The interest rate charged to banks for these so-called *discount loans* is called the *discount rate.* By making discount loans to banks, the Fed can increase reserves in the banking system.

Member banks are required to own stock in the Federal Reserve bank in their district, and this stock ownership entitles them to a specified dividend. Any additional profit earned by the Reserve banks is turned over to the U.S. Treasury.

Banking During the Great Depression

From 1913 to 1929, both the Federal Reserve System and the national economy performed relatively well. Then the stock market crash of 1929 was followed by the Great Depression, bringing a new set of problems for the Federal Reserve System. Frightened depositors wanted their money back, precipitating bank runs. But the Fed failed to respond to the crisis; it failed to act as a lender of last resort—that is, it did not lend banks the money they needed to satisfy deposit withdrawals in cases of runs on otherwise sound banks. Between 1930 and 1933, about 9,000 banks failed in the United States—roughly half the banks in the nation.

The Federal Reserve System had been established precisely to prevent such panics and to add stability to the banking system. What went wrong? In a word, everything. Between 1930 and 1933, the support offered by the Federal Reserve System seemed to crumble in stages. As businesses failed, they were unable to repay their loans. These defaults on loans led to the initial bank failures. As the crisis deepened, the public grew more concerned about the safety of bank deposits, so cash withdrawals increased. To satisfy the increased demand for currency, banks were forced to sell their holdings of stocks and bonds. But with many banks trying to sell and with few buyers, securities markets collapsed, sharply reducing the market value of these bank assets. Many banks did not have the resources to survive.

Because the Fed failed to understand the extent of the problem and its role as the lender of last resort, it failed to extend loans on a large scale to banks experiencing short-run shortages of cash (in contrast, the Fed was a ready source of loans a half century later during the stock market crash of 1987). The Fed failed to act because it did not understand either the gravity of the situation or its own power to assist troubled banks. The Fed viewed bank failure as a regrettable but inevitable consequence of poor management or prior speculative excesses, or simply as the effect of a collapsing economy. The Fed did not seem to understand that the banking system's instability was contributing to the deterioration of the economy. For example, the stock market collapsed between 1929 and 1933 in part because many banks were trying to sell their securities at the same time. And the collapse came just when banks were badly in need of cash. Fed officials appeared concerned primarily with the solvency of the Federal Reserve banks. They did not realize that because Federal Reserve banks had unlimited money-creating power, they could not fail.

Roosevelt's Reforms

In his first inaugural address, President Franklin D. Roosevelt said, "The only thing we have to fear is fear itself," a view that was especially applicable to a fractional reserve banking system. Most banks were sound as long as people had confidence in the safety of their deposits. *But if many people became frightened and tried to withdraw their money, they could not do so because each bank held reserves amounting to only a fraction of its deposits.*

Upon taking office in early 1933, President Roosevelt attempted to soothe prevailing fears by declaring a "banking holiday," which closed all banks for a week. A national suspension of banking business for a week was unprecedented, yet it was welcomed as a sign that something would be done. Roosevelt also proposed the Banking Acts of 1933 and 1935 and other measures aimed at shoring up the banking system and centralizing the power of the Federal Reserve in Washington. Let's consider the most important features of this legislation.

Board of Governors. The Federal Reserve Board was renamed the Board of Governors and became responsible for setting and implementing the nation's monetary policy. *Monetary policy* is the regulation of the economy's money supply to promote macroeconomic objectives. All 12 Reserve banks came under the authority of the Board of Governors, which consists of seven members appointed by the president and confirmed by the Senate. Each governor serves a 14-year term, with terms staggered so that one governor is appointed every two years. The president also appoints one of the governors to chair the board for a 4-year term. A president bent on changing the direction of monetary policy could be sure of changing only two members in a single presidential term. Board membership is relatively stable, and in one 4-year term a president has only limited control over the board's monetary policy. *The idea was to insulate monetary authorities from short-term political pressure by elected officials.*

Open-market operations
Purchases and sales of government securities by the Federal Reserve in an effort to influence the money supply

Federal Open Market Committee. Originally, the power of the Federal Reserve was vested in each of the 12 Reserve banks. The Banking Acts established the *Federal Open Market Committee (FOMC)* to consolidate decisions about the most important tool of monetary policy—**open-market operations,** which are purchases and sales of U.S. government securities by the Fed (open-market operations and other tools of monetary policy will be examined in the next chapter). The FOMC consists of the seven board governors plus five of the 12 presidents from the Reserve banks; the group is headed by the chair of the Board of Governors. Open-market operations are carried out by the New York Federal Reserve bank, and the president of the New York Fed is always on the FOMC. The organizational structure of the Federal Reserve System as it now stands is presented in Exhibit 2. That exhibit shows that the presidential appointment of Board members is subject to Senate confirmation. The FOMC and the Federal Advisory Committee (which consists of a commercial banker from each of the 12 Reserve districts) advise the Board.

Regulating the Money Supply. As we saw earlier, because reserves amount to only a fraction of deposits, we have a *fractional reserve* banking system. Specific reserve requirements had been established by the Federal Reserve Act of 1914. Member banks were required to hold reserves equal to a certain percentage of their deposits, say from 3 percent to 12 percent depending on the type of deposit and the type of bank. The Banking Acts of 1933 and 1935 authorized the

EXHIBIT 2

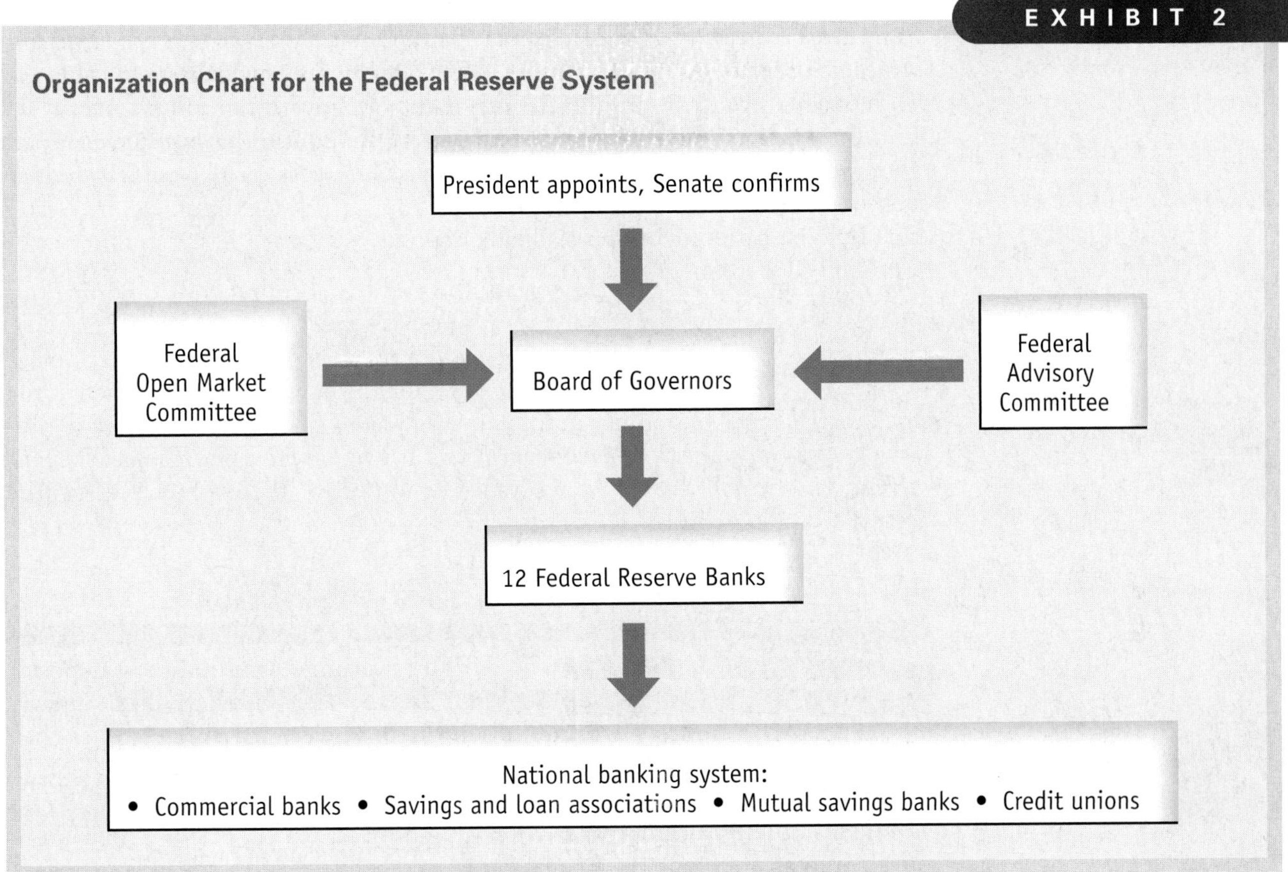

Board of Governors to vary reserve requirements within a range, thereby giving the Fed an additional tool of monetary policy.

Thus, as of 1935, the Federal Reserve System had a variety of tools to regulate the money supply, including *(1) conducting open-market operations—buying and selling U.S. government securities; (2) setting the discount rate—the interest rate charged by Reserve banks for loans to member banks; and (3) setting legal reserve requirements for member banks.* We will explore these tools in greater detail in the next chapter.

Deposit Insurance. One cause of bank failures during the depression was the lack of confidence in the safety of bank deposits. The Federal Deposit Insurance Corporation (FDIC) was established in 1933 to insure the first $2,500 of each deposit account. Today the insurance ceiling is $100,000 per account. Members of the Federal Reserve System are required to purchase FDIC insurance; the program is voluntary for other banks. About 97 percent of commercial banks and about 90 percent of savings and loan associations are insured by the FDIC. The rest are insured by private companies or state reserve funds. *Deposit insurance, by calming fears about the safety of deposits, worked wonders to reduce bank runs.*

Restricting Bank Investment Practices. As part of the Banking Act of 1933, commercial banks were forbidden to buy or sell corporate stocks and bonds. The belief was that when commercial banks hold assets that fluctuate widely in value, the stability of the banking system is endangered. *The act limited bank assets primarily to loans and to government securities—bonds issued by federal, state, and local governments.* A *bond* is an IOU promising the lender an annual interest payment and full repayment of the loan on a certain date, so a government bond is an IOU from the government. Also, bank failures were thought to have resulted in part from interest-rate competition among banks for customer deposits. To reduce such competition, the Fed was empowered to set the maximum interest rates that could be paid on commercial bank deposits.

Objectives of the Fed. Over the years, the Fed has accumulated additional objectives. Six goals are frequently mentioned as objectives of the Fed's policies: (1) a high level of employment in the economy, (2) economic growth, (3) price stability, (4) stability in interest rates, (5) stability in financial markets, such as the stock market, and (6) stability in foreign-exchange markets. *We can boil these goals down to high employment, economic growth, and stability in prices, interest rates, financial markets, and exchange rates.* As we will see, not all of these objectives can be achieved simultaneously.

From the Great Depression to Deregulation

Restrictions imposed on depository institutions during the 1930s made banking a heavily regulated industry. The federal government insured most deposits. Depository institutions lost much of their freedom to wheel and deal. The assets they could acquire were carefully limited, as were the interest rates they could offer depositors. Households typically left their money in savings deposits earning 4 percent interest or less; checking deposits earned no interest. Banks and thrifts quietly accepted these deposits and made loans, earning their profit on the interest differential.

Federal Reserve ceilings on interest rates reduced interest-rate competition for deposits *among* depository institutions. As long as the interest-rate ceilings were at or above prevailing market rates of interest, the banking system as a whole did not have to worry about outside competition for customer deposits. When market interest rates rose above the ceiling that banks and thrifts could offer, however, many savers withdrew their deposits and put them into higher-yielding alternatives.

Money market mutual fund A collection of short-term interest-earning assets purchased with funds collected from many shareholders

The surge of inflation during the 1970s increased interest rates in the economy, and banking has not been the same since. In 1972, Merrill Lynch, a major brokerage house, introduced an account combining a **money market mutual fund** with check-writing privileges. Money market mutual fund shares are claims on a portfolio, or collection, of short-term interest-earning assets. By pooling the funds of many shareholders, the managers of a mutual fund can acquire a diversified portfolio of assets offering shareholders higher rates of interest than those available at most depository institutions. Money market mutual funds proved to be stiff competition for bank deposits, especially demand deposits, which paid no interest.

Depository institutions use savers' deposits to make loans; when savers withdrew their deposits, banks and thrifts had to replace the funds needed to support their loans by borrowing at prevailing interest rates, which were typically higher than the rates they earned on their existing loans. Because their loans were typically for short periods, commercial banks got in less trouble than thrifts when interest rates rose. But thrifts had made loans for long-term mortgages, loans that would not be fully repaid for decades. *Because thrifts had to pay more interest to borrow funds than they were earning on these mortgages, they were in big trouble and many failed.*

Bank Deregulation

In response to the loss of deposits and other problems of depository institutions, Congress tried to ease regulations, thereby giving banks and thrifts greater discretion in their operations. For example, the interest-rate ceilings for deposits were eliminated, and all depository institutions were authorized to offer checking accounts. Thrifts were given wider latitude in making loans and in the kinds of assets they could acquire. Additionally, all depository institutions were allowed to offer money market deposit accounts, whose value jumped from only \$8 billion in 1978 to \$200 billion in 1982.

Some states, such as California and Texas, largely deregulated state-chartered savings and loan associations. The combination of deposit insurance, unregulated interest rates, and wider latitude in the kinds of assets that could be purchased gave savings and loan associations a green light to compete for large deposits in national markets and to acquire assets as they pleased. Once-staid financial institutions moved into the fast lane.

Thus thrifts could wheel and deal, but with the benefit of deposit insurance. The combination of deregulation and deposit insurance encouraged some thrifts already in financial trouble to take big risks—to "bet the bank"—because their depositors would be protected by deposit insurance. This created a so-called *moral hazard,* which in this case is the tendency of bankers to take unwarranted risks when they believe the government is providing a safety net. Banks that were already virtually bankrupt—so-called "zombie" banks—were able to attract additional deposits because of deposit insurance. Zombie banks, by offering higher interest rates, also attracted deposits away from healthy banks.

Meanwhile, since deposits were insured, most depositors paid little attention to their bank's health. *Thus deposit insurance, originally introduced during the Great Depression to prevent bank panics, caused depositors to become complacent about the safety of their deposits. Worse still, it caused those who ran the banks and thrifts to take unwarranted risks because they were gambling with other people's money.*

Bailing Out the Thrifts

Losses in the savings and loan industry topped \$10 billion in 1987 and \$20 billion in 1988. The result was a disaster, and depository institutions, particularly thrifts, failed at record rates. Thrift failures began growing in the mid-1980s, peaking at 327 in 1989. The insolvency and collapse of a growing number of thrifts prompted Congress, in August 1989, to approve the largest financial bailout of any industry in history—a measure that would eventually cost about \$250 billion. Taxpayers paid nearly two-thirds of the total, and the thrift industry paid the remaining third through higher deposit insurance premiums. The money was spent to shut down failing thrifts and pay off insured depositors.

Part of the cleanup involved selling more than \$450 billion of office buildings, shopping malls, apartment buildings, land, and other assets formerly taken over by insolvent thrifts because of bad loans. A glut of such properties dragged down market values and reduced the federal government's ability to recoup its losses from deposit insurance. Still, the mess was cleaned up in the early 1990s and the number of failures dropped sharply. Exhibit 3 shows failures by year.

EXHIBIT 3

Annual Failures of U. S. Thrift Institutions

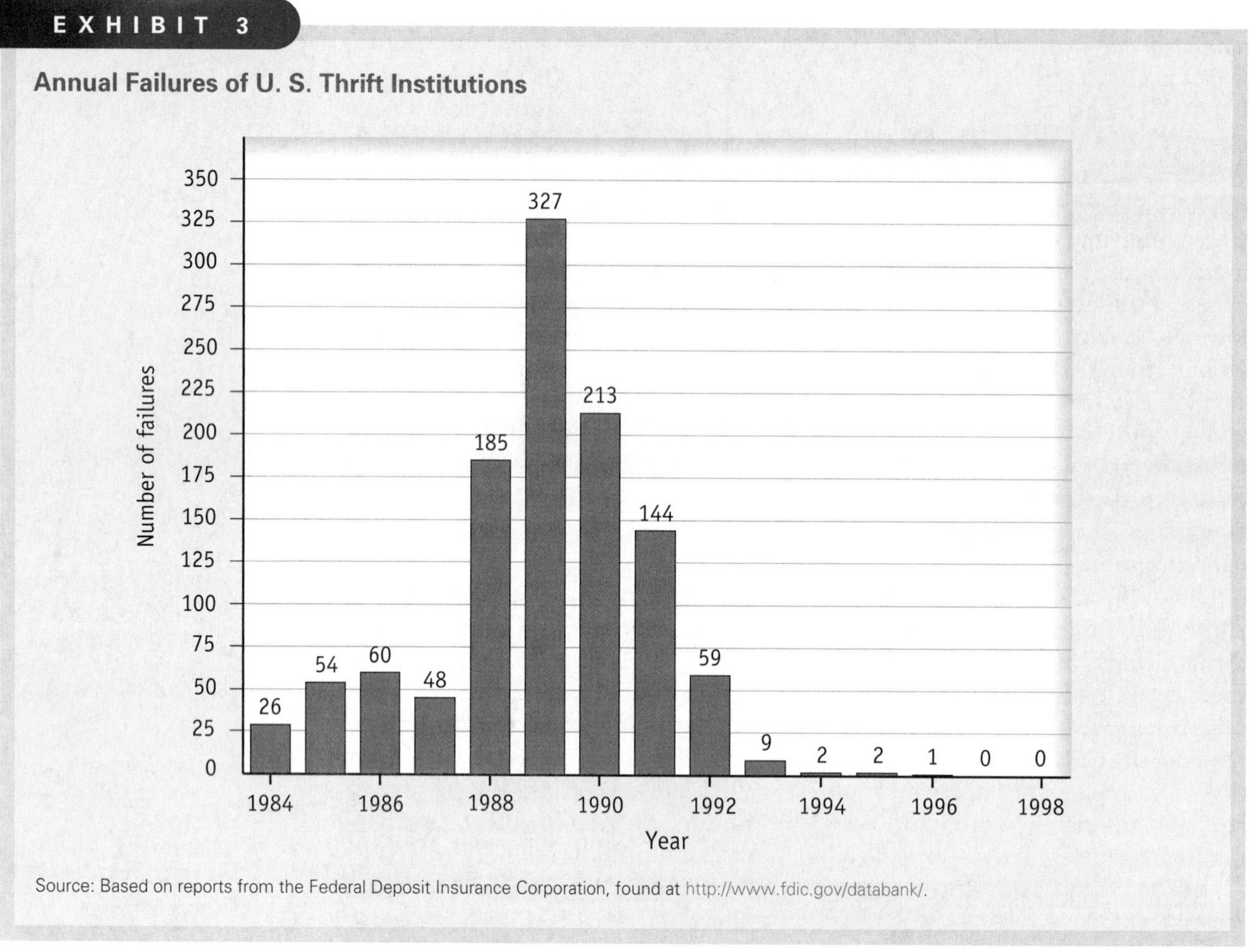

Source: Based on reports from the Federal Deposit Insurance Corporation, found at http://www.fdic.gov/databank/.

From their peak of 327 in 1989, the number of thrift failures dropped to zero in 1997 and 1998. Because of failures and mergers, the number of thrift institutions dropped from about 3,700 in 1986 to under 1,900 in 1998.

Commercial Banks Were Also Failing

The U.S. banking system experienced more change and upheaval during the 1980s and early 1990s than at any other time since the Great Depression. As they had in the case of thrifts, risky decisions based on deposit insurance coupled with the slump in property values also hastened the demise of many commercial banks. Hundreds of troubled banks, such as Continental Illinois, First Republic Bank of Dallas, and the Bank of New England, were taken over by the FDIC or forced to merge with healthier competitors. Banks in Texas and Oklahoma failed when loans to oil drillers and farmers went sour. Banks in the Northeast failed because falling real estate values caused borrowers to default. Exhibit 4 shows the number of bank failures per year since 1935. The rising tide of failures during the 1980s is clear.

The United States was not alone in experiencing banking problems in the 1980s and 1990s. A wave of banking trouble swept around the world. Countries

EXHIBIT 4

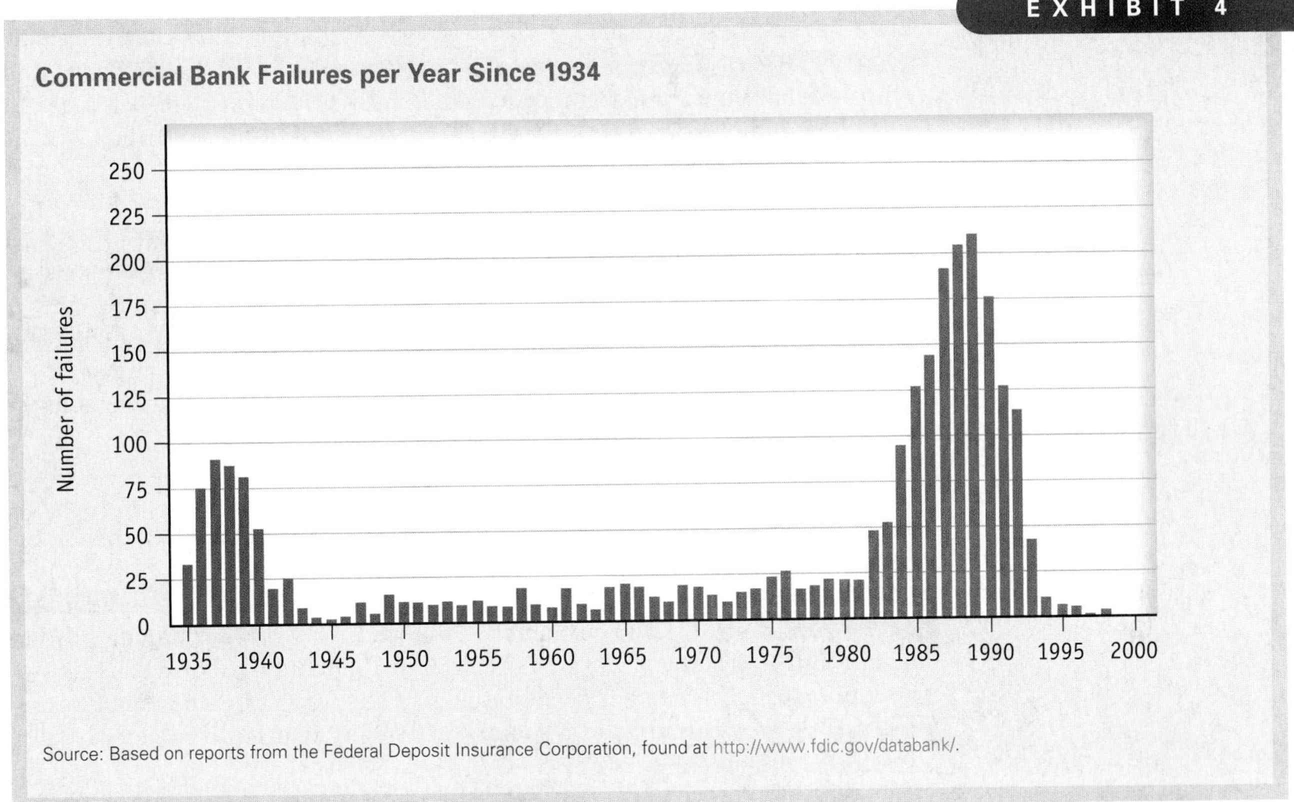

where huge bank losses occurred include Argentina, Chile, Venezuela, Mexico, Brazil, Finland, Uruguay, Sweden, Colombia, Norway, Russia, and countries in Eastern Europe.

The Structure of U.S. Banking

The United States now has about 9,000 commercial banks—more than any other country, but down from 14,500 in 1984. Other industrial countries have fewer than 1,000 commercial banks, and Japan has fewer than 100. The 10 largest U.S. commercial banks hold less than half the U.S. banking industry assets. In contrast, as few as a half dozen banks hold over half the assets in other developed countries, such as Australia, Canada, Japan, and the United Kingdom. *So the United States has more banks than other countries, and U.S. bank assets are distributed more evenly across banks.*

The large number of banks in this country reflects past government restrictions on *branches,* which are additional offices that carry out banking operations. The combination of intrastate and interstate restrictions on branching spawned the many commercial banks that exist today, most of which are relatively small. *Restrictions on interstate banking create inefficiencies, since banks cannot achieve optimal size and cannot as easily diversify their portfolio of loans among different regions.*

Bank holding company A corporation that owns banks

In recent years, two developments have allowed banks to get around branching restrictions: bank holding companies and mergers. A **bank holding company** is a corporation that may own several different banks. Many states now permit holding companies to cross state lines, thereby skirting federal prohibitions against interstate banking. Moreover, a holding company can provide other services that banks are not authorized to offer, such as financial advising, leasing, insurance, issuing credit cards, and selling securities. Holding companies have blossomed in recent years, and the nation's major banks are all owned by holding companies. More than three-quarters of the nation's checking deposits are in banks owned by holding companies.

Another important development that has allowed banks to expand their geographical reach is mergers, which have spread the presence of some banks across the country. Banks are merging because they want more customers and expect the higher volume of transactions to reduce operating costs per customer. Nationwide banking is also seen as a way of avoiding the concentration of bad loans that sometimes occur in one geographical area. The merger movement was fueled by a rising stock market during the 1990s and by federal legislation passed in 1994 that facilitates consolidation of merged banks.

NationsBank and BankAmerica merged in 1998 to create Bank of America, the nation's largest bank and the first one to stretch coast to coast. The new bank in 1998 held $1 of every $12 Americans put in banks; its 4,800 branch offices and 14,000 ATMs spanned 27 states and 38 countries.

U.S. bank profits increased to record levels by the mid-1990s, so the industry has turned around. As shown in Exhibit 4, the number of bank failures dropped to only three in 1998, down from well over 200 in 1988. But a national banking system is no guarantee that banks will not fail. The following case study discusses recent banking problems in Japan, a country with fewer than 100 commercial banks.

CaseStudy

Other Times, Other Places

During the Japanese banking crisis, Fuji Bank survived by restructuring while the Nippon Credit Bank was taken over by the government. How are they doing now? Go to their English language home pages at http://www.fujibank.co.jp/eng/fb/home.html for Fuji Bank and http://www.ncb.co.jp/lr/English/1998/index.html for the Nippon Credit Bank. Review some of their recent news releases. What plans does the Japanese government have for the Nippon Credit Bank? Does the government intend to privatize the bank or has it already done so?

Banking Troubles in Japan

Prior to the 1980s, financial markets in Japan were heavily regulated, with severe restrictions on interest rates that banks could offer. As a result of financial deregulation, banks became more aggressive in attracting deposits and more willing to make riskier loans, particularly in the real estate sector. For example, the Kizu Credit Cooperative, by offering high interest rates on deposits, increased deposits from $2 billion in 1988 to $12 billion by 1995. Kizu lent these deposits to finance real estate loans.

When Japanese property values collapsed in the 1990s, banks were in trouble. As the bad loans piled up, Japan experienced its first bank failures since World War II. Banks that grew the fastest during the go-go era, such as Kizu, became some of the first casualties. According to the Japanese finance minister, bank losses in the country totaled $350 billion by 1997.

Although many Japanese banks failed, regulatory officials appeared reluctant to close down banks that were financially insolvent. Regulators seemed to be following a "too-big-to-fail" philosophy by promising that none of the nation's 21 largest banks would be allowed to fail. But that approach was violated in late 1997 when Hokkaido Takushuku Bank, Japan's tenth largest, failed. After the failure, the Japanese government immediately extended emergency central bank loans and arranged for another bank to take over the failed bank's deposits and outstanding loans. All deposits were protected, but the bank's shareholders lost their investment. Following that bank's collapse, some other Japanese banks found it difficult to borrow.

Even after such bank failures, much of the Japanese banking system consists of zombies, living-dead banks kept alive only by transfusions from the Bank of Japan, the central bank. As the economy worsened in 1998, with GDP contracting by 3.3 percent, the stock of bad loans soared to an estimated 30 percent of GDP. This makes Japan's banking problem about five times bigger, in relative terms, than America's savings-and-loan problem.

One problem with the banking crisis in Japan is that nobody knows how bad off banks really are because reporting requirements there are much looser than in the United States. This so-called *lack of transparency* in accounting magnifies the impact of the information that does become public. For example, in September 1998, Fuji Bank reported that its problem loans were 50 percent larger than it had previously disclosed. Fuji also said that the reserves it set aside to cover these loans were far below what most observers believed would be sufficient. The effect of these announcements was a huge drop in Fuji's share price, along with share prices of other banks. To resolve its banking crisis, the Japanese government in 1998 began using public funds to bail out troubled banks. By early 1999, about $75 billion had been earmarked to shore up 15 major banks. But with Japan stuck in its worst recession in decades, banking troubles were expected to continue.

Sources: David Sanger, "Japanese Tell U.S. That Their Banks Are in Big Trouble," *New York Times* (5 October 1998); Bill Spindle, Norihiko Shirouzu, and Jason Sapsford, "Bleak Economy Emerges from Japanese Survey," *Wall Street Journal* (1 October 1998); "Time to Wake Up," *Economist* (26 September 1998), pp. 21–23; and Houtan Bassiri, "Japan Banks Step Toward Recovery with More Public Funds," *Dow-Jones Newswire* (14 February 1999).

CONCLUSION

Money has grown increasingly more abstract over time, moving from commodity money to paper money that represented a claim on some commodity such as gold, to paper money with no intrinsic value. As you will see, paper money constitutes only a fraction of the money supply. Most modern money consists of electronic entries in the banking system's computers. So money has changed from a physical commodity to an electronic entry. Money today not so much changes hands as changes computer accounts.

Money and banking have been intertwined ever since the early goldsmiths offered to hold customers' valuables for safekeeping. Banking has since evolved from one of the most staid industries to one of the most competitive. Deregulation and branching innovations have increased competition and have expanded the types of bank deposits. Reforms have given the Fed more uniform control over all depository institutions and have given the institutions greater access to the services provided by the Fed. Thus all depository institutions can compete on more equal footing.

Deregulation provides greater freedom not only to prosper but also to fail. Failures of depository institutions create a special problem, however, because these institutions provide the financial underpinning of the nation's money supply, as you will see in the next chapter. There we will examine more closely how banks operate and supply the nation's money.

SUMMARY

1. Barter was the first form of exchange. As specialization grew, it became more difficult to discover the double coincidence of wants required for barter. The time and inconvenience associated with barter led even simple economies to introduce money.

2. Anything that acquires a high degree of acceptability throughout an economy as a medium of exchange thereby becomes money. The first moneys were commodities, such as salt or gold. Eventually what changed hands was a piece of paper that could be redeemed for something of value, such as gold. As paper money became widely accepted, governments introduced fiat money, which is paper money that cannot be redeemed for anything other than more paper money. Fiat money is given its status as money by law, or by fiat. Most currencies throughout the world today are fiat money. People accept fiat money because they believe others will do so as well.

3. The value of money depends on how much it will buy. If money fails to serve as a medium of exchange, traders will resort to some second-best means of exchange, such as barter, a careful system of record-keeping, or some informal commodity money. If a monetary system breaks down, more time must be devoted to exchange, leaving less time for production, so the economy's efficiency suffers.

4. The Federal Reserve System was established in 1914 to stabilize the banking system. After many banks failed during the Great Depression, the Fed's powers were increased and centralized. Its control over all depository institutions was extended by legislation passed during the 1980s. The primary powers of the Fed are to (1) conduct open-market operations (buying and selling U.S. government securities to control the money supply), (2) set the discount rate (the rate at which depository institutions can borrow from the Fed), and (3) establish and enforce reserve requirements for depository institutions.

5. Regulations introduced during the Great Depression turned banking into a closely regulated and largely predictable industry. But high interest rates during the 1970s disturbed the quiet life of depository institutions. Reforms in the 1980s were designed to give depository institutions greater flexibility in competing with other kinds of financial intermediaries. Many thrifts used this flexibility to gamble on investments, but these gambles often failed, causing hundreds of thrifts to go bankrupt. In 1989, Congress approved a measure to close failing thrifts, pay off insured deposits, and regulate more closely the operations of remaining thrifts. Commercial banks also experienced record numbers of failures during the 1980s, but their problems were not as serious as those affecting the thrifts. By the mid-1990s, commercial banks and thrifts were thriving once again in the United States, although they remained troubled in Japan. Mergers of banks are creating a national banking system.

QUESTIONS FOR REVIEW

1. *(Barter)* Define a double coincidence of wants and explain its role in a barter system.

2. *(Money Versus Barter)* "Without money, everything would be more expensive." Explain this statement. Then take a look at a Web page devoted to barter at http://www.ex.ac.uk/~RDavies/arian/barter.html. What are some current developments in barter exchange?

3. *(Functions of Money)* What are the three important functions of money? Define each of them.

4. *(Functions of Money)* "If an economy had only two goods (both *nondurable*), there would be no need for money because exchange would always be between those two goods." What important function of money does this statement disregard?

5. *(Characteristics of Money)* Why is universal acceptability such an important characteristic of money? What other characteristics can you think of that might be important to market participants?

6. *(Commodity Money)* Why do you think rice was chosen to serve as money in medieval Japan? What would happen to the price level if there was a particularly good rice harvest one year?

7. *(Commodity Money)* Early in U.S. history, tobacco was used as money. If you were a tobacco farmer and had two loads of tobacco that were of different qualities, which would you use for money and which for smoking? Under what conditions would you use both types of tobacco for money?

8. *(Origins of Banking)* Discuss the various ways in which London goldsmiths functioned as early banks.

9. *(Types of Money)* Complete each of the following sentences:
   a. If the face value of a coin exceeds the cost of coinage, the resulting revenues to the issuer of the coin are known as ________.
   b. A product that serves both as money and as a commodity is ________.
   c. Coins and paper money circulating in the United States have face values that exceed the value of the material from which they are made. Therefore, they are forms of ________.
   d. If the government declares that creditors must accept a form of money as payment for debts, the money becomes ________.
   e. A common unit for measuring the value of every good or service in the economy is known as a(n) ________.

10. *(Fiat Money)* Most economists believe that the better fiat money serves as a store of value, the more acceptable it is. What does this statement mean? How could people lose faith in money?

11. *(The Value of Money)* When the value of money was based on its gold content, new discoveries of gold were frequently followed by periods of inflation. Explain.

12. *(Case**Study:** When the Monetary Systems Break Down)* In countries where the monetary system has broken down, what are some alternatives to which people have resorted to carry out transactions?

13. *(Depository Institutions)* What is a depository institution and what types of depository institutions are found in the United States? How do they act as intermediaries between savers and borrowers? Why do they play this role?

14. *(Federal Reserve System)* What are the main powers and responsibilities of the Federal Reserve System?

15. *(Bank Deregulation)* Some economists argue that deregulated deposit rates combined with deposit insurance led to the insolvency of many depository institutions. On what basis do they make such an argument?

16. *(The Structure of U.S. Banking)* Discuss the impact of bank mergers on the structure of American banking. Why do banks wish to merge?

17. *(Case**Study:** Banking Troubles in Japan)* Discuss problems with the banking system in Japan. In what ways are they similar to U.S. banking problems in the late 1980s and early 1990s? What is the current status of bank restructuring in Japan?

EXPERIENTIAL EXERCISES

18. *(When Money Performs Poorly)* Visit Glyn Davies' History of Money site at http://mirrors.org.sg/money/llyfr.html. Click on "A Comparative Chronology of Money" and check the years since 1939. How many hyperinflations are mentioned for those years? What does that tell you about the relationship between monetary systems and economic well-being?

19. *(Bank Deregulation)* The Federal Reserve Bank of Philadelphia's *Business Review* often runs informative articles that are accessible to introductory economics students. Read the article by Ted Temzelides entitled "Are Bank Runs Contagious?" in the November/December 1997 issue at http://www.phil.frb.org/econ/br/brnd97in.html. What is his conclusion and how does it relate to the discussion of banking regulation in this chapter?

20. The *Wall Street Journal* prints several features that track key interest rates. The daily Money Rates box lists the current prime lending rate, along with a variety of short-term rates. The weekly Key Interest Rates table reports on Treasury securities. And a weekly Consumer Savings Rates List shows the rates paid by 100 large banks. Take a look at these sources—you can find them on the Money and Credit Markets pages—and determine the extent to which all these interest rates move together.

CHAPTER

14 Banking and the Money Supply

What role do banks play in creating money? Why are banks more likely to be called First Trust, Security National, or Federal Savings rather than Benny's Bank, Easy Money Bank and Trust, or Loans 'R' Us? Why are we so interested in banks, anyway? After all, isn't banking a business like any other—dry cleaning, auto manufacturing, or home remodeling? Why not devote this chapter to the home-remodeling business? Answers to these and related questions are addressed in this chapter, which examines banking and the money supply.

In this chapter, we take a closer look at the role banks play in the economy. Banks are special in macroeconomics because, like the London goldsmith, they can convert a borrower's IOU into money, and an adequate supply of money is a key ingredient in a healthy economy. Since regulatory reforms have elimi-

Visit the McEachern Interactive Study Center for this chapter at http://mcisc.swcollege.com

nated many of the distinctions between commercial banks and thrift institutions, and since thrifts represent a dwindling share of depository institutions, from here on, all depository institutions will usually be referred to more simply as *banks.*

We first consider the role of banks in the economy and the types of deposits they hold. We then examine how banks work and see how the money supply expands through the creation of deposits. We also consider the operation of the Federal Reserve System in more detail. As we will see, the Federal Reserve, or the Fed, attempts to control money supply indirectly by controlling bank reserves. Topics discussed in this chapter include:

- Checkable deposits
- Monetary aggregates
- Balance sheets
- Money creation process
- Money multipliers
- Tools of the Fed

BANKS, THEIR DEPOSITS, AND THE MONEY SUPPLY

Banks attract funds from savers and lend these funds to borrowers. Savers need a safe place for their money and borrowers need credit; banks try to earn a profit by serving both groups. To inspire depositor confidence, banks present an image of sober dignity—an image meant to foster trust and assurance. For example, they are more apt to be called First Trust, Security National, or Federal Savings rather than Benny's Bank, Easy Money Bank and Trust, or Loans 'R' Us. In contrast, *finance companies* are financial intermediaries that do not get their funds from depositors, so they can choose names aimed more at borrowers—names such as Household Finance and The Money Store.

Banks Are Financial Intermediaries

By bringing together the two sides of the market, banks serve as financial intermediaries, or as go-betweens. They gather various amounts from savers and repackage these funds into the amounts demanded by borrowers. Usually savers want to save relatively small amounts, while borrowers want to borrow relatively large amounts, so banks repackage the various small savings into larger amounts for borrowers. Some savers need their money back next week, some next year, some only after retirement. Likewise, different borrowers want to borrow for different lengths of time. Banks, as intermediaries, offer desirable durations to both savers and borrowers.

Coping with Asymmetric Information. Banks, as lenders, try to identify borrowers who are willing to pay interest and are able to repay the loans. But borrowers have more reliable information about their own credit history and financial plans than do lenders. Thus in the market for loans there is **asymmetric information:** a disparity in the information known by each party to the transaction. This asymmetry would not create a problem if borrowers could be trusted to report relevant details to lenders. Some borrowers, however, have an incentive to suppress critical information, such as other debts, a troubled financial history, or plans to invest the borrowed funds in a risky venture. Because they have experience and expertise in evaluating the creditworthiness of loan applicants, banks have a greater ability to cope with asymmetric information than an individual saver would. Moreover, because banks have experience in

Asymmetric information
Unequal information known by each party to a transaction; borrowers usually have more information about their creditworthiness than do lenders

drawing up and enforcing contracts with borrowers, they can do so more cheaply than could an individual saver. Thus savers are better off dealing with banks than making loans directly to the ultimate borrower. *The economy is more efficient because banks develop expertise in evaluating borrowers, structuring loans, and enforcing loan contracts.*

Reducing Risk Through Diversification. By developing a diversified portfolio of assets rather than lending funds to a single borrower, banks reduce the risk to each individual saver. A bank, in effect, lends a tiny fraction of each saver's deposits to each of its many borrowers. If one borrower fails to repay a loan, this failure will hardly affect a large, diversified bank. Certainly such a default does not represent the personal disaster it would if one saver's entire nest egg had been loaned directly to that defaulting borrower.

The Narrow Definition of Money: M1

Suppose you have some cash in your pocket. If you deposit this cash in a checking account, you can then write checks directing your bank to pay someone from your account. When you think of money, what most likely comes to mind is currency—dollar bills and coins. Indeed, dollar bills and coins are money, but money consists primarily of a particular class of bank liabilities—**checkable deposits,** or deposits against which checks can be written. Banks hold a variety of checkable deposits. The most important over the years have been *demand deposits,* which are held by commercial banks and do not earn interest. In recent years, financial institutions have developed other kinds of accounts that carry check-writing privileges but also earn interest, such as negotiable order of withdrawal (NOW) accounts.

Checkable deposits Deposits in financial institutions against which checks can be written

Monetary aggregates are various measures of the money supply defined by the Federal Reserve. The most narrowly defined money supply is **M1,** which consists of currency (including coins) held by the nonbanking public, checkable deposits, and travelers checks. Note that currency sitting in bank vaults is not included as part of the money supply, because it is not being used as a medium of exchange. But checkable deposits are money because their owners can write checks against them.

Monetary aggregates Measures of the economy's money supply

M1 A measure of the money supply consisting of currency and coins held by the nonbanking public, checkable deposits, and travelers checks

Currency has been declared *legal tender* by the federal government; this means that if currency is offered as payment, it must be accepted or the debt is canceled. Checkable deposits are the liabilities of the issuing banks, which stand ready to convert these deposits into currency. Checks are *not* legal tender, so sellers need not accept them, as signs that say "No Checks!" attest. Yet checks are so widely accepted as a medium of exchange that checkable deposits are counted as part of M1, the narrow definition of the money supply.

The primary currency circulating in the United States consists of Federal Reserve notes, which are issued by, and are liabilities of, the Federal Reserve banks. In fact, over three-fourths of the Fed's liabilities consist of Federal Reserve notes. Since Federal Reserve notes are redeemable for nothing other than more Federal Reserve notes, U.S. currency is *fiat money,* as noted in Chapter 13. The other component of currency is coins, manufactured and distributed by the U.S. Mint. Our coins are token coins because their metal value is less—usually much less—than their face value.

So the Fed supplies the nation's currency, which is printed by the U.S. Bureau of Engraving and Printing. But currency attracts counterfeiters. The following case study discusses recent trends in counterfeiting Federal Reserve notes and the measures taken to thwart them.

CaseStudy

Public Policy

Visit the "$100 Information" page from the U.S. Treasury Department at http://www.treas.gov/currency/hundred.html for a detailed explanation of the new design and security features of the $100 Franklin note. What has happened to the Federal Reserve Seal that traditionally identifies the issuing bank? Will all the new currency designs get the same level of protection as the $100? Who is paying for these design changes?

Tracking the Supernote

Until recently, U.S. currency had changed little—so little, in fact, that on the back of a $10 bill the car driving by the Treasury building dates back to the 1920s. Since 1879, Crane & Company, of Dalton, Massachusetts, has been the exclusive supplier of U.S. currency paper. That paper is 75 percent cotton and 25 percent linen, with embedded red and blue fibers.

Of the $500 billion or so in Federal Reserve notes now in circulation, more than half are in foreign hands. On U.S. soil, the Secret Service, by tracking suspicious purchases of paper and ink, has been able to seize an estimated 90 percent of counterfeit money before it gets into circulation. But foreign counterfeiting poses a problem for the Secret Service, which is primarily a domestic police force (only a small fraction of its 2,000 agents work abroad). Most counterfeit money seized in the United States is printed abroad, and the volume of seizures outside the United States has been growing.

The biggest threat to the integrity of U.S. currency is the so-called supernote, which is a counterfeit $100 bill of extremely high quality that began showing up around 1990. The supernote is a remarkable forgery, including sequential serial numbers and a polymer security thread that had taken Crane years to develop. The supernote can fool currency scanning machines at the nation's 12 Federal Reserve banks by perfectly emulating the magnetic field generated by ferrous oxide inked into Benjamin Franklin's portrait.

Supernotes are ubiquitous abroad, especially in Europe. Up to one-fifth of the $100 bills circulating in Russia in a recent year were believed to be supernotes. German banks reportedly no longer accept $100 bills from Russian citizens. More generally, because of the supernote, merchants and bank tellers in Europe and the Far East have grown reluctant to accept $100 bills.

In 1996, a newly designed $100 bill was issued, the first major change of the currency since 1929. The new bill is the same size as the old one and is printed on the same Crane paper in the same green and black ink. Modifications include a new off-center portrait, a watermark, the number "100," which shifts from green to black when viewed from different angles, and microprinting around the oval portrait of Franklin repeating the phrase "THE UNITED STATES OF AMERICA." Another addition to thwart copy machines is a new security thread that glows red under ultraviolet light. The thread has "USA 100" repeated in print 42-thousandths of an inch tall; this lettering is visible when held up to the light but is not reproducible in a photocopier. By September 1998, a new $50 bill and a new $20 bill were also introduced, each with its own security features. For example, under ultraviolet light, the security strip glows yellow in the $50 bill and glows green in the $20 bill.

After the $1 bill, the $20 bill is the most used bill, especially in the nation's 190,000 ATMs. The $20 bill is three times more popular than the $10 bill. To ensure acceptance of the new $20 bill, $8 million was budgeted for a publicity campaign.

The United States has a policy of never recalling existing currency for fear that the world's hoarders of dollars might switch to euros or yen. Over time, preference for the new currency and the replacement of old bills as they pass through the Fed will eventually eliminate the old bills. Since the process could take years, there will be two types of currency in circulation for some time. To give you an idea how long this may take, for decades the Fed has been destroying $500 bills and $1,000 bills whenever they get deposited in the banking system. But even after a decades-long eradication program, these denominations still show up from time to time, after having been stashed away for a good part of the century.

Sources: Frances Taylor, "Jackson Gets a Face Lift," *Hartford Courant* (7 September 1998); Frederic Dannen and Ira Silverman, "The Supernote," *New Yorker* (23 October 1995), pp. 50–55; and Peter Brimelow, "Going Underground," *Forbes* (21 September 1998), pp. 206–207. The U.S. Treasury has a Web site providing information about the new bills at www.moneyfactory.com/currency/facts1.cfm.

Broader Money Aggregates

We regard currency and checkable deposits as money because each serves as a medium of exchange; each is also a unit of account and a store of value. Some other kinds of assets perform the store-of-value function and sometimes can be readily converted into currency or to checkable deposits. Because these financial assets are so close to money, we call them money under broader definitions.

Savings deposits Deposits that earn interest but have no specific maturity date

Savings deposits earn interest but have no specific maturity date. Banks often allow depositors to shift funds from savings accounts to checking accounts by simply making a phone call or pressing a few buttons on an ATM, so distinctions between the narrower and broader definitions of money have become blurred.

Time deposits Deposits that earn a fixed rate of interest if held for the specified period, which can range anywhere from several months to several years

Time deposits (also called *certificates of deposit,* or *CDs*) earn a fixed rate of interest if held for the specified period, which can range from several months to several years. Premature withdrawals are penalized by forfeiture of several months' interest. Neither savings deposits nor time deposits serve directly as a medium of exchange, so they are not included in M1, the narrowest definition of money.

Money market mutual fund accounts, discussed in Chapter 13, represent another component of money when defined more broadly. But, because of restrictions on the minimum balance, on the number of checks that can be written per month, and on the minimum amount of each check, these popular accounts are not viewed as money when narrowly defined.

M2 A monetary aggregate consisting of M1 plus savings deposits, small-denomination time deposits, and money market mutual funds

M3 A monetary aggregate consisting of M2 plus large-denomination time deposits

Recall that M1 consists of currency (including coins) held by the nonbanking public, checkable deposits, and travelers checks. **M2** is a monetary aggregate that includes M1 as well as savings deposits, small-denomination time deposits, and money market mutual fund accounts. **M3** includes M2 plus large-denomination time deposits. In subsequent discussions when we refer to the "money supply," we will usually be talking about M1, the narrow definition of money.

The size and relative importance of each monetary aggregate are presented in Exhibit 1. As you can see, M2 is about four times larger than M1, and M3 is more than five times larger. Thus the narrow definition of money describes only a fraction of broader aggregates. And distinctions between M1 and M2 become less meaningful as banks allow depositors to transfer funds from one account to another.

EXHIBIT 1

Alternative Measures of the Money Supply (January 1999)

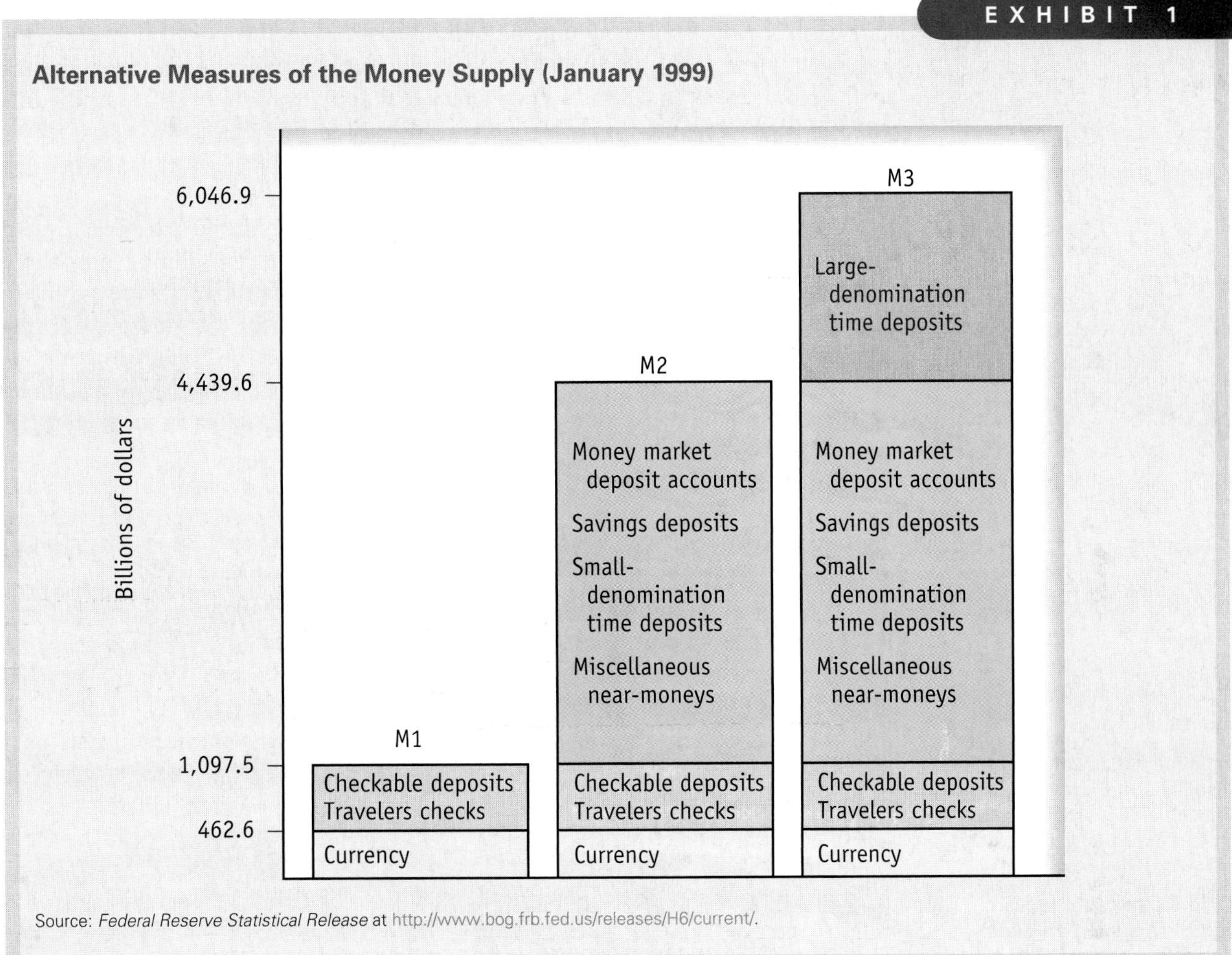

Source: *Federal Reserve Statistical Release* at http://www.bog.frb.fed.us/releases/H6/current/.

You may be curious why the definitions of money do not include credit cards, such as VISA and MasterCard. After all, most sellers accept credit cards as readily as they accept cash or checks (some even prefer credit cards to checks). Shouldn't credit cards be included in any definition of money? Credit cards themselves are not money; they are simply a means of obtaining a short-term loan from the card issuer. If you use a credit card to purchase plane tickets from a travel agent, the transaction is not complete until the card issuer pays for the tickets. The credit card has not eliminated the use of money; it has merely postponed the travel agent's receipt of money.

HOW BANKS WORK

Banks are profit-making institutions in the business of taking people's money on deposit, lending out a large portion of that money, and earning a profit on the difference between the interest paid on deposits and the interest received from loans.

We could consider the operation of any type of depository institution (commercial bank, savings and loan, mutual savings bank, or credit union), but we will focus on commercial banks because they are the most important in terms of total assets. Moreover, the operating principles that apply to money creation in commercial banks generally apply to other depository institutions as well.

Starting a Bank

Let's begin with the formation of a bank. Suppose some business leaders in your hometown decide to form a commercial bank called Home Bank. To obtain a *charter,* or the right to operate, they must apply to the state banking authority, in the case of a state bank, or to the U.S. Comptroller of the Currency in the case of a national bank. When the chartering agency reviews the application, it considers the quality of the bank's management, the amount of money the owners plan to invest, the need for an additional bank in the region, and the likely success of the bank.

Suppose the founders plan to invest $100,000 in the bank, and they so indicate on their application for a national charter. If their application is approved, they issue themselves shares of stock—certificates indicating ownership. Thus they exchange $100,000 in cash for shares of stock in the bank. These shares are called the *owners' equity,* or the **net worth,** of the bank. Part of the $100,000, say $20,000, is used to buy shares in their district Federal Reserve bank. So Home Bank is now a member of the Federal Reserve System. With the remaining $80,000, the owners acquire and furnish the bank building.

Net worth Assets minus liabilities

To focus our discussion, we will examine the bank's **balance sheet,** presented in Exhibit 2. As the name implies, a balance sheet shows a balance between the two sides of the bank's accounts. The left-hand side lists the bank's assets. An **asset** is any physical property or financial claim owned by the bank. At this early stage, assets include the building and equipment owned by Home Bank plus its stock in the district Federal Reserve bank. The right-hand side lists the bank's liabilities and net worth. A **liability** is an amount the bank owes. So far the right-hand side includes only the net worth of $100,000. The two sides of the ledger must always be equal, or in *balance*—hence the name *balance sheet.* Since the two sides must be in balance, assets must equal liabilities plus net worth:

Balance sheet A financial statement that shows assets, liabilities, and net worth at a given point in time; since assets must equal liabilities plus net worth, the statement is in balance.

Asset Anything of value that is owned

Liability Anything that is owed to another individual or institution

$$\text{assets} = \text{liabilities} + \text{net worth}$$

The bank is now ready to open. Opening day is the bank's lucky day, because its first customer comes in with a briefcase full of $100 bills and puts $1,000,000 into a checking account. When a bank accepts a deposit, it promises to repay the depositor that amount. The deposit therefore is an amount the bank owes—it is a

EXHIBIT 2

Home Bank's Balance Sheet

Assets		Liabilities and Net Worth	
Building and furniture	$ 80,000	Net worth	$100,000
Stock in district Fed	20,000		
Total	$100,000	Total	$100,000

EXHIBIT 3

Home Bank's Balance Sheet After $1,000,000 Deposit

Assets		Liabilities and Net Worth	
Cash	$1,000,000	Checkable deposits	$1,000,000
Building and furniture	80,000	Net worth	100,000
Stock in district Fed	20,000		
Total	$1,100,000	Total	$1,100,000

liability of the bank. As a result of this deposit, the bank's assets increase by $1,000,000 in cash, and its liabilities increase by $1,000,000 in checkable deposits. Exhibit 3 shows the effects of this transaction on Home Bank's balance sheet. The customer has deposited $1,000,000 in the bank, so the bank owes the customer the amount deposited. On the right-hand side there are now two kinds of claims on the bank's assets: claims by the owners, called net worth, and claims by non-owners, called liabilities, which at this point consist of checkable deposits.

Reserve Accounts

Where do we go from here? As mentioned in Chapter 13, banks are required by the Fed to set aside, or to hold in reserve, an amount equal to a certain percentage of their deposits. The **required reserve ratio** dictates the minimum *proportion* of deposits the bank must hold in reserve. Suppose the required reserve ratio on checkable deposits is 10 percent. Home Bank must therefore hold reserves equal to 10 percent of its checkable deposits. The dollar amount that must be held in reserve is called **required reserves**—deposits multiplied by the required reserve ratio. All depository institutions are subject to the reserve requirements established by the Fed. Home Bank must therefore hold $100,000 as required reserves, which equals checkable deposits of $1,000,000 multiplied by 0.10. A bank must hold reserves either as cash in its vault or as deposits at the Fed, but neither earns the bank any interest income.

Required reserve ratio The ratio of reserves to deposits that banks are required, by regulation, to hold

Required reserves The dollar amount of reserves a bank is legally required to hold

Suppose Home Bank deposits $100,000 in a reserve account with its district Federal Reserve bank. Home Bank's reserves are now divided between $100,000 in required reserves on deposit with the Fed and $900,000 in **excess reserves** as cash in the vault. So far Home Bank has not earned a penny. Excess reserves, however, can be used to make loans or to purchase interest-bearing assets, such as government bonds. By law, the bank's interest-bearing assets are limited primarily to loans and government bonds.

Excess reserves Bank reserves in excess of required reserves

Liquidity Versus Profitability

Like the early goldsmiths, modern banks must be prepared to satisfy depositors' requests for funds. A bank loses reserves whenever a depositor withdraws cash or writes a check that is deposited in another bank. The bank wants to be in a position to satisfy all depositor demands, even if many depositors ask for their money at the same time or even if many checks are written against its checkable deposits. A bank could fail if it lacked sufficient reserves to meet all depositor requests for funds. Required reserves are not meant to be used to meet depositor requests for funds, so banks often hold excess reserves or hold some assets that can be easily converted to cash to satisfy any unexpected demand for funds. Banks may also want to have excess reserves on hand in case a valued customer needs an immediate loan.

The bank manager must therefore structure the portfolio of assets with an eye toward liquidity but must not forget that the bank's survival also depends on profitability. **Liquidity** is the ease with which an asset can be converted into cash without a significant loss of value. *The objectives of liquidity and profitability are at odds.* For example, the bank will generally find that the assets offering a higher interest rate are less liquid than other assets offering a lower interest rate. The most liquid asset is bank reserves, either in the bank's vault as cash or on account with the Fed, but reserves earn no interest.

Liquidity A measure of the ease with which an asset can be converted into money without significant loss in its value

At one extreme, suppose a bank is completely liquid, holding all its assets as cash reserves. Such a bank would clearly have no difficulty meeting depositors' demands for funds. The bank is playing it safe—too safe. Since it holds no interest-earning assets, it will earn no income and will fail. At the other extreme, suppose a bank uses all its excess reserves to acquire high-yielding but illiquid assets, such as long-term loans. Such a bank will run into problems whenever withdrawals exceed new deposits. The bank portfolio manager's task is to strike just the right balance between liquidity, or safety, and profitability.

Since reserves earn no interest, banks usually try to keep their excess reserves to a minimum. Banks continuously "sweep" their accounts to find excess reserves that can be put to some interest-bearing use. They do not let excess reserves remain idle even overnight. The **federal funds market** provides for day-to-day lending and borrowing among banks of excess reserves on account at the Fed; these funds usually do not leave the Fed—they shift among accounts. For example, suppose that at the end of the business day Home Bank has excess reserves of $50,000 on account at the Fed and wants to loan that amount to another bank that finished the day with a reserve deficiency of $50,000. These two banks are brought together by a broker who specializes in the market for federal funds—that is, the market for excess reserves at the Fed. The interest rate paid on this loan is called the **federal funds rate,** and it is this rate the Fed targets as a tool of monetary policy, but more on that later.

Federal funds market A market for overnight lending and borrowing of reserves among banks; the market for reserves on account with the Fed

Federal funds rate The interest rate prevailing in the federal funds market; the interest rate banks charge one another for overnight borrowing

Let's now discuss how Home Bank and the banking system as a whole can create money.

HOW BANKS CREATE MONEY

This chapter is really about how fiat money is created. We are now in a position to examine how an individual bank and the banking system as a whole can create money. Our discussion will focus on the behavior of commercial banks because these are the largest and most important depository institutions, although thrifts can carry out similar activities.

Creating Money Through Excess Reserves

As we shall see, excess reserves are the raw material the banking system employs to support the creation of money. The Fed can influence the amount of excess reserves by (1) buying or selling U.S. government bonds, (2) extending discount loans to banks, and (3) changing the required reserve ratio. By far the most important of these is buying or selling U.S. government bonds, bonds originally issued by the U.S. Treasury.

Assume there are no excess reserves in the banking system initially and that the reserve requirement on checkable deposits is 10 percent. To get our analysis rolling, suppose the Federal Reserve buys a $1,000 U.S. government bond from Home Bank. To pay for the bond, the Fed simply increases Home Bank's reserve account with the Fed by $1,000. Where does the Fed get these reserves? It makes them up—creates them out of electronic ether, out of thin air!

In the transaction, Home Bank has exchanged one asset, a U.S. bond, for another asset, reserves on deposit with the Fed. So far the money supply has not changed, because neither U.S. bonds nor Home Bank's reserves are part of the money supply. But the increase in excess reserves fuels an increase in the money supply.

The story, in brief, is this. A bank's lending is limited to the amount of its excess reserves. Suppose Home Bank makes a loan by increasing the borrower's checkable deposits by $1,000. Since checkable deposits are money, the bank, by making the loan, has created money in the amount of $1,000. These borrowed funds eventually get spent and end up as $1,000 in someone else's checkable deposits, perhaps in another bank, so the money supply remains $1,000 higher. That bank, after setting aside required reserves of, say, $100, can lend out its excess reserves of $900 by increasing a new borrower's checkable deposits, thereby adding $900 more to the money supply, or M1. The money supply continues to expand in this fashion until no excess reserves are left in the banking system. Let's look at the deposit creation process in greater detail in the following series of rounds.

Round One. We begin with the Fed buying a $1,000 U.S. bond from Home Bank. After selling that bond, Home Bank has $1,000 in excess reserves. Rather than sit on these reserves and earn no interest, Home Bank can make loans for the full amount of excess reserves. Suppose Home Bank is your regular bank and you apply for a $1,000 student loan. Home Bank approves your loan and consequently increases your checking account by $1,000. *Home Bank has converted your promise to repay the loan, your IOU, into a $1,000 checkable deposit. Because checkable deposits are part of M1, this action increases the money supply by $1,000.* In the process, Home Bank's excess reserves have become required reserves. As shown in Exhibit 4, Home Bank's assets increase by $1,000, as do its liabilities. On the asset side, loans increase by $1,000 because your IOU becomes an asset to the bank. On the liability side, checkable deposits increase by $1,000 because Home Bank has increased your account by that amount. Home Bank has created money based on your promise to repay the loan.

EXHIBIT 4

Changes in Home Bank's Balance Sheet After Home Bank Lends You $1,000

Home Bank's Balance Sheet

Assets		**Liabilities and Net Worth**	
Loans	+ 1,000	Checkable deposits	+ 1,000

Round Two. When you write a $1,000 check for tuition, your college promptly deposits the check in its checking account at College Bank. College Bank then increases the college's account by $1,000 and presents your check to the Fed. The Fed reduces Home Bank's reserve account by $1,000 and increases College Bank's reserve account by the same amount. The Fed then sends the check to Home Bank, which reduces your checkable deposits by $1,000. The Fed has "cleared" your check by settling the claim that College Bank had on Home Bank. So far, the $1,000 in checkable deposits, the newly created money, has simply shifted from Home Bank to College Bank.

But College Bank now has $1,000 more in reserves on deposit with the Fed. After setting aside $100, or 10 percent of your college's increase in deposits, as required reserves, College Bank has $900 in excess reserves. College Bank can thus make a loan or purchase some other interest-bearing asset. Suppose the bank lends $900 to an enterprising business student who plans to open an all-night bait-and-bagel shop to lure early morning anglers on their way to a nearby fishing spot. College Bank extends the loan by providing this student with a checking account balance of $900. As shown in Exhibit 5, College Bank's assets increase by the $900 loan, and its liabilities increase by the $900 added to the student's checkable deposits. *College Bank has converted the student's promise to repay the loan into a checkable deposit, which is money.*

Suppose the student writes a $900 check for equipment purchased at a hardware store, which deposits the check into an account at Merchants Trust. Merchants Trust increases the hardware store's checkable deposits by $900 and sends the check to the Fed, which increases Merchants Trust's reserves by $900 and decreases College Bank's reserves by the same amount. The Fed then sends the check to College Bank, which reduces the student's checkable deposit account by $900. So deposits at the Fed and checkable deposits decrease by $900 at College Bank and increase by that amount at Merchants Trust.

At this point, checkable deposits in the banking system total $1,900 more than before we started: Your college still has $1,000 more in checkable deposits at College Bank because you paid tuition, and the hardware store has $900 more in its account at Merchants Trust because of the enterprising student's equipment purchase.

Round Three and Beyond. Merchants Trust sets aside $90 of the $900 deposited as required reserves, leaving $810 in excess reserves. Suppose it loans $810 to an English major who is starting a new venture called "Note This," a note-taking service for students in large classes. Exhibit 6 shows that Merchants Trust's assets are up by $810 in loans, and its liabilities are up by the same amount in checkable deposits.

EXHIBIT 5

Changes in College Bank's Balance Sheet After the Bank Makes a $900 Loan

Assets		Liabilities and Net Worth	
Loans	+ 900	Checkable deposits	+ 900

EXHIBIT 6

Changes in Merchants Trust's Balance Sheet After an $810 Loan to English Major

Assets		Liabilities and Net Worth	
Loans	+ 810	Checkable deposits	+ 810

The loan of $810 is spent at the college bookstore on notebooks and computer software. The bookstore then deposits the check in its account at Fidelity Bank. Fidelity Bank credits the bookstore's checkable deposits with $810 and sends the check to the Fed for clearance. The Fed reduces Merchants Trust's reserves by $810 and increases Fidelity Bank's by the same amount. The Fed then sends the check to Merchants Trust, which reduces the English major's checkable deposits by $810. So deposits at the Fed and checkable deposits are down by $810 at Merchants Trust and up by the same amount at Fidelity Bank.

At this point checkable deposits in the banking system, and the money supply in the economy, are up by $2,710: your college's $1,000 checkable deposit at College Bank, plus the hardware store's $900 checkable deposit at Merchants Trust, plus the bookstore's $810 checkable deposit at Fidelity Bank. We could continue the deposit expansion process with Fidelity Bank, which sets aside $81 in required reserves and uses the $729 in excess reserves as a basis for additional loans, but by now you get the idea.

Notice the pattern of deposits and loans emerging from the analysis. Each time a bank receives a new deposit, 10 percent is set aside to satisfy the reserve requirement. The rest becomes excess reserves, which can be left idle or can serve as a basis for making loans or purchasing government bonds. In our example, excess reserves support loans that were then spent by the borrowers. This spending became another bank's checkable deposits, thereby generating excess reserves to support still more loans. Thus the excess reserves created initially by the Federal Reserve's purchase of U.S. bonds were passed from one bank to the next in the chain. Each bank set aside 10 percent of new deposits as required reserves, then used the remaining 90 percent to support additional lending.

An individual bank can lend no more than its excess reserves. When the borrower spends the amount loaned, reserves at one bank usually fall, but total reserves in the banking system do not. A check drawn against one account will typically be deposited in another account—if not in the same bank, then in another. Thus when a bank makes a loan and creates checkable deposits, the excess reserves on which that loan was based usually find their way back into the banking system. The recipient bank uses most of the new deposit to extend more loans and create more checkable deposits. The potential expansion of checkable deposits in the banking system therefore equals some multiple of the initial increase in excess reserves. Note that our example assumes that banks do not allow excess reserves to sit idle and that the public does not choose to hold some of the newly created money as cash. If excess reserves remained just that, they obviously would not fuel an expansion of the money supply. And if people choose to hold some of the newly created money as cash rather than in checking accounts, then the borrowed funds would not provide additional reserves in the banking system.

Summary of Rounds

To review: *The initial and most important step in the process described in the preceding section is the Fed's injection of $1,000 in new reserves into the banking system.* In our example, this resulted from the Fed's $1,000 bond purchase, but Home Bank's excess reserves would also increase if it had borrowed $1,000 in the form of a discount loan from the Fed, or if the Fed freed up $1,000 in excess reserves by lowering the reserve requirement.

Home Bank uses this $1,000 in excess reserves to support its loan to you. You pay your tuition bill, and your college deposits the check in its bank. This deposit precipitates a series of rounds that expand the money supply. These rounds are summarized in Exhibit 7, where the banks are listed along the left-hand margin. Column (1) lists the increase in checkable deposits at each bank, column (2) lists the increase in required reserves resulting from the increase in checkable deposits, and column (3) lists the increase in loans each bank extends as a result of the increase in excess reserves. As you can see, the increase in loans equals the increase in checkable deposits minus the increase in required reserves. Each bank lends out an amount equal to its excess reserves. Checkable deposits increase by a total of $10,000, which consists of the $1,000 deposited by your college into College Bank plus the $9,000 in the banking system as a result of College Bank's $900 in excess reserves. Incidentally, Home Bank is not on the list because the $1,000 checking account they created for you shifted to College Bank when you paid your tuition. If you had allowed the $1,000 you borrowed to idle in your account, the money-creation process would have stopped right there.

The increase in College Bank's checkable deposits is the change in the money supply arising from the first round. This $1,000 deposit translates into $100 in required reserves, leaving $900 in new loans. The $900 lent by College Bank ends up as checkable deposits in Merchants Trust, which sets aside $90 in required reserves and lends the balance of $810. The loan is spent and ends up in an account at Fidelity Bank, which sets aside $81 as reserves and lends the balance. Theoretically, the process will continue until there are no more excess reserves in the system to serve as a basis for additional loans. Because this example began with the Fed creating $1,000 in excess reserves, the Fed can rightfully claim that "The buck starts here," which is a slogan on New York Fed T-shirts.

EXHIBIT 7

Summary of the Credit Expansion Process Resulting from the Fed's Purchase of a $1,000 U.S. Government Bond from Home Bank

Bank	Increase in Checkable Deposits (1)	Increase in Required Reserves (2)	Increase in Loans (3) = (1) − (2)
1. College Bank	$ 1,000	$ 100	$ 900
2. Merchants Trust	900	90	810
3. Fidelity Bank	810	81	729
All remaining rounds	7,290	729	6,561
Totals	$10,000	$1,000	$9,000

What if, instead of buying the $1,000 U.S. bond from Home Bank, the Fed buys it from a bond dealer, paying with $1,000 in Federal Reserve notes. The Fed has increased the money supply by $1,000 by exchanging Federal Reserve notes, which become part of the money supply when in the hands of the public, for a U.S. bond, which is not part of the money supply. Once the bond dealer puts this cash into a checkable deposit—or spends the cash, so the money ends up in someone else's checkable deposit—the banking system's money expansion process is off and running.

Excess Reserves, Reserve Requirements, and Money Expansion

The banking system as a whole eliminates excess reserves by expanding the money supply. With a 10 percent reserve requirement, an initial injection of $1,000 in new reserves by the Fed could support, at most, $10,000 in new checkable deposits in the banking system as a whole, *assuming no bank holds excess reserves and nobody withdraws cash.* We can think of the $1,000 injection as the source of the $1,000 in reserves required to support the expansion of $10,000 in new checkable deposits.

The multiple by which the money supply increases as a result of an increase in the banking system's excess reserves is called the **money multiplier.** The **simple money multiplier** equals the reciprocal of the required reserve ratio, or $1/r$, where r is the reserve ratio. In our example the reserve ratio was 10 percent, or 0.1, so the reciprocal is 1/0.1, which equals 10. The formula for the multiple expansion of checkable deposits can be written as

Money multiplier The multiple by which the money supply increases as a result of an increase in excess reserves in the banking system

Simple money multiplier The reciprocal of the required reserve ratio, or $1/r$; the maximum multiple of excess reserves by which the money supply can increase

$$\text{change in checkable deposits} = \text{change in excess reserves} \times 1/r$$

The simple money multiplier assumes that banks hold no excess reserves, that borrowers do not let the funds sit idle, and that the public withdraws no cash. The higher the reserve requirement, the greater the fraction of deposits that must be held as reserves, and the smaller the money multiplier. If the reserve requirement were 20 percent instead of 10 percent, each bank would have to set aside twice as much for required reserves. The simple money multiplier in this case would be $1/0.2 = 5$, and the maximum possible increase in checkable deposits resulting from an initial $1,000 increase in excess reserves would therefore be $1,000 × 5 = $5,000. Deposits in the banking system could be expanded by only half as much as when the reserve requirement was 10 percent. *Excess reserves fuel the deposit expansion process, and a higher reserve requirement drains this fuel from the banking system, thereby reducing the amount of new money that can be created.*

On the other hand, with a reserve requirement of only 5 percent, banks would set aside less for required reserves, leaving more excess reserves available for loans. The simple money multiplier in that case would be $1/0.05 = 20$. With $1,000 in new reserves and a 5 percent reserve requirement, the banking system could increase the money supply by a maximum of $1,000 × 20 = $20,000. Thus the change in the required reserve ratio affects the banking system's ability to create money.

In summary, money creation can begin with an injection of new reserves into the banking system by the Fed. An individual bank lends an amount no greater than its excess reserves. The borrower spends the proceeds of this loan, and the seller deposits the receipts in a checking account. The reserves thereby created serve as a basis for additional loans. An increase in bank reserves kicks off a multiple expansion of checkable deposits, and checkable deposits are money. *The fractional reserve requirement is the key to the multiple expansion of checkable deposits.* If each deposit had to be backed by 100 percent reserves, each $1 injected into reserves could create at most a $1 expansion of the money supply.

Limitations on Money Expansion

Various leakages from the multiple expansion process reduce the size of the money multiplier, which is why $1/r$ is called the *simple* money multiplier. Let's consider leakages. Our example assumed that borrowers do something with the money and also that people do not choose to increase their cash holdings. The first assumption is easy to defend. Why would people borrow money if they didn't plan to spend it? The second assumption is trickier. Cash may sometimes be preferable to checking accounts since cash is more versatile, so people may choose to withdraw some of the newly created money as cash. *To the extent that people prefer to hold cash, the actual money multiplier will be smaller than the simple money multiplier because cash withdrawals reduce reserves in the banking system.* With reduced reserves, banks have less ability to make loans or buy bonds. Finally, a third assumption is that banks do not let excess reserves sit idle. If banks chose to do nothing with excess reserves, these reserves would not fuel expansion of the money supply. Incidentally, for the money multiplier to operate, the bank need not use excess reserves in a specific way; it could use them to pay all its employees a Christmas bonus, for that matter.

Multiple Contraction of the Money Supply

We have already outlined the money creation process, so the story of how the Federal Reserve System can reduce bank reserves, thereby reducing the money supply, can be a brief one. Again, we begin by assuming there are no excess reserves in the system and the reserve requirement is 10 percent. Suppose that, rather than buy government bonds, the Fed *sells* Home Bank a $1,000 U.S. bond. Home Bank might want to buy it because such bonds pay interest and are considered safe. Home Bank pays with reserves on account at the district Federal Reserve bank. So Home Bank's deposits with the Fed are down by $1,000, and the bond account is up by that amount.

Since Home Bank had no excess reserves at the outset, something has to give. To replenish reserves, Home Bank must recall loans (ask for repayment before the due date), sell some other asset, or borrow additional reserves. Suppose the bank calls in loans amounting to $1,000, and those who repay the loans do so with checks written against College Bank. When the checks clear, Home Bank's reserves are up by $1,000, just enough to satisfy its reserve requirement, but College Bank's reserves are down by $1,000. Since we assumed that there were no excess reserves at the outset, the loss of $1,000 in reserves leaves College Bank short of its required level of reserves. Specifically, in keeping with the legal reserve requirement, College Bank had $100 in required reserves supporting the $1,000 checkable deposits, so its reserves are now $900 below the required level. College Bank must therefore recall $900 in loans or otherwise try to replenish the $900 in required reserves.

And so it goes down the line. The Federal Reserve's sale of government bonds reduces bank reserves, forcing banks to recall loans or to somehow replenish reserves. *The maximum possible effect is to reduce the money supply by the amount of the original reduction in bank reserves times the simple money multiplier, which again equals 1 divided by the reserve requirement, or 1/*r. In our example, the Fed's sale of $1,000 in U.S. bonds to Home Bank could reduce the money supply by as much as $10,000.

Now that we have some idea how fractional-reserve banking works, we are in a position to summarize the Federal Reserve's role in the economy.

FED TOOLS OF MONETARY CONTROL

As mentioned in the previous chapter, in its capacity as a bankers' bank, the Fed clears checks for, extends loans to, and holds deposits of banks. The Fed, through its regulation of financial markets, tries to prevent major disruptions and financial panics. For example, during the stock market crash of 1987, Fed Chairman Alan Greenspan worked behind the scenes to ensure that banks had sufficient liquidity to calm the panic. In 1989 and 1998, when similar crashes threatened, the Fed again stepped in to ensure the necessary liquidity.

As noted already, about two-thirds of the money supply, as narrowly defined (M1), consists of checkable deposits, and it is the Fed's control over the creation of these deposits that most affects the money supply. The Fed's control over checkable deposits works indirectly through its control over reserves in the banking system. You are already familiar with the Fed's three tools for controlling excess reserves: (1) conducting **open-market operations,** or the buying and selling of U.S. government bonds; (2) setting the **discount rate,** which is the interest rate the Fed charges for loans it makes to banks; and (3) setting the required reserve ratio, which is the minimum fraction of reserves that banks must hold against deposits. Let's examine each of these in more detail.

NetBookmark

For an on-line introduction to the Federal Reserve System and a monetary policy link to the New York Federal Reserve Bank, go to the welcome page at http://www.ny.frb.org/introduce/. This site provides a very readable overview of the Fed's structure and operations. It includes links giving more details about particular terms. Be sure to take a peek inside the gold vault.

Open-Market Operations

The Fed carries out open-market operations whenever it buys or sells U.S. government bonds in the open market. To increase the money supply, the Fed directs the New York Fed to buy bonds. The purchase of bonds by the Fed is called an **open-market purchase**. To reduce the money supply, the Fed can carry out an **open-market sale**. Policy decisions about open-market operations are made by the Federal Open Market Committee, or FOMC, which meets every six weeks. Open market operations are relatively easy to carry out. They require no change in laws or regulations and can be executed in any amount—large or small—chosen by the Fed. Their simplicity and ease of use make them the tool of choice for the Fed.

Open-market operations Purchases or sales of U.S. government bonds in an effort to influence the money supply

Discount rate The interest rate charged by the Fed for loans to banks

Open-market purchase The purchase of U.S. government bonds by the Fed for the purpose of increasing the money supply

Open-market sale The sale of U.S. government bonds by the Fed for the purpose of reducing the money supply

The Discount Rate

The second monetary policy tool available to the Fed is changes in the discount rate, which is the interest rate the Fed charges on loans it makes to banks. Banks borrow from the Fed when they need reserves to satisfy their reserve requirements. If the Fed extends loans to banks, reserves increase, allowing the banking system to increase lending and thereby increase the money supply.

By lowering or raising the discount rate, the Fed encourages or discourages banks from borrowing, which alters reserves and affects the money supply. A lower discount rate reduces the cost of borrowing, encouraging banks to borrow reserves from the Fed. More bank reserves usually result in more bank lending and an increased money supply. On the other hand, a higher discount rate increases the cost of borrowing reserves from the Fed, resulting in less bank lending and a reduced money supply. The Fed's Board of Governors (not the FOMC) sets the discount rate by majority vote.

The Fed uses the discount rate more as a signal to financial markets about its monetary policy than as a tool for increasing or decreasing the money supply. The discount rate might also be thought of as an emergency tool for injecting liquidity into the banking system in the event of some financial crisis, such as a stock market crash.

The discount rate is a relatively imperfect tool for monetary policy because there is no guarantee that banks will necessarily borrow more even if the discount rate is reduced. If business prospects look poor and if banks view lending as risky, then even a lower discount rate may not entice banks to borrow from the Fed. Still, changes in the discount rate signal the Fed's intentions about monetary policy.

Reserve Requirements

The Fed also influences the money supply through reserve requirements, which are regulations regarding the minimum amount of reserves that banks must hold against deposits. Reserve requirements influence how much money the banking system can create with each dollar of reserves. If the Fed increases the reserve requirement, then banks must hold more reserves, reducing the amount of each dollar on deposit that can be lent out, which has the effect of reducing the money supply. On the other hand, a decrease in the reserve requirement increases the fraction of each dollar on deposit that can be lent out, which has the effect of increasing the money supply. Reserve requirements can be changed by a simple majority vote by the Board of Governors. But since changes in the reserve requirement are disruptive to the banking system, the Fed seldom employs them as a tool of monetary policy.

The Fed Is a Money Machine

Over three-fourths of the Federal Reserve's assets are U.S. government bonds. These bonds, the result of open-market operations, are IOUs from the federal government and assets of the Fed. *Over three-fourths of the Fed's liabilities are Federal Reserve notes in circulation.* These notes—U. S. currency—are IOUs from the Fed and are therefore liabilities of Fed. The Fed's primary asset—U.S. government bonds—earns interest, whereas the Fed's primary liability—Federal Reserve notes—requires no interest payments by the Fed. *The Fed is therefore both literally and figuratively a money machine. It is literally a money machine because it supplies the economy with Federal Reserve notes, and it is figuratively a money machine because its main asset earns interest but its main liability requires no interest payments.* The Fed also earns revenue from various services it provides. After financing its operating costs, the Fed turns over any remaining income to the U.S. Treasury to help fund the federal government.

We will learn more about the Fed's monetary policy in the next chapter. For a change of pace, let's close with a case study that looks at new developments in banking sparked by the revolution in personal computers and the Internet.

Banking on the Net

The Security First Network Bank (SFNB) never closes. It's open 24 hours a day, 365 days a year. Bank customers can pay bills, check account balances, and buy financial services from anywhere in the world—anywhere they have access to a personal computer and the Internet. SFNB was the nation's first "virtual" bank, authorized by regulators to offer full banking services on the Internet. Accounts are insured by the Federal Deposit Insurance Corporation. And the bank can accept deposits from customers in all 50 states. Deposits are accepted through the mail, direct deposit (such as with payroll checks), and electronic transfers. Depositors can also use ATM cards to carry out transactions or get cash at thousands of locations.

Incidentally, Internet banking is not quite the same thing as home banking. Internet banking requires no special software beyond your browser, nor is any banking data stored on your hard drive. The Internet customer need only log on to benefit from all the features of a bank. In contrast, home banking may require special software, and customers may be able to access their accounts only through computers on which the application is installed.

With hundreds of banks now accessible via the Internet, customers are increasingly shopping nationwide, even worldwide, for the best rates for deposits, credit cards, or loans. So a customer in St. Louis can get a housing mortgage in Atlanta, a car loan in Phoenix, a credit card in Boston, and a checking account in Chicago. And most banks offer an on-screen calculator so potential customers can figure out what size loan they can afford.

The Internet could become the biggest market in history, and banks want to become part of the picture. Over the long run, the Internet offers convenience for customers and potential cost savings for banks. Like telephone banking, which now accounts for one-fourth of all bank transactions, the Internet reduces the need for branches and branch personnel. Citibank, for example, encourages on-line use by eliminating fees for those who bank via computer. By 2005, three-quarters of U.S. households are expected to be doing some form of on-line banking.

Sources: Saul Hansell, "Online Banking Doesn't Always Cover the Basics," *New York Times* (10 November 1997); Peter Truell, "Industry Trend Seen as Citicorp, Travelers Plan Major Layoffs," *New York Times* (18 September 1998). SFNB's Internet address is http://www.sfnb.com. For access to hundreds of banking sites on the Internet see "Banks," USA Online at http://www.usaol.com/YP/banks/banks.html.

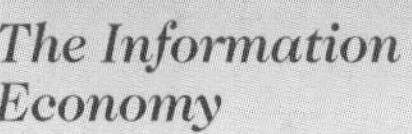

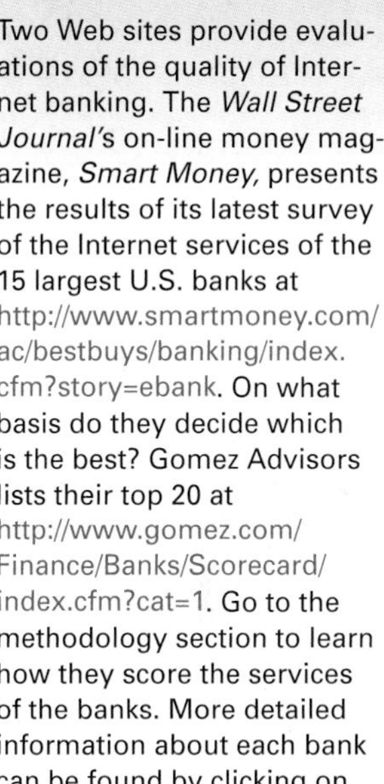

The Information Economy

Two Web sites provide evaluations of the quality of Internet banking. The *Wall Street Journal*'s on-line money magazine, *Smart Money*, presents the results of its latest survey of the Internet services of the 15 largest U.S. banks at http://www.smartmoney.com/ac/bestbuys/banking/index.cfm?story=ebank. On what basis do they decide which is the best? Gomez Advisors lists their top 20 at http://www.gomez.com/Finance/Banks/Scorecard/index.cfm?cat=1. Go to the methodology section to learn how they score the services of the banks. More detailed information about each bank can be found by clicking on the bank's name.

CONCLUSION

Banks play a unique role in the economy because they can transform someone's IOU into a checkable deposit, and a checkable deposit is money. The banking system's ability to expand the money supply depends on the amount of excess reserves in that system. Through open-market operations, changes in the discount rate, or changes in reserve requirements, the Fed can vary the amount of excess reserves in the banking system. In our example, it was the purchase of a $1,000 U.S. bond that started the ball rolling. The Fed can also increase reserves by lowering the discount rate enough to stimulate bank borrowing from the Fed (although the Fed uses changes in the discount rate more to signal its policy goals than to alter the money supply). And, by reducing the required reserve ratio, the Fed not only instantly creates excess reserves in the banking system but also increases the money multiplier. In practice, the Fed rarely changes the reserve requirement because of the disruptive effect of such a change on the banking system. *To control the money supply, the Fed relies primarily on open-market operations.*

Open-market operations can have a direct affect on the money supply, as when the Fed buys bonds from the public for cash. But the Fed's primary effect on the money supply is indirect, as when the Fed's bond purchase increases bank reserves, which then serve as fuel for the money multiplier. In the next chapter, we will consider the effects of the money supply on the economy.

SUMMARY

1. Banks are unlike other businesses because they can turn a borrower's IOU into money—they can create money. Banks match the different desires of savers and borrowers. Banks also evaluate loan applications and diversify portfolios of assets to reduce the risk to any one saver.
2. The money supply is narrowly defined as M1, which consists of currency held by the nonbanking public plus checkable deposits and travelers checks. Broader monetary aggregates include other kinds of deposits. M2 includes M1 plus savings deposits, small-denomination time deposits, and money market mutual funds. M3 includes M2 plus large-denomination time deposits.
3. In acquiring portfolios of assets, banks attempt to maximize profits while maintaining enough liquidity to satisfy depositors' demands for funds.
4. Any single bank can expand the money supply by the amount of its excess reserves. For the banking system as a whole, the maximum expansion of the money supply equals a multiple of excess reserves. The simple money multiplier equals the reciprocal of the reserve ratio. The money multiplier is reduced to the extent that borrowers sit on their proceeds, the public withdraws cash from the banking system, and banks allow excess reserves to remain just that.
5. The key to changes in the money supply is the Fed's impact on excess reserves in the banking system. To increase excess reserves and, hence, to increase the money supply, the Fed can buy U.S. government bonds, reduce the discount rate, or lower the reserve requirement. To reduce excess reserves and, hence, to reduce the money supply, the Fed can sell U.S. government bonds, increase the discount rate, or increase the reserve requirement. By far the most important monetary tool for the Fed is open-market operations—buying or selling U.S. bonds.

QUESTIONS FOR REVIEW

1. *(Banks as Financial Intermediaries)* In acting as financial intermediaries, what needs and desires of savers and borrowers must banks consider?
2. *(Case**Study**: Tracking the Supernote)* Why did the U.S. government consider it important to redesign the $100 bill in order to combat the effects of the "supernote"?
3. *(Monetary Aggregates)* Determine whether each of the following is included in any of the M1, M2, or M3 measures of the money supply:
   a. Currency held by the nonbanking public
   b. Available credit on credit cards held by the nonbanking public
   c. Savings deposits

d. Large-denomination time deposits
e. Money market mutual fund accounts

4. *(Monetary Aggregates)* Suppose that $1,000 is moved from a savings account at a commercial bank to a checking account at the same bank. Which of the following statements are true and which are false?
   a. The amount of currency in circulation will fall.
   b. M1 will increase.
   c. M2 will increase.

5. *(Bank Deposits)* Explain the differences among checkable deposits, demand deposits, savings deposits, and time deposits. Explain whether each of these deposits represents a bank asset or a bank liability.

6. *(Reserve Accounts)* Explain why a reduction in the required reserve ratio cannot, at least initially, increase total reserves in the banking system. Is the same true of lowering the discount rate? What would happen if the Fed bought U.S. bonds from, or sold them to, the banking system?

7. *(Liquidity Versus Profitability)* Why must a bank manager strike a balance between liquidity and profitability on the bank's balance sheet?

8. *(Creating Money)* Often it is claimed that banks create money by making loans. How can commercial banks create money? Is the government the only institution that can legally create money?

9. *(Fed Tools of Monetary Control)* What three tools can the Fed can use to change the money supply? Which tool is used most frequently? What are two limitations on the money expansion process?

10. *(Discount Rate)* What is the difference between the federal funds rate and the discount rate? What is the ultimate impact on the money supply of an increase in the discount rate?

11. *(Federal Funds Market)* What is the federal funds market? How does it help banks strike a balance between liquidity and profitability?

12. *(The Fed Is a Money Machine)* Why is the Fed both literally and figuratively a money machine?

13. (**CaseStudy:** *Banking on the Net*) What impact is increased Internet banking likely to have on money's function as a medium of exchange?

PROBLEMS AND EXERCISES

14. *(Monetary Aggregates)* Calculate M1, M2, and M3 using the following information:

Large-denomination time deposits	$304 billion
Currency and coin held by non-banking public	$438 billion
Checkable deposits	$509 billion
Small-denomination time deposits	$198 billion
Travelers checks	$18 billion
Savings deposits	$326 billion
Money market mutual fund accounts	$637 billion

15. *(Money Creation)* Show how each of the following *initially* affects bank assets, liabilities, and reserves. Do *not* include the results of bank behavior resulting from the Fed's action. Assume a required reserve ratio of 0.05.
    a. The Fed purchases $10 million worth of U.S. government bonds from a bank.
    b. The Fed loans $5 million to a bank.
    c. The Fed raises the required reserve ratio to 0.10.

16. *(Money Creation)* Show how each of the following would initially affect a bank's assets and liabilities.
    a. Someone makes a $10,000 deposit.
    b. A bank makes a loan of $1,000 by establishing a checking account for $1,000.
    c. The loan described in part (b) is spent.
    d. A bank must write off a loan because the borrower defaults.

17. *(Reserve Accounts)* Suppose that a bank's customer deposits $4,000 in her checking account. The required reserve ratio is 0.25. What are the required reserves on this new deposit? What is the largest loan that the bank can make on the basis of the new deposit? If the bank chooses to hold reserves of $3,000 on the new deposit, what are the excess reserves on the deposit?

18. *(Money Multiplier)* Suppose that the Federal Reserve lowers the required reserve ratio from 0.10 to 0.05. How does this affect the simple money multiplier, assuming that excess reserves are held to zero and there are no currency leakages? What are the money multipliers for required reserve ratios of 0.15 and 0.20?

19. *(Money Creation)* Suppose Bank A, which faces a reserve requirement of 10 percent, receives a $1,000 deposit from a customer.

a. Assuming that it wishes to hold no excess reserves, determine how much the bank should lend. Show your answer on Bank A's balance sheet.
b. Assuming that the loan shown in Bank A's balance sheet is redeposited in Bank B, show the changes in Bank B's balance sheet if it lends out the maximum possible.
c. Repeat this process for three additional banks: C, D, and E.
d. Using the simple money multiplier, calculate the total change in the money supply resulting from the $1,000 initial deposit.
e. Assume Banks A, B, C, D, and E each wish to hold 5 percent excess reserves. How would holding this level of excess reserves affect the total change in the money supply?

20. *(Monetary Control)* Suppose the money supply is currently $500 billion and the Fed wishes to increase it by $100 billion.
    a. Given a required reserve ratio of 0.25, what should it do?
    b. If it decided to change the money supply by changing the required reserve ratio, what change should it make?

EXPERIENTIAL EXERCISES

21. *(Fed Tools of Monetary Control)* Review the Fed's on-line brochure on the Federal Open Market Committee at http://www.bog.frb.fed.us/pubs/frseries/frseri2.htm, especially the sections entitled "The Decision-making Process" and "Reports." What information does the FOMC consider as it plans open-market operations? Look at the minutes of the most recent meeting to determine what kinds of open-market operations are going on now.

22. *(CaseStudy: Banking on the Net)* The *Journal of Internet Banking and Commerce* at http://www.arraydev.com/commerce/jibc/current.htm is a Web-based magazine devoted to Internet banking and related issues. Take a look at the current edition and see if you can determine what effect electronic banking is having on the Fed's ability to control the U.S. money supply. Also see what you can learn about the status of Internet banking outside the United States.

23. *(Wall Street Journal)* If you have access to the Interactive Edition of the *Wall Street Journal,* you can use the Briefing Books feature to obtain data on over 10,000 public companies. Use this feature to locate the Briefing Book on a large commercial bank in your area. Look at some of its press releases to determine how this bank has been influenced by Federal Reserve regulations and monetary policy operations.

CHAPTER

15 Monetary Theory And Policy

Why do people maintain checking accounts and have cash in their pockets, purses, wallets, desk drawers, coffee cans—wherever? In other words, why do people hold money? More fundamentally, what impact does money have on the economy? How does the supply of money in the economy affect your chances of finding a job, your ability to finance a new car, the interest rate you pay on credit cards, the ease of securing a student loan, and the interest rate on that loan? What have economic theory and the historical record taught us about the relationship between the quantity of money in the economy and other macroeconomic variables? Answers to these and related questions are addressed in this chapter, which examines monetary theory and policy.

'isit the McEachern eractive Study Center for this chapter at ://mcisc.swcollege.com

The supply of money in the economy affects you in a variety of ways, but to understand those effects we must dig a little deeper. Thus far we have focused on how the banking system creates money. But a more fundamental question is how the money supply affects the economy. The Fed's role in supplying money to the economy is called *monetary policy.* The study of the effect of money on the economy is called *monetary theory.* A central concern of monetary theory is the effect of the money supply on the economy's price level and on the level of output.

Until now, we have not emphasized differences among competing theories of how the economy works. Traditionally, economists have maintained that there are two channels through which a change in the money supply may affect aggregate demand: an indirect channel, working through changes in the interest rate, and a direct channel, where changes in the supply of money directly affect how much people want to spend. There was a time when the major debate among macroeconomists involved the relative importance of each channel. One group of economists believed the indirect channel was more important and the other believed the direct channel was more important. Most economists now find some validity with each channel.

In this chapter, we consider the theory behind each channel. Note that although these two theories are different, they are not mutually exclusive. Each traces a different path between changes in the money supply and changes in aggregate demand, and both paths could operate at the same time. Topics discussed in this chapter include:

- Demand and supply of money
- Indirect and direct channels to aggregate demand
- Equation of exchange
- Velocity of money
- Monetary targets

MONEY AND THE ECONOMY: THE INDIRECT CHANNEL

Let's begin by reviewing the important distinction between the *stock of money* and *the flow of income.* How much money do you have with you right now? That amount is a *stock.* Income, in contrast, is a *flow,* indicating how much money you earn per period of time. Income has no meaning unless the time period is specified. You would not know whether to be impressed that a friend earned $100 unless you knew whether this was earnings per week, per day, or per hour.

Demand for money The relationship between how much money people want to hold and the interest rate

The **demand for money** is a relationship between how much money people want to hold and the interest rate. Keep in mind that the quantity of money held is a stock measure. It may seem odd at first to be talking about the demand for money. You might think people would demand all the money they could get their hands on. But remember that money, the stock, is not the same as income, the flow. People express their demand for income by selling their labor and other resources. People express their demand for money by holding some of their wealth as money rather than holding other assets that would earn more interest.

But we are getting ahead of ourselves. The question we want to ask initially is why people demand money. Why do people maintain checking accounts and have cash in their pockets, purses, wallets, desk drawers, coffee cans—wherever? The most obvious reason people demand money is that it is a convenient medium of exchange. *People demand money to carry out market transactions.*

The Demand for Money

Because barter represents an insignificant portion of exchange in the modern industrial economy, households, firms, governments, and foreigners need money to conduct their daily transactions. Consumers need money to buy products, and firms need money to buy resources. *Money allows people to carry out their economic transactions more easily.* When credit cards are involved, the payment of money is delayed briefly, but all accounts must eventually be settled with money.

The greater the value of transactions to be financed in a given period, the greater the demand for money. So the more active the economy is—that is, the greater the volume of exchange as reflected by the level of real output—the greater the demand for money. Also, the higher the price level, the greater the demand for money. The more things cost on average, the more money is required to purchase them.

Your demand for money supports expenditures you expect in the course of your normal economic affairs plus various unexpected expenditures. If you plan to buy lunch tomorrow, you will carry enough money to pay for it. But you also may want to be able to pay for other possible contingencies. For example, you could have car trouble or you could come across an unexpected sale on a favorite item. You may have a little extra money with you right now for who knows what. Even *you* don't know.

The demand for money is rooted in money's role as a medium of exchange. But as we have seen, money is more than a medium of exchange; it is also a store of value. Because a household's income and expenditures are not perfectly matched each period, purchasing power is often saved to finance future expenditures. People save for a new home, for college, for retirement. The view of money that emphasizes the indirect channel focuses on two ways in which people can store their purchasing power: (1) in the form of money and (2) in the form of other financial assets, such as corporate and government securities. When people purchase bonds and other financial assets, they are lending their money and are paid interest for doing so.

The demand for any asset is based on the flow of services it provides. The big advantage of money as a store of value is its liquidity: Money can immediately be exchanged for whatever is for sale. In contrast, other financial assets, such as corporate or government bonds, must first be *liquidated*, or exchanged for money, which can then be used to buy goods and services. Money, however, has one major disadvantage when compared to other types of financial assets. Money in the form of currency and travelers checks earns no interest, and the interest rate earned on checkable deposits is typically below that earned on other financial assets. So those who hold their wealth in the form of money forgo some interest that they could earn by holding some other financial asset. For example, suppose a corporation could earn 3 percent more by holding financial assets other than money. The opportunity cost of holding \$10 million as money rather than as some other financial asset would amount to \$300,000 per year. *The interest forgone is the opportunity cost of holding money.*

Money Demand and Interest Rates

When the market interest rate is low, other things constant, the cost of holding money—the cost of maintaining liquidity—is low, so people hold a larger fraction of their wealth in the form of money. When the market interest rate is

EXHIBIT 1

Demand for Money

The demand for money curve, D_m, slopes downward. As the interest rate falls, so does the opportunity cost of holding money; the quantity of money demanded increases.

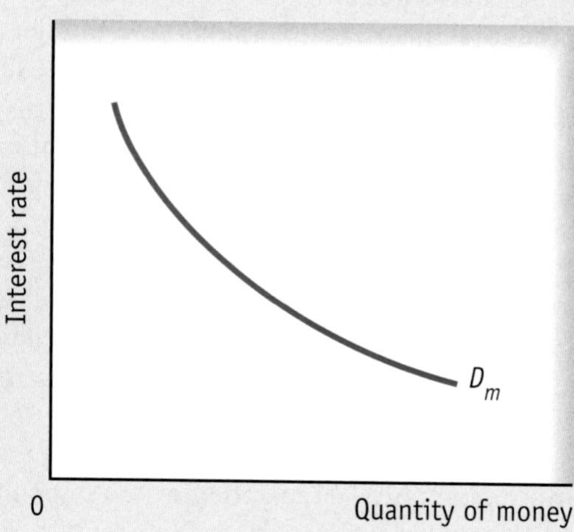

high, the cost of holding money is high, so people hold less of their wealth in money and more of their wealth in other financial assets that pay more interest. Thus, *other things constant, the quantity of money demanded varies inversely with the market interest rate.*

The money demand curve, D_m, in Exhibit 1 shows the quantity of money people in the economy demand at alternative interest rates, other things constant. Both the quantity of money and the interest rate are in nominal terms. *The money demand curve slopes downward because the lower the interest rate, the lower the opportunity cost of holding money.* Movements along the curve reflect the effects of changes in the interest rate on the quantity of money demanded, other things constant. The quantity of money demanded is inversely related to the price of holding money, which is the interest rate. *Held constant along the curve are the price level and real GDP. If either increases, the demand for money increases, as reflected by a shift to the right in the entire money demand curve.*

Supply of Money and the Equilibrium Interest Rate

The supply of money—the stock of money available in the economy at a particular time—is determined primarily by the Fed through its control over currency and over excess reserves in the banking system. The supply of money, S_m, is depicted as a vertical line, as in Exhibit 2. *A vertical supply curve implies that the quantity of money supplied is independent of the interest rate.*

The intersection of the supply of money, S_m, and the demand for money, D_m, determines the equilibrium interest rate, *i*—the interest rate that equates the quantity of money supplied in the economy with the quantity of money demanded. At interest rates above the equilibrium level, the opportunity cost of holding money is higher, so the quantity of money people want to hold is less than the quantity supplied. At interest rates below the equilibrium level, the opportunity cost of holding money is lower, so the quantity of money people want to hold is greater than the quantity supplied.

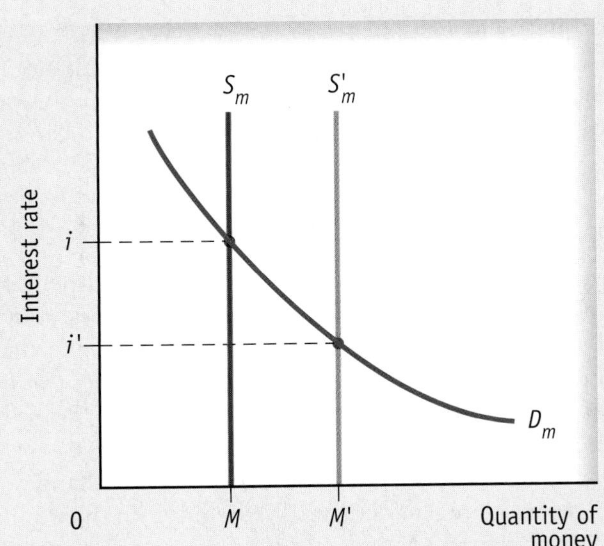

EXHIBIT 2

Effect of an Increase in the Money Supply

Since the supply of money is determined by the Federal Reserve, it can be represented by a vertical line. The intersection of the supply of money, S_m, and the demand for money, D_m, determines the equilibrium interest rate, i. Following an increase in the money supply to S'_m, the quantity of money supplied exceeds the quantity demanded at the original interest rate, i. People who are holding more money than they would like attempt to exchange money for bonds or other financial assets. In doing so, they drive the interest rate down to i', where quantity demanded equals the new quantity supplied.

If the Fed increases the money supply, the money supply curve shifts to the right, as shown by the movement from S_m to S'_m in Exhibit 2. The quantity supplied now exceeds the quantity demanded at the original interest rate, i. Because of the increased supply of money, there is now more money in the hands of the public, so people are *able* to hold a greater quantity of money. But at interest rate i they are *unwilling* to hold that much. Since people are now holding more of their wealth as money than they would like, they exchange some money for other financial assets, such as bonds.

As people try to exchange money for bonds, the market rate of interest falls. As the demand for bonds increases, bond issuers can pay less interest yet still attract enough buyers. The interest rate falls until the quantity demanded just equals the quantity supplied. With the decline in the interest rate to i' in Exhibit 2, the opportunity cost of holding money falls enough so the public is willing to hold the now-larger stock of money. *For a given demand for money curve, increases in the supply of money drive down the market interest rate, and decreases in the supply of money drive up the market interest rate.*

Now that you have some idea how money demand and supply determine the market interest rate, you are ready to see how money fits into the model of the macroeconomy developed thus far. Specifically, let's see how changes in the supply of money affect aggregate demand and equilibrium output.

*Net*Bookmark

Bloomberg.com's financial news network provides quick links to the latest key interest rates and currency exchange rates at its markets Web site at http://www.bloomberg.com/markets/index.html. Bloomberg also offers numerous other resources over the Web, including BloombergTV financial news.

MONEY AND AGGREGATE DEMAND

Monetary policy influences the market interest rate, which, in turn, affects the level of planned investment, a component of aggregate demand. This is the indirect channel of money, where money affects the economy through changes in the interest rate. Let's work through the chain of causation in a specific economic setting.

Interest Rates and Planned Investment

Suppose the Federal Reserve believes that the economy is operating well below its potential level of output and decides to increase the money supply to stimulate output and employment. Recall from the previous chapter that the Fed can expand the money supply by (1) purchasing U.S. government bonds, (2) lowering the discount rate, the rate at which banks can borrow from the Fed, or (3) lowering the reserve requirement.

The four panels of Exhibit 3 trace the links between changes in the money supply and changes in aggregate demand. We begin with the equilibrium interest rate i, which is determined in panel (a) by the intersection of the demand for money, D_m, with the supply of money, S_m. This intersection is identified by point a. Suppose the Fed purchases U.S. government bonds and thereby increases the money supply, as shown in panel (a) by the shift to the right in the money supply curve from S_m to S'_m. After the increase in the supply of money, people are holding more of their wealth in money than they would prefer at the initial interest rate i, so they try to exchange one form of wealth, money, for other financial assets. This greater willingness to lend has no direct effect on aggregate demand, but it does reduce the market interest rate.

A decline in the interest rate to i', other things constant, reduces the opportunity cost of financing new plants and equipment, thereby making new business investment more profitable. Likewise, a lower interest rate reduces the cost of mortgages on new housing, so housing investment increases. Thus the decline in the rate of interest increases the quantity of investment demanded. Panel (b) shows the demand for investment, D_I, first introduced in Chapter 9. When the interest rate falls from i to i', investment spending increases from I to I'.

The aggregate expenditure line in panel (c) shifts upward by the increase in planned investment, from AE to AE'. The spending multiplier magnifies this increase in investment, leading to a greater increase in the quantity of real GDP demanded at each price level. The quantity demanded increases from Y to Y', as reflected in panel (c) by the intersection of the new aggregate expenditure function with the 45-degree line. This same increase is also reflected in panel (d), given price level P, by the horizontal shift in the aggregate demand curve from AD to AD'.

The sequence of events can be summarized as follows:

$$M\uparrow \rightarrow i\downarrow \rightarrow I\uparrow \rightarrow AE\uparrow \rightarrow AD\uparrow$$

An increase in the money supply, M, reduces the interest rate, i. The lower interest rate stimulates investment spending, I, which shifts up the aggregate expenditure line. This increase in the quantity of real GDP demanded at a particular price level is reflected by a shift to the right in the aggregate demand curve,

EXHIBIT 3

Effects of an Increase in the Money Supply on Interest Rates, Investment, Aggregate Expenditure, and Aggregate Demand

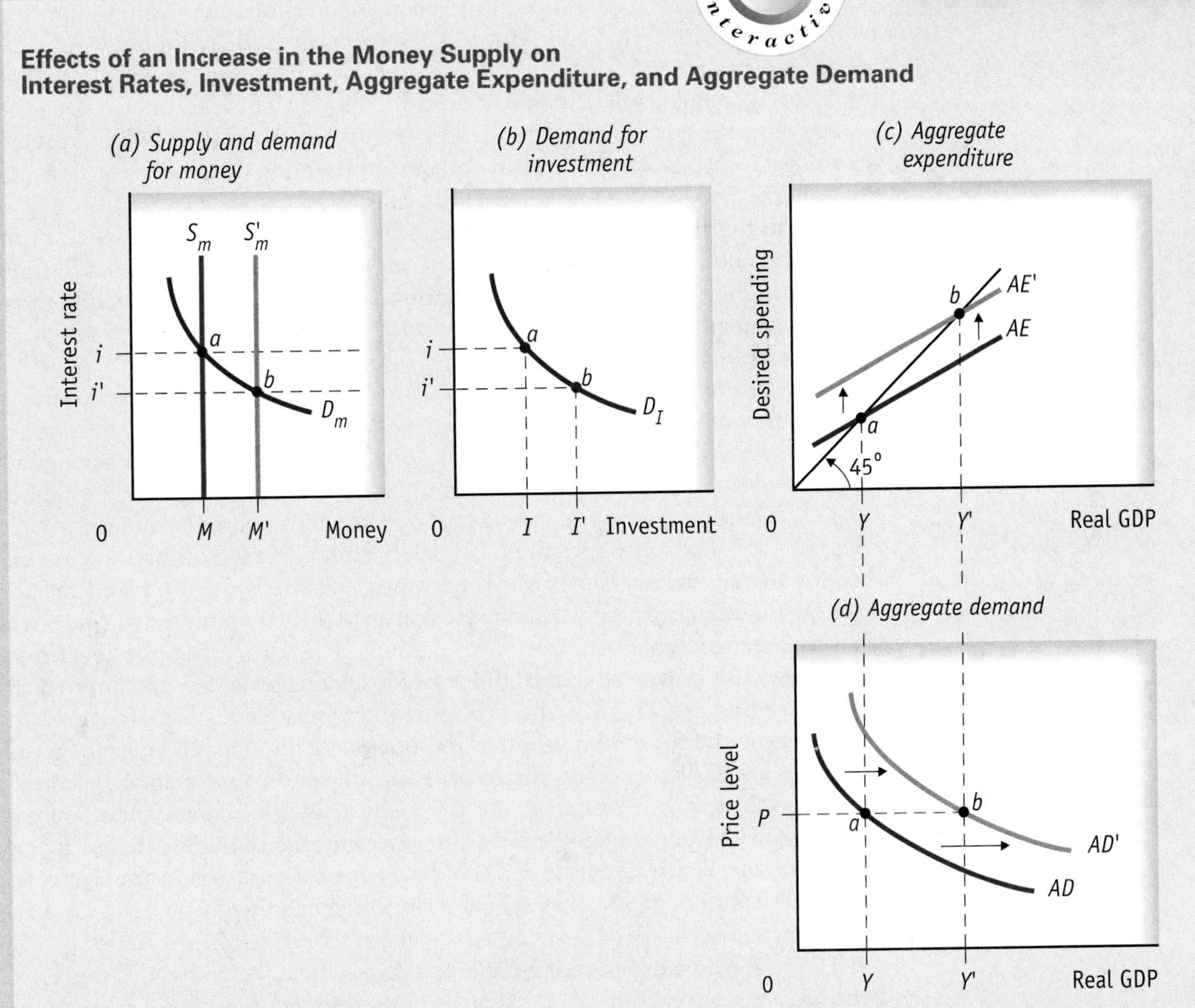

In panel (a), an increase in the money supply drives the interest rate down to *i'*. With the cost of borrowing now lower, the level of investment spending increases from *I* to *I'*, as shown in panel (b). More investment spending drives aggregate expenditure up from *AE* to *AE'*, as shown in panel (c). The increased expenditure sets off the multiplier process, so the quantity of aggregate output demanded increases from *Y* to *Y'*. The increase is shown by the shift to the right in the aggregate demand curve in panel (d).

from *AD* to *AD'*.[1] The entire sequence is also traced out in each panel by the movement from points *a* to *b*.

1 The graphs are actually more complicated than those presented here. Since the demand for money depends on the level of real GDP, an increase in real GDP would shift the money demand curve to the right in panel (a). For simplicity, we have not shown a shift in the money demand curve. If we had shifted the money demand curve, the equilibrium interest rate would still have fallen, but not by as much, so investment and aggregate demand would not have increased by as much.

Let's now consider the effect of a Fed-orchestrated reduction in interest rates. In Exhibit 3 such a policy can be traced by moving from point *b* to point *a* in each panel, but we will dispense with a blow-by-blow discussion of the graphs. Suppose the Federal Reserve decides to reduce the money supply to cool down an overheated economy. A decrease in the money supply would create an excess demand for money at the initial interest rate, so people will attempt to exchange other financial assets for money. These efforts to get more money raise the market interest rate, or the opportunity cost of holding money. The interest rate increases until the quantity of money demanded declines just enough to equal the now-lower quantity of money supplied.

At the higher interest rate, businesses find it more costly to finance plants and equipment, and households find it more costly to finance new homes. Hence a higher rate of interest reduces investment. The resulting decline in investment is magnified by the spending multiplier, leading to a greater decline in aggregate demand.

As long as the interest rate is sensitive to changes in the money supply, and as long as the quantity of investment is sensitive to changes in the interest rate, changes in the supply of money affect planned investment. The extent to which a given change in planned investment affects aggregate demand depends on the size of the spending multiplier.

Let's examine a recent example of a Fed-orchestrated reduction in interest rates. At 2:15 P.M. on September 29, 1998, immediately following a regular meeting of the Federal Open Market Committee, the Fed announced that "to cushion the effects on prospective growth in the United States of increasing weakness in foreign economies," it planned to increase the money supply enough to push down the federal funds rate from a target of 5.5 percent to a target of 5.25 percent. This was the Fed's first interest rate cut since January 1996. As you know, the federal funds rate is the one that banks charge one another for overnight loans. The next day, major banks around the country announced they would lower their prime interest rate, the interest rate they charge their best customers, by 0.25 percentage points. Thus, by announcing a cut in the federal funds rate, the Fed was able to reduce the prime interest rate in the economy. We will learn more about interest rate changes later in the chapter.

Adding Aggregate Supply

Even after tracing the effect of a change in the money supply on aggregate demand, we still have only half the story. To determine the effects of monetary policy on the equilibrium level of real GDP in the economy, we need the supply side. An aggregate supply curve can help show how a given shift in the aggregate demand curve affects real GDP and the price level. In the short run, the aggregate supply curve slopes upward, so the quantity supplied will expand only if the price level increases. *For a given shift in the aggregate demand curve, the steeper the short-run aggregate supply curve, the smaller the increase in real GDP and the larger the increase in the price level.*

Assume the economy is producing at point *a* in Exhibit 4, where the aggregate demand curve, *AD*, intersects the short-run aggregate supply curve, AS_{130}, yielding a short-run equilibrium output of $7.8 trillion and a price level of 125. As you can see, the actual price level of 125 is below the expected price level of 130, so the short-run equilibrium output of $7.8 trillion is below the economy's potential of $8.0 trillion, yielding a contractionary gap of $0.2 trillion.

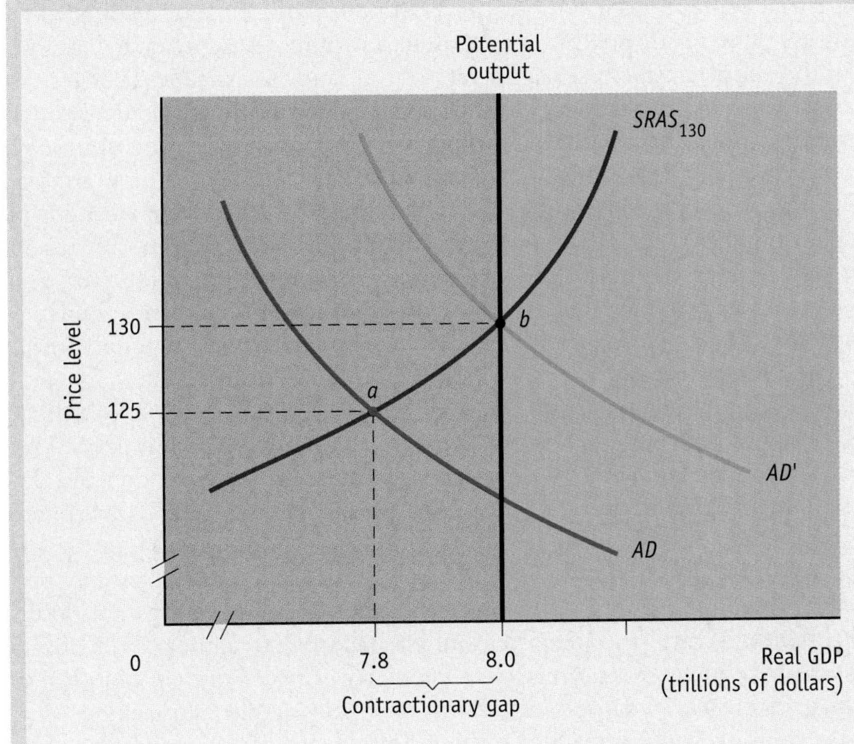

EXHIBIT 4

Expansionary Monetary Policy to Correct a Contractionary Gap

At point *a*, the economy is producing below potential. There is a contractionary gap equal to $0.2 trillion. If the Federal Reserve increases the money supply, the aggregate demand curve shifts to *AD*'. Equilibrium will be reestablished at point *b*, with price level 130 and output at the potential level of $8.0 trillion.

The Fed can wait to see whether natural market forces close the gap as the short-run aggregate supply curve shifts to the right, or it can intervene and attempt to close the gap with an expansionary monetary policy. For example, in 1992 and 1993 the Fed aggressively increased the money supply in order to lower interest rates and stimulate aggregate demand. If the Fed increases the money supply by exactly the appropriate amount, this increases the aggregate demand curve enough to achieve a new equilibrium at point *b*, where the economy is producing its potential output. Given all the connections in the chain of causality between changes in the money supply and changes in equilibrium output, however, it would actually be quite remarkable for the Fed to execute monetary policy so precisely—but more on that later.

To review: *The indirect effect of an increase in the money supply is to reduce the market interest rate, resulting in an increase in planned investment and a consequent increase in aggregate demand. As long as the short-run aggregate supply curve slopes upward, the short-run effect of an increase in the money supply is an increase in both real output and the price level.*

Fiscal Policy with Money

Now that we have considered the indirect effect that money has on aggregate demand and equilibrium output, we can take another look at fiscal policy. Suppose there is an increase in government purchases, other things constant. In Chapter 12, we found that an increase in government purchases increases aggregate demand and, in the short run, leads to both a greater output and a higher price level. Once money enters the picture, however, we must recognize that an increase in either real output or the price level increases the demand for money.

Thus an increase in government purchases increases aggregate demand, which in the short run increases aggregate output and the price level. Increases in aggregate output and the price level cause increases in money demand since more money is needed for additional transactions. For a given supply of money, an increase in money demand leads to a higher interest rate. And a higher interest rate *reduces* investment spending. We therefore say that the fiscal stimulus of government purchases *crowds out* some investment. This reduction in investment will, to some extent, dampen the expansionary effects of fiscal policy on real output. Hence *the inclusion of money in the fiscal framework introduces yet another reason why the simple spending multiplier overstates the increase in real output arising from any given fiscal stimulus.*

Likewise any fiscal policy designed to reduce aggregate demand will be tempered by monetary effects. Suppose that, in an attempt to cool inflation, income taxes are increased, which reduces consumption. As aggregate demand declines, equilibrium output and the price level fall in the short run. With a lower level of output and a lower price level, less money is needed to carry out transactions, so the demand for money falls. Again, with the supply of money unchanged, a drop in the demand for money leads to a lower interest rate. This drop in the interest rate stimulates investment spending, to some extent offsetting the effects of lower taxes. Thus, *given the supply of money, the impact of changes in the demand for money on interest rates reduces the effectiveness of fiscal policy.*

When we look at the impact of money on the economy through the indirect channel, we see that money influences aggregate demand and equilibrium output through its effect on the interest rate. Another framework focuses more directly on the effects of changes in the money supply on aggregate demand. We next examine this direct channel.

MONEY AND THE ECONOMY: THE DIRECT CHANNEL

The indirect channel assumes that the only alternative to holding money as a store of value is holding other *financial* assets. In this view, an increased supply of money makes people want to exchange money for other financial assets, which lowers the interest rate and stimulates investment. Thus changes in the money supply affect aggregate demand through changes in the interest rate.

Another view of the effect of money sees a more direct channel for money in aggregate spending. In the more direct channel, money is just one asset among many that can serve as a store of value. In addition to other financial assets, people hold *real* assets, such as real estate and automobiles. An increase in the money supply means that, at the initial interest rate, the quantity of money supplied exceeds the quantity demanded. People are therefore holding more of their wealth in the form of money than they would like. As they attempt to reduce their money holdings, people increase their demand for all kinds of assets, including homes and other durable goods. So, in the direct channel, an increase in the supply of money increases the demand for both financial assets and real assets. This increased demand for real assets increases aggregate demand directly. The direct channel relies on a framework called the equation of exchange, which we examine next.

The Equation of Exchange

Every transaction in the economy involves a two-way swap: The seller surrenders goods and services for money, and the buyer surrenders money equal in value to the agreed-upon price. One way of expressing this relationship among key variables in the economy is the **equation of exchange,** first developed by classical economists. Although this equation can be arranged in different ways depending on the variables to be emphasized, the basic version is

Equation of exchange The quantity of money, *M*, multiplied by its velocity, *V*, equals nominal GDP, which is the product of the price level, *P*, and real GDP, *Y*.

$$M \times V = P \times Y$$

where M is the quantity of money in the economy; V is the velocity of money, or the average number of times per year each dollar is used to purchase goods and services; P is the price level; and Y is real national output, or real GDP. The equation of exchange says that the quantity of money in circulation, M, multiplied by the number of times that money turns over (changes hands), V, equals the average price level of products sold, P, times real output, Y. The price level, P, times real output, Y, equals the economy's nominal income and output, or nominal GDP.

Imagine a simple economy in which total sales during the year consist of 1,000 bags of popcorn priced at $1 each and 1,000 six-packs of Pepsi priced at $3 each. The total output, Y, equals 2,000 units, and the average price level, P, is $2 per unit. The nominal value of output, $P \times Y$, equals $\$2 \times 2{,}000$, or $4,000, which also equals the income received by resource suppliers. Suppose the total money supply in this economy is $500. How often is each dollar used on average to pay for final goods and services during the year? In other words, what is the **velocity of money?** We can derive the velocity by rearranging the equation of exchange to yield

Velocity of money The average number of times per year a dollar is used to purchase final goods and services

$$V = \frac{P \times Y}{M} = \frac{\$4{,}000}{\$500} = 8$$

Given the value of total output and the money supply, the average dollar must have been spent eight times to finance final goods and services. There is no other way these market transactions could occur. The specific value of velocity is implied by the values of the other variables. Incidentally, velocity measures spending on only final goods and services—not on intermediate products, secondhand goods, or financial assets, even though such spending also takes place in the economy.

Classical economists developed the equation of exchange as a way of explaining the economy's price level. The equation says that total spending ($M \times V$) is always equal to total receipts ($P \times Y$), as was the case in our circular flow analysis. As described thus far, however, the equation of exchange is simply an *identity*—a relationship expressed in such a way that it is true by definition. Another example of an identity would be a relationship equating miles per gallon to the distance driven divided by the gasoline required.

The Quantity Theory of Money

Those who point to the direct channel of money on aggregate demand, a group called *monetarists,* claim that velocity is relatively stable, at least in the short term. To the extent that velocity varies over time, monetarists maintain that it varies in a predictable manner unrelated to changes in the money supply. By arguing that velocity is predictable, monetarists transform the equation of exchange

Quantity theory of money If the velocity of money is stable or at least predictable, then changes in the money supply have predictable effects on nominal GDP.

from an identity into a theory—the quantity theory of money. The **quantity theory of money** states that if the velocity of money is stable or at least predictable, then the equation of exchange can be used to predict the effects of changes in the money supply on *nominal* GDP, $P \times Y$. For example, if M is increased by 10 percent and if V remains constant, then $P \times Y$, which measures nominal GDP, must also increase by 10 percent.

Thus an increase in the money supply results in more spending, and that increase in spending results in a higher nominal GDP. How is this increase in $P \times Y$ divided between changes in the price level and changes in real GDP? The answer does not lie in the quantity theory, for that theory is stated only in terms of nominal GDP. The answer lies in the shape of the aggregate supply curve. In the short run, the aggregate supply curve slopes upward, as was illustrated in Exhibit 4, so a shift to the right in the aggregate demand curve will increase both real output and the price level. If there is much unemployment and much idle production capacity, short-run changes in the price level may be relatively small. If the economy is already exceeding potential output, short-run changes in the price level will be relatively large. So, *in the short run, changes in nominal GDP are divided between changes in real GDP and changes in the price level.*

In the long run, the aggregate supply curve is vertical at the economy's potential level of output. If the economy is already operating at its potential output, then a rightward shift of the aggregate demand curve will in the long run increase only the price level, leaving output unchanged at potential GDP. Note that the economy's potential output level is not affected by changes in the money supply. Thus, *in the long run, increases in the money supply result only in higher prices.*

What is the long-run relationship between increases in the money supply and inflation? Since the Federal Reserve System was established in 1914, the United States has suffered three major episodes of high inflation, and each was preceded and accompanied by a corresponding increase in the rate of growth in the money supply. These inflation episodes occurred from 1914 to 1920, 1939 to 1948, and 1967 to 1980. The following case study examines evidence linking growth in the money supply with inflation around the world.

CaseStudy

Other Times, Other Places

The latest economic statistics and reports on the Argentine economy are available in English from the Ministry of Economics at http://www.mecon.ar/cabinet/default1.htm.

Check out the latest inflation trends in Israel at "Economic Trends in Israel" at

The Money Supply and Inflation

If we look around the world, what's the link between inflation and changes in the money supply? According to the quantity theory, there is a direct relation between the percentage change in the money supply and the percentage change in the price level. Panel (a) in Exhibit 5 illustrates the relationship between the average annual growth rate in M2 from 1980 to 1990 and the average annual inflation rate from 1980 to 1990 for the 85 countries for which complete data are available. As you can see, the points fall rather neatly along the trend line, showing a

EXHIBIT 5

Annual Inflation and Money Growth in 85 Countries: 1980–1990

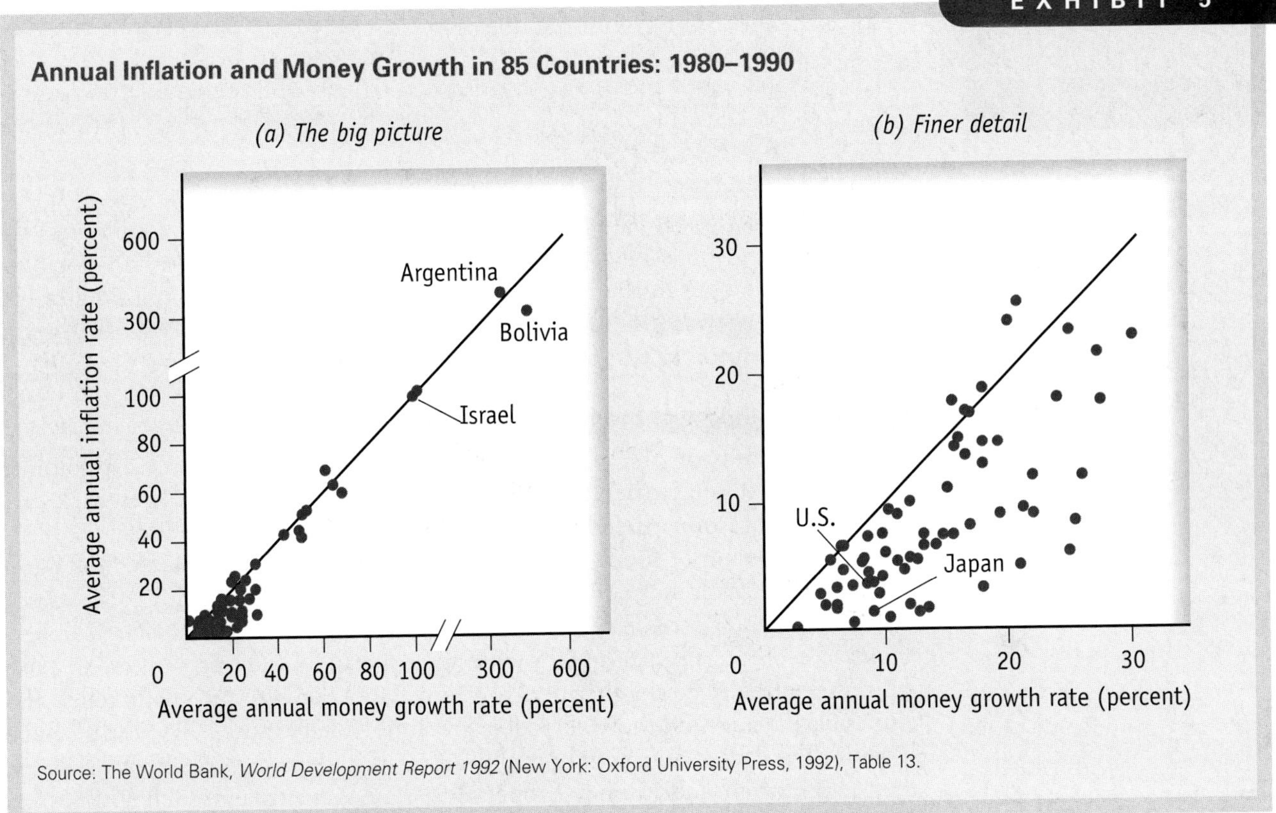

Source: The World Bank, *World Development Report 1992* (New York: Oxford University Press, 1992), Table 13.

positive relation between money growth and inflation. Since most countries are bunched below an inflation rate of 20 percent, these points are broken out in finer detail in panel (b). Although panel (a) shows a sharper link between money growth and inflation than does panel (b), in both panels countries with higher rates of money growth tend to experience higher rates of inflation.

In panel (a), Argentina, Bolivia, and Israel—three countries with annual inflation averaging more than 100 percent—also had an annual growth in the money supply exceeding 100 percent. Hyperinflation is largely a 20th-century phenomenon, and in every case it was accompanied by extremely rapid growth in the supply of paper money. For example, Argentina, which had the highest average annual inflation rate over the 10-year period in the sample, at 395 percent, also had the highest average annual rate of growth in the money supply, at 369 percent.

How do hyperinflations end? Monetary authorities must convince the public they are committed to halting the rapid growth in the money supply. The most famous hyperinflation was in Germany between August of 1922 and November of 1923, when inflation averaged 322 percent *per month*. Inflation was halted when the German government created an independent central bank that issued a new currency convertible on demand into gold. Argentina, Bolivia, and Israel all managed to tame inflation during the 1990s; for each country, the inflation rate in 1998 was under 5 percent per year. Incidentally, households in all

http://www.bank.co.il/trends/indexEng.html. What economic factors are cited to explain the current inflation trend? What are the expectations for future inflation?

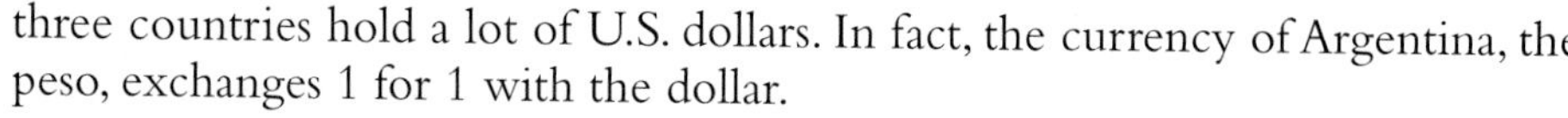

three countries hold a lot of U.S. dollars. In fact, the currency of Argentina, the peso, exchanges 1 for 1 with the dollar.

Sources: Michael Salemi, "Hyperinflation," *The Fortune Encyclopedia of Economics*, D. R. Henderson, ed. (New York: Warner Books, 1993): 208–211; Central Intelligence Agency, *World Factbook* (Washington, D.C.: Brassey's, 1995); *World Development Report 1997*, World Bank (Oxford: Oxford University Press, 1997); and "Emerging Market Indicators," *Economist* (26 September 1998): 108.

To review: *What turns the equation of exchange from an identity into a theory is the monetarist assertion that velocity is relatively stable, or at least predictable.* If velocity is predictable, changes in the money supply affect nominal GDP in a predictable way. Velocity is therefore a key component of the quantity theory of money. Let's consider some factors that might influence velocity.

What Determines the Velocity of Money?

Velocity depends on the customs and conventions of commerce. In colonial times, money might be tied up in transit for days as a courier on horseback carried a payment from a merchant in Boston to one in Baltimore. Today the electronic transmission of funds takes only seconds, so the same stock of money can move around much more quickly to finance many more transactions. *The velocity of money has also been increased by a variety of commercial innovations that have facilitated exchange.* For example, a wider use of charge accounts and credit cards has reduced the need for shoppers to carry cash. Likewise, automatic teller machines have made cash more accessible any time. What's more, ATM cards can be used as *debit cards* at a growing number of retail outlets, so people have reduced their "walking around" money. Monetarists argue that although such changes can affect velocity, financial innovations do not occur suddenly or frequently, and their effects are predictable, so the quantity theory remains a useful model.

Another institutional factor that determines velocity is the frequency with which workers get paid. Suppose a worker earns \$26,000 per year and is paid \$1,000 every two weeks. Earnings are spent evenly during the two-week period and are gone by the end of the period. In that case a worker's average money balance during the pay period is \$500. If a worker earns the same \$26,000 per year but, instead, gets paid \$500 weekly, the average money balance during the week falls to \$250. Thus, the more often workers get paid, other things constant, the lower their average money balances, so the more active the money supply and the greater its velocity. Again, payment practices change slowly over time, and the effects of these changes on velocity are predictable.

The better money serves as a store of value, the more money people want to hold, so the lower its velocity. For example, the introduction of interest-bearing checking accounts made money a better store of value, and this financial innovation reduced velocity. When inflation increases unexpectedly, money is not as good a store of value. People become more reluctant to hold money; they try to exchange it for some asset that retains its value during inflation. This reduction in people's willingness to hold money during periods of high inflation increases the velocity of money. During hyperinflations, workers usually get paid daily, boosting velocity. Thus *velocity increases with a rise in the inflation rate, other things constant.* Money becomes a hot potato.

The usefulness of the modern quantity theory hinges on how stable and predictable the velocity of money is. Even a small unexpected change in velocity could undermine the ability of the equation of exchange to predict nominal GDP. For example, if velocity turned out to be 5 percent lower than expected, then nominal GDP would also be 5 percent lower than expected. Let's examine the stability of velocity over the years.

How Stable Is Velocity?

Exhibit 6 graphs velocity since 1915, measured both as nominal GDP divided by M1 and as nominal GDP divided by M2. Based on this exhibit, is it reasonable to conclude that the velocity of M1 is relatively stable? That depends on the time period we consider and what we mean by "relatively stable." As you can see, from 1915 to 1947 the velocity of M1 fluctuated a fair amount, but the trend was downward. From 1947 to 1979 the trend was upward, with less variability than before. In fact, between 1973 and 1979 velocity grew each year at a rate of between 3.0 and 4.3 percent. *Velocity growth appeared so stable during this six-year stretch that some economists began to talk about an economic law relating the money supply to nominal GDP.* More attention was thus accorded the direct channel of money during the latter part of the 1970s. Whereas the decade of the 1960s was the high point for supporters of the indirect channel, which worked through changes in interest rates, the period of the late 1970s was perhaps the high point for supporters of the direct channel.

EXHIBIT 6

Historical Record of Velocity

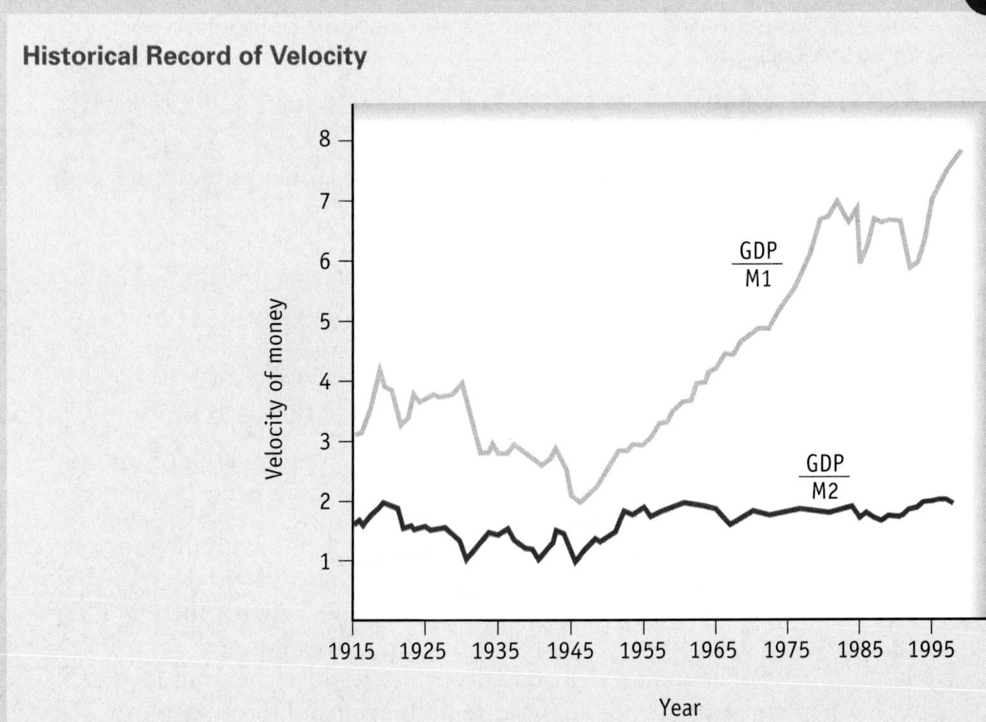

Sources: *Long-Term Economic Growth, 1860–1970* (Washington, D.C.: U.S. Government Printing Office, 1973); and *Economic Report of the President*, February 1999.

After 1979, however, the velocity of M1 became more erratic. For example, after jumping 4.2 percent in 1981, it dropped 2.5 percent during the recession year of 1982, the largest decline since 1946. That swing meant that nominal GDP was 6.7 percent lower in 1982 than it would have been had velocity continued to grow in 1982 as it had in 1981. The decline in velocity, coupled with a slower growth in the money supply, has been viewed by some economists as the cause of the deepest recession since the Great Depression.

The velocity of M1 has continued to be volatile in the 1990s. The equation of exchange has consequently become less reliable as a short-run predictor of the effects of a change in M1 on nominal GDP. There is less talk now about economic laws relating changes in the money supply to changes in nominal GDP. Some economists believe that the link between the money supply and nominal GDP has been disturbed only temporarily. Others aren't so sure.

The deregulation of the interest paid on checkable deposits is a possible source of the demise of a predictable relationship between M1 and nominal GDP. Prior to 1980, with minor exceptions, interest was not paid on checkable deposits. Since after 1980 people could earn interest on their checking accounts, they choose to hold more money in checking accounts, thus halting the growth in the velocity of M1.

Since the mid-1950s, the velocity of M2 has been more stable than the velocity of M1, as you can see in Exhibit 7. In setting objectives for monetary growth, the Fed in 1987 switched from a focus on M1 to a focus on M2. But even M2 velocity became volatile between 1991 and 1994, though it has stabilized since then. The Fed announced in 1993 that monetary aggregates, including M2, were no longer considered reliable guides for monetary policy.

MONEY SUPPLY VERSUS INTEREST RATE TARGETS

According to the indirect channel, monetary policy affects the economy largely by influencing the interest rate. Monetarists think the linkage is more direct—that changes in the money supply affect how much people want to spend. The indirect channel suggests that monetary authorities should worry about interest rates; the direct channel suggests authorities should focus on the money supply. Thus the debate focuses on whether monetary authorities should be concerned with keeping interest rates stable or with keeping the money stock stable. As we will see, the Fed lacks the tools to do both at the same time.

Contrasting Policies

To demonstrate the effects of different policies, we begin with the money market in equilibrium at point *e* in Exhibit 7. The interest rate is *i* and the money stock is *M*, values the monetary authorities find appropriate. Suppose there is an increase in the demand for money in the economy, perhaps because of an increase in nominal GDP. The money demand curve shifts to the right, from D_m to D'_m.

When confronted with an increase in the demand for money, monetary authorities can choose to do nothing, thereby allowing the interest rate to rise, or they can increase the supply of money in an attempt to keep the interest rate constant. If monetary authorities do nothing, the quantity of money in the economy will remain at M, but the interest rate will rise because the greater demand for money will increase the equilibrium from point e up to point e'. Alternatively, monetary authorities can try to keep the interest rate at its initial level by increasing the supply of money from S_m to S'_m. In terms of possible combinations of the money stock and the interest rate, monetary authorities must choose from points lying along the new money demand curve D'_m.

A growing economy usually needs a growing money supply to pay for the increase in aggregate output. If monetary authorities maintain a constant growth in the money supply, the interest rate will probably fluctuate unless the growth in the supply of money each period just happens to match the growth in the demand for money (as in the movement from e to e'' in Exhibit 7). Alternatively, monetary authorities could try to adjust the money supply each period by the amount needed to keep the interest rate stable. In this approach, changes in the money supply would have to offset any changes in the demand for money.

Interest rate fluctuations could be harmful if they created undesirable fluctuations in investment. For interest rates to remain stable during economic expansions, the money supply should grow at the same rate as the demand for money. Likewise, for interest rates to remain stable during economic contractions, the money supply should shrink at the same rate as the demand for money. Hence, for monetary authorities to maintain the interest rate at some specified level, the money supply must increase during periods of economic expansion and decrease during periods of economic contraction. But an increase in the money supply during an expansion would increase aggregate demand even more, and a decrease in the money supply during a contraction would reduce aggregate demand even more. *Such changes in the money supply would thus*

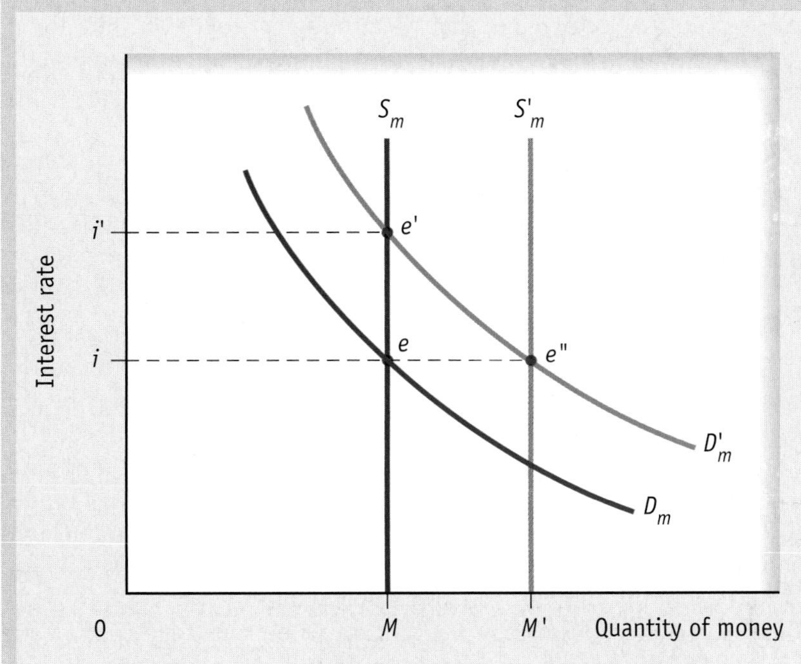

EXHIBIT 7

Targeting Interest Rates Versus the Supply of Money

An increase in the price level or in real GDP increases the demand for money from D_m to D'_m. If the Federal Reserve holds the money supply at S_m the interest rate will rise from i (at point e) to i' (at point e'). Alternatively, the Fed could hold the interest rate constant by increasing the supply of money to S'_m. The Fed may choose any point along the money demand curve, D'_m.

tend to reinforce fluctuations in economic activity, thereby adding more instability to the economy. With this in mind, let's examine monetary policy in recent years.

Targets Until 1982

Between World War II and October 1979, the Fed attempted to stabilize interest rates. Stable interest rates were viewed as a prerequisite for an attractive investment environment and, thus, for a stable economy. Milton Friedman, the Nobel prize winner and father of modern monetarism, argued that this exclusive attention to interest rates made monetary policy a major source of instability in the economy because changes in the money supply reinforced fluctuations in the economy. Monetarists said that the Fed should pay less attention to interest rates and instead should focus on a steady and predictable growth in the money supply.

The debate raged during the 1970s, and monetarists made some important converts. Amid growing concern about the rising inflation rate, the Fed, under its new chairman, Paul Volcker, announced in October 1979 that it would de-emphasize interest rates and would instead target the growth in specific monetary aggregates. Not surprisingly, the interest rate became much more volatile.

But many observers believe that a sharp reduction in money growth in the latter half of 1981 caused the recession of 1982. Inflation declined rapidly, but the unemployment rate jumped to over 10 percent. People were worried. As you might expect, the Fed was widely criticized for its monetary policy. Volcker was denounced by farmers, politicians, and businesspeople. Emotions ran high. Volcker was reportedly even given Secret Service protection. In October 1982, three years after the focus on interest rates was dropped, Volcker announced that the Fed would pay attention to both interest rates *and* money growth. In effect, the Fed returned to a policy of smoothing interest rates.

Monetarists do not acknowledge that the attempt to focus on the money supply was a failure. Rather, they argue that the Fed never really implemented a policy of steady, predictable growth in the money supply, so the three-year period should not be viewed as a test of the effectiveness of monetarism. Some monetarists even believe that the Fed espoused monetarism simply as a smoke screen for putting the brakes on inflation rates that exceeded 12 percent in 1979 and 1980. According to this argument, Congress would have objected if the Fed had announced an explicit policy of raising interest rates to cool inflation.

Targets After 1982

The Fed is always feeling its way, looking for signs about the direction of the economy. The rapid pace of financial innovations and deregulation during the 1980s made the definition and measurement of the money supply more difficult. What's more, as we have seen, the relationship between M1 and economic activity began to break down. In 1987, the Fed announced it would no longer set targets for M1 growth. The Fed switched the focus to M2, which appeared to have a more stable link to economic activity. But by the early 1990s, the link between M2 and economic activity had also deteriorated.

Alan Greenspan, who became the Fed chairman in 1987, said that, in the short run, changes in the money supply "are not linked closely enough with those of nominal income to justify a single-minded focus on the money supply."[2] In 1993, he testified in Congress that the Fed would no longer target monetary aggregates as a guide to monetary policy. The Fed's focus in the last few years has been on short-term interest rates as the tool of monetary policy, in particular, the federal funds rate (the interest rate on funds loaned overnight between banks). For example, to stimulate the economy, the Fed lowered its target interest rate for federal funds from 8 percent in 1990 to 3 percent in 1992, where it remained for 18 months. But in 1994, fearing that a strengthening economy would increase inflation, the Fed began a series of increases that doubled the federal fund rate to 6 percent over the next year. The Fed in 1994 also, for the first time, began announcing after each FOMC meeting whether the target interest rate would increase, decrease, or remain unchanged. With such concrete news coming after each meeting, these sessions became media events.

What's happened lately? The federal funds rate declined to 5.25 percent in early 1996 and remained in the 5.25 to 5.5 percent range until the last quarter of 1998, when it dropped to 4.75 percent. The Fed now tracks a variety of indicators of inflationary pressure to chart a proper course, including the growth in real GDP and the unemployment rate. One of Chairman Greenspan's favorite measures is the employment cost index, which records changes in the cost of labor. An increase in labor cost without an increase in labor productivity signals to Greenspan that inflationary pressure is building in the economy.

Thus far we have confined the discussion of monetary policy to domestic issues, but international transactions complicate the picture. The Fed is at times an active trader in foreign exchange markets. Foreign currency operations are carried out by the New York Fed's foreign trading desk in cooperation with the U.S. Treasury. For example, in order to influence foreign exchange rates, the Fed can sell Japanese bonds and receive yen in exchange, which can then be used to buy dollars from a U.S. bank. These transactions increase both the supply of yen and the demand for dollars, thereby increasing the value of the dollar relative to the yen. Let's look at the Fed's international role in the following case study.

The World of Finance

CaseStudy

Other Times, Other Places

How has the Fed engaged in international policy coordination recently? The minutes of the Federal Open Market Committee reveal the Fed's recent thinking and activities. These are posted on the Web at http://www.bog.frb.fed.us/FOMC/minutes/. Read recent issues of the minutes to find what the Fed has been doing to coordinate U.S. monetary policy with those of other G7 countries.

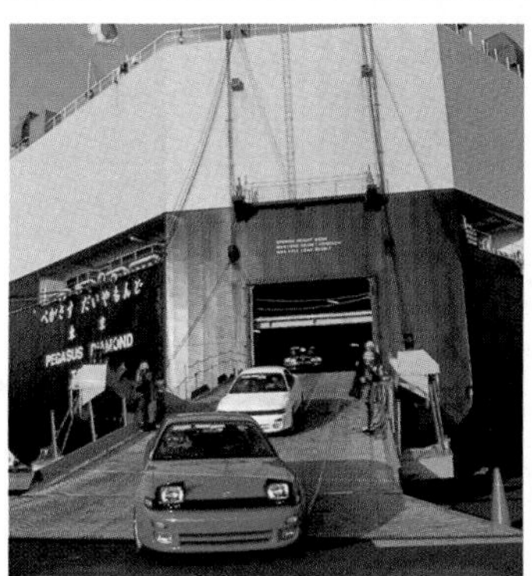

Savers throughout the world have an incentive to find the highest real interest rate, adjusted for risk, that they can earn. For a Japanese saver, for example, the alternatives might be buying Japanese corporate bonds paying, say, 4 percent annually or buying U.S. corporate bonds paying, say, 7 percent. To purchase U.S. corporate bonds, that Japanese saver would first have to purchase U.S. dollars with Japanese yen. Therefore, relatively high interest rates in the United States cause foreigners to exchange their own currencies for dollars. This increase in the

2 As quoted in "Greenspan Asks That Fed Be Allowed to Pay Interest," *Wall Street Journal* (11 March 1992).

demand for dollars causes the dollar to increase in value (appreciate) relative to other currencies.

Between 1980 and 1985, real interest rates in the United States were higher than foreign interest rates, and the U.S. dollar appreciated by about 55 percent relative to other currencies. Interest rates, therefore, affect not only domestic investment but also the value of the dollar on world currency markets. A higher-valued dollar means that U.S. residents find foreign goods cheaper and foreigners find U.S. goods more expensive, so imports increase and exports decrease. The result is a reduction in the demand for U.S. output. A stronger dollar contributed to a decline in American competitiveness in world markets.

At the time, Chairman Volcker said the dollar was too expensive on world markets. In 1985 and 1986, the Fed pursued an expansionary monetary policy, aimed at reducing real interest rates. Real interest rates in the United States began a sharp decline in early 1985, a decline that continued until 1987. When U.S. interest rates fall relative to foreign interest rates, the foreign demand for U.S. dollars also falls and the dollar tends to depreciate. By 1987, the value of the dollar had fallen nearly to its 1980 level. A lower value of the dollar means that U.S. residents find foreign goods more expensive and foreigners find U.S. goods cheaper, so imports decrease and exports increase. The result is an increase in net exports and thus an increase in the demand for U.S. output. The Fed's actions were coordinated with central banks in other countries. Such *international policy coordination* has grown.

Sources: "1997 Monetary Policy Objectives," *Summary Report of the Federal Reserve Board* (22 July 1997); *OECD Economic Outlook 64* (December 1998); and *Economic Report of the President*, February 1999.

CONCLUSION

This chapter has described two ways of viewing the effects of money on the economy's performance, but we should not overstate the differences. In the model that focuses on the indirect channel, an increase in the money supply means that people are holding more money than they would like at prevailing interest rates, so they exchange one form of wealth, money, for other financial assets, such as corporate or government securities. This increased demand for other financial assets has no direct effect on aggregate demand, but it does reduce the interest rate, and this lower interest rate stimulates investment. The increase in planned investment is magnified by the spending multiplier, increasing aggregate demand. The ultimate effect of this increase in demand on real output and the price level depends on the shape of the aggregate supply curve.

In the model that focuses on the direct channel, changes in the money supply act more directly on both output and prices. If velocity is relatively stable or at least fairly predictable, then changes in the money supply will have a predictable effect on nominal income and output in the economy. The mechanism through which changes in money translate into changes in nominal income is no more complicated than the equation of exchange. Increase the supply of money in the economy, and people try to reduce their money balances by exchanging money for other assets, including houses and cars. This greater spending leads to an increase in aggregate demand and to a greater nominal output.

Each model employs a different perspective to examine the way the economy works. The indirect approach uses the income-expenditure model, with the components of aggregate spending as basic building blocks. The direct approach uses the equation of exchange, with the elements of that equation as basic building blocks. To understand why these are alternative ways of viewing the same thing, consider the following analogy.

Suppose city officials, concerned about traffic congestion, ask their planners and engineers to estimate the total number of trips made from the suburbs to the city each month. The city planners estimate that those suburbanites who commute to work make 700,000 trips per month, shoppers make 500,000 trips per month, and joyriders make 300,000 trips per month, for a total of 1.5 million trips. In contrast, the city engineers check with the state department of motor vehicles and find that 100,000 cars are registered to suburban residents. They then estimate that each car makes an average of 15 trips to the city per month, for a total of 1.5 million trips.

The city planners focus not on the number of cars in the suburbs but on the different sources of trips to the city by suburban residents. Likewise, the indirect channel focuses not on the money stock but on the spending by various sectors in the economy. In contrast, the engineers focus on the number of cars and the average number of trips taken by each. Likewise, to arrive at total spending, the direct channel focuses on the money supply and the average number of "trips" each dollar takes—that is, the average number of times each dollar gets spent. Note that the engineers count all registered vehicles, even though some may sit idle in garages. Similarly, the direct channel counts all dollars, even though some remain idle in checking accounts or piggy banks.

SUMMARY

1. The opportunity cost of holding money is the higher interest forgone by not holding other financial assets instead. Along a given money demand curve, the quantity of money demanded is inversely related to the interest rate. The demand for money itself increases as a result of an increase in either the price level or in real GDP.

2. The supply of money is determined by the Fed, and quantity supplied is assumed to be independent of the interest rate. The intersection of the supply and demand for money curves determines the equilibrium interest rate. According to the approach that emphasizes the indirect channel, an increase in the supply of money reduces the interest rate, which increases investment spending. This increase in investment increases aggregate demand, which increases real output and the price level.

3. The approach that emphasizes the direct channel, also called monetarism, focuses on the role of money through the equation of exchange, which states that the money stock, M, multiplied by velocity, V, which is the average number of times each dollar is used to pay for final output, equals the price level, P, multiplied by real GDP, Y. So $M \times V = P \times Y$.

4. The two approaches agree that an increase in the supply of money results in a lower interest rate and greater investment. But the direct-channel approach also claims

that when the supply of money increases, people exchange money for other assets including real assets such as homes and cars. If velocity is stable enough, the effect of changes in the money supply on nominal output can be predicted.

5. During most of the 1970s, velocity appeared relatively predictable, but since 1979 the velocity of M1 has been so variable that economists began to question the usefulness of the quantity theory, at least in the short run. Velocity has been more stable for M2 than for M1, but in the early 1990s even M2 velocity became more volatile. The Fed no longer focuses on the growth of monetary aggregates and instead pays more attention to targeting short-term interest rates, particularly the federal funds rate.

QUESTIONS FOR REVIEW

1. *(Demand for Money)* Determine whether each of the following would lead to an increase, a decrease, or no change in the quantity of money people wish to hold. Also determine whether there is a shift in the money demand curve or a movement along a given money demand curve.
   a. A decrease in the price level
   b. An increase in real output
   c. An improvement in money's ability to act as a store of value
   d. An increase in the market interest rate
2. *(Demand for Money)* If money is so versatile and can buy anything, why don't people demand all the money they can get their hands on?
3. *(Indirect Channel for Monetary Policy)* Through the indirect channel for monetary policy, what is the impact of a decrease in the required reserve ratio on aggregate demand? Explain each step by which aggregate demand is affected.
4. *(Fiscal Policy with Money)* Explain why incorporating money into our macroeconomic framework moderates the effects of fiscal policy. That is, how does the existence of the supply and demand for money moderate the effects of increased government spending?
5. *(Equation of Exchange)* Using the equation of exchange, show why fiscal policy alone cannot increase nominal GDP if the velocity of money is constant.
6. *(Velocity of Money)* Why do some economists believe that higher expected inflation will lead to a rise in velocity?
7. *(Velocity of Money)* Determine whether each of the following would lead to an increase or a decrease in the velocity of money:
   a. Increasing the speed of funds transfers
   b. Decreased use of credit cards
   c. Decreasing the frequency with which workers are paid
   d. Increased customer use of ATM, or debit, cards at retailers
8. *(Quantity Theory of Money)* The quantity theory states that the impact of money on nominal GDP can be determined without details about the *AD* curve, so long as the velocity of money is predictable. Discuss the reasoning behind this claim.
9. ***(CaseStudy:** The Money Supply and Inflation)* According to Exhibit 5 in this chapter, what is the relationship between the rate of money supply growth and the inflation rate? How does this explain the hyperinflation experienced in some economies?
10. *(How Stable Is Velocity?)* How did lifting the prohibition against paying interest on checkable deposits affect the opportunity cost of holding currency? What was the effect on the opportunity cost of holding checkable deposits? Were currency leakages and the money multiplier also affected?
11. *(Indirect Channel Versus Direct Channel)* The main difference between the indirect and direct channels of monetary policy is their underlying assumptions about alternatives to holding money as a store of value. Explain this difference. What do the different assumptions imply about how changes in the money supply influence aggregate demand?
12. *(Money Supply Versus Interest Rate Targets)* In recent years the Fed's monetary target has been the federal funds rate. How does the Fed raise or lower that rate, and how is that rate related to other interest rates in the economy such as the prime rate?
13. ***(CaseStudy:** The World of Finance)* What was the relationship between the U.S. real interest rate and the international value of the U.S. dollar during the 1980s? Explain this relationship.

PROBLEMS AND EXERCISES

14. *(Money Demand)* Suppose that you never carry cash. Your paycheck of $1,000 per month is deposited directly into your checking account, and you spend your money at a constant rate so that at the end of each month your checking account balance is zero.
    a. What is your average money balance during the pay period?
    b. How would each of the following changes in assumptions affect your average monthly balance?
        i. You are paid $500 twice monthly rather than $1,000 each month.
        ii. You are uncertain about your total spending each month.
        ii. You spend a lot at the beginning of the month (e.g., for rent) and little at the end of the month.
        iv. Your monthly income increases.

15. *(Money and Aggregate Demand)* According to the indirect channel, would each of the following increase, decrease, or have no impact on the ability of open-market operations to affect aggregate demand. Explain your answers.
    a. Investment demand becomes less sensitive to changes in the interest rate.
    b. The marginal propensity to consume rises.
    c. The money multiplier rises.
    d. Banks desire to hold additional excess reserves.
    e. The demand for money becomes more sensitive to changes in the interest rate.

16. *(Money Demand and Interest Rates)* Exhibit 2 in this chapter shows the impact of an increase in the money supply on the interest rate. Considering the demand for money and the impact of money on aggregate demand as illustrated in Exhibit 3, why is the new interest rate shown in Exhibit 2 likely to be too low to be a new short-run equilibrium rate? (Hint: See footnote 1 in this chapter.)

17. *(Monetary Policy and Aggregate Supply)* Assume that the economy is initially in long-run equilibrium. Using an *AD–AS* diagram, illustrate and explain the short-run and long-run impacts of an increase in the money supply.

18. *(Monetary Policy and an Expansionary Gap)* Suppose the Fed wishes to use monetary policy to close an expansionary gap. Assume the indirect channel.
    a. Should the Fed increase or decrease the money supply?
    b. If the Fed uses open-market operations, should it buy or sell government securities?
    c. Determine whether each of the following increases, decreases, or remains unchanged in the short run: the market interest rate, the quantity of money demanded, investment spending, aggregate demand, potential output, the price level, and equilibrium real GDP.

19. *(Equation of Exchange)* Calculate the velocity of money if real GDP is 3,000 units, the average price level is $4 per unit, and the quantity of money in the economy is $1,500. What happens to velocity if the average price level drops to $3 per unit? What happens to velocity if the average price level remains at $4 per unit but the money supply rises to $2,000? What happens to velocity if the average price level falls to $2 per unit, the money supply is $2,000, and real GDP is 4,000 units?

20. *(Quantity Theory of Money)* What basic assumption about the velocity of money transforms the equation of exchange into the quantity theory of money?
    a. According to the quantity theory, what will happen to nominal income if the money supply increases by 5 percent and velocity does not change?
    b. What will happen to nominal income if, instead, the money supply decreases by 8 percent and velocity does not change?
    c. What will happen to nominal income if, instead, the money supply increases by 5 percent and velocity decreases by 5 percent?
    d. What happens to the price level in the short run in each of these three situations?

21. *(Money Supply Versus Interest Rate Targets)* Assume that the economy's real GDP is growing.
    a. What will happen to money demand over time?
    b. If the Fed leaves the money supply unchanged, what will happen to the interest rate over time?
    c. If the Fed changes the money supply to match the change in money demand, what will happen to the interest rate over time?
    d. What would be the effect of the policy described in part (c) on the economy's stability over the business cycle?

22. *(Targets After 1982)* One of the Fed's objectives is maintaining relative stability in foreign exchange rates. What has happened to foreign exchange rates lately, and what, if anything, has the Fed done to promote stability? In particular, what has been happening lately to the exchange rate between the dollar and the yen and between the dollar and the euro? (A good source for the data is http://www.american.edu/academic.depts/cas/econ/econdata.htm.)

EXPERIENTIAL EXERCISES

23. *(Money Supply Versus Interest Rate Targets)* A favorite activity of many macroeconomists is Fed-watching. Go to the Federal Reserve Board's Web site and look for the most recent Congressional testimony of the Board Chairperson at http://www.bog.frb.fed.us/boarddocs/testimony/. Is the Fed targeting interest rates, the money supply, or something else?

24. *(Targets After 1982)* The Federal Reserve Bank of Cleveland's monthly publication *Economic Trends* at http://www.clev.frb.org/research/ is available online. Choose a recent issue and click on "Monetary Policy." What are some current developments in monetary policy? See if you can illustrate them using the *AD–AS* model.

25. *(Wall Street Journal)* The Federal Reserve Report appears in each Friday's *Wall Street Journal*. You can find it in the Money and Investing section. In addition to the weekly report, a monthly chart shows the recent performance of money supply indicators, compared with Fed targets. Does it look as if the Fed has been hitting its targets over the last year?

CHAPTER

16 The Policy Debate: Active or Passive?

Does the private sector work fairly well on its own or does it require active government intervention? If people expect government intervention to prod the economy along, does this expectation affect people's behavior? Does government intervention do more harm than good? What is the relationship between unemployment and inflation in the short run and in the long run? Answers to these and other questions are provided in this chapter, which examines the policy debate regarding the appropriate role for government in economic stabilization.

You have now studied both fiscal and monetary policy and are in a position to take a broader view of the impact of public policy on the U.S. economy. This chapter distinguishes between two approaches: the *active approach* and the *passive approach*. The active approach views the private sector as relatively unstable and

'isit the McEachern
eractive Study Center
'or this chapter at
://mcisc.swcollege.com

unable to recover from shocks when they occur. According to advocates of an active approach, economic fluctuations arise primarily from the private sector, particularly investment, and natural market forces may not be much help when the economy gets off track. To move the economy to its potential output, the active approach calls for the use of discretionary policy.

The passive approach, on the other hand, considers the private sector to be relatively stable and able to recover from shocks when they occur. According to advocates of a passive approach, when the economy gets off track, natural market forces nudge it back on course. Not only is active government intervention unnecessary, but such activism, according to advocates of the passive approach, often does more harm than good.

In this chapter, we will consider the pros and cons of *active* intervention in the economy versus *passive* reliance on natural market forces. We will also examine the role that expectations play in determining the effectiveness of stabilization policy. You will learn why unanticipated stabilization policies have more impact on employment and output than do anticipated ones. Finally, the chapter explores the trade-off between unemployment and inflation. As you read, keep in mind that issues of macroeconomic policy remain the most widely debated of economic questions. Topics discussed in this chapter include:

- Active versus passive policies
- Self-correcting mechanisms
- Rational expectations
- Policy rules and policy credibility
- The time-inconsistency problem
- Short-run and long-run Phillips curves
- Natural rate hypothesis

ACTIVE POLICY VERSUS PASSIVE POLICY

According to the *active approach,* discretionary fiscal or monetary policy can reduce the costs imposed by an unstable private sector. According to the *passive approach,* discretionary policy contributes to the instability of the economy and is therefore part of the problem, not part of the solution. The two approaches differ in their assumptions about how well natural market forces operate.

Closing a Contractionary Gap

Perhaps the best way to describe each approach is by examining a particular macroeconomic problem. Suppose the economy is in short-run equilibrium at point *a* in panel (a) of Exhibit 1, with a real GDP of $7.8 trillion, which is below the economy's potential output of $8.0 trillion. The contractionary gap of $0.2 trillion drives unemployment above the natural rate (the rate of unemployment when the economy is producing its potential output). This gap could have resulted from lower than expected aggregate demand or some adverse supply shock that temporarily decreased short-run aggregate supply. What should public officials do when confronted with this gap?

Those who subscribe to the passive approach, like their classical predecessors, have more faith in the *self-correcting mechanisms* of the economy than do those who favor the active approach. In what sense is the economy self-correcting? According to the passive approach, wages and prices are flexible enough to adjust within a reasonable period to labor shortages or surpluses. The high unemployment in panel (a) will cause wages to fall, which will reduce production

EXHIBIT 1

Closing a Contractionary Gap

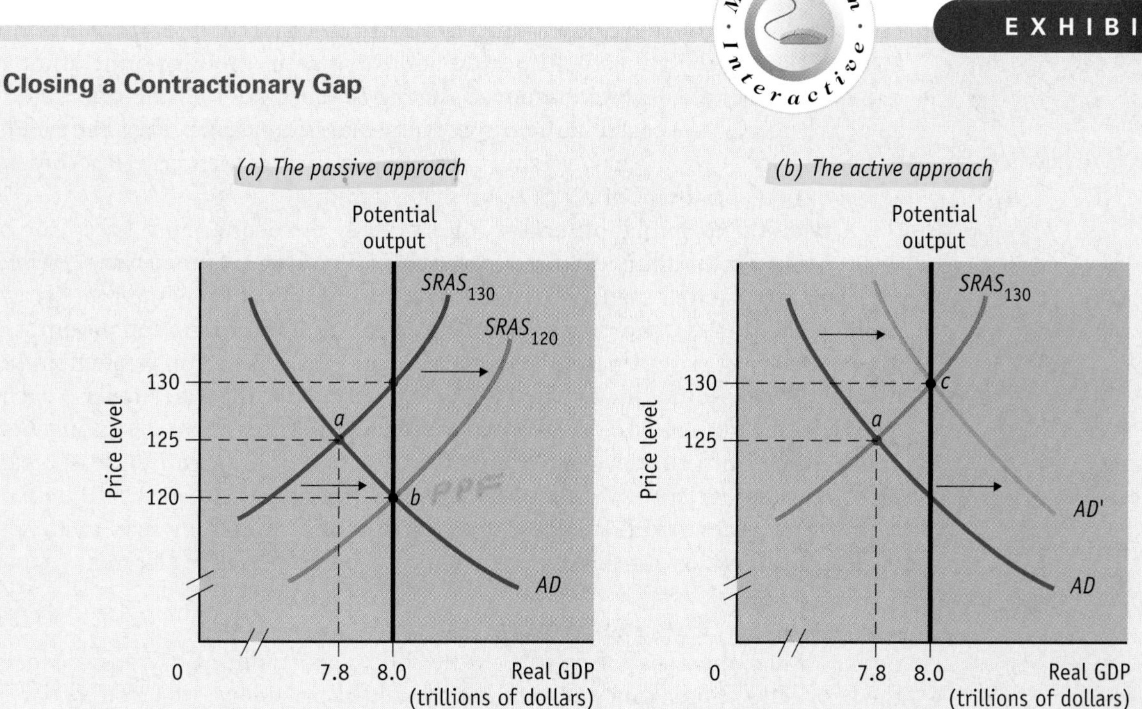

At point *a* in both panels, the economy is in short-run equilibrium, with unemployment above the natural rate. According to the passive approach, that high unemployment will eventually cause wages to fall, reducing firms' cost of doing business. The decline in costs will cause the short-run aggregate supply curve to shift out to $SRAS_{120}$, moving the economy to its potential level of output at point *b* in panel (a). In panel (b), the government employs an active approach to shift the aggregate demand curve from *AD* to *AD'*. If the policy works, the economy moves to its potential level of output at point *c*.

costs, which will shift the short-run aggregate supply curve rightward. (Money wages need not actually fall; money wage increases may simply lag behind increases in the price level, so that real wages fall.) According to the passive approach, the short-run aggregate supply curve will, within a reasonable period, shift from $SRAS_{130}$ to $SRAS_{120}$, moving the economy to its potential level of output at point *b*. *According to the passive approach, the economy is inherently stable, gravitating in a reasonable amount of time toward potential GDP. Consequently, advocates of passive policy see little reason for active government intervention.* The passive approach is to let natural market forces close the contractionary gap. So the prescription of passive policy is to do nothing special.

Advocates of an active approach, on the other hand, believe that prices and wages are not very flexible, particularly in the downward direction. They think that when adverse supply shocks or sagging demand result in unemployment that exceeds the natural rate, the economy does not quickly adjust to eliminate this unemployment. Advocates of the active approach argue that even when there is much unemployment in the economy, the renegotiation of long-term wage contracts in line with a lower expected price level may take a long time.

If so, the wage reductions required to shift the short-run aggregate supply curve outward may also take a long time, even years. The longer it takes natural market forces to lower unemployment to the natural rate, the greater the output forgone during the adjustment period and the greater the economic and psychological costs to those unemployed during that period. Because advocates of an active policy associate a high cost with the passive approach, they believe that the economy needs an active stabilization policy to alter aggregate demand and achieve the natural rate of output and price stability.

A decision by public officials to intervene in the economy to speed the return to potential output—that is, a decision to use discretionary policy—reflects an active approach. In panel (b) of Exhibit 1, we begin at the same point *a* as in panel (a). At point *a*, short-run equilibrium output is below potential output, so the economy is experiencing a contractionary gap. Through monetary policy, fiscal policy, or some mix of the two, active policy attempts to increase aggregate demand from *AD* to *AD*', moving equilibrium from point *a* to point *c* and closing the contractionary gap. One cost of such a policy is an increase in the price level, or inflation. To the extent that the stimulus to aggregate demand worsens the federal budget deficit, another cost of active policy is an increase in the national debt, a cost that will be examined more closely in the next chapter.

Closing an Expansionary Gap

Let's consider the situation in which the short-run equilibrium output exceeds the economy's potential. Suppose that the actual price level of 135 exceeds the expected price level of 130, causing an expansionary gap of $0.2 trillion, as shown in Exhibit 2. The passive approach argues that natural market forces will prompt firms and workers to negotiate higher wages. These higher nominal wages will increase production costs, shifting the short-run supply curve up and to the left, from $SRAS_{130}$ to $SRAS_{140}$, as shown in panel (a). This leads to a higher price level and lowers output to the economy's potential. So the natural adjustment process will result in a higher price level, or inflation.

An active approach sees discretionary policy as a way of returning the economy to its potential output without an increase in the price level, or inflation. Advocates of active policy believe that if aggregate demand can be reduced from *AD*" to *AD*', as shown in panel (b) of Exhibit 2, then the equilibrium point will move down along the initial aggregate supply curve from *d* to *c*. *Whereas the passive approach relies on natural market forces to close an expansionary gap through a decrease in the short-run aggregate supply curve, the active approach relies on just the right discretionary policy to close the gap through a decrease in aggregate demand.* The passive approach results in a higher price level, but the active approach results in a lower price level. Thus the correct discretionary policy can relieve the inflationary pressure associated with an expansionary gap. Whenever the Fed attempts to cool an overheated economy, as it did in 1994, it employs an active monetary policy to close an expansionary gap. In 1994, the economy was flying high, with output exceeding potential, and the Fed was trying to orchestrate a so-called soft landing.

Problems with Active Policy

The timely adoption and implementation of an appropriate active policy is not easy. One problem is identifying the economy's potential output level and the unemployment at that level. Suppose the natural rate of unemployment is 5

EXHIBIT 2

Policy Responses to an Expansionary Gap

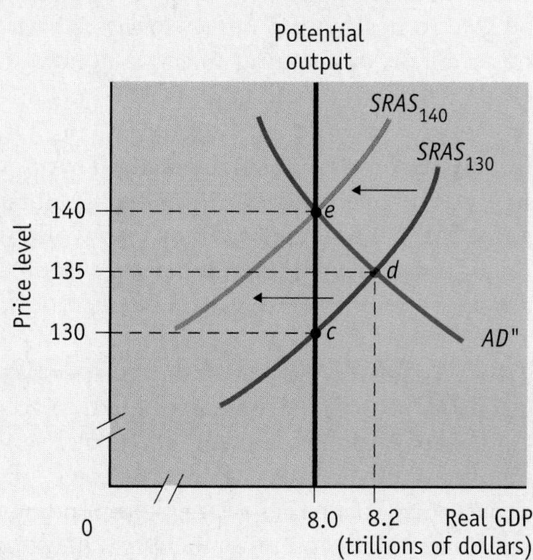

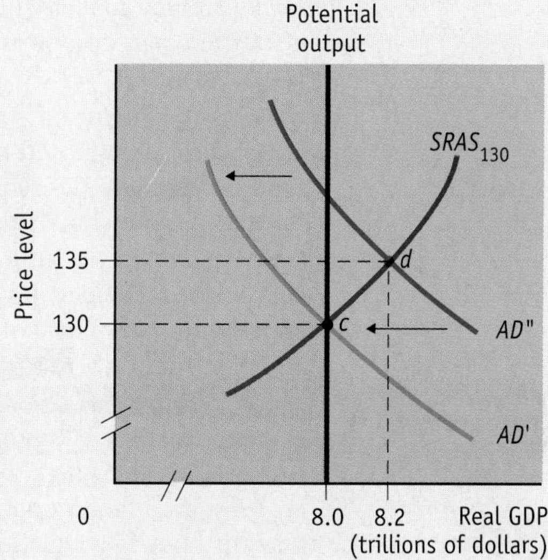

At point *d* in both panels, the economy is in short-run equilibrium, producing $8.2 trillion. Unemployment is below the natural rate. In the passive approach reflected in panel (a), the government makes no change in policy, so natural market forces will eventually bring about a higher negotiated wage, shifting the short-run supply curve up to $SRAS_{140}$. The new equilibrium at point *e* will result in a higher price level and a lower level of output and employment. An active policy might be able to reduce aggregate demand, shifting the equilibrium from point *d* to point *c* in panel (b), thus closing the expansionary gap without increasing the price level.

percent, but policy makers believe it is 4 percent. As they pursue their elusive objective of 4 percent, they will find that output is constantly pushed beyond its potential, creating higher prices in the long run but no permanent reduction in unemployment. Recall that in the short run, if output is pushed beyond the economy's potential, an expansionary gap opens up, which will cause an upward shift in the short-run aggregate supply curve until the economy returns to its potential level of output at a higher price level.

Even if policy makers can accurately estimate the economy's potential level of output, formulating an effective policy requires detailed knowledge of current and future economic conditions. To pursue an effective active policy, policy makers must *first* be able to forecast what aggregate demand and aggregate supply would be without government intervention. Simply put, they must be able to predict what would happen with a passive policy. *Second,* policy makers must have the tools necessary to achieve the desired result relatively quickly. *Third,* policy makers must be able to forecast the effects of an active policy on the economy's key performance measures. *Fourth,* policy makers must work together. Congress and the president pursue fiscal policy while the Fed directs monetary policy; these groups often fail to coordinate their efforts. To the extent that an active policy requires coordination, the policy may not work as desired. In early 1995, for example, Congress was considering an expansionary tax cut at the same time the Fed was pursuing a contractionary monetary policy. *Fifth,* policy makers must be able to implement the appropriate policy, even if that policy involves short-term political costs. For example, during inflationary times the optimal policy may call for a tax increase or a tighter monetary policy, policies that may be unpopular because they increase unemployment. *Finally,* policy makers must be able to deal with a variety of lags. As we will see next, these lags compound the problems of pursuing an active policy.

The Problem of Lags

So far we have ignored the time required to implement policy. That is, we have assumed that the desired policy was selected and implemented instantaneously. We have also assumed that, once implemented, the policy will work as advertised—again, in no time. Actually, there may be long, sometimes unpredictable, lags at several stages in the process. These lags reduce the effectiveness and increase the uncertainty of active policies.

Recognition lag The time needed to identify a macroeconomic problem and assess its seriousness

First, there is a **recognition lag,** which is the time it takes to identify a problem and determine how serious it is. For example, time is required to accumulate evidence that the economy is indeed performing below its potential. Even if initial data spell trouble, these data are often subsequently revised. Therefore, policy makers must await additional evidence of trouble rather than risk responding to what may turn out to be a false alarm. Since a recession is not identified until more than six months after it begins and since the average recession lasts about a year, a typical recession will be more than half over before it is officially recognized as such.

Decision-making lag The time needed to decide what to do once a macroeconomic problem has been identified

Even after enough evidence has accumulated, policy makers usually take additional time deciding what to do, so there is a **decision-making lag.** In the case of discretionary fiscal policy, Congress and the president must develop and agree upon an appropriate course of action. Fiscal legislation usually takes months to approve; it could take more than a year. On the other hand, the Fed can decide on the appropriate monetary policy more quickly, so the decision-making lag is shorter for monetary policy.

Implementation lag The time needed to introduce a change in monetary or fiscal policy

Once a decision has been made, the new policy must be introduced, which often involves an **implementation lag.** Again, monetary policy has the advantage: After a policy has been adopted, the Fed can buy or sell U.S. bonds, change the discount rate, or alter reserve requirements relatively quickly. The implementation lag is longer for fiscal policy. For example, if tax rates change, new tax forms must be printed and distributed. If government spending changes, the appropriate government agencies must get involved. The implementation of fiscal policy can take more than a year. For example, in February 1983, the nation's unemployment rate reached 10.3 percent, with 11.5 million unemployed. The following month, Congress passed the Emergency Jobs Appropriation Act, providing $9 billion to create what supporters claimed would be hundreds of thousands of new jobs. Fifteen months later, only $3.1 billion had been spent and only 35,000 new jobs had been created, according to a U.S. General Accounting Office study. By that time, the economy had recovered on its own, reducing the unemployment rate to 7.1 percent and adding 6.2 million jobs! So this public spending program was implemented only after the recession had bottomed out. Likewise, in the spring of 1993, President Clinton proposed a $16 billion stimulus package to help boost what appeared to be a sluggish recovery. The measure was defeated because it would have added to a large federal deficit, yet the economy still gained 5.6 million jobs between January of 1993 and December of 1994.

Once a policy has been implemented, there is an **effectiveness lag** before the full impact of the policy registers on the economy. One problem with monetary policy is that the lag between a change in the money supply and its effect on aggregate demand and output is long and variable, ranging from several months up to three years. Fiscal policy, once enacted, usually requires 3 to 6 months to take effect and between 9 and 18 months to register its full effect.

Effectiveness lag The time necessary for changes in monetary or fiscal policy to have an effect on the economy

These various lags make active policy difficult to execute. The more variable the lags, the harder it is to predict when a particular policy will take hold and what the state of the economy will be at that time. To advocates of passive policy, these lags are reason enough to avoid discretionary policy. *Advocates of a passive approach argue that an active stabilization policy imposes troubling fluctuations in the price level and real GDP because it often takes hold only after self-correcting market forces have already returned the economy to its potential output level.*

Talk in the media about "jump-starting" the economy reflects the active approach, which views the economy as a sputtering machine that can be fixed by an expert mechanic. The passive approach views the economy as more like a supertanker on automatic pilot. The policy question then becomes whether to trust that automatic pilot (the self-correcting tendencies of the economy) or to try to override the mechanism with active discretionary policies.[1]

Review of Policy Perspectives

The active and passive approaches embody different views about the natural stability of the economy and the ability of Congress or the Fed to implement appropriate discretionary policies. Hence they disagree about the role of public policy in the economy. As we have seen, advocates of an active approach think that the natural adjustments of wages and prices can be excruciatingly slow, particularly when unemployment is high, as it was during the Great Depression. Prolonged high unemployment means that much output must be sacrificed, and the unemployed must suffer personal hardship during the slow adjustment period. If high unemployment lasts a long time, labor skills may grow rusty, and some long-term unemployed workers may drop out of the labor force. Therefore prolonged unemployment may cause the economy's potential GDP to fall, as the case study of hysteresis in Chapter 11 suggested.

Thus, active policy associates a high cost with the failure to pursue a discretionary policy. And, despite the lags involved, advocates of active policy prefer action—through fiscal policy, monetary policy, or some combination of the two—to inaction. Passive policy advocates, on the other hand, believe that uncertain lags and ignorance about how the economy works prevent policy makers from accurately determining and effectively implementing the appropriate active policy. Therefore the passive approach, rather than pursuing a misguided activist policy, relies more on the economy's natural ability to correct itself and on the government's automatic stabilizers.

Differences between active and passive approaches emerged during the presidential campaign of 1992, when the economy was slow to recover from a recession, as is discussed in the following case study.

1 This analogy was contributed by J. W. Mixon, Jr., to *The Teaching Economist*, Issue 4 (Spring 1992): 3, W. A. McEachern, ed.

CaseStudy

Public Policy

President Bush's last State of the Union address was on January 28, 1992—a time when the country had been experiencing a mild recession. The text of his speech is available from the Bush Presidential Library at http://www.csdl.tamu.edu/bushlib/papers/1992/92012801.html. Read it to determine whether he was in favor of an active or passive approach to dealing with the recession. President Clinton's State of the Union address can be found under "Read Speeches by the President" at the White House Web site, http://www.pub.whitehouse.gov/WH/Publications/html/Publications.html. Given current economic conditions, how activist does Clinton appear to be? Is he seeking additional government programs and targeted tax cuts? For what purposes?

Active Versus Passive Presidential Candidates

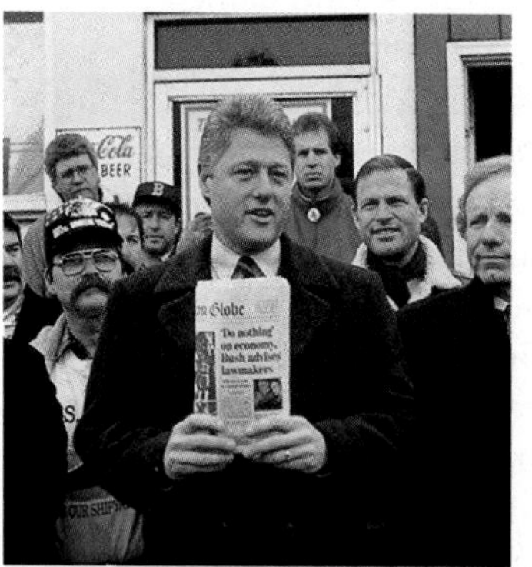

During the third quarter of 1990, after the longest peacetime expansion this century, the U.S. economy slipped into a recession, touched off by the uncertainty generated when Iraq invaded Kuwait. Because of the large federal deficit prevailing at the time, policy makers were reluctant to employ discretionary fiscal policy to stimulate the economy. That task was left to monetary policy. The Fed supplied enough additional reserves to the banking system to lower the federal funds rate. The Fed also cut the discount rate several times. These moves were aimed at stimulating spending. The recession lasted only nine months, but the recovery was sluggish.

That sluggish recovery was the economic setting for the presidential election of 1992 between Republican President George Bush and Democratic challenger Bill Clinton. Since monetary policy did not seem to be providing a sufficient kick, was an additional fiscal stimulus a viable option? With the federal budget deficit in 1992 already nearing $300 billion, a record level, would a higher deficit do more harm than good?

Bush's biggest liability during the campaign was the sluggish recovery and ballooning federal deficit; these were Clinton's biggest political assets. Clinton's economic positions were that (1) Bush had not done enough to revive the economy; (2) Bush and his predecessor, President Reagan, were responsible for the huge federal deficits; and (3) Bush could not be trusted because he broke his 1988 campaign pledge of no new taxes by signing a tax increase in 1990 to reduce the deficits. Clinton called for raising the marginal tax rate on the top 2 percent of taxpayers and cutting taxes for the middle class. He also promised to create jobs through government spending that would "invest in America."

Bush tried to point out that, technically, the recession was over and the economy was on the right track. He blamed a Democratic Congress for blocking his recovery proposals, and he renewed his pledge of no new taxes (saying he really meant it this time). In fact, Bush promised to cut taxes by 1 percent, arguing that this would reallocate spending from government back to households.

Although both candidates were short on specifics, Clinton saw a stronger role for government, and Bush saw a stronger role for the private sector. Clinton's approach was more *active,* and Bush's approach was more *passive.* In the end, the negative economic reports that dominated the news during the campaign made people willing to gamble on Clinton. Evidently, during hard times, an active policy has more voter appeal than a passive one. Ironically, the economy at the time was much stronger than was conveyed by the media and by challenger Clinton. The growth in real GDP in 1992 turned out to be 2.7 percent, which is quite respectable by current standards and better than the average real GDP growth of 2.6 percent achieved during Clinton's first term.

Sources: David Wessel, "Wanted: Fiscal Stimulus Without Higher Taxes," *Wall Street Journal* (5 October 1992); Herbert Stein, "The Inane Campaign Gives Me a Pain," *Wall Street Journal* (7 October 1992); and *Economic Report of the President*, February 1999.

ROLE OF EXPECTATIONS

The effectiveness of a particular government policy depends in part on what people expect. As we saw in Chapter 11, the short-run aggregate supply curve is drawn for a given expected price level reflected in long-term wage contracts. If workers and firms expect continuing inflation, their wage agreements will reflect these inflationary expectations. One approach in macroeconomics, called **rational expectations,** argues that people form expectations on the basis of all available information, including information about the probable future actions of policy makers. Thus aggregate supply depends on what sort of macroeconomic course policy makers are expected to pursue. For example, if people were to observe that policy makers try to stimulate aggregate demand every time real output falls below potential, people will come to anticipate the effects of this policy on the price level and output. Robert Lucas, of the University of Chicago, won the 1995 Nobel prize for his work in rational expectations.

Rational expectations A school of thought that claims people form expectations based on all available information, including the probable future actions of government policy makers

Monetary authorities are required to testify before Congress regularly, indicating the monetary policy they plan to pursue. The Fed also announces any changes in interest rate targets after each meeting, held every six weeks. We will consider the role of expectations in the context of monetary policy by examining the relationship between policy pronouncements and equilibrium output. We could employ a similar approach with fiscal policy, but active discretionary fiscal policy over the last two decades was hobbled by high federal deficits. To be sure, there were still tax increases, as in 1993, and tax cuts, as in 1997, and now that the federal deficit has been erased policy makers will turn once again to discretionary fiscal policy. Still, monetary policy has been at center stage for the last two decades.

Monetary Policy and Expectations

Suppose the economy is producing the potential rate of output. At the beginning of the year, firms and employees must negotiate wage agreements. While labor negotiations are under way, the Fed announces that throughout the year its monetary policy will aim at serving the money needs of an economy producing at the potential level. Thus the Fed plans to keep the price level constant. This seems to be the appropriate policy since unemployment is already at the natural rate. Until the year is under way and monetary policy is actually implemented, however, the public cannot be sure what the Fed will do. Firms and workers understand that the Fed's constant-price plan appears optimal under the circumstances, since an expansionary monetary policy would result simply in higher inflation in the long run.

As long as wage increases do not exceed the growth in labor productivity, the Fed's plan of a constant price level should work out. Alternatively, workers could try for higher wage growth, but that option would ultimately lead to inflation. Suppose workers and firms believe the Fed's pronouncements and agree on wage settlements based on expectations of a constant price level. If the Fed follows through, as promised, then the price level will turn out as expected. Output will remain at the economy's potential, and unemployment will remain at the natural rate. The situation is depicted in Exhibit 3, where the short-run aggregate supply curve, $SRAS_{130}$, is based on wage contracts reflecting an expected price level of 130. If the Fed follows the announced course, aggregate demand

EXHIBIT 3

Short-Run Effects of an Unexpected Expansionary Monetary Policy

At point *a*, firms and workers expect the price level to be 130; supply curve $SRAS_{130}$ reflects those expectations. If the Federal Reserve unexpectedly pursues an expansionary monetary policy, the aggregate demand curve will be *AD'* rather than *AD*. Output will temporarily rise above the potential rate (at point *b*), but in the long run it will fall back to the potential rate at point *c*. The short-run effect of monetary policy is a higher level of output, but the long-run effect is just an increase in the price level.

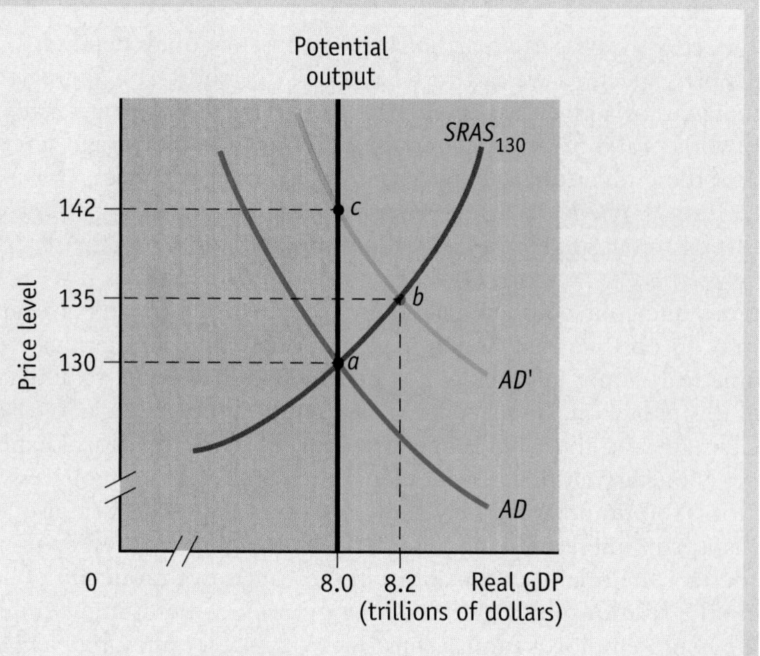

will be *AD* and equilibrium will be at point *a*, where the price level is as expected and the economy is producing $8.0 trillion, the potential level of output.

Suppose, however, that after workers and firms have agreed on nominal wages—that is, after the short-run aggregate supply curve has been determined—public officials become dissatisfied with the prevailing level of unemployment. Perhaps election-year concerns about unemployment or a false alarm about the onset of a recession prompts elected officials to persuade the Fed to stimulate aggregate demand.

An expansionary monetary policy increases aggregate demand from *AD*, the level anticipated by firms and employees, to *AD*'. This unexpected policy stimulates output and employment in the short run to equilibrium point *b*. Output increases to $8.2 trillion, and the price level increases to 135. This temporary boost in output and reduction in unemployment lasts perhaps long enough to help public officials get reelected.

So the price level is now higher than workers expected, which means that the wage they agreed to buys less in real terms. At their next opportunity, they will negotiate higher wages. These higher wage agreements will eventually cause the short-run aggregate supply curve in Exhibit 3 to shift up to the left, intersecting *AD*' at point *c*, the economy's potential output. (To keep the diagram less cluttered, the shifted short-run aggregate supply curve is not shown.) So output once again returns to the economy's potential GDP, but in the process the price level rises to 142.

Thus the unexpected expansionary monetary policy causes a short-run increase in output and employment. But in the long run the increase in the aggregate demand results only in a higher price level, and a higher inflation rate, than had been expected. After a short-run surge in output, the short-run aggregate supply curve shifts to the left, the price level climbs, and output returns once again to the economy's potential.

The **time-inconsistency problem** arises when policy makers have an incentive to announce one policy to influence expectations but then pursue a different policy once those expectations have been formed and acted on. As we shall see in the next section, one solution to the time-inconsistency problem is to take discretion away from the policy makers so that once a policy is announced, it cannot be changed.

Time-inconsistency problem The problem that arises when policy makers have an incentive to announce one policy to influence expectations but then pursue a different policy once those expectations have been formed and acted on

Anticipating Monetary Policy

Workers may be fooled once by the Fed's actions, but they won't be fooled again. Suppose Fed policy makers become alarmed by the high inflation. The next time around, the Fed once again announces that it plans a monetary policy that will hold the price level constant at 142, a policy aimed at keeping real GDP at its potential. From their previous experience, however, workers and firms have learned that the Fed is willing to accept higher inflation in exchange for a temporary reduction in unemployment. Consequently, they take the Fed's announcement with a grain of salt. Workers, in particular, do not want to get caught again with their real wages down should the Fed implement a stimulative monetary policy, so a high wage-increase settlement is reached.

In effect, workers and firms are betting that monetary authorities will pursue an expansionary monetary policy regardless of their pronouncement to the contrary. The short-run aggregate supply curve reflecting these high wage-increase agreements is depicted by $SRAS_{152}$ in Exhibit 4, where 152 is the expected price level. Note that AD' is the aggregate demand that would result if the Fed's announced constant-price-level policy were pursued; that demand curve intersects the potential output line at point *c,* where the price level is 142. But AD'' is the aggregate demand that firms and workers expect based on an expansionary policy. They have agreed to wage settlements that will produce the economy's potential level of output if the Fed behaves as *expected,* not as *announced.* Thus, a price level of 152 is based on rational expectations. In effect, workers and firms expect the expansionary policy to shift aggregate demand from AD' to AD''.

Monetary authorities must now decide whether to stick with their announced plan of holding the price level constant or follow a more expansionary monetary policy. If they pursue the constant-price-level policy, aggregate demand will turn out to be AD' and short-run equilibrium will occur at point *d.* Short-run output will fall below the economy's potential, resulting in unemployment exceeding the natural rate. If monetary authorities want to keep the economy performing at its potential, they have only one alternative—to match expectations. Monetary authorities *must* pursue an expansionary monetary policy, a course of action that reinforces public skepticism of policy announcements. This expansionary policy will result in an aggregate demand of AD'', leading to an equilibrium at point *e,* where the price level is 152 and output equals the economy's potential.

Thus firms and workers enter their negotiations with the realization that the Fed has an incentive to pursue an expansionary monetary policy. Therefore workers and firms agree to high wage increases, and the Fed follows with an expansionary policy, one that results in more inflation. Once workers and firms

EXHIBIT 4

Short-Run Effects of the Fed Pursuing a More Expansionary Policy than Announced

The Fed announces a monetary policy that will keep the price level at 142. Firms and workers, however, do not believe the announcement; they think the monetary policy will be expansionary. The short-run aggregate supply curve, $SRAS_{152}$, reflects their forecasts of the price level. The Fed must then decide what to do. If it follows the noninflationary policy, aggregate demand will be AD', and output will fall below potential to point *d*. To keep the economy performing at its potential, the Fed must increease the money supply by as much as workers and firms expected.

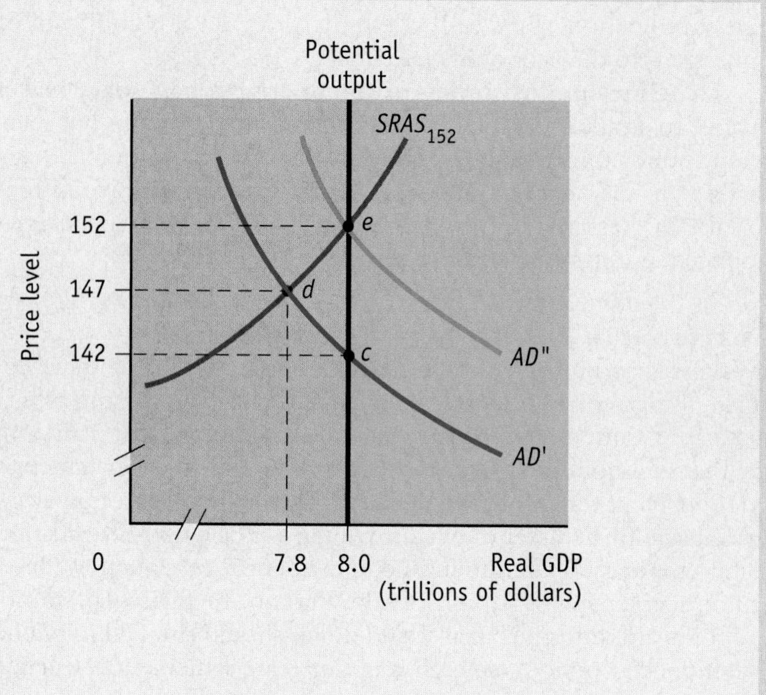

come to expect an expansionary monetary policy and the resulting inflation, such a policy does not spur even a temporary boost in output beyond the economy's potential. *Economists of the rational expectations school believe that if the economy is already producing its potential output, an expansionary monetary policy, if fully and correctly anticipated, will have no effect on output or employment. Only unanticipated or incorrectly anticipated changes in policy can temporarily influence output and employment.*

Policy Credibility

If the economy is already producing its potential output, an unexpected expansionary monetary policy would increase output and employment temporarily. The costs, however, include not only inflation in the long term but also a loss of credibility the next time around. Is there any way out of this? For the Fed to pursue a policy consistent with a constant price level, its announcements must somehow be *credible,* or believable. Firms and workers must believe that when the time comes to make a hard decision, the Fed will follow through as promised. Perhaps the Fed could offer some sort of insurance policy to make everyone believe that policy makers who deviate from the set course will pay dearly—for example, the chairman of the Fed could promise to resign if the Fed does not pursue the announced course. Ironically, policy makers are often more credible and therefore more effective if they have their discretion taken away. In this case, a hard-and-fast rule could be substituted for a policy maker's discretion. Policy rules will be considered in the next section.

Consider the problems facing central banks in countries that have experienced hyperinflation. For an anti-inflation policy to succeed at the least possible cost in forgone output, the public must believe the announcements of central bankers. How do they establish credibility? Some economists believe that the most efficient anti-inflation policy is **cold turkey,** which is to announce and execute tough measures to stop inflation, such as halting the growth in the money supply. For example, in 1985 the annual rate of inflation in Bolivia was running at 20,000 percent when the new government announced a stern policy. The restrictive measures worked and inflation was stopped within a month, with only a 5 percent loss on output. Around the world, credible anti-inflation policies have been successful.[2] Drastic measures may involve costs. For example, some economists argue that the Fed's dramatic efforts to curb high U.S. inflation during the early 1980s precipitated the worst recession since the Great Depression. Some say that the Fed's pronouncements were not credible and therefore resulted in a recession.

Cold turkey The announcement and execution of tough measures to reduce high inflation

Much depends on the Fed's time horizon. If policy makers take the long view of their duties, they will be reluctant to risk their long-run policy effectiveness for a temporary reduction in unemployment. If Fed officials realize that their credibility is hard to develop but easy to undermine, they will be reluctant to pursue policies that will ultimately increase inflation.

Often Congress tries to pressure the Fed to stimulate the economy. By law the Fed must "promote effectively the goals of maximum employment, stable prices, and moderate long-term interest rates." The law leaves it up to the Fed to determine how best to pursue these goals. The Fed does not rely on congressional appropriations, so Congress cannot attempt to influence the Fed by withholding funds. In fact, the Fed makes a "profit" of nearly $20 billion a year, which it turns over to the U.S. Treasury. Thus, although the U.S. president appoints members of the Board of Governors, and these appointments must be approved by the Senate, the Fed operates fairly independently of the president and Congress. Consider central bank independence around the world in the following case study.

Central Bank Independence and Price Stability

Public Policy

Argentina limited its central bank's ability to issue new currency by creating a currency board, which required that each new peso be backed by one U.S. dollar held in reserve by the bank. "Are Currency Boards a Cure for All Monetary Problems?" is an article from the IMF publication, *Finance and Development*, which explores the use of independent currency boards to control the supply of money in advanced industrial countries. It can be found

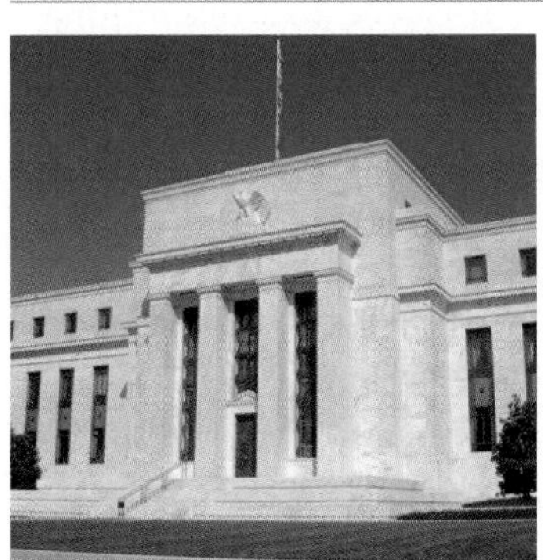

Some economists argue that the Fed would do better in the long run if it were committed to the single goal of price stability. Look, for example, at the Japanese experience. Since 1975, the Japanese central bank has had a strong commitment to low inflation, and inflation in Japan since 1975 has averaged only half the U.S. rate.

Some economists argue that to focus on price stability, a central bank should be insulated from political influence. When the Fed was established, several features insulated it from the ordinary political process—the 14-year terms with staggered appointments, for example. Also, the Fed is prohibited from purchasing securities directly from the

2 For a discussion about how four hyperinflations in the 1920s ended, see Thomas Sargent, "The Ends of Four Big Inflations," *Inflation: Causes and Consequences*, Robert Hall, ed. (Chicago: University of Chicago Press, 1982): 41–98.

at http://imfnt1x.imf.org/external/pubs/ft/fandd/1998/12/enoch.htm. What are the benefits of imposing such strict rules? How does a currency board derive its own credibility?

U.S. Treasury (the Fed purchases these securities in so-called secondary markets). What's more, since the Fed has its own source of income (interest on government securities and discount loans), it does not rely on Congress for a budget.

Does this independence affect performance? When central banks for 17 advanced industrial countries were ranked from least independent to most independent, inflation turned out to be the lowest in countries with the most independent central banks and highest in countries with the least independent central banks. For example, the most independent central banks were in Germany and Switzerland, and their inflation rates from 1973 to 1988 averaged about 3 percent per year. The least independent banks during that period were in Spain, New Zealand, Australia, and Italy, where inflation averaged 11.5 percent per year. The U.S. central bank is considered relatively independent; our inflation rate, which averaged 6.5 percent per year between 1973 and 1988, fell between the most independent and least independent groups.

The tendency around the world is toward greater central bank independence. Since 1988, for example, Australia and New Zealand have amended laws governing their central banks to make price stability the primary goal. Chile, Colombia, and Argentina, developing countries that recently experienced hyperinflation, have legislated more central bank independence. And the Maastricht agreement, which defined the framework for establishing a single European currency, the euro, identified price stability as the main objective of the new European central bank.

Sources: Alberto Alesina and Lawrence Summers, "Central Bank Independence and Macroeconomic Performance: Some Comparative Evidence," *Journal of Money, Credit and Banking*, 25 (May 1993): 151–162; Paul Lewis, "Bundesbank Puts Politicians on Notice," *New York Times* (23 October 1997); and Patricia Pollard, "Central Bank Independence and Economic Performance," *Federal Reserve Bank of St. Louis* (July/August 1993): 21–36.

POLICY RULES VERSUS DISCRETION

As noted earlier, the active approach views the economy as inherently unstable and in need of discretionary policy to eliminate excessive unemployment when it arises. The passive approach views the economy as so stable that discretionary policy is not only unnecessary but may actually cause destabilizing swings in aggregate demand that ultimately lead to more inflation. In place of discretionary policy, the passive approach often calls for predetermined rules to guide the actions of policy makers. In the context of fiscal policy, these rules take the form of automatic stabilizers, such as unemployment insurance, a progressive income tax, and transfer payments, all of which are aimed at offsetting the effects of business fluctuations. In this section, we examine the arguments for rules versus discretion in the context of monetary policy.

Rationale for Rules

The rationale for passive rules rather than the use of active discretion arises from different views of how the economy works. One view holds that *the economy is so complex and economic aggregates interact in such obscure ways and with such varied lags that policy makers cannot comprehend what is going on well enough to pursue an active monetary or fiscal policy.* Milton Friedman is perhaps the best-known advocate of this position. He argues that although there is a link between money growth and the growth in nominal GDP, the exact relationship is hard to pin down because of long lags in the response of economic activity to changes in money growth. If the central bank adopts a discretionary policy that is based on an incorrect estimate of the lag structure, the money supply may expand just when a tighter monetary policy would be more appropriate. To avoid the timing problem, Friedman recommends that the Fed follow a fixed-growth-rate monetary policy year after year, such as an annual growth rate of 3 percent in the money supply. Changes in the financial structure of the economy since the early 1980s have made reliance on the fixed-growth-rate rule problematic. But the argument is that the Fed should announce and then pursue some clear, identifiable policy rule.

A comparison of economic forecasters and weather forecasters may help shed light on the position of those who advocate the use of a passive rule. Suppose you are in charge of the heating and cooling system at a major shopping mall. You realize that weather forecasters have a poor record in your area, particularly in the early spring, when days can be either warm or cold. Each day you must guess what the temperature will be and, based on that guess, decide whether to fire up the heater, turn on the air conditioner, or leave them both off. Because the mall is so large, you must start up the system long before you know for sure what the weather will be. Once the system has been turned on, it cannot be turned off until much later in the day.

Suppose you guess the day will be cold, so you turn on the heat. If the day turns out to be cold, your policy is correct and the mall temperature will be just right. But if the day turns out to be warm, the heater will make the mall unbearable. You would have been better off with nothing. In contrast, if you turn on the air conditioner expecting a warm day but the day turns out to be cold, the mall will be freezing. The lesson is that if you are unable to predict the weather, you should use neither heat nor air conditioning. Similarly, if monetary officials cannot predict the course of the economy, they should not try to fine-tune monetary policy. Complicating the prediction problem is the fact that monetary officials are not sure about the lags involved with monetary policy. The situation is comparable to your not knowing for sure when you turn the switch to "on" how long the system will actually take to come on.

This analogy applies only if the cost of doing nothing—using neither heat nor air conditioning—is relatively low. In the early spring, you can assume that there is little risk of the weather being so cold that water pipes freeze or so hot that the walls sweat. A similar assumption in the passive view is that the economy is inherently stable and periods of prolonged unemployment are unlikely. In such an economy, the costs of *not* intervening are relatively low. In contrast, advocates of active policy believe that there can be wide and prolonged swings in the economy (analogous to wide and prolonged swings in temperature), so doing nothing involves significant risks.

NetBookmark

The Region, a publication of the Minneapolis Federal Reserve Bank, has conducted interviews with Nobel prize winners and other noted economists. These are all now available on-line at http://minneapolisfed.org/pubs/region/int.html. Be sure to check out the interviews with Milton Friedman, the most important contemporary monetarist, Robert Lucas, and James Buchanan.

Rules and Rational Expectations

Another group of economists also advocates passive rules, but not because they believe we know too little about how the economy works. Proponents of the rational expectations approach, introduced earlier in this chapter, claim that people on average have a pretty good idea about how the economy works and what to expect from government policy makers. Individuals and firms know enough about the monetary and fiscal policies pursued in the past to forecast, with reasonable accuracy, future policies and their effects on the economy. Some individuals will forecast too high and some too low, but on average forecasts will turn out to be about right. *To the extent that monetary policy is fully anticipated by workers and firms, it has no effect on the level of output; it affects only the price level.* Thus only unexpected changes in policy can bring about short-run changes in output.

Since, in the long run, changes in the money supply affect only the rate of inflation, not real output, followers of the rational expectations theory believe that the Fed should not try to pursue a discretionary monetary policy. Instead, the Fed should follow a predictable monetary rule. A monetary rule would reduce monetary surprises and keep output near the natural rate. *Whereas Friedman advocates a rule because of the Fed's ignorance about the lag structure of the economy, rational expectations theorists advocate a predictable rule to avoid monetary surprises, which result in unnecessary departures from the natural rate of output.*

Despite support by some economists for explicit rules rather than discretion, central bankers appear reluctant to follow hard-and-fast rules about the course of future policy. Discretion appears to rule the day. As Paul Volcker, the former Fed chairman, argued:

> *The appeal of a simple rule is obvious. It would simplify our job at the Federal Reserve, make monetary policy easy to understand, and facilitate monitoring of our performance. And if the rule worked, it would reduce uncertainty. . . . But unfortunately, I know of no rule that can be relied on with sufficient consistency in our complex and constantly evolving economy.*[3]

Thus far we have looked at active stabilization policy, which focuses on shifts in the aggregate demand curve, and passive stabilization policy, which relies more on natural shifts in the short-run aggregate-supply curve. In the final section we focus on an additional model, the Phillips curve, which sheds more light on the relationship between aggregate demand and aggregate supply.

THE PHILLIPS CURVE

At one time, policy makers thought they faced a fairly stable long-run tradeoff between inflation and unemployment. This view was suggested by the research of New Zealand economist A.W. Phillips, who in 1958 published an article that examined the historical relation between inflation and unemployment in the United Kingdom.[4] Based on about 100 years of evidence, his data traced out an inverse relationship between the unemployment rate and the rate of change in money wages (serving as a measure of inflation). This relationship implied that the opportunity cost of reducing unemployment was higher inflation, and the opportunity cost of reducing inflation was higher unemployment.

Phillips curve A curve showing possible combinations of the inflation rate and the unemployment rate

The possible options with respect to unemployment and inflation are illustrated by the hypothetical **Phillips curve** in Exhibit 5. The unemployment rate is measured along the horizontal axis and the inflation rate along the vertical axis. Let's begin at point *a,* which depicts one possible combination of unemployment and inflation. Fiscal or monetary policy could be used to stimulate output and

3 Statement of Paul Volcker, then chairman of the Board of Governors of the Federal Reserve System, before the Committee on Banking, Finance, and Urban Affairs, U.S. House of Representatives, August 1983.

4 A.W. Phillips, "Relation Between Unemployment and the Rate of Change in Money Wage Rates in the United Kingdom, 1861–1957," *Economica* 25 (November 1958): 283–299.

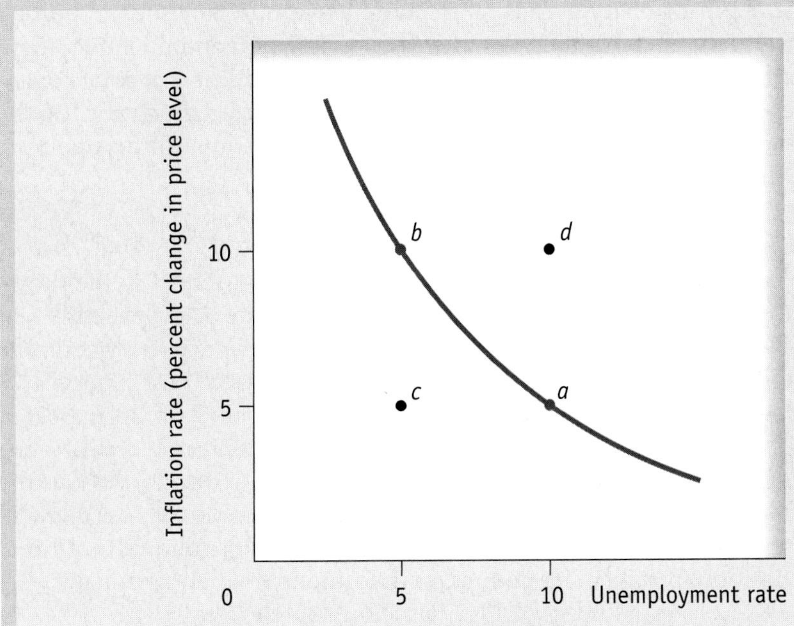

EXHIBIT 5

Hypothetical Phillips Curve

Points *a* and *b* lie on the Phillips curve and represent alternative combinations of the inflation rate and the unemployment rate that are attainable as long as the curve itself does not shift. Points *c* and *d* are off the curve; they are not attainable combinations.

thereby reduce unemployment, moving the economy from point *a* to point *b*. Notice, however, that the reduction in unemployment comes at the cost of higher inflation. A reduction in unemployment with no change in inflation would be represented by point *c*. But as you can see, this alternative is not an option available on the curve. Thus policy makers were thought to face a difficult trade-off: They could choose either lower inflation or lower unemployment, but not both.

Not everyone accepted the implications of the Phillips curve, but during the 1960s, policy makers increasingly came to believe that they faced a stable, long-run trade-off between unemployment and inflation. The Phillips curve was based on an era when inflation was low and the primary disturbances in the economy were shocks to aggregate demand. Changes in aggregate demand can be viewed as movements along a given short-run aggregate supply curve. If aggregate demand increased, the price level increased, but unemployment fell. If aggregate demand decreased, the price level decreased, but unemployment increased. Many economists therefore assumed that there was a trade-off between inflation and unemployment. Hence, with appropriate demand-management policies, government policy makers could choose any point along the Phillips curve.

The 1970s proved this view wrong for two reasons. First, some of the biggest disturbances were adverse *supply* shocks, such as those created by the oil embargoes and worldwide crop failures. These shocks shifted the aggregate supply curve to the left. A reduction in aggregate supply led to both higher inflation *and* higher unemployment. This stagflation was at odds with the Phillips curve. Second, economists learned that when short-run equilibrium output exceeds potential output, an expansionary gap opens. As this gap is closed by the upward movement of the short-run aggregate supply curve, the results are greater inflation *and* higher unemployment—again, results inconsistent with a given Phillips curve.

The combination of high inflation and high unemployment resulting from stagflation and expansionary gaps is represented by an outcome such as point *d* in Exhibit 5. By the end of the 1970s, increases in inflation and unemployment suggested either that the Phillips curve had shifted outward or that it no longer described economic reality. The situation called for a reexamination of the Phillips curve, a reexamination that led economists to distinguish between the short-run Phillips curve and the long-run Phillips curve.

The Short-Run Phillips Curve

To discuss the underpinnings of the Phillips curve, we must return to the short-run aggregate supply curve. Let's begin by assuming that the price level this year is reflected by a price index of, say, 100. Suppose that people expect prices to be about 3 percent higher next year. So the price level expected for next year is 103. Workers will therefore negotiate wage contracts based on an expected price level of 103, which is 3 percent higher than the current price level. As the short-run aggregate supply curve in panel (a) of Exhibit 6 indicates, if *AD* is the aggregate demand curve and the price level is 103, as expected, output will equal the economy's potential GDP, shown here to be $8.0 trillion. Recall that when the economy produces its potential GDP, unemployment is equal to the natural rate.

The short-run relationship between inflation and unemployment is presented in panel (b) of Exhibit 6 under the assumption that people expect the inflation rate to be 3 percent. The unemployment rate is measured along the horizontal axis and the inflation rate along the vertical axis. Panel (a) shows that when the inflation rate is 3 percent, the economy produces its potential GDP. When the economy produces its potential GDP, unemployment is at the natural rate, which we assume to be 5 percent in panel (b). The combination of 3 percent inflation and 5 percent unemployment is reflected by point *a* in panel (b), which corresponds to point *a* in panel (a).

What if aggregate demand turns out to be greater than expected, as indicated by *AD*' in panel (a)? In the short run, the greater demand results in equilibrium at point *b,* with a price level of 105 and an output level of $8.1 trillion. Since the price level is greater than the level reflected in wage contracts, the inflation rate is also greater than expected. Specifically, the inflation rate turns out to be 5 percent, not 3 percent. Output now exceeds potential, so the unemployment rate falls below the natural rate to 4 percent. This combination of a higher inflation rate and a lower level of unemployment is depicted by point *b* in panel (b), which corresponds to point *b* in panel (a).

What if aggregate demand turns out to be lower than expected, as indicated by *AD*" in panel (a)? In the short run, the lower demand results in equilibrium at point *c,* where the price level of 101 is lower than the expected level reflected in labor contracts, and output of $7.9 trillion is below potential GDP. With a lower-than-expected price level, the inflation rate is 1 percent rather than the expected 3 percent. With output below the economy's potential, the unemployment rate is 6 percent, which exceeds the natural rate. This combination of lower-than-expected inflation and higher-than-expected unemployment is reflected by point *c* on the curve in panel (b).

Note that the short-run aggregate supply curve in panel (a) can be used to establish the inverse relationship between the inflation rate and the level of

EXHIBIT 6

Relationship Between the Short-Run Aggregate Supply Curve and the Short-Run Phillips Curve

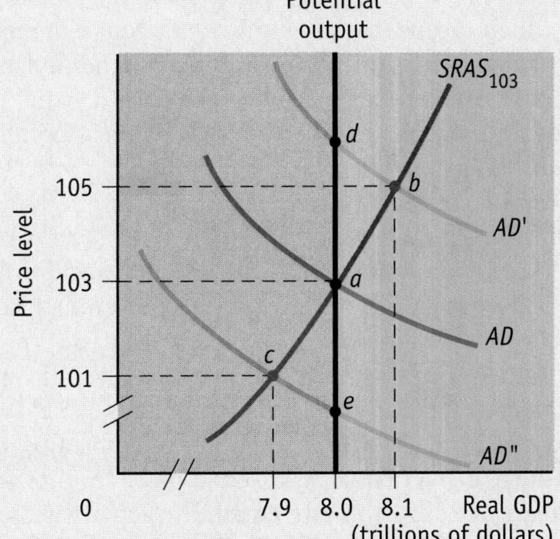

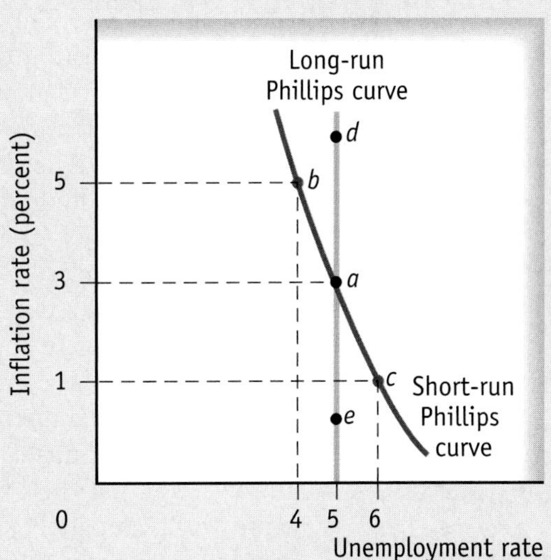

If people expect a price level of 103, which is 3 percent higher than the current level, and if *AD* is the aggregate demand curve, then the price level will actually be 103 and output will be at the potential rate. Point *a* in both panels represents this situation. Unemployment will be at the natural rate, 5 percent

If aggregate demand is higher than expected (*AD'* instead of *AD*), the economy will be at point *b* in both panels. If aggregate demand is less than expected (*AD"* rather than *AD*), short-run equilibrium will be at point c; the price level, 101, will be lower than expected, and output will be below the potential rate. The lower inflation rate and higher unemployment rate are shown as point *c* in panel (b). In panel (b), points *a, b,* and *c* trace the short-run Phillips curve.

In the long run, the actual price level equals the expected price level and output is at the potential level, $8.0 trillion, in panel (a), and unemployment is at the natural rate, 5 percent, in panel (b). Points *a, d,* and *e* represent that situation; they lie on the vertical long-run Phillips curve.

unemployment illustrated in panel (b). This latter curve is called a **short-run Phillips curve,** and it is generated by the intersection of alternative aggregate demand curves along a given short-run aggregate supply curve. *The short-run Phillips curve is based on labor contracts that reflect a given expected price level, which implies a given expected rate of inflation.* The short-run Phillips curve in panel (b) is based on an expected inflation rate of 3 percent. If inflation turns out as expected, unemployment equals the natural rate. If inflation is higher than expected, unemployment in the short run falls below the natural rate. If inflation is lower than expected, unemployment in the short run exceeds the natural rate.

Short-run Phillips curve A curve, based on an expected inflation rate, that reflects an inverse relationship between the inflation rate and the level of unemployment

The Long-Run Phillips Curve

If inflation is higher than was expected, output can exceed the economy's potential in the short run but not in the long run. Labor shortages and worker dissatisfaction with shrinking real wages will lead to higher wage agreements during the next round of negotiations. The short-run aggregate supply curve will shift up to the left until it passes through point *d* in panel (a) of Exhibit 6, returning the economy to its potential level of output. Point *d* corresponds to a higher price level, and hence a higher rate of inflation. But notice that the higher inflation is no longer associated with reduced unemployment.

With the closing of the expansionary gap, the economy experiences both higher unemployment and higher inflation. At point *d* in panel (a) the economy is producing its potential GDP, which means that unemployment equals the natural rate. This combination of the natural rate of unemployment and higher inflation is depicted by point *d* in panel (b). The unexpectedly higher aggregate demand curve has no lasting effect on output or unemployment. Note that whereas points *a, b,* and *c* are on the same short-run Phillips curve, point *d* is not.

To trace the long-run effects of a lower-than-expected price level, let's return to point *c* in panel (a) of Exhibit 6. At this point, the actual price level is below the expected level, so output is below potential GDP. If firms and workers negotiate lower money wages (or if the growth in nominal wages trails inflation), the short-run aggregate supply curve will shift to the right until it passes through point *e,* where the economy returns once again to its potential level of output. Both inflation and unemployment will fall, as reflected by point *e* in panel (b).

Note that points *a, d,* and *e* in panel (a) depict long-run equilibrium points, in the sense that the expected price level equals the actual price level. At those same points in panel (b), the expected inflation rate equals the actual rate, so unemployment equals the natural rate. We can connect points *a, d,* and *e* in panel (b) to form what is called the **long-run Phillips curve.** *When employers and workers have the time and the ability to adjust fully to any unexpected change in aggregate demand, the long-run Phillips curve is a vertical line drawn at the economy's natural rate of unemployment,* as shown in panel (b). As long as prices and wages are flexible, the rate of unemployment, in the long run, is independent of the rate of inflation. *Thus, according to proponents of this type of analysis, in the long run, policy makers cannot choose between unemployment and inflation. They can choose only among alternative rates of inflation.*

Long-run Phillips curve A vertical line drawn at the economy's natural rate of unemployment that traces equilibrium points that can occur when employers and workers have the time to adjust fully to any unexpected change in aggregate demand

The Natural Rate Hypothesis

As defined in Chapter 11, the natural rate of unemployment is the rate that is consistent with the economy's potential level of output, which we have discussed extensively already. An important idea that emerged from this reexamination of the Phillips curve is the **natural rate hypothesis,** which states that in the long run the economy tends toward the natural rate of unemployment. This natural rate is largely independent of the level of the *aggregate demand* stimulus provided by monetary or fiscal policy. Policy makers may be able to push the economy beyond its natural, or potential, rate of production temporarily, but only if the public does not anticipate the resulting level of aggregate demand and the resulting price level. The natural rate hypothesis implies that *regardless of policy makers' concerns about unemployment, the policy that results in low inflation is generally going to be the optimal policy in the long run.*

Natural rate hypothesis The natural rate of unemployment is largely independent of the stimulus provided by monetary or fiscal policy.

Evidence of the Phillips Curve

What has been the actual relationship between unemployment and inflation in the United States? In Exhibit 7, each year since 1960 is represented by a point, with the unemployment rate measured along the horizontal axis and the infla-

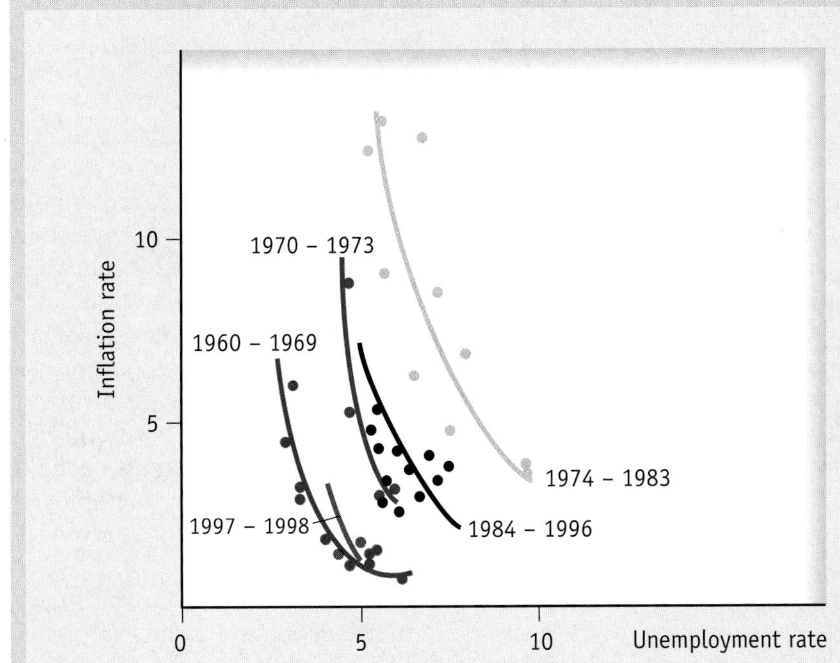

EXHIBIT 7

Short-Run Phillips Curves Since 1960

The figure shows U.S. unemployment-inflation rate combinations since 1960. Note that the short-run Phillips curve has shifted as inflation expectations have changed.

tion rate measured along the vertical axis. Superimposed on these points is a series of short-run Phillips curves showing patterns of unemployment and inflation during five distinct periods since 1960. Remember, each short-run Phillips curve is drawn for a given *expected rate of inflation*. A change in inflationary expectations results in a shift of the short-run Phillips curve.

The clearest trade-off between unemployment and inflation occurred between 1960 and 1969; the points for those years fit neatly along the curve. In the early part of the decade, inflation was low but unemployment was high; as the 1960s progressed, unemployment declined but actual inflation increased. The inflation rate during the decade averaged only 2.5 percent, and the unemployment rate averaged 4.8 percent.

The short-run Phillips curve shifted up to the right for the period from 1970 to 1973, when inflation and unemployment both climbed to an average of 5.2 percent. In 1974, sharp increases in oil prices and crop failures around the world reduced aggregate supply, which sparked another shift in the Phillips curve. Although points for the decade between 1974 and 1983 do not lie as neatly along the curve as points for earlier periods do, a trade-off between inflation and unemployment is still evident. During the 1974–1983 period, inflation rose on average to 8.2 percent and unemployment climbed on average to 7.5 percent.

After recessions in the early 1980s, the short-run Phillips curve seems to have shifted downward since 1983. Average inflation for 1984–1996 fell to 3.7 percent and average unemployment fell to 6.1 percent. Finally, data for 1997 and 1998 suggest that a new, lower short-run Phillips curve may be forming, with average inflation of only 1.6 percent and average unemployment of 4.7.

Thus the Phillips curve shifted outward between the 1960s and the early 1980s. Since then, the Fed has learned more about how to control inflation, thereby shifting the Phillips curve back to about where it was during the 1960s.

CONCLUSION

This chapter examined the implications of active and passive policy. The important question is whether the economy is (1) essentially stable and self-correcting when it gets off track or (2) essentially unstable and in need of active intervention. Advocates of active policy believe that the Fed or Congress should reduce economic fluctuations by stimulating aggregate demand when output falls below its potential level and by dampening aggregate demand when output exceeds its potential level. Advocates of active policy argue that government attempts to insulate the economy from the ups and downs of the business cycle may be far from perfect but are better than nothing. Some activists also believe that high unemployment may be self-reinforcing, because some unemployed workers lose valuable job skills and grow to accept unemployment as a way of life, as has happened in Europe.

Advocates of passive policy, on the other hand, believe that discretionary policy may contribute to the cyclical swings in the economy, leading to higher inflation in the long run with no permanent boost in either output or employment. This group favors passive rules for monetary policy and automatic stabilizers for fiscal policy.

The active-passive debate in this chapter has focused primarily on monetary policy because discretionary fiscal policy, until quite recently, had been hampered by large federal deficits that ballooned the national debt. In the next chapter, we will take a closer look at the federal budget, recent federal deficits, and federal debt.

SUMMARY

1. Advocates of active policy view the private sector—particularly fluctuations in investment—as the main source of economic instability in the economy. Activists argue that the return to potential output can be slow and painful, so the Fed or Congress should intervene with monetary or fiscal policy to stimulate aggregate demand when actual output falls below potential output.

2. Advocates of passive policy argue that the economy has a natural resiliency that will cause output to return to its potential level within a reasonable amount of time if upset by some shock. They point to the variable and uncertain lags associated with discretionary policy as reason enough to steer clear of active intervention.

3. The passive policy approach suggests that the government should follow clear and predictable policies and avoid trying to stimulate or dampen aggregate demand over the business cycle. Passive policies are reflected in automatic fiscal stabilizers and in explicit monetary rules, such as a fixed rate of growth in the money supply.

4. At one time, public officials thought they faced a stable trade-off between higher unemployment and higher inflation. Recent evidence suggests that if there is a trade-off, it exists only in the short run, not in the long run. Expansionary fiscal or monetary policies, if unexpected, can stimulate output and employment in the short run. But if the economy is already at or near its potential output, these expansionary policies will, in the long run, result only in higher inflation.

QUESTIONS FOR REVIEW

1. *(Active Versus Passive Policy)* Contrast the passive policy view of the behavior of wages and prices during a contractionary gap to the active policy view.

2. *(Active Policy)* Why do proponents of active policy recommend government intervention to close an expansionary gap?

3. *(Active Versus Passive Policy)* According to advocates of passive policy, what variable naturally adjusts in the labor market, shifting the short-run aggregate supply curve to restore unemployment to the natural rate? Why does the active policy approach assume that the short-run aggregate supply curve shifts upward more easily and quickly than it shifts downward?

4. *(Review of Policy Perspectives)* Why may an active policy approach be more politically popular than a passive approach, especially during a recession?

5. *(Macroeconomic Policy)* Some economists argue that only unanticipated increases in the money supply can affect real GDP. Explain why this may be the case.

6. *(Anticipating Monetary Policy)* In 1993 the Fed began announcing its interest rate targets immediately following each meeting of the Federal Open Market Committee. Prior to that, observers were left to draw inferences about Fed policy based on the results of that policy. What is the value of this new openness?

7. *(Policy Credibility)* What is policy credibility and how is it relevant to the problem of reducing the inflation rate? How is credibility related to the time-inconsistency problem?

8. *(Case**Study**: Central Bank Independence and Price Stability)* One source of independence for the Fed, as suggested in Chapter 13, is the length of term for members of the Board of Governors. In Chapter 15, we learned that the Fed is a "money machine." Does this suggest another source of Fed independence from Congress?

9. *(Rationale for Rules)* Some economists call for predetermined rules to guide the actions of government policy makers. What are the two rationales that have been given for such rules?

10. *(Rational Expectations and Policy)* Suppose that people in an election year believe that public policy makers are going to pursue expansionary policies to enhance their reelection prospects. How could such expectations put pressure on officials to pursue expansionary policies even if they hadn't been planning to?

11. *(Short-Run Phillips Curve)* Why does a movement leftward and upward along the short-run Phillips curve imply a declining real wage for workers? Would workers allow this decline to continue unabated? How would the short-run Phillips curve eventually adjust to changes in workers' perceptions about their real wages?

12. *(Potential GNP)* Why is it hard for policy makers to decide if the economy is operating at its potential output level? Why is this uncertainty a problem?

13. *(Phillips Curves)* Describe the different policy trade-offs implied by the short-run Phillips curve and the long-run Phillips curve. What forces shift the long-run Phillips curve?

PROBLEMS AND EXERCISES

14 *(Active Versus Passive Policy)* Discuss the role each of the following plays in the debate between the active and passive approaches:
   a. The speed of adjustment of the nominal wage
   b. The speed of adjustment of expectations about inflation
   c. The existence of lags in policy creation and implementation
   d. Variability in the natural rate of unemployment over time

15. *(Case**Study**: Active versus Passive Presidential Candidates)* What were the main differences between candidates Bush and Clinton in the 1992 presidential campaign? Illustrate their ideas using the aggregate supply and demand model.

16. *(Problems with Active Policy)* Use an *AD-AS* diagram to illustrate and explain the short-run and long-run effects on the economy of the following situation: Both the natural rate of unemployment and the actual rate of unemployment are 5 percent. However, the government

believes that the natural rate of unemployment is 6 percent and that the economy is overheating. Therefore, it introduces a policy to reduce aggregate demand.

17. *(Policy Lags)* What lag in discretionary policy is described in each of the following statements? Why do long lags make discretionary policy less effective?
    a. The time from when the government determines that the economy is in recession until a tax cut is approved to reduce unemployment
    b. The time from when the money supply is increased until the resulting effect on the economy is felt
    c. The time from the start of a recession until the government identifies the existence and severity of the recession
    d. The time from when the Fed decides to reduce the money supply until the money supply actually declines

18. *(Rational Expectations)* Using an *AD-AS* diagram, illustrate the short-run effects on prices, output, and unemployment of an increase in the money supply that is correctly anticipated by the public. Assume that the economy is initially at potential output.

19. *(Long-Run Phillips Curve)* Suppose the economy is at point *d* on the long-run Phillips curve shown in Exhibit 6. If that inflation rate is unacceptably high, how can policy makers get the inflation rate down? Would rational expectations help or hinder their efforts?

EXPERIENTIAL EXERCISES

20. *(Active Versus Passive Policy)* The Federal Reserve Bank of Minneapolis's *The Region* at http://woodrow.mpls.frb.fed.us/pubs/region/int.html features an ongoing series of interviews with prominent U.S. policy makers. Choose a Fed governor or a regional Reserve Bank president and try to determine whether that person leans more toward an active or a passive policy view. What specific policy views does that person advocate?

21. *(CaseStudy: Central Bank Independence and Price Stability)* The Bank for International Settlements maintains a list of links to central banks around the world at http://www.bis.org/cbanks.htm. Many of those banks maintain English-language Web pages. Choose one or two nations and explore their central bank Web pages. How much independence do those banks have? To what extent are their functions and goals similar to those of the U.S. Federal Reserve System?

22. *(Wall Street Journal)* A good source for the latest information regarding macroeconomic policy is the Economy column that appears in the daily *Wall Street Journal.* Take a look at today's issue and review the latest hot topics. Then turn to the editorial pages, where the *Journal's* editorial board, contributors, and letter writers have their say.

HAPTER

17

Federal Budgets and Public Policy

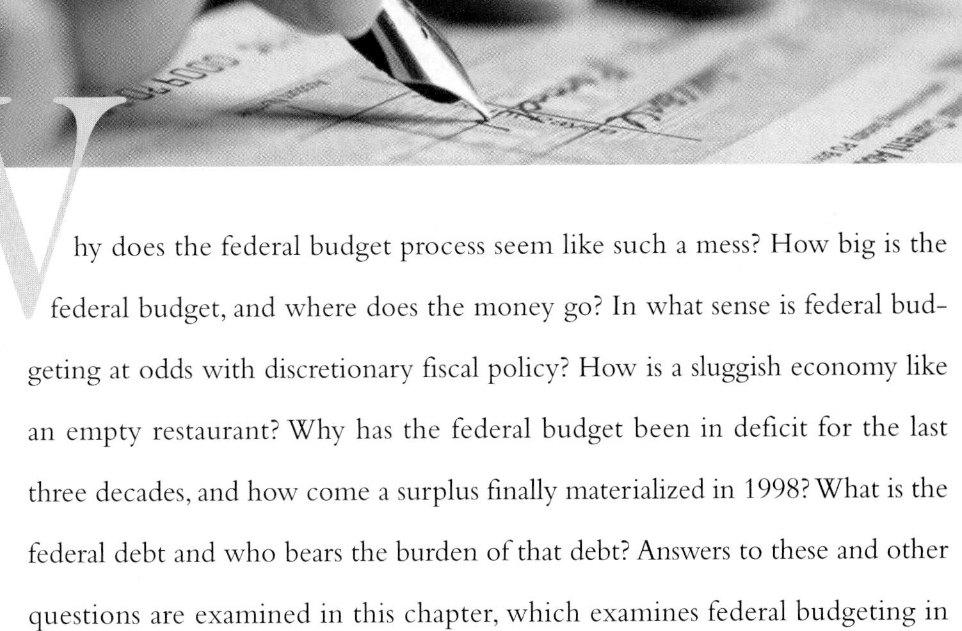

Why does the federal budget process seem like such a mess? How big is the federal budget, and where does the money go? In what sense is federal budgeting at odds with discretionary fiscal policy? How is a sluggish economy like an empty restaurant? Why has the federal budget been in deficit for the last three decades, and how come a surplus finally materialized in 1998? What is the federal debt and who bears the burden of that debt? Answers to these and other questions are examined in this chapter, which examines federal budgeting in theory and practice.

sit the McEachern
ractive Study Center
or this chapter at
/mcisc.swcollege.com

The word *budget* derives from the Old French word *bougette,* which means "little bag." The annual federal budget now exceeds $1,800,000,000,000.00— over $1.8 trillion dollars a year. That's big money! If this "little bag" contained

$100 bills, it would weigh over 19,000 *tons*! These $100 bills would fill over 670 trailer trucks or they could paper over a 10-lane highway stretching from Bangor, Maine, to San Diego, California. This budget could cover every U.S. family's mortgage and car payment every month. If the president's sole function were to pay the bills by writing million-dollar checks, to keep up with federal spending, our chief executive would have to write over three checks a minute, 24 hours a day, 365 days a year.

Government budgets have a tremendous impact on the economy. Government outlays at all levels amount to about one-third the size of GDP. Our focus in this chapter will be the federal budget, beginning with an examination of the federal budget process. We then consider budget deficits of the last three decades along with the resulting explosion of national debt. We will look at the source of the deficits, the effects of deficits on the economy, and why the deficits disappeared as of 1998. We also examine the impact of a higher national debt. Topics discussed in this chapter include:

- The budget process
- Rationale for deficits
- Impact of deficits
- Crowding out and crowding in
- The miraculous budget surplus
- The burden of the federal debt

Federal budget A plan for federal government outlays and revenues for a specified period, usually a year

THE FEDERAL BUDGET PROCESS

The **federal budget** is a plan for government outlays and revenues for a specified period, usually a year. Outlays include both government purchases (which we have referred to as *G*) and transfer payments. Social Security, Medicare, and welfare payments made up about half of federal outlays in fiscal year 1998. National defense accounted for 15.8 percent of the budget (down from 28.1 percent in 1987). And interest payments on the debt soaked up 14 percent of the budget, or about one in seven federal dollars, up from 7 percent in 1975.

The period covered by the federal budget is called the *fiscal year;* it runs from October 1 of one year to September 30 of the following year. Exhibit 1 shows the composition of federal outlays by major category since 1959. As you can see, defense spending has declined as a percentage of federal outlays, while Social Security and Medicare, programs aimed primarily at the elderly, have increased and now account for over one-third of the federal budget. For the last two decades, welfare spending, which consists of cash and in-kind transfer payments, has remained relatively constant as a share of all federal outlays, accounting for one-seventh of the federal budget.

NetBookmark

Policy.com at www.policy.com is ". . . a comprehensive public policy resource and community. Policy.com is non-partisan and free to users." The site provides daily news headlines and links to other on-line resources organized by issue and group. One such group is the Center on Budget and Policy Priorities, at http://www.cbpp.org/index.html, which describes itself as a nonpartisan research organization and policy institute that conducts research and analysis on a range of government policies and programs, with an emphasis on those affecting people with low and moderate incomes.

The Presidential Role in the Budget Process

Before 1921, the federal budget played a minor role in the economy, with federal outlays, except during wartime, amounting to less than 3 percent of GDP (versus 19.2 percent in 1998). Federal agencies made budget requests directly to Congress, bypassing the president entirely. Legislation in 1921 created the Office of Management and Budget (OMB) to examine agency budget requests and to help the president develop a budget proposal.

The Employment Act of 1946 created the Council of Economic Advisers to forecast economic activity and assist the president in formulating an appro-

EXHIBIT 1

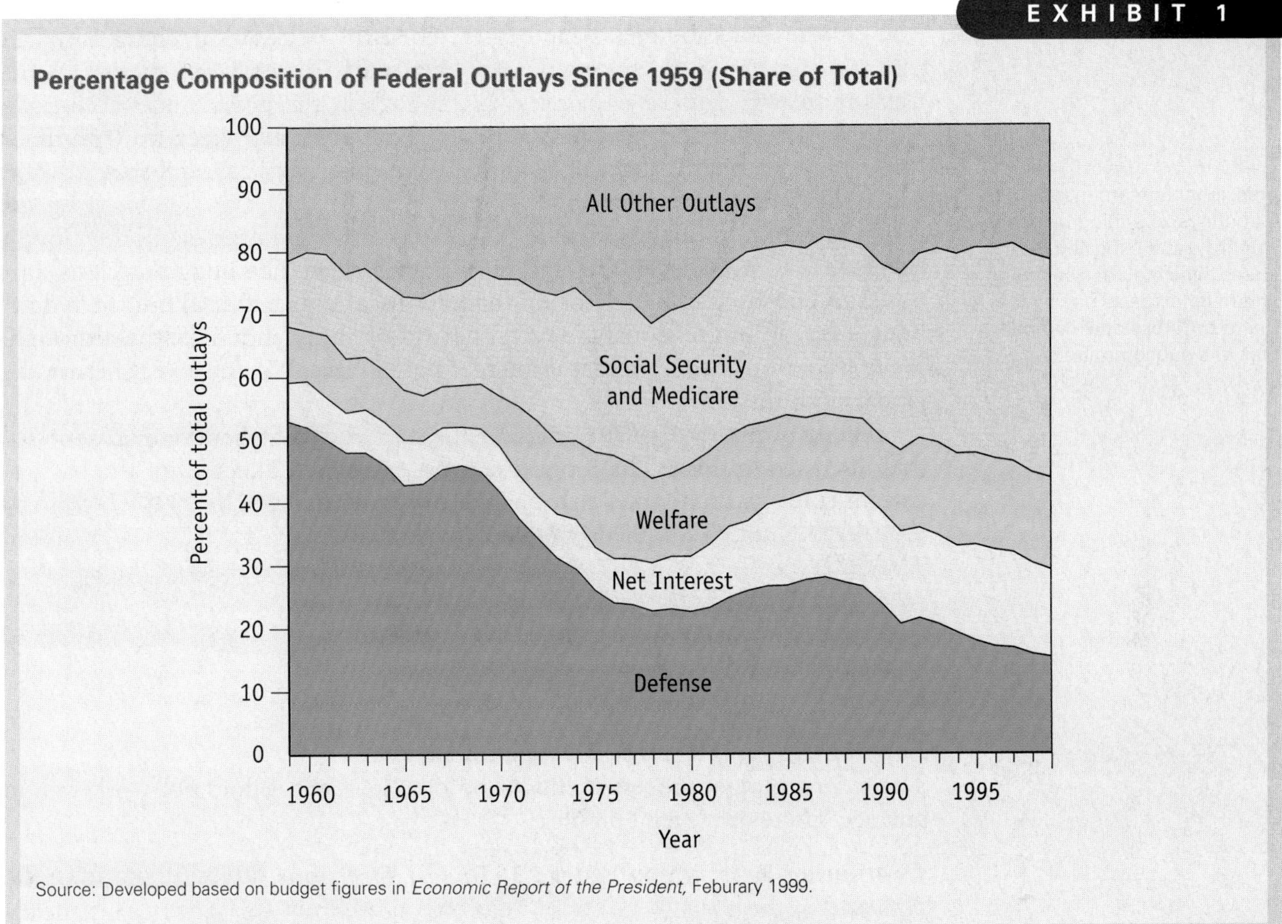

Source: Developed based on budget figures in *Economic Report of the President,* Feburary 1999.

priate fiscal policy. During the 1960s and 1970s, various measures were introduced by the executive branch to improve the evaluation of government programs. By the mid-1970s, the president had in place the staff and the procedures to translate policy into a budget proposal to be presented to Congress.

Development of the president's budget begins a year before it is submitted to Congress, with each agency preparing a budget request. The formal budget process begins early in the calendar year, when the president submits to Congress a pile of books called *The Budget of the United States Government* (the 1999 budget filled four volumes). This document details the president's proposals about what should be spent in the upcoming fiscal year and how this spending should be financed. At this stage, the president's budget is little more than detailed suggestions for congressional consideration. Soon after a budget is proposed, the *Economic Report of the President* is also transmitted to Congress. This report, required under the Employment Act of 1946 and written by the Council of Economic Advisers, reflects the administration's views about the state of the economy and includes fiscal policy recommendations for fostering "maximum employment, production, and purchasing power."

The Congressional Role in the Budget Process

The congressional budget cycle begins when the president presents a budget to Congress—in late January or early February. Budget committees in the House and the Senate then rework the President's budget and eventually agree on total outlays, spending by major category, and expected revenues. Once an overall budget outline has been approved by Congress as a **budget resolution,** this resolution is supposed to discipline the many congressional committees and subcommittees that authorize spending by establishing a framework to guide spending and revenue decisions. The budget cycle is supposed to end by October 1, when the new fiscal year begins. Thus the federal budget has a congressional gestation period of about nine months, although, as we have noted, the president's budget begins taking shape a year before the January submission.

Budget resolution A congressional agreement about total outlays, spending by major category, and expected revenues, which guides spending and revenue decisions by the many congressional committees and subcommittees

The spending side of the budget is usually outlined in much greater detail than the revenue side. That's because most taxes are collected on the basis of certain rules and schedules that change infrequently. Of special interest is the bottom line, the relationship between *budgeted* outlays and *projected* revenues. The difference between outlays and revenues is one measure of the budget's fiscal impact. *When outlays exceed revenues, the budget is in deficit. A larger deficit stimulates aggregate demand. Alternatively, when revenues exceed outlays, the budget is in surplus. A larger surplus dampens aggregate demand.*

Problems with the Budget Process

The federal budget process sounds good on paper, but it does not work well in practice. There are several problems.

Continuing Resolutions Instead of Budget Decisions. The budget timetable discussed in the preceding section is often ignored by Congress. Because deadlines are frequently missed, budgets typically run from year to year based on **continuing resolutions,** which are agreements to allow agencies, in the absence of an approved budget, to spend at the rate of the previous year's budget. Poorly conceived programs continue through sheer inertia; successful programs cannot be expanded. On occasion, the president must shut down some government functions temporarily because not even the continuing resolution can be approved on time. For example, in late 1995 and early 1996, two government shutdowns closed most government offices for 27 days. Congress also failed to approve a continuing resolution before the start of the 1999 fiscal year.

Continuing resolutions Budget agreements that allow agencies, in the absence of an approved budget, to spend at the rate of the previous year's budget

Overlapping Committee Authority. Overlaps in budget authority among the many congressional committees and subcommittees require the executive branch of government to defend the same section of the president's budget before several committees in both the House and the Senate. Those responsible for running the federal government end up spending much of their time testifying before assorted congressional committees. Because several committees have jurisdiction over the same area, no committee really has final authority, so matters often remain unresolved even after extensive committee deliberations.

Lengthy Budget Process. You can imagine the difficulty of using the budget as a tool of fiscal policy when the budget process takes so long. Given that the average recession lasts only about a year and that budget preparations begin more than a year and a half before the budget goes into effect, planning discretionary fiscal measures to address economic fluctuations is difficult. That's one reason why attempts to stimulate an ailing economy often seem so half-hearted; by the time Congress agrees on a fiscal remedy, the economy has often taken a turn for the better on its own.

Uncontrollable Budget Items. Congress has only limited control over much of the budget. Some budget items, such as interest on the national debt, cannot be changed in the near term. *About three-quarters of the budget outlays are determined by existing laws.* For example, once Congress establishes eligibility criteria, **entitlement programs,** such as Social Security and Medicare, take on a life of their own, with each annual appropriation simply reflecting the amount required to support the expected number of entitled beneficiaries. Congress has no say in such appropriations unless it chooses to change the eligibility criteria or the level of benefits. Most entitlement programs have such politically powerful constituencies that Congress is reluctant to mess with the structure.

Entitlement programs
Guaranteed benefits for those who qualify under government transfer programs such as Social Security and Medicare

Overly Detailed Budget. The federal budget is divided into thousands of accounts and subaccounts, which is why it fills four volumes. To the extent that the budget is a way of making political payoffs, such micromanagement allows elected officials to reward friends and punish enemies with great precision. For example, in recent budgets Congress has found $2.7 million for a freshwater catfish farm in Arkansas, $2.5 million to remove asbestos from a meat-packing plant in Iowa, and $10 million to build a ramp to the Milwaukee Brewers' stadium parking lot. Congress tends to budget in such minute detail that the big picture gets lost. *This detailed budgeting is not only time-consuming, but it also reduces the flexibility of the budget as a tool for discretionary fiscal policy.* When economic conditions change or when there is a shift in the demand for certain kinds of publicly provided goods, the federal government cannot easily reallocate funds from one account to another.

Suggested Budget Reforms

Several reforms have been suggested to improve the budget process. First, the annual budget could be converted into a two-year budget, or *biennial budget.* As it is, Congress spends nearly all of the year working on the budget. The executive branch is always dealing with three budgets: administering an approved budget, defending a proposed budget before congressional committees, and preparing the next budget for submission to Congress. If decisions were made for two years at a time, Congress would not be continually involved with budget deliberations, and executive branch heads could run their agencies rather than march from committee hearing to committee hearing. A two-year budget, however, would require longer-term economic forecasts of the economy and would be even less useful than a one-year budget as a tool of discretionary fiscal policy.

Another possible reform would be for Congress to simplify the budget document by concentrating on major groupings and eliminating line items. Each agency head could then be given an overall budget, along with the discretion to allocate funds in a manner consistent with the perceived demands for agency services. The drawback is that agency heads may have different priorities than those of elected representatives.

Another way of making more sense of the budget and its impact would be to sort federal spending into a capital budget and an operating budget. As it is, Congress approves a single budget that throws together the cost of new federal building with the payroll cost of federal employees. A *capital budget* would include spending on physical capital such as buildings, highways, dams, computers, and other government infrastructure. An *operating budget* would include spending on the payroll, building maintenance, computer paper, paper clips, and other ongoing expenses. We will return to this issue.

FEDERAL BUDGET DEFICITS

When government outlays—that is, government purchases plus transfer payments—exceed government revenue, the result is a *budget deficit,* a term first introduced in Chapter 5. Although the federal budget experienced a surplus in 1998, it had been in deficit every year but one since 1960. That's nearly four decades of deficits. To place deficits in perspective, let's first examine the economic rationale for deficit financing.

Rationale for Deficits

Deficit financing has been justified for outlays that increase the economy's productivity—capital outlays for investments such as highways, waterways, and dams. The cost of these capital projects should be borne in part by future taxpayers, who will also benefit from these investments. Hence there is some justification for borrowing to finance capital projects so that future taxpayers can help pay for them. This rationale is used to fund capital projects at the state and local level. But, as noted already, the federal government does not budget capital projects separately, so there is no link between deficits and capital budgets.

Before the Great Depression, federal deficits occurred only during wartime. Because wars involved much hardship, public officials were understandably reluctant to increase taxes much to finance war-related spending. Deficits incurred during wars were largely self-correcting, however, because after each war government spending dropped faster than government revenues.

The Depression led John Maynard Keynes to argue that government spending should compensate for any drop in investment spending. As you know, the Keynesian prescription for fighting an economic slump is for the federal government to stimulate aggregate demand through deficit spending. As a result of the Depression, automatic stabilizers were also introduced, which increased government outlays during recessions and decreased them during expansions. The federal deficit therefore increases during recessions because, as economic activity slows, unemployment rises, increasing government outlays for unemployment benefits and for other transfer payments. Furthermore, tax revenues decline during recessions. For example, as a result of the 1990–1991 recession, annual tax revenues from corporations fell by $14 billion between 1989 and 1992, while transfer payments for "income security" jumped by $60 billion. An economic expansion is the other side of the coin. As business activity expands, so do jobs, personal income, and corporate profits, causing federal revenue to swell. With reduced joblessness, transfer payments decline. Thus the federal deficit shrinks.

Budget Philosophies and Deficits

Several budget philosophies have emerged over the years. Fiscal policy prior to the Great Depression aimed at maintaining an **annually balanced budget,** except during wartime. Since tax revenues rise during expansions and fall during recessions, the annually balanced budget means the federal government must increase spending during expansions and reduce spending during recessions. But such spending will worsen fluctuations in the business cycle, overheating the economy during expansions and increasing unemployment during recessions.

A second budget philosophy calls for a **cyclically balanced budget,** which means budget deficits during recessions and budget surpluses during expansions. Fiscal policy would thereby dampen swings in the business cycle without increasing the national debt. Nearly all state governments have established "rainy day" funds to build up budget surpluses during the good times for use during hard times.

A third budget philosophy is **functional finance,** which says that policy makers should be less concerned with balancing the budget annually, or even over the business cycle, than with ensuring that the economy produces its potential output. This philosophy argues that one of the federal government's primary responsibilities is to promote stability at the economy's potential level of output. If the budgets needed to keep the economy operating at its potential GDP involve chronic deficits, so be it. Since the Great Depression, budgets in this country have seldom balanced. *Although budget deficits have been larger during recessions than during expansions, the federal budget has been in deficit in all but nine years since 1931.*

Annually balanced budget Budget philosophy prior to the Great Depression; aimed at equating revenues with outlays, except during times of war

Cyclically balanced budget A budget philosophy calling for budget deficits during recessions to be financed by budget surpluses during expansions

Functional finance A budget philosophy aiming fiscal policy at achieving potential GDP, rather than balancing budgets either annually or over the business cycle

Deficits in the 1980s

In 1981, President Reagan secured a three-year budget resolution that included a large tax cut along with increases in defense spending. Some so-called *supply-side* economists argued that tax cuts would stimulate enough economic activity to keep tax revenues from falling. The congressional budget resolution adopted in 1981 was based on an assumption that unspecified spending cuts would bring the two sides of the budget into balance, but the promised cuts in spending never materialized.

Moreover, overly optimistic revenue projections—so-called rosy scenarios—were built into the budget. For example, the budget projected that real GDP would grow by 5.2 percent in 1982, but the economy fell into a recession and, instead, output dropped by 2.1 percent. The recession caused the automatic stabilizers to kick in, thereby reducing revenues and increasing spending still more. Since spending was underestimated and revenue overestimated, the deficit in 1982 amounted to about 4 percent of GDP, at the time one of the largest peacetime deficits in U.S. history.

The deficit served as a backdrop for budget debates in the early 1980s. President Reagan's budget strategy called for increases in defense spending, but he promised to veto any new taxes or any cuts in Social Security. The deficit climbed to 6.1 percent of GDP in 1983. In short, the government had cut tax rates but did not cut expenditures. *Federal revenues declined relative to GDP, but federal spending rose relative to GDP.* Exhibit 2 shows federal budget deficits and the lone surplus since 1970 relative to GDP. As you can see, the deficit as a percentage of GDP climbed in the early 1980s, declined somewhat as the economy improved after the recession of 1982, then increased in 1990 with the onset of another recession. But after bottoming out in 1991, the deficit decreased each year until blooming into a surplus in 1998. That's the short history of modern deficits. The longer story comes next.

EXHIBIT 2

U.S. Federal Budget Deficits and Surplus Relative to GDP

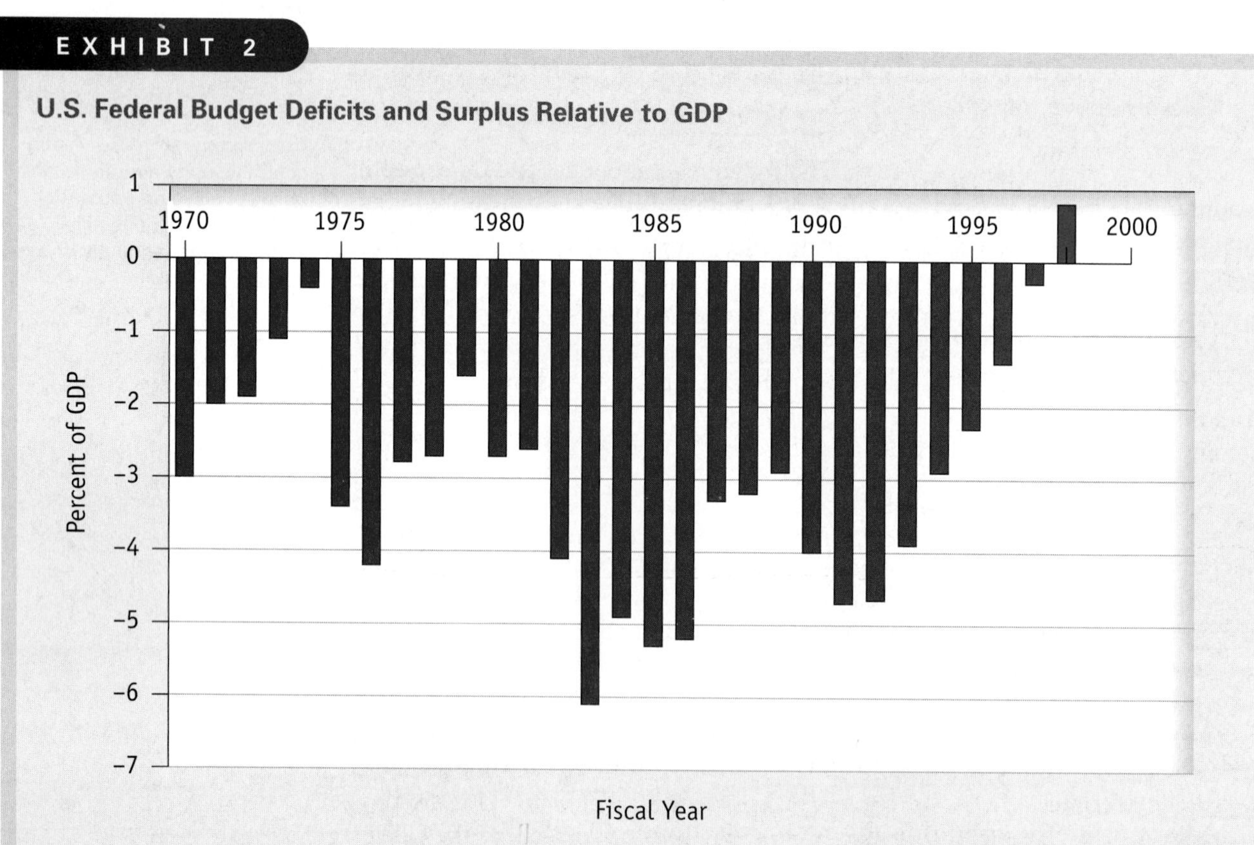

Source: Based on data found in the *Economic Report of the President,* February 1999.

Why Did Deficits Persist So Long?

As we have seen, the huge deficits of the 1980s and early 1990s were caused by a combination of tax cuts and spending increases. But why has the budget been in deficit for all but nine years since 1931? Why did federal budget deficits become so much a part of the federal budget scene? The most obvious answer is that Congress is not required to balance the budget. In contrast, in 49 states the legislatures are required to balance their budgets.

Let's consider one widely accepted model of the public sector. Elected officials attempt to maximize political support, including votes and campaign contributions. Voters like public spending programs but hate paying taxes, so spending programs win support and taxes lose support. Because of this asymmetry, candidates attempt to maximize their chances of getting elected by offering a budget that is long on benefits but short on taxes.

Moreover, the many fragmented congressional committees push their favorite programs with little concern about the overall budget. For example, a defense bill recently included 18 F-14D fighter jets and 36 V-22 Osprey aircraft because the planes were produced by firms located in key congressional districts. The Pentagon did not want the planes.

The Relationship Between Deficits and Other Aggregate Variables

During the era of high deficits, there was much talk in the news media about the relationships among deficits, interest rates, and inflation. To develop a clearer understanding of these links, let's go back to our model of aggregate demand and aggregate supply. We begin with a balanced federal budget and an economy producing its potential GDP (point *a* in Exhibit 3). The short-run aggregate supply curve is based on long-term labor contracts reflecting an expected price level of 130.

Suppose an unexpected decline in private-sector spending reduces aggregate demand. Recent research suggests that each percentage point added to the unemployment rate cuts output by two percentage points. As employment and output decline, the automatic stabilizers kick in, reducing tax revenues and increasing transfer payments. These stabilizers keep aggregate demand from falling as much as it would without them. Still, the aggregate demand curve shifts from *AD* to *AD*', resulting in a short-run equilibrium with an output of $7.8 trillion. This combination of reduced tax revenues and increased government outlays results in a budget deficit. According to research, every 1 percent increase in the unemployment rate increases the federal deficit by over $30 billion.

Now let's consider the association between this deficit, triggered as it is by automatic stabilizers, and what happens to real output, the price level, and interest rates. You can see from Exhibit 3 that a deficit resulting from a decline in private-sector spending occurs with falling real output and a falling price level, or reduced inflation. With regard to the interest rate, when output and the price level decline, the transactions demand for money declines as well, so the interest rate tends to fall. Thus, *a decline in private-sector spending triggers automatic stabilizers that result in a federal budget deficit. This deficit is associated with a lower price level, lower output, and lover interest rates.*

EXHIBIT 3

Deficits and Other Measures of the Economy's Performance

At point *a*, the federal budget is in balance and output is at potential. A decline in aggregate demand to *AD*' triggers automatic stabilizers. Tax revenues fall, transfer payments increase, and the budget moves to a deficit position. In this case, the deficit is associated with falling output and a falling price level.

With the economy now at point *b*, suppose policy makers stimulate aggregate demand through expansionary fiscal policy. Tax revenues fall, government expenditures increase, and the deficit grows larger. Here the deficit is associated with rising output and a rising price level.

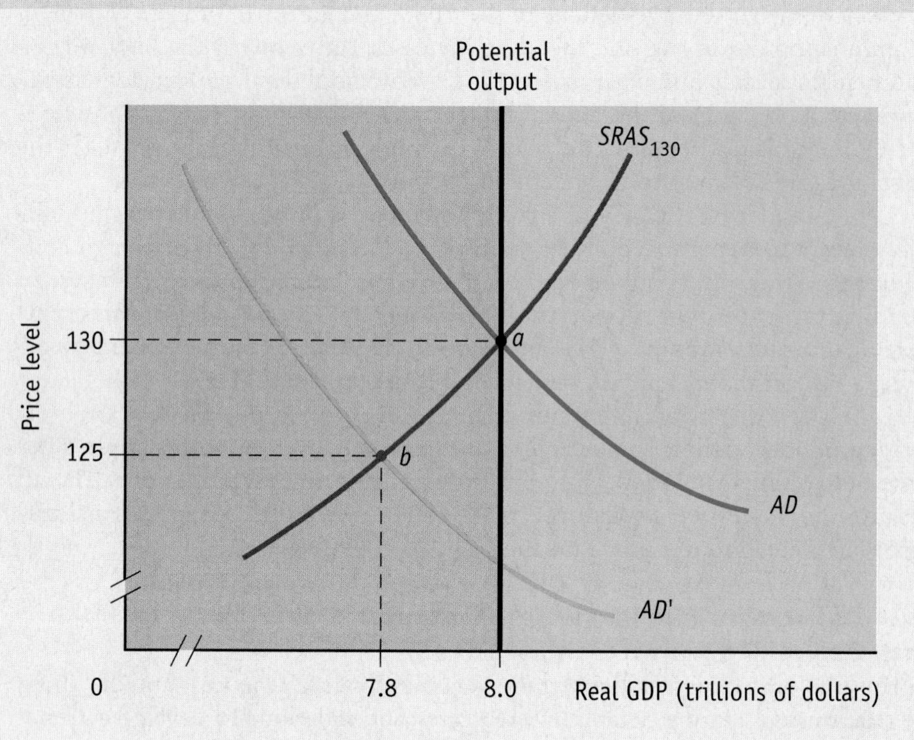

At point *b*, the economy is in recession, with a short-run equilibrium output that is below the economy's potential. Policy makers can either do nothing, waiting for natural market forces to correct the problem of unemployment, or they can intervene in some way. Recall that activists believe that if government takes no action, the movement back to potential output could be long and painful, with much unemployment and much forgone output. Advocates of passive policy believe that government intervention involves unpredictable lags and may affect aggregate demand only after the economy has naturally returned to its potential.

Suppose the government increases its spending, financing this increase by selling bonds to the public, a move that puts upward pressure on interest rates. According to the activist view, the appropriate increase in government spending could stimulate aggregate demand just enough to return the economy to its potential GDP. The effects of this policy would be represented in Exhibit 3 by a movement from point *b* back to point *a*. In essence, increased government demand offsets the decline in private-sector demand.

What is the relationship between the higher deficit that results from this discretionary fiscal policy and the other macroeconomic measures? This higher deficit is associated with greater output and a higher price level. The interest rate rises not only because the Treasury sells bonds to finance the deficit but also because the higher price and output levels increase the demand for money.

Thus, *a deficit that arises from discretionary fiscal policy is associated with a higher real output, a higher price level, and a higher interest rate.*

We can conclude that there is no necessary relationship between deficits and various measures of economic performance. Deficits resulted initially from automatic stabilizers and then from discretionary fiscal policy, but the results of each deficit on real output, the price level, and interest rates differ. The results differ because the source of the deficit differs.

Crowding Out and Crowding In

Why do we care about the effect deficits have on interest rates? Recall that interest rates are a key determinant of investment, and investment is critical to economic growth. What's more, year-to-year fluctuations in investment spending are the primary source of shifts in aggregate demand. Let's look at the impact of deficit spending on business investment.

Suppose the federal government decides to expand the interstate highway system with a construction program that involves deficit spending of $10 billion. To pay for the new system, the Treasury sells government securities, or IOUs. The government's increased demand for credit raises interest rates in the market for loanable funds. Higher interest rates in turn discourage, or *crowd out,* some private investment, reducing the deficit expansionary effect. The extent of **crowding out** is a matter of debate. Some argue that although government borrowing may displace some private-sector borrowing, discretionary fiscal policy will result in a net increase in aggregate demand, leading to greater output and employment in the short run. Others believe the crowding out is more extensive, so borrowing from the public in this way could result in little or no net increase in aggregate demand and output.

Crowding out The displacement of interest-sensitive private investment that occurs when increased government deficit spending drives up interest rates

Although crowding out is likely to occur to some degree, there is another possibility. If the economy is operating well below its potential, the additional fiscal stimulus provided by deficit spending could encourage firms to invest more and could thus result in a higher level of investment. Recall that an important determinant of investment spending is business expectations. A government deficit could stimulate a weak economy, increasing aggregate demand, boosting employment, and putting a sunny face on business expectations. As business expectations grow more favorable, firms could become more willing to invest. The Japanese government has recently proposed deficit spending as a way of stimulating private-sector spending. This ability of government deficits to stimulate private investment is sometimes called **crowding in,** to distinguish it from crowding out.

Crowding in The potential for government spending to stimulate private investment in an otherwise sluggish economy

Were you ever unwilling to patronize a restaurant because it was too crowded? You simply did not want to put up with the hassle and long wait and were thus "crowded out." As that baseball-player-turned-philosopher Yogi Berra said, "No one goes there nowadays. It's too crowded." Similarly, large government deficits may "crowd out" some investors by driving up interest rates. On the other hand, did you ever pass up an unfamiliar restaurant because the place seemed dead—it had few customers? Perhaps you wondered why so few people chose to eat there. If you had seen just a few more customers, you might have stopped in—you might have been willing to "crowd in." Similarly, businesses may be reluctant to invest in a seemingly lifeless economy. The economic stimulus resulting from deficit spending could encourage some investors to "crowd in."

The Twin Deficits

To finance the huge deficits of the early 1980s, the U.S. Treasury had to sell a lot of bonds, driving up the market interest rate. With U.S. interest rates relatively high, foreigners were more willing to buy dollar-denominated bonds. To buy them, foreigners had to exchange their currencies for dollars. This greater demand for dollars caused the dollar to appreciate relative to foreign currencies during the first half of the 1980s. The rising value of the dollar made foreign goods cheaper in the United States and U.S. goods more expensive abroad. Thus, U.S. imports increased and U.S. exports decreased, so the foreign trade deficit increased.

The higher trade deficits meant that foreigners were accumulating dollars. With these dollars, they purchased U.S. assets, including U.S. government bonds, and thereby helped fund the giant federal deficits. The increase in funds from abroad in the 1980s was both good news and bad news for the U.S. economy. The good news was that the supply of foreign funds increased investment in the United States over what would have occurred in the absence of these funds. Ask people what they think of foreign investment in their town; they will likely say it's great.

But the foreign supply of funds to some extent simply offsets a decline in U.S. saving. Such a pattern could pose problems in the long run. The United States has surrendered a certain amount of control over its economy to foreign investors. And the return on foreign investments in the United States flows abroad.

The Miraculous Budget Surplus

In 1990 federal outlays were 22.4 percent as large as GDP; federal revenue was 18.8 percent the size of GDP. The difference represented a substantial deficit of 3.6 percent relative to GDP. By 1998 federal revenue exceeded federal outlays, yielding a surplus of $70 billion, or 0.8 percent relative to GDP. What happened between 1990 and 1998 that erased the deficit?

Tax Increases. With concern about the deficit growing, Congress and President Bush agreed to the 1990 Budget Enforcement Act, a package of spending cuts and tax increases aimed at trimming the projected deficit. Ironically, that tax increase not only may have cost President Bush reelection in 1992, but it also helped create the surplus in 1998, which President Clinton took credit for. President Clinton, for his part, increased taxes substantially on high-income households in 1993. The highest marginal tax rate jumped from 31 percent to 39.6 percent. Certain exemptions for high-income households were also reduced or eliminated, raising the effective marginal rate at the top to about 42 percent. Meanwhile the economy experienced a vigorous recovery during the 1990s, fueled by growing consumer spending and the strongest stock market in history. The combined effects of these tax increases and a strengthening economy raised federal revenue from 18.8 percent of GDP in 1990 to 21.8 percent in 1998.

Reduced Growth in Federal Outlays. Because of spending restrictions imposed by the 1990 Budget Enforcement Act, the rate of growth in federal outlays slowed compared to the 1980s. The collapse of the Soviet Union reduced U.S. military commitments abroad and resulted in a 30 percent drop in defense spending between 1990 and 1998 in inflation-adjusted dollars. The size of the armed forces dropped from 2.1 million people in 1990 to 1.4 million in 1998. The number of nondefense federal employees declined by 62,000, or about 5 percent, between 1990 and 1998. Part of the impetus for slower growth came from Republicans, who attained a congressional majority in 1994. Since then, inflation-adjusted domestic spending has been flat. Another beneficial factor has been the decline in interest rates on U.S. government securities. By late 1998, these rates had declined to their lowest level in 30 years, saving the federal government billions in interest charges on the national debt. Federal outlays dropped from 22.4 percent relative to GDP in 1990 to 21.0 percent in 1998.

Not-Quite-Perfect Picture. Thanks to the tax-rate increases and the strong economy, tax revenues gushed into Washington, growing an average of 8.0 percent per year between 1993 and 1998. Meanwhile, federal outlays remained in check, growing only 3.8 percent per year. By 1998 that combination created a federal budget surplus of $70 billion, a reversal of fortune from a deficit that had topped $290 billion only six years earlier.

But the results are not quite as rosy as they appear, so hold the champagne for now. The first surplus in three decades would have been a $30 billion deficit had it not been for about $100 billion in surplus generated by the Social Security program, as discussed in the following case study.

Reforming Social Security

*Case***Study**

Public Policy

The National Academy of Social Insurance is a nonpartisan research organization formed to study Social Security and Medicare. Its Web site includes a "Social Security Sourcebook" page at http://www.nasi.org/source/reso.htm. Read "Social Security Briefs" to learn more about particular reforms suggested for Social Security. There is also a glossary of terms to help you sort out the jargon.

Social Security is a federal redistribution program that collects payroll taxes from current workers to provide pensions for current retirees. Annual benefits in 1998 averaged $8,772 for individual retirees and $15,456 for couples. Social Security consists of two plans, each with its own tax structure. The pension program is paid from the old-age, survivors, and disability insurance (OASDI) tax, which in 1998 applied at a rate of 6.2 percent each on employee and employer to the first $68,400 earned, so the combined maximum tax that year was $8,881.60. Hospital care for the elderly is paid from the Medicare tax, which applies at a rate of 1.45 percent each on employee and employer, with no cap on the earnings taxed, so the Medicare tax on Harrison Ford's earnings of $20 million per movie totals $580,000.

During the first 50 years of the program, whenever tax revenues exceeded the cost of the program, Congress either raised benefits, expanded eligibility, or spent the surplus on something else. In the early 1980s, analysts began to fathom the tremendous impact of the baby boom generation on such a pay-as-you-go program. When baby boomers begin retiring in large numbers around 2020, the pension and Medicare costs will explode. To head off this problem, reforms adopted in 1983 increased the tax rate, expanded the tax base by the rate of inflation, gradually increased the retirement age from 65 to 67, increased the penalty for early retirement, and provided more incentives for delaying retirement.

The reforms ensured that revenues would exceed program costs while baby boomers were in the work force. To help pay for baby boomer retirements, the 1983 reform began accumulating the resulting surplus in the Social Security Trust Fund. Each year's surplus is lent to the U.S. Treasury in return for Treasury bonds. By 1998 the Trust Fund totaled $750 billion. That fund is projected to peak at $3.8 trillion in 2020, when baby boomers begin retiring in large numbers.

But here's the problem. By the year 2030, only ten years after the fund peaks, the fund will be empty—spent to help pay benefits for retired baby boomers. Not only will the trust fund be erased, but the flow of Social Security taxes will then cover only three-quarters of projected retirement outlays. The huge sucking sound will be a Social Security operating deficit amounting to nearly a trillion dollars a year.

What to do, what to do? Social Security has been called the "third rail" of American politics: electrically charged and untouchable. Lobbying groups supporting Social Security are so well organized that any legislator who proposes limiting benefits or increasing payroll taxes risks instant electrocution. Still, more than a dozen reform plans are under consideration in Congress—including higher payroll taxes, reduced benefits, increasing the retirement age, and privatizing part of the system. Any effort to place a larger burden on future workers or reduce the benefits of retirees threatens the viability of the program, not to mention the tenure of the legislators involved.

As noted earlier, the $70 billion federal budget surplus for 1998 would have been a $30 billion deficit were it not for a $100 billion surplus generated by the Social Security program in 1998. Without counting revenue from Social Security payroll taxes, the federal budget will not experience a true surplus until 2006. Thus, when you hear politicians debating about how to spend the new-found surplus, you should realize there is no surplus. Worse yet, the Social Security program is set on a course for bankruptcy.

Sources: Glenn Burkins, "Labor Organizations Are Gearing Up for 1999 Debate on Social Security," *Wall Street Journal* (28 September 1998); Richard Stevenson, "With Deficit Gone, Benefits of Surplus Are Debated," *New York Times* (1 October 1998); Linda Feldmann, "Linking Social Security to Stocks: A Good Idea?" *Christian Science Monitor* (10 September 1998); and the Concord Coalition's Web site on Social Security at www.concordcoalition.org.

So the federal deficit has been squeezed down, at least temporarily. Let's turn our attention to an unintended consequence of the high deficits—the huge federal debt accumulated during the last quarter century.

THE NATIONAL DEBT

Federal deficits add up. It took 39 presidents, six wars, the Great Depression, and more than 200 years for the federal debt to reach $1 trillion, as it did in 1981. It took only three presidents and another 15 years for that debt to top $5 trillion, as it did in 1996. (In constant 1996 dollars, the national debt in 1981 was about

$3.1 trillion.) Ironically, the biggest growth in debt occurred primarily under President Reagan, who was first elected on a promise to balance the budget.

The federal deficit is a flow variable measuring the amount by which outlays exceed revenues in a particular year. The federal debt, or the **national debt,** is a stock variable measuring the accumulation of past deficits. In this section we want to put the national debt in perspective by looking at (1) changes over time, (2) U.S. debt levels compared to those in other countries, (3) interest on the debt, and (4) some other fiscal issues.

National debt The net accumulation of federal budget deficits

In talking about the national debt, we distinguish between the gross debt and debt held by the public. The *gross debt* includes U.S. Treasury securities purchased by various federal agencies, such as the Social Security Trust Fund. Since this is debt the federal government owes to itself, we often ignore it and focus on *debt held by the public,* which includes debt held by households, firms, banks (including Federal Reserve banks), and foreign entities. As of the end of 1998, the gross federal debt stood at about $5.5 trillion and the debt held by the public stood at $3.7 trillion.

The National Debt Since World War II

In constant 1998 dollars, the national debt held by the public doubled between 1946 and 1998, *increasing from about $1.4 trillion to about $3.7 trillion* in 1998. Another way to measure debt over time is relative to the economy's production and income, or GDP (just as a bank might compare the size of a mortgage to a borrower's income). Exhibit 4 shows federal debt held by the public relative to

EXHIBIT 4

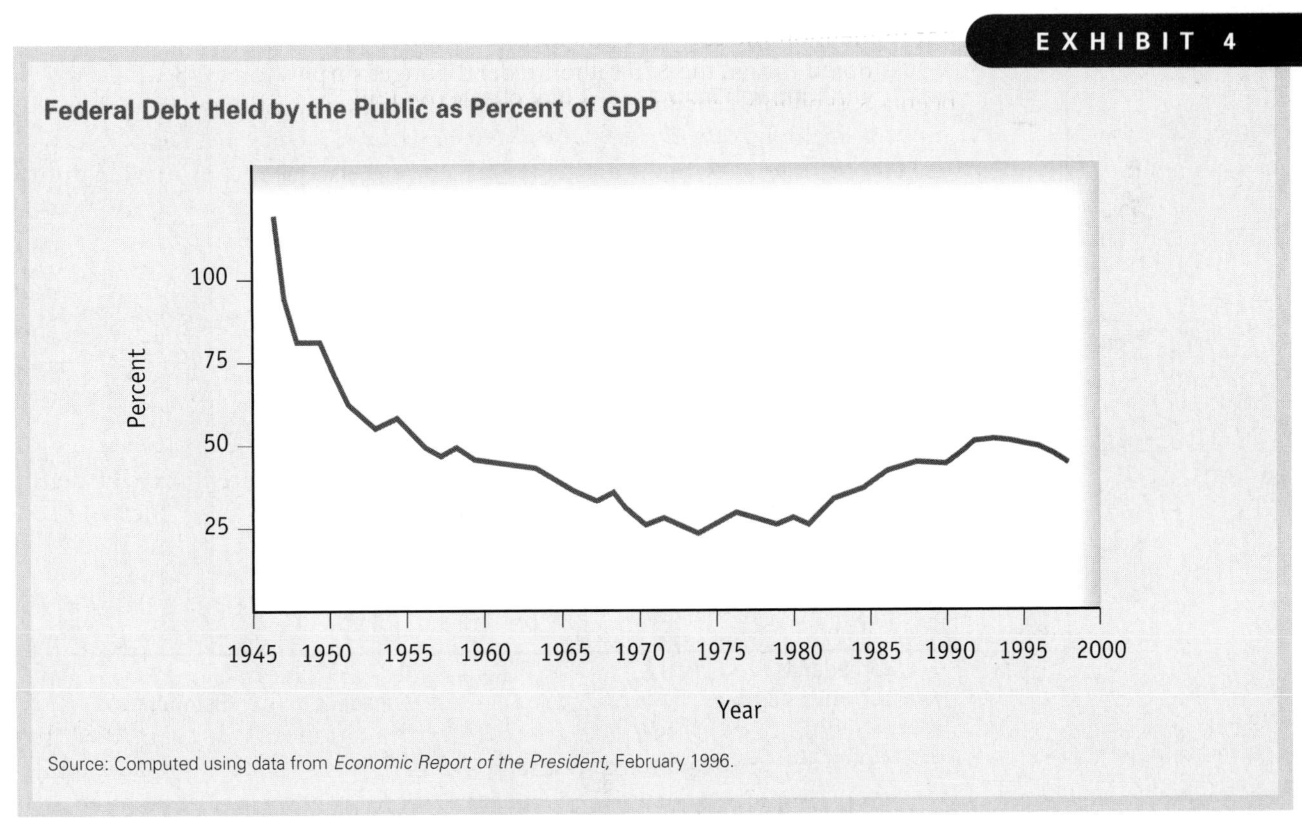

Source: Computed using data from *Economic Report of the President,* February 1996.

GDP. In 1946, the national debt was 109 percent of GDP. Between 1946 and 1980, debt relative to GDP declined to only 26 percent, but climbed to 50 percent by 1993, then backed off to 44 percent by 1998. Thus, between 1946 and 1998, the federal debt held by the public more than doubled in constant dollars but dropped by more than half relative to GDP.

An International Perspective on National Debt

Exhibit 5 compares the U.S. public-sector debt levels in 1998 relative to GDP with those of nine other industrial countries. Two measures of debt are used: total debt and net debt. *Total debt* includes all outstanding liabilities of federal, state, and local governments. *Net debt* subtracts the government's financial assets, such as loans to students and farmers, stock shares, cash on hand, and foreign exchange on reserve.

As you can see in Exhibit 5, despite the huge increase in federal debt since 1980, the United States ranks in about the middle for industrial countries, with total debt in 1998 for all levels of government combined amounting to

EXHIBIT 5

Government Debt at All Levels as Percent of GDP in 1998

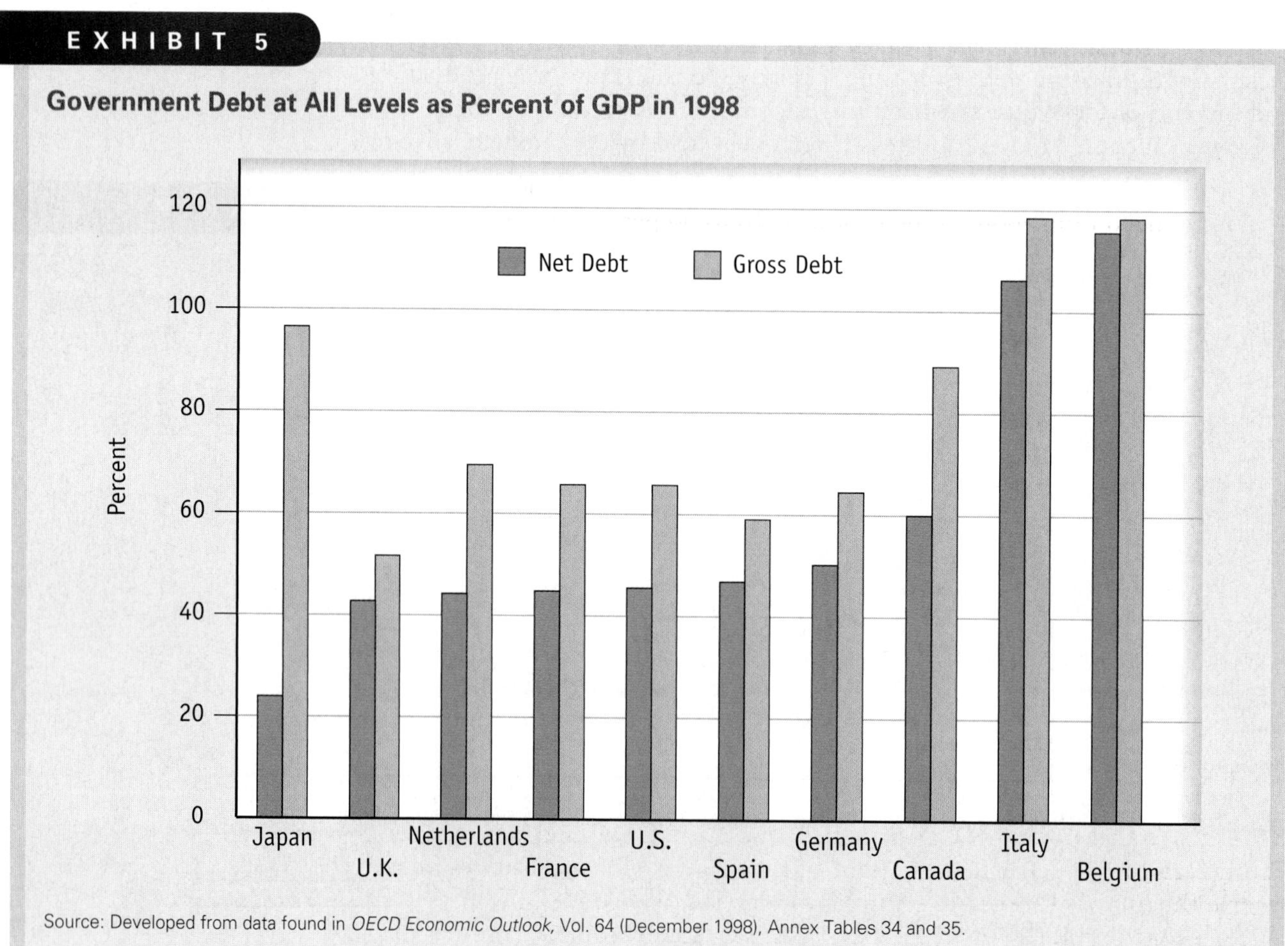

Source: Developed from data found in *OECD Economic Outlook*, Vol. 64 (December 1998), Annex Tables 34 and 35.

60.3 percent of GDP and net debt amounting to 45.5 percent. Italy's net debt in 1998 stood at 106.2 percent of its GDP, the highest among the G-7 countries and second to Belgium among all industrial countries. Because political power in Italy is fragmented among a dozen parties, a government can be formed only through coalitions among several parties. That resulting coalition has been so fragile that it could not easily withstand the fallout from raising taxes or cutting spending; hence, deficits in Italy until quite recently persisted, adding to the debt. Lately, as a condition for joining the European Monetary Union, countries have been forced to reduce their federal deficits. Italy, for example, has cut its deficit from 9.0 percent of GDP in 1993 to only 1.9 percent in 1998.

Interest on the Debt

Purchasers of government securities range from individuals who buy $25 savings bonds to institutions that buy $1 million Treasury bonds. When these securities mature, the government issues more securities to pay them off. Because most government securities are short term, the national debt "turns over" rapidly—about 45 percent of the debt is refinanced every year. With over $150 billion coming due each month, debt service payments are quite sensitive to movements in interest rates. Based on a $3.7 trillion debt held by the public, a 1-percentage-point increase in the nominal interest rate ultimately increases annual interest costs by $37 billion.

Interest payments increased from 8 percent of the federal budget in 1978 to 13 percent in 1998. Interest payments as a percentage of federal income tax collections jumped from about 20 percent in 1978 to 30 percent in 1998.

Who Bears the Burden of the Debt?

Deficit spending is a way to increase current expenditures without raising taxes. The national debt raises moral questions about the right of one generation of taxpayers to bequeath to the next generation the burden of its own borrowing. To what extent do budget deficits shift the burden to future generations? Let's examine two arguments about the burden of the debt.

We Owe It to Ourselves. It is often argued that the debt is not a burden to future generations because, although future generations must service the debt, those same generations will receive the debt service payments. It's true that if U.S. citizens forgo present consumption to buy bonds, they or their heirs will receive the interest payments, so debt service payments will stay in the country. Thus future generations will both pay the interest on the debt and receive those same interest payments. In that sense, the debt is not a burden on future generations.

Foreign Ownership of Debt. But the "we owe it to ourselves" argument does not apply to that portion of the national debt that is purchased by foreigners. Foreigners who buy U.S. government bonds forgo present consumption and receive the future benefits. An influx of foreign savings reduces the amount of current consumption that Americans must sacrifice to finance the national debt. *A reliance on foreigners, however, increases the burden of the debt on future gen-*

erations because future debt service payments no longer remain in the country. Foreigners are owed about one-fifth of the debt held by the public.

Crowding Out and Capital Formation

We have seen that government borrowing can drive up interest rates, crowding out some private investment by making it more costly. The long-run effects of deficit spending depend on how the government spends the borrowed dollars. If additional outlays are oriented toward investments such as improving interstate highways or educating the workforce, the public investment may be as productive as any private investment forgone. Hence, there may be no harmful effects on the economy's long-run productive capabilities. If, however, the additional borrowed dollars go toward current consumption, such as farm subsidies or federal retirement benefits, the economy's capital formation will be less than it would otherwise be. With less investment today, there will be a smaller endowment of capital equipment and technology for future generations. U.S. private investment declined from about 16 percent of GDP in 1984 to 12 percent in 1991. But since 1991 private investment has rebounded to about 16 percent of GDP in 1998. So private investment increased as the federal deficit decreased.

Ironically, despite the large federal deficits of the 1980s and early 1990s, government investments in roads, bridges, and airports—so-called *public capital*—has declined. In 1970, the value of the nation's public capital stock was about 50 percent of GDP; this figure has declined to about 40 percent today. So public investment has declined. Some argue that declining investment in the public infrastructure serves as a drag on productivity growth. For example, the failure to invest sufficiently in airports and in the air traffic control system has resulted in congested airports and flight delays.

Thus government deficits of one generation can affect the standard of living of the next. And some argue that our current measure of the national debt does not capture all burdens passed on to future generations. For example, Martin Feldstein, a Harvard economist, believes that unfunded liabilities of government retirement programs, such as Social Security, should be included in the debt. Such an inclusion would triple the measure of the national debt. A model that considers some intergenerational issues is discussed in the following case study.

Across Generations is an archive of articles from *Pioneer Press* (St. Paul, MN) dealing with intergenerational issues, Social Security in particular. Link to http://www.pioneerplanet.com/archive/gen/index.htm and explore the numerous themes listed along the right-side menu

An Intergenerational View of Deficits and Debt

Robert Barro, another economist from Harvard, has developed a model that assumes parents are concerned about the welfare of their children, who, in turn, are concerned about the welfare of *their* children, and so on for generations. Thus, the welfare of all generations is tied together. According to Barro, parents concerned about future generations will reduce the burden of federal debt on future generations and reduce the stimulative effect of deficit spending.

Here's his argument. When the government incurs deficits, this keeps current taxes lower than they would otherwise be, but taxes in the future must increase to service the resulting debt. If there is no regard for the welfare of future generations, then the older people are, the more attractive debt becomes relative to taxes. Older people can enjoy the benefits of public spending now, but will not live long enough to finance the debt through higher taxes or lower benefits. If people are concerned about their children's welfare, however, they will be more reluctant to run deficits now and thereby raise future taxes.

Parents can undo the harm that deficit financing imposes on their children by consuming less now and saving more. As governments substitute deficits for taxes, parents will consume less and save more to increase gifts and bequests to their children. If increases in household saving just offset increases in federal deficits, deficit spending will not increase aggregate demand, because the decline in consumption will negate the fiscal stimulus provided by deficits. This intergenerational transfer offsets the future burden of higher debt and neutralizes the effect of deficit spending on aggregate demand, output, and employment.

The large budget deficits of the last two decades, caused in part by tax cuts, seem to provide a natural experiment for testing Barro's theory of government debt. The evidence fails to support his theory, since the large federal deficits coincided with low national saving rates. Yet defenders of Barro's view say that maybe the saving rate was low because people were optimistic about future economic growth, an optimism that was reflected by a huge increase in the stock market. Or maybe the saving rate was low because people believed the tax cuts would result not in higher future taxes but in lower government spending, as President Reagan promised.

But there are other reasons to be skeptical about Barro's theory. First, individuals without children may not be concerned about the welfare of future generations. Second, the theory assumes that people are well informed about federal spending and tax policies and about the future consequences of current policies; most people are in fact poorly informed about such matters. One survey found that only one in ten adults polled had any idea about the size of the federal deficit. In the poll taken in 1995, when the federal deficit was around $165 billion, only one in ten adults said correctly that the deficit was between $100 billion and $400 billion.

Sources: Robert J. Barro, "Are Government Bonds Net Worth?" *Journal of Political Economy* 82 (November/December 1974): 1095–1117; Robert J. Barro, "The Ricardian Approach to Budget Deficits," *Journal of Economic Perspectives* 3 (Spring 1989): 37; and Jay Mathews, "How High Is the Deficit, the Dow? Most in Survey Didn't Know," *Hartford Courant* (19 October 1995).

bar. The site also provides links to additional Internet resources such as the Third Millenium at http://www.thirdmil.org/, an organization of generation Xers proposing solutions to long-term problems facing the U.S.

CONCLUSION

John Maynard Keynes introduced the idea that federal deficit spending is an appropriate fiscal policy when private aggregate demand is insufficient to achieve potential output. The federal budget has not been the same since. Until the last year or so, the federal budget had been in deficit every year but one since 1960.

And beginning in the early 1980s, giant federal deficits dominated the fiscal policy debate. But after peaking at $290 billion in 1992, the deficit came down because of higher tax rates on high-income households, reduced federal outlays (especially for defense), and a rip-roaring economy and stock market. Whether chronic deficits have been eliminated remains to be seen.

SUMMARY

1. The federal budget process suffers from a variety of problems, including overlapping committee jurisdictions, lengthy budget deliberations, extensive use of continuing resolutions, budgeting in too much detail, and a lack of year-to-year control over most of the budget. Suggested improvements include instituting a biennial budget, budgeting in less detail, and distinguishing between a capital budget and an operating budget.

2. Deficits usually rise during wars and severe recessions, but deficits remained large during the economic expansion of the 1980s. The deficits arose from a combination of tax cuts during the early 1980s and growth in federal spending. As a percentage of GDP, the national debt has doubled since 1980.

3. There is no clear, consistent relationship between deficits and other measures of macroeconomic performance, such as output, the price level, and interest rates. If a fall in aggregate demand results in a recession, deficits increase because of automatic stabilizers, but output, the inflation rate, and the interest rate all decline. If discretionary fiscal policy is used to rekindle aggregate demand, deficits increase; so do output, the price level, and the interest rate.

4. To the extent that deficits crowd out private capital formation, this decline in private investment reduces the economy's ability to grow. Foreign holdings of debt also impose a burden on future generations because future payments to service this debt are paid to foreigners and consequently are not available to U.S. citizens. Thus the deficits of one generation can reduce the standard of living of the next.

5. After peaking at $290 billion in 1992, the federal deficit turned into a surplus by 1998 because of higher tax rates, reduced outlays especially for defense, declining interest rates, and a strengthening economy.

QUESTIONS FOR REVIEW

1. *(The Federal Budget Process)* The budgets passed by Congress and signed by the president show the relationship between *budgeted* expenditures and *projected* revenues. Why does the budget require a forecast of the state of the economy? Under what circumstances would the actual government spending and tax revenue fail to match the budget as approved?

2. *(The Federal Budget Process)* In what sense is the executive branch of the U.S. government always dealing with three budgets?

3. *(Problems with the Budget Process)* In terms of the policy lags described in Chapter 16, discuss the following problems with the budget process:
   a. Continuing resolutions
   b. Overlapping committee authority
   c. Uncontrollable budget items
   d. An overly detailed budget

4. *(Budget Philosophies)* Explain the differences among an annually balanced budget, a cyclically balanced budget, and functional finance. How does each affect economic fluctuations?

5. *(Budget Philosophies)* One alternative to balancing the budget annually or cyclically is to produce a government budget that would be balanced if the economy were at potential output. Given the cyclical nature of government tax revenues and spending, how would the resulting budget deficit or surplus vary over the business cycle?

6. *(Budget Philosophies)* The functional finance approach to budget deficits would set the federal budget to promote

an economy operating at potential output. What problems would you expect if the country were to employ this kind of budgetary philosophy?

7. *(Deficits and Other Aggregate Variables)* Distinguish between (1) the short-run changes in real output, the price level, and the interest rate associated with deficits caused by automatic stabilizers and (2) the short-run effects associated with deficits caused by discretionary fiscal policy. .

8. *(Crowding Out)* Is it possible for U.S. federal budget deficits to crowd out investment spending in other countries? How could German or British investment be hurt by large U.S. budget deficits?

9. *(Crowding Out)* How might federal deficits crowd out private domestic investment? How could this crowding out affect future living standards?

10. *(Interest on the Debt)* The percentage of federal income tax revenues necessary to service the debt increased from 20 percent in 1978 to 30 percent in 1998. What problems has that created for public officials and spending programs?

11. *(Burden of the Debt)* Suppose that government budget deficits are financed to a considerable extent by foreign sources. How does this create a potential burden for the domestic economy in the future?

12. *(The Twin Deficits)* How is the U.S. budget deficit related to the trade deficit?

13. *(The Miraculous Budget Surplus)* Why did the federal budget go from a huge deficit in 1992 to a surplus in 1998? Explain the factors that contributed to the turnaround.

14. *(**CaseStudy:** Reforming Social Security)* Why is the Social Security program headed for trouble? When will the trouble begin? What possible solutions have been proposed?

15. *(Crowding Out and Capital Formation)* In earlier chapters, we've seen that the government can increase GDP in the short run by running a government budget deficit. What are some of the longer-term effects of deficit spending?

16. *(**CaseStudy:** An Intergenerational View of Deficits and Debt)* Explain why Robert Barro argues that if parents are concerned about the future welfare of their children, the effects of deficit spending will be neutralized.

PROBLEMS AND EXERCISES

17. *(The National Debt)* Try the following exercises to better understand how the national debt is related to the government's budget deficit.
    a. Assume that the gross national debt initially is equal to $3 trillion and the federal government then runs a deficit of $300 billion:
       i. What is the new level of gross national debt?
       ii. If 100 percent of the deficit is financed by the sale of securities to federal agencies, what happens to the amount of debt held by the public? What happens to the level of gross debt?
       iii. If GDP increased by 5 percent in the same year that the deficit is run, what happens to gross debt as a percent of GDP? What happens to the level of debt held by the public as a percent of GDP?
    b. Now suppose that the gross national debt initially is equal to $2.5 trillion and the federal government then runs a deficit of $100 billion:
       i. What is the new level of gross national debt?
       ii. If 100 percent of this deficit is financed by the sale of securities to the public, what happens to the level of debt held by the public? What happens to the level of gross debt?
       iii. If GDP increases by 6 percent in the same year as the deficit is run, what happens to gross debt as a percent of GDP? What happens to the level of debt held by the public as a percent of GDP?

EXPERIENTIAL EXERCISES

18. *(Federal Budget Deficits)* Try your hand at balancing the federal budget. Visit the National Budget Simulation at UC Berkeley's Center for Community Economic Research at http://socrates.berkeley.edu:3333/budget/budget.html.
    a. Develop a budget and see what happens. Were you successful in balancing the budget? If not, how much of a deficit or surplus did you end up with? What does this exercise tell you about the process of creating a balanced budget?
    b. Reexamine the budget cuts or increases you made. What problems would such changes pose for a politician facing reelection?
    c. This budget simulator allows you only to change spending and tax expenditures over a one-year period. What problems does this pose to finding a realistic economic solution for balancing the budget?

19. *(**CaseStudy:** Reforming Social Security)* Visit South-Western College Publishing's EconDebates Online at http://www.swcollege.com/bef/mceachern/mceachern.html. Review the materials on "Will Social Security survive into the 21st century?" What are some of the macroeconomic implications of Social Security reform?

20. *(Wall Street Journal)* You learned that the government pays billions of dollars in interest each year to finance the national debt. Those debt payments are sensitive to changes in the nominal interest rate. Check the "Treasury Issues" table in the Money and Investing section of today's *Wall Street Journal*. Have interest rates on Treasury bonds and bills been increasing or decreasing lately? What are the implications of interest rate changes for bond prices and for debt finance?

CHAPTER

18 Elasticity of Demand and Supply

Why did visits to Microsoft's on-line magazine, *Slate*, drop 95 percent when the access charge increased from zero to $20 a year? Why did total usage by subscribers of America Online explode when the company switched from an hourly charge to a flat monthly fee? Why do higher cigarette taxes cut teenage smoking more than smoking by other groups? Why is a bountiful harvest often bad news for farmers? Answers to these and other questions are explored in this chapter, which considers the effects of price changes on quantity demanded and quantity supplied.

As we learned back in Chapter 1, macroeconomics concentrates on aggregate markets—on the big picture. But the big picture is a mosaic pieced together from individual decisions made by households, firms, governments, and

Visit the McEachern Interactive Study Center for this chapter at http://mcisc.swcollege.com

the rest of the world. To understand how a market economy works, we must take a closer look at these individual decisions, especially at the role played by prices. In a market economy, prices inform producers and consumers about the relative scarcity of products and resources.

A downward-sloping demand curve and an upward-sloping supply curve combine to form a powerful analytical tool. But to make best use of this tool, you must learn more about the shapes of demand and supply curves. The more you know about their shapes, the better you can predict the effects of a change in the price on quantity demanded or supplied. Decision makers are willing to pay dearly for such information. For example, Taco Bell would like to know what happens to taco sales if the price decreases. Public officials would like to know the effect of higher cigarette taxes on teenage smoking. College officials would like to know how tuition hikes affect enrollments. And public transportation officials would like to know the impact of fare cuts on ridership. To answer such questions, we must determine how *responsive* consumers and producers are to price changes. *Elasticity* is a tool used to measure such *responsiveness*. Topics discussed in this chapter include:

- Price elasticity of demand
- Determinants of price elasticity
- Price elasticity and total revenue
- Price elasticity of supply
- Income elasticity of demand
- Cross-price elasticity of demand

PRICE ELASTICITY OF DEMAND

Just before a recent Thanksgiving weekend, Delta Airlines, in an attempt to boost ticket sales, announced fare cuts of up to 50 percent. Was this a good idea? For Delta's total revenue to increase, the growth in the number of tickets sold would have to more than offset the decline in ticket prices. A firm's success or failure often depends on how much it knows about the market for its product.

Likewise, the operators of Taco Bell would like to know what would happen to sales if the price of a taco increased from, say, $0.90 to $1.10. The law of demand says that a higher price will reduce quantity demanded, but by how much? How sensitive is quantity demanded to a change in price? Would the number sold decline by only a little or by a lot? After all, if quantity demanded declined just a little, a price increase might be a profitable move for Taco Bell.

Let's get more specific about the sensitivity of changes in quantity demanded to changes in price. Consider the two demand curves in Exhibit 1. In each panel, we begin with a price of $0.90 per taco and a quantity demanded of 105,000 tacos per day. Now suppose the taco price increases to $1.10. Note that quantity demanded decreases to 95,000 tacos per day in panel (a), where the demand is less responsive, but to 75,000 tacos per day in panel (b). In response to the price increase, consumers in panel (b) cut their quantity demanded more than do consumers in panel (a). The numerical measure of this responsiveness is called the **price elasticity of demand.** *Elasticity* is simply another word for *responsiveness*.

Price elasticity of demand
A measure of the responsiveness of quantity demanded to a price change; the percent change in quantity demanded divided by the percent change in price

EXHIBIT 1

Demand Curves of Different Elasticities

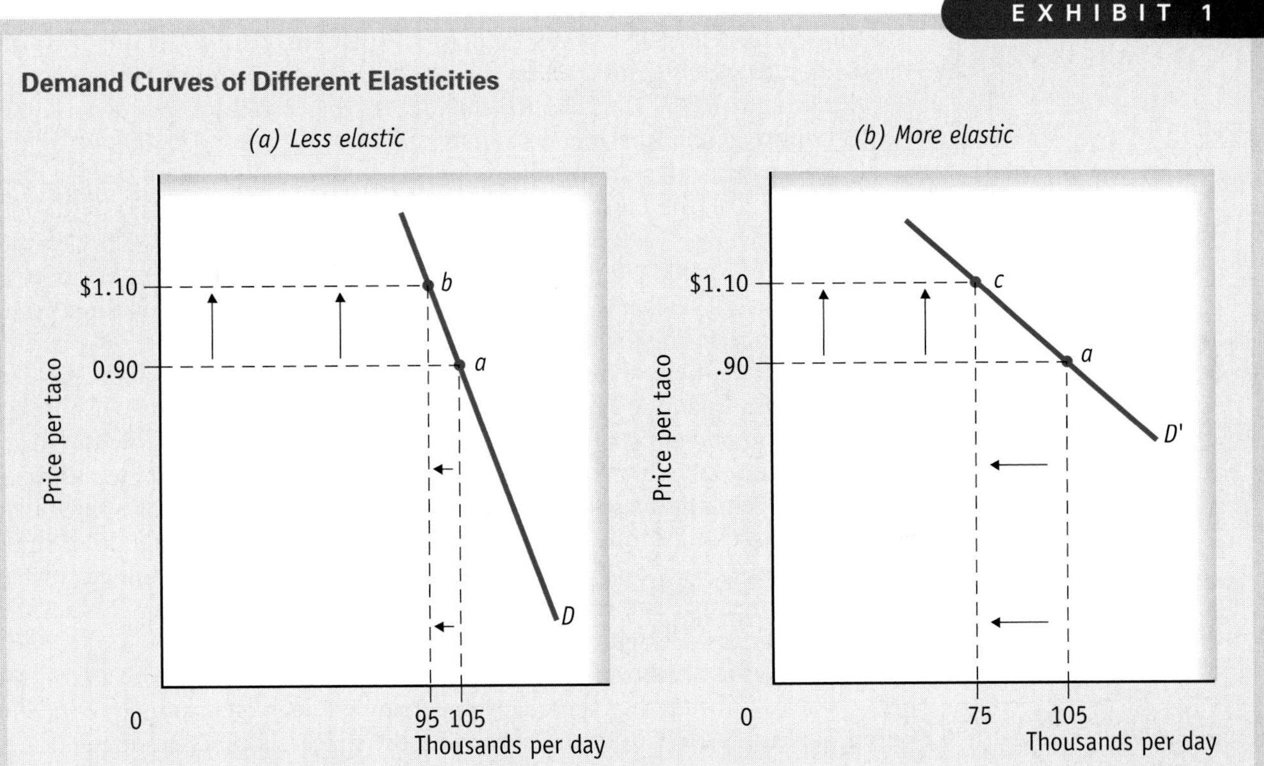

For a given change in price, the less elastic the demand, the smaller the change in quantity demanded. In panel (a), a 20 percent increase in price leads to a 10 percent decrease in quantity demanded. In panel (b), with more elastic demand *D'*, the same 20 percent price increase leads to a 33 percent decrease in quantity demanded.

Calculating Price Elasticity of Demand

In simplest terms, the price elasticity of demand is the percent change in quantity demanded divided by the percent change in price, or

$$\text{Price elasticity of demand} = \frac{\text{percent change in quantity demanded}}{\text{percent change in price}}$$

Recall that the law of demand states that price and quantity demanded are inversely related, so the change in price and the change in quantity demanded will move in opposite directions. Hence in the elasticity formula the numerator and the denominator have opposite signs, so the price elasticity of demand has a negative sign.

To compute the percent change in price or in quantity demanded, we use as a base the average of the initial value and the new value. For example, in Exhibit 1, the price increases from $0.90 to $1.10, an increase of $0.20. The base used to calculate the percent change is the average of $0.90 and $1.10, which is $1.00. The percent change in price is therefore $0.20/$1.00, or 20 percent.

The same holds for changes in quantity demanded. In panel (a), the quantity demanded decreases from 105,000 to 95,000 tacos per day, so the base used to calculate the percent change is the average, or 100,000. The percent change in quantity demanded is therefore −10,000/100,000, or −10 percent. The resulting price elasticity of demand is the percent change in quantity demanded, −10 percent, divided by the percent change in price, 20 percent, or −10%/20%, which is −0.5. So in panel (a) the price elasticity of demand between points *a* and *b* is −0.5.

If the quantity demanded falls from 105,000 to 75,000 tacos per day, as it does in panel (b), the base used for computing the percent change is 90,000, which is the average of 105,000 and 75,000. So the percent change in quantity demanded is −30,000/90,000, or −33 percent. The resulting price elasticity of demand is −33%/20%, or −1.65. Demand in panel (b) is about three times more responsive to the price increase than is demand in panel (a).

Note that elasticity expresses a relationship between two amounts: the percent change in quantity demanded and the percent change in price. Since the focus is on the percent change, we need not be concerned with how output or price is measured. For example, suppose the good in question is apples. It makes no difference in the elasticity formula whether the measure of apples is in pounds, bushels, or even tons. All that matters is the percent change in quantity demanded, not how quantity demanded is measured. Nor does it matter whether we measure the price in U.S. dollars, Mexican pesos, French francs, or Botswanan thebes. All that matters is the percent change in price.

Price elasticity formula Percent change in quantity divided by the percent change in price; the average quantity and the average price are used as bases for computing percent changes in quantity and in price

Let's develop a more general price elasticity formula. Suppose that if the price increases from p to p', the quantity demanded decreases from q_D to q'_D. The **price elasticity formula** for calculating the price elasticity of demand, E_D, between the two points is the percent change in quantity demanded divided by the percent change in price, or

$$E_D = \frac{q'_D - q_D}{(q'_D + q_D)/2} \div \frac{p' - p}{(p' + p)/2}$$

The 2s cancel out to yield

$$E_D = \frac{q'_D - q_D}{q'_D + q_D} \div \frac{p' - p}{p' + p}$$

Incidentally, because the average quantity and average price are used as a base for computing percent change, the same elasticity measure results whether the change is from the higher price to the lower price or the other way around.

Categories of Price Elasticity of Demand

Inelastic demand The type of demand that exists when a change in price has relatively little effect on quantity demanded; the percent change in quantity demanded is less than the percent change in price

Price elasticity of demand can be divided into three general categories, based on how responsive quantity demanded is to a change in price. In terms of absolute values, if the percent change in quantity demanded is smaller than the percent change in price, the resulting price elasticity has a value between 0 and −1.0. That portion of the demand curve is said to be **inelastic,** meaning that quantity demanded is relatively *unresponsive* to a change in price. For example, the elasticity derived in Exhibit 1 (a) between points *a* and *b* is −0.5, so that portion of the demand curve is inelastic. If the percent change in quantity demanded just equals the percent change in price, the resulting price elasticity has a value of −1.0, and that portion of the curve is said to exhibit unit elastic demand. Finally, if the percent change in quantity demanded exceeds the percent change in price, the resulting price elasticity is more negative than −1.0, and that portion of the demand curve is said to be **elastic.** For example, the elasticity derived in panel (b) of Exhibit 1 is −1.65, so between points *a* and *c*, the demand curve is elastic. In summary, *the price elasticity of demand is inelastic if it is between 0 and −1.0, unit elastic if equal to −1.0, and elastic if more negative than −1.0.*

Elastic demand The type of demand that exists when a change in price has a relatively large effect on quantity demanded; the percent change in quantity demanded exceeds the percent change in price

Elasticity and Total Revenue

Knowledge of price elasticity is especially valuable to producers because it tells them what happens to their total revenue when the price changes. **Total revenue** (*TR*) is the price multiplied by the quantity sold at that price, or $TR = p \times q$. What happens to total revenue when the price decreases? Well, according to the law of demand, if the price falls, the quantity demanded increases. The lower price means producers get less per unit, which tends to decrease total revenue. But the increased quantity demanded that results from a lower price tends to increase total revenue. The overall change in total revenue resulting from a lower price is the net result of these opposite effects. *If the positive effect of a greater quantity demanded exceeds the negative effect of a lower price, total revenue will rise.* More specifically, when demand is *elastic*, the percent increase in quantity demanded exceeds the percent decrease in price, so total revenue increases. When demand is *unit elastic*, the percent increase in quantity demanded just offsets the percent decrease in price, so total revenue remains unchanged. Finally, when demand is *inelastic*, the percent increase in quantity demanded is less than the percent decrease in price, so total revenue decreases.

Total revenue Price multiplied by the quantity sold at that price

NetBookmark

A report on projected demand for air traffic in Britain up to the year 2015 shows how elasticity is used in economic analysis. Go to the Content page for *Air Traffic Forecasts for the United Kingdom 1997* at http://www.aviation.detr.gov.uk/aed/air/aircont.htm and read the Introduction and Section VIII - Sensitivity Tests. What are the forecasts used for? What is the rationale for imposing a fuel tax? Which test is implicitly measuring income elasticity of demand? Which ones are using price elasticity of demand? Why would the channel tunnel be expected to affect demand for air traffic?

Price Elasticity and the Linear Demand Curve

The price elasticity of demand usually varies along a demand curve. An examination of the elasticity along a particular type of demand curve, the linear demand curve, will tie together the concepts examined thus far. A **linear demand curve** is simply a straight-line demand curve. Panel (a) of Exhibit 2 presents a linear demand curve, and panel (b) shows the total revenue generated at each price-quantity combination along the demand curve. Recall that total revenue equals price times quantity.

Since the demand curve in panel (a) is linear, the slope is constant, so a given decrease in price always causes the same unit increase in quantity demanded. For example, a $10 drop in price always increases quantity demanded by 100 units. But *the price elasticity of demand is greater on the higher-price end of the demand curve than on the lower-price end.* Here is why. Because quantity demanded is smaller at the upper end of the demand curve than at the lower end, a 100-unit increase in quantity demanded represents a greater percent change in quantity demanded at the upper end than at the lower end. And because the price is higher at the upper end than at the lower end of the curve, a $10 decrease in price represents a smaller percent change in price at the upper end than at the lower end. Thus at the upper end of the demand curve, the percent increase in quantity demanded is relatively large and the percent decrease in price is relatively small, so the price elasticity of demand is relatively large. At the lower end of the demand curve, the percent increase in quantity demanded is relatively small and the percent decrease in price is relatively large, so the price elasticity of demand is relatively small.

Linear demand curve A straight-line demand curve; such a demand curve has a constant slope

EXHIBIT 2

Demand, Price Elasticity, and Total Revenue

Where demand is elastic in panel (a), total revenue in panel (b) increases following a price decrease. Total revenue attains its maximum value at the level of output where demand is unit elastic. Where demand is inelastic, further decreases in price cause total revenue to fall.

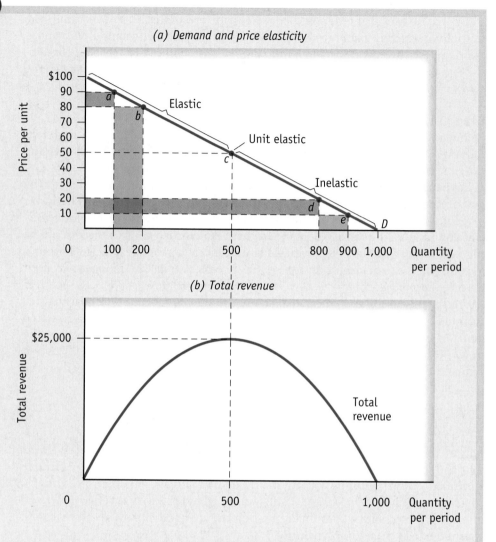

(a) Demand and price elasticity

Price per unit: $100, 90, 80, 70, 60, 50, 40, 30, 20, 10, 0

Elastic

Unit elastic

Inelastic

a b c d e D

Quantity per period: 0, 100, 200, 500, 800, 900, 1,000

(b) Total revenue

Total revenue: $25,000

Total revenue

Quantity per period: 0, 500, 1,000

Consider a movement from point *a* to point *b* on the upper end of the demand curve in Exhibit 2. The 100-unit increase in quantity demanded is a percent change of 100/150, or 67 percent. The \$10 price drop is a percent change of −10/85, or about −12 percent. Therefore, the price elasticity of demand between points *a* and *b* is 67%/−12%, which equals −5.6. Between points *d* and *e* on the lower end, however, the 100-unit quantity increase is a percent change of 100/850, or only 12 percent, and the \$10 price decrease is a percent change of −10/15, or −67 percent. The price elasticity of demand is 12%/−67%, or −0.18. In other words, *if the demand curve is linear, consumers are more responsive to a given price change when the initial price is high than when the price is low.*

Demand becomes less elastic as we move down the curve. At a point halfway down the linear demand curve in Exhibit 2, the elasticity is equal to −1.0. *This halfway point divides a linear demand curve into an elastic upper half and an inelastic lower half.* You can observe the clear relationship between the elasticity of demand in the upper diagram and total revenue in the lower diagram. Note that where demand is elastic, a decrease in price will increase total revenue because the gain in revenue from selling more units (represented by the large blue rectangle in the top panel) exceeds the loss in revenue from selling at the lower price (the small red rectangle). Where demand is inelastic, a price decrease reduces total revenue because the gain in revenue from selling more units (the small blue rectangle) is less than the loss in revenue from selling at the lower price (the large red rectangle). Where demand is unit elastic, the gain and loss of revenue exactly cancel each other out, so total revenue at that point remains constant (hence, total revenue "peaks" in the lower portion of the exhibit).

In summary, total revenue increases as the price declines until the midpoint of the linear demand curve is reached, where total revenue peaks. In Exhibit 2, total revenue peaks at $25,000 when quantity demanded equals 500 units. Below the midpoint of the demand curve, total revenue declines as the price falls. More generally, regardless of whether the demand curve is a straight line or a curve, there is a relationship between the price elasticity of demand and total revenue: A price decline *increases* total revenue if demand is elastic, *decreases* total revenue if demand is inelastic, and *has no effect* on total revenue if demand is unit elastic. Finally, note that a downward-sloping linear demand curve has a constant slope but a varying elasticity, so *the slope of a demand curve is not the same as the price elasticity of demand.*

Constant-Elasticity Demand

Again, price elasticity measures the responsiveness of consumers to a change in price. This responsiveness varies along a linear demand curve unless the demand curve is horizontal or vertical, as in panels (a) and (b) of Exhibit 3. These two demand curves, along with the special demand curve in panel (c), are called *constant-elasticity demand curves* because the elasticity does not change along the curves.

Perfectly Elastic Demand. The horizontal demand curve in panel (a) indicates that consumers will demand all that is offered for sale at the given price p. If the price rises above p, however, the quantity demanded drops to zero. This demand curve is said to be **perfectly elastic**, and its numerical elasticity value is minus infinity, a number too negatively large to be defined. You may think this is an odd sort of demand curve: Consumers, as a result of a small increase in price, go from demanding as much as is available to demanding nothing. Consumers are so sensitive to price changes that they cannot tolerate any increase. As you will see later, this reflects the demand for the output of any individual producer when many producers are selling identical products. The shape of the demand curve for a firm's product is an important ingredient in the pricing and output decision.

Perfectly elastic demand curve A horizontal line reflecting a situation in which any price increase reduces quantity demanded to zero; the elasticity value is minus infinity

Perfectly Inelastic Demand. The vertical demand curve in panel (b) of Exhibit 3 represents the situation in which quantity demanded does not vary at all when the price changes. This demand curve expresses consumers' sentiment that "price is no object." For example, if you were very rich and needed insulin injections to stay alive, price would be no object. No matter how high the price, you would continue to demand the amount necessary to stay well. As Ben Franklin said, "Necessity never made a good bargain." And if the price of insulin

EXHIBIT 3

Three Constant-Elasticity Demand Curves

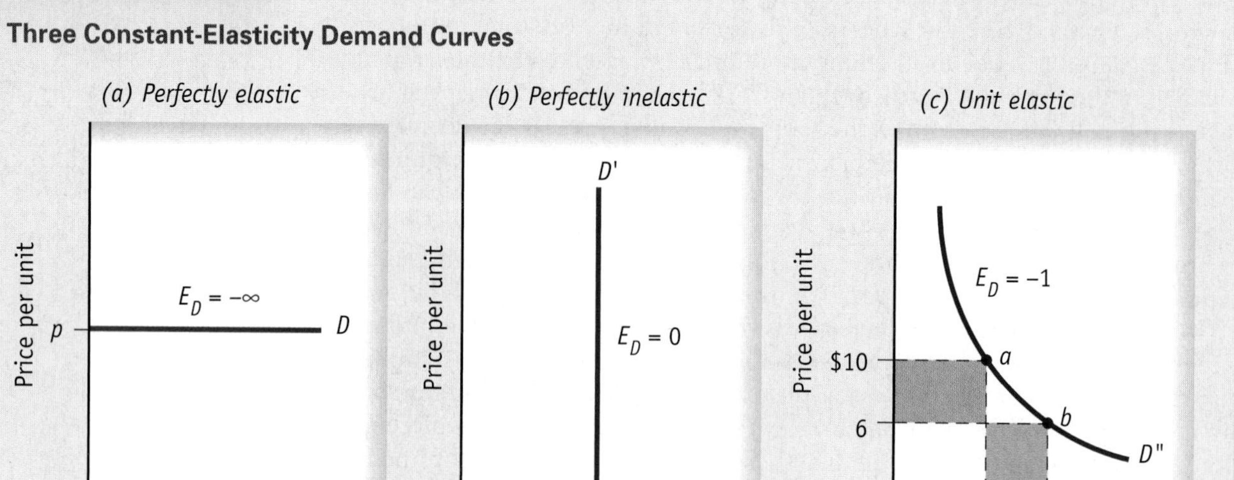

Along the perfectly elastic (horizontal) demand curve of panel (a), consumers will purchase all that is offered for sale at price *p*. Along the perfectly inelastic (vertical) demand curve of panel (b), consumers will purchase quantity *Q* regardless of price. Along the unit-elastic demand curve of panel (c), total revenue is the same for every price-quantity combination.

dropped, you would not demand any more of it. Vertical demand curves are called **perfectly inelastic** because price changes do not affect quantity demanded, at least not over the range of prices shown by the demand curve. Since the percent change in quantity demanded is zero for any given percent change in price, the numerical value of the price elasticity is zero.

Perfectly inelastic demand curve A vertical line reflecting a situation in which price change has no effect on the quantity demanded; the elasticity value is zero

Unit-elastic demand The type of demand that exists when a percent change in price causes an equal (but of opposite sign) percent change in quantity demanded; the elasticity value is minus one

Unit-Elastic Demand. Panel (c) in Exhibit 3 presents a demand curve that is unit elastic everywhere. **Unit-elastic demand** means that a percent change in price will always result in an identical percent change in quantity demanded but of opposite sign. Because percent changes in price and in quantity will be equal and offsetting, total revenue will be the same for every price-quantity combination along the curve. For example, when the price falls from $10 to $6, the quantity demanded increases from 60 to 100 units. The red shaded rectangle represents the loss in total revenue because all units are sold at the lower price; the blue shaded rectangle represents the gain in total revenue because more units are sold when the price drops. Because the demand curve is unit elastic, the revenue gained by selling more units just equals the revenue lost by lowering the price on all units, so total revenue is unchanged at $600. A demand curve that is unit elastic everywhere would actually be quite rare.

Constant-elasticity demand curve The type of demand that exists when price elasticity is the same everywhere along the curve; the elasticity value is constant

Each of the demand curves in Exhibit 3 is called a **constant-elasticity demand curve** because the elasticity is the same all along the curve. In contrast, the downward-sloping linear demand curve examined earlier had a different elasticity value at each point along the curve. Exhibit 4 lists the values of the five categories of price elasticity we have discussed, summarizing the varying

EXHIBIT 4

Summary of Price Elasticity of Demand

Effects of a 10 Percent Increase in Price

Price Elasticity Value	Type of Demand	What Happens to Quantity Demanded	What Happens to Total Revenue
$E_D = 0$	Perfectly inelastic	No change	Increases by 10 percent
$-1 < E_D < 0$	Inelastic	Drops by less than 10 percent	Increases by less than 10 percent
$E_D = -1$	Unit elastic	Drops by 10 percent	No change
$-\infty < E_D < -1$	Elastic	Drops by more than 10 percent	Decreases
$E_D = -\infty$	Perfectly elastic	Drops to 0	Drops to 0

effects of a 10 percent increase in the price on quantity demanded and on total revenue. Give this exhibit some thought, and see if you can draw a demand curve to reflect each type of elasticity.

DETERMINANTS OF THE PRICE ELASTICITY OF DEMAND

Thus far we have explored the technical properties of demand elasticity. But we have not yet considered why price elasticities of demand vary for different goods. Several characteristics influence the price elasticity of demand for a good. We will examine each of these in detail.

Availability of Substitutes

As we saw in Chapter 3, your particular wants can be satisfied in a variety of ways. A rise in the price of pizza makes other foods relatively cheaper. If close substitutes are available, an increase in the price of pizza will encourage consumers to shift to these substitutes. But if nothing else satisfies like pizza, the quantity of pizza demanded will not decline as much. *The greater the availability of substitutes for a good and the closer these substitutes, the more elastic the demand.*

The number and similarity of substitutes depend on how we define the good. *The more broadly we define a good, the fewer substitutes there will be and the less elastic the demand will be.* For example, the demand for shoes is less elastic than the demand for running shoes because there are few substitutes for shoes but several substitutes for running shoes, such as sneakers, tennis shoes, cross-trainers, and the like. The demand for running shoes, however, is less elastic than the demand for Nike running shoes because the consumer has more substitutes for Nikes, including Reeboks, New Balance, and so on. Finally, the demand for Nike running shoes is less elastic than the demand for a specific model of Nikes, such as Visi-Zoom Air or Air Max Triax Plus.

For some goods, such as insulin for a diabetic, there are simply no close substitutes. The demand for such goods tends to be less elastic than for goods with close substitutes. Much advertising is aimed at establishing in the consumer's mind the uniqueness of a particular product—an effort to convince consumers "to accept no substitutes." Why might a firm want to make the demand for its product less elastic?

As an example of the substitute principle, consider the pattern of commercial breaks during TV movies. When the movie first begins, viewers have several possible substitutes for it, including other shows and perhaps movies on other channels. To keep viewers from switching channels, the first movie segment is longer than usual, perhaps 20 or 30 minutes without a commercial break. But after viewers get hooked on the movie, shows on other channels are no longer close substitutes, so broadcasters inject commercials with greater frequency without fear of losing many viewers.

Proportion of the Consumer's Budget Spent on the Good

Recall that a higher price reduces quantity demanded in part because a higher price causes consumers' real spending power to decline. A demand curve reflects both the *willingness* and *ability* to purchase a good at alternative prices. Because spending on some goods represents a large share of the consumer's budget, a change in the price of such a good has a substantial impact on the quantity that consumers are *able* to purchase. An increase in the price of housing, for example, reduces consumers' ability to purchase housing. The income effect of a higher price reduces the quantity demanded. In contrast, the income effect of an increase in the price of, say, paper towels is trivial because paper towels represent such a small proportion of any budget. *The more important the item is as a proportion of the consumer's budget, other things constant, the greater will be the income effect of a change in price, so the more elastic will be the demand for the item.* The smaller the spending on the item as a proportion of the budget, other things constant, the smaller the income effect of a change in price, so the less elastic is the demand for the item. Hence the quantity of housing demanded will be more responsive to a given percentage change in price than the quantity of paper towels demanded.

A Matter of Time

Consumers can substitute lower-priced goods for higher-priced goods, but finding substitutes usually takes time. Suppose your college announces a substantial increase in room and board fees, effective immediately. Some students will move off campus as soon as they can; others will wait until the next school year. And, over time, fewer students may apply for admission, and more incoming students will choose off-campus housing. Thus *the longer the adjustment period allowed, the greater is consumers' ability to substitute away from relatively higher-priced products toward lower-priced substitutes. Hence, the longer the period of adjustment, the more responsive the change in quantity demanded is to a given change in price.* As another example, between 1973 and 1974, the OPEC cartel raised the price of oil sharply. As a result, the price of gasoline increased 45 percent, but the quantity demanded decreased by only 8 percent. As more time passed, however, people purchased smaller cars and made more use of public transportation. Since the price of oil used to fire power generators and to heat homes had increased as well, people bought more energy-efficient appliances and added more insulation to their homes. Again, the change in quantity demanded was greater as consumers had more time to respond to the price increase.

Exhibit 5 demonstrates how demand becomes more elastic over time. Given an initial price of $1.00, let D_w be the demand curve one week after a price change; D_m, one month after; and D_y, one year after. If the price increases from $1.00 to $1.25, the more time consumers have to respond to the price increase, the greater the reduction in quantity demanded. For example, the demand curve D_w shows that one week after the price increase, the quantity demanded per day has not declined much—in this case, from 100 to 95. The demand curve D_m indicates a reduction to 75 after one month, and demand curve D_y shows a reduction to 50 after one year. Notice that among these demand curves and over the range starting from the point of intersection, the flatter the demand curve, the more price elastic the demand. Here elasticity appears to be linked to the slope because we are starting from the same point—the same price-quantity combination.

Elasticity Estimates

Let's review some estimates of the price elasticity of demand for particular goods and services. As we have noted, the substitution of relatively lower-priced goods for a good whose price has just increased often takes time. Thus, when estimating price elasticity, economists often distinguish between a period during which consumers have little time to adjust—let's call it the *short run*—and a period during which consumers can fully adjust to a price change—let's call it the *long run*. Exhibit 6 provides some short-run and long-run price elasticity estimates for selected products.

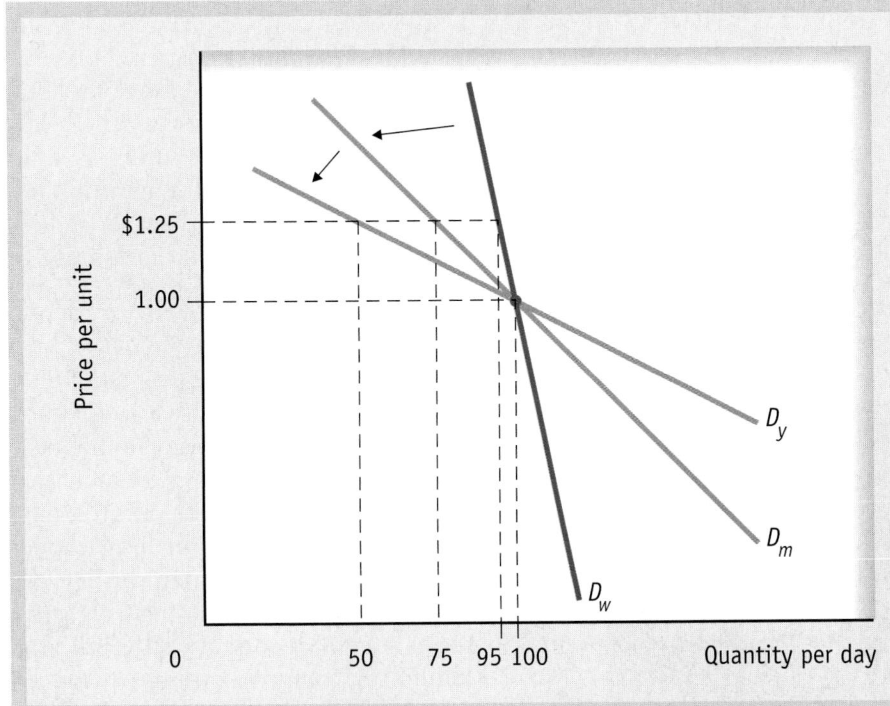

EXHIBIT 5

Demand Becomes More Elastic over Time

D_w is the demand curve one week after a price increase from $1.00 to $1.25. Along this curve, quantity demanded per day falls from 100 to 95. One month after the price increase, quantity demanded has fallen to 75 along D_m. One year after the price increase, quantity demanded has fallen to 50 along D_y. At any given price, D_y is more elastic than D_m, which is more elastic than D_w.

EXHIBIT 6

Selected Price Elasticities of Demand

Product	Short Run	Long Run
Cigarettes (among adults)	—	−0.4
Electricity (residential)	−0.1	−1.9
Air travel	−0.1	−2.4
Medical care and hospitalization	−0.3	−0.9
Gasoline	−0.4	−1.5
Milk	−0.4	—
Fish (cod)	−0.5	—
Wine	−0.7	−1.2
Movies	−0.9	−3.7
Natural gas (residential)	−1.4	−2.1
Automobiles	−1.9	−2.2
Chevrolets	—	−4.0

Sources: F. Chaloupka, "Rational Addictive Behavior and Cigarette Smoking," *Journal of Political Economy,* (August 1991); Hsaing-tai Cheng and Oral Capps, Jr., "Demand for Fish," *American Journal of Agricultural Economics* (August 1998); J. Johnson et al., "Short-Run and Long-Run Elasticities for Canadian Consumption of Alcoholic Beverages," *Review of Economics and Statistics* (February 1992); R. Archibald and R. Gillingham, "The Review of the Short-Run Consumer Demand for Gasoline Using Household Survey Data," *Review of Economics and Statistics* 62 (November 1980); J. Griffin, Energy Conservation in the OECD, 1980–2000 (Cambridge, Mass.: Balinger, 1979); H. Houthakker and L. Taylor, *Consumer Demand in the United States: Analysis and Projections,* 2nd ed. (Cambridge, Mass.: Harvard University Press, 1970); and G. Lakshmanan and W. Anderson, "Residential Energy Demand in the United States," *Regional Science and Urban Economics* 10 (August 1980).

The price elasticity is greater in the long run because consumers have more time to adjust. For example, if the price of electricity rose today, consumers in the short run might cut back a bit in their use of electrical appliances, and those with electric heat might lower the thermostat a bit in winter. Over time, however, consumers would switch to more energy-efficient appliances and might convert from electric heat to oil or natural gas. So demand is more elastic in the long run than in the short run, as is reflected in Exhibit 6. In fact, in every instance where values for both the short run and the long run are listed, the long run is more elastic than the short run. Notice also that the long-run price elasticity of demand for Chevrolets exceeds the price elasticity for automobiles in general. There are many more substitutes for Chevrolets than for automobiles. There are no close substitutes for cigarettes, even in the long run, so the demand for cigarettes among adults is price inelastic. Such elasticity measures can be of more than just academic interest, as discussed in the following case study.

McEachern Interactive

CaseStudy

Public Policy

Smoking rates among teens are higher in Alaska than in the rest of the U.S., and are even higher for Native Alaskans according to "Tobacco Use among Alaska Youth," an article in the State of Alaska's

Deterring Young Smokers

As the U.S. Surgeon General warns on each pack of cigarettes, smoking can be hazardous to your health. Researchers estimate that smoking causes many times more deaths than traffic accidents do. Deaths from lung cancer have doubled among older women since 1980. A recent federal study found that cigarette smoking costs the U.S. economy $130 billion a year: $80 billion in foregone output because of smoking-related illness and death and $50 billion because of health care costs resulting from smoking-related disease. That's more than was spent on all U.S. public higher education in 1998.

Health-related issues and the addictive nature of cigarettes have created a growing public policy concern about smoking, especially smoking by young people, which jumped one-third during the 1990s. A federal study of 16,000 U.S. students in grades 9 through 12 found cigarette smoking rose from 27.5 percent of those surveyed in 1991 to 36.4 percent in 1997. Among black youths, the rate nearly doubled from 12.6 percent to 22.7 percent. Reasons offered for the jump include a stable price for cigarettes (prices did not increase between 1992 and 1997) and the greater glamorization of smoking in movies and television. (For example, in the movie *Titanic*, the two young, attractive, leading characters smoked cigarettes.)

One way to reduce smoking is to raise the price of cigarettes through higher cigarette taxes. Researchers have found the price elasticity of demand for cigarettes among young smokers to be −1.3, so a 10 percent increase in the price of cigarettes would reduce smoking by 13 percent. As noted earlier, among adult smokers, the estimated price elasticity of demand was only −0.4.

Why are teenagers more responsive to price changes than adults? *First*, recall that one of the factors affecting price elasticity of demand is the importance of the item in the consumer's budget. The proportion of income that a young smoker spends on cigarettes usually exceeds the proportion for adult smokers. *Second*, peer pressure is much more influential in the young person's decision to smoke than in an adult's decision to continue smoking. (If anything, adults face negative peer pressure.) Because of peer pressure, the effects of higher price get multiplied among young smokers because a higher price reduces smoking by peers. With fewer peers smoking, there is less pressure to smoke. And *third*, since smoking is addictive, young people who are not yet hooked are more sensitive to price increases than are adult smokers who are already hooked. Addicts by definition are less sensitive to a price change than those not addicted.

If a price elasticity of −1.3 remains constant over the relevant range of price changes, a price increase of $1.80 per pack would reduce smoking among young people by 60 percent. To be fully effective, the price increase must be introduced quickly, not, as was proposed in Congress, phased in over five years. The experience from other countries supports the effectiveness of higher prices. For example, a large tax increase on cigarettes in Canada during the 1980s cut youth smoking by two thirds.

Sources: David Wessel and Jeanne Cummings, "U.S. to Release Analysis Showing Smoking Costs $130 Billion a Year," *Wall Street Journal* (25 March 1998); Sheryl Gay Stolberg, "Smoking by Black Youths Is Up Sharply, Study Finds," *New York Times* (3 April 1998); Marlene Cimons, "Tobacco Use Soars Among Teenagers," *Hartford Courant* (3 April 1998); "Prepared Statement of Frank J. Chaloupka, Ph.D., Before the Senate Judiciary Committee," *Federal News Service* (29 October 1997).

Epidemiology Bulletin at http://www.epi.hss.state.ak.us/bulletins/topics/docs/b1997_05.htm. The report uses estimates of elasticity to predict decreases in smoking as a result of increases in cigarette taxes. What missteps can you detect in the way in which the report uses price elasticity? Alaska did increase the tax on a pack of cigarettes to $1.

Let's turn now to the price elasticity of supply.

PRICE ELASTICITY OF SUPPLY

Prices are signals to both sides of the market about the relative scarcity of products; high prices discourage consumption but encourage production. The price elasticity of demand measures how responsive consumers are to a price change.

Price elasticity of supply A measure of the responsiveness of quantity supplied to a price change; the percent change in quantity supplied divided by the percent change in price

Similarly, the **price elasticity of supply** measures how responsive producers are to a price change. This elasticity is calculated in the same way as price elasticity of demand, but by using the percent change in quantity supplied instead of the percent change in quantity demanded. In simplest terms, the price elasticity of supply equals the percent change in quantity supplied divided by the percent change in price. Since the higher price usually results in an increased quantity supplied, the percent change in price and the percent change in quantity supplied move in the same direction, so the price elasticity of supply is usually positive.

Exhibit 7 depicts a typical upward-sloping supply curve. As you can see, if the price increases from p to p', the quantity supplied increases from q_S to q'_S. Price and quantity supplied move in the same direction. Let's look at the elasticity formula for the supply curve. The price elasticity of supply, E_S, is

$$E_S = \frac{q'_S - q_S}{(q'_S + q_S)/2} \div \frac{p' - p}{(p' + p)/2}$$

Again, the 2s cancel out so the formula reduces to

$$E_S = \frac{q'_S - q_S}{(q'_S + q_S)} \div \frac{p' - p}{(p' + p)}$$

Categories of Supply Elasticity

The terminology for supply elasticity is the same as for demand elasticity: If supply elasticity is less than 1.0, supply is *inelastic*; if its value is equal to 1.0, supply is

EXHIBIT 7

Price Elasticity of Supply

If the price increases from p to p', the quantity supplied increases from q_s to q'_s. Price and quantity supplied move in the same direction, so the price elasticity of supply is a positive number.

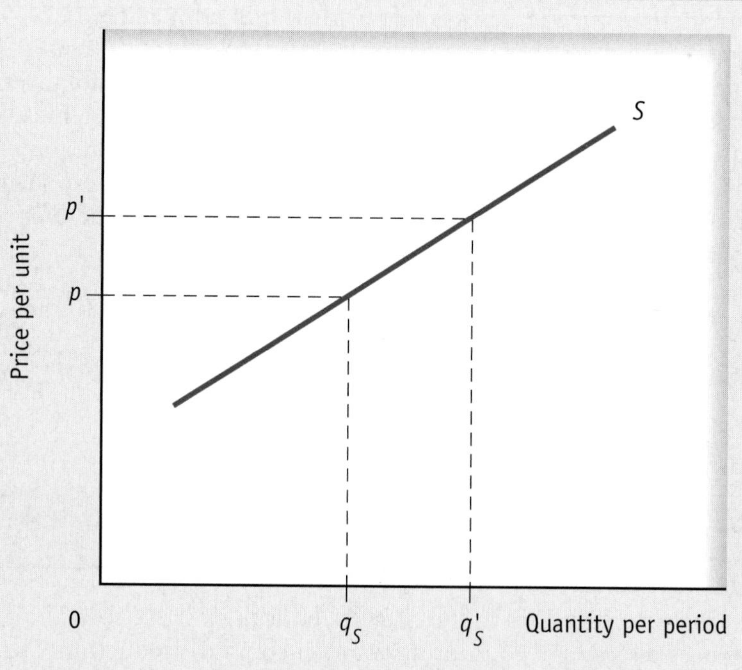

unit elastic; and if its value is greater than 1.0, supply is *elastic*. There are also some special values of supply elasticity to consider.

Perfectly Elastic Supply. At one extreme is the horizontal supply curve, such as supply curve *S* in panel (a) of Exhibit 8. In this case, producers will supply none of the good at a price below *p* but will supply any amount at a price of *p*. The quantity actually supplied at price *p* will depend on the amount demanded at that price. Because a tiny increase from a price just below *p* to a price of *p* will result in an unlimited quantity supplied, this curve is said to reflect **perfectly elastic supply,** which has a numerical value of infinity. As individual consumers, we typically face perfectly elastic supply curves. When we go to the supermarket, we usually can buy as much as we want at the prevailing price but none at a lower price. This is not to say that all consumers together could buy an unlimited amount at the prevailing price. (Recall the fallacy of composition: What is true for any individual consumer is not necessarily true for all consumers as a group.)

Perfectly elastic supply curve A horizontal line reflecting a situation in which any price decrease reduces the quantity supplied to zero; the elasticity value is infinity

Perfectly Inelastic Supply. The most unresponsive relationship between price and quantity supplied is the one in which there is no change in the quantity supplied regardless of the price. Such a case is represented by the vertical supply curve *S'* in panel (b) of Exhibit 8. Because the percent change in quantity supplied is zero, regardless of the change in price, the value of the supply elasticity equals zero. This curve reflects **perfectly inelastic supply.** Any good that is in fixed supply, such as Picasso paintings or 1978 Dom Perignon champagne, will have a perfectly inelastic supply curve.

Perfectly inelastic supply curve A vertical line reflecting a situation in which a price change has no effect on the quantity supplied; the elasticity value is zero

EXHIBIT 8

Three Constant-Elasticity Supply Curves

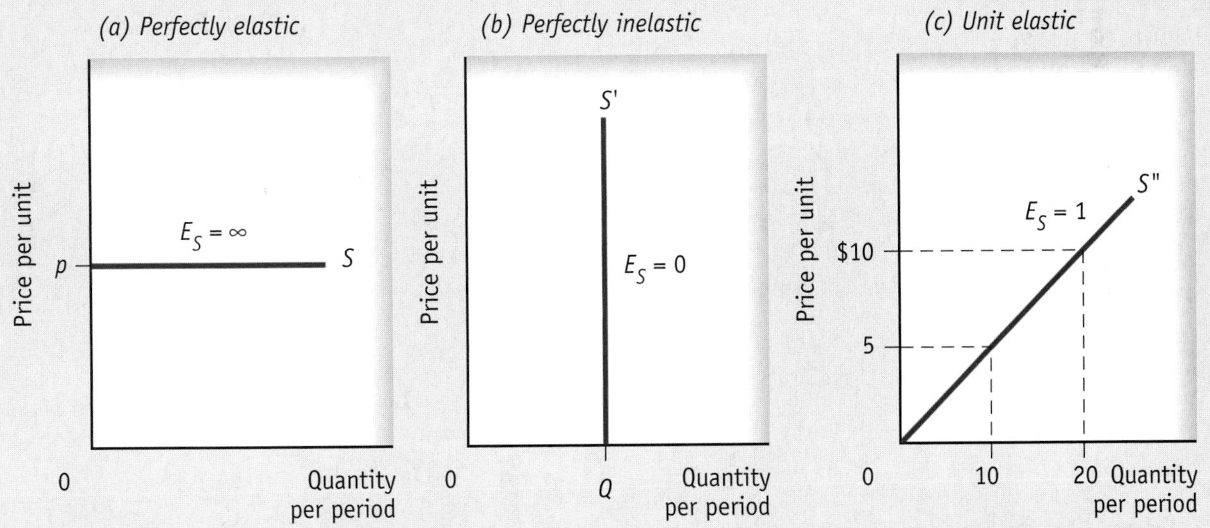

Supply curve *S* in panel (a) is perfectly elastic (horizontal). Along *S*, firms will supply any amount of output demanded at price *p*. Supply curve *S'* is perfectly inelastic (vertical). *S'* shows that the quantity supplied is independent of the price. In panel (c), *S"* is a ray, which has a unit-elastic price elasticity of supply. Any percentage change in price will result in the same percentage change in quantity supplied.

Unit-elastic supply curve A percent change in price causes an identical percent change in quantity supplied; depicted by a supply curve that is a straight line from the origin; the elasticity value is one

Unit-Elastic Supply. Any supply curve that can be represented as a straight line from the origin—such as S" in panel (c) of Exhibit 8—is a **unit-elastic supply curve.** This means that a percent change in price will always result in an identical percent change in quantity supplied. For example, along S" a doubling of the price results in a doubling of the quantity supplied. Note that unit elasticity is determined not by the slope of the line but by the fact that the linear supply curve emanates from the origin.

Determinants of Supply Elasticity

The elasticity of supply indicates how responsive producers are to a change in price. Their responsiveness depends on how easy or difficult it is to alter output as a result of a change in price. If the cost of supplying an additional unit rises sharply as output expands, then a higher price will elicit little increase in quantity supplied, so supply will tend to be inelastic. But if the additional cost rises slowly as output expands, the lure of a higher price will prompt a large increase in output. In this case, supply will tend to be more elastic.

One determinant of supply elasticity is the length of the adjustment period under consideration. Just as demand becomes more elastic over time as consumers adjust to price changes, supply also becomes more elastic over time as producers adjust to price changes. The longer the time period under consideration, the more able producers are to adjust to changes in relative prices. Exhibit 9 presents a different supply curve for each of three time periods. S_w is the supply curve when the period of adjustment is a week. As you can see, a higher price will not elicit much of a response in quantity supplied because firms have little time to adjust. Thus such a supply curve will tend to slope steeply, reflecting inelastic supply.

EXHIBIT 9

Market Supply Becomes More Elastic over Time

The supply curve one week after a price increase, S_w, is less elastic, at a given price, than the curve one month later, S_m, which is less elastic than the curve one year later, S_y. Given a price increase from $10 to $12, quantity supplied per day increases to 55 units af-ter one week, to 70 units after one month, and to 100 units after one year.

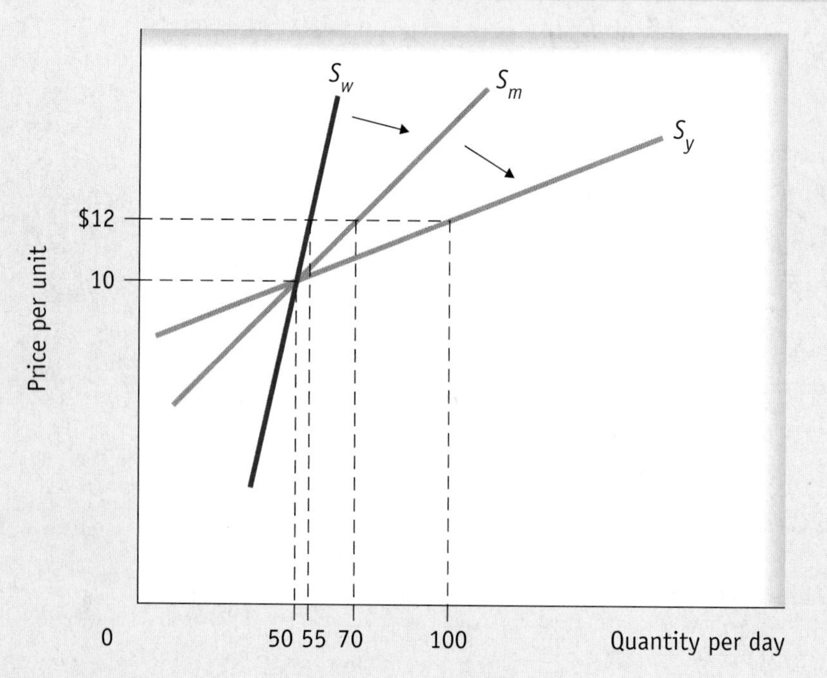

S_m is the supply curve when the adjustment period under consideration is a month. In a month, firms can more easily adjust the rate at which they employ some resources. As a result, firms have a greater ability to vary output. Thus supply is more elastic when the adjustment period is a month than when it is a week. Supply is even more elastic when the adjustment period is a year, as is shown by S_y. If firms can vary all inputs in a year, they can more easily respond to a higher price.

So a given price increase will elicit a greater quantity supplied, the longer the adjustment period. For example, if the price of oil increases, oil producers in the short run can try to pump more from existing wells, but in the long run they can try to discover more oil in the remote jungles of the Amazon or the stormy waters of the North Sea. Empirical research confirms the positive link between the price elasticity of supply and the length of the adjustment period. *The elasticity of supply is typically greater the longer the period of adjustment.* Firms' ability to alter quantity supplied in response to price changes differs across industries. The response time will be slower for producers of electricity, oil, and timber—where production capacity may take years to develop—than for window washing, lawn maintenance, and hot-dog vending—where a production capacity can be increased overnight.

OTHER ELASTICITY MEASURES

The price elasticities of demand and supply are frequently used in economic analysis, but other elasticities also provide useful information—information about how demand responds to a change in consumer income or to a change in the price of a related good.

Income Elasticity of Demand

What happens to the demand for new cars, garden supplies, or computer software if consumer income increases by, say, 10 percent? The answer to this question is of great interest to producers of these goods because it helps them predict the effect of changing income on quantity sold and on total revenues. The **income elasticity of demand** measures how consumer demand at a given price changes in response to a change in income. More specifically, *the income elasticity of demand measures the percent change in demand divided by the percent change in income that caused it.*

Income elasticity of demand The percent change in demand (at a given price) divided by the percent change in income

As we noted in Chapter 3, the demand for some products, such as bus rides and laundromat services, actually declines as income increases. Thus, the income elasticity of demand for such products will be negative. Goods with an income elasticity less than zero are called *inferior goods*. The demand for most goods increases as income increases. These goods are called *normal goods*, and they have an income elasticity greater than zero.

Let's take a closer look at normal goods. Suppose demand increases as income increases but by a smaller percent than income increases. In such cases the value of income elasticity is greater than zero but less than 1. For example, people buy more food as their incomes rise, but the percent increase in demand is less than the percent increase in income. Normal goods with an income elasticity less than 1 are said to be *income inelastic*. *Necessities* such as food, housing, and clothing often have an income elasticity less than 1.

Goods with an income elasticity greater than 1 are said to be *income elastic*. *Luxuries*, such as fine cars, vintage wine, and meals at fancy restaurants, have an income elasticity greater than 1. For example, during 1990 and 1991, the U.S. economy experienced a recession, meaning that national income declined; as a result, the demand for meals at fancy restaurants declined, and some restaurants went out of business. During the same period, the demand for basic foods such as bread, sugar, and cheese changed very little. Incidentally, the terms *inferior goods, necessities,* and *luxuries* are not meant to imply some value judgment about the merit of particular goods; these terms are simply convenient definitions economists use to classify economic behavior.

Exhibit 10 presents some income elasticity estimates for various goods and services. The figures indicate that as income increases, consumers spend proportionately more on items such as private education, automobiles, wine, owner-occupied housing, furniture, dental service, and restaurant meals. For items such as food, cigarettes, gasoline, rental housing, and beer, consumer spending increases as income increases, but less than proportionately. So as income rises, the demand for owner-occupied housing increases more in percentage terms than the demand for rental housing and the demand for wine increases more in percentage terms than the demand for beer. Flour has negative income elasticity, indicating that the demand for flour declines as income increases. As income increases, consumers switch from home baking to purchasing baked goods.

As we have seen, the demand for food is income inelastic. The demand for food also tends to be price inelastic. This combination of income inelasticity

EXHIBIT 10

Selected Income Elasticities of Demand

Product	Income Elasticity	Product	Income Elasticity
Private education	2.46	Physicians' services	0.75
Automobiles	2.45	Coca-Cola	0.68
Wine	2.19	Beef	0.62
Owner-occupied housing	1.49	Food	0.51
Furniture	1.48	Coffee	0.51
Dental service	1.42	Cigarettes	0.50
Restaurant meals	1.40	Gasoline and oil	0.48
Shoes	1.10	Rental housing	0.43
Chicken	1.06	Beer	0.27
Spirits ("hard" liquor)	1.02	Pork	0.18
Clothing	0.92	Flour	−0.36

Sources: F. Gasmi et al., "Econometric Analyses of Collusive Behavior in a Soft-Drink Market," *Journal of Economics and Management Strategy* (Summer 1992); J. Johnson et al., "Short-Run and Long-Run Elasticities for Canadian Consumption of Alcoholic Beverages," *Review of Economics and Statistics* (February 1992); H. Houthakker and L. Taylor, *Consumer Demand in the United States: Analyses and Projections*, 2d ed. (Cambridge, Mass.: Harvard University Press, 1970); C. Huang et al., "The Demand for Coffee in the United States, 1963–77," *Quarterly Review of Economics and Business* (Summer 1980); and G. Brester and M. Wohlgenant, "Estimating Interrelated Demands for Meats Using New Measures for Ground and Table Cut Beef," *American Journal of Agricultural Economics* (November 1991).

and price inelasticity creates special problems in agricultural markets, as described in the following case study.

The Market for Food and "The Farm Problem"

Despite decades of federal support through various farm-assistance programs, the number of farmers continues to drop. Farm employment dropped by more than two-thirds from 10 million in 1950 to about 3 million today. The demise of the family farm can be traced to the price and income elasticities of demand for farm products and to technological breakthroughs that increased production.

Many of the forces that determine farm production are beyond the farmer's control. Temperature, rain, insects, and other external forces affect crop size and quality. For example, 1995 offered especially favorable growing conditions and crop production increased by 16 percent. Such swings in production create special problems for farmers because the demand for most farm crops, such as milk, eggs, corn, potatoes, oats, sugar, and beef, is price inelastic.

The effect of inelastic demand on farm revenue is illustrated in Exhibit 11. Suppose that in a normal year, farmers supply 10 billion bushels of grain at a market price of $5 per bushel. Annual revenue, which is price times quantity, totals $50 billion in our example. What if more favorable growing conditions increase crop production to 11 billion bushels, an increase of 10 percent? Because demand is price inelastic, the average price in our example must fall by

What are the forces shaping U.S. agriculture today? The Economics Research Service of the U.S. Dept. of Agriculture provides some answers with its briefing book at http://www.econ.ag.gov/briefing/forces/. Check to find out what the latest edition says about the current state of the American farm family. How have farm size and the number of family farms been changing? How does farm family income compare to average household income? What percent of farm income is a result of government farm support policies?

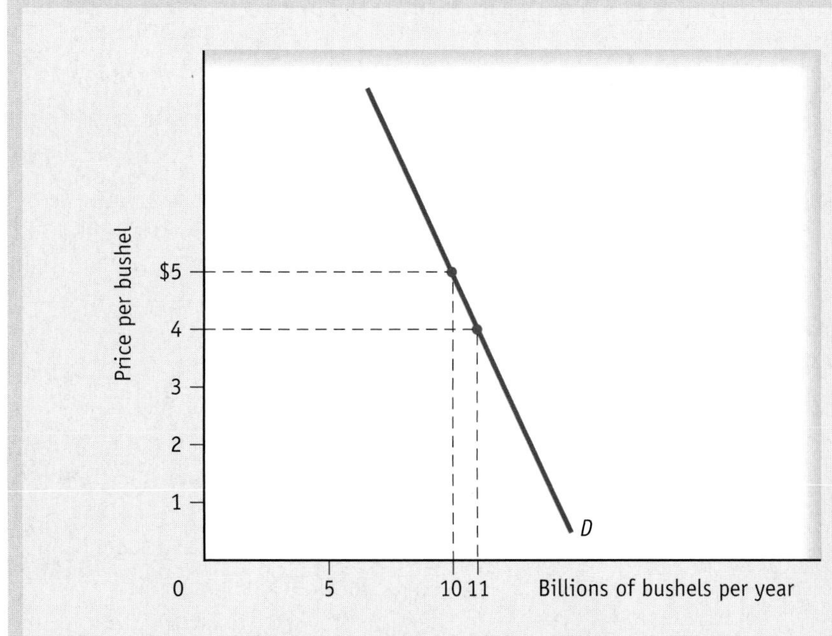

EXHIBIT 11

The Demand for Grain

The demand for grain tends to be price inelastic. As the market price falls, total revenue also falls.

more than 10 percent to, say, $4 per bushel, in order to clear the market of the additional billion bushels. Thus the 10 percent increase in farm production can be sold only if the price drops by 20 percent.

Because, in percentage terms, the drop in price exceeds the increase in output, total revenue declines from $50 billion to $44 billion. So farm revenue drops by over 10 percent, despite the 10 percent increase in production. *Since demand is price inelastic, an increase in output reduces total revenue.* Of course, for farmers, the up side of inelastic demand is that a lower-than-normal crop results in a proportionately higher price and a higher total revenue. For example, because of the drought of 1988, corn prices rose by more than 50 percent and net farm income was up sharply. So weather-generated changes in farm production create substantial year-to-year swings in farm revenue.

Problems created by fluctuations in farm revenue are compounded in the long run by the *income inelasticity* of demand for grain and, more generally, for food. As household incomes grow over time, spending on food may increase because people substitute prepared foods and restaurant meals for home cooking. But this switch has little effect on the total demand for farm products. Thus, as the economy grows over time and real incomes rise, the demand for farm products tends to increase but by less than the increase in real income. This is reflected by the shift of the demand curve from *D* to *D*' in Exhibit 12.

Because of technological improvements in production, the supply of farm products has increased sharply. Farm output per worker is about *eight times* greater now than in 1950 because of such factors as more sophisticated machines, better fertilizers, and healthier seed strains. Exhibit 12 shows the supply of grain increasing from *S* to *S*'. Since the increase in supply exceeds the increase in demand, the price of grain has declined. And because the demand for

EXHIBIT 12

The Effect of Increases in Supply and Demand on Farm Revenue

Over time, technological advances in farming have sharply increased the supply of grain. In addition, increases in household income over time have increased the demand for farm products. But because increases in the supply of grain have exceeded increases in demand, the combined effect has been a drop in the market prices and a fall in total farm revenue.

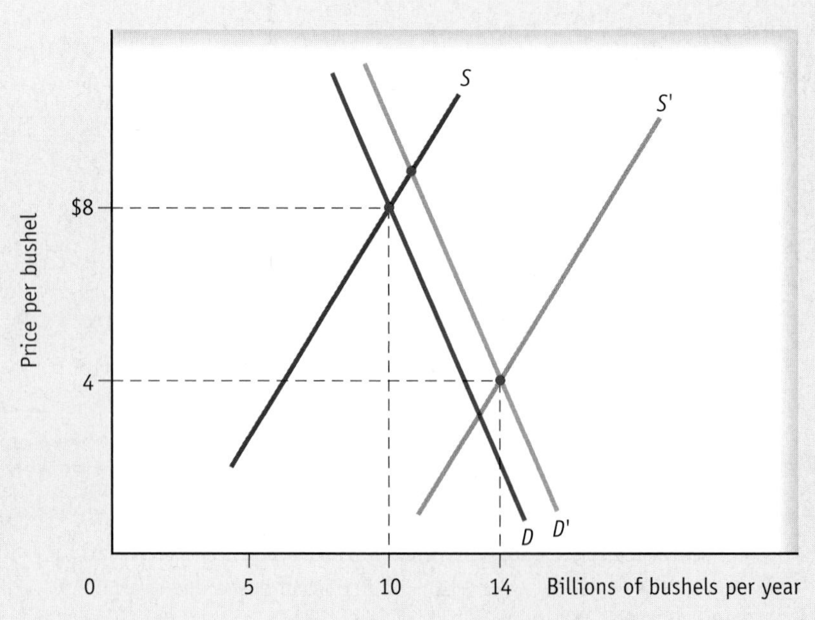

grain is price inelastic, the percent drop in price exceeds the percent increase in output. The combined effect in our example is lower total farm revenue. In fact, net income (adjusted for inflation) to all U.S. farmers combined is now only half what it was in the early 1950s.

Another wild card in the farm-revenue equation is unstable foreign demand. Foreign demand for U.S. crops depends on foreign production and prices, on the exchange rate between the dollar and foreign currencies, and on public policy with regard to foreign trade. Thus many of the forces that shape the market for farm products are beyond the farmer's control. And demand that is both price inelastic and income inelastic means that greater farm output may result in lower total revenue.

Sources: Bruce L. Gardner, "Changing Economic Perspective on the Farm Problem," *Journal of Economic Literature* 30 (March 1992): 62–105; Ching-Fun Cling and James Peale, "Income and Price Elasticities," in *Advances in Econometrics Supplement*, Henri Theil, ed. (Greenwich, Conn.: JAI Press, 1989); and *Economic Report of the President*, February 1999, Tables B–97 to B–102.

Cross-Price Elasticity of Demand

Since a corporation often produces an entire line of products, it has a special interest in how a change in the price of one product will affect the demand for another. For example, the Coca-Cola Corporation needs to know how changing the price of Cherry Coke will affect sales of Classic Coke. Similarly, Procter & Gamble wants to know how changing the price of Safeguard soap will affect sales of its Ivory soap. The responsiveness of the demand for one good to changes in the price of another good is called the **cross-price elasticity of demand**. It is defined as the percent change in the demand of one good (holding the price constant) divided by the percent change in the price of another good. Its numerical value can be positive, negative, or zero, depending on whether the two goods in question are substitutes, complements, or unrelated, respectively.

Cross-price elasticity of demand The percent change in the demand of one good as a result of the percent change in the price of another good

Substitutes. If an increase in the price of one good leads to an increase in the demand for another good, the value of their cross-price elasticity is positive, and the goods are considered *substitutes*. For example, an increase in the price of Coke, other things constant, will increase the demand for Pepsi, reflecting the fact that the two are substitutes. In fact, the cross-price elasticity between Coke and Pepsi is about 0.7, indicating that a 10 percent increase in the price of one will increase the demand for the other by 7 percent.[1]

Complements. If an increase in the price of one good leads to a decrease in the demand for another good, the value of their cross-price elasticity is negative, and the goods are considered *complements*. For example, an increase in the price of gasoline, other things constant, will reduce the demand for tires because people will drive less and so will replace their tires less frequently. Gasoline and tires have a negative cross-price elasticity and are complements.

In summary, when the change in demand for one good has the same sign as the change in price of another good, the two goods are substitutes; when the change in demand for one good has the opposite sign from the change in price

1 This estimate was reported in F. Gasmi, J. Laffont, and Q. Vuong, "Econometric Analysis of Collusive Behavior in a Soft-Drink Market," *Journal of Economics and Management Strategy* (Summer 1992).

of another good, the goods are complements. Most pairs of goods selected at random are *unrelated*, so the value of their cross-price elasticity is approximately zero.

CONCLUSION

Because this chapter has been more quantitative than earlier chapters, you may have been preoccupied with the mechanics of the calculations and thus may have overlooked the intuitive appeal and the neat simplicity of the notion of elasticity. *An elasticity measures the willingness and ability of buyers and sellers to alter their behavior in response to a change in their economic circumstances*. For example, if the price of a good falls, consumers may be able but not willing to increase their consumption of the good. In that case the demand would be perfectly inelastic.

Firms try to estimate the price elasticity of demand for their products. Since a corporation often produces an entire line of products, it also has a special interest in certain cross-price elasticities. Governments also have an ongoing interest in various elasticities. For example, state governments want to know the effect of a 1 percent increase in the sales tax on total tax receipts, and local governments want to know how an increase in income will affect the demand for real estate and, hence, the revenue generated by a property tax. International groups are interested in elasticities; for example, the Organization of Petroleum Exporting Countries (OPEC) is concerned about the price elasticity of demand for oil. Many questions can be answered by referring to particular elasticities. Some corporate economists estimate elasticities for a living.

SUMMARY

1. The price elasticities of demand and supply show how sensitive buyers and sellers are to changes in the price of a good. More elastic means more responsive, and less elastic means less responsive.
2. If demand is price elastic—that is, if the percent change in quantity demanded exceeds the percent change in price—a price increase will reduce total revenue and a price decrease will increase total revenue. If demand is price inelastic—that is, if the percent change in quantity is less than the percent change in price—then a price increase will increase total revenue and a price decrease will reduce total revenue. And if demand is unit elastic—that is, if the percent change in quantity just equals the percent change in price—a price change will not affect total revenue.
3. Along a linear, or straight-line, downward-sloping demand curve, the elasticity of demand falls steadily as the price falls. But constant-elasticity demand curves have the same elasticity everywhere.
4. Demand will be more elastic (1) the greater the availability of substitutes and the more closely they resemble the good in question; (2) the more narrowly the good is defined; (3) the larger the proportion of the consumer's budget spent on the good; and (4) the longer the time allowed for adjustment to a change in price.
5. The price elasticity of supply uses a similar approach to the price elasticity of demand, but since price and quantity supplied are directly related, price elasticity of supply is a positive number. Price elasticity of supply depends on how quickly production cost changes as output changes. If such cost rises sharply as output expands, quantity supplied will be less responsive to price increases and, hence, less elastic. The longer the time period producers have to adjust to price changes, the more elastic the supply.
6. The income elasticity of demand measures the responsiveness of demand to changes in consumer income. This elasticity is positive for normal goods and negative for inferior goods.
7. The cross-price elasticity of demand measures the responsiveness of demand to changes in the price of another product. Two goods are defined as substitutes, complements, or unrelated, depending on whether the value of their cross-price elasticity of demand is positive, negative, or equal to zero, respectively.

QUESTIONS FOR REVIEW

1. *(Categories of Price Elasticity of Demand)* For each of the following values of price elasticity of demand, indicate whether demand is elastic, inelastic, perfectly elastic, perfectly inelastic, or unit elastic. In addition, determine what would happen to total revenue if a firm raised its price in each elasticity range identified.
   a. $E_D = -2.5$
   b. $E_D = -1.0$
   c. $E_D = -\infty$
   d. $E_D = -0.8$
2. *(Elasticity and Total Revenue)* Explain the relationship between the price elasticity of demand and total revenue.
3. *(Price Elasticity and the Linear Demand Curve)* How is it possible for many price elasticities to be associated with a single demand curve?
4. *(Determinants of Price Elasticity)* Why is the price elasticity of demand for Coca-Cola greater than the price elasticity of demand for soft drinks generally?
5. *(Determinants of Price Elasticity)* What factors help determine the price elasticity of demand? What factors help determine the price elasticity of supply?
6. *(Cross-Price Elasticity)* Using supply and demand curves, predict the impact on the price and quantity demanded of Good 1 of an increase in the price of Good 2 if the two goods are substitutes. What if the two goods are complements?
7. *(Other Elasticity Measures)* Complete each of the following sentences:
   a. The income elasticity of demand measures, for a given price, the ______ in quantity demanded divided by the ______ income from which it resulted.
   b. If a decrease in the price of one good causes a decrease in demand for another good, the two goods are ______.
   c. If the value of the cross-price elasticity of demand between two goods is approximately zero, they are considered ______.

PROBLEMS AND EXERCISES

8. *(Calculating Price Elasticity of Demand)* Suppose that 50 units of a good are demanded at a price of $1 per unit. A reduction in price to $0.20 results in an increase in quantity demanded to 70 units. Show that these data yield a price elasticity of −0.25. By what percentage would a 10 percent rise in the price reduce the quantity demanded assuming price elasticity remains constant along the demand curve?
9. *(Price Elasticity and Total Revenue)* Fill in values for each point listed in the following table. What relationship have you depicted?

P	Q	Price Elasticity	Total Revenue
$8	2	______	______
7	3	______	______
6	4	______	______
5	5	______	______
4	6	______	______
3	7	______	______
2	8	______	______

10. *(Income Elasticity of Demand)* Calculate the income elasticity of demand for each of the following goods:

	Quantity Demanded When Income = $10,000	Quantity Demanded When Income = $20,000
Good 1	10	25
Good 2	4	5
Good 3	3	2

11. *(Price Elasticity of Supply)* Calculate the price elasticity of supply for each of the following combinations of price and quantity supplied. Determine whether supply is elastic, inelastic, perfectly elastic, perfectly inelastic, or unit elastic in each case.
    a. Price falls from $2.25 to $1.75; quantity supplied falls from 600 units to 400 units.
    b. Price falls from $2.25 to $1.75; quantity supplied falls from 600 units to 500 units.
    c. Price falls from $2.25 to $1.75; quantity supplied remains at 600 units.
    d. Price increases from $1.75 to $2.25; quantity supplied increases from 466.67 units to 600 units.

Use the following diagram to answer the next two questions.

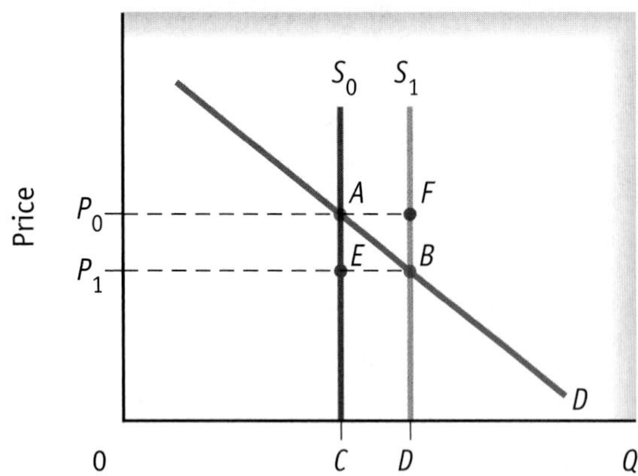

12. *(CaseStudy: The Demand for Food and "The Farm Problem")* Interpret this diagram as showing the market supply and demand curves for agricultural products. Suppose that supply increased from S_0 to S_1 and that demand is inelastic over the relevant range of prices. What areas in the figure would you use to illustrate the net change in farmers' total revenue as a result of the increase in supply?

13. *(CaseStudy: The Demand for Food and "The Farm Problem")* Again suppose that this diagram represents the market for agricultural products and that supply has increased from S_0 to S_1. To aid farmers, the federal government decides to stabilize the price at P_0 by buying up surplus farm products. Show on the diagram how much this would cost the government. By how much would farm income change compared to what it would have been without government intervention?

14. *(Cross-Price Elasticity)* Rank the following in order of increasing (from negative to positive) cross-price elasticity of demand with coffee. Explain your reasoning.

    Bleach
    Tea
    Cream
    Cola

EXPERIENTIAL EXERCISES

15. *(CaseStudy: Deterring Young Smokers)* Policy.com has a Web page devoted to tobacco-related policy issues. Review the articles at their site at http://policy.com/issues/issue 126.html. Choose one and interpret the analysis using supply and demand curves and the concept of elasticity. For additional background information in the form of the transcript of a five-part television series, check *The Tobacco Wars* by Walter Adams and James Brock (Cincinnati, OH: South–Western College Publishing Co., 1999).

16. *(CaseStudy: The Demand for Food and the "Farm Problem")* Farm problems are not unique to the United States. Alan Matthews at Trinity College, Dublin has an interesting Web page devoted to "The Farm Problem and Farm Policy Objectives" at http://www.economics.tcd.ie/amtthews/AgEcCourse/FarmProblem/pagetwo.html. Review the material presented there and determine to what extent agricultural issues in the European Union (EU) are similar to those experienced in the United States. What role does economics play in the analysis of EU farm policy?

17. *(Wall Street Journal)* In the computer industry, cross-elasticities of demand are quite important. For example, we know that computers and computer software are complements, and the cross-elasticity of demand would tell us how strong that relationship is. Read the "Personal Technology" column in Thursday's *Wall Street Journal* and find a story that describes pricing of computer hardware or software. Based on what you know about the relationships among different types of computers, among different types of software, and between computers and software, try to predict the effects of the price change. How will the change affect the quantity demanded of the item described? How will it affect the demand for substitutes and complements to that item?

CHAPTER

19 Consumer Choice and Demand

Why does Universal Studios in Orlando offer second-day admission free? Why are newspapers sold in vending machines that allow you to take more than one copy? How much do you eat when you can eat all you want? What's a cure for spring fever? Why is water cheaper than diamonds even though water is essential to life? To answer these and other questions, we take a closer look at the law of demand, a key building block in economics.

You have already learned two reasons why demand curves slope downward. The first is the *substitution effect* of a price change. When the price of a good falls, consumers substitute that now-cheaper good for other goods. The second is the *income effect* of a price change. When the price of a good falls, the real

isit the McEachern
ractive Study Center
or this chapter at
/mcisc.swcollege.com

incomes of consumers increase, so they will purchase more of the good as long as the good is normal.

Demand is so important that we must know more about it. In this chapter, we develop the law of demand based on the satisfaction derived from consumption. As usual, we assume that consumer choice in a world of scarcity is motivated by the desire to maximize satisfaction. The point of this chapter is not to tell you how to maximize satisfaction. That comes naturally. But understanding the theory behind this behavior helps us understand the implications of that behavior, making predictions more accurate. Topics discussed in this chapter include:

- Total and marginal utility
- The law of diminishing marginal utility
- Measuring utility
- Utility-maximizing conditions
- Consumer surplus
- The role of time in demand
- Money price and time price

UTILITY ANALYSIS

Suppose you and a friend dine together. After dinner, your friend asks how you liked your meal. You might say, "It was delicious," or "I liked it better than my last meal here." You would not say, "I liked mine twice as much as you liked yours." Nor would you say, "It deserves a rating of 86 on the consumer satisfaction index." The utility, or satisfaction, you derived from that meal cannot be measured objectively. You cannot give your meal an 86 satisfaction rating and your friend's meal a 43. Although you can't make comparisons with other people's experience, you can say whether one of your personal experiences was more satisfying than another, and we can draw inferences from your behavior. For example, we can conclude that you likes apples more than oranges if, when the two are priced the same, you always buy apples.

Tastes and Preferences

As was mentioned in Chapter 4, *utility* is the sense of pleasure, or satisfaction, that comes from consumption. Utility is subjective. The utility you derive from consuming a particular good depends on your **tastes,** which are your attitudes toward and preferences for different goods and services—your likes and dislikes in consumption. Some goods are extremely appealing to you and others are not. You may not understand, for example, why someone would pay good money for raw oysters, chicken livers, polka music, martial arts movies, the Psychic Friends Network, or an Electric Tongue Cleaner from Sharper Image. Why are nearly all baby carriages sold in the United States navy blue, whereas they are yellow in Italy and chartreuse in Germany? And why do Australians like chicken-flavored potato chips and chicken-flavored salt?

Tastes A consumer's preferences for different goods and services

Economists actually have little to say about the origin of tastes or why tastes seem to differ across individuals, across households, across regions, and across countries. *Economists assume simply that tastes are given and are relatively stable—that is, different people may have different tastes but an individual's tastes are not constantly in flux.* To be sure, tastes for some products do change over time (for example, hiking and work boots are replacing running shoes as preferred footwear among college students), but economists believe tastes to be stable enough to allow for the study of such matters as the relationship between price and quantity demanded. If tastes were not reasonably stable, then we could not make the assumption in demand analysis that "other things remain constant."

The Law of Diminishing Marginal Utility

Suppose it's a hot summer day and you are extremely thirsty after jogging four miles. You pour yourself a glass of cold water. That first glass is wonderful, and it puts a serious dent in your thirst; the next one is not quite as wonderful, but it is still pretty good; the third is just fair; and the fourth glass you barely finish. Let's talk about the *utility,* or satisfaction, you get from consuming water.

We want to distinguish between total utility and marginal utility. **Total utility** is the total satisfaction a consumer derives from consumption. For example, total utility is the total satisfaction you get from consuming the four glasses of water. **Marginal utility** is the change in total utility resulting from a one-unit change in consumption of a good. For example, the marginal utility of the third glass of water is the change in total utility resulting from consuming that third glass of water.

Total utility The total satisfaction a consumer derives from consumption; it could refer either to the total utility of consuming a particular good or the total utility from all consumption

Marginal utility The change in total utility derived from a one-unit change in consumption of a good

Law of diminishing marginal utility The more of a good consumed per period, the smaller the increase in total utility from consuming one more unit, other things constant

Your experience with water reflects a basic principle of utility analysis: the **law of diminishing marginal utility.** This law states that the more of a good an individual consumes per time period, other things constant, the smaller the increase in total utility from additional consumption—that is, the smaller the marginal utility of each additional unit consumed. The marginal utility you derive from each additional glass of water declines as your consumption increases. You enjoy the first glass a lot, but each additional glass provides less and less marginal utility. If someone forced you to drink a fifth glass, you probably would not have enjoyed it; your marginal utility from a fifth glass would likely have been negative.

Diminishing marginal utility is a feature of all consumption. A second Big Mac may provide some marginal utility, but, for most people, the marginal utility of a third one during the same meal would be slight or even negative. You may still enjoy a second video movie on Friday night, but a third and fourth one would be numbing. More generally, the expression "Been there, done that" conveys the idea that, for many activities, things start to get old after the first time.

Marginal utility does not always decline right away or very quickly. For example, you may eat many potato chips before the marginal utility of additional chips begins to fall. After a long winter, that first warm day of spring is something special and is the cause of "spring fever." The fever is "cured" by many warm days like the first. By the time August rolls around, people attach much less marginal utility to yet another warm day. For some goods, the drop in marginal utility with additional consumption is more pronounced. A second copy of the same daily newspaper would likely provide you with no marginal utility (in fact, the design of newspaper vending machines relies on the fact that you will not want to take more than one paper).[1] Likewise, a second viewing of the same movie at one sitting usually yields no additional utility. A second day at Orlando's Universal Studios may provide few additional thrills, which is why the theme park can safely offer the second day free without being overrun with people.

1 This example appeared in Marshall Jevons, *The Fatal Equilibrium* (Cambridge, MA: MIT Press, 1985).

MEASURING UTILITY

So far our descriptions of utility have used such words as "wonderful," "good," and "fair." We cannot push the analysis very far if we limit ourselves to such subjective language. If we want to predict behavior based on changes in the economic environment, we must develop a consistent way of viewing utility.

Units of Utility

Let's go back to the water example. Although there really is no objective way of measuring utility, if pressed you might be able to be more specific about how much you enjoyed each glass of water. For example, you might say the first glass was twice as good as the second, the second was twice as good as the third, the third was twice as good as the fourth, and you passed up a fifth glass because you expected no additional utility. In order to get a handle on this description of your satisfaction, let's assign arbitrary numbers to the amount of utility from each quantity consumed, so that the pattern of numbers reflects the pattern of your satisfaction. Let's say the first glass of water provides you with 40 units of utility, the second glass yields 20, the third yields 10, and the fourth yields 5. A fifth glass, if you were forced to drink it, would yield negative utility, in this case, say, −2 units of utility. *Developing numerical values for utility allows us to be more specific about the utility derived from consumption.* If it would help, you could think of units of utility more playfully as kicks, thrills, or jollies—as in, getting your jollies from consumption.

By attaching a numerical measure to utility, we can compare the total utility a particular consumer gets from different goods as well as the marginal utility that same consumer gets from additional consumption. Thus we can employ units of utility to evaluate a consumer's preferences for various units of a good or even various units of different goods. Note, however, that we should not try to compare units of utility across consumers. *Each individual has a uniquely subjective utility scale.*

The first column of Exhibit 1 lists possible quantities of water you might consume after running four miles on a hot day; the second column presents the total utility derived from that consumption; and the third column shows the

EXHIBIT 1

Utility You Derive from Water After Jogging Four Miles

Units of Water Consumed (8-ounce glass)	Total Utility	Marginal Utility
0	0	—
1	40	40
2	60	20
3	70	10
4	75	5
5	73	−2

marginal utility of each additional glass of water consumed. Recall that marginal utility is the change in total utility that results from consuming an additional unit of the good. You can see from the second column that total utility increases with each of the first four glasses, but by smaller and smaller amounts. The third column shows that the first glass of water yields 40 units of utility, the second glass yields an additional 20 units, and so on. Marginal utility declines after the first glass of water, becoming negative with the fifth glass. At any level of consumption, marginal utilities up to and including that level sum to total utility. Total utility is graphed in panel (a) of Exhibit 2. Again, because of diminishing marginal utility, each glass adds less to total utility, so total utility increases for the first four glasses but at a decreasing rate. Marginal utility is presented in panel (b).

Utility Maximization in a World Without Scarcity

Economists assume that your purpose for drinking water, as with all consumption, is to *maximize total utility*. So how much water do you consume? If the price of water is zero, you drink water as long as each additional glass increases

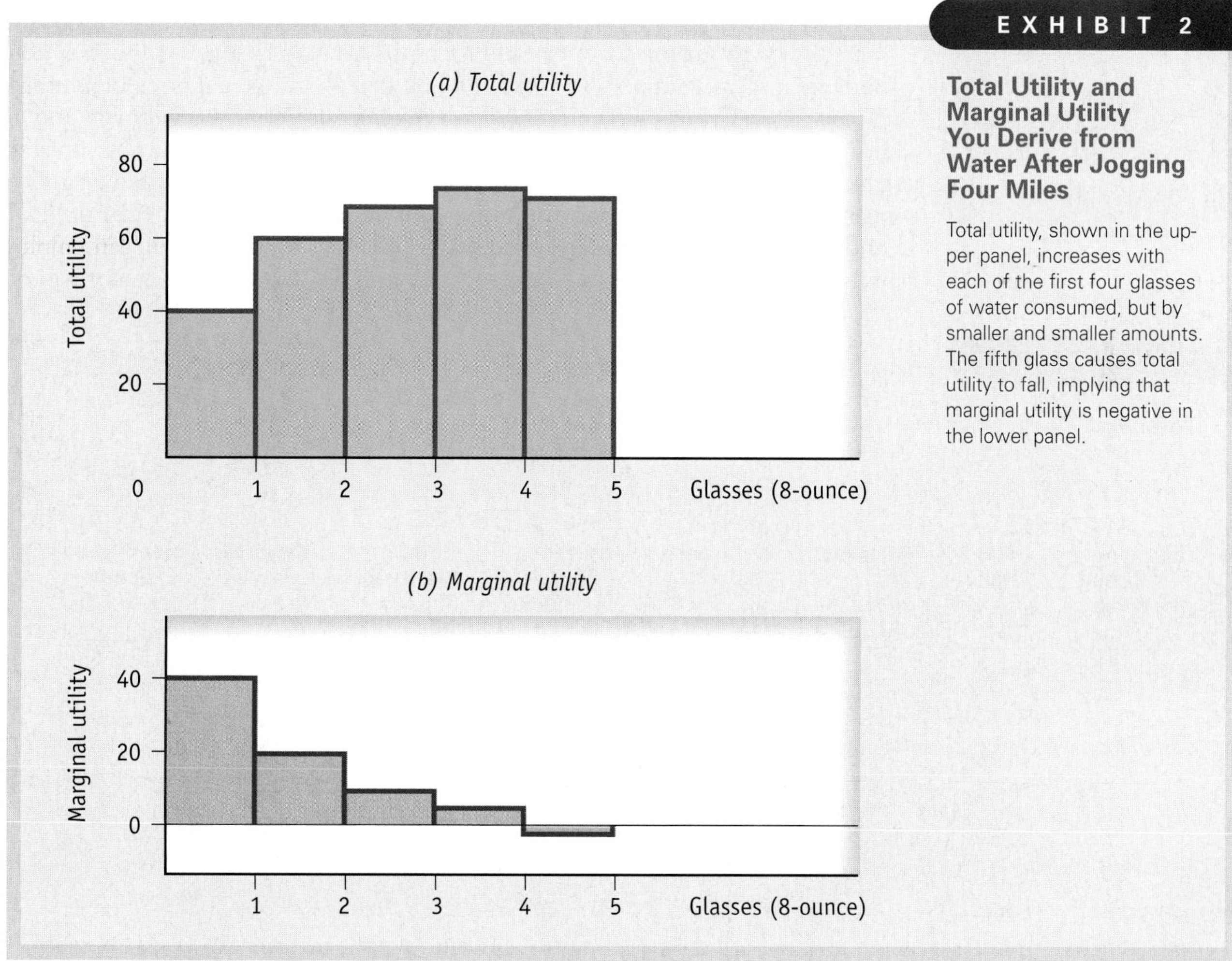

EXHIBIT 2

Total Utility and Marginal Utility You Derive from Water After Jogging Four Miles

Total utility, shown in the upper panel, increases with each of the first four glasses of water consumed, but by smaller and smaller amounts. The fifth glass causes total utility to fall, implying that marginal utility is negative in the lower panel.

total utility, which means you consume four glasses of water. *So when a good is free, you increase consumption as long as additional units provide positive marginal utility.*

Let's extend the analysis of utility to discuss the consumption of pizza and video rentals. We will continue to translate the relative satisfaction you receive from consumption into units of utility. Given your tastes and preferences, suppose your total and marginal utility from consumption are as presented in Exhibit 3. The first four columns apply to pizza and the second four to videos. Please spend a little time right now becoming familiar with each column.

Notice from columns (3) and (7) that both goods exhibit diminishing marginal utility. Given this set of preferences, how much of each good would you consume? At a zero price, you would increase consumption as long as you derived positive marginal utility from additional units of each good. Thus you would consume at least the first six pizzas and first six videos per week because both generate positive marginal utility at that level of consumption. Did you ever go to a party where the food and drinks were free? How much did you eat and drink? You probably ate and drank until you didn't want any more—that is, until the marginal utility of each good consumed declined to zero.

Utility Maximization in a World of Scarcity

Alas, scarcity is our lot, so we should focus on how a consumer chooses when goods are not free. Suppose the price of a pizza is \$8, the rental price of a movie video is \$4, and your income is \$40 per week. You still want to maximize utility, but now subject to the conditions that income is limited and prices are greater than zero. Under these conditions, the utility you receive from different goods relative to their prices determines how you allocate your income. In the real world, consumption depends on tastes (as reflected by the marginal utilities), prices, and your income.

EXHIBIT 3

Total and Marginal Utility from Pizza and Video Rentals

Pizzas Consumed per Week (1)	Total Utility of Pizza (2)	Marginal Utility of Pizza (3)	Marginal Utility of Pizza per Dollar Expended (price = \$8) (4)	Video Rentals per Week (5)	Total Utility of Videos (6)	Marginal Utility of Videos (7)	Marginal Utility of Videos per Dollar Expended (price = \$4) (8)
0	0	—	—	0	0	—	—
1	56	56	7	1	40	40	10
2	88	32	4	2	68	28	7
3	112	24	3	3	88	20	5
4	130	18	$2\frac{1}{4}$	4	100	12	3
5	142	12	$1\frac{1}{2}$	5	108	8	2
6	150	8	16	6	114	6	$1\frac{1}{2}$

How do you allocate income between the two goods so as to maximize utility? Suppose you start off with some combination of pizzas and videos. If you can increase your utility by reallocating expenditures, you will do so, and you will continue to make adjustments as long as you can increase your utility. There may be some trial and error at first, but, by learning from your mistakes, you move toward the utility-maximizing position. When no further utility-increasing moves are possible, you have settled on the combination that maximizes your utility, given your tastes, prices, and your income—*you have arrived at the equilibrium combination.* Once you achieve this utility-maximizing equilibrium, you will maintain this consumption pattern unless there is a change in your tastes, your income, or the prices you face.

To get the process rolling, suppose you start off spending your entire budget of $40 on pizza, purchasing 5 pizzas a week, which yields a total of 142 units of utility a week. You soon realize that if you buy one less pizza, you free up enough income to rent 2 movies. Would total utility increase? You give up 12 units of utility, the marginal utility of the fifth pizza, to get 68 units of utility from the first 2 videos. Total utility thereby increases from 142 to 198 units of utility per week. Then you notice that if you reduce purchases to 3 pizzas, you give up 18 units of utility from the fourth pizza but gain 32 units of utility from the third and fourth videos. This is another utility-increasing move. Further reductions in pizza, however, would reduce your total utility because you would give up 24 units of utility from the third pizza but gain only 14 units of utility from the fifth and sixth videos. Thus, by trial and error, you find that the utility-maximizing equilibrium combination is 3 pizzas and 4 videos per week, for a total utility of 212. This involves an outlay of $24 on pizza and $16 on videos. *You are in equilibrium when consuming this combination because any affordable change would reduce your total utility.* Note that you consume fewer units now than when they were free.

The Utility-Maximizing Conditions

As you can see from the previous example, once equilibrium has been achieved, any shift in spending from one good to another will decrease utility. *Once a consumer is in equilibrium, there is no way to increase utility by reallocating the budget.* We will now examine a special property of the utility-maximizing combination: In equilibrium, the last dollar spent on each good yields the same utility. More specifically, *utility is maximized when the budget is completely spent and the marginal utility of a good divided by its price is identical for the last unit of each good purchased.* In short, the consumer gets the same bang per last buck spent on each good.

Let's see how this works. Columns (4) and (8) in Exhibit 3 indicate the marginal utility of each dollar's worth of pizza and videos, respectively. Column (4) shows the marginal utility of pizza divided by its price of $8. Column (8) shows the marginal utility of videos divided by its price of $4. You can see that the equilibrium choice of 3 pizzas and 4 videos exhausts the $40 budget and yields 3 units of utility for the last dollar spent on each good. **Consumer equilibrium** is achieved when the budget is completely spent and the last dollar spent on each good yields the same utility, or the marginal utility of pizza divided by its price equals the marginal utility of videos divided by its price. This equality can be expressed as

Consumer equilibrium
The condition in which an individual consumer's budget is completely spent and the last dollar spent on each good yields the same marginal utility; therefore, utility is maximized

$$\frac{MU_p}{p_p} = \frac{MU_v}{p_v}$$

where MU_p is the marginal utility of pizza, p_p is the price of pizza, MU_v is the marginal utility of videos, and p_v is the price of videos. Although we have considered only two goods, the logic of utility maximization applies to any number of goods. The consumer will reallocate spending until the last dollar spent on each product yields the same marginal utility.

In equilibrium, higher-priced goods must yield more marginal utility than lower-priced goods—enough additional utility to compensate for their higher price. In our example, since a pizza costs twice as much as a video, the marginal utility of the final pizza purchased must, in equilibrium, be twice that of the final video rented. In fact, 24 units of utility, the marginal utility of the third pizza, is twice as much as 12 units of utility, the marginal utility of the fourth video rented. Economists do not claim that you consciously equate the ratios of marginal utility to price, but they do claim that you act as if you had made such calculations. *Thus, you decide how much of each good to purchase by considering your relative preferences for the alternative goods, the prices of the alternative goods, and your income.*

Thus consumers maximize utility by equalizing the marginal utility per dollar of expenditure across goods. This equality resolved what had been an economic puzzle, as discussed in the following case study.

CaseStudy

The World of Business

Water, Water, Everywhere

Almost any question you might have about water supply and use in the United States can be answered by visiting the Water Q&A at the U.S. Geological Survey's Web site at http://wwwga.usgs.gov/edu/qausage.html. Various terms are linked to pages with additional information. What is the number one use of water in the U.S.? How does domestic use rate in importance? From which sources is most of the water in your state drawn—surface or groundwater supplies? How does water supply and use in the U.S. compare with the rest of the world. Find the answer in "Water: Critical Shortages Ahead?" from the World Resources Institute at http://www.wri.org/wr-98-99/water.htm.

Centuries ago economists puzzled over the price of diamonds relative to the price of water. Diamonds are mere baubles—certainly not a necessity of life in any sense. Water is essential to life and has a huge number of uses. Yet diamonds are expensive, while water is cheap. For example, the $10,000 spent on a one-carat diamond could instead buy about ten million gallons of municipally-supplied water (which typically sells for about 10 cents per hundred gallons). However measured, diamonds are extremely expensive relative to water. For the price of a one-carat diamond, you could buy enough water to last four lifetimes.

How can the price of something as useful as water be so much lower than something of such limited use as diamonds? Adam Smith discussed in 1776 what has come to be called the *diamonds-water paradox*. What explains this paradox? Because water is so essential to life, the total utility derived from water greatly exceeds the total utility derived from diamonds. But the market value of a good is based, not on its total utility, but on what consumers are willing and able to pay for an additional unit of the good—that is, on its marginal utility. Since water is so abundant in nature, the marginal utility of the last gallon purchased is relatively low. Since diamonds are so scarce in nature, the marginal utility of the last diamond purchased is relatively high. Thus water is cheap and diamonds expensive.

Speaking of water, let's examine the recent surge in the demand for bottled water. In the past decade, sales of bottled water gushed 144 percent—faster than any other beverage segment—creating a $4 billion industry in the United States. Annual consumption of bottled water increased from 5 gallons to 11 gallons per capita. The United States offers the world's largest market for bottled water—some of it imported from places such as Italy, France, Sweden, Wales, even Fiji. And there are even "water bars" in Boston, New York and Los Angeles, where the primary attraction is bottled water.

Why would consumers pay a premium for bottled water when they can draw water from the tap for virtually nothing? First, many people do not view the two options as good substitutes. About half of respondents in a recent Gallup Poll said they won't drink water straight from the tap. They have concerns about the safety of tap water, such as possible contamination by e-coli bacteria, and they view bottled water as a healthy alternative. Second, even those who have no problem with tap water consider bottled water a convenient alternative when away from home.

According to the theory of utility maximization, people who buy bottled water apparently feel the additional benefit offsets the additional cost. Bottled-water sales are expected to continue growing. Pepsi's Aquafina brand is sold around the country, and Coke is launching its own brand.

Sources: Corby Kummer, "What's In the Water?" *New York Times Magazine*, 30 (August 1998), pp. 38, 42, 59, 61; Christopher Williams "US Filter, Water Stocks Up; New Report on Drinking Water Cited," Dow Jones Newswire, 21 (October 1998); "Lax Oversight Raises Tap Water Risks," *USA Today*, 21 (October 1998); and Nikhil Deogun, "The Really Real Thing: Coke to Peddle Brand of Purified Bottled Water in U.S." *Wall Street Journal*, 3 (November 1998). The Web site for the International Bottled Water Association is www.bottledwater.org.

The Law of Demand and Marginal Utility

The purpose of utility analysis is to provide information about quantity demanded. How does the previous analysis relate to your demand for pizza? It yields a single point on your demand curve for pizza: At a price of $8, you demand 3 pizzas per week. This point is based on a given income of $40 per week, a given rental price of $4 per video, and the tastes reflected by your utility schedules in Exhibit 3.

This single point, in itself, offers no inkling about the shape of your demand curve. To generate another point, let's change the price of pizza, keep other things constant (such as income, tastes, and the price of videos), then see what happens to the quantity demanded. Suppose the price of a pizza drops from $8 to $6. What will happen to your consumption, given the preferences already outlined in the discussion of Exhibit 3? Exhibit 4 is the same as Exhibit 3, except the price per pizza has been reduced from $8 to $6.

Your original choice was 3 pizzas and 4 video rentals. At that combination and with the price of pizza now $6, the marginal utility per dollar expended on the third pizza is 4, but the marginal utility per dollar spent on the fourth video is 3. The marginal utilities of the last dollar spent on each good are no longer equal across goods. What's more, if you maintained the original combination, you would have $6 remaining in your budget because you would be spending only $18 on pizza. So you could still buy your original bundle but have $6 left over (this, incidentally, is the income effect of a lower price of pizza). You can increase your utility by consuming a different bundle.

EXHIBIT 4

Total and Marginal Utility from Pizza and Video Rentals After Price of Pizza Decreases from $8 to $6

Pizzas Consumed per Week (1)	Total Utility of Pizza (2)	Marginal Utility of Pizza (3)	Marginal Utility of Pizza per Dollar Expended (price = $6) (4)	Video Rentals per Week (5)	Total Utility of Videos (6)	Marginal Utility of Videos (7)	Marginal Utility of Videos per Dollar Expended (price = $4) (8)
0	0	—	—	0	0	—	—
1	56	56	$9\frac{1}{3}$	1	40	40	10
2	88	32	$5\frac{1}{3}$	2	68	28	7
3	112	24	4	3	88	20	5
4	130	18	3	4	100	12	3
5	142	12	2	5	108	8	2
6	150	8	$1\frac{1}{3}$	6	114	6	$1\frac{1}{2}$

Take a moment to see if you can figure out what the new equilibrium bundle should be.

In light of your utility schedules in Exhibit 4, you would increase your consumption to 4 pizzas per week. This increase exhausts your budget and equates the marginal utilities of the last dollar expended on each good. Your video purchases remain the same (although they could have changed due to the income effect of the price change). But as your consumption increases to 4 pizzas per week, the marginal utility of the fourth pizza, 18, divided by the price of $6, yields 3 units of utility per dollar of expenditure, which is the same as for the fourth video. You are in equilibrium once again. Your total utility increases by the 18 units of utility you receive from pizza. Hence you are clearly better off as a result of the price decrease.

We now have a second point on your demand curve for pizza—when the price of pizza is $6, your quantity demanded is four pizzas. The two points are presented as *a* and *b* in Exhibit 5. We could continue to change the price of pizza and thereby generate additional points on the demand curve, but you get some idea of the demand curve's downward slope from these two points. The shape of the demand curve for pizza conforms to our expectations based on the law of demand: Price and quantity demanded are inversely related. (Try to estimate the price elasticity of demand between points *a* and *b.* Hint: What does total expenditure tell you?)

We have gone to some length to see how you (or any consumer) maximize utility. Given prices and your income, your tastes and preferences naturally guide you to the most preferred bundle. You are not even conscious of your behavior. The urge to maximize utility is like the force of gravity—both work whether or not you understand them. Even animals seem to behave in a way that appears consistent with the law of demand.

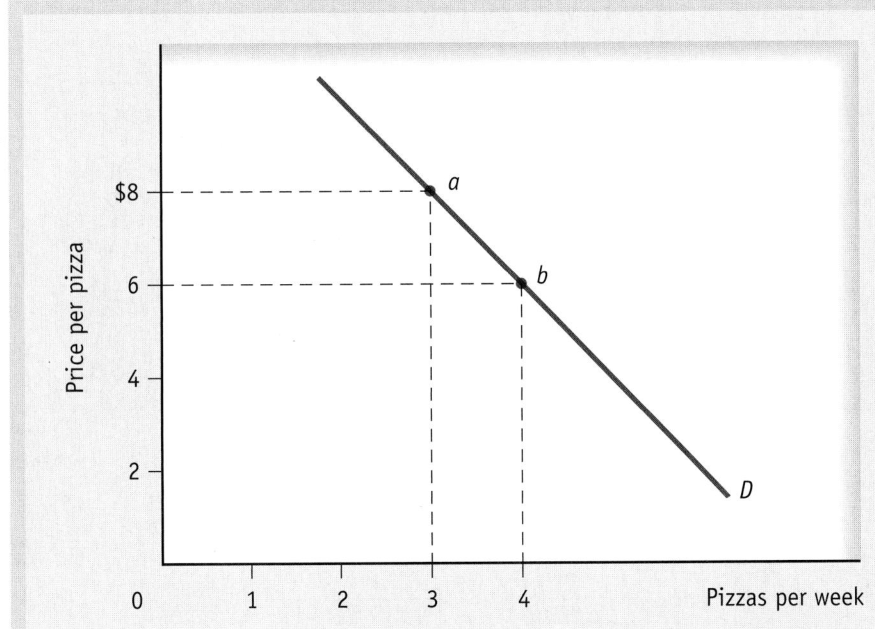

EXHIBIT 5

Demand for Pizza Generated from Marginal Utility

At a price of $8 per pizza, the consumer is in equilibrium when consuming 3 pizzas (point *a*). Marginal utility per dollar is the same for all goods consumed. If the price falls to $6, the consumer will increase consumption to 4 pizzas (point *b*). Points *a* and *b* are two points on this consumer's demand curve for pizza.

Certain animal behavior in the wild appears consistent with the idea that resources are valued more when they are relatively scarce. When food is naturally abundant in the environment, some species devote little or no energy to establishing and defending food sources. Wolves, for example, exhibit no territorial concerns when game is plentiful. But when game is scarce, wolves carefully mark their territory and defend it against interlopers.

Now that you have some idea of utility, let's consider an application of utility analysis.

Consumer Surplus

In our earlier example, total utility increased when the price of pizza fell from $8 to $6. In this section, we'll take a closer look at how consumers benefit from a lower price. Suppose your demand for foot-long Subway sandwiches is as shown in Exhibit 6, which measures on the horizontal axis the number of Subways you are willing and able to buy each month. Recall that in constructing an individual's demand curve, we hold tastes, income, and the prices of related goods constant; only the price of Subways varies.

At a price of $8 or above, you find that the marginal utility of other goods that you could buy for $8 is higher than the marginal utility of a Subway. Consequently, you buy no Subways. At a price of $7, you are willing and able to buy one per month, so the marginal utility of that first Subway exceeds the marginal utility you expected from spending that money on your best alternative—say, a movie ticket. A price of $6 prompts you to buy two Subways a month. The second is worth at least $6 to you. At a price of $5, you buy three Subways, and at $4, you buy four. *In each case, the value to you of the last Subway purchased must at least equal the price; otherwise, you wouldn't buy it.* Along the

EXHIBIT 6

Consumer Surplus from Subway Sandwiches

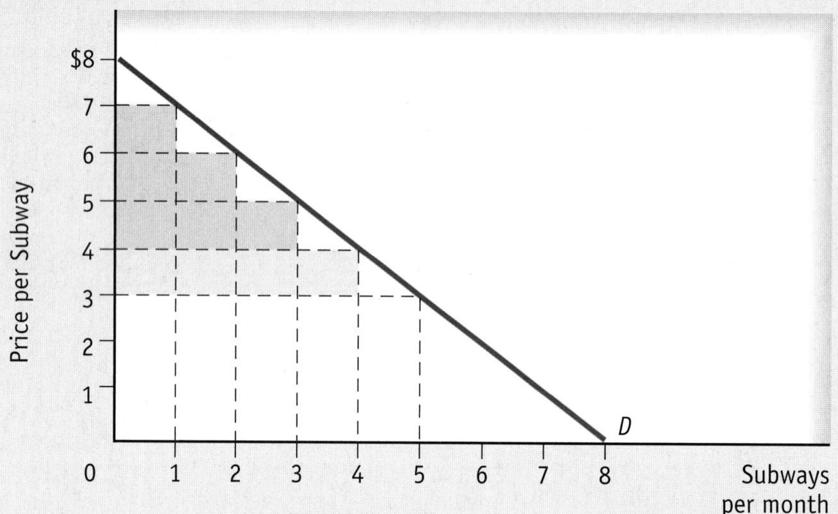

At a given quantity of Subway sandwiches, the height of the demand curve shows the value of the last one purchased. The area under the demand curve up to a specific quantity shows the total value the consumer places on that quantity. At a price of $4, the consumer purchases four Subways. The first one is valued at $7, the second at $6, the third at $5, and the fourth at $4. The consumer values four at $22. Since the consumer pays $4 per Subway, all four can be obtained for $16. The difference between what the consumer would have been willing to pay ($22) and what the consumer actually pays ($16) is called consumer surplus. When the price is $4, the consumer surplus is represented by the dark shaded area under the demand curve above $4. When the price of Subways falls to $3, consumer surplus increases by $4, as is reflected by the lighter shaded area.

Marginal valuation The dollar value of the marginal utility derived from consuming each additional unit of a good

Consumer surplus The difference between the maximum amount that a consumer is willing to pay for a given quantity of a good and what the consumer actually pays

demand curve, therefore, the price reflects your **marginal valuation** of the good, or the dollar value of the marginal utility derived from consuming each additional unit.

Notice that when the price is $4, you can purchase each of the four Subways for that price even though you would have been willing to pay more than $4 for each of the first three Subways. The first sandwich provides marginal utility that you value at $7; the second, marginal utility valued at $6; and the third, marginal utility valued at $5. In fact, if you had to, you would have been willing to pay $7 for the first, $6 for the second, and $5 for the third. The value of the total utility of the first four sandwiches is $7 + $6 + $5 + $4 = $22. But when the price is $4, you get all four for $16. Thus, a price of $4 confers a **consumer surplus,** or a consumer bonus, equal to the difference between the maximum amount you would have been willing to pay ($22) rather than go without Subways and what you actually paid ($16). When the price is $4, your consumer surplus is $6, as shown by the six darker shaded blocks in Exhibit 6. The consumer surplus equals the total utility you receive from consuming the sandwiches minus your total spending on them. Consumer surplus is the area under the demand curve but above the price.

If the price falls to \$3, you purchase five Subways a month. Evidently you feel that the marginal benefit you receive from the fifth one is worth at least \$3. The lower price means that you get to buy all five for \$3 each even though most are worth more to you than \$3. Your consumer surplus when the price is \$3 is the value of the total utility conferred by the first five, which is \$7 + \$6 + \$5 + \$4 + \$3 = \$25, minus your cost, which is \$3 × 5 = \$15. Thus, your consumer surplus totals \$25 − \$15 = \$10, as indicated by both the dark and the light shaded blocks in Exhibit 6. If the price declines to \$3, you are able to purchase all Subways for less, so your consumer surplus increases by \$4, as reflected by the four lighter-shaded blocks in Exhibit 6. You can see how consumers benefit from lower prices.

Market Demand and Consumer Surplus

Let's talk more generally now about the market demand for a good, assuming the market consists of you and two other consumers. *The market demand curve is simply the horizontal sum of the individual demand curves for all consumers in the market.* Exhibit 7 shows how the demand curves for three consumers in the market for Subway sandwiches are summed horizontally to yield the market demand. At a price of \$4, for example, you demand 4 Subways per month, Brittany demands 2, and Chris demands none. The market quantity demanded at a price of \$4 is therefore 6 sandwiches. At a price of \$2, you demand 6 per month, Britanny, 4, and Chris, 2, for a market quantity demanded of 12 sandwiches. *The market demand curve shows the total quantity demanded per period by all consumers at various prices.*

The idea of consumer surplus can be used to examine market demand as well as individual demand. *At a given price, consumer surplus for the market is the difference between the amount consumers are willing to pay for that quantity and the total amount they do pay.*

EXHIBIT 7

Summing Individual Demands to Derive the Market Demand for Subway Sandwiches

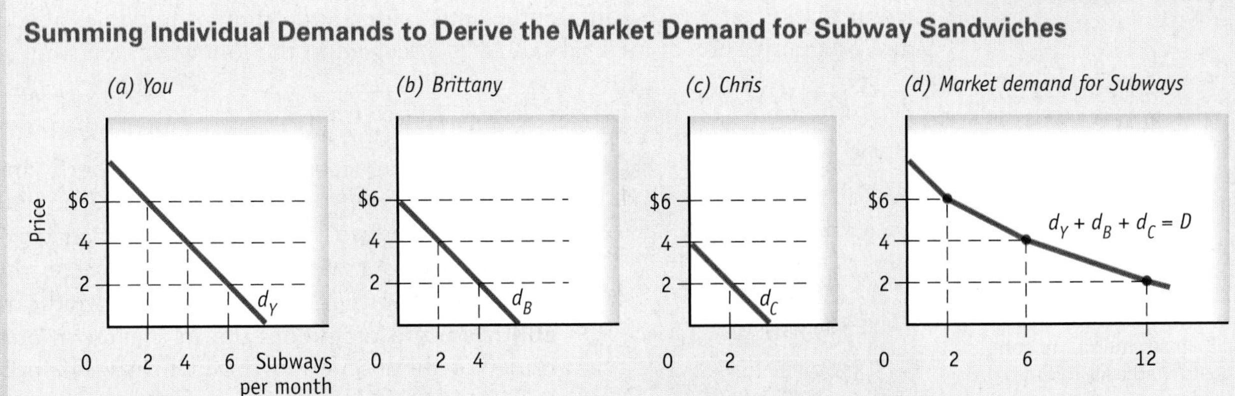

At a price of \$4 per Subway, you demand 4 per month, Brittany demands 2, and Chris demands none. Total market demand at a price of \$4 is 4 + 2 + 0 = 6 Subways per month. At a lower price of \$2, you demand 6, Brittany demands 4, and Chris demands 2. Market demand at a price of \$2 is 12 Subways. The market demand curve D is the horizontal sum of individual demand curves d_Y, d_B, and d_C.

EXHIBIT 8

Market Demand and Consumer Surplus

Consumer surplus at a price of $2 is shown by the darker area. If the price falls to $1, consumer surplus increases to include the lighter area.

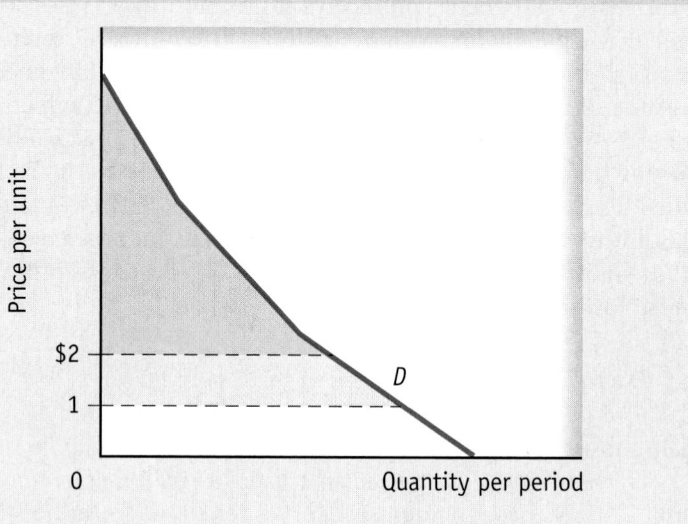

Instead of just three consumers in the market, suppose there are many. Exhibit 8 presents market demand for a good when there are millions of consumers. If the price is $2 per unit, each person adjusts his or her quantity demanded until the marginal valuation of the last unit purchased equals $2. But each consumer gets to buy all the other units for $2 as well. In Exhibit 8, the dark shading, bounded above by the demand curve and below by the price of $2, depicts the market consumer surplus when the price is $2. The light shading shows the increase in consumer surplus if the price drops to $1. Note that if this good were given away, the consumer surplus would not be that much greater than when the price is $1.

Consumer surplus is the net benefit consumers get from market exchange. It can be used to measure economic welfare and to compare the effects of different market structures, different tax structures, and different public expenditure programs, such as medical care, as is discussed in the following case study.

*Case***Study**

Public Policy

This case study points out that patients have little incentive to monitor physician behavior when they do not pay the bill. In an attempt to control costs Medicare reduces the reimbursement rate for services provided by the physicians. How do you suppose that they respond? The Health Care Financing Administration's auditors examined physician behavior and found

The Marginal Value of Free Medical Care

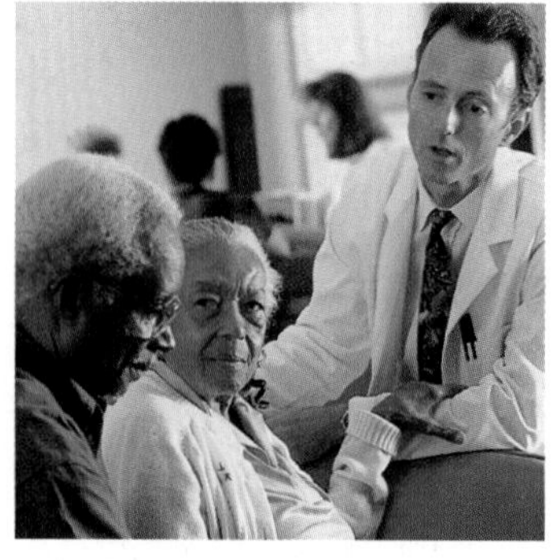

Certain Americans, such as the elderly and those on welfare, are provided government-subsidized medical care. State and federal taxpayers spent over $400 billion in 1998 on the medical care provided to 75 million Medicare and Medicaid recipients, for an average annual outlay of about $5,000 per beneficiary. The dollar cost to most beneficiaries of these programs was usually little or nothing. The problem with giving something away is that beneficiaries consume it up to the point where their marginal benefit from the final unit is zero, although the marginal cost to taxpayers can be substantial.

This is not to say that beneficiaries derive no benefit from free medical care. Even though they may attach little or no value to marginal units, they likely derive a substantial consumer surplus from the other units they consume. For example, suppose that the previous exhibit, Exhibit 8, represents the demand for medical care by Medicare and Medicaid beneficiaries. If the price to them is zero, they consume up to the point where the demand curve intersects the horizontal axis, so their consumer surplus is the entire area under the demand curve.

One way to reduce the taxpayer cost of such programs without significantly harming beneficiaries is to charge a nominal price—say $1 per physician visit. As a result, beneficiaries would eliminate visits they value less than $1. This would yield significant savings to taxpayers, yet would still leave beneficiaries with adequate health care and with a substantial consumer surplus (measured in Exhibit 8 as the area under the demand curve but above the $1 price). As a case in point, one Medicaid experiment in California required a group of beneficiaries to pay $1 per visit for their first two office visits per month (after two visits, the price of additional visits reverted to zero). Few could argue that a cost of at most $2 per month represents a substantial burden on recipients. A control group continued to receive completely free medical care. The $1 charge reduced office visits by 8 percent compared to the control group.

Medical care, like other goods and services, is also sensitive to the time component of the cost (a topic to be examined in the next section). For example, a 10 percent increase in the average travel time required to visit a free outpatient clinic reduced visits by 10 percent. Similarly, when the relocation of a free clinic at one college campus increased students' walking time by ten minutes, student visits declined by 40 percent.

These findings do not mean that certain groups do not deserve low-cost medical care. The point is that when something is free, people consume it until their marginal valuation is zero. Even a modest money or time cost will reduce consumption yet will still leave beneficiaries with a substantial consumer surplus. A second problem with giving something away is that beneficiaries are less vigilant about getting honest value for their money when they pay little or nothing for the good. This increases the possibility of fraud and abuse by health care providers. According to experts, about 10 percent of government spending on health care is wasted because of padded bills, fake claims, and other activities that would be less tolerated if the beneficiaries were paying their own bills. For example, in one case the government was billed for round-the-clock cardiac monitoring when the patient was in fact monitored only 30 minutes a month. Such abuse by health care providers translates into a waste of at least $40 billion per year.

Sources: Steven Rhoads, "Marginalism," *The Fortune Encyclopedia of Economics*, D. R. Henderson, ed. (New York: Warner Books, 1993): 31–33; Joseph White, "Paying the Right Prices: What the United States Can Learn from Health Care Abroad," *Brookings Review* (Spring 1994) 6–11; Paul Gertler and Jacques van der Gaag, *The Willingness to Pay for Medical Care* (Baltimore: Johns Hopkins University Press, 1990); and L. J. Davis, "Medscam," *Mother Jones* (March/April 1995).

that they increase the volume and intensity of work in response to declining prices in order to maintain revenue. Their easy-to-read report on physician response, which includes several real examples, can be found at http://www.hcfa.gov/pubforms/behavoff/behavoff.htm.

THE ROLE OF TIME IN DEMAND

Because consumption does not occur instantaneously, time also plays an important role in demand analysis. Consumption takes time and, as Benjamin Franklin said, time is money—time has a positive value for most people. Consequently,

*Net*Bookmark

For an example of pricing that uses the law of marginal utility, visit the on-line ticket purchase page for Universal Studios Florida at http://www.usf.com/tickets/index_2dfree.html. Find the prices for one-day, two-day and three-day passes. How much does each additional day cost? What special promotions are being offered? What restrictions are there on getting a second day free? Compare these to the restrictions on using the second day of a two-day pass. Also try comparing a three-day pass to an annual pass. Which is cheaper?

the cost of consumption has two components: the *money price* of the good and the *time price* of the good. Goods are demanded because of the benefits they offer. Your demand for medicine is based on its ability to cure you; your interest is not in the medicine itself but in the benefit it provides. Thus, you may be willing to pay more for medicine that works more quickly. Similarly, it is not the microwave oven, personal computer, or airline trip that you value, but the benefits they provide. Other things constant, the good that provides the same benefit in less time is preferred. That's why we are willing to pay more for seedless grapes, seedless oranges, and seedless watermelon.

Your willingness to pay a premium for time-saving goods and services depends on the opportunity cost of your time. Differences in the value of time among consumers help explain differences in the consumption patterns observed in the economy. Consider the alternative ways to get to Europe. You could, for example, take the Concorde or a regular airline. Your mode of travel will depend in part on your opportunity cost of time. The Concorde takes less than half the time of other flights, but because the Concorde is much more expensive, only travelers with an extremely high opportunity cost of time, such as busy corporate executives and celebrities, will pay such a premium for faster service. Students on their summer vacations are more inclined to opt for some discount excursion fare or even standby status; for them, the lower money cost more than compensates for the higher time cost.

A retired couple is likely to have a lower opportunity cost of time and so will purchase fewer time-saving goods, such as microwave ovens and frozen dinners, than a working couple in the fast lane. The retired couple may clip coupons and search the newspapers for bargains, sometimes going from store to store for particular grocery items on sale that week. The working couple will usually ignore the coupons and sales and will often eat out or purchase items at convenience stores, where they pay extra for the "convenience." The retired couple will be more inclined to drive across the country on vacation, whereas the working couple will fly to a vacation destination.

Just inside the gates at Anaheim's Disneyland, Orlando's Disney World, and Orlando's Universal Studios are signs posting the waiting times of each attraction and ride. Since, at that point, the dollar cost of admission has already been paid, the dollar cost of each ride and attraction is zero. The posting of waiting times offers menus of the time costs of each ride or attraction. Incidentally, people who are willing to pay up to $55 an hour at Disney World and $60 an hour at Disneyland (plus the price of admission) can take VIP tours that eliminate the lines.[2]

Differences in the opportunity cost of time among consumers shape consumption patterns and add another dimension to our analysis of demand.

CONCLUSION

We have developed a utility-based analysis of consumer choice. Our focus was on the utility, or satisfaction, that consumers receive from consumption. In observing consumer behavior, we assume that for a particular individual, utility

2 Nancy Keates, "Tourists Learn How to Mouse Around Disney's Long Lines," *Wall Street Journal* (27 March 1998).

can be measured in some systematic way, even though different consumers' utility levels cannot be compared. Our ultimate objective is to predict how consumer choice is affected by such variables as a change in price. We judge a theory not by the realism of its assumptions but by the accuracy of its predictions. Based on this criterion, the theory of consumer choice presented in this chapter has proven to be quite useful.

Again, we stress that consumers do not have to understand the material presented in this chapter in order to maximize utility. Economists assume that rational consumers attempt to maximize utility naturally and instinctively. In this chapter, we simply tried to analyze that process using a model of consumer choice based on utility analysis. A more general approach to consumer choice and utility analysis, an approach that does not require a specific measure of utility, is developed in the appendix to this chapter.

SUMMARY

1. Utility is the sense of pleasure or satisfaction that comes from consumption; it is the want-satisfying power of goods, services, and activities. The utility you receive from consuming a particular good depends on your tastes. We distinguish between the total utility derived from consuming a good and the marginal utility derived from consuming one more unit of that good. The law of diminishing marginal utility says that the greater the amount of a particular good consumed per time period, other things constant, the smaller the increase in total utility received from each additional unit consumed.
2. Any assessment of the want-satisfying power of consumption must be made by each individual consumer—utility is subjective. By translating an individual's subjective measure of satisfaction into units of utility, we can predict the effect of a change in price on quantity demanded.
3. The consumer's objective is to maximize utility within the limits imposed by income and prices. In a world without scarcity, utility would be maximized by consuming goods until the marginal utility of the last unit of each good consumed was zero. In the real world, a world shaped by scarcity, utility is maximized when the final unit of each good consumed yields the same utility per dollar spent. Put another way, utility is maximized when the marginal utility divided by the price is identical for each good consumed.
4. Utility analysis can be used to construct an individual consumer's demand curve. By changing the price and observing the utility-maximizing levels of consumption, we can generate points along the demand curve.
5. When the price of a good drops, other things constant, the consumer is able to buy all units of the good at the lower price. Consumers typically receive a surplus, or a bonus, from consumption, and this surplus grows as the price falls.
6. The market demand curve is simply the horizontal sum of the individual demand curves for all consumers in the market. Consumer surplus for the market demand curve can be measured as the difference between the maximum amount consumers would pay for a given quantity of the good and the amount paid.
7. There are two components to the cost of consumption: the money price of the good and the time price of the good. People with a higher opportunity cost of time will pay a higher money price for goods and services that save time.

QUESTIONS FOR REVIEW

1. *(Law of Diminishing Marginal Utility)* Some restaurants offer "all you can eat" meals. How is this practice related to diminishing marginal utility? What restrictions must the restaurant impose on the customer in order to make a profit?
2. *(Law of Diminishing Marginal Utility)* Complete each of the following sentences:
   a. Your tastes determine the _______ you derive from consuming a particular good.

b. _______ utility is the change in _______ utility resulting from a _______ change in the consumption of a good.

c. As long as marginal utility is positive, total utility is _______ .

d. The law of diminishing marginal utility states that as an individual consumes more of a good during a given time period, other things constant, total utility _______ .

3. *(Marginal Utility)* Is it possible for marginal utility to be negative while total utility is positive? If yes, under what circumstances is it possible.

4. *(Utility-Maximizing Conditions)* For a particular consumer, the marginal utility of cookies equals the marginal utility of candy. If the price of a cookie is less than the price of candy, is the consumer in equilibrium? Why or why not? If not, what should the consumer do to attain equilibrium?

5. *(Utility-Maximizing Conditions)* Suppose that marginal utility of Good X = 100, the price of X is $10 per unit, and the price of Y is $5 per unit. Assuming that the consumer is in equilibrium and is consuming both X and Y, what must the marginal utility of Y be?

6. *(Utility-Maximizing Conditions)* Suppose that the price of X is twice as high as the price of Y. You are a utility maximizer who allocates your budget between those two goods. What must be true about the equilibrium relationship between the marginal utility levels of the last unit consumed of each good? What must be true about the equilibrium relationship between the marginal utility levels of the last dollar spent on each good?

7. *(Consumer Surplus)* The height of the demand curve at a given quantity reflects the marginal valuation of the last unit of that good consumed. For a normal good, an increase in income will shift the demand curve to the right and therefore increase its height at any quantity. Does this mean that consumers get greater marginal utility from each unit of this good than they did before? Explain.

8. *(Consumer Surplus)* Suppose that a good is in perfectly elastic supply at a price of $5. The market demand curve for this good is linear, with zero quantity demanded at a price of $25. If the slope of this linear demand curve is −0.25, draw a supply and demand graph to illustrate the consumer surplus that occurs when the market is in equilibrium.

9. *(Case**Study**: The Marginal Value of Free Medical Care)* Medicare recipients pay a monthly premium for coverage, must meet an annual deductible, and have a copayment for doctor's office visits. There is no coverage for prescription medications. What impact would an increase in the monthly premium have on their consumer surplus? What would be the impact of a reduction in their copayments? What would be the impact on the quantity demanded and consumer surplus if Medicare started providing coverage for prescription medications?

10. *(Role of Time in Demand)* In many amusement parks, you pay an admission fee to the park but you do not need to pay for individual rides. How do people choose which rides to go on?

11. *(Case**Study**: Water, Water Everywhere)* What is the diamonds–water paradox, and how is it explained? Use the same reasoning to explain why bottled water costs so much more than tap water?

PROBLEMS AND EXERCISES

12. *(Utility Maximization)* The following tables illustrate Eileen's utilities from watching first-run movies in a theater and from renting movies from a video store. Suppose that she has a monthly entertainment budget of $36, each movie in a theater costs $6, and each video rental costs $3.

Movies in a Theater

Q	TU	MU	MU/P
0	0	______	______
1	200	______	______
2	290	______	______
3	370	______	______
4	440	______	______
5	500	______	______
6	550	______	______
7	590	______	______

Movies from a Video Store

Q	TU	MU	MU/P
0	0	______	______
1	250	______	______
2	295	______	______
3	335	______	______
4	370	______	______
5	400	______	______
6	425	______	______
___	___	______	

a. Complete the tables.
b. Do these tables show that Eileen's preferences obey the law of diminishing marginal utility? Explain your answer.
c. How much of each good will Eileen consume in equilibrium?
d. Suppose the prices of both types of movies drop to $1 while Eileen's entertainment budget shrinks to $10. How much of each good will she consume in equilibrium?

13. *(Utility Maximization)* Suppose that a consumer has a choice between two goods, X and Y. If the price of X is $2 per unit and the price of Y is $3 per unit, how much of X and Y will the consumer purchase, given an income of $17? Use the following information about marginal utility:

Units	MU_X	MU_Y
1	10	5
2	8	4
3	2	3
4	2	2
5	1	2

14. *(The Law of Demand and Marginal Utility)* Daniel allocates his budget of $24 per week among three goods. Use the following table of the marginal utilities for Good A, Good B, and Good C to answer the questions below:

Q_A	MU_A	Q_B	MU_B	Q_C	MU_C
1	50	1	75	1	25
2	40	2	60	2	20
3	30	3	40	3	15
4	20	4	30	4	10
5	15	5	20	5	7.5

a. If the price of A is $2, the price of B is $3, and the price of C is $1, how much of each will Daniel purchase in equilibrium?
b. If the price of A rises to $4 while other prices and Daniel's budget remain unchanged, how much of each will he purchase in equilibrium?
c. Using the information from parts (a) and (b), draw the demand curve for Good A. Be sure to indicate the price and quantity demanded for each point on the curve.

15. *(Consumer Surplus)* Suppose the linear demand curve for shirts slopes downward and that consumers buy 500 shirts per year when the price of a shirt is $30 and 1,000 shirts per year when their price is $25.
a. Compared to the prices of $30 and $25, what can you say about the marginal valuation that consumers place on the 300th shirt, the 700th shirt, and the 1,200th shirt they might buy each year?
b. With diminishing marginal utility, are consumers deriving any consumer surplus if the price is $25 per shirt? Explain.
c. Use a market demand curve to illustrate the change in consumer surplus if the price drops from $30 to $25.

EXPERIENTIAL EXERCISES

16. *(Consumer Surplus)* Access a copy of "Creating Value and Destroying Profits? Three Measures of Information Technology's Contributions," by Loren Hitt and Erik Brynjolfsson at http://ccs.mit.edu/CCSWP183.html. Use your "find" function to search for the words "consumer surplus" in this paper. How do Hitt and Brynjolfsson use the concept of consumer surplus to measure the value of information technology?

17. *(**CaseStudy:** The Marginal Value of Free Medical Care)* To learn more about economic issues related to health care, visit the McEachern Web page http://mceachern.swcollege.com, click on Econ-Debate Online, and find the debate "Is there a need for health care reform?" What are some economic issues related to health care reform?

18. *(The Role of Time in Demand)* To learn more about the economics of consumption, read Jane Katz's "The Joy of Consumption: We Are What We Buy," in the Federal Reserve Bank of Boston's *The Region* at http://www.bos.frb.org/economic/nerr/katz97_1.htm. What evidence does Katz cite about how the rising value of time has affected consumer spending patterns?

19. *(Wall Street Journal)* In this chapter, you learned that the cost of consumption involves both a money price and a time price. Turn to the Wednesday *Wall Street Journal* and find the "Work and Family" column. See if you can find some examples of changes in new goods, services, government policies, or institutional arrangements that work by reducing the time price of a product. How do you think that change will affect the demand for the product? Will demand for any related products be affected?

Appendix

INDIFFERENCE CURVES AND UTILITY MAXIMIZATION

The approach used in the main part of the chapter, marginal utility analysis, requires some numerical measure of utility in order to determine the optimal bundle of goods and services. Economists have developed another, more general, approach to utility and consumer behavior, one that does not require that numbers be attached to specific levels of utility. All the new approach requires is that consumers be able to rank their preferences for various combinations of goods. For example, the consumer should be able to say whether combination A is preferred to combination B, combination B is preferred to combination A, or both combinations are equally preferred. This approach is more general and more flexible than the approach developed in the body of the chapter. We begin by examining consumer preferences.

CONSUMER PREFERENCES

Indifference curve analysis is an approach to the study of consumer behavior that does not require a numerical measure of utility. An **indifference curve** shows all combinations of goods that provide the consumer with the same satisfaction, or the same utility. Thus the consumer finds all combinations on a curve equally preferred. Since each of the alternative bundles of goods yields the same level of utility, the consumer is *indifferent* about which combination is actually consumed. We can best explain the use of indifference curves through the following example.

In reality consumers choose from among thousands of goods and services, but to keep the analysis manageable, suppose there are only two goods available: pizzas and movie videos. In Exhibit 9, the horizontal axis measures the quantity of pizzas you consume per week, and the vertical axis measures the quantity of videos you rent per week. Point *a*, for example, shows the consumption bundle consisting of 1 pizza and 8 video rentals. Suppose you are given a choice of the combination at point *a* or some other combination along the curve. The question is: Holding your total utility constant, how many video rentals would you be willing to give up to get a second pizza? As we can see, in moving from point *a* to point *b*, you are willing to give up 4 videos to get a second pizza. Total utility is the same at points *a* and *b*. The marginal utility of that additional pizza per week is just sufficient to compensate you for the utility lost from decreasing your video watching by 4 movies per week. Thus, at point *b*, you are eating 2 pizzas and watching 4 movies a week and are indifferent between this combination and the combination represented by point *a*, since total utility is the same at both points.

EXHIBIT 9

An Indifference Curve

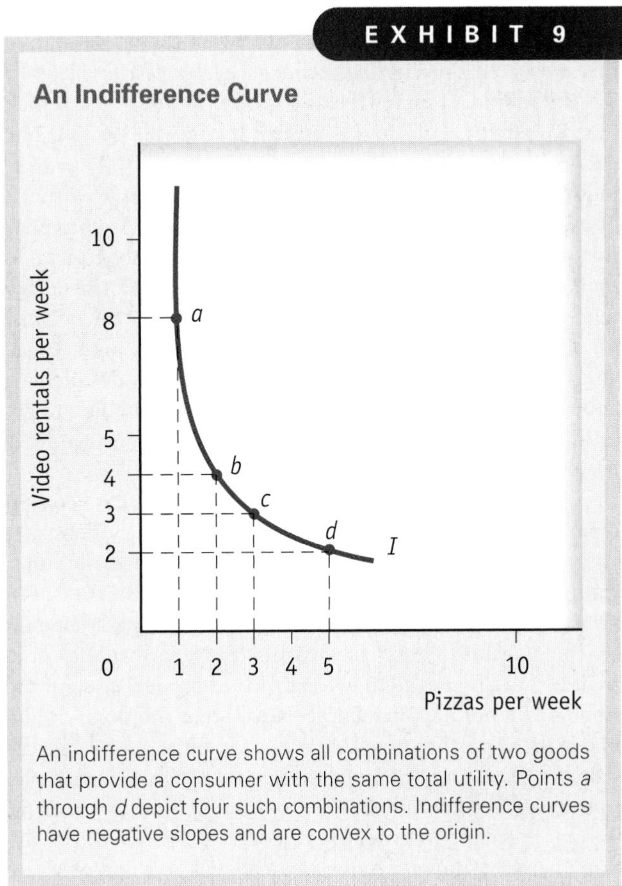

An indifference curve shows all combinations of two goods that provide a consumer with the same total utility. Points *a* through *d* depict four such combinations. Indifference curves have negative slopes and are convex to the origin.

In moving from point *b* to point *c*, again total utility is constant; you are now willing to give up only 1 video to get another pizza. At point *c*, your consumption bundle consists of 3 pizzas and 3 videos. Once at point *c*, you are willing to give up another video only if you get two more pizzas in return. Combination *d* therefore consists of 5 pizzas and 2 videos.

Points *a*, *b*, *c*, and *d* are connected to form an indifference curve, *I*, which represents possible combinations of pizza and videos that would keep you at the same level of total utility. Since points on the curve offer the same total utility, you are indifferent among them—hence the name *indifference curve*. Note that we don't know, nor do we need to know, the value you attach to the utility reflected by the indifference curve—that is, there is no particular number attached to the total utility along *I*. *Combinations of goods along an indifference curve reflect some constant, though unspecified, level of total utility.*

For you to remain indifferent among consumption combinations, the decrease in your utility from watching fewer videos must be just offset by the increase in your utility from eating more pizza. Thus, along an indifference curve, there is an inverse relationship between the quantity of one good consumed and the quantity of another consumed. Because of this inverse relationship, *indifference curves slope downward.*

Indifference curves are also *convex to the origin,* which means that they are bowed inward toward the origin. The curve gets flatter as you move down it. Here is why. Your willingness to substitute pizza for videos depends on how much of each is in your current consumption bundle. At combination *a,* for example, you rent 8 videos and eat only 1 pizza, so there are many videos relative to pizza. Because movies are relatively abundant in your consumption bundle, you are willing to give up watching 4 movies to get another pizza. Once you reach point *b,* your pizza consumption has doubled, so you are not quite so willing to give up movie-watching to get a third pizza. In fact, you will forgo only 1 video to get 1 more pizza. This moves you from point *b* to point *c.*

The **marginal rate of substitution,** or **MRS,** between pizza and video rentals indicates the number of videos that you are willing to give up to get one more pizza, neither gaining nor losing utility in the process. Because the MRS measures your willingness to trade videos for pizza, it depends on the amount of each good you already have at the time. Mathematically, the MRS is equal to the absolute value of the slope of the indifference curve. Recall that the slope of any line is the vertical change between two points on the line divided by the corresponding horizontal change. For example, in moving from combination *a* to combination *b* in Exhibit 9, you are willing to give up 4 videos to get 1 more pizza; the slope between those two points equals -4, so the MRS is 4. In the move from *b* to *c,* the slope is -1, so the MRS is 1. And from *c* to *d,* the slope is $-\frac{1}{2}$, so the MRS is $\frac{1}{2}$.

The **law of diminishing marginal rate of substitution** says that as your consumption of pizza increases, the number of videos that you are willing to give up to get another pizza declines. This law applies to most pairs of goods. Because your marginal rate of substitution of videos for pizza declines as your pizza consumption increases, the indifference curve has a diminishing slope, meaning that it is convex when viewed from the origin. As you move down the indifference curve, your pizza consumption increases, so your marginal utility of additional pizza decreases. Conversely, the number of movies you rent decreases so your marginal utility of movies increases. Thus, in moving down the indifference curve, you require more pizza to offset the loss of each video.

We have focused on a single indifference curve, which indicates some constant but unspecified level of utility. We can use the same approach to generate a series of indifference curves, called an **indifference map.** An indifference map is a graphical representation of a consumer's tastes. Each curve in the indifference map reflects a different level of utility. Part of such a map is shown in Exhibit 10, where indifference curves for a particular consumer, in this case you, are labeled I_1, I_2, I_3, and I_4. Each consumer has a unique indifference map based on his or her preferences.

Because both goods yield utility, you, the consumer, prefer more of each, rather than less. Thus, curves farther from the origin represent greater consumption levels and, therefore, higher levels of total utility. The total utility level along I_2 is higher than that along I_1. I_3 reflects a higher level of utility than I_2, and so on. We can show this best by drawing a ray from the origin and following it to higher indifference curves. Such a ray has been included in Exhibit 10. By following that ray to higher and higher indifference curves, we can see that the combination on each successive indifference curve reflects greater amounts of *both* goods. Since you value both goods, the greater amounts of each good reflected on higher indifference curves represent higher levels of utility.

Indifference curves in a consumer's indifference map do not intersect. Exhibit 11 shows why. If indifference curves crossed, as at point *i,* then every point on indifference

EXHIBIT 10

An Indifference Map

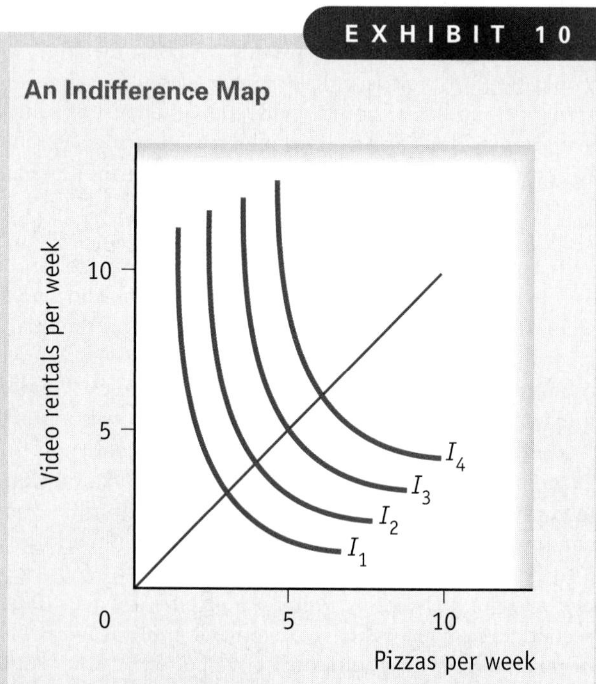

Indifference curves I_1 through I_4 are four examples from a consumer's indifference map. Indifference curves farther from the origin depict higher levels of utility. A ray intersects each higher indifference curve, reflecting more of both goods.

EXHIBIT 11

Indifference Curves Do Not Intersect

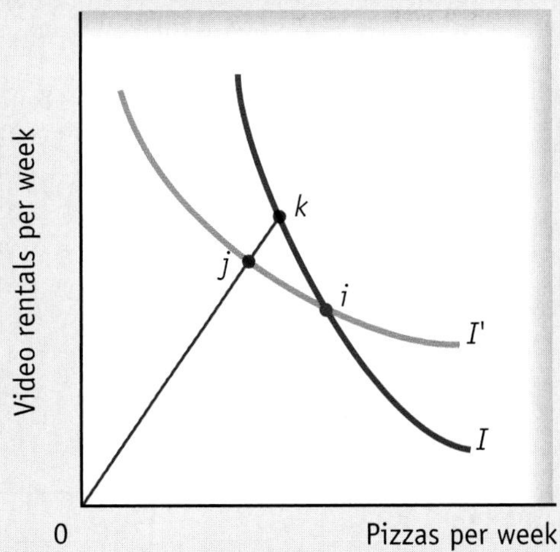

If indifference curves crossed, as at point *i*, then every point on indifference curve *I* and every point on curve *I'* would have to reflect the same level of utility as at point *i*. But point *k* is a combination with more pizza and more videos than point *j* and so must represent a higher level of utility. This contradiction means that indifference curves cannot intersect.

curve *I* and every point on curve *I'* would have to reflect the same level of utility as at point *i*. But point *k* in Exhibit 11 is a combination with more pizza and more videos than point *j* and so must represent a higher level of utility. This contradiction means that indifference curves cannot intersect.

Let's summarize the properties of indifference curves.

1. *A particular indifference curve reflects a constant level of utility, so the consumer is indifferent among all consumption combinations along a given curve.*
2. *If total utility is to remain constant, an increase in the consumption of one good must be offset by a decrease in the consumption of the other good, so each indifference curve slopes downward.*
3. *Because of the law of diminishing marginal rate of substitution, indifference curves are bowed in toward the origin.*
4. *Higher indifference curves represent higher levels of utility.*
5. *Indifference curves do not intersect.*

Given a consumer's indifference map, how much of each good will be consumed? To determine that, we must consider the relative prices of the goods and the consumer's income. In the next section we focus on the consumer's budget.

THE BUDGET LINE

The **budget line** depicts all possible combinations of pizza purchases and movie rentals, given prices of pizzas and videos and your budget. Suppose a pizza sells for $8, movies rent for $4, and your budget, or income, for these items is $40 per week. If you spend the entire $40 on videos, you can afford to watch 10 videos per week. Alternatively, if you spend the entire $40 on pizzas, you can afford to eat 5 per week. In Exhibit 12, your budget line meets the vertical axis at 10 video rentals and meets the horizontal axis at 5 pizzas. We can connect the axis intercepts to form the budget line. You can purchase any combination on your budget line, or your budget constraint. You might think of the budget line as your *consumption possibilities frontier.*

Let's find the slope of the budget line. At the point where the budget line meets the vertical axis, the maximum number of videos you can rent equals your income divided by the video rental price, or I/p_v, where I is income and p_v is the rental price. At the point where the budget line meets the horizontal axis, the maximum quantity of pizzas that you can

EXHIBIT 12

A Budget Line

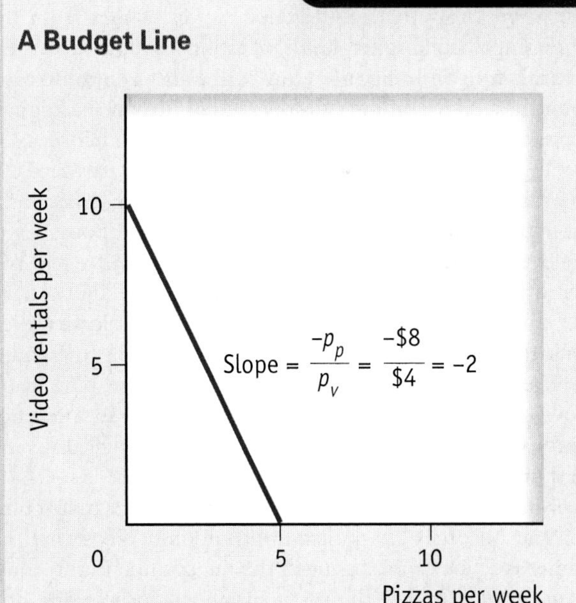

The budget line shows all combinations of pizza and videos that can be purchased at fixed prices with a given amount of income. If all income is spent on vidoes, 10 can be purchased. If all income is spent on pizzas, 5 can be purchased. Points between the vertical intercept and the horizontal intercept represent combinations of some pizza and some videos. The slope of the budget line is −2, illustrating that the cost of 1 pizza is 2 videos.

purchase equals your income divided by the price of a pizza, or I/p_p, where p_p is the price of pizza. The slope of the budget line between the vertical intercept in Exhibit 12 and the horizontal intercept equals the vertical change, or $-I/p_v$, divided by the horizontal change, or I/p_p:

$$\text{Slope of budget line} = -\frac{I/p_v}{I/p_p} = -\frac{p_p}{p_v}$$

In our example it is −$8/$4, which equals −2. The slope of the budget line indicates what it costs you in terms of forgone video rentals to get another pizza. You must give up 2 videos for each additional pizza. *Note that the income term cancels out, so the slope of a budget line depends only on relative prices, not on the level of income.*

The indifference curve indicates what you are *willing* to buy. The budget line shows what you are *able* to buy. We must therefore bring together the indifference curve and the budget line to find out what quantities of each good you are both *willing* and *able* to buy.

CONSUMER EQUILIBRIUM AT THE TANGENCY

As always, the objective of consumption is to maximize utility. We know that indifference curves farther from the origin represent higher levels of utility. You, as a utility-maximizing consumer, therefore will select a combination along the budget line in Exhibit 13 that lies on the highest attainable indifference curve. Given prices and income, you maximize utility at the combination of pizza and videos depicted by point *e* in Exhibit 13, where indifference curve I_2 just touches, or *is tangent to,* your budget line. At point *e*, you buy 3 pizzas at $8 each and rent 4 videos at $4 each. You thereby spend your budget of $40 per week. Other attainable combinations along the budget line reflect lower levels of utility. For example, point *a* is on the budget line and is therefore a combination you are *able* to purchase, but *a* is on a lower indifference curve, I_1. Other, "better," indifference curves, such as I_3, lie completely above the budget line and are thus unattainable.

Since you maximize your utility at point *e*, that combination becomes an equilibrium outcome. Note that the indifference curve is tangent to the budget line at the equilibrium point, and at the point of tangency the slope of a curve equals the slope of a line drawn tangent to that curve. At point *e*, the slope of the indifference curve equals the slope of the budget line. Recall that the absolute value of the slope of the indifference curve is your marginal rate of substitution, and the absolute value of the slope of the budget line equals the price ratio. In equilibrium, therefore, your marginal rate of substitution between video rentals and pizza, MRS, must equal the ratio of the price of pizza to the price of video rentals, or

EXHIBIT 13

Utility Maximization

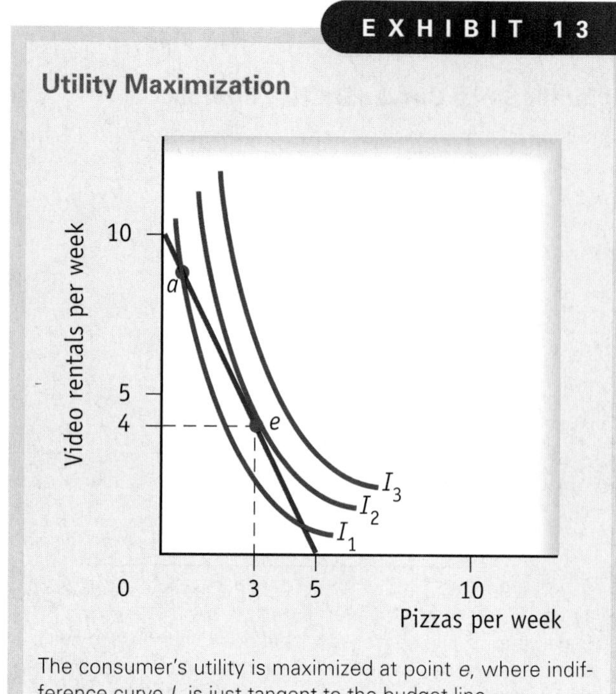

The consumer's utility is maximized at point *e*, where indifference curve I_2 is just tangent to the budget line.

$$\text{MRS} = \frac{p_p}{p_v}$$

What is the relationship between indifference curve analysis and the marginal utility theory introduced in the chapter? The marginal rate of substitution of pizza for video rentals can also be found from the marginal utilities of pizza and videos presented in the chapter. Exhibit 3 indicated that, at the consumer equilibrium, the marginal utility you derived from the third pizza was 24 and the marginal utility you derived by the fourth video was 12. Since the marginal utility of pizza (MU_p) is 24 and the marginal utility of videos (MU_v) is 12, in moving to that equilibrium, you were willing to give up 2 videos to get 1 more pizza. Thus, the marginal rate of substitution of pizza for videos equals the ratio of pizza's marginal utility (MU_p) to video's marginal utility (MU_v), or

$$\text{MRS} = \frac{MU_p}{MU_v}$$

In fact, the absolute value of the slope of the indifference curve equals MU_p/MU_v. Since the absolute value of the slope of the budget line equals p_p/p_v, the equilibrium condition for the indifference curve approach can be written as

$$\frac{MU_p}{p_p} = \frac{MU_v}{p_v}$$

This equation is the same equilibrium condition for utility maximization presented in the chapter using marginal utility analysis. The equality says that in equilibrium—that is, when the consumer maximizes total utility—the last dollar spent on each good yields the same marginal utility. If this equality does not hold, the consumer can increase total utility by adjusting consumption until the equality occurs.

EFFECTS OF A CHANGE IN PRICE

What happens to your equilibrium consumption when there is a change in price? The answer can be found by deriving the demand curve. We begin at point *e*, our initial equilibrium, in panel (a) of Exhibit 14. At point *e*, you eat 3 pizzas and watch four videos per week. Suppose that the price of pizzas falls from \$8 to \$6 per unit, other things constant. The price drop means that if the entire budget were devoted to pizza, you could purchase 6.67 pizzas (40/6). Since the rental price of videos has not changed, however, 10 remains the maximum number you can rent. Thus the budget line's vertical intercept remains fixed at 10 videos, but the lower end of the budget line rotates out.

After the price of pizza changes, the new equilibrium position occurs at *e*", where pizza purchases increase from 3 to 4, and, as it happens, video rentals remains at 4. Thus, price and the quantity of pizza demanded are inversely related. The demand curve in panel (b) of Exhibit 14 shows how price and quantity demanded are related. Specifically, when the price of pizza falls from \$8 per unit to \$6 per unit, other things constant, your quantity demanded increases from 3 to 4. Since you are on a higher indifference curve at *e*", you are clearly better off after the price reduction (your consumer surplus has increased).

EXHIBIT 14

Effect of a Drop in the Price of Pizza

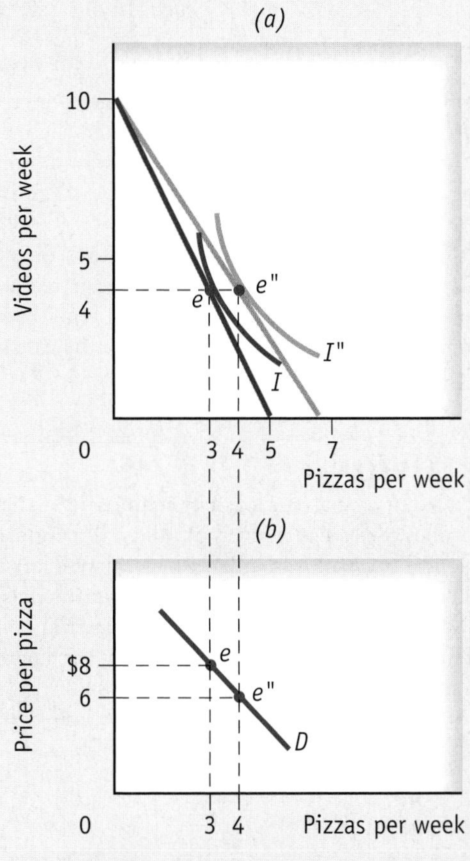

A reduction in the price of pizza rotates the budget line outward in panel (a). The consumer is back in equilibrium at point *e*" along the new budget line. Panel (b) shows that a drop in the price of pizza from \$8 per unit to \$6 leads to an increase in quantity demanded from 3 to 4. Price and quantity demanded are inversely related.

INCOME AND SUBSTITUTION EFFECTS

The law of demand was originally explained in terms of an income effect and a substitution effect. You now have the analytical tools to examine these two effects more precisely. Suppose the price of pizza falls from \$8 to \$4, other things constant. You can now purchase a maximum of 10 pizzas with a budget of \$40 per week. As shown in Exhibit 15, the budget line intercept rotates out from 5 to 10 pizzas. After the price change, the quantity of pizzas demanded increases from 3 to 5. The increase in utility shows that you benefit from the price decrease.

The increase in the quantity of pizzas demanded can be broken down into the substitution effect and the income effect of a price change. When the price of pizza falls, the change in the ratio of the price of pizza to the price of video rentals shows up through the change in the slope of the budget line. In order to derive the substitution effect, let's assume that you must maintain the same level of utility after the price change as before. In other words, let's suppose your utility level has not yet changed but the relative prices you face have changed. We want to learn how you would adjust to the price change. A new budget line reflecting just the change in relative prices, not a change in utility, is shown by the dashed line, *CF*, in Exhibit 15. Given the new set of relative prices, you would increase the quantity of pizzas demanded to the point on indifference curve *I* where the indifference curve is just tangent the dashed budget line. That tangency keeps utility at the initial level but reflects the new set of relative prices. Thus we adjust your budget line to correspond to the new relative prices, but adjust your income level so that your utility remains unchanged.

EXHIBIT 15

Substitution and Income Effects of a Drop in the Price of Pizza from \$8 to \$4 Each

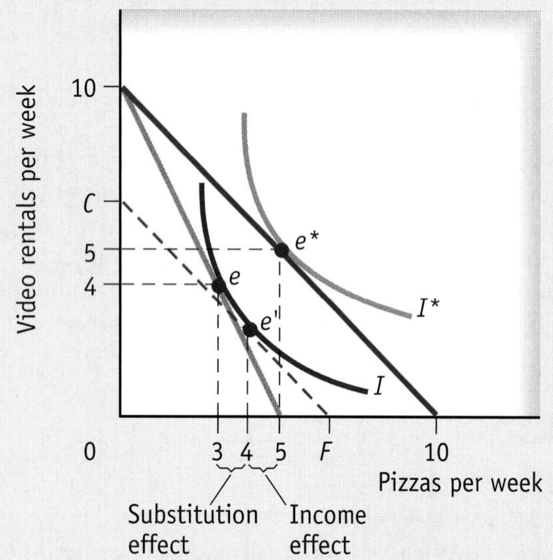

A reduction in the price of pizza moves the consumer from point *e* to point *e**. This movement can be decomposed into a substitution effect and an income effect. The substitution effect (from *e* to *e'*) reflects a reaction to a change in relative prices along the original indifference curve. The income effect (from *e'* to *e**) moves the consumer to a higher indifference curve at the new relative price ratio.

You move down along indifference curve *I* to point *e'*, renting fewer videos but buying more pizza. These changes in quantity demanded reflect the *substitution effect* of lower pizza prices. The substitution effect always increases the quantity demanded of the good whose price has dropped. Since consumption bundle *e'* represents the same level of utility as consumption bundle *e*, you are neither better off nor worse off at point *e'*.

But at point *e'*, you have not spent your full budget. The drop in the price of pizza has increased the quantity of pizza you can buy, as shown by the expanded budget line that runs from 10 video rentals to 10 pizzas. Your *real income* has increased because of the lower price of pizza. As a result, you are able to attain point *e*★ on indifference curve *I*★. At this point, you buy 5 pizzas and rent 5 videos. Because prices are held constant during the move from *e'* to *e*★, the change in consumption is due solely to a change in real income. Thus, the change in the quantity of pizza demanded reflects the *income effect* of the lower pizza price.

We can now distinguish between the substitution effect and the income effect of a drop in the price of pizza. The substitution effect is shown by the move from point *e* to point *e'* in response to a change in the relative price of pizza, with your utility held constant along *I*. The income effect is shown by the move from *e'* to *e*★ in response to an increase in your real income, with relative prices held constant.

The overall effect of a change in the price of pizza is the sum of the substitution effect and the income effect. In our example, the substitution effect accounts for a one-unit increase in the quantity of pizza demanded, as does the income effect. Thus, the income and substitution effects combine to increase the quantity of pizza demanded by 2 units when the price falls from \$8 to \$4. The income effect is not always positive. For inferior goods, the income effect is negative, so as the price falls, the income effect can cause consumption to fall, offsetting part or even all of the substitution effect. Incidentally, notice that as a result of the increase in your real income, video rentals increase as well—from 4 to 5 rentals per week in our example, though it will not always be the case that the income effect is positive.

CONCLUSION

Indifference curve analysis does not require us to attach numerical values to particular levels of utility, as marginal utility theory does. The results of indifference curve analysis confirm the conclusions drawn from our simpler models. Indifference curves provide a logical way of viewing consumer choice, but consumers need not be aware of this approach in order to make rational choices. The purpose of the analysis in this chapter is to predict consumer behavior—not to advise consumers how to maximize utility.

APPENDIX QUESTIONS

1. *(Consumer Preferences)* The absolute value of the slope of an indifference curve equals the marginal rate of substitution. If two goods were *perfectly* substitutable, what would the indifference curves look like? Explain.

2. *(Effects of a Change in Price)* Chris has an income of $90 to allocate between Goods A and B. Initially, the price of A is $3 and the price of B is $4.
   a. Draw Chris's budget line, indicating its slope if units of A are measured on the horizontal axis and units of B are on the vertical axis.
   b. Add an indifference curve to your graph and label the point of consumer equilibrium. Indicate Chris's consumption levels of A and B. Why is this a consumer equilibrium?
   c. Now assume that the price of A rises to $4. Draw the new budget line, a new point of consumer equilibrium, and the consumption levels of Goods A and B. What is Chris's marginal rate of substitution at the new equilibrium point?
   d. Draw the demand curve for good A, labeling the different price and quantity demanded combinations determined in parts (b) and (c).

CHAPTER

20 Production and Cost in the Firm

Why is fast food is so fast? Why do too many cooks spoil the broth? Why do movie theaters have so many screens? Why don't they add even more? If you go into business for yourself, how much must you earn just to break even? Why might your grade point average fall even though your grades improved from the previous term? Answers to these and other questions are discovered in this chapter, which introduces production and cost in the firm.

The previous chapter explored the consumer behavior underlying the demand curve. This chapter examines the producer behavior underlying the supply curve. More specifically, we will examine a firm's production and cost of operation as a prelude to our analysis of supply. In the previous chapter, you were asked to think like a consumer, or demander. In this chapter, you must

Visit the McEachern Interactive Study Center for this chapter at *http://mcisc.swcollege.com*

think like a producer, or supplier. You may feel more natural as a consumer (after all, you *are* a consumer), but you know more about producers than you may realize. You have been around producers all your life—bookstores, video stores, department stores, grocery stores, doughnut shops, convenience stores, dry cleaners, gas stations, auto dealers, restaurants, farms, factories, offices, and thousands of other producers in the *Yellow Pages* and on the Internet.

Although you may not yet have been a producer yourself, you already have some idea how businesses operate. They all have the same goal: *maximum profit.* Profit equals revenue minus cost. In this chapter we introduce the cost side of the profit equation. Topics discussed in this chapter include:

- Explicit and implicit costs
- Economic and normal profit
- Increasing and diminishing returns
- Short-run costs
- Long-run costs
- Economies and diseconomies of scale

COST AND PROFIT

When we examined demand, we assumed that consumers try to maximize utility, a goal that provides the motivation for consumer behavior. When we turn to supply, we assume that producers try to maximize *profit*—that is, the difference between the total revenue from the sale of output and the opportunity cost of resources. Over time, the firms that survive and grow are those that are the most profitable. Firms that are unprofitable year after year eventually fail.

Firms transform inputs or resources into outputs or products to earn a profit. Each year throughout the world, millions of new firms enter the marketplace, and nearly as many leave. The firm's decision makers must choose what goods and services to produce and what resources to employ. They must make plans while confronting uncertainty about consumer demand, resource availability, and the intentions of other firms in the market. *The lure of profit is so strong, however, that eager entrepreneurs are always ready to pursue their dreams.*

Explicit and Implicit Costs

To hire resources, producers must pay resource owners at least their *opportunity cost*—that is, what the resources could earn in their best alternative use. For resources purchased in resource markets, the corresponding cash payments approximate the opportunity cost. For example, the $3 per pound that Domino's Pizza pays for cheese reflects a price the cheese supplier could get elsewhere. Some resources, however, are owned by the firm (or the firm's owners), so there are no direct cash payments for their use. For example, the firm pays no rent to operate in a company-owned building. Similarly, the owner and operator of the corner dry cleaner usually does not pay himself or herself an hourly wage. But these resources are not free. *Whether resources are hired in resource markets or owned by the firm, resources have an opportunity cost.* The company-owned building could likely be sold or rented to another user; the dry cleaner could find another job.

A firm's **explicit costs** are its actual cash payments for resources purchased in resource markets: wages, rent, interest, insurance, taxes, and the like. In addition to these direct cash outlays, or explicit costs, the firm also faces **implicit costs,** which are the opportunity costs of using resources owned by the firm or

Explicit cost Opportunity cost of a firm's resources that takes the form of cash payments

Implicit cost A firm's opportunity cost of using its own resources or those provided by its owners without a corresponding cash payment provided by the firm's owners. Examples include the use of a company-owned building, use of company funds, or the time of the firm's owners. Like explicit costs, implicit costs are opportunity costs. But unlike explicit costs, implicit costs require no cash payment and no entry in the firm's *accounting statement,* which records its revenues, explicit costs, and accounting profit.

Alternative Measures of Profit

A particular example may help clarify the distinction between implicit and explicit costs. Meet Wanda Wheeler, an aeronautical engineer who earns $40,000 a year working for the Skyhigh Aircraft Company. On her way home from work one day, she gets an idea for a rounder, more friction-resistant airplane wheel. She decides to quit her job and start a business, which she calls Wheeler Dealer. To buy the necessary machines and equipment, she withdraws savings of $20,000 from her bank account, where it had been earning interest of $1,000 a year. She hires an assistant and starts producing the wheel in a spare bay in her garage, a bay that she had been renting to a neighbor for $100 per month.

Sales are slow at first—people keep telling her she is just trying to reinvent the wheel—but her wheel eventually gets rolling. When Wanda and her accountant examine the firm's performance after the first year, they are quite pleased. As you can see in the top part of Exhibit 1, company revenue in 1999 was $95,000. After paying the assistant's salary and the cost of materials and equipment, the firm shows an accounting profit of $54,000. **Accounting profit** equals total revenue minus explicit costs. This is the profit used by accountants to determine a firm's taxable income.

Accounting profit A firm's total revenue minus its explicit cost

But accounting profit ignores the opportunity cost of Wanda's own resources used in the firm. First is the opportunity cost of her time. Remember, she quit a $40,000-a-year job to work full time on her business, thereby forgoing that salary. Second is the $1,000 annual interest she passes up by financing the operation with her own savings. And third, by using the spare bay in her garage for the business, she forgoes $1,200 per year in rental income. The forgone salary, interest, and rental income are implicit costs because, although Wanda makes no explicit payment for the resources, she no longer earns income generated from

EXHIBIT 1

Accounts of Wheeler Dealer, 1999

Total revenue		$95,000
Less explicit costs:		
Assistant's salary	−21,000	
Material and equipment	−20,000	
Equals accounting profit		$54,000
Less implicit costs:		
Wanda's forgone salary	−$40,000	
Forgone interest on savings	−1,000	
Forgone garage rental	−1,200	
Equals economic profit		$11,800

their best alternative uses. **Economic profit** equals total revenue minus all costs, both implicit and explicit; *economic profit takes into account the opportunity cost of all resources used in production.* In Exhibit 1, accounting profit of $54,000 less implicit costs of $42,200 equals economic profit of $11,800.

Economic profit A firm's total revenue minus its explicit and implicit costs

What would happen to the accounting statement if Wanda decided to pay herself a salary of $40,000 per year? Explicit costs would increase by $40,000, implicit costs would decrease by $40,000, and accounting profit would decrease by $40,000. Economic profit would not change, however, since it already reflects both implicit and explicit costs.

There is one other important profit measure to consider: the accounting profit required to induce the firm's owners to employ their resources in the firm. The accounting profit just sufficient to ensure that *all* resources used by the firm earn their opportunity cost is called a **normal profit.** Wanda's firm earns a normal profit when accounting profit equals the sum of the salary she gave up at her regular job ($40,000), the interest she gave up by using her own savings ($1,000), and the rent she gave up on her garage ($1,200). Thus, if the accounting profit is $42,200 per year—the opportunity cost of resources Wanda supplies to the firm—the company earns a normal profit. *Any accounting profit in excess of a normal profit is economic profit.*

Normal profit The accounting profit required to persuade a firm's owners to employ their resources in the firm; the accounting profit earned when all resources used by the firm earn their opportunity cost

If accounting profit is large enough, it can be divided into normal profit and economic profit. The $54,000 in accounting profit earned by Wanda's firm consists of (1) a normal profit of $42,200, which just covers the opportunity cost of Wanda's resources supplied to the firm, and (2) an economic profit of $11,800, which is over and above what these resources could earn in their best alternative use. As long as economic profit is positive, Wanda is better off running her own firm than working for the Skyhigh Aircraft Company. If total revenue had been only $50,000, accounting profit of only $9,000 would cover less than one-fourth of Wanda's salary, to say nothing of her forgone rent and interest. Since Wanda would not be earning even a normal profit, she would be better off back in her old job.

To understand profit maximization, you must develop a feel for both revenue and cost. In this chapter, we will begin learning about the cost of production, beginning first with the relationship between inputs and outputs.

PRODUCTION IN THE SHORT RUN

We shift now from a discussion of profit to a discussion of how firms operate. Suppose a new McDonald's has just opened in your neighborhood and business is booming far beyond expectations. The manager responds to the unexpected demand by quickly hiring more workers. But cars are still backed up into the street waiting for a parking space. The solution is to add a drive-through window, but such an expansion takes time.

Fixed and Variable Resources

Some resources, such as labor, are called **variable resources** because they can be varied quickly to change the output rate. Adjustments in some other resources, however, take more time. The size of the building, for example, cannot easily be altered. Such resources are therefore called **fixed resources.** When considering the time required to alter the quantity of resources employed,

Variable resource Any resource that can be varied in the short run to increase or decrease the rate of output

Fixed resource Any resource that cannot be varied in the short run

Short run A period during which at least one of a firm's resources is fixed

Long run A period during which all resources under the firm's control are variable

economists distinguish between the short run and the long run. In the **short run,** at least one resource is fixed. In the **long run,** no resource is fixed.

Output can be changed in the short run by adjusting variable resources, but the size, or *scale,* of the firm is fixed in the short run. In the long run, however, all resources can vary. The length of the long run differs from industry to industry because the nature of the production process differs. For example, the size of a McDonald's restaurant can be increased more quickly than can the size of an electric power plant. Thus, the long run for McDonald's is shorter than the long run for an electric company. As the length of time required to plan and construct a new building increases, so does the length of the long run.

The Law of Diminishing Marginal Returns

Let's focus on the short-run link between resource use and the rate of production by considering a hypothetical moving company called Smoother Mover. Suppose the company's fixed resources are already in place and consist of a warehouse, a moving van, and moving equipment. In this example, labor will be the only variable resource.

Exhibit 2 relates the amount of labor employed to the amount of output produced. Labor is measured in worker-days, which is one worker for one day, and output is measured in tons of furniture moved per day. The column to the left shows the amount of labor employed, which ranges from 0 to 8. The center column shows the tons of furniture moved, or the **total product**, at each rate of employment. The relationship between the amount of resources employed and total product is called the firm's *production function*. The right column shows the **marginal product** of each worker—that is, the amount by which the total product changes with each additional unit of labor, assuming all other resources remain unchanged. Spend a little time acquainting yourself with each column.

Total product The total output produced by a firm

Marginal product The change in total product that occurs when the use of a particular resource increases by one unit, all other resources constant

Increasing Marginal Returns. Without labor, nothing gets moved, so when the quantity of labor is 0, the total product is 0. Now look what happens when labor gets into the act. If only one worker is employed, that worker alone must do all

EXHIBIT 2

The Short-Run Relationship Between Units of Labor and Tons of Furniture Moved

Units of the Variable Resource (worker-days)	Total Product (tons moved per day)	Marginal Product (tons moved per day)
0	0	—
1	2	2
2	5	3
3	9	4
4	12	3
5	14	2
6	15	1
7	15	0
8	14	−1

the driving, packing, crating, and moving. Some of the larger pieces of furniture, such as couches and beds, cannot easily be moved by one worker. Still, in our example one worker manages to move 2 tons of furniture per day.

When a second worker is hired, some division of labor in packing is possible, and two workers can lift the larger household items much more easily than just the one worker could, so total production more than doubles, reaching 5 tons per day. The marginal product resulting from adding a second worker is 3 tons per day. Adding a third worker allows for a better division of labor, which contributes to increased output. For example, one worker can specialize in packing fragile objects while the other two do the heavy lifting. The total product of three workers is 9 tons per day, which is 4 tons more than that of two workers. Because the marginal product increases, the firm experiences **increasing marginal returns** to labor as each of the first three workers is added. Marginal returns to labor increase because additional workers can specialize and can thereby make more efficient use of the fixed resources.

Diminishing Marginal Returns. The addition of a fourth worker adds to the total product, but not as much as was added by a third worker. Adding still more workers increases total product by successively smaller amounts, so the marginal product in Exhibit 2 declines after three workers. With four workers, the **law of diminishing marginal returns** takes hold. This law states that as additional quantities of the variable resource are combined with a given amount of fixed resources, a point is eventually reached where each additional unit of the variable resource yields a smaller marginal product. *The law of diminishing marginal returns is the most important feature of production in the short run.*

As additional units of the variable resource are added, total output may eventually turn negative. For example, when Smoother Mover hires eight workers per day, the working area becomes so crowded that workers get in each other's way. Transporting so many people to and from moving sites cuts into production because workers take up valuable space in the moving van. As a result, the total product actually declines if an eighth worker is added, so the marginal product turns negative. Likewise, a McDonald's outlet can add only so many workers before congestion in the work area causes marginal product to decline. As more workers are added, marginal product will at some point turn negative. ("Too many cooks spoil the broth.")

The Total and Marginal Product Curves

Panels (a) and (b) of Exhibit 3 illustrate the relationship between total product and marginal product, using the data from Exhibit 2. Note that because of increasing marginal returns, marginal product in panel (b) increases as each of the first three workers is added. With marginal product increasing, total product in panel (a) increases at an increasing rate (although this is hard to see). But when decreasing marginal returns set in, which occurs with the fourth worker, marginal product begins to decline. Total product continues to increase, although at a decreasing rate. As long as marginal product is positive, total product increases. At the output rate where marginal product turns negative, total product begins to decrease.

Note that Exhibit 3 sorts production into three ranges: increasing marginal returns, diminishing but positive marginal returns, and negative marginal returns. These ranges correspond with total product that increases at an increasing rate, total product that increases at a decreasing rate, and total product that declines.

*Net*Bookmark

Unit labor cost is the term used to describe the cost of labor per unit of output. Since labor costs generally represent the largest share of costs, this value is closely watched by business people and analysts at the Federal Reserve. Look for the most recent data on unit labor costs at http://stats.bls.gov/news.release/prod2.toc.htm from the Bureau of Labor Statistics. What is the current trend? What forces may be pushing unit labor cost downward? What does this mean for the profitability of firms?

Increasing marginal returns Marginal product increases experienced by a firm when another unit of a particular resource is employed, all other resources constant

Law of diminishing marginal returns When more and more of a variable resource is added to a given amount of a fixed resource, the resulting change in output will eventually diminish and could become negative

EXHIBIT 3

The Total and Marginal Product Labor

When marginal product is rising, total product is increasing by increasing amounts. When marginal product is decreasing but is still positive, total product is increasing by decreasing amounts. When marginal product equals 0, total product is at a maximum. Finally, when marginal product is negative, total product is falling.

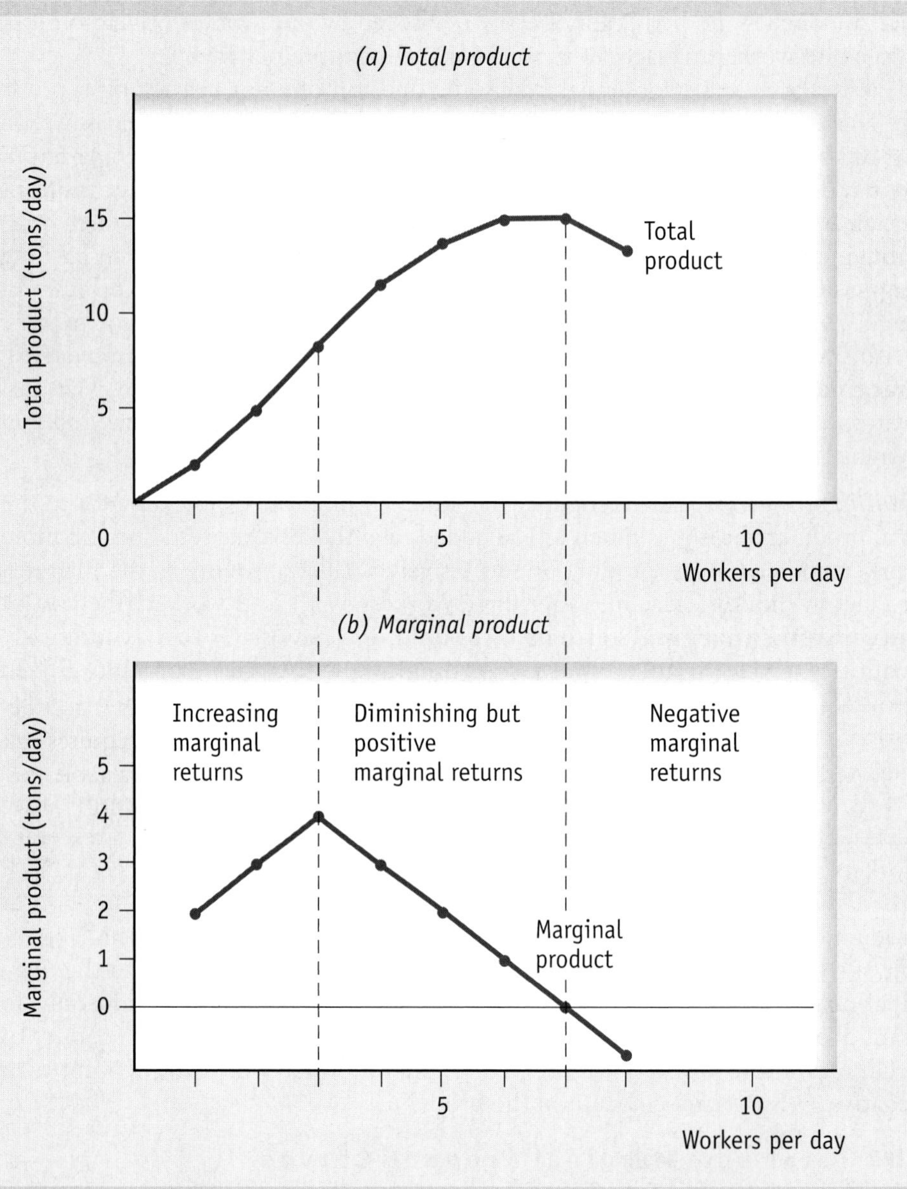

COSTS IN THE SHORT RUN

Now that we have examined the relationship between the amount of resources used and the rate of output, we can consider how the firm's cost of production varies as its rate of output varies. Short-run cost is divided into two categories: fixed cost and variable cost. Simply put, fixed cost is incurred for fixed resources and variable cost is incurred for variable resources. A firm must pay a **fixed cost** even if no output is produced. Even if Smoother Mover hires no labor and moves no furniture, it must pay for property taxes, insurance premiums, vehicle registration, and maintenance, plus principal and interest on any loans for its

Fixed cost Any production cost that is independent of the firm's rate of output

warehouse, van, and equipment. By definition, fixed cost is just that: fixed—it does not vary with output in the short run. Another name for fixed cost is *sunk cost* because this cost is incurred in the short run even if the firm decides to produce nothing. Let's assume that the firm's *fixed cost* amounts to $200 per day.

Variable cost, as the name implies, is the cost of variable resources. When no variable resource is employed, output is 0, as is variable cost. As more variable resources are employed, output increases, as does variable cost. The amount by which variable cost increases depends on the amount of variable resources employed and the prices of those resources. In our example, variable cost consists of labor cost. Suppose the firm can hire labor at a cost of $100 per worker-day. This firm's *variable cost*, therefore, equals $100 times the quantity of labor employed.

Variable cost Any production cost that changes as output changes

Total Cost and Marginal Cost in the Short Run

Exhibit 4 presents cost data for Smoother Mover. The table lists the daily cost of production associated with alternative rates of output per day. Column (1) shows possible rates of output in the short run, measured in tons of furniture moved per day.

Total Cost. Column (2) indicates the fixed cost (FC) for each rate of output. Note that fixed cost remains constant at $200 per day regardless of the rate of output. Column (3) shows the amount of labor required to produce each rate of output and is based on the productivity measures reported in the previous two exhibits. (Only the first 6 units of labor are listed because units 7 and beyond added nothing to total product.) For example, moving 2 tons requires one worker, 5 tons requires two workers, and so on. Column (4) lists variable cost (VC) per day, which equals $100 times the number of workers. For example, the variable cost of moving 9 tons of furniture per day is $300, since three workers are employed. Column (5) lists the **total cost** (TC) of each rate of output, which is the sum of fixed cost and variable cost: $TC = FC + VC$. Note that at 0 units of output, variable cost is $0, so total cost equals only the fixed cost of $200. Since total cost is the opportunity cost of all resources employed by the firm, total cost includes a normal profit.

Total cost The sum of fixed cost and variable cost; the opportunity cost of all resources employed by the firm

EXHIBIT 4

Short-Run Cost Data for Smoother Mover

Tons Moved per Day (q) (1)	Fixed Cost (FC) (2)	Workers per Day (3)	Variable Cost (VC) (4)	Total Cost ($TC = FC + VC$) (5)	Marginal Cost $\left(MC = \frac{\Delta TC}{\Delta q}\right)$ (6)
0	$200	0	$ 0	$200	—
2	200	1	100	300	$ 50.00
5	200	2	200	400	33.33
9	200	3	300	500	25.00
12	200	4	400	600	33.33
14	200	5	500	700	50.00
15	200	6	600	800	100.00

Marginal cost The change in total cost resulting from a one-unit change in output; the change in total cost divided by the change in output

Marginal Cost. Of special interest to the firm is how total cost changes as output changes. More specifically, what is the marginal cost of producing another unit? The **marginal cost** of production listed in column (6) is simply the change in total cost divided by the change in output, or $MC = \Delta TC/\Delta q$, where Δ means "change in". For example, increasing output from 0 to 2 tons increases total cost by \$100 (= \$300 − \$200). The marginal cost of each of the first 2 tons is the change in total cost, \$100, divided by the change in output, 2 tons, or \$100/2, which equals \$50. The marginal cost of each of the next 3 tons is \$100/3, or \$33.33.

Notice in column (6) that marginal cost first decreases, then increases. *Changes in marginal cost reflect changes in the marginal productivity of the variable resource employed.* Recall from Exhibit 2 that the first three workers contributed to increasing marginal returns, with each additional worker producing more than the last. This greater productivity of labor results in a falling marginal cost for the output produced by the first three workers. As more labor is hired beyond three workers, however, the firm experiences diminishing marginal returns to labor, so the marginal cost of output increases. *When the firm experiences increasing marginal returns, the marginal cost of output decreases; when the firm experiences diminishing marginal returns, the marginal cost of output increases.*

Thus, the marginal cost in Exhibit 4 first falls and then rises, because of first increasing and then diminishing marginal returns. The labor employed by Smoother Mover shows increasing marginal returns for the first 9 tons of furniture moved and decreasing marginal returns thereafter.

Total and Marginal Cost Curves. Exhibit 5 shows the cost curves for the data in Exhibit 4. Since fixed cost does not vary with output, the fixed cost curve is a horizontal line at the \$200 level in panel (a). Variable cost is \$0 when output is 0, so the *variable cost curve* starts from the origin. For reasons that we will get to soon, variable cost increases slowly at first, then increases sharply. The *total cost curve* is derived by *vertically* summing the variable cost curve and the fixed cost curve. Because a constant amount of fixed cost is added to variable cost, the total cost curve is the variable cost curve shifted vertically by the amount of fixed cost.

We have already discussed the reasons for the pattern of marginal cost. In panel (b) of Exhibit 5, marginal cost declines until the ninth unit of output and then increases, reflecting labor's increasing and then diminishing marginal returns. There is a geometric relationship between panels (a) and (b) because the change in total cost resulting from a one-unit change in production equals the marginal cost. With each successive unit of output, the total cost increases by the marginal cost of that unit. Thus, *the slope of the total cost curve at each rate of output equals the marginal cost at that rate of output.* The total cost curve can be divided into two sections, based on what happens to marginal cost:

1. Because of increasing marginal returns from the variable resource, marginal cost at first declines, so total cost initially increases by successively smaller amounts and the total cost curve gets flatter.
2. Because of diminishing marginal returns from the variable resource, marginal cost begins to increase after the ninth unit of output, leading to a steeper total cost curve.

Keep in mind that economic analysis is marginal analysis. Marginal cost is key to economic decisions made by firms. The firm operating in the short run has

EXHIBIT 5

Total and Marginal Cost Curves for Smoother Mover

In panel (a), fixed cost is constant at all levels of output. Variable cost starts from the origin and increases slowly at first as output increases. When the variable resource generates diminishing marginal returns, variable cost begins to increase more rapidly. Total cost is the vertical sum of fixed cost and variable cost. In panel (b), marginal cost first declines, reflecting increasing marginal returns, and then increases, reflecting diminishing marginal returns.

(a) Total cost curves

Total dollars
$1,000
500
200
0
Total cost
Variable cost
Fixed cost
Fixed cost
3 6 9 12 15 Tons per day

(b) Marginal cost curve

Cost per ton
$100
50
25
0
Marginal cost
3 6 9 12 15 Tons per day

no control over its fixed cost, but, by varying output in the short run, the firm alters its variable cost and hence its total cost. *Marginal cost indicates how much total cost will increase if one more unit is produced or how much total cost will drop if production is reduced by one unit.*

Average Cost in the Short Run

Although total cost and marginal cost are of the greatest analytical interest, the average cost per unit of output is also useful. There are average cost measures corresponding to variable cost and to total cost. These average costs are shown

EXHIBIT 6

Short-Run Cost Data for Smoother Mover

Tons Moved per Day (q) (1)	Variable Cost (VC) (2)	Total Cost ($TC = FC + VC$) (3)	Marginal Cost $\left(MC = \frac{\Delta TC}{\Delta q}\right)$ (4)	Average Variable Cost $\left(AVC = \frac{VC}{q}\right)$ (5) = (2)/(5)	Average Total Cost $\left(ATC = \frac{TC}{q}\right)$ (6) = (3)/(1)
0	$ 0	$200	$ 0	——	∞
2	100	300	50.00	$50.00	$150.00
5	200	400	33.33	40.00	80.00
9	300	500	25.00	33.33	55.55
12	400	600	33.33	33.33	50.00
14	500	700	50.00	35.71	50.00
15	600	800	100.00	40.00	52.33

Average variable cost Variable cost divided by output

Average total cost Total cost divided by output

in columns (5) and (6) of Exhibit 6. Column (5) lists **average variable cost,** or *AVC,* which equals variable cost divided by output, or $AVC = VC/q$. The final column lists **average total cost,** or *ATC,* which is total cost divided by output, or $ATC = TC/q$. Both average variable cost and average total cost first decline as output expands and then increase.

The Relationship Between Marginal Cost and Average Cost

To understand the relationship between marginal cost and average variable cost, let's begin with an analogy of college grades. Think about how your grades each term, which we can think of as your marginal grades, affect your cumulative grade point average, or your average grades. Suppose you do well your first term, starting your college career with a grade point average of 3.4. Your grades for the second term drop to 2.8, reducing your average to 3.1. You slip again in the third term to 2.2, lowering your average to 2.8. Your grades for the fourth term improve a bit to 2.4, but your average continues to slide to 2.7. In the fifth term, your grades improve to 2.7, leaving your average unchanged at 2.7. And in the sixth term, you get a 3.3, boosting your average to 2.8.

Notice that when your term grades are below your average grades, your average falls. When your performance for the term improves, your average does not improve until your term grades *exceed* your average grades. Your term grades at first pull down your average and then pull up your average.

Let's now take a look at the relationship between marginal cost and average cost. In Exhibit 6, marginal cost has the same relationship to average cost as your term grades have to your grade point average. You can observe this marginal-average relationship in columns (4) and (5). Because of increasing marginal returns from the first three workers, the marginal cost falls for the first 9 tons of furniture moved. Where marginal cost is below average cost, marginal cost pulls

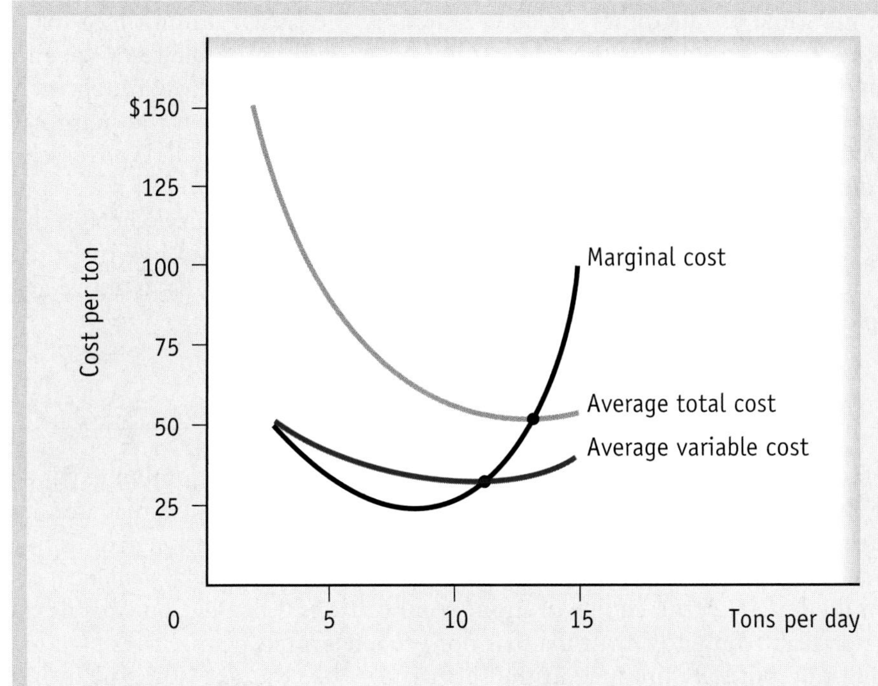

EXHIBIT 7

Average and Marginal Cost Curves for Smoother Mover

Average variable cost and average total cost drop, reach low points, and then rise; overall, they take on U shapes. When marginal cost is below average variable cost, average variable cost is falling. When marginal cost equals average variable cost, average variable cost is at its minimum value. When marginal cost is above average variable cost, average variable cost is increasing. The same relationship holds between marginal cost and average total cost.

down average cost. Marginal cost and average cost are equal where output equals 12 tons, and marginal cost exceeds average cost where output exceeds 12 tons, so marginal cost pulls up average cost.

Exhibit 7 shows the same marginal cost curve first presented in Exhibit 5, along with average cost curves based on data in Exhibit 6. At low rates of output, marginal cost declines as output expands because of increasing marginal returns. As long as marginal cost is below average cost, average cost falls as output expands. At higher rates of output, marginal cost increases because of diminishing marginal returns. Where marginal cost exceeds average cost, marginal cost pulls up the average. Because marginal cost first pulls down average cost and then pulls up average cost, this explains why the average cost curves have a U shape. The shape of the average variable cost curve and average total cost curve are determined by the shape of the marginal cost curve, and each is shaped by increasing and diminishing marginal returns.

Notice also that the rising marginal cost curve intersects both the average variable cost curve and the average total cost curve where these average curves are at their minimum. This occurs because the marginal pulls down the average where the marginal is below the average and pulls up the average where the marginal is above the average. One more thing: The distance between the average variable cost curve and the average total cost curve is *average fixed cost*, which gets smaller as the rate of output increases.

Summary of Short-Run Cost Curves

The law of diminishing marginal returns and the prices of resources determine the shape of short-run cost curves. The shape of the marginal product curve discussed earlier in the chapter determines the shape of the marginal cost curve. And the shape of the marginal product curve is determined by the law of diminishing marginal productivity, which is the relationship between the variable resource and output. Thus, the marginal cost curve depends ultimately on how much each unit of the variable resource, in this case labor, produces. When the marginal product of labor increases, the marginal cost of output must fall. Conversely, once diminishing marginal returns set in, the marginal cost of output must rise. Thus marginal cost first falls, then rises. And the marginal cost curve dictates the shapes of the average variable cost and average total cost curves. When marginal cost is less than average cost, average cost falls; when marginal cost is above average cost, average cost rises.

COSTS IN THE LONG RUN

Thus far our analysis has focused on how costs vary as the rate of output expands in the short run for a firm of a given size. In the long run, all inputs that are under the firm's control can be varied, so there is no fixed cost. The long run is not just a succession of short runs. The long run is best thought of as a *planning horizon*. In the long run, the choice of input combinations is flexible, but this flexibility is available only to a firm that has not yet acted on its plans. Firms plan for the long run, but they produce in the short run. Once the size of the plant has been selected and the concrete has been poured, the firm has fixed costs and is once again back in the short run. We turn now to long-run cost curves.

The Long-Run Average Cost Curve

Suppose that, because of the special nature of technology in the industry, a firm's plant can be one of only three possible sizes: small, medium, or large. Exhibit 8 presents this simple case. The short-run average total cost curves for the three

EXHIBIT 8

Short-Run Cost Curves and the Long-Run Planning Curve

Curves *SS'*, *MM'*, and *LL'* show short-run average total costs for smal, medium, and large plants, respectively. For output less than q_a average cost is lowest when the plant is small. Between q_a and q_b cost is lowest with a medium-size plant. If output exceeds q_b the large plant is best. The long-run average-cost curve is *SabL'*.

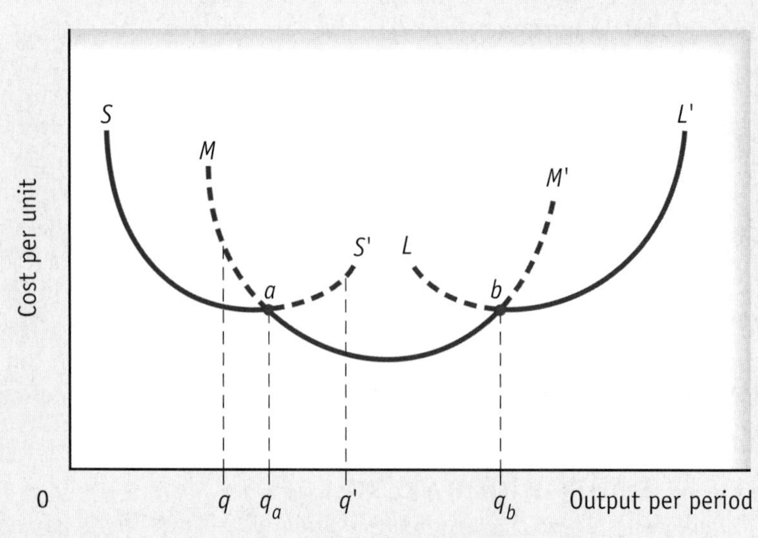

plant sizes are SS', MM', and LL'. Which size plant should the firm build to minimize the average cost of production? The appropriate size, or scale, for the plant depends on how much the firm wants to produce. For example, if q is the desired production rate in the long run, the average cost per unit will be lowest with a small plant. If the desired output rate is q', the medium plant size ensures the lowest average cost.

More generally, for any output less than q_a, average cost of output is lowest when the plant is small. For output rates between q_a and q_b, the average cost is lowest when the plant is of medium size. And for output rates that exceed q_b, the average cost is lowest when the plant is large. The **long-run average cost curve** connects portions of the three short-run average cost curves that are lowest for each output rate. In Exhibit 8, that curve consists of the line segments connecting *S, a, b,* and *L'*.

Long-run average cost curve A curve that indicates the lowest average cost of production at each rate of output when the firm's size is allowed to vary; also called the planning curve and the envelope curve

Now suppose there are many possible plant sizes. Exhibit 9 presents a sample of possible short-run average total cost curves. The long-run average cost curve is created by connecting the points on the various short-run average cost curves that represent the lowest per-unit cost for each rate of output. Each of the short-run cost curves is tangent to the long-run average cost curve, which is sometimes called the firm's *planning curve,* or *envelope curve.* An envelope curve is the long-run curve tangent to each of a family of short-run curves. If we could display enough short-run cost curves, we would have a different plant size for each rate of output. *These points of tangency represent the least-cost way of producing each particular rate of output, given the technology and resource prices.* For example, the short-run average cost curve ATC_1 is tangent to the planning curve at point *a,* indicating that the least-cost way of producing output rate q is with the plant size associated with ATC_1. No other size plant would produce output rate q at as low a cost per unit. Note, however, that other output rates along ATC_1

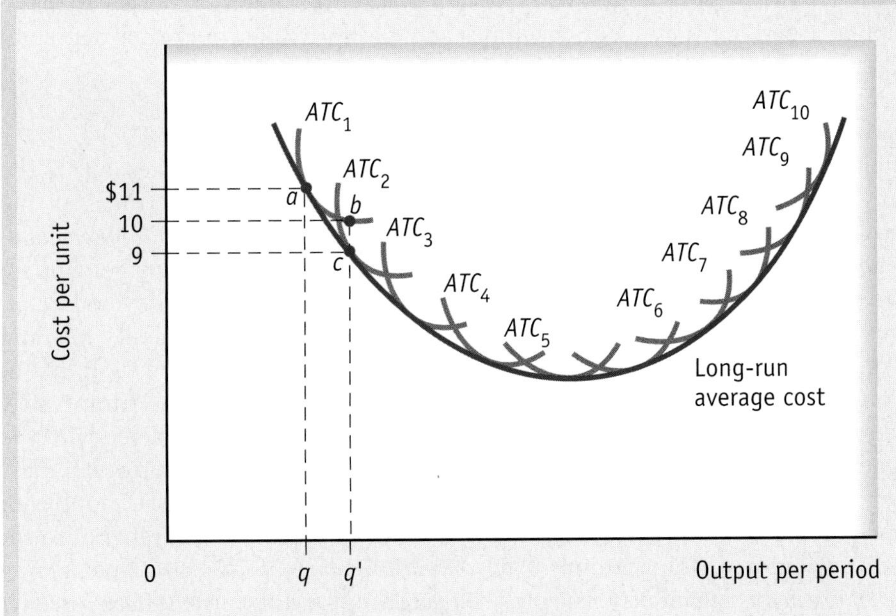

EXHIBIT 9

Family of Many Short-Run Cost Curves Forming a Firm's Long-Run Planning Curve

With many possible plant sizes, the long-run average cost curve is the envelope of portions of the short-run average cost curves. Each short-run curve is tangent to the long-run average cost curve, or long-run planning curve. Each point of tangency represents the least-cost way of producing a particular level of output.

have a lower average cost of production. In fact, for output rate q' at point *b*, the average cost per unit is only \$10, compared to an average cost per unit of \$11 for producing q at point *a*. Point *b* depicts the lowest average cost along ATC_1. So although the point of tangency represents the least-cost way of producing a particular rate of output, it does not in this case represent a least-cost output rate for this particular plant size.

If the firm decides to produce output rate q', which size plant should it choose to minimize the average cost of production? Output rate q' could be produced at point *b*, which represents the minimum average cost along ATC_1. However, the firm could achieve a lower average cost with a larger plant. Specifically, if the firm built a plant of the size associated with ATC_2, the average cost of producing q' would be minimized at \$9 per unit at point *c*. *Each point of tangency between a short-run average cost curve and the long-run average cost curve, or planning curve, represents the least-cost way of producing that particular rate of output.*

Economies of Scale

Economies of scale Forces that cause a reduction in a firm's average cost as the scale of operation increases in the long run

Like short-run average cost curves, the long-run average cost curve is U-shaped. Recall that the shape of the short-run average total cost curve is determined primarily by the law of diminishing marginal returns. A different principle shapes the long-run cost curve. A firm experiences **economies of scale** if long-run average cost falls as output expands. Consider some sources of economies of scale. *A larger size often allows for larger, more specialized machines and greater specialization of labor.* For example, compare a household-sized kitchen of a small restaurant with the kitchen at McDonald's. At low rates of output, say 15 meals a day, the smaller kitchen produces meals at a lower average cost than does McDonald's. But if production in the smaller kitchen increases beyond, say, 100 meals per day, a kitchen on the scale of McDonald's would have a lower average cost. Thus, because of economies of scale, the long-run average cost for a restaurant may fall as firm size increases. A larger scale of operation allows firms to employ larger, more efficient, machines and allows workers a greater degree of specialization.

Diseconomies of Scale

Diseconomies of scale Forces that cause a firm's average cost to increase as the scale of operation increases in the long run

Often another force, called **diseconomies of scale**, eventually takes over as the firm expands, increasing long-run average cost as output expands. As the amount and variety of resources employed increase, so does the *task of coordinating all these inputs*. As the work force grows, additional layers of management are needed to monitor production. In the thicket of bureaucracy that develops, *communication may become garbled*. The top executives have more difficulty keeping in touch with the shop floor because information is distorted as it passes through the chain of command. Indeed, in very large organizations, rumors may become a primary source of information, thereby reducing the efficiency of the organization and increasing average cost. For example, IBM undertook a massive restructuring program because the firm was experiencing diseconomies of scale, particularly in management. IBM's solution was to decentralize into six smaller decision-making groups. *Note that diseconomies of scale result from a larger firm size, whereas diminishing marginal returns result from using more variable resources in a firm of a given size.*

In the long run, the firm can vary the inputs under its control. Some inputs, however, are not under the firm's control, and the inability to vary these inputs may be a source of diseconomies of scale. Consider economies and diseconomies of scale at the movies in the following case study.

At the Movies

CaseStudy

The World of Business

With substantial economies of scale in the movie theater industry, a few chains now operate thousands of theaters. Their corporate Web sites provide information on current plans and include histories of how they grew to be so large. Browse through the following sites: AMC theatres at http://www.amctheatres.com/amc_info/index.html, General Cinema at http://www.generalcinema.com/default.asp?ID=0801, and Regal Cinemas at http://www.regalcinemas.com/corporate/facts.html. Can you find the average number of screens per theater for each corporation? What is a megaplex? Where can megaplexes be found?

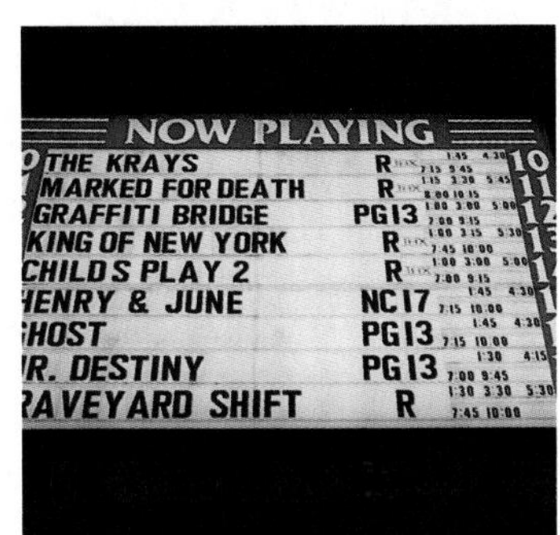

Movie theaters experience both economies and diseconomies of scale. A movie theater with one screen needs someone to sell tickets, someone to operate the concession stand (concession stand sales, incidentally, account for well over half the profit at most theaters), and someone to operate the projector. If another screen is added, the same staff can perform these tasks for both screens. Thus the ticket seller becomes more productive by selling tickets for both movies. Furthermore, construction costs per screen are reduced because only one lobby and one set of rest rooms are required. The theater can run bigger, more noticeable, newspaper advertisements and can spread the cost over more films. This is why we see theater owners adding more and more screens at the same location; they are taking advantage of economies of scale. In the last decade the number of screens in the United States increased from 18,000 to 27,000, or by 50 percent, a rate of increase that exceeded the growth rate in the number of theater locations.

But why stop at, say, 12 screens per movie theater? Why not 20 or 30 screens, particularly in thickly populated urban areas with sufficient demand for such a high rate of output? One problem with expanding the number of screens is that the public roads leading to the theaters are a resource that theaters cannot control. The congestion around the theater grows with the number of screens at that location. Also, the supply of popular films may not be sufficiently large at any one time to fill so many screens.

Finally, time itself is a resource that the firm cannot easily control. Only certain hours are popular with moviegoers. Scheduling becomes more difficult because the manager must space out starting and ending times to avoid the road congestion that occurs when too many customers arrive and depart at the same time. No more additional "prime time" can be created. Thus theater owners lack control over such inputs as the size of public roads, the supply of films, and the amount of "prime time" in the day, and this lack of control may contribute to an increase in the long-run average cost as output expands, or to diseconomies of scale.

Sources: Leonard Klady, "Theaters Scramble to Fit in Summer Pix," *Variety* (6 August 1995); Bruce Orwall, "Cineplex-Leows Merger Is Backed By Regulators, with Theater Sales," *Wall Street Journal* (17 April 1998); William Echikson, "Europe's Film Industry Could Use a Dose of Realism," *Business Week*, International Edition (9 March 1998); and *Statistical Abstract of the United States 1997*, Bureau of the Census, (Hoover's Business Press, 1997), Tables 408 and 418.

It is possible for average cost to neither increase nor decrease with changes in firm size. If neither economies of scale nor diseconomies of scale are apparent, the firm experiences *constant long-run average costs.* Perhaps economies and diseconomies of scale exist simultaneously in such a firm but have offsetting effects.

EXHIBIT 10

A Firm's Long-Run Average Cost Curve

Up to output level *A*, the long-run average cost curve has a negative slope; the firm is experiencing economies of scale. Output level *A* is the minimum efficient scale—the lowest rate of output at which the firm takes full advantage of economies of scale. Between *A* and *B*, the average cost is constant. Beyond output level *B*, the long-run average cost curve has a positive slope, reflecting diseconomies of scale.

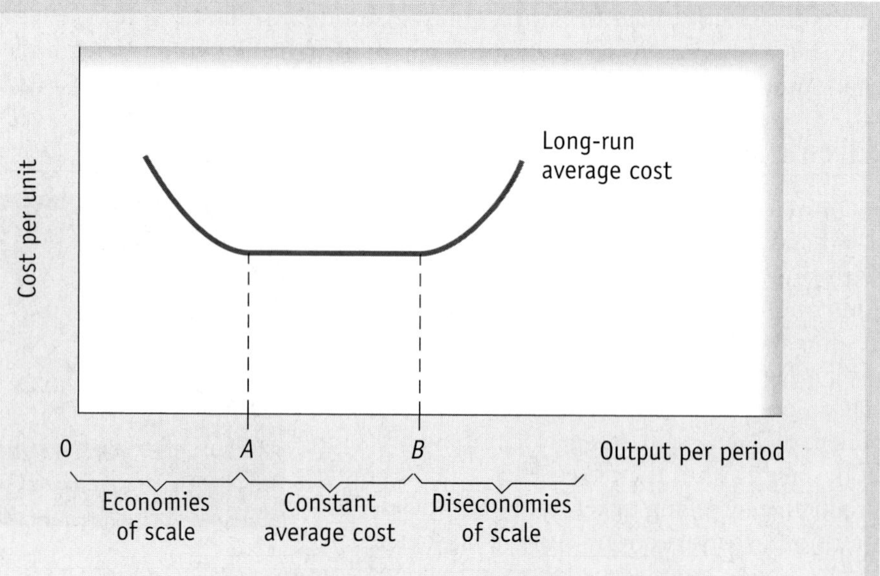

Exhibit 10 presents a firm's long-run average cost curve, which is divided into segments reflecting economies of scale, constant long-run average cost, and diseconomies of scale. The rate of production must reach quantity *A* for the firm to achieve the **minimum efficient scale**, which is the lowest rate of output at which long-run average cost is at a minimum. From output rate *A* to rate *B*, average cost is constant. Beyond output rate *B*, diseconomies of scale increase long-run average cost.

Minimum efficient scale The lowest rate of output at which a firm takes full advantage of economies of scale

Economies and Diseconomies of Scale at the Firm Level

Our discussion so far has referred to a particular plant—a movie theater or a restaurant, for example. But a firm could also be a collection of plants, such as the thousands of McDonald's restaurants. More generally, we can distinguish between economies and diseconomies of scale at the *plant level*—that is, at a particular location—and at the *firm level*, where the firm is a collection of plants. We'll explore issues of multi-plant scale economies and diseconomies in the following case study.

CaseStudy

The World of Business

McDonald's uses the term "corporate alliances" to describe its placement of restaurants in service stations and Wal-marts. View the Web page devoted to this new strategy

Billions and Billions of Burgers

McDonald's experiences economies of scale at the plant, or restaurant, level because of its specialization of labor and machines, but it also benefits from economies of scale at the company level. Experience gained from decades of selling hamburgers can be shared with new managers through centralized management training programs. More efficient production techniques can be shared across thousands of locations. For example, the new campaign "Made for you . . . at the speed of McDonald's," involves new high-tech holding cabinets with special moisture controls to keep cooked beef and chicken patties hot and juicy for up to 20 minutes (it took three years to decide on an exact temperature for the holding cabinets). And the cost of advertising and promoting McDonald's can be spread across the more than 13,000 U.S. locations and the more than 10,000 locations in 110 foreign countries.

Some diseconomies also arise in such large-scale operations. The fact that the menu must be reasonably uniform across thousands of locations means that if customers in some parts of the country or the world do not like a product, it may not get on the menu regardless of its popularity elsewhere. Another problem with a uniform menu is that the ingredients must be available around the world and cannot be subject to droughts or sharp swings in price. One burger chain decided not to add bacon strips as an option on its burgers because the price of pork bellies fluctuated so much.

Because McDonald's has moved aggressively overseas (10 percent of the beef sold in Japan is in McDonald's hamburgers), menu planning has grown increasingly complex. For example, when McDonald's went into Russia, the company had to develop supply sources for beef, potatoes, lettuce, and other ingredients. In some cases, the company had to train farmers to grow products to specifications. Thus when a firm expands to multiple firms and to multiple countries, it experiences both economies of scale and diseconomies of scale.

Change comes slowly in large firms, but it does come. McDonald's in 1997 reorganized its U.S. operation into five regions, allowing managers in each region more leeway in pricing and promotion. McDonald's has also become more flexible by putting mini-restaurants in airports, gas stations, and Wal-Marts. These so-called satellite restaurants recently accounted for half of the company's new U.S. outlets openings. This flexibility in product and pricing across regions and in restaurant structure is an effort by McDonald's officials to overcome some diseconomies of scale.

Sources: Bruce Horovitz, "Re-inventing McDonald's Fast-Food Giant's New Plan: Hot Juicy, Made to Order," *USA Today* (20 February 1998); Richard Gibson and Matt Moffitt, "McDonald's to Expand Overseas, Making a Dynamic Market Push," *Wall Street Journal* (23 October 1997);"McDonald's Testing 'Big Xtra' Hamburger," *Reuters* (27 December 1997); and *Golden Arches East: McDonald's in East Asia*, James L. Watson, ed. Palo Alto, CA: Stanford University Press, 1998). An Internet site featuring McDonald's restaurants in Austria is at http://www.mcdonalds.co.at/mcdonalds/.

at http://www.mcdonalds.com/corporate/alliances/index.html. How many alliances has it developed? McDonald's now reaches the four corners of the globe. Surf the world of McDonald's at http://www.mcdonalds.com/surftheworld/index.html. Since tastes vary, so does the McDonald's menu. Can you find the country where they serve the Rhode Island McFeast Menu? If you can read a foreign language, try to find a McDonald's page for a country where it is spoken.

CONCLUSION

By considering the relationship between production and cost, we have developed the foundations for a theory of firm behavior. The chapter appendix presents an alternative way of determining a firm's most efficient combination of resources. Despite what may appear to be a tangle of short-run and long-run cost curves, *only two relationships between resources and outputs underlie all the curves. In the short run, it is increasing and diminishing returns to the variable resource. In the long run, it is economies and diseconomies of scale.* If you understand the sources of these two phenomena, you have grasped the central ideas of the chapter. Our examination of the relationship between resource use and the amount produced in both the short run and the long run will help us derive an upward-sloping supply curve in the next chapter.

SUMMARY

1. Explicit costs are opportunity costs of a firm's resources that take the form of cash payments. Implicit costs are the opportunity costs of using resources owned by the firm or provided by the firm's owners. A firm is said to be earning a normal profit if total revenue just covers all implicit and explicit costs. Economic profit equals total revenue minus both explicit and implicit costs.

2. Resources that can quickly be varied to increase or decrease the output level are called variable resources. In the short run, at least one resource is fixed. In the long run, all resources are variable.

3. Short-run increases in a variable resource initially may result in increasing marginal returns as the firm takes advantage of increased specialization of the variable resource. The law of diminishing marginal returns indicates that a point is eventually reached where additional units of the variable resource, combined with the fixed resources, yield an ever-smaller marginal product.

4. The law of diminishing marginal returns is the most important feature of production in the short run and explains why the marginal cost curve eventually slopes upward as output expands. The law of diminishing marginal returns also explains why average cost eventually increases as output increases in the short run.

5. In the long run, all inputs under the firm's control are variable, so there are no fixed costs. The firm's long-run average cost curve is an envelope formed by a series of short-run average total cost curves. The long run is best thought of as a planning horizon.

6. In the long run, the firm selects the most efficient size for the desired rate of output. Once the size of the firm has been selected and resources have been committed, some resources become fixed, so the firm is back operating in the short run. Thus the firm plans for the long run but produces in the short run.

7. The long-run average cost curve, like the short-run average total cost curve, is U-shaped. As output expands, average cost at first declines because of economies of scale—a larger plant size allows for more specialized machinery and a more extensive division of labor. Eventually, average cost stops falling. Average cost may be constant over some range. If output expands still further, the plant may encounter diseconomies of scale as the cost of coordinating resources grows.

QUESTIONS FOR REVIEW

1. *(Explicit and Implicit Costs)* Amos McCoy is currently raising corn on his 100-acre farm and earning an accounting profit of $100 per acre. However, if he raised soybeans, he could earn $200 per acre. Is he currently earning an economic profit? Why or why not?

2. *(Explicit and Implicit Costs)* Determine whether each of the following is an explicit or an implicit cost:
   a. Payments for labor purchased in the labor market
   b. A firm's use of a warehouse that it owns and that could be rented to another firm
   c. Rent paid for the use of a warehouse not owned by the firm
   d. The wages that owners could earn if they did not work for themselves

3. *(Alternative Measures of Profit)* Calculate the accounting profit or loss as well as the economic profit or loss in each of the following situations:
   a. A firm with total revenues of $150 million, explicit cost of $90 million, and implicit costs of $40 million
   b. A firm with total revenues of $125 million, explicit cost of $100 million, and implicit costs of $30 million
   c. A firm with total revenues of $100 million, explicit cost of $90 million, and implicit costs of $20 million
   d. A firm with total revenues of $250,000, explicit cost of $275,000, and implicit costs of $50,000

4. *(Alternative Measures of Profit)* Why is it reasonable to think of normal profit as a type of cost to the firm?

5. *(Short Run Versus Long Run)* What distinguishes a firm's short-run period from its long-run period?

6. *(Law of Diminishing Marginal Returns)* As a farmer, you must decide how many times during the year you will plant a new crop. Also, you must decide how far apart to space the plants. Will diminishing returns be a factor in your decision making? If so, how will it affect your decisions?

7. *(Marginal Cost)* What is the difference between fixed cost and variable cost? Do both types of costs affect short-run marginal cost? If yes, explain how each affects marginal cost. If no, explain why each does or does not affect marginal cost.

8. *(Marginal Cost)* Explain why the marginal cost of production *must* increase if the marginal product of the variable resource is decreasing.

9. *(Costs in the Short Run)* What effect would each of the following have on a firm's short-run marginal cost curve and its total fixed cost curve?
   a. An increase in the wage rate
   b. A decrease in property taxes
   c. A rise in the purchase price of new capital
   d. A rise in energy prices

10. *(Costs in the Short Run)* Identify each of the curves in the following graph:

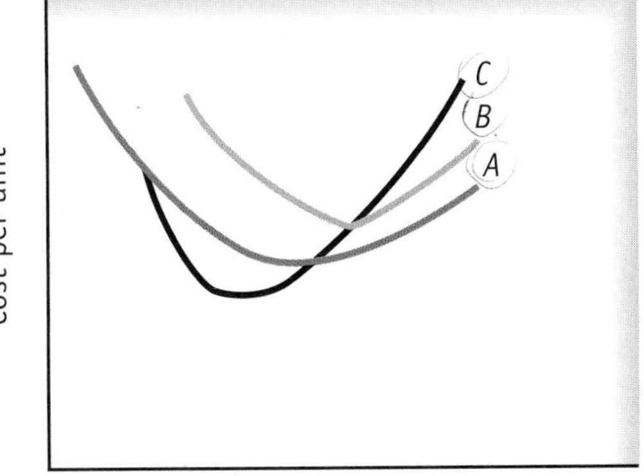

11. *(Marginal Cost and Average Cost)* Explain why the marginal cost curve must intersect the average total cost curve and the average variable cost curve at their minimum points. Why do the average total cost and average variable cost curves approach one another as output increases?

12. *(Marginal and Average Cost)* In Exhibit 7 in this chapter, the output level where average total cost is at a minimum is greater than the output level where average variable cost is at a minimum. Why is this the case?

13. *(Long-Run Average Cost Curve)* What types of changes could shift the long-run average cost curve? How would these changes also affect the short-run average total cost curve?

14. *(Long-Run Average Cost Curve)* Explain the shape of the long-run average cost curve. What does "minimum efficient scale" mean?

15. *(**CaseStudy:** At the Movies)* The case study notes that the concession stand accounts for well over half the profits at most theaters. Given this, what are the benefits of the staggered movie times allowed by multiple screens? What is the benefit to a multiscreen theater of locating at a shopping mall?

16. *(**CaseStudy:** Billions and Billions of Burgers)* How does having a menu that is uniform around the country provide McDonald's with economies of scale? Why is menu planning made more complex by expanding into other countries?

PROBLEMS AND EXERCISES

17. *(Production in the Short Run)* Complete the following table. At what point do diminishing marginal returns set in?

Units of the Variable Resource	Total Product	Marginal Product
0	0	—
1	10	____
2	22	____
3	____	9
4	____	4
5	34	____

18. *(Total Cost and Marginal Cost)* Complete the following table, assuming that each unit of labor costs $75 per day.

Quantity of Labor per Day	Output per Day	Fixed Cost	Variable Cost	Total Cost	Marginal Cost
0	____	$300	$____	$____	$____
1	5	____	75	____	15
2	11	____	150	450	12.5
3	15	____	____	525	____
4	18	____	300	600	25
5	20	____	____	____	37.5

a. Graph the fixed cost, variable cost, and total cost curves for these data.
b. What is the marginal product of going from two to three units of labor?
c. What is average total cost when output is 18 units per day?

19. *(Total Cost and Marginal Cost)* Complete the following table, where *L* is units of labor, *Q* is units of output and MP is the marginal product of labor.

L	Q	MP	VC	TC	MC	ATC
0	0	____	$ 0	$12	____	____
1	6	____	3	15	____	____
2	15	____	6	____	____	____
3	21	____	9	____	____	____
4	24	____	12	____	____	____
5	26	____	15	____	____	____

a. At what level of labor input do the marginal returns to labor begin to diminish?
b. What is the average variable cost when $Q = 24$?
c. What is this firm's fixed cost?
d. What is the wage rate?

20. *(Relationship Between Marginal Cost and Average Cost)* Assume that labor and capital are the only inputs used by a firm. Capital is fixed at 5 units, which cost $100 each. Workers can be hired for $200 each. Complete the following table to show average variable cost (AVC), average total cost (ATC), and marginal cost (MC).

Quantity of Labor	Total Output	AVC	ATC	MC
0	0	____	____	____
1	100	____	____	____
2	250	____	____	____
3	350	____	____	____
4	400	____	____	____
5	425	____	____	____

21. *(Long-Run Costs)* Suppose that a firm has only three possible scales of production, as shown below.

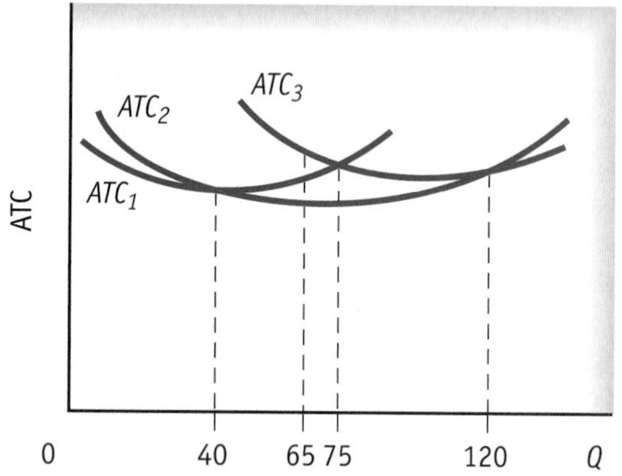

a. Which scale of production is best when $Q = 65$?
b. Which scale of production is best when $Q = 75$?
c. Trace out the long-run average cost curve on the diagram.

EXPERIENTIAL EXERCISES

22. *(Short- and Long-Run Costs)* The terms "diminishing returns" and "economies of scale" are often referred to in everyday discussions and in the popular press. Using an Internet search engine, search for the "diminishing returns" or for "economies of scale." Check the first five sites you find and, in each case, decide whether the term is being used correctly or incorrectly. If the latter, see if you can determine the nature of the writer's confusion. For example, check "The Concepts of Diminishing and Increasing Returns" (http://www.useit.com/alertbox/increasingreturns.html), in which the author manages to compare a short-run concept—diminishing (marginal) returns—with a long-run concept—increasing returns (to scale).

23. *(Costs in the Long Run)* Find Erik Brynjolfsson and Shinkyu Yang's "Information Technology and Productivity: A Review of the Literature," available on-line at http://ccs.mit.edu/ccswp202/. Using the concepts you learned in this chapter, try to explain the expected long-run impact of information technology on productivity and costs.

24. *(Wall Street Journal)* A firm's cost curves are based on the prices of the inputs it uses and on the firm's technology. Technology is the way the inputs are combined to produce a product. The "Technology" column in the Marketplace section of the *Wall Street Journal* describes many interesting technological innovations. Pick one and see if you can determine how it might affect a firm's cost curves. Will it cause one resource to be substituted in place of another? Try to guess both the short-run and long-run effects.

Appendix

A CLOSER LOOK AT PRODUCTION AND COSTS

This appendix develops a model for determining how a profit-maximizing firm will combine resources to produce a particular amount of output. The quantity of output that can be produced with a given amount of resources depends on the existing *state of technology,* which is the prevailing knowledge of how resources can be combined. Therefore, let's begin by considering the technological possibilities available to the firm.

THE PRODUCTION FUNCTION AND EFFICIENCY

The ways in which resources can be combined to produce output are summarized by a firm's production function. The *production function* identifies the maximum quantities of a particular good or service that can be produced per time period with various combinations of resources, for a given level of technology. The production function can be presented as an equation, a graph, or a table.

The production function summarized in Exhibit 11 reflects, for a hypothetical firm, the output resulting from particular combinations of resources. This firm uses only two resources: capital and labor. The amount of capital used is listed in the left-hand column of the table, and the amount of labor employed is listed across the top. For example, if 1 unit of capital is combined with 7 units of labor, the firm can produce 290 units of output per month.

The firm produces the maximum possible output given the combination of resources employed; that same output could not be produced with fewer resources. Since the production function combines resources efficiently, 290 units is the most that can be produced with 7 units of labor and 1 unit of capital. Thus we say that production is **technologically efficient.**

We can examine the effects of adding additional labor to an existing amount of capital by starting with any level of capital and reading across the table. For example, when 1 unit of capital and 1 unit of labor are employed, the firm produces 40 units of output per month. If the amount of labor is increased by 1 unit and the amount of capital employed is held constant, output increases to 90 units, so the marginal product of labor is 50 units. If the amount of labor employed increases from 2 to 3 units, other things constant, output goes to 150 units, yielding a marginal product of 60 units. By reading across the table, you will discover that the marginal product of labor first rises, showing increasing marginal returns from the variable resource (labor), and then declines, showing diminishing marginal returns. Similarly, by holding the amount of labor constant and following down the column, you will find that the marginal product of capital also reflects first increasing marginal returns, then diminishing marginal returns.

EXHIBIT 11

A Firm's Production Function Using Labor and Capital: Production per Month

Units of Capital Employed per Month	Units of Labor Employed per Month						
	1	2	3	4	5	6	7
1	40	90	150	200	240	270	290
2	90	140	200	250	290	315	335
3	150	195	260	310	345	370	390
4	200	250	310	350	385	415	440
5	240	290	345	385	420	450	475
6	270	320	375	415	450	475	495
7	290	330	390	435	470	495	510

ISOQUANTS

Notice from the tabular presentation of the production function in Exhibit 11 that some different combinations of resources yield the same rate of output. For example, several combinations of labor and capital yield 290 units of output per month. (Try to find all four combinations.) Some of the information provided in Exhibit 11 can be presented more clearly in graphical form. In Exhibit 12, the quantity of labor employed is measured along the horizontal axis and the quantity of capital along the vertical axis. Combinations that yield 290 units of output are presented in Exhibit 12 as points *a, b, c,* and *d*. These points can be connected to form an *isoquant,* Q_1, which shows the possible combinations of the two resources that produce 290 units of output per month. Likewise, Q_2 shows combinations of inputs that yield 415 units of output, and Q_3 shows combinations that yield 475 units of output. (The colors of the isoquants match those of the corresponding entries in the production function table in Exhibit 11.)

An **isoquant**, such as Q_1 in Exhibit 12, is a curve that shows all the technologically efficient combinations of two resources, such as labor and capital, that produce a certain rate of output. *Iso* is from the Greek word meaning "equal," and *quant* is short for "quantity"; so *isoquant* means "equal quantity." Along a particular isoquant, such as Q_1, the rate of output produced remains constant, in this case 290 units per month, but the combinations of resources vary. To produce a particular rate of output, the firm can use resource combinations ranging from much capital and little labor to much labor and little capital. For example, a paving contractor can put in a new driveway with 10 workers using shovels, wheelbarrows, and hand rollers; the same job can also be done with only 2 workers, a road grader, and a paving machine. A Saturday-afternoon charity car wash to raise money to send the school band to Disney World is labor-intensive, involving perhaps a dozen workers per car, plus buckets, sponges, and hose. In contrast, a professional car wash is fully automated, requiring only one worker to turn on the machine and collect the money. An isoquant shows such alternative combinations of resources for producing the same rate of output. Let's consider some properties of isoquants.

EXHIBIT 12

Isoquants

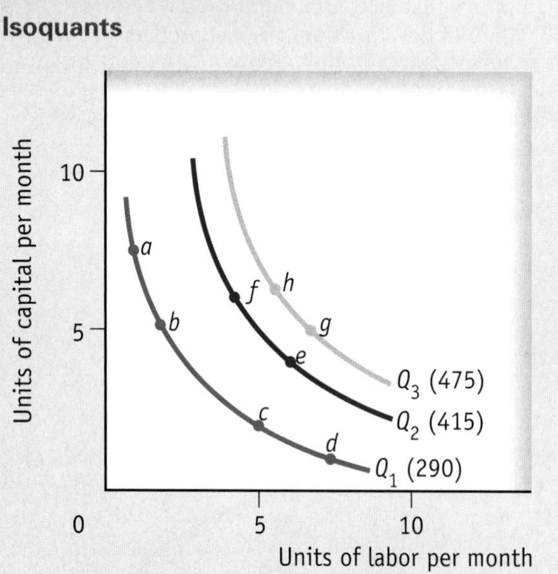

Isoquant Q_1 shows all technologically efficient combinations of labor and capital that can be used to produce 290 units of output. Isoquant Q_2 is drawn for 415 units, and Q_3 for 475 units. Each isoquant has a negative slope and is convex to the origin.

Isoquants Farther from the Origin Represent Greater Output Rates Although we have included only three isoquants in Exhibit 12, there is a different isoquant for every quantity of output depicted in Exhibit 11. Indeed, there is a different isoquant for every output rate the firm could possibly produce, with isoquants farther from the origin indicating higher rates of output.

Isoquants Slope Down to the Right Along a given isoquant, the quantity of labor employed is inversely related to the quantity of capital employed, so isoquants have negative slopes.

Isoquants Do Not Intersect Since each isoquant refers to a specific rate of output, no two isoquants intersect, for such an intersection would indicate that the same combination of resources could, with equal efficiency, produce two different amounts of output.

Isoquants Are Usually Convex to the Origin Isoquants are usually convex to the origin, meaning that any isoquant gets flatter as you move down along the curve. The slope of an isoquant measures the ability of additional units of one resource—in this case, labor—to substitute in production for another—in this case, capital. As noted already, the isoquant has a negative slope. The absolute value of the slope of the isoquant is the **marginal rate of technical substitution,** or **MRTS,** between two resources. The MRTS is the rate at which labor can be substituted for capital without affecting output. When much capital and little labor are used, the marginal productivity of labor is relatively great and the marginal productivity of capital is relatively small, so one unit of labor will substitute for a relatively large amount of capital. For example, in moving from point *a* to *b* along isoquant Q_1 in Exhibit 12, 1 unit of labor substitutes for 2 units of capital, so the MRTS between points *a* and *b* equals 2. But as more labor and less capital are employed, the marginal product of labor declines and the marginal product of capital increases, so it takes more labor to make up for a one-unit reduction in capital. For example, in moving from point *c* to point *d* in Exhibit 12, 2 units of labor substitute for 1 unit of capital; hence, the MRTS between points *c* and *d* equals $\frac{1}{2}$.

The extent to which one input substitutes for another, as measured by the marginal rate of technical substitution, is directly linked to the marginal productivity of each input. For example, between points *a* and *b,* 1 unit of labor replaces 2 units of capital, yet output remains constant. So labor's marginal product, MP_L—that is, the additional output resulting from an additional unit of labor—must be twice as large as capital's marginal product, MP_C. In fact, *anywhere along the isoquant, the marginal rate of technical substitution of labor for capital equals the marginal product of labor divided by the marginal product of capital, which also equals the absolute value of the slope of the isoquant.* Thus we can say that

$$|\text{Slope of isoquant}| = \text{MRTS} = MP_L/MP_C$$

where the vertical lines on either side of "Slope of isoquant" mean the absolute value. For example, between points *a* and *b* the slope equals -2, which has an absolute value of 2, which equals the marginal rate of substitution of labor for capital and the ratio of marginal productivities. Between points *b* and *c*, 3 units of labor substitute for 3 units of capital, while holding output constant at 290. Thus, the slope between *b* and *c* is $-3/3$, for an absolute value of 1. Note that the absolute value of the isoquant's slope declines as we move down the curve because larger increases in labor are required to offset the decline in capital. Put another way, as less capital is employed, its marginal product increases, and as more labor is employed, its marginal product decreases.

If labor and capital were perfect substitutes in production, the rate at which labor substituted for capital would remain fixed along the isoquant, so the isoquant would be a downward-sloping straight line. Since most resources are *not* perfect substitutes, however, the rate at which one substitutes for another changes along an isoquant. As we move down along an isoquant, more labor is required to offset each 1-unit decline in capital, so the isoquant gets flatter, yielding an isoquant that is convex to the origin.

Let's summarize the properties of isoquants.

1. *Isoquants farther from the origin represent higher rates of output.*
2. *Isoquants slope downward.*
3. *Isoquants never intersect.*
4. *Isoquants are bowed toward the origin.*

ISOCOST LINES

Isoquants graphically illustrate a firm's production function for all quantities of output the firm could possibly produce. Given these isoquants, how much should the firm produce? But here we are interested in what combination of resources should be employed to minimize the cost of producing a given rate of output. The answer depends on the cost of resources.

Suppose a unit of labor costs the firm \$1,500 per month, and a unit of capital costs \$2,500 per month. The total cost (TC) of production is

$$TC = (w \times L) + (r \times C)$$
$$= \$1{,}500L + \$2{,}500C$$

where w is the monthly wage rate, L is the quantity of labor employed, r is the monthly cost of capital, and C is the quantity of capital employed. An **isocost line** identifies all combinations of capital and labor the firm can hire for a given total cost. Again, *iso* is Greek for "equal," so an isocost line is a line representing resource combinations of equal cost. In Exhibit 13, for example, the line $TC = \$15{,}000$ identifies all combinations of labor and capital that cost the firm a total of \$15,000. The entire \$15,000 could pay for 6 units of capital per month; if the entire budget is spent on only labor, 10 workers per month could be hired; or the firm could employ any other combination of resources along the isocost line.

Recall that the slope of any line is the vertical change between two points on the line divided by the corresponding horizontal change. At the point where the isocost line meets the vertical axis, the quantity of capital that can be purchased equals the total cost divided by the monthly cost of a unit of

EXHIBIT 13

Firm's Isocost Lines

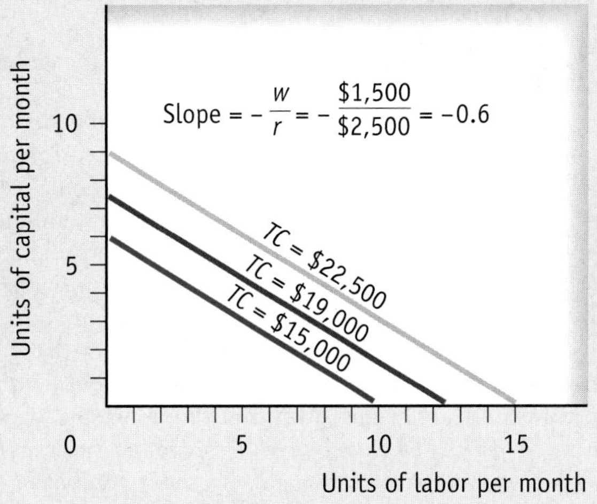

Each Isocost line shows combinations of labor and capital that can be purchased for a fixed amount of total cost. The slope of each is equal to minus the wage rate divided by the rental rate of capital. Higher levels of cost are represented by isocost lines farther from the origin.

capital, or TC/r. At the point where the isocost line meets the horizontal axis, the quantity of labor that can be hired equals the firm's total cost divided by the monthly wage, or TC/w. The slope of any isocost line in Exhibit 13 can be calculated by considering a movement from the vertical intercept to the horizontal intercept. That is, we divide the vertical change $(-TC/r)$ by the horizontal change (TC/w), as follows:

$$\text{Slope of isocost line} = -\frac{TC/r}{TC/w} = -\frac{w}{r}$$

The slope of the isocost line equals minus the price of labor divided by the price of capital, or $-w/r$, which indicates the relative prices of the inputs. In our example, the absolute value of the slope of the isocost line equals w/r, or

$$|\text{Slope of isocost line}| = w/r$$
$$= 1{,}500/2{,}500$$
$$= 0.6$$

The wage rate of labor is 0.6 of the monthly cost of a unit of capital, so hiring one more unit of labor, without incurring any additional cost, implies that the firm must employ 0.6 fewer units of capital.

A firm is not confined to a particular isocost line. This is why in Exhibit 13 we include three isocost lines, each corresponding to a different total budget. In fact, there is a different isocost line for every possible budget. *These isocost lines are parallel because each reflects the same relative resource price.* Resource prices in our example are assumed to be constant regardless of the amount of each resource the firm employs.

Optimal Combinations of Inputs

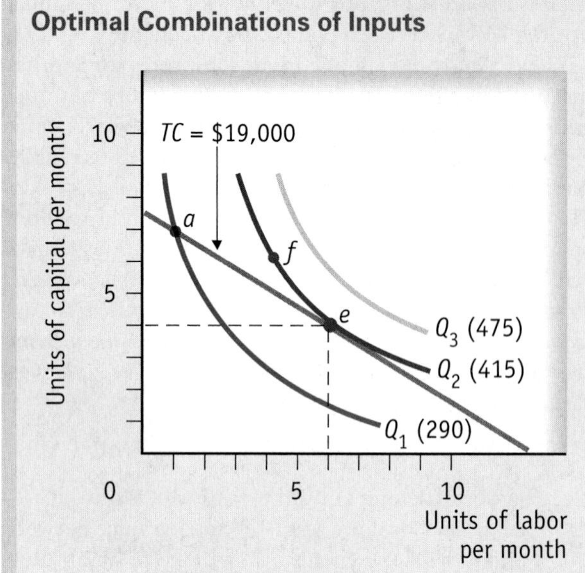

At point e, isoquant Q_2 is tangent to the isocost line. The optimal combination of inputs is 6 units of labor and 4 units of capital. The maximum output that can be produced for \$19,000 is 415 units. Alternatively, point e determines the minimum-cost way of producing 415 units of output.

THE CHOICE OF INPUT COMBINATIONS

We bring the isoquants and the isocost lines together in Exhibit 14. Suppose the firm has decided to produce 415 units of output and wants to minimize the total cost of doing so. It could select point f, where 6 units of capital are combined with 4 units of labor. This combination, however, would cost \$21,000 at prevailing prices. Since the profit-maximizing firm wants to produce its chosen output at the minimum cost, it tries to find the isocost line closest to the origin that still touches the isoquant. At a point of tangency, a movement in either direction along an isoquant shifts the firm to a higher cost. So *the point of tangency between the isocost line and the isoquant shows the minimum cost required to produce a given output.*

Look at what's going on at the point of tangency. At point e in Exhibit 14, the isoquant and the isocost line have the same slope. As mentioned already, the absolute value of the slope of an isoquant equals the *marginal rate of technical substitution* between labor and capital, and the absolute value of the slope of the isocost line equals the *ratio of the input prices*. So when a firm produces output in the least costly way, the marginal rate of technical substitution must equal the ratio of the resource prices, or

$$\text{MRTS} = w/r = 1{,}500/2{,}500 = 0.6$$

This equality shows that the firm adjusts resource use so that the rate at which one input can be substituted for another in production—that is, the marginal rate of technical substitution—equals the rate at which one resource can be exchanged for another in resource markets, which is w/r. If this equality does not hold, the firm could adjust its input mix to produce the same output for a lower cost.

THE EXPANSION PATH

Imagine a set of isoquants representing each possible rate of output. Given the relative cost of resources, we could then draw isocost lines to determine the optimal combination of resources for producing each rate of output. The points of tangency in Exhibit 15 show the least-cost input combinations for producing several output rates. For example, output rate Q_2 can be produced most cheaply using C units of capital and L units of labor. The line formed by connecting these tangency points is the firm's **expansion path**. The expansion path need not be a straight line, although it will generally slope upward, implying that firms will expand the use of both resources in

EXHIBIT 15

Isoquants

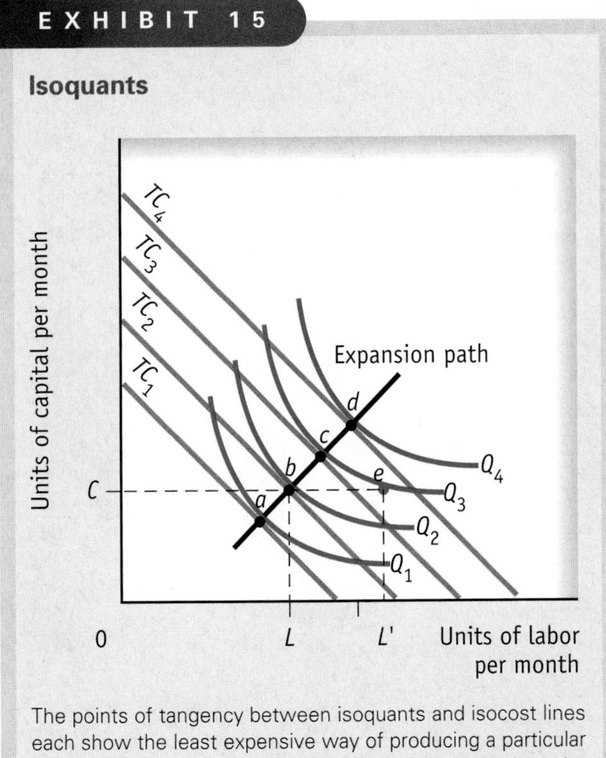

The points of tangency between isoquants and isocost lines each show the least expensive way of producing a particular level of output. Connecting these tangency points gives the firm's expansion path.

the long run as output increases. Note that we have assumed that the prices of inputs remain constant as the firm varies output along the expansion path, so the isocost lines at the points of tangency are parallel—that is, they have the same slope.

The expansion path indicates the lowest long-run total cost for each rate of output. For example, the firm can produce output rate Q_2 for TC_2, output rate Q_3 for TC_3, and so on. Similarly, the firm's long-run average cost curve indicates, at each rate of output, the total cost divided by the rate of output. The firm's expansion path and the firm's long-run average cost curve represent alternative ways of portraying costs in the long run, given resource prices and technology.

We can use Exhibit 15 to distinguish between short-run and long-run adjustments in output. Let's begin with the firm producing Q_2 at point *b*, which requires *C* units of capital and *L* units of labor. Now suppose that in the short run, the firm wants to expand output to Q_3. Since capital is fixed in the short run, the only way to expand output to Q_3 is by increasing the quantity of labor employed to *L'*, which requires moving to point *e* in Exhibit 15. Point *e* is not the cheapest way to produce Q_3 in the long run, for it is not a tangency point. In the long run, capital usage is variable, and if the firm wishes to produce Q_3, it should adjust capital and shift from point *e* to point *c*, thereby minimizing the total cost of producing Q_3.

One final point: If the relative prices of resources change, the least-cost combination of those resources will also change, so the firm's expansion path will change. For example, if the price of labor increases, capital becomes cheaper relative to labor. The efficient production of any given rate of output will therefore call for less labor and more capital. With the cost of labor higher, the firm's total cost for each rate of output rises. Such a cost increase would also be reflected by an upward shift in the average total cost curve.

SUMMARY

A firm's *production function* specifies the relationship between resource use and output, given prevailing technology. An *isoquant* is a curve that illustrates the possible combinations of resources that will produce a particular rate of output. An *isocost* line presents the combinations of resources the firm can employ, given resource prices and the firm's total budget.

For a given rate of output—that is, for a given isoquant—the firm minimizes its total cost by choosing the lowest isocost line that just touches, or is tangent to, the isoquant. The least-cost combination of resources will depend on the productivity of resources and the relative cost of resources.

APPENDIX QUESTIONS

1. *(Choice of Input Combination)* Suppose that a firm's cost per unit of labor is \$100 per day and its cost per unit of capital is \$400 per day.
   a. Draw the isocost line for a total cost per day of \$2000.
   b. If this firm is producing efficiently, what is the marginal rate of technical substitution between labor and capital?
   c. Demonstrate your answer to part (b) using isocost lines and isoquant curves.
2. *(The Expansion Path)* How are the expansion path and the long-run average cost curve related?

CHAPTER

21 Perfect Competition

What does a bushel of wheat have in common with a share of Amazon.com stock? Why might a firm continue to operate even though it's losing money? Why do firms, even in the most competitive of industries, sometimes earn economic profit? In what sense can it be said that the more competitive the industry, the less individual firms compete with each other? To answer these and other questions, we examine our first market structure, perfect competition.

The previous chapter developed cost curves for an individual firm in both the short run and the long run. In light of these costs, how much should a firm produce and what price should it charge? To discover the firm's profit-maximizing output and price, we revisit an old friend: demand. Demand and production costs, or supply, together guide the firm to maximum economic profit.

Visit the McEachern Interactive Study Center for this chapter at *http://mcisc.swcollege.com*

In the next few chapters we will examine how firms respond to their economic environments in deciding what to produce, in what quantities, and at what price. No matter what the market structure, we assume that firms try to maximize economic profit. Topics discussed in this chapter include:

- Market structure
- Price takers
- Marginal revenue
- Golden rule of profit maximization
- Loss minimization
- Firm and industry short-run supply curve
- Industry's long-run supply curve
- Competition and efficiency
- Producer surplus
- Gains from exchange

AN INTRODUCTION TO PERFECT COMPETITION

First, a few words about terminology. An industry consists of all firms that supply output to a particular market, such as the auto market, the shoe market, or the wheat market. The terms *industry* and *market* are used interchangeably throughout this chapter. Many of the firm's decisions depend on the structure of the market in which it operates. **Market structure** describes the important features of a market, such as the number of firms (are there many or few?), the product's degree of uniformity (do firms in the market supply identical products or are there differences across firms?), the ease of entry into the market (can new firms enter easily or are they blocked by natural or artificial barriers?), and the forms of competition among firms (do firms compete only through prices or are advertising and product differentiation common as well?). The various features will become clearer as we examine each type of market structure in the next few chapters.

Market structure Important features of a market, such as the number of firms, uniformity of product among firms, ease of entry and exit, and forms of competition

Perfectly Competitive Market Structure

We begin with **perfect competition,** in some ways the most basic of market structures. A *perfectly competitive* market is characterized by the following: (1) there are many buyers and sellers, so many that each buys or sells only a tiny fraction of the total amount exchanged in the market; (2) firms sell a standardized, or *homogeneous,* product such as bushels of wheat or a share of Amazon.com stock; (3) buyers and sellers are fully informed about the price and availability of all resources and products; and (4) firms and resources are freely mobile—that is, over time they can easily enter or leave the industry, with no obstacles to block entry or exit, such as patents, licenses, high capital costs, or ignorance about available technology.

Perfect competition A market structure in which there are large numbers of fully informed buyers and sellers of a homogeneous product, with no obstacles to entry or exit of firms in the long run

If these conditions are present in a market, individual participants have no control over the price. Price is determined by market supply and demand. A perfectly competitive firm is called a **price taker** because it must "take," or accept, the market price—as in "take it or leave it." Once the market establishes the price, each individual firm is free to supply whatever amount maximizes that firm's profit. A perfectly competitive firm is so small relative to the size of the market that the firm's choice of what quantity to supply has no perceptible effect on the market price.

Price taker A firm that faces a given market price and whose actions have no effect on that market price

Examples of perfectly competitive markets include markets for stocks and bonds; markets for basic commodities such as gold and silver; markets for foreign exchange; and markets for most agricultural products such as wheat, corn, and livestock. Again, there are so many buyers and sellers that the actions of any one cannot influence the market price. For example, about 150,000 farmers in the United States raise hogs.

The model of perfect competition allows us to make a number of predictions that hold up when we examine the real world. Perfect competition is also an important benchmark for evaluating the efficiency of other types of markets. Let's look at demand under perfect competition.

Demand Under Perfect Competition

Suppose the market in question is the world market for wheat and the firm in question is a wheat farm. In the world market for wheat, there are tens of thousands of farms, so any one farm produces only a tiny fraction of market output. For example, the thousands of wheat farmers in Kansas together produce less than 3 percent of the world's supply of wheat.

In Exhibit 1, the market price of wheat of $5 per bushel is determined in panel (a) by the intersection of the market demand curve, *D*, and the market supply curve, *S*. Once the market price is established, any farmer can sell all he or she wants at that market price. *The demand curve as it appears to an individual farmer is therefore a horizontal line drawn at the market price.* In our example, the demand curve facing the farmer, identified as *d* in panel (b), is drawn at the market price of $5 per bushel, indicating that this farmer can sell any quantity he or she desires at the market price. Thus each farmer faces a horizontal, or *perfectly elastic*, demand curve.

Each farm is so small relative to the market that each has no impact on the market price; each farmer is a *price taker*. Because all farmers supply identical goods, bushels of wheat in this case, anyone who charges more than the market

EXHIBIT 1

Market Equilibrium and the Firm's Demand Curve in Perfect Competition

(a) Market equilibrium

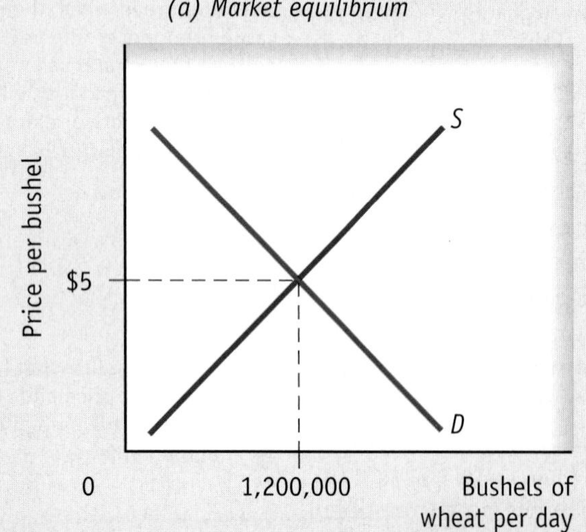

(b) Firm's demand

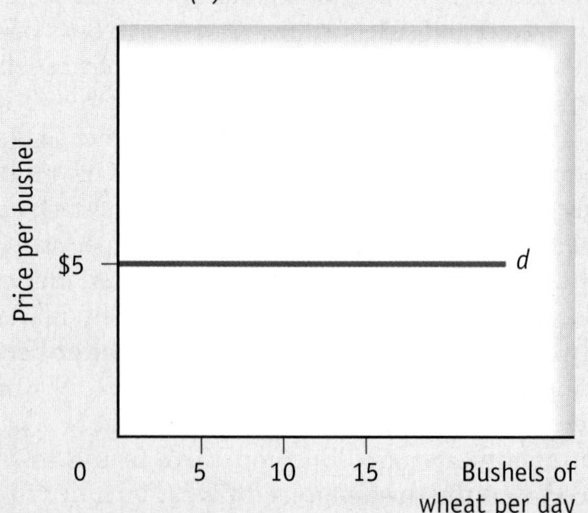

In panel (a), the market price of $5 is determined by the intersection of the market demand and supply curves. The individual perfectly competitive firm can sell any amount at that price. The demand curve facing the competitive firm is horizontal at the market price, as shown by demand curve *d* in panel (b).

price will sell no output. For example, if a farmer charged $5.25 per bushel, buyers would simply turn to other suppliers. Of course, any farmer is free to charge less than the market price, but why do that when all wheat can be sold at the market price? Farmers are not stupid; if they were, they would not last long.

It has been said, "In perfect competition there is no competition." Ironically, two neighboring wheat farmers in perfect competition are not really rivals. They both sell as much wheat as they want to at the market price. The amount one sells has no effect on the price the other receives.

SHORT-RUN PROFIT MAXIMIZATION

We assume that firms (farms are the firms in this example) try to maximize economic profit. Firms that ignore this strategy will not be around long. Economic profit equals total revenue minus total opportunity cost, including both explicit and implicit costs. Implicit cost, you will recall, is the opportunity cost of resources owned by the firm and includes a normal profit; economic profit is any profit above normal profit. How do firms maximize profit? You have already learned that the perfectly competitive firm has no control over price. What the firm does control is the amount produced, the rate of output. The question then boils down to: *What rate of output will maximize economic profit?*

Total Revenue Minus Total Cost

The firm maximizes economic profit by finding the rate of output at which total revenue exceeds total cost by the greatest amount. Total revenue for a perfectly competitive firm is simply the rate of output times the price per unit. Column (1) in Exhibit 2 shows an individual farmer's output possibilities in bushels of wheat per day. Column (2) shows the market price per bushel of $5, a price that does not vary with output. Column (3) shows total revenue, which is output times price, or column (1) times column (2). And column (4) shows the total cost of output. Total cost already includes a normal profit, so total cost includes all opportunity costs. Although the exhibit does not distinguish between fixed and variable costs, fixed cost must equal $15 per day, since total cost is $15 when output is zero. The fact that this farm incurs a fixed cost indicates that at least one resource must be fixed, so the farm must be operating in the short run.

Total revenue in column (3) minus total cost in column (4) yields the economic profit or economic loss per period, which is presented in column (7). As you can see, at low and high rates of output, total cost exceeds total revenue, so the farm incurs an *economic loss* at low and high rates of output. Between 7 and 14 bushels per day, total revenue exceeds total cost, so the farm earns an *economic profit.* Economic profit is maximized at $12 per day when the farm produces 12 bushels of wheat per day (the $12 and 12 bushel combination is just a coincidence).

These results are graphed in panel (a) of Exhibit 3, which shows the total revenue and total cost curves. As output increases by 1 bushel, total revenue increases by $5, so the farm's total revenue curve is a straight line emanating from the origin, with a slope of 5. The short-run total cost curve has a backward S shape reflecting first increasing marginal returns, then diminishing marginal returns from changes in the amount of variable resource employed. Total cost

EXHIBIT 2

Short-Run Costs and Revenues for a Perfectly Competitive Firm

Bushels of Wheat per day (q) (1)	Marginal Revenue (Price) (p) (2)	Total Revenue ($TR = q \times p$) (3) = (1) × (2)	Total Cost (TC) (4)	Marginal Cost $\left(MC = \frac{\Delta TC}{\Delta q}\right)$ (5)	Average Total Cost $\left(ATC = \frac{TC}{q}\right)$ (6) = (4) ÷ (1)	Economic Profit or Loss = $TR - TC$ (7) = (3) − (4)
0	—	$ 0	$15.00	—	∞	−$15.00
1	$5	5	19.75	$ 4.75	$19.75	−14.75
2	5	10	23.50	3.75	11.75	−13.50
3	5	15	26.50	3.00	8.83	−11.50
4	5	20	29.00	2.50	7.25	−9.00
5	5	25	31.00	2.00	6.20	−6.00
6	5	30	32.50	1.50	5.42	−2.50
7	5	35	33.75	1.25	4.82	1.25
8	5	40	35.25	1.50	4.41	4.75
9	5	45	37.25	2.00	4.14	7.75
10	5	50	40.00	2.75	4.00	10.00
11	5	55	43.25	3.25	3.93	11.75
12	**5**	**60**	**48.00**	**4.75**	**4.00**	**12.00**
13	5	65	54.50	6.50	4.19	10.50
14	5	70	64.00	9.50	4.57	6.00
15	5	75	77.50	13.50	5.17	−2.50
16	5	80	96.00	18.50	6.00	−16.00

always increases as the rate of output expands. Note that the shape of the total cost curve is independent of the market structure.

Comparing total revenue and total cost is one way to find the profit-maximizing rate of output. At rates of output less than 7 bushels or greater than 14 bushels, total cost exceeds total revenue, resulting in an economic loss, which is measured by the vertical distance between the two curves. Total revenue exceeds total cost between 7 and 14 bushels per day; at these rates of output the farm earns an economic profit. *Profit is maximized at the rate of output where total revenue exceeds total cost by the greatest amount.* We already know that profit is greatest when 12 bushels are produced per day.

Marginal Cost Equals Marginal Revenue in Equilibrium

Both total revenue and total cost change when output changes, which is why the profit-maximizing choice is not immediately apparent. A second way to find the profit-maximizing rate of output is to focus on marginal revenue and marginal

EXHIBIT 3

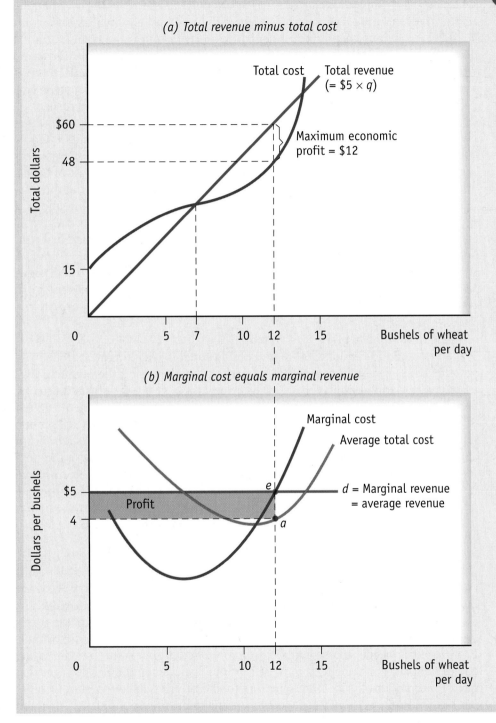

(a) Total revenue minus total cost

Total cost

Total revenue
(= $5 × *q*)

Maximum economic
profit = $12

Total dollars

$60
48
15
0

5 7 10 12 15

Bushels of wheat
per day

(b) Marginal cost equals marginal revenue

Marginal cost

Average total cost

d = Marginal revenue
= average revenue

Profit

e

a

Dollars per bushels

$5
4
0

5 10 12 15

Bushels of wheat
per day

Short-Run Profit Maximization

In panel (a), the total revenue curve for a competitive firm is a straight line with a slope equal to the market price of $5. Total cost increases with output, first at a decreasing rate and then at an increasing rate. Profit is maximized at 12 bushels of wheat per day, where total revenue exceeds total cost by the greatest amount. In panel (b), marginal revenue is a horizontal line at the market price of $5. Profit is maximized at 12 bushels of wheat per day, where the marginal cost equals marginal revenue (point *e*). Profit per day is output (12 bushels) multiplied by the difference between price ($5) and average total cost ($4), as shown by the shaded rectangle.

cost. Column (2) of Exhibit 2 presents the farm's marginal revenue schedule. **Marginal revenue** is the change in total revenue divided by the change in output, or $MR = \Delta TR/\Delta q$. In perfect competition each firm is a price taker, so if one

Marginal revenue The change in total revenue resulting from a one-unit change in sales; in perfect competition, marginal revenue equals the market price

more unit is sold, total revenue increases by an amount equal to the market price. Thus, *in perfect competition, marginal revenue equals the market price.* In this example, marginal revenue, the revenue from selling one more bushel of wheat, is $5.

In the previous chapter you learned that *marginal cost* is the change in total cost divided by the change in output. Column (5) of Exhibit 2 presents the farm's marginal cost of each bushel of wheat. Marginal cost first declines, reflecting increasing marginal returns in the short run as more of the variable resource is employed. Marginal cost then increases, reflecting diminishing marginal returns.

The firm will expand output as long as each additional unit sold adds more to total revenue than to total cost—that is, as long as marginal revenue exceeds marginal cost. Comparing columns (2) and (5) in Exhibit 2, we see that marginal revenue exceeds marginal cost for each of the first 12 units of output. The marginal cost of bushel 13, however, is $6.50, compared to its marginal revenue of $5. Producing the thirteenth bushel would reduce economic profit by $1.50. Since we assume the goal is maximum profit, the farm will limit its output rate to 12 bushels per day.

A firm will expand output as long as marginal revenue exceeds marginal cost, and it will stop expanding before marginal cost rises above marginal revenue. A shorthand expression for this approach is the **golden rule of profit maximization,** which states that the firm produces where marginal cost equals marginal revenue. The golden rule flows from our assumption about profit maximization.

Golden rule of profit maximization To maximize profit or minimize loss, a firm should produce at the rate of output at which cost equals marginal revenue; this rule holds for all market structures.

Economic Profit in the Short Run

Per-unit cost and revenue data are graphed in panel (b) of Exhibit 3. Since marginal revenue in perfect competition equals the market price, the marginal revenue is a horizontal line at the market price of $5, which is also the perfectly competitive firm's demand curve. Since the perfectly competitive firm can get $5 for each bushel sold, the price of $5 is the marginal revenue from selling one more bushel and also the average revenue for each bushel sold. At any point along the demand curve, marginal revenue equals the price. Because the perfectly competitive firm can sell all output for the same market price, marginal revenue equals **average revenue,** which is the total revenue divided by the rate of output. Regardless of the rate of output, therefore, the following equality holds at all points on a perfectly competitive firm's demand curve:

Average revenue Total revenue divided by output; in all market structures, average revenue equals the market price

$$\text{market price} = \text{marginal revenue} = \text{average revenue}$$

The marginal cost curve intersects the marginal revenue (and demand) curve at point *e,* where the rate of output is about 12 bushels per day. At lower rates of output, marginal revenue exceeds marginal cost, so the farm could increase profit by expanding output. At higher rates of output, marginal cost exceeds marginal revenue, so the farm could increase profit by reducing output. Profit itself appears as the shaded rectangle. The height of that rectangle, *ea,* equals the price, or average revenue, $5, minus the average total cost, $4, at that rate of output. Thus, price minus average total cost yields an average profit of $1 per bushel. Profit per day, $12, equals the average profit per bushel, $1 (denoted by *ea*), times the 12 bushels produced.

Note that with total cost and total revenue curves, we measure economic profit by the vertical *distance* between the two curves. But with per-unit curves, we measure economic profit by an *area*—that is, by multiplying the average profit of $1 per bushel times the 12 bushels sold.

MINIMIZING SHORT-RUN LOSSES

An individual firm in perfect competition has no control over the market price. Sometimes the price is so low that no rate of output will yield an economic profit. Faced with losses at all rates of output, the firm can continue to produce at a loss or can temporarily shut down production, such as when an auto plant responds to slack demand by temporarily halting production for weeks or months, or when Dairy Queen shuts down for the winter. Even if the firm shuts down, it cannot in the short run go out of business or produce something else. The short run is by definition a period too short to allow existing firms to leave or new firms to enter this industry. In a sense, firms are trapped in this industry in the short run.

Fixed Cost and Minimizing Losses

Your instincts probably tell you that, rather than produce at a loss, the firm should shut down. But it's not that simple. Keep in mind that the firm has two types of cost in the short run: fixed cost, which must be paid in the short run even if the firm produces nothing, and variable cost, which depends on the rate of output. If the firm shuts down, it must still pay fixed costs, such as property taxes, fire insurance, interest on any loans, and other expenses incurred, even though output is zero. *There may be some positive rate of output at which the firm's revenue will not only cover variable cost but also cover a portion of fixed cost.* A firm will produce if the revenue thus generated exceeds the variable cost of production; revenue in excess of variable cost is used to pay a portion of fixed cost.

Consider the same cost data presented in Exhibit 2, but now suppose the market price has fallen from $5 to $3 per bushel of wheat. This new situation is presented in Exhibit 4. Because of the lower price, total revenue and economic profit are lower at all rates of output. Column (8) indicates that each output rate results in a loss. If the firm produces nothing, its loss is the fixed cost of $15 per day. But if it produces between 6 and 12 bushels per day, it loses less than $15 per day. From column (8), you can see that the loss is minimized at $10 per day when 10 bushels are produced, so the farmer minimizes the loss by producing 10 units per day rather than shutting down. Total cost per day increases from $15 at zero output to $40 at 10 bushels. So total cost increases by $25, which is the variable cost of producing 10 bushels. Since total revenue from selling 10 bushels is $30, the farmer covers the variable cost of $25, leaving $5 toward fixed cost.

Panel (a) of Exhibit 5 presents the firm's total cost and total revenue curves from the data in Exhibit 4. The total cost curve has not changed and remains the same as in Exhibit 3. The drop in price from $5 to $3 per unit changes the slope of the total revenue curve from 5 to 3, so the curve is now flatter than in Exhibit 3. Notice that the total revenue curve now lies below the total cost curve at all output rates. The vertical distance between the two curves measures the loss at each rate of output. If the farmer produces nothing, the loss is the fixed cost of $15 per day. The vertical distance between the two curves is minimized at an output rate of about 10 bushels, where the loss is $10 per day.

Marginal Cost Equals Marginal Revenue

We get the same result using marginal analysis. The per-unit data from Exhibit 4 are presented in panel (b) of Exhibit 5. *The firm will produce rather than shut down if marginal cost equals marginal revenue at a rate of output where the price exceeds or is equal*

EXHIBIT 4

Minimizing Losses in the Short Run

Bushels of Wheat per day (q) (1)	Marginal Revenue (Price) (p) (2)	Total Revenue ($TR = q \times p$) (3) = (1) × (2)	Total Cost (TC) (4)	Marginal Cost $\left(MC = \frac{\Delta TC}{\Delta q}\right)$ (5)	Average Total Cost $\left(ATC = \frac{TC}{q}\right)$ (6) = (4) ÷ (1)	Average Variable Cost $\left(AVC = \frac{TVC}{q}\right)$ (7)	Economic Profit or Loss = $TR - TC$ (8) = (3) − (4)
0	—	$ 0	$15.00	—	∞	—	−$15.00
1	$3	3	19.75	$ 4.75	$19.75	$4.75	−16.75
2	3	6	23.50	3.75	11.75	4.25	−17.50
3	3	9	26.50	3.00	8.83	3.83	−17.50
4	3	12	29.00	2.50	7.25	3.50	−17.00
5	3	15	31.00	2.00	6.20	3.20	−16.00
6	3	18	32.50	1.50	5.42	2.92	−14.50
7	3	21	33.75	1.25	4.82	2.68	−12.75
8	3	24	35.25	1.50	4.41	2.53	−11.25
9	3	27	37.25	2.00	4.14	2.47	−10.25
10	**3**	**30**	**40.00**	**2.75**	**4.00**	**2.50**	**−10.00**
11	3	33	43.25	3.25	3.93	2.57	−10.25
12	3	36	48.00	4.75	4.00	2.75	−12.00
13	3	39	54.50	6.50	4.19	3.04	−15.50
14	3	42	64.00	9.50	4.57	3.50	−22.00
15	3	45	77.50	13.50	5.17	4.17	−32.50
16	3	48	96.00	18.50	6.00	5.06	−48.00

to the average variable cost. In Exhibit 5, the marginal cost and marginal revenue curves intersect at point *e,* where the output rate is about 10 bushels per day and the price of $3 exceeds the average variable cost per bushel of $2.50.

Because the price of $3 per bushel exceeds average variable cost, the farmer is able to cover variable cost and a portion of fixed cost. Specifically, $2.50 of the price pays the average variable cost, and $0.50 covers a portion of the average fixed cost of $1.50 (average fixed cost is average total cost of $4.00 minus average variable cost of $2.50). This still leaves a loss of $1 per bushel. A loss of $1 per bushel multiplied by 10 bushels yields an economic loss of $10 per day, which is identified in panel (b) by the shaded rectangle. Why is the farmer better off operating with this loss rather than shutting down?

Shutting Down in the Short Run

As long as the loss that results from producing is less than the shutdown loss, the farmer will remain open for business in the short run. You may have read or heard about firms that report a loss; most firms reporting a loss continue to op-

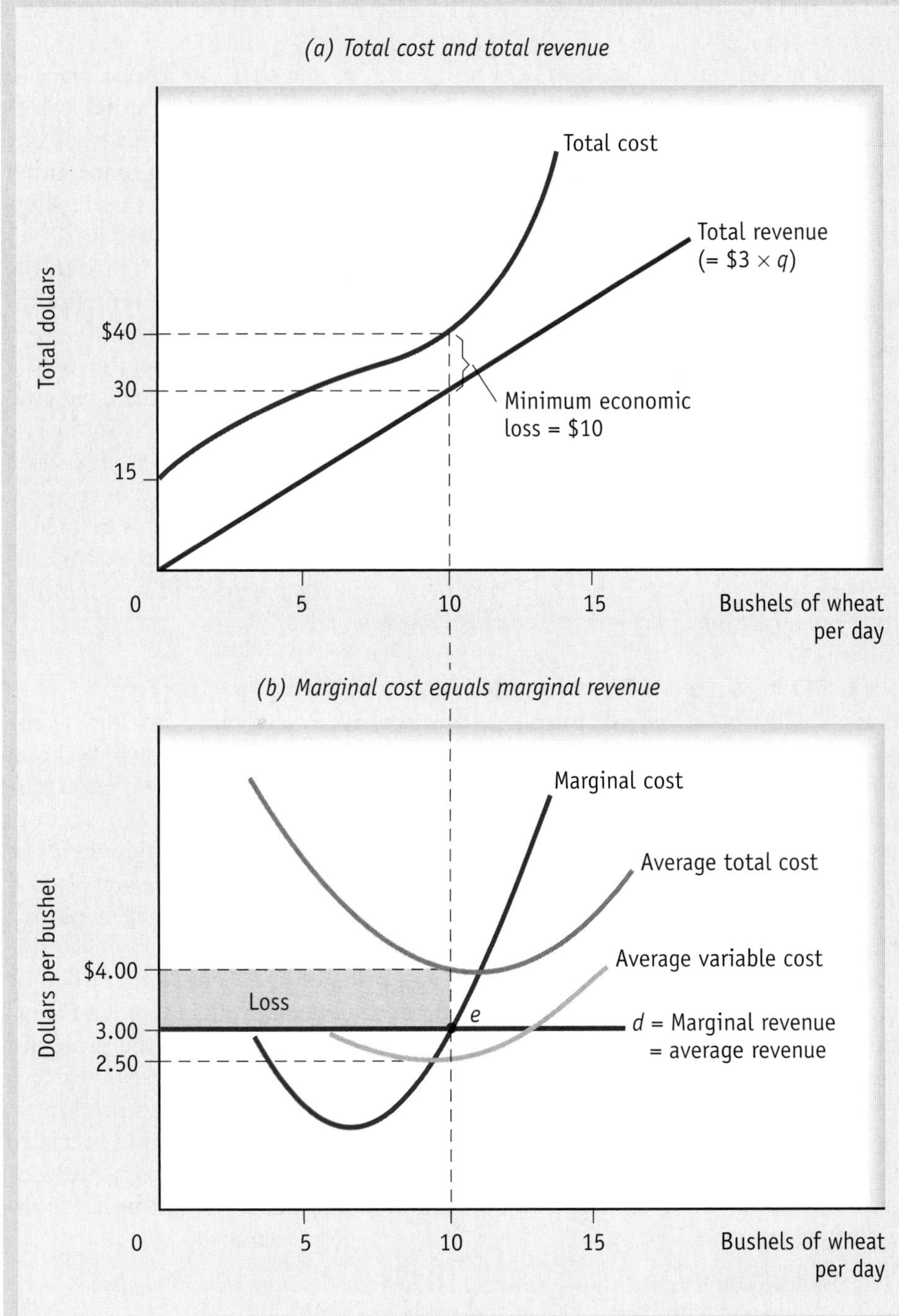

EXHIBIT 5

Minimizing Short-Run Losses

Since total cost always exceeds total revenue in panel (a), the firm suffers a loss at every rate of output. The loss is minimized at 10 bushels per day. Panel (b) shows that marginal cost equals revenue at point *e*. The loss is equal to output (10) multiplied by the difference between average total cost ($4) and price ($3). Since price exceeds average variable cost ($2.50), the firm is better off continuing to produce in the short run.

erate. In fact, most new firms lose money for the first year or two. But *if the average variable cost of production exceeds the price at all rates of output, the firm will shut down*. After all, why produce if doing so only increases the short-run loss? For example, suppose the price of wheat falls to $2 per bushel. As you can see from column (7) of Exhibit 4, average variable cost exceeds $2 at all rates of output. By shutting down, the farmer must pay only fixed cost, not fixed cost plus a portion of variable cost.

From column (7) of Exhibit 4 you can also see that the lowest price at which the farmer would cover average variable cost is $2.47 per bushel, which is the average variable cost when output is 9 bushels per day. At this price, the farmer will be indifferent between producing and shutting down, since either way the loss is the outlay of $15 for fixed cost. Any price above $2.47 will allow the farmer, by producing, to cover some portion of fixed cost.

Note that shutting down is not the same as going out of business. In the short run, a firm keeps its productive capacity intact—paying the rent, fire insurance, and property taxes, keeping water pipes from freezing in the winter, and so on. (Think, again, about Dairy Queen shutting down for the winter months.) The firm does not escape fixed cost by shutting down, since fixed cost, by definition, is cost that does not vary with output. If prices should rise enough or costs should fall enough, the firm will resume operation. If market conditions look grim and are not expected to improve, the firm will consider going out of business, but that's a long-run decision. The short run is defined as a period during which some resources and some costs are fixed, so a firm cannot escape those costs in the short run, no matter what it does. *Fixed cost is sunk cost in the short run, no matter what decision the firm makes.*

The Firm and Industry Short-Run Supply Curves

A firm will vary its rate of output as the market price changes. As long as the price exceeds average variable cost, the firm will produce where marginal cost equals marginal revenue. But if average variable cost is everywhere above the price, the firm will shut down. The effects of various prices on the firm's output decision are summarized in Exhibit 6. Points 1, 2, 3, 4, and 5 indicate where the marginal cost curve intersects various demand, or marginal revenue, curves.

At a price as low as p_1, the firm will shut down rather than produce at point 1 because no output rate generates revenue sufficient to cover average variable cost; so the loss-minimizing output rate at a price of p_1 is zero, as identified by q_1. At a price of p_2, the firm will be indifferent between producing q_2 and shutting down because either way the loss will equal fixed cost since the price just covers average variable cost. Point 2 is called the *shutdown point.* If the price is p_3, the firm will produce q_3 to minimize its loss. At p_4, the firm will produce q_4 to earn just a normal profit, since price equals average total cost. Point 4 is called the *break-even point.* If the price rises to p_5, the firm will earn a short-run economic profit by producing q_5 (see if you can identify economic profit in the diagram when price is p_5).

Short-run firm supply curve A curve that indicates the quantity a firm supplies at each price in the short run; that portion of a firm's marginal cost curve that intersects and rises above the low point on its average variable cost curve

The Short-Run Firm Supply Curve. *As long as the price is high enough to cover average variable cost, the firm will supply the quantity resulting from the intersection of its upward-sloping marginal cost curve and its marginal revenue, or demand, curve.* Thus, that portion of the firm's marginal cost curve that intersects and rises above the lowest point on its average variable cost curve becomes the **short-run firm supply curve.** *In Exhibit 6, the short-run supply curve is the upward-sloping portion of the marginal cost curve, beginning at point 2, the shutdown point.* The solid short-run supply curve indicates the quantity the firm is willing and able to supply in

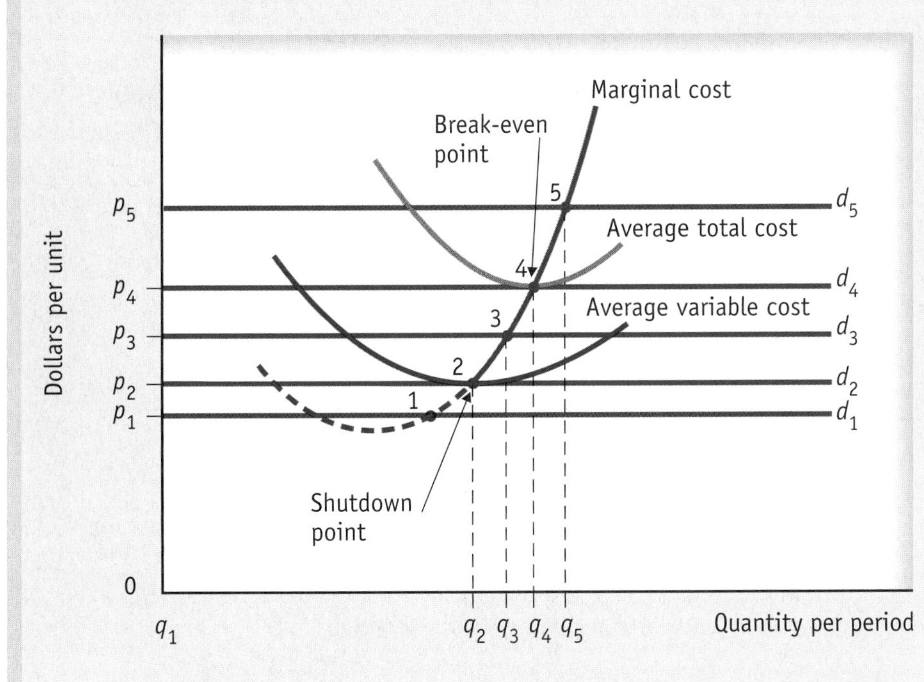

EXHIBIT 6

Summary of Short-Run Output Decisions

At price p_1, the firm produces nothing because p_1 is less than the firm's average variable cost. At price p_2, the firm is indifferent between shutting down and producing q_2 units of output, because in either case the firm would suffer a loss equal to its fixed cost. At p_3, it produces q_3 units and suffers a loss that is less than its fixed cost. At p_4, the firm produces q_4 and just breaks even, since p_4 equals average total cost. Finally, at p_5, the firm produces q_5 and earns an economic profit. The firm's short-run supply curve is that portion of its marginal cost curve at or rising above the minimum point of average variable cost (point 2).

the short run at each alternative price. The quantity supplied when the price is p_2 or higher is determined by the intersection of the firm's marginal cost curve and its demand, or marginal revenue, curve. The firm shuts down if the price is below p_2.

The Short-Run Industry Supply Curve. Exhibit 7 presents an example of how supply curves for just three firms with identical marginal cost curves can be summed horizontally to form the short-run industry supply curve. (In perfectly competitive markets, there will be many more firms.) The **short-run industry supply curve** is the horizontal sum of all firms' short-run supply curves. At a price below *p*, no output is supplied. At a price of *p*, 10 units are supplied by each of the three firms, for a market supply of 30 units. At a price above *p*, say *p*', 20 units are supplied by each firm, so the market supply is 60 units.

Short-run industry supply curve A curve that indicates the quantity supplied by the industry at each price in the short run; the horizontal sum of each firm's short-run supply curve

Firm Supply and Industry Equilibrium. Exhibit 8 shows the relationship between the short-run profit-maximizing output of the individual firm and market equilibrium price and quantity. We assume there are 100,000 identical wheat farmers in this industry. Their individual supply curves (represented by the portions of the marginal cost curve at or rising above the average variable cost) are summed horizontally to yield the market, or industry, supply curve shown in panel (b), where the market price of $5 per bushel is determined. At that market

EXHIBIT 7

Aggregating Individual Supply to Form Market Supply

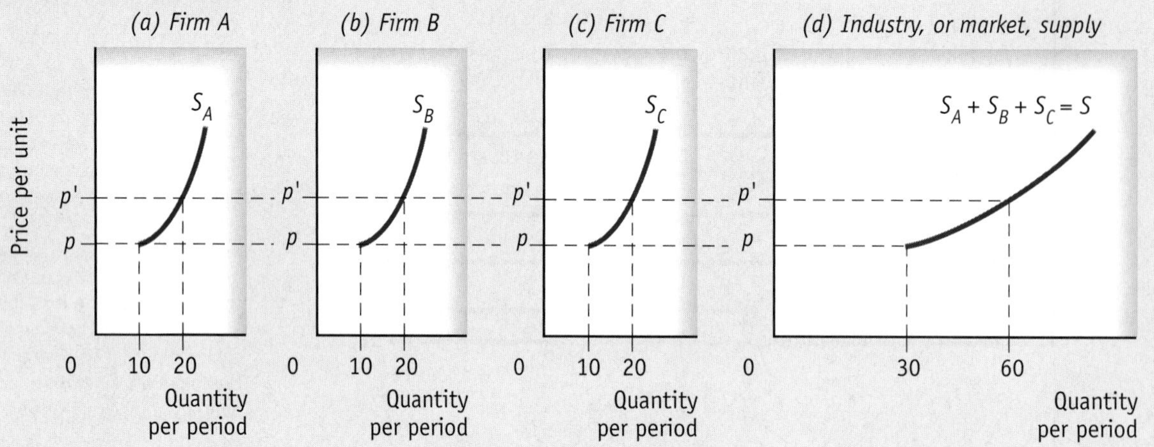

At price *p*, firms A, B, and C each supply 10 units of output. Total market supply is 30 units. In general, the market supply curve, panel (d), is the horizontal summation of the individual firm supply curves S_A, S_B, and S_C.

EXHIBIT 8

Relationship Between Short-Run Profit Maximization and Market Equilibrium

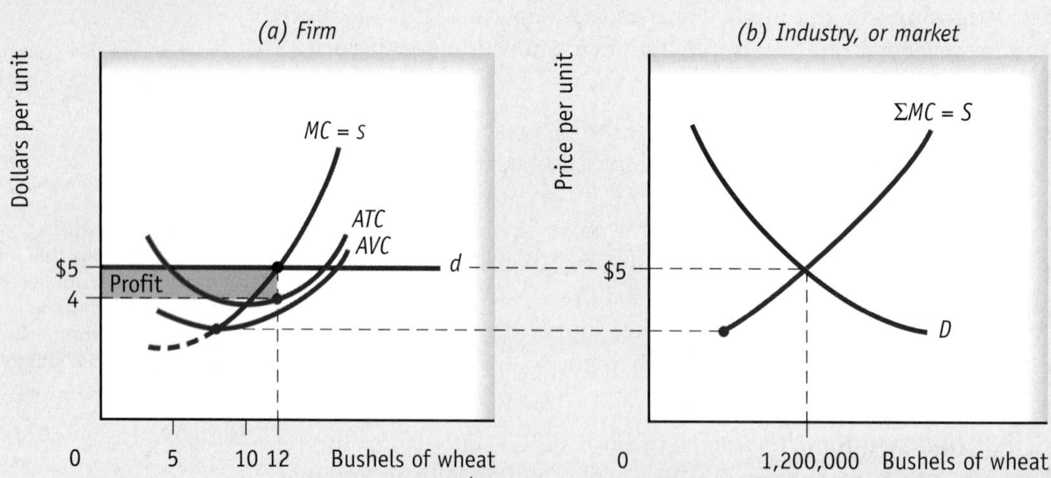

The market supply curve *S* in panel (b) is the horizontal sum of the supply curves of all firms in the industry. The intersection of *S* with the market demand curve *D* determines the market price, $5. That price, in turn, determines the height of the perfectly elastic demand curve facing the individual firm in panel (a). That firm produces 12 bushels per day (where marginal cost equals marginal revenue of $5) and earns an economic profit of $1 per bushel, or $12 in total per bushels per day.

price, each farmer supplies 12 bushels per day, as shown in panel (a), for a total quantity supplied of 1,200,000 bushels per day, as shown in panel (b). Each farmer in the short run earns an economic profit of $12 per day, represented by the shaded rectangle in panel (a).

In summary, *a perfectly competitive firm selects the short-run output rate that maximizes profit or minimizes loss. When confronting a loss, a firm either will produce an output that minimizes that loss or will shut down temporarily.*

Given the conditions for perfect competition, the market will converge toward equilibrium. But how is that equilibrium actually reached? In the real world, markets operate based on customs and conventions, which vary across markets. For example, the rules acceptable on the New York Stock Exchange are not the same as those followed in the market for flowers. In the following case study, we consider one of the oldest market mechanisms for reaching equilibrium—auctions.

Auction Markets

The World of Business

Are you fast enough to compete in the Dutch Flower Auction? Try your hand in a Java-based computer simulation run by the University of Mississippi at http://cypress.mcsr.olemiss.edu/~ccjimmy/auction/. How often did a winning bid appear before the price fell to the point where you could earn a profit? Did you lose out on any profitable opportunities? Were you tempted to bid faster and too high after losing out a few times? If so, you can return to the entry page to choose a slower clock speed. If you think you can go faster, try increasing the speed.

Five days a week in a huge building ten miles outside Amsterdam, some 2,500 buyers gather to participate in the world's largest flower auction. About 14 million flowers from 5,000 growers are auctioned off each day in the largest commercial building in the world, spread across the equivalent of 100 football fields. Flowers are grouped and auctioned off by type—long-stemmed roses, tulips, and so on. Hundreds of buyers are seated in the theater-like setting with their fingers on buttons. Once the flowers are presented, a clock-like instrument starts ticking off descending prices until a buyer stops it by pushing a button. The winning bidder gets to choose how many and which items to take. The clock starts again until another buyer stops it, and so on, until all flowers are sold. Flower auctions occur swiftly; on average a transaction occurs every four seconds.

This is an example of a *Dutch auction,* which starts at a high price and works down. Dutch auctions are more common when there are multiple lots of similar, though not identical, items to be sold, such as flowers in Amsterdam, tobacco in Canada, and fish in seaports around the world. Because there is some difference among the products for sale in a given market—for example, some flower lots are in better condition than others—this is not quite perfect competition, since perfectly competitive markets sell homogeneous products.

More common than the Dutch auction is the *English open outcry auction,* where bidding opens at a low price and moves up until only one buyer remains. Products sold this way include stocks, bonds, wine, art, antiques, livestock, and automobiles. For example, on commodity markets, such as the Chicago Board of Trade, market prices for homogeneous commodities like coffee, wheat, and gold are continuously determined in the trading pits using variations of an open outcry auction.

The birth of the Internet has breathed new life into auctions. Web sites such as eBay, Auction Interactive 2000, Onsale, Internet Auction List, Z Auction, and hundreds more hold on-line auctions. Individual sites specialize in old maps, used computers, wine, airline tickets, antiques, military memorabilia, comic books, paperweights, Beanie Babies, you name it. The largest auction site is eBay, which sells more than one thousand categories in a forum that mimics a live auction. Internet auctions allow specialized sellers to reach a world of customers.

Computers are taking over markets in other ways. In New York, Chicago, Philadelphia, London, and Frankfurt, hand-waving traders in what seem like mosh pits are gradually being replaced by electronic trading. On the Matif, the French futures exchange, when electronic trading was added as an option to the open-outcry system, electronic trading dominated within a matter of months.

Sources: Ken Bensinger and Dustan Prial, "On-Line Auction Sites Gain in Credibility and Popularity," *Wall Street Journal* (31 July 1998); Saul Hansell, "Auctions of Goods and Services Thrive on Internet," *New York Times* (2 April 1998); and David Barboza, "Cold, Efficient Screens Threaten Traditional 'Outcry' Trading," *New York Times* (12 June 1998). On the Internet, eBay's address is http://www.ebay.com.

NetBookmark

Quick links to numerous on-line auctions, such as eBay, can be found at the most popular search engines. Excite offers auctions at http://www.classifieds2000.com/, Lycos has http://www.lycos.com/auctions/ and Yahoo! presents http://auctions.yahoo.com/. HotBot offers a list of particular on-line auctions at http://shop.hotbot.com/index.html?section=auction. What are the most frequently listed types of goods available through on-line auctions? Are these the types of goods you would expect to find offered in a perfectly competitive market? Can you distinguish which goods are fads? Some of the search engines bring you directly to auctions for particular goods, but are they running the auction? Who is "powering" the auction processes? Does the auctioning business appear to be perfectly competitive?

PERFECT COMPETITION IN THE LONG RUN

In the short run, variable resources can be altered, but other resources, which mostly determine firm size, are fixed. In the long run, however, firms have time to enter and exit and to adjust their size—that is, to adjust the scale of their operations. In the long run, there is no distinction between fixed and variable costs because all resources under the firm's control are variable.

Short-run economic profit will attract new entrants and will encourage existing firms to expand the scale of their operations. Economic profit will attract resources from industries where firms are earning only normal profit or may be suffering losses. An increase in the number and size of firms will increase market supply in the long run, and an increase in market supply will reduce the price. New firms will continue to enter a profitable industry and existing firms will continue to increase in size as long as economic profit is positive. Entry and expansion will stop only when the increase in supply has reduced the market price to the point where economic profit is zero. *Short-run economic profit will attract new entrants and may cause existing firms to expand; market supply will thereby increase, driving down the market price until economic profit is eliminated.*

On the other hand, a short-run loss will prompt some firms to leave the industry or to reduce their scale of operation. In the long run, departures and reductions in scale will reduce market supply and increase market price until remaining firms just break even—that is, earn just a normal profit.

Zero Economic Profit in the Long Run

In the long run, firms in perfect competition will earn just a normal profit, which means zero economic profit. Exhibit 9 shows the individual firm and the market in long-run equilibrium. In the long run, market supply adjusts as firms enter or leave the market or change the scale of their operations; *this process continues until the market supply curve intersects the market demand curve at a price that equals the lowest point on each firm's long-run average cost curve, or LRAC curve.* A higher price would generate economic profit in the short run and would therefore attract new entrants in the long run. In the case of wheat farming, economic profit encourages existing farmers to expand the scale of their operation and will

EXHIBIT 9

Long-Run Equilibrium for the Firm and the Industry

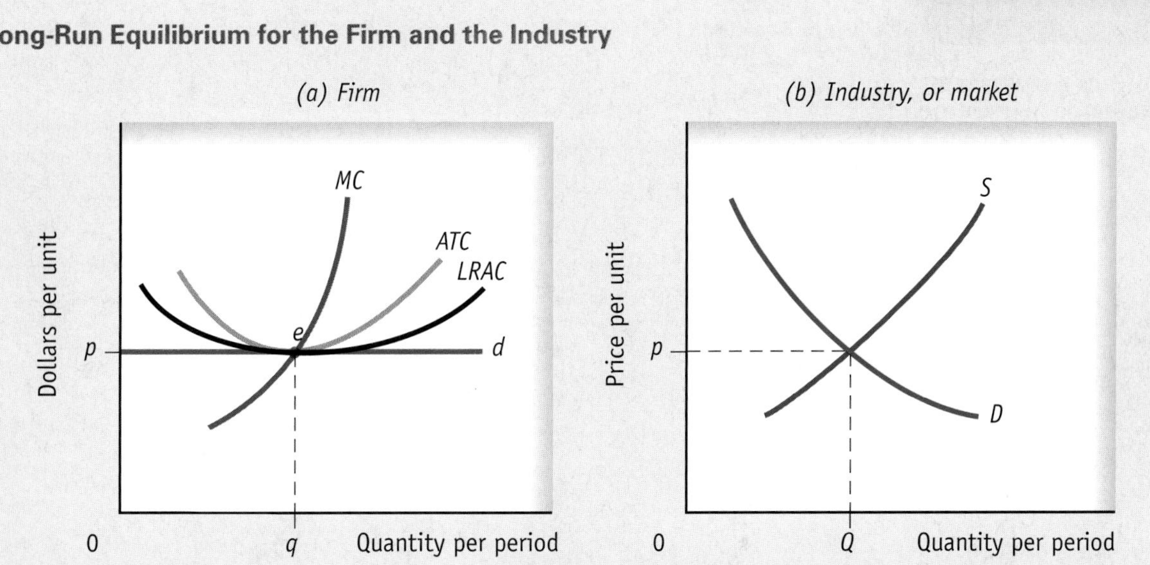

In long-run equilibrium, the firm produces *q* units of output per period and earns a normal profit. At point *e,* price, marginal cost, short-run average total cost, and long-run average cost are all equal. There is no reason for new firms to enter or for existing firms to leave the market. Thus, the market supply curve, *S,* in panel (b) does not shift. As long as market demand, *D,* is stable, the industry will continue to produce a total of *Q* units of output at price *p.*

attract new wheat farmers, perhaps some who had been raising other crops. A lower price would create a loss in the short run, causing some farmers in the long run to scale back their wheat production or give up wheat farming altogether.

Perfect competition in the long run cuts economic profit to zero. Because the long run is a time period during which all resources under the firm's control are variable and because firms try to maximize profit, *firms in the long run will adjust their scale of operation until their average cost of production is minimized.* Firms that fail to minimize costs will not survive in the long run. At point *e* in panel (a) of Exhibit 9, the firm is in equilibrium, producing *q* units and earning just a normal profit. At point *e,* price, marginal cost, short-run average total cost, and long-run average cost are all equal. No firm in the market has any reason to alter its output and no outside firm has any incentive to enter this industry, since each firm in the market is earning normal, but not economic, profit.

The Long-Run Adjustment to a Change in Demand

To explore the long-run adjustment process, let's consider how a firm and an industry respond to an increase in market demand. This firm is representative of all firms in the industry. Assume that the costs facing each individual firm do not depend on the number of firms in the industry (this assumption will be explained soon).

Effects of an Increase in Demand. Exhibit 10 shows a perfectly competitive firm and industry in long-run equilibrium, with the market supply curve intersecting the market demand curve at point *a* in panel (b). The market-clearing price is

EXHIBIT 10

Long-Run Adjustment to an Increase in Demand

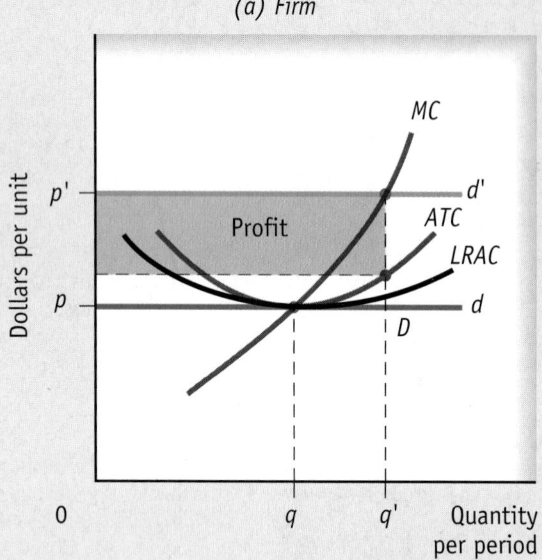

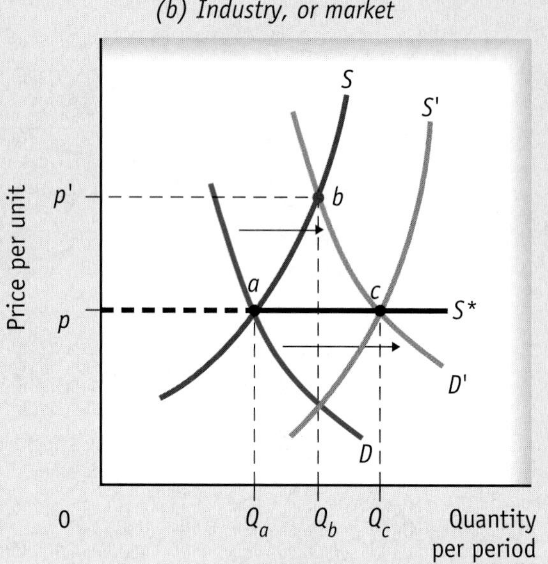

An increase in market demand from *D* to *D*' in panel (b) moves the short-run equilibrium point from *a* to *b*. Output rises to Q_b and price increases to *p*'. The rise in market price causes the demand curve facing the firm to rise from *d* to *d*' in panel (a). The firm responds by increasing output to *q*' and earns an economic profit, identified by the shaded rectangle. With existing firms earning economic profit, new firms enter the industry in the long run. Market supply shifts out to *S*' in panel (b). Output rises further, to Q_c, and price falls back to *p*. In panel (a), the firm's demand curve shifts back to *d*, eliminating economic profits. The short-run adjustment is from point *a* to point *b* in panel (b), but the long-run adjustment is from point *a* to point *c*.

p and the market quantity is Q_a. The individual firm, shown in panel (a), supplies *q* units at that market price, earning a normal profit in long-run equilibrium. This representative firm produces where price, or marginal revenue, equals marginal cost, short-run average total cost, and long-run average cost. (Remember, a normal profit is included in the firm's average total cost curve.)

Now suppose the market demand for this product increases from *D* to *D*' in panel (b), causing the market price to increase in the short run to *p*'. Each firm responds to the higher price by expanding output along its short-run supply, or marginal cost, curve until the quantity supplied increases to *q*'. At that rate of output, the firm's marginal cost curve intersects the new marginal revenue curve, which is also the firm's new demand curve, *d*'. Because all firms expand production, industry output increases to Q_b, where the change in industry output is the sum of the changes of all the individual firms in the industry. Note that in the short run, each firm is now earning economic profit, shown by the shaded rectangle in panel (a).

In the long run, economic profit attracts new firms. Their entry adds additional supply to the market, shifting out the market supply curve, which causes the market price to fall. Firms continue to enter as long as they can earn economic profit. The market supply curve eventually shifts out to *S*', where it intersects *D*' at point *c*, returning the price to its initial equilibrium level, *p*. The decline in the market price has dropped the demand curve facing the individual firm from *d*' back down to *d*. As a result, each firm reduces output from *q*' back to *q* and once again each earns just a normal profit. Notice that although industry output increases from Q_a to Q_c, each firm's output returns to *q*. In this case, the additional output comes from new firms attracted to the industry rather than from greater output by existing firms, since existing firms could not expand without increasing their long-run average costs.

New firms are attracted to the industry by short-run economic profits arising from the increase in demand. The resulting increase in market supply, however, forces the price down until economic profit disappears. In Exhibit 10(b), the short-run adjustment to increased demand is from point *a* to point *b;* in the long run, market equilibrium moves to point *c*.

Effects of a Decrease in Demand. Next, let's consider the effect of a decrease in demand on the long-run market adjustment process. The initial long-run equilibrium situation in Exhibit 11 is the same as in Exhibit 10. Market demand and supply curves intersect at point *a* in panel (b), yielding an equilibrium price of *p* and an equilibrium quantity of Q_a. The firm in panel (a) earns a normal profit

EXHIBIT 11

Long-Run Adjustment to a Decrease in Demand

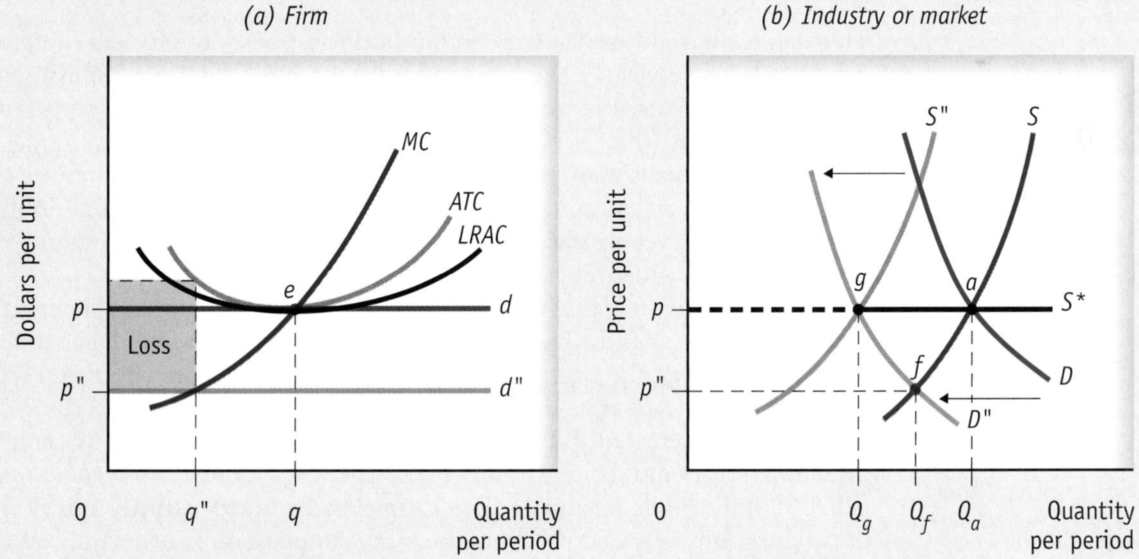

A decrease in demand to *D*" in panel (b) disturbs the long-run equilibrium at point *a*. Prices are driven down to *p*" in the short run; output falls to Q_f. In panel (a), the firm's demand curve shifts down to *d*". Each firm reduces its output to *q*" and suffers a loss. As firms leave the industry in the long run, the market supply curve shifts left to *S*". Market prices rise to *p* as output falls further to Q_g. At price *p*, the remaining firms once again earn zero economic profit. Thus, the short-run adjustment is from point *a* to point *f* in panel (b); the long-run adjustment is from point *a* to point *g*.

in the long run by producing output rate q, where price, or marginal revenue, equals marginal cost, short-run average cost, and long-run average cost.

Now suppose that the demand for this product declines, as reflected in panel (b) by the shift to the left in the market demand curve, from D back to D''. In the short run, this decline in demand reduces the market price to p''. As a result, the demand curve facing each individual firm drops from d to d''. Each firm responds in the short run by cutting its output to q'', where marginal cost equals the now-lower marginal revenue, or price. Market output falls to Q_f. Since the lower market price is below short-run average total cost, each firm operates at a loss. This loss is shown in panel (a) by the shaded rectangle (although the price must still be above average variable cost, since the firm's short-run supply curve, MC, is defined as that portion of the firm's marginal cost curve at or above its average variable cost curve).

In the long run, continued losses force some firms out of the industry. As firms leave, market supply decreases so the market price increases. Firms continue to leave until the market supply curve decreases to S'', where it intersects D'' at point g. Market output has fallen to Q_g, and price has returned to p. With the price back up to p, the remaining firms once again earn a normal profit. At the conclusion of the adjustment process, each remaining firm produces q, the initial equilibrium quantity, but because some firms have left the industry, market output has fallen from Q_a to Q_g. Note, again, that the adjustment process involves the departure of firms from the industry rather than a reduction in the scale of firms; a reduction in scale would have increased each firm's long-run average cost.

THE LONG-RUN INDUSTRY SUPPLY CURVE

Thus far, we have looked at firm and industry responses to changes in demand, distinguishing between a short-run adjustment and a long-run adjustment. In the short run, firms alter quantity supplied by moving up or down their marginal cost curves (that portion at or rising above average variable cost) until marginal cost equals marginal revenue, or price. If price does not cover minimum average variable cost, firms shut down in the short run. The long-run adjustment, however, involves the entry or exit of firms until the resulting equilibrium price provides remaining firms with a normal profit.

In Exhibits 10 and 11, we began with an initial long-run equilibrium point and were able to identify two more long-run equilibrium points generated by the intersection of the shifted demand curve and the shifted short-run market supply curve. In each case, the price remained the same in the long run, but industry output increased in Exhibit 10 and decreased in Exhibit 11. Connecting these long-run equilibrium points yields the *long-run industry supply curve,* labeled $S^\star$ in Exhibits 10 and 11. The **long-run industry supply curve** shows the relationship between price and quantity supplied once firms fully adjust to any short-term economic profit or loss resulting from a shift in market demand.

Long-run industry supply curve A curve that shows the relationship between price and quantity supplied by the industry once firms fully adjust to any change in market demand

Constant-cost industry An industry that can expand or contract without affecting the long-run, per-unit cost of production; the long-run industry supply curve is horizontal

Constant-Cost Industries

The industry we have studied thus far is called a **constant-cost industry** because the firm's long-run average cost curve does not shift up or down as industry output changes. Resource prices and other production costs remain constant in the long run as industry output increases or decreases. In a constant-cost industry, each firm's per-unit production costs are independent of the number of firms in the industry, so a firm's long-run average cost curve remains constant in the long run as firms enter or leave the industry. *The long-run supply curve for a constant-cost industry is horizontal,* as is depicted in Exhibits 10 and 11.

A constant-cost industry is most often characterized as one that uses such a small portion of the resources available in resource markets that increasing industry output does not bid up resource prices. For example, output in the pencil industry can expand without bidding up the prices of wood, graphite, and synthetic rubber, since the pencil industry uses such a small share of the market supply of these resources.

Increasing-Cost Industries

The firms in some industries encounter higher average costs as industry output expands in the long run. Firms in these **increasing-cost industries** find that expanding output bids up the prices of some resources or otherwise increases per-unit production costs, and these higher production costs shift each firm's cost curves upward. For example, an industry-wide expansion of oil production could bid up the price of drilling equipment and the wages of petroleum engineers and geologists, raising per-unit production costs for each firm. Likewise, more housing construction could bid up what building contractors must pay for land, lumber, other building materials, and carpenters.

Increasing-cost industry
An industry that faces higher per-unit production costs as industry output expands in the long run; the long-run industry supply curve slopes upward

To illustrate the equilibrium adjustment process for an increasing-cost industry, we begin again in long-run equilibrium in panel (b) of Exhibit 12, where the industry demand curve, *D*, intersects the short-run industry supply curve, *S*, at equilibrium point *a* to yield the market price p_a and the market quantity Q_a. When the price is p_a, the demand (and marginal revenue) curve facing each firm is d_a in panel (a). The firm produces the rate of output at which marginal cost equals marginal revenue, shown by point *a* in panel (a). At the firm's equilibrium rate of output, *q*, average total cost is at a minimum, so average total cost equals the price and the firm earns no economic profit in this long-run equilibrium.

Suppose an increase in the demand for this product shifts the market demand curve to the right from *D* to *D'* in panel (b). The new demand curve intersects the short-run market supply curve *S* at point *b*, yielding the short-run equilibrium price p_b and quantity Q_b. With an increase in the equilibrium price, each firm's demand curve shifts from d_a up to d_b in panel (a). The new short-run equilibrium occurs at point *b* in panel (a), where the marginal cost curve intersects the new demand curve, which is also the marginal revenue curve. Each firm produces output q_b. In the short run, each firm earns an economic profit equal to q_b times the difference between the price, p_b, and the average total cost at that rate of output. So far, the sequence of events is the same as for a constant-cost industry.

Economic profit attracts new entrants like bears to honey. Because this is an increasing-cost industry, the new entrants' increased demand for resources drives up the cost of production, raising each firm's marginal and average cost curves. In panel (a) of Exhibit 12, *MC* and *ATC* shift up to *MC'* and *ATC'*. (We assume for simplicity that the new average cost curves are parallel to the old curves, so the minimum efficient plant size remains the same.)

EXHIBIT 12

An Increasing-Cost Industry

McEachern Interactive

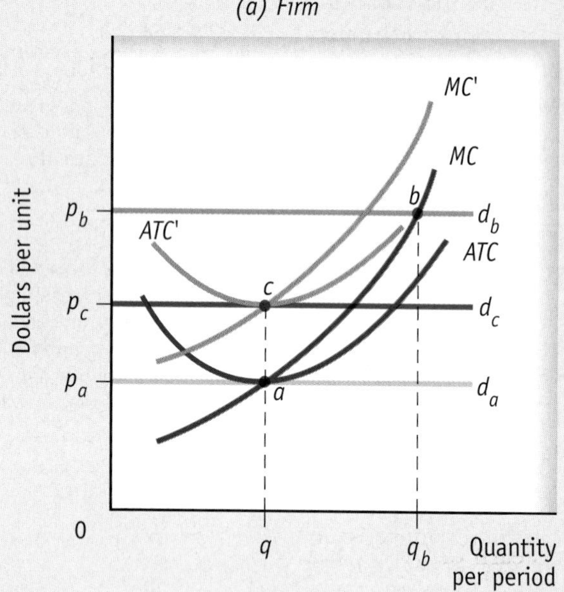

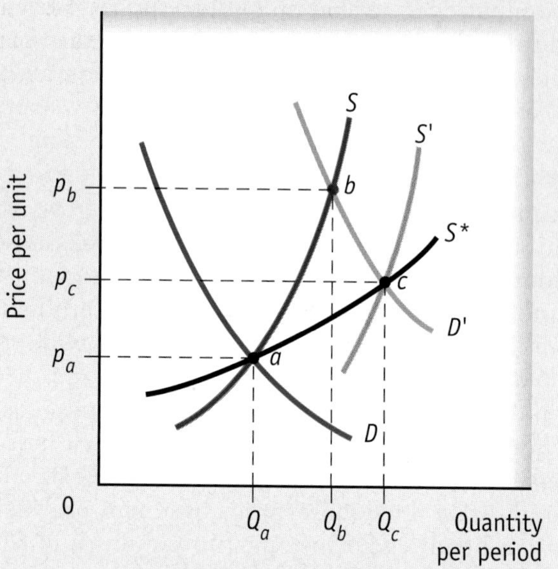

An increase in demand to *D'* in panel (b) disturbs the initial equilibrium at point *a*. A short-run equilibrium is established at point *b*, where *D'* intersects the short-run market supply curve, *S*. At the higher price p_b, the firm's demand curve shifts up to d_b, and its output increases to q_b in panel (a). At point *b*, the firm is earning an economic profit. New firms enter to try to capture some of the profits. As they do so, input prices are bid up, so each firm's marginal and average cost curves rise. The intersection of the new market supply curve, *S'*, with *D'*, determines the market price, p_c. At p_c, individual firms are earning zero economic profit. Point *c* is a point of long-run equilibrium. By connecting long-run equilibrium points *a* and *c* in panel (b), we obtain the upward-sloping long-run market supply curve, *S** for this increasing-cost industry.

The entry of new firms also shifts the short-run industry supply curve outward, thus reducing the market price of output. *New firms enter the industry until the combination of a higher production cost and a lower output price squeezes economic profit to zero.* This long-run equilibrium occurs when entry of new firms has shifted the short-run industry supply curve out to *S'*, which lowers the price until it equals the minimum on each firm's new average total cost curve. The market price does not fall back to the initial equilibrium level because each firm's average total cost curve has shifted up. The intersection of the new short-run market supply curve, *S'*, and the new market demand curve, *D'*, determines the new long-run market equilibrium point, identified as point *c* in panel (b). Points *a* and *c* are on the *upward-sloping* long-run supply curve, denoted as *S** for this increasing-cost industry.

In constant-cost industries, each firm's costs depend simply on the scale of its plant and its rate of output. For firms in increasing-cost industries, costs depend also on the *number of firms in the market.* By bidding up the price of resources, long-run expansion increases each firm's average cost. The long-run supply curve for an increasing-cost industry slopes upward, like S^* in Exhibit 12.

Decreasing-Cost Industries

Firms in some industries may experience a lower average cost as output expands in the long run, although this is considered rare. Firms in **decreasing-cost industries** find that as industry output expands, the per-unit cost of production falls, causing a downward shift in each firm's cost curves. For example, in the coal-mining industry, a major production cost is pumping ground water from the mine shafts. As more mines in the same area operate pumps, the water table in the area falls, so each mine's pumping costs go down.

Decreasing-cost industry The rare case in which an industry faces lower per-unit production costs as industry output expands in the long run; the long-run industry supply curve slopes downward

An increase in market demand results in a higher price in the short run, so firms earn economic profit. This profit attracts new entrants in the long run, reducing average cost for all firms in the industry. Decreasing-cost industries have long-run supply curves like the one depicted in Exhibit 13, where point *a* is the initial equilibrium, point *b* is the short-run adjustment to an increase in demand, and point *c* is the long-run equilibrium adjustment as new firms are attracted by short-run profits. In the long run, the price, p_c, falls below the initial price, p_a. Entry eliminates economic profit by driving down the price.

In summary, firms in perfect competition can earn an economic profit, a normal profit, or an economic loss in the short run, but in the long run the entry or exit of firms drives economic profit to zero, so firms earn only a normal profit. This is true whether the industry in question exhibits constant costs, increasing costs, or decreasing costs in the long run. Notice that, regardless of

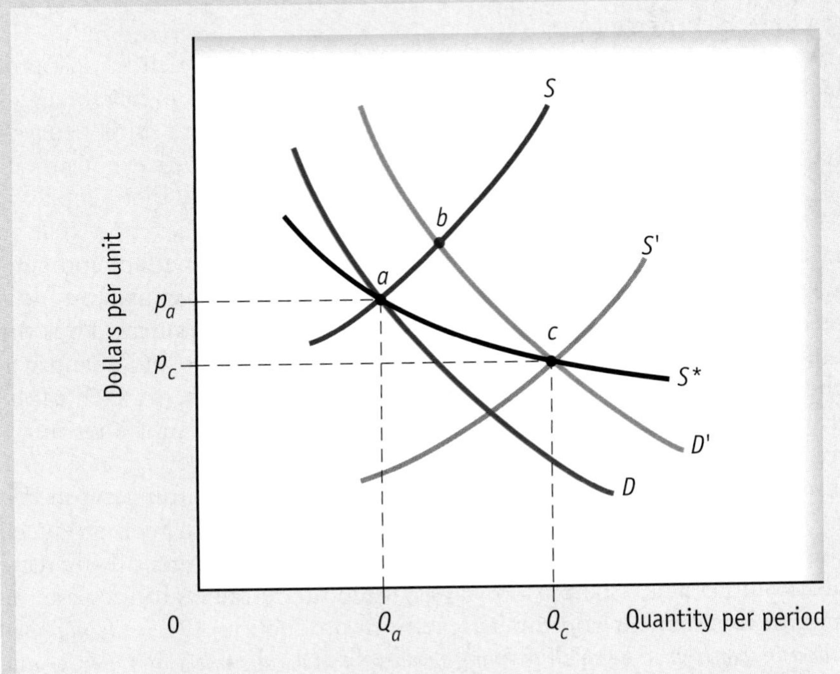

EXHIBIT 13

A Decreasing-Cost Industry Adjusts to an Increase in Demand

An increase in market demand moves the industry from starting point *a* to short-run equilibrium at point *b*. With each firm earning an economic profit, new firms begin to enter. If entry drives down the average cost of production, long-run equilibrium will be reestablished at point *c*, with a lower price than at point *a*. Connecting long-run equilibrium points *a* and *c* yields the downward-sloping long-run market supply curve, S^* for this decreasing-cost industry.

the nature of costs in the industry, the industry supply curve is less elastic in the short run than in the long run. In the long run, firms can adjust all their resources, so they are better able to respond to changes in price.

As mentioned at the outset, perfect competition serves as a useful benchmark for evaluating the efficiency of markets. Let's examine the qualities of perfect competition that make it so useful.

PERFECT COMPETITION AND EFFICIENCY

How does perfect competition perform in terms of the efficient allocation of resources? There are two concepts of efficiency used in judging market performance. The first, called *productive efficiency,* refers to producing output at the least possible cost. The second, called *allocative efficiency,* emphasizes producing the output that consumers value the most. Perfect competition guarantees both productive efficiency and allocative efficiency.

Productive Efficiency

Productive efficiency The condition that exists when output is produced with the least-cost combination of inputs, given the level of technology

Productive efficiency occurs when the firm produces at the minimum point on its long-run average-cost curve, so the market price equals the minimum average total cost. In the long run in perfect competition, the entry and exit of firms and any adjustment in the scale of each firm ensure that each firm produces at the minimum point on its long-run average cost curve. Firms whose size does not reach minimum long-run average cost must either change their size or leave the industry to avoid continued losses. Thus, the long-run industry output in perfect competition is produced at the least possible cost per unit.

Allocative Efficiency

Allocative efficiency The condition that exists when firms produce the output that is most preferred by consumers; the marginal cost of each good just equals the marginal benefit that consumers derive from that good

Allocative efficiency occurs when firms produce the output that is most preferred by consumers. How do we know that perfect competition guarantees allocative efficiency? The answer lies with the market demand and supply curves. You'll recall that the demand curve reflects the marginal value that consumers attach to each unit, so the market price is the amount of money that people are willing and able to pay for the final unit they consume. We also know that, in both the short run and the long run, the equilibrium price in perfect competition equals the marginal cost of supplying the last unit sold. Marginal cost measures the opportunity cost of using resources employed by the firm. Thus the supply and demand curves intersect at the combination of price and quantity at which the marginal value, or the marginal benefit, that consumers attach to the last unit of output purchased just equals the opportunity cost of the resources employed to produce that unit of output.

As long as marginal cost equals marginal benefit, the last unit produced is valued as much as, or more than, any other good that could have been produced using those same resources. There is no way to reallocate resources to increase the value of output. Thus, there is no way to reallocate resources to increase the total utility or total benefit consumers reap from production. *When the marginal cost of producing each good equals the marginal benefit that consumers derive from that good, the market is said to be allocatively efficient.*

What's So Perfect About Perfect Competition?

If the marginal cost to firms of supplying the good just equals the marginal benefit to consumers, does this mean that market exchange confers no net benefits on participants? No. Market exchange usually benefits both consumers and producers. Recall that consumers garner a surplus from market exchange because the maximum amount they would be willing to pay for each unit of the good exceeds the amount they in fact pay. Exhibit 14 depicts a market in short-run equilibrium. The *consumer surplus* in this exhibit is represented by the blue shaded area, which is the area below the demand curve but above the market-clearing price of $10.

Producers in the short run also usually derive a net benefit, or a surplus, from market exchange, because the amount they receive for their output exceeds the minimum amount they would require to supply that amount in the short run. Recall that the short-run market supply curve is the sum of that portion of each firm's marginal cost curve at or above the minimum point on its average variable cost curve. Point *m* in Exhibit 14 is the minimum point on the market supply curve; it indicates that at a price of $5, firms are willing to supply 100,000 units. At prices below $5, quantity supplied is zero because firms could not cover variable costs and would shut down. At point *m*, firms in this industry gain no net benefit from production in the short run, because the total industry revenue derived from selling 100,000 units at $5 each just covers the variable cost incurred by producing that amount of output.

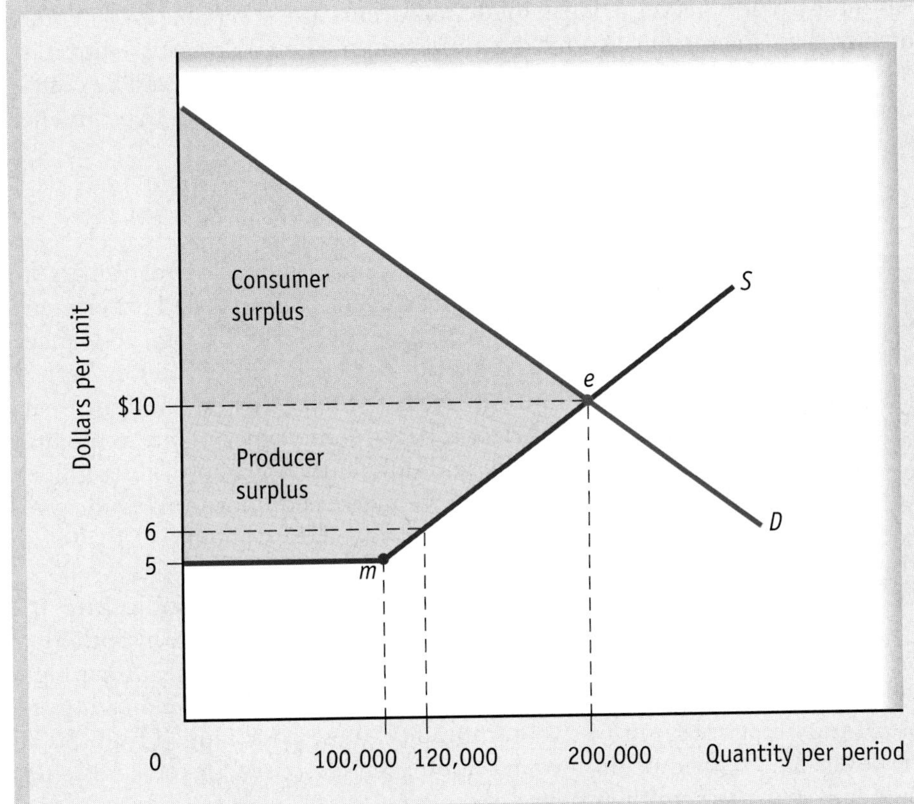

EXHIBIT 14

Consumer Surplus and Producer Surplus for a Competitive Market in the Short Run

Consumer surplus is represented by the area above the market-clearing price of $10 per unit and below the demand curve; it is shown as a blue triangle. Producer surplus is represented by the area above the short-run market supply curve and below the market-clearing price of $10 per unit; it is shown by the gold shading. At a price of $5 per unit, there is no producer surplus. At a price of $6 per unit, producer surplus is the shaded area between $5 and $6.

If the price increases to \$6, firms increase their quantity supplied until their marginal cost equals \$6. Market output increases from 100,000 to 120,000 units, and total revenue increases from \$500,000 to \$720,000. Part of the increased revenue covers the higher marginal cost of production. But the balance of the increased revenue is a bonus to producers, who would have been willing to supply 100,000 units for only \$5 each. When the price is \$6, they get to sell these 100,000 units for \$6 each rather than \$5 each. Thus producer surplus at a price of \$6 is the shaded area between \$5 and \$6.

Producer surplus The amount by which total revenue from production exceeds total variable cost

In the short run, **producer surplus** is the total revenue producers are paid minus their total variable cost of production. In Exhibit 14, the market-clearing price is \$10 per unit, and the producer surplus is depicted by the shaded area under the price but above the market supply curve. That area represents the market price minus the marginal cost of each unit produced.

The combination of consumer surplus and producer surplus shows the gains from voluntary exchange. Productive and allocative efficiency in the short run occurs at point *e,* which is the combination of price and quantity that maximizes the sum of consumer surplus and producer surplus. Even though marginal cost equals marginal benefit in equilibrium, both consumers and producers usually get a surplus, or bonus, from market exchange.

Note that producer surplus is not the same as economic profit. Any price that exceeds average variable cost will result in a short-run producer surplus, even though that price could result in a short-run economic loss. The definition of producer surplus ignores fixed cost, because fixed cost is irrelevant to the firm's short-run production decision. Fixed cost is *sunk* in the short run because the firm must pay it whether or not production occurs. Only variable cost matters. For each firm, the marginal cost is the increase in total variable cost as output increases, and the sum of the marginal costs for all units is the total variable cost.

The gains from market exchange have been examined in an experimental setting, as is discussed in the following case study.

The World of Business

Vanderbilt University's Market.Econ brings "experimental economics to the Internet" at http://market.econ.vanderbilt.edu/. By supplying your e-mail address, you can receive a password and play one of their games on-line. Be sure to carefully read through any rules. Rules of and results of a variety of other games are available at http://eeps.caltech.edu/ from Caltech's Laboratory for Experimental Economics and Political Science. The Director is Charles

Experimental Economics

Economists have limited opportunities to carry out the kind of controlled experiments available in the physical and biological sciences. But about four decades ago, Professor Vernon Smith (pictured at left), now at the University of Arizona, began some experiments to see how quickly and efficiently a group of test subjects could achieve market equilibrium. His original experiment involved 22 students, 11 of whom were designated as "buyers" and 11 as "sellers." Each buyer was given a card indicating the value of purchasing one unit of a hypothetical commodity; these values ranged from \$3.25 downward to \$0.75, forming a downward-sloping demand curve. Each seller was given a card indicating the cost of providing one unit of that commodity; these costs ranged from \$0.75 upward to \$3.25, forming an upward-sloping supply curve. Buyers and sellers knew only what was on their own cards.

To provide market incentives, participants were told they would receive a cash bonus at the end of the experiment based on the difference between their cost or their value and the price they negotiated in the open market. As a way of trading, Smith employed a system in which any buyer or seller announced a bid or an offer to the entire group—a system called a *double continuous auction*—based on rules similar to those governing stock markets and commodity exchanges. A transaction occurred whenever any buyer accepted an offer or when any seller accepted a bid. *Smith found that the price quickly converged to the market-clearing level,* which in his experiment was $2.00.

Economists have since performed thousands of experiments testing the properties of markets. The experiments show that under most circumstances, markets are extremely efficient in moving goods from the lowest-cost producers to the consumers who place the highest value on the goods. This maximizes the sum of consumer and producer surplus and thus maximizes social welfare. One surprising finding is how few participants are required to establish a market price. Market experiments sometimes use only four buyers and four sellers, each capable of trading several units. Some experiments use only two sellers, yet the competitive equilibrium model performs quite well under double-auction rules.

Incidentally, most U.S. retail markets, such as supermarkets and department stores, use *posted-offer pricing*—that is, the price is marked, not negotiated. Experiments show that posted pricing does not adjust to changing market conditions as quickly as does a double-continuous auction. Despite their slow response times, posted prices may be the choice for large, relatively stable markets, because such pricing involves low transaction costs. In contrast, continuous-auction pricing involves high transaction costs, requiring in the case of stock and commodity markets thousands of people in full-time negotiations to maintain prices at their equilibrium levels (although, as discussed in the previous case study, the Internet has reduced the transaction costs of establishing prices through continuous auctions).

Experiments have provided empirical support for economic theory and have yielded insights about how market rules affect market outcomes. They have also helped shape markets that did not exist, such as the market for pollution rights or for broadcast spectrum rights. Finally, experiments offer a safe and inexpensive way for those in emerging market economies, such as Poland, Russia, and Hungary, to learn how markets work.

Sources: Vernon Smith and Arlington Williams, "Experimental Market Economics," *Scientific American* (December 1992): 116–121; Vernon Smith, "Experimental Methods in Economics," *The New Palgrave Dictionary of Economics*, Vol. 2, J. Eatwell et al., eds. (New York: Stockton Press, 1987): 241–249; Vernon Smith, "Economics in the Laboratory," *Journal of Economic Perspectives* 8 (Winter 1994): 113–134; and T. C. Bergstrom and J. H. Miller, *Experiments with Economic Principles* (New York: McGraw-Hill, 1997).

Plott, an early innovator of experimental economics. Be sure to check out the Jaws animation, a QuickTime video presentation of changing equilibrium prices. Charles Holt of the University of Virginia, an innovator in using games in the classroom maintains a Web site with instructions and game sheets for some experiments at http://theweb.badm.sc.edu/laury/games.html.

CONCLUSION

Let's review the assumptions of a perfectly competitive market and see how they relate to ideas developed in this chapter. *First,* there must be many buyers and many sellers. This is necessary so that no individual buyer or seller is large enough to influence the price (although recent experiments show that the large-number assumption may be stronger than is necessary). *Second,* firms must produce a homogeneous product. If consumers could distinguish among the output of different producers, they might prefer one firm's product even at a higher price, so different producers could sell at different prices. In that case, not every firm would be a price taker—that is, each firm's demand curve would no longer be horizontal. *Third,* all market participants must have full information about all prices and all production processes. Otherwise, some producers could charge more than the market price, and some uninformed consumers would pay that higher price. Also, through ignorance, some firms might select outdated technology or fail to recognize the opportunity for short-run economic profits. *Fourth,* all resources must be mobile in the long run, and there must be no obstacles preventing new firms from moving into profitable markets. Otherwise, some firms could earn economic profit in the long run.

Perfect competition is not the market structure most commonly observed in the real world. The markets for agricultural products, stocks, commodities such as gold and silver, and foreign exchange come close to being perfect. But even if not a single example of perfect competition could be found, the model would be a useful tool for analyzing market behavior. As you will see in the next two chapters, perfect competition provides a valuable benchmark for evaluating the efficiency of other market structures.

SUMMARY

1. Market structure describes important features of the economic environment in which firms operate. These features include the number of buyers and sellers, the ease or difficulty of entering the market, the similarities or differences in the output that is produced by each firm, and the forms of competition among firms. As we will see in the next two chapters, there are four types of market structure. This chapter examined perfect competition.

2. Perfectly competitive markets are characterized by (1) a large number of buyers and sellers, each too small to influence market price; (2) production of a homogeneous product; (3) full information about the availability and prices of all resources, goods, and technologies; and (4) free and complete mobility of resources in the long run. Firms in such markets are said to be price takers because no individual firm can influence the price. Individual firms can vary only the amount they choose to sell at the market price.

3. The market price in perfect competition is determined by the intersection of the market demand and market supply curves. Each firm then faces a demand curve that is a horizontal line drawn at the market price. Because this demand curve is horizontal, it represents the average revenue and the marginal revenue the firm receives at each rate of output. Firms in perfect competition are price takers.

4. That portion of the firm's marginal cost curve at or above the average variable cost curve is the perfectly competitive firm's short-run supply curve. The horizontal summation of all firms' supply curves forms the market supply curve. Each perfectly competitive firm maximizes profit or minimizes loss by producing where marginal cost equals marginal revenue. Fixed costs are irrelevant to the short-run production decision.

5. Because firms are not free to enter or leave the market in the short run, economic profit or loss is possible in the short run. In the long run, however, some firms will adjust their scale of operations and other firms will enter or leave the market until economic profit or loss is driven to zero. In the long run, each firm will produce at the lowest point on its long-run average cost curve. At this rate of output, marginal cost, marginal revenue, price, and average total cost are all equal. Firms that fail to produce at this least-cost combination will not survive in the long run.

6. In the short run, a firm alters quantity supplied in response to a change in price by moving up or down its marginal cost curve. The long-run industry adjustment

to a change in demand involves firms entering or leaving the market until the remaining firms in the industry earn just a normal profit. As the industry expands or contracts in the long run, the long-run industry supply curve has a shape that reflects either increasing costs, constant costs, or decreasing costs.

7. Perfectly competitive markets exhibit both productive efficiency, because output is produced using the most efficient combination of resources available, and allocative efficiency, because the goods produced are those most valued by consumers. In equilibrium, perfectly competitive markets allocate goods so that the marginal cost of the last unit produced equals the marginal value that consumers attach to that last unit purchased. Voluntary exchange in competitive markets maximizes the sum of consumer surplus and producer surplus.

QUESTIONS FOR REVIEW

1. *(Market Structure)* Define "market structure." What factors are considered in determining the market structure of a particular industry?
2. *(Demand Under Perfect Competition)* What type of demand curve does a perfectly competitive firm face? Why?
3. *(Total Revenue)* Look back at Exhibit 3(a) in this chapter. Explain why the total revenue curve is a straight line from the origin, whereas the slope of the total cost curve changes.
4. *(Profit in the Short Run)* Look back at Exhibit 3(b) in this chapter. Why doesn't the firm choose the output that maximizes average profit (i.e., the output for which average cost is the lowest)?
5. *(The Short-Run Firm Supply Curve)* An individual competitive firm's short-run supply curve is the portion of its marginal cost curve that equals or rises above the average variable cost. Explain why.
6. *(**CaseStudy:** Auction Markets)* Which of the characteristics of the perfectly competitive market structure are found in the Amsterdam flower market?
7. *(Long-Run Industry Supply)* Why does the long-run industry supply curve for an increasing-cost industry slope upward? What causes the increasing costs in an increasing-cost industry?
8. *(Perfect Competition and Efficiency)* Define productive efficiency and allocative efficiency. What conditions must be met in order to achieve them?
9. *(**CaseStudy:** Experimental Economics)* In the University of Arizona experiment, which "buyers" ended up with a surplus at the market-clearing price of $2? Which "sellers" had a surplus? Which "buyers" or "sellers" did not engage in a transaction?

PROBLEMS AND EXERCISES

10. *(Short-Run Profit Maximization)* A perfectly competitive firm has the following fixed and variable costs in the short run. The market price for the firm's product is $150.

Output	FC	VC	TC	TR	Profit/ Loss
0	$100	$ 0	___	___	___
1	100	100	___	___	___
2	100	180	___	___	___
3	100	300	___	___	___
4	100	440	___	___	___
5	100	600	___	___	___
6	100	780	___	___	___

a. Complete the table.
b. At what output rate does the firm maximize profit or minimize loss?
c. What is the firm's marginal revenue at each positive level of output? Its average revenue?
d. What can you say about the relationship between marginal revenue and marginal cost for output rates below the profit-maximizing (or loss-minimizing) rate? For output rates above the profit-maximizing (or loss-minimizing) rate?

11. *(The Short-Run Firm Supply Curve)* Use the following data to answer the questions below:

Q	TVC	MC	AVC
1	$10	___	___
2	16	___	___
3	20	___	___
4	25	___	___
5	31	___	___
6	38	___	___
7	46	___	___
8	55	___	___

a. Calculate the marginal cost and average variable cost for each level of production.
b. How much would the firm produce if it could sell its product for $5? for $7? for $10?
c. Explain your answers.
d. Assuming that its fixed cost is $3, calculate the firm's profit at each of the production levels determined in part (c).

12. *(The Short-Run Firm Supply Curve)* Each of the following situations could exist for a firm in the short run. In each case, indicate whether the firm should produce in the short run or shut down in the short run, or whether additional information is needed to determine what it should do in the short run.

a. Total cost exceeds total revenue at all output levels.
b. Total variable cost exceeds total revenue at all output levels.
c. Total revenue exceeds total fixed cost at all output levels.
d. Marginal revenue exceeds marginal cost at the current output level.
e. Price exceeds average total cost at all output levels.
f. Average variable cost exceeds price at all output levels.
g. Average total cost exceeds price at all output levels.

13. *(Perfect Competition in the Long Run)* Draw the short- and long-run cost curves of a competitive firm in long-run equilibrium. Indicate the long-run equilibrium price and quantity.

a. Discuss the firm's short-run response to a reduction in the price of a variable resource.
b. Assuming that this is a constant-cost industry, describe the process by which the industry returns to long-run equilibrium following a change in market demand.

14. *(The Long-Run Industry Supply Curve)* A normal good is being produced in a constant-cost, perfectly competitive industry. Initially, each firm is in long-run equilibrium.

a. Graphically illustrate and explain the short-run adjustments of the market and the firm to a decrease in consumer incomes. Be sure to discuss any changes in output levels, prices, profits, and the number of firms.
b. Next, show on your graph and explain the long-run adjustment to the income change. Be sure to discuss any changes in output levels, prices, profits, and the number of firms.

15. *(The Long-Run Industry Supply Curve)* The following graph shows possible long-run market supply curves for a perfectly competitive industry. Determine which supply curve indicates a constant-cost industry, an increasing-cost industry, and a decreasing-cost industry.

a. Explain the difference between a decreasing-cost industry and an increasing-cost industry.
b. Distinguish between the long-run impact of an increase in market demand in a decreasing-cost industry and the impact in an increasing-cost industry.

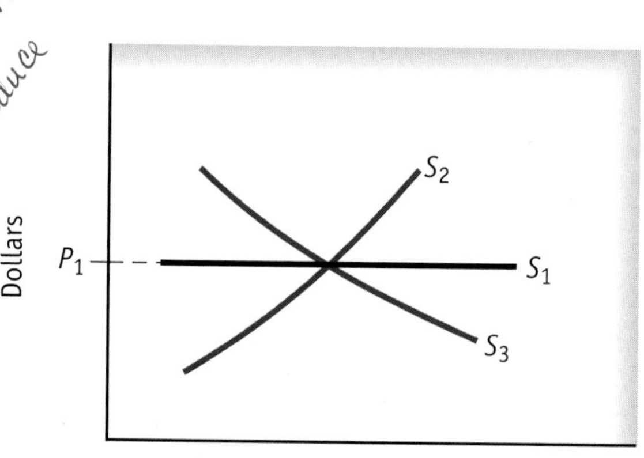

16. *(What's So Perfect About Perfect Competition)* Use the following data to answer the questions.

Quantity	Marginal Cost	Marginal Valuation
0	—	—
1	$ 2	$10
2	3	9
3	4	8
4	5	7
5	6	6
6	8	5
7	10	4
8	12	3

a. For the product shown, assume that the minimum point of each firm's average variable cost curve is at $2. Construct a supply and demand diagram for the product and indicate the equilibrium price and quantity.

b. On the graph, label the area of consumer surplus as *f*. Label the area of producer surplus as *g*.

c. If the equilibrium price were $2, what would be the amount of producer surplus?

EXPERIENTIAL EXERCISES

17. Economics America's EconEd link has an interesting module on the economics of Internet access at **http://www.economicsamerica.org/econedlink/newsline/internet/index.html**. Review the materials provided (including video if you have the right software available). Is provision of Internet access a competitive industry? How would you use the tools of supply and demand to model recent developments in Internet pricing?

18. *(**CaseStudy:** Auction Markets)* Rent the movie *Trading Places,* starring Eddie Murphy and Dan Ackroyd. Enjoy the movie and pay special attention to the scene near the end when Billy Ray and Louis participate in an auction of orange-juice futures. How does the arrival of new information affect the price of those futures contracts? Try to model the situation, using supply and demand curves.

19. *(Wall Street Journal)* Financial markets are quintessential examples of perfectly competitive markets. And, of course, the *Wall Street Journal* features in-depth coverage of these markets. Turn to the Money and Investing section of today's *Wall Street Journal* and choose one or two articles that seem interesting to you. Then, try to determine how financial markets contribute to productive and allocative efficiency in the U.S. economy.

CHAPTER

22 Monopoly

Why aren't all markets monopolized? Why don't monopolies charge the highest price possible? Why don't most monopolies last? Why do some firms offer discounts to students, senior citizens, and other groups? Why do airlines charge less if you stay over Saturday night? Why are diamonds so expensive even though they aren't especially rare either in nature or in jewelry stores? These and other questions are answered in this chapter, which examines monopoly—a market structure quite different from perfect competition.

Monopoly is from the Greek, meaning "one seller." In some parts of the country, monopolists sell electricity, cable TV service, and local phone service. Monopolists also sell postage stamps, food at sports arenas, patented products, and other goods and services with no close substitutes. You have probably heard

Visit the McEachern Interactive Study Center for this chapter at *http://mcisc.swcollege.com*

about the evils of monopoly. You may have even played the board game, Monopoly, on a rainy day.

Like perfect competition, pure monopoly is not as common as other market structures. But by understanding monopoly, you will grow more familiar with the market structures that lie between the two extremes of perfect competition and pure monopoly. In this chapter we examine (1) the sources of monopoly power, (2) how a monopolist maximizes profit, (3) the difference between monopoly and perfect competition in terms of efficiency, and (4) why a monopolist often charges different prices for the same product. Topics discussed in this chapter include:

- Barriers to entry
- Price elasticity and marginal revenue
- Economic profit in the short run and the long run
- Monopoly and resource allocation
- Welfare cost of monopoly
- Price discrimination
- Perfect price discrimination

*Net***Bookmark**

For more information about patents—their purpose, what can be patented, how to apply, what rights are included—go to the Patent Office's Web page on General Information Concerning Patents at http://www.uspto.gov/web/offices/pac/doc/general/. How does the Patent Office treat the information provided about a new invention? Why do you suppose that some firms prefer not to seek patent protection for new inventions? What types of intellectual property, other than new machines and processes, can be protected by patents?

BARRIERS TO ENTRY

As noted in Chapter 4, a *monopoly* is the sole supplier of a product with no close substitutes. Why do some markets come to be dominated by a single supplier? Perhaps the most important characteristic of a monopolized market is *barriers to entry*—new firms cannot profitably enter that market in the long run. **Barriers to entry** are restrictions on the entry of new firms into an industry. We will examine three types of barriers: legal restrictions, economies of scale, and the monopolist's control of an essential resource.

Barrier to entry Any impediment that prevents new firms from competing on an equal basis with existing firms in an industry

Legal Restrictions

One way to prevent new firms from entering a market is to make entry illegal. Patents, licenses, and other legal restrictions imposed by the government provide some producers with legal protection against competition.

Patents and Invention Incentives. In the United States, a **patent** awards an inventor the exclusive right to produce a good or service for 20 years. Originally enacted in 1790, the patent laws encourage inventors to invest the time and money required to discover and develop new products and processes. If others could simply copy successful products, inventors would be less inclined to incur the up-front costs of developing new products. Patents also provide the stimulus to turn an invention into a marketable product, a process called **innovation.**

Patent A legal barrier to entry that conveys to its holder the exclusive right to supply a product for 20 years

Innovation The process of turning an invention into a marketable product

Licenses and Other Entry Restrictions. Governments often confer monopoly status by awarding a single firm the exclusive right to supply a particular good or service. Federal licenses give certain firms the right to broadcast radio and TV signals. State licenses are required to provide services such as medical care, haircuts, and legal assistance. A license is not a monopoly, but it often confers the ability to charge a price above what would be the competitive level; hence, a license can serve as an effective barrier to new firms. Governments confer monopoly rights to sell hot dogs at civic auditoriums, collect garbage, provide bus and cab service in and out of town, and supply services ranging from electricity to cable TV. The government itself may claim the right to provide certain products by outlawing competitors. For example, many states are monopoly sellers of liquor and lottery tickets, and the U.S. Postal Service has the exclusive right to deliver first-class mail.

Economies of Scale

A monopoly sometimes emerges naturally when a firm experiences *economies of scale,* as reflected by the downward-sloping, long-run average cost curve shown in Exhibit 1. When this is the case, a single firm can satisfy market demand at a lower average cost per unit than could two or more firms operating at smaller rates of output. Thus a single firm will emerge from the competitive process as the sole seller in the market. Even though the production of electricity has grown more competitive, the *transmission* of electricity still exhibits economies of scale. Once wires are run throughout the community, the marginal cost of linking additional households to the power source is relatively small. Consequently, the average cost per household declines as more and more households are wired for electricity.

Because such a monopoly emerges from the nature of supply, it is called a *natural monopoly,* to distinguish it from the artificial monopolies created by government patents, licenses, and other legal barriers to entry. A new entrant cannot sell enough output to experience the economies of scale enjoyed by an established natural monopolist, so entry into the market is naturally blocked. We will have more to say about the regulation of natural monopolies in a later chapter, where we examine government regulation of markets.

EXHIBIT 1

Economies of Scale as a Barrier to Entry

A monopoly sometimes emerges naturally when a firm experiences economies of scale as reflected by a downward-sloping, long-run average cost curve. An individual firm can satisfy market demand at a lower average cost per unit than could two or more firms operating at smaller rates of output.

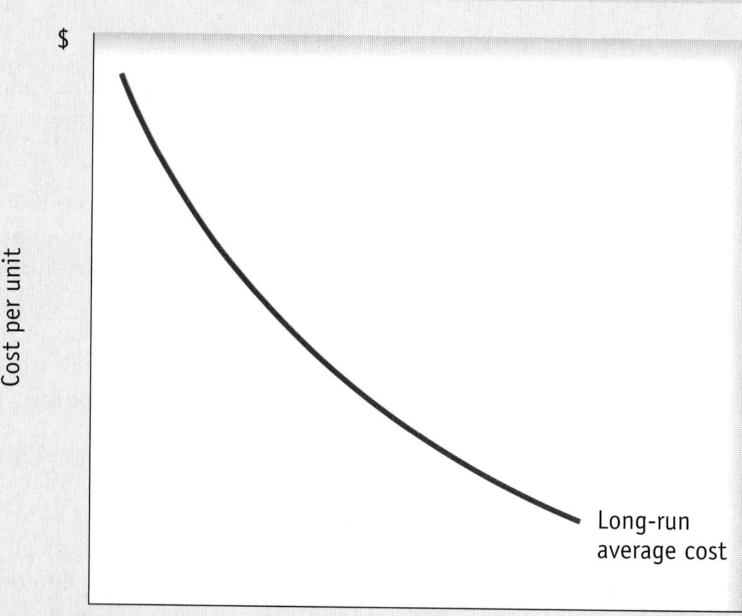

Control of Essential Resources

Sometimes the source of monopoly power is a firm's control over some nonreproducible resource critical to production. For example, professional sports leagues try to block the formation of competing leagues by signing the best athletes to long-term contracts and by seeking the exclusive use of sports stadiums and arenas. Likewise, Alcoa was the sole U.S. manufacturer of aluminum from the late 19th century until World War II; its monopoly power was initially due to production process patents that expired in 1909, but for the next three decades its monopoly power stemmed from its control of U.S. bauxite supplies. Similarly, the world's diamond trade is operated primarily by De Beers Consolidated Mines, which controls most of the world's supply of rough diamonds, as is discussed in the following case study.

Are Diamonds Forever?

The World of Business

At www.adiamondisforever.com you can learn about buying diamonds but you will not learn much about the sponsoring firm—De Beers. For information about the company check http://www.edata.co.za./DeBeers/ from E-Data. In particular, look at the Primary Activities section and the Corporate Report supplied by Financial Mail, a South African business newspaper. What are the current prospects for De Beers' grip on the diamond market? De Beers is not standing idly by while Canadian diamonds come into the market. The company has set up operations in Canada. What have they accomplished there? Find out at the De Beers Canada Web site at http://www.debeers.ca/index.html.

In 1866, a child walking along the Orange River in South Africa picked up an interesting-looking pebble that turned out to be a 21-carat diamond. That discovery on a farm owned by Johannes De Beers sparked the development of the largest diamond mine in history. De Beers Consolidated Mines eventually expanded from mining diamonds to buying rough diamonds mined elsewhere around the world. By controlling the supply of rough diamonds, De Beers has tried to maintain a worldwide monopoly for more than six decades.

De Beers now controls three-quarters of the world's diamond trade—not quite a monopoly, but close to it. The company keeps prices high by carefully limiting supply and promoting market demand through advertising. Several times a year, De Beers invites wholesalers to London, where they are offered a box of diamonds for a set price—no negotiating. If the box of diamonds is not purchased, the buyer may not be invited back next time. Because De Beers tries to reduce market competition, the company cannot operate in the United States due to antitrust legislation (which is why U.S. buyers go to London).

It may surprise you that diamonds are not rare gems, either in nature or in jewelry stores. Nearly all jewelry stores offer more diamonds for sale than any other gem. Diamonds may be the most common natural cut gemstone. Jewelers are willing to hold large inventories of diamonds because they are confident that, because of De Beers' supply controls and marketing efforts, the price will not plummet tomorrow. De Beers' slogan "A diamond is forever" implies both that diamonds retain their value and that diamonds should stay in the family. This slogan helps keep secondhand diamonds, which are good substitutes for newly cut diamonds, off the market, where they could otherwise increase supply and drive down the price. De Beers spends over $200 million a year convincing people that diamonds are scarce and valuable. One promotional coup was to persuade the producers of "Baywatch," a TV show viewed widely around the world, to devote an entire episode to a story about the purchase of a diamond engagement ring. The story played up the company line that the ring should cost two months' salary.

But De Beers has recently lost control of some rough diamond suppliers and the average price has declined. Russians have apparently been selling half their diamonds to independent dealers. A major diamond mine in Australia has also broken away from De Beers. And in October 1998, Canada began operations expected eventually to mine 10 percent of the world's gem-quality diamonds; the prospecting company has not yet promised to sell to De Beers. A monopoly that relies on the control of a key resource, as De Beers does, loses its monopoly status once that control slips away. Perhaps reflecting the growing uncertainty in this monopoly's grip, prices of some diamonds have slipped lately, and De Beers's stock price dropped by 40 percent between mid-1997 and April 1999.

Sources: Jon Ashworth, "Diamond Chief Looks Forward to Keeping the Dream Alive," *Times* (24 January 1998); "Glass with Attitude," *Economist* (20 December 1997); and "First World-Class Diamond Mine in North America," *Journal Inquirer* (17 June 1998). The De Beers home page is at http://www.adiamondisforever.com/.

Local monopolies are more common than national or international monopolies. In rural areas, monopolies may include the only grocery store, movie theater, or restaurant for miles around. But long-lasting monopolies are rare because, as we will see, a profitable monopoly attracts competitors offering close substitutes. Also, over time, technological change tends to break down barriers to entry. For example, the development of wireless transmission of long-distance telephone calls attracted competitors to AT&T. Wireless transmission will soon erase the monopoly held by local cable TV providers and even local phone service. Likewise, fax machines, e-mail, the Internet, and firms such as Federal Express now compete with the U.S. Postal Service's monopoly on first-class mail, as we will see in a later case study. And the ability to produce synthetic diamonds will eventually create additional problems for De Beers.

REVENUE FOR THE MONOPOLIST

Because a monopoly, by definition, supplies the entire market, the demand for goods or services produced by a monopolist is also the market demand. The demand curve for the monopolist's output therefore slopes downward, reflecting the law of demand—price and quantity demanded are inversely related. Let's first take a look at the monopolist's revenue schedule and revenue curves.

Revenue Schedule

Suppose that De Beers controls the entire diamond market, and the market demand for 1-carat diamonds is as presented in the first two columns of Exhibit 2. The first column lists the quantity of diamonds demanded per day, and the second column lists the corresponding price, or average revenue. The two columns together represent the demand schedule facing De Beers for 1-carat diamonds. The monopolist's *total revenue,* which equals price times quantity, appears in the third column. Notice that total revenue increases for the first 15 diamonds sold per day, but then tops out and begins to decline with 17 diamonds.

Marginal revenue, the change in total revenue as a result of selling one more diamond, is listed in the fourth column. For all units of output except the first,

EXHIBIT 2

Revenue for De Beers, a Monopolist

1-Carat diamonds per day (Q) (1)	Price (average revenue) (p) (2)	Total Revenue ($TR = Q \times p$) (3) = (1) × (2)	Marginal Revenue $\left(MR = \frac{\Delta TR}{\Delta Q}\right)$ (4)
0	$7,750	0	—
1	7,500	$ 7,500	$7,500
2	7,250	14,500	7,000
3	7,000	21,000	6,500
4	6,750	27,000	6,000
5	6,500	32,500	5,500
6	6,250	37,500	5,000
7	6,000	42,000	4,500
8	5,750	46,000	4,000
9	5,500	49,500	3,500
10	5,250	52,500	3,000
11	5,000	55,000	2,500
12	4,750	57,000	2,000
13	4,500	58,500	1,500
14	4,250	59,500	1,000
15	4,000	60,000	500
16	3,750	60,000	0
17	3,500	59,500	−500

marginal revenue is less than the price, and the gap between the two grows larger as the price declines. As the price declines, marginal revenue falls for two reasons: (1) the amount of revenue received from selling another diamond declines (since the price drops), and (2) the revenue forgone by selling all diamonds at this lower price increases. For example, to sell a second diamond, the price must drop from $7,500 to $7,250. Total revenue from selling two diamonds is $14,500 and marginal revenue is $7,000 (= $14,500 − $7,500), so marginal revenue is below the price of $7,250.

Revenue Curves

The data in Exhibit 2 are graphed in Exhibit 3, which shows the demand and marginal revenue curves in the upper panel and the total revenue curve in the lower panel. Total revenue, recall, equals price times quantity. Note that the marginal revenue curve is below the demand curve and that total revenue is at a maximum when marginal revenue is zero. Take a minute to study these relationships—they are important.

Total revenue divided by quantity is *average revenue per unit.* Average revenue equals the price for any level of sales, so *the demand curve is also the*

EXHIBIT 3

Monopoly Demand and Marginal and Total Revenue

Where demand is price elastic, marginal revenue is positive, so total revenue increases as the price falls. Where demand is price inelastic, marginal revenue is negative, so total revenue decreases as the price falls. Where demand is unit elastic, marginal revenue is zero, so total revenue is at a maximum, neither increasing nor decreasing.

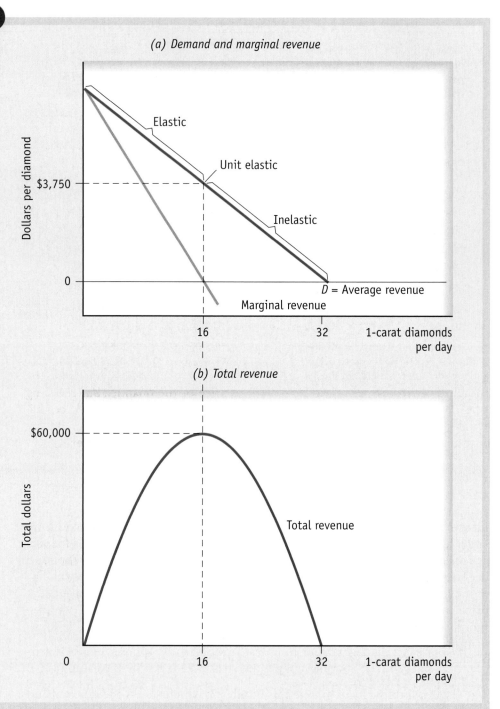

(a) Demand and marginal revenue

Dollars per diamond
$3,750
0
Elastic
Unit elastic
Inelastic
D = Average revenue
Marginal revenue
16
32
1-carat diamonds per day

(b) Total revenue

Total dollars
$60,000
Total revenue
0
16
32
1-carat diamonds per day

monopolist's average-revenue curve (just as the perfectly competitive firm's demand curve is also that firm's average-revenue curve). Earlier you learned that the price elasticity for a straight-line demand curve decreases as you move down the curve. Where demand is elastic—that is, where the percent increase in quantity demanded more than offsets the percent decrease in price—a decrease in price will increase total revenue. Therefore, *where demand is elastic, marginal revenue is positive, so in that region total revenue increases as the price falls.* On the other hand, where demand is inelastic, the increase in quantity demanded from a lower price is not enough to make up for the loss in revenue resulting from selling all diamonds for the lower price, so total revenue will decline if the price falls. *Where demand is inelastic, marginal revenue is negative, so total revenue decreases as the price falls.* From Exhibit 3, you can see that marginal revenue becomes negative if the price drops below $3,750, indicating an inelastic demand at prices below $3,750.

In this example, demand is unit elastic at the price of $3,750. At that price, marginal revenue is zero and total revenue is at a maximum. Your understanding of elasticity will help as we discover the price and output combination that maximizes the monopolist's profit.

THE FIRM'S COSTS AND PROFIT MAXIMIZATION

Given the demand curve, the important question is: How will this monopolist choose among the price-quantity alternatives? We assume that the objective of De Beers, like that of other firms, is to *maximize economic profit.* In the case of perfect competition, the firm's choice is confined to *quantity* because the price is already determined by the market. The perfect competitor is a *price taker.* The monopolist, however, can choose either the price or the quantity, but choosing one determines the other. Because the monopolist can select the price that maximizes profit, we say the monopolist is a *price searcher.* More generally, any firm that has some control over the price it charges is a **price searcher.**

Price searcher A firm that has some control over the price it charges because its demand curve slopes downward

Profit Maximization

Exhibit 4 repeats the revenue data from Exhibits 2 and 3 and also includes short-run cost data reflecting costs similar to those already introduced in the two previous chapters. Please take a little time right now to become familiar with Exhibit 4. Then ask yourself what price-quantity combination maximizes profit.

There are two approaches to profit maximization—the total approach and the marginal approach.

Total Revenue Minus Total Cost. The profit-maximizing monopolist employs the same decision rule as the competitive firm. *The monopolist must find the production rate where total revenue exceeds total cost by the greatest amount.* Economic profit appears in the right-hand column of Exhibit 4. As you can see, the maximum profit is $12,500 per day, which occurs when output is 10 diamonds per day and price is $5,250. At that rate of output, total revenue is $52,500 and total cost is $40,000.

Marginal Cost Equals Marginal Revenue. De Beers, as a profit-maximizing monopolist, increases output as long as selling additional diamonds adds more to total revenue than to total cost. So De Beers expands output as long as marginal revenue exceeds marginal cost but will stop before marginal cost exceeds marginal revenue. Again, profit is maximized at $12,500 when output is 10 diamonds per day. The marginal revenue from the 10th diamond is $3,000; its marginal cost

EXHIBIT 4

Short-Run Costs and Revenue for a Monopolist

Diamonds per day (Q) (1)	Price (average revenue) (p) (2)	Total Revenue ($TR = Q \times p$) (3) = (1) × (2)	Marginal Revenue $\left(MR = \frac{\Delta TR}{\Delta Q}\right)$ (4)	Total Cost (TC) (5)	Marginal Cost $\left(MC = \frac{\Delta TC}{\Delta Q}\right)$ (6)	Average Total Cost $\left(ATC = \frac{TC}{Q}\right)$ (7)	Total Profit or Loss = $TR - TC$ (8)
0	$7,750	0	—	$15,000	—	—	−$15,000
1	7,500	$ 7,500	$7,500	19,750	$ 4,750	$19,750	−12,250
2	7,250	14,500	7,000	23,500	3,750	11,750	−9,000
3	7,000	21,000	6,500	26,500	3,000	8,830	−5,500
4	6,750	27,000	6,000	29,000	2,500	7,750	−2,000
5	6,500	32,500	5,500	31,000	2,000	6,200	1,500
6	6,250	37,500	5,000	32,500	1,500	5,420	5,000
7	6,000	42,000	4,500	33,750	1,250	4,820	8,250
8	5,750	46,000	4,000	35,250	1,500	4,410	10,750
9	5,500	49,500	3,500	37,250	2,000	4,140	12,250
10	**5,250**	**52,500**	**3,000**	**40,000**	**2,750**	**4,000**	**12,500**
11	5,000	55,000	2,500	43,250	3,250	3,930	11,750
12	4,750	57,000	2,000	48,000	4,750	4,000	9,000
13	4,500	58,500	1,500	54,500	6,500	4,190	4,000
14	4,250	59,500	1,000	64,000	9,500	4,570	−4,500
15	4,000	60,000	500	77,500	13,500	5,170	−17,500
16	3,750	60,000	0	96,000	18,500	6,000	−36,000
17	3,500	59,500	−500	121,000	25,000	7,120	−61,500

is $2,750. Because an 11th diamond has a marginal cost of $3,250 but a marginal revenue of only $2,500, producing that additional unit would lower profit from $12,500 to $11,750. As you can see, at output rates in excess of 10 diamonds per day, marginal cost exceeds marginal revenue. For simplicity, we say that *the profit-maximizing output occurs where marginal cost equals marginal revenue,* which, you will recall, is the golden rule of profit maximization.

Graphical Solution. The cost and revenue data in Exhibit 4 are reflected in Exhibit 5, with per-unit cost and revenue curves in the upper panel and total cost and revenue curves in the lower panel. The intersection of the two marginal curves at point *e* in the lower panel indicates that profit is maximized when 10 diamonds are sold. At that rate of output, we move up to the demand curve to find the profit-maximizing price of $5,250. The average total cost of $4,000 is

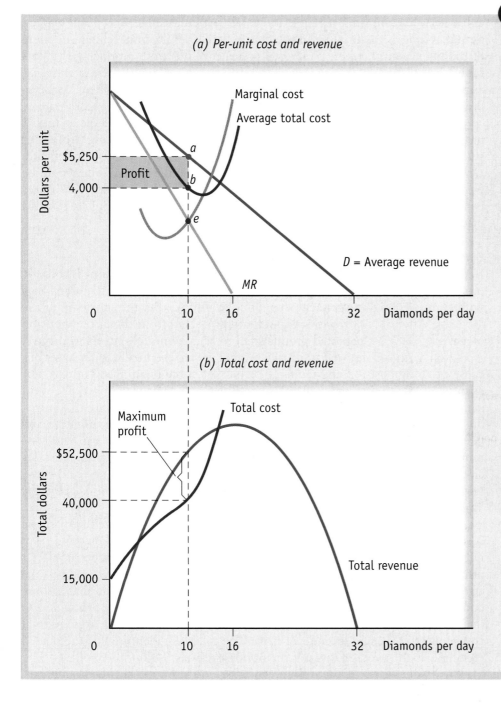

(a) Per-unit cost and revenue

Dollars per unit

$5,250

4,000

Profit

Marginal cost

Average total cost

a

b

e

D = Average revenue

MR

0 10 16 32 Diamonds per day

(b) Total cost and revenue

Total dollars

Maximum profit

Total cost

$52,500

40,000

15,000

Total revenue

0 10 16 32 Diamonds per day

EXHIBIT 5

Monopoly Costs and Revenue

The monopolist produces 10 diamonds per day and charges a price of $5,250. Total profit, shown by the blue rectangle in panel (a), is $12,500, the profit per unit multiplied by the number of units sold. In panel (b), profit is maximized where total revenue exceeds total cost by the greatest amount, which occurs at an output rate of 10 diamonds per day. Profit is total revenue ($52,500) minus total cost ($40,000), or $12,500.

identified by point *b*. The average profit per diamond equals the price of $5,250 minus the average total cost of $4,000. Economic profit is the average profit per unit of $1,250 multiplied by the 10 units sold, for a total profit of $12,500 per day, as identified by the shaded rectangle. *So the profit-maximizing rate of output is found where the rising marginal cost curve intersects the marginal revenue curve.*

In the lower panel, the firm's profit or loss is measured by the vertical distance between the total revenue and total cost curves. De Beers will expand output as long as the increase in total revenue that results from selling one more diamond exceeds the increase in total cost that results from producing that diamond. *The profit-maximizing firm will produce the rate of output where total revenue exceeds total cost by the greatest amount.* Again, profit is maximized where De Beers produces 10 diamonds per day.

One common myth about monopolies is that they will charge as high a price as possible. But the monopolist is interested in maximizing profit, not price. The amount the monopolist can charge is limited by consumer demand. De Beers could charge a price of $7,500 per diamond, but only one would be purchased at that price. Indeed, the monopolist could charge $8,000 or $10,000 per diamond, but none would be purchased. So charging the highest possible price is not consistent with maximizing profit.

Short-Run Losses and the Shutdown Decision

Being a monopolist provides no guarantee of profit. A monopolist is the sole producer of a good with no close substitutes, but the demand for that good may not be great enough to generate economic profit in either the short run or the long run. After all, many new products are protected from direct competition by patents, yet most patented products fail to attract enough buyers to survive. And even a monopolist that is initially profitable may eventually suffer losses because of rising costs, falling demand, or market entry of similar products. For example, Coleco, the original mass producer of Cabbage Patch dolls, went bankrupt after that craze died down. And Cuisinart, the company that introduced the food processor in the early 1980s, soon faced many imitators and filed for bankruptcy before the end of the decade. In the short run, the loss-minimizing monopolist, like the loss-minimizing perfect competitor, must decide whether to produce or to shut down. *If the price covers average variable cost, the firm will operate. If no price covers average variable cost, the firm will shut down, at least in the short run.*

Loss minimization is illustrated graphically in Exhibit 6, where the marginal cost curve intersects the marginal revenue curve at point *e*. At the equilibrium rate of output, Q, the price, *p*, is read off the demand curve at point *b*. That price exceeds average variable cost (found at point *c*) but is below average total cost (found at point *a*). Since price covers average variable cost and makes some contribution to average fixed cost, this monopolist loses less by producing Q than by shutting down. The loss per diamond is *ab*, which is the average total cost minus the average revenue, or price. The total loss, identified by the shaded rectangle, is the average loss per diamond, *ab*, times the number sold, Q. The firm will shut down if the average variable cost curve is above the demand curve, or average revenue curve, at all output rates.

Recall that for a perfectly competitive firm, that portion of the marginal cost curve at or above the average variable cost curve shows how much the firm supplies at each price. Thus that portion of the marginal cost curve represents a perfect competitor's supply curve. For the monopolist, unlike the perfectly competitive firm, marginal revenue does not equal the price. The price at the profit-maximizing (or loss-minimizing) rate of output is found on the demand

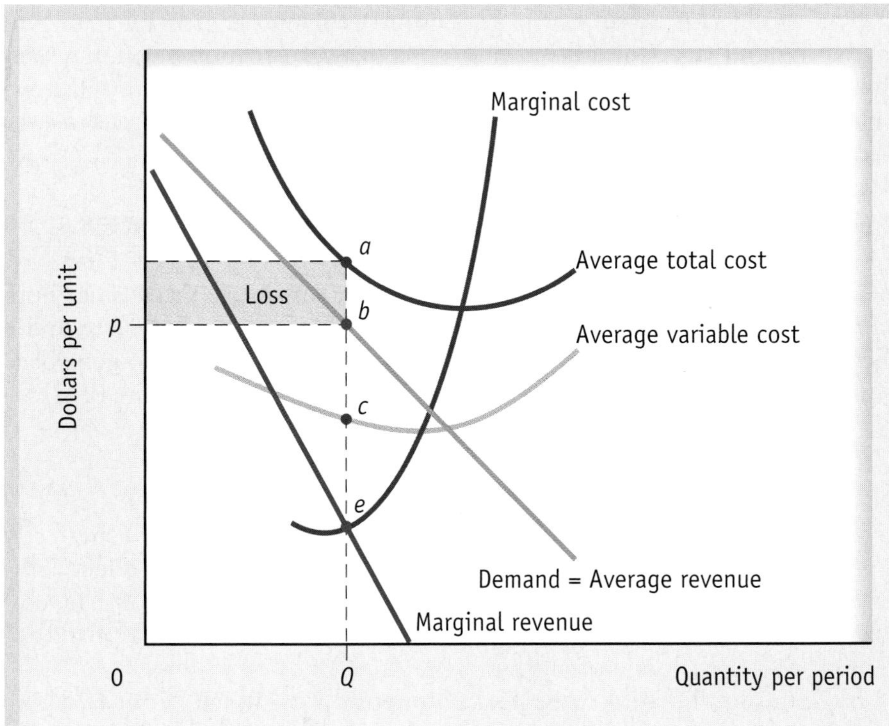

EXHIBIT 6

The Monopolist Minimizes Losses in the Short Run

Marginal cost equals marginal revenue at point *e*. At quantity *Q*, price *p* (at point *b*) is less than average total cost (at point *a*), so the monopolist is suffering a loss. The monopolist will continue to produce in the short run because price is greater than average variable cost (at point *c*).

curve, which lies *above* the marginal revenue and marginal cost curves at that quantity. The intersection of a monopolist's marginal cost and marginal revenue curves identifies the profit-maximizing (or loss-minimizing) quantity, but the price must be read off the demand curve. So each point along the monopolist's marginal cost curve does not identify a price-quantity combination, as was the case for a perfectly competitive firm. Hence, there is no curve that reflects combinations of price and quantity the monopolist is willing and able to supply, so *there is no monopolist supply curve.*

Long-Run Profit Maximization

For perfectly competitive firms, the distinction between the short run and the long run is important, because in the long run entry and exit of firms can occur, erasing any economic profit or loss. For the monopolist, the distinction between the short and long run is less important. *If a monopoly is insulated from competition by high barriers that block new entry, then economic profit can persist in the long run.*

Yet short-run profit is no guarantee of long-run profit. For example, if the monopoly power rests on a patent, patents last only a specified time and even while a product is under patent, the monopolist often must defend the patent in court (patent litigation has increased by more than half in the last decade).

A monopolist that earns economic profit in the short run may find that profit can be increased in the long run by adjusting its scale of production.

A monopolist that suffers a loss in the short run may be able to eliminate that loss in the long run by adjusting to a more efficient size or by trying to increase demand through advertising (most start-up firms lose money initially). A monopolist that is unable to erase a loss in the long run will leave the market.

MONOPOLY AND THE ALLOCATION OF RESOURCES

If monopolists are no more greedy than perfectly competitive firms (since both maximize profit), if monopolists do not charge the highest possible price, and if monopolists are not guaranteed a profit, then what's the problem? To get a handle on the problem, we will compare monopoly with that benchmark established in the previous chapter: perfect competition.

Price and Output Under Perfect Competition

Let's begin with the long-run equilibrium price and output for a perfectly competitive market. Suppose the long-run market supply curve in perfect competition is horizontal, as shown by S_c in Exhibit 7. Since this is a constant-cost industry, the horizontal long-run supply curve also shows marginal cost and average total cost at each rate of output.

Long-run equilibrium in perfect competition occurs at point *c*, where market demand and market supply intersect to yield price p_c and quantity Q_c. Remember, the demand curve reflects the marginal benefit from each unit purchased. In competitive equilibrium, this marginal benefit also equals the marginal cost to society of producing the final unit sold. Because consumers are able to purchase Q_c units at price p_c, they enjoy a net benefit from con-

EXHIBIT 7

Perfect Competition and Monopoly

A perfectly competitive industry would produce output Q_c determined at the intersection of market demand curve *D* and supply curve S_c. The price would be p_c. A monopoly that could produce output at the same minimum average cost would produce output Q_m, determined at point *b*, where marginal cost and marginal revenue intersect. It would charge price p_m. Hence, output is lower and price is higher under monopoly than under perfect competition.

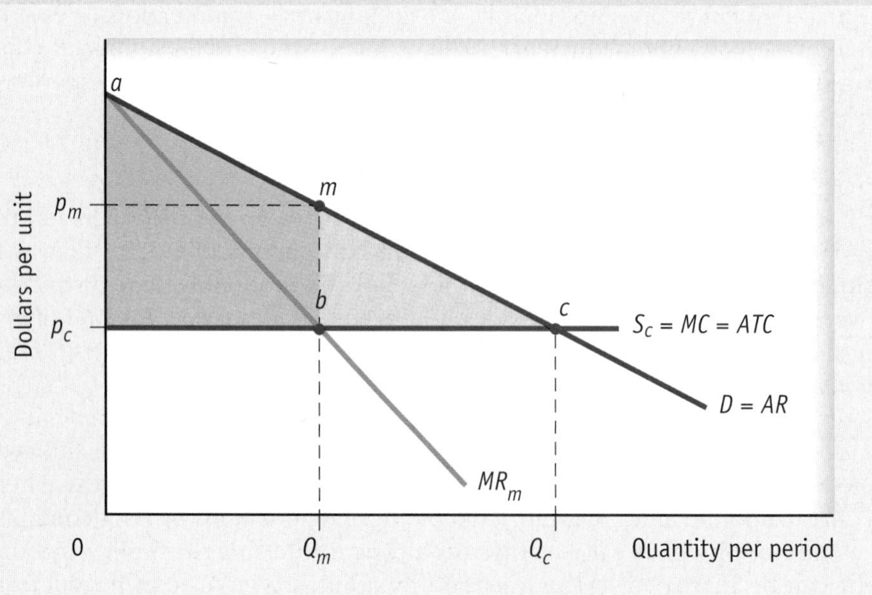

sumption, or a consumer surplus, which is measured by the entire shaded triangle acp_c.

Price and Output Under Monopoly

When there is only one firm in the industry, the industry demand curve becomes the monopolist's demand curve, so the price the monopolist charges determines how much is sold. Because the monopolist's demand curve slopes downward, the marginal revenue curve also slopes downward, as is indicated by MR_m in Exhibit 7. Suppose the monopolist can produce at the same constant long-run average cost as can the competitive industry. The monopolist maximizes profit in the long run by equating marginal cost with marginal revenue. Marginal cost equals marginal revenue at point *b*, yielding equilibrium output Q_m at price p_m. The consumer surplus at that price is triangle amp_m. The consumers' marginal benefit, identified as point *m*, exceeds the monopolist's marginal cost, identified as point *b*. Society would be better off if output were expanded beyond Q_m, because the marginal value consumers attach to additional units exceeds the marginal cost of producing those additional units.

Allocative and Distributive Effects

Consider the allocative and distributive effects of monopoly versus perfect competition. In Exhibit 7, the monopolist earns economic profit equal to the rectangle $p_m mbp_c$. Consumer surplus under perfect competition was the large triangle acp_c; under monopoly, it shrinks to the smaller triangle amp_m, which in this example is only one-fourth as large. By comparing the situation under monopoly with that under perfect competition, you can see that economic profit comes entirely from what was consumer surplus under perfect competition. Because the profit rectangle reflects a transfer from consumer surplus to monopoly profit, this amount is not lost to society and so is not considered a welfare loss of monopoly.

Notice, however, that consumer surplus has been reduced by more than the profit rectangle. Consumers have also lost the triangle *mcb,* which was part of the consumer surplus under perfect competition. The *mcb* triangle is called the **deadweight loss,** or *welfare loss,* of monopoly because it is a loss to consumers that is a gain to nobody. *The triangle* mcb *measures the welfare loss arising from the higher price and reduced output of the monopolist.* This triangle is a deadweight loss because it represents consumer surplus forgone on units of output that are not produced. Empirical estimates of the U.S. annual welfare cost of monopoly have ranged from about 1 percent to about 5 percent of national income. Applied to national income data for 1999, these estimates imply a welfare cost that could range from about $90 billion to $440 billion.

Deadweight loss A loss of consumer surplus and producer surplus that is not transferred to anyone else; it can result from monopolization of an industry

PROBLEMS ESTIMATING THE WELFARE COST OF MONOPOLY

The actual cost of monopoly could differ from the welfare loss described in the previous section. We will first consider why the welfare loss of monopoly might be lower than that measured in Exhibit 7 and then consider why it might be higher.

Why the Welfare Loss of Monopoly Might Be Lower

If firms in an industry experience economies of scale, a monopolist may be able to produce output at a lower cost per unit than could competitive firms. Therefore, the price, or at least the cost of production, could be lower under monopoly than under competition. If there are no economies of scale, the monopolist may still keep the price below the profit-maximizing level to avoid attracting new competitors. For example, before World War II, Alcoa was the only U.S. manufacturer of aluminum. Some observers claim the company kept prices low to discourage potential rivals from entering the industry.

The welfare loss shown in Exhibit 7 may also overstate the true cost of monopoly because monopolists may, in response to public scrutiny and political pressure, keep prices below what the market could bear. Although monopolists would like to earn as great an economic profit as possible, they realize that if the public outcry over high prices and high profits grows loud enough, some sort of government intervention could reduce or even eliminate profits. For example, the prices and profits of drug companies, which individually are monopoly producers of patented medicines, came under scrutiny by President Clinton, who threatened to regulate drug prices. Firms may try to avoid such treatment by keeping prices below the level that would maximize economic profit.

Why the Welfare Loss of Monopoly Might Be Higher

Another line of thought suggests that the welfare loss of monopoly may, in fact, be greater than shown in our simple diagram. *If resources must be devoted to securing and maintaining a monopoly position, monopolies may involve more of a welfare loss than simple models suggest.* For example, consider radio and TV broadcasting rights, which confer on the recipient the exclusive right to use a particular band of the scarce broadcast spectrum. In the past, these rights have been given away by government agencies to the applicants deemed most deserving. Because these rights are so valuable, numerous applicants spend a bundle on lawyers' fees, lobbying expenses, and other costs associated with making themselves appear the most deserving. The efforts devoted to securing and maintaining a monopoly position are largely a social waste because they use up scarce resources but add not one unit to output. Activities undertaken by individuals or firms to influence public policy in a way that will directly or indirectly redistribute income to themselves are referred to as **rent seeking.**

Rent seeking Activities undertaken by individuals or firms to influence public policy in a way that will directly or indirectly redistribute income to them

The monopolist, insulated from the rigors of competition in the marketplace, may also grow fat and lazy—and become inefficient. Since some monopolies could still earn an economic profit even if output were not produced at the least possible cost, corporate executives may waste resources in creating a more comfortable life for themselves. Long lunches, afternoon golf, plush offices, corporate jets, and extensive employee benefits may make company life more enjoyable, but these additional expenses also increase the average cost of production.

Monopolists have also been criticized for being slow to adopt the latest production techniques, being reluctant to develop new products, and generally lacking innovativeness. Because monopolists are largely insulated from the rigors of competition, they may take it easy. It's been said that "The best of all monopoly profits is a quiet life." The following case study discusses the performance of one of the oldest monopolies in the United States, the U.S. Postal Service.

The Mail Monopoly

The U.S. postal monopoly was established in 1775 and has operated under federal protection ever since. In 1971, Congress converted the Post Office Department into an independent agency called the U.S. Postal Service, with revenue of about $60 billion in 1998. It has a legal monopoly in delivering first-class letters; it also has the exclusive right to the use of the space inside mailboxes. The 760,000 Postal Service employees handle over half a billion pieces of mail a day—nearly half the world's total.

The Postal Service monopoly has suffered in recent years because of higher postal rates and competition from new technologies. The price of a first-class stamp climbed from 6 cents in 1970 to 33 cents by 1999, more than double the increase in inflation and triple the increase in telephone rates. Emerging technologies such as fax machines and e-mail also compete with the Postal Service (e-mail messages now greatly outnumber first-class letters).

The United Parcel Service (UPS) is more mechanized and more containerized than the Postal Service and thus has lower costs and less breakage. The Postal Service has tried to emulate UPS, but with only limited success. Postal employees are also paid more on average than employees at UPS or other private-sector delivery services, such as Federal Express.

Despite threatened legal actions by the Postal Service, Federal Express and others have captured 90 percent of the overnight mail business. Since the Postal Service has no monopoly except for regular first-class mail, it has lost huge chunks of the other classes to private firms offering lower rates and better service. For example, in the last 20 years, UPS and others have taken away 95 percent of fourth-class mail—parcel post business. When the Postal Service recently raised third-class ("junk" mail) rates, third-class mailers shifted to other forms of advertising, including cable TV and telemarketing. The Postal Service is losing its first-class monopoly because of competition from overnight mail and from new technologies. Things could be worse: Russia's Post Office went broke in 1998, and trainloads full of mail were held hostage by the state Railway Ministry waiting to get paid.

Source: Richard John, *Spreading the News: The American Postal System from Franklin to Morse* (Harvard University Press, 1996); Matt Lake, "Focus on Productivity and Profit at Internet World," *New York Times* (9 October 1998); and Michael Wines, "At Russian Post Office, Check Isn't in the Mail," *New York Times* (3 October 1998). The home page of the U.S. Postal Service is at http://www.usps.com/welcome.htm.

CaseStudy

Public Policy

How has the Postal Service dealt with competition and change? A chapter in its on-line history, at http://www.usps.gov/history/his3_5.htm#CHANGE, describes the reforms made in the 1990s to compete with for-profit firms and e-mail. How does the Postal Service set rates now that it is no longer a monopoly? The process is described at http://www.usps.gov/fyi/welcome.htm. What role do forces of competition play in rate setting? On-line cost calculators are provided by both USPS at http://www.usps.gov/business/calcs.htm and UPS (United Parcel Service) at http://www.usps.gov/business/calcs.htm. Try finding the cost of sending a letter to Uruguay. Which is cheaper? Why?

Not all economists believe that monopolies, especially private monopolies, manage their resources with any less vigilance than perfect competitors do. Some argue that because monopolists are protected from rivals, they are in a good position to capture the fruits of any innovation and therefore will be more innovative than competitive firms. Other economists believe that if a private monopolist strays from the path of profit maximization, the value of the firm's stock will drop. This lower stock price provides an incentive for outsiders to buy a controlling share of the firm's stock, shape up the operation, and watch profits—as well as the value of the firm's stock—grow. This market for corporate control is thus said to direct monopolists along the path of efficient production.

MODELS OF PRICE DISCRIMINATION

Price discrimination Increasing profit by selling the same good for different prices to different consumers for reasons unrelated to cost

In the model of monopoly developed so far, to sell more output, a monopolist must lower the price for all output sold. In reality, a monopolist can sometimes increase economic profit by charging higher prices to people who value the output more. This practice of charging different prices to different consumers for identical output is known as **price discrimination.** For example, some firms offer discounts to senior citizens. Children pay lower admission prices to sporting events, movies, plays, and other shows. As a student, you also qualify for reduced prices for a variety of products. Firms offer certain groups reduced prices because doing so enhances profits. Let's see how and why.

Conditions for Price Discrimination

To practice price discrimination, certain conditions must exist. First, the demand curve for the product must slope downward, indicating that the producer is a price searcher—the producer has some market power, some control over the price. Second, there must be at least two classes of consumers, with different price elasticities of demand. Third, the producer must be able, at little cost, to identify each class of consumers and charge them different prices. Finally, the producer must be able to prevent those who pay the lower price from reselling the product to those who pay the higher price.

Examples of Price Discrimination

Let's consider some examples of price discrimination. Because businesspeople face unpredictable yet urgent demands for travel and communication, and because such expenses are paid by the company, businesspeople are less sensitive to changes in the price of travel and communication than are householders. In other words, businesspeople have a less elastic demand for business travel and telephone use than do householders, so airlines and telephone services try to maximize profits by charging business customers higher rates than residential customers.

But how do firms distinguish between classes of customers? Telephone companies are able to sort out their customers by charging different rates based on the time of day. Long-distance charges are often higher during normal *business* hours than during evenings and weekends, when householders, who presumably have a higher price elasticity of demand, make social calls. Airlines try to distinguish between business customers and household customers based on the terms under which tickets are purchased. Householders plan their trips well in advance and often stay over Saturday night. They have more flexibility about when they travel and are more sensitive to price than are business travelers. Business travel, on the other hand, is more unpredictable, more urgent, and seldom involves a weekend stay. The airlines separate business travelers from vacationers by requiring purchasers of "super-saver" fares to buy tickets well in advance and to stay over Saturday.

Major amusement parks, such as Disney World, often think of customers as falling into two distinct groups with different elasticities: local residents and out-of-towners. Out-of-towners typically spend a substantial amount on airlines and lodging just to get there, so they are less sensitive to the price of admission than are local residents, who can go any time. The problem is how to charge a lower price to local residents. The parks do this by making discount coupons available at local businesses, such as dry cleaners, which tourists are not likely to visit.

A Model of Price Discrimination

Exhibit 8 shows the effects of price discrimination. Consumers are divided into two groups with distinctly different demands. *At a given price level,* the price elasticity of demand in panel (b) is greater than that in panel (a). Think of panel (b) as reflecting the demand of college students, senior citizens, or some other group that tends to be more sensitive to the price.

The exhibit also shows the marginal cost curve. For simplicity, we assume that the monopolist produces at a constant long-run average cost of $1 and that this cost is the same for both groups. The monopolist maximizes profit by finding the output in each market that equates marginal cost with marginal revenue. In panel (a), the resulting price is $3 per unit; in panel (b), that price is $1.50 per unit. So profit maximization results in charging a lower price to the group with more elastic demand. Note that, despite the price difference, the monopolist collects the same marginal revenue from the last unit sold to each group.

EXHIBIT 8

Price Discrimination with Two Groups of Consumers

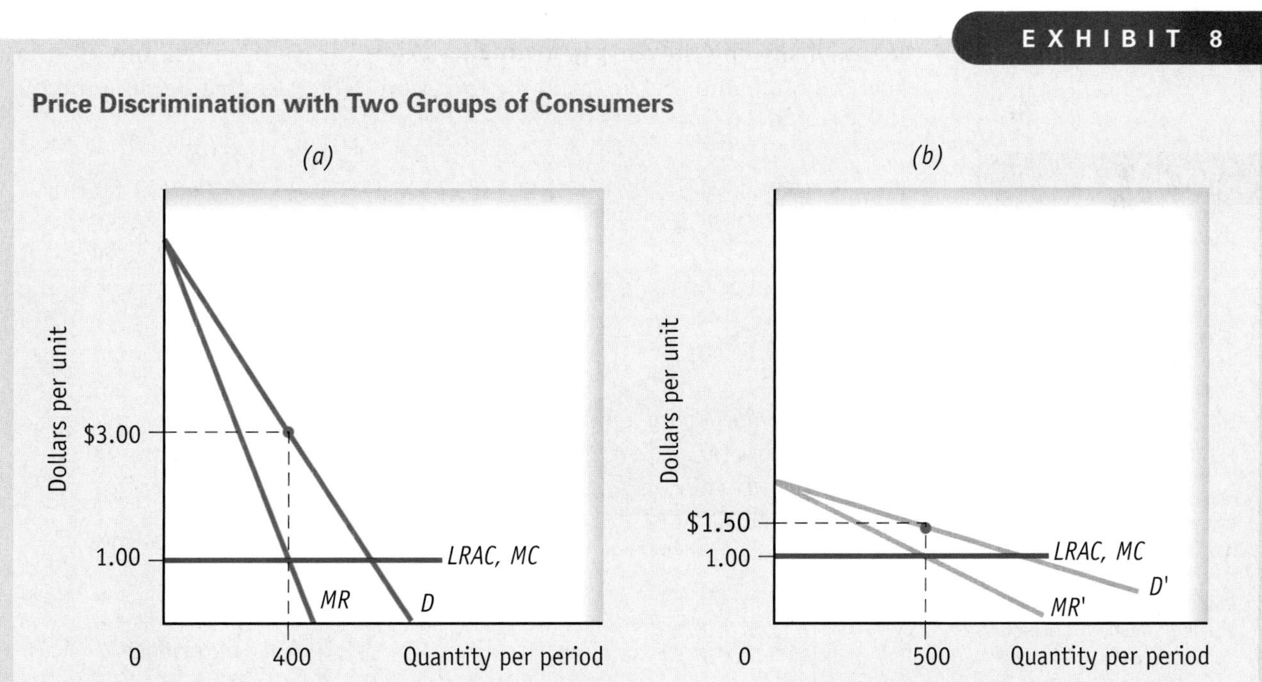

A monopolist that faces two groups of consumers with different demand elasticities may be able to practice price discrimination. With marginal cost the same in both markets, the firm sells 400 units to the high-marginal-value consumers in panel (a) and charges them a price of $3 per unit. It sells 500 units to the low-marginal-value consumers in panel (b) and charges them a price of $1.50.

Perfect Price Discrimination: The Monopolist's Dream

The demand curve shows the marginal value of each unit consumed, which is also the maximum amount consumers would pay for each unit. If the monopolist could charge a different price for each unit sold—a price reflected by the height of the demand curve—the firm's marginal revenue from selling one more unit would equal the price of that unit. Thus, the demand curve would become the firm's marginal revenue curve. The **perfectly discriminating monopolist** charges a different price for each unit of the good.

Perfectly discriminating monopolist A monopolist who charges a different price for each unit of the good

In Exhibit 9, the monopolist is assumed to produce at a constant average cost in the long run. A perfectly discriminating monopolist, like any producer, would maximize profit by finding the output rate where marginal cost equals marginal revenue. Since the demand curve is now the marginal revenue curve, the profit-maximizing output occurs at the point where the demand curve intersects the marginal cost curve, identified at point *e* in Exhibit 9. Price discrimination is a way of increasing profit. The perfectly discriminating monopolist's economic profit is defined by the area of the shaded triangle *aec*.

By charging a different price for each unit of output, the perfectly discriminating monopolist is able to convert every dollar of consumer surplus into economic profit. Although it may seem unfair to consumers, perfect price discrimination gets high marks based on allocative efficiency. In fact, because we have assumed that this is a constant-cost industry, *Q* is the same rate of output that would result from perfect competition (though under perfect competition, consumer surplus would equal the triangle *aec*). As in the perfectly competitive outcome, the marginal cost of the last unit of output produced just equals the marginal benefit consumers attach to that unit. And although perfect price discrimination yields no consumer surplus, the total benefits consumers derive from consumption just equal the total amount they paid for the good. Note also that because the mo-

EXHIBIT 9

Perfect Price Discrimination

If a monopolist can charge a different price for each unit sold, it may be able to practice perfect price discrimination. By setting the price of each unit equal to the maximum amount consumers are willing to pay for that unit (shown by the height of the demand curve), the monopolist can achieve a profit equal to the area of the shaded triangle. Consumer surplus is zero.

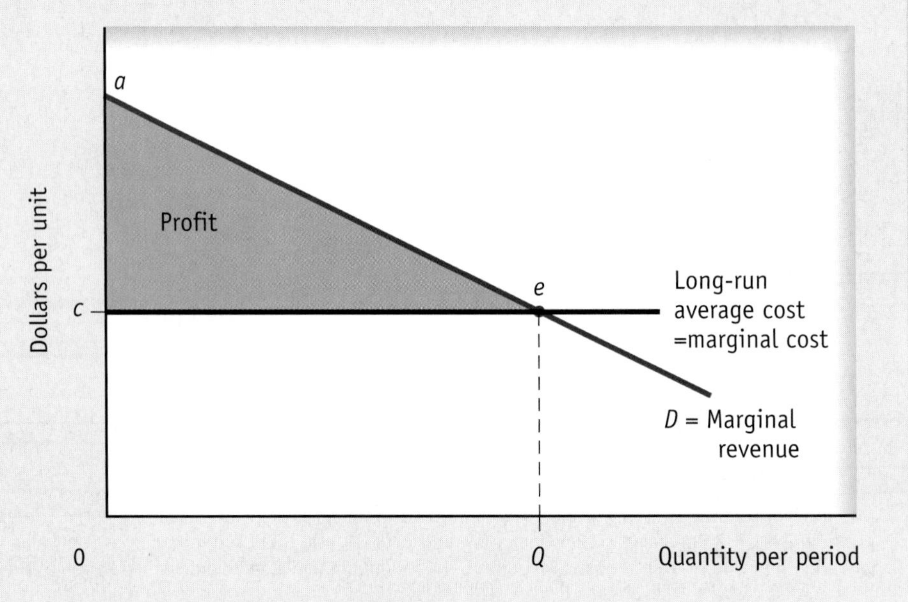

nopolist does not restrict output, there is no deadweight loss of monopoly—no welfare-loss triangle. Hence perfect price discrimination enhances social welfare when compared with monopoly output in the absence of price discrimination. The problem is that the monopolist reaps all net gains from production and consumers just break even, since their total cost equals their total benefit.

CONCLUSION

Pure monopoly, like perfect competition, is not that common. Perhaps the best examples are firms producing patented items with unique characteristics, such as certain prescription drugs. Some firms may have monopoly power in the short run, but the lure of economic profit encourages rivals to hurdle seemingly high entry barriers. Changing technology also works against monopoly in the long run. The railroad monopoly was erased by the interstate highway system. AT&T's monopoly on long-distance phone service crumbled as microwave technology replaced copper wire. The U.S. Postal Service's legal monopoly on first-class mail delivery is being eroded by express delivery, fax machines, and e-mail. And cable TV may soon lose its local monopoly status to technological breakthroughs in fiber-optics technology and wireless communications.

Although perfect competition and pure monopoly are relatively rare, our examination of them yields a framework that will help us view market structures that lie between the two extremes. As we will see, many firms have some degree of monopoly power—that is, they face downward-sloping demand curves. In the next chapter, we will consider two market structures that lie in the gray region between perfect competition and monopoly.

SUMMARY

1. A monopolist sells a product with no close substitutes. Economic profit earned by a monopolist can persist in the long run only if the entry of new firms into the market is blocked. Three barriers to entry are (1) legal restrictions, such as patents and operating licenses; (2) economies of scale, which lower average cost as output expands in the long run; and (3) control over a key resource.

2. Because a monopolist is the sole supplier, the monopolist's demand curve is also the market demand curve. Since the monopolist can sell more only if the price falls, the marginal revenue is less than the price. When demand is elastic, marginal revenue is positive and total revenue increases as the price falls. When demand is inelastic, marginal revenue is negative and total revenue decreases as the price falls.

3. If, at some positive rate of output, the monopolist can at least cover variable cost, profit is maximized or loss is minimized in the short run by finding the output rate that equates marginal cost with marginal revenue.

4. In the short run, the monopolist, like the perfect competitor, can earn economic profit but will shut down unless price is at or above average variable cost. In the long run, the monopolist, unlike the perfect competitor, can continue to earn economic profit as long as the entry of new firms is blocked.

5. Resources are not allocated as efficiently under unregulated monopoly as under perfect competition. If costs are similar, the monopolist will charge a higher price and supply less output than will a perfectly competitive industry. Monopoly usually results in a net welfare loss when compared to perfect competition because the loss in consumer surplus under monopoly exceeds the gain in monopoly profit.

6. To increase profit through price discrimination, the monopolist must have at least two identifiable types of consumers with different elasticities of demand and must be able to prevent those consumers charged the lower price from reselling to those charged the higher price. A perfect price discriminator charges a different price for each unit of the good, thereby converting all consumer surplus into economic profit. Perfect price discrimination seems unfair because the monopolist "cleans up," but it gets high marks in terms of allocative efficiency.

QUESTIONS FOR REVIEW

1. *(Barriers to Entry)* Complete each of the following sentences:
   a. Patents and licenses are examples of government-imposed ______ that prevent entry into an industry.
   b. A U.S. ________ awards inventors the exclusive right to production for 20 years.
   c. When economies of scale make it possible for a single firm to satisfy market demand at a lower cost per unit than could two or more firms, the single firm is considered a ________.
   d. A potential barrier to entry is a firm's control of a(n) ______ resource critical to production in the industry.
2. *(Barriers to Entry)* Explain how economies of scale can be a barrier to entry.
3. *(**CaseStudy:** Are Diamonds Forever?)* How does the De Beers cartel maintain control of the price in the diamond market? How might this control be threatened?
4. *(Revenue for the Monopolist)* How does the demand curve faced by a monopolist differ from the demand curve faced by a perfectly competitive firm?
5. *(Revenue Schedule)* Explain why the marginal revenue curve for a monopolist lies below its demand curve, rather than coinciding with the demand curve, as is the case for a perfectly competitive firm. Is it ever possible for a monopolist's marginal revenue curve to coincide with its demand curve?
6. *(Revenue for the Monopolist)* Why is it impossible for a profit-maximizing monopolist to choose any price *and* any quantity it wishes?
7. *(Revenue Curves)* Why would a monopoly firm never knowingly produce on the inelastic portion of its demand curve?
8. *(Profit Maximization)* Review the following graph (upper right) showing the short-run situation of a monopolist. What output level will the firm choose in the short run? Why?

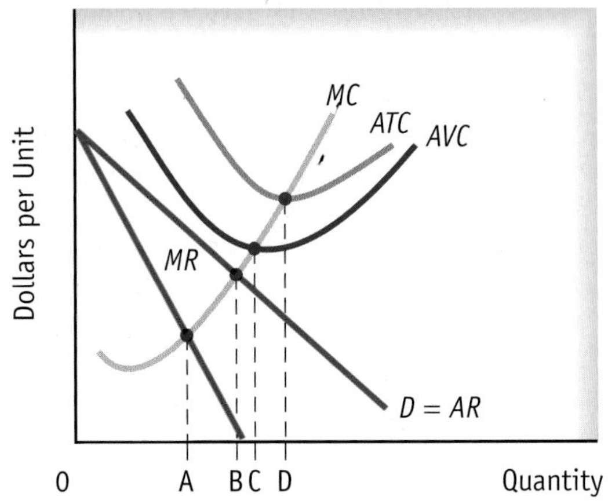

9. *(Allocative and Distributive Effects)* Why is society worse off under monopoly than under perfect competition, even if both market structures face the same constant long-run average cost curve?
10. *(Welfare Cost of Monopoly)* Explain why the welfare loss of a monopoly may be smaller or larger than the loss shown in Exhibit 7 in this chapter.
11. *(**CaseStudy:** The Mail Monopoly)* Can the U.S. Postal Service be considered a monopoly in first-class mail? Why or why not? What has happened to the price elasticity of demand for first-class mail in recent years?
12. *(Conditions for Price Discrimination)* What conditions must be met in order for a monopolist to price discriminate successfully?
13. *(Price Discrimination)* Explain how it may be profitable for South Korean manufacturers to sell new autos at a lower price in the United States than in South Korea, even with transportation costs included.
14. *(Perfect Price Discrimination)* Why is the perfectly discriminating monopolist's marginal revenue curve identical to the demand curve it faces?

PROBLEMS AND EXERCISES

15. *(Short-Run Profit Maximization)* Answer the following questions on the basis of the monopolist's situation illustrated in the following graph.
    a. At what output level and price will the monopolist operate?
    b. In equilibrium, what will be the firm's total cost and total revenue?
    c. What will be the firm's profit or loss in equilibrium?

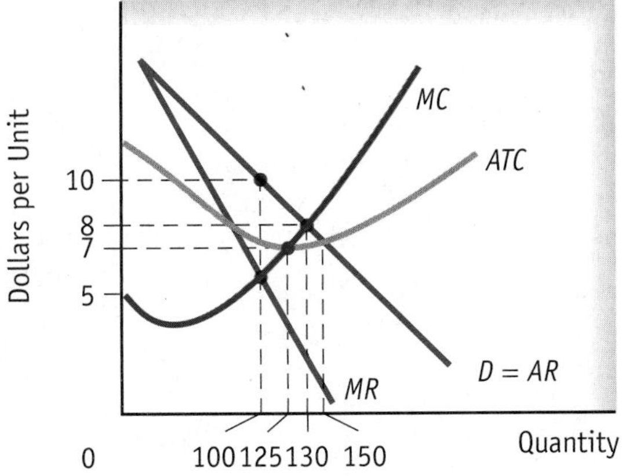

16. *(Monopoly)* Suppose that a certain manufacturer has a monopoly on the sorority and fraternity ring business (a constant-cost industry) because it has persuaded the "Greeks" to give it exclusive rights to their insignia.
    a. Using demand and cost curves, draw a diagram depicting the firm's profit-maximizing price and output level.
    b. Why is marginal revenue less than price for this firm?
    c. On your diagram, show the deadweight loss that occurs because the output level is determined by a monopoly rather than by a competitive market.
    d. What would happen if the Greeks decided to charge the manufacturer a royalty fee of $3 per ring?

EXPERIENTIAL EXERCISES

17. *(The Welfare Cost of Monopoly)* In many larger U.S. cities monopoly owners of sports franchises have been lobbying local governments for new, publicly financed sports stadiums. Is this a form of rent seeking? Go to the Heartland Institute's Sports Stadium Madness page at http://www.heartland.org/studies/sports/index.html and look at one of the papers collected there. Is there convincing evidence of rent seeking? If so, how does that relate to the welfare cost of monopoly?

18. *(Price Discrimination)* The Robinson-Patman Act is a federal statute that outlaws certain forms of price discrimination. Review the main provisions of the Act as outlined by RPAMall http://www.lawmall.com/rpa/. Then visit a local supermarket and look for evidence of price discrimination. Are the conditions for price discrimination, as outlined in this chapter, met there? Do you think the forms of price discrimination you found are legal under the Robinson-Patman Act?

19. *(Wall Street Journal)* The Legal Beat column, found in the Marketplace section of the *Wall Street Journal* chronicles court decisions and legal trends that affect American businesses. In the legal arena, firms and the government often struggle over monopoly power. Find an article describing a firm seeking to restrict competition or a government action aimed at reducing monopoly power. See if you can use the monopoly model to understand the issues involved.

CHAPTER

23 Monopolistic Competition and Oligopoly

Why are some panty hose sold in egg-shaped cartons? Why do some pizza makers deliver? Why is some shampoo sold only in beauty salons? Why do airlines sometimes engage in airfare warfare? Why was the oil cartel, OPEC, created and why has it failed? To answer these and other questions, we turn in this chapter to the vast gray area that lies between perfect competition and monopoly.

Perfect competition and pure monopoly represent the two extreme market structures. Under perfect competition, many suppliers offer a homogeneous commodity to a market where firms in the long run can enter and leave the industry with ease. A monopoly sells a product with no close substitutes; would-be competitors are blocked by natural or artificial barriers to entry. These polar

Visit the McEachern Interactive Study Center for this chapter at *http://mcisc.swcollege.com*

market structures are logically appealing and are useful in describing the workings of some markets observed in the economy.

But most firms operate in markets that are not well described by either model. Some firms are in markets that have many sellers producing goods that vary slightly, such as the many radio stations that vie for your attention or the video rental stores that abound. Other firms are in markets consisting of a small number of sellers that in some cases produce homogeneous goods (such as the markets for oil, steel, or aluminum) and in other cases produce differentiated goods (such as the markets for automobiles, breakfast cereals, or cigarettes). In this chapter, we examine the two additional market structures that together include the majority of firms in the economy. Topics discussed in this chapter include:

- Monopolistic competition
- Product differentiation
- Excess capacity
- Models of oligopoly
- Firm interdependence
- Mergers

MONOPOLISTIC COMPETITION

During the 1920s and 1930s, economists began formulating models to fit between perfect competition and pure monopoly. Two models of *monopolistic competition* were developed independently. In 1933 at Harvard University, Edward Chamberlin published *The Theory of Monopolistic Competition.* Across the Atlantic that same year, Cambridge University's Joan Robinson published *The Economics of Imperfect Competition.* Although the theories differed, their underlying principles were similar. We will discuss Chamberlin's approach.

Characteristics of Monopolistic Competition

As the expression **monopolistic competition** suggests, this market structure contains elements of both monopoly and competition. Chamberlin used the term to describe a market in which many producers offer products that are close substitutes but are not viewed as identical by consumers. Examples include the many convenience stores scattered throughout a metropolitan area or the dozens of radio stations vying for listeners. Because the products of different suppliers differ slightly—for example, some convenience stores are closer to you than others—the demand curve for each is not horizontal but rather slopes downward. Each producer therefore has some power over the price it charges. Thus the firms that populate this market are not *price takers,* as they would be under perfect competition, but are *price searchers.*

Monopolistic competition
A market structure characterized by a large number of firms selling products that are close substitutes, yet different enough that each firm's demand curve slopes downward

Because barriers to entry are low, firms in monopolistic competition can enter or leave the market with ease. Consequently, there are enough sellers that they behave competitively. There are also enough sellers that each tends to get lost in the crowd. For example, in a large metropolitan area, an individual restaurant, gas station, drugstore, video rental store, dry cleaner, or convenience store tends to act *independently.* In other market structures, there may be only two or three sellers in each market, so they keep an eye on one another; they act *interdependently.* You will understand the significance of the distinction between independent and interdependent behavior later in the chapter.

Product Differentiation

In perfect competition, the product is homogeneous, such as a bushel of wheat or a share of stock. In monopolistic competition, the product differs among sellers, as with the difference between a Big Mac and a Whopper or between one rock radio station and another. Sellers differentiate their products in four basic ways.

Physical Differences. The most obvious way products differ is in their physical appearance and their qualities. Product differentiation is seemingly endless: size, weight, color, taste, texture, and so on. Shampoos, for example, differ in color, scent, thickness, lathering ability, and bottle design. Particular brands aim at consumers with dandruff and those whose hair is normal, dry, or oily. Packaging is also designed to make a product stand out in a crowded field, such as panty hose in a plastic egg shell (L'Eggs®), instant soup in a cup (Cup O' Soup®), and baseball cards in a can (Pinnacle®).

Location. The number and variety of locations where a product is available are another means of differentiation. Some products seem to be available everywhere, including the Internet; finding other products requires some search and travel. If you live in a metropolitan area, you are no doubt accustomed to a large number of convenience stores. Each wants to be closest to you when you need that gallon of milk or bag of Doritos—hence the proliferation of stores. As the name says, these mini grocery stores are selling *convenience.* Their prices are higher and their selections are more limited than those of regular grocery stores, but they are likely to be nearer customers, don't have long lines, and stay open later.

Services. Products also differ in terms of their accompanying services. For example, some pizza sellers, such as Domino's, and some booksellers, such as Amazon, deliver; others do not. Some retail stores offer helpful product demonstrations by a well-trained sales staff; other stores are essentially self-service. Some products come with on-line support and toll-free numbers; other products leave you on your own. Some offer a money-back guarantee; others say "no returns."

Product Image. A final way products differ is in the image the producer tries to foster in the consumer's mind. For example, footwear and clothing pro-du-cers often rely on endorsements from athletes and other celebrities. Some producers try to demonstrate high quality based on where products are sold, such as shampoo that is sold only in beauty salons. Some products try to appeal to environmental concerns by emphasing the use of recycled packaging material.

Short-Run Profit Maximization or Loss Minimization

Because each monopolistic competitor offers a product that differs somewhat from other products in the industry, each seller has some control over the price charged. This *market power* means that the product's demand curve for the product slopes downward. Since many firms are selling close substitutes, any firm that raises its price can expect to lose some (but not all) customers to rivals. By way of comparison, a monopolist has no close rivals and loses fewer customers when the price increases, whereas a perfect competitor who raises the price can expect to lose *all* customers. Therefore, a monopolistic competitor faces a demand curve that is more elastic than a monopolist's and less elastic than a perfect competitor's.

Recall that the number and similarity of available substitutes for a given product are important determinants of the price elasticity of demand. Therefore, the elasticity of the monopolistic competitor's demand depends on (1) the number of rival firms that produce similar products and (2) the firm's ability to differentiate its product from those of its rivals. *A firm's demand curve will be more elastic the greater the number of competing firms and the less differentiated the firm's product.*

Marginal Cost Equals Marginal Revenue. From our study of monopoly, we know that the downward-sloping demand curve means the marginal revenue curve also slopes downward and lies below the demand curve. Exhibit 1 depicts demand and marginal revenue curves for a monopolistically competitive firm. The exhibit also presents cost curves. Remember that the forces that determine the cost of production are independent of the forces that shape demand, so there is nothing special about a monopolistic competitor's cost curves.

In the short run, if a firm can at least cover its variable cost, it will increase output as long as marginal revenue exceeds marginal cost. A monopolistic competitor maximizes profit in the short run just as a monopolist does: *the profit-maximizing rate of output occurs where marginal cost equals marginal revenue; the profit-maximizing price is found on the demand curve at that rate of output.* Exhibit 1 shows the price and output combinations that maximize short-run profit in panel (a) and minimize short-run loss in panel (b). In each panel, the marginal

EXHIBIT 1

The Firm in Monopolistic Competition in the Short Run

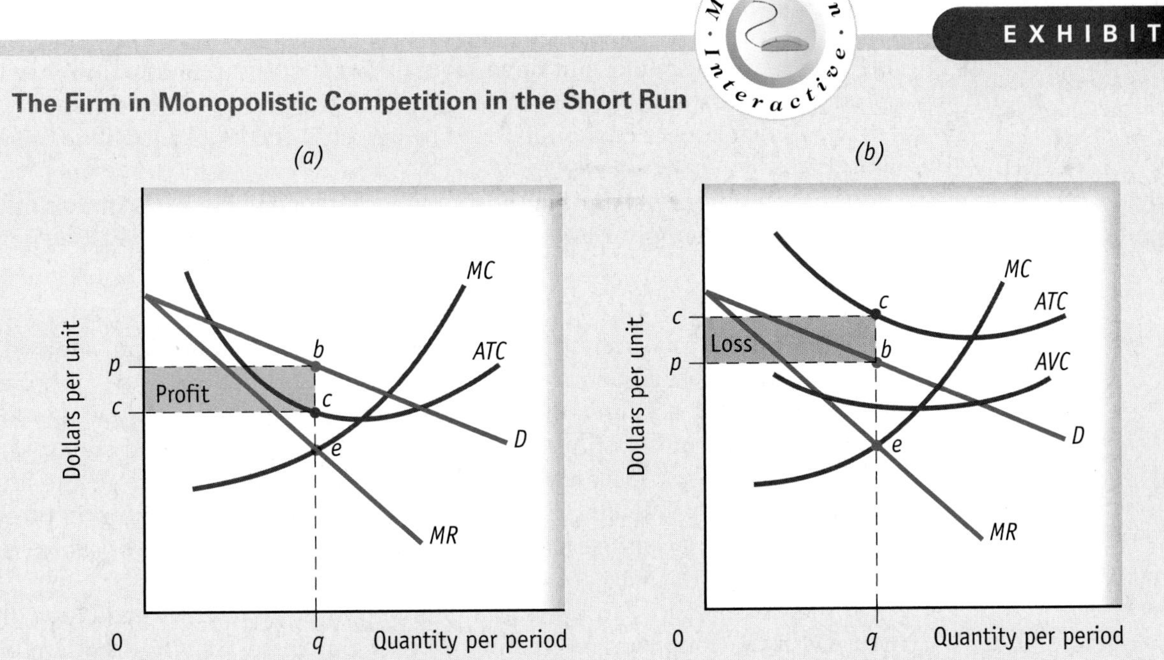

The monopolistically competitive firm produces the level of output at which marginal cost equals marginal revenue (point *e*) and charges the price indicated by point *b* on the downward-sloping demand curve. In panel (a), the firm produces *q* units, sells them at price *p*, and earns a short-run economic profit equal to (*p* – *c*) multiplied by *q*, shown by the blue rectangle. In panel (b), the average total cost exceeds the price at the optimal level of output. Thus the firm suffers a short-run loss equal to (*c* – *p*) multiplied by *q*, represented by the red rectangle.

cost and marginal revenue curves intersect at point *e,* yielding equilibrium output *q*, equilibrium price *p,* and average total cost *c.* Demand is greater in panel (a) than in panel (b).

Maximizing Profit or Minimizing Loss in the Short Run. Recall that the short run is a period too brief to allow firms to enter or leave the market. The demand and cost conditions shown in panel (a) of Exhibit 1 indicate that this firm will earn an economic profit in the short run. At the firm's profit-maximizing rate of output, average total cost, measured as *c* on the vertical axis, is below the price, *p.* As noted earlier, the difference between the two is the firm's profit per unit, which, when multiplied by the quantity sold, yields the economic profit, shown by the blue shaded rectangle in panel (a). Again, quantity supplied is found by the intersection of the marginal cost and marginal revenue curves, and the price is found on the demand curve at that quantity. Hence a monopolistic competitor, like a monopolist, has no supply curve—that is, *there is no curve that uniquely relates price and quantity supplied.*

The monopolistic competitor, like other firms, has no guarantee of earning economic profit. The firm's demand curve is the same in panel (b) as in panel (a), but the average total cost curve is higher in panel (b). Because the firm's average total cost curve lies above the demand curve, no rate of output would allow the firm to break even. In such a situation, the firm must decide whether to produce or to shut down temporarily. The rule here is the same as with perfect competition and monopoly: As long as the price is at or above average variable cost, the firm should produce in the short run, thereby covering its variable cost and at least a portion of its fixed cost. If the price fails to cover average variable cost, the firm should shut down. Recall that the halt in production may be only temporary; shutting down is not the same as going out of business. However, firms that expect economic losses to persist in the long run will leave the industry.

Short-run profit maximization in monopolistic competition is quite similar to that under monopoly. But the stories differ in the long run, as we'll see next.

Zero Economic Profit in the Long Run

Since there are no barriers to entry in monopolistic competition, short-run economic profit will attract new entrants in the long run. Because new entrants offer products that are similar to those offered by existing firms, they draw some customers away from existing firms, thereby reducing the demand facing each firm and increasing the elasticity of demand. Entry will continue in the long run until the demand facing each firm falls enough to erase economic profit. *Because of the ease of entry, monopolistically competitive firms will tend toward zero economic profit in the long run.*

If they incur short-run losses, some monopolistic competitors will leave the industry in the long run, redirecting their resources to activities that are expected to earn at least a normal profit. As firms leave the industry, their customers will switch to the remaining firms, increasing the demand for each remaining firm's product. Firms will continue to leave in the long run until the remaining firms have enough customers to earn normal profit but not economic profit (since economic profit would attract more firms to the industry).

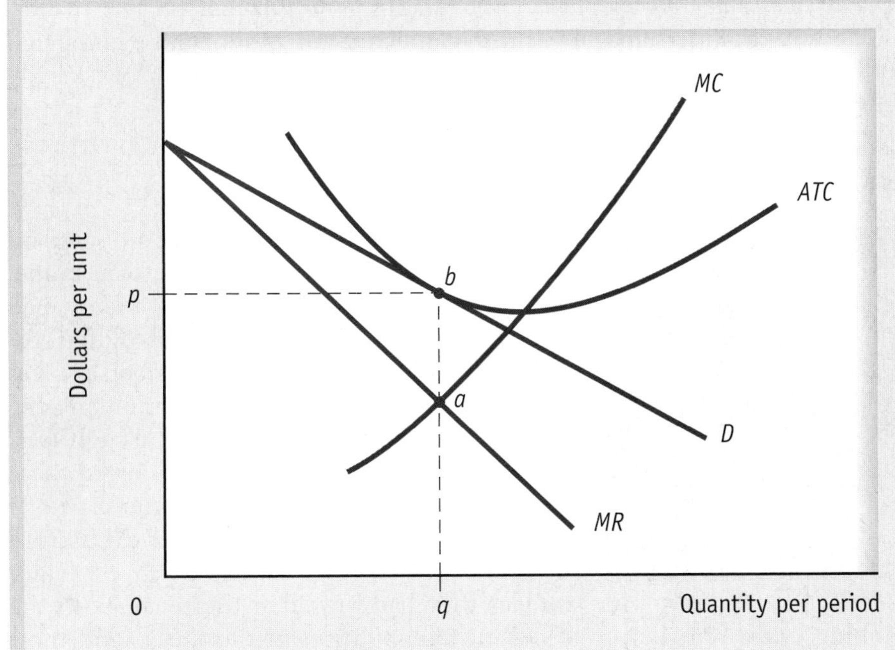

EXHIBIT 2

Long-run Equilibrium in Monopolistic Competition

If existing firms are earning economic profits, new firms will enter the industry. The entry of firms reduces the demand facing each firm. In the long run, demand is reduced until marginal revenue equals marginal cost (point *a*) and the demand curve is tangent to the average total cost curve (point *b*). Profit is zero at output *q*. With zero economic profit, no new firms enter, so the industry is in long-run equilibrium.

Exhibit 2 shows the long-run equilibrium for a typical monopolistic competitor. In the long run, entry and exit will alter each firm's demand curve until economic profit disappears—that is, until average total cost equals the price. This long-run outcome is shown in Exhibit 2, where the marginal cost curve intersects the marginal revenue curve at point *a*. At the equilibrium rate of output, *q*, the average total cost curve is tangent to the demand curve at point *b*. Since average total cost equals the price, *p*, the firm earns no economic profit.[1] At all other rates of output, the firm's average total cost is above its demand curve, so the firm would lose money if it reduced or increased its output.

Thus if entry is easy, short-run economic profit will draw new entrants into the industry in the long run. The demand curve facing each firm shifts left until economic profit disappears and firms earn only a normal profit. A short-run economic loss will prompt some firms to leave the industry in the long run. The demand curve facing each firm shifts right until the loss disappears and remaining firms earn just a normal profit. In summary, *monopolistic competition is like pure monopoly in the sense that firms in both industries face demand curves that slope*

1 You may wonder why average cost equals the price at the same rate of output where marginal cost equals marginal revenue. The explanation relies on total cost and total revenue curves, which are not shown. Recall that the slope of the total cost curve equals the firm's marginal cost, and the slope of the total revenue curve equals the firm's marginal revenue. Where average cost equals price, the firm earns a normal profit but no economic profit. Where there is no economic profit, the total cost curve is tangent to the total revenue curve, so both total curves have the same slope at that rate of output. Therefore, marginal cost must equal marginal revenue at that rate of output.

downward. Monopolistic competition is like perfect competition in the sense that easy entry and exit eliminate economic profit or economic loss in the long run.

One way to understand how short-run economic profit can be competed away by new firms in the long run is to consider the evolution of a newly emerging industry, as is discussed in the following case study.

CaseStudy

The World of Business

A history of Blockbuster Video is maintained by the firm at http://www.blockbuster.com/company/. A FORTUNE magazine profile of Bill Fields, the person chosen to be Blockbuster's CEO in 1996, is at http://www.pathfinder.com/fortune/1996/961125/blo.html. Try reading both of these to get a feel for how the firm has developed. When did Blockbuster's rapid growth grind to a halt? What were Fields' plans for reviving the company? How long did he remain CEO? What change of direction can you discern following the hiring of John Antioco as CEO?

Fast Forward

Video recorders have now become standard equipment in the typical American home. These recorders fueled demand for videotaped movies. The first videotape rental outlets required tape deposits, imposed membership fees of up to $100, and rented tapes for as much as $5 per day. Despite the high prices and high fees, the exploding number of VCRs allowed these early rental stores to thrive. What's more, part of the initial surge in rental demand came from consumers who were catching up on older movies they had missed at the theaters. In the beginning, most rental stores faced no competition in their area, and most earned short-run economic profit.

But this profit attracted competitors. Since entry was relatively easy, many new rental stores opened for business. Other types of stores—convenience stores, grocery stores, bookstores, even drugstores—also began renting tapes as a sideline. The growth rate of new rental outlets soon exceeded the growth rate of VCRs. Between 1982 and 1987, for example, the number of outlets renting tapes increased fourfold. And once consumers caught up with the backlog of movies, demand came to focus primarily on new releases.

Thus, the supply of rental movies increased faster than the demand. Worse yet for video stores, cable television with 40 to 50 channels and pay-per-view options plus direct sale of movie videos to consumers all substituted for video rentals. The greater supply of rentals along with the increased availability of substitutes had the predictable effect on market prices. Rental rates dropped sharply—to as little as 99 cents per night—and membership fees and tape deposits disappeared. Some rental stores could not survive at such a low price, and they folded. In fact, so many failed that a market developed to buy and resell their tape inventories. The "shakeout" in the industry is still going on—tape rental revenue declined 3 percent industry-wide in 1997. Many existing rental stores will fail. As the market evolves, one large firm, Blockbuster, has grown to over 4000 U.S. stores, accounting for 25 percent of market rentals in 1998. If that firm comes to dominate the market, tape rentals could change from monopolistic competition to oligopoly, a market structure to be examined later in the chapter. But Blockbuster faces its own growing pains, including an "excess inventory" of tapes and a failed effort to sell books, magazines, and snacks at its rental stores.

Sources: John Kirkpatrick, "Troubles Cut Blockbuster Performance," *Dallas Morning News* (2 July 1997); Chris Olson, "Curtain to Rise on Video Sites," *Omaha World-Herald* (6 August 1997); Eban Shapiro, "Blockbuster's Chief Executive Says the Viacom Unit Is on Fast Forward," *Wall Street Journal*, (7 April 1998); and Ed Hulse, "Roaming the Aisles," *Video Business* (29 September 1997).

Monopolistic Competition and Perfect Competition Compared

How does monopolistic competition compare with perfect competition in terms of efficiency? In the long run, neither a perfect competitor nor a monopolistic competitor can earn economic profit, so what's the difference? The difference arises because of the different demand curves facing individual firms in each of the two market structures. Exhibit 3 presents the long-run equilibrium price and quantity for firms in each of the two market structures, assuming the two firms have identical cost curves. In each case, the marginal cost curve intersects the marginal revenue curve at the rate of output where the average total cost curve is tangent to the demand curve faced by the firm.

The demand curve for the firm in perfect competition is a horizontal line drawn at the market price, as shown in panel (a). This demand curve is tangent to the lowest point of the long-run average total cost curve. Thus a perfect competitor produces at the lowest possible average cost in the long run. In panel (b), a monopolistic competitor faces a downward-sloping demand curve because its product differs somewhat from that of other producers. In the long run, the monopolistic competitor produces less than the amount necessary to achieve the lowest possible average cost. Thus, the price and average cost under monopolistic competition, identified in panel (b) as p', exceed the price and average cost under perfect competition, identified in panel (a) as p. *If firms have the same*

EXHIBIT 3

Monopolistic Competition Versus Perfect Competition

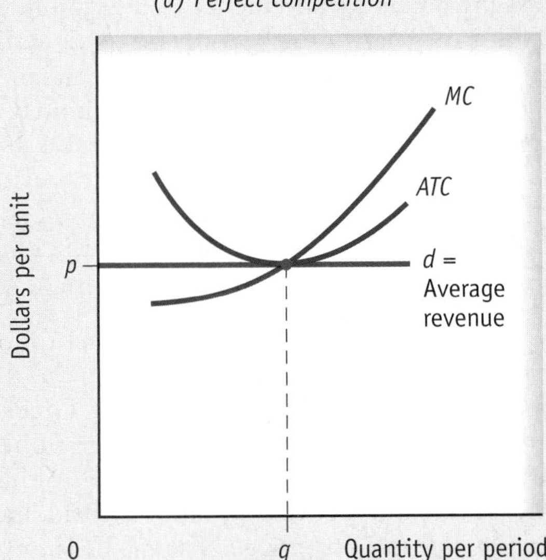

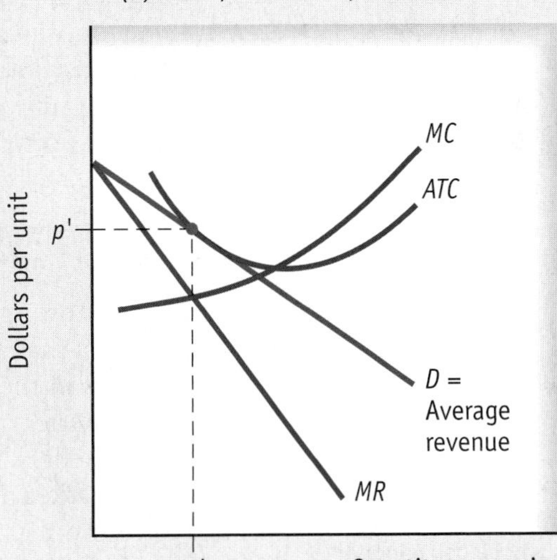

The perfectly competitive firm of panel (a) faces a demand curve that is horizontal at market price *p*. Long-run equilibrium occurs at output *q*, where the demand (average revenue) curve is tangent to the average total cost curve at its lowest point. The monopolistically competitive firm of panel (b) is in long-run equilibrium at output *q*', where demand is tangent to average total cost. However, since the demand curve slopes downward, the tangency does not occur at the minimum point of average total cost. Hence the monopolistically competitive firm produces less output at a higher price than does a perfectly competitive firm facing the same cost conditions.

cost curves, the firm under monopolistic competition produces less and charges more than the firm under perfect competition.

Excess capacity The difference between the rate of output at a firm's minimum average cost and the profit-maximizing rate of output

Firms in monopolistic competition do not produce at minimum average cost. They are said to have **excess capacity,** since production is short of the rate that would achieve the lowest average cost. Excess capacity means that producers could easily satisfy a greater demand and in the process would lower the average cost of production. Because the marginal value of production exceeds the marginal cost of production, then the marginal value of increased output would exceed its marginal cost, thereby increasing economic welfare. Such excess capacity exists with gas stations, drugstores, convenience stores, restaurants, motels, bookstores, flower shops, and firms in other monopolistic competitive industries. A good example is the funeral home business. Industry analysts argue that the nation's 23,000 funeral homes could efficiently handle 4 million funerals a year, but only about 2.5 million people die. So the industry operates at only about 60 percent of capacity, resulting in a higher average cost per funeral because valuable resources are idle much of the time.

There is another difference between perfect competition and monopolistic competition that does not show up in Exhibit 3. Although the cost curves drawn in each panel of Exhibit 3 are identical, firms in monopolistic competition in fact spend more on advertising and other promotional expenses to differentiate their products than do firms in perfect competition. These higher costs shift up their average cost curves.

Some economists have argued that monopolistic competition results in too many suppliers and in product differentiation that is often artificial. The counter argument is that consumers are willing to pay a higher price for having a greater selection. According to this latter view, consumers benefit from the wider choice among gas stations, restaurants, convenience stores, clothing stores, drugstores, economics textbooks, and many other goods and services. For example, what if half of the restaurants were to close just so the remaining ones could operate at full capacity? Some consumers would be disappointed if their favorite or most convenient restaurant went out of business.

AN INTRODUCTION TO OLIGOPOLY

Perfect competitors and monopolistic competitors are so numerous in their respective markets that an action by any one of them has little effect on the behavior of others in the market. Another important market structure in the gray area between perfect competition and monopoly is *oligopoly,* a Greek word meaning "few sellers." When you think of "big business," you are thinking of **oligopoly,** a market dominated by just a few firms. Perhaps three or four firms account for more than half the market output. Many industries, including steel, automobiles, oil, breakfast cereals, and tobacco, are *oligopolistic.* Because an oligopolistic market has only a few firms, each firm must consider the effect of its own policies on competitors' behavior. Oligopolists are therefore *interdependent.*

Oligopoly A market structure characterized by a small number of firms whose behavior is interdependent

Varieties of Oligopoly

In some oligopolistic industries, such as steel and oil, the product is homogeneous—an ingot of steel or a barrel of oil. In other industries, such as automobiles and breakfast cereal, the product is differentiated across producers—Ford versus Toyota or Wheaties versus Kellogg's Corn Flakes. The more homogeneous the products, the greater the interdependence among the few dominant firms in the industry. For example, because steel ingots are essentially identical, steel producers are quite sensitive to each other's pricing policies. A small rise in the one producer's price will send customers to a rival. But in markets where the product is differentiated, such as the auto industry, producers are not quite as sensitive about each other's pricing policies as are steel producers.

Because of this interdependence among firms in an industry, the behavior of any particular firm is difficult to analyze. *Each firm knows that any changes in its product quality, price, output, or advertising policy may prompt a reaction from its rivals. And each firm may react if another firm alters any of these features.* Monopolistic competition is like a golf tournament, where each player is striving for a personal best; oligopoly is more like a tennis match, where each player's actions depend on how and where the opponent hits the ball.

Why have some industries evolved into an oligopolistic market structure, dominated by only a few firms, whereas other industries have not? Although the reasons are not always clear, *an oligopolistic market structure can often be traced to some form of barrier to entry, such as economies of scale, legal restrictions, brand names built up by years of advertising, or control over an essential resource.* In the previous chapter, we examined barriers to entry as they applied to monopoly. The same principles apply to oligopoly. In the following case study, we consider some barriers to entry in the airline industry.

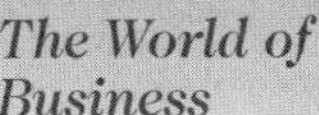

The World of Business

The Government Accounting Office (GAO) prepares reports on competition in the domestic airline industry. For example, read "Barriers to Entry Continue to Limit Benefits of Airline Deregulation" at http://www.bts.gov/ntl/data/rc97120t.pdf. This report includes data on the concentration of ownership of landing slots at the major U.S. airports. What particular barriers to entry does GAO cite? Current statistics on air travel are available in the annual reports of the Air Transport Association at http://www.air-transport.org/data/ff.htm. Try clicking through the series of graphs showing recent trends in the airline industry. What trends do you find in prices, number of passengers, and percent of Americans who have never flown?

The Unfriendly Skies

At one time, airline routes were straight lines from one city to another. Now they radiate like the spokes of a wagon wheel from a "hub" city. From 29 hub airports across the country, the airlines send out planes along the spokes to about 400 commercial airports, then quickly bring them back to the hubs. The major airlines dominate hub airports. For example, American and United dominate Chicago's O'Hare International, which is a big, centrally located airport. A new airline trying to enter the industry would have to secure a hub airport as well as landing rights at crowded airports around the country—not an easy task, since all the viable hubs are taken, as are the landing rights at those airports. So landing rights are the first barrier to entry in the airline industry. Studies show that ticket prices involving airports dominated by a single airline average about 5 percent higher than tickets at more competitive airports.

Another barrier to entry is frequent flyer mileage programs. The biggest airlines fly more national and international routes, so they offer greater opportunities to accumulate frequent flyer miles and to use the accumulated mileage for free flights. Hence the biggest airlines have the most attractive programs.

These factors—landing slots and frequent flyer programs—create barriers for potential entrants and create barriers to expansion for smaller airlines already

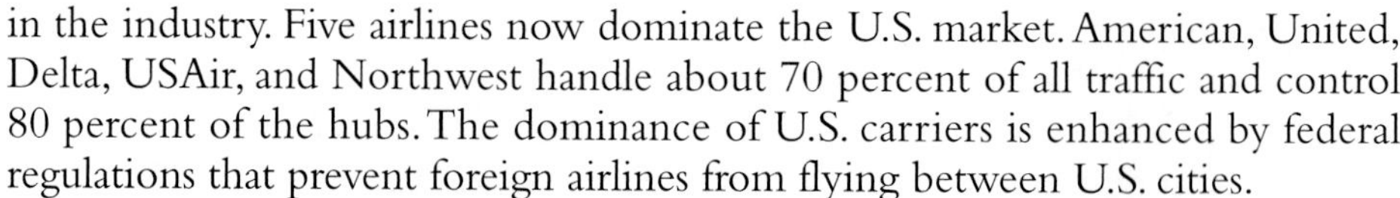

in the industry. Five airlines now dominate the U.S. market. American, United, Delta, USAir, and Northwest handle about 70 percent of all traffic and control 80 percent of the hubs. The dominance of U.S. carriers is enhanced by federal regulations that prevent foreign airlines from flying between U.S. cities.

Until quite recently, another barrier to entry was the computerized reservation systems used by travel agents. American Airlines offered the Sabre system and United the Apollo system. These two airlines have now spun off their computer systems into separate entities, so the systems are available to all airlines. Airline Internet sites also allow individuals to buy tickets on-line.

Sources: "US Airways Plans Computer Deal with Sabre," *Los Angeles Times* (29 January 1998); "Medium-sized Airports Need Landing Slots, Gates, Terminals," *Business Wire* (25 June 1997); Kenneth Li, "Web's Got the Ticket," *New York Daily News* (9 November 1997); Matthew Wald, "U.S. Seeks to Curb Unfair Practices of Major Airlines," *Wall Street Journal* (7 April 1998); and Steven Morrison and Clifford Winston, *The Evolution of the Airline Industry*, (Washington, D.C.: Brookings Institution, 1995).

Economies of Scale

Perhaps the most significant barrier to entry is economies of scale. Recall that the minimum efficient scale is the lowest rate of output at which the firm takes full advantage of economies of scale. If a firm's minimum efficient scale is relatively large compared to industry output, then only a few firms are needed to produce the total output demanded in the market. A good example is the auto industry. Research shows that an automobile plant of minimum efficient scale could produce enough cars to supply nearly 10 percent of the U.S. market. If there were 100 auto plants, each would supply such a tiny portion of the market that the average cost per car would be higher than if only 10 plants manufactured autos.

In the automobile industry, economies of scale are a barrier to entry. To compete with existing producers, a new entrant must sell enough automobiles to reach a competitive scale of operation. Exhibit 4 presents the long-run average cost curve for a typical firm in the industry. If a new entrant sells only S cars, the average cost per unit, c_a, far exceeds the average cost, c_b, of a firm that has reached the rate of output, M, achieved at the minimum efficient size. If autos sell for a price less than c_a, a potential entrant can expect an economic loss, and this prospect will discourage entry.

High Cost of Entry

Potential entrants into oligopolistic industries may face another problem. The total investment needed to reach the minimum efficient size is often gigantic (a new auto plant or new semiconductor plant can cost over $1 billion). The average cost of developing and testing a new drug exceeds $300 million. Advertising a new product enough to compete with established brands may also require an enormous initial outlay. High start-up costs and established brand names can create substantial barriers to entry, especially since the fortunes of a new product are uncertain. In fact, eight of ten new consumer products don't survive. An unsuccessful attempt at securing a place in the market could result in crippling losses for upstart firms. The prospect of such losses turns away many potential entrants. Most new products come from existing firms, which can better with-

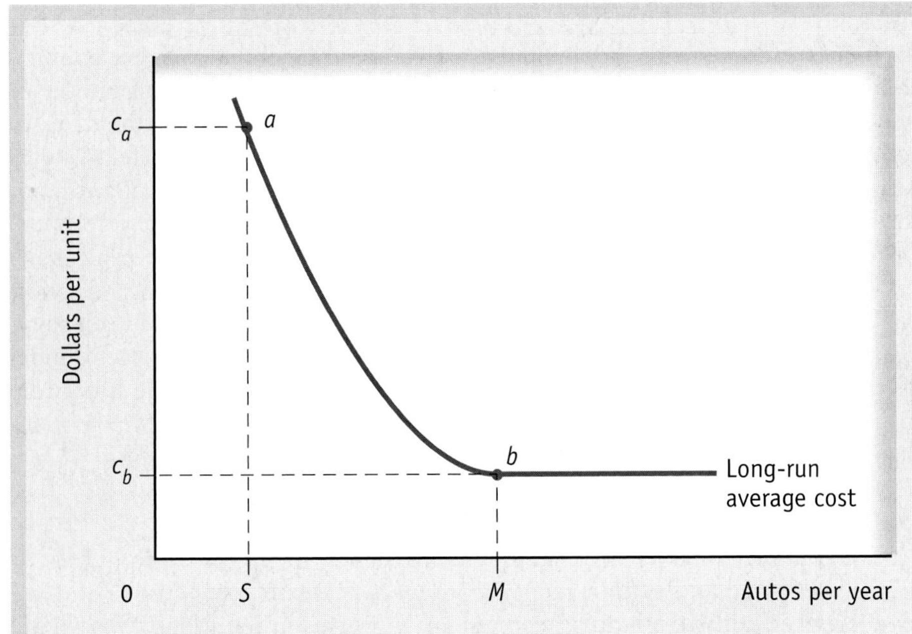

EXHIBIT 4

Economies of Scale as a Barrier to Entry

At point *b*, an existing firm can produce *M* automobiles at an average cost of c_b. A new entrant that can hope to sell only *S* automobiles will incur a much higher average cost of c_a at point *a*. If cars sell for less than c_a, the new entrant will suffer a loss. In this case, economies of scale serve as a barrier to entry, protecting the existing firms from new competitors.

stand the possible losses. For example, Colgate-Palmolive spent $100 million introducing Total toothpaste, as did McDonald's in its failed attempt to sell America the Arch Deluxe. And Unilever lost $160 million when its new detergent, Power, failed to crack into the market.

In perfect competition, all firms sell identical products. There is no incentive to advertise or to promote a particular product since consumers know that all products are the same. Moreover, producers already can sell all they want at the prevailing market price, so why advertise? In an oligopoly, however, firms often spend millions and sometimes billions differentiating their products. Some of these expenditures have the beneficial effects of providing valuable information to consumers and offering them a wider array of products. But some forms of product differentiation are of little value. Slogans such as "Generation Next" or "Always Cola-Cola" convey little information, yet Pepsi and Coke have spent huge sums on such messages (Coke spent $1.6 billion on advertising in 1997).

Product differentiation expenditures create barriers to entry. Oligopolies often compete with existing rivals and try to block new entry by offering a variety of models or products. For example, several cereal makers offer more than a dozen products each, and seven of the top-selling cereals are from Kellogg.[2] One study of 25,500 new products introduced in 1996 found only 7 percent really offered new or added benefits.[3] With the proliferation of brands, retail shelf space grows scarce, blocking out potential competitors.

2 Rankings are for 1997 sales according to the Food Marketing Policy Center at the University of Connecticut.
3 The study was carried out by Market Intelligence Service and was reported in "Market Makers," *The Economist* (14 March 1998).

MODELS OF OLIGOPOLY

Since oligopolists are interdependent, analyzing their behavior gets complicated. Because of this interdependence, we should not expect any *one* model of oligopoly theory to explain all oligopoly behavior. At one extreme, the firms in the industry may try to coordinate their behavior so they act collectively as a single monopolist, forming a cartel, such as the Organization of Petroleum Exporting Countries (OPEC). At the other extreme, oligopolists may compete so fiercely that price wars erupt, as with airfare warfare and cigarette price wars.

Many theories have been developed to explain oligopoly pricing behavior. We will study four of the better-known models: (1) cartels, (2) price leadership, (3) game theory, and (4) the kinked demand curve. As you will see, each model has some relevance in explaining observed behavior, although none is entirely satisfactory as a general theory of oligopoly. Thus *there is no general theory of oligopoly, but a set of theories, each based on the diversity of observations.*

Collusion

Collusion An agreement among firms to divide the market or to fix the market price to maximize economic profit

Cartel A group of firms that agree to coordinate their production and pricing decisions to maximize cartel profits, thereby behaving as a monopolist

In an oligopolistic market there are few firms; hence, they may try to *collude,* or to agree on price and output rates, in order to decrease competition and increase profit. **Collusion** is an agreement among firms in the industry to divide the market up and fix the price. A **cartel** is a group of firms that agree to collude so they can act as a single monopolist and earn monopoly profits. Cartels are more likely when the good supplied is homogeneous, as with oil or steel. A cartel provides benefits to member firms—greater certainty about the behavior of "competitors," an organized effort to block new entry, and, as a result, increased profit. Colluding firms, when compared to competing firms, usually reduce output, increase price, and block the entry of new firms. Consumers suffer because prices are higher as a result of limited output, and potential entrants suffer because of lost opportunities for profit. Collusion and cartels are both illegal in this country; some other countries are more tolerant. Some countries even promote cartels, as with OPEC.

Monopoly profit can be so tempting that U.S. firms sometimes break the law. During the 1950s, for example, there was evidence of extensive collusion among electrical equipment producers, and some executives went to jail for their participation in the scheme. Some cartels are worldwide in scope, such as the now-familiar oil cartel, OPEC. If OPEC held a meeting in the United States, its members would be arrested for price fixing. Cartels can operate worldwide (even though they are outlawed in some countries) because there are no international laws to stop them.

Suppose that the firms in an industry establish a cartel. The market demand curve, D, appears in Exhibit 5. What price will maximize the cartel's profit, and how will market output be divided among participating firms? The first task of the cartel is to determine the marginal cost of production for the cartel as a whole. Since the cartel acts as if it were a single monopoly operating many plants, the marginal cost curve in Exhibit 5 is the horizontal sum of the marginal cost curves of all firms in the cartel. The cartel's marginal cost curve intersects the marginal revenue curve to determine the price and output that maximize the cartel's profit. This intersection yields price p , industry output Q, and marginal cost of production, identified as c. So far, so good. To maximize

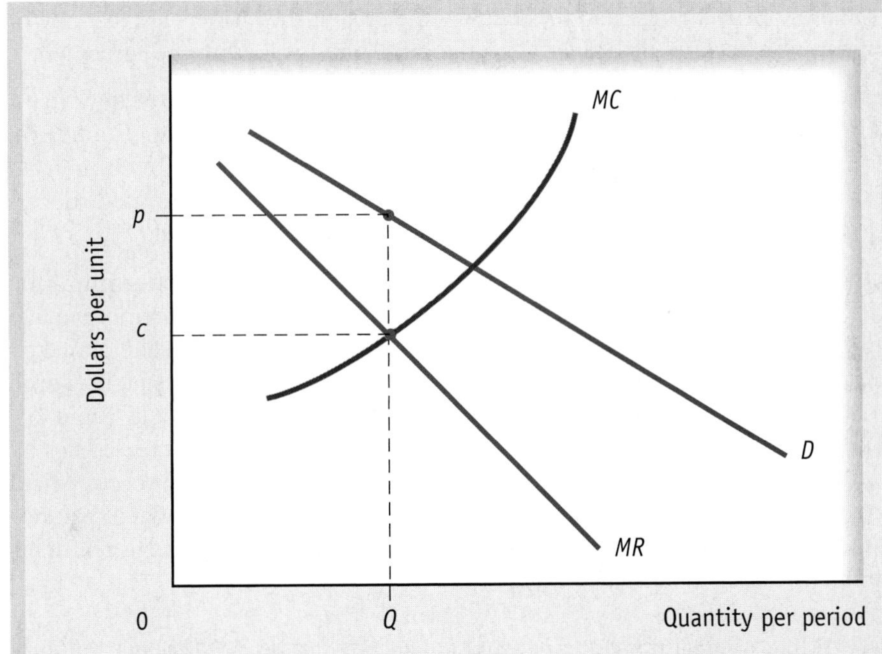

EXHIBIT 5

Cartel Model Where Firms Act as a Monopolist

A cartel acts like a monopolist. Here *D* is the market demand curve, *MR* the associated marginal revenue curve, and *MC* the horizontal sum of the marginal cost curves of cartel members. Cartel profits are maximized when the industry produces quantity *Q* and charges price *p*.

cartel profits, output Q must be allocated among firms so that each cartel member's marginal cost equals *c*; otherwise some firms would be producing where the marginal cost of output exceeds *c*, and this higher marginal cost would lower cartel profits. Thus *for cartel profit to be maximized, output must be allocated so that the marginal cost of production is identical across firms.* All this is easier said than done. Let's look at the problems with maintaining a successful cartel.

Differences in Cost. If all firms have identical cost curves, output and profit are easily allocated across firms (each firm produces the same output), but if costs differ, as they usually do, problems arise. The greater the differences in average costs across firms, the greater will be the differences in economic profits among firms. If cartel members try to equalize each firm's total economic profit, a high-cost firm would need to sell more than a low-cost firm. But this allocation scheme would violate the profit-maximizing condition for the cartel, which is that the marginal cost be identical across firms. Thus, *if average costs differ across firms, the quantity allocation that maximizes cartel profit will yield unequal profit across cartel members.* If the cartel allocates less output to high-cost firms than they want, they could drop out of the cartel, thereby undermining it. Usually, the allocation of output is the result of haggling among cartel members. Firms that are more influential or more adept at bargaining will get a larger share of output. Allocation schemes are sometimes based on geography or on the historical division of output among firms. OPEC allocates output among member countries based on their estimated oil reserves.

Number of Firms in the Cartel. The greater the number of firms in the industry, the more difficult it is to negotiate an acceptable allocation of output among them.

Consensus becomes harder to achieve as the number of firms in the industry grows. And the more firms there are in the industry, the greater the chances are that one or more firms will become dissatisfied with the cartel and break with the agreement.

New Entry into the Industry. If a cartel cannot block the entry of new firms into the industry, new entry will eventually force the price down, squeezing economic profit. The profit of the cartel attracts entry, entry increases market supply, and increased supply forces the price down. A cartel's continued success therefore depends on barriers that block the entry of new firms.

Cheating. Perhaps the biggest problem in keeping the cartel running smoothly is the powerful temptation to cheat on the agreement. By offering a price slightly below the established price, a firm can usually increase its sales and economic profit. Because oligopolists usually operate with excess capacity, some may cheat on the established price. Even if cartel members keep an eagle eye on each firm's price, a firm, rather than lowering the price, can increase sales by offering extra services, rebates, or other concessions. The incentive to cut prices is particularly strong when industry sales are in a slump. Typically, when production is low, so is the marginal cost of producing more output. Cartel agreements collapse if cheating becomes widespread.

In summary, *establishing and maintaining an effective cartel will be more difficult (1) if the product is differentiated among firms, (2) if costs differ among firms, (3) if there are a large number of suppliers in the industry, (4) if entry barriers in the industry are low, and (5) if cheating on the agreement becomes widespread.* The problems of establishing and maintaining a cartel are reflected in the spotty history of OPEC. In 1985, the average price of oil reached $34 a barrel. By 1998, because of competition among the world's oil producers, the price dropped to less than half that. Many of the 11 OPEC members are poor countries that rely on oil as a major source of revenue, so they argue over the price and their market share. OPEC members also cheat on the cartel.

Like other cartels, OPEC has experienced difficulty with new entrants. The high prices resulting from OPEC's early success back in the 1970s attracted new oil suppliers from the North Sea, Mexico, and elsewhere. Nearly two-thirds of the world's oil supply now comes from non-OPEC countries. Most observers doubt that OPEC will ever regain its former power. Efforts to cartelize the world supply of a number of products, including bauxite, copper, and coffee, have failed so far.

Price Leadership

Price leader A firm whose price is adopted by the rest of the industry

An informal, or *tacit,* type of collusion occurs in industries that contain **price leaders,** who set the price for the rest of the industry. A dominant firm or a few firms establish the market price, and other firms in the industry follow that lead, thereby avoiding price competition. The price leader also initiates any change in the price, and others follow.

Historically, the steel industry has been an example of the price-leadership form of oligopoly. Typically, U.S. Steel, the largest firm in the industry, would set the price for various products, and other firms would follow. Congressional investigations into the pricing policy in this industry indicate that smaller steel producers relied on the price schedules of U.S. Steel. Public pressure on U.S.

Steel not to raise the price shifted the price-leadership role onto smaller producers, resulting in a rotation of the leadership function among firms. Although the rotating price leadership did reduce price conformity among firms in the industry, particularly during the 1970s, prices in the steel industry were still higher than they would have been with no price leadership.

Like other forms of collusion, price leadership is subject to a variety of obstacles. First, the practice usually violates U.S. antitrust laws. Second, the greater the product differentiation among sellers, the less effective price leadership will be as a means of collusion. Third, there is no guarantee that other firms will follow the leader. If other firms in the industry do not follow a price increase, the leading firm must either roll back prices or risk losing sales to lower-priced competitors. Fourth, as with formal cartels, some firms will try to cheat on the agreement by cutting the price to increase sales and profits. And finally, unless there are barriers to entry, a profitable price will attract entrants into the market, which could destabilize the price leadership agreement.

Game Theory

How will firms act when they recognize their interdependence but either cannot or do not collude? Because oligopoly involves interdependence among a few firms, we can think of interacting firms as like players in a poker game. **Game theory** examines oligopolistic behavior as a series of strategic moves and counter-moves among rival firms. It analyzes the behavior of decision makers, or players, whose choices affect one another. The focus is on the players' incentives either to cooperate or to compete.

Game theory A model that analyzes oligopolistic behavior as a series of strategic moves and counter-moves by rival firms

As an example, consider the market for gasoline in a rural community with only two gas stations, Mobil and Exxon. Here we focus on an oligopoly consisting of two firms, or a **duopoly.** Suppose customers are indifferent between the two brands and consider only the price when choosing between stations. To keep the analysis manageable, suppose only two prices are possible: a high price or a low price. If both gas stations charge the high price, they split the total quantity demanded and each gas station earns a profit of $700 per day. If they both charge the low price, they also split the market, but profit drops to only $400 per day. If one charges the high price but the other charges the low price, the low-price station earns a profit of $500 per day. But the high-price station has virtually no customers and loses $200 per day.

Duopoly A market with only two producers, who compete with each other; a type of oligopoly market structure

What price will each gas station charge? The answer depends on the assumptions about firm behavior—that is, what *strategy* each player pursues. A **strategy** reflects a player's operational plan. Exhibit 6 shows the *payoff matrix* for the two gas stations, with the price strategy that Mobil pursues shown along the left-hand margin and the price strategy that Exxon pursues shown along the top. A **payoff matrix** is a table listing the profits, or payoff, that each of the two rival firms can expect based on the strategy that each firm adopts. As we have seen already, each firm can charge either a "high price" or a "low price." Each cell of the matrix reports each firm's earnings, depending on the combination of strategies pursued by each seller. For example, the upper left-hand cell indicates that if both firms charge the high price, then each will earn $700 per day.

Strategy In game theory, the operational plan pursued by a player; for example, one strategy is to avoid the worst outcome

Payoff matrix In game theory, a table listing the payoffs that each player can expect based on the strategy that each player pursues

Given this payoff matrix, what does each firm do? Again, the answer depends on each firm's strategy. Suppose you are running the Mobil station and are trying to decide what to do. If you charge a high price, you will earn $700

EXHIBIT 6

A Payoff Matrix

		Exxon's Strategy High Price		*Exxon's Strategy* Low Price	
Mobil's Strategy	High Price	Mobil's profit = $700	Exxon's profit = $700	Mobil's loss = $200	Exxon's profit = $500
Mobil's Strategy	Low Price	Mobil's profit = $500	Exxon's loss = $200	Mobil's profit = $400	Exxon's profit = $400

per day as long as the Exxon station charges a high price as well, but you will lose $200 a day if your rival charges a low price. If you charge a low price and your rival does too, you both earn $400 per day. If you charge a low price and your rival charges a high price, you really clean up, earn $500 per day. What to do, what to do?

One common game-theory strategy is to avoid the worst outcome. The worst outcome is to lose $200 per day by being the only gas station charging the high price. You avoid that outcome by charging the low price. If each gas station tries to avoid the worst outcome, both will charge the low price and each will earn $400 per day, as is reflected by the cell in the lower right-hand corner. Both would be better off if they each agreed to charge a high price.

Avoiding the worst outcome is only one of several strategies we could consider in analyzing oligopoly markets in terms of game theory. Outcomes can be as volatile as the personalities involved. Some players are more conservative, and some are more willing to take risks. Price wars sometimes break out among oligopolists. For example, in the summer of 1997, auto makers aggressively matched and exceeded one another's price cuts, leaving cars more affordable relative to consumers' average income than they had been in a decade.[4] And just before a recent Thanksgiving weekend, a price war erupted in airfares. American Airlines first announced holiday discounts. TWA quickly cut fares even more, then Delta topped them both with cuts of up to 50 percent. Within hours, American, United, and other major carriers said they would match Delta's reductions. So go sporadic price wars.

The Kinked Demand Curve

Prices in some oligopolistic industries appear to be stable even during periods when altered cost conditions suggest that a price change would be appropriate. An often-cited case of price stability occurred in the sulfur industry, where the price remained at $18 per ton for a dozen consecutive years, despite major changes in the cost of production. One oligopoly model that sheds light on this

4 Keith Bradsher, "Price War Leaves Cars Positively Affordable," *New York Times* (3 July 1997).

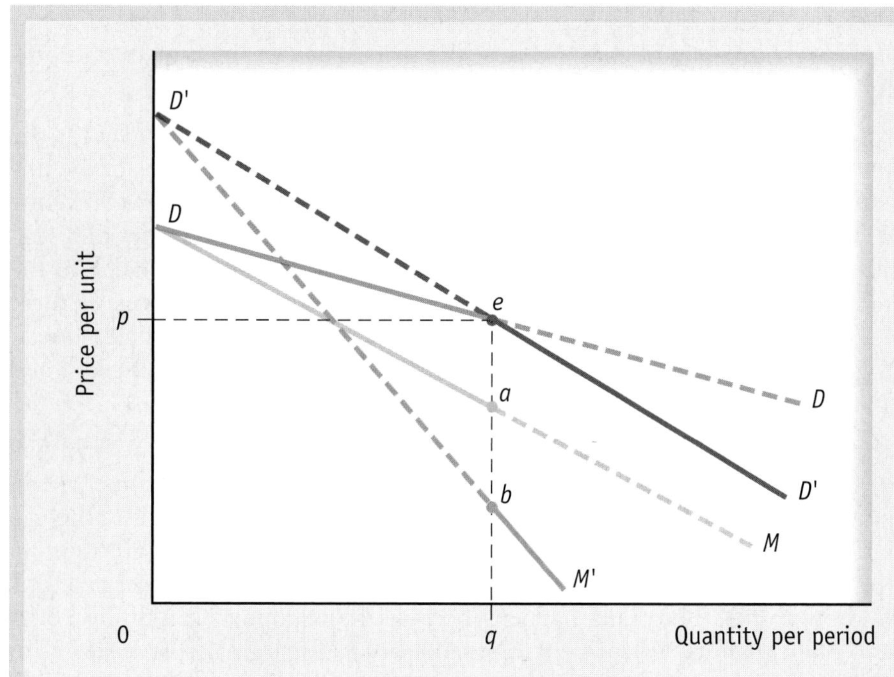

EXHIBIT 7

The Kinked Demand Model of Oligopoly

In the initial situation, an oligopolist is at point *e*, selling *q* units at price *p*. The firm's demand curve is *DD* if its competitors do not match its price changes; its demand curve is *D'D'* if competitors do match price changes. Assuming that the firm's rivals match price cuts but not price increases, the relevant demand curve is *DeD'*, with a kink at quantity *q*. *DabM'* is the associated marginal revenue curve, with a gap at quantity *q*.

apparent price stability relies on the simple idea that if a firm cuts its price, other firms will cut theirs as well to avoid losing customers to the price cutter. But if a firm raises its price, other firms will stand pat, hoping to attract customers away from the price raiser. If an oligopolist expects such responses from competitors, the **kinked demand curve** describes the oligopolist's pricing strategy. Firms in the tire industry have been said to have a kinked demand curve.[5]

Kinked demand curve A demand curve that illustrates price stickiness; if one firm cuts its prices, other firms in the industry will cut theirs as well, but if the firm raises its prices, other firms will not change theirs

To develop the kinked demand curve model, we start at point *e* in Exhibit 7, with the firm producing *q* units at price *p*. The firm's demand curve will depend on whether other firms follow price moves or ignore them. Demand curve *DD* assumes that rivals will not follow a change in price. Alternatively, demand curve *D'D'* assumes that rivals will match any change in price. Notice that *DD* is flatter than *D'D'*. To see why, suppose that Michelin raises its prices, but other tire makers do not. In this situation, Michelin will lose far more sales than if other producers also raised their prices. Likewise, if Michelin cuts prices but others do not, Michelin will pick up more sales than if other producers also cut prices. Thus, if rivals do not follow price changes, any price increase will drive away more customers and any price decrease will attract more customers than if rivals matched price changes. Therefore, Michelin's demand curve is flatter when rivals do not follow price changes than when they do.

If rivals follow a price decrease but do not follow a price increase, the oligopolist's demand curve consists of the two solid segments shown in Exhibit 7 by *DeD'*. That solid portion of the demand curve reflecting a price increase, *De,*

5 See the remarks of economist Dennis Byrne in Miles Moore's "Tire Oligopoly Leaves Dealers in Tough Spot," *Tire Business* (17 March 1997).

is flatter than that solid portion of the demand curve reflecting a price decrease, *eD'*. Because rivals match a price decrease but not a price increase, this oligopolist's demand curve, *DeD'*, has a *kink* at the firm's current price-quantity combination, point *e*.

Marginal Revenue. To find the marginal revenue curve associated with the kinked demand curve, we simply piece together the relevant portions of the underlying marginal revenue curves. The solid segment *Da* is the marginal revenue curve applicable to portion *De* of the kinked demand curve. And the solid segment *bM'* is the marginal revenue curve associated with the portion *eD'* of the kinked demand curve. The marginal revenue curve is thus *DabM'*. Because there is a kink in the demand curve, the marginal revenue curve is not a single line; it has a gap at the currently produced quantity, *q*. The kinked demand curve and the corresponding marginal revenue curve appear in Exhibit 8.

Price Rigidity. Within the gap in the marginal revenue curve, *ab,* the firm will not respond to small shifts in the marginal cost curve. Suppose that curve *MC* in Exhibit 8 is the initial marginal cost curve. The point where *MC* crosses the gap in the marginal revenue curve identifies the profit-maximizing rate of output, *q*, and price, *p*. What happens to equilibrium price and quantity if the marginal cost curve drops to *MC'*? Nothing happens, because the oligopolist can do no better than to offer quantity *q* at price *p*. The same holds if marginal cost increases to *MC"*—again, there is no change in the equilibrium price and quantity. *Since changes in the marginal cost curve do not necessarily affect the price, the price tends to be rigid, or stable, in oligopolistic industries if firms behave in the manner described by the kinked demand curve.* It takes a greater shift in the marginal cost curve to produce a change in equilibrium price and quantity. Specifically, to change the equilibrium price and quantity, the marginal cost curve must change enough to intersect the marginal revenue curve above point *a* or below point *b* in Exhibit 8.

EXHIBIT 8

Demand and Marginal Revenue Curves for the Kinked Demand Model

If *MC* is the initial marginal cost curve, the firm will produce quantity *q* (where marginal cost equals marginal revenue) at price *p*. Marginal cost could fall to *MC'* or increase to *MC"* without affecting the quantity produced. Likewise, price *p* will be rigid if marginal cost for output *q* varies between *a* and *b*.

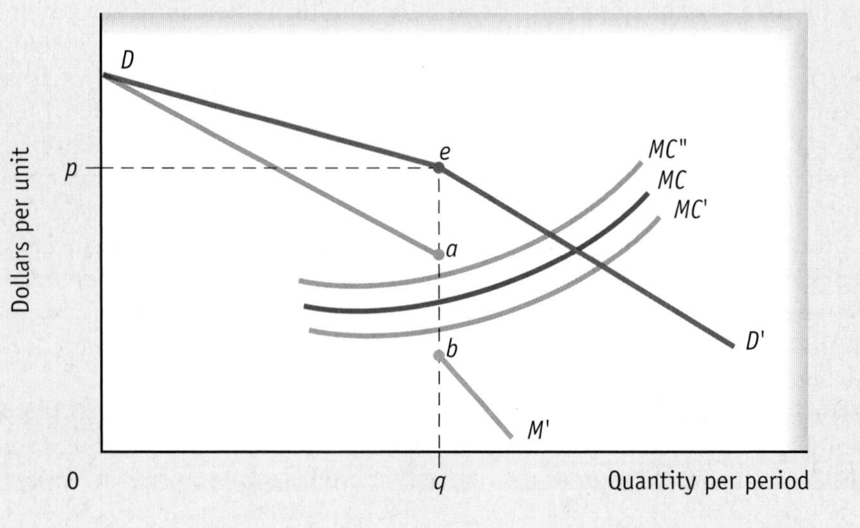

Although the kinked demand model offers a possible explanation for the price stickiness observed over the years, it says nothing about how the equilibrium price and quantity are initially determined. That's a major weakness of the model. What's more, not all prices in oligopolies are rigid. For example, during the inflationary periods of the 1970s and early 1980s, some oligopolies increased prices frequently. In fact, some oligopolies change prices more often than some monopolies, even though the kinked demand model predicts just the opposite.

Summary of Oligopoly Models

Each of the oligopoly models we have considered helps explain certain phenomena observed in oligopolistic markets. Interdependence, which these models explain, gives rise to all kinds of behavior, so many models exist. The *cartel,* or *collusion,* model shows why oligopolists might want to cooperate to determine market price and output; that model also explains why cartels are hard to establish and maintain. The *price-leadership* model explains why and how firms may act in unison on prices without actually establishing a formal cartel. *Game theory* models show that, because of firm interdependence, market strategies can range from cooperation to price wars. Finally, the *kinked demand curve* explains why some oligopoly prices tend to remain unchanged for long periods even while costs are changing.

Comparison of Oligopoly and Perfect Competition

As we have seen, each oligopoly model explains a piece of the oligopoly puzzle. Each model has limitations, however, and none provides a complete depiction of all oligopoly behavior. Consequently, since there is no typical, or representative, model of oligopoly, "the" oligopoly model cannot be compared with the competitive model. We might, however, imagine an experiment in which we took the hundreds of firms that populate a competitive industry and, through a series of giant mergers, combined them to form, say, four firms. We would thereby transform the industry from perfect competition to oligopoly. How would the behavior of firms in this industry differ before and after the massive merger?

Price Is Usually Higher Under Oligopoly. With fewer competitors after the merger, remaining firms would become more interdependent. Oligopoly models presented in this chapter suggest that the firms may act in concert in their pricing policies. *If the oligopolists engaged in some sort of implicit or explicit collusion, industry output would be smaller and the price would be higher than under perfect competition.* Even if oligopolists did not collude but simply operated with excess capacity, the long-run average cost of production would be higher with oligopoly than with perfect competition. The price could become temporarily lower under oligopoly compared to perfect competition only if a price war broke out among oligopolists.

Higher Profits Under Oligopoly. In the long run, easy entry prevents perfect competitors from earning more than a normal profit. With oligopoly, however, there are presumably barriers to entry, such as economies of scale or brand names, that allow firms in the industry to earn long-run economic profits. Such barriers could be insurmountable for a new entrant. Therefore, *we should expect profit rates in the long run to be higher under oligopoly than under perfect competition.*

Profit rates do in fact appear to be higher in industries where a few firms account for a high proportion of industry sales. Some economists view these higher profit rates as troubling evidence of market power. But not all economists share this view. Some note that the largest firms in oligopolistic industries tend to earn the highest rate of profit. Hence, the higher profit rates observed in oligopolistic industries stem not necessarily from market power per se. Rather, these higher profit rates stem from the greater efficiency arising from economies of scale in these large firms.[6] Many of these issues will be examined later, when we explore the government's role in regulating markets.

CONCLUSION

This chapter moves us from the extremes of perfect competition and pure monopoly to the gray area inhabited by most firms. Firms in monopolistic competition and firms in oligopoly face a downward-sloping demand curve for their products. In choosing the profit-maximizing price-output combination, a monopolistically competitive firm is not concerned much about the effects of this choice on the behavior of competitors. There are so many firms in the market that each individual firm tends to get lost in the crowd. But oligopolistic firms are interdependent and therefore must consider the effects their pricing and output decisions will have on other firms. This interdependence complicates the analysis of oligopoly, leaving open a wide array of possible models.

The analytical results derived in this chapter are not as neat as those derived for the polar cases of perfect competition and pure monopoly, but we can still point to general conclusions, using perfect competition as our benchmark. In the long run, perfect competitors operate at minimum average cost, while the other types of firms usually operate with some excess capacity. Therefore, given identical cost curves, monopolistic competitors and oligopolists tend to charge higher prices than perfect competitors, especially in the long run. In the long run, monopolistic competitors, like perfect competitors, earn only a normal profit because entry barriers are low. But oligopolists can earn economic profit in the long run if new entry is somehow restricted. In a later chapter, we will examine how government policy is often aimed at making industries more competitive. *Regardless of the market structure, however, profit maximization prompts firms to produce the output rate at which marginal cost equals marginal revenue.*

SUMMARY

1. Whereas the pure monopolist produces a product that has no close substitutes, a monopolistic competitor must contend with many rivals offering close substitutes. Because there are some differences among the products offered by different firms, even if the difference stems just from the location of the seller, each monopolistic competitor faces a downward-sloping demand curve.

2. Sellers in monopolistic competition differentiate their products through (1) physical qualities, (2) sales locations,

6 For this argument, see Harold Demsetz, "Industry Structure, Market Rivalry, and Public Policy," *Journal of Law and Economics* 16 (April 1973): 1–10.

(3) services provided with the product, and (4) the image of the product established in the consumer's mind.

3. In the short run, monopolistic competitors that can at least cover their average variable costs will maximize profits or minimize losses by producing where marginal cost equals marginal revenue. In the long run, free entry and exit of firms ensure that monopolistic competitors earn only a normal profit, which occurs where the average total cost curve is tangent to the firm's downward-sloping demand curve.

4. An oligopoly is an industry dominated by a few sellers, some of which are large enough relative to the entire market to influence price. In some oligopolistic industries, such as steel or oil, the product is homogeneous; in other oligopolistic industries, such as automobiles or breakfast cereal, the product differs.

5. Because an oligopolistic industry consists of just a few firms, each firm may react to another firm's changes in quality, price, output, services, or advertising policy. Because of this interdependence, the behavior of oligopolists is difficult to analyze. No single model of behavior characterizes oligopolistic markets.

6. In this chapter, we considered four models of oligopoly behavior: (1) the cartel, through which firms collude to behave like a monopolist; (2) price leadership, whereby one or a few firms set the price for the industry and other firms follow the leaders; (3) game theory, which focuses on each firm's strategy, based on the expected response of rivals; and (4) the kinked demand curve, which assumes that a firm's rivals follow price decreases but do not follow price increases.

QUESTIONS FOR REVIEW

1. *(Characteristics of Monopolistic Competition)* Why does the demand curve facing a monopolistically competitive firm slope downward in the long run, even after the entry of new firms?

2. *(Product Differentiation)* What are four ways in which a firm can differentiate its product? What role can advertising play in product differentiation? How can advertising become a barrier to entry?

3. *(Zero Economic Profit in the Long Run)* In the long run, a monopolistically competitive firm earns zero economic profit, which is exactly what would occur if the industry were perfectly competitive. Assuming that the cost curves for each firm are the same whether the industry is perfectly or monopolistically competitive, answer the following questions.
   a. Why don't perfectly and monopolistically competitive industries produce the same equilibrium quantity in the long run?
   b. Why is a monopolistically competitive industry said to be economically inefficient?
   c. What benefits might cause us to prefer the monopolistically competitive result to the perfectly competitive result?

4. *(Varieties of Oligopoly)* Do the firms in an oligopoly act independently or interdependently? Explain your answer.

5. ***(CaseStudy:** The Unfriendly Skies)* One complaint frequently heard about airfares is that flying from an airline's hub city airport is more expensive than flying from a nearby city that is not a hub. How may this reflect a different level of competition in hub city airports?

6. *(Collusion and Cartels)* Why would each of the following induce some members of OPEC to cheat on their cartel agreement?
   a. Newly joined cartel members are less-developed countries.
   b. The number of cartel members doubles from 10 to 20.
   c. International debts of some members grow.
   d. Expectations grow that some members will cheat.

7. *(Price Leadership)* Why might a price-leadership model of oligopoly not be an effective means of collusion in an oligopoly?

8. *(The Kinked Demand Curve)* If a firm believes that it is facing a kinked demand curve, what assumptions is it making about its rivals' reactions to its own price changes? How would the firm react to changes in its production costs?

9. *(Market Structures)* Determine whether each of the following is a characteristic of perfect competition, monopolistic competition, oligopoly, and/or monopoly:
   a. A large number of sellers
   b. A homogeneous product
   c. Advertising by firms
   d. Barriers to entry
   e. Firms that are price searchers

PROBLEMS AND EXERCISES

10. *(Short-Run Profit Maximization)* A monopolistically competitive firm has the following demand and cost structure in the short run:

Output	Price	FC	VC	TC	TR	Profit/Loss
0	$100	$100	$ 0	___	___	___
1	90	___	50	___	___	___
2	80	___	90	___	___	___
3	70	___	150	___	___	___
4	60	___	230	___	___	___
5	50	___	330	___	___	___
6	40	___	450	___	___	___
7	30	___	590	___	___	___

a. Complete the table.
b. What is the best profit or loss available to this firm?
c. Should the firm operate or shut down in the short run? Why?
d. What is the relationship between marginal revenue and marginal cost as the firm increases output?

11. ***(CaseStudy:** Fast Forward)* Use a cost-and-revenue graph to illustrate and explain the short-run profits in the video rental business. Then use a second graph to illustrate the long-run situation. Explain fully.

12. *(Monopolistic Competition Versus Perfect Competition)* Illustrated below are the marginal cost and long-run average total cost curves for a small firm.
a. Locate the long-run equilibrium price and quantity if the firm is perfectly competitive.
b. Label the price and quantity P_1 and Q_1.
c. Draw in a demand and marginal revenue curve to illustrate long-run equilibrium if the firm is monopolistically competitive. Label the price and quantity P_2 and Q_2.

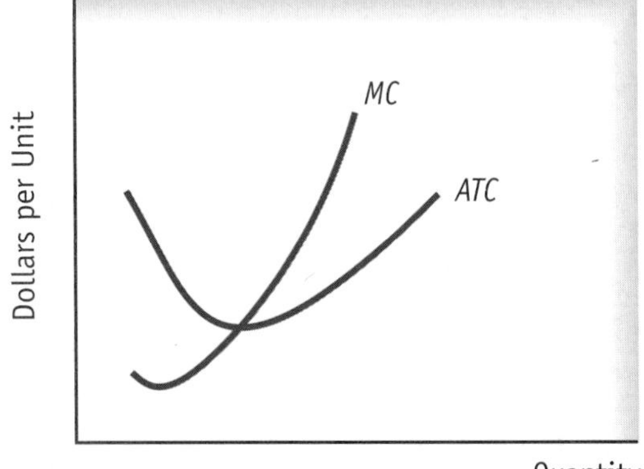

d. How do the monopolistically competitive firm's price and output compare to those of the perfectly competitive firm?
e. How do long-run profits compare for the two types of firms?

13. *(Collusion and Cartels)* Use revenue and cost curves to illustrate and explain the sense in which a cartel behaves like a monopolist.

14. *(Game Theory)* Suppose there are only two automobile companies, Ford and Chevrolet. Ford believes that Chevrolet will match any price it sets. Use the following price and profit data to answer the following questions.

If Ford sells for	and Chevrolet sells for	Ford's profits (millions)	Chevrolet's profits (millions)
$ 4,000	$ 4,000	$ 8	$ 8
4,000	8,000	12	6
4,000	12,000	14	2
8,000	4,000	6	12
8,000	8,000	10	10
8,000	12,000	12	6
12,000	4,000	2	14
12,000	8,000	6	12
12,000	12,000	7	7

a. What price will Ford charge?
b. What price will Chevrolet charge?
c. What is Ford's profit after Chevrolet's response?
d. If the two firms collaborated to maximize joint profits, what prices would they set?
e. Given your answer to part (d), how could undetected cheating on price cause the cheating firm's profit to rise?

EXPERIENTIAL EXERCISES

15. *(Product Differentiation)* One important way monopolistic competitors differentiate their products is by location. Review John Campbell's article, "Time to Shop: The Geography of Retailing," from the Federal Reserve Bank of Boston's *The Region* at http:/www.bos.frb.org/economic/nerr/camp96_3.htm. What locational strategies are retailers using? What does the theory of monopolistic competition predict about the success of such strategies in the short run and in the long run?

16. *(OPEC)* OPEC is the economist's favorite cartel to study. That is partly because it had such a spectacular short-run success and partly because oligopoly theory could be used to predict how OPEC pricing actually evolved. Take a look at the U.S. Department of Energy's OPEC Fact Sheet at http://www.eia.doe.gov/emeu/cabs/opec.html. What are some recent developments in petroleum pricing? How relevant are the factors listed in this chapter as affecting the difficulty of maintaining a cartel?

17. *(Wall Street Journal)* If you look carefully, you can often find evidence of price leadership. For example, the *Wall Street Journal* frequently runs stories about airfares. Typically, one airline will raise its fares—on certain routes or across the board—and other airlines match those changes within a day or two. As you read through the *Wall Street Journal* this week, be on the lookout for such stories. They are typically reported on the front page—in the What's News column. When you find such a story, check back over the next few days. Did other airlines match the leader, or was the leader forced to back off its price changes?

CHAPTER

24 Resource Markets

Why does Charles Schulz, the cartoonist, earn $25 million a year for drawing *Peanuts,* while Charles Schultze, the economist, earns peanuts, relatively speaking, for drawing conclusions about the economy? Why do surgeons earn twice as much as general practitioners? Why do tractor-trailer drivers earn more than rickshaw drivers? Why did a 30-second ad on the final episode of *Seinfeld* cost $2 million, when the prime-time average was only $120,000? Why does prime Iowa corn acreage sell for more than scrubland in the Texas panhandle? Why are the buildings in downtown Chicago taller than those in the farm towns of southern Illinois? To answer these and other questions, we turn in this chapter to the supply and demand for resources.

Visit the McEachern Interactive Study Center for this chapter at *http://mcisc.swcollege.com*

You say you've been through demand and supply already? True. But the earlier discussion focused on the product market—that is, the market for final goods and services. Goods and services, however, are produced by resources—labor, capital, land, and entrepreneurial ability. Demand and supply in resource markets determine the price and employment of resources. The distribution of resource ownership determines the distribution of income throughout the economy.

Because your earnings depend on the market value of your resources, you should find resource markets particularly interesting. Certainly one key element in your career decision is the expected income associated with various careers. The next three chapters will examine how demand and supply interact to establish market prices for various resources. Topics discussed in this chapter include:

- Demand and supply of resources
- Opportunity cost and economic rent
- Marginal revenue product
- Marginal resource cost
- Shifts in resource demand
- Distribution of resource earnings

THE ONCE OVER

Just to prove you already know a lot more about resource markets than you may think, try answering the questions in the following paragraphs.

Resource Demand

We begin with the demand for labor. The manager of Wal-Mart estimates that hiring one more sales clerk would increase total cost by $400 per week but would increase total revenue by $500 per week. Should an additional sales clerk be hired? Sure. The additional clerk would increase Wal-Mart's profit by $100 per week. *As long as the additional revenue from employing another worker exceeds the additional cost, the firm should hire that worker.*

How about capital? Suppose that you operate a lawn-and-garden service during the summer, earning an average of $20 per lawn. You mow about 15 lawns a week, for a total revenue of $300. You are considering upgrading to a larger, faster mower called the Lawn Monster, which would cost an extra $200 per week. The bigger mower would cut your time per lawn in half, enabling you to mow 30 lawns per week, so your total revenue would double to $600. Should you make the switch? Since the additional revenue of $300 exceeds the additional cost of $200, you should move up to the Monster.

What about land? A neighbor offers Farmer Jones the opportunity to lease 100 acres of farmland. Jones figures that farming the extra land would cost $70 per acre but would yield $60 per acre in additional revenue. Should he lease the extra land? What do you think? Since the additional cost of farming that land would exceed the additional revenue, the answer is no.

These examples show that *a firm demands an additional unit of a resource as long as the marginal revenue generated by that additional unit exceeds its marginal cost.*

Resource Supply

You likely also understand the economic logic behind resource supply. Suppose you are deciding between two jobs that are identical except that one pays more than the other. Is there any question which job you will take? If the working conditions of both jobs are equally attractive, you will choose the higher-paying job. Now consider your choice between two jobs that pay the same; one has normal nine-to-five hours, but the other starts at 5:00 A.M., an hour when your body tends to reject conscious activity. Which would you choose? You would select the job more in accord with your natural body rhythms.

Resource owners will supply their resources to the highest-paying alternative, other things equal. Since other things are not always equal, resource owners must often be paid more to supply their resources to certain uses. In the case of labor, the worker's utility depends on both monetary and nonmonetary aspects of the job. People must be paid more to work in jobs that are dirty, dangerous, dull, exhausting, of low status, that have no future, and that involve inconvenient hours than to work in jobs that are clean, safe, stimulating, of high status, have bright prospects, and involve convenient hours.

NetBookmark

What makes a good job good? Working for a good employer might be one factor. Each year *FORTUNE* magazine lists the 100 best employers at http://www.pathfinder.com/fortune/bestcompanies/intro. What factors other than compensation are cited in the report as creating a favorable work environment? What are the best and worst jobs? Search the Web for news and reviews of the *National Business Employment Weekly's* Jobs Rated Almanac; it ranks 250 jobs. Your Web site manager had the top rated job for 1999! Fishing ranked 248 yet most fishing grounds are overfished. Why do so many people want to fish for a living, when others consider this to be one of the worst jobs?

THE DEMAND AND SUPPLY OF RESOURCES

In the market for goods and services—that is, in the product market—households are the demanders and firms are suppliers. Households demand the goods and services that maximize utility, and firms supply the goods and services that maximize profit. In the resource market, the roles of demander and supplier are reversed: Firms are demanders and households are suppliers. Firms demand resources so as to maximize profit and households supply resources so as to maximize utility. *Any differences between the profit-maximizing goals of firms and the utility-maximizing goals of households are reconciled through voluntary exchange in markets.*

Exhibit 1 presents the market for a particular resource—in this case, carpenters. As you can see, the demand curve slopes downward and the supply curve slopes upward. *Like the demand and supply for final goods and services, the demand and supply for resources depend on the willingness and the ability of buyers and sellers to participate in market exchange.* This market will converge to the equilibrium wage rate, or the market price, for this type of labor.

The Market Demand for Resources

Why does a firm employ resources? Resources are used to produce goods and services, which the firm tries to sell for a profit. The firm does not value any resource itself but rather that resource's ability to produce goods and services that can be sold for a profit. Because the value of any resource depends on the value of what it produces, the demand for a resource is said to be a **derived demand**—derived from the demand for the final product. For example, a carpenter's pay derives from the market demand for the carpenter's output, such as a cabinet or a new deck; a professional baseball player's pay derives from the market demand for ball games; a truck driver's pay derives from the market demand for transporting goods. The derived nature of resource demand helps explain why professional

Derived demand The demand for a resource derived from the demand for the product the resource produces

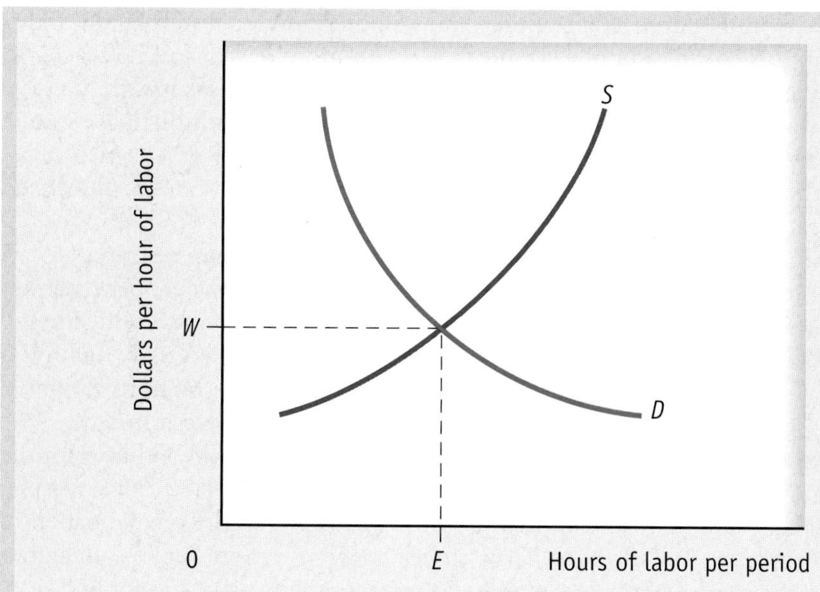

EXHIBIT 1

Resource Market for Carpenters

The intersection of the upward-sloping supply curve of carpenters with the downward-sloping demand curve determines the equilibrium wage rate, *W*, and the level of employment, *E*.

baseball players usually earn more than professional hockey players, why brain surgeons earn more than tree surgeons, why drivers of big rigs earn more than drivers of delivery vans, and why a 30-second TV ad during the Superbowl costs more than one during a typical game.

The market demand for a particular resource is the sum of demands for that resource in all its different uses. For example, the market demand for carpenters adds together the demands for carpenters in residential and commercial construction, remodeling, cabinet making, and so on. Similarly, the market demand for the resource, timber, sums the demand for timber as lumber, railway ties, firewood, furniture, pencils, toothpicks, paper products, and so on. The demand curve for a resource, like the demand curves for the goods produced by that resource, slopes downward, as depicted in Exhibit 1.

As the price of a resource falls, producers are more willing and able to employ that resource. Consider first the producer's greater *willingness* to hire resources as the resource price falls. In developing the demand curve for a particular resource, we assume the prices of other resources remain constant. So if the price of a particular resource falls, it becomes relatively cheaper compared to other resources the firm could use to produce the same output. Firms therefore are more willing to hire this resource rather than hire other, now relatively more costly, resources. Thus, we observe *substitution in production*—coal for oil, security alarms for security guards, and backhoes for grave diggers, as the relative prices of coal, security alarms, and backhoes fall.

A lower price for a resource also increases a producer's *ability* to hire that resource. For example, if the resource price falls, a firm can hire more of the resource for the same total cost. The lower resource price means the firm is *more able* to buy the resource.

The Market Supply for Resources

The market supply curve of a resource sums all the individual supply curves for that resource. Resource suppliers tend to be both more *willing* and more *able* to supply the resource as the resource price increases, so the market supply curve slopes upward, as the supply curve for carpenters does in Exhibit 1. Resource suppliers are more *willing* because the higher the market price of a particular resource, other things constant, the more goods and services can be purchased with the earnings obtained from supplying the resource.

Resource prices are signals about the rewards for supplying resources to alternative activities. A high resource price tells the resource owner, "The market really values your resource and is willing to pay you well for what you supply." Higher resource prices will draw resources from lower-valued uses, including leisure. For example, as the wage for carpenters increases, the quantity supplied will increase; some carpenters will give up leisure to work more hours.

The second reason a resource supply curve slopes upward is that resource owners are *able* to supply more of the resource at a higher price. For example, higher paper prices increase the market price of timber used to make paper, so logging companies can afford to harvest trees in more remote regions. A higher resource price *enables* resource suppliers to increase their quantity supplied.

Temporary and Permanent Resource Price Differences

Resource owners have a strong interest in selling their resources where they are most valued. *Resources tend to flow to their highest-valued use.* If carpenters, for example, can earn more by building homes than making furniture, then carpenters will shift from making furniture to building homes until wages in the two activities are equal. Because resource owners seek the highest pay, *other things constant,* the prices paid for identical resources should tend toward equality.

For example, suppose the wage paid to carpenters engaged in home building is $25 per hour, which is $5 more than the wage paid to carpenters who work as furniture makers. This difference is shown in Exhibit 2 by a wage of $25 per hour in panel (a) and a wage of $20 per hour in panel (b). This wage difference will encourage some carpenters to move from furniture making to home building. This shift will decrease the wage in home building and increase the wage in furniture making. Carpenters will move into home building until wages equalize. In Exhibit 2, supply shifts until the wage is $24 in both markets. Note that in the adjustment process, 2,000 hours of labor per week move from furniture making to home building. *As long as the nonmonetary benefits of supplying resources to alternative uses are identical and as long as resources are freely mobile, resources will adjust across uses until they earn the same in their alternative uses.*

Sometimes earnings appear to differ between seemingly similar resources. For example, corporate economists on average earn more than academic economists, and land in the city sells for more than land in the country. As you will now see, these differences reflect the workings of demand and supply.

Temporary Differences in Resource Prices. Resource prices sometimes differ temporarily across markets because market adjustment takes time. For example, there are sometimes wage differentials among workers who appear equally qualified. As we have seen, however, a difference between the prices of similar resources prompts resource owners and firms to make adjustments that drive

Market for Carpenters in Alternative Uses: Home Building and Furniture Making

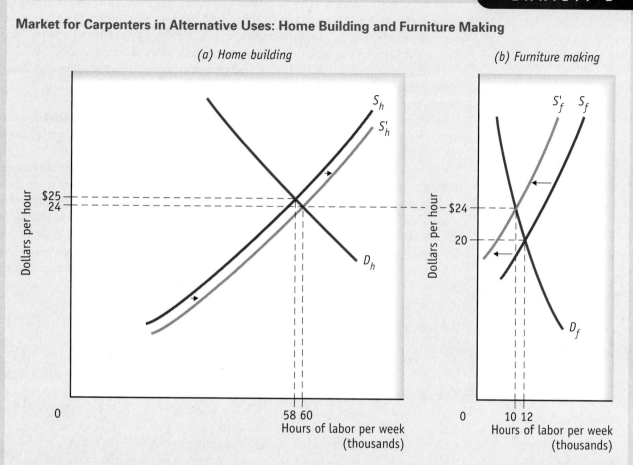

(a) Home building

(b) Furniture making

Suppose the wage offered carpenters is $25 per hour in home building but only $20 per hour in furniture making. As a result of the wage differential, some carpenters will shift from furniture making to home building, and this will continue until the wage offered carpenters is identical in both alternative uses. In panel (b), the reduction in the supply of carpenters to furniture making increases the equilibrium wage from $20 per hour to $24 per hour. In panel (a), the increase in the supply of carpenters to home building decreases the equilibrium wage from $25 per hour to $24 per hour. A total of 2,000 carpenter hours per week are shifted from furniture making to home building.

resource prices toward equality, as with the carpenters in the previous exhibit. The process may take years, but when resource markets are free to adjust, price differences trigger the reallocation of resources, which equalizes payments for similar resources.

Permanent Differences in Resource Prices. Not all resource price differences cause a reallocation of resources. For example, land along New York's Fifth Avenue sells for as much as $36,000 a *square yard!* For that amount, you could buy several acres of land in upstate New York. Yet such a differential does not prompt land owners in upstate New York to supply their land to New York City—obviously that's impossible. The price per acre of farmland varies widely, reflecting differences in the land's productivity and location. Such differences do not trigger actions that result in price equality. Similarly, certain wage differentials stem in part from the different costs of acquiring the education and training required to perform particular tasks. This difference explains why brain surgeons earn more than tree surgeons, why ophthalmologists earn more than optometrists, and why airline pilots earn more than truck drivers.

Other earning differentials reflect differences in the nonmonetary aspects of similar jobs. For example, other things constant, most people require higher pay to work in a grimy factory than in a pleasant office. Similarly, corporate economists earn more than academic economists in part because corporate economists typically have less freedom in their daily schedules, their attire, their choices of research topics, or even their public statements.

Temporary price differentials are just that, for they spark the movement of resources away from lower-paid uses toward higher-paid uses. Permanent price differentials cause no such reallocations. Permanent price differentials are explained by *a lack of resource mobility* (rural land versus urban land), *differences in the inherent quality of the resource* (scrubland versus fertile land), *differences in the time and money involved in developing the necessary skills* (file clerk versus certified public accountant), and *differences in nonmonetary aspects of the job* (prison guard at San Quentin versus lifeguard at Malibu Beach).

Opportunity Cost and Economic Rent

Shaquille O'Neal reportedly earned over $25 million in 1998, mostly from product endorsements. But he would likely be willing to play basketball and to endorse products for less money. The question is, how much less? What is his best alternative? Suppose his best alternative is to devote his energy full time to becoming a rap artist, something he now pursues in his spare time. Suppose as a full-time rap artist he could earn $2 million per year, including endorsements. Assume too that, if it weren't for the pay difference, he would be indifferent between rap and basketball, so the nonmonetary aspects of the two jobs balance out. Thus he must earn at least $2 million to remain a basketball player. This amount represents his *opportunity cost*—the amount he must be paid to prevent him from supplying his time to rap. *The opportunity cost of a resource is what that resource could earn in its best alternative use.*

Economic rent The portion of a resource's total earnings above its opportunity cost; earnings above the amount necessary to keep the resource in its present use

The amount O'Neal earns in excess of his opportunity cost is called *economic rent*. **Economic rent** is that portion of a resource's total earnings that is not necessary to keep the resource in its present use; it is, as the saying goes, "pure gravy." In O'Neal's case, economic rent is $25 million minus $2 million, or $23 million. Economic rent is a form of producer surplus earned by resource suppliers. The *division* of earnings between opportunity cost and economic rent depends on the resource owner's elasticity of supply. *In general, the less elastic the resource supply, the greater the economic rent as a proportion of total earnings.* To develop a feel for the difference between opportunity cost and economic rent, consider the following three cases.

Case A: All Earnings Are Economic Rent. If the supply of a resource to a particular market is perfectly inelastic, that resource has no alternative uses. Hence, there is no opportunity cost, and all returns are economic rent. For example, scrubland in the high plains of Montana has no use other than for cattle grazing. The supply of this grazing land is depicted by the vertical line in panel (a) of Exhibit 3, which indicates that the 10 million acres have no alternative use. Since the supply is fixed, the amount paid to rent this land for grazing has no effect on the quantity supplied. The land has no alternative use, so the opportunity cost is zero and all earnings are economic rent, shown by the blue shaded area. Here, *fixed supply determines the equilibrium quantity of the resource, but demand determines the equilibrium price.*

Case B: All Earnings Are Opportunity Costs. At the other extreme is the case in which a resource can earn as much in its best alternative use as in its present use. This situation is illustrated by the perfectly elastic supply curve in panel (b) of Exhibit 3. Suppose this figure depicts the market for janitors in the local school system. The school system can employ as many janitors as it wants at the market wage of $10 per hour; here, schools demand 1,000 hours of labor per week. If the wage offered janitors falls below $10 per hour, they will find jobs elsewhere, perhaps in nearby factories, where the wage is $10 per hour. In this case, all earnings equal opportunity costs because any reduction in the wage reduces the quantity of labor supplied to this particular use to zero. In this case, *the horizontal supply curve determines the equilibrium wage, but demand determines the equilibrium quantity.*

Case C: Earnings Include Both Economic Rent and Opportunity Costs. If the resource supply curve slopes upward, most resource suppliers will earn economic rent in addition to their opportunity cost. For example, if the wage for unskilled work in your college community increases from $5 to $10 per hour, the quantity of labor supplied will increase, as will the economic rent earned by resource suppliers. This situation occurs in panel (c) of Exhibit 3, where the pink area identifies opportunity costs and the blue area identifies economic rent. If the wage increases from $5 to $10, the quantity supplied per week will increase by 5,000 hours. For those resource suppliers who had been offering their services at a wage of $5 per hour, the difference between $5 and $10 is economic rent. These workers did not require the higher price to supply their services, but they certainly are not going to turn it down. *In the case of an upward-sloping supply curve and a downward-sloping demand curve, both demand and supply determine the equilibrium price and quantity.*

Note that specialized resources tend to earn a higher proportion of economic rent than do resources with many alternative uses. Thus, Shaquille O'Neal earns a greater *proportion* of his income as economic rent than does the janitor who cleans the Los Angeles Lakers' locker room. O'Neal would take a huge pay cut if he didn't play professional basketball, but the Lakers' janitor could find another unskilled job that would pay nearly as much.

To review: Given a resource demand curve that slopes downward, when the resource supply curve is vertical (perfectly inelastic), all earnings are economic rent; when that supply curve is horizontal (perfectly elastic), all earnings reflect opportunity cost; and when that supply curve slopes upward (an elasticity greater than zero but less than infinity), earnings divide between opportunity cost and economic rent. Remember, *the opportunity cost of a resource is what that resource could earn in its best alternative use. Economic rent is earnings in excess of opportunity cost.*

EXHIBIT 3

Opportunity Cost and Economic Rent

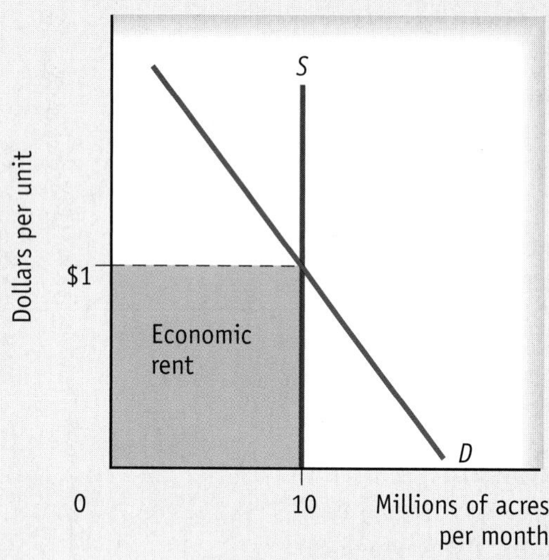

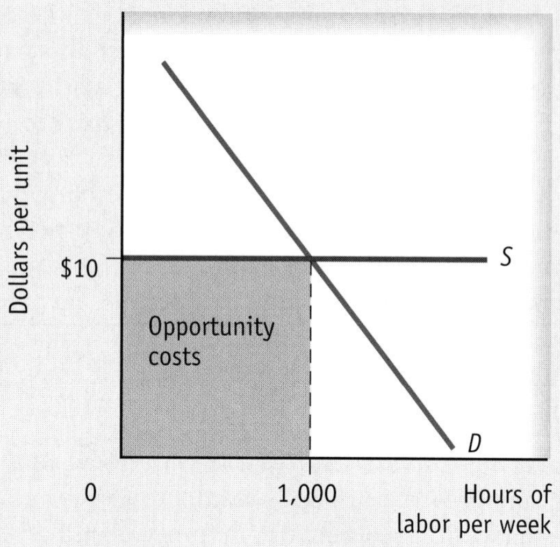

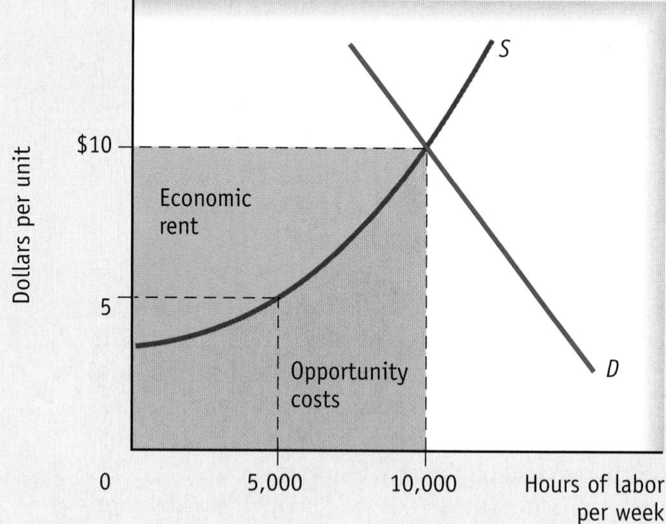

In panel (a), the resource supply curve is vertical, indicating that the resource has no alternative use. The price is demand-determined, and all earnings are in the form of economic rent. In panel (b), the supply curve is horizontal, indicating that the resource can earn $10 in its best alternative use. Employment is demand-determined, and all earnings are opportunity costs. Panel (c) shows an upward-sloping supply curve. At the equilibrium wage of $10, resource earnings are partly opportunity costs and partly economic rent. Both supply and demand determine the equilibrium price and quantity.

This completes our introduction to resource supply. In the balance of this chapter, we take a closer look at the demand side of resource markets. The determinants of the demand for a resource are largely the same whether we are talking about labor, capital, or land. The supply of different resources, however, has certain peculiarities depending on the resource, so the supply of specific resources will be taken up in the next two chapters.

A CLOSER LOOK AT RESOURCE DEMAND

Although production usually involves many inputs, we will cut the analysis down to size by focusing on a single resource, assuming that the quantities of other resources are constant. As usual, we assume that firms try to maximize profit and households try to maximize utility.

The Firm's Demand for a Resource

You may recall that when the firm's costs were first introduced, we considered a moving company, where labor was the only variable resource in the short run. By varying the amount of labor employed, we examined the relationship between the quantity of labor employed and the amount of furniture moved per day. We use the same approach in Exhibit 4, where all but one of the firm's inputs remain constant. The first column in the table lists possible employment levels of the variable resource, in this case measured as workers per day. The second column presents the total output, or total product, and the third column

EXHIBIT 4

The Marginal Revenue Product When a Firm Sells in a Competitive Market

Workers Per Day (1)	Total Product (2)	Marginal Product (3)	Product Price (4)	Total Revenue (5) = (2) × (4)	Marginal Revenue Product (6)
0	0	—	$20	$ 0	—
1	10	10	20	200	$200
2	19	9	20	380	180
3	27	8	20	540	160
4	34	7	20	680	140
5	40	6	20	800	120
6	45	5	20	900	100
7	49	4	20	980	80
8	52	3	20	1040	60
9	54	2	20	1080	40
10	55	1	20	1100	20
11	55	0	20	1100	0
12	53	−2	20	1060	−40

presents the marginal product. The *marginal product* of labor indicates how much additional output each additional unit of labor produces.

When one worker is employed, total product is 10 units and so is the marginal product. The marginal product of adding the second worker is 9 units. As the firm hires more workers, the marginal product of labor declines, reflecting the law of diminishing marginal returns. In Exhibit 4, diminishing marginal returns set in immediately—that is, right after the first worker is employed.

Although labor is the variable resource here, we could examine the marginal product of any resource. For example, we could consider how many lawns could be cut per week by varying the quantity of capital employed. We might start off with very little capital—imagine cutting grass with a pair of scissors—then moving up to a push mower, a power mower, and the Lawn Monster. By holding labor constant and varying the quantity of capital employed, we could compute the marginal product of capital. Likewise, we could compute the marginal product of land by examining crop production for varying amounts of land, holding other inputs, such as the amount of farm labor and capital, constant.

Marginal Revenue Product

The important question is, what happens to the firm's *revenue* as a result of hiring additional workers? The first three columns of Exhibit 4 show what happens to output as the firm hires more workers. The *marginal revenue product* of labor indicates how total revenue changes as more labor is employed, other things constant. The **marginal revenue product** of any resource is the change in the firm's total revenue resulting from employing an additional unit of the resource, other things constant. You could think of the marginal revenue product as the firm's "marginal benefit" from hiring one more unit of the resource. A resource's marginal revenue product depends on (1) how much additional output the resource produces and (2) the price at which output is sold.

Marginal revenue product
The change in total revenue when an additional unit of a resource is hired, other things constant

Selling Output as a Price Taker. The calculation of marginal revenue product is simplest when the firm sells output in a perfectly competitive market, which is the assumption underlying Exhibit 4. Since an individual firm in perfect competition can sell as much as it wants without affecting the product's price, a perfectly competitive firm is said to be a *price taker.* That firm must accept, or "take," the market price for its product. The marginal revenue product, listed in column (6), is the change in total revenue that results from changing input usage by one unit. For the perfectly competitive firm, the marginal revenue product is simply the marginal product of the resource multiplied by the product price of $20. Note that because of diminishing returns, the marginal revenue product falls steadily as the firm employs additional units of the resource.

Selling Output as a Price Searcher. If the firm has some market power in the product market—that is, some ability to set the price—the demand curve for that firm's output slopes downward. To sell more output, the firm must lower its price. The firm, consequently, must search for the price that maximizes profit. Such a firm is called a *price searcher.* Exhibit 5 reproduces the first two columns of Exhibit 4; the remaining columns reflect the revenue of a firm selling as a price searcher. Total output multiplied by the price at which that output sells yields the firm's total revenue, which appears in column (4).

EXHIBIT 5

The Marginal Revenue Product When a Firm Sells as a Price Searcher

Workers Per Day (1)	Total Product (2)	Product Price (3)	Total Revenue (4) = (2) × (3)	Marginal Revenue Product (5)
0	0	—	—	—
1	10	$40.00	$400.00	$400.00
2	19	35.20	668.80	268.80
3	27	31.40	847.80	179.00
4	34	27.80	945.20	97.40
5	40	25.00	1000.00	54.80
6	45	22.50	1012.50	12.50
7	49	20.50	1004.50	−8.00
8	52	19.00	988.00	−16.50
9	54	18.00	972.00	−16.00
10	55	17.50	962.50	−9.50
11	55	17.50	962.50	0.00

The marginal revenue product of labor, which is the change in total revenue resulting from a 1-unit change in the quantity of labor employed, appears in column (5). For example, the first worker produced 10 units per day, which sell for $40 each, yielding total revenue of $400. Hiring the second worker adds 9 more units to the total product, but to sell 9 more units, the firm must lower the price of all units from $40 to $35.20. Total revenue increases to $668.80, which means the marginal revenue product from hiring a second worker is $268.80.

Again, *the marginal revenue product is the additional revenue that results from employing each additional worker.* The profit-maximizing firm should be willing and able to pay as much as the marginal revenue product for an additional unit of the resource, hence *the marginal revenue product curve can be thought of as the firm's demand curve for that resource.* You could think of the marginal revenue product curve as the marginal benefit to the firm of hiring each additional unit of the resource.

To review, whether a firm is a price taker or a price searcher, the marginal revenue product of a resource is the change in total revenue resulting from a 1-unit change in that resource, other things held constant. The marginal revenue product curve of a resource is the demand curve for that resource—it shows the most a firm would be willing and able to pay for each successive unit of the resource. *For a price taker, the marginal revenue product curve declines only because of diminishing marginal returns. For a price searcher, the marginal revenue product curve declines both because of diminishing returns and because additional output can be sold only if the price declines.* For both price takers and price searchers, the marginal revenue product is the change in total revenue resulting from hiring an additional unit of the resource.

Marginal Resource Cost

Marginal resource cost
The change in total cost when an additional unit of a resource is hired, other things constant

Given the firm's marginal revenue product, can we determine how much labor the firm should employ to maximize profit? Not yet, because we must also know how much labor costs the firm. Specifically, what is the **marginal resource cost**—that is, what is the additional cost to the firm of employing one more unit of labor? The typical firm hires such a tiny fraction of the available resource that its employment decision has no effect on the market price of the resource. Thus, each firm usually faces a given market price for the resource and decides only on how much to hire at that price.

For example, panel (a) in Exhibit 6 shows the market for factory workers, measured in workers per day. The intersection of market demand and supply determines the equilibrium wage of $100 dollars per day. Panel (b) shows the situation for the individual firm. The market-determined wage for factory workers of $100 per day becomes the marginal resource cost of labor to the firm regardless of how many workers the firm employs. The *marginal resource cost* curve appears as the horizontal line drawn at the $100 level in panel (b); this is the labor supply curve to the firm. Panel (b) also shows the marginal revenue product curve, or resource demand curve, based on the schedule presented in Exhibit 4. The marginal revenue product curve indicates the additional revenue the firm receives as a result of employing each additional unit of labor.

EXHIBIT 6

Market Equilibrium for a Resource and the Firm's Employment Decision

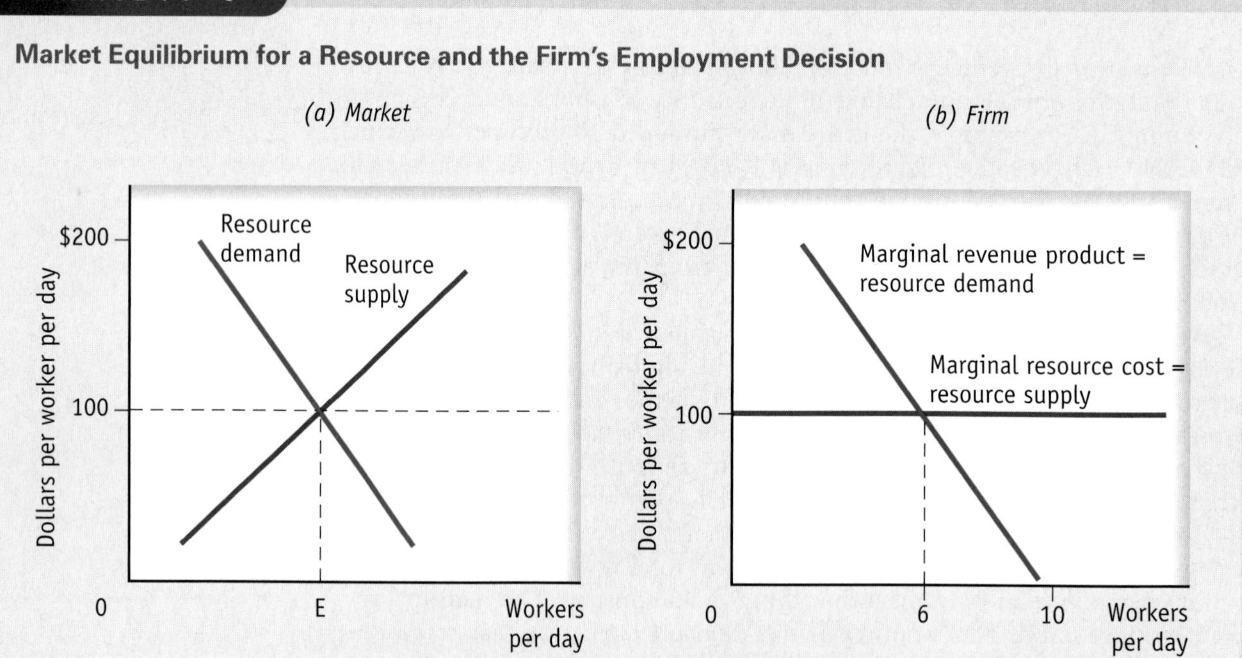

Market demand and supply determine the equilibrium price and quantity. Given the market price of the resource, the individual firm employs as much as it wants at the market price, so the market price is the firm's marginal resource cost. The firm's demand curve for the resource is based on that resource's marginal revenue product. The firm maximizes profit by hiring up to the point where the marginal revenue product equals the marginal resource cost.

Given a marginal resource cost of $100 per worker per day, how much labor will the firm employ to maximize profit? *The firm will hire more labor as long as doing so adds more to revenue than to cost—that is, as long as the marginal revenue product exceeds the marginal resource cost. The firm will stop hiring labor only when the two are equal.* If marginal resource cost is a constant $100 per worker, the firm will hire 6 workers per day because the marginal revenue product from hiring a sixth worker equals $100. Thus, the firm should hire additional inputs up to the level at which

marginal resource cost = marginal revenue product

or MRC = MRP. This equality holds for all resources employed, whether the firms sells output as a price taker or a price searcher. The profit-maximizing employment occurs where the market wage, or the market-determined resource price, equals the marginal revenue product. Based on data presented thus far, we cannot determine the firm's actual profit because we don't yet know about the firm's other costs. We do know, however, that in Exhibit 6 a seventh worker would add $100 to cost but would add less than that to revenue, so hiring a seventh worker would reduce the firm's profit (or increase its loss).

Whether the firm sells output as a price taker or as a price searcher, the profit-maximizing level of employment occurs where the marginal revenue product of labor equals its marginal resource cost. Similarly, the profit-maximizing employment of other resources, such as land and capital, occurs where their respective marginal revenue products equal their marginal resource costs. Each resource must "pull its own weight"—it must yield a marginal revenue at least equal to its marginal cost.

In an earlier chapter, we developed a rule for determining the profit-maximizing level of output. Maximum profit (or minimum loss) occurs at the output level where the marginal cost of producing *output* equals the marginal revenue from selling that *output*. Likewise, maximum profit (or minimum loss) occurs at the resource level where the marginal cost of employing a *resource* equals the marginal revenue that *resource* yields. Although the first rule focuses on output and the second on input, the two approaches are equivalent ways of deriving the same principle of profit maximization. For example, in Exhibit 6, the firm maximizes profit by hiring 6 workers when the wage is $100 per day. The details of production were provided in Exhibit 4: Employing a sixth worker adds 5 more units to output, which sell for $20 per unit, for a marginal revenue product of $100. The marginal cost of that output is the change in total cost, $100, divided by the change in output, 5 units; so the marginal cost of output is $100/5, or $20. The marginal revenue of that output is simply its price of $20. Thus, *in equilibrium, the marginal cost of output equals its marginal revenue.*

Now that you have some idea of how to derive the demand for a resource, let's determine what could shift resource demand.

Shifts in the Demand for Resources

As we have seen, a resource's marginal revenue product consists of two components: the resource's marginal product and the price at which that product is sold. A resource's marginal product will change following a change in the amount of other resources employed or a change in technology. The output's selling price will change due to a change in demand for that output. Let's first consider changes that could affect marginal product, then changes that could affect the demand for the final product.

Other Inputs Employed. Although our analysis thus far has focused on a single input, in practice the marginal product of any resource depends on the quantity and quality of other resources used in the production process. Sometimes resources are *substitutes.* For example, coal substitutes for oil in generating electricity. And automatic teller machines substitute for tellers in handling bank transactions. If two resources are substitutes, an increase in the price of one will increase the demand for the other. An increase in the price of oil will increase the demand for coal, and an increase in the wage of tellers will increase the demand for ATMs.

Sometimes resources are *complements,*—trucks and truck drivers, for example. If the relationship is complementary, an increase in the price of one reduces the demand for the other. If the price of tractor-trailer trucks increases, the quantity demanded decreases, which will reduce the demand for truck drivers.

One reason why U.S. truck drivers earn about $20 an hour and why rickshaw drivers in the Far East earn less than $1 per hour is the *truck.* The rickshaw driver pulls a cart worth maybe $100; the cart can carry relatively little and can move only as fast and as far as the driver's legs will take it. The truck driver is behind the wheel of a $200,000 machine that can haul huge amounts great distances at high speeds. The truck makes the driver more productive.

A valuable resource is one that helps other resources become more productive. In sports, the "most valuable player" is typically the team member who not only contributes directly but makes other players on the team more productive as well. For example, Michael Jordan scored so easily that opponents typically "double-teamed" him—that is, had two players try to prevent him from scoring. This allowed Jordan to "assist" other team members left open for a shot. More generally, *the greater the quantity and quality of complementary resources used in production, the greater the marginal productivity of the resource in question and the greater the demand for that resource.*

Changes in Technology. *Technological improvements can enhance the productivity of some resources and can make others obsolete.* The development of computer-controlled machines increased the demand for computer-trained machinists, but decreased the demand for machinists without computer skills. The development of synthetic fibers, such as rayon and orlon, increased the demand for these synthetic fibers, but reduced the demand for natural fibers, such as cotton and wool. Breakthroughs in fiber-optic and satellite communication increased the demand for fiberglass and satellites and reduced the demand for copper wire.

New computer programs are changing job prospects in the fields of law, medicine, accounting, architecture, computer programming, banking, and insurance, to name a few. For example, the computer program *WillMaker* has written more wills than any lawyer alive. In medicine, a program called *Iliad* can, in response to a series of questions, help diagnose about 1,000 diseases plus another 1,500 intermediate conditions in a chain of diagnostic deductions. Web page construction is now as easy as other forms of desktop publishing with programs such as *Fusion*, *Texture*, and *FrontPage*. And in accounting, programs like *TurboTax* and *Quicken* reduce the demand for CPAs. As the software gets cheaper and better, the demand for some professional skills will diminish, although the demand for those who write new software will increase.

Changes in the Demand for the Final Product. Because the demand for a resource *derives* from the demand for the final output, any change in the demand for output will affect resource demand. For example, an increase in the demand for automobiles will increase their market price and thereby increase the marginal revenue product of auto workers. Let's look at the derived demand for architects in the following case study.

The Derived Demand for Architects

The big drop in real estate prices, particularly commercial real estate prices, that occurred in the late 1980s and early 1990s cut demand for new construction, and in so doing reduced the demand for resources used in construction, such as builders and architects. Consider what happened to the demand for architects. In New York City, the number of classified ads for architectural positions declined from 5,000 in 1987 to 500 in 1991. Similar drops took place in other major cities. Employment at one national architectural firm shrank from 1,600 to 700 between 1988 and 1992.

Among entry-level architects, job losses were compounded because of improved technology. Drafting jobs long represented the traditional entry-level positions for new architects, but computer-assisted design programs coupled with more powerful and cheaper computers reduced the demand for new architects. Programs such as *Auto-Architect* and *3D Manager* help configure all aspects of a structure and create plans that can be manipulated in three-dimensional space, something impossible with traditional drawings. Programs also help estimate the cost of structures. Design software such as *Design Your Own Home*, *Planix Home Design Kit*, and *This Old House Kitchen & Home Architect* even help amateurs with designs and may have an accompanying Web site and on-line help desk. Whereas construction-grade blueprints drafted by an architect cost about $550 a set, do-it-yourself design CDs sell for $40 to $70. Thus new software substitutes for entry-level architectural positions.

The declining demand for architects had an interesting impact on the demand for higher education, which itself is a derived demand. Enrollment in undergraduate classes in architecture declined as entry-level positions disappeared. Enrollment in graduate courses, however, remained relatively stable. Apparently many out-of-work architects decided to pursue graduate study, since the poor job market reduced their opportunity cost of time. The exception that proves the rule about derived demand is that those architectural firms that specialize in the health-care industry flourished, because health care became the fastest-growing sector of the economy.

Sources: Tracie Rozhou, "At Hospitals, Construction Is Regaining Its Health," *New York Times* (7 July 1997); D. W. Dunlap, "Recession Is Ravaging Architects' Firms," *New York Times* (17 May 1992); Paul Stern, "Remodel Your House with Your Home Computer: Click to Fix," *Hartford Courant* (3 December 1998); Steven Ross, "Will Amateur CAD Put Residential Architects Out of Business?" *Architectural Record* (April 1994); and Internet site http://www.softdesk.com/index.html.

CaseStudy

The World of Business

What is the current demand for architects? The American Institute of Architects maintains a career center with a job board at http://www.e-architect.com/career/jobboard/job_SearchP.asp. How many architect positions are available in your part of the country? What is the employment outlook for future professional architects? You can find analysis and forecasts of future employment trends for many jobs in the Bureau of Labor Statistics' *Occupational Outlook Handbook.* The prospectus for architects is at http://www.bls.gov/oco/ocos038.htm. What is the typical size of a firm that hires architects? What does this tell you about search costs for both job seekers and employers?

In summary, the demand for a resource depends on its marginal revenue product. Any change that increases a resource's marginal revenue product will increase resource demand.

Optimal Use of More than One Resource

As long as the marginal revenue product exceeds the marginal resource cost, the firm can increase profit by employing more of a resource. The firm will increase resource use until the marginal revenue product just equals the marginal resource cost, or

$$\text{marginal revenue product} = \text{marginal resource cost}$$

Rearranging terms yields:

$$\frac{\text{marginal revenue product}}{\text{marginal resource cost}} = 1$$

This holds for each resource employed. Profit-maximizing employers will hire each resource up to the point at which the last unit hired adds as much to revenue as it does to cost.

Recall that at the outset of the chapter, you were asked why the buildings at the center of Chicago are taller than those farther out. Land and capital, to a large extent, substitute in the production of building space. Since land is more expensive at the center of the city, builders there substitute additional capital for land, building up instead of out. Hence, buildings are taller when they are closer to the center of the city and are tallest in cities where the land is most expensive. Buildings in Chicago and New York City are taller than buildings in Salt Lake City and Tucson, for example.

The high price of land in metropolitan areas has other implications for the efficient employment of resources. For example, in New York City, as in many large cities, vending carts on street corners specialize in everything from hot dogs to ice cream. Why are there about 4,100 licensed pushcarts in New York City? Consider the resources used to supply hot dogs: land, labor, capital, entrepreneurial ability, plus intermediate goods such as hot dogs, buns, and other ingredients. Which of these do you suppose is most expensive in New York City? Retail space along Madison Avenue rents for an average of $550 a year per square foot.[1] Since operating a hot dog cart requires about four square yards, it could cost up to $20,000 a year to rent the required commercial space. Aside from the necessary public permits, however, space on the public sidewalk is free to vendors. Profit-maximizing street vendors substitute public sidewalk space, which is free to them, for costly commercial rental space.

Government policy can affect resource allocation in other ways, as is discussed in the following case study.

1 As reported by Leslie Eaton in "Madison Ave. Strip Now Has Highest Store Rents," *New York Times* (27 November 1998).

The McMinimum Wage

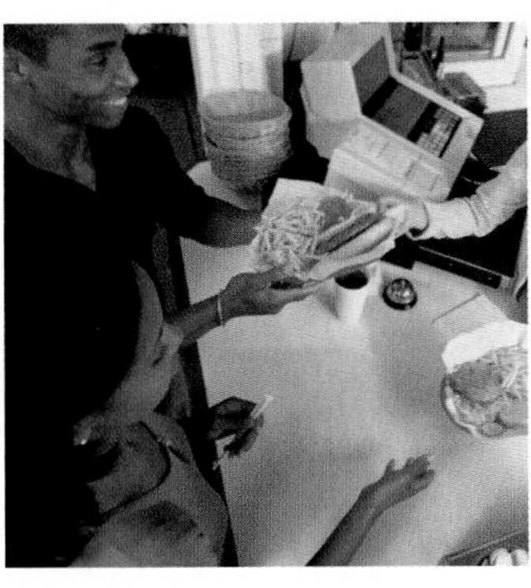

In March 1998, President Clinton proposed raising the minimum wage by $1.00 to $6.15 over two years. Ever since a federal minimum wage of 25 cents was established in 1938, economists have debated the benefits and costs of the law. The federal law initially covered only 43 percent of the work force—primarily workers in large firms involved in interstate commerce. Over the years, the minimum wage has been raised and the coverage has been broadened, so that by 1998 the law covered 86 percent of the work force (groups still not covered include domestic workers and those in small retail establishments and small restaurants).

At the time of Clinton's proposed increase, about 12 million workers earned between $5.15 and $6.15 an hour, and thus could potentially be affected by an increase. This group included many young workers, the majority working part time, primarily in service and sales occupations. Advocates of minimum-wage legislation argue that an appropriately applied minimum wage can increase the income of the poorest workers at little or no cost to overall employment. Critics argue that a minimum wage set above the market-clearing level causes employers either to cut nonwage compensation or to scale back employment.

There have been over 40 U.S. studies published since 1970 looking at the effect of changes in the minimum wage on employment. A few found a small positive effect of the minimum wage on employment, but most found either no effect or a negative effect, particularly among teenage workers. One reason an increase in the minimum wage may not always have the expected negative effect on total employment is that employers often react to a wage increase by substituting part-time jobs for full-time jobs, by substituting more-qualified minimum-wage workers (such as college students) for less-qualified workers (such as high-school dropouts), and by adjusting some nonwage features of the job to reduce costs or increase productivity.

Here are some of the nonwage job features that an employer could alter in response to a higher minimum wage: the convenience of work hours, expected work effort, on-the-job training, time allowed for lunch and for breaks, vacation days, paid holidays, sick leave policy, health-care benefits, tolerance for tardiness, parking provisions, air conditioning, dress code, and so on. Of most concern to economists is a possible reduction in the provision of on-the-job training to young workers, particularly those with little education.

A higher minimum wage also raises the opportunity cost of staying in school. For example, one study found that an increase in the minimum wage encouraged some 16- to 19-year-olds to quit school to seek work, although many failed to find a job. And those who had already left school were more likely to become unemployed because of a higher minimum wage. Thus there may be a significant enrollment effect associated with an increase in the minimum wage.

CaseStudy

Public Policy

The US Department of Labor maintains a Minimum Wage page at http://www.dol.gov/dol/esa/public/minwage/main.htm with questions and answers about the legal aspects and history of the minimum wage. Be sure to view the chart showing the real value of the minimum wage. In what year was it greatest? A link to Questions and Answers about the economic impact of the minimum wage is provided by the Employment Policies Institute at http://www.epionline.org/minimum_frame.htm. There are also links to several research reports on the impacts of minimum wage laws. The liberal view can be found at the Economic Policy Institute's Web page on labor markets at http://epinet.org/subjectpages/labor.html. In particular, look for the report on Making Work Pay. What percent of those receiving the minimum wage are supporting families?

In one survey of 193 labor economists, 87 percent believed "a minimum wage increases unemployment among young and unskilled workers." Minimum-wage increases, however, have broad public support. According to one recent poll, the highest support, 81 percent, came from those aged 18 to 29, the group most likely to be affected by a hike in the minimum wage. The typical college student has a part-time job that pays the minimum wage or close to it. The unemployment rate is usually twice as high for high-school dropouts as for college students. An increase in the minimum wage would benefit college students more than high-school dropouts.

Sources: Louis Uchitelle, "Better Pay vs. Job Stability in Wage Debate," *New York Times* (20 March 1998); "$6.15 Minimum Wage Approved in Hartford," *New York Times* (24 April 1998); Jane Blotzer, "Closing the Gap: A How-To Guide," *Pittsburgh Post-Gazette* (3 May 1998); "Review Symposium: Myth and Measurement: The New Economics of the Minimum Wage," *Industrial and Labor Relations Review* 48 (July 1995): 827–849; and Robert Whaples, "Is There Consensus Among American Labor Economists? Survey Results of Forty Propositions," *Journal of Labor Research* 27 (Fall 1996): 725–734.

DISTRIBUTION OF U.S. RESOURCE EARNINGS

This chapter showed that firms increase resource employment as long as a resource's marginal revenue product exceeds its marginal resource cost. This employment rule results in an allocation of earnings based on each resource's marginal productivity. So *earnings in a market economy are based on the marginal productivity of resources*. Resources that are more productive earn more, sometimes much more, than resources that are less productive. Not everyone is happy with the market outcome, especially those whose resources are not highly valued in the market. In this final section, we examine the distribution of earnings across different kinds of resources in the United States.

Exhibit 7 shows the percentage share of national income that goes to (1) wages and salaries, (2) proprietors' income, (3) corporate profits, (4) interest, and (5) rent. Proprietors' income consists of incomes of farmers, doctors, lawyers, small-business owners, and other unincorporated business owners. Over time, wages and salaries have claimed by far the largest share of national income, accounting most recently for 71.8 percent of the total during the 1990s. But this understates the proportion going to labor, because a large portion of proprietors' income consists of labor income as well. During the 1990s, labor's share declined slightly and profit's share increased.

Exhibit 7 also shows the decline over time in the share of national income received by proprietors. A generation ago, the income from the corner store was proprietors' income; these stores were named after the owner-operator, such as "Phil's Market" and "Pam's Pantry." Today these corner stores are more likely to be called "7-Eleven" or "Circle K," and the cashier who rings up your Pepsi and Cheetos typically earns a wage paid by the corporate chain. Note that wages and salaries combined with proprietors' income have remained relatively constant at about 80 percent for the entire century.

The column headings "Corporate Profits," "Interest," and "Rent" do not correspond exactly to the terms *profit, interest,* and *economic rent* used by economists, but the definitions in Exhibit 7 are similar enough to make the table useful. *The most important conclusion to draw from Exhibit 7 is that labor's share of total*

EXHIBIT 7

Functional Distribution of Income: Percentage Share of Each Source of National Income by Decade

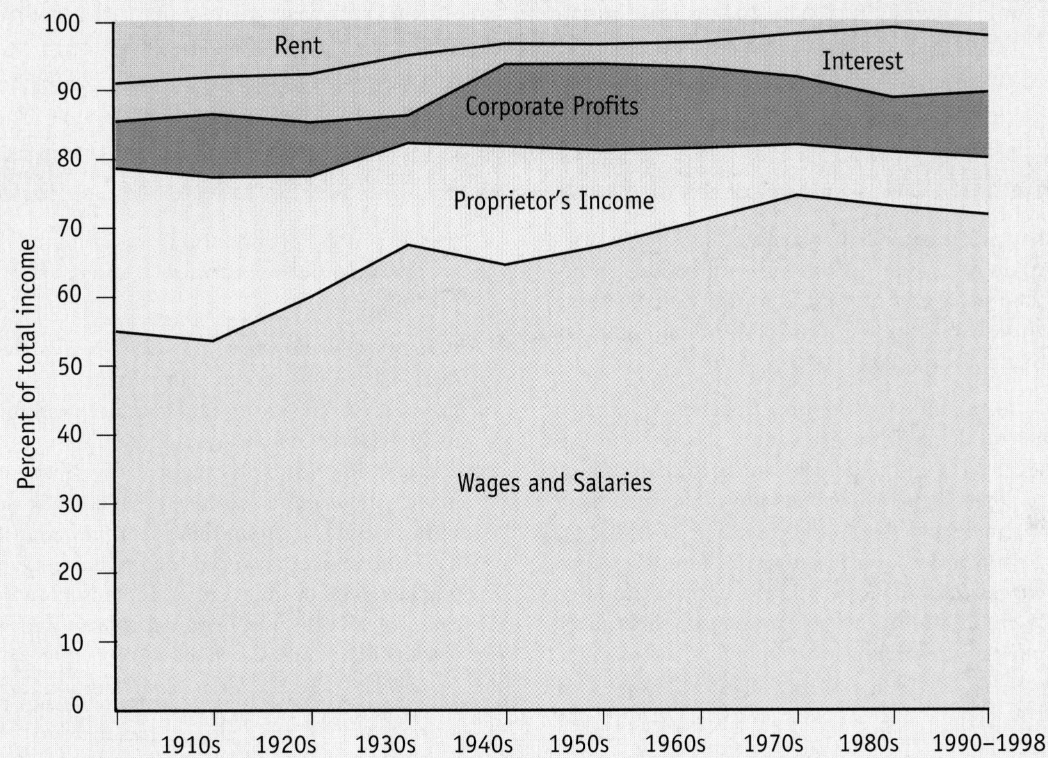

Source: Irving Kravis, "Income Distribution: Functional Shares," *International Encyclopedia of Social Sciences* 7 (The Free Press, 1968), and *Economic Report of the President,* February 1999.

income is relatively large and has grown during this century. This conclusion still holds even if the definitions of some other income categories do not exactly match our economic definitions. Labor's share has grown primarily because proprietors' income has decreased, as reflected, for example, by the shift from owner-operators to corporate chains.

CONCLUSION

The framework we have developed focuses on the marginal analysis of resource use to determine equilibrium price and quantity. The firm uses each resource up to the point where the marginal revenue product of that resource equals its marginal cost. The objective of profit maximization ensures that to produce any given level of output, firms will employ the least-cost combination of resources and will thereby use the economy's resources most efficiently. If this were not so, firms could produce the same output at a lower cost by adjusting the resource mix.

Although our focus has been on the marginal productivity of each resource, we should keep in mind that resources combine to produce output, so the marginal productivity of a particular resource will depend in part on what other resources are employed. For example, a baseball player whose teammates get on base more frequently will have more runs batted in during the season and will thereby be considered more productive.

SUMMARY

1. Firms demand resources to maximize profits. Households supply resources to maximize utility. The profit-maximizing goals of firms and the utility-maximizing goals of households are harmonized through voluntary exchange in resource markets.
2. Because the value of any resource depends on what it produces, the demand for a resource is a derived demand—derived from the demand for the final product. Resource demand curves slope downward because firms are more willing and able to increase their quantity demanded as the price of a resource declines. Resource supply curves tend to slope upward because resource owners are more willing and able to increase their quantity supplied as their reward for supplying the resource increases.
3. Some differentials in the market prices of similar resources trigger the reallocation of resources to equalize those prices. Other price differentials do not cause a shift in resources among uses because of a lack of resource mobility, differences in the inherent quality of the resources, differences in the time and money involved in developing necessary skills, and differences in nonmonetary aspects of jobs.
4. Resource earnings divide between (1) earnings that reflect the resource's opportunity cost, the amount that must be paid to get a resource owner to supply that resource to a particular use, and (2) economic rent, that portion of a resource's total earnings that exceeds the resource's opportunity cost. If a resource has no alternative uses, earnings consist entirely of economic rent; if a resource has other uses of similar value, opportunity cost predominates.
5. A firm's demand curve for a resource is the resource's marginal revenue product curve, which shows the change in total revenue that results from each one-unit increase in the amount of the resource employed, other things constant. If a firm sells output in a perfectly competitive market, the marginal revenue product curve slopes downward because of diminishing marginal returns. If a firm has some market power in the product market, the marginal revenue product curve slopes downward both because of diminishing marginal returns and because the product price must fall to sell more output.
6. The demand curve for a resource will shift to the right if there is an increase either in its marginal productivity or in the price of the output. An increase in the use of a complementary resource or a decrease in the use of a substitute resource will increase a resource's marginal productivity.
7. Marginal resource cost is the change in total cost resulting from employing one more unit of a resource. A firm maximizes profit by employing each resource up to the point where the marginal revenue product equals its marginal resource cost.
8. Wages and salaries have grown as a percentage of total resource income this century and proprietors' income has fallen.

QUESTIONS FOR REVIEW

1. *(Resource Demand and Supply)* Answer each of the following questions about the labor market:
   a. Which economic decision makers determine the demand for labor? What is their goal and what decision criteria do they use in trying to reach that goal?
   b. Which economic decision makers determine the supply of labor? What is their goal and what decision criteria do they use in trying to reach that goal?
   c. In what sense is the demand for labor a derived demand?

2. *(Market Supply of a Resource)* Explain why the market supply curve of a resource slopes upward.

3. *(Resource Price Differences)* Distinguish between the market reaction to a temporary difference in prices for the same resource and the market reaction to a permanent difference. Why do the reactions differ?

4. *(Opportunity Cost and Economic Rent)* On-the-job experience typically enhances a person's productivity in that particular job. If the person's salary increases to reflect increased experience but if the additional experience has no relevance for other jobs, does this higher salary reflect an increase in opportunity cost or in economic rent?

5. *(Firm's Demand for a Resource)* How does the law of diminishing marginal productivity affect a firm's demand for labor?

6. *(Shifts in Resource Demand)* Many countries are predominantly agrarian. How would changes in the supply of fertilizer affect the marginal product, and thus the income, of farmers in such countries?

7. *(Optimal Use of More Than One Resource)* Explain the rule for determining optimal resource use when a firm employs more than one resource.

8. *(Distribution of Resource Earnings)* What resource employment rule determines the allocation of earnings in a market economy? In the United States, which resource receives the largest share of national income? What has happened to this resource's share of income during the 20th century?

PROBLEMS AND EXERCISES

9. *(Opportunity Cost and Economic Rent)* Define economic rent. In the graph below, assume that the market demand curve for labor is initially D_1.

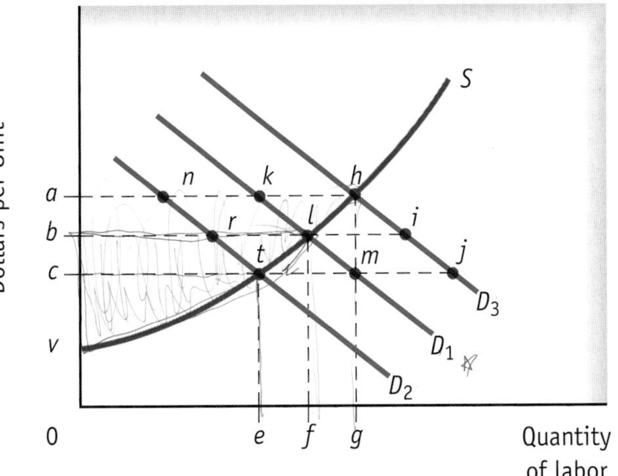

   a. What are the equilibrium wage rate and level of employment? What is the amount of economic rent?
   b. Next assume that the price of a substitute resource increases, other things constant. What happens to demand for labor? What are the new equilibrium wage rate and level of employment? What happens to the amount of economic rent?
   c. Suppose instead that demand for the final product drops, other things constant. Using labor demand curve D_1 as your starting point, what happens to demand for labor? What are the new equilibrium wage rate and level of employment? Does the amount of economic rent change?

10. *(Firm's Demand for a Resource)* Use the following data to answer the questions below. Assume a perfectly competitive output market.

Units of Labor	Units of Output
0	0
1	7
2	13
3	18
4	22
5	25

   a. Calculate the marginal revenue product for each additional unit of labor if output sells for $3 per unit.
   b. Draw the demand curve for labor based on the above data and the $3 per unit output price.
   c. If the wage rate is $15 per hour, how much labor will be hired?
   d. Using your answer to part (c), compare the firm's total revenue to the total amount paid for labor. Who gets the difference?
   e. What would happen to your answers to parts (b) and (c) if the price of output increased to $5 per unit, other things constant?

11. *(Selling Output as a Price Taker)* If a competitive firm hires another full-time worker, total output will increase from 100 units to 110 units per week. Suppose the market price of output is $25 per unit. What is the maximum weekly wage at which the firm would hire that additional worker?

12. *(Shifts in Resource Demand)* A local pizzeria hires college students to prepare pizza, wait on tables, take telephone orders, and deliver pizzas. For each situation described, determine whether the demand for student employees by the restaurant would increase, decrease, or remain unchanged. Explain each answer.
    a. The demand for pizza increases.
    b. Another pizzeria opens up next door.
    c. An increase in the minimum wage raises the cost of hiring student employees.
    d. The restaurant buys a computer system for taking telephone orders.

13. ***(CaseStudy:** The Derived Demand for Architects)* Use a supply-and-demand diagram to illustrate the change in the market for entry-level architects as described in the case study. Explain your conclusions.

EXPERIENTIAL EXERCISES

14. *(A Closer Look at Resource Demand)* The *Occupational Outlook Handbook* (OOH) is a U.S. Department of Labor publication that projects employment trends. Using the search feature available at the OOH Web site at http://stats.bls.gov/ocohome.htm, search several occupations. What factors seem to be affecting employment prospects in those fields? What role does derived demand play? How about technological change?

15. ***(CaseStudy:** The McMinimum Wage)* In the absence of legislated changes, the federal minimum wage decreases in real terms whenever the economy experiences inflation. Go to the Department of Labor's Minimum Wage page at http://dol.gov/dol/esa/public/minwage/chart2.htm and look at Chart 2. How would these changes in the inflation-adjusted minimum wage affect the market for low-skilled workers? Use a labor supply and demand diagram to illustrate your conclusions.

16. *(Wall Street Journal)* Review the Work Week column on the front page of Tuesday's *Wall Street Journal*. Choose an interesting article, read it, then try to interpret it using the tools developed in this chapter. Did labor supply, labor demand, or both change? Was only a single labor market affected, or were the effects felt in several markets simultaneously? Be sure that your explanation accounts for what happened to both the wage rate and the level of employment.

CHAPTER

25 Labor Markets and Labor Unions

How do we allocate our time among different possible uses, especially between work and leisure? What factors other than the wage rate are important in the decision to supply labor? Why do some people choose to work *less* if the wage rate increases sharply? For example, why do unknown rock groups perform for hours for hardly anything, while famous ones perform much less for much more. More generally, what determines the wage structure in the economy?

You don't need a course in economics to figure out why corporate presidents earn more than file clerks, or why heart surgeons earn more than registered nurses. But why do lawyers earn more than accountants, and schoolteachers more than truck drivers? Will we observe similar patterns ten years

Visit the McEachern Interactive Study Center for this chapter at //mcisc.swcollege.com

from now? You can be sure of one thing: Demand and supply play a central role in the wage structure. In this chapter, we focus on labor markets to dig more deeply into wage determination.

You have already examined the demand for resources. Demand depends on a resource's marginal productivity. In the first half of this chapter, we focus on the supply of labor, then bring demand and supply together to arrive at the market wage. In the latter part of the chapter, we consider the role that labor unions play in labor markets. We examine the economic effects of unions and review recent trends in union membership. Topics discussed in this chapter include:

- Theory of time allocation
- Backward-bending supply curve for labor
- Nonwage factors and labor supply
- Why wages differ
- Unions and collective bargaining
- Union wages and employment
- Recent trends in union membership

LABOR SUPPLY

As a resource supplier, you have a labor supply curve for each of the many possible uses of your labor. To some markets, your quantity supplied is zero over the realistic range of wages. The qualifier "over the realistic range" is added because, for a high enough wage (say, $1 million per hour), you might supply labor to just about *any* activity. In most labor markets, your quantity supplied may be zero either because you are *willing* but *unable* to perform the job (for example: airline pilot, professional golfer, novelist) or because you are *able* but *unwilling* to do so (for example: soldier of fortune, prison guard, gym teacher).

So you have as many supply curves as there are labor markets, just as you have as many demand curves as there are markets for goods and services. Your labor supply to each market depends, among other things, on your ability, your taste for the job in question, and the opportunity cost of your time—how much you could earn in other activities. Your supply to a particular labor market assumes that wages in other markets are constant, just as your demand for a particular product assumes that other prices are constant.

Labor Supply and Utility Maximization

Recall the definition of economics: *the study of how people use their scarce resources in an attempt to satisfy their unlimited wants.* That is, individuals attempt to use their scarce resources so as to maximize their utility. Two sources of utility are of special interest to us in this chapter: the consumption of goods and services and the enjoyment of leisure. The utility derived from consuming goods and services is obvious and serves as the foundation for consumer demand. Another valuable source of utility is leisure—time spent relaxing, sleeping, eating, and in recreational activities. Leisure is a normal good that, like other goods, is subject to the law of diminishing marginal utility. Thus, the more leisure time you have, the less you value each additional unit of leisure. Sometimes you may have so much leisure that you "have time on your hands" and are "just killing time." As that sage of the comic page Garfield the cat once lamented, "Spare time would be more fun if I had less to spare." Or as Shakespeare wrote, "If all the year were playing holidays, to sport would be as tedious as to work." Leisure's diminishing marginal utility explains why some of the so-called idle rich grow bored in their idleness.

Three Uses of Time. Some of you are at a point in your career when you have few resources other than time. Time is the raw material of life. You can use your time in three ways. First, you can undertake **market work**—selling your time in the labor market in return for income. When you supply labor, you usually surrender control of your time to the employer in return for a wage. Second, you can undertake what we will call **nonmarket work**—using time to produce your own goods and services. Nonmarket work includes the time you spend doing your laundry, preparing your meals, or typing your term paper. Nonmarket work also includes the time spent acquiring skills and education that enhance your future productivity. Although the time spent studying and attending class provides little immediate payoff, you are betting that the knowledge and perspective you gain will pay off in the future. Third, you can convert time directly into **leisure**—nonwork uses of your time.

Market work Time sold as labor in return for a money wage

Nonmarket work Time spent producing goods and services in the home or acquiring an education

Leisure Time spent on nonwork activities

Work and Utility. Unless you are one of the fortunate few, work is not a pure source of utility, as it often generates some boredom, discomfort, or aggravation. In short, time spent working can be "a real pain," a source of *disutility*—the opposite of utility. And work is subject to increasing marginal disutility—the more you work, the greater the marginal disutility of working another hour. You work nonetheless, because your earnings buy goods and services. You expect the utility from these goods and services to more than offset the disutility of work. Thus, the *net utility of work*—the utility of the consumption made possible through work minus the disutility of the work itself—usually makes some amount of work an attractive use of your time. In the case of market work, your income buys goods and services. In the case of nonmarket work, either you produce goods and services directly, as in making yourself a tuna sandwich, or you invest your time in education with an expectation of higher future earnings and higher future consumption. The additional utility you expect from the tuna sandwich and higher future consumption resulting from education are the marginal benefits of nonmarket work.

Utility Maximization. Within the limits of a 24-hour day, seven days a week, you balance your time among market work, nonmarket work, and leisure so as to maximize utility. As a rational consumer, *you attempt to maximize utility by allocating your time so that the expected marginal utility of the last unit of time spent in each activity is identical.* Thus, in the course of a week or a month, the marginal utility of the last hour of leisure equals the net marginal utility of the last hour of market work, which equals the net marginal utility of the last hour of nonmarket work. In the case of time devoted to acquiring skills, you must consider the marginal utility expected from the future increase in earnings that will result from your enhanced productivity.

Perhaps at this point you are saying, "Wait a minute. I don't allocate my time with that sort of precision or logic. I just sort of go along, doing what feels good." Economists do not claim that you are even aware of making such marginal calculations. But as a rational decision maker, you allocate your scarce time to satisfy your wants, or to maximize utility. And utility maximization, or "doing what feels good," implies that you act *as if* you allocated your time to derive the same expected net marginal utility from the last unit of time spent in each alternative use.

You probably have settled into a rough plan (for meals, work, entertainment, study, sleep, and so on) that fits your overall objectives and seems reasonable. This plan is probably in constant flux as you make expected and unexpected adjustments in the use of your time. For example, this morning you may have slept later than you planned because you were up late last night; last weekend you may have failed to crack a book, despite good intentions. Over a week or a month, however, your use of time is roughly in line with an allocation that maximizes utility as you perceive it. Put another way, given the various constraints on your time, money, energy, and other resources, if you could change your use of time to increase your utility, you would do so. Nobody is stopping you! You may emphasize immediate gratification over long-term goals, but that's your choice and you bear the consequences. *This time-allocation process ensures that at the margin, the expected net utilities from the last unit of time spent in each activity are equal.*

Because information is costly and because the future is uncertain, you sometimes make mistakes in allocating time; you do not always get what you expect. Some mistakes are minor, such as going to a movie that proves to be a waste of time. But other mistakes can be costly. For example, you may now be studying for a field that will grow crowded by the time you graduate, or you may be acquiring skills that will become obsolete because of new computer software.

Implications. The model of time allocation described thus far has several implications for individual choice. First, consider the choice among market work, nonmarket work, and leisure. The higher your market wage, other things constant, the higher your opportunity cost of leisure and nonmarket work. For example, individuals with a high market wage will spend less time on nonmarket work, other things constant. Surgeons are less likely to mow their own lawns than are butchers. And among those earning the same market wage, people who are handy around the house and are good cooks will tend to do more for themselves and hire fewer household services. Conversely, those who are all thumbs around the house and who have difficulty boiling water will hire more household services and will eat out more frequently. In short, *utility maximization implies that individuals will spend time in nonmarket work if they can produce goods and services more cheaply than the market can.* By the same logic, the higher the expected earnings right out of high school, other things constant, the higher the opportunity cost of attending college.

Most young, successful movie stars do not go to college. Some, such as Tom Cruise, are high-school dropouts. And the most promising athletes "turn pro" right after high school or before completing college. Top players who never attended college include Ken Griffey, Jr., and Mark McGwire in baseball; Kobe Bryant and Kevin Garnett in basketball; Mario Lemieux and Wayne Gretsky in hockey; and most top tennis players. But the vast majority of people do not face such a high opportunity cost of higher education. As one fellow explained, "Since my wife left me, my kids joined a cult, and my dog died, now would be a good time to go back and get my MBA."

Wages and Individual Labor Supply

To breathe life into the time-allocation problem, consider your choices for the summer. If you can afford to, you can take the summer off, spending it entirely on leisure, perhaps as a fitting reward for a rough academic year. Or you can supply your time to market work. Or you can undertake nonmarket work, such as cleaning the basement or attending summer school. As a rational decision maker, you will select that combination of leisure, market work, and nonmarket work that you expect will maximize your utility. And the optimal combination is likely to involve allocating some time to each activity. For example, even if you work during the summer, you might still consider taking one or two summer courses.

Suppose the only summer job available is some form of unskilled labor, such as working in a fast-food restaurant or for the town parks department. For simplicity, let's assume that you view all such jobs as equally attractive (or unattractive) in terms of their nonmonetary aspects, such as working conditions, working hours, and so on. (These nonmonetary aspects are discussed in the next section.) If there is no difference among these unskilled jobs, the most important question for you in deciding how much market labor to supply is: What is the market wage for unskilled labor?

Suppose the wage is $6 per hour. At a wage that low, you might decide to work around the house, attend summer school full-time, take a really long nap, travel across the country to find yourself, or perhaps do some combination of these. In any case, you supply no market labor at such a low wage. The market wage must rise to $7 per hour before you supply any market labor. Suppose that at a wage of $7 per hour, you supply 20 hours per week, perhaps taking fewer summer courses and shorter naps.

As the wage increases, this raises your opportunity cost of time spent in other activities, so you substitute market work for other uses of your time. You decide to work 30 hours per week at a wage of $8 per hour, 40 hours at $9 per hour, 48 hours at $10 per hour, and 55 hours at $11 per hour. At a wage of $12 you go to 60 hours per week; you are starting to earn serious money—$720 per week.

If the wage hits $13 per hour, a wage you consider to be very attractive indeed, you decide to cut back to 58 hours per week, so you earn $754 per week—more than when the wage was $12 per hour. Finally, if the wage hits $14 per hour, you cut back to 55 per week and earn $770. To explain why you may eventually reduce the quantity of labor supplied, let's consider the impact of wage increases on your allocation of time.

Substitution and Income Effects. An increase in the wage rate affects your choice between market work and other uses of your time in two ways. First, a higher wage provides you with an incentive to work more, since each hour of work now buys more goods and services. As the wage increases, the opportunity cost of other uses of your time, such as leisure, also increases. Thus, as the wage increases, you substitute market work for other activities; this is the **substitution effect of a wage increase.** But a higher wage means a higher income for the same number of hours, and a higher income means that you demand more of all normal goods. Since leisure is a normal good, a higher income increases your demand for leisure, thereby reducing your allocation of

Substitution effect of a wage rate increase When the wage increases, workers substitute market work for other activities, which now have a higher opportunity cost

Income effect of a wage increase A higher wage rate increases workers' real income, increasing their demand for all normal goods, including leisure, so the quantity of labor supplied decreases

time to market work. This **income effect of a wage increase** tends to reduce the quantity of market labor supplied.

As the wage rate increases, the substitution effect causes you to supply more time to market work, but the income effect causes you to demand more leisure and, hence, to supply less time to market work. In our example, the substitution effect exceeds the income effect for wage rates up to $12 per hour, resulting in a greater quantity of market labor supplied as the wage increases. When the wage rises above $12 per hour, however, the income effect exceeds the substitution effect, causing a net reduction in the quantity of labor supplied to market work.

Backward-bending supply curve of labor Occurs if the income effect of a higher wage dominates the substitution effect

Backward-Bending Labor Supply Curve. The labor supply curve just described appears in Exhibit 1. As you can see, this supply curve slopes upward until a wage of $12 per hour is reached, then it begins to bend backward. The **backward-bending supply curve** gets its shape as the income effect of a higher wage eventually exceeds the substitution effect, reducing the quantity of labor supplied as the wage increases. We see evidence of a backward-bending supply curve, particularly among high-wage individuals, who reduce their work and consume more leisure as the wage increases. For example, doctors often play golf on a weekday afternoon. Entertainers typically perform less as they become more successful. Unknown bands play hours for hardly anything; famous bands play much less for much more. Despite top pay, the cast from *Seinfeld* decided to call it quits in 1998, in part to take more leisure. The income effect of rising real wages helps explain the decline in the U.S. work week from an average of 60 hours in 1900 to less than 40 hours today.

EXHIBIT 1

Individual Labor Supply Curve for Market Work

When the substitution effect of a wage increase outweighs the income effect, the quantity of labor supplied increases with the wage rate. Above some wage (here, $12), the income effect dominates. Above that wage, the supply curve bends backward; further increases in the wage rate reduce the quantity of labor supplied.

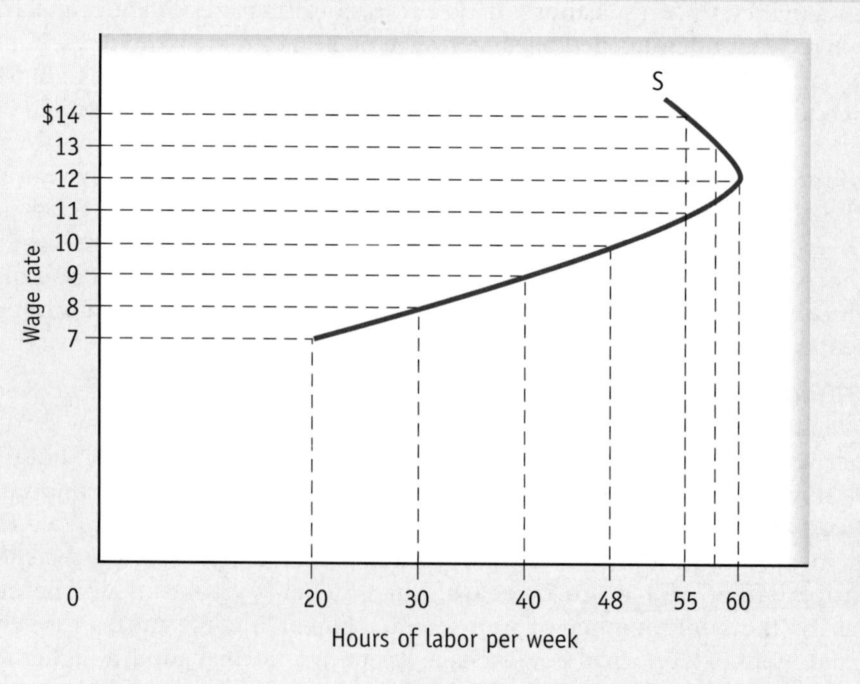

Flexibility of Hours Worked. The model we have been discussing assumes that workers have some control over the number of hours they work per week. Opportunities for part-time work and overtime allow workers to put together their preferred quantity of hours (for instance, 30 hours in a restaurant and 15 hours at the college bookstore). Workers also have some control over the timing and length of their vacations. More generally, individuals can control the length of time they stay in school, when and to what extent they enter the workforce, and when they choose to retire. Thus, they actually have more control over the number of hours worked than you might think if you focused on the benchmark of, say, 40 hours per week.

Nonwage Determinants of Labor Supply

The supply of labor to a particular market depends on a variety of factors other than the wage rate, just as the demand for a particular good depends on factors other than the price. As we have already seen, the supply of labor to a particular market depends on wage rates in other labor markets. So what are the nonwage factors that shape a college student's labor supply for the summer?

Other Sources of Income. Although some jobs are rewarding in a variety of nonmonetary ways, the primary reason people work is to earn money to buy goods and services. Thus the willingness to supply time to a labor market depends on income from other sources, including savings, borrowing, family support, and scholarships. A student who receives a generous scholarship, for example, may feel less pressure to earn additional income. More generally, wealthy people have less incentive to work. For example, multimillion-dollar lottery winners often quit their jobs after hitting the jackpot.

Nonmonetary Factors. Labor is a special kind of resource. Unlike capital and land, which can be supplied regardless of the whereabouts of the resource owners, time supplied to market work usually requires the seller of that time to be on the job. Because the individual must be physically present to supply labor, such *nonmonetary factors* as the difficulty of the job and the quality of the work environment have important effects on the labor supply. For example, deckhands on fishing boats in the winter waters of the Bering Sea off Alaska earn over $3,000 for five days' work, but the temperature seldom gets above zero and daily shifts are 21 hours long, allowing only three hours for sleep. Consider the different working conditions you might encounter. If you are a college student, a library job that allows you to study much of the time is more attractive than a job that affords no study time. Some jobs have flexible hours; others impose rigid work schedules. Is the workplace air-conditioned or do you have to sweat it out? The more attractive the working conditions, the more labor you will supply to that particular market, other things constant.

The Value of Job Experience. All else equal, you are more inclined to take a job that provides valuable experience. Serving as the assistant treasurer for a local business provides better job experience and looks better on a résumé than serving hash at the college cafeteria. Some people are willing to accept relatively low wages now because of the promise of higher wages later. For example, new lawyers are eager to fill clerkships for judges, although the pay is low and the hours long, because these positions provide experience and contacts valued by future employers. Likewise, athletes who play in the minor leagues do so because they hope the experience so gained will move them up to the major leagues. Thus *the more a job enhances future earning possibilities, the greater the supply of labor to that occupation, other things constant.* Because of the greater supply of labor to such positions, other things constant, the pay is usually lower than for similar jobs that impart less experience.

Taste for Work. Just as the tastes for goods and services differ, tastes for work also differ among labor suppliers. Some people prefer physical labor and would avoid a desk job. Some become surgeons; others can't stand the sight of blood. Some become airline pilots; others are afraid to fly. Many struggling writers, artists, actors, and dancers could earn more elsewhere, but apparently the satisfaction of the creative process and the chance, albeit slim, of hitting it big more than offset the low pay. Some people evidently have such a strong preference for certain jobs that they do them for free, such as auxiliary police officers or volunteer fire fighters.

As with the taste for goods and services, economists do not attempt to explain the origin of taste for work. They simply argue that your supply of labor will be greater to those jobs that are more in accord with your tastes. Voluntary sorting based on tastes allocates workers among different jobs in a way that tends to minimize the disutility of work. This is not to say that everyone will end up in his or her most preferred occupation. The cost of acquiring information about jobs and the cost of changing jobs may prevent some matchups that might otherwise seem desirable. But in the long run, people tend to find jobs that suit them. We are not likely to find tour directors who hate to travel, zoo keepers who are allergic to animals, or garage mechanics who can't stand getting their hands dirty.

Market Supply of Labor

In the previous section we considered those factors, both monetary and nonmonetary, that influence individual labor supply. *The supply of labor to a particular market is the horizontal sum of all the individual supply curves.* The horizontal sum is found by adding the quantities supplied by each individual supplier at each particular wage rate. If an individual supply curve of labor bends backward, does this mean that the market supply curve for labor also bends backward? Not necessarily. Since different individuals have different opportunity costs and different tastes for work, the bend in the supply curve occurs at different wages for different individuals. And, for some individuals, the labor supply curve may not bend backward over the realistic range of wages. Exhibit 2 shows how just three individual labor supply curves sum to yield a market supply curve that slopes upward.

Why Wages Differ

Just as both blades of a pair of scissors contribute equally to cutting cloth, both demand and supply determine the market wage. Therefore, wage differences across markets can be traced to differences in labor demand, in labor supply, or in both. In the previous chapter we discussed the elements that influence the demand for resources, and we examined labor in particular. In brief, *a profit-maximizing firm*

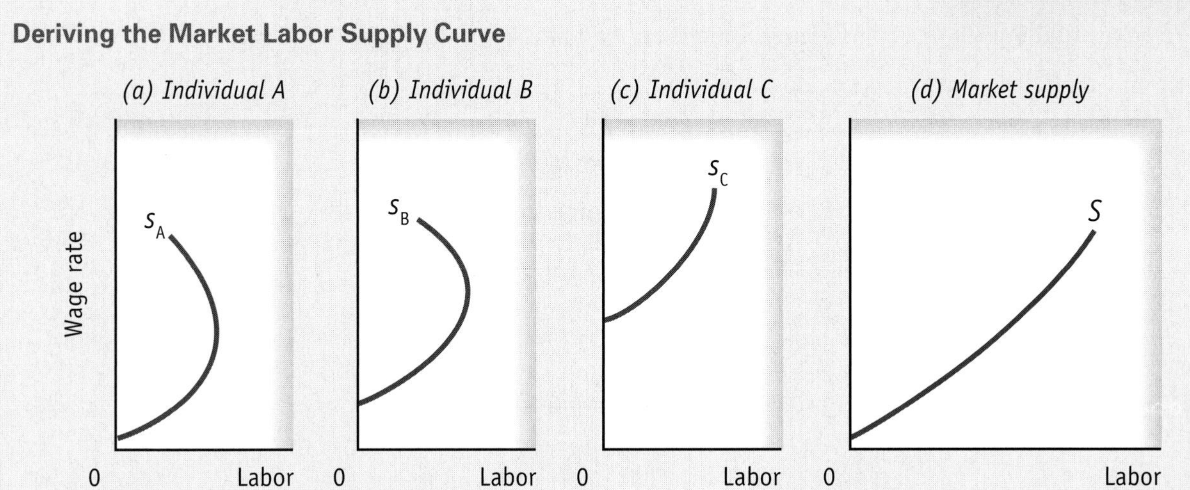

The individual labor supply curves in panels (a) and (b) each bend backward. The market supply curve, however, still slopes upward over the relevant range of wage rates.

hires labor up to the point where labor's marginal revenue product equals its marginal resource cost—that is, where the last unit employed earns the firm just enough to cover its cost (MRP = MRC). Since we have already discussed the forces that affect the demand for labor, let's focus here primarily on market supply.

Differences in Training, Education, Age, and Experience. Some jobs pay more than others because they require a long and costly training period. Costly training reduces market supply because fewer individuals are willing to incur the time and expense. But the training increases the productivity of labor, thereby increasing the demand for these skills. Reduced supply and increased demand both have a positive effect on the market wage. Certified public accountants earn more than file clerks both because the extensive training of CPAs limits the supply to this field and because this training increases the productivity of CPAs compared to file clerks.

Exhibit 3 shows how education and experience affect average earnings based on education and age. Age groups are indicated on the horizontal axis and average annual earnings on the vertical axis. The lines are labeled to reflect the highest level of education achieved and range from no high school degree at the bottom to a doctorate at the top.

The relationship between income and education is clear. At every age, those with more education earn more. For example, among the 45-to-54 age group, those with a doctorate earn on average three times as much as high school graduates and more than four times as much as those with no high school degree. Age itself also has an important effect on income. For most of their careers, earnings increase as workers acquire valuable job experience, get promoted, and assume added responsibility. Average earnings rise more sharply with age for more educated workers. Earnings begin to fall as workers reach retirement age,

EXHIBIT 3

Average Annual Earnings of Americans Based on Age and Highest Degree Earned

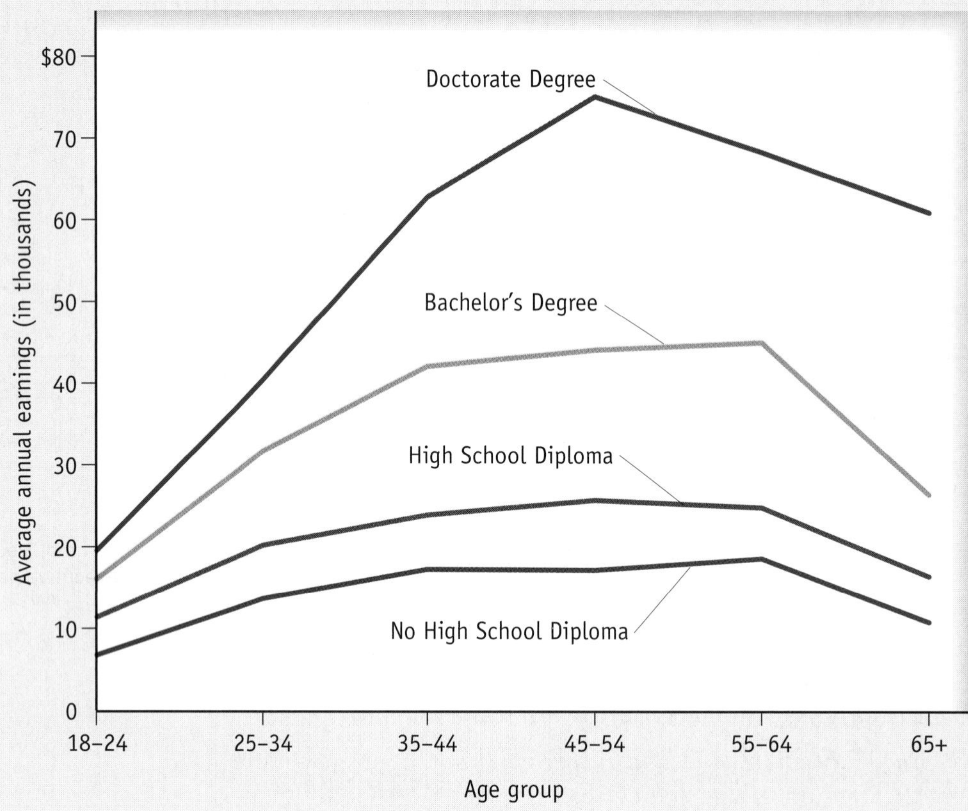

Source: U.S. Bureau of the Census, *Statistical Abstracts of the United States: 1997* (117th edition), Washington, D.C., Table 246. Earnings are for 1996.

although even among those 65 and over, those with a doctorate degree earn twice as much as those with bachelor's degrees, nearly five times as much as those with high school diplomas, and six times as much as those without a high school diploma. Differences in earnings reflect the normal workings of resource markets, whereby workers are rewarded according to their marginal productivity.

Differences in Ability. Because they are more able and talented, some individuals earn more than others with the same training and education. Two lawyers may have an identical education, but one earns more because of differences in underlying ability. Most executives have extensive training and business experience, but only a few become chief executives of large corporations. In major-league sports, some players earn up to 50 times more than others. From lawyers to executives to professional athletes, pay differences often reflect differing abilities. The following case study examines why the premium awarded greater ability has grown in the last two decades.

Winner-Take-All Labor Markets

Each year *Forbes* magazine reports on the multimillion-dollar pay of top entertainers and professional athletes. Entertainment and sports have come to be called "winner-take-all" labor markets because a few key people critical to the overall success of an enterprise are rewarded substantially. For example, the credits at the end of a movie list the dozens of people directly involved in the production. Hundreds, sometimes thousands, more are employed behind the scenes. Despite a cast and crew of thousands, the difference between a movie's financial success and failure depends primarily on the performance of just a few people in crucial roles—the leads, the director, and the screenwriters. Competition for these top few people bids up their pay to extremely high levels, such as the $20 million per movie garnered by top stars. The same happens in sports. Even though thousands of players compete each year in professional tennis, the value of television time, ticket sales, and endorsements is based on the drawing power of just the top players. In professional basketball, attendance and TV ratings were significantly higher for games in which Michael Jordan played. Thus, top performers generate a high marginal revenue product.

But high marginal productivity alone is not enough. To be paid the value of that marginal product, there must be an open competition for the talents of the top people. Before the free-agency rule was introduced in professional sports (which allows players to go to the highest bidder), top players could not move on their own from team to team. They were, in a sense, trapped with their team and, consequently, earned only a fraction of today's pay, despite their huge economic value to a team.

So relatively high pay in entertainment and sports is not that new. What is new is the proliferation of winner-take-all pay structures to other markets in the United States. The "star" treatment has spread to such fields as management, law, banking, finance, even academia. Consider, for example, what has happened to the pay of top U.S. executives in the last two decades. In 1974 the chief executive officers (CEOs) of the 200 largest U.S. corporations earned on average about $310,000, or about 35 times the $8,820 earned by the average U.S. production worker. By 1997, average pay for this top group had increased twelvefold to about $4 million, versus a mere tripling of production-worker pay to $26,600, so CEO pay in 1997 averaged 150 times production worker pay. Comparable multiples were only 21 in Germany and 16 in Japan. Why the big jump in the U.S. multiple?

Robert Frank and Philip Cook argue in their book *The Winner-Take-All Society* that the relatively higher pay for top U.S. performers resulted from three developments. First, breakthroughs in communications, production, and transportation allowed talented performers to serve wider markets, thereby increasing the value of their services. For example, a well-run U.S. company supplying a valued product can now sell that product around the world.

Second, greater market freedom has enhanced competition for the top performers, so these top people earn closer to their marginal productivity. For

CaseStudy

The World of Business

For current news stories about executive compensation, visit *Forbes* magazine's subsection about trends in this area at http://www.forbes.com/forbes/SubSect/Executiv.htm. What is the latest explanation for the pay differential? Who are the highest-paid CEOs? For a union's view on the executive pay differential, read the United Auto Workers' article on unionization and executive compensation at http://www.uaw.org/publications/jobs_pay/1098/jpe_02.html. How does having a unionized work force affect executive pay, according to the UAW?

example, in the 1970s, U.S. businesses usually selected their CEOs from company ranks, promoting mainly from within (a practice still alive today in Germany and Japan). Because other firms were not trying to bid away the most talented executives, companies were able to retain executives for just a fraction of the pay that now prevails in a more competitive market. Today top executives are attracted from outside the firm and even outside the industry. This wider competition for the top people has ratcheted up the average pay. A final reason cited by Frank and Cook is that large salaries have become more socially acceptable in the United States than they once were. High salaries are still frowned upon in some countries.

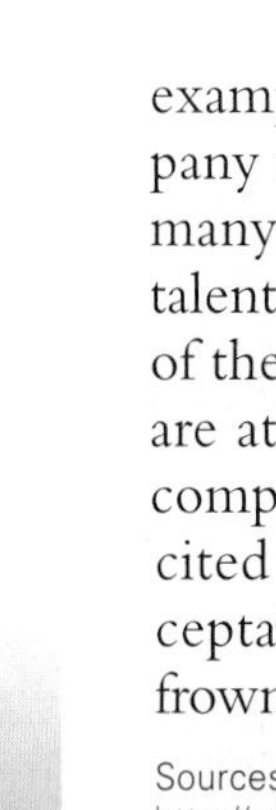

Sources: Robert Frank, "Talent and the Winner-Take-All Society," *American Prospect* 17 (Spring 1994): 97–107 http://epn.org/prosect/17/17fran.html; Robert H. Frank and Philip J. Cook, *The Winner-Take-All Society*, The Free Press, 1995; "Who Gets Paid What," *Forbes* (18 May 1998): 234–266; "The Forbes 500s," *Forbes* (20 April 1998): 246–342; and *Economic Report of the President*, February 1999.

Differences in Risk. Research indicates that jobs with a higher probability of injury or death, such as coal mining, pay more, other things constant. Workers also earn more, other things constant, in fields such as construction, where the risks of unemployment are greater.

Geographic Differences. People have a strong incentive to sell their resources in the market where they earn the most, other things constant. For example, place kickers come to the United States from around the world for the attractive salaries available in the National Football League. Likewise, because physicians earn more in the United States than elsewhere, thousands of foreign-trained physicians migrate here each year. The flow of labor is not all one way: Some Americans seek their fortune abroad. Basketball players not quite talented enough to excel in the NBA head for the high pay in Europe; likewise, baseball players go to Japan. Most workers face migration hurdles if they seek higher pay in another country. Any reduction in these hurdles would reduce wage differentials across countries.

Job Discrimination. Sometimes individuals earn different wages because of racial or gender discrimination in the job market. Although such discrimination is illegal, history shows that certain groups—including blacks, Hispanics, and women—have systematically earned less than others of apparently equal ability.

Union Membership. Other things equal, members of organized labor tend to earn more than nonmembers. The balance of this chapter discusses the effects of unions on the market for labor.

UNIONS AND COLLECTIVE BARGAINING

Few aspects of the labor market make the news more often than the activities of labor unions. Labor negotiations, strikes, picket lines, confrontations between workers and employers—all fit neatly into TV's "action news" format. Despite media attention, only about one out of seven workers belongs to a union and well over 95 percent of union agreements are reached without a strike. For the balance of this chapter, we will study the tools that unions employ to seek higher pay and other benefits for their members.

Kinds of Unions

A **labor union** is a group of workers who join together to improve their terms of employment. Labor unions in the United States date back to the early days of national independence, when employees in various crafts, such as carpenters, shoemakers, and printers, formed local groups to seek higher wages and shorter hours. Such **craft unions** confined their membership to workers with a particular skill, or craft. These craft unions eventually formed their own national organization, the *American Federation of Labor* (*AFL*). The AFL, founded in 1886 under the direction of Samuel Gompers, was not a union itself but rather an organization of national unions, with each retaining its autonomy.

Labor union A group of employees who join together to improve their terms of employment

Craft union A union whose members have a particular skill or work at a particular craft, such as plumbers or carpenters

By the beginning of World War I, the AFL, still under Gompers, was viewed as the voice of labor. The Clayton Act of 1914 exempted labor unions from antitrust laws, meaning that *unions at competing companies could join forces in an attempt to raise wages.* Unions were also tax exempt. Union membership jumped during World War I but dropped after the war as the government retreated from its support of union efforts. Membership dropped by half between 1920 and 1933.

The *Congress of Industrial Organizations* (*CIO*) was established in 1935 to serve as a national organization of unions in mass-production industries, such as autos and steel. Whereas the AFL had organized workers in particular crafts, such as plumbers and carpenters, the CIO was made up of unions whose membership embraced all workers in a particular industry. These **industrial unions** included unskilled, semiskilled, and skilled workers in an industry, such as all autoworkers or all steelworkers.

Industrial union A union of both skilled and unskilled workers from a particular industry, such as autoworkers or steelworkers

Collective Bargaining

Collective bargaining is the process by which representatives from the union and management negotiate a mutually agreeable contract specifying wages, employee benefits, and working conditions. Once a tentative agreement has been reached, union representatives must present it to the membership for a vote. If the agreement is rejected, the union can strike or continue negotiations.

Collective bargaining The process by which union and management negotiate a labor agreement

Mediation and Arbitration. If negotiations over a contract reach an impasse and the public interest is involved, government officials may ask an independent mediator to step in. A **mediator** is an impartial observer who listens to both sides separately then suggests how each side could adjust its position to resolve differences. If a resolution appears possible, the mediator brings the parties together to iron out a contract. The mediator has no power to impose a settlement on the parties.

Mediator An impartial observer who helps resolve differences between union and management

In certain critical sectors, such as police and fire protection, where a strike could seriously harm the public interest, an impasse in negotiations is sometimes settled through **binding arbitration,** whereby a neutral third party evaluates both sides of the dispute and issues a ruling that the parties are committed to accept. Some disputes skip the mediation and arbitration steps and go directly from impasse to strike.

Binding arbitration Negotiation in which both parties in a union-management dispute agree to accept an impartial observer's resolution of the dispute

The Strike

A major source of union power in the bargaining relationship is the threat of a **strike,** which is the union's attempt to withhold labor from the firm. The purpose of a strike is to stop production, thereby forcing the firm to accept the

Strike A union's attempt to withhold labor from a firm

union's position. But strikes can also impose significant costs on union members, who forgo pay and benefits for the duration of the strike and risk losing their jobs. Union funds and other sources, such as unemployment benefits in some states, may provide support during a strike, but the typical striker's income falls substantially. The threat of a strike hangs over labor negotiations and can serve as a real spur to reach an accord. *Although neither party usually wants a strike, both sides, rather than concede on key points, typically act as if they could and would endure a strike.*

The strike's success depends on blocking the supply of labor. Unions usually picket the targeted employer to prevent or discourage so-called strikebreakers, or "scabs," from crossing the picket lines to work. But the firm, by hiring temporary workers and nonstriking union workers, can sometimes continue production.

NetBookmark

Does it make any difference to the quality of your job if your workplace is unionized? The AFL-CIO, an umbrella organization of most of the nations' unions, certainly believes it makes a difference. A Web page making the argument that better pay, benefits, and stability come to union members can be found at http://www.aflcio.org/uniondifference/index.htm. A short history of the labor movement is available at http://www.unionweb.org/.

UNION WAGES AND EMPLOYMENT

Union members, like everyone else, have unlimited wants, but no union can regularly get everything it desires. Because resources are scarce, choices must be made. A menu of union desires includes higher wages, more benefits, greater job security, better working conditions, and so on. To keep the analysis manageable, let's focus on a single objective: higher wages. We will examine three possible ways unions might increase wages: (1) by forming an inclusive, or industrial, union; (2) by forming an exclusive, or craft, union; and (3) by increasing the demand for union labor.

Inclusive, or Industrial, Unions

With the *inclusive, or industrial,* approach, the union tries to negotiate an industry-wide wage for each class of labor. In panel (a) of Exhibit 4, the market demand and supply for a particular type of labor are presented as *D* and *S*. In the absence of a union, the equilibrium wage is *W* and the equilibrium employment level is *E*. At the market wage, each individual employer faces a horizontal, or perfectly elastic, supply of labor, as reflected by *s* in panel (b) of Exhibit 4. Thus, each firm, as a labor price taker, can hire as much labor as it wants at the market wage of *W*. The firm hires labor up to the point where the marginal revenue product equals the marginal resource cost; this amount is represented by quantity *e* in panel (b). As we saw earlier, in equilibrium each worker hired is paid a wage just equal to the marginal revenue product.

Now suppose that the union is able to negotiate a wage above the market-clearing wage. Specifically, suppose the wage negotiated is *W'*, meaning that no labor will be supplied at a lower wage, but any amount desired by the firms, up to the quantity identified at point *a* in panel (a) of Exhibit 4, will be supplied at the wage floor. In effect, the supply of union labor is perfectly elastic at the union wage up to point *a*. If more than *E"* workers are demanded, however, the wage floor no longer applies; the upward-sloping portion, *aS*, becomes the relevant part of the labor supply curve. For an industry facing a wage floor of *W'*, the entire labor supply curve is *W'aS*, which has a kink where the wage floor joins the upward-sloping portion of the original supply curve.

Effect of a Union's Wage Floor

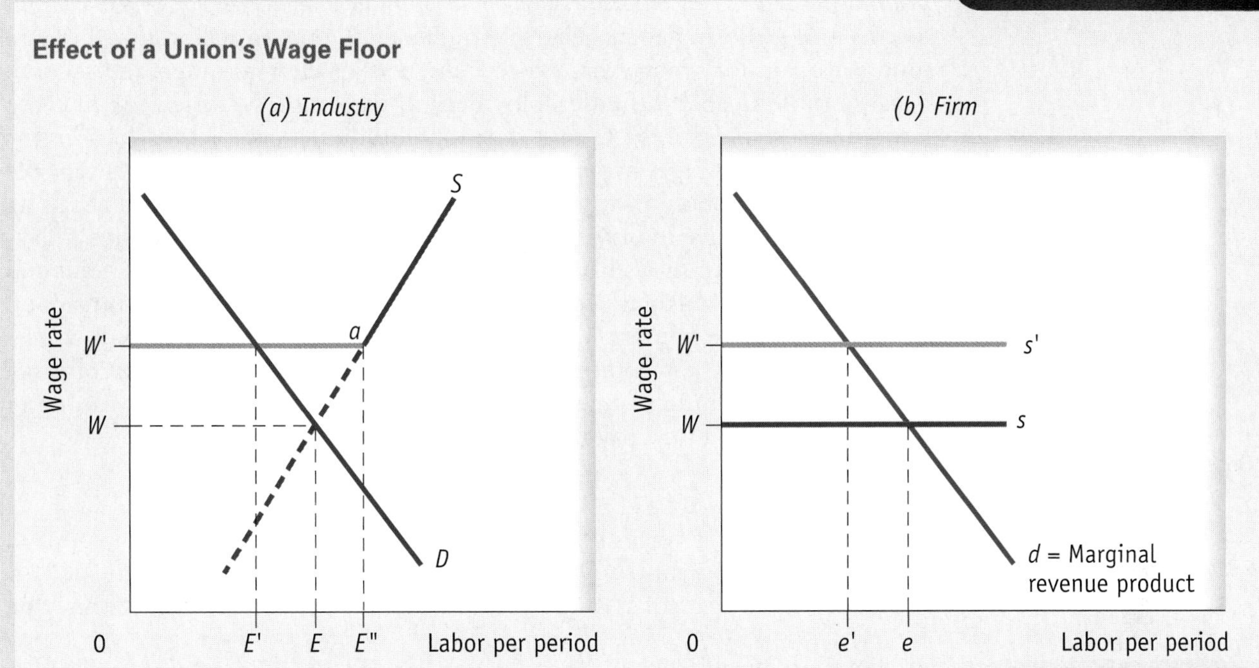

In panel (a), the equilibrium wage rate in the absence of a labor union is *W*. At that wage, the individual firm of panel (b) hires labor up to the point where the marginal revenue product equals *W*. Each firm hires quantity *e;* total employment is *E*. If a union can negotiate a wage *W*' above the equilibrium level, the supply curve facing the firm shifts up to *s*'. The firm hires fewer workers, *e*', and total employment falls to *E*'. At wage *W*' there is an excess supply of labor equal to *E*' – *E*".

Once this wage floor has been established, each firm faces a horizontal supply curve of labor at the collectively bargained wage, *W*'. Since the wage is now higher, the quantity of labor demanded by each employer declines, as reflected by the reduction in employment from *e* to *e*' in panel (b) of Exhibit 4. Consequently, the higher wage leads to a reduction in total employment; the quantity demanded by the industry drops from *E* to *E*' in panel (a). Notice that since the wage is set above the market-clearing wage, the demand curve dictates the quantity of labor employed.

At wage *W*', the amount of labor workers would like to supply, *E*", exceeds the amount demanded, *E*'. In the absence of a union, this excess quantity of labor supplied would cause unemployed workers to lower their asking wage. But union members agree *collectively* to a wage, so individual workers cannot offer to work for less, nor can employers hire them at a lower wage. Because the number of union members willing and able to work exceeds the number of jobs available, the union must develop some mechanism for rationing available jobs, such as awarding jobs based on worker seniority or connections within the union. *With the inclusive, or industrial, union, which negotiates with the entire industry, the wage rate is higher and total employment lower than they would be in the absence of a union.*

Those who cannot find union employment will look for jobs in the nonunion sector. *This increased supply of labor in the nonunion sector drives down the nonunion wage.* So wages are relatively higher in the union sector: first, because unions bargain for a wage that exceeds the market-clearing wage, and second, because those unable to find employment in the union sector crowd into the nonunion sector. A survey of more than 200 studies concluded that unions increased members' wages by an average of about 15 percent above the wages of similarly skilled nonunion workers.[1] Unions tend to be less successful at raising wages in competitive industries and more successful in less-competitive industries. For example, unions have little impact on the wages in the garment and textile industries, which are competitive industries, but have greater impact on the wages in airline, auto, steel, mining, and transportation industries, which historically have been less-competitive industries. Competitive firms cannot easily pass along higher union wages as higher product prices. New firms can enter the competitive industry, pay nonunion wages, and sell the product for less.

Exclusive, or Craft, Unions

One way to increase wages while avoiding an excess quantity of labor supplied is for the union to somehow shift the supply curve of labor to the left, as is shown in panel (a) of Exhibit 5. Successful supply restrictions of this type

EXHIBIT 5

Effect of Reducing Supply or Increasing Labor Demand

(a) Reducing labor supply

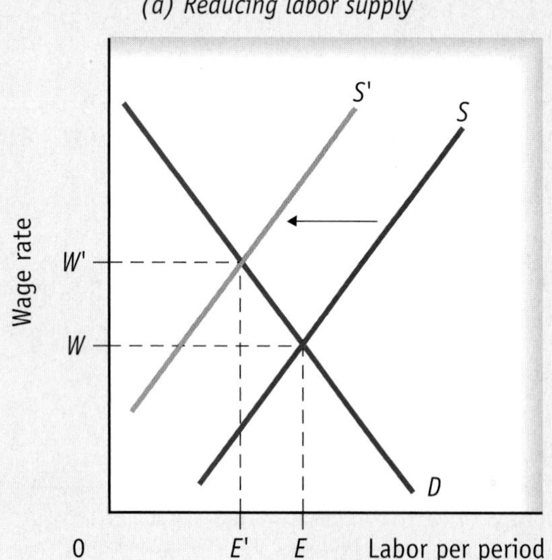

(b) Increasing labor demand

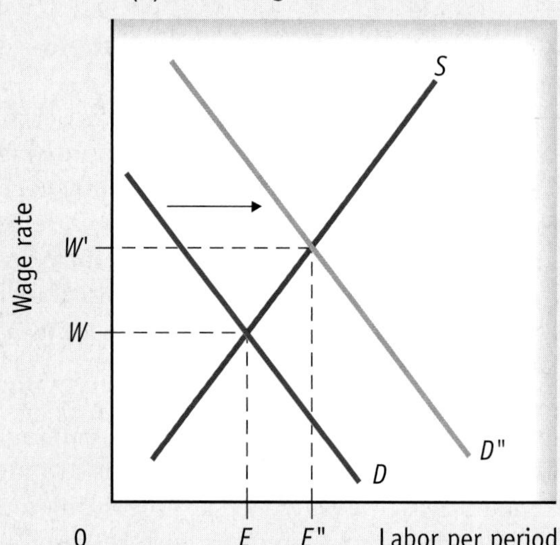

If a union can restrict labor supply to an industry, the supply curve shifts to the left from *S* to *S'*, as in panel (a). The wage rate rises from *W* to *W'*, but at the cost of a reduction in employment from *E* to *E'*. In panel (b), an increase in labor demand from *D* to *D"* raises both the wage and the level of employment.

1 See H. Gregg Lewis, *Union Relative Wage Effects: A Survey* (Chicago: University of Chicago Press, 1986).

require that the union first limit its membership and second force all employers in the industry to hire only union members. The union can restrict membership with high initiation fees, long apprenticeship periods, difficult qualification exams, restrictive licensing requirements, and other devices aimed at slowing down or discouraging new membership. But even if unions can restrict membership, unions have difficulty requiring all firms in the industry to hire only union workers.

Whereas wage setting is more typical of the industrial unions, restricting supply (and employment) is more characteristic of the craft unions, such as unions of carpenters, plumbers, and bricklayers. Groups of professionals such as doctors, lawyers, and accountants also impose entry restrictions through education and examination standards. Such restrictions, usually defended on the grounds that they protect the public, are often no more than self-serving attempts to increase wages by restricting supply.

Increasing Demand for Union Labor

A third way to increase the wage is to increase the demand for union labor by somehow shifting the labor demand curve outward as from D to D'' in panel (b) of Exhibit 5. This approach is an attractive alternative *because it increases both the wage rate and employment,* so there is no need to ration jobs. Here are some ways unions try to increase the demand for union labor.

Increase Demand for Union-Made Goods. The demand for union labor may be increased through a direct appeal to consumers to buy only union-made products. Because the demand for labor is a derived demand, an increase in the demand for union-made products will increase the demand for union labor.

Restrict Supply of Nonunion-Made Goods. Another way to increase the demand for union labor is to restrict the supply of products that compete with union-made products. Again, this approach relies on the derived nature of labor demand. The United Auto Workers (UAW) have, for example, supported restrictions on imported cars. Fewer imported cars means a greater demand for cars produced by U.S. workers, who are mostly union members. Now that Japanese and German automakers also build cars in the United States, the UAW has a trickier problem trying to limit imports.

Increase Productivity of Union Labor. Some observers claim that the efficiency with which unions organize and monitor the labor-management relationship increases the demand for union labor. According to this theory, unions increase worker productivity by minimizing conflicts, resolving differences, and at times even straightening out workers who are goofing off. In the absence of a union, a dissatisfied worker may simply look for another job, thereby causing job turnover, which is costly to the firm. With a union, however, workers usually have grievance and arbitration channels through which they can complain, and the negotiated responses they receive may reduce their urge to leave the firm. Quit rates are in fact significantly lower among union workers (although this could be due to the higher pay). If unions increase the productivity of workers in this way, the demand for union labor will increase.

Featherbedding Union efforts to force employers to hire more workers than demanded for the task

Featherbedding. Still another way unions attempt to increase the demand for union labor is by **featherbedding,** which is an attempt to ensure that more union labor is hired than producers would prefer. For example, union rules require that each Broadway theater have a permanent "house" carpenter, electrician, and property manager. Once the show run begins, these workers appear only on payday. The box office must be staffed by three people. And the musicians' union requires that from 9 to 22 musicians be employed at each theater staging a musical, even if the show calls for fewer musicians.

Featherbedding does not create a true increase in demand, in the sense of shifting the demand curve to the right; instead, it forces firms to hire more labor than they really want, thus moving the firm to a point to the right of its true labor demand curve. The union tries to limit a firm to an all-or-none choice: either hire the number the union requires, or a strike will halt production. Thus, with featherbedding, *the union attempts to dictate not only the wage but also the quantity that must be hired at that wage, thereby moving employers to the right of their labor demand curve.*

We have examined three ways in which unions can try to raise members' wages: (1) by negotiating a wage floor above the equilibrium wage for the industry and somehow rationing the limited jobs among union members, (2) by restricting the supply of labor, and (3) by increasing the demand for union labor. Unions try to increase the demand for union labor in several ways: (1) through a direct public appeal to buy only union-made products, (2) by restricting the supply of products made by nonunion labor, (3) by reducing labor turnover and thereby increasing productivity, and (4) through featherbedding, which forces employers to hire more union workers than they would prefer.

Recent Trends in Union Membership

In 1955, about one-third of nonfarm wage and salary workers belonged to unions. Union membership as a fraction of the work force has declined since then; now only one in seven workers belongs to a union. The decline in union membership in recent decades is due partly to an increase in product market competition, particularly from imports. Increased competition from nonunion employers, both foreign and domestic, has also reduced the ability of unionized firms to pass on higher labor costs as higher prices.

Another factor in the decline of the union movement is structural changes in the economy. Unions have long been more important in the industrial sector than in the service and agricultural sectors. But employment in the industrial sector, including manufacturing, mining, and construction, has declined from 37 percent of the nonfarm work force in 1960 to 20 percent today. Over the same period, service-sector employment increased from 63 percent to 80 percent. These days, membership rates are highest among government employees, over one-third of whom are unionized, compared to only one-eighth of the private sector. Union workers are now more likely brain-workers than brawn-workers. A typical union member now is a schoolteacher.

The bar graph in Exhibit 6 indicates recent U.S. union membership rates by age and gender. The rates for men, shown by the dark shaded bars, are higher than the rates for women, in part because men tend to be employed more in manufacturing and women more in the service sector, where union membership historically has been lower. The highest membership rates are for middle-

EXHIBIT 6

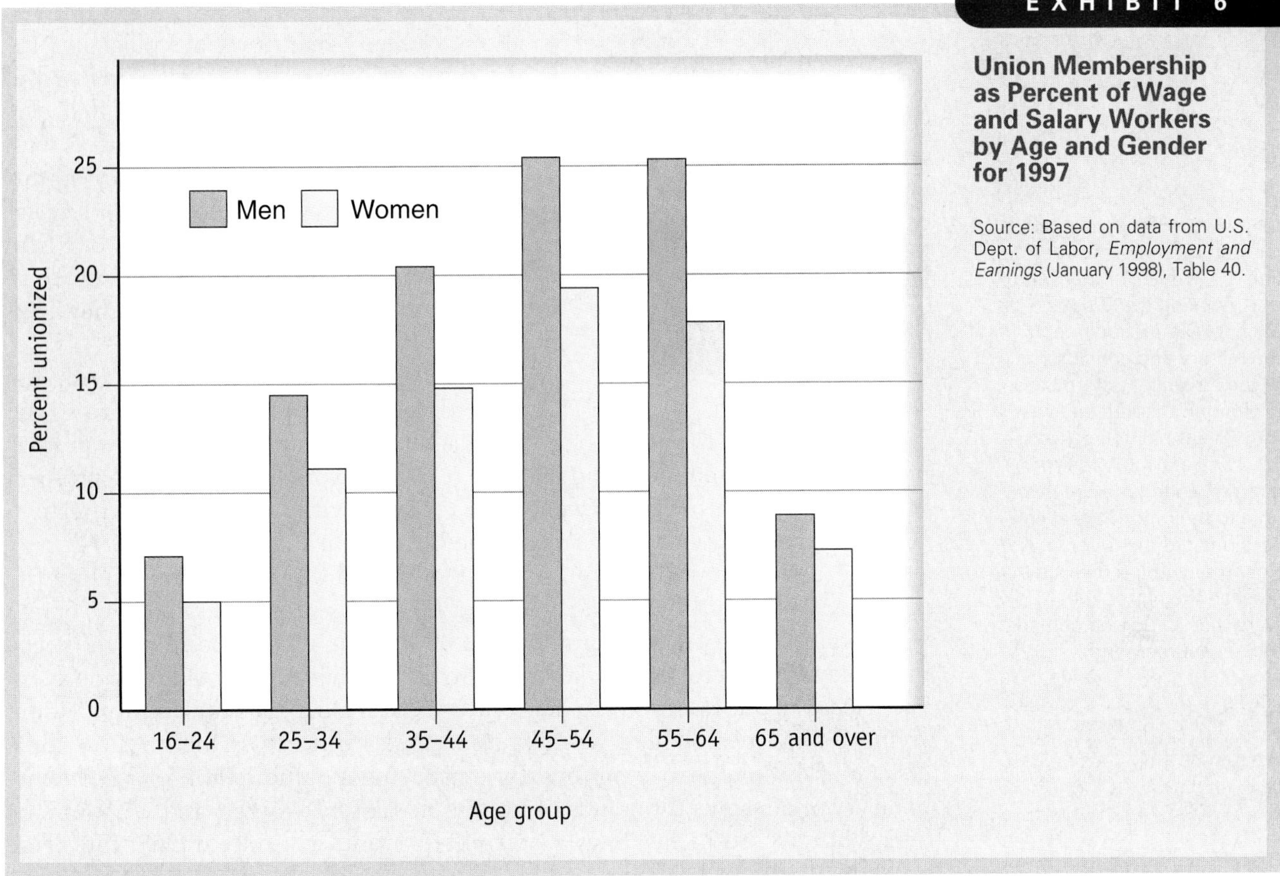

Union Membership as Percent of Wage and Salary Workers by Age and Gender for 1997

Source: Based on data from U.S. Dept. of Labor, *Employment and Earnings* (January 1998), Table 40.

aged males. Although the exhibit does not show it, blacks have a higher union membership rate than whites (20 percent versus 15 percent), in part because blacks are more often employed by government and by heavy industries such as autos and steel, where union membership rates tend to be higher. In fact, black women have a higher union membership rate (18 percent) than white men (17 percent). Union membership among those of Hispanic origin, who can be of any race, is only 14 percent.

Union membership rates also vary greatly across states. Rates in 1998 were 20 percent or more in the industrial states of the North and 8 percent or less in the South. The highest rate was 29 percent in New York; the lowest was 4 percent in South Carolina. Compared with those of other industrialized countries, the union participation rate in the United States ranks relatively low.

During the 1970s, there were nearly 300 strikes a year in the United States involving 1,000 or more workers. But there were only 29 such strikes in 1997, or only about 10 percent of strike levels of two decades ago. Let's close this section with the following case study, which helps explain why unions have grown more reluctant to strike.

CaseStudy

The World of Business

In the Fall 1998 issue of the US Department of Labor's online magazine *Compensation and Working Conditions,* Michael Cimini documents the history and conclusion of the strike in "Caterpillar's Prolonged Dispute Ends" at http://www.bls.gov/opub/cwc/1998/Fall/art1full.pdf. What contract changes were favorable to the union? What concessions did the union make? How many union members crossed the picket lines? How were they to be treated under the new agreement?

Hardball at Caterpillar

Labor troubles began for Caterpillar in November 1991, when the company refused to accept the job-security provisions that the United Auto Workers (UAW) negotiated with Deere & Co., a rival firm in the heavy equipment industry. In a system called *pattern bargaining,* a union reaching a settlement with one firm in an industry could expect that contract to serve as a model for agreements with other firms in the industry.

Caterpillar's refusal to go along with the Deere settlement prompted the UAW to strike. Five months after the strike began, management threatened to replace permanently any union member who failed to return to work. Faced with the prospect of lost jobs, union members went back to work without a contract. After two years of wrangling with the company, the UAW struck again in June 1994.

The UAW showed its commitment to the 13,000 strikers by tripling the usual level of monthly strike pay to $1,200. This sweetened strike pay, which would ultimately cost the union over $200 million, was aimed in part at keeping strikers from crossing picket lines. Strikers believed their skills made them irreplaceable, but as the strike dragged on, Caterpillar introduced more labor-saving techniques. Skilled workers also came from across the country for a chance at these high-paying jobs. By employing a combination of 5,600 temporary workers, plus thousands of nonunion salaried workers and UAW members who crossed picket lines, Caterpillar's production rate during the strike exceeded prestrike levels.

In December 1995, some 17 months after the walkout began and with no evidence that the company was about to give in, union officials decided that the 8,700 members still on strike were "available immediately and unconditionally for return to work." This unconditional surrender by the union was a crushing defeat for a union movement badly in need of a victory. Each striking worker had lost on average about $37,000 in wages during the strike. Union members worked without a contract until March 1998, when they ratified a contract that provided pay increases but allowed the company to introduce greater flexibility in scheduling and to pay new workers 30 percent less.

During the long labor dispute, Caterpillar restructured its manufacturing process to utilize all resources more efficiently, particularly labor. Profits increased to record levels, boosting Caterpillar's share price fourfold. The company's performance apparently refuted the conventional wisdom that both sides suffer during a long strike.

Sources: Robert Rose and Carl Quintanilla, "Caterpillar Touts Its Gains as UAW Battle Ends," *Wall Street Journal* (24 March 1998); "UAW Members Back Contract with Caterpillar, First Since '91," *New York Times* (23 March 1998); and Carl Quintanilla, "Caterpillar Posts Record Earnings," *Wall Street Journal* (20 April 1998).

The experience at Caterpillar underscores two reasons why unions have grown more reluctant to strike: (1) the increased willingness of employers to hire strikebreakers and (2) the increased willingness of workers—both union and nonunion—to cross picket lines. With fewer voters belonging to labor unions, the political climate is also less supportive of unions. Similar strike scenarios have played out at Phelps–Dodge Copper, Continental Airlines, and Hormel Meatpacking—all companies that successfully broke strikes by hiring replacement workers. Thus the strike and the threat of a strike has become less important, and this has diminished the power of unions.

CONCLUSION

The first half of this chapter focused on the supply of labor and explained why wages differ both across occupations and among individuals within occupations. The interaction of the demand and supply for labor determines wage rates and the level of employment. The second half of the chapter explored the effect of unions on the labor market. At one time unions dominated some key industries. But as global competition intensifies, employers have a harder time passing higher union labor costs along to consumers. What's more, the decline of production workers relative to service workers and the growing reluctance to strike have eroded union strength. Both in the United States and in other industrial economies, union members represent a dwindling segment of the labor force.

SUMMARY

1. The demand for labor is the relationship between the wage rate and the quantity of labor producers are willing and able to hire, other things constant. The supply of labor is the relationship between the wage rate and the quantity of labor workers are willing and able to supply, other things constant. The intersection of demand and supply curves determines the equilibrium wage rate.

2. There are three uses of time: market work, nonmarket work, and leisure. People allocate their time so as to maximize utility. The higher the market wage, other things constant, the more goods and services can be purchased with that wage, so a higher wage encourages labor suppliers to substitute market work for other uses of time. But the higher the wage, the higher the income, and as income increases, people consume more of all normal goods, including leisure. The net effect of a higher wage on an individual's quantity of market labor supplied depends on both the substitution effect and the income effect.

3. The supply of labor depends on factors other than the wage, including (1) other sources of income, (2) job amenities, (3) the value of job experience, and (4) worker tastes.

4. Market wages differ because of (1) differences in training and education requirements, (2) differences in the skill and ability of workers, (3) differences in the riskiness of the work, both in terms of the workers' safety and the chances of getting laid off, (4) geographic differences, (5) racial and gender discrimination, and (6) union membership.

5. Unions and employers attempt to negotiate a mutually agreeable labor contract through collective bargaining. A major source of union power has been the threat of a strike, which is an attempt to withhold labor from the firm.

6. Inclusive, or industrial, unions attempt to establish a wage floor that exceeds the competitive market wage. But a wage above the market-clearing level creates an excess quantity of labor supplied, so the union must somehow ration jobs among its members. Exclusive, or craft, unions try to raise the wage by restricting the supply of labor. Another way to raise union wages is to increase the demand for union labor.

7. Union membership as a percentage of the labor force has been decreasing for decades. Today, only one-seventh of the nonfarm labor force is unionized, compared to

one-third in 1955. Unions' problems have included a shift in employment from goods production to service production, more intense global competition, a greater willingness of firms to hire replacements for striking workers, a greater willingness of union members and others to cross picket lines, and less political support for the labor movement.

QUESTIONS FOR REVIEW

1. *(Uses of Time)* Describe the three possible uses of an individual's time, and give an example of each.
2. *(Work and Utility)* Explain the concept of the "net utility of work." How is it useful in developing the labor supply curve?
3. *(Utility Maximization)* How does a rational consumer allocate time among competing uses?
4. *(Substitution and Income Effects)* Suppose that the substitution effect of an increase in the wage rate exactly offsets the income effect as the hourly wage increases from $12 to $13. What would the supply of labor curve look like over this range of wages? Why?
5. *(Substitution and Income Effects)* Suppose that the cost of living increases, thereby reducing the purchasing power of your income. If your money wage doesn't increase, you may work *more* hours because of this cost-of-living increase. Is this an income or substitution effect response? Explain.
6. *(Nonwage Determinants of Labor Supply)* Suppose that two jobs are exactly the same except that one is performed in an air-conditioned workplace. How could you measure the value workers attach to such a job amenity?
7. *(Why Wages Differ)* Why might permanent wage differences occur between different markets for labor or within the same labor market?
8. *(Mediation and Arbitration)* Distinguish between mediation and binding arbitration. Under what circumstances do firms and unions use these tools? What is the role of strikes in the bargaining process?
9. *(The Strike)* Why might firms in industries with high fixed costs be inclined to prevent strikes or end strikes quickly?
10. *(Industrial Unions)* Why are unions more effective in oligopolistic industries than in competitive industries?
11. *(Craft Unions)* Both industrial unions and craft unions attempt to raise their members' wages, but each goes about it differently. Explain the difference in approaches and describe the impact these differences have on excess quantity of labor supplied.
12. *(**CaseStudy:** Hardball at Caterpillar)* What is *pattern bargaining?* What were the consequences of the decision by Caterpillar to "break the pattern"?

PROBLEMS AND EXERCISES

13. *(Market Supply of Labor)* The following table shows the number of hours per week supplied to a particular market by three individuals at various wage rates. Calculate the total hours per week (Q_T) supplied to the market.

Hourly Wage	Hours per Week Q_1	Q_2	Q_3	Q_T
$ 5	20	0	0	___
$ 6	25	0	0	___
$ 7	35	10	0	___
$ 8	45	25	10	___
$ 9	42	40	30	___
$10	38	37	45	___

Which individuals, if any, have backward-bending supply curves in the wage range shown? Does the market supply curve bend backward in this wage range?

14. *(Inclusive Unions)* Review the logic underlying Exhibit 4. Then determine the effect, on the industry and a typical firm, of an increase in the demand for industry output. Show your conclusions on a graph. Does the magnitude of the increase in demand make a difference?

EXPERIENTIAL EXERCISES

15. *(Wages and Labor Supply)* Interview five of your classmates to determine the nature of their labor supply curves for a summer job. Ask each of them how many hours of work he or she would be willing to supply at wage rates of $10, $15, $20, $25, and $30 per hour. Plot the results on a labor supply diagram. Do any of these individuals exhibit a backward-bending labor supply curve? Is the market supply curve for these five individuals backward bending?

16. ***(CaseStudy:** Winner-Take-All Labor Markets)* Robert Frank's "Talent and the Winner-Take-All-Society" appeared in *The American Prospect* (Spring, 1994) at http://epn.org/prospect/17/17fran.html. Read this nontechnical article. What are some of the problems that Frank identifies?

17. *(Unions and Collective Bargaining)* Visit the AFL-CIO home page at http://www.aflcio.org/publ/estatements/index.htm and look at some recent Executive Council actions. Choose one such action and depict its intended effects, using the models developed in this chapter.

18. *(Wall Street Journal)* It shouldn't be too hard to find a *Wall Street Journal* story dealing with labor unions. Check the Economy page in the First Section, the Work Week report on the front page of the Tuesday *Journal*, or the Legal Beat column inside the Marketplace section. What's going on in the world of organized labor? Is the example you found consistent with the trends described in this chapter?

CHAPTER

26 Capital, Interest, and Corporate Finance

Why do first-run movie theaters charge more for admission than other theaters? Why do you burn your mouth eating pizza? What determines the interest rate a bank charges you? Why would that bank charge IBM less? These and other questions are answered in this chapter, which concerns investment.

So far, our discussion of resource markets has focused primarily on labor. This emphasis is appropriate because labor claims most resource income. The rewards to labor, however, depend in part on the amount and quality of the other resources employed, particularly capital. A farmer plowing a field with a tractor is more productive than one scraping the soil with a stick. A CPA using spreadsheet software is more productive balancing the company books than a high-school–trained bookkeeper using pencil and

Visit the McEachern Interactive Study Center for this chapter at http://mcisc.swcollege.com

paper. In this chapter, you will examine the role of capital in production—its cost and its expected return. You will learn about optimal employment of capital and how firms finance that investment.

First a note of caution. Earlier we distinguished between opportunity cost (the payment necessary to attract a resource to a particular use) and economic rent (a payment in excess of opportunity cost). Often economists refer to the return on land as rent, because land is typically thought to be in fixed supply; and the return on a resource in fixed supply consists entirely of economic rent. Describing the earnings on land as rent is quite appropriate, but land as a resource will not receive special treatment in this book. Topics discussed in this chapter include:

- Consumption, saving, and time
- Production, saving, and time
- Optimal investment
- Loanable funds market
- Present value and discounting
- Corporate finance
- Corporate ownership and control

THE ROLE OF TIME IN CONSUMPTION AND PRODUCTION

Time plays an important role in both production and consumption. In this section, we first consider the effect of time on the production decision and show why firms are willing to pay for the use of household savings. Next we consider time in the consumption decision and show why households must be rewarded for saving, or for deferring consumption. Then, bringing together the desires of borrowers and the desires of savers, we examine the market rate of interest.

Production, Saving, and Time

Suppose Jones is a primitive farmer in a simple economy. Isolated from any neighbors or markets, he literally scratches out a living on a plot of land, using only crude sticks as farm implements. While a crop is growing, none of it is available for current consumption. Since production takes time, Jones must rely on food saved from prior production to support himself while the new crop grows. The longer the growing season, the more saving is required. Thus even in this simple example, it is clear that *production cannot occur without saving.*

Suppose that with his current resources, consisting of land, labor, seed corn, fertilizer, and some crude sticks, Jones grows about 500 bushels of corn per year. He soon realizes that if he had a plow—a type of investment good, or capital—his productivity would increase. Making a plow in such a crude setting, however, would be time-consuming, keeping him away from the fields for a year. Thus the plow has an opportunity cost of 500 bushels of corn. Jones will be unable to sustain such a temporary drop in production unless he has saved enough food from previous harvests.

The question is, should he invest his time in making the plow? The answer depends on the costs and benefits of the plow. We already know that the cost is 500 bushels—the forgone output. The benefit depends on how much the plow will increase crop production and how long it will last. Jones figures that the plow will increase production by 200 bushels per year and will last his lifetime. In making the investment decision, he compares current costs to future benefits.

Suppose he decides the benefit of increasing corn production by 200 bushels per year exceeds the one-time cost of 500 bushels sacrificed to make the plow.

In making the plow, he engages in *roundabout production*. Rather than working the soil with his crude sticks, the farmer produces capital, which will increase his future productivity. An increased amount of roundabout production in an economy means that more capital accumulates, so more consumer goods (and more capital goods) can be produced in the future. Advanced industrial economies are characterized by much roundabout production and abundant capital accumulation.

You can see why production cannot occur without saving. *Production requires saving because both direct and roundabout production require time—time during which goods and services are not available from current production.* Now let's modernize the example by introducing the ability to borrow. Many farmers visit the bank each spring to borrow enough "seed money" to finance production until their crop is grown and sold. Likewise, other businesses often borrow at least a portion of the start-up funds they need to get going. Thus, in a modern economy, producers do not rely exclusively on their own prior saving. Banks and other financial institutions serve as *intermediaries* between savers and borrowers. As you will see later, financial markets for trading stocks and bonds also help channel savings to producers. Let's take a look at saving incentives.

Consumption, Saving, and Time

Did you ever burn the roof of your mouth by biting into a slice of pizza that hadn't cooled sufficiently? Have you done this more than once? Why do you persist in such self-mutilation? You persist because that bite of pizza is worth more to you now than the same bite five minutes from now. In fact, you are willing to risk burning your mouth rather than wait until the pizza has lost its destructive properties. In a small way, this phenomenon reflects the fact that you and other consumers value *present* consumption more than *future* consumption. You and other consumers have a **positive rate of time preference.**

Positive rate of time preference A characteristic of consumers, who value present consumption more highly than future consumption

Because present consumption is more valuable than future consumption, you are willing to pay more to consume something now rather than later. And prices often reflect this greater willingness to pay. Consider the movies. You pay more to see a movie at a first-run theater rather than wait until it appears at other theaters. If you are patient, you can wait until it comes out on video or appears on TV. The same is true for books. By waiting for a new book to come out in paperback, you can save more than half the hardback price. Photo developers, dry cleaners, fast-food restaurants, convenience stores, and other producers tout the speed of their services, knowing that consumers are willing to pay more for earlier availability, other things constant.

Thus *impatience* is one explanation for a positive rate of time preference. Another explanation is *uncertainty*. If you wait, something may intervene to prevent your consumption of the good. There is a T-shirt slogan that perhaps captures this point best: "Life is uncertain. Eat dessert first."

Because present consumption is valued more than future consumption, households must be rewarded to postpone consumption. In other words, saving must be rewarded. Saving equals income minus consumption. By saving a portion of their income in financial institutions such as banks, households refrain from spending on present consumption in return for the promise of a greater ability to consume in the future. Interest is the reward offered households for forgoing present consumption. The **interest rate** is the interest per year as a percentage of the amount saved. For example, if the interest rate is 5 percent, the interest is $5 per year for each $100 saved. The higher the interest rate, other things constant, the more consumers are rewarded for saving, so the greater the amount they are willing to save. You will read more on this later in the chapter.

Interest rate The amount of money paid per year to savers as a percentage of the amount saved

Optimal Investment

In a market economy characterized by specialization and exchange, Farmer Jones no longer needs to produce his own capital, nor does he need to rely on his own savings. He can purchase capital using borrowed funds.

Suppose he is interested in buying farm equipment and he estimates its expected productivity. Column (1) in panel (a) of Exhibit 1 identifies six pieces of farm equipment, ranked from most productive, a Tractor-Tiller, to least productive, a Post-Hole Digger. The total product of each piece of farm equipment is listed in column (2) and its marginal product is listed in column (3). Note that other resources are assumed to be constant (in this case, the farmer's labor, land, seeds, and fertilizer).

With no equipment, Jones can grow 1,000 bushels of corn per year. Jones figures that the purchase of a Tractor-Tiller would allow him to increase production to 2,000 bushels per year. Thus the Tractor-Tiller would yield a marginal product of 1,000 bushels per year. The addition of a Combine would increase total output to 2,800 bushels a year, thus yielding a marginal product of 800 bushels. Note that in this example, diminishing marginal returns set in immediately. Marginal product continues to decrease as more capital is added, dropping to zero for a Post-Hole Digger.

Suppose Jones sells corn in a perfectly competitive market, so he is a price taker in the market for corn. He can sell all he wants at the market price of $4 per bushel. This price is multiplied by the marginal product from column (3) to yield capital's *marginal revenue product* in column (4). The marginal revenue product in this example is the marginal product times the price, or the change in total revenue resulting from adding another piece of farm equipment

Suppose each piece of farm equipment costs $10,000. Thus, the marginal resource cost is $10,000, as listed in column (5). Suppose also that the equipment is so durable that it lasts indefinitely, that operating expenses are negligible, and that the price of corn is expected to remain at $4 per bushel in the future. This farm equipment will increase revenue not only in the first year but in every year into the future. Since the equipment costs a sum of money now but yields a stream of revenue this year and in the future, the optimal investment solution requires Jones to take *time* into account. He can't simply equate marginal resource cost with marginal revenue product, because the marginal cost is for capital expected to last indefinitely, whereas the marginal product is an annual amount this year and each year in the future. As we will see, *markets bridge time by use of the interest rate.*

Jones must decide how much to invest in farm equipment. The first task in determining the optimal investment is to compute the *marginal rate of return* that could be earned each year by investing in equipment. Given the scenario described thus far, the **marginal rate of return on investment** is capital's marginal revenue product as a percentage of its marginal resource cost.

Marginal rate of return on investment The marginal revenue product of capital expressed as a percentage of its marginal cost

EXHIBIT 1

Marginal Rate of Return on Investment in Farm Equipment

The marginal rate of return shown in column (6) of panel (a) equals the marginal revenue product of each additional piece of farm equipment divided by its marginal resource cost. The marginal rate of return curve in panel (b) consists of line segments showing the relationship between the market rate of interest and the amount invested in farm equipment. This curve is the demand for investment.

(a)

Farm Equipment (1)	Total Product (bushels) (2)	Marginal Product (bushels) (3)	Marginal Revenue Product (4) = (3) × $4	Marginal Resource Cost (5)	Marginal Rate of Return (6) = (4)/(5)
No equipment	1,000	—	—	—	—
Tractor-Tiller	2,000	1,000	$4,000	$10,000	40%
Combine	2,800	800	3,200	10,000	32
Irrigator	3,400	600	2,400	10,000	24
Harrow	3,800	400	1,600	10,000	16
Crop Sprayer	4,000	200	800	10,000	8
Post-Hole Digger	4,000	0	0	10,000	0

(b)

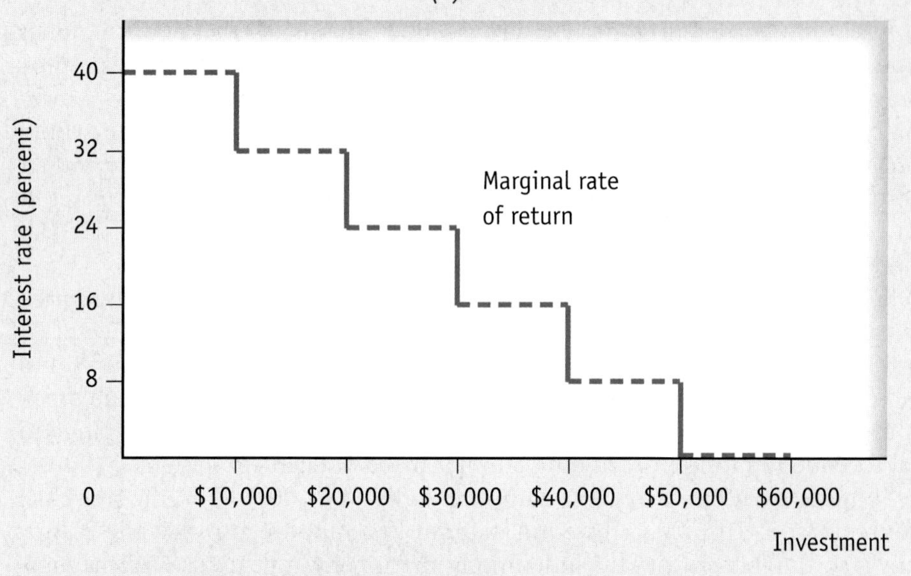

The Tractor-Tiller yields a marginal revenue product of $4,000 per year and has a marginal resource cost of $10,000. As long as Jones has that $10,000 invested in the Tractor-Tiller, the rate of return earned on that investment is $4,000/$10,000, or 40 percent per year. Thus this investment yields a *marginal rate of return* of 40 percent per year, as shown in column (6). The Combine yields a marginal revenue product of $3,200 per year and has a marginal cost of $10,000, so its marginal rate of return equals $3,200/$10,000, or 32 percent per year. Dividing the marginal revenue product of capital in column (4) by the marginal resource cost of that capital in column (5) yields the marginal rate of return in column (6) for each piece of equipment.

Given the marginal rate of return, how much should Jones invest in order to maximize profit? Suppose he borrows the money, paying the *market rate of interest*. Jones will invest in more equipment as long as its marginal rate of return exceeds the market rate of interest. He will not buy an additional piece of equipment if its marginal rate of return falls below the market rate of interest.

For example, if the market interest rate is 20 percent, Jones will invest $30,000 buying three pieces of equipment. The marginal rate of return on the last item purchased, an Irrigator, is 24 percent. Investing another $10,000 to buy a Harrow would yield a marginal return of only 16 percent, a rate below his cost of borrowing. If the market interest rate were 10 percent, Jones would invest in the Harrow as well. If the interest rate were 6 percent, Jones would buy the Crop Sprayer.

Farmer Jones should increase his investment as long as the marginal rate of return on that investment exceeds the market rate of interest. The marginal rate of return reflects the marginal benefit of the investment and the market rate of interest reflects the marginal cost of that investment, so Jones is simply maximizing profit (or minimizing the loss) by investing up to the point where the marginal benefit equals the marginal cost. The data in column (6) are depicted in panel (b) of Exhibit 1 as a step-like curve, where the solid lines reflect the amount that should be invested based on the market interest rate. The curve steps down to reflect the diminishing marginal productivity of additional farm equipment. For example, if the market interest rate is between 32 percent and 40 percent, a Tractor-Tiller should be purchased. If the interest rate is between 24 percent and 32 percent, a Combine should be added. Since the marginal rate of return curve shows how much should be invested at each interest rate, this step-like curve represents the farmer's *demand for investment*. This demand is a derived demand, based on each additional piece of equipment's marginal productivity.

Would the example change if Jones already had the money saved and did not need to borrow? Not as long as he can save at the market rate of interest. For example, suppose Jones has $50,000 in savings that is earning a market rate of interest of 10 percent. In that case, Jones should invest $40,000 in capital, with the Harrow, which earns a marginal rate of return of 16 percent, the last piece purchased. The 10 percent Jones earns on his remaining $10,000 in savings exceeds the 8 percent he could have earned if he had invested that money in the Crop Sprayer. Thus as long as he can borrow and save at the same interest rate, Jones ends up with the same equipment whether he borrows funds or draws on his own savings. *Whether Jones borrows the money or uses savings on hand, the market rate of interest represents his opportunity cost of funds.*

Let's review the procedure used to determine the optimal amount of investment. First, compute the marginal revenue product of capital. Next, divide the marginal revenue product by the marginal resource cost to determine the marginal rate of return. A firm should invest more in capital as long as the marginal rate of return on capital exceeds the market interest rate. The market interest rate reflects the opportunity cost of investing either borrowed funds or savings. Finally, the marginal rate of return curve is a firm's demand curve for capital—that is, it shows the amount a firm is willing and able to invest at each alternative interest rate.

The Market for Loanable Funds

We have now examined why producers are willing to pay interest to borrow money: *money provides a command over resources that makes roundabout production possible.* The simple principles developed for Farmer Jones can be generalized to other producers. The major demanders of loans are firms that borrow to invest in capital goods, such as computers, machines, trucks, and buildings. At any time, each firm has a variety of possible investment opportunities. Each firm ranks its opportunities from highest to lowest, based on the expected marginal rates of return on the investments. Firms will increase their investment until their expected marginal rate of return just equals the market rate of interest. With other inputs held constant, as they were on the farm, the demand curve for investment slopes downward.

But firms are not the only demanders of loans. As we have seen, households value present consumption more than future consumption; they are often willing to pay extra to consume now rather than later. One way to ensure that goods and services are available now is to borrow money for present consumption. Mortgages, car loans, college loans, and credit-card purchases are examples of household borrowing. The household's demand curve for loans, like the firm's, slopes downward, reflecting consumers' greater ability and greater willingness to borrow at lower interest rates, other things constant. The government sector and the rest of the world are also demanders of loans.

Banks are willing to pay interest on consumer savings because the banks can, in turn, lend these savings to those who need credit, such as farmers, home buyers, and entrepreneurs looking to start a new business. Banks play the role of *financial intermediaries* in what is known as the market for loanable funds. The **loanable funds market** brings together savers, or suppliers of loanable funds, and borrowers, or demanders of loanable funds, to determine the market rate of interest. The **supply of loanable funds** curve reflects the positive relationship between the market rate of interest and the quantity of savings, other things constant, as reflected by the usual upward-sloping supply curve. This upward-sloping supply curve is shown as *S* in Exhibit 2.

Loanable funds market The market in which savers (suppliers of funds) and borrowers (demanders of funds) come together to determine the market rate of interest

Supply of loanable funds The relationship between the market interest rate and the quantity of loanable funds supplied to the economy, other things constant

Demand for loanable funds The relationship between the market interest rate and the quantity of loanable funds demanded, other things constant

For the economy as a whole, if the amount of other resources and the level of technology are fixed, diminishing marginal productivity causes the marginal rate of return curve, which is the demand curve for investment, to slope downward. The **demand for loanable funds** curve is based on the expected marginal rate of return these borrowed funds yield when invested in capital. Each firm has a downward-sloping demand curve for loanable funds, reflecting a declining marginal rate of return on investment. With some qualifications, the demand for loanable funds by each firm can be summed horizontally to yield the demand for loanable funds by all firms, as shown by *D* in Exhibit 2. Factors assumed constant along this demand curve include the prices of other resources, the level of technology, and the tax laws.

By bringing the demand and supply for loanable funds together, as in Exhibit 2, we can determine the market interest rate. In this case, the equilibrium interest rate of 8 percent is the only rate that will exactly match the wishes of borrowers and savers. The equilibrium quantity of loanable funds is $100 billion per year. Any change in the supply or demand for loanable funds will change the equilibrium interest rate. For example, a major technological breakthrough that increases the productivity of capital will increase its marginal rate of return

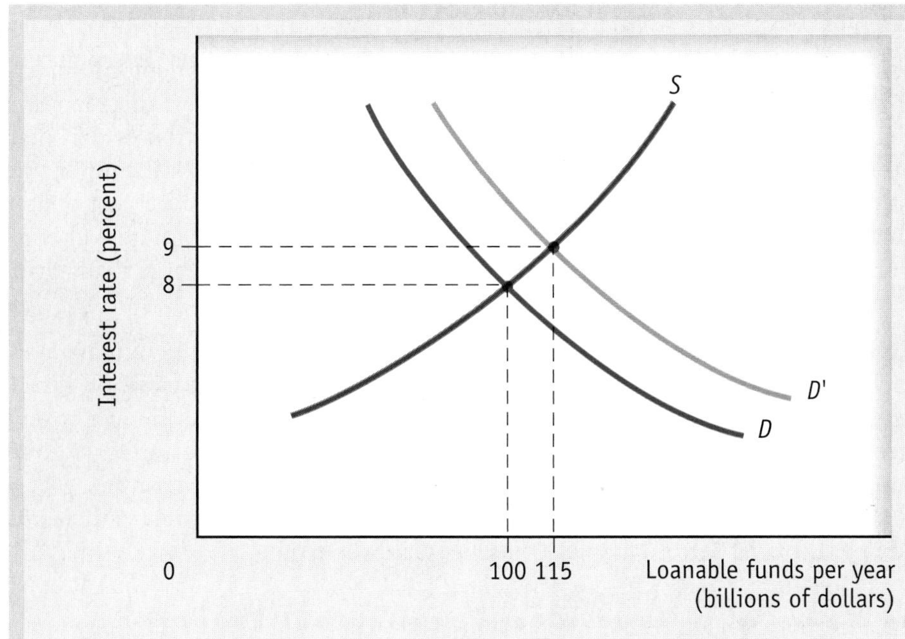

EXHIBIT 2

Market for Loanable Funds

Because of the declining marginal rate of return on capital, the quantity of loanable funds demanded is inversely related to the rate of interest. The equilibrium rate of interest, 8 percent, is determined at the intersection of the demand and supply curves for loans. An increase in the demand for loans from *D* to *D'* leads to an increase in the equilibrium rate of interest from 8 percent to 9 percent.

and shift out the demand curve for loanable funds, as shown in the movement from *D* to *D'* in Exhibit 2. Such an increase in the demand for loanable funds would raise the equilibrium interest rate to 9 percent and increase the quantity of loanable funds to $115 billion per year.

Why Interest Rates Differ

So far, we have been talking about *the* market rate of interest, implying that only one interest rate prevails in the loanable funds market. At any particular time, however, a range of interest rates can be found in the economy. For example, there are different interest rates on home mortgages, car loans, student loans, and credit cards, as well as the so-called *prime rate,* which is offered to the most trustworthy borrowers. Let's see why interest rates differ.

Risk. Some borrowers are more likely than others to repay their loans. Differences in the risk associated with various borrowers are reflected in differences in the interest rate negotiated. As loans become more risky, lenders are less willing to supply loanable funds, so the market interest rate on these loans rises, reflecting the higher risk. For example, the interest rate charged on a home mortgage is lower than on a car loan in part because a home serves as better collateral for the loan than does a car, which depreciates faster and can be driven away.

Duration of the Loan. The future is uncertain, and the further into the future a loan is to be repaid, the more uncertain that repayment becomes. Thus as the duration of a loan increases, lenders are less willing to supply funds. Hence loans extended for longer periods usually involve a higher interest rate to compensate the lender for this greater risk. The **term structure of interest rates** is the relationship between the duration of a loan and the interest rate charged. This

Term structure of interest rates The relationship between the duration of a loan and the interest rate charged

term structure usually indicates that the interest rate increases as the duration of loans increases.

Cost of Administration. The costs of executing the loan agreement, monitoring the conditions of the loan, and collecting the payments on the loan are called the *administration costs* of the loan. These costs, as a proportion of the total amount of the loan, decrease as the size of the loan increases. For example, the cost of administering a $100,000 loan will be less than 10 times the cost of administering a $10,000 loan. Consequently, that portion of the interest charge reflecting the cost of administering the loan will be smaller for large loans than for small loans.

Tax Treatment. Differences in the tax treatment of different types of loans will also affect the market rate of interest. For example, the interest earned on funds loaned to state and local governments is not subject to federal income taxes. Since lenders are interested in their after-tax rate of interest, state and local governments can pay lower interest rates than those paid by other borrowers.

We have now discussed investing in capital. We close this section with a case study on a special form of capital—intellectual property.

CaseStudy

The Information Economy

For a comprehensive Internet resource on technology law, containing pages on patent, copyright, trademark, and Internet legal issues, visit http://www.bitlaw.com/. Also visit the Web site of *The Industry Standard,* an on-line magazine about the Internet economy, at http://www.industrystandard.net/ on. What are the current issues in these fields? What can you learn about protecting music copyright with the advent of MP3 and other music digitizing technologies?

The Value of a Good Idea—Intellectual Property

One potentially valuable capital asset is information, or so-called *intellectual property*. But information is an unusual commodity. On the demand side, consumers are uncertain about the value of information until they acquire it. But they can't acquire it until they pay for it. So there is a circularity problem. There is also a problem on the supply side. Information is costly to produce, but it can be transmitted at relatively low cost. For example, the first copy of a new software program may cost $100 million to develop. But each additional copy may cost only $1 to produce.

Because of these demand and supply problems, producers of information may have difficulty appropriating its value through the sale of information. As soon as the producer sells information, that first customer, because of the low cost of transmitting information, becomes a potential supplier of the information. For example, a producer could invest millions developing a new software application, then sell a single copy. The buyer could, in turn, make copies and give or sell the software to others (are you using any "pirated" software?). The original producer has difficulty preventing nonpaying beneficiaries from consuming the good. As a result of these problems in the market for information, creators have less incentive to invest time and money to develop new ideas and new inventions.

To address these problems, the law grants property rights to the creators of new ideas and new inventions. By conferring monopoly power on such creators, those originators are better able to appropriate the value of their creations and thus have more incentive to develop new ideas and new inventions. The *patent system* establishes ownership rights to inventions and other technical advances. The *copyright system* confers ownership rights to the original expression of an idea by an author, artist, or composer. And the *trademark system* establishes property in unique commercial marks and symbols, such as the Nike swoosh or McDonald's golden arches.

Granting copyright protection is one thing, but enforcing it is quite another. Many of the CDs, movie videos, and software programs sold in other countries, especially China, are pirated editions of products originally developed in the United States. In fact, some movie videos are sold on the black market before the movie is released in theaters. So enforcement of these property rights is costly, and this diminishes the incentive to create new ideas.

Revisions have adapted copyright laws to a changing world. For example, computer software is now protected by copyright laws. The courts have also granted copyright protection for the wiring and circuitry design that make up a computer chip. The Internet has given rise to some special problems of intellectual property, since someone can download the contents of a site, change the headings, and derive commercial benefit from that content. Some digital gurus have argued that the ease of duplicating data on the Internet spells an end to copyright benefits. They say that anything that can be reduced to bits can be copied. But several companies are now developing software and hardware that, through the use of encryption and passwords, allow producers of information to specify how digital works can be used. Each new generation of technology has created new ways of communicating ideas and thus has called for new ways to help protect the rights of the creators of those ideas.

Sources: *Journal of Intellectual Property Law* (http://www.lawsch.uga.edu/~jipl/); "World Wide Web Link Creation, Intellectual Property, Copyrights and Trademarks," *Computerworld* (www.computerworld.com/links/970505linklinks.html); Mark Stefik, "Trusted Systems," *Scientific American* (March 1997) (www.sciam.com/0397issue/0397stefik.html); and Peter Burrows, "A Nest of Software Spies," *Business Week,* (19 May 1997) (www.businessweek.com/1997/20/b352792.htm).

PRESENT VALUE AND DISCOUNTING

Because present consumption is valued more than future consumption, present and future consumption cannot be directly compared. What we need is a yardstick to compare present and future amounts. A way of standardizing the discussion is to measure all consumption in terms of its present value. **Present value** is the current value of a payment or payments that will be received in the future. For example, how much would you pay now for the right to receive $100 one year from now? Put another way, what is the *present value* to you of receiving $100 one year from now?

Present value The value today of income or an income stream to be received in the future

Present Value of Payment One Year Hence

Suppose that the market interest rate is 10 percent, so you can either lend or borrow money at that rate. One way to determine how much you would pay for the opportunity to receive $100 one year from now is to ask how much you would have to save now, at the market interest rate, to end up with $100 one year from now. Here is the problem we are trying to solve: What amount of money, if saved at a rate of 10 percent, will accumulate to $100 one year from now? We can calculate the answer with a simple formula. We can say

$$\text{present value} \times 1.10 = \$100$$

or

$$\text{present value} = \frac{\$100}{1.10} = \$90.91$$

Thus if the interest rate is 10 percent, \$90.91 is the present value of receiving \$100 one year from now; it is the most you would be willing to pay today to receive \$100 one year from now. Rather than pay more than \$90.91, you could simply deposit your \$90.91 at the market rate of interest and end up with \$100 a year from now. The procedure of dividing the future payment by 1 plus the prevailing interest rate in order to express it in today's dollars is called **discounting.** The interest rate used to discount future payments is called the **discount rate.**

Discounting Determining the present value of income to be received in the future

Discount rate The interest rate used to convert income to be received in the future into present value

The present value of \$100 to be received one year from now depends on the interest rate, or discount rate. The more that present consumption is preferred to future consumption, the higher the interest rate that must be offered savers to defer consumption. *The higher the interest rate, or discount rate, the more the future payment is discounted and the lower its present value.* Put another way, the higher the interest rate, the less you need to save now to yield a given amount in the future. For example, if the interest rate is 15 percent, the present value of receiving \$100 one year from now is \$100/1.15, which equals \$86.96.

Conversely, the less present consumption is preferred to future consumption, the less savers need be paid to defer consumption and the lower the interest rate. The lower the interest rate, or discount rate, the less the future income is discounted and the greater its present value. A lower interest rate means that you must save more now to yield a given amount in the future. As a general rule, the present value of receiving an amount one year from now is

$$\text{present value} = \frac{\text{amount received one year from now}}{1 + \text{interest rate}}$$

For example, when the interest rate is 5 percent, the present value of receiving \$100 one year from now is

$$\text{present value} = \frac{\$100}{1 + 0.05} = \frac{\$100}{1.05} = \$95.24$$

Present Value for Payments in Later Years

Now consider the present value of receiving \$100 two years from now. What amount of money, if deposited at the market rate of interest of 5 percent, would yield \$100 two years from now? At the end of the first year, the value would be the present value × 1.05, which would then earn the market rate of interest during the second year. At the end of the second year, the deposit would have accumulated to the present value × 1.05, × 1.05. Thus, we have the equation

$$\text{present value} \times 1.05 \times 1.05 = \text{present value} \times (1.05)^2 = \$100$$

Solving for the present value yields

$$\text{present value} = \frac{\$100}{(1.05)^2} = \frac{\$100}{1.1025} = \$90.70$$

If the $100 were to be received three years from now, we would discount the payment over three years:

$$\text{present value} = \frac{\$100}{(1.05)^3} = \$86.38$$

If the interest rate is i, the present value formula of a payment of M dollars t years from now is

$$\text{present value} = \frac{M}{(1 + i)^t}$$

Because $(1 + i)$ is greater than 1, the more times it is multiplied by itself (as determined by t), the greater the denominator will be and the smaller the present value will be. Thus *the present value of a given payment will be smaller the further in the future that payment is to be received.*

Present Value of an Income Stream

The previous method is used to compute the present value of a single sum to be paid at some point in the future. Most investments, however, yield a stream of income over time. In cases where the income is received over a period of years, the present value of each receipt can be computed individually, and the results summed to yield the present value of the entire income stream. For example, the present value of receiving $100 next year and $150 the year after is simply the present value of the first year's receipt plus the present value of the second year's receipt. If the interest rate is 5 percent,

$$\text{present value} = \frac{\$100}{1.05} + \frac{\$150}{(1.05)^2} = \$231.29$$

Present Value of an Annuity

A given sum of money received each year for a specified number of years is called an **annuity.** Such an income stream is called a *perpetuity* if it continues indefinitely into the future, as it would in our earlier example of the productivity gain stemming from the purchase of indestructible farm equipment. The present value of receiving a certain amount forever seems like it should be a very large sum indeed. But because future income is valued less the more distant into the future it is to be received, the present value of receiving a particular amount forever is not much more than that of receiving it for, say, 20 years.

Annuity A given sum of money received each year for a specified number of years

To determine the present value of receiving $100 each year forever, we need only ask how much money must be deposited in a savings account to yield $100 in interest each year. When the interest rate is 10 percent, a deposit of $1,000 will earn $100 per year. Thus, the present value of receiving $100 a year indefinitely when the interest rate is 10 percent is $1,000. More generally, the present value equals the amount received each year divided by the interest rate, or discount rate.

The concept of present value is useful in making investment decisions. Farmer Jones, by investing $10,000 in the Crop Sprayer, expected to earn $800 more per year. Thus, his marginal rate of return was 8 percent. At a market interest rate of 8 percent, the present value of a cash flow of $800 per year discounted at that rate would be $800/0.08, which equals $10,000. Thus, *Jones was willing to invest in capital an amount that, at the margin, would yield a cash stream with a present value just equal to the marginal amount invested.*

What about your decision to invest in human capital—to go to college? In the previous chapter you learned that individuals with at least a college degree earn about twice as much throughout their working life as those with only a high school education. We could compute the present value of each level of education by discounting earnings based on that level of education, then summing the total earnings over your working life. Even without carrying out those calculations, we can say with reasonable certainty that the present value of at least a college education will be about twice that of just a high school education. You also learned way back in Chapter 1 that some college majors earn more than others. For example, based on a survey of those 35 to 44 years of age with a college degree as their highest degree, males who majored in economics had median earnings that were 55 percent higher than those who majored in philosophy. Among females, that advantage was 91 percent for the same majors. If such an advantage prevailed throughout all working years, the present value of a degree in economics would be 55 percent higher than the present value of a degree in philosophy for males and 91 percent higher for females.

To develop a hands-on appreciation for present value and discounting, consider the following case study.

CaseStudy

Public Policy

Lottery winners in Virginia can receive either a series of annual payments over 25 years or a lump sum in cash (cash option). For details, visit the Virginia Lottery Web site at http://www.valottery.com/cashopt.htm. How does the Virginia Lottery determine the value of the jackpot? What interest rate does it use?

The Million-Dollar Lottery

Since New Hampshire introduced the first modern state-run lottery, 36 states and the District of Columbia have followed suit, generating profits of $12 billion in 1997. Multimillion-dollar prizes are now ho-hum. Some winners expect to be handed a check for the prize. Instead, they are usually paid in installments. For example, a million-dollar prize-winner gets $50,000 a year for 20 years. You now know that such a payment stream has a present value of less than the advertised million. To put this payment schedule in perspective, keep in mind that at a discount rate of 10 percent, the $50,000 received in the twentieth year has a present value of only $7,432. If today you deposited $7,432 in an account earning 10 percent interest, you would wind up with $50,000 in 20 years.

If the discount rate is 10 percent, the present value of a $50,000 annuity for the next 20 years is $425,700. Thus the present value of the actual payment stream is less than half of the promised million, which is why lottery officials pay it out in installments (the multi-state Powerball lottery pays out over 25 years, but offers winners the choice of a much smaller lump-sum payment).

Incidentally, we might consider the present value of receiving $50,000 per year forever. Using the formula for an annuity discussed earlier, the present value when the interest rate is 10 percent is $50,000/0.10 = $500,000. Since the present value of receiving $50,000 for 20 years is $425,700, continuing the $50,000 annual payment forever adds only $74,300 to the present value. This shows the dramatic effect of discounting on the present value of payments beyond year 20.

In some states, lottery winners are allowed to sell their jackpots. Winners typically receive only 40 cents on the dollar for the 20-year annuity. So a million-dollar pot, if sold by the winner, would fetch only $400,000. At tax rates prevailing in 1998, federal income taxes on $400,000 for a single tax filer amount to at least $140,000. State and local income taxes could add an additional $50,000. All told, because of time and taxes, the much-touted million could shrink to about $200,000 in after-tax income—only one-fifth the amount advertised.

Sources: Adam Wolfson, "Life Is a Gamble," *Wall Street Journal* (14 August 1998); Lin Bixby, "A Ticket to Paradise? Don't Bet on It," *Hartford Courant* (28 June 1998); and Michelle Malkin, "The State's Lottery Ads Are Hazardous to Your Health," *Seattle Times* (6 May 1997). Internet links to lottery sites can be found at www.state.wv.us/lottery/links.htm.

This discussion of present value and discounting concludes our treatment of capital and interest. We now have the tools to consider how firms, especially corporations, are financed.

CORPORATE FINANCE

During the Industrial Revolution, labor-saving machinery made large-scale production more profitable, so construction of the huge factories to house this heavy machinery began to require large capital investments. The corporate structure became the easiest way to finance these large investments, and by 1920 corporations accounted for most employment and output in the U.S. economy. Way back in Chapter 4, you learned about the pros and cons of the corporate form of business organization, but thus far little has been said about corporate finance.

As was noted in Chapter 4, a corporation is a legal entity, distinct from its shareholders. The corporation may own property, earn a profit, sue or be sued, and incur debt. Stockholders, the owners of the corporation, are liable only to the extent of their investment in the firm. Use of the abbreviation "Inc." or "Corp." in the company name serves as a warning to potential creditors that stockholders will not accept unlimited personal liability for the debts the company incurs.

Corporate Stock and Retained Earnings

Corporations acquire funds for investment in three ways: by issuing stock, by retaining part of their profit, and by borrowing. Corporations *issue and sell stock* to raise money for operations and for new plant and equipment. Suppose you have developed a recipe for a hot, spicy chili that your friends have convinced you will be a

NetBookmark

Louis Rukeyser has been hosting his weekly television program, *Wall Street Week*, since 1970. He has written several popular books about economics and finance and produces a monthly newsletter available through the show's Web site at http://www.pbs.org/mpt/rukeyser/index.html. From there you can also view his latest opening commentary and experience his dry wit yourself. David Gardner, a former writer for Rukeyser, went on to found one of the most popular and witty Web sites devoted to investing and economic news and information—the Motley Fool. You can find the Fools and their investing philosophy and suggestions at http://www.fool.com/index.htm. Look for the CEO Wealth Meter to see what the shares of top U.S. executives in their own firms are worth.

best-seller. You decide to incorporate and raise $1 million by issuing stock in the company, which you call the Six-Alarm Chili Corporation. To do this, you sell 10,000 shares for $100 per share. This initial sale of stock to the public is called an **initial public offering,** or an **IPO.** A *share* of **stock** represents a claim on the net income and assets of a corporation, as well as the right to vote on corporate directors and on other important matters. A person who buys 1 percent of the shares issued thereby owns 1 percent of the corporation, is entitled to 1 percent of any profit, and gets to cast 1 percent of the votes.

Initial public offering (IPO) The initial sale of stock to the public

Stock A certificate reflecting part ownership of a corporation

Dividends After-tax corporate profits that are paid to stockholders rather than reinvested in the firm

Retained earnings After-tax corporate profits that are reinvested in the firm rather than paid to stockholders as dividends

Corporations must pay corporate income taxes on any profits. After-tax profits are either paid as **dividends** to shareholders or reinvested in the corporation. Reinvested profits, or **retained earnings,** allow the firm to finance expansion. Stockholders expect dividends, but the corporation is not bound by contract to pay dividends. Once shares are issued, their price tends to fluctuate directly with the firm's profit prospects. People buy stock because of the dividends and because they usually expect the value of the stock to increase in the future.

Corporate Bonds

Again, your corporation can acquire funds by issuing stock, by retaining earnings, or by borrowing. The corporation can go to a bank for a loan or can issue and sell bonds. A **bond** is the corporation's promise to pay back the holder a fixed sum of money on the designated *maturity date* plus make annual interest payments until that date of maturity. For example, a corporation might sell for $1,000 a bond that promises to make an annual interest payment of, say, $100 and to repay the $1,000 at the end of 20 years.

Bond A certificate reflecting a firm's promise to pay the holder periodic interest until the date of maturity, then to pay a fixed sum of money on the designated maturity date

The payment stream for bonds is more predictable than that for stocks. Unless this corporation goes bankrupt, it is obliged to pay bondholders the promised amounts. In contrast, stockholders are last in line when resource holders get paid, so bondholders get paid before stockholders. Investors usually consider bonds less risky than stocks, although bonds involve risk as well.

Securities Exchanges

Once stocks and bonds have been issued and sold, owners of these securities are free to resell them on *security exchanges.* In the United States, there are seven security exchanges registered with the *Securities and Exchange Commission,* or *SEC,* the federal body that regulates securities markets. The New York Stock Exchange is the largest, trading the securities of over 2,000 major companies and accounting for well over half of U.S. securities trades. Nearly all the securities traded each day are *secondhand securities* in the sense that they have already been sold by the issuing company. So the bulk of the daily transactions do not provide funds to firms in need of investment capital. Most money goes from a securities seller to a securities buyer. *Institutional investors,* such as banks, insurance companies, and mutual funds, account for over half the trading volume on the New York Stock Exchange. By providing a *secondary market* for securities, exchanges enhance the *liquidity* of these securities—that is, the exchanges make the securities more readily exchangeable for cash and thus more attractive to investors.

The secondary markets for stocks also determine the current market value of the corporation. The market value of a firm at any given time can be found by multiplying the share price times the number of shares outstanding. For example, if your chili company's stock price increases from $100 to $150 per share, the market value of the firm, or *market capitalization*, would equal $150 times the 10,000 outstanding shares, or $1.5 million. The share price reflects the present value of the discounted stream of expected profits. Just to give you some idea, the market capitalization of the top-valued U.S. firm, Microsoft, exceeded $400 billion in May 1999, and the total market capitalization of all firms on U.S. exchanges exceeded $14 trillion.

Securities prices give the firm's management some indication of the wisdom of raising new capital through retained earnings, new stock issues, or new bond issues. The more profitable the company is expected to be, other things constant, the higher the value of shares on the stock market and the lower the interest rate that would have to be paid on new bond issues. *Thus, securities markets allocate funds more readily to successful firms than to firms in financial difficulty.* Some firms may be in such poor financial shape that they cannot sell new securities. Securities markets usually promote the survival of the fittest.

So one function of securities markets is to allocate investment funds to those firms that appear capable of making the most profitable use of those funds. Securities markets also help determine the ownership and control of corporations. We examine this function next.

CORPORATE OWNERSHIP AND CONTROL

As the founder of the Six-Alarm Chili Corporation, you are that firm's entrepreneur. An **entrepreneur** is a profit-seeking decision maker who organizes an enterprise and assumes the risk of operation. An entrepreneur pays resource owners for the opportunity to use those resources in the firm. The entrepreneur need not actually manage the firm's resources as long as he or she has the power to hire and fire the manager—that is, as long as the entrepreneur controls the manager.

Entrepreneur A profit-seeking decision maker who organizes an enterprise and assumes the risk of its operation

Managerial Behavior in Large Corporations

Up to this point, we have assumed that firms attempt to maximize profits. In a small firm, there is usually little danger that the hired manager will not follow the wishes of the owner; the manager and owner are often the same person. As the modern corporation has evolved, however, its ownership has become widely distributed among many stockholders, often leaving no single stockholder with either the incentive or the ability to control the manager.

Ownership has become widely distributed in part because individual stockholders prefer to diversify their portfolios across different types of assets rather invest in just a single company. A **portfolio** is an individual's collection of stocks, bonds, and other financial assets. The exact composition of the portfolio depends on the individual's financial needs and attitude toward risk. For example, a young family may prefer a portfolio that yields no current income but will grow to finance college costs. An older couple, on the other hand, would prefer a portfolio that provides a reliable stream of retirement income. Even an individual who is wealthy enough to purchase a large fraction of a particular firm usually prefers to buy a small fraction of many firms instead. That way, if a particular firm performs poorly and its share price drops, the portfolio

Portfolio A collection of stocks, bonds, and other financial assets

still retains most of its value. Simply put, investors choose diversified portfolios to avoid putting all their eggs in one basket. The upshot is that the ownership of most firms is spread across many stockholders.

Separation of ownership from control The situation that exists when no single stockholder or unified group of stockholders owns enough shares to control the management of a corporation

Economists since the days of Adam Smith have been concerned with what is known as the **separation of ownership from control** in the large corporation. Various economists have formulated theoretical models suggesting that, when freed from the control of a dominant stockholding influence, managers might attempt to pursue their own selfish goals rather than those of the firm's owners. The alternatives vary from model to model, but emphasis has focused on such goals as maximizing the firm's size or increasing the discretionary resources available to the managers, such as attractive surroundings, private dining rooms, corporate jets, and other amenities. A manager may try to increase the firm's size, by, for example, acquiring other firms, even if profits suffer in the process, because managers want the power, security, and status associated with a larger firm. They want to appear on the cover of *Business Week*. As goals other than profit are pursued, so the argument goes, the firm's resources are used less efficiently, resulting in a lower level of profit. Thus, stockholders—the owners of the firm—suffer because managers are not pursuing the owners' best interests.

Constraints on Managerial Discretion

Analysts have identified a variety of constraints that can serve as checks on wayward managers. The nature and effectiveness of each constraint will be examined next.

Economics of Natural Selection. Some economists argue that even if managers are freed from the control of a dominant stockholder, the rigors of competition in the product market will force them to maximize profits. This "economics of natural selection" theoretically ensures that only the most efficient firms will survive; inefficient firms will not earn enough profit to attract and retain resources and so will eventually go out of business.

The problem with this argument is that although pressure to pursue profits may arise when firms sell their products in competitive markets, many large corporations are at least partially insulated from intense product competition. Either because government regulations protect their firms from competition or because their firms enjoy some degree of market power, many managers have a certain amount of discretion in how they use their firms' resources. Such managers could divert corporate resources into activities reflecting their own interests, yet still earn enough profit to ensure their firms' survival.

Managerial Incentives. Other economists have examined the manager's incentive structure. If executive pay is linked closely to the firm's profit, the compensation scheme may encourage the manager to pursue profit even in the absence of a dominant stockholder or competition in the product market. Evidence suggests that at least a portion of the typical manager's compensation is tied to the firm's profitability through some type of bonus pay scheme or stock option plan. But even if the manager's income is tied to profit, the manager will not necessarily attempt to maximize profit. The manager in a large corporation who diverts profit to other ends will simply forgo some income. This profit diversion may be "cheap" in view of the small fraction of the firm's shares typically owned by management. For example, if a manager who owns 1 percent of the firm's shares diverts $50,000 of potential profit to buy an antique desk for the executive suite, this diversion will cost the manager only $500 in forgone pretax profit. After corporate taxes and personal income taxes are figured in, the cost is less than half that. Thus, the existence of a link between executive pay and firm profit is not necessarily evidence that managers will attempt to maximize profit; it is only evidence that profit diversion will involve some personal cost, but that cost may be quite small.

Stockholder Voting. Each year stockholders have an opportunity to attend the company meeting and elect the board of directors. Couldn't stockholders join forces to oust an inefficient manager? Chances of an effective stockholder revolt are slim. The average stockholder does not have the information, the resources, or the incentive to challenge management. Most shareholders either ignore the election or dutifully pass their proxy votes to the managers. Dissatisfied stockholders, however, do have one very important alternative. They can "fire" the manager and the firm simply by selling their shares in the corporation. As dissatisfied stockholders sell their holdings, the share price drops and the firm becomes more attractive as a target for a reform-minded entrepreneur. An outside individual or another firm can buy a controlling interest in the firm at a relatively low price, reform or replace the management, and then benefit as the firm's rising profits lead to an increase in the value of shares. Some firms specialize in acquiring, then shaping up, other firms that do not appear to be performing up to their potential.

Institutional Investors. A growing fraction of corporate shares are purchased not by individual investors but by institutional investors such as mutual funds, who purchase these shares as part of a portfolio. Large institutional investors can exercise corporate control either directly through the election of the board of directors or indirectly through buying and selling corporate shares. Some top executives have been ousted by institutional investors.

CONCLUSION

This chapter introduced you to capital, interest, and corporate finance. Capital is a more complicated resource than this chapter has conveyed. For example, the demand curve for investment is a moving target, not the stable relationship drawn in Exhibit 1. An accurate depiction of the investment demand curve calls for knowledge of the marginal product of capital and the price of output in the future. But capital's marginal productivity changes with breakthroughs in technology and with changes in the employment of other resources. And the future price of the product can also vary widely. Consider, for example, the dilemma of a firm contemplating an investment in drilling rigs in recent years, when oil prices fluctuated between $10 and $36 per barrel.

One final point. When economists talk about investing they have in mind purchases of new capital, such as new machines and new buildings. When business journalists talk about investing, they usually mean buying stocks and bonds. To an economist, Farmer Jones is investing only when he purchases new capital, not when he buys corporate stocks and bonds.

SUMMARY

1. Production cannot occur without savings because both direct production and roundabout production require time—time during which the resources required for production must be paid. Because present consumption is valued more than future consumption, consumers must be rewarded to defer consumption. Interest is the reward paid to savers for forgoing present consumption and is the cost paid by borrowers to increase present consumption.

2. Choosing the profit-maximizing level of capital is complicated because capital purchased today yields a stream of benefit for years into the future. The marginal rate of return on a capital investment equals the marginal revenue product of capital as a percentage of the marginal resource cost of capital. The profit-maximizing firm invests up to the point where its marginal rate of return on capital equals the market rate of interest, which is the opportunity cost of investing savings or borrowed funds.

3. The demand and supply for loanable funds determine the market rate of interest. At any given time, market rates of interest may differ because of differences in risk, maturity, administrative costs, and tax treatment.

4. Corporations secure investment funding from three sources: new stock issues, retained earnings, and borrowing (either directly from a lender or by issuing bonds). Once new stocks and bonds are issued, these securities are then bought and sold on securities exchanges. Securities prices tend to vary directly with the firm's expected profitability.

5. The ownership of a large corporation is typically fragmented among many stockholders, with no stockholder owning a dominant share. The fact that a poorly performing firm can be bought at a bargain price, shaped up, and sold for a profit is said to keep management behavior in accord with stockholders' interests.

QUESTIONS FOR REVIEW

1. *(Role of Time)* Complete the following sentences:
   a. If Bryan values current consumption more than future consumption, he has a ________.
   b. The reward to households for forgoing current consumption is ________.
   c. Producing capital goods rather than producing final goods is known as ________ .

2. *(Consumption, Saving, and Time)* Explain why the supply of loanable funds curve slopes upward to the right.

3. *(Why Interest Rates Differ)* At any given time, a range of interest rates prevails in the economy. What are some factors that contribute to differences among interest rates?

4. *(Present Value of an Annuity)* Why is $10,000 a close approximation of the price of an annuity that pays $1,000 each year for 30 years at 10 percent annual interest?

5. *(Present Value of an Annuity)* Suppose you are hired by your state government to determine the profitability of a lottery offering a grand prize of $10 million paid out in equal annual installments over 20 years. Show *how* to calculate the cost to the state of paying out such a prize. Assume payments are made at the end of each year.

6. *(Case* **Study:** *The Million-Dollar Lottery)* In many states with lotteries, people can take their winnings in a single, discounted, lump-sum payment or in a series of annual payments for 20 years. What factors should a winner consider in determining how to take the money?

7. *(Corporate Finance)* Describe the three ways in which corporations acquire funds for investment.

8. *(Securities Exchanges)* What role do securities exchanges play in financing corporations?

9. *(Managerial Behavior in Large Corporations)* How could the separation of ownership from control lead to lower profits for a firm?

10. *(Constraints on Managerial Discretion)* The separation of ownership from control in a large corporation can allow managers to follow goals other than profit maximization. Discuss reasons why managers may continue to maximize profits. Why might these reasons be insufficient to ensure profit maximization?

PROBLEMS AND EXERCISES

11. *(Optimal Investment)* Look back at Exhibit 1 in this chapter. If the marginal resource cost rose to $24,000 what would be the optimal investment at a market interest rate of 10 percent? If the interest rate then rose to 16.6 percent, what would be the optimal level of investment?

12. *(Market for Loanable Funds)* Using a supply-demand for loanable funds diagram, show the effect on the market interest rate of each of the following:
    a. An increase in the marginal resource cost of capital
    b. An increase in the marginal productivity of capital
    c. A shift in preferences toward present consumption and away from future consumption

13. *(Present Value)* Calculate the present value of each of the following future payments. (For some of these problems you may wish to use the on-line calculator available at http://www.datachimp.com/articles/finworks/fmpresval.htm.
    a. A $10,000 lump sum received 1 year from now if the market interest rate is 8 percent
    b. A $10,000 lump sum received 2 years from now if the market interest rate is 10 percent
    c. A $1,000 lump sum received 3 years from now if the market interest rate is 5 percent
    d. A $25,000 lump sum received one year from now if the market interest rate is 12 percent
    e. A $25,000 lump sum received one year from now if the market interest rate is 10 percent
    f. A perpetuity of $500 per year if the market interest rate is 6 percent

14. *(Present Value of an Income Stream)* Suppose the market interest rate is 10 percent. Would you be willing to lend $10,000 if you were guaranteed to receive $1,000 at the end of each of the next 12 years plus a $5,000 payment 15 years from now? Why or why not?

EXPERIENTIAL EXERCISES

15. *(**CaseStudy:** The Value of a Good Idea)* MIT's Michael Kremer has suggested an interesting way to encourage innovation in drug development. The basic idea is explained in a nontechnical article in the June 15, 1996 issue of *The Economist* at http://rider.wharton.upenn.edu/~faulhabe/790/patent_cure-all.html. Take a look at the article and determine how Kremer places a value on an innovation.

16. *(Corporate Ownership and Control)* Read Jane Katz, "Who Should Be in Charge," in the Federal Reserve Bank of Boston's *Regional Review* at http://www.bos.frb.org/economic/nerr/katz97_4.htm. What are some of the current issues in corporate finance outlined by Katz?

17. *(Wall Street Journal)* The *Wall Street Journal* is the quintessential source for information about U.S. financial markets. Most of the Money & Investing section is devoted to reporting on individual firms' financial activities and on the stock and bond markets generally. This section is worth scanning every day, but today try to find an article related to corporate ownership and control. Are there any examples of takeover attempts in which a firm or a group of institutional investors is trying to buy up shares of another firm? What factors are motivating this behavior?

CHAPTER

27

Transaction Costs, Imperfect Information, and Market Behavio

General Motors offers car loans and issues credit cards, so why don't some banks make automobiles? Why do some firms, such as Domino's Pizza, specialize in a single product, while other firms, such as General Electric, make hundreds of different products? Why stop at hundreds of different products? Why not thousands? In fact, why isn't there one giant firm that produces everything? Why does buying a used car make us nervous? Why is proper spelling so important on your résumé? Answers to these and other seemingly unrelated questions are addressed in this chapter, which digs deeper into some assumptions made about firms, households, and the role that information plays in market interaction.

Visit the McEachern Interactive Study Center for this chapter at *http://mcisc.swcollege.com*

Little has been said so far about the internal structure of the firm. We have ignored the internal workings of the firm because our objective has been to understand how the price system coordinates resource allocation. In the first half of this chapter, we will step inside the factory gates to reconsider some assumptions made about the firm.

We have also assumed thus far that consumers have all the information they need to make informed choices, including knowledge of the price, availability, and quality of the goods and services they demand. As you will see in the second half of the chapter, participants in most markets do not operate with complete information about the variables that matter most, such as price and quality. To further complicate matters, at times sellers know more than do buyers about the quality of the product; at times it's the other way around. The second half of this chapter examines how a lack of information affects the behavior of market participants and shapes market outcomes. Overall, this chapter should help you develop a better understanding of market behavior. Topics discussed in this chapter include:

- Transaction costs and the firm
- Vertical integration
- Economies of scope
- Optimal search
- Winner's curse
- Asymmetric information
- Adverse selection
- Signaling and screening
- Principal-agent problems

RATIONALE FOR THE FIRM AND ITS SCOPE OF OPERATION

The competitive model assumes that all participants in the market know everything they need to know about the price and availability of all inputs, outputs, and production processes. Perfect competition assumes that the firm is headed by a decision maker with a computer-like ability to calculate all the relevant marginal productivities. This individual knows everything necessary to solve complex production and pricing problems.

The irony is that if the marginal products of all inputs could be measured easily and if prices for all inputs could be determined without cost, there would be little reason for production to take place in firms. In a world characterized by perfect competition, perfect information, constant returns to scale, and costless exchange, the consumer could bypass the firm to deal directly with resource suppliers, purchasing inputs in the appropriate amounts. Someone who wanted a table could buy timber, have it milled, contract with a carpenter, contract with a painter, and end up with a finished product. The consumer could carry out transactions directly with each resource supplier.

Firms Reduce Transaction Costs

This section explores why production is carried out within firms. More than 60 years ago, in a classic article entitled "The Nature of the Firm," Nobel prize winner Ronald Coase asked the fundamental question, "Why do firms exist?"[1]

1 *Economica* 4 (November 1937): 386–405.

Why do people organize in the hierarchical structure of the firm and coordinate their decisions through a manager rather than simply relying on market exchange? His answer would not surprise today's students of economics: *Organizing activities through the hierarchy of the firm is often more efficient than market exchange, because production requires the coordination of many transactions among many resource owners. The firm is the favored means of production when the transaction costs involved in using the price system exceed the costs of organizing those same activities through direct managerial controls within a firm.*

Consider again the example of purchasing a table by contracting directly with all the different resource suppliers, from the grower of timber to the individual who paints the table. Using resource markets directly involves (1) the cost of determining what inputs are needed and how they should be combined and (2) the cost of negotiating a separate agreement with each resource owner for each specific contribution to production *over and above* the direct costs of the timber, nails, machinery, paint, and labor required to make the table. Where inputs are easily identified, measured, priced, and hired, production can be carried out through a price-guided "do-it-yourself" approach using the market. For example, getting your house painted is a relatively simple production task: You can buy the paint and brushes and hire painters by the hour. In this case you, the consumer, become your own painting contractor, hiring inputs in the market and combining these inputs to do the job.

Where the costs of identifying the appropriate inputs and negotiating a contract for each specific contribution are high, the consumer minimizes transaction costs by purchasing the finished product from a firm rather than hiring all the inputs directly through markets. For example, although some people serve as their own contractor to get their house painted, few do so when building a house; most hire general contractors. The more complicated the task, the greater the ability to economize on transaction costs through specialization and centralized control. For example, attempting to buy a car by contracting with the hundreds of resource suppliers required to assemble one would be time-consuming and costly. What type of skilled labor should be hired and at what wages? How much steel, aluminum, plastic, glass, paint, and other materials should be purchased? How should the resources be combined and in what proportions? The task is impossible for someone who lacks specialized engineering knowledge of auto production. Consequently, it is more efficient for a consumer to buy a car produced by a firm than to contract separately with each resource supplier.

At the margin there will be some activities that could go either way, with some consumers using firms and some hiring resources directly in the markets. The choice will depend on each consumer's skill and opportunity cost of time. For example, some people may not want to be troubled with hiring all the inputs to get their house painted; instead, they will simply contract with a firm to do the entire job for an agreed-upon price—they will hire a contractor. As you will see later in the chapter, however, hiring a contractor may give rise to other problems of quality control.

The Bounds of the Firm

So far, the chapter has explained why firms exist: *Firms minimize both the transaction costs and the production costs of economic activity.* The next question is, What are the efficient bounds of the firm? The theory of the firm described in earlier chapters is largely silent on questions concerning the boundaries of the firm—that is, on the appropriate degree of vertical integration. **Vertical integration** is the expansion of a firm into stages of production earlier or later than those in which it has previously specialized. For example, a steel company may decide (1) to integrate backward by mining its own iron ore or even mining the coal used to smelt ore (e.g., U.S. Steel owns coal mines in Kentucky) or (2) to integrate forward by forming raw steel into various components. A large manufacturer employs an amazing variety of production processes, but on average about half of the cost of production goes to purchasing inputs from other firms. For example, General Motors spends well over $60 billion a year on parts and raw materials, an amount that exceeds the annual output of some countries.

Vertical integration The expansion of a firm into stages of production earlier or later than those in which it has specialized, such as a steel producer that buys a coal mine

How does the firm determine which activities to undertake and which to purchase from other firms? Should IBM manufacture its own computer chips or buy them from another firm? The answer depends on a comparison of the costs and benefits of internal production versus market purchases. The point bears repeating: *Internal production and markets are alternative ways of organizing transactions.* The choice will depend on which form of organization is the more efficient way to carry out the transaction in question. Keep in mind that market prices coordinate transactions *between* firms, whereas managers coordinate activities *within* firms. The market coordinates resources by harmonizing the independent plans of separate decision makers, but a firm coordinates resources through the conscious direction of managers.

The usual assumption is that transactions will be organized by market exchange unless markets pose problems. Market exchange allows each firm to benefit from specialization and comparative advantage. For example, IBM can specialize in making computers and buy from chip makers who specialize in what they do best. But sometimes the item to be purchased in the market is not standardized or the exact performance requirements are hard to specify. For example, suppose one firm wants another firm to supply research and development services. The uncertainty involved in the purchase of such a nonspecific service makes it difficult to write, execute, and enforce a purchase agreement covering all possible contingencies that could arise. What if the R&D supplier, in the course of fulfilling the agreement, makes a valuable discovery for an application in an unrelated field? Who has the right to that new application—the firm that purchased the R&D service or the firm that supplied it? And who determines if the field is unrelated? Since incomplete contracts create potentially troublesome situations, conducting research and development *within the firm* often involves a lower transaction cost than purchasing it in the market.

At this point, it might be useful to discuss specific criteria the firm considers when deciding whether to purchase a particular input from the market, thereby benefiting from another producer's comparative advantage, or to produce the input internally.

Bounded Rationality of Managers. To direct and coordinate activity in a conscious way in the firm, a manager must understand how all the pieces of the puzzle fit together. As the firm takes on more and more activities, however, the manager starts losing track of things and the quality of managerial decisions suffers. The more production tasks the firm takes on, the longer the lines of

Bounded rationality The notion that there is a limit to the amount of information an economic agent, such as a manager, can comprehend

communication between the manager and production workers who must implement the decision. One constraint on vertical integration is the manager's **bounded rationality,** which limits the amount of information the manager can comprehend about the firm's operation. When the firm takes on additional functions, coordination and communication become more difficult. The firm can experience diseconomies similar to those it experiences when it expands output beyond the efficient scale of production. The solution is for the firm to reduce its functions to those it does best. Such cutbacks occurred when automakers increased the proportion of parts they purchased from other firms.

Minimum Efficient Scale. As noted when firm costs were first discussed, the *minimum efficient scale* is the minimum level of output at which economies of scale have been fully exploited. For example, suppose that minimum efficient scale in the production of personal computers is achieved when output reaches 1 million computers per year, as shown by the long-run average cost curve in panel (a) of Exhibit 1. Suppose also that this output rate turns out to be the amount the firm wants to produce to maximize profit. Since the computer chip is an important component in the personal computer, should the PC maker integrate backward into chip production? Suppose that the minimum efficient scale in chip production is not achieved until production reaches a rate of 5 million chips per year, so a PC manufacturer needs only 20 percent of the chips produced at the minimum efficient scale. As you can see in panel (b) of Exhibit 1, if only 1 million chips were produced per year, the cost per chip would be high relative to the cost that could be achieved at minimum efficient scale in chip production. The PC manufacturer therefore minimizes production costs by buying chips from a chip firm of optimal size. More generally, *other things constant, a firm should buy an input if the price is below what it would cost the firm to make.*

Easily Observable Quality. If an input is well defined and its quality is easily determined at the time of purchase, that input is more likely to be purchased in the market than produced internally, other things equal. For example, a flour mill will typically buy wheat in the market rather than grow its own, as the quality of the wheat can be easily assessed by inspection. In contrast, the quality of certain inputs can be determined only during the production process. Firms whose reputations depend on the operation of a key component are likely to produce that component, especially if the quality of that component varies widely across producers over time and cannot be easily observed by inspection. For example, suppose that the manufacturer of a sensitive measuring instrument requires a crucial gauge, the quality of which can be observed only as the gauge is assembled. If the firm produces the gauge itself, it can closely monitor quality.

Producers sometimes integrate backward so they can offer consumers a guarantee about the quality of the components or ingredients in a product. For example, Frank Perdue can talk about the health and quality of the chickens he sells because he raises his own. Kentucky Fried Chicken, however, does not discuss the family background of its chickens because the company makes no claim about raising them. Instead, KFC ads focus on such aspects as the secret ingredients used to fry the chicken and the fact that, by specializing in chicken preparation, the company does a better job than other fast-food franchises that sell much more than chicken.

EXHIBIT 1

Minimum Efficient Scale and Vertical Integration

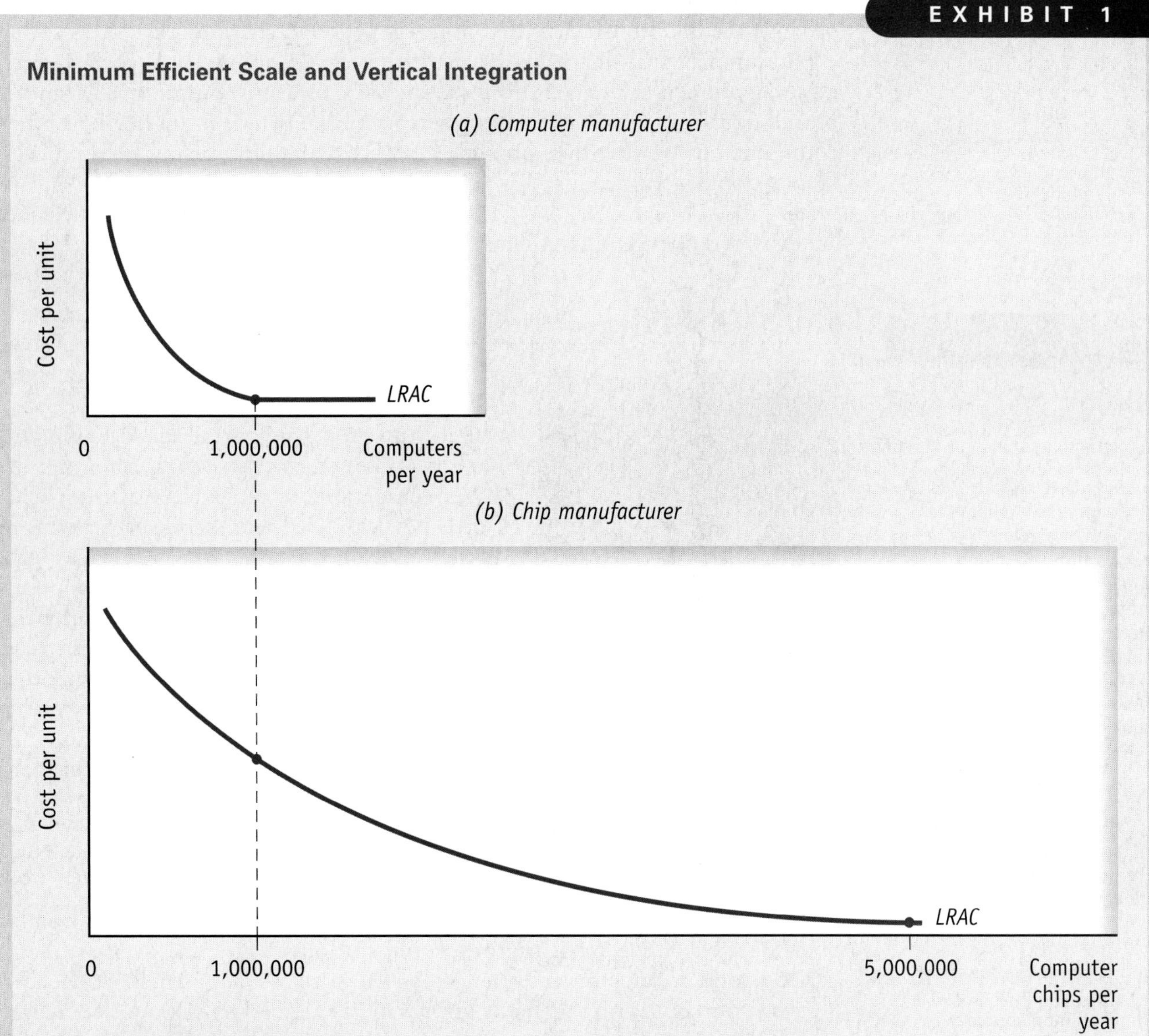

The computer manufacturer in panel (a) is producing at the minimum efficient scale of 1,000,000 units per period. That level of production requires 1,000,000 computer chips. If the manufacturer produced its own chips, the cost would be much higher than if it purchased them from a chip manufacturer operating on a much larger scale. As panel (b) shows, at 1,000,000 chips, economies of scale in chip production are far from exhausted.

Number of Suppliers. A firm wants an uninterrupted source of component parts. When there are many interchangeable suppliers of a particular input, a firm is more likely to purchase that input in the market than produce it internally, other things constant. Not only does the existence of many suppliers ensure a dependable source of components, but competition among these suppliers keeps the component price down. If the resource market is so unstable that the firm cannot rely on a consistent supply of components, the firm may produce the item to insulate itself from the vagaries of that market.

In summary, if a firm relies on market purchases of inputs rather than vertical integration, it can benefit from the specialization and comparative advantage of individual suppliers. Other things constant, the firm is more likely to buy a component part rather than produce it if (1) the item can be purchased for less than it could be if produced by the firm, (2) the item is well defined and its quality easily observable, or (3) there are many possible suppliers. These issues are discussed further in the following case study.

CaseStudy

The World of Business

Should a firm hire an outside consulting firm to help manage its outsourcing? There are now firms that specialize in helping other firms with outsourcing. For example, Everest provides outsourcing management services. Visit its site at http://www.outsourcing-mgnt.com/index.html. Look under Outsourcing and browse through some of its reports, such as "How to Avoid a Multi-Million Dollar Mistake?" The Outsourcing Institute provides information on the hows and whys of outsourcing at http://www.outsourcing.com/howandwhy/. What do these reports say about how outsourcing is defined and why firms might outsource?

The Trend Toward Outsourcing

Outsourcing occurs when a firm buys products, such as auto parts, or services, such as data processing, from outside suppliers. The firm relies on the division of labor and the law of comparative advantage to focus on what it does best, while depending on other firms to supply component parts, payroll services, data processing, building security, and other inputs that are beyond that firm's "core competency." Firms, particularly manufacturing firms, have long purchased some components from other firms, but the outsourcing movement extended these purchases to a broader range of products and activities that typically had been produced internally. Japanese firms pioneered outsourcing to reduce production costs and enhance quality. In the United States, outsourcing blossomed in manufacturing during the 1980s and spread to virtually every industry. The boom in outsourcing has created many new firms that specialize in supplying what some firms no longer want to do for themselves.

For example, faced with outdated computer hardware and software, Bethlehem Steel executives realized they could no longer hire and retain enough skilled people to keep up with the changes in such a dynamic field. So Bethlehem outsourced its management information system. Dell Computer, a large mail-order personal computer vendor, turned over all shipping responsibility to an outside firm. Du Pont outsourced responsibility for shipping all imports and exports. And a growing number of computer makers are outsourcing computer assembly.

Outsourcing A firm sticks to its core competency, while buying inputs such as auto parts from outside suppliers

Amazon.com offers more than a million book titles plus CDs and videos, but it has no inventory and no real store—its bookstore being a virtual one on the Internet. Many Internet companies are just order-takers that pass these orders along to a local retailer. TopsyTail sells millions of its simple hair-styling gadgets, but the company has only a few employees. Nearly everything the company does—design, production, marketing, forecasting, packaging, and distribution—is carried out by subcontractors. The founder says the company could not have grown so fast any other way.

What are the limits to outsourcing? One cost of outsourcing can be a loss of control. For example, when Compaq Computer outsourced some laptop-computer production to a Japanese producer, problems mushroomed in design, production, cost, and quality. Compaq now has a separate management team to oversee outsourced activities. Some companies fear that outsourcing can weaken ties with customers. For example, several auto manufacturers had to recall a total of 8 million vehicles because of faulty seat belts from a Japanese supplier. Customers blamed the auto companies for the recall, not the subcontractor.

Recently, there has been a modest move back to more in-house production. For example, because of better software and cheaper computers, some companies are now "insourcing" many of the data processing activities once supplied by other firms. Insourcing reduces the number of times that records must be handled, improving data quality and reducing errors. Chrysler, before it merged with Daimler-Benz, considered outsourcing its data processing, but its own division was the low bidder. Because computer software has made Harley-Davidson more efficient, the company now makes more of its own motorcycle components. By taking back or keeping key production steps in house, some managers think they can respond more flexibly to custom orders and changing market conditions.

Sources: Julia King, "Farming Out Everything: TopsyTail Focus," *Computerworld* (23 March 1998); Saul Hansell, "On the Internet Clock, Middlemen Are Turning into Manufacturers," *New York Times* (26 July 1998); and Loise Lee, "Hiring Outside Firms to Run Computers Isn't Always a Bargain," *Wall Street Journal* (18 May 1995). Amazon Books can be found at www.amazon.com.

Economies of Scope

Thus far we have considered issues affecting the optimal degree of vertical integration in producing a particular product. Even with outsourcing, the focus is on how best to produce a particular product, such as an automobile or a computer. But sometimes firms branch out into product lines that do not have a vertical relationship. **Economies of scope** exist when it is cheaper to combine two or more product lines in one firm than to produce them in separate firms. For example, General Electric produces hundreds of different products ranging from light bulbs to jet engines, because outlays for research and development and marketing can be minimized when spread over different products. Ford Motor Company owns Hertz Rent-A-Car. Travelers Insurance and Citibank merged to offer consumers a worldwide smorgasbord of financial services. Or consider economies of scope on the farm. A farmer often grows a variety of crops and raises different kinds of farm animals—animals that recycle damaged crops and food scraps into useful fertilizer. With economies of *scale,* the average cost per unit of output falls as the *scale* of the firm increases; *with economies of scope, average costs per unit fall as the scope of the firm increases—that is, as the firm produces more types of products.* The cost of some fixed resources, such as specialized knowledge, can be spread across product lines.

Economies of scope Forces that make it cheaper for a firm to produce two or more different products rather than just one

Some combinations of production don't work out. For example, in 1994 The Quaker Oats Company paid $1.7 billion for the Snapple drink business. Over the next three years, Snapple sales dropped. Quaker sold its Snapple division in 1997 for $300 million, or less than one-fifth the purchase price. Likewise, AT&T bought NCR for $7.5 billion in 1991 and spent another $2 billion trying to make the marriage work. In 1997, NCR was sold for $3.4 billion—a huge loss. In short, many mergers of firms in different business lines do not yield the expected economies of scope.

Our focus thus far has been on why firms exist, why they often integrate vertically, why they outsource, and why they often produce a whole range of products. These steps toward greater realism move us beyond the simple depiction of the firm employed earlier. The rest of the chapter challenges some simplifying assumptions about how much information is available to market participants.

MARKET BEHAVIOR WITH IMPERFECT INFORMATION

For the most part, our analysis of market behavior has assumed that market participants have full information about products and resources. For consumers, full information involves knowledge about a product's price, quality, and availability. For firms, full information includes knowledge about the marginal productivity of various resources, about the appropriate technology for combining them, and about the demand for the firm's product. In reality, *reliable information is costly for both consumers and producers.* What's more, in some markets, one side of a transaction has better information than does the other side of the transaction. This section examines the impact of less-than-perfect information on market behavior.

NetBookmark

For most American households, their house is the single biggest investment they will ever make. The larger the investment, the more worthwhile it is to gather information. The search process is made easier with http://www.realtor.com, the official Web site of the National Association of Realtors. What types of information are provided on the introductory Web page? From there you can search for homes for sale in any part of the country, filtering the selection according to various criteria. Try finding a home you might like. Notice that the listings do not include an address for the house. Why do you suppose this most important fact is not given? Information about how to buy a house also abounds on the Web. For example, Microsoft gives free home buying advice at http://homeadvisor.msn.com/ie/.

Optimal Search with Imperfect Information

Suppose you want to buy a new computer. You need information about the quality and features of each model and the prices of each model at various retail outlets, mail-order firms, and Internet sites. To learn more about your choices, you may read promotional brochures and computer publications and visit the Web. You may also talk with experts.

Once you narrow your choice to one or two models, you may price-shop by going from store to store or by letting your fingers do the walking through the *Yellow Pages,* computer catalogs, Internet search engines, newspaper ads, and the like. Searching for the lowest price involves a cost, primary the opportunity cost of your time. This cost will obviously vary from individual to individual and from item to item. Some people actually enjoy shopping, but this "shop-'til-you-drop" attitude does not necessarily carry over to all items. *For most of us, the process of gathering consumer information can be considered nonmarket work.*

Marginal Cost of Search. In your quest for product information, you gather the easy and obvious information first, such as the range of products on the market and where these products are sold. For example, you may check on the price and availability at the few computer stores at the mall. But as your search widens, the *marginal cost* of acquiring additional information increases, both because you may have to travel greater distances to check prices and services and because the opportunity cost of your time increases as you spend more time acquiring information. Consequently, the marginal cost curve for additional information slopes upward, as is shown in Exhibit 2. Note the assumption in Exhibit 2 is that some amount of information, as shown by I_f, is common knowledge and is freely available.

Marginal Benefit of Search. The *marginal benefit* from acquiring additional information is any improvement you uncover in the quality of the product of a given price or any reduction in the price of a product of given quality. The marginal benefit is relatively large at first, but as you gather more information and

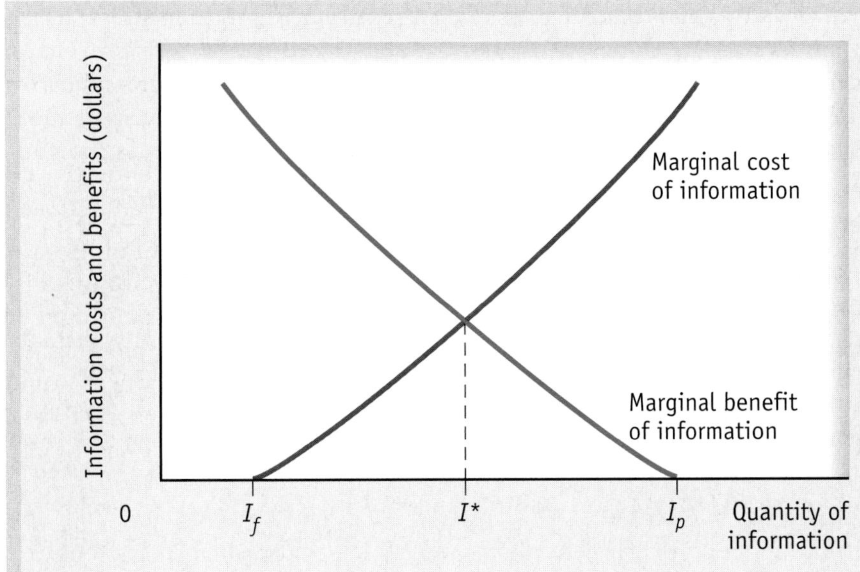

EXHIBIT 2

Optimal Search with Imperfect Information

When information is costly, additional information is acquired as along as its marginal benefit exceeds its marginal cost. Equilibrium, or optimal search, occurs where marginal benefit equals marginal cost.

grow more acquainted with the market, additional information yields less and less additional benefit. For example, the likelihood of uncovering valuable information, such as an attractive feature or a lower price, at the second store visited is greater than finding this information at the twentieth store visited. Thus the marginal benefit curve for additional information slopes downward, as is shown in Exhibit 2.

Optimal Search. Market participants will continue to gather information as long as the marginal benefit of additional information exceeds its marginal cost. *Optimal search occurs where the marginal benefit just equals the marginal cost,* which in Exhibit 2 occurs where the two curves intersect. Note that at search levels exceeding the equilibrium amount, the marginal benefit of additional information is still positive, but it's below the marginal cost. Note also that at some point the value of additional information reaches zero, as identified by I_p on the horizontal axis. This level of information could be identified as complete information or *perfect information*. The high marginal cost of acquiring I_p, however, makes it impractical to become perfectly informed. Thus firms and consumers, by gathering the optimal amount of information, I^*, have less-than-perfect information about the price, availability, and quality of products and resources.

Implications. The search model we have presented was developed by George Stigler, winner of the Nobel prize in 1982. Nearly four decades ago, he showed that the price of a product can differ among sellers because some consumers are unaware of lower prices offered by some sellers.[2] Thus, *search costs result in price dispersion, or different prices, for the same product.* Some sellers call attention to price dispersions by claiming to have the lowest prices around and by promising to

2 George Stigler, "The Economics of Information," *Journal of Political Economy* (June 1961): 213–225.

match any competitor's price. *Search costs also lead to quality differences across sellers, even for identically priced products, because consumers find it too costly to shop for a higher-quality product.*

There are other implications of Stigler's search model. The more expensive the commodity, the greater the price dispersion in dollar terms. Thus, the more expensive the item, the greater the incentive to shop around. Also, as the consumer's wage rises, the opportunity cost of time increases. This increases the marginal cost of additional information, resulting in less search and more price dispersion in the market. On the other hand, any change in technology that lowers the marginal cost of information will reduce the marginal cost of additional information, resulting in more information and less price dispersion. For example, some Internet search engines identify the lowest price for products offered by booksellers, airlines, computers, and dozens of other products. Some Internet sellers, such as Buycomp, maintain the lowest prices on the Web as a way of attracting customers carrying out such searches.

The Winner's Curse

In 1996 the federal government auctioned off leases to valuable space on the scarce radio spectrum. The space can be used for newly invented personal communications services, such as pocket telephones, portable fax machines, and wireless computer networks. The bidding was carried out in the face of much uncertainty about future competition in the industry, the potential size of the market, and future technological change. Thus bidders had little experience with the potential value of such leases. At the time, 89 companies made winning bids for 493 licenses, totaling $10.2 billion. But by 1998 it became clear that many of the winning bidders could not pay, and dozens of licenses were tied up in bankruptcy proceedings.[3] The auction eventually raised only half the amount of the winning bids. In auctions for products of uncertain value, such as wireless communications licenses or drilling rights in the Gulf of Mexico, why do many "winners" end up losers?

The actual value of space on the radio spectrum was unknown and could only be estimated. For example, suppose the average bid price was $10 million, with some companies bidding more and others bidding less. Suppose also that the winning bid was $20 million. The winning bid was not the average bid, which may have been the most reliable estimate of the true value, but the highest bid, which was the most optimistic estimate. Winners of such bids are said to experience the **winner's curse** because they often lose money after winning the bid. The winner's curse applies to all cases of bidding in which the true value is unknown at the outset. For example, movie companies often bid up the price of screenplays to what many argue are unrealistic values. Likewise, publishers get into bidding wars over book manuscripts and even book proposals that are little more than titles. Sports team owners bid for free agents and often overpay. CBS lost money on the 1998 Winter Olympics, and NBC may have overbid by offering $2.3 billion for the rights to broadcast the Olympics in the years 2002, 2006, and 2008; at the time of the bid, Olympic cities had not yet been selected. If there were perfect information about the market value of a resource, potential buyers would never bid more than the market value. But when

Winner's curse The plight of the winning bidder for an asset of uncertain value who has overestimated the asset's true value

3 See Scott Ritter, "FCC Says Several Bidders to Return Wireless Licenses," *Wall Street Journal* (18 June 1998).

competitive bidding is coupled with imperfect information, the winning bidder often loses money on the deal.

ASYMMETRIC INFORMATION IN PRODUCT MARKETS

Thus far we have considered the effects of costly information and limited information on market behavior. The issue becomes more complicated when one side of the market has more reliable information than does the other side, a situation in which there is **asymmetric information.** This section examines several examples of asymmetric information in the product market and the effect on market efficiency.

Asymmetric information A situation in which one side of the market has more reliable information than the other side does

There are two types of information that a market participant may want but lack. First, one side of the market may know more about *characteristics* of the product for sale than the other side knows. For example, the seller of a used car knows more about that car's record of reliability than does the buyer. Likewise, the buyer of a health insurance policy knows more about his or her general state of health than does the insurance company. When one side of the market knows more than the other side about product characteristics that are important in the transaction, the asymmetric information problem involves **hidden characteristics.**

Hidden characteristics A type of asymmetric information problem in which one side of the market knows more than the other side about product characteristics that are important to the other side of the market

A second type of asymmetric information problem occurs when one side of a transaction can pursue an *action* that affects the other side but that cannot be observed by the other side. For example, the mechanic you hire to check out that strange noise in your car engine may undertake unneeded repairs, charging three hours' work for a job that should have taken only 10 minutes. Whenever one side of an economic relationship can take a relevant action that the other side cannot observe, the situation is described as one of **hidden actions.**

Hidden actions A type of asymmetric information when one side of an economic relationship can take a relevant action that the other side cannot observe

Hidden Characteristics: Adverse Selection

One type of hidden-characteristic situation occurs when sellers know more about the quality of the product than do buyers, such as with the market for used cars. The seller of a used car normally has abundant experience with important *characteristics* of that car: breakdowns, accidents, gas mileage, record of maintenance, performance in bad weather, and so on. A prospective buyer can only guess at these based on the car's appearance and perhaps a test drive. The buyer cannot really know how good the car is without driving it for several months under varying traffic and weather conditions. So buyers of used cars have less information than sellers do.

To simplify the problem, suppose there are only two types of used cars for sale: good ones and bad ones, or "lemons." Again, only the seller knows which type is for sale. Suppose that a buyer who is certain about a car's type would be willing to pay $10,000 for a good used car but only $4,000 for a lemon. A buyer who believes that half the used cars on the market are good ones and half are lemons would be willing to pay, say, $7,000 for a car of unknown type (the average perceived value of cars on the market). Would $7,000 be the equilibrium price of used cars?

So far, the analysis has ignored the actions of potential sellers, who know which type of cars they have. Since sellers of good cars can get only $7,000 for cars they know to be worth $10,000 on average, many will choose not to sell their cars or will sell them to friends or relatives. But sellers of lemons will find $7,000 an attractive price, since they know their cars are worth only $4,000 on average. As a result, the proportion of good cars on the market will fall and the proportion of lemons will increase, reducing the average value of available used cars.

As buyers come to realize that the mix has shifted toward lemons, they will reduce the amount they are willing to pay for a car of unknown quality. As the market price of used cars falls, potential sellers of good cars become even more reluctant to sell at such a low price, so the proportion of lemons increases still more, leading to lower prices still. The process could continue until there were very few good cars sold on the open market. More generally, *when sellers have better information about a product's quality than buyers do, lower-quality products tend to dominate the market.*

Adverse selection A situation in which those on the informed side of the market self-select in a way that harms the uninformed side of the market

When those on the informed side of the market self-select in a way that harms the uninformed side of the market, the problem is one of **adverse selection.** In our example, car sellers, the informed parties, self-select—that is, decide whether to offer their cars for sale—in a way that increases the percentage of lemons for sale. Because of this adverse selection, car buyers, the uninformed side of the market, end up trading primarily with owners of lemons—exactly the group buyers do not want to deal with.

Hidden Actions: Principal-Agent Problem

In this age of specialization, there are many tasks we do not do for ourselves because others do them better and because others have a lower opportunity cost of time. Suppose your objective is to get your car repaired, but you don't know how to repair it yourself. The mechanic you hire may have other objectives, such as maximizing on-the-job leisure or maximizing the garage's revenue. But the mechanic's actions are hidden from you. Even though your car may have only a loose electrical wire, the mechanic could inflate the bill by charging you for "repairs" that were not really needed or that were not performed. This asymmetric information problem occurs because one side of a transaction can pursue *hidden actions* that affect the other side. When buyers have difficulty monitoring and evaluating the quality of goods or services purchased, some suppliers may substitute poor-quality resources or exercise less diligence in providing the service.

Principal-agent problem A situation in which the agent's objectives differ from those of the principal's objectives and the agent can pursue hidden actions

Principal A person who enters into a contractual agreement with an agent in the expectation that the agent will act on behalf of the principal

Agent A person who performs work or provides a service on behalf of another person, the principal

The problem that arises from hidden actions is called the **principal-agent problem,** which describes a relationship in which one party, known as the **principal,** makes a contractual agreement with another party, known as the **agent,** in the expectation that the agent will act on behalf of the principal. *The problem arises when the goals of the agent are incompatible with those of the principal and when the agent can pursue hidden actions.* You could confront a principal-agent problem when you deal with a doctor, lawyer, auto mechanic, or financial advisor, to name a few. Any employer-employee relationship could potentially be a source of a principal-agent problem. The owners of a corporation are the principals and the managers are the agents. Again, the problem arises because the agent's objectives are not the same as the principal's *and* because the agent's actions are hidden. Not all principal-agent relationships pose a problem. For example, when you hire someone to mow your lawn or cut your hair, there are no hidden actions and you are able to judge the results.

Asymmetric Information in Insurance Markets

Asymmetric information also creates problems in insurance markets. For example, from an insurance company's point of view, ideal candidates for health insurance are those who will lead long, healthy lives, then die peacefully in their sleep. But many people are poor risks for health insurers because of hidden characteristics (bad genes) or hidden actions (smoking and drinking excessively, getting exercise only on trips to the refrigerator, and thinking a seven-course meal consists of beef jerky and a six-pack of beer). In the insurance market, it is the buyers, not the sellers, who have more information about the characteristics and actions that predict their likely need for insurance in the future.

If the insurance company has no way of distinguishing among applicants, it must charge those who are poor health risks the same premiums as those who are good health risks. This rate is attractive to poor health risks, but will seem too high to good health risks, some of whom will choose to self-insure. As the number of healthy people who self-insure increases, the insurance pool becomes less healthy on average, so rates must rise, making insurance even less attractive to healthy people. Because of adverse selection, insurance buyers tend to be less healthy than the population as a whole. Adverse selection has been used as an argument for a universal national health insurance program.

The insurance problem is compounded by the fact that once people buy insurance, their behavior may change in a way that increases the probability that a claim will be made. For example, after buying theft insurance, people may take less care of their valuables. This incentive problem is referred to as *moral hazard*. **Moral hazard** occurs when an individual's behavior changes in a way that increases the likelihood of an unfavorable outcome.

Moral hazard A situation in which one party to a contract has an incentive after the contract is made to alter behavior in a way that harms the other party to the contract

More generally, *moral hazard is a principal-agent problem since it occurs when those on one side of a transaction have an incentive to shirk their responsibilities because the other side is unable to observe them*. The responsibility could be to repair a car or to safeguard valuables. In the car-repair example, the mechanic is the agent; in the insurance example, the policy buyer is the principal. Both the mechanic and the policy buyer may take advantage of the ignorant party. Thus moral hazard arises on the part of the party that can undertake hidden action; this could be either the agent or the principal, depending on the circumstance.

Coping with Asymmetric Information

There are ways of reducing the consequences of asymmetric information. An incentive structure or an information-revealing system can be developed to reduce the problems associated with the lopsided availability of information. For example, some states have passed "lemon laws" that offer compensation to buyers of new or used cars that turn out to be lemons. Used-car dealers also usually offer warranties to reduce the buyer's risk of getting stuck with a lemon. Some auto-repair garages provide written estimates before a job is done and return the defective parts to the customer as evidence that the repair was necessary and was carried out. Consumers often get multiple estimates for major expenditures and may seek second and third opinions on medical procedures.

Health insurance companies deal with adverse selection and moral hazard in a variety of ways. Most require applicants to take a physical exam and to answer questions about their medical histories. A policy often covers all those in a group, such as all company employees, not just those who would otherwise self-select. Such group policies avoid the problem of adverse selection. Insurers reduce moral hazard by making the policyholder pay, say, the first $250 of a claim as a "deductible" or by requiring the policyholder to pay a certain percentage of a claim. Also, the premiums on some automobile and theft policies go up, and policies may be canceled as more claims are filed.

ASYMMETRIC INFORMATION IN LABOR MARKETS

Our market analysis for particular kinds of labor typically assumed that workers are identical. In equilibrium, each worker in a particular labor market is assumed to be paid the same wage, a wage that is equal to the marginal revenue product of the last unit of labor hired. But what if ability differs across workers?

Differences in worker ability present no particular problem as long as these differences can be readily observed by the employer. If the productivity of each particular worker is easily quantified through a measure such as the quantity of oranges picked, the number of garments sewed, or the number of cars sold, that measure itself can and does serve as the basis for pay. But because production often takes place through the coordinated efforts of several workers, the employer may not be able to attribute specific outputs to each particular worker. Because information about each worker's marginal productivity is hard to come by, employers usually pay workers by the hour rather than keep track of each worker's contribution to total output.

Often the pay is some combination of an hourly rate and incentive pay linked to a measure of productivity. For example, a sales representative typically receives a base salary plus a commission tied to the amount sold. At times, the task of evaluating performance is left to the consumer rather than to the firm. Workers who provide personal services, such as waiters and waitresses, barbers and beauticians, pizza deliverers, and bellhops, are paid partly in tips. Since these services are by definition "personal," customers are in the best position to judge the quality and timeliness of service and to tip accordingly.

Adverse-Selection Problems in Labor Markets

An adverse-selection problem arises in the labor market when labor suppliers have better information about their own productivities than do employers, because a worker's ability is not easily observed prior to employment. Before the individual is hired, a worker's true abilities—motivation, work habits, skills, ability to get along with others, and the like—are, to a large extent, *hidden characteristics.*

Suppose an employer wants to hire a program coordinator for a new project, a job that calls for imagination, organizational skills, and the ability to work independently. The employer would like to attract the most qualified person in the market, but the qualities demanded are not directly observable. The employer offers a market wage for such a position. Individual workers have a good idea of their own intelligence and creativity and are able to evaluate this wage in view of their own abilities and opportunities. Talented people will find that wage to be below the true value of their abilities and will be less inclined to apply for the job. Less-talented individuals, however, will find that the offered wage exceeds their marginal productivity, so they will be more likely to seek the job. Because of adverse selection, the employer ends up with a pool of applicants of below-average ability. In a labor market with hidden characteristics, employers might be better off offering a higher wage. The higher the wage, the more attractive the job is to more-qualified workers. Paying a higher wage also encourages workers not to goof off or otherwise do anything that would risk losing an attractive job. So paying a high wage gets at the problem of hidden actions by workers. Paying a higher wage to attract and retain more-productive workers is called paying **efficiency wages,** a theory also discussed in macroeconomics.

Efficiency wage theory The idea that offering high wages attracts a more talented labor pool, making it easier for firms to hire more productive workers; also a higher wage that encourages those more productive workers to do a good job

Signaling and Screening

The side of the market with hidden characteristics and hidden actions has an incentive to say the right thing. For example, a job applicant might say, "Hire me because I am hard-working, reliable, prompt, highly motivated, and just an all-around great employee." Or a producer might say, "At Ford, quality is job one." But such direct claims of quality appear self-serving and therefore are not necessarily believable. So both sides of the market have an incentive to develop credible ways of communicating reliable information.

Therefore, adverse selection may give rise to **signaling,** which is the attempt by the informed side of the market to communicate information that the other side would find valuable. Consider signaling in the job market. Because the true requirements for many jobs are qualities that are unobservable on a résumé or in an interview, job applicants offer evidence of the unobservable features by relying on proxy measures, such as years of education, college grades, and letters of recommendation. A proxy measure is called a *signal,* which is an observable indicator of some hidden characteristic. A signal is sent by the informed side of the market to the uninformed side and will serve as a useful way of sorting out applicants as long as less qualified applicants have more difficulty sending the signal.

Signaling Using a proxy measure to communicate information about unobservable characteristics; the signal is more effective if more productive workers find it easier to send the signal than do less productive workers

In order to identify the best workers, employers try to *screen* applicants. **Screening** is the attempt by the uninformed side of the market to uncover the relevant but hidden characteristics of the informed party. An initial screen might be to check each résumé for spelling and typographical errors. Although not important in themselves, such errors indicate a lack of attention to detail—attention to detail that could prove important on the job. The uninformed party must find signals that less-productive individuals will have more difficulty sending. A signal that can be sent with equal ease or difficulty by all workers, regardless of their productivity, does not provide a useful way of screening applicants. But if, for example, more productive workers find it easier to succeed in college than do less-productive workers, a good college record is a measure worth using to screen workers. In this case, education may be valuable, not so much because of its effects on a worker's productivity, but because it enables employers to distinguish among types of workers. To summarize, an employer often cannot directly measure the potential productivity of job applicants, so the employer must rely

Screening The process used by employers to select the most qualified workers based on readily observable characteristics, such as level of education and course grades

on some proxy to screen applicants. The most valuable proxy is one that best reflects future productivity.

The problems of adverse selection, signaling, and screening are discussed in the following case study of McDonald's.

CaseStudy

The Information Economy

McDonald's maintains a Web site devoted to information about obtaining a franchise at http://www.mcdonalds.com/corporate/franchise/index.html. Look over the FAQ file. How much cash does a potential franchisee currently need in order to qualify? How many partners can be involved in a franchise? Who selects the sites and who constructs the building? For more detail on life as a franchisee, download the franchising brochures available in PDF format.

The Reputation of a Big Mac

McDonald's has over 15,000 restaurants and is opening more than 500 a year. The secret to their success is that customers can count on product consistency whether they are buying a Big Mac in Anchorage, Moscow, or Singapore. McDonald's has grown because it has attracted competent and reliable franchise owners and has provided these owners with appropriate incentives and constraints.

To avoid adverse selection, McDonald's seldom advertises for franchisees, but it still averages more than 10 applicants for each new franchise. To be granted an interview, applicants must show sufficient financial resources and adequate business experience. Those who pass an initial screening must come up with a security deposit and must complete the 12- to 18-month training program. During this period, the individual is paid nothing, not even expenses. Some who complete the training are rejected for a franchise. Those accepted may wait up to three years for their own restaurants. Once the restaurant opens, a franchisee is required to work full-time in its daily operation and is also encouraged to become involved in community service.

Franchisees make a huge commitment of time and money. Forty percent of the $400,000 to $675,000 cost of a new restaurant must come from the franchisee's own savings, not from borrowed funds. Thus the franchisee has a clear financial stake in the success of the operation. And the fact that the potential franchisee saved so much reflects some financial competence.

The franchisee cannot sell the restaurant without prior approval and the company retains the right to better any offer for the restaurant. Any buyer must have company approval and must complete the same training program as all other franchisees.

Because each franchisee gets a large share of the restaurant's operating profit, there is a strong incentive to be efficient. As a further reward, successful operators may get additional restaurants. If all goes well, the franchise is valid for 20 years and renewable after that, but it can be canceled *at any time* if the restaurant fails the company's standards of quality, pricing, cleanliness, hours of operation, and so on. Thus, the franchisee is bound to the company by highly specific investments of money and time, such as the time required to learn McDonald's operating system. The loss of a franchise could represent the loss of the individual's life savings. In selecting and monitoring franchisees, McDonald's has successfully addressed problems stemming from hidden characteristics and hidden actions.

Source: D. L. Noren, "The Economics of the Golden Arches," *American Economist* (Fall 1990): 60–64; Richard Gibson, "McDonald's Sales Fail to Meet Projected Plans and Ad Outlays, *Wall Street Journal Interactive Edition* (10 April 1998); Dana Canedy, "McDonald's Alters System for Kitchens," *New York Times* (27 March 1998); and McDonald's home page at http://www.mcdonalds.com/.

CONCLUSION

The firm has evolved through a natural selection process as the form of organization that minimizes both transaction and production costs. According to this theory of natural selection, those forms of organization that are most efficient will be selected by the economic system for survival. Attributes that yield an economic profit will thrive, and those that do not will fall by the wayside. The form of organization selected may not be optimal in the sense that it cannot be improved upon, but it will be the most efficient of those that have been tried. If there is a way to organize production that is more efficient than the firm, some entrepreneur will stumble upon it one day and will be rewarded with greater profit. Thus the improvement may not be the result of any conscious design. Once a more efficient way of organizing production is uncovered, others will imitate the successful innovation.

Problems created by asymmetric information are not reflected in the simple account of how markets work. In conventional demand-and-supply analysis, trades occur in impersonal markets, and the buyer has no special concern about who is on the selling side. But with asymmetric information, the mix and characteristics of the other side of the market become important. When the problem of adverse selection is severe enough, some markets may cease to function. Market participants try to overcome the limitations of asymmetric information by signaling, screening, and trying to be quite explicit and transparent about the terms of the transaction.

SUMMARY

1. According to Ronald Coase, firms exist because production often can be accomplished more efficiently through the hierarchy of the firm than through a series of market transactions. Because production requires the extensive coordination of transactions among many resource owners, all this activity can usually be carried out more efficiently under the direction of a manager in a firm than by consumers specifying detailed performance contracts with many separate suppliers.

2. The extent to which a firm integrates vertically will depend on both the transaction and the production costs of economic activity. Other things constant, the firm is more likely to buy a component part than to produce it if (1) the item can be purchased for less than the firm would spend to make it, (2) the item is well defined and its quality is easily observable, and (3) there are many suppliers of the item. Economies of scope exist when it is cheaper to produce two or more types of products in one firm than to produce them in separate firms.

3. A buyer acquires additional information as long as the marginal benefit exceeds the marginal cost of searching for that information. In equilibrium, the marginal cost of information equals the marginal benefit. Because information is costly, the same good may be offered for different prices by different sellers.

4. Asymmetric information occurs when one side of the market is better informed about the quality of a product than the other side. The uninformed party may not know about hidden characteristics or about hidden actions. Because of adverse selection, those on the uninformed side of the market may find they are dealing with exactly the wrong people.

5. When the productivity of potential employees is not directly observable, employers sometimes try to screen workers based on some signal that more productive workers can send more easily than less productive workers can.

QUESTIONS FOR REVIEW

1. *(Rationale for the Firm)* Explain Ronald Coase's theory of why firms exist. Why isn't all production consolidated in one large firm?

2. *(Bounds of the Firm)* Define vertical integration. What factors should a firm consider when determining the degree of vertical integration to undertake?

3. *(Bounds of the Firm)* Ashland Oil, Inc., is an oil refiner that buys its crude oil in the market. Larger oil companies, such as Texaco, have their own crude oil production facilities. Why do some oil companies drill for their own crude oil and others buy crude oil in the market?

4. **(CaseStudy:** *The Trend Toward Outsourcing)* In the movement to downsize government, advocates often recommend turning over some government services to private firms hired by the government. What are the potential benefits and costs of such outsourcing? Prepare your answer by reviewing The Outsourcing Institute's "Top 10 Reasons Companies Outsource" at http://www.outsourcing.com/howandwhy/top10.

5. *(Economies of Scope)* Distinguish between economies of scale and economies of scope. Why do some firms produce multiple product lines, while others produce only one?

6. *(Search with Imperfect Information)* Fifty years ago, people shopped by mail using catalogs from large mail-order houses. In the last few years, catalog shopping has again become a widely used method of buying. On-line shopping is also growing. What reasons can you suggest for the growth in these forms of shopping?

7. *(Asymmetric Information)* Define asymmetric information. Distinguish between hidden characteristics and hidden actions. Which type of asymmetric information contributes to the principal-agent problem?

8. *(The Principal-Agent Problem)* Discuss the nature of the principal-agent problem. Determine which is the principal and which is the agent in each of the following relationships:
   a. A firm that produces export goods and the export management company that helps market its goods
   b. The management of a firm and its stockholders
   c. A homeowner and the plumber hired to make repairs
   d. A dentist and a patient
   e. An employee-pension management firm and the company using its services

9. *(Adverse Selection and Moral Hazard)* Describe the problems faced by health insurance companies as a result of adverse selection and moral hazard. How do insurance companies try to reduce these problems?

10. *(Signaling)* Give an example of signaling in each of the following situations:
    a. Choosing a doctor
    b. Applying to graduate school
    c. Filling out a form for a dating service

11. *(Signaling and Screening)* What roles do signaling and screening play in a labor market with asymmetric information?

12. **(CaseStudy:** *The Reputation of a Big Mac)* Explain how the time and financial requirements involved in obtaining a McDonald's franchise relate to the hidden-characteristics problem. Why would each franchise owner have an interest in the maintenance of high application standards for new franchise owners?

PROBLEMS AND EXERCISES

13. *(Search with Imperfect Information)* The following questions concern the accompanying graph.
    a. Identify the two curves shown on the graph, and explain their upward or downward slopes.
    b. Why does curve A intersect the horizontal axis?
    c. What is the significance of quantity *d*?
    d. What does point *e* represent?
    e. How would the optimal quantity of information change if the marginal benefit of information increased; that is, if the marginal benefit curve shifted upward?

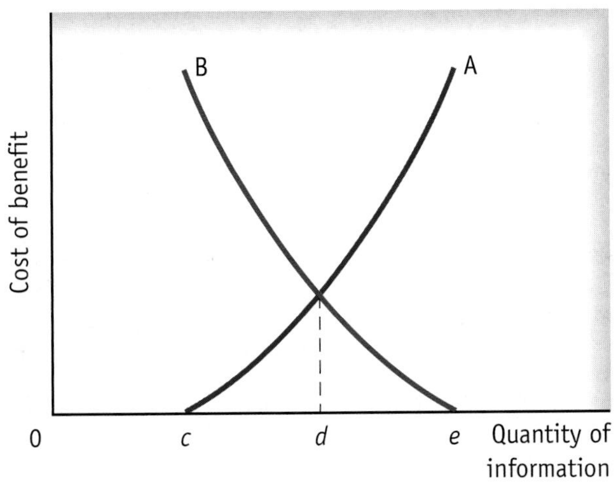

14. *(Search with Imperfect Information)* Determine the effect of each of the following on the optimal level of search.
    a. The consumer's income increases.
    b. One seller guarantees to offer the lowest price on the market.
    c. The technology of gathering and transmitting information improves.

EXPERIENTIAL EXERCISES

15. *(Market Behavior with Imperfect Information)* Kenneth Arrow, a Nobel laureate, has contributed many important ideas in the economics of information. Read the interview with Arrow in *The Region* at http://woodrow.mpls.frb.fed.us/pubs/region/int9512.html. What does he think are the policy implications that arise because of imperfect information?

16. *(Adverse Selection)* Adverse selection is a serious problem for health insurers. As an example, read the brief analysis in "Medical Savings Accounts for Medicare" at http://www.public-policy.org/~ncpa/ba/bal183.html. What is the mechanism by which adverse selection can make health insurance unprofitable for private insurers to provide?

17. *(Wall Street Journal)* Once you learn about the economics of asymmetric information, you begin to see examples all around you. To demonstrate this point, check today's *Wall Street Journal*. It should not be too hard to find a story that describes some new development that is a response to an asymmetric information problem. Look on the Economy page in the First Section or in the Marketplace section. When you've found an article, try to analyze it using the ideas developed in this chapter.

CHAPTER

28 Economic Regulation and Antitrust Activity

If the invisible hand of competition yields such desirable results for the economy, why does the government need to stick its nose into people's business? When is monopoly good for the economy and when is it harmful? Who benefits most when government tries to regulate monopoly? Why is government so interested in Microsoft? Is the U.S. economy more competitive now than it used to be? Answers to these and other questions are addressed in this chapter, which discusses government regulation of business.

It has been said that business people praise competition but love monopoly. They praise competition because it harnesses the diverse and often conflicting objectives of various market participants and channels them into the efficient production of goods and services. And competition does this "as

Visit the McEachern Interactive Study Center for this chapter at *http://mcisc.swcollege.com*

if by an invisible hand." Business people love monopoly because it provides the surest path to economic profit in the long run—and, after all, profit is the name of the game. The fruits of monopoly are so tempting that firms sometimes try to eliminate the competition or to conspire with them. As Adam Smith remarked more than 200 years ago, "People of the same trade seldom meet together, even for merriment or diversion, but the conversation ends in a conspiracy against the public, or in some contrivance to raise prices."

The tendency of firms to seek monopolistic advantage is understandable, but the pursuit of monopoly often harms the economy. Public policy can play a role by promoting competition in those markets where competition seems desirable and by reducing the harmful consequences of monopolistic behavior in those markets where the output can be most efficiently produced by one or a few firms. Topics discussed in this chapter include:

- Market power
- Regulating natural monopolies
- Theories of economic regulation
- Deregulation
- Antitrust activity
- Per-se illegality
- Rule of reason
- Merger movements
- Competitive trends

BUSINESS BEHAVIOR AND PUBLIC POLICY

You'll recall that a monopolist supplies a product with no close substitutes and so can charge a higher price than would prevail with more competition. When a few firms account for most of the sales in a market, those firms are sometimes able to coordinate their actions, either explicitly or implicitly, to approximate the behavior of a monopolist. This ability of one or more firms to maintain a price above the competitive level is termed **market power.** The presumption is that a monopoly or firms acting together as a monopoly will restrict output and charge a higher price than a competitive firm would. With output restricted, the marginal benefit of the final unit produced exceeds its marginal cost, so social welfare could be increased by expanding output. By failing to expand output to the point where marginal benefit equals marginal cost, monopoly misallocates resources.

Market power The ability of one or a few firms to maintain a price above the competitive level

Other distortions have also been associated with monopolies. For example, because monopolies are insulated from competition, many critics argue that they are not as innovative as aggressive competitors would be. Worse yet, because of their size and economic importance, monopolies have been said to exert a disproportionate influence on the political system, which they use to protect and enhance their monopoly power.

Social regulation Government regulations aimed at improving health and safety

Economic regulation Government regulations aimed at controlling prices, output, market entry and exit, and product quality in situations in which, because of economies of scale, average production costs are lowest when the market is served by only one or a few firms

Government Regulation of Business

There are three kinds of government policies designed to alter or control firm behavior: social regulation, economic regulation, and antitrust activity. **Social regulation** consists of government measures designed to improve health and safety, such as control over unsafe working conditions and dangerous products. **Economic regulation** is concerned with controlling the price, the output, the entry of new firms, and the quality of service *in industries in which monopoly appears inevitable or even desirable.* The regulation of *natural monopolies*, such as local electricity transmission and local phone service, is an example of this type of regulation. Several other industries, such as land and air transportation, have also been regulated, for reasons that will be discussed later in this chapter. Economic regulation is carried out by various regulatory bodies at the federal, state, and local levels.

Antitrust activity Government activity aimed at preventing monopoly and fostering competition in markets where competition is desirable

Antitrust activity attempts to prohibit firm behavior aimed at monopolizing, or cartelizing, markets where competition is desirable. Antitrust activity is pursued in the courts by government attorneys and by individual firms that charge other firms with violating antitrust laws

Both economic regulation and antitrust activity will be examined in this chapter. The first type of economic regulation we consider is the regulation of natural monopolies.

REGULATING NATURAL MONOPOLIES

Because of economies of scale, natural monopolies have a downward-sloping long-run average-cost curve over the entire range of market demand. This means that the lowest average cost is achieved when one firm serves the entire market. Local electricity transmission is an example of a good provided by a natural monopoly. If two competing electric transmission companies both strung their own wires throughout the community, the average cost per household would be higher than if a single provider wired the community.

Unregulated Profit Maximization

Exhibit 1 shows the demand and cost conditions for a natural monopoly. A natural monopoly usually faces large capital costs, such as those associated with laying the tracks for a railroad, putting a satellite in orbit, installing a natural gas pipeline, or stringing the wires to transmit electricity, local phone service, or cable TV signals. Because of heavy capital outlays, average cost tends to fall as production increases, so the average-cost curve slopes downward over a broad range of output. In this situation, the average cost of production is minimized when a single firm produces the market output.

We know that a monopolist, if unregulated, will choose the price-quantity combination that maximizes profit. In Exhibit 1, the monopolist maximizes profit by producing where marginal cost equals marginal revenue, which occurs at output level Q. The monopolist will charge price p and earn the economic profit identified by the purple-shaded rectangle. The problem is that the monopolist's choice of price and output is inefficient in terms of social welfare: Consumers pay a price that exceeds the marginal cost of producing the good. Economic welfare would improve if output were to expand, because the marginal value of additional output exceeds the marginal cost of that output.

Government has four options when dealing with a natural monopoly. First, government can do nothing. If left alone, a monopolist will maximize profits, as at price p in Exhibit 1, so inefficiency results. Second, government can sell the monopoly right to this market, such as the right to run concession stands at the municipal stadium. The winning bidder would still maximize profit at price p in Exhibit 1, but at least the winning monopolist would pay for the privilege, in the process increasing government revenue, which can be used to fund public goods or reduce taxes. Third, the government can own and operate the monopoly, as with the Tennessee Valley Authority, many urban electricity and transit systems, and state-run lotteries and liquor stores. And fourth, government can *regulate* a privately operated monopoly, as it does with local phone services. Government-owned or -regulated industries are called *public utilities.* The focus in this chapter will be on government regulation rather than government ownership, although the issues discussed are similar whether the government operates as a monopoly or regulates the monopoly. Many facets of a natural monopoly have been regulated, but the object of regulation that captures the most attention is the monopolist's price-output combination.

Setting Price Equal to Marginal Cost

Let's assume that government regulators decide to make the monopolist produce at the level of output that is allocatively efficient—that is, where price, or marginal value, equals marginal cost. Such a price-output combination is depicted as point *e* in Exhibit 1, where price equals marginal cost, yielding a price *p*' and quantity *Q*'. Consumers will clearly prefer this outcome because the

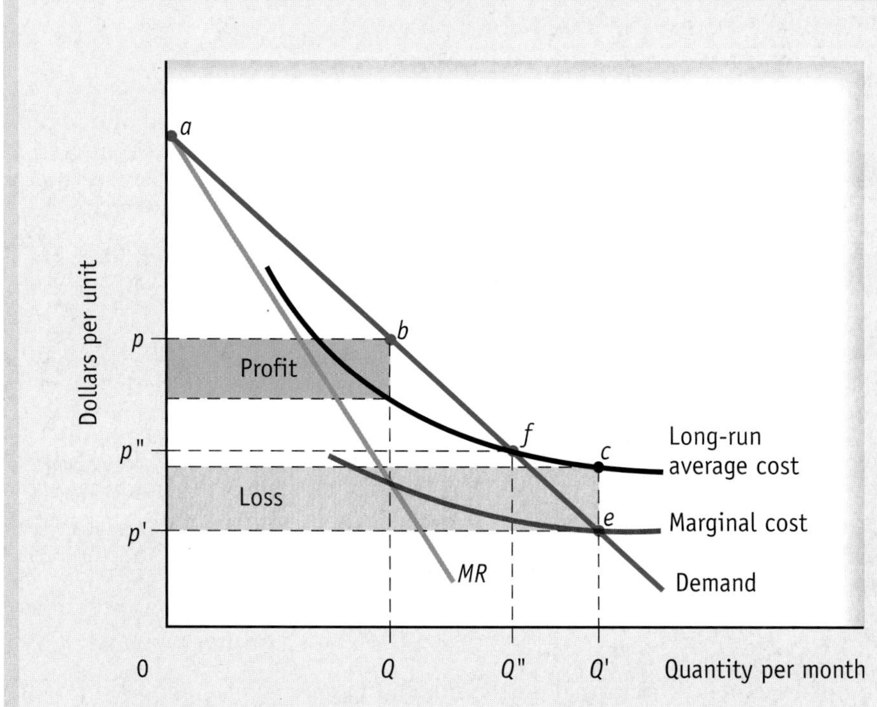

EXHIBIT 1

Regulating the Natural Monopoly

In a natural monopoly, the long-run average-cost curve slopes downward at its point of intersection with the market-demand curve. The unregulated firm produces output *Q* (where marginal cost equals marginal revenue) and charges price *p*. This situation is inefficient because price, or marginal benefit, exceeds marginal cost. To obtain the efficient level of output, government could regulate the monopolist's price. At price *p*', the monopoly would produce output *Q*'—an efficient solution. However, at that price and quantity, the firm would suffer a loss and require a subsidy. As an alternative, the government could set a price of *p*". The monopoly would produce output *Q*"—an inefficient level. Since *p*" equals the average cost, the firm would earn a normal profit and no subsidy would be required.

price is lower than when the monopolist is free to maximize profit. The consumer surplus, a measure of consumers' net gain from consuming this good, increases from triangle *abp* with profit maximization to *aep*' with regulation.

Notice, however, that the monopolist now has a problem. At output level Q', the regulated price, *p*', is below the firm's average total cost, identified as point *c*. Rather than earning a profit, the monopolist now suffers a loss, identified by the red-shaded rectangle. *Forcing the natural monopolist to produce where marginal cost equals price results in an economic loss.* In the long run, the monopolist would go out of business rather than continue suffering such a loss.

Subsidizing the Natural Monopolist

How can regulators encourage the monopolist to stay in business and yet produce where marginal cost equals price? One way is for the government to compensate the monopolist for the losses—to *subsidize* the firm so that it earns a normal profit. Bus and subway fares are typically set below the average cost of providing the service; the difference is made up through a government subsidy. For example, in 1996 the Washington, D.C., subway system received over $200 million in subsidies from the federal government; Amtrak also receives substantial federal subsidies. One problem with the subsidy solution is that, to provide the subsidy, the government must raise taxes, borrow more, or forgo spending in some other area.

Setting Price Equal to Average Cost

Although some public utilities are subsidized, most are not. Instead, the regulators attempt to establish a price that will provide the monopolist with a "fair return." Recall that the average-total-cost curve includes a normal profit. Thus, *setting price equal to average total cost* provides a normal, or "fair," profit for the monopolist. In Exhibit 1, the demand curve and the average cost curve intersect at point *f*, yielding a price of *p*" and a quantity of Q". Such a price will allow the monopolist to stay in business without a subsidy.

Setting price equal to average total cost enhances economic welfare relative to the unregulated situation, but the regulated monopolist would rather earn an economic profit. If given no other choice, however, the monopolist will continue to operate with a normal profit, since that is what could be earned if the resources were redirected to their most profitable alternative uses. Also, the marginal value that consumers attach to output level Q" exceeds the marginal cost of that output level. Therefore social welfare could be enhanced by expanding output until consumers' marginal value equals the marginal cost of production at *e*.

The Regulatory Dilemma

Setting price equal to marginal cost yields the *socially optimal* allocation of resources because *the marginal cost of producing the last unit sold equals the consumers' marginal value of that last unit.* For example, suppose the price of subway tokens is 50 cents, which is the marginal cost per rider on the subway system. With this pricing policy, however, the monopolist will face recurring losses unless a subsidy is provided. These losses disappear if price is set equal to average cost, which for the subway system is, say, $1.50. That higher price ensures that the monopolist earns a normal profit, but ridership is much lower than would be socially optimal. Thus the dilemma facing regulators is whether to require a price equal to marginal cost, which is socially optimal but which would require a subsidy, or to allow the monopolist to break even by setting price equal to average cost but thereby restrict ridership well below the socially optimal level. There is no right answer. Compared to point *b*, the outcome without regulation, either point *f* or point *e* reduces price, increases output, increases consumer surplus, eliminates economic profit, and increases social welfare.

Although Exhibit 1 neatly lays out the options, regulators usually face an unclear picture of things. Demand and costs can only be estimated, and the regulated firm may not always be completely forthcoming about cost information. For example, a utility may overstate its costs so it can charge a higher price and earn more profit.

ALTERNATIVE THEORIES OF ECONOMIC REGULATION

Why does government regulate certain markets? Why not let market forces allocate resources? There are two views of government regulation. The first view has been implicit in the discussion thus far—namely, that economic regulation is in the *public interest*. Economic regulation is designed to promote social welfare by controlling the price and output when a market is most efficiently served by one or just a few firms. A second view of economic regulation is that it is not in the public's, or consumers', best interest, but rather is in the *special interest* of producers. According to this view, *well-organized producer groups expect to profit from economic regulation and are able to persuade public officials to impose the restrictions existing producers find attractive, such as limiting entry into the industry or preventing competition among existing firms.* Individual producers have more to gain or lose from regulation than do individual consumers; producers typically are also better organized and more focused than consumers and therefore better able to bring about regulations that are favorable to them.

Producers Have a Special Interest in Economic Regulation

To understand how producer interests could influence public regulation, think back to the last time you got your hair cut. Most states regulate the training and licensing of hair professionals. If any new regulations affecting the profession are proposed, such as higher entry restrictions or longer training requirements, who do you suppose has more interest in the outcome of that legislation, you or a person who cuts hair for a living? *Producers have a strong interest in matters that affect their source of income, so they play a disproportionately large role in trying to influence such legislation.* If there are public hearings on haircut regulations, the industry will provide expert witnesses, while consumers will largely ignore the proceedings.

As a consumer, you do not specialize in getting haircuts. You purchase haircuts, socks, soft drinks, software, underwear, and thousands of other goods and services. You have no *special interest* in legislation affecting hair cutting. Some critics argue that because of this asymmetry between the interests of producers and consumers, business regulations often favor producer interests rather than consumer interests. Well-organized producer groups, as squeaky wheels in the legislative system, receive the most grease in the form of favorable regulations.

Legislation favoring producer groups is usually introduced under the guise of advancing consumer interests. Producer groups may argue that unbridled competition in their industry would lead to results that are undesirable for consumers. For example, the alleged problem of "cutthroat" competition among taxi drivers has led to regulations that eliminate price competition and limit the number of taxis in most large metropolitan areas. Or regulation may appear under the guise of quality control, as in the case of state control of professional groups such as barbers, doctors, and lawyers, in which case regulations are viewed as necessary to keep unlicensed "quacks" out of these professions.

The special-interest theory may be valid even when the initial intent of the legislation is in the consumer interest. Over time, the regulatory machinery may begin to act more in accord with the special interests of producers, because producers' political power and strong stake in the regulatory outcome lead them, in effect, to "capture" the regulating agency and prevail upon it to serve producers. This *capture theory* of regulation was best explained by George Stigler, the Nobel prize winner mentioned in the previous chapter, who argued that "as a general rule, regulation is acquired by the industry and is designed and operated for its benefit."[1]

Perhaps it would be useful at this point to discuss in some detail the direction that economic regulation and, more recently, deregulation has taken in a particular industry—airlines.

*Case*Study

Public Policy

A review of the history of airline deregulation from a conservative viewpoint is available online from the Heritage Foundation's magazine at http://www.heritage.org/library/backgrounder/bg1173es.html. What actions was the Department of Transportation considering at the time this review was written? What non-regulatory alternatives does the author suggest? The concerns of airline pilots about employment security and getting what they see as their fair share of industry revenues are presented through the Airline Pilots' Association Web site at http://www.alpa.org/. What particular issues related to industry structure are of current concern to the pilots?

Airline Regulation and Deregulation

The interstate airline business was once closely regulated by the Civil Aeronautics Board (CAB), established in 1938. Any potential entrant interested in serving an interstate route had to persuade the CAB that the route needed another airline, a task that proved impossible. During the 40 years prior to deregulation, more than 150 applications for long-distance routes were submitted by potential entrants, *but not a single new interstate airline was allowed*. The CAB also forced strict compliance with regulated prices. A request to lower prices on any route would result in a rate hearing, during which the request was scrutinized by both the CAB and competitors. In effect, the CAB had created a cartel that fixed prices among the 10 existing major airlines.

Although the CAB prohibited price competition in the industry, *nonprice competition flourished*. Airlines competed on the basis of the frequency of flights, the quality of meals, the width of the seats, even the friendliness of the staff. For example, American Airlines put Wurlitzer pianos in its jumbo jet lounges. United Airlines countered with wine tastings and guitarists. Such competition

1 George Stigler, "The Theory of Economic Regulation," *Bell Journal of Economics and Management Science* (Spring 1971):3.

increased operating costs. Costs rose until firms in the industry earned only a normal rate of return. Thus, *air fares set above competitive levels, coupled with entry restrictions, were no guarantee of economic profit as long as airlines were free to compete in other ways, such as in the frequency of flights.*

The CAB did not regulate airlines that flew *intrastate* routes. The record shows that fares on intrastate airlines were about 50 percent below fares on identical routes flown by regulated airlines. So regulated airlines were more costly to consumers.

Airline Deregulation. In 1978, despite opposition from the major airlines and relevant labor unions, Congress passed the Airline Deregulation Act, which reduced restrictions on price competition and on new entry. By 1990, airline fares in inflation-adjusted dollars were about 10 to 18 percent lower because of deregulation. The fall in fares contributed to a doubling of passenger miles flown. The savings to travelers are estimated to exceed $12 billion per year. The airlines could afford to lower fares because they became more productive by adding more seats to planes and by filling a greater percentage of seats. The hub-and-spoke system developed under deregulation also allowed airlines to route planes more efficiently. Airline routes used to be straight lines from one city to another. Now they radiate like the spokes of a wagon wheel from a "hub" city. From 29 hub airports across the country, airlines send out planes along the spokes to the 400 commercial airports, then quickly bring them back to the hubs.

The insulation from price competition provided by regulation allowed firms to pay higher wages than they would have in a more competitive industry. The Air Line Pilots Association, the union that represented pilots for all the major airlines prior to deregulation, had been able to negotiate extremely attractive wages for its members, annual wages that reached into six digits for working less than two weeks a month (many pilots had so much free time, they pursued second careers). Just how attractive a pilot's position was became apparent after deregulation. America West Airlines, a nonunion firm that sprouted from deregulation, paid its pilots only $32,000 a year and required them to work 40 hours a week, performing dispatch and marketing tasks when they were not flying. Yet America West received more than 4,000 applications for its 29 pilot openings.

Some critics of deregulation were concerned that the government would lose the control it had, under regulation, over the quality and safety of airline service. Despite the demise of the CAB, however, the Federal Aviation Administration (FAA) still regulates the safety and quality of air service. And the Department of Transportation has the authority to stop any unfair practices. Research indicates that between 1979 and 1990, accident rates declined by anywhere from 10 to 45 percent, depending on the specific measure used. What's more, the lower fares encouraged more people to fly rather than drive, thereby saving lives that would have been lost driving (per passenger mile, flying is about twenty times safer than driving).

Another concern was that smaller communities would no longer be served by a deregulated industry. This has not been a problem; commuter airlines have replaced major airlines in servicing smaller communities. Because of the hub-and-spoke system, the number of scheduled departures from smaller cities and rural communities has actually increased by 35 percent.

Airport Capacity Has Restricted Competition. But competitive trends in the airline industry in recent years raise some troubling questions. Although airline traffic nearly doubled in the 1980s, no new airports were opened during that decade (Denver has since opened a new airport) and the air traffic control system did not expand. Airports and air traffic controllers are provided by the government. Thus, *the government did not follow up deregulation with an expansion of airport capacity.* Consequently, departure gates and landing rights became the scarce resources in the industry. Those airlines unable to secure such facilities at major airports went out of business. Some argue that the major airlines have not pushed for an expansion of airport facilities because additional capacity could encourage new entry and greater competition. Deregulation initially promoted a wave of new entry by such upstarts as People Express and New York Air. By the early 1990s, however, most of the new entrants had disappeared or had been absorbed by larger airlines. *New entrants could not acquire the necessary departure gates and landing slots at key airports.* A landing slot can sell for hundreds of thousands of dollars. The market share of the five largest airlines climbed from 63 percent before deregulation to 70 percent during the 1990s, and most key airports came to be dominated by a one or two airlines. For example, United and American control 82 percent of the landing slots at Chicago's O'Hare Airport, up from 66 percent in 1986. American and Delta control 83 percent of the slots at New York's Kennedy Airport, up from 43 percent in 1986. This concentration at certain hubs gives airlines some market power to raise prices; prices average about 5 percent more for trips involving concentrated hubs than more competitive airports

Foreign airlines can fly to and from U.S. cities from abroad, but cannot operate between U.S. cities. British-owned Virgin Atlantic, for example, would like to launch a low-cost airline in the United States but so far is prevented by law from doing so.

The federal government is concerned that some airlines may have acquired more landing slots and more long-term gate leases than they need simply as a way to block possible competitors from entering that market. In 1998 several major airlines announced plans to form alliances. Northwest bought a controlling interest in Continental. United planned an alliance with Delta. And American planned to tie its networks to Delta's. These airlines control 85 percent of the U.S. market.

Despite concerns about recent anticompetitive trends in the industry, deregulation has been quite beneficial for consumers. Few economists are calling for reregulation of the industry.

Sources: Steven Morrison and Clifford Winston, *The Evolution of the Airline Industry* (Washington, D.C.: Brookings Institution, 1995); "Come Fly with Me," *Economist* (20 June 1998); Bruce Ingersoll, "Administration's Plan for Hubs Is Target of Airlines' Media Blitz," *Wall Street Journal* (19 June 1998); and Matthew L. Wald, "U.S. Seeks to Curb Unfair Practices of Major Airlines," *New York Times* (7 April 1998).

The course of regulation and deregulation raises some interesting questions about the true objective of regulation. Recall the competing views of regulation: one holds that regulation is in the public, or consumer, interest; the other holds that regulation is in the special, or producer, interest. In the airline industry, regulation appeared more in accord with producer interests, and producer groups fought deregulation.

This concludes our discussion of economic regulation, which tries to reduce the harmful consequences of monopolistic behavior in those markets where the output can be most efficiently produced by one or a few firms. We now turn to antitrust activity, which aims to promote competition in those markets where competition seems desirable.

ANTITRUST LAW AND ENFORCEMENT

Although competition typically ensures the most efficient use of the nation's resources, an individual firm would prefer to operate as a monopoly. If left alone, some competing firms might try to create a monopolistic environment by driving competitors out of business, by merging with competitors, or by colluding with competitors. In the United States, *antitrust policy* is an attempt to curb these anticompetitive tendencies by (1) promoting the sort of market structure that will lead to greater competition and (2) reducing anticompetitive behavior. *Antitrust laws attempt to promote socially desirable market performance.*

NetBookmark

A Web site devoted entirely to antitrust issues is http://www.antitrust.org/ sponsored by the Owen Graduate School of Management at Vanderbilt University. Its stated mission includes exposing lawyers to relevant economic research, exposing economists to the legal issues that arise in antitrust cases and teaching students about antitrust. For each type of issue, there are links to relevant economic research. Learn about the role of economics in antitrust suits by playing some of the merger simulation games.

Origins of Antitrust Policy

A variety of economic developments that occurred in the last half of the 19th century created a political climate supportive of antitrust legislation. Perhaps the two most important developments were (1) technological breakthroughs that led to more extensive use of capital and a larger optimal plant size in manufacturing industries and (2) reduced transportation cost as railroads increased from 9,000 miles of track in 1850 to 167,000 miles by 1890. *Economies of scale in production and the cheaper cost of transporting goods extended the geographical reach of markets.* So firms grew larger and reached wider markets.

Declines in the national economy in 1873 and in 1883, however, caused panics among these large manufacturers, who were now committed to large-scale production with heavy fixed costs. Their defensive reaction was to lower prices in an attempt to stimulate sales. Price wars erupted, creating economic turmoil. Firms desperately sought ways to stabilize their markets. One solution was for competing firms to form a *trust* by transferring their voting stock to a single board of trustees, which would vote in the interest of the entire group. Early trusts were formed in the sugar, tobacco, and oil industries. Although the activity of these early trusts is still a matter of debate today, they allegedly pursued anticompetitive practices to develop and maintain a dominant market position. Gradually the word "trust" came to represent any firm or group of firms that tried to monopolize a market.

These practices provoked widespread criticism and earned creators of trusts the derisive title of "robber barons." Public sentiment lay on the side of the smaller competitors. Farmers, especially, resented the higher prices of manufactured goods, which resulted from the trusts' activities, particularly since farm prices were declining through the latter part of the 19th century. At the time, agriculture accounted for 40 percent of the U.S. workforce and thus had political clout. Eighteen states, primarily agricultural, enacted *antitrust* laws in the 1880s, prohibiting the formation of trusts. But these laws were largely ineffective because the trusts could simply move across state lines to avoid them.

Sherman Antitrust Act of 1890. In 1888, the major political parties put antitrust planks in their platforms. This consensus culminated in the passage of the *Sherman Antitrust Act* of 1890, the first national legislation in the world against monopoly. The law prohibited the creation of trusts, restraint of trade, and monopolization, although it failed to define what constituted such activities. Enforcement of the law was hampered by its vague language.

Clayton Act of 1914. Ambiguous language in the Sherman Act let much anticompetitive activity slip by. The *Clayton Act* of 1914 was passed to outlaw certain practices not prohibited by the Sherman Act and to help government stop a potential monopoly before it developed. For example, the Clayton Act prohibits *price discrimination* when this practice tends to create a monopoly. You'll recall that price discrimination is charging different customers different prices for the same good or charging the same customer different prices for different quantities of a good. The Clayton Act also prohibits *tying contracts* and *exclusive dealing* if they substantially lessened competition. **Tying contracts** require the buyer of one good to purchase another good as well. For example, a seller of a patented machine might require customers to purchase other supplies from the seller as part of the deal. **Exclusive dealing** occurs when a producer will sell a product only if the buyer agrees not to purchase from other manufacturers. For example, a computer-chip maker might sell chips to a computer maker only if the computer maker agrees not to purchase chips elsewhere. The law also prohibited **interlocking directorates,** whereby the same individual serves on the boards of directors of competing firms. Finally, mergers through the acquisition of the stock of a competing firm were outlawed in cases in which the merger would substantially lessen competition. More on mergers later.

Tying contract An arrangement in which a seller of one good requires buyers to purchase other goods as well

Exclusive dealing The situation that occurs when a producer prohibits customers from purchasing from other sellers

Interlocking directorate An arrangement whereby one individual serves on the boards of directors of competing firms

Federal Trade Commission Act of 1914. The *Federal Trade Commission (FTC)* was established in 1914 to help enforce antitrust laws. The commission consists of five full-time commissioners appointed by the president for seven-year terms and assisted by a staff of mostly lawyers and economists.

The Sherman, Clayton, and FTC acts provided the antitrust framework, a framework that has been clarified and embellished by subsequent amendments. A loophole in the Clayton Act was closed in 1950 with the passage of the *Celler-Kefauver Anti-Merger Act,* which prevents one firm from buying the assets of another firm if the effect is to reduce competition. This law can block both **horizontal mergers**, or the merging of firms that produce the same product, such as a merger between Coke and Pepsi, and **vertical mergers**, or the merging of firms where one supplies inputs to the other or demands output from the other, such as a merger between Microsoft and Dell Computer.

Horizontal merger A merger in which one firm combines with another firm that produces the same product

Vertical merger A merger in which one firm combines with another from which it purchases inputs or to which it sells output

Antitrust Law Enforcement

Any law's effectiveness depends on the vigor and vigilance of enforcement. The pattern of antitrust enforcement goes something like this. Either the Antitrust Division of the Justice Department or the Federal Trade Commission charges a firm or group of firms with breaking the law. These government agencies are often acting on a complaint by a customer or a competitor. At that point, those charged with the wrongdoing may be able, without admitting guilt, to sign a **consent decree** whereby they agree not to continue doing what they had been charged with. If the charges are contested, evidence from both sides is pre-

Consent decree A legal agreement through which the accused party, without admitting guilt, agrees to refrain in the future from certain illegal activity if the government drops the charges

sented in a court trial, and a decision is rendered by a judge. Certain decisions may be appealed all the way to the Supreme Court, and in such cases the Court may render new interpretations of existing law.

Per-Se Illegality and the Rule of Reason

The courts have interpreted antitrust laws in essentially two ways. One set of practices has been declared **per se illegal**—that is, without regard to economic rationale or consequences. For example, under the Sherman Act, all formal agreements among competing firms to fix prices, restrict output, or otherwise restrain the forces of competition are viewed as illegal *per se*. In order for the defendant to be found guilty under a per-se rule, the government need only show that the offending practice took place; thus, the government need only examine the firm's *behavior*.

Per se illegal A category of illegality in antitrust law, applied to business practices that are deemed illegal regardless of their economic rationale or their consequences

Another set of practices falls under the **rule of reason.** Here the courts engage in a broader inquiry into the facts surrounding the particular offense—namely, the reasons why the offending practices were adopted and the effect of these practices on competition. The rule of reason was first set forth in 1911, when the Supreme Court held that Standard Oil had illegally monopolized the petroleum refining industry. Standard Oil allegedly had come to dominate 90 percent of the market by acquiring more than 120 former rivals and by implementing **predatory pricing** tactics to drive remaining rivals out of business, such as by temporarily selling below cost or dropping the price only in certain markets. In finding Standard Oil guilty, the Court focused on both the company's *behavior* and the *market structure* that resulted from that behavior. Based on this approach, the Court found that the company had behaved *unreasonably*.

Rule of reason A principle used by a court to examine the reasons for certain business practices and their effects on competition before ruling on their legality

Predatory pricing Pricing tactics employed by a dominant firm to drive competitors out of business, such as temporarily selling below cost or dropping the price only in certain markets

But in 1920 the rule of reason led the Supreme Court to find U.S. Steel not guilty of monopolization. In that case, the Court ruled that not every contract or combination in restraint of trade was illegal—only those that "unreasonably" restrained trade violated antitrust laws. The Court said that *mere size was not an offense*. Although U.S. Steel clearly possessed market power, the company was not in violation of antitrust laws because, in the Court's view, it had not unreasonably used that power. The Court switched positions again 25 years later in reviewing the charges against the Aluminum Company of America (Alcoa). In a 1945 decision, the Supreme Court held that although a firm's conduct might be reasonable and legal, the mere possession of market power—Alcoa controlled 90 percent of the aluminum ingot market—violated the antitrust laws. Here the Court was using *market structure* rather than firm *behavior* as the test of legality.

Mergers and Public Policy

Some firms have pursued rapid growth by merging with other firms. In some industries, the *merging,* or joining together, of two firms has created oligopolies. Much of what the Antitrust Division does is approve or deny proposed mergers and acquisitions. In determining the possible detrimental effects a merger might have on competition, one important consideration is its impact on the share of sales accounted for by the largest firms. If a few firms account for a relatively large share of sales, the industry is considered to be *concentrated*. As a measure of sales concentration, the Justice Department uses the **Herfindahl index,** which is calculated by squaring the percent market share of each firm in the market and then adding those squares. For example, if the industry consists of 100 firms of

Herfindahl index The sum of the squared percentages of market share of all firms in an industry; a measure of the level of market concentration in that industry

equal size, the Herfindahl index is 100 [= 100 × $(1)^2$]. If the industry is a pure monopoly, the index is 10,000 [= $(100)^2$], the largest possible value. The more firms there are in the industry and the more equal in size the firms are, the smaller the Herfindahl index. This index gives greater weight to firms with larger market shares, as can be seen for the three examples presented in Exhibit 2. Note that the index for Industry III is nearly triple that for the two other industries.

The Justice Department's guidelines also sort all mergers into two types: *horizontal mergers*, which involve firms in the same market, and *nonhorizontal mergers*, which include all others. Of greatest interest for antitrust purposes are horizontal mergers, such as a merger between competing oil companies like Mobil and Exxon. The Justice Department generally challenges any merger in an industry where two conditions are met: (1) the post-merger Herfindahl index would exceed 1,800 and (2) the merger would increase the index by more than 100 points. Mergers in an industry that would have a post-merger index of less than 1,000 are seldom challenged. Other factors such as the ease of entry into the market are considered for intermediate cases.

Merger Movements

Over the last century there have been four major merger waves in this country. These merger waves are outlined in Exhibit 3. The first occurred between 1887 and 1904. Some of today's largest firms, including U.S. Steel and Standard Oil, were formed during this first merger movement. These tended to be horizontal mergers. For example, the firm that is today U.S. Steel was created in 1901 through a billion-dollar merger that involved dozens of individual steel producers and two-thirds of the industry's productive capacity. During this first wave, similar mergers occurred in Canada, Great Britain, and elsewhere, creating dominant firms, some of which still exist today.

EXHIBIT 2

Computation of the Herfindahl Index Based on Market Share in Three Industries

	Industry I		Industry II		Industry III	
Firm	**Market Share (percent)**	**Market Share Squared**	**Market Share (percent)**	**Market Share Squared**	**Market Share (percent)**	**Market Share Squared**
A	23	529	15	225	57	3,249
B	18	324	15	225	1	1
C	13	169	15	225	1	1
D	6	36	15	225	1	1
Remaining 40 firms (at 1 percent each)	1 each	40	1 each	40	1 each	40
Herfindahl Index		1,098		940		3,292

EXHIBIT 3

Merger Waves in the Past Century

Wave	Years	Dominant Type of Merger	Examples
First	1887–1904	Horizontal	U.S. Steel, Standard Oil
Second	1916–1929	Vertical	Copper refiners with fabricators
Third	1948–1969	Conglomerate	Litton Industries
Fourth	1982–present	Horizontal & Vertical	Banking, telecommunications, health services, insurance

The second merger wave took place between 1916 and 1929, when vertical mergers were more common. A vertical merger, recall, is the merging of one firm with a firm that either supplies its inputs or demands its outputs: it is the merging of firms at different stages of the production process. For example, a steel firm might merge with a firm that mines iron ore or a copper refiner might merge with a firm that fabricates copper parts.

The third merger wave was from 1948 to 1969. More than 200 of the 1,000 largest firms in 1950 had disappeared by the early 1960s as a result of mergers. In that period, many large firms were absorbed by other, usually larger, firms. The third merger wave culminated in the peak merger activity of 1964 to 1969, when **conglomerate mergers,** which join firms in different industries, accounted for four-fifths of all mergers. For example, Litton Industries combined firms that made calculators, appliances, electrical equipment, and machine tools.

Conglomerate merger
A merger involving the combination of firms in different industries

The fourth merger wave, which is still underway today, began with the "deal decade" of the 1980s. This wave involves both horizontal and vertical mergers. Some of the big conglomerate mergers that occurred during the 1960s were dissolved in the 1980s as the core firm sold off unrelated operations. About one-third of mergers in the 1980s resulted from *hostile takeovers*, where one firm would buy control of another against the wishes of the target firm's management. Hostile takeovers dwindled to less than 10 percent of all mergers during the 1990s. Most mergers of the 1990s were financed by the exchange of corporate stock and were fueled by a booming stock market (just like mergers during the 1920s).

Merger activity gained momentum during the latter half of the 1990s. The $1 trillion in mergers in 1997 exceeded the 1996 level by 50 percent. The five largest mergers in U.S. history were proposed between April and December 1998. Sectors with heavy merger activity during the 1990s included banking, radio and television, insurance, telecommunications, and health services.

During the 1990s there was little objection to mergers on antitrust grounds either from academics or regulatory officials. The government shifted from rules that restrict big mergers to a more flexible economic approach that allows big companies to merge. Notable exceptions include the $4-billion merger proposed in 1997 between Staples and Office Depot, the nation's two largest office-supply retailers. Evidence showed that consumers in areas with only one office superstore paid higher prices than consumers in areas with more competition. On the other hand, the government approved Boeing's $15 billion acquisition of McDonnell Douglas, the commercial aircraft manufacturer, because the key customers of the airplanes, the airlines, said it made no difference to them whether or not the two combined. As one Justice Department official said, "We have very flexible guidelines. Bigness in and of itself doesn't tell me much. I want to know about the market, the players and what competition exists to judge."[2] The Chairman of the Federal Trade Commission said in 1998 that "the mergers we see these days make more sense" than earlier mergers.[3] He also said, "I do not believe that size alone is a basis to challenge a merger transaction."[4] Only 2 percent of all proposed mergers in the 1990s were ultimately challenged by regulators.

Mergers during the 1990s were for strategic concerns, where companies often merged to achieve a stronger competitive position in global markets. The end of the Cold War stabilized world markets and expanded capitalism around the world. The combination of a surging stock market and relatively low interest rates reduced the cost of funding mergers through stock swaps.

One industry where mergers seem to be having anticompetitive effects is local phone service. In 1996 Congress enacted a law designed to reduce the monopoly power of local phone companies by allowing long-distance carriers, cable operators, and other telecommunications providers to enter the local market. But rather than enhancing more competition, the 1996 act spawned a wave of mergers among local providers as they raced to span the country. For example, in May 1998 SBC Communications offered $62 billion for Ameritech. The proposed merger, if approved by regulators, would give the resulting company control over one-third of the 178 million local phone lines.[5]

COMPETITIVE TRENDS IN THE U.S. ECONOMY

For years there has been concern about the sheer size of some firms because of the real or potential power these firms might exercise in both the economic and the political arenas. One way to measure the power of the largest corporations is to calculate the share of the nation's corporate assets controlled by the 100 largest firms. What percentage of the nation's manufacturing assets do the top 100 manufacturing companies own, and how has this share changed over time?

The largest 100 manufacturers now control about half of all production assets in the United States, up from a 40 percent share after World War II. We should recognize, however, that size alone is not synonymous with market power. A very big firm, such as a large oil company, may face stiff competition from other very big oil companies both foreign and domestic; on the other hand, the only movie theater in an isolated community may be able to raise its price with less concern about competition.

2 As quoted by Leslie Wayne in "Wave of Mergers Recasts the Face of Business," *New York Times* (19 January 1998).
3 As quoted by John R. Wilke in "Greenspan Questions Governments Antitrust-Enforcement Campaigns," *Wall Street Journal*, (17 June 1998).
4 As quoted by Leslie Wayne in "Wave of Mergers Recasts the Face of Business," *New York Times* (19 January 1998).
5 See Stephanie N. Mehta, "SBC-Ameritech Deal, Formally Unveiled, Draws Criticism from Rival Carriers," *Wall Street Journal* (12 May 1998).

Market Competition over Time

More important than the size of the largest firms in the nation is the market structure in each industry. Various studies have examined the level of competition and change in industry structure over the years. All have used some measure of market share, such as the Herfindahl index, as a point of departure, sometimes supplementing these measures with data from each industry. Among the most comprehensive of these studies is the research of William Shepherd, of the University of Massachusetts, who relied on many sources to determine the competitiveness of each industry in the U.S. economy.[6]

Shepherd sorted industries into four groups: (1) pure monopoly, in which a single firm controlled the entire market and was able to block entry; (2) dominant firm, in which a single firm had over half the market share and had no close rival; (3) tight oligopoly, in which the top four firms supplied more than 60 percent of market output, with stable market shares and evidence of cooperation; and (4) effective competition, in which firms in the industry exhibited low concentration, low entry barriers, and little or no collusion.

Exhibit 4 presents Shepherd's breakdown of all U.S. industries into the four categories for the years 1939, 1958, and 1988. The table shows a modest trend toward greater competition between 1939 and 1958, with the percentage of those industries rated as "effectively competitive" growing from 52.4 percent to 56.3 percent of all industries. Between 1958 and 1988, however, there was a sharp rise in competitiveness in the economy, with the percentage of effectively competitive industries jumping from 56.3 to 76.7 percent.

According to Shepherd, the growth in competition from 1958 to 1988 can be traced to three primary causes: *competition from imports, deregulation, and antitrust activity*. Foreign imports between 1958 and 1988 resulted in increased competition in 13 major industries, including autos, tires, and steel. According to Shepherd, the growth in imports accounted for one-sixth of the overall increase in competition. Imports were attractive to consumers because of their superior quality and lower price. Because they were competing with U.S. producers that often had been tightly knit domestic oligopolies, foreign competitors found these U.S. markets relatively easy to penetrate. Finding themselves at a cost and technological disadvantage, domestic producers initially responded by seeking protection from foreign competitors through trade barriers, such as quotas and tariffs.

According to Shepherd, deregulation accounted for one-fifth of the increase in competition. Trucking, airlines, and telecommunications were among the industries deregulated between 1958 and 1988. We have already discussed some of the effects of this deregulation in airlines, particularly in reducing barriers to entry and in eliminating uniform pricing schedules. With regard to telecommunications, in 1982 AT&T was forced to divest itself of 22 companies that provided most of the country's local phone service. Between 1984 and 1996, AT&T's share of the long-distance market declined from 88 to 54 percent. This enhanced competition reduced long-distance rates. But, as noted

6 William G. Shepherd, "Causes of Increased Competition in the U.S. Economy, 1939–1980," *Review of Economics and Statistics* 64 (November 1982); and William G. Shepherd, *The Economics of Industrial Organization*, 3rd ed. (Englewood Cliffs, NJ: Prentice Hall, 1990): 15.

EXHIBIT 4

Competitive Trends in the U.S. Economy

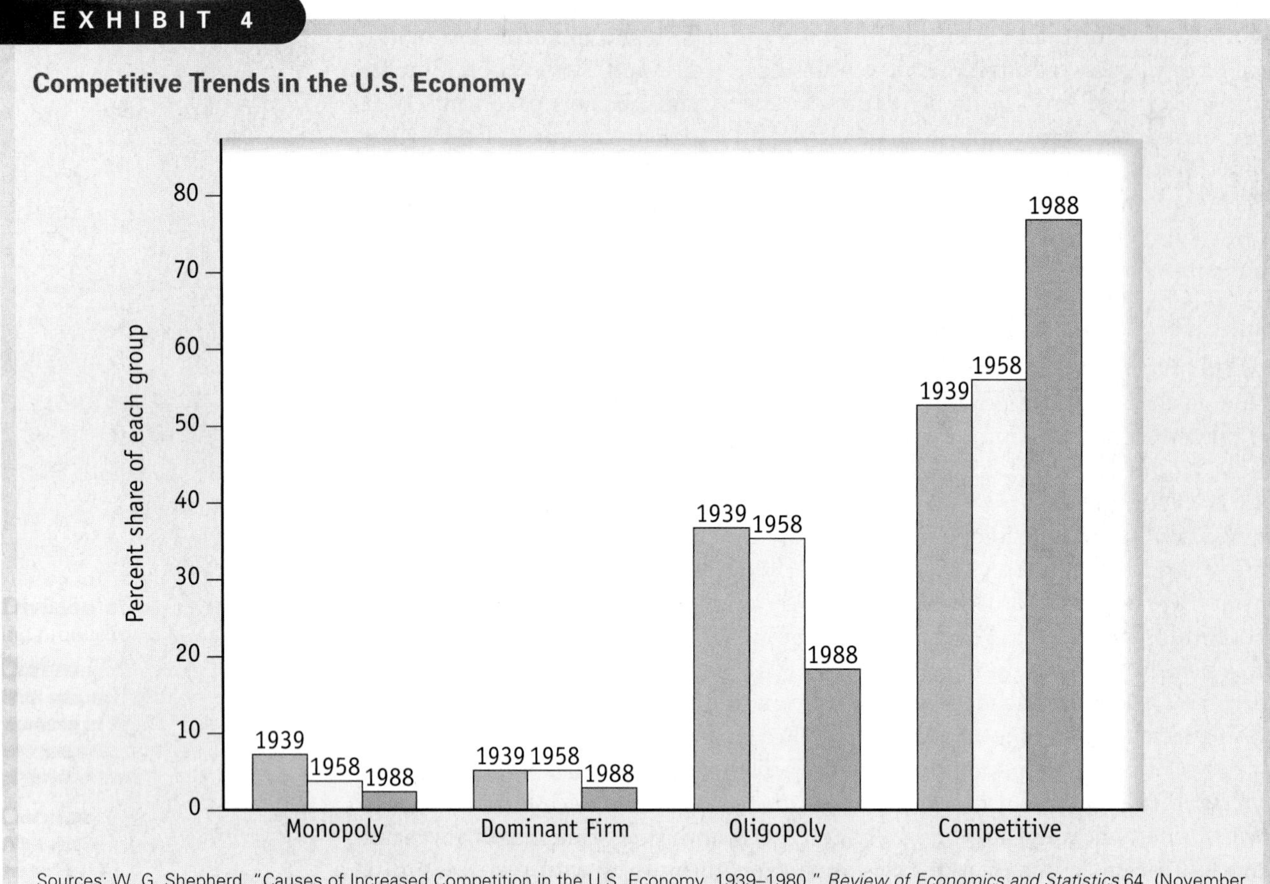

Sources: W. G. Shepherd, "Causes of Increased Competition in the U.S. Economy, 1939–1980," *Review of Economics and Statistics* 64, (November 1982); and W. G. Shepherd, *The Economics of Industrial Organization*, 3rd ed. (Englewood Cliffs, N.J.: Prentice Hall, 1990): 15.

earlier, local service providers are starting to join forces again. Deregulation has also occurred in securities trading and banking.

Although it is difficult to attribute an increase in competition to specific antitrust cases, Shepherd concludes that about two-fifths of the increase in competition between 1958 and 1988 could be credited to the effects of antitrust activity.

Recent Competitive Trends

What has been the recent trend in competition? Growing world trade has increased competition in the U.S. economy. Until the 1970s, for example, the so-called big three auto makers—General Motors, Ford, and Daimler-Chrysler—controlled 80 percent of the U.S. auto market. By 1997 their market share had dropped to about 60 percent. And federal action to deregulate international phone service should force down the average price of international phone calls from 88 cents a minute in 1997 to 20 cents a minute by 2002.

Other major markets are also growing more competitive in part as a result of technological change. In the last two decades, the prime-time audience share controlled by the three major television networks (NBC, CBS, and ABC) dropped from 91 percent to 46 percent, as satellite and cable technology brought in many more networks. Despite Microsoft's dominance in operating systems, the packaged software market for personal computers barely existed in 1980 but has flourished in a technology-rich environment now populated by more than 7,800 producers with sales in 1997 of $30 billion. And the Internet has opened possibilities for enhanced competition in a number of industries, from on-line stock trading to all kinds of electronic commerce.

But some deregulation has hit bumps in the road. Airlines are now more concentrated than they were before deregulation, although plane service is still cheaper and safer than during the regulation era. The bankruptcy of many savings institutions has been blamed in part on deregulation. And the recent federal measure to promote competition in local phone service seems to have backfired, as local providers merge with other local providers across the country. Despite these setbacks, the trend toward deregulation continues, both here and abroad, with the deregulation of electricity generation being the most recent development.

Problems with Antitrust Legislation

There is growing doubt about the economic value of some of the lengthy antitrust cases pursued in the past. One case against Exxon was in the courts for 17 years before the company was cleared of charges in 1992. Another case began in 1969 when IBM, with nearly 70 percent of domestic sales of electronic data-processing equipment, was accused of monopolizing that market. IBM responded that its large market share was based on its innovative products and on its economies of scale. The trial began in 1975, and the government took nearly three years to present its case. Litigation dragged on for years. In the meantime, many other computer manufacturers emerged both in this country and abroad to challenge IBM's dominance. In 1982, the government dropped the case, noting that the threat of monopoly had diminished enough that the case was "without merit."

Too Much Emphasis on the Competitive Model. Joseph Schumpeter argued half a century ago that competition should be viewed as a dynamic process, one of "creative destruction." Firms are continually in flux—introducing new products, phasing out old products, trying to compete for the consumer's dollar in a variety of ways. In light of this, antitrust policy should not necessarily be aimed at increasing the number of firms in each industry. In some cases, firms will grow large because they are more efficient than rivals at offering what consumers want. Accordingly, firm size should not be the primary concern. Moreover, as noted in the case study in the chapter on perfect competition, economists have shown through market experiments that most of the desirable properties of perfect competition can be achieved with a relatively small number of firms.[7]

7 See, for example, Vernon Smith, "Markets as Economizers of Information: Experimental Examinations of the 'Hayek Hypothesis'," *Economic Inquiry* 20 (1982); and Douglas Davis and Charles Holt, *Experimental Economics* (Princeton, N.J.: Princeton University Press, 1993).

Abuse of Antitrust. Parties that can show injury from firms that have violated antitrust laws can sue the offending company and recover three times the amount of the damages sustained. These so-called *treble damage* suits increased after World War II; more than 1,000 cases are initiated each year. Courts have been relatively generous to those claiming to have been wronged. But studies show that such suits can be used to intimidate an aggressive competitor or to convert a contract dispute between, say, a firm and its supplier into treble damage payoffs. The result can have a chilling effect on competition. Many economists now believe that the anticompetitive costs from this abuse of treble damage suits may exceed the procompetitive benefits of these laws.

Growing Importance of International Markets. Finally, a standard approach to measuring the market power of a firm is its share of the market. With the growth of international trade, however, the local or even the national market share becomes less relevant. General Motors may dominate U.S. auto manufacturing, accounting for half of sales in the United States by domestically owned firms. But when auto sales by Japanese and European producers are included, GM's share of the U.S. auto market falls to less than one-third. GM's share of world production has declined steadily since the mid-1950s. *Where markets are open to foreign competition, antitrust enforcement that focuses on domestic producers makes less economic sense.*

We close this chapter by looking at the most visible antitrust case of the decade

McEachern Interactive

CaseStudy

The Information Economy

The *New York Times* maintains an archive of its articles about the lawsuit at http://www.nytimes.com/library/tech/reference/index-microsoft.html. Microsoft maintains its own archive of articles at its Freedom to Innovate Web site at http://www.microsoft.com/presspass/doj/background.htm. Check Bill Gates's response to the *Economist* magazine's editorial supporting the filing of the lawsuit. You can access the original complaint, other court filings, and transcripts at the Department of Justice's Antitrust Division Web site at http://www.usdoj.gov/atr/cases/ms_index.htm. From information at these sites, can you find what remedy or relief the government was seeking for Microsoft's alleged anticompetitive behavior?

Windows 98 Sold With Microsoft Browser

Microsoft released its long-awaited Windows 98 operating system in June 1998 under a cloud. The U.S. Justice Department and 20 state attorneys general had filed lawsuits a month earlier alleging that Microsoft engaged in a pattern of predatory conduct to protect its operating-system monopoly and to extend that monopoly into Internet software. Windows software is used on 90 percent of the nation's desktop computers. The plaintiffs charged that Microsoft's integration of its browser, Internet Explorer, into Windows 98 was not, as the company claimed, solely to make life easier for customers, but was aimed at boosting the browser's market share. A dominance in browser software is important, because controlling the gateway to the Internet is a big step in directing traffic and commerce in cyberspace. Government officials wanted Microsoft customers to be free to choose a browser. Microsoft disputed the charges and said the government was interfering with its right to create new products that benefit consumers.

Prior to any judicial ruling on the suit, Microsoft's choices were (a) to separate its Internet browser from Windows 98, a task the company claimed would take "months if not years;" (b) ship their major rival's browser, Netscape, as well as their own browser, with Windows 98—a task Bill Gates likened to "requiring Coca-Cola to include three cans of Pepsi in every six-pack it sells;" or (c) release Windows 98 with Microsoft's browser bundled in the software. Microsoft chose (c), which involved some risk, since if the practice was ultimately found to be anticompetitive, other companies could try to sue Microsoft for treble damages.

The trial began in October 1998, with 24 witnesses scheduled. Frederick Warren-Boulton, an economist hired by the government, testified that Microsoft holds monopoly power because it has the ability to set prices for its products in a way that excludes competitors: "I believe Microsoft has raised prices over the competitive level" because of its lack of rivals. He said that Microsoft had engaged in predatory practices aimed at harming competitors (the company's actions would be considered illegal only if it is found to possess monopoly power). Warren-Boulton argued that Microsoft's actions were "predatory" because they were aimed not at adding revenue but at winning the browser war. For example, Microsoft's decision to give away its Internet Explorer browser sacrificed revenue but was viewed as a way of beating Netscape. With Microsoft's browser on more than 60 percent of new Internet users' computers, the company may become dominant in the browser market, he said.

Microsoft, for its part, characterized itself as an aggressive but legal player in a fiercely competitive industry. Lawyers detailed Microsoft's frequent efforts to improve its operating system software all the way from MS-DOS to Windows 98. They said that the product would not have such a huge share of the market if it failed to improve quality and value with each new version. They argued that the high market share "does not begin to reflect the intense competitive dynamic in the software industry." Even such a lead is "susceptible to rapid deterioration should the market leader fail to innovate at a rapid and competitive pace." The company said it planned to invest $3 billion in fiscal year 1999 on research and development.

Bill Gates was not among the 24 witnesses scheduled to testify live. But he was interrogated by government lawyers for 20 hours during a videotaped deposition, parts of which were show during the trial to support the government's case. The federal judge presiding at the trial said "I think it is evident to every spectator that, for whatever reasons, in many respects, Mr. Gates has not been particularly responsive to his deposition."

A report by the Software and Information Industry Association, the nation's largest software-industry trade group, recommended to the Justice Department that Microsoft be restructured. As a cure for what the report says is a lack of competition in the software industry, the report argued that Microsoft should be broken into three companies. The first company would be Microsoft's operating systems business, including Windows. The second would get Microsoft's software applications such as Word, Excel, and PowerPoint. The third would get their Internet-related business. According to the report, the problem is that companies now competing with Microsoft in the applications business very much need the company's cooperation in sharing its operating system technology. Software not compatible with Microsoft's operating system simply doesn't survive. As a consequence, competition in the applications business is blunted by the dominance of Microsoft's operating system.

For the latest developments in the case, check the Web sites mentioned in the margin at the beginning of this case study.

Sources: Bryan Gruley and Keith Perine, "U.S. Witness Criticizes Microsoft for Operating System Monopoly," *Wall Street Journal* (19 November, 1998); John R. Wilke, "Witness Cites Microsoft Monopoly Power," *Wall Street Journal* (2 December 1998); "Judge Finds Gates Unresponsive," *New York Times* (20 November 1998); and Steve Lohr, "On Breaking Up Microsoft Into 'Baby Bills,'" *New York Times* (5 March 1999). For a library of *Wall Street Journal* articles about the case and for a discussion forum on the case, see http://interactive.wsj.com/pages/microsft.htm.

CONCLUSION

Competition has been growing in recent decades because of changing technology, greater international trade, industry deregulation, and antitrust activity. The current merger wave could ultimately diminish competition, but the jury is still out on that question.

Federal Reserve Chairman Alan Greenspan, testifying in 1998 before Congress about antitrust policy, expressed skepticism about the need for antitrust intervention, arguing that changes in market conditions and technologies tend to undermine monopolies over time. He called for "a higher degree of humility when enforcers make . . . projections" about the lasting effects of monopoly power. But, at the same hearing, Joel Klein, the antitrust chief for the Justice Department, said "we reject categorically the notion that markets will self-correct and we should sit back and watch."[8] So goes the public policy debate.

SUMMARY

1. In this chapter, we examined two forms of government regulation of business: (1) economic regulation, such as the regulation of natural monopolies, and (2) antitrust activity, which promotes competition and prohibits efforts to monopolize, or to cartelize, an industry.
2. Natural monopolies are regulated by government so that output is greater and prices lower than they would be if the monopolist were allowed to maximize profits. One problem with regulation is that the price that maximizes social welfare results in an economic loss, whereas the price that allows the firm to earn a normal profit does not maximize social welfare.
3. There are two views of economic regulation. The first is that economic regulation is in the public interest because it controls natural monopolies where production by one or a few firms is most efficient. A second view is that regulation is not in the public's, or consumer's, best interest, but is more in the special interest of regulated producers as a means of fixing the price and blocking entry.
4. The airline industry was regulated for much of this century. Regulation had the effect of restricting entry and fixing prices. Deregulation in 1978 stimulated new entry and reduced prices overall, though the industry once again is growing more concentrated because new entrants have difficulty securing landing rights at the nation's major airports.
5. Antitrust laws are aimed at promoting competition and prohibiting efforts to cartelize, or monopolize, an industry. The Sherman, Clayton, and FTC acts provided the basic framework for antitrust enforcement, a framework that has been clarified and embellished by subsequent amendments and judicial decisions.
6. Research indicates that competition in U.S. industries has been increasing since World War II. Four reasons for the growth in competition are foreign trade, deregulation, antitrust activity, and technological change.

8 As quoted in John R. Wilke, "Greenspan Questions Government's Antitrust-Enforcement Campaigns," *Wall Street Journal* (17 June 1998).

QUESTIONS FOR REVIEW

1. (*Business Behavior and Public Policy*) Define market power, then discuss the rationale for government regulation of firms with market power.
2. (*Government Regulation of Business*) What three types of government policies are used to alter or control firm behavior? Determine which type of regulation is used for each of the following:
   a. Preventing a merger that the government believes would lessen competition.
   b. The activities of the Food and Drug Administration.
   c. Regulation of fares charged by a municipal bus company.
   d. Occupational safety and health regulations that affect working conditions.
3. (*Regulating Natural Monopolies*) What is the "regulatory dilemma?" That is, what tradeoffs do regulators have to consider when deciding how to control a natural monopoly?
4. (*Theories of Regulation*) Compare and contrast the public-interest and special-interest theories of economic regulation. Which better describes the case of airline deregulation? Which better explains the U.S. government's case against Microsoft?
5. (**CaseStudy:** *Airline Regulation and Deregulation*) Since the Airline Deregulation Act of 1978, has concentration in the airline industry increased or decreased? Explain why.
6. (*Antitrust Law and Enforcement*) Discuss the difference between *per se* illegality and the rule of reason.
7. (*Antitrust Activity*) "The existence of only three or four big U.S. auto manufacturers is evidence that the market structure is anticompetitive and that antitrust laws are being broken." Evaluate this assertion.
8. (*Mergers and Public Policy*) Under what circumstances, and why, would the government be opposed to a merger of two firms? How does the Justice Department decide which mergers to challenge?
9. (*Competitive Trends in the U.S. Economy*) William Shepherd's study of U.S. industries showed a clear increase in competition in the U.S. economy between 1958 and 1988. How did Shepherd explain this trend?

PROBLEMS AND EXERCISES

10. (*Regulating Natural Monopolies*) The following graph represents a natural monopoly.
    a. Why is this firm considered a natural monopoly?
    b. If the firm is unregulated, what price and output would maximize its profit? What would be its profit or loss?

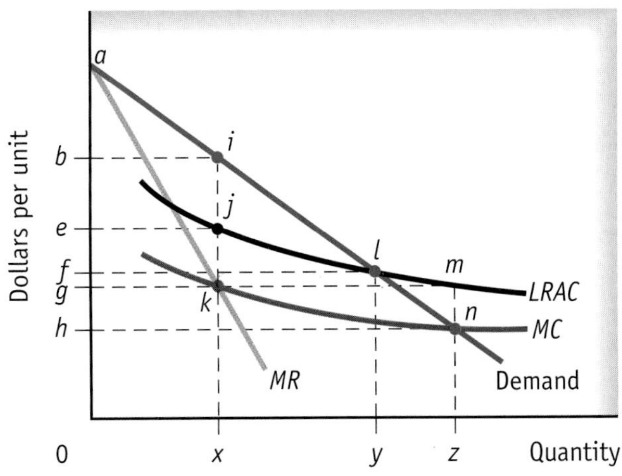

    c. If a regulatory commission establishes a price with the goal of achieving allocative efficiency, what would be the price and output? What would be the firm's profit or loss?
    d. If a regulatory commission establishes a price with the goal of allowing the firm a "fair return," what would be the price and output? What would be the firm's profit or loss?
    e. Which of the prices in parts b, c, and d maximizes consumer surplus? What problem, if any, occurs at this price?
11. (*Origins of Antitrust Policy*) Identify the type of anticompetitive behavior illustrated by each of the following:
    a. A university requires buyers of season tickets for its basketball games to buy season tickets for its football games as well.
    b. Dairies that bid on contracts collude to artificially inflate the price of milk sold to school districts.
    c. The same individual serves on the boards of directors of General Motors and Ford.

d. A large retailer sells merchandise below cost in certain regions in order to drive competitors out of business.
e. A producer of carbonated soft drinks sells to a retailer only if the retailer agrees not to buy from the producer's major competitor.

12. (*Mergers and Public Policy*) Calculate the Herfindahl index for each of the following industries. Which of the industries is the most concentrated?
    a. An industry with five firms that have the following market shares: 50 percent, 30 percent, 10 percent, 5 percent, and 5 percent
    b. An industry with five firms that have the following market shares: 60 percent, 20 percent, 10 percent, 5 percent, and 5 percent
    c. An industry with five firms, each of which has a 20 percent market share.

EXPERIENTIAL EXERCISES

13. (*Mergers and Public Policy*) Find the Department of Justice and Federal Trade Commission merger guidelines at http://www.antitrust.org/law/mg.html. How does the government use the Herfindahl index to determine which proposed mergers to allow and which to challenge? Do these guidelines indicate that the Justice Department is using the *per se* illegality or rule of reason approach to antitrust enforcement?

14. (*Case***Study:** *Windows 98 Sold with Microsoft Browser*)The latest information on the Justice Department's case against Microsoft is available at http://www.usdoj.gov/atr/cases/ms_index.htm. To get the other side of the story, check Microsoft's PressPass page at http://microsoft.com/presspass/. What has happened in this case since this textbook went to press?

15. (*Wall Street Journal*) The best place for finding late breaking information about antitrust activity is in the Legal Beat column of the *Wall Street Journal*. You can find it inside the Marketplace section. Try to find at least one relevant article and determine the basis for the antitrust action. Were the Justice Department guidelines and the Herfindahl index mentioned in the article?

CHAPTER

29 Public Goods and Public Choice

How do public goods differ from private goods? Why do most people remain largely ignorant about what's happening in the public sector? Why is voter turnout so low? Why do politicians cater to special interests? Why are elected officials more likely than challengers to support campaign spending limits? Answers to these and related questions are discussed in this chapter, which focuses on the public sector—both the rationale for public goods and public choices about those goods.

The effects of government are all around us. Stitched into the clothes you put on this morning are government-regulated labels providing washing instructions. The prices of the milk and sugar you put on your cereal were propped up by government price supports. The condition of the vehicle in

Visit the McEachern Interactive Study Center for this chapter at http://mcisc.swcollege.com

*Net*Bookmark

The Cato Institute, at http://www.cato.org/, and the Heritage Foundation, at http://www.heritage.org/, are conservative organizations that promote limited government and free markets. Their Web sites provide news, analysis and commentaries reflecting their view of why big government is bad and how it can be limited. Nobel laureate in Economics, James Buchanan has been one of the most influential proponents of this philosophy. He tells his story in an interview with *The Region* at http://minneapolisfed.org/pubs/region/int959.html.

which you rode to campus was regulated by the government, as were the speed and sobriety of the driver. Your education has been subsidized by the public sector in a variety of ways. Government has a pervasive influence on all aspects of your life and on the economy. Yes, government is big business. The federal government alone spends over $1,800,000,000,000.00 a year—over $1.8 *trillion*—more than $1 million on paper clips alone. State and local governments raise and spend another $1 trillion on their own.

The role of government has been discussed throughout this book. For the most part, the discussion has assumed that government makes optimal decisions in response to the shortcomings of the private sector—that is, when confronted with a market failure, government adopts and implements the appropriate program to address the problem. But there are limits to the effectiveness of government activity, just as there are limits to the effectiveness of market activity. In this chapter, we look at the pros and cons of government activity. We begin with public goods, discuss the decision-making process, then examine the limitations of that process. Topics discussed in this chapter include:

- Private versus public goods
- Representative democracy
- Rational ignorance
- Special-interest legislation
- Rent seeking
- Underground economy
- Bureaucratic behavior
- Private versus public production

OPTIMAL PROVISION OF PUBLIC GOODS

Throughout most of this book, we have been talking about *private goods*. As noted in Chapter 4, private goods have two important features. First, private goods are *rival* in consumption, meaning that the amount consumed by one person is unavailable for others to consume. For example, when you and a friend share a pizza, each slice your friend eats is one less available for you. A second key feature of private goods is that suppliers can easily *exclude* those who don't pay. Only paying customers get pizzas from Domino's. Thus private goods are said to be *exclusive*.

Private Goods, Public Goods, and In Between

In contrast to private goods, public goods, such as national defense, a lighthouse, or a neighborhood mosquito-control program, are *nonrival* in consumption. One person's consumption does not diminish the amount available to others. Once produced, such goods are available to all in equal amount; the marginal cost of providing the good to an additional consumer is zero. But once a public good is produced, suppliers cannot easily deny the good to those who fail to pay for it. For example, if a company sprays a community for mosquitoes, all households in the community benefit from having fewer mosquitoes. But the firm would be unable to exclude those households that failed to pay for the service. The mosquito spraying is *nonexclusive*—it is available to all households, regardless of who pays and who doesn't. Producers find it difficult or impossible to charge people for nonexclusive goods. So recipients figure, "Why bother paying if you can enjoy the benefits without paying?"

In short, public goods are both *nonrival* and *nonexclusive*. Once produced, public goods are available for all to consume, regardless of who pays and who doesn't. As a consequence, private firms cannot profitably sell public goods. There are no vending machines for public goods. In this case of market failure, government comes to the rescue by providing public goods and paying for them through enforced taxation.

But the economy consists of more than just private goods and public goods. Some goods are *nonrival* but *exclusive*. For example, additional households can watch a TV show without affecting the TV reception of other viewers. It's not as if there's only a limited amount of TV signal to go around. Television signals are nonrival in consumption. Yet the program's producers, should they choose to, could use cable boxes to charge each household for the show, as with pay-per-view. Along the same lines, short of the point of congestion, additional people can benefit from a golf course, swimming pool, rock concert, or bridge crossing without diminishing the benefit to other users. These goods, when not congested, are nonrival. Yet producers can, with relative ease, exclude those who don't pay the green fee, pool admission, ticket price, or bridge toll. A good that is nonrival but exclusive is called a **quasi-public good**. If congestion sets in, however, these goods become rival—space is scarce on a backed-up golf course, in a crowded swimming pool, at a jam-packed rock concert, or on a traffic-laden bridge. Essentially, once congestion sets in these quasi-public goods become private goods—both rival and exclusive.

Quasi-public good A good that is nonrival but exclusive, such as cable TV

Some other goods are *rival* but *nonexclusive*. The fish in the ocean are rival, in the sense that every fish caught is not available for others to catch; the same goes for migrating birds. But fish and game are nonexclusive, in that it would be costly or impossible for a private firm to prevent access to these goods. A good that is rival but nonexclusive is called an **open-access good** since it would be difficult and costly to prevent individuals from using the good. Problems that arise with open-access goods are examined in the next chapter.

Open-access good A good that is rival but nonexclusive, such as fish in the sea

Exhibit 1 offers a matrix that sorts out the four types of goods discussed. Across the top, goods are categorized as either *rival* or *nonrival*, and along the

EXHIBIT 1

Categories of Private and Public Goods

	Rival	Nonrival
Exclusive	1. Private Goods —pizza —crowded swimming pool	2. Quasi-Public Goods —Cable TV —uncrowded swimming pool
Nonexclusive	3. Open-Access Goods —ocean fish —migratory birds	4. Public Goods —national defense —mosquito control

left-hand margin, goods are categorized as either *exclusive* or *nonexclusive*. Box 1 shows *private goods*, such as a pizza or a crowded swimming pool. These goods, by definition, are both rival and exclusive. Box 2 shows *quasi-public goods*, such as cable TV or an uncrowded swimming pool; these goods are nonrival but exclusive. Box 3 shows *open-access goods*, such as fish in the ocean or migrating birds, which are rival but nonexclusive. And Box 4 shows public goods, such as national defense or mosquito control, which are both nonrival and nonexclusive. Private goods are usually provided by the private sector. Quasi-public goods are sometimes provided by government, as with a municipal golf course, and sometimes provided by the private sector, as with a private golf course. Open-access goods are usually regulated by government, as you will see in the next chapter. And public goods are usually provided by government.

Optimal Provision of Public Goods

Because private goods are rival in consumption, the market demand for a private good is the sum of the quantities demanded by each consumer. For example, the market quantity of pizza demanded when the price is $5 is the quantity demanded by Alan plus the quantity demanded by Maria plus the quantity demanded by all other consumers in the market. The market demand curve for a private good is the *horizontal* sum of individual demand curves. The efficient quantity of a private good occurs where the market demand curve intersects the market supply curve.

But since a public good is nonrival in consumption, that good, once produced, is available to all consumers in an identical amount. For example, the market demand for a given level of mosquito control reflects the marginal benefit that Alan gets from the good plus the marginal benefit that Maria gets plus the marginal benefit that all others in the community get from the good. Therefore, the market demand curve for a public good is the *vertical* sum of each consumer's demand for the public good. To arrive at the efficient level of provision of the public good, we find where the market demand curve intersects the marginal cost curve—that is, where the sum of the marginal valuations equals the marginal cost.

Suppose the public good in question is mosquito control in a neighborhood, which, for simplicity consists of only two houses, one headed by Alan and the other by Maria. Alan spends a lot of time in the yard and thus values a mosquito-free environment more than does Maria, who spends more time away from home. Their demand curves are shown in Exhibit 2 as D_a and D_m, reflecting the marginal benefits that Alan and Maria get, respectively, at each rate of output. Quantity is measured here as hours of mosquito spraying per week.

For example, when the town sprays two hours a week, Maria is willing to pay $5 for the second hour and Alan is willing to pay $10 for the second hour. To derive the sum of the marginal benefits for the neighborhood, we simply add each resident's marginal benefit to get $15, as identified by point *e*. By vertically summing marginal valuations at each rate of output, we derive the neighborhood demand curve, *D*, for mosquito spraying.

How much of this public good should be produced? Suppose the marginal cost of spraying is a constant $15 an hour, as shown in Exhibit 2. The efficient level of output is found where the marginal benefit to the neighborhood equals the marginal cost, which occurs where the neighborhood demand curve inter-

EXHIBIT 2

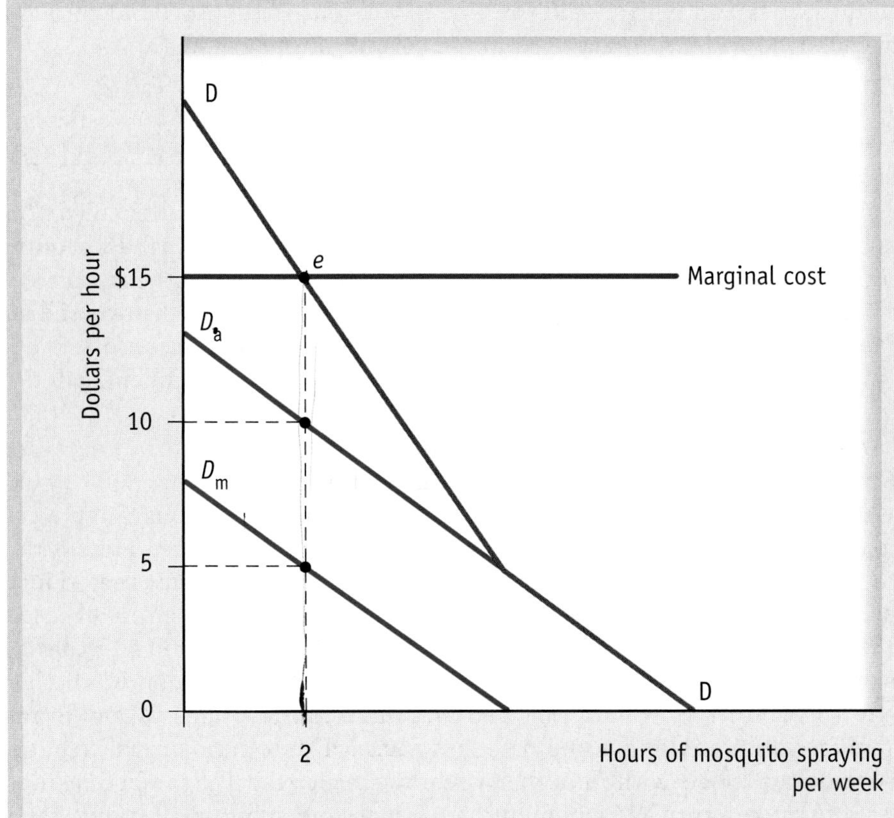

Market for Public Goods

Because public goods, once produced, are available to all in identical amounts, the demand for a public good is the vertical sum of each individual's demand. Thus, the market demand for mosquito spraying is the vertical sum of Maria's demand, D_m, and Alan's demand, D_a. The efficient level of provision is found where the marginal cost of mosquito spraying equals its marginal benefit. This occurs where the marginal cost curve intersects the market demand curve, *D*, resulting in point *e*.

sects the marginal cost curve. In our example, these curves intersect where output is two hours per week.

The government pays for the mosquito spray through taxes, user fees, or some combination of the two. The most straightforward approach might be to impose a tax on each resident equal to his or her marginal valuation. Simple enough, but there are at least two problems with this. First, once people realize their taxes are based on how much the government thinks they value the good, they tend to understate their true valuation. Why admit you really value the good if, as a result, you get smacked with a higher tax bill? Thus taxpayers are reluctant to offer information about their true valuation of public goods. But even if the government had accurate information about marginal valuations, some households earn much higher incomes than other households and thus have a greater ability to pay taxes. In our example, Alan valued mosquito control more because he spent more time around the house than did Maria. What if Alan was around the house more because he couldn't find a job. Should his taxes be double those of Maria, who, say, has a good job?

Once the public good is produced, only that rate of output is available. Since only one quantity is produced, each individual's consumption is limited to that particular quantity. In contrast, with private goods, each consumer is free to purchase any quantity he or she prefers. Thus public goods are much more complicated than private goods in terms of what goods should be provided, in what quantities, and who should pay. These decisions are thrashed out through public choices, which are examined in the balance of this chapter.

PUBLIC CHOICE IN A REPRESENTATIVE DEMOCRACY

Government decisions about the provision of public goods and the collection of tax revenues are *public choices*. In a democracy, public choices usually require approval by a majority of voters. As it turns out, we can frequently explain the choice of the electorate by focusing on the preferences of the median voter. The *median voter* is the voter whose preferences lie in the middle of the set of all voters' preferences. For example, if the issue is the size of the government, half the voters prefer a larger government and half prefer a smaller one.

Median Voter Model

Median voter model Under certain conditions, the preference of the median, or middle, voter will dominate other public choices

The **median voter model** predicts that under certain conditions, the preference of the median, or middle, voter will dominate other choices. Here is the logic behind the model. Suppose you and two roommates have just moved into an apartment, and the three of you must decide on furnishings. You all agree that the common costs will be shared equally by the three of you and that majority rule will prevail, with one vote per person. The issue at hand is whether to buy a TV and, if so, of what size. The problem is that you each have different preferences. Your studious roommate considers a TV an annoying distraction and would rather go without; otherwise, the smaller the TV, the better. Your other roommate, a real TV fan, prefers a 48-inch screen but would settle for a smaller size rather than go without. Although you are by no means a TV addict, you enjoy watching TV as a relief from the rigors of academe; a 26-inch screen is your first choice, but you prefer the 48-inch screen to no TV. What to do, what to do?

You all agree to make the decision by voting on two alternatives at a time, then pairing the winning alternative against the remaining alternative until one choice dominates the others. When the 26-inch set is paired with the no-TV option, the 26-inch set wins because this option gets both your vote and the TV fan's vote. When the 26-inch screen is then paired with the 48-inch screen, the 26-inch screen wins a majority again, this time because your studious roommate sides with you rather than voting for the super screen.

Majority voting in effect delegates the public choice to the person whose preference is the median for the group. You, as the median voter in this case, can have your way; if you preferred a 12-inch screen or a 36-inch screen, you could have received majority support for either. Similarly, *the median voter in an electorate often determines public choices. Political candidates try to get elected by appealing to the median voter.* This is one reason why candidates often seem so much alike.

Note that under majority rule, only the median voter gets his or her way. Other voters are required to go along with what the median voter wants. Thus other voters usually end up paying for what they consider to be either too much or too little of the public good.

People vote directly on issues at New England town meetings and on the occasional referendum, but direct democracy is not the most common means of public choice. When you consider the thousands of public choices made on behalf of individual voters, it becomes clear that direct democracy through referenda would be unwieldy and impractical. Rather than make decisions by direct referenda, voters elect *representatives*, who, at least in theory, make public choices that reflect their constituents' views. Under certain conditions, the resulting public choices reflect the preferences of the median voter. Some complications of making public choices through representative democracy will be explored next.

Goals of the Participants

We assume that consumers maximize utility and firms maximize profit, but what about governments? As noted in Chapter 4, there is no common agreement about what governments maximize or, more precisely, what elected officials maximize, if anything. One theory that parallels the rational self-interest assumption employed in private choices is that elected officials attempt to *maximize their political support*.

It is possible that elected representatives will cater to special interests rather than serve the interests of the majority. The problem arises because of the asymmetry between special interests and the public interest, an idea introduced in the previous chapter. Consider only one of the thousands of decisions that are made each year by elected representatives: funding an obscure federal program that subsidized U.S. wool production. Under the wool-subsidy program, the federal government guarantees that a floor price is paid to sheep farmers for each pound of wool they produced, a subsidy that costs taxpayers over $75 million per year. During deliberations to renew the program, the only person to testify before Congress was a representative of the National Wool Growers Association, who claimed that the subsidy was vital to the nation's economic welfare. Why didn't a single taxpayer challenge the subsidy? Why were sheep farmers able to pull the wool over the taxpayers' eyes?

Rational Ignorance

Households consume so many different public and private goods and services that they have neither the time nor the incentive to understand the effects of public choices on every one of these products. What's more, voters realize that each of them has only a tiny possibility of influencing the outcome of public choices. And even if an individual voter is somehow able to affect the outcome, the impact on that voter is likely to be small. For example, even if a taxpayer could successfully stage a grass-roots campaign to eliminate the wool subsidy, the taxpayer would save, on average, less than $1 per year in federal income taxes. Therefore, unless voters have a special interest in the legislation, they adopt a stance of **rational ignorance**, which means that they remain largely oblivious to the costs and benefits of the thousands of proposals considered by elected officials. The cost to the typical voter of acquiring and acting on such information is typically greater than any expected benefit.

Rational ignorance A stance adopted by voters when they find that the cost of understanding and voting on a particular issue exceeds the benefit expected from doing so

In contrast, consumers have a greater incentive to gather and act on information about decisions they make in private markets because they benefit directly from the knowledge so acquired. *Since information and the time required to acquire and digest it are scarce, consumers concentrate on private choices rather than public choices because the payoff in making wise private choices is usually more immediate, more direct, and more substantial*. For example, a consumer in the market for a new car has an incentive to examine the performance records of different models, test-drive a few, and check prices at dealerships and on the Internet. That same individual has less incentive to examine the performance records of candidates for public office because that single voter has virtually no chance of deciding the election. What's more, political candidates, who aim to please the median voter, will often take positions that are quite similar anyway.

Distribution of Costs and Benefits

Let's turn now to how the costs and benefits of public choices are spread across the population. The costs imposed by a particular legislative measure may be either narrowly or widely distributed over the population, depending on the issue. Likewise, the benefits may be conferred on only a small group or on much of the population. The possible combinations of costs and benefits yield four alternative types of distributions: (1) widespread costs and widespread benefits, (2) widespread costs and concentrated benefits, (3) concentrated costs and concentrated benefits, and (4) concentrated costs and widespread benefits.

Traditional public goods, such as national defense and a system of justice, have widespread costs and widespread benefits—nearly everyone pays and nearly everyone benefits from this category of distribution. Traditional public goods usually have a positive impact on the economy because the sum of the benefits outweighs the costs.

Special-interest legislation Legislation that generates concentrated benefits but imposes widespread costs

With **special-interest legislation**, benefits are concentrated but costs are widespread. For example, as you'll see shortly, price supports for dairy products mean consumers pay a higher price for milk than would result from normal market forces. The program benefits are concentrated on dairy farmers. The costs are widespread across consumers and taxpayers. And the total cost far exceeds the total benefit. Legislation that caters to special interest groups usually harms the economy, on net, because total costs exceed total benefits.

Competing-interest legislation Legislation that imposes concentrated costs on one group and provides concentrated benefits to another group

Competing-interest legislation involves both concentrated costs and concentrated benefits. For example, restrictions on sugar imports boost the price of U.S. sugar to twice the world price,[1] thereby benefiting growers of sugarcane and sugar refiners. But major sugar-using manufacturers such as Hershey and M&M Mars must pay these higher sugar prices, which cut into their profits. The issue pits sugar growers against sugar buyers—two special interests.

The fourth possible combination of costs and benefits involves concentrated costs but widespread benefits. If legislators try to impose costs in a concentrated way so as to confer benefits widely, the group getting hit with the concentrated costs will object strenuously. Meanwhile, those who benefit usually remain rationally ignorant of the proposed legislation, so they provide little political support. For example, whenever Congress considers imposing a tax on a particular industry, that industry floods Washington with lobbyists, phone calls, faxes, e-mail, snail mail, and telegrams, usually claiming that the tax will lead to economic ruin, not to mention the decline of Western civilization as we know it. Here, for example, is a recent account from The *New York Times*:

1 See "Sugar Battle Brews in Congress," *New York Times* (13 June 1998).

A lobbying blitz by some of the biggest names in corporate America has succeeded in maintaining a lucrative tax break for multinational corporations—one that allows them to avoid U.S. taxes and reduce their foreign tax bill, too. . . . Business succeeded through a combination of arm-twisting, letter-writing, and hiring some of the best tax-lobbying talent in Washington, including many who helped create the tax law.[2]

Thus legislation that imposes costs on a small group but confers benefits widely has less chance of approval than do measures that confer benefits narrowly but spread costs widely.

In the following case study, we consider the redistributive and efficiency effects of a particular special-interest program—supports for milk prices.

Farm Subsidies

CaseStudy

Public Policy

Provisions of the Federal Agriculture Improvement and Reform Act of 1996, available at http://www.econ.ag.gov/epubs/pdf/aib729/, describes new legislation aimed at reducing farmer reliance on price support programs. You can learn about its impact on the dairy sector by reading the summary of *The Structure of Dairy Markets: Past, Present and Future* at http://www.econ.ag.gov/epubs/htmlsum/aer757.htm. Which type of firm buys most of the fluid milk produced by dairy farmers? What does the future hold for dairy markets? More reports on the marketing of dairy products are at http://www.inform.umd.edu/EdRes/Topic/AgrEnv/ndd/marketin/ from the U.S. National Dairy Database maintained by the University of Maryland.

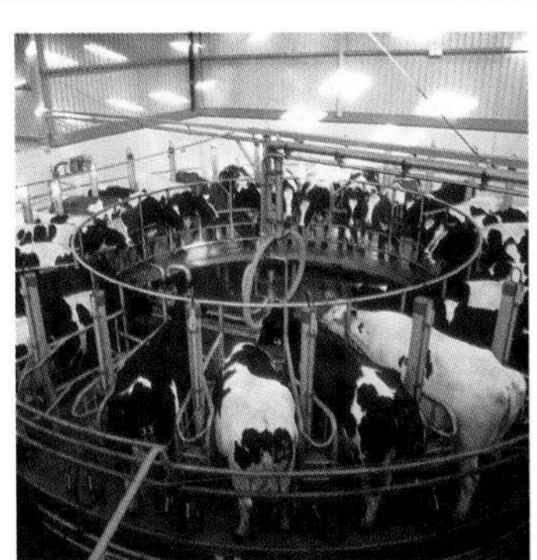

The Agricultural Marketing Agreement Act became law in 1937 to prevent what was viewed as "ruinous competition" among farmers. In the years since, the government introduced a variety of policies to set floor prices for a wide range of farm products. Until the federal government began scaling back farm subsidies in 1996, direct costs exceeded $10 billion a year for dozens of agricultural products. Support programs for milk and sugar persist.

In most parts of the country, milk prices are the most heavily regulated of farm products. Explaining the intricacies of the complicated milk-price support program takes up three volumes of the *Code of Federal Regulations*, and administering the regulations employs 500 people at the U.S. Department of Agriculture—as many as oversee the entire federal budget in the Office of Management and Budget. These rules cost consumers an estimated $1.7 billion a year, according to Agriculture Department studies.

Let's see how price supports worked in the dairy industry using a hypothetical example. Exhibit 3 depicts a simplified view of the market for milk. Suppose that, in the absence of government intervention, the market price of milk would average $1.50 per gallon and the equilibrium quantity would average 100 million gallons per week. In long-run equilibrium, dairy farmers would earn a normal rate of return. Consumers as a group would capture the consumer surplus shown by the blue shaded area. Recall that consumer surplus is the difference between the most that consumers would have been willing to pay and the amount actually paid.

But suppose that dairy farmers persuade Congress that the free-market price is too low, so legislation establishes a price floor for milk of, say, $2.50 per gallon. The higher price floor provides farmers with an incentive to increase the quantity supplied to 150 million gallons per week. In response to the higher price, however, consumers reduce their quantity demanded to 75 million gallons per week. To make the higher price stick, the government must buy the 75 million

2 This is the lead paragraph in a story by Leslie Wayne, "Tax Break Intact for Now After Fight By Business," *New York Times* (12 July 1998).

gallons of "surplus" milk generated by the floor price or somehow get dairy farmers to restrict their output to 75 million gallons per week. For example, the government could pay dairy farmers not to produce or could buy cows from farmers to reduce production (as was done in the 1980s).

Consumers end up paying dearly to subsidize the farmers. First, the price per gallon increases by $1. Second, consumers, as taxpayers, must pay for the surplus milk or otherwise pay farmers not to produce that milk. And third, if the government buys the surplus milk, taxpayers must then pay for storage. So the consumer pays $2.50 per gallon for milk purchased on the market; the consumer as an average taxpayer also pays another $2.50 for each gallon the government buys, plus, say, an extra $0.50 per gallon to convert surplus milk into powder and to store it. Instead of paying just $1.50 for a gallon of milk, which is the price in the absence of government price supports, the typical consumer-taxpayer in our example pays $5.50 per gallon, or an extra outlay of $4.00 per gallon of milk actually consumed.

How do the farmers make out? Each farmer receives an extra $1 per gallon in additional revenue over the price that would have prevailed in a free market. As farmers increase their output, however, the marginal cost of production increases; at the margin, the higher price the farmer receives is just offset by higher production costs. Still, farmers gain an increase in producer surplus because of the subsidy program, identified in Exhibit 3 by the area above the supply curve that is between the market price of $1.50 and the floor price of $2.50.

EXHIBIT 3

Effects of Milk Price Supports

In the absence of government intervention, the market price of milk is $1.50 per gallon and 100 million gallons are sold per week. If Congress establishes a floor price of $2.50 per gallon, then the quantity supplied will increase and the quantity demanded will decrease. To maintain the higher price, the government must buy up the excess quantity at $2.50 per gallon.

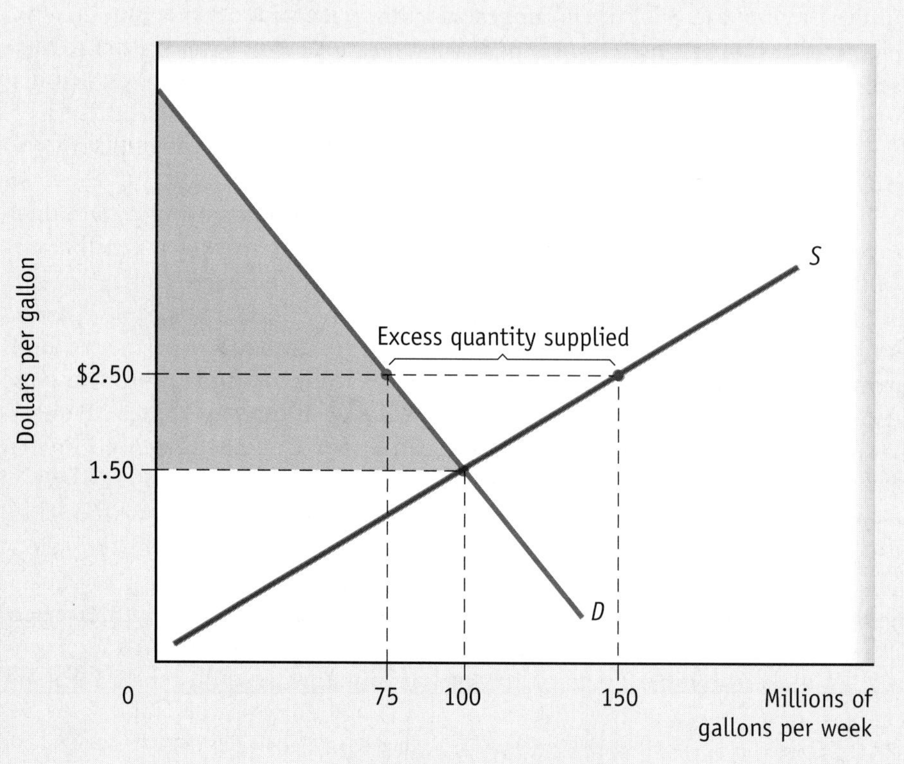

The subsidy will increase the value of resources specialized to dairy farming, such as cows and grazing land, and farmers who own these resources when the subsidy program goes into effect will benefit. Farmers who purchase these resources after the subsidy has been introduced will pay more and will end up earning just a normal rate of return on that investment. So with free entry into the dairy industry, most farmers in the long run earn just a normal rate of return, despite the billions spent on farm subsidies.

If the extra $1 per gallon that farmers receive for milk were pure profit, farm profits would increase by $150 million per week. But consumer-taxpayer costs would increase by $300 million per week ($75 million for the higher price of each of the 75 million gallons consumers purchase, plus $187.5 million in higher taxes for the 75 million surplus gallons purchased by the government, plus $37.5 million to store the 75 million surplus gallons). Thus, consumer-taxpayer costs are double the farmers' maximum possible gain of $150 million. The government subsidy therefore has a negative impact on the economy, as the losses outweigh the gains. This does not mean nobody gains—those who owned specialized resources gained when the subsidy was first introduced. But once the price of farm resources increases, new farmers must pay more to get in a position to reap the subsidies. Ironically, subsidies aimed at preserving the family farm raise the costs of a young person entering the industry.

Over the years, federal price support programs bought up the surplus, paid dairy farmers not to produce, and bought cows from farmers. By the mid-1980s, dairy herds had expanded so much that the government spent more than $1 billion to reduce herd size (herds are now growing again). Since 1980, U.S. milk prices have averaged twice the price on world markets, yet imports are restricted. Federal regulations also limit farmers in one part of the country from selling their milk in another part of the country. For decades minimum milk prices in each region around the country were determined by a complicated formula based on the distance from Eau Claire, Wisconsin.

The dairy industry is supported in other ways. Some state programs support even higher prices. Other laws promote the consumption of dairy products. For example, laws in many states prohibit restaurants from serving margarine unless customers specifically request it instead of butter. Margarine has faced a long history of discrimination dating back a century.

In November 1997 a federal judge threw out the federal regulations on milk pricing, but the battle to deregulate milk prices is not over. The U.S. Department of Agriculture is appealing the judge's ruling, and dairy farmers in some parts of the country are trying to bypass the ruling by forming their own interstate pricing agreements. For example, the New England states approved a milk-price compact that establishes minimum prices to farmers, prices that average 5 percent to 22 percent above the mandated minimum prices under existing federal legislation. Dairy farmers in other states are looking to follow New England's example.

The profound long-run problem for dairy farmers is that technological breakthroughs, such as genetically engineered hormones that stimulate milk production, have made dairies far more productive. Yet milk consumption remains flat (despite the widely advertised "Got milk?" and milk-mustache campaigns). The combination of increased supply and stagnant demand is a recipe for excess quantity supplied.

Everyone would be better off if the government made a direct transfer payment to farmers, a payment not tied to milk production or price. Although a direct transfer payment to dairy farmers would be more efficient, such a transparent special-interest proposal could attract the public's attention and be doomed. Special-interest legislation is often promoted under the cover of some greater good. The ostensible goal of farm subsidies, for example, is to save the family farm, but farm households on average earn more than nonfarm households and are wealthier. And business failure rates are lower in agriculture than the average for all industries.

Sources: Bruce L. Gardner, "Changing Economic Perspectives on the Farm Problem," *Journal of Economic Literature* 30 (March 1992): 62–101; Scott Kilman, "Byzantine Method of Pricing Milk Won't Be Simplified Anytime Soon," *Wall Street Journal* (25 November 1997); "Consumer Prices Vary Widely," *New York Times* (18 April 1998); and Kim Archer, "U.S. House Defeats Sugar, Milk Amendments in Ag Debate," *Dow Jones Newswire* (24 June 1998).

Rent Seeking

An important feature of representative democracy is the incentive and political power it offers participants to employ legislation that increases their wealth, either through direct transfers or through favorable public expenditures and regulations. Special-interest groups, such as sugarcane growers, dairy farmers, or trial lawyers, try to persuade elected officials to approve measures that provide the special interest with some market advantage or some outright transfer or subsidy. Such benefits are sometimes called *rents*. The term in this context implies that the government transfer or subsidy constitutes a payment to the resource owner that exceeds the earnings necessary to call forth that resource—*a payment exceeding opportunity cost*. The activity that interest groups undertake to elicit these special favors from government is called *rent seeking*.

The government frequently bestows some special advantage on a producer or group of producers, and abundant resources are expended to secure these rights. For example, *political action committees*, known more popularly as *PACs*, contribute millions to congressional campaigns. More than 4,000 PACs try to shape federal legislation; the top contributors recently included the tobacco lobby and the American Trial Lawyers Association. Tobacco interests would like to influence cigarette legislation and lawyers fear legal reforms that would limit liability lawsuits.

To the extent that special-interest groups engage in rent-seeking activities, they shift resources from productive endeavors that create income to activities that focus more on transferring income. *Resources employed in an attempt to get government to redistribute income or wealth are unproductive because they do nothing to increase output and usually end up reducing it.* Often many firms compete for the same government advantage, thereby wasting still more resources. If the advantage conferred by government on some special-interest group requires higher income taxes, the net return individuals expect from working and investing will fall, so less work and less investment may occur. If this happens, productive activity will decline.

As a firm's profitability becomes more and more dependent on decisions made in Washington, resources are diverted from productive activity to rent seeking, or lobbying efforts to gain special advantage. One firm may thrive because it secured some special advantage at a critical time; another firm may fail because its managers were more concerned with productive efficiency than with rent seeking.

Special-interest groups have little incentive to make the economy more efficient. In fact, special-interest groups will usually support legislation that transfers wealth to them even if the measure reduces the economy's overall efficiency. For example, suppose that the American Trial Lawyers Association is able to push through product-liability legislation that has the effect of increasing lawyers' incomes by a total of $1 billion per year, or about $1,900 for each lawyer in private practice. Suppose, too, that this measure drives up insurance premiums, raising the total cost of production by, say, $5 billion per year. Lawyers themselves will have to bear part of this higher cost, but since they account for only about 1 percent of the spending in the economy, they will bear only about 1 percent of the $5 billion in higher costs, or a total of $50 million, which amounts to about $100 per lawyer per year. Thus, the legislation is a bargain for lawyers because it increases the income of each by an average of about $1,900 per year but increases the cost each faces by an average of only about $100 a year.

Think of the economy's output in a particular period as depicted by a pie. The pie is the total value of goods and services produced. In deciding on answers to the "what," "how," and "for whom" questions introduced in Chapter 2, policy makers have three alternatives: (1) they can introduce changes that will yield a bigger pie (that is, positive-sum changes), (2) they can decide simply to carve up the existing pie differently (redistribution of income), or (3) they can start fighting over the pie, causing some of it to end up on the floor (negative-sum changes). Much special-interest legislation leads to a net reduction in social welfare. Some of the nation's best minds are occupied with devising schemes to avoid taxes or divert income to favored groups at the expense of market efficiency. For example, the pursuit of tax loopholes fills the days of some of the brightest lawyers and accountants.

There are hundreds of special-interest groups representing farmers, physicians, lawyers, teachers, manufacturers, barbers, and so on. One way special interests try to gain access to the political process is through campaign contributions. The elusive issue of campaign-finance reform is discussed in the following case study.

Public Policy

You can find a comprehensive list of Web sites on campaign reform compiled by the Electronic Policy Network at http://epn.org/camfinre.html. Among these you will find the Brookings Institution, a Washington, DC thinktank at http://www.brook.edu/gs/campaign/cfr_hp.htm and Common Cause, a nonpartisan lobbying group promoting accountable government at http://www.commoncause.org/issue_agenda/campaign_finance.htm. What bills are pending?

Campaign Finance Reform

Critics of the current campaign finance system have argued that American politics is awash in special-interest money. Most Americans seem to agree. In one poll, two-thirds of those surveyed said they would be willing to have their tax dollars used for campaigns if this meant the elimination of financing by large private donations and organized interest groups. Since the 1970s, presidential campaigns have been publicly funded, but not Congressional races (the Clinton and Dole campaigns each received $62 million during the 1996 presidential election).

A campaign finance reform measure proposed recently in the House of Representatives would establish a $600,000 voluntary spending limit for House candidates and sharply reduce special-interest influence by restricting PAC contributions, large individual contributions, and contributions from lobbyists. Proposed legislation would also restrict individual contributions that exceed $200 (since 1974, contributions to candidates have been limited to $1,000 per person.) If candidates voluntarily agree to limit their spending, they would get public money and cut-rate television time.

Limits on special-interest contributions may help reduce their influence in the political process, but such limits would heighten the current advantage of incumbency. The overwhelming majority of congressional incumbents are re-elected. For example, 380 of the 405 Congress members who ran for reelection in 1996 won, yielding a reelection rate of 94 percent. Observers claim that this results from the unfair advantages that incumbents have in the electoral process, especially because of taxpayer-funded staff and free mailing privileges (campaign literature masquerading as official communications).

Limits on campaign spending would magnify the advantages of incumbency by reducing a challenger's ability to appeal directly to voters. Some liberal *and* conservative thinkers agree that the supply of political money should be increased, not decreased. As Curtis Gans of the Committee for the Study of the American Electorate argues, "The overwhelming body of scholarly research . . . indicates that low spending limits will undermine political competition by enhancing the existing advantages of incumbency." *Money matters more to challengers than to incumbents* since the public knows less about challengers than about incumbents. Challengers must be able to spend enough to get their message out. One study found a positive relationship between spending by challengers and election success but found no relationship between spending by incumbents and their reelection success. So a limit on spending favors incumbents.

Although many decry the amount spent on campaigns, spending is a relative concept. For example, total direct campaign spending for all congressional races in 1994 averaged about $3 per eligible voter. All 1993–1994 PAC contributions for all federal races would not cover the cost of the movie *Titanic.*

The U.S. Supreme Court has struck down mandatory campaign spending limits. According to the Constitution, "Congress shall make no law . . . abridging freedom of speech." The Supreme Court ruled that "dollars are not stuffed in ballot boxes . . . The mediating factor that turns money into votes is speech. . . . Advocacy cannot be proscribed because it's effective."

The point is that legislation often has unintended consequences. Efforts to limit campaign spending may or may not reduce the influence of special-interest groups, but a limit would reduce a challenger's ability to reach the voters and thereby increase the advantage of incumbency.

Sources: Jill Abramson, "When $10 Million Is in Trough, Few Want to Overturn It," *New York Times* (15 June 1998); Stanley Brubaker, "The Limits of Campaign Spending Limits," *Public Interest* (Fall 1998): 33–54; Edward Crane, "Testimony before the Committee on House Oversight, U.S. House of Representatives," 16 November 1995; Alison Mitchell, "House Votes to Consider 258 Amendments to Campaign Bill," *New York Times* (19 June 1998); and James Dao, "Shay Leads Battle in House for Campaign Finance Bill," *New York Times* (22 June 1998).

The Underground Economy

A government subsidy promotes production, as we saw in the case study on milk price supports. Conversely, a tax discourages production. Perhaps it would be more accurate to say that when government taxes productive activity, less production is *reported*. If you have worked as a waitress or waiter, did you faithfully report all your tips to the Internal Revenue Service? To the extent that you did not, your income became part of the underground economy. The **underground economy** is a term used for all market activity that goes unreported to the government either to avoid taxes or because the activity itself is illegal. Thus income arising in the underground economy ranges from unreported tips to the earnings of a drug dealer.

Underground economy Economic activity that goes unreported to the government either to avoid taxes or because the activity is illegal

The introduction of a tax on productive activity has two effects. First, resource owners may supply less of the taxed resource because the tax reduces the net return from supplying the resource. Second, in an attempt to evade taxes, some people will divert their economic activity from the formal, reported economy to an underground, "off-the-books" economy. Thus, when the government taxes market exchange or the income it generates, less market activity is reported.

We should take care to distinguish between tax *avoidance* and tax *evasion*. Tax avoidance is a legal attempt to arrange one's economic affairs so as to pay the least tax possible, such as buying municipal bonds because they yield tax-free interest. Tax evasion is illegal; it takes the form of either failing to file a tax return or filing a fraudulent return by understating income or overstating deductions. Research around the world indicates that the underground economy grows (1) when government regulations increase, (2) when the tax burden increases, and (3) where government corruption is more widespread.[3]

Although there are no official figures on the size of the underground economy, federal agencies try to make estimates based on other data. The Commerce Department estimates that official figures capture only 90 percent of U.S. income. An Internal Revenue Service survey estimated that only 87 percent of tax liabilities are paid. These studies suggest an underground economy amounting to between $675 billion and $900 billion in 1999.

Those who pursue rent-seeking activity and those involved in the underground economy view government from opposite perspectives. Rent seekers want government to become actively involved in transferring wealth to them, but those in the underground economy want to avoid government contact. *Subsidies and other advantages bestowed by government draw some groups closer to government; taxes drive others underground.*

BUREAUCRACY AND REPRESENTATIVE DEMOCRACY

Elected representatives approve legislation, but the task of implementing that legislation is typically left to various government departments and agencies. The organizations charged with implementing legislation are usually referred to as **bureaus,** which are government agencies whose activities are financed by appropriations from legislative bodies.

Bureaus Government agencies charged with implementing legislation and financed by appropriations from legislative bodies

Ownership and Funding of Bureaus

We can get a better feel for government bureaus by comparing them to corporations. Ownership of a corporation is based on the shares owned by stockhold-

3 For a summary of these studies, see Simon Johnson, et al., "Regulatory Discretion and the Unofficial Economy," *American Economic Review* 88 (May 1988): 387–392.

ers. Stockholders are the residual claimants of any profits or losses arising from the firm's operations. Ownership in a corporation is *transferable:* the shares can be sold in the stock market. In contrast, taxpayers are in a sense the "owners" of government bureaus in the jurisdiction in which they live. If the bureau earns a "profit," taxes will be reduced; if the bureau operates at a "loss," as most do, this loss must be covered by taxes. Each taxpayer has just one vote, regardless of the taxes paid. Ownership in the bureau is surrendered only if the taxpayer dies or moves out of the jurisdiction; ownership is not transferable—it cannot be bought and sold directly.

Whereas firms receive their revenue when customers voluntarily purchase their products, bureaus are typically financed by a budget appropriation from the legislature. Most of this budget comes from taxpayers. On occasion, bureaus earn revenue through user charges, such as admission fees to state parks or tuition at state colleges, but supplementary funds for these activities often come from budget appropriations. Because of these differences in the forms of ownership and in the sources of revenue, bureaus have different incentives than do profit-making firms, so they are likely to behave differently as well.

Ownership and Organizational Behavior

A central assumption of economics is that people behave rationally and respond to economic incentives. The more tightly compensation is linked to individual incentives, the more people will behave in accordance with those incentives. If a letter carrier's pay is based on the customers' satisfaction, the carrier will make a greater effort to deliver mail promptly and intact.

The private firm receives a steady stream of consumer feedback. If the price is too high or too low to clear the market, the firm will see surpluses or shortages develop. Not only is consumer feedback abundant, but the firm's owners have a profit incentive to act on that information in an attempt to satisfy consumer wants. The promise of profits also creates incentives to produce output at minimum cost. Thus, the firm's owners stand to gain from any improvement in customer satisfaction or in production efficiency.

Since public goods and services are not sold in markets, government bureaus receive less consumer feedback and are less sensitive to the feedback they do receive. There are no prices and no obvious shortages or surpluses. For example, how would you know whether there was a shortage or a surplus of police protection in your community? (Would gangs of police officers hanging around the doughnut shop indicate a surplus?) Not only do bureaus receive less consumer feedback than do firms, they also have less incentive to act on the information available. Because any "profits" or "losses" arising in the bureau are spread among all taxpayers, and because there is no transferability of ownership, bureaus have less incentive to satisfy customers or to produce their output using the least-cost combination of resources. (Laws prevent bureaucrats from taking home any "profit.")

Some pressure for customer satisfaction and cost minimization may be communicated by voters to their elected representatives and thereby to the bureaus. But this discipline is not very precise, particularly since any gains or losses in efficiency are diffused among all taxpayers. For example, suppose that you are one of a million taxpayers in a jurisdiction and you know about an inefficiency that wastes a million dollars a year. If you undertake measures that succeed in correcting the shortcoming, you save yourself about a dollar per year in taxes.

Voters can also leave a jurisdiction if they believe government is inefficient. Yet this mechanism, whereby people "vote with their feet" by moving to a more responsive jurisdiction, is a rather crude way to approximate voter satisfaction. Moreover, voters dissatisfied with the national government cannot easily vote with their feet.

Because of differences between public and private organizations—in the owners' ability both to transfer ownership and to appropriate profits—we expect bureaus to be less concerned with satisfying consumer demand and minimizing costs than private firms are. A variety of empirical studies has attempted to compare costs for products that are provided by both public bureaus and private firms, such as garbage collection. Of those studies that show a difference, some find public bureaus to be more efficient, but the majority find private firms to be more efficient.

Bureaucratic Objectives

Assuming that bureaus are not simply at the beck and call of the legislature—that is, assuming that bureaucrats have some autonomy—what sort of objectives will they pursue? The traditional view is that bureaucrats are "public servants," who try to serve the public as best they can. No doubt many public employees do just that, but is this a realistic assumption for bureaucrats more generally? Why should we assume self-sacrificing behavior by public-sector employees when we make no such assumption about private-sector employees?

One widely discussed theory of bureaucratic behavior has been proposed by William Niskanen. He argues that bureaus attempt to *maximize their budgets,* for along with a bigger budget comes size, prestige, amenities, staff, and pay—all features that are valued by bureaucrats.[4] How do bureaucrats maximize the bureau's budget? According to Niskanen, bureaus are monopoly suppliers of their output to the legislature. Rather than charge a price per unit, bureaus offer the legislature the entire amount as a package deal in return for the requested appropriation. According to this theory, the legislature has little ability to dig into the budget and cut particular items (no line-item veto). If the legislature proposes cuts in the bureau's budget, the bureau may threaten to make those cuts as painful to the legislature and constituents as possible. For example, if city officials attempt to reduce the school budget, school bureaucrats, rather than increase teaching loads, may threaten to eliminate kindergarten, abolish the high-school football team, or cut textbook purchases. If such threats are effective in forcing the legislature to back off from any cuts, the government budget turns out to be larger than most taxpayers would prefer. *Budget maximization results in a budget larger than that desired by the median voter.* The key to this argument is that bureaus are monopoly suppliers. If taxpayers have alternatives in the private sector, the monopoly power of the bureau is diminished.

Private Versus Public Production

Simply because some goods and services are financed by the government does not mean that they must be produced by the government. Elected officials may contract directly with private firms to produce public output. For example, a city council may contract with a firm to handle garbage collection for the city.

4 William A. Niskanen, Jr., *Bureaucracy and Representative Government* (Chicago: Aldine-Atherton, 1971).

Profit-making firms now provide everything from fire protection to prisons to local education. Elected officials may also use some combination of bureaus and firms to produce the desired output. For example, the Pentagon, a giant bureau, hires and trains military personnel, yet contracts with private firms to develop and produce various weapon systems. State governments typically hire private contractors to build roads but employ state workers to maintain roads. The mix of firms and bureaus varies over time and across jurisdictions, but the trend is toward increased *privatization,* or production by the private sector, of government goods and services. For example, among a sample of a dozen services provided by local governments, the share of services privatized increased from 24 percent in 1987 to 34 percent in 1992.[5]

When governments produce public goods and services, they are using *the internal organization of the government*—the bureaucracy—to supply the product. When governments contract with private firms to produce public goods and services, they are using *the market* to supply the product. Legislators might prefer dealing with bureaus rather than with firms for two reasons. First, in situations where it is difficult to specify a contract that clearly spells out all the possible contingencies, the internal organization of the bureau may be more responsive to the legislature's concerns than the manager of a firm would be. Second, to the extent that bureaus are vehicles for political patronage, legislators may prefer bureaus because bureaus provide opportunities to reward friends and supporters with jobs.

Using market competition to supply services that are not well defined, such as the guidance provided by a social worker, may lead to poor service. A private firm that wins the contract might be tempted to skimp on quality, particularly if the quality of the service can be determined only by direct observation when the service is provided. For example, suppose that government puts social work out for bid, selects the lowest bidder, then attempts to monitor the quality of the service through direct observation. The government would find direct monitoring quite costly. These services thus might best be provided by a government bureau. Because the bureau is less concerned with minimizing costs, it has less reason to lower the quality to reduce cost.

CONCLUSION

This chapter examined public goods and how preferences are reflected in public choices. After examining public goods, we discussed the problems arising from representative democracy and then examined bureaus, the organizations that usually implement public choices. We also considered indirect income transfers, or rent seeking, which arise because of changes in the rules governing economic activity in the private sector. Price supports, import restrictions, and other indirect transfers are not reflected fully in the government budget but often have profound effects on the economy. Whenever governments become involved in the workings of the economy to favor one group over another, some resources are shifted from productive activity to rent-seeking activity—that is, efforts to persuade the government to confer benefits on certain groups.

5 Robert Barro, "The Imperative to Privatize," *Wall Street Journal* (29 June 1995).

Individual incentives may also be distorted in a way that reduces the economy's output.

Governments attempt to address market failures in the private economy. But simply turning problems of perceived market failure over to government may not always be the best solution, because government has failings of its own. Participation in markets is based on voluntary exchange. Governments, however, have the legal power to enforce public choices. We should employ at least as high a standard in judging the performance of government, where allocations have the force of law, as we do in judging the private market, where allocations are decided by voluntary exchange between consenting parties.

SUMMARY

1. Private goods are rival and exclusive, such as a pizza. Public goods are nonrival and nonexclusive such as national defense. Goods that are in between include quasi-public goods, which are nonrival but exclusive, such as cable TV, and open-access goods, which are rival but nonexclusive, such as fish in the sea. Since private-sector producers cannot easily exclude nonpayers from consuming a public good, such goods are typically provided by government, which has the power to impose taxes.
2. Public choice based on majority rule usually reflects the preferences of the median voter. Other voters often must "buy" either more or less of the public good than they would prefer.
3. Producers have an abiding interest in any legislation that affects their livelihood. Consumers, however, purchase thousands of different goods and services and have no special interest in legislation affecting any particular product. Most consumers adopt a posture of rational ignorance about producer-oriented legislation, because the costs of keeping up with special-interest issues usually outweigh the expected benefits.
4. The intense interest that producer groups express in relevant legislation, coupled with the rational ignorance of voters on most issues, leaves government officials vulnerable to rent seeking by special interests. Elected officials interested in maximizing their political support may tend to serve producer interests rather than consumer interests—that is, to serve special interests at the expense of the public interest.
5. Bureaus differ from firms in the amount of consumer feedback they receive, in their incentive to minimize costs, and in the transferability of their ownership. Because of these differences, bureaus may not be as efficient or as sensitive to consumer preferences as private firms are.

QUESTIONS FOR REVIEW

1. *(Private and Public Goods)* Distinguish among private goods, quasi-public goods, open-access goods, and public goods. Provide examples of each.
2. *(Median Voter Model)* In a single-issue majority vote, such as the TV example in this chapter, will the median voter always get his or her most preferred outcome?
3. *(Representative Democracy)* Major political parties typically produce "middle-of-the-road" platforms rather than take extreme positions. Is this consistent with the concepts of the median voter and rational ignorance discussed in this chapter?
4. *(Distribution of Costs and Benefits)* Why are consumer interest groups usually less effective than producer lobbies in influencing legislation?
5. *(Distribution of Costs and Benefits)* Which groups typically bear the costs and which groups enjoy the benefits of (a) traditional public goods, (b) special-interest legislation, and (c) competing-interest legislation?
6. *(Case**Study:** Farm Subsidies)* "Subsidizing the price of milk or other agricultural products is not very expensive considering how many consumers there are in the

United States. Therefore, there is little harmful effect from such subsidies." Evaluate this statement.

7. *(**CaseStudy:** Farm Subsidies)* Subsidy programs are likely to have a number of secondary effects in addition to the direct effect on dairy prices. What impact do you suppose such subsidies are likely to have on the following?
   a. Housing prices
   b. Technological change in the dairy industry
   c. The price of dairy product substitutes

8. *(Rent Seeking)* Explain how rent seeking can lead to a drop in production. What role might the underground economy play in lessening the drop in productive activities?

9. *(The Underground Economy)* What is the underground economy? What is the impact on the underground economy of instituting a tax on a certain productive activity?

10. *(Bureaucracy and Representative Democracy)* How do the incentives and feedback for government bureaus differ from those for profit-making firms?

11. *(Bureaucracy and Representative Government)* Earlier in the text, the firm was described as combining managerial coordination with market exchange in order to produce its good or service. Does similar behavior occur in government bureaus? Explain.

PROBLEMS AND EXERCISES

12. *(Optimal Provision of Public Goods)* Using at least two individual consumers, show how the market demand curve is derived from individual demand curves (1) for a private goods and (2) for a public good. Once you have derived the market demand curve in each case, introduce a market supply curve and then show the optimal level of production.

13. *(Median Voter Model)* Suppose that the voters on a school property tax issue can be divided into three groups: A, B, and C. The graph at the right illustrates the preferences of these groups for the size of the school budget. If the budget decision is made by voting on two alternatives at a time, what is the most likely result of the vote?

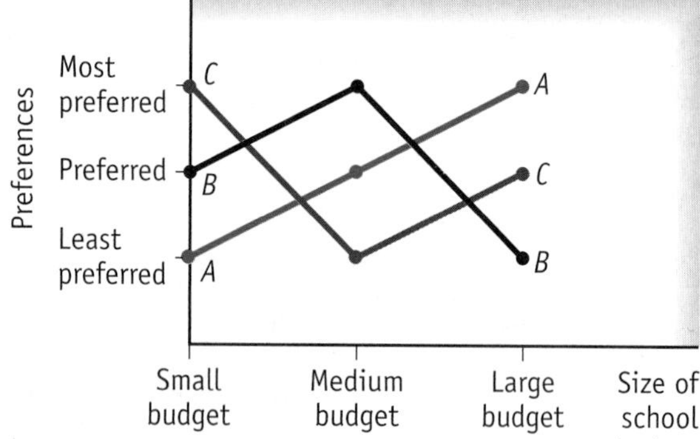

14. *(Distribution of Costs and Benefits)* Suppose that the government decides to guarantee an above-market price for a good by buying up any surplus at that above-market price. Using a conventional supply-demand diagram, illustrate the following gains and losses from such a price support:
   a. The loss of consumer surplus
   b. The gain of producer surplus in the short run
   c. The cost of running the government program (assuming no storage costs)
   d. What is the total cost of the program to consumers?
   e. Are the costs and benefits of the support program widespread or concentrated?

EXPERIENTIAL EXERCISES

15. *(**CaseStudy:** Campaign Finance Reform)* The Economic Policy Network's briefing book on campaign finance reform at http://epn.org/camfinre.html provides numerous links to information on the issues. Try to determine which individuals, firms, and PACs have been the major contributors in your local congressional district. Based on your knowledge of these groups, what specifically are they trying to accomplish by contributing to a congressional campaign?

16. *(Rational Ignorance)* Loren Lomasky, in "The Booth and Consequences" at http://www.magnolia.net/~leonf/sc/tbac.html wrestles with the question of why people bother to vote. Read the article and decide for yourself: Is voting rational?

17. *(Wall Street Journal)* The Politics & Policy column in the First Section of the Wall Street Journal is a good source for articles on politics at every level. Choose one such article and decide whether it describes special-interest or general-interest legislation. Then, classify the benefits and the costs as either concentrated or widespread.

HAPTER

30 Externalities and the Environment

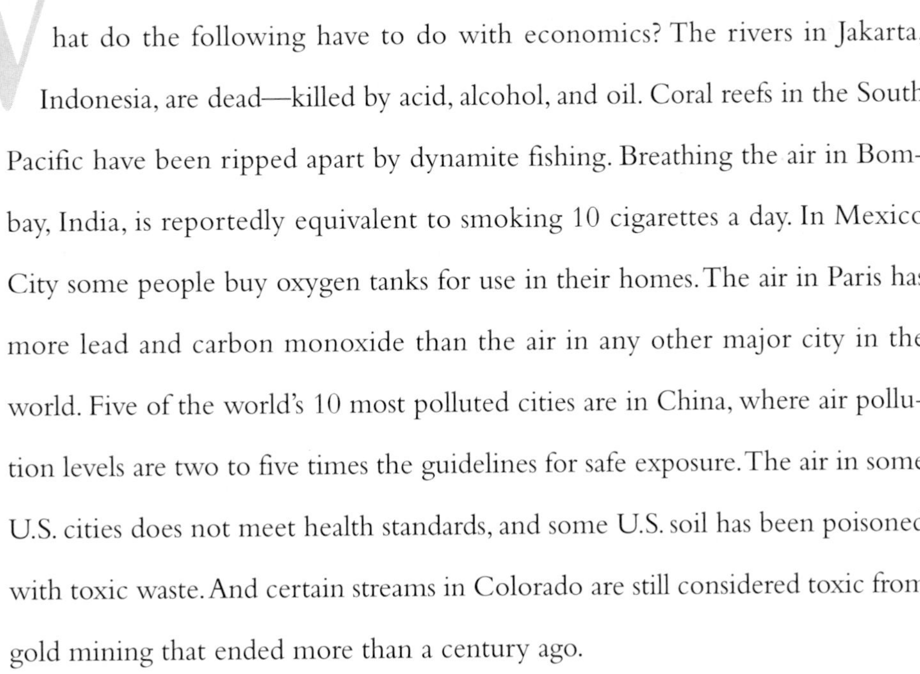

What do the following have to do with economics? The rivers in Jakarta, Indonesia, are dead—killed by acid, alcohol, and oil. Coral reefs in the South Pacific have been ripped apart by dynamite fishing. Breathing the air in Bombay, India, is reportedly equivalent to smoking 10 cigarettes a day. In Mexico City some people buy oxygen tanks for use in their homes. The air in Paris has more lead and carbon monoxide than the air in any other major city in the world. Five of the world's 10 most polluted cities are in China, where air pollution levels are two to five times the guidelines for safe exposure. The air in some U.S. cities does not meet health standards, and some U.S. soil has been poisoned with toxic waste. And certain streams in Colorado are still considered toxic from gold mining that ended more than a century ago.

sit the McEachern
ractive Study Center
or this chapter at
'mcisc.swcollege.com

What does all that have to do with economics? Plenty! Market prices can efficiently allocate resources only as long as property rights are well defined and can be easily enforced. But property rights to clean water, air, and soil, to fish in the ocean, to peace and quiet, and to scenic vistas are hard to establish and enforce. *This chapter examines the difficulty of assigning property rights to some key resources, and why the lack of property rights results in inefficient use.*

As you learned in Chapter 4, externalities, which are unpriced byproducts of production or consumption, may be either negative (for example, air pollution) or positive (for example, the general improvement in the civic climate that results from better education). This chapter concentrates mostly on negative externalities. The focus is on how externalities affect resource allocation and on how well-designed public policies can promote greater efficiency. Topics discussed in this chapter include:

- Exhaustible resources
- Renewable resources
- The common-pool problem
- Private property rights
- Optimal pollution
- Marginal social cost
- Marginal social benefit
- The market for pollution permits
- The Coase theorem
- Environmental protection

EXTERNALITIES AND THE COMMON-POOL PROBLEM

Let's begin our discussion by distinguishing between *exhaustible* resources and *renewable* resources. An **exhaustible resource,** such as oil, coal, or copper ore, does not renew itself, and so is available in a finite amount. Each gallon of oil burned is gone forever. Sooner or later, all oil wells will run dry. The world's oil reserves are exhaustible.

Exhaustible resource A resource available in fixed supply, such as crude oil or copper ore

Renewable Resources

A resource is **renewable** if, when used conservatively, the resource can be drawn on indefinitely. Thus timber is a renewable resource if felled trees can be replaced at rates that provide a steady supply. The atmosphere and rivers are renewable resources to the extent that they can absorb and neutralize a certain level of pollutants. More generally, biological resources such fish, game, forests, rivers, grasslands, and agricultural soil are renewable if managed appropriately.

Renewable resource A resource that can regenerate itself and so can be used periodically for an indefinite period of time if used conservatively, such as a properly managed forest

Some renewable resources are also *open-access goods*, an idea introduced in the previous chapter, meaning that the good is rival in consumption but exclusion is costly. For example, fish caught in the ocean are not available for others to catch, yet it would be costly for an individual to own the fish in the sea and prevent someone from catching them. An open-access good is often subject to the **common-pool problem,** which results because such a good will be used until the marginal value of additional use drops to zero. Consequently, open-access goods are often overused or overharvested.

Common-pool problem Unrestricted access to a resource that results in overuse until the marginal value of additional use drops to zero

Because the atmosphere is an open-access resource, we use the air as a dump for unwanted gases. Air pollution is a negative externality imposed by polluters on society. As noted already, *negative externalities* are unpriced byproducts of production or consumption that impose costs on other consumers or other firms. For example, some spray cans release fluorocarbons into the atmosphere; these gases are said to cause a thinning of the ozone layer that protects us from the sun's ultraviolet rays.

In a market system, specific individuals usually own the rights to resources and therefore have a strong interest in using those resources efficiently. **Private property rights** allow individuals to control the use of certain resources and to charge others for their use. Private property rights are defined and enforced by government, by informal social actions, and by ethical norms. But because specifying and enforcing property rights to certain resources is quite costly, not all resources are owned as private property. For example, how could specific individuals claim and enforce a right to the air, to the fish in the ocean, or to migrating birds? There are usually no individual property rights to such resources because no individual can (1) easily exclude others from using the resource and (2) easily capture the value of the resource by "consuming" it all or selling it all. Thus we say that some resources are both *nonexclusive* (preventing someone from using the resource is costly if not impossible) and *nonappropriable* (no individual can easily capture the entire value of the resource).

Private property rights
The right of an owner to use, rent, or sell, property

Pollution and other negative externalities arise because there are no practical, enforceable, private property rights to open-access resources, such as the air. Market prices usually fail to include the costs that negative externalities impose on society. For example, the cost of a can of hair spray powered by fluorocarbons does not reflect the effect of gas emissions on the atmosphere's ozone layer. The price you pay for a gallon of gasoline does not reflect the costs imposed by the dirtier air and the traffic congestion your driving creates. And electric rates in the Midwest do not reflect the negative externalities, or *external* costs, that sulfur-dioxide emissions impose on people living downwind from power plants. Note that externalities are unintended side effects of actions that are themselves useful and purposeful. Electricity producers, for example, did not go into business to pollute.

Resolving the Common-Pool Problem

Because property rights are not attached to open-access resources, individual users of fresh air, clean water, wildlife, or other open-access goods tend to ignore the effects of their activities on the resource's renewal ability. As stocks diminish from overuse or overharvesting, the resource grows more scarce. A lack of regulation in the fishing industry allowed decades of massive harvesting of the ocean's bounty, which depleted the stock of fish. For example, Georges Bank, off New England, long one of the world's most productive fishing grounds, has been so depleted by overfishing that by the 1990s the catch was down 85 percent from peak years.[1] The United Nations says 11 of the world's 15 primary fishing grounds are seriously depleted.

The common-pool problem of resource exploitation can be reduced if some central authority imposes restrictions on resource use. By restricting output or by imposing an appropriate depletion tax, a regulatory authority can force competitive firms to use the resource at a rate that is socially optimal. For example, in the face of the tendency to overfish and to catch fish before they are sufficiently mature, the government has imposed a variety of restrictions on the fishing industry. There are limits on the total amount of the catch, on the

1 See Deborah Cramer, "Troubled Waters," *Atlantic Monthly* (June 1995): 22-26.

NetBookmark

The history of the U.S. Environmental Protection Agency is documented at its Web site at http://www.epa.gov/oppe/25year/. Look under the New Directions section for evidence of the role of market-based incentives in environmental policy. The Acid Rain program is often cited by economists as an example of how such incentives can be implemented. This program is well documented at http://www.epa.gov/acidrain/ardhome.html. For introductory information about almost any environmental problem, go to the EPA's student section at http://www.epa.gov/students/.

size of fish caught, on the length of the fishing season, on the equipment used, and on other aspects of the business.

More generally, *when imposing and enforcing private property rights would be too costly, government regulations may improve allocative efficiency.* For example, stop signs and traffic lights allocate the scarce road space at an intersection, minimum-size restrictions control lobster fishing, hunting seasons control the stock of game, and official study hours may calm the din in the dormitory.

But not all regulations are equally efficient. For example, fishing authorities sometimes limit the *total* industry catch and allow all firms to fish until that total is reached. Consequently, when the fishing season opens, there is a mad scramble to catch as much as possible before the industry limit is reached. Since time is of the essence, firms make no effort to fish selectively. And the catch reaches fish processors all at once, creating a problem for all segments of the industry. Also, each firm has an incentive to expand its fishing fleet to catch more in those precious few weeks. Thus, large fleets of technologically efficient fishing vessels sit in port for most of the year, except during the beginning of the fishing season. *Each firm is acting rationally, but the collective effect of the regulation is grossly inefficient in terms of social welfare.* Consider the complicated and sometimes confounding nature of fishing regulations in Iceland:

> *The Icelandic government realized that it would have to curb the capacity of its own fleet. But the fishermen compensated by buying more trawlers. Then the government restricted the size of the fleet and the number of days at sea; the fishermen responded by buying larger, more efficient gear. The cod stocks continued to decline. In 1984, the government introduced quotas on species per vessel per season. This was a controversial and often wasteful system. A groundfish hauled up from fifty fathoms [300 feet] is killed by the change in pressure. But if it is a cod and the cod quota has been used up, it is thrown overboard. Or if the price of cod is low that week and cod happens to come in the haddock or plaice net, the fishermen will throw them overboard because they do not want to use up their cod quota when they are not getting a good price.*[2]

Fish remain a common-pool good because the technology has not yet been developed to establish and enforce rights to particular schools of fish. But advances in technology may some day allow the creation of private property rights to ocean fish, migrating birds, and even the air we breathe. At one time, establishing property rights to cattle on the Great Plains seemed impossible, but the invention of barbed wire allowed ranchers to fence the range. In a sense, barbed wire tamed the "wild West."

OPTIMAL LEVEL OF POLLUTION

Research suggests (though the issue is far from resolved) that the sulfur dioxide emitted by coal-fired power plants during electricity production mixes with moisture in the air to form sulfuric acid, which is carried by the prevailing winds and falls as acid rain. Many argue that acid rain has killed lakes and forests and has corroded buildings, bridges, and other structures. Electricity produc-

2 Quoted from Mark Kurlansky, *Cod: A Biography of the Fish that Changed the World,* Walker & Co., 1997, p. 172.

tion, therefore, involves the external cost of using the atmosphere as a gas dump. In this section we show how to analyze this externality problem.

External Costs with Fixed Technology

Suppose the demand curve for electricity in the Midwest is depicted by *D* in Exhibit 1. Recall that the demand curve reflects consumers' marginal benefit for each level of consumption. The lower horizontal line reflects the *marginal private cost* of production incurred by electricity producers. If producers base their pricing and output decisions on their private marginal costs, the equilibrium quantity of electricity used per month is 50 million kilowatt hours and the equilibrium price is $0.10 per kilowatt hour. At that price and output level, the marginal private cost of production just equals the marginal benefit enjoyed by consumers of electricity.

Electricity production involves not only the private marginal cost of the resources employed but also the external cost of using the atmosphere as a gas dump. Suppose that the marginal external cost imposed on the environment by the generation of electricity is $0.04 per kilowatt hour. If the only way of reducing the emission of sulfur is by reducing the generation of electricity, then the relationship between the production of electricity and the production of pollution is a fixed one. Thus we say that pollution in this case occurs with **fixed-production technology.**

Fixed-production technology The relationship between output rate and the generation of an externality is a fixed one; the only way to the reduce the externality is to reduce the output rate.

The marginal external cost of $0.04 per kilowatt hour is shown by the vertical distance between the marginal private cost curve and the marginal social

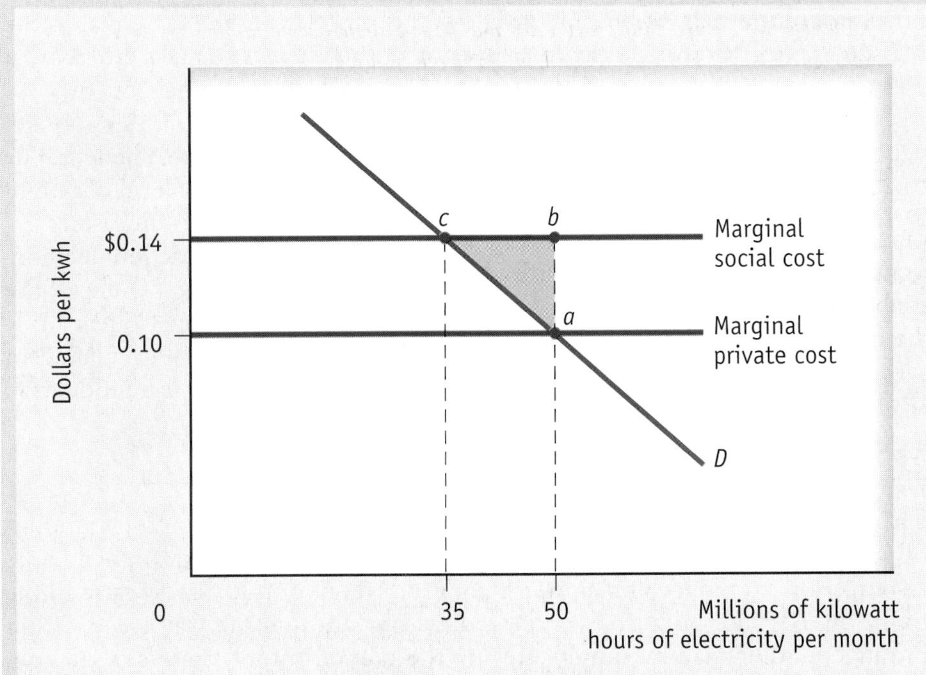

EXHIBIT 1

Negative Externalities: The Market for Electricity in the Midwest

If producers base their output on marginal private cost, 50 million kilowatt hours of electricity are produced per month. The marginal external cost of electricity production reflects the cost of pollution imposed on society. The marginal social cost curve includes both the marginal private cost and the marginal external cost. If producers base their output decisions on marginal social cost, only 35 million kilowatt hours are produced, which is the optimal level of output. The total social gain from basing production on marginal social cost is reflected by the blue triangle.

Marginal social cost The sum of the marginal private cost and the marginal external cost of production or consumption

cost curve in Exhibit 1. The **marginal social cost** includes both the marginal private cost and the *marginal external cost* that production imposes on society. Because the marginal external cost is assumed to be constant, the two cost curves are parallel. Notice that at the private-sector equilibrium output level of 50 million kilowatt hours, the marginal social cost, identified at point *b,* exceeds society's marginal benefit from that unit of electricity, identified at point *a* on the demand curve. The last kilowatt hour of electricity produced costs society $0.14 to produce but has a marginal benefit of only $0.10. Because the marginal cost to society exceeds the marginal benefit, the firm's choice of output results in a *market failure.* Too much electricity is generated, and too much pollution is produced in the process. What's more, the price of electricity is too low because it fails to reflect the social cost.

The efficient level of output from society's point of view is where the demand, or marginal benefit, curve intersects the marginal social cost curve—a point identified as *c* in Exhibit 1. How could output be restricted to the socially efficient level of 35 million kilowatts per month? If government policy makers knew the demand curve and the marginal cost curves, they could simply require electric utilities to produce no more than the optimal level. Or they could impose on each unit of output a *pollution tax* equal to the marginal external cost of generating electricity. If correctly determined, such a tax would raise the industry supply curve up to the marginal social cost curve, so the marginal private cost of electricity would equal the marginal social cost. The externality would, in effect, be internalized.

With the appropriate tax, the equilibrium combination of price and output moves from point *a* to point *c*. The price rises from $0.10 to $0.14 per kilowatt hour, and output falls to 35 million kilowatt hours. Setting the tax equal to the marginal external cost results in a level of output that is socially efficient; at point *c,* the marginal social cost of production equals the marginal benefit.

Notice that pollution is not eliminated at point *c,* but the utilities no longer generate electricity whose marginal social cost exceeds its marginal benefit. The total social gain from reducing production to the socially optimal level of output is shown by the blue shaded triangle in Exhibit 1. This triangle also measures the total social cost of ignoring the negative externalities in the production decision; it reflects the total amount by which the social cost exceeds the benefit of the good if 50 million kilowatt hours are produced. Although Exhibit 1 offers a tidy solution, the external costs of pollution often cannot be easily calculated or taxed. At times, government intervention may result in more or less production than the optimal solution calls for.

External Cost with Variable Technology

Variable technology The amount of externality generated at a given rate of output can be reduced by altering the production process rather than by simply reducing the rate of output.

The preceding example assumes that the only way to reduce the total amount of pollution is to reduce output. But power companies can usually change the resource mix to reduce emissions for a given level of output, particularly in the long run. Because pollution can be reduced by altering the way electricity is produced rather than by simply altering the rate of output, these externalities are said to be produced under conditions of **variable technology**.

To examine the optimal amount of pollution under variable technology, consider Exhibit 2. The horizontal axis measures air quality. If all firms made their production decisions based simply on their private cost—that is, if the cost

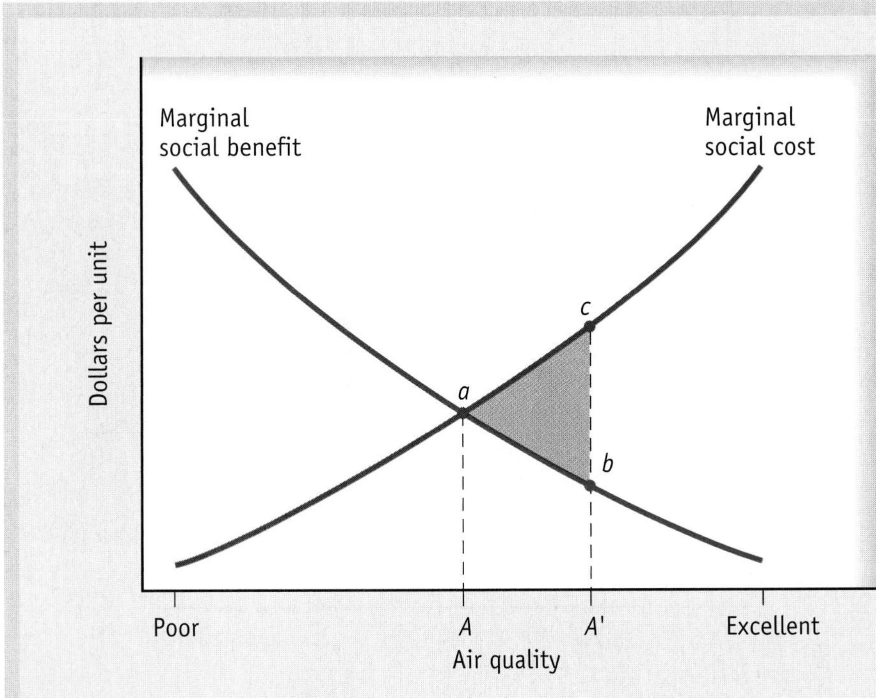

EXHIBIT 2

The Optimal Level of Air Quality

The optimal level of air quality is found at point *a,* where the marginal social cost of cleaner air equals its marginal social benefit. If some higher level of air quality were dictated by the government, the marginal social cost would exceed the marginal social benefit, and social waste would result. The total social waste resulting from a higher-than-optimal air quality is indicated by the red shaded triangle.

of pollution is external to the firm—then the firm would have no incentive to search for production methods that would reduce pollution, so too much pollution as a by-product of production would occur.

But air quality can be improved by adopting cleaner production technology. For example, coal-burning plants can be fitted with smoke "scrubbers" to reduce toxic emissions. Yet the production of cleaner air, like the production of other goods, is subject to diminishing returns. Cutting emissions of the largest particles may involve simply putting a screen over the smokestack, but eliminating successively finer particles requires more sophisticated and more expensive processes. Thus, the marginal social cost curve of cleaning the air slopes upward, as shown in Exhibit 2.

Marginal social benefit The sum of the marginal private benefit and the marginal external benefit of production or consumption

The **marginal social benefit** curve reflects the additional benefit society derives from improving air quality. When air quality is poor, an improvement can save lives and will be valued by society more than when air quality is excellent. Cleaner and cleaner air, like other goods, has a declining marginal benefit to society (though the total benefit still increases). The marginal social benefit curve from cleaner air therefore slopes downward, as shown in Exhibit 2.

The optimal level of air quality is found at point *a,* where the marginal social cost of cleaner air equals the marginal social benefit. In this example, the optimal level of air quality is *A*. What if the government decreed that the level of air quality should exceed *A*? For example, suppose a law were passed setting *A*' as the minimum acceptable level. The marginal social cost, identified as *c*, of achieving that improved level of air quality exceeds the marginal social benefit, identified as *b*. The total social waste associated with imposing a greater-than-optimal

EXHIBIT 3

Effect of Changes in Costs and Benefits on the Optimal Level of Air Quality

Either a reduction in the marginal social cost of cleaner air, as shown in panel (a), or an increase in the marginal social benefit of cleaner air, as shown in panel (b), will increase the optimal level of air quality.

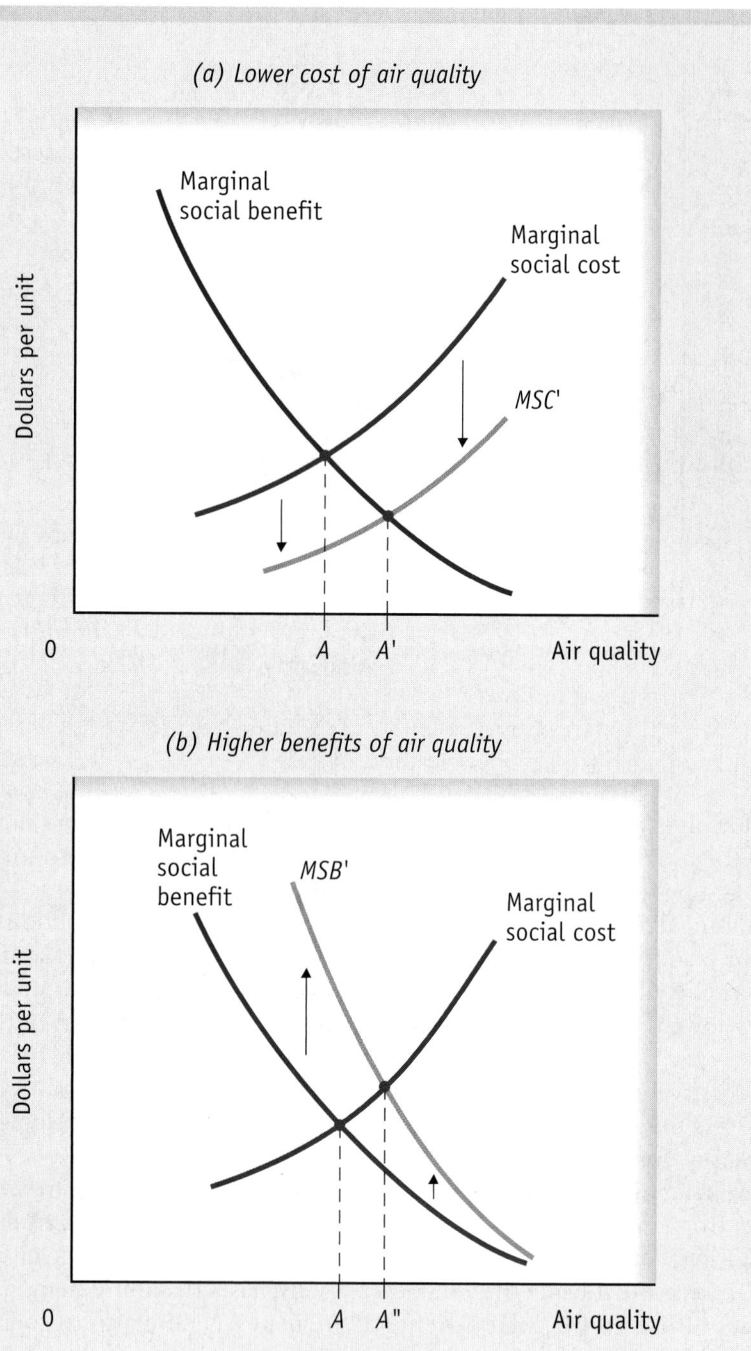

level of air quality is represented by the red shaded triangle, *abc*. This is the total amount by which the additional social costs of cleaner air (associated with a move from *A* to *A*') exceed the additional social benefits.

The idea that all pollution should be eliminated is a popular misconception. Usually some pollution is consistent with efficiency. *Improving air quality benefits society as a whole as long as the marginal benefit of cleaner air exceeds its marginal cost.*

What would happen to the optimal level of air quality if either the marginal cost or the marginal benefit of cleaner air changed? Suppose, for example, that some technological breakthrough reduces the marginal cost of cleaning the air. As shown in panel (a) of Exhibit 3, the marginal social cost curve of reducing pollution would shift down to MSC', thereby increasing the optimal level of air quality from A to A'. The simple logic is that the *lower the marginal cost of reducing pollution, other things constant, the greater the optimal level of air quality.*

An increase in the marginal benefit of air quality would have a similar effect. For example, what if we discovered that bad air quality increases the incidence of certain types of cancer? The perceived marginal benefit of cleaner air would increase, as reflected in panel (b) of Exhibit 3 by a shift upward in the marginal social benefit curve to MSB'. As a result, the optimal level of air quality would increase. *The greater the marginal benefit of air quality, other things constant, the greater the optimal level of air quality.*

The atmosphere has the ability to cleanse itself of some emissions, but the destruction of the tropical rain forest has reduced this ability, as discussed in the following case study.

Destruction of the Tropical Rain Forest

The tropical rain forests have been called "the lungs of the world" because they naturally recycle carbon dioxide by transforming it into oxygen and wood, thus helping to maintain the world's atmospheric balance. The Amazon rain forest contains the largest collection of plant and animal life on Earth, along with 20 percent of the world's water supply. But the high world demand for timber has caused loggers to cut down much of the tropical forest. Worse yet, farmers burn down these forests to create farmland and pastures. Burning the world's forests has a triple-barreled effect. The loss of trees reduces the atmosphere's ability to cleanse itself, the burning adds yet more harmful gases to the atmosphere, and the forest subsoil usually contains huge quantities of carbon subject to oxidization when the trees are removed. Since the world's atmosphere is a common pool, the costs of deforestation are imposed on people around the globe.

Forest acreage throughout the world has declined by 15 percent over the last decade. The Amazon has lost 260,000 square miles of rain forest, an area the size of Texas. The north coast of South America contains one of the world's largest unspoiled tropical rain forests, but the governments of Guyana and Suriname have opened huge tracts of forest for logging by companies from Korea, Indonesia, and Malaysia. In Central America, the forests have been cleared for cattle ranches. Commercial logging has been so extensive in the African countries of Ghana and the Ivory Coast that the business is already winding down, leaving behind poverty and devastation. According to the World Bank, two-thirds of the countries that export tropical forest products are running out of trees.

McEachern Interactive

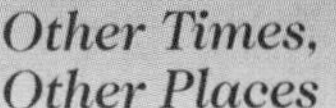

*Case***Study**

Other Times, Other Places

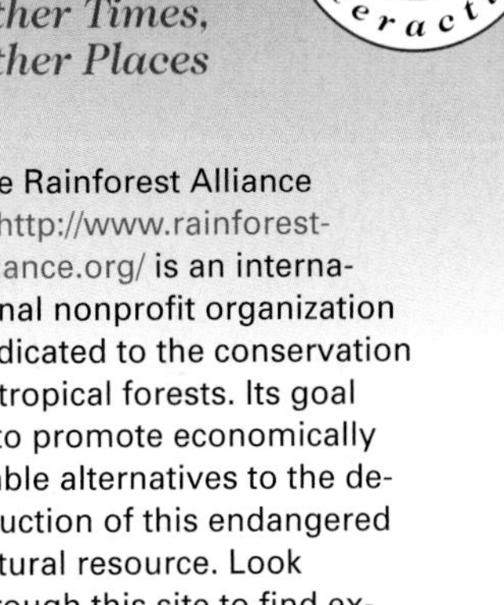

The Rainforest Alliance at http://www.rainforest-alliance.org/ is an international nonprofit organization dedicated to the conservation of tropical forests. Its goal is to promote economically viable alternatives to the destruction of this endangered natural resource. Look through this site to find examples of the role economics plays in the projects and research the group supports. The Rainforest Action Network is another group devoted to rainforest conservation but focuses more on citizen activism. Visit its site at http://www.ran.org/ran/ and compare and contrast the approaches of these two groups.

The loss of the tropical forests causes other negative externalities as well. As long as the tropical forest has its canopy of trees, it remains a rich, genetically diverse ecosystem. Tropical forests cover only 6 percent of the Earth's land surface (down from 12 percent 50 years ago), but they contain *half* of the world's species of plants and animals, and thus represent an abundant source of fruits, crops, and medicines. One-fourth of the prescription drugs used in the United States are derived from tropical plants, such as seeds that may help cure some types of cancer. Biologists estimate that 50,000 species are condemned to extinction each year because of deforestation. Yet most tropical plants have not been tested for their medicinal properties.

Small farmers and wood gatherers and big lumber companies are stripping the tropical forests. Once the forests are cut down, the tropical soil is eroded by rains and baked by the sun and soon runs out of nutrients. When the nutrients are lost, the system is not very resilient. It takes a century for a clear-cut forest to return to its original state. The policy of cutting down everything in sight is of benefit only to loggers, who usually do not own the land and thus have little interest in its future.

The world's rain forests are located in countries that are relatively poor: Brazil, Peru, Indonesia, Zaire, and the Philippines. Environmental quality is a normal good, meaning that as incomes rise, the demand for it increases. In poor countries, however, the priority is not environmental quality but food and shelter. Brazil and other developing countries are destroying their forests to provide jobs. But since the soil quickly loses its nutrients to erosion and the sun, few settlers have become successful farmers.

The tropical rain forests, by serving as the lungs of the world, confer benefits around the globe. But the positive effects that the trees have on the atmosphere tend to be ignored in the decision to clear the land. Worse yet, the taking of timber is often "first come, first served," and government investment programs frequently subsidize the harvesting of timber. *It is not the greed of peasants and timber companies that leads to inefficient, or wasteful, uses of resource, but the fact that the atmosphere, and, indeed, the rain forests are open-access resources that can be degraded with little immediate personal cost to those who clear the forests.*

What to do? Those who benefit from the tropical rain forest should be willing to pay for the benefits. Government programs that encourage selective cutting and replanting would allow the forest to remain an air filter and a renewable source of forest products. For example, with help from the World Bank and the World Wildlife Fund, Brazil announced plans in 1998 to protect an area of rain forest the size of Colorado. Other ideas are on the drawing board, but a systematic solution is still a long way off.

Sources: Edmund Andrews, "For Europeans, Greenhouse-Gas Issue Is How Much to Cut," *New York Times* (4 December 1997); "Brazil to Set Aside 62 Million Acres of Forest Lands," *Minneapolis Star Tribune* (30 April 1998); Thomas C. Schelling, "Some Economics of Global Warming," *American Economic Review* 82 (March 1992): 1–14; "Argentina Makes Plans to Aid Reduction of Global Warming," *Hartford Courant* (12 November 1998); and "Saving Rain Forests," *San Francisco Examiner* (24 April 1998)

The Coase Analysis of Externalities

The traditional analysis of externalities assumes that market failures arise because people ignore the external effects of their actions. Suppose a research laboratory that tests delicate equipment is located next to a manufacturer of heavy machinery. The vibrations caused by the manufacturing process throw off the delicate machinery in the lab next door. Professor Ronald Coase, who won the Nobel prize in 1991, would point out that the negative externality in this case is not necessarily imposed by the machinery producer on the testing lab—rather, *it arises from the incompatible activities of the two parties.* The externality is the result both of vibrations created by the factory *and* of the location of the testing lab next door. One efficient solution to this externality problem might be to modify the machines in the factory; others might be to make the equipment in the testing lab more shock resistant or to move the lab elsewhere.

According to Coase, the efficient solution to an externality problem depends on which party can avoid the problem at the lower cost. Suppose the factory has determined that it would cost $2 million to reduce vibrations enough to allow the lab to function normally. For its part, the testing lab has concluded that it cannot easily alter its equipment to reduce the effects of the vibrations, so its only recourse would be to move the lab elsewhere at a cost of $1 million. Based on these costs, the least-cost, or most efficient, resolution to the externality problem is for the testing lab to relocate.

Coase argues that when property rights are assigned to one party or another, the two parties will agree on the efficient solution to an externality problem as long as transaction costs are low. This efficient solution will be achieved regardless of which party is assigned the property right. Suppose the testing lab is granted the right to operate free of vibrations from next door, so the testing lab has the right to ask the factory to reduce its vibration. Rather than cut vibrations at a cost of $2 million, the factory can offer to pay the lab to relocate. Any payment by the factory owners that is greater than $1 million but less than $2 million will make both firms better off, since the lab will receive more than its moving cost and the factory will pay less than its cost of reducing vibrations. Thus the lab will move, which is the efficient outcome.

Alternatively, suppose the factory is granted the right to generate vibrations in its production process. For the factory, this means business as usual. The lab may consider paying the factory to alter its production method, but since the minimum payment the factory would accept is $2 million, the lab would rather move at a cost of $1 million. Thus whether property rights are granted to the lab or to the factory, the lab will move, which is the most efficient, or least-cost, solution. The **Coase theorem** says that as long as bargaining costs are small, the assignment of property rights will generate an efficient solution to an externality problem regardless of which party is assigned the property rights. A particular assignment of property rights determines only who incurs the externality costs, not the efficient outcome.

Coase theorem As long as bargaining costs are small, an efficient solution to the problem of externalities will be achieved by assigning property rights.

Inefficient outcomes do occur, however, when the transaction costs of arriving at a solution are high. For example, an airport located in a populated area would have difficulty negotiating with all the surrounding residents about noise levels. Or a power plant emitting sulfur dioxide would have trouble negotiating with the millions of people scattered across the downwind states. Or a would-be farmer contemplating clearing a portion of the tropical rain forest cannot negotiate with the millions, and perhaps, billions, of people ultimately affected by that decision. When the number of parties involved in the transaction is large, the chance for a voluntary agreement is small.

A Market for Pollution Rights

According to Coase, the assignment of property rights is often sufficient to resolve the market failure typically associated with externalities. Additional government intervention is not necessary. If pollution can be easily monitored and polluters easily identified, the government may be able to achieve an efficient solution to the problem of pollution simply by assigning the right to pollute. For example, firms that dump waste into a river evidently value the ability to discharge their waste matter in this way. For them, the river provides an inexpensive outlet for pollutants that otherwise would have to be disposed of at greater cost. The river provides disposal services, and the demand curve for this pollutant transportation system slopes downward just like the demand for other resources.

The demand for the river as a discharge system is presented as *D* in Exhibit 4. The horizontal axis measures the amount of pollutants dumped into the river per day, and the vertical axis measures firms' marginal benefits of disposing of their waste in this way. The demand curve thus measures the marginal value to firms of using the river as a resource for discharging pollutants. With no restrictions on river pollution—that is, if all are free to discharge their wastes into the river—the daily discharge rate would occur where the private marginal value of discharging wastes falls to zero, which is at output level Q in Exhibit 4. Dumping will continue as long as it yields some private marginal benefit. If dumping remains unregulated, the river must carry away whatever polluters choose to dump there.

The river, like the atmosphere and the soil, can absorb and neutralize a certain amount of pollution per day without deteriorating in quality. Suppose

EXHIBIT 4

Optimal Allocation of Pollution Rights

Suppose the demand for a river as an outlet for pollution is *D*. In the absence of any environmental controls, pollution will occur up to point *Q*, where the marginal benefit of further pollution equals zero. If regulatory authorities establish *Q** as the maximum allowable level of pollution and then sell the rights to pollution, the market for these pollution rights will clear at price *p*. If the demand for pollution rights increases to *D'*, the market-clearing price will rise to *p'*.

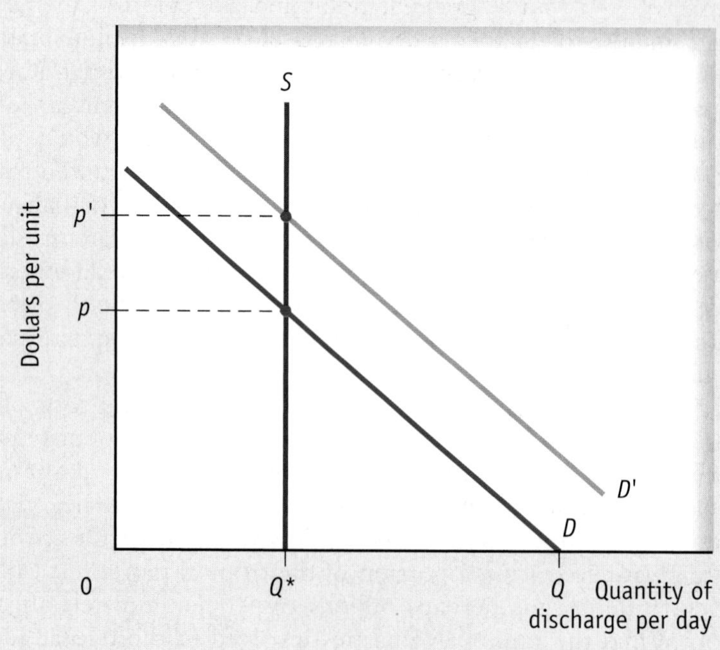

voters in the jurisdiction that encompasses the river make the public choice that the river should be clean enough for swimming and fishing. The maximum level of waste discharge that is consistent with this quality is Q^* in Exhibit 4. Hence, if the river is to be preserved at the specified level of quality, the "supply" of the river available as a discharge resource must be fixed at S.

If government regulators can easily identify polluters and monitor their behavior, authorities can allocate an amount of pollution permitted equal to Q^*. If polluters are simply given these permits (that is, if the price of permits is zero), there will be an excess demand for them, since the quantity supplied is Q^* but the quantity demanded at a price of zero would be Q. An alternative is to *sell* the specified quantity of pollution permits at the market-clearing price. The intersection of the supply curve, S, and the demand curve, D, yields a permit price, p, which is the marginal value of dumping quantity Q^* into the river each day. To most purchasers, the marginal value of a permit will exceed p.

The beauty of this system is that those producers that value the discharge rights the most will ultimately end up with them. Producers that attach a lower marginal value to river dumping obviously have cheaper ways of resolving their waste problems, including changing production techniques. And if conservation groups wish to maintain a higher river quality than the government's standard, they can purchase pollution permits but not exercise them.

What if additional firms locate along the river and want to discharge wastes? This added demand for discharge rights is reflected in Exhibit 4 by the higher level of demand, D'. This greater demand would bid up the market price of pollution permits to p', so some existing permit owners will sell to those who value the permits more. Regardless of the comings and goings of would-be polluters, the total quantity of discharge rights is restricted to Q^*, so the river's quality will be maintained. Thus the value of pollution permits, but not the total amount of pollution, may fluctuate over time.

If the right to pollute could be granted, monitored, and enforced, then what had been a negative externality problem could be solved through market allocation. Historically, the U.S. government has relied on setting discharge standards and fining offenders, and has used pollution rights only in some metropolitan areas. But in 1989, a pollution-rights market for fluorocarbon emissions was established and was followed in 1990 by a market for sulfur dioxide. The price for the right to emit a ton of sulfur dioxide was recently \$140. So the market for pollution rights is alive and growing.[3]

Unfortunately, legislation dealing with pollution is affected by the same problems of representative democracy that trouble other public policy questions. Polluters have a special interest in government proposals relating to pollution, and they fight measures to limit pollution. But members of the public remain rationally ignorant about pollution legislation. So pollution regulations may be less in accord with the public interest than with the special interests of polluters. This is why pollution permits are often given free to existing firms. For example, under the sulfur-dioxide program, the nation's 101 dirtiest power plants receive credits equal to between 30 and 50 percent of the pollution they

3 For a discussion of the market for sulfur dioxide emissions, see Paul Joskow, Richard Schmalensee, and Elizabeth Bailey, "The Market for Sulfur-Dioxide Emissions," *American Economic Review* 88 (September 1998): 669–685.

emitted prior to the program. Because they receive something of value, polluters are less inclined to fight the institution of the program. Once the permits are granted, some recipients find it profitable to sell their permits to other firms that value them more. Thus a market emerges that leads to an efficient allocation of pollution permits. According to some analysts, the sulfur program saves up to $3 billion annually compared to the old system.[4] More generally, a system of marketable pollution rights can reduce the cost of pollution abatement by as much as 75 percent.

Now that you know something about the theory of externalities, let's turn to the primary application of the theory—environmental protection.

ENVIRONMENTAL PROTECTION

Federal efforts to address the common-pool problem of air, water, and soil are coordinated by the *Environmental Protection Agency* (*EPA*). Four federal laws and subsequent amendments underpin U.S. efforts to protect the environment: the Clean Air Act of 1970, the Clean Water Act of 1972, the Resource Conservation and Recovery Act of 1976 (which governs solid waste disposal), and the *Superfund* law of 1980, legislation focusing on toxic waste dumps. In 1970, the EPA had about 4,000 employees and a budget of $200 million. By the 1990s, the EPA had about 18,000 employees and a budget of $5 billion.

According to EPA estimates, compliance with pollution-control regulations costs U.S. producers and consumers an amount equivalent to 2 percent of gross domestic product,[5] the market value of all final goods and services produced in the economy in a given year. We can divide pollution-abatement spending into three main categories: spending for air-pollution abatement, spending for water-pollution abatement, and spending for solid-waste disposal. About 40 percent of the pollution-abatement expenditures in the United States goes toward cleaner air, another 40 percent goes toward cleaner water, and 20 percent goes toward disposing of solid waste. In this section we will consider, in turn, air pollution, water pollution, Superfund activities, and disposing of solid waste.

Air Pollution

In the Clean Air Act of 1970 and in subsequent amendments, Congress set national standards for the amount of pollution that could be emitted into the atmosphere. Congress thereby recognized the atmosphere as an economic resource, which, like other resources, has alternative uses. The air can be used as a source of life-giving oxygen, as a prism for viewing breathtaking vistas, or as a dump for carrying away unwanted soot and gases. The 1970 act gave Americans the right to breathe air of a certain quality and at the same time gave producers the right to emit certain specified pollutants.

4 This saving was estimated by Paul R. Portney, "Air Pollution Policy," in P. R. Portney, Ed., *Public Policies for Environmental Protection* (Washington, D.C.: Resources for the Future 1990): 27-96.

5 Other researchers estimate that clean-air and clean-water regulations reduced GDP in 1990 to be about 6 percent less than what it would have been in the absence of such regulations. See Michael Hazilla and Raymond Kopp, "Social Cost of Environmental Quality Regulations: A General Equilibrium Analysis," *Journal of Political Economy* 98 (August 1990): 544-551.

Smog is the most visible form of air pollution. Automobile emissions account for 40 percent of smog. Another 40 percent comes from consumer products, such as paint thinner, fluorocarbon sprays, dry-cleaning solvents, and baker's yeast by-products. Surprisingly, only 15 percent of smog comes from manufacturing. The 1970 Clean Air Act mandated a reduction of 90 percent in auto emissions, leaving it to the auto industry to achieve this target. At the time, auto makers complained that the objective was impossible. Between 1970 and 1990, however, average emissions of lead fell 97 percent, carbon monoxide emissions fell 41 percent, and sulfur oxide emissions fell 25 percent. In fact, a recent EPA study concluded that because auto emissions and industrial smoke have been reduced, air pollution now runs two to five times higher indoors than outdoors. U.S. air quality is good compared to the air quality in some parts of the world.

Efforts are underway to improve air quality on a global scale. A tentative accord reached in Kyoto, Japan, in December 1997, would require the 38 industrial countries to reduce emissions of carbon dioxide and other so-called greenhouse gases by one-third over ten years. The measure would impose a carbon tax on coal, natural gas and oil. The cost to the U.S. economy could reach $300 billion a year, according to one study. Only industrial economies would be required to reduce emissions; developing countries need not participate. Thus even if industrial nations meet their Kyoto targets, carbon dioxide emissions would continue to rise since most of the projected global increase would come from exempted countries. The treaty requires approval by legislative bodies in the United States and in the other countries, which appears doubtful at this point.

Critics of the treaty argue that cleaner air requires a greater commitment from the developing world, such as China and India, which are major polluters. Argentina is the first developing nation offering to voluntarily cut back greenhouse emissions. The following case study examines the problem of cleaning up the polluted air in one developing country.

CaseStudy

Other Times, Other Places

GAIA, a collaborative effort of European research centers and universities, builds multimedia tools for environmental education and management. It presents an interesting case study, "Urban Air Pollution in Mexico City," at http://www.ess.co.at/GAIA/CASES/MEX/index.html. What are the major sources of air pollutants in Mexico City, and what are their primary effects? What plans are there to control emissions? A photographic essay illustrating the problem is archived by the National Geographic Society at //www.nationalgeographic.com/features/96/mexico/a011.html.

City in the Clouds

Mexico City has a metropolitan population of 24 million, ranking it the second-largest city in the world. There are 41,000 people per square mile, about four times the density of New York City. More than half of Mexico's industrial output is produced in or near Mexico City. Millions of vehicles and tens of thousands of small, poorly regulated businesses spew a soup of pollution into the atmosphere. For example, brickmakers fire their kilns with old rubber tires and with sawdust soaked in kerosene—fuels that generate black, acrid smoke. A recent study suggests that leaks from tanks of liquefied gas used widely for cooking and heating are the primary source of smog over the city. In all, an estimated 12,000 tons of pollutants are released into the atmosphere each day.

Pollution problems are compounded by the city's geography and altitude. Mexico City is surrounded on three sides by mountains, so the wind that blows in from the north (the open side) traps pollution over the city. Worse yet, the city's high altitude reduces the oxygen content of the atmosphere by about one-quarter. The combination of high pollution and low oxygen makes for unhealthy air. In the last decade, the number of days when the city's air quality fell below acceptable levels has doubled. Winter smog sends thousands to the city's hospitals with respiratory problems. Some medical specialists claim that living in Mexico City is equivalent to smoking a pack of cigarettes a day. Pollution also contributes to a high infant death rate. Foreign countries advise their diplomats not to have babies while stationed there. Some foreigners who are stationed in Mexico City earn a 10-percent premium as hardship pay.

City officials have taken steps to address the common-pool problem, but their efforts have been halfhearted. The price of gasoline in Mexico City is among the lowest in the world, so price is not much of a check on fuel consumption. Unleaded gas has been introduced but accounts for less than half of the total used. New regulations prohibit half of the city's three million cars from traveling the streets during weekdays, yet fuel consumption has actually increased. And, although stricter regulations have been imposed on business activity, enforcement has been lax.

Part of the problem is that low income levels in Mexico make environmental protection there costly luxury. After adjusting for differences in the cost of living, per capita income there was less than 30 percent of the U.S. level in 1997.

Sources: "Pollution Costs Mexico Millions, Official Says," *St. Louis Post-Dispatch* (30 May1998); Sam Howe Verhovek, "Pollution Problems Fester South of the Border," *New York Times* (4 July 1998); "Mexico City Pollution Link to Infant Deaths Is Studied," *Chicago Tribune* (7 May 1998); and *World Development Report: Knowledge for Development 1998/99* (World Bank, Oxford University Press, 1999).

Water Pollution

Two major sources of water pollution are sewage and chemicals. For decades, U.S. cities had an economic incentive to dump their sewage directly into waterways rather than incur the expense of cleaning it up first. Frequently, the current or tides would carry the waste away to become someone else's problem. Although each community found it rational, based on a narrow view of the situation, to dump into the river or sea, the combined effect of these individual choices was polluted waterways. Water pollution is a negative externality imposed by one community on other communities.

Most federal money over the years has funded sewage treatment plants, and real progress has been made in lessening sewage-related water pollution. Hundreds of once-polluted waterways have been cleaned up enough to permit swimming and fishing. The majority of U.S. cities now have modern sewage control. Notable exceptions include Boston, which still dumps sewage directly into Boston Harbor, and New York City, which teams up with New Jersey to dump raw sewage into the Atlantic Ocean, using a discharge point 106 miles off Cape May, New Jersey. At a huge cost, Boston is in the process of cleaning up its harbor. By the year 2000, the typical Boston resident's water and sewer bill is expected to be more than four times higher than it was in 1990.

Chemicals are another source of water pollution. Chemical pollution may conjure up an image of a chemical company dumping in a river, but only about

10 percent of water pollution comes from *point* pollution, which means pollution from factories and other fixed industrial sites. About two-thirds of chemical pollutants in water come from what is called *nonpoint* pollution, derived mostly from runoff of agricultural pesticides and fertilizer. Congress has been reluctant to limit the use of pesticides, although pesticides pollute water and contaminate food. Industrial America seems an easier target than Old MacDonald's farm.

In 1970, Congress shifted control of pesticides from the U.S. Department of Agriculture to the newly formed Environmental Protection Agency (EPA). But the EPA already had its hands full administering the Clean Water Act, so it turned pesticide regulation over to the states. Most states handed the job to their departments of agriculture. But these state agencies often *promote* the interests of farmers, not *restrict* what farmers can do. The EPA now reports that in most states pesticides have fouled some groundwater. The EPA also argues that pesticide residues on food pose more health problems than do toxic waste dumps or air pollution. The EPA's Inspector General said in 1998 that federal and state officials failed to enforce the nation's clean air and water laws. For example, for three quarters of the streams in Missouri, the state failed to adopt the Clean Water Act's central goal of making the water clean enough for swimming.[6]

Hazardous Waste and the Superfund

The U.S. synthetic chemical industry has flourished in the last 40 years, and about 55,000 chemicals are now in common use. Some have harmful effects on humans and other living creatures. These chemicals can pose risks at every stage of their production, use, and disposal. New Jersey manufactures more toxic chemicals than any other state and, not surprisingly, has the worst toxic waste burden. Prior to 1980, the disposal of toxic waste created get-rich-quick opportunities for anyone who could rent or buy a few acres of land to open a toxic waste dump. One site in New Jersey took in 71 million gallons of hazardous chemicals during a three-year period.[7]

Prior to 1980, once a company paid someone to haul away its hazardous waste, the company was no longer responsible. The Comprehensive Environmental Response, Compensation, and Liability Act of 1980, known more popularly as the *Superfund* law, now requires any company that generates, stores, *or* transports hazardous wastes to pay to clean up any wastes that are improperly disposed of. A producer or hauler that is the source of even one barrel of pollution dumped at a site can be held liable for cleaning up the entire site.

The Superfund law gives the federal government authority over sites contaminated with toxins. But to get an offending company to comply with its edicts, the EPA frequently must sue the company. The process is slow, and nearly half the budget goes to lawyers, consultants and administrators rather than to site cleanups. As of 1997, fewer than 200 of the 1400 sites identified under the Superfund law had actually been cleaned up. The law does not require that benefits exceed costs or even that such comparisons be attempted.[8] A General

6 As reported by John Cushman in "E.P.A. and States Found to Be Lax on Pollution Law," *New York Times* (7 June 1998).
7 See Jason Zweig, "Real-Life Horror Story," *Forbes* (12 December 1988).
8 For a fuller discussion of the costs and benefits of environmental protection, see Maureen L. Cropper and Wallace E. Oates, "Environmental Economics: A Survey," *Journal of Economic Literature* 30 (June 1992): 675–740.

Accounting Office study says that the number of cleanup sites could reach 4,000 and the cost could reach $40 billion. An Office of Technology Assessment study says the site total could reach 10,000 and the cost could climb to $100 billion.

But a recent EPA study concluded that the health hazards of Superfund sites have been vastly exaggerated. Chemicals in the ground often move slowly, sometimes taking years to travel a few feet, so any possible health threat may be confined to the site itself. In contrast, air pollution represents a more widespread threat because the air is so mobile and polluted air is drawn directly into the lungs. Those who are neighbors of toxic waste sites know it and can exert political pressure to get something done. But those who may in the future develop some disease from air- or water-borne pollution do not know it now. Thus most people see no reason to press public officials for legislation that mandates clean air and clean water. *Because of their greater media appeal and political urgency, toxic waste dumps tend to receive more attention than air or water pollution.*

Solid Waste: "Paper or Plastic?"

Throughout most of history, households tossed their trash outside as fodder for pigs and goats. New York City, like other cities, had no trash collection, so domestic waste was thrown into the street, where it mixed with mud and horse manure; decades of such behavior explains why the oldest Manhattan streets are anywhere from 3 to 15 feet above their original levels. About 200 years ago, people began to bury their trash near their homes or take it to the town dump. Now U.S. households generate about 4.3 pounds of garbage per resident per day—more than twice the quantity produced in 1960 and the largest amount per capita in the world. Much of our solid waste consist of packaging material. The question is how to dispose of the more than 200 million tons of household garbage generated in this country each year.

Advanced economies produce and buy more than less-developed economies, so there is more to throw away. And because of higher incomes in advanced economies, the opportunity cost of time is higher, so there is a tendency to discard items rather than repair or recycle them. A broken toaster, for example, is more likely to be sent to the dump than to the repair shop. It's cheaper to buy a new toaster for $25 than to pay up to $40 an hour to have it repaired, assuming you can find a repair shop. (Look up "Appliance Repair, Small" in the *Yellow Pages* on the Internet's BigBook and see if you can find even one such repair shop in your area.)

About 70 percent of the nation's garbage is bulldozed and covered with soil in landfills. Although a well-managed landfill poses few environmental concerns, at one time communities dumped all kinds of toxic materials in them, materials that could leach into the soil, contaminating wells and aquifers. So landfills developed a bad reputation. The prevailing attitude with landfills is *Nimby* (Not in my back yard!). Everybody wants the garbage picked up but nobody wants it put down anywhere nearby.

As the cost of solid-waste disposal increases, state and local governments are instituting economizing measures, such as requiring households to sort their trash, charging households by the pound for trash pickups, and requiring returnable bottles. A little over one third of U.S. households participate in curbside recycling programs. **Recycling** is the process of converting waste products into reusable material. Still, according to the EPA, only about 15 percent of the

Recycling The process of converting waste products into reusable material

200 million tons of garbage generated annually in the United States gets recycled. About 15 percent is incinerated and the remaining 70 percent goes into landfills. Of the recycled material, three quarters consists of corrugated boxes, newspapers, and office paper. Some of the paper product is shipped to Korea and Taiwan, where it becomes packaging material for U.S. imports such as VCRs, CD players, and computer components.

Most of the 15 percent of garbage that is incinerated each year is burned in trash-to-energy plants, which generate electricity using the heat from incineration. Until recently, such plants looked like the wave of the future, but a decline in energy prices, less favorable tax treatment, and environmental concerns over the siting of incinerators (Nimby) have taken the steam out of the trash-to-energy movement.

So about 70 percent of our garbage goes to landfills, and only 30 percent is incinerated or recycled. In contrast, the Japanese recycle 40 percent of their waste and incinerate 33 percent, leaving only 27 percent to be deposited in landfills. Japanese households sort their trash into as many as 21 categories. Because land is more scarce in Japan—we know this because it costs relatively more—it is not surprising that the Japanese deposit a smaller share of their garbage in landfills.

Some recycling is clearly economical—such as aluminum cans, which are a cheap source of aluminum compared to producing new aluminum. About two out of three aluminum cans now get recycled. Recycling paper and cardboard is also economical and occurred long before the environmental movement. Still, despite promotional efforts, curbside programs account for only one-seventh of U.S. recycling. Such old standbys as paper drives, drop-off bins, and redemption centers still collect more tonnage than curbside programs. Most recycling results from salvaging scrap material from business and industry, a practice that goes back decades.

Governments have tried to stimulate demand for recycled material—for example, by requiring newspapers to use a certain amount of recycled newsprint. Other recycled products are not in such demand. In fact, some recycled products have become worthless and must be hauled to the dump.[9] Plastic containers, for example, have limited recycling potential.

Recycling imposes its own cost on the environment. Curbside recycling requires fleets of trucks that pollute the air. Newsprint must first be de-inked, creating a sludge that must be disposed of. But greater environmental awareness has made consumers more receptive to more efficient packaging material. For example, liquid laundry detergent is now available in a more concentrated "ultra" form, which cuts volume in half. And labels for all kinds of products proudly identify the recycled content of the packaging.

POSITIVE EXTERNALITIES

Until now, we have considered only negative externalities. Externalities can sometimes be positive, or beneficial. *Positive externalities* occur when the unpriced by-product of consumption or production benefits other consumers or other firms.

9 For example, see the discussion by Jeff Bailey, "Curbside Recycling Comforts the Soul, But Benefits Are Scant," *Wall Street Journal* (19 January 1995).

For example, people who get inoculated against a disease reduce their own likelihood of contracting the disease, but in the process they also reduce the chances of transmitting the disease to others. Inoculations thus provide *external benefits* to others. Education also confers external benefits on society as a whole because those who acquire more education become better citizens, can read road signs, are better able to support themselves and their families, and are less likely to require public assistance or to resort to crime for income. Education confers private benefits but it also confers additional social benefits to others.

The effect of external benefits on the optimal level of consumption is illustrated in Exhibit 5, which presents the supply and demand for education. The demand curve, *D*, represents the private demand for education, which reflects the *marginal private benefit* for those who acquire the education. More education is demanded at a lower price than at a higher price.

The benefit of education, however, spills over to others in society. If we add this positive externality, or *marginal external benefit,* to the marginal private benefit of education, we get the marginal social benefit of education. The *marginal social benefit* includes all the benefit society derives from education, both private and public. The marginal-social-benefit curve is above the private demand curve in Exhibit 5. At each level of education, the marginal social benefit exceeds the marginal private benefit by the amount of marginal external benefit generated by that particular unit of education.

If education were a strictly private decision, the amount purchased would be determined by the intersection of the private demand curve, *D*, with the

EXHIBIT 5

Education and Positive Externalities

In the absence of government intervention, the quantity of education demanded is *E*, at which the marginal cost equals the marginal private benefit of education. However, education also confers a positive externality on the rest of society, so the marginal social benefit exceeds the private benefit. At quantity *E*, the marginal social benefit exceeds the marginal cost, so more education is in society's best interest. In such a situation, government will try to encourage an increase in the quantity of education to *E'*, at which point the marginal cost equals the marginal social benefit.

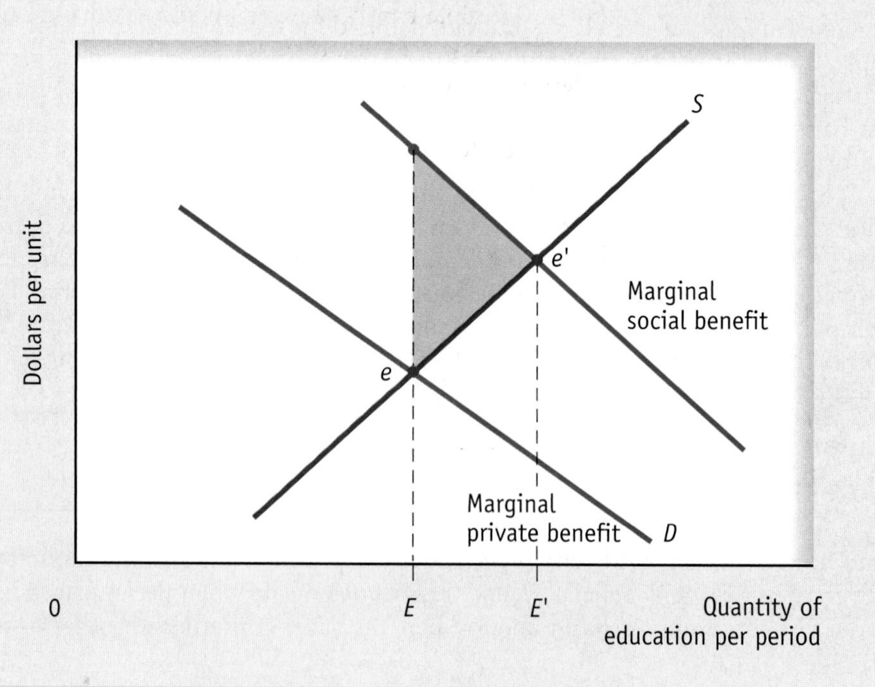

supply curve, *S*. The supply curve reflects the marginal cost of producing each unit of the good. This intersection, identified as point *e*, yields education level *E*, where the marginal cost of education equals the marginal private benefit.

But at level *E* the marginal social benefit of education exceeds its marginal cost. Net social welfare will increase if education is expanded beyond *E*. *As long as the marginal social benefit of education exceeds its marginal cost, social welfare is increased by expanding education.* Social welfare is maximized at point *e*' in Exhibit 5, where *E*' units of education are provided—that is, where the marginal social benefit equals the marginal cost, as reflected by the supply curve. The blue-shaded triangle identifies the net increase in social welfare that results from increasing the quantity of education to *E*'.

Thus, society is better off if the amount of education provided exceeds the private equilibrium. *When positive externalities are present, decisions based on private marginal benefits result in less than the socially optimal quantity of the good.* Hence, like negative externalities, positive externalities typically point to *market failure,* which is why government often gets into the act. When there are external benefits, public policy tries to increase the level of output beyond the private optimum. For example, government attempts to encourage education by providing free primary and secondary education, by requiring students to stay in school until they reach 16 years of age, and by subsidizing public higher education.

CONCLUSION

Six billion people inhabit the globe, whose population increases by about 90 million each year. World population is projected to increase 50 percent by the middle of the 21st century, with most of this growth occurring in less-developed countries, where most people barely eke out a living. Growing population pressure coupled with a lack of incentives to preserve open-access resources results in deforestation, dwindling fish stocks, and polluted air, land, and water.

Ironically, because of tighter pollution controls, industrial countries tend to be less polluted than developing countries, where there is more pollution per capita from what little industry there is. Most developing countries have such profound economic problems that environmental quality is not high on their list of priorities. The air in places such as Mexico City and Lagos, Nigeria, is dangerous. Residents of China's cities cover their mouths with masks when the smog is especially thick. The average Chinese car produces 10 to 15 times more emissions than the average U.S. car.[10] Farmers in Central America douse their crops with pesticides long banned in the United States.

Market prices can direct the allocation of resources only as long as property rights are well defined and can be enforced at a reasonable cost. Pollution of air, land, and water arises not so much from the greed of producers and consumers as from the fact that these open-access resources are subject to the common-pool problem.

10 As noted by Elisabeth Rosenthal, "China Finally Confronts Its Air-Pollution Crisis," *New York Times* (14 June 1998).

SUMMARY

1. Private choices will result in too little output when positive externalities exist and too much output when negative externalities exist. Public policy should subsidize or otherwise promote production that generates positive externalities and should tax or otherwise discourage production that generates negative externalities.

2. The optimal amount of environmental quality occurs where the marginal social cost of higher quality equals its marginal social benefit. A decrease in the marginal cost or an increase in the marginal benefit of environmental quality increases the optimal level of environmental quality.

3. The world's tropical rain forests have served to recycle noxious gases and convert them into oxygen and wood. The destruction of these forests reduces the environment's ability to cleanse itself.

4. The Coase theorem argues that as long as bargaining costs are small, assigning property rights to one party leads to an efficient solution to the problem of externalities. An example of the Coase theorem in action is the market for pollution permits.

5. In the last two decades, progress has been made in cleaning up the nation's air and waterways. The air is cleaner because of stricter emissions standards for motor vehicles; the water is cleaner because of billions spent on sewage treatment facilities. Although much of the federal attention and federal budget goes toward cleaning up toxic waste dumps, this pollution source does not pose as great a health threat to the population as a whole as do other forms of pollution, such as smog and pesticides.

QUESTIONS FOR REVIEW

1. *(Types of Resources)* Complete each of the following sentences:
   a. Resources that are available only in a finite amount are ______resources.
   b. The possibility that a nonexcludable resource will be used until the net marginal value of additional use equals zero is known as the _____.
   c. Resources for which periodic use can be continued indefinitely are known as ________ resources.
   d. If no individual can easily capture the value of a resource, it is termed________.

2. *(Resolving the Common-Pool Problem)* Why have authorities found it so difficult to regulate the fishing catch to allow for a sustainable yield?

3. *(Optimal Level of Pollution)* Explain the difference between fixed-technology production and variable-technology production. Should the government set a goal of reducing the marginal social cost of pollution to zero in industries with fixed technology? Should they do so in industries with variable technology?

4. ***(Case*****Study:** *Tropical Rain Forests)* Why does a solution to the overharvesting of timber in the tropical rain forests require some form of international cooperation? Would this be a sufficient solution to the deforestation problem?

5. *(Coase Analysis of Externalities)* Suppose a firm pollutes a stream that has a recreational value only when pollution is below a certain level. If transaction costs are low, why does the assignment of property rights to the stream lead to the same(efficient) level of pollution whether the firm or the recreational users own the stream?

6. *(Coase Analysis of Externalities)* Ronald Coase points out that a market failure does not arise simply because people ignore the external cost of their actions. What other condition is necessary? What did Coase consider to be efficient solution to a negative externality?

7. *(Positive Externalities)* The value of a home depends in part on how attractive other homes and yards in the neighborhood are. How do local zoning ordinances try to promote land uses that generate external benefits for neighbors?

PROBLEMS AND EXERCISES

8. *(External Costs with Fixed Technology)* Review the situation illustrated in Exhibit 1 in this chapter. If the government sets the price of electricity at the socially optimal level, why is the net gain equal to triangle *abc* even though consumers now pay a higher price for electricity? What would the net gain be if the government set the price above the optimal level?

9. *(Negative Externalities)* Suppose you wish to reduce a negative externally by imposing a tax on the activity that creates that externality. If the amount of the externality produced per unit of output increases as output increases, show the correct tax can be determined by using a supply-demand diagram. Assume that the marginal-private-cost curve slopes upward.

10. *(External Costs)* Use this data to answer the following questions.

Quantity	Marginal Private Benefit (Demand)	Marginal Private Cost (Supply)	Marginal Social Cost
0	—	$ 0	$ 0
1	$10	2	4
2	9	3	5
3	8	4	6
4	7	5	7
5	6	6	8
6	5	7	9
7	4	8	10
8	3	9	11
9	2	10	12
10	1	11	13

a. What is the external cost per unit of production?
b. What level will be produced if there is no regulation of the externality?
c. What level should be produced to achieve economic efficiency?
d. Calculate the dollar value of the net gain to society from correcting the externality.

11. *(External Costs with Variable Technology)* Think of an industry that pollutes the water and has access to variable technology for reducing that water pollution. Graphically illustrate and explain the impact of each of the following, other things constant, on the optimal level of water quality:
    a. New evidence is discovered of a greater risk of cancer from water pollution.
    b. The cost of pollution-abatement equipment increases.
    c. A technological improvement reduces the cost of pollution abatement.

12. *(Market for Pollution Rights)* The following graph shows the market for pollution rights.
    a. If there are no restrictions on pollution, what will be the amount of discharge?
    b. What will be the quantity supplied and the quantity demanded if the government restricts the amount of discharge to Q^* but gives the permits away?
    c. Where is market equilibrium if the government sells the permits? Illustrate this on the graph.
    d. What happens to market equilibrium if the government reduces the amount of permitted discharged to Q^{**}? Illustrate this on the graph.

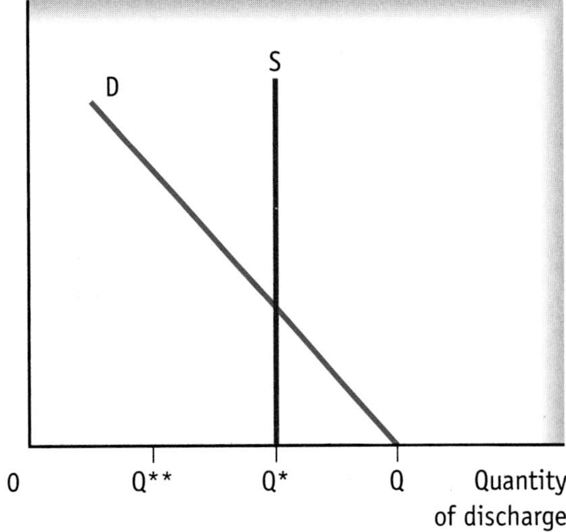

EXPERIENTIAL EXERCISES

13. *(Case***Study:** *City in the Clouds)* Suppose you are the mayor on Mexico City. How can you use some of the techniques outlined in this chapter to control pollution there? (For background information check http:cesimo.ing.ul.ve/GAIA/CASES/MEX)

14. *(The Common-Pool Problem)* Garret Hardin's 1968 article,"The Tragedy of the Commons," is available on-line at http://www.aloha.net/~jhanson/page95.htm. Download and read this clearly written article. Then describe some examples of the common-pool problem or, as he calls it, the tragedy of the commons.

15. *(External Costs with Fixed Technology)* Download Betty Joyce Nash, "Pollution Allowances Help Clear the Air" at http://www.rich.frb.org/cross/cross134/2.html. Based on what you've learned in this chapter, evaluate Nash's case for pollution allowances as a way of controlling negative exteranlities.

16. *(Wall Street Journal)* The Marketplace section of the *Wall Street Journal* is a good place to look for information related to externalities. On a given day, see how many stories you can find that deal with externalities—positive or negative. Are businesses taking steps to "internalize" externalities? What role does technology play in controlling negative externalities?

CHAPTER

31 Income Distribution and Poverty

Why are some families poor even in the most productive nation on Earth? Who are the poor and how did they get that way? What has been the trend in poverty rates over time? What has been the impact of the changing family structure on that trend? What programs are aimed at reducing poverty and how have they changed over time? Answers to these and related questions are addressed in this chapter, which examines poverty in the United States.

To establish a reference point, we first examine the distribution of income in the United States, paying special attention to poverty in recent years. We then discuss and evaluate the "social safety net"—government programs aimed at helping the poor. We also consider the impact of the changing family structure on the incidence of poverty, focusing in particular on the increase in female

sit the McEachern
ractive Study Center
or this chapter at
/mcisc.swcollege.com

householders. We will explore the effects of discrimination on the distribution of income and close the chapter by examining recent welfare reforms. Topics discussed in this chapter include:

- Distribution of income
- The official poverty level
- Public policy and poverty
- The feminization of poverty
- Poverty and discrimination
- Recent welfare reforms

THE DISTRIBUTION OF HOUSEHOLD INCOME

In a market economy, income depends primarily on earnings, which depend on the productivity of one's resources. The problem with allocating income according to productivity is that some people have difficulty earning income. Those born with mental or physical disabilities tend to be less productive and may be unable to earn a living. Others may face limited job choices and reduced wages because of advanced age, poor education, discrimination, or the demands of caring for small children.

Income Distribution by Quintiles

As a starting point, let's consider the distribution of income in the economy and see how it has changed over time, focusing on the household as the economic unit. After dividing the total number of households into five groups of equal size, or *quintiles*, ranked according to income, we can examine what percentage of income is received by each group. Such a division is presented in Exhibit 1 by decade since 1967. Take a moment to look over this exhibit. Notice that households in the lowest, or poorest, fifth of the population received only 4.0 percent of the income in 1967, whereas households in the highest, or richest, fifth received 43.8 percent of the income. Income here is measured after cash transfer payments have been received but before taxes have been paid.

In recent years, the share of income going to the top fifth has increased and the share going to the bottom fifth has declined slightly. The richest group's share of income increased from 43.8 percent in 1967 to 49.4 percent in 1997. So most recently, the top fifth received over 13 times as much income as the bottom fifth. A primary contributor to the growing share of income going to highest group has been the growth of two-earner households in the top group and the growth of single-parent households in the bottom group.

Also shown in Exhibit 1 is the share of income going to the top 5 percent of households; that share jumped between 1987 and 1997, and accounts for the jump in income going to the top 20 percent of households.

A College Education Pays Relatively More

Also contributing the dominance of the top group is a growing pay premium for individuals with a college education. Between 1980 and 1996, for example, the median wage (adjusted for inflation) for those with only a high school diploma declined 6 percent, while the median wage of college graduates rose 12 percent. Why have more educated workers done better? First, new computer-based information technologies have increased the demand for skilled labor—for knowledge workers—relative to unskilled labor. Second, trends such as industry deregulation, declining unionization, and freer international trade have reduced the demand for

EXHIBIT 1

Share of Aggregate Household Income by Quintile: 1967, 1977, 1987, and 1997

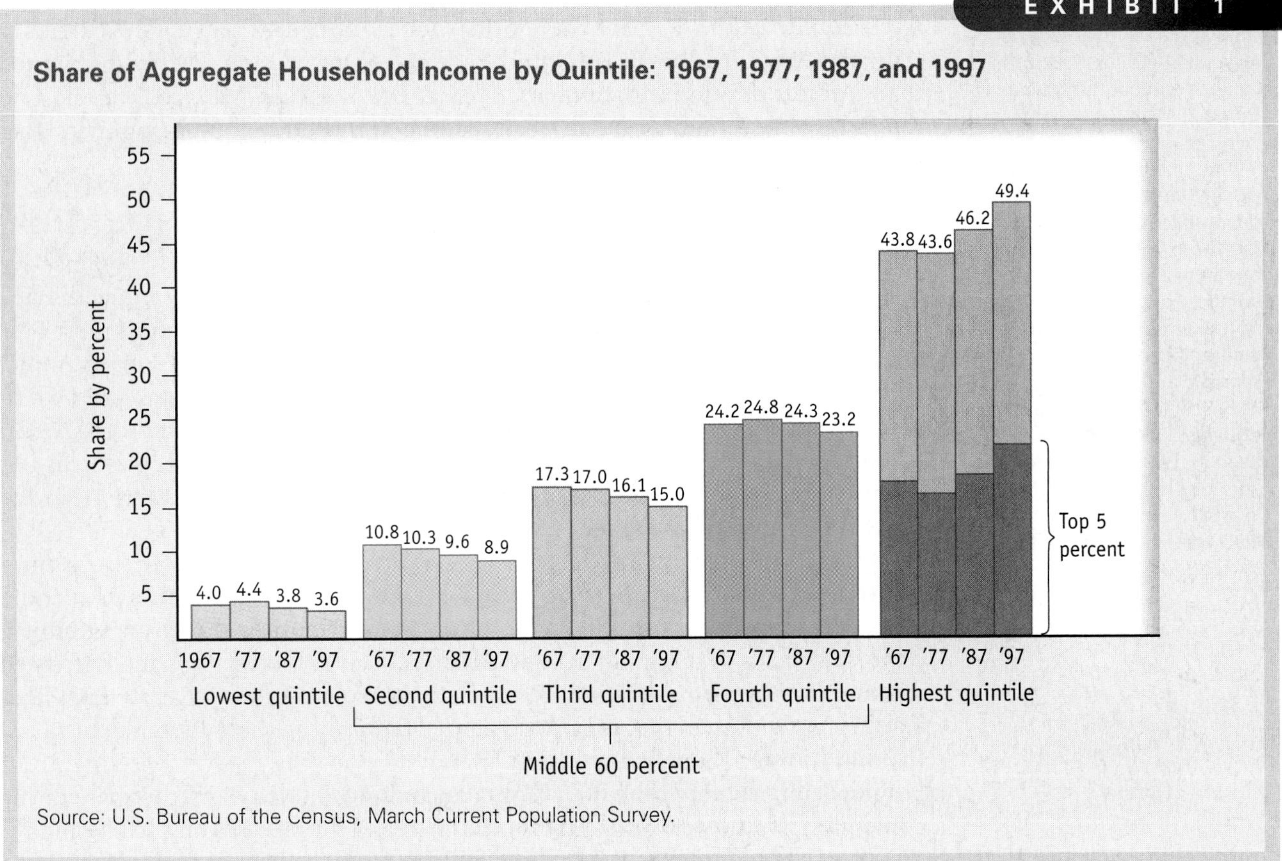

Source: U.S. Bureau of the Census, March Current Population Survey.

workers with less education. Labor unions, for example, help to increase the wages of many workers who would otherwise end up in the bottom half of the income distribution. The share of the labor force that is unionized declined from 26 percent in 1973 to only 15 percent in 1998.

Third, recent U.S. immigrants have tended to be less well-educated than existing residents, thus increasing the supply of relatively poorly educated workers and depressing their wages. For example, the U.S. Hispanic population roughly doubled in size between 1980 and 1996, and during that time the percentage of Hispanics who are foreign-born has grown. Only 62 percent of Hispanics aged 25 to 29 had at least a high school education in 1996, compared to 88 percent of whites and 86 percent of blacks.[1]

So economic developments in recent years have benefited the better educated, and this helps explain the growing disparity in household income. Note that it is not necessarily the same households who remain rich or poor over time. Some households drop out of high-income ranks and are replaced by others. Likewise, some households work their way out of poverty to be replaced, for example, by families headed by young unmarried women who become mothers. So we are not talking about the same households getting richer or poorer over time.

1 As reported by Rick Green in "Education Gap Closes for Blacks and Whites," *Hartford Courant* (29 June 1998).

NetBookmark

Data and analytical reports about income distribution can be found at the Census Bureau's Web Site at http://www.census.gov/hhes/www/income.html. The income site includes a link to a page devoted to income inequality. There you can find data on the distribution of income by quintile and a report examining trends in income distribution since World War II, *A Brief Look at Postwar U.S. Income Inequality.* What measure is used in this report to measure income distribution? In what year was income least unequal? What is the current trend?

Income in the United States is less evenly distributed than in other developed countries throughout the world, such as Canada, France, Great Britain, Italy, and Australia. But income in the United States is more evenly distributed than in most developing countries, such as Brazil, Chile, Mexico, Nigeria, and the Philippines. More than half of all income in most developing countries goes to the richest 20 percent of the population.

Problems with Distributional Benchmarks

One problem with examining income distributions is that there is no objective standard for evaluating them. The usual assumption is that a more equal distribution of income is more desirable, but is a perfectly even distribution most preferred? If not, then how uneven should the distribution be? For example, among major league baseball players, about 54 percent of the pay goes to 20 percent of the players. Earnings in professional basketball are even more skewed toward the top players. So income among baseball and basketball players is less evenly distributed than household income in the economy. Does this mean the economy as a whole is "fairer" than these professional sports?

Households receive income from two primary sources: resource earnings and transfer payments from the government. Exhibit 1 measures money income after cash transfers but before taxes. Thus the distribution shown in Exhibit 1 omits the effects of taxes and in-kind transfers, such as food stamps and free medical care for poor families. The tax system as a whole is progressive, meaning that families with higher incomes pay a larger fraction of their incomes in taxes. In-kind transfers benefit the lowest-income groups the most. Consequently, if Exhibit 1 incorporated the effects of taxes and in-kind transfers, the share of income going to the lower groups would increase, the share going to the higher groups would decrease, and income would be more evenly distributed.

Finally, the income distribution estimates include only reported sources of income. If people receive payment "under the table" to evade taxes, or if they earn money through illegal activities, their actual income will exceed their reported income. The omission of unreported income will distort the data in Exhibit 1 only if unreported income as a percentage of total family income differs across income levels.

Why Do Household Incomes Differ?

Median income The middle income in a series of incomes ranked from smallest to largest

The **median income** of all households is the middle income when incomes are ranked from lowest to highest. In any given year, half the households are above the median income and half are below it. We have already seen one reason why incomes differ across households, namely that some workers are better educated than others. Income differences across households also stem from differences in the *number* of workers in each household. Thus *another reason household incomes differ is that the number of household members who are working differs.* For example, among households in the bottom 20 percent based on income, only one household in five has a full-time, year-round worker. Over two-thirds of households in the bottom 20 percent are headed by unmarried females.

The median income for households with two earners is about 82 percent higher than for households with only one earner and nearly *four times* higher than for households with no earners. Incomes also differ for all the reasons labor incomes differ, such as differences in education, ability, job experience, and so on. At every age, those with more education earn more, on average. For example, according to the U.S. Census Bureau, males with a professional degree had average earnings of $109,206 in 1997, or about four times the average of $28,307 earned by males with only a high school education. Age itself also has an important effect on income. As workers mature, they acquire valuable job experience, get promoted, and earn more.

Differences in earnings based on age and education reflect the normal *life-cycle* pattern of income. In fact, most income differences across households reflect the normal workings of resource markets, whereby workers are rewarded according to their productivity. A high-income household usually consists of a well-educated couple who are both employed. A low-income household is usually headed by single parent who is young, female, poorly educated, and not employed. Low incomes are a matter of public concern, especially when children are involved, as we will see in the next section.

POVERTY AND THE POOR

Since poverty is such a relative concept, how do we measure it objectively and how do we ensure that our measure can be applied with equal relevance over time? The federal government has developed a method for calculating an official poverty level; this level has become the benchmark for poverty analysis in the United States.

Official Poverty Level

To derive the **U.S. official poverty level**, the U.S. Department of Agriculture first estimates the cost of a nutritionally adequate diet. Then, based on the assumption that the poor spend about one-third of their income on food, the official poverty level is calculated by multiplying these food costs by three. Adjustments are made for family size and for inflation over time. The official poverty threshold of money income for a family of four was $16,400 in 1997; a family of four at or below that income threshold was regarded as living in poverty. Poverty thresholds in 1997 ranged from $8,350 for a person living alone to $32,566 for a family with nine or more members. The poverty definition is based on pretax money income, including cash transfers, but it excludes the value of noncash transfers such as food stamps, Medicaid, subsidized housing, or employer-provided health insurance.

U.S. official poverty level
Benchmark level of income computed by the federal government to track poverty over time, based on three times the cost of a nutritionally adequate diet

Each year since 1959, the Census Bureau has conducted a survey comparing individual families' annual cash incomes to the annual poverty threshold applicable to that family. Results of this survey are presented in Exhibit 2, which indicates both the millions of people living below the official poverty level and the percentage of the U.S. population below that level. Periods of U.S. recession are also shown (a recession is defined as two or more successive quarters of declining gross domestic product). Note that beginning in the early 1970s, poverty increased during recessions.

The biggest decline in poverty occurred prior to 1970; *the poverty rate dropped from 22.4 percent in 1959 to 12.1 percent in 1969*. During that period, the number of poor people dropped from about 40 million to 24 million. The poverty rate bottomed out during the 1970s, then rose between 1979 and 1983. After a modest decline between 1983 and 1989, the rate turned up in 1990 and

EXHIBIT 2

Number and Percent of U.S. Population in Poverty: 1959–1997

Source: Census Bureau, March 1998 Current Population Survey, http://census.gov/hhes/poverty/poverty/pov.97.html

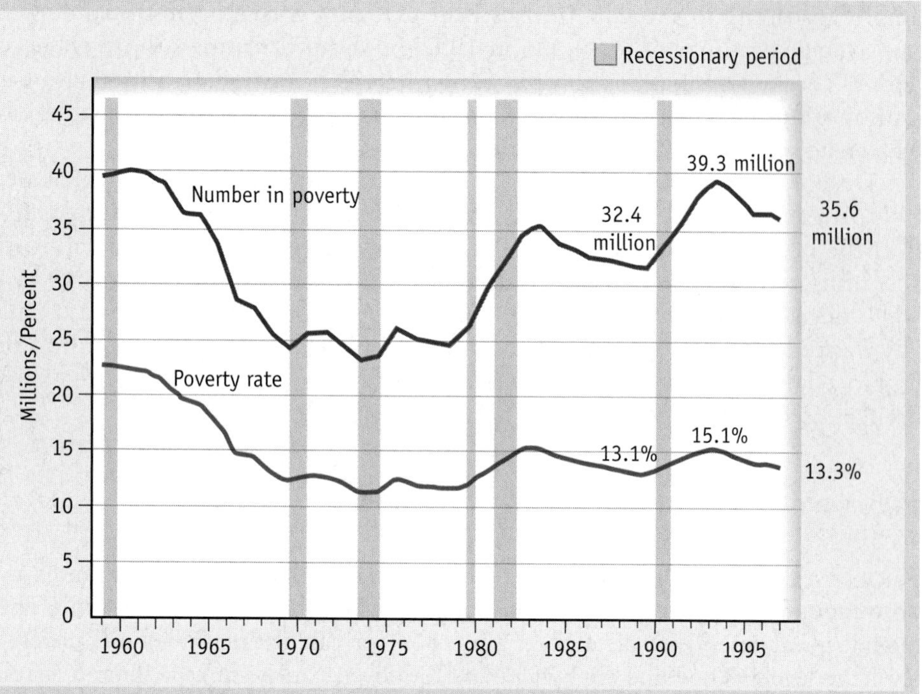

topped out in 1993 at 15.1 percent before falling to 13.3 percent in 1997. The 35.6 million people in poverty in 1997 is down from 39.3 million in 1993.

Poverty is a relative term. If we examined the distribution of income across countries, we would find huge gaps between rich and poor nations. The official U.S. poverty level of income is many times greater than the average income for three-fourths of the world's population.[2] For example, the U.S. minimum wage in 1998 was $5.15 per hour; in Mexico the minimum wage was the equivalent of $3.40 *per day!*

An income at the U.S. poverty level today provides a standard of living that would have been considered attractive by most people who lived in the United States in 1900, when only 15 percent of families had flush toilets, only 3 percent had electricity, and only 1 percent had central heating. Finally, the official definition of poverty ignores a household's other assets, such as owner-occupied housing or automobiles. According to one study carried out in the 1980s, three in ten households identified as poor owned their own home and half owned a motor vehicle.

Programs to Help the Poor

What should society's response to poverty be? *Families with a full-time worker are nine times more likely to escape poverty than are families with no workers.* Thus the government's first line of defense in fighting poverty is to promote a healthy economy. Yet even when the unemployment rate is relatively low, some people may remain poor because they lack marketable skills, must care for small children, or face discrimination in the labor market.

2 See World Bank, *World Development Report 1998/99* (New York: Oxford University Press, 1998), Table 30.

Although some government programs to help the poor involve direct market intervention, such as minimum-wage laws, the most visible programs redistribute income after the market has provided an initial distribution. Since the mid-1960s, social welfare expenditures at all levels of government have increased significantly. We can divide social welfare programs into two major categories: social insurance and income assistance.

Social Insurance. Social insurance programs are designed to replace the lost income of those who worked but are now retired, temporarily unemployed, or unable to work because of disability or work-related injury. The major social insurance program is **Social Security**, established during the Great Depression of the 1930s to supplement retirement income to those with a work history and a record of contributing to the program. **Medicare**, another social insurance program, provides health insurance for short-term medical care to about 37 million Americans mostly aged 65 and older, regardless of income. Other social insurance programs include *unemployment insurance* and *worker's compensation*, which supports workers injured on the job; both programs require that beneficiaries have a prior record of employment.

The social insurance system deducts "insurance premiums" from workers' pay to provide benefits to other retired, disabled, and unemployed individuals. These programs protect some families from poverty, particularly the elderly receiving Social Security, but they are aimed more at those with a work history. Still, the social insurance system tends to redistribute income from rich to poor and from young to old. Most current Social Security beneficiaries receive far more in benefits than they paid into the program, especially those with a brief work history or a record of low wages.

Social Security By far the largest social insurance program; supplements retirement income to those with a record of contributing to the program during their working years

Medicare Social insurance program providing health insurance for short-term medical care to older Americans, regardless of income

Income Assistance. **Income assistance programs**—what we usually call "welfare"—provide money and in-kind assistance to the poor. Unlike social insurance programs, income assistance programs do not require the recipient to have a work history or to have contributed to the program. Income assistance programs are means tested. In a **means-tested program,** a household's income and assets must lie below a certain level to qualify for benefits. The federal government funds two-thirds of welfare spending, and state and local governments fund one-third. Nearly half of all welfare spending pays for medical care for the poor.

The two primary *cash transfer* programs are **Temporary Assistance for Needy Families (TANF)**, which provides cash to poor families with dependent children, and **Supplemental Security Income (SSI)**, which provides cash to the elderly poor and the disabled. Cash transfers vary inversely with family income from other sources. In July 1997, TANF replaced Aid for Families with Dependent Children (AFDC), which began during the Great Depression and was originally aimed at providing support for widows with young children. Whereas AFDC was a federal *entitlement* program, meaning that anyone who met the criteria was *entitled* to benefits, TANF is under the control of each state government and carries no federal entitlement. The federal government provides each state a fixed grant to help fund TANF programs.

The Supplemental Security Income program provides support for the elderly and disabled poor. SSI is the fastest-growing cash transfer program, with outlays increasing from $8 billion in 1980 to nearly $30 billion in 1998. SSI coverage has been broadened to include those addicted to drugs and alcohol,

Income assistance programs Welfare programs that provide money and in-kind assistance to the poor; benefits do not depend on prior contributions.

Means-tested program To be eligible for such a program, an individual's income and assets must not exceed specified levels.

Temporary Assistance for Needy Families (TANF) An income assistance program run by the states that provides cash transfer payments to poor families with dependent children.

Supplemental Security Income (SSI) An income assistance program that provides cash transfer payments to the elderly poor and the disabled; a uniform federal payment is supplemented by transfers that vary across states.

children with learning disabilities, and, in some cases, the homeless. The federal portion of this program is uniform across states, but states can supplement federal aid. Benefit levels in California average nearly twice those in Alabama. Most states also offer modest *General Assistance* aid to those who are poor but do not qualify for TANF or SSI.

The federal government also provides an *earned income tax credit* to the working poor. For example, a family with two children and earnings of $13,000 in 1998 would not only pay no federal income tax but would also receive a cash transfer of $3,600. More than 12 million workers received transfers under the program.

Medicaid In-kind transfer program that provides medical care for poor people; by far the most costly welfare program

In addition to cash transfer programs, a variety of *in-kind transfer* programs provide health care, food stamps, and housing assistance to the poor. **Medicaid** pays for medical care for those with incomes below a certain level who are aged, blind, disabled, or are living in families with dependent children. Medicaid is by far the largest welfare program, costing nearly twice as much as all cash transfer programs combined. It has grown more than any other poverty program, quadrupling in the last decade and accounting for one-fifth of the typical state's budget (though states receive federal grants covering half or more of their Medicaid budget). The qualifying level of income is set by each state, and some states are quite strict. Therefore, the proportion of poor covered by Medicaid varies greatly across states. In 1998, about 36 million individuals received Medicaid; outlays averaged about $4,200 per recipient. Spending on the 3.5 million beneficiaries aged 65 and older averaged about $8,000 per year. For many elderly, Medicaid pays for long-term nursing care (Medicaid pays half the nation's nursing home costs). Although half the nation's welfare budget goes for health care, nearly 40 million U.S. residents still have no health insurance.

Food stamps An in-kind transfer program that offers low-income households vouchers redeemable for food; benefit levels vary inversely with household income.

Food stamps are vouchers that can be redeemed for food. The program is aimed at reducing hunger and providing nutrition to poor families. The cost is paid by the federal government, and benefits are uniform across states. About 1 in 10 Americans received food stamps in 1998, with an average monthly benefit per recipient of about $80.

Housing assistance programs include direct assistance for rental payments and subsidized low-income housing. Spending for housing assistance has doubled since 1990. About 10 million people receive some form of housing assistance.[3] Other in-kind programs include the *school lunch program* for poor children; supplemental food vouchers for pregnant women, infants, and children; *energy assistance* to help pay the energy bills of poor families; and *education and training assistance* for poor families, such as Head Start and the Job Training Partnership Act. In all, there are about 75 means-tested federal welfare programs.

WHO ARE THE POOR?

Who are the poor, and how has the composition of this group changed over time? We will slice poverty statistics in several ways to examine the makeup of the group. Keep in mind that we are relying on official poverty estimates, which ignore the value of in-kind transfers and to that extent overstate poverty.

3 This is an increase of about 50 percent over the number receiving benefits in 1980. About 60 percent of the families in public housing in 1990 had incomes below the poverty level.

Poverty and Age

Earlier we looked at the poverty rate among the entire population. Now we focus on poverty and age. Exhibit 3 presents the poverty rates for three age groups since 1959: those less than 18 years old, those between 18 and 64, and those 65 and older. The poverty rates for each group declined between 1959 and 1968. Between the mid-1970s and the early 1980s, the rate among those under 18 years of age trended upward. In 1997, the poverty rate among people under 18 years of age was 19.9 percent—nearly twice the rate of those 18 and over.

In 1959, the elderly were the poorest group, with a poverty rate about 35 percent. Since then, poverty among the elderly has fallen steadily; in 1997, the rate was 10.5 percent, slightly below the rate of 10.9 percent for those 18 to 64 years of age. This reduction in poverty among the elderly can be attributed to a tremendous growth in Social Security and Medicare spending, which in real terms grew tenfold from $60 billion in 1959 to about $600 billion in 1998 (measured in 1998 dollars). Social Security and Medicare spending is now *triple* what the federal government spends on income assistance, or welfare, programs. *Although not welfare programs in a strict sense, Social Security and Medicare have been extremely successful in reducing poverty among the elderly.*

Poverty and Public Choice

In a democratic country such as ours, public policies depend very much on the political power of the interest groups involved. In recent years, the elderly have become a strong political force. Unlike most interest groups, the elderly are a group we all expect to join one day. The elderly actually are represented by four constituencies: (1) the elderly themselves, (2) those under 65 who are concerned about the current benefits to their parents or other elderly relatives, (3) those

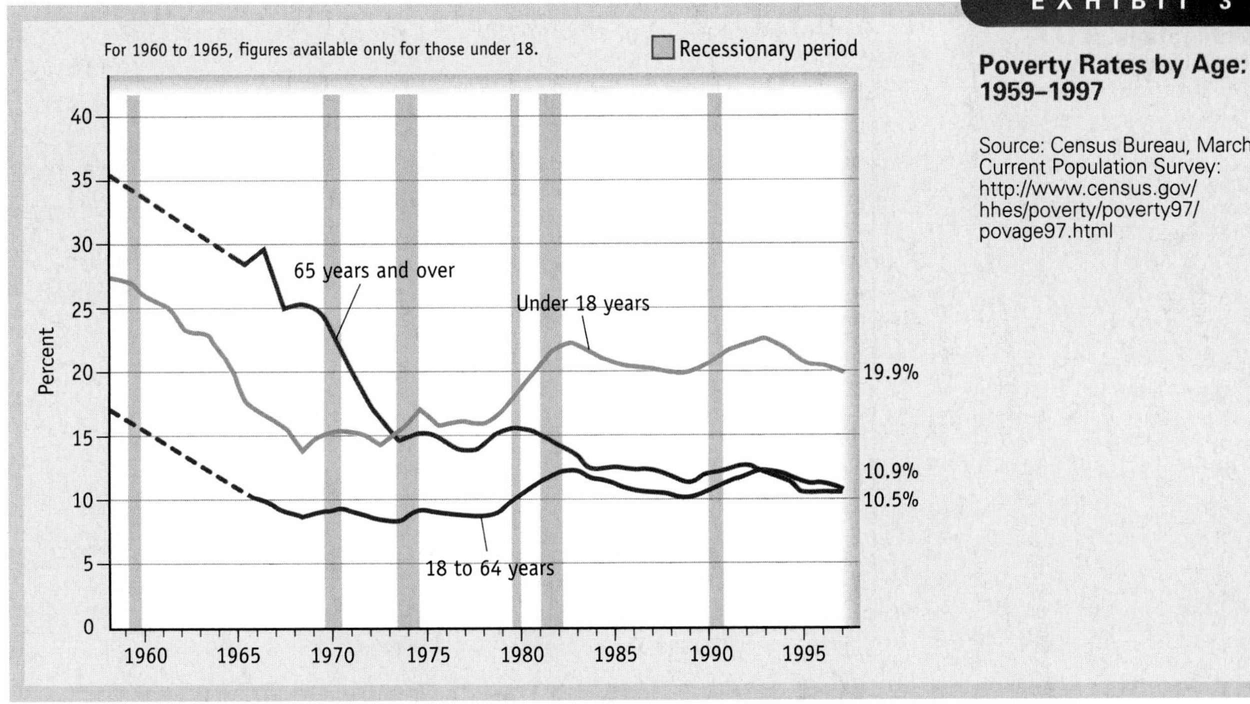

EXHIBIT 3

Poverty Rates by Age: 1959–1997

Source: Census Bureau, March Current Population Survey: http://www.census.gov/hhes/poverty/poverty97/povage97.html

under 65 who are concerned about their own benefits in the future, and (4) those who earn their living by caring for the elderly, such as doctors and nursing home operators. So the elderly have a broad constituency.

Moreover, the voter participation rate of those 65 and over is higher than that of other age groups. For example, voter participation of those 65 years of age and older is typically triple that of those between 18 and 24 and four times that of welfare recipients. The political muscle of the elderly has been flexed whenever a question of Social Security benefits has come up for a vote.

The Feminization of Poverty

One way of classifying the incidence of poverty is by age. Another way is based on the marital status and race of the household head. Exhibit 4 compares, for white, black, and Hispanic families, the poverty rates for married couples with the rates among families headed by females. Three trends are unmistakable. First, married couples have poverty rates only about one-third the rates of female householders. Second, Hispanic families have the highest poverty rates (individuals of Hispanic origin may be of any race) followed by black families, then white families. And third, since the early 1980s, rates have remained relatively unchanged among white and Hispanic families, but have fallen among black families. Specifically, among black married couples the poverty rate declined from about 15 percent in the early 1980s to 8 percent in 1997. Among black female householders, poverty rates declined from about 54 percent to 40 percent.

Not shown in the exhibit are poverty rates among male householders, which are higher than among married couples but still only about half the rates of female householders. The findings show that regardless of race or Hispanic

EXHIBIT 4

Percentage of U.S. Families in Poverty by Type of Household

Developed from data found in U.S. Bureau of the Census Home Page, Income and Poverty, Table 4, 1998, at http://www.census.gov/hhes/poverty/histpov/hstpov4.html

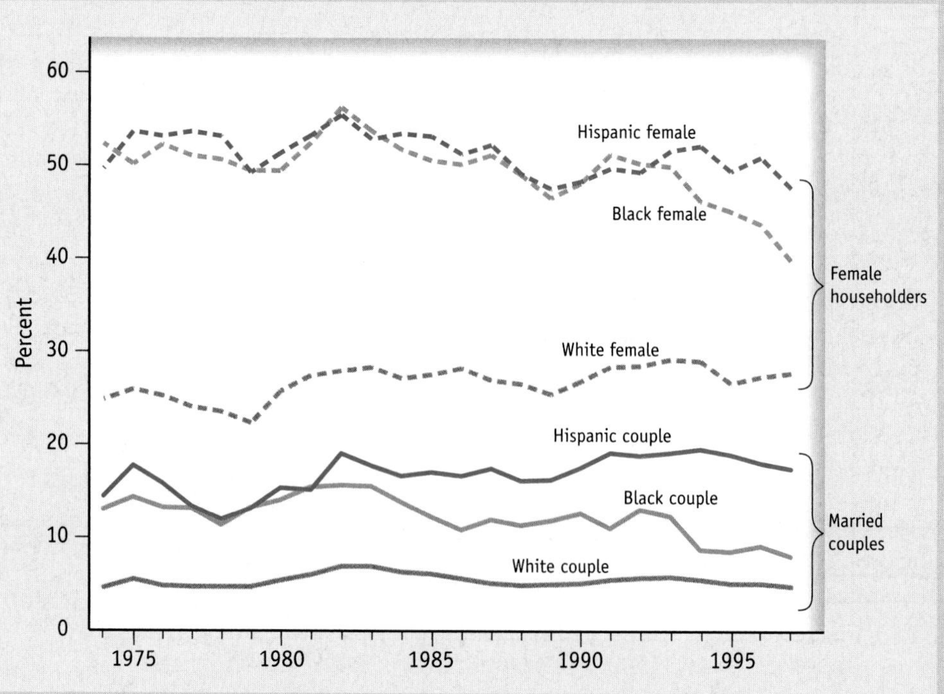

origin, people living in two-parent families are much less likely to be poor than those living in one-parent families.

Though poverty rates among female householders are high, *these rates have increased little since 1969.* What has increased is the *number* of female householders in the economy. The percentage of births to unmarried mothers is five times greater today than in 1960. In 1960, only one in 200 children lived with a single parent who had never married. Today, one in ten children lives with a single parent who has never married.

The United States has the highest teenage pregnancy rate in the developed world—twice the rate of Great Britain and 15 times that of Japan. Since the father in such cases typically assumes little responsibility for child support, children born outside marriage are likely to be poorer than other children. The divorce rate has also increased since 1960. Because of the higher divorce rate, even children born to married couples now face a greater likelihood of living in a one-parent household before they grow up. Divorce usually reduces the resources available to the children. *Children of female householders are five times more likely to live in poverty than are other children.*

Increases in the number of unwed mothers and in the divorce rate increased the number of female householders by 126 percent between 1969 and 1997. With this came a similar increase in the number of poor people from such families. Thus, even though the poverty *rate* among female householder has remained relatively constant at about 32 percent since 1969, the *number* of poor female householders has increased because the *number* of female householders has increased. Whereas the number of female householders jumped 126 percent between 1969 and 1998, the number of other families grew only 27 percent and their poverty rate *declined* from 6.9 percent to 5.7 percent.

Between 1969 and 1997, the number of poor families in the United States increased by 2.3 million, or 46 percent. Poverty among families with female householders increased 2.2 million, or 119 percent. Poverty in other families increased only 0.1 million, or 5 percent. Thus female householders accounted for nearly all of the increase in poor families since 1969. *The growth in the number of poor families since 1969 resulted overwhelmingly from the growth in the number of female householders.* Since 1969, the U.S. economy has generated 50 million new jobs. Families with a female householder were in the worst position to take advantage of this job growth.

Young, single motherhood is a recipe for instant poverty. Often the young mother drops out of school, which reduces her future earning possibilities when and if she seeks work outside the home. Even a strong economy is little aid to households with nobody in the labor force. Worse yet, young, single mothers-to-be are less likely to seek adequate medical care; the result is a higher proportion of premature, underweight babies. This is one reason why the U.S. infant mortality rate exceeds many other industrialized countries. Compared to two-parent families, children in one-parent families are twice as likely to drop out of school, and girls from one-parent families are twice as likely to become single mothers themselves.

Each year, about 1.2 million children in the United States are born to single mothers. There is a clear link between unwed parenthood and welfare dependency. Two-thirds of all out-of-wedlock births are to 15- to 24-year olds. Only 57 percent of these mothers have a high-school diploma, and only 28 percent ever worked full time (another 9 percent worked part time). Because of a lack of education and limited job skills, most unwed mothers go on welfare. Prior to recently imposed lifetime limits on welfare, the average never-married mother was on welfare for a decade, twice as long as divorced mothers on welfare. Of all births to teenage girls, the proportion who were unmarried was 13 percent in 1950, 30 percent in 1970, 67 percent in 1990 and 76 percent in 1994.[4]

Poverty has therefore become increasingly feminized, mostly because female householders have become more common. Children from mothers who finished high school, married before having a child, and gave birth after age twenty are ten times less likely to be poor than children from mothers who fail to do these things.[5] Because the number of female householders has grown more rapidly among blacks, the feminization of poverty has been more dramatic in black households. Seventy percent of all black births in 1994 were to unmarried women, compared to 43 percent of all births among those of Hispanic origin and 25 percent of births among whites.[6]

Poverty and Discrimination

Is the lower family income and greater incidence of poverty among minorities the result of discrimination in job markets, or are there other explanations? We should note that discrimination can occur in many ways: in school funding, in housing, in employment, in career advancement. Also, discrimination in one area can affect opportunities in another. For example, housing discrimination may reduce job opportunities if a black family cannot move within commuting distance of the best employers. Moreover, the legacy of discrimination can affect career choices long after discrimination has ceased. Someone whose father and grandfather found job avenues blocked may be less inclined to pursue an education or to accept a job that requires a long training program. Thus discrimination is a complex topic, and we cannot do it justice in this brief section.

Job-market discrimination can take many forms. An employer may fail to hire a black job applicant because the applicant lacks training. But this lack of training may arise from discrimination in the schools, in union apprenticeship programs, or in training programs run by other employers. For example, evidence suggests that black workers receive less on-the-job training than otherwise similar white workers.

Let's first consider the difference between the earnings of nonwhite and white workers. After adjusting for a variety of factors that could affect the wage, such as education and work experience, research shows that whites earn more than blacks, but the wage gap between the two narrowed between 1940 and 1976 to the point where blacks earned only 7 percent less than white workers. The gap then widened a bit,[7] but has narrowed since 1993.

Could explanations besides job discrimination account for the wage gap? Though the data adjust for *years* of schooling, some research suggests that black

4 As noted by James Q. Wilson, "Human Remedies for Social Disorder," *Public Interest* (Spring 1998): 27.

5 As noted by James Q. Wilson, p. 28.

6 These figures are from *Statistical Abstracts of the United States: 1997,* U.S. Bureau of the Census (Austin, Texas: Hoover's Business Press, 1997), Table 89.

7 See the evidence in M. Boozer, A. Krueger, and S. Wolken, "Race and School Quality Since Brown v. Board of Education," *Brookings Papers on Economic Activity: Microeconomics,* 1992: 269–326.

workers received a lower *quality* of schooling than white workers. For example, black students are less likely to use computers in school. Inner-city schools often have more problems with classroom discipline, which takes time and attention away from instruction. Such quality differences could account for at least a portion of the remaining gap in standardized wages. Although any differences attributable to a poorer-quality education would not necessarily reflect job discrimination, they might well reflect discrimination in the funding of schools.

Evidence of discrimination comes from audit studies, where otherwise similar white and minority candidates are sent to the same source to seek jobs, rent apartments, or apply for mortgage loans. For example, a white and a black job applicant with similar qualifications and résumés applied for the same job. These studies find that employers are less likely to interview or offer a job to minority applicants. Minority applicants also tend to be treated less favorably by real estate agents and lenders. The President's Council of Economic Advisers concluded in 1998 that discrimination against members of racial and ethnic minorities, while "far less pervasive and overt" than it was, still persists.[8]

Affirmative Action

The Equal Employment Opportunity Commission, established by the Civil Rights Act of 1964, monitors cases involving unequal pay for equal work and unequal access to promotion. Executive Order 11246, signed by President Lyndon Johnson, required all companies doing business with the federal government to set numerical hiring, promotion, and training goals to ensure that these firms did not discriminate in hiring on the basis of race, sex, religion, or national origin. For three decades, the order governed employment practices in firms that accounted for one-third of all jobs. Black employment increased in those firms required to file affirmative-action plans.[9] The fraction of the black labor force employed in white-collar jobs increased from 16.5 percent in 1960 to 40.5 percent in 1981—an increase that greatly exceeded the growth of white-collar jobs in the labor force as a whole. Research also suggests that civil-rights legislation played a role in narrowing the black-white earnings gap between 1960 and the mid-1970s.[10]

Attention focused on hiring practices and equality of opportunity at the state and local levels as well, as governments introduced so-called set-aside programs to guarantee minorities a share of contracts. But in 1989, the U.S. Supreme Court rejected Richmond, Virginia's, set-aside program, which had reserved 30 percent of construction work for minorities. Within a year of the ruling, many local affirmative action programs, including Richmond's, had been suspended or eliminated.

A 1995 U.S. Supreme Court decision challenged affirmative-action programs more broadly, ruling that Congress must meet a rigorous legal standard in order to justify any contracting or hiring practice based on race, especially programs that reserve job slots for minorities and women. Programs must be shown to be in response to injustices created by past discrimination, said the

8 See the *Economic Report of the President,* February 1998, p. 152.

9 See the evidence provided in James Smith and Finis Welch, "Black Economic Progress After Myrdal," *Journal of Economic Literature* 27 (June 1989): 519–563.

10 See David Card and Alan Krueger, "Trends in Relative Black-White Earnings Revisited," *American Economic Review* 83 (May 1993): 85–91.

Court. The ruling could affect the 200,000 federal contractors operating under Executive Order 11246.

In summary, evidence suggests that blacks earn less than whites after adjustment for other factors that could affect wages, such as education and job experience. Part of this wage gap may reflect differences in the quality of education, differences that could themselves be the result of discrimination. Keep in mind that unemployment rates are twice as high among blacks as among whites and are higher still among black teenagers, the group most in need of job skills and job experience. *But we should also note that black families are not a homogeneous group. In fact, the distribution of income is more uneven among black families than it is among the population as a whole.*

On the upside, according to the 1998 *Economic Report of the President*, the median income of black families has risen faster since 1993 than that of whites. The proportion of black families living below the poverty line fell to a record low by 1997. And the ratio of black-to-white average income for married couples increased from 0.71 in 1967 to 0.80 in 1997; for female-headed families, that ratio increased from 0.63 to 0.73.

There is also a growing middle class among black households. The number of black-owned businesses increased by 46 percent between 1987 and 1992, according to the Census Bureau. Some of the progress among blacks stems from their steady advances in education. In 1975, the percentage of young blacks without a high school diploma was 12.3 percentage points above that of whites (27.0 percent versus 14.7 percent). By 1995, the percentage of young blacks without diplomas had fallen to within 2 percentage points of whites (15.8 percent versus 13.8 percent). In 1960, the average black adult had only a junior high school education; by 1990, a high school education was the average. In 1980, only 7 percent of middle-aged blacks had a college degree; by 1990, that figure had jumped to 17 percent. More generally, since 1970, the number of black doctors, nurses, college teachers, and newspaper reporters has more than doubled; the number of black engineers, computer programmers, accountants, managers, and administrators has more than tripled; the number of black elected officials has quadrupled; and the number of black lawyers has increased sixfold.

UNINTENDED CONSEQUENCES OF INCOME ASSISTANCE

On the plus side, antipoverty programs increase the consumption possibilities of poor families, and this is significant, especially since children are the largest poverty group. But programs to assist the poor may have secondary effects that limit their ability to reduce poverty. Here we consider some unintended consequences.

Work Disincentives

Society, through government, tries to provide families with an adequate standard of living, but society also wants to ensure that only those in need receive benefits. As we have seen, income assistance consists of a bundle of cash and in-kind transfer programs. Because these programs are designed to help the poor and only the poor, the level of benefits is inversely related to income from other sources. This has resulted in a system in which transfers decline sharply as earned income increases, in effect imposing a high marginal tax rate on that earned income. An increase in earnings may cause a decline in benefits received from TANF, Medicaid, food stamps, housing assistance, energy assistance, and other programs. If a bite is taken from each transfer program as earned income increases, working may result in little or no increase in total income. In fact, over certain income ranges, the welfare recipient may lose well over $1 in transfer benefits for each $1 increase in earnings. The *marginal tax rate* on earned income could exceed 100 percent.

Since holding even a part-time job involves additional expenses, such as transportation and child-care costs, not to mention the loss of free time, such a system of perverse incentives can frustrate those trying to work their way off welfare. *This high marginal tax rate discourages employment and self-sufficiency.* In many cases, the value of welfare benefits exceeds the disposable income resulting from full-time employment. For example, according to one study, the value of welfare benefits in most states exceeded the full-time earning of a janitor or the starting salary for a secretary.[11]

Just how much the higher marginal tax rates reduced the incentive to work remains unclear. We do know that prior to recent welfare reforms only about one of every 20 persons receiving welfare was employed. Twice as many welfare recipients worked in the mid-1970s. These high marginal tax rates also encouraged welfare recipients to conceal earned income; some worked "off the books" for cash or became involved in illegal activities.

The longer people are out of the labor force, the more their job skills deteriorate, so when they do seek employment, their productivity and their pay are lower than when they were last employed. This lowers their expected wage and makes work less attractive. Some economists argue that in this way, welfare benefits can lead to long-term dependency. While welfare seems to be a rational choice in the short run, it has an unfavorable long-term outcome both for the family and for society.

Does Welfare Cause Dependency?

Does the system of incentives created by high marginal tax rates create dependency among welfare recipients? How could we examine such a question? A relatively brief average stay on welfare would be evidence of little dependency. If, however, the same families were found to be poor year after year, this would be a matter of concern.

To explore the possibility of welfare dependency in the United States, a University of Michigan study tracked 5,000 families over a number of years, paying particular attention to economic mobility both from year to year and from one generation to the next.[12] The study first examined poverty from year to year, or dependency within a generation. It found that most recipients received welfare for less than a year, but about 30 percent of all welfare recipients remained on welfare for at least eight years. Thus there was a core of long-term recipients.

11 See Michael Tanner and Stephen Moore, "Why Welfare Pays," *Wall Street Journal* (28 September 1995).

12 Greg J. Duncan, Richard D. Coe, et al., *Years of Poverty, Years of Plenty* (Ann Arbor: University of Michigan Press, 1984).

A second and more serious concern is whether the children of the poor end up in poverty as well. Is there a cycle of poverty? Why might we expect such a transmission mechanism? Children in welfare households may learn the ropes about the welfare system and may come to view welfare as a normal way of life rather than as a temporary bridge over a rough patch. Research indicates that daughters from welfare families are more likely than daughters in families not on welfare to participate in the welfare system themselves and are more likely to have premarital births.[13] The evidence is weaker when it comes to sons from welfare families. What's difficult to say is whether welfare "caused" the link between mother and daughter, since the same factors that contributed to a mother's welfare status could also have contributed to her daughter's welfare status.

WELFARE REFORM

There has been much dissatisfaction with the welfare system, both among those who pay for the programs and among direct beneficiaries. A variety of welfare reforms has been introduced in recent years aimed mostly at reducing long-term dependence on poverty.

Recent Reforms

Some analysts believe that one way to reduce poverty is to provide welfare recipients with job skills and make them find jobs. Even before the 1996 federal reform of welfare, to be discussed shortly, some sort of "workfare" component for welfare recipients operated in over 35 states. In such states, as a condition of receiving welfare, the head of the household had to participate in education and training programs, search for work, or take some paid or unpaid position. The idea was to acquaint those on welfare with the job market. Evidence from various states indicates that programs involving mandatory job searches, short-term unpaid work, and training could operate at low cost and increase employment. The government saved money because those in welfare-to-work programs left welfare rolls sooner.

Reforms at the state level set the stage for federal reform. By far the biggest reform in the welfare system in the last 60 years came with the 1996 Personal Responsibility and Work Reconciliation Act, which replaced the Aid to Families with Dependent Children (AFDC) entitlement program with Temporary Assistance for Needy Families (TANF). Whereas the AFDC program set eligibility rules and left federal costs open-ended through a matching grant to the state, TANF offers a block grant called the Family Assistance Grant to the states to run their welfare programs. States ended AFDC and began TANF by July 1, 1997. The total Family Assistance Grant is fixed at $16.4 billion per year from 1997 to 2002, though supplementary grants will go to the states with the highest population growth.

Under the new system, states are granted wide latitude to run their own welfare programs. But concerns about welfare dependency fostered some special provisions. The act imposes a lifetime limit of five years that a recipient can

13 See Robert Moffit, "Incentive Effects of the U.S. Welfare System: A Review," *Journal of Economic Literature* 30 (March 1992): 37.

be on welfare. All able-bodied recipients on welfare for two years must participate in welfare-to-work programs. When fully implemented, states must have half their welfare recipients working at least 30 hours per week.

Provisions of the act limit benefits for noncitizens and for teenage mothers not living at home. States must also be more aggressive in enforcing child support from fathers of children on welfare. Finally the act tightens eligibility requirements for disabled children receiving Supplemental Security Income, extending aid only to those who suffer from "marked or severe" disabilities. Food Stamps, Supplemental Security Income, and Medicaid continue as federal entitlement programs.

Given the structure of the new program, states now have an incentive to constrain the growth of welfare rolls. Under the old system the federal government helped fund each dollar of spending, with the state paying from 22 to 50 cents per dollar, depending on its per capita income. For example, Mississippi spent 22 cents per dollar of welfare and Connecticut spent 50 cents per dollar. Under the new system, each state must pay 100 percent of any welfare costs above its Family Assistance Grant.

Aside from the time limits and work participation rates imposed by the federal government, states are free to set benefit levels and experiment however they choose. About half the states imposed time limits shorter than five years; 10 states have a two-year limit. In 33 states, all cash benefits are lost if recipients fail to comply with work requirements. Some observers fear that states now have a strong incentive to keep welfare costs down by cutting benefits. To avoid becoming destinations for poor people—that is, to avoid becoming "welfare magnets"—states may be tempted to offer relatively low levels of benefits.

The fear is that states will undercut benefit levels in what has been called a "race to the bottom." Another concern with ending federal entitlements and capping grants to states is what will happen should the economy enter a recession. One economist estimates that a 1-percent increase in unemployment will increase the welfare rolls by 2.5 percent and increase public spending on welfare by 3 percent.[14] Since state tax revenue drops during a recession, budgeters may be forced to cut welfare benefits, causing hardship for poor families.

The following case study surveys some results of welfare reform so far.

Is Welfare-to-Work Working?

Here are some preliminary conclusions based on the course of welfare reform as of 1998. Work requirements *do* seem to yield substantial declines in caseloads. In 1994 the number of welfare recipients peaked at 14 million, mostly single women with children. By 1998 the rolls had dropped by nearly one-third. Exhibit 5 shows the percentage of the U.S. population on welfare since 1960, where welfare includes Aid to Families with Dependent Children and, more recently, Temporary Assistance to Needy

14 See the analysis by Elizabeth Powers, "Welfare Reform and the Cyclicality of Welfare Programs," *Economic Commentary* (June 1996).

CaseStudy

Public Policy

The Urban Institute is a policy research organization working to increase citizens' awareness of important public choices. According to its report "Does Work Pay?," at http://newfederalism.urban.org/html/anf28.html, going to work improves the standard of living for low-income single mothers on welfare, so long as other benefit programs continue to provide assistance. What are some of these other assistance programs and policies? What happens to income when wages increase but benefits decrease? For more reports about welfare to work, visit the following Web sites: Idea Central's recommended links on Welfare and Families at http://epn.org/idea/welf-bkm.html#2.

Families. Notice the sharp decline in recent years. The percentage of the population on welfare in 1998 was lower than at any time since 1968. Fortunately the reforms occurred during an expanding economy, with jobs plentiful, and the unemployment rate the lowest it had been in three decades. But welfare rolls declined both in good economies, such as in Wisconsin, and in lagging economies, such as in New York City, where the unemployment rate was more than twice the national average.

Many of those on welfare had other ways to support themselves. One expert who counted everything from food stamps to income from unreported jobs said cash transfers accounted for about 34 percent of the average welfare recipient's income, food stamps provided about 25 percent, and 36 percent came from unreported sources such as secret jobs, boyfriends, contributions from relatives, or private charities. (Medicaid was not counted as income although it costs taxpayers more than any other welfare program).

Despite the "welfare-to-work" slogan, only about half those leaving welfare found jobs. In Massachusetts, 50 percent of former recipients said they had jobs. Job rates were 52 percent in Idaho, 56 percent in New Mexico, 50 percent in Tennessee, and 66 percent in Maryland. This is not much of an improvement compared to employment rates prior to the reforms. Remember that even before the recent reforms, most beneficiaries remained on welfare only temporarily.

Since most people on welfare are poorly educated and have few job skills, wage levels for those who find jobs remain low. For example, annual earnings for individuals who found jobs in Maryland averaged $8,300 (the poverty level for a family of three in 1997 was $12,800). Part-time work is also common, as is job loss among those who initially found jobs. Tennessee surveyed 205 welfare recipients who had found jobs. Three months later, one-quarter had lost their jobs and only about half were working full time. On the plus side, the earned income tax credit adds up to $3,650 a year in additional income to low-income workers. Most of those working can also receive food stamps, child care, and Medicaid.

Because the welfare rolls declined but the federal grant to the states remained constant, there has been a significant increase in welfare spending per recipient. Most states are combining tough new rules with an expanded menu of welfare services. States have made large investments in work-related services such as job placement, transportation, and especially child care. Because of the increase in state outlays for child care, expected day-care shortages never materialized.

Finally, one effect of the work requirements of welfare reform has been to raise the "price" of welfare to the recipients. Raising the price of going on welfare reduced the amount of welfare demanded. As one welfare director noted, a lot of people who are leaving welfare are saying, "It's not worth the hassle." We might say that the demand curve for welfare is downward sloping, with "hassle" measured on the vertical axis. The greater the "hassle," the less welfare is demanded. What's more, welfare rolls declined more in states where efforts to get people to work are the greatest. For example, Wisconsin and Minnesota had similar economies as reflected by identical unemployment rates, but Wisconsin's much more aggressive work requirements cut welfare rolls there three times faster than in Minnesota.

Sources: Jason DeParle, "U.S. Welfare System Dies as State Programs Emerge," *New York Times* (30 June 1997); Michael Grunwald, "Welfare-to-Work: The Challenge Grows Harder," *Boston Globe* (20 April 1998); Joe Sexton, "In a Part of Brooklyn, the New Welfare Rules Change Everything," *New York Times* (10 March 1997); and Joe Sexton, "Only Severely Troubled Children Need Apply," *New York Times* (22 December 1997).

EXHIBIT 5

Welfare Recipients Since 1960 as Percentage of U.S. Population by Year

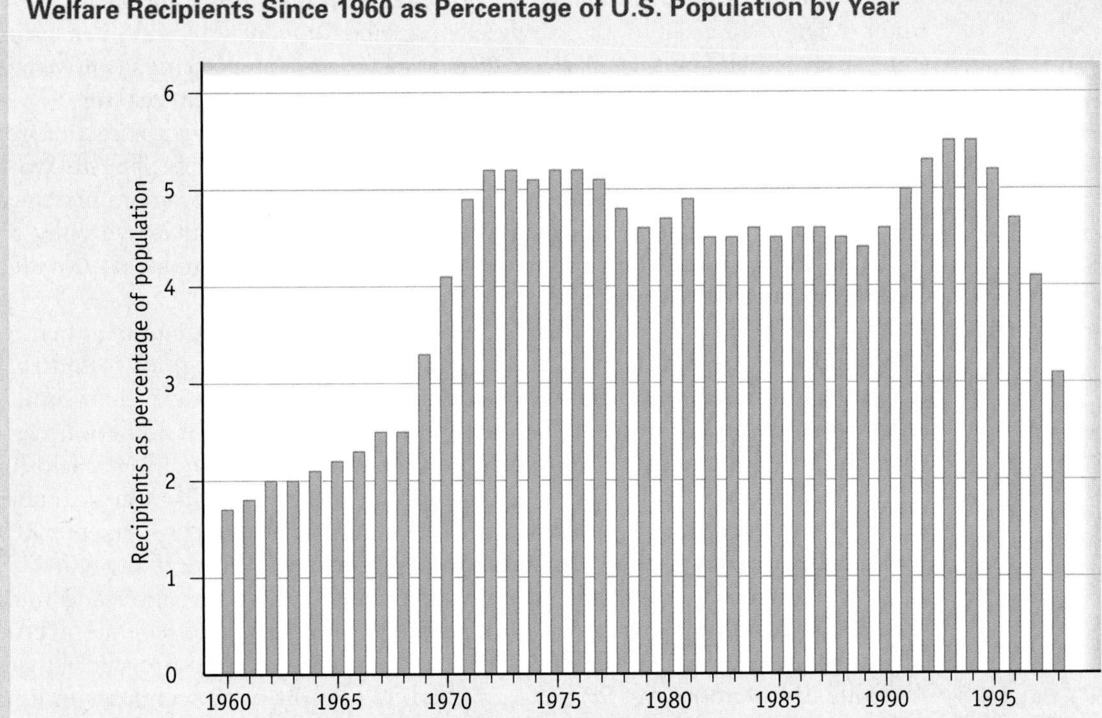

Source: U.S. Department of Health and Human Services, August 1998, at http://www.acf.dfhhs.gov/news/6097rf.htm. Figure for 1998 is as of June 1998.

Perhaps the most successful welfare reform in the country is taking place in Oregon, which is discussed in this final case study.

CaseStudy

Public Policy

Visit Oregon's Healthcare, Human Services and Labor Policy Web site at http://www.governor.state.or.us/governor/hhslp/index.html for progress reports on welfare reform policy. Notice that the policy is referred to as "social support." The site includes a link to a quarterly newsletter. Read the report, "The Oregon Strategy for Social Support," for details about how the policy is being implemented. What is the difference between support and services? In what ways is the state considering changing how services are delivered?

Oregon's Program of "Tough Love"

Oregon's welfare caseload fell from 43,600 in March 1994 to 18,000 by February 1999. The drop came not as a result of strict time limits or tougher eligibility standards, but by providing strong work incentives and working more closely with clients. TANF in Oregon provided $460 a month in 1998 for a family of three, a benefit level in the upper third for all states. The typical family on welfare and food stamps was living at about 75 percent of the poverty level in 1998.

After leaving TANF for work, people in Oregon continue to qualify for health benefits for at least a year, for day care until income reaches 200 percent of the federal poverty level, for food stamps for those who are income-eligible, and for the federal earned income tax credit, which in effect raises the wage by about $1 an hour. By working at even the state's minimum wage of $6 an hour, the family's living standard increases to 130 percent of the poverty level. The average starting wage in the first job placement off welfare in fact exceeded $7 an hour. Thus work is attractive compared to welfare.

One federal study tracked 5,500 welfare applicants and recipients in Oregon over a two-year period. Half the group participated in the welfare-to-work program and half did not. Taking part in the welfare-to-work program increased employment by 18 percent, raised average earnings over the two years by 35 percent, and boosted the proportion of individuals with employer-provided health insurance by 71 percent.

Oregon became the first state to require drug addicts to attend treatment as a condition of receiving welfare. An evaluation of that program found that clients who completed drug treatment earned 65 percent more than similar clients in a comparison group. Those completing treatment for addiction were 45 percent less likely to be arrested and only half as likely to be investigated for child abuse or neglect. The study also found that for every dollar Oregon spent on drug treatment it saved at least $5.60 on other social services. The approach in most other states is simply to ban recent drug felons from receiving aid.

The Oregon program offers abundant services, but welfare applicants must first spend a month looking for work before getting help. The federal government requires states to enroll 50 percent of their recipients in job-related activity by 2002. By October of 1997, Oregon had 89 percent of its recipients in job-related activity, including unpaid workfare jobs to develop experience and wage-subsidized jobs for those who could not otherwise find work. Perhaps the most persuasive evidence that Oregon's approach of tough love is working is that after 18 months, only 8 percent of those who left welfare returned to the rolls.

Sources: Jason DeParle, "Newest Challenge for Welfare: Helping the Hard-Core Jobless," *New York Times* (20 November 1997); "Oregon Welfare Reform Fact Sheet," Oregon Department of Human Resources (June 1998); Gary Weeks, "Oregon a Success Story in Welfare Reform," *Business Journal of Portland* (1 July 1996); and "Oregon's Welfare-to-Work Efforts Bring National Recognition," Oregon Department of Human Services (23 June 1998).

CONCLUSION

Government redistribution programs have been most successful at reducing poverty among the elderly. But poverty rates among children have increased since 1970 because of the growth in the number of female householders. We might ask why transfer programs have reduced poverty rates among the elderly but not among female householders. Transfer programs do not encourage people to get old; that process occurs naturally and is independent of the level of transfers. But the level and availability of transfer programs at the margin influences some young unmarried women as they are deciding whether to have a child and may, at the margin, influence a married mother's decision to get divorced.

Most transfers in the economy are not from the government but rather are in-kind transfers within the family, from parents to children. Thus any change in a family's capacity to earn income has serious consequences for dependent children. Family structure appears to be a primary determinant of family income. One-fifth of the children in the United States live in poverty. Children are the innocent victims of the changing family structure.

SUMMARY

1. Money income (before taxes but after cash transfers) in the United States became somewhat less evenly distributed between 1967 and 1997. Since 1959, poverty rates have dropped most among the elderly.
2. Young, single motherhood is a recipe for instant poverty. Often the young mother drops out of school, which reduces her future earning possibilities when and if she seeks work outside the home. Growth in the number of female householders has increased poverty among children.
3. The wage gap between blacks and whites narrowed between 1940 and 1975, widened until the early 1990s, and has been narrowing again since 1993. Affirmative-action programs seem to have increased employment opportunities among blacks.
4. Among the undesirable effects of income assistance is a high marginal tax rate on earned income, which discourages employment and encourages welfare dependency. According to one survey, about 30 percent of families on welfare remain there for eight years or more.
5. Welfare reforms introduced by the states set the stage for federal welfare reforms aimed at promoting the transition from welfare to work. The states have been experimenting with different systems aimed at promoting greater personal responsibility. The welfare rolls dropped by about one-third between 1994 and 1998.

QUESTIONS FOR REVIEW

1. *(Distribution of Household Income)* Look back at Exhibit 1 in this chapter. How would you explain the shift in the U.S. income distribution in the last two decades?
2. *(Official Poverty Level)* Although the poverty rate among single mothers has remained constant at 32 percent for the last three decades, the number of poor children from such families has more than doubled. Explain.
3. *(Official Poverty Level)* How does the U.S. Department of Agriculture calculate the official poverty level? What government assistance programs does the Census Bureau consider when calculating a household's income? What programs are ignored?
4. *(Income Differences)* List some reasons why household incomes differ. Which factors are the most important?
5. *(Programs to Help the Poor)* Distinguish between social insurance programs and income assistance programs. Identify the key examples of each.
6. *(Poverty and Age)* Poverty among the elderly fell dramatically between 1959 and 1974 and has continued to decline since then. However, poverty among that portion of the U.S. population that is less than 18 years old is higher today that in the mid-1970s. Why have the experiences of these two age groups differed?
7. *(Poverty and Public Choice)* Why is it difficult to pass legislation to reduce Social Security or Medicare benefits?
8. *(Poverty and Discrimination)* Which types of discrimination can drive a wedge between what whites earn and what nonwhites earn? Consider discrimination in schooling, for example. How could you detect such discrimination?
9. *(Work Disincentives)* How does the implicit tax on earned income (in the form of lost benefits from government assistance programs) affect work incentives? How do some people avoid the implicit tax?
10. *(Welfare Reform)* What has happened to the welfare caseload in recent years? Discuss some differences in results across states.
11. *(Case**Study**: Is Welfare-to-Work Working?)* Discuss the key features of welfare reforms introduced by the federal government in 1996. Why were policy makers worried that turning welfare over to the states would result in a "race to the bottom"?

EXPERIENTIAL EXERCISES

12. *(Poverty and the Poor)* Visit the Census Bureau's page on poverty statistics at www.census.gov/hhes/www/poverty.html. Look at the Small Area Income and Poverty Estimates and find the latest poverty estimate for your county. How does the poverty rate there compare to the overall rate in your state and in the United States as a whole?

13. *(CaseStudy: Oregon's Program of "Tough Love")* The National Governors' Association maintains a page on state-level welfare reform efforts at http://www.nga.org/Welfare/WelfareDocs/WelfareStateWebLinks.htm. Look up Oregon and see how the state's program is evolving. Has it been a success?

14. *(Wall Street Journal)* The front page of the Marketplace section of the *Wall Street Journal* often carries articles on income distribution and the personal impact of poverty. Pay particular attention to the Work & Family and Business and Race columns in the Wednesday paper. How are the actions of U.S. businesses affecting income distribution and poverty?

CHAPTER

32 International Trade

This morning you pulled up your Levi jeans from Mexico, pulled over your Benetton sweater from Italy, and laced up your Nikes from Indonesia. After a breakfast that included bananas from Honduras and coffee from Brazil, you climbed into your Volvo from Sweden fueled by Saudi Arabian oil and headed for a lecture by a visiting professor from Hungary. If the United States is such a rich and productive nation, why do we import so many goods and services? Why don't we produce everything ourselves? And why do some groups try to restrict foreign trade? Answers to these and other questions are addressed in this chapter.

The world is a giant shopping mall, and Americans are big spenders. Americans buy Japanese cars, French wine, Swiss clocks, European vacations, and

/isit the McEachern
eractive Study Center
for this chapter at
//mcisc.swcollege.com

thousands of other goods and services from around the globe. But foreigners spend a lot on American products too—grain, personal computers, aircraft, movies, trips to Disney World, and thousands of other goods and services. In this chapter, we examine the gains from international trade and the effects of trade restrictions on the allocation of resources. The analysis is based on the familiar tools of supply and demand. Topics discussed in this chapter include:

- Gains from trade
- Absolute and comparative advantage revisited
- Tariffs
- Import quotas
- Welfare loss from trade restrictions
- Arguments for trade restrictions

THE GAINS FROM TRADE

A family from Virginia that sits down for a meal of Kansas prime rib, Idaho potatoes, and California string beans, with Georgia peach cobbler for desert is benefiting from interstate trade. You already understand why the residents of one state trade with those of another. Back in Chapter 2, you learned about the gains arising from specialization and exchange. You may recall the discussion of how you and your roommate could maximize output by specializing in typing or ironing. The law of comparative advantage says that the individual with the lowest opportunity cost of producing a particular output should specialize in producing that output. Just as individuals benefit from specialization and exchange, so do states and, indeed, nations. To reap the gains that arise from specialized production, countries engage in international trade. *With trade, each country can concentrate on producing those goods and services that involve the least opportunity cost.*

A Profile of Imports and Exports

Some nations are more involved in international trade than others, just as some states are more involved in interstate trade than others. For example, exports account for about half of the gross domestic product (GDP) in Holland; about one-third of the GDP in Germany, Sweden, and Switzerland; and about one-quarter of the GDP in Canada and the United Kingdom. Despite the perception that Japan has a giant export sector, only about 13 percent of Japanese production is exported.

In the United States, exports of goods and services amounted to about 11 percent of GDP in 1998. Although small relative to GDP, exports play a growing role in the U.S. economy. The four main U.S. exports are (1) high-technology manufactured products, such as computer software and hardware, aircraft, telecommunication equipment, and military equipment; (2) industrial supplies and materials; (3) agricultural products, especially corn and soybeans; and (4) entertainment products, such as movies and recorded music.

The United States depends on imports for some key inputs. For example, our position as the world's largest producer of aluminum depends on our importing vast amounts of bauxite. Most of our platinum and chromium and all of our manganese, mica, diamonds, and nickel are imported. Two-thirds of U.S. imports are (1) manufactured consumer goods, such as automobiles from Japan and Germany and electronic equipment from Taiwan, and (2) capital goods, such as high-tech printing presses from Germany. *U.S. imports of goods and services amounted to about 13 percent relative to GDP in 1998.*

The big change in U.S. exports over the last 25 years has been a growth in the dollar value of machinery exports; nearly half of the capital goods produced in the United States are exported. The primary change in U.S. imports over the last 25 years has been the increase in spending on foreign oil. Canada is our largest trading partner, followed by Japan and Mexico. Other important trading partners include Germany, Great Britain, South Korea, France, Hong Kong, Italy, and Brazil.

Production Possibilities Without Trade

The rationale behind some international trade is obvious. The United States grows no coffee beans because our climate is not suited to coffee. It is more revealing, however, to examine the gains from trade where the cost advantage is not so obvious. Suppose that just two goods—food and clothing—are produced and consumed and that there are only two countries in the world—the United States, with a labor force of 100 million workers, and the mythical country of Izodia, with 200 million workers. The conclusions we derive from this simple model will have general relevance to the pattern of international trade.

Exhibit 1 presents each country's production possibilities table, based on the size of the labor force and the productivity of workers in each country. We assume a given technology and that labor is fully and efficiently employed. Since no trade occurs between countries, Exhibit 1 presents each country's *consumption possibilities* table as well, reflecting each country's consumption alternatives.

The production numbers imply that each worker in the United States can produce either 6 units of food or 3 units of clothing per day. If all 100 million U.S. workers produce food, 600 million units can be produced per day, as reflected by combination U_1 in part (a) of Exhibit 1. If all U.S. workers produce clothing, U.S. output would be 300 million units per day, as reflected by combination U_6.

EXHIBIT 1

Production Possibilities Schedules for the United States and Izodia

(a) United States

	Units Produced (per worker per day)	Production Possibilities with 100 Million Workers (millions of units per day)					
		U_1	U_2	U_3	U_4	U_5	U_6
Food	6	600	480	360	240	120	0
Clothing	3	0	60	120	180	240	300

(b) Izodia

	Units Produced (per worker per day)	Production Possibilities with 200 Million Workers (millions of units per day)					
		I_1	I_2	I_3	I_4	I_5	I_6
Food	1	200	160	120	80	40	0
Clothing	2	0	80	160	240	320	400

Combinations in between represent alternatives if some workers produce food and some produce clothing. Because a U.S. worker can produce either 6 units of food or 3 units of clothing, *his opportunity cost of 1 more unit of food is ½ unit of clothing.*

Suppose Izodian workers are less educated, work with less capital, and farm less fertile land than U.S. workers. So each Izodian can produce only 1 unit of food or 2 units of clothing per day. If all 200 million Izodian workers specialize in food, they can produce 200 million units of food per day, as reflected by combination I_1 in part (b) of Exhibit 1. If all Izodian workers produce clothing, total output is 400 million units of clothing per day, as reflected by combination I_6. Some intermediate production possibilities are also listed in the exhibit. Because an Izodian worker can produce either 1 unit of food or 2 units of clothing, *her opportunity cost of 1 more unit of food is 2 units of clothing.*

We can convert the data in Exhibit 1 to a production possibilities frontier for each country, as is shown in Exhibit 2. In each diagram, the amount of food produced is measured on the vertical axis and the amount of clothing is measured on the horizontal axis. U.S. combinations are shown in panel (a) by U_1, U_2, and so on; Izodian combinations are designated in panel (b) by I_1, I_2, and so on. Because we assume that resources are perfectly adaptable to the production of each commodity, each production possibilities curve is a straight line reflecting constant opportunity cost.

Autarky A situation of national self-sufficiency in which there is no economic interaction with foreigners

Exhibit 2 illustrates—in red—the possible combinations of food and clothing that residents of each country can produce and consume if all resources are fully and efficiently employed and there is no trade between the two countries. **Autarky** is the situation of national self-sufficiency, in which there is no economic interaction with foreigners. Suppose that U.S. producers maximize profit

EXHIBIT 2

Production Possibilities Frontiers for the United States and Izodia Without Trade (in millions of units per day)

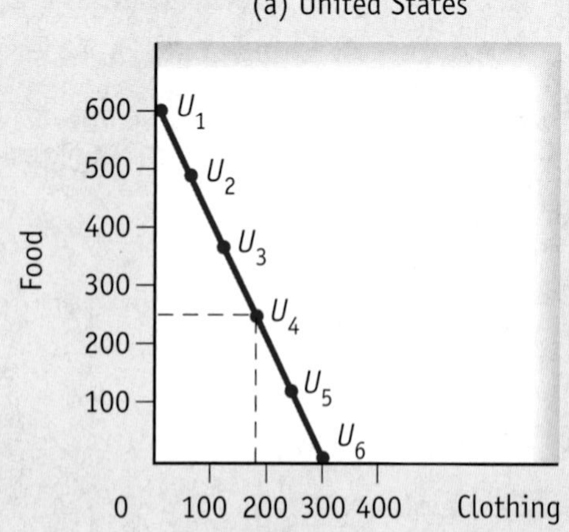

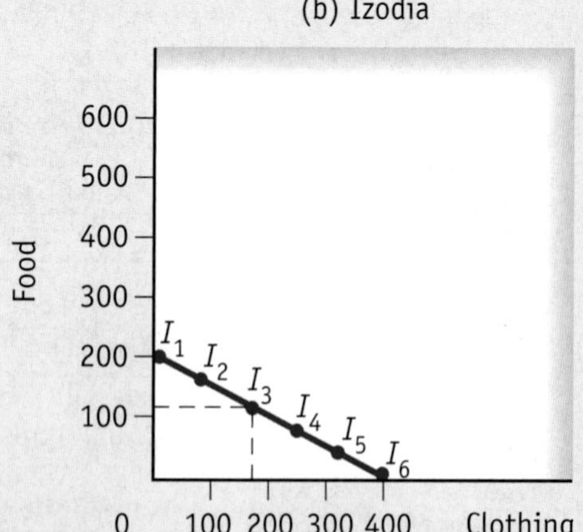

Panel (a) shows the U.S. production possibilities curve; its slope indicates that the opportunity cost of an additional unit of food is 1/2 unit of clothing. Panel (b) shows production possibilities in Izodia; an additional unit of food costs 2 units of clothing. Food is relatively cheaper to produce in the United States.

and U.S. consumers maximize utility with the combination of 240 million units of food and 180 million units of clothing—combination U_4. This combination will be called the *autarky equilibrium*. Suppose also that Izodians have an autarky equilibrium, identified as combination I_3, of 120 million units of food and 160 million units of clothing.

Consumption Possibilities Based on Comparative Advantage

In our example, each U.S. worker can produce both more clothing and more food per day than can each Izodian worker. U.S. workers therefore have an *absolute advantage* in the production of both goods because a U.S. worker can produce each good in less time than can an Izodian worker. With an absolute advantage in the production of both commodities, should the U.S. economy remain in autarky—that is, self-sufficient in both food and clothing productions—or could there be gains from trade?

As long as the opportunity cost of the two goods differs between the two countries, there are gains from specialization and trade. The opportunity cost of producing 1 more unit of food in the United States is ½ unit of clothing, compared to 2 units of clothing in Izodia. *According to the law of comparative advantage, each country should specialize in producing the good with the lower opportunity cost.* Since the opportunity cost of producing food is lower in the United States than in Izodia, both countries will gain if the United States specializes in producing food and exports some to Izodia, and Izodia specializes in producing clothing and exports some to the United States.

Before countries can trade, they must somehow determine how much of one good will be exchanged for another—that is, they must establish the **terms of trade.** Suppose that market forces shape terms of trade whereby 1 unit of clothing exchanges for 1 unit of food. Based on those terms of trade, Americans trade 1 unit of food to Izodians for 1 unit of clothing. To produce 1 unit of clothing Americans would have to sacrifice 2 units of food. Likewise, Izodians sacrifice 1 unit of clothing by trading clothing to Americans for 1 unit of food, which is only half what Izodians would sacrifice to produce 1 unit of food themselves.

Terms of trade How much of one good exchanges for a unit of another good

Exhibit 3 shows that with 1 unit of food trading for 1 unit of clothing, Americans and Izodians can consume anywhere along or below their blue consumption possibilities frontiers. *The consumption possibilities frontier* shows a nation's alternative combinations of goods available as a result of production and foreign trade. (Note that the U.S. consumption possibilities curve does not extend to the right of 400 million units of clothing, since that is the most the Izodians can produce.) The amount each country actually consumes will depend on its relative preferences for food and clothing. Suppose Americans select point *U* in panel (a) and Izodians select point *I* in panel (b).

Without trade, the United States produced and consumed 240 million units of food and 180 million units of clothing. With trade, the United States specializes in food by producing 600 million units; Americans eat 400 million units and exchange the remaining 200 million for 200 million units of Izodian clothing. This consumption combination is reflected by point *U* in panel (a). Through exchange, Americans increase their consumption of both food and clothing.

EXHIBIT 3

Production (and Consumption) Possibilities Frontiers with Trade (in millions of units per day)

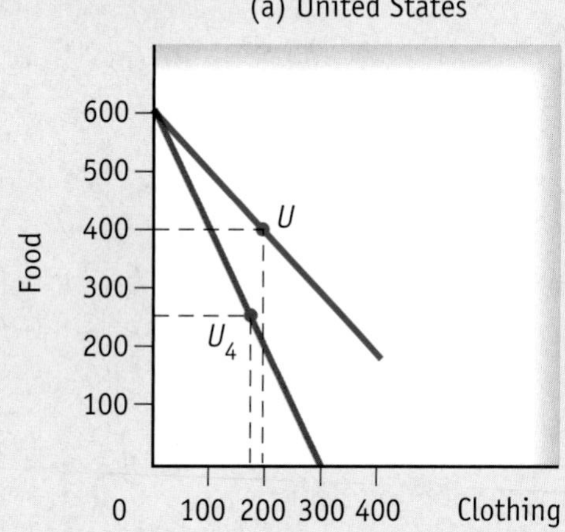

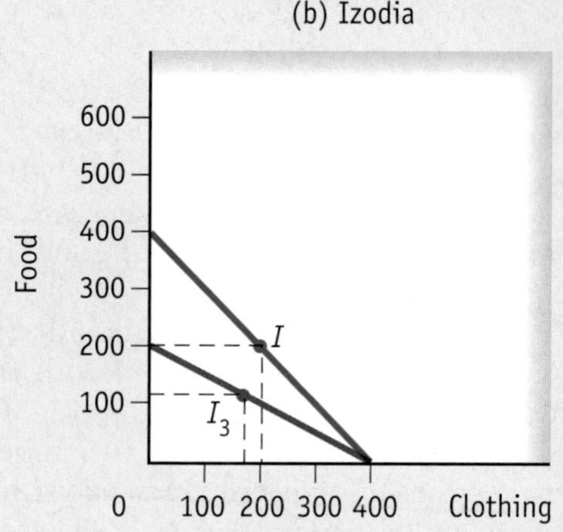

If Izodia and the United States can trade at the rate of 1 unit of clothing for 1 unit of food, both can benefit. Consumption possibilities at those terms of trade are shown by the blue lines. The United States was previously producing and consuming combination U_4. By trading with Izodia, it can produce only food and still consume combination U—a combination that contains more food and more clothing than combination U_4 does. Likewise, Izodia can attain the preferred combination I by trading its clothing for U.S. food. Both countries are better off as a result of international trade.

Without trade, Izodians produced and consumed 120 million units of food and 160 million units of clothing. With trade, Izodians specialize in clothing to produce 400 million units; Izodians wear 200 million units of clothing and exchange the remaining 200 million units for 200 million units of food. This consumption combination is shown by point *I* in panel (b). Izodians, like Americans, are able to increase their consumption of both food and clothing through trade. How is this possible?

Since Izodians are relatively more efficient in the production of clothing and Americans relatively more efficient in the production of food, total output increases when each country specializes. Specifically, without specialization, total world production was 360 million units of food and 340 million units of clothing. With specialization, food production increases to 600 million units and clothing production increases to 400 million units. The only constraint on trade is that, for each good, *total world production must equal total world consumption.* In our two-country world, this means that the amount of food the United States exports must equal the amount of food Izodia imports. The same goes for Izodia's exports of clothing.

Thus, both countries have more goods and services after trade. *Although the United States has an absolute advantage in both goods, differences in the opportunity cost of production between the two nations ensure that specialization and exchange will result in mutual gains.* Remember that comparative advantage, not absolute advantage, is the source of gains from trade.

We simplified trade relations in our example to highlight the gains from specialization and exchange. We assumed that each country would completely specialize in producing a particular good, that resources were equally adaptable to the production of either good, that the costs of transporting the goods from one country to another were inconsequential, and that there were no problems in arriving at the terms of trade. The world is not that simple (for example, we don't expect a country to produce just one good), but the law of comparative advantage still points to gains from trade.

Reasons for International Specialization

Countries trade with one another—or, more precisely, people and firms in one country trade with those in another—because each side expects to gain from the exchange. How do we know what each country should produce and what goods should be traded?

Differences in Resource Endowments. Trade is often prompted by differences in resource endowments. Two key resources are labor and capital. Countries differ not only in their amounts of labor and capital but in the qualities of those resources. A well-educated and well-trained labor force is more productive than an uneducated and unskilled one. Similarly, capital that reflects the most recent technological developments is more productive than nonexistent or obsolete capital. Some countries, such as the United States and Japan, have an educated labor force and an abundant stock of modern capital. Both resources result in greater productivity per worker, making each nation quite competitive in producing goods that require skilled labor and sophisticated capital.

Some countries are blessed with an abundance of fertile land and favorable growing seasons. The United States, for example, has been called the "breadbasket of the world" because of its rich farmland. Honduras has the ideal climate for growing bananas. Coffee is grown best in the climate and elevation of Colombia, Brazil, and Jamaica. Thus, the United States exports corn and imports coffee and bananas. Differences in the seasons across countries also serve as a basis for trade. For example, during the winter months, Americans import fruit from Chile and Canadian tourists travel to Florida for sun and fun. During the summer months, Americans export fruit to Chile and American tourists travel to Canada for fishing and camping.

Mineral resources are often concentrated in particular countries: oil in Saudi Arabia, bauxite in Jamaica, diamonds in South Africa. The United States has abundant coal supplies, but not enough oil to satisfy domestic demand. Thus the United States exports coal and imports oil. More generally, *countries export those products that they can produce more cheaply in return for those that are unavailable domestically or are more costly to produce than to buy from other countries.*

Economies of Scale. If production is subject to *economies of scale*—that is, if the average cost falls as the rate of production increases—countries can gain from trade if each nation specializes. Such specialization allows each nation to produce at a greater output rate, which reduces average production costs. The primary reason for establishing the single integrated market in Western Europe is to offer European producers a large, open market of over 320 million consumers so that producers can increase production, experience economies of scale, and in the process become more competitive in international markets.

Differences in Tastes. Even if all countries had identical resource endowments and combined those resources with equal efficiency, each country would still gain from trade as long as tastes and preferences differed among countries. Consumption patterns differ. For example, the per-capita consumption of beer in Germany is more than double that in Portugal or Sweden. The French drink three times as much wine as Danes do. The Danes consume twice as much pork as Americans do. Americans consume twice as much chicken as Hungarians do. Soft drinks are four times more popular in the United States than in Western Europe. The English like tea; Americans coffee. Algeria has an ideal climate for growing grapes, but its large Muslim population abstains from alcohol. Thus Algeria exports wine.

NetBookmark

What goods and services does the United States trade? With whom? Who are our largest trading partners? Answers to these and many other trade-related questions can be found by cruising through the U.S. Census Bureau's Trade Data Web site at http://www.census.gov/foreign-trade/www/tradedata.html.

TRADE RESTRICTIONS

Despite the benefits of international trade, nearly all countries at one time or another erect barriers to impede or block free trade among nations. Trade restrictions usually benefit domestic producers but harm domestic consumers. In this section, we will consider the effects of restrictions and the reasons they are imposed.

Consumer and Producer Surplus

Before we consider the net effect of world trade on social welfare, let's develop a framework for describing the benefits that consumers and producers derive from exchange. To do this, let's consider a hypothetical market for chicken shown in Exhibit 4. The height of the demand curve reflects the amount that consumers are willing and able to pay for each additional pound of chicken. In effect, the height of the demand curve shows the *marginal benefit* consumers expect from each pound of chicken. For example, the demand curve indicates that some consumers are willing to pay $1.50 or more per pound for the first few pounds of chicken. But all consumers get to buy chicken at the market-clearing price, which in Exhibit 4 is only $0.50 per pound. The blue shaded triangle below the demand curve and above the market price reflects the *consumer surplus,* which is the difference between the maximum sum of money consumers would pay for 60 pounds of chicken per day and the actual sum they do pay. Consumers thus get a bonus, or a surplus, from market exchange. We all enjoy a consumer surplus from most products we consume.

There is a similar surplus on the producer side. The height of the supply curve reflects the minimum amount of money that producers are willing and able to accept for each additional pound of chicken. That is, the height of the supply curve shows the *marginal cost* producers incur in supplying each additional pound of chicken. For example, the supply curve indicates that some producers incur a marginal cost of $0.25 or less per pound for supplying the first few pounds of chicken. But all producers get to sell chicken for the market-clearing price—in this case, $0.50 per pound. The gold shaded triangle above the supply curve and below the market price reflects the *producer surplus,* which is the difference between the actual sum of money producers receive for 60 pounds of chicken and the minimum sum they would accept for that quantity.

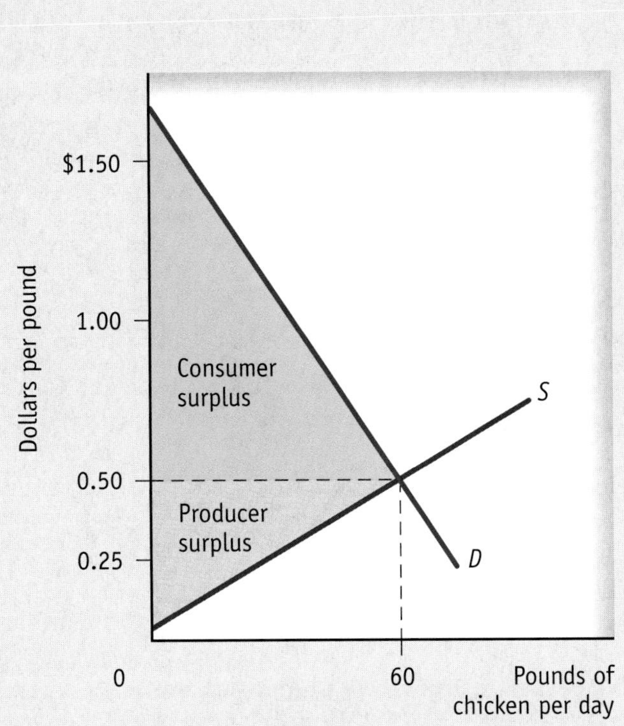

EXHIBIT 4

Consumer Surplus and Producer Surplus

Consumer surplus, shown by the blue shaded triangle, shows the net benefits consumers reap by being able to purchase 60 pounds of chicken at $0.50 per pound. Some consumers would have been willing to pay $1.50 or more per pound for the first few pounds. Consumer surplus measures the difference between the maximum sum of money consumers would pay for 60 pounds of chicken and the actual sum they pay. Producer surplus, shown by the gold shaded triangle, shows the net benefits producers reap by being able to sell 60 pounds of chicken at $0.50 per pound. Some producers would have been willing to supply chicken for $0.25 per pound or less. Producer surplus measures the difference between the actual sum of money producers receive for 60 pounds of chicken and the minimum amount they would accept for this amount of chicken.

The point is that market exchange usually yields a surplus, or a bonus, to both producers and consumers. In the balance of the chapter, we focus on how restrictions on international trade affect consumer surplus and producer surplus.

Tariffs

A *tariff,* a term first introduced in Chapter 4, is a tax on imports. (Tariffs can also be applied to exports, but we will focus on import tariffs.) A tariff can be either *specific,* such as a tariff of $5 per barrel of oil, or *ad valorem,* a percentage of the price of imports at the port of entry. Consider the effects of a specific tariff on a particular good. In Exhibit 5, *D* is the domestic demand for sugar and *S* is the supply provided by domestic producers. Suppose that the world price of sugar is $0.10 per pound, as it was in 1998. The **world price** is the price determined by the world supply and world demand for a product. It is the price at which any supplier can sell output on the world market and at which any demander can purchase output on the world market.

World price The price at which a good is traded internationally; determined by the world supply and demand for the good

EXHIBIT 5

Effect of a Tariff

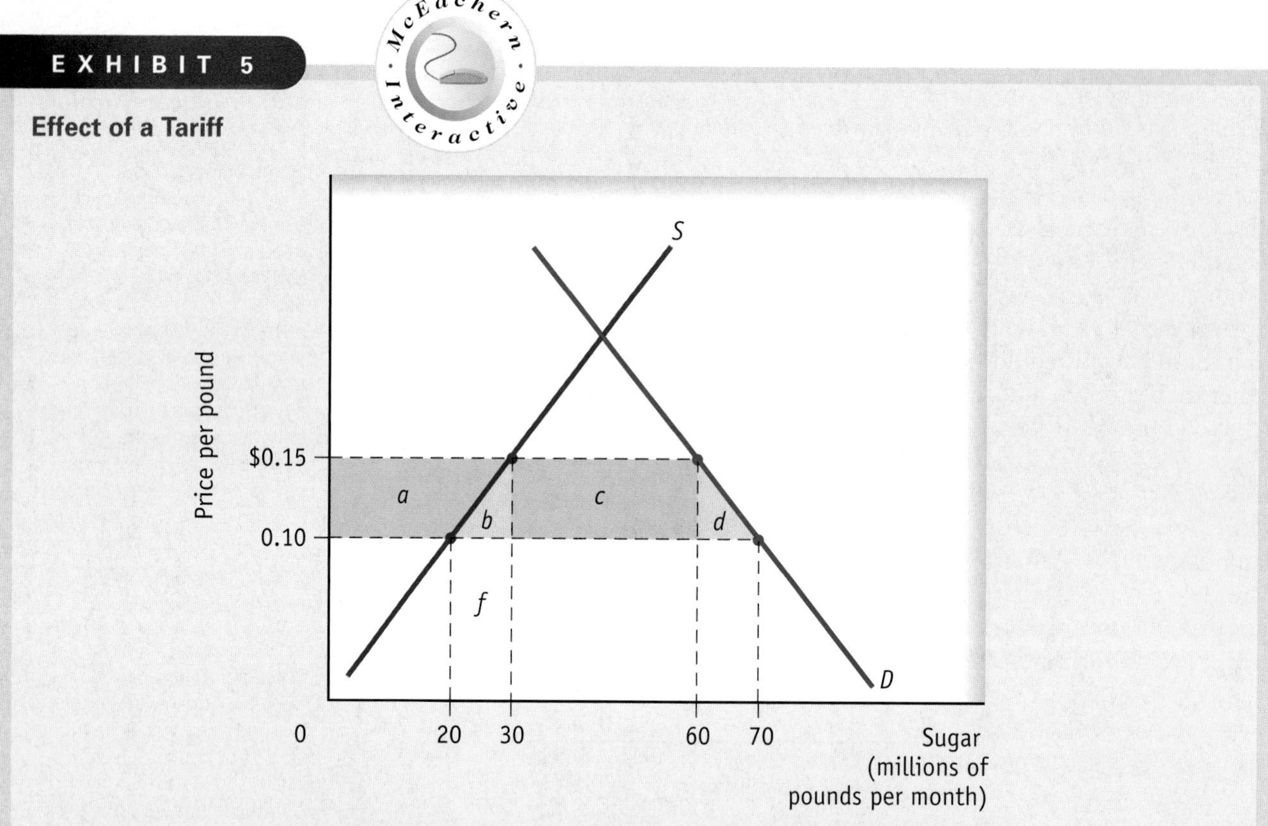

At a world price of $0.10 per pound, domestic consumers demand 70 million pounds per month and domestic producers supply 20 million pounds per month; the difference is imported. With the imposition of a $0.05 per pound tariff, the domestic price rises to $0.15 per pound, domestic producers increase production to 30 million pounds, and domestic consumers cut back to 60 million pounds. Imports fall to 30 million pounds. At the higher domestic price, consumers are worse off; their loss of consumer surplus is the sum of areas *a, b, c,* and *d.* Area *a* represents an increase in producer surplus: a transfer from consumers to producers. Areas *b* and *f* reflect the portion of additional revenues to producers that is just offset by the higher production costs of expanding domestic output by 10 million pounds. Area *c* shows government revenue from the tariff. The net welfare loss to society is the sum of area *d,* which reflects the loss of consumer surplus resulting from the drop in consumption, and area b, which reflects the higher marginal cost of domestically producing output that could have been produced more cheaply abroad.

With free trade, domestic consumers can buy any amount desired at the world price, so the quantity demanded is 70 million pounds per month, of which 20 million pounds are supplied by domestic producers and 50 million pounds are imported. Domestic producers cannot charge more than the world price, since domestic buyers can purchase as much sugar as they want at $0.10 per pound in the world market.

Now suppose that a specific tariff of $0.05 is imposed on each pound of sugar imported, raising the price of imported sugar from $0.10 to $0.15 per pound. Domestic producers can therefore raise their price to $0.15 per pound as well without losing sales to imports. At the higher price, the quantity supplied by domestic producers increases to 30 million pounds per month, but the quantity demanded by domestic consumers declines to 60 million pounds per month. Because the quantity demanded has declined and the quantity supplied by domestic producers has increased, imports decline from 50 million to 30 million pounds per month.

Since the price is higher after the tariff, consumers are worse off. The loss in consumer surplus is identified in Exhibit 5 by the blue and red shaded areas. Because both the domestic price and the quantity of sugar supplied by domestic producers have increased, the total revenue received by domestic producers increases by the areas *a* plus *b* plus *f*. But only the light-blue shaded area, *a*, represents an increase in producer surplus. The increase in revenue represented by the areas *b* plus *f* merely offsets the higher marginal cost of expanding domestic production from 20 million to 30 million pounds. The red shaded triangle, *b*, represents part of the net welfare loss to the domestic economy, because those 10 million pounds could have been purchased from abroad for $0.10 per pound rather than produced domestically at a higher marginal cost.

Government revenue from the tariff is identified by the light-blue shaded area, *c*, which equals the tariff of $0.05 per pound multiplied by the 30 million pounds that are imported, or $1.5 million per month. Tariff revenue represents a loss to consumers, but since the tariff is revenue to the government, this loss can potentially be offset by a reduction in taxes or an increase in public services. The red-shaded triangle, *d*, shows a loss in consumer surplus resulting from the fact that less sugar is consumed at the higher price. This loss in consumer surplus is not redistributed as a gain to anyone else, so area *d* reflects part of the net welfare loss of the tariff. Therefore, the two red-shaded triangles, *b* and *d*, show the domestic economy's net welfare loss of the tariff; the *two triangles measure a net loss in consumer surplus that is not offset by a net gain to anyone else.*

Of the total loss in consumer surplus (areas *a*, *b*, *c*, and *d*) resulting from the tariff, area *a* is redistributed from consumers to domestic producers, area *c* becomes tariff revenue for the government, and the two red-shaded triangles, *b* and *d*, reflect a net loss in social welfare because of the tariff.

Import Quotas

An *import quota* is a legal limit on the quantity of a particular commodity that can be imported. Quotas often target exports from certain countries. For example, a quota may limit automobile imports from Japan or shoe imports from Brazil. To have an impact on the market, or to be *effective*, a quota must restrict imports to less than the amount imported with free trade.

Let's consider the impact of a quota on the domestic market for sugar. In panel (a) of Exhibit 6, the domestic supply curve of sugar is *S* and the domestic demand curve is *D*. Suppose again that the world price of sugar is $0.10 per pound. With free trade, that price would prevail in the domestic market, and a total of 70 million pounds per month would be demanded. Domestic producers would supply 20 million pounds and importers would supply 50 million pounds. With a quota of 50 million pounds or more per month, the domestic price would remain the same as the world price of $0.10 per pound, and domestic sales would be 70 million pounds per month. In short, a quota of at least 50 million pounds would have no effect. A more stringent quota, however, would reduce the supply of imports, which, as we will see, would raise the domestic price.

Suppose that a quota of 30 million pounds per month is established. As long as the price in the U.S. market is at or above the world price of $0.10 per pound, foreign producers supply 30 million pounds to the U.S. market. So at

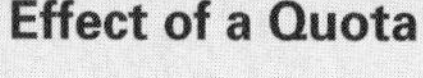

Effect of a Quota

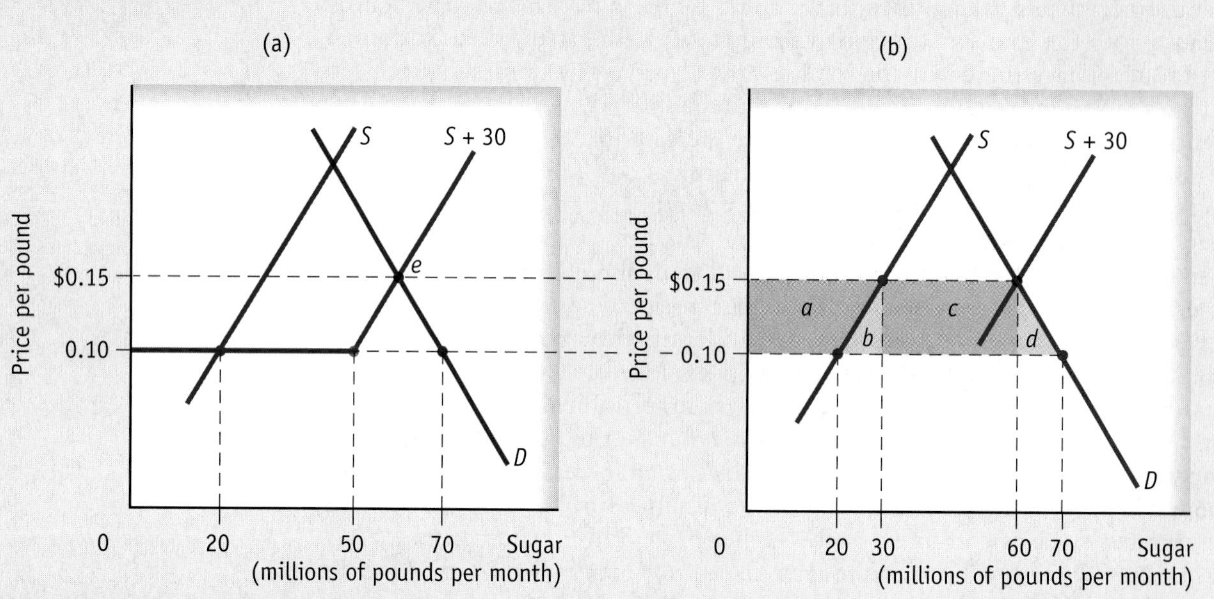

In panel (a), *D* is the domestic demand curve and *S* is the domestic supply curve. When the government establishes a sugar quota of 30 million pounds per year, the supply curve from both domestic production and imports becomes horizontal at the world price of $0.10 per pound and remains horizontal until the supply reaches 50 million pounds. For higher prices, the supply curve equals the horizontal sum of the domestic supply curve, *S*, and the quota. The new domestic price, $0.15 per pound, is determined by the intersection of the new supply curve, *S* + 30, with the domestic demand curve, *D*. Panel (b) shows the welfare effect of the quota. As a result of the higher domestic price, consumer surplus is reduced by the amount of shaded area. Area *a* represents a transfer from domestic consumers to domestic producers. Rectangular area *c* shows the gain to those who can import sugar at the world price and sell it at the higher domestic price. Triangular area *b* reflects a net loss; it represents the amount by which the cost of producing an extra 10 million pounds of sugar in the United States exceeds the cost of buying it from abroad. Area *d* also reflects a net loss—a reduction in consumer surplus as consumption falls. Thus, the blue-shaded areas illustrate the loss in consumer surplus that is captured by domestic producers and those who are permitted to fulfill the quota, and the red-shaded triangles illustrate the minimum net welfare cost.

prices at or above $0.10 per pound, the total supply of sugar to the domestic market is found by adding 30 million pounds of sugar to the amount supplied by domestic producers. At the world price of $0.10 per pound, domestic producers supply 20 million pounds, and importers supply the quota of 30 million pounds, for a total quantity supplied of 50 million pounds. At prices above $0.10, domestic producers can and do expand their quantity supplied in the U.S. market, but imports are restricted to the quota of 30 million pounds.

Domestic and foreign producers will never sell their output for less than $0.10 per pound in the U.S. market because they can always sell for that price on the world market. Thus the supply curve that sums both domestic production and imports becomes horizontal at the world price of $0.10 per pound and remains horizontal until the quantity supplied reaches 50 million pounds. For prices above $0.10 per pound, the supply curve equals the horizontal sum of the supply curve of domestic producers, *S*, and the quota of 30 million pounds. The domestic price is found where this new supply curve intersects the domestic demand curve, which in panel (a) of Exhibit 6 occurs at point *e*. *An effective quota, by limiting imports, raises the domestic price of sugar above the world price and reduces quantity below the free-trade level.* (Note that to compare more readily the effects of tariffs and quotas, this quota was designed to yield the same equilibrium price and quantity as the tariff we examined earlier.)

Panel (b) of Exhibit 6 focuses on the distributional and efficiency effects of the quota. The decline in consumer surplus after the imposition of the quota is depicted by the blue-and red-shaded areas. The loss in consumer surplus represented by the blue-shaded area *a* is converted into the gain in producer surplus resulting from the higher price. Because the value of area *a* is simply transferred from domestic consumers to domestic producers, area *a* involves no loss in domestic welfare. The blue-shaded rectangle *c* shows the gain to those permitted by the quota to sell 30 million pounds per month at the domestic price of $0.15 per pound. To the extent that the gains from the quota go to foreign exporters rather than to domestic importers, area *c* reflects a net loss in domestic welfare.

The red-shaded triangle *b* shows the amount by which the marginal cost of producing another 10 million pounds in the United States exceeds the world price of the good. This triangular area represents a welfare loss to the domestic economy, because sugar could have been purchased abroad for $0.10 per pound, and the domestic resources employed to increase sugar production could have been used more efficiently in the production of other goods. The red-shaded triangle *d* also represents a welfare loss, because it reflects a reduction in consumer surplus (resulting from the fact that less sugar is consumed at the higher price) with no offsetting gain to anyone. Thus, the two red-shaded triangles in panel (b) of Exhibit 6 measure the minimum welfare cost imposed on the domestic economy by an effective quota. To the extent that the profit from quota rights (area *c*) accrues to foreigners, the welfare loss imposed on the domestic economy includes area *c*.

Quotas in Practice

The United States has granted quotas to specific countries. These countries, in turn, award these rights to their exporters through a variety of means. *By rewarding domestic producers with higher prices and foreign producers with the right to sell goods to the United States, the quota system creates two groups intent on securing and perpetuating these quotas.* Lobbyists for foreign producers work the halls of Congress seeking the right to export to the United States. This strong support from producers, coupled with a lack of opposition from consumers (who remain largely unaware of all this), has resulted in quotas that have lasted for decades. Apparel quotas have been in effect for over 30 years, and sugar quotas for over 50 years.

Some economists have argued that if quotas are to be used, the United States should auction off quota allocations to foreign producers, thereby capturing the difference between the world price and the U.S. price. Auctioning off quotas would not only increase federal revenue but also reduce the attractiveness of quotas to foreign sellers, thereby reducing pressure on Washington to perpetuate quotas.

Consider the similarities and differences between a quota and a tariff, which in our example were designed to increase the domestic price of sugar by the same amount. Since the tariff and the quota in our example had identical effects on the price, they reflect the same change in quantity demanded. In both cases, domestic consumers suffer the same loss in consumer surplus and domestic producers reap the same gain in producer surplus. The net welfare loss of both restrictions is the loss in consumer surplus. The primary difference between the two restrictive policies is that the revenue resulting from the tariff goes to the domestic government, whereas the revenue resulting from the quota goes to whoever secures the right to sell foreign goods in the domestic market. *If quota rights accrue to foreigners, then the domestic economy is worse off with a quota than with a tariff.* But even if quota rights go to domestic importers, quotas, like tariffs, still increase the domestic price, restrict quantity, and thereby reduce consumer surplus.

Other Trade Restrictions

Besides tariffs and quotas, a variety of other measures affect free trade. A country may provide *export subsidies* to encourage firms to export, or *low-interest loans* to foreign buyers to promote exports of large capital goods. Some countries impose *domestic content requirements* specifying that a certain percentage of a final good's value must be produced domestically. Other requirements concerning health, safety, or technical standards often discriminate against foreign goods. For example, European countries prohibit imports of beef from hormone-fed cattle, a measure aimed at U.S. beef producers. Purity laws in Germany bar importing many non-German beers. Until uniform standards were adopted by members of the European Community, differing technical standards forced manufacturers to make as many as seven different models of the same TV for that market. Even though the U.S. and Mexico have a free trade agreement, Mexican customs agents usually inspect every package crossing the border. For example, if a shipment contains 20 VCRs, all in identical boxes, customs officials open every box rather than sample them. This inconveniences shippers and slows down free trade. Sometimes exporters will voluntarily agree to limit exports, as when Japanese auto makers agreed to restrain auto exports to the United States. *The point is that tariffs and quotas are only two of many devices that restrict foreign trade.*

Recent research on the cost of protectionism points to the fact that international trade barriers prevent new goods and new technologies from being introduced into an economy. So rather than simply raising the cost of goods that are currently available, the cost of protection is much higher and helps explain why highly protected developing economies remain poor.

Freer Trade by Multilateral Agreement

Mindful of the welfare loss from trade restrictions, the United States, after World War II, invited its trading partners to negotiate less stringent restrictions. The result was the **General Agreement on Tariffs and Trade (GATT),** an international trade treaty adopted in 1947 by 23 countries, including the United States. Each member of GATT agreed to (1) treat all member nations equally with respect to trade, (2) reduce tariff rates through multinational negotiations, and (3) reduce import quotas. The agreement resulted in thousands of tariff reductions.

General Agreement on Tariffs and Trade (GATT)
An international tariff-reduction treaty adopted in 1947 that resulted in a series of negotiated "rounds" aimed at freer trade; the Uruguay Round created GATT's successor, the World Trade Organization (WTO).

The greatest improvements in trade liberalization have come through trade negotiations among many countries, or "trade rounds," under the auspices of GATT. Trade rounds offer a package approach rather than an issue-by-issue approach to trade negotiations. Concessions that are necessary but otherwise difficult to defend in domestic political terms can be made more acceptable in the context of a package that also contains politically and economically attractive benefits. Most early GATT trade rounds aimed at reducing tariffs. The Kennedy Round in the mid-1960s included new provisions against **dumping,** which is selling a commodity abroad at a price that is below its cost of production or below the price charged in the home market. The Tokyo Round of the 1970s was a more sweeping attempt to extend and improve the system.

Dumping Selling a commodity abroad at a price that is below its cost of production or below the price charged in the domestic market

The most recent round of negotiations was launched in Uruguay in September 1986 and ratified by 123 participating countries in April 1994 with 550 pages of legal text spelling out the results of the negotiations. This so-called Uruguay Round, the most comprehensive of the eight postwar multilateral trade negotiations, called for a phased reduction in tariffs on 85 percent of world trade and eventual elimination of quotas. The Uruguay Round also created the World Trade Organization to take over from GATT. The new organization is discussed in the following case study.

World Trade Organization (WTO) The legal and institutional foundation of the multilateral trading system that succeeded GATT in 1995

The World Trade Organization

Other Times, Other Places

The **World Trade Organization (WTO)** now provides the legal and institutional foundation for the multilateral trading system. The WTO offers the platform on which trade relations among member countries can evolve through collective debate. Whereas GATT was a multilateral agreement with no institutional foundation, the WTO is a permanent institution with its own secretariat, located in Geneva, Switzerland. With a staff of 450 headed by a director general and four deputies, the secretariat's responsibilities include supporting WTO delegate bodies, providing trade policy analysis, and assisting in the resolution of trade disputes involving the interpretation of WTO rules and precedents. The staff has a special responsibility of providing technical support to the member countries that are least developed.

Whereas GATT involved only merchandise trade, the WTO includes services and trade-related aspects of intellectual property, such as books, movies, and computer programs. For example, the agreement ensures that computer programs will be protected as literary works and specifies which databases should be protected by copyright. The agreement also requires that a 20-year patent protection be available for all inventions in almost all fields of technology, whether of products or processes (developing-country members that do not currently provide patent protection have up to 10 years to introduce such protection).

Under the *most-favored-nation* clause, each WTO member must offer all other member countries the same trade concessions offered to any member country. While quotas will eventually be outlawed by the WTO, tariffs and customs duties remain legal. Tariff reductions made by the Uruguay Round are contained in some 22,500 pages of national tariff schedules that are considered

The World Trade Organization's Web site describes its role and functions and explains the value of reducing trade barriers. The basic principles underlying the most recent trade agreement can be found at http://www.wto.org/wto/about/facts2.htm#mfn. What policies support the goal of nondiscriminatory trade? For an example of how one industry has been affected, read the case study on agriculture at http://www.wto.org/wto/about/agmnts3.htm. How is the concept of distortion defined, and why is it important in this case? What will happen to agricultural quotas under the new agreement?

an integral part of the WTO. Tariff reductions, in most cases phased in over five years, will result in a drop in the average tariff level from 6.3 percent to 3.8 percent (when GATT began in 1947, the average tariff was 40 percent). If the negotiated reforms are implemented by all 123 participating countries, by the year 2005 (the target date for full implementation) world income is projected to be $510 billion a year higher because of the Uruguay Round.

Dispute settlements under WTO are expected to be faster, more automatic, and less susceptible to blockage than under the GATT system. The WTO extends and clarifies previous GATT rules regarding two forms of "unfair" competition: dumping and export subsidies. Whereas GATT relied on voluntary cooperation, the WTO has a permanent dispute settlement body.

Countries that were not parties to the Uruguay Round must negotiate conditions of entry if they want to join the WTO. For example, China is trying to join the WTO as a developing country (thereby getting a longer grace period to comply with provisions such as patent laws). But the U.S. government would like China admitted only as a developed country, because of concern about China's violations of human rights, the widespread pirating of American products there, and restrictions imposed on the entry of U.S. firms into China's markets. As a developed country, China would have less time to comply with WTO standards.

So far, the United States is the major user of the WTO's dispute settlement system. Charges brought by the United States include accusing Japan of unfair liquor taxes, Canada of discrimination against magazine publishers, Pakistan of violating pharmaceutical copyrights, and Turkey of excessive taxation of U.S. movies. In all, the United States filed about one-third of the cases brought in the first two years of the WTO and was successful in nearly all of them.

Sources: Boris Aliabyev, "Gabunia Key to Russia's WTO Bid," *Moscow Times* (14 May 1998): Paul Meller, "E.U. Requests WTO Panel on U.S. Export Subsidies," *Dow Jones Newswire* (1 July 1998); Paul Meller, "Clinton: U.S. Demands for China WTO Entry Won't Soften," *Dow Jones Newswire* (30 June 1998); and Anne Swardson, "Trial for the Trade Police," *Washington Post* (16 October 1996.)

Common Markets

Some countries have looked to the success of the U.S. economy, which is essentially a free-trade zone across 50 states, and have developed free-trade pacts of their own. The largest and best known is the European Union, which began in 1958 with a half-dozen countries and has now expanded to more than a dozen. The idea was to create a barrier-free European market like the United States in which goods, services, people, and capital are free to flow to their highest-valued use without restrictions. Eleven members of the European Union introduced a common currency, the euro, in 1999; the euro will replace national currencies by 2002.

Another trading bloc has formed among the newly industrialized nations of East Asia. The United States, Canada, and Mexico have developed a free-trade pact called the North American Free Trade Agreement, (NAFTA). And South Africa and its four neighboring countries have formed the Southern African Customs Union. Regional trading bloc agreements such as NAFTA and the European Union require an exception to World Trade Organization rules because bloc members can make special deals among themselves and can then discriminate against outsiders. Recall that under the WTO's most-favored nation clause, any trade concession granted one country must be given to *all other* WTO members.

Through NAFTA, Mexico hopes to increase U.S. investment in Mexico by guaranteeing to those who build manufacturing plants in Mexico duty-free access to U.S. markets, which is where over two-thirds of Mexico's exports go. The United States is interested in NAFTA because Mexico's 100 million people represent an attractive export market for U.S. producers, and because Mexico's huge oil reserves could ease U.S. energy problems. The United States would also like to bolster Mexico's move toward a more market-oriented economy, as is reflected, for example, by Mexico's privatization of its phone system and banks.

ARGUMENTS FOR TRADE RESTRICTIONS

Trade restrictions often appear to be little more than welfare programs for the domestic industries they protect. Given the welfare loss that results from these restrictions, it would be more efficient simply to transfer money from domestic consumers to domestic producers. But such a blatant transfer would be politically unpopular. Arguments for trade restrictions avoid mention of transfers to domestic producers and instead cite loftier concerns. As we shall now see, some of these arguments are more valid than others.

National Defense Argument

Certain industries are said to be in need of protection from import competition because their production is vital in time of war. Products such as strategic metals and weapons of war are sometimes insulated from foreign competition by trade restrictions. Thus national defense considerations outweigh concerns about efficiency and equity.

How valid is this argument? Trade restrictions may shelter the defense industry, but other methods of sheltering it, such as government subsidies to U.S. producers, might be more efficient. Or the government could stockpile basic military hardware so that maintaining an ongoing productive capacity would become less essential, though technological change soon makes many weapons obsolete. Since most industries can make some claim to being vital to national defense, instituting trade restrictions on this basis can get out of hand. For example, one reason U.S. wool producers benefited from protective policies is that wool was said to be critical for military uniforms.

Infant Industry Argument

The infant industry argument was formulated as a rationale for protecting emerging domestic industry from foreign competition. According to this argument, in industries where a firm's average cost per unit falls as production expands, new domestic firms may need protection from foreign competitors until those domestic firms reach sufficient size to be competitive. Trade restrictions are thus defended as temporary devices for allowing domestic firms to achieve sufficient economies of scale needed to compete with established foreign producers.

One problem is how to identify which industries merit protection. And when do domestic firms become old enough to look after themselves? The very existence of protection may foster inefficiencies that firms may not be able to outgrow. The immediate cost of such restrictions is the net welfare loss from higher domestic prices. These costs may become permanent if the industry never realizes the expected economies of scale and thus never becomes competitive. As with the national defense argument, policy makers should be careful in adopting trade restrictions based on the infant industry argument. Here again, production subsidies may be more efficient than import restrictions.

Antidumping Argument

As we have noted already, *dumping* is selling a commodity abroad at a price that is below its cost of production or below the price charged in the home market. Exporters may be able to sell the good for less overseas because of export subsidies, or firms may simply find it profitable to charge lower prices in foreign markets, where there are more competitors. Critics of dumping recommend imposing a tariff to raise the price of dumped goods.

Why should U.S. consumers be prevented from buying products for as little as possible even if these low prices are the result of a foreign subsidy? If the dumping is *persistent,* the lower price may increase consumer surplus by an amount that will more than offset losses to domestic producers. *There is no good reason why consumers should not be allowed to buy imports for a persistently lower price.*

An alternative form of dumping, termed *predatory dumping,* is the *temporary* sale of an export at a lower price in order to drive out competing producers in that foreign market. Once the competition has been eliminated, so the story goes, the exporting firm can raise the price in the foreign market. Predatory dumping may also be a way to discourage production in the country that buys these goods for less. Firms in this importing country would not find entry into this industry attractive because they would not be able to sell at the low price that results from dumping. By driving out established firms or by discouraging domestic entry, the dumpers try to monopolize the market. The trouble with this argument is that if dumpers try to take advantage of their monopoly position by sharply increasing the price, then other firms, either domestic or foreign, may enter the market and sell for less. There are few documented cases of predatory dumping.

Sometimes dumping may be *sporadic,* as firms occasionally sell at a discount to unload excess inventories; retailers hold periodic "sales" for the same reason. Sporadic dumping can be unsettling for domestic industry, but the economic impact is not a matter of great public concern. Regardless, all dumping is prohibited in the United States by the Trade Agreements Act of 1979, which calls for the imposition of tariffs when a good is sold for less in the United States than in its home market. In addition, WTO rules allow for the imposition of offsetting tariffs when products are sold for "less than fair value" and when there is "material injury" to domestic producers. U.S. producers of lumber and beer have accused their Canadian counterparts of dumping.

Jobs and Income Argument

One rationale for trade restrictions that is commonly heard in the United States today is that they protect U.S. jobs and wage levels. Using trade restrictions to protect domestic jobs is a strategy that dates back centuries. One problem with such a policy is that other countries will likely retaliate by restricting *their* imports to save *their* jobs, so international trade is reduced, jobs are lost in export industries, and potential gains from trade fail to materialize.

Wage rates in other countries, especially developing countries, are often a small fraction of wages in the United States. Looking simply at differences in wage rates, however, narrows the focus too much. Wages represent just one component of the total production cost and may not necessarily be the most important. Employers are interested in the labor cost per unit of output, which depends on both the wage rate and labor productivity.

Wage rates are high in the United States partly because U.S. labor productivity remains the highest in the world. This high productivity can be traced to education and training and to the abundant computers, machines, and other physical capital that make workers more productive. Workers in the United States also benefit from a business climate that is relatively stable and that offers appropriate incentives to produce.

But how about the lower wages in many competing countries? These low wages can often be linked to workers' lack of education and training, the meager amount of physical capital available to each worker, and a business climate that is less stable and less attractive. In industries where higher U.S. wages are supported by higher U.S. output per worker, the labor cost per unit of output may be as low, or lower, in the United States as in many countries with low wages and low productivity. For example, although total hourly compensation is more than twice as high at Birmingham Steel, a U.S. corporation, as at South Korean steel plants, Birmingham's labor productivity is four times greater, so the labor cost per ton of steel is lower for Birmingham.

Once multinational firms build plants and provide technological know-how in developing countries, however, U.S. workers lose some of their competitive edge, and their relatively high wages could price some U.S. products out of the world market. This has already happened in the stereo and consumer electronics industries, and General Motors is planning to make more cars in Mexico.

Over time, as labor productivity in developing countries increases, wage differentials among countries will narrow, much as wage differentials between northern and southern U.S. states have narrowed. As technology and capital spread, U.S. workers, particularly unskilled workers, cannot expect to maintain wage levels that are far above those in other countries. The U.S. government may promote research and development to keep U.S. producers on the cutting edge of technological developments, but staying ahead in the technological game is a constant battle.

Domestic producers do not like to compete with foreign producers whose costs are lower, so they often push for trade restrictions. But if restrictions negate any cost advantage a foreign producer might have, the law of comparative advantage becomes inoperative, and domestic consumers are denied access to the lower-priced goods.

Declining Industries Argument

Where an established domestic industry is in jeopardy of being displaced by lower-priced imports, there could be a rationale for *temporary* import restrictions to allow the orderly adjustment of the domestic industry. After all, domestic producers employ many industry-specific resources—both specialized machines and specialized labor. This physical and human capital is worth less in its best alternative use. If the extinction of the domestic industry is forestalled through trade restrictions, specialized machines can be allowed to wear out naturally and specialized workers can retire voluntarily or can gradually pursue more promising careers.

Thus in the case of declining domestic industries, trade protection can be a temporary measure that helps lessen shocks to the economy and allows for an orderly transition to a new industrial mix. But the protection offered should not be so generous as to encourage continued investment in the industry. Protection should be of specific duration and should be phased out over that period.

The clothing industry is an example of a declining U.S. industry. The 22,000 U.S. jobs saved as a result of trade restrictions paid an average of about $23,000 per year. But a Congressional Budget Office study estimated that because of higher domestic prices, U.S. consumers paid between $39,000 and $74,000 per year for each textile and apparel job saved. Trade restrictions in the U.S. clothing and textile industry are scheduled to be phased out under the Uruguay Round of trade agreements.

Free trade may displace some U.S. jobs through imports, but it also creates U.S. jobs through exports. And even where foreign competition appears to have displaced U.S. workers, many foreign companies have built plants in the United States and employ U.S. workers. For example, a dozen foreign television manufacturers and all major Japanese automobile manufacturers now have plants in the United States.

The number of jobs in the United States has more than doubled since 1960. To recognize this job growth is not to deny the problems facing workers who are displaced by imports. Some displaced workers, particularly those in blue-collar jobs in steel and other unionized industries, are not likely to find jobs that will pay as well as the jobs they lost. As with infant industries, however, the problems posed by declining industries need not be solved by trade restrictions. To support the affected industry, the government could offer wage subsidies or special tax breaks that decline over time. The government could also fund programs to retrain workers for jobs that are in greater demand.

Problems with Protection

Trade restrictions raise a number of problems in addition to the ones already mentioned. First, protecting one stage of production often requires protecting downstream stages of production. Protecting the U.S. textile industry from foreign competition, for example, may raise the cost of cloth to U.S. clothing manufacturers, reducing their competitiveness. Thus if the government protects domestic textile manufacturers, it should also protect the domestic garment industry. Otherwise, foreign manufacturers will fashion lower-priced foreign textiles into garments for export to the United States, where they will sell for less than U.S.-made garments fashioned from higher-priced U.S. textiles.

Second, the cost of protection includes not only the welfare loss arising from the higher domestic price, but also the cost of the resources used by domestic producers and groups to secure the favored protection. The cost of *rent seeking*—lobbying fees, propaganda, legal actions—can equal or exceed the direct welfare loss from restrictions. A third problem with imposing trade restrictions is that other countries often retaliate, thus shrinking the gains from trade. Retaliation can set off still greater trade restrictions, leading to an outright trade war. A final problem with trade restrictions is the costs of enforcing the myriad quotas, tariffs, and other restrictions. These policing and enforcement costs are discussed in the following case study.

Enforcing Trade Restrictions

CaseStudy

Other Times, Other Places

The U.S. Customs Service maintains a Web page devoted to its enforcement activities at http://www.customs.treas.gov/enforce/index.htm. What enforcement topics are currently listed? Information about protecting copyrighted material can be found under the Importing and Exporting category of the Customs Service's main Web page.

The United States is the richest, most attractive market in the world. Trade restrictions often make U.S. markets even more appealing to foreign producers because U.S. prices exceed world prices. With thousands of different quota and tariff classifications and with tariffs ranging from zero to over 100 percent, the U.S. Customs Service has difficulty keeping things straight. Customs operates 24 hours a day, 365 days a year and must also process the 435 million people who enter the country each year. From Mexico alone, some 300,000 rail cars enter the United States each year through eight border crossings.

We should not be surprised that some importers try to skirt trade restrictions, either evading restrictions by redefining the product slightly or illegally importing goods that are restricted by quotas. For example, lumber from Canada is subject to quota restrictions. But take a 2-by-4, which is considered lumber, and drill a few small holes in it for electrical wiring, and that 2-by-4 is no longer classified as lumber but as "carpentry," which is not subject to quotas. A diverse array of goods is imported in violation of quotas, including clothing, sugar, coffee, gems, and steel pipes. It has been estimated that more than 10 percent of all imports are illegal.

Restrictions affect not only the quantity of imports but also the quality. Nearly all schemes to import clothing illegally involve fraudulent documents intended to misrepresent the clothing so that it fits into some quota or qualifies for a lower tariff. Sometimes the garments are altered to evade detection. For example, because imports of men's running shorts were controlled by a quota, manufacturers often added a flimsy inner lining so the shorts could pass for swimming trunks, which faced no quotas.

Because the United States allows some countries more generous quotas than others, exporters in a country under tight control sometimes ship their goods through a country with a liberal ceiling. For example, Japan makes so little clothing for export that the United States imposes no clothing quota for imports from Japan. As a result, clothing made in Korea is often shipped through Japan to evade U.S. quotas on Korean goods. Similarly, because Nepal is not subject to a clothing quota but India is, India ships clothing to the United States through Nepal. And China ships clothing through Macau, a tiny island next to Hong Kong.

Some foreign producers and U.S. importers engage in "port shopping," or testing various ports to see where inspections are most lax. Documents are often forged. U.S. Customs inspectors are responsible for policing all this activity.

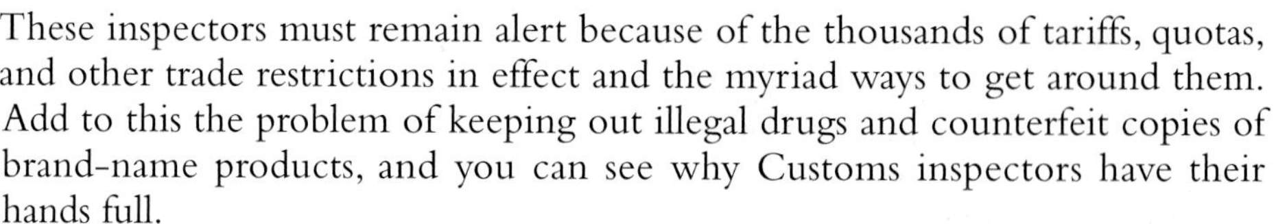

These inspectors must remain alert because of the thousands of tariffs, quotas, and other trade restrictions in effect and the myriad ways to get around them. Add to this the problem of keeping out illegal drugs and counterfeit copies of brand-name products, and you can see why Customs inspectors have their hands full.

Sources: "U.S. Customs Service Hearing of the Trade Subcommittee of the House Ways and Means Committee," *Federal News Service* (30 April 1998); Richard Lawrence, "US, EU Smooth Over Differences on Country-of-Origin Regulations," *Journal of Commerce* (15 April 1998); and David Parkinson, "U.S. Formally Imposes Quotas on Canadian Pre-drilled Studs," *Dow Jones Newswire* (29 June 1998).

CONCLUSION

Comparative advantage, specialization, and trade allow people to use their scarce resources most efficiently to satisfy their unlimited wants. International trade arises from voluntary exchange among buyers and sellers pursuing their self-interest. Since 1950 the volume of world output has risen 7-fold, while the volume of world trade has increased 17-fold.

World trade offers many advantages to the trading countries: the chance to take advantage of economies of scale, the opportunity to utilize abundant resources, the improvements that come with competitive pressure, more ready access to information about markets and technology, and lower prices for consumers.

Despite the clear gains from free trade, restrictions on international trade date back hundreds of years, and pressure to impose trade restrictions continues today. For example, in 1997 Congress refused to grant President Clinton so-called fast-track negotiating authority on trade agreements, a privilege that had been granted to previous presidents. And China restricts imports with high tariffs, taxes, and non-tariff measures such as limitations on which enterprises can import goods. Billions of dollars have been lost to Americans because of Chinese pirating of CDs and software.

Those who benefit from trade restrictions are the domestic producers (and their resource suppliers) who are able to sell their output for a higher price because of the restrictions. Protection insulates an industry from the rigors of global competition, in the process stifling innovation and leaving the industry vulnerable to technological change in other countries. Under a system of quotas, the winners also include those who have secured the right to import goods at the world prices and sell them at the domestic prices.

Consumers who must pay higher prices for protected goods suffer from trade restrictions, as do the domestic producers who use imported resources. Other losers are U.S. exporters, who face higher trade barriers if foreigners retaliate. Even if other countries do not retaliate, U.S. trade restrictions reduce the gains from comparative advantage and thereby reduce world income. With world income lower, U.S. exporters find that their foreign markets have shrunk. Some of these exporters may go out of business; others may never even start producing.

Trade restrictions are often imposed gradually over a period of years. Because the domestic adjustments to restrictions are slow and because those who lose out are scattered throughout the economy, the losers frequently do not know that they are losers or they fail to connect their troubles with trade policy. On the other hand, those who benefit from trade restrictions are usually a well-defined group of producers who can clearly identify the source of their gains. *One reason trade restrictions get introduced is that most of those harmed by restrictions do not know they are losers, whereas beneficiaries know what's at stake.*

Producers have an interest in trade legislation, but consumers remain largely ignorant. Consumers purchase thousands of different goods and thus have no special interest in the effects of trade policy on any particular good. Congress tends to support the group that makes the most noise, so trade restrictions persist, despite the clear gains from free trade.

SUMMARY

1. Even if a country has an absolute advantage in producing all goods, that country should specialize in producing the goods in which it has a comparative advantage. If each country specializes and trades according to the law of comparative advantage, all countries will have greater consumption possibilities.
2. Tariff revenues go to the government and could be used to lower taxes. Quotas confer benefits on those with the right to buy the good at the world price and sell it at the higher domestic price. Both restrictions harm domestic consumers more than they help domestic producers, although tariffs at least yield domestic government revenue.
3. Despite the gains from free trade and the net welfare losses arising from tariffs and quotas, trade restrictions have been a part of trade policy for hundreds of years. The General Agreement on Tariffs and Trade (GATT) was an international treaty ratified in 1947 to reduce tariffs. Subsequent rounds of negotiations promoted lower tariffs and discouraged trade restrictions. The Uruguay Round, ratified by 123 countries in 1994, created the World Trade Organization (WTO) to succeed GATT.
4. Reasons given for instituting trade restrictions include promoting national defense, giving infant industries time to grow, preventing foreign producers from dumping goods in domestic markets, protecting domestic jobs, and allowing declining industries time to phase out.

QUESTIONS FOR REVIEW

1. *(Profile of Imports and Exports)* What are the major U.S. exports and imports? How does international trade affect consumption possibilities?

2. *(Gains from Trade)* Complete each of the following sentences:
   a. When a nation has no economic interaction with foreigners and produces everything it consumes, the nation is in a state of ________.
   b. According to the law of comparative advantage, each nation should specialize in producing the goods in which it has the lowest ________.
   c. The amount of one good that a nation can exchange for one unit of another good is known as the ________.
   d. Specializing according to comparative advantage and trading with other nations results in ________.
3. *(Reasons for International Specialization)* What determines which goods a country should produce and export?
4. *(Tariffs)* High tariffs usually lead to black markets and smuggling. How is government revenue reduced by such activity? Relate your answer to the graph in Exhibit 5 in this chapter. Does smuggling have any social benefits?
5. *(Trade Restrictions)* Exhibits 5 and 6 show net losses to the economy of a country that imposes tariffs or quotas on imported sugar. What kinds of gains and losses would occur in the economies of countries that export sugar?
6. ***(CaseStudy:** The World Trade Organization)* What is the World Trade Organization (WTO) and how does it help foster multilateral trade? (Check the WTO website at http://www.wto.org/).
7. *(Arguments for Trade Restrictions)* Explain the national defense, declining industries, and infant industry arguments for protecting a domestic industry from international competition.

8. *(Arguments for Trade Restrictions)* Firms hurt by cheap imports typically argue that restricting trade will save U.S. jobs. What's wrong with this argument? Are there ever any reasons to support such trade restrictions?

9. *(Case***Study:** *Enforcing Trade Restrictions)* Increasingly, goods are manufactured using a variety of domestic and imported parts or resources. What problem does this create in enforcing such trade restrictions?

PROBLEMS AND EXERCISES

10. *(Comparative Advantage)* Suppose that each U.S. worker can produce 8 units of food or 2 units of clothing daily. in Fredonia, which has the same number of workers, each worker can produce 7 units of food or 1 unit of clothing daily. Why does the United States have an absolute advantage in both goods? Which country enjoys a comparative advantage in food? Why?

11. *(Comparative Advantage)* The consumption possibilities frontiers shown in Exhibit 3 assume terms of trade of 1 unit of clothing for 1 unit of food. What would the consumption possibilities frontiers look like if the terms of trade were 1 unit of clothing for 2 units of food?

12. *(Import Quotas)* What is an effective import quota? Using a supply-and-demand diagram, illustrate and explain the net welfare loss from imposing such a quota. Under what circumstances would the net welfare loss from an import quota exceed the net welfare loss from an equivalent tariff (one that results in the same price and import level as the quota)?

13. *(Trade Restrictions)* Suppose that the world price for steel is below the U.S. domestic price, but the government requires that all steel used in the United States be domestically produced.
    a. Use a diagram like the one in Exhibit 5 to show the gains and loses from such a policy.
    b. How could you estimate the net welfare loss (deadweight loss) from such a diagram?
    c. What response to such a policy would you expect from industries (like automobile producers) that use U.S. steel?
    d. What government revenues are generated by this policy.

EXPERIENTIAL EXERCISES

14. *(Arguments for Trade Restrictions)* Visit the Office of the U.S. Trade representative at http://www.ustr.gov/. The U.S. Trade Representative is a Cabinet member who acts as the principal trade advisor, negotiator, and spokesperson for the president on trade and related investment matters. Look at some of the most recent press releases. What are some of the trade-related issues the United States is currently facing?

15. *(Antidumping Argument)* Thomas Klitgaard and Karen Schiele have analyzed dumping in their article "Free Trade or Fair Trade: The Dumping Issue." Current Issues in Economics and Finance, (August 1998). Download this article at http://www.ny.frb.org/rmaghome/curr-iss/ci4-8.htm. How can we tell whether foreign firms are selling products in the U.S. at a price below the cost of production?

16. *(Wall Street Journal)* The *Wall Street Journal* is one of the world's best sources of information regarding international trade. A good place to look is the International page inside the First Section of each day's *Journal*. Look at today's issue and find an article dealing with trade barriers—tariffs, quotas, and so on. Model the trade barrier using a graph, and try to determine who are the beneficiaries and who bears the costs. If you are lucky, the article will provide sufficient information to allow you to actually estimate costs and benefits in dollar terms.

CHAPTER

33 International Finance

What do we mean when we talk about a "strong dollar"? How come U.S. consumers favor a strong dollar more than U.S. producers? Should we worry when we hear about a rising U.S. trade deficit? And what about the new European currency, the euro? Answers to these and other questions are explored in this chapter, which focuses on international finance.

A U.S. firm that plans to buy a German printing press will be quoted a price in euros. Suppose that machine costs one million euros. How many dollars is that? The cost in dollars will depend on the current exchange rate. When buyers and sellers from two countries trade, two currencies are usually involved. Supporting the flows of goods and services are flows of currencies that connect all international transactions.

isit the McEachern
ractive Study Center
or this chapter at
/mcisc.swcollege.com

The *exchange rate* between two currencies—the price of one in terms of the other—is the means by which the price of a good produced in one country gets translated into the price to the buyer in another country. The willingness of buyers and sellers to strike deals, therefore, depends on the rate of exchange between currencies. In this chapter we examine the international transactions that determine the relative value of one currency in terms of another. Topics discussed in this chapter include:

- Balance of payments
- Trade deficits and surpluses
- Foreign exchange markets
- Floating exchange rates
- Purchasing power parity
- Fixed exchange rates
- The international monetary system
- Managed float
- Bretton Woods agreement

BALANCE OF PAYMENTS

A country's gross domestic product measures the flow of economic activity that occurs within that country during a given period. To account for dealings abroad, countries also keep track of their international transactions. A country's *balance of payments,* as introduced in Chapter 4, summarizes all economic transactions that occur during a given time period between residents of that country and residents of other countries. *Residents* include individuals, firms, and governments.

International Economic Transactions

Balance-of-payments statements measure economic transactions that occur between countries, whether they involve goods and services, real or financial assets, or transfer payments. Because it reflects the volume of transactions that occur during a particular time period, usually a year, the balance of payments measures a *flow.*

Some transactions included in the balance-of-payments account do not involve payments of money. For example, if *Time* magazine ships a new printing press to its Australian subsidiary, no payment occurs, yet an economic transaction involving another country has taken place and must be included in the balance-of-payments account. Similarly, if CARE sends food to Africa, or if the Pentagon sends military assistance to Israel, these transactions must be captured in the balance of payments. So remember, although we speak of the *balance of payments,* a more descriptive phrase would be the *balance of economic transactions.*

Balance-of-payments accounts are maintained according to the principles of *double-entry bookkeeping,* in which entries on one side of the ledger are called *debits,* and entries on the other side are called *credits.* As we will see, the balance-of-payments accounts are made up of several individual accounts; a deficit in one or more accounts must be offset by a surplus in the other accounts. Thus the total debits must be in balance with, or equal to, the total credits—hence the expression *balance* of payments. The balance of payments involves a comparison during a given time period, such as a year, between the outflow of payments to the rest of the world, which are entered as debits, and the inflow of receipts from the rest of the world, which are entered as credits. The next few sections describe the major accounts in the balance of payments.

Merchandise Trade Balance

The *merchandise trade balance,* a term first introduced in Chapter 4, equals the value of merchandise exported minus the value of merchandise imported. The merchandise account reflects trade in tangible products (stuff you can drop on your toe), such as French wine and U.S. computers, and is often referred to simply as the *trade balance.* The value of U.S. merchandise exports is listed as a credit in the U.S. balance-of-payments account because U.S. residents must *be paid* for the exported goods. The value of U.S. merchandise imports is listed as a debit in the balance-of-payments account because U.S. residents must *pay* for the imported goods.

If the value of merchandise exports exceeds the value of merchandise imports, there is a *surplus* in the merchandise trade balance, or, more simply, a *trade surplus.* If the value of merchandise imports exceeds the value of merchandise exports, there is a *deficit* in the merchandise trade balance, or a *trade deficit.* The merchandise trade balance, which is reported monthly, influences foreign exchange markets, the stock market, and other financial markets. The trade balance depends on a variety of factors, including the relative strength and competitiveness of the domestic economy compared to other economies and the relative value of the domestic currency compared to other currencies.

The U.S. merchandise trade balance since 1979 is presented in Exhibit 1. Because imports have exceeded exports every year, the balance has been in deficit, as is reflected by the bottom line. Note that during recessions, which are indicated by shading, imports growth are relatively flat, as is the trade deficit. Between 1983 and 1990, and since 1991, the U.S. economy has expanded. *When the domestic economy expands, spending on all goods increases, so imports have increased.* In 1998 the merchandise trade deficit exceeded $300 billion, a record level.

NetBookmark

The Bureau of Economic Analysis reports data on U.S. international accounts at http://www.bea.doc.gov/bea/ai1.htm. Review the most recent edition of U.S. International Transactions. What are the trends in the current and capital accounts, and in trade in goods and services? Which are in deficit, which in surplus? How has the value of the dollar been changing? What relationship is there between the state of these accounts and the value of the dollar?

Balance on Goods and Services

The merchandise trade balance focuses on the flow of goods, but services are also traded internationally. *Services* are intangibles, such as transportation, insurance, banking, consulting, and tourist expenditures. Services also include the income earned from foreign investments less the income earned by foreigners from their investment in the U.S. economy. Services are often called "invisibles," because they are not tangible—not something you can drop on your toe. The value of U.S. service exports, such as when an Irish tourist visits New York City, is listed as a credit in the U.S. balance-of-payments account because U.S. residents receive payments for these services. The value of U.S. service imports, such as when a computer specialist in Ireland enters policy information for a Connecticut insurer, is listed as a debit in the balance of payments account because U.S. residents must pay for the imported services.

The **balance on goods and services** is the difference between the value of exports of goods and services and the value of imports of goods and services. Currently-produced goods and services that are sold or otherwise provided to foreigners form part of U.S. output. The production of these goods and services generates income during the current period. Conversely, imports of goods and services form part of the nation's current expenditures—part of consumption, investment, and government expenditures. Allocating imports to each of the

Balance on goods and services The section of a country's balance of payments account that measures the difference in value between a country's exports of goods and services and its imports of goods and services

EXHIBIT 1

Merchandise Trade Balance (billions of 1992 dollars)

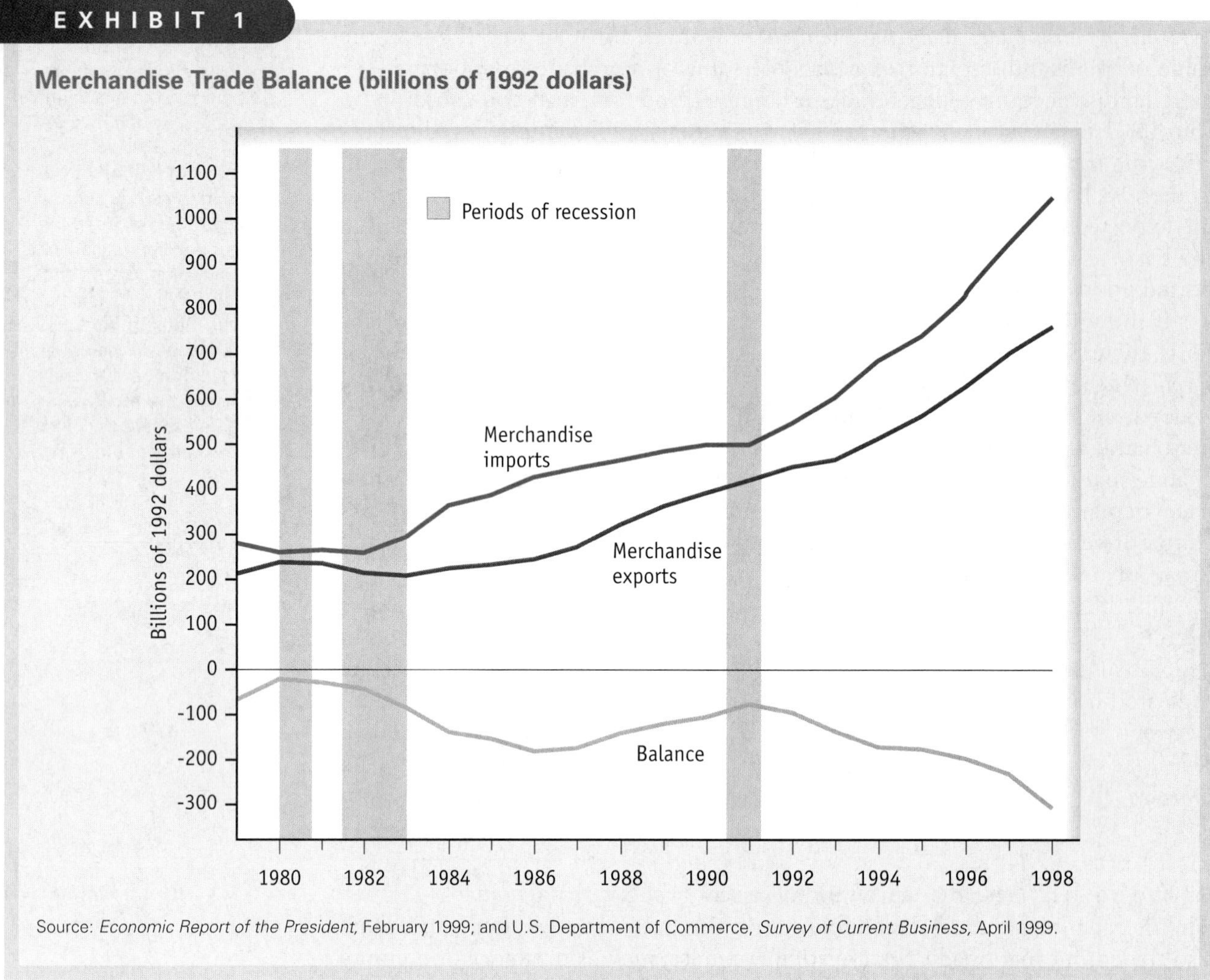

Source: *Economic Report of the President,* February 1999; and U.S. Department of Commerce, *Survey of Current Business,* April 1999.

major expenditure components is an accounting nightmare, so we usually just subtract imports from exports to yield *net exports.* Thus the U.S. gross domestic product in a given year equals total expenditures for consumption, investment, government purchases, and net exports.

Unilateral Transfers

Net unilateral transfers The unilateral transfers (gifts and grants) received from abroad by residents of a country minus the unilateral transfers residents send abroad

Unilateral transfers consist of government transfers to foreign residents, foreign aid, personal gifts to friends and relatives abroad, personal and institutional charitable donations, and the like. For example, money sent abroad by a U.S. resident to friends or relatives would be included in U.S. unilateral transfers and would be a debit in the balance of payments account. U.S. **net unilateral transfers** equal the unilateral transfers received from abroad by U.S. residents minus the unilateral transfers sent to foreign residents. U.S. net unilateral transfers have been negative each year since World War II, except for 1991, when the U.S. government received sizable transfers from foreign governments to support the Persian Gulf war.

The United States places no restrictions on money sent out of the country.[1] Other countries, particularly developing countries, strictly limit the amount of money that may be sent abroad. More generally, developing countries often restrict the convertibility of their currency into other currencies.

When we add net unilateral transfers to the exports of goods and services minus the imports of goods and services, we get the **balance on current account,** which is reported quarterly. Thus, *the current account includes all transactions in currently produced goods and services plus net unilateral transfers.* It can be negative, reflecting a current account deficit; positive, reflecting a current account surplus; or zero.

Balance on current account The section of a country's balance-of-payments account that measures the sum of the country's net unilateral transfers and its balance on goods and services

Capital Account

Whereas the current account records international transactions involving the flows of goods, services, and unilateral transfers, the **capital account** records international transactions involving the flow of financial assets, such as borrowing, lending, and investments. For example, U.S. investors purchase foreign assets in order to earn a higher rate of return and to diversify their portfolios. When economists talk about capital, they usually mean the physical and human resources employed to produce goods and services. But sometimes *capital* is used as another word for *money*—money used to acquire financial assets, such as stocks, bonds, bank balances, and money used to make direct investments in foreign plants and equipment. U.S. capital outflows result when Americans purchase foreign assets. U.S. capital inflows result from foreign purchases of U.S. assets.

Capital account The record of a country's international transactions involving purchases or sales of financial and real assets

Between 1917 and 1982, the United States was a net capital exporter, and the net return on all this foreign investment over the years improved our balance on current account. In 1983, high real interest rates in the United States (relative to those in the rest of the world) resulted in a net inflow of capital for the first time in 65 years. A net inflow of capital shows up as a surplus in the capital account. Since then, U.S. imports of capital have exceeded exports of capital nearly every year, meaning that Americans owe foreigners more and more. *The United States is now the world's largest net debtor nation.* This is not as bad as it sounds, since foreign investment in the United States adds to America's productive capacity and promotes employment. But the return on foreign investment in the United States flows to foreigners, not to Americans.

The **official reserve transactions account** indicates the net amount of international reserves that shift among central banks to settle international transactions. (Many government publications show this not as a separate account but as part of the capital account.) International reserves consist of gold, dollars, euros, other major currencies, and a special-purpose reserve currency called *Special Drawing Rights*, or *SDRs*.

Official reserve transactions account The section of a country's balance-of-payments account that reflects the flow of gold, Special Drawing Rights, and currencies among central banks

Statistical Discrepancy

As we have seen, the U.S. balance of payments is a record of all transactions between U.S. residents and foreign residents over a specified period. It is easier to

1 Federal authorities do, however, require reporting the source of cash exports of $10,000 or more. This measure is aimed at reducing money laundering overseas.

describe this record than to compile it. Despite efforts to capture all international transactions, some go unreported. Yet as the name *balance of payments* suggests, debits must equal credits—the entire balance of payments account must by definition be in balance. This idea that debits equal credits is expressed in a double-entry bookkeeping system in which debits are recorded on one side of the ledger and credits are recorded on the other side. To ensure that the two sides of the ledger balance, a residual account called the *statistical discrepancy* was created. An excess of credits in all other accounts is offset by an equivalent debit in the statistical discrepancy account, or an excess of debits in all other accounts is offset by an equivalent credit in the discrepancy account. So you might think of the statistical discrepancy as the "fudge factor." The statistical discrepancy provides analysts with both a measure of the net error in the balance of payments data and a means of satisfying the double-entry bookkeeping requirement that total debits must equal total credits.

Deficits and Surpluses

Nations, like households, operate under a cash-flow constraint. Expenditures cannot exceed income plus cash on hand and borrowed funds. We have distinguished between *current* transactions, which are the income and expenditures from exports, imports, and unilateral transfers, and *capital* transactions, which reflect international investments and borrowing. Any surplus or deficit in one account must be balanced by other changes in the balance of payments accounts. The current account has been in deficit since 1982, meaning that the sum of U.S. imports and unilateral transfers to foreigners has exceeded the sum spent by foreigners on our exports and sent as unilateral transfers to us.

Exhibit 2 presents the U.S. balance of payments statement for 1998. All transactions requiring payments from foreigners to U.S. residents are entered as credits, indicated by a plus sign (+), because they result in a flow of funds from foreign residents to U.S. residents. All transactions requiring payments to foreigners from U.S. residents are entered as debits, indicated by a minus sign (−), because they result in a flow of funds from U.S. residents to foreign residents. As you can see, a surplus in the capital account offsets deficits in the current account, in the official reserve transactions account, and in the statistical discrepancy.

Foreign exchange is the currency of another country that is needed to carry out international transactions. A country runs a deficit in its current account when the amount of foreign exchange that country gets from exporting goods and services and from receipts of unilateral transfers falls short of the amount needed to pay for its imports and to make unilateral transfers. The additional foreign exchange required must come from either a net capital inflow (international borrowing, foreign purchases of domestic stocks and bonds, and so forth) or through official government transactions in foreign currency. If a country runs a current account surplus, the foreign exchange received from selling exports and from unilateral transfers exceeds the amount required to pay for imports and to make unilateral transfers. This excess foreign exchange could be held in a bank account, converted to the domestic currency, or used to purchase foreign stocks, bonds, or other foreign investments.

When all transactions are considered, the balance of payments must always balance, though specific accounts may not. A deficit in a particular account

EXHIBIT 2

U.S. Balance of Payments: 1998 (billions of dollars)

Item	
Current Account	
1. Merchandise exports	+671.0
2. Merchandise imports	−919.0
3. Trade balance (1 + 2)	−248.0
4. Service exports	+503.0
5. Service imports	−446.6
6. Goods and services balance (3 + 4 + 5)	−191.6
7. Net unilateral transfers	−41.9
8. Current account balance (6 + 7)	−233.5
Capital Account	
9. Outflow of U. S. capital	−297.8
10. Inflow of foreign capital	+564.6
11. Capital account balance (9 + 10)	+266.8
Official Reserve Transactions Account	
12. Change in U. S. official assets abroad	−7.6
13. Change in foreign official assets in U. S.	−22.1
14. Official reserve balance (12 + 13)	−29.7
15. Statistical discrepancy	−3.6
TOTAL (8 + 11 + 14 + 15)	**0.0**

Source: *Survey of Current Business,* U. S. Department of Commerce, April 1999.

should not necessarily be viewed as a source of concern, nor should a surplus be a source of satisfaction. The deficit in the U.S. current account in recent years has been offset by a net inflow of capital from abroad. As a result of the net inflow of capital, foreigners are acquiring more claims on U.S. assets.

FOREIGN EXCHANGE RATES AND MARKETS

Now that you have some idea about the international flow of products and investment funds, we can take a closer look at the forces that determine the underlying value of the currencies involved in these transactions. We begin by looking at exchange rates and the market for foreign exchange.

Foreign Exchange

Foreign exchange, recall, is foreign currency needed to carry out international transactions. The **exchange rate** is the price of one currency measured in terms of another currency. Exchange rates are determined by the interaction of the households, firms, private financial institutions, governments, and central banks that buy and sell foreign exchange. The exchange rate fluctuates to equate

Exchange rate The price of one country's currency measured in terms of another country's currency

the quantity of foreign exchange demanded with the quantity supplied. Typically, foreign exchange is made up of bank deposits denominated in the foreign currency. When foreign travel is involved, foreign exchange may consist of foreign paper money.

The foreign exchange market incorporates all the arrangements used to buy and sell foreign exchange. This market is not so much a physical place as it is a network of telephones and computers connecting large banks all over the world. Perhaps you have seen pictures of foreign exchange traders in New York, Frankfurt, London, or Tokyo amid a tangle of phone lines. The foreign exchange market is like an all-night diner—it never closes. Some trading center is always open somewhere in the world.

We will consider the market for the euro in terms of the dollar. But first a bit about the euro, since it may be new to you. In January 1999, the euro became the official common currency of eleven European countries, now known collectively as the euro zone or *Euroland*. By 2002, the national currencies of Germany, France, Italy, Austria, Spain, Portugal, Finland, Ireland, Belgium, Luxembourg, and the Netherlands are scheduled to disappear. In the mean time, the euro will be interchangeable with the local currency at a fixed rate.

The price, or exchange rate, of the euro in terms of the dollar is the number of dollars required to purchase one euro. An increase in the number of dollars needed to purchase a euro indicates a weakening, or a **depreciation,** of the dollar. A decrease in the number of dollars needed to purchase a euro indicates a strengthening, or an **appreciation,** of the dollar. Put another way, a decrease in the number of euros needed to purchase a dollar is a depreciation of the dollar, and an increase in the number of euros needed to purchase a dollar is an appreciation of the dollar.

Currency depreciation
With respect to the dollar, an increase in the number of dollars needed to purchase 1 unit of foreign exchange

Currency appreciation
With respect to the dollar, a decrease in the number of dollars needed to purchase 1 unit of foreign exchange

Since the exchange rate is a price, it can be determined using the conventional tools of supply and demand: the equilibrium price of foreign exchange is the one that equates quantity demanded with quantity supplied. To simplify the analysis, let's suppose that the United States and Euroland make up the entire world, so the supply and demand for euros is the supply and demand for foreign exchange from the U.S. perspective.

Demand for Foreign Exchange

U.S. residents need euros to pay for goods and services produced in Euroland, to invest in assets there, to make loans to Euroland, or simply to send cash gifts to friends or relatives there. Whenever U.S. residents need euros, they must buy them in the foreign exchange market, which could be their local bank, paying for them with dollars.

Exhibit 3 depicts a market for foreign exchange—in this case, for euros. The horizontal axis identifies the quantity of foreign exchange, measured here in millions of euros. The vertical axis identifies the price per unit of foreign exchange, measured here as the number of dollars required to purchase each euro. The demand curve for foreign exchange, identified as *D,* shows the inverse relationship between the dollar price of the euro and the quantity of euros demanded, other things constant. Some of the factors held constant along the demand curve are the incomes and preferences of U.S. consumers, the expected inflation rates in the United States and Euroland, the euro price of goods in Euroland, and interest rates in the United States and Euroland. People have many

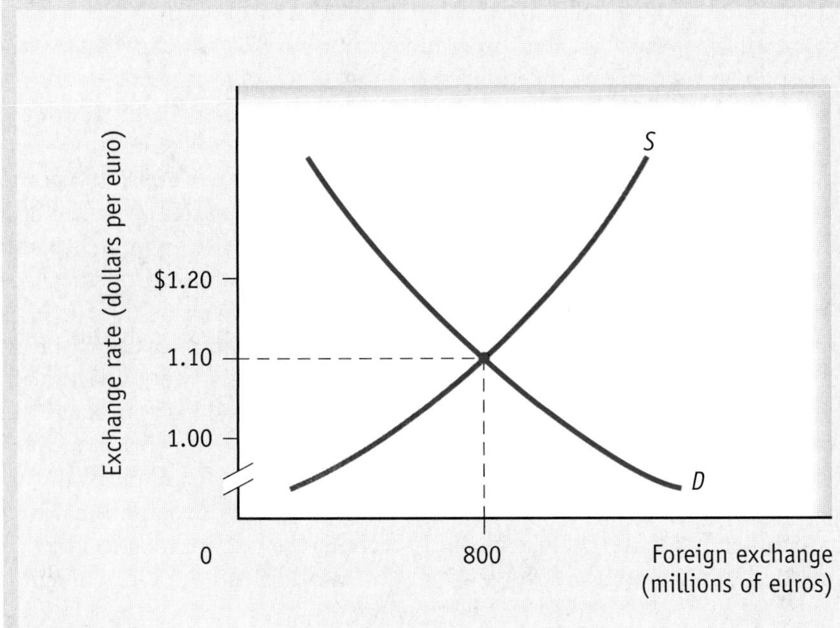

EXHIBIT 3

The Foreign Exchange Market

The fewer dollars needed to purchase 1 unit of foreign exchange, the lower the price of foreign goods and the greater the quantity of foreign goods demanded. The greater the demand for foreign goods, the greater the amount of foreign exchange demanded. The demand curve for foreign exchange slopes downward. An increase in the exchange rate makes U.S. products cheaper for foreigners. The increased demand for U.S. goods implies an increase in the quantity of foreign exchange supplied. The supply curve of foreign exchange slopes upward.

different reasons for demanding foreign exchange, but in the aggregate, the lower the dollar price of foreign exchange, other things constant, the greater the quantity demanded.

A drop in the dollar price of foreign exchange, in this case the euro, means that fewer dollars are needed to purchase each euro, so the dollar prices of Euroland products (such as German cars, Italian shoes, French wine, along with investments in Euroland), which have price tags listed in euros, become cheaper. The cheaper it is to buy euros, the lower the dollar price of Euroland products to U.S. residents, so the greater the quantity of euros demanded by U.S. residents, other things constant. For example, a cheap enough euro might persuade you to tour Rome, climb the Austrian Alps, wander the museums of Paris, or crawl the pubs of Dublin.

Supply of Foreign Exchange

The supply of foreign exchange is generated by the desire of foreign residents to acquire dollars—that is, to exchange euros for dollars. Foreign residents want dollars to buy U.S. goods and services, to buy U.S. assets, to make loans in dollars, or to make cash gifts in dollars to their U.S. friends and relatives. Also, citizens of countries suffering from economic and political turmoil, such as Malaysia, Indonesia, and South Korea, may want to buy dollars as a hedge against the depreciation and instability of their own currencies. The dollar has long been accepted as an international medium of exchange. It is also the currency of choice in the world markets for oil and for illegal drugs. But the euro may challenge that dominance, in part because the largest euro denomination, the 500 euro note, is worth about five times more than the top dollar note, the

$100 bill (hence, with euro notes, it would be five times easier to smuggle, say, a million dollars).

Europeans supply euros in the foreign exchange market to acquire the dollars they need. An increase in the dollar-per-euro exchange rate, other things constant, makes U.S. products cheaper for foreigners, since foreign residents need fewer euros to get the same number of dollars. For example, suppose a Dell computer sells for $1,100. If the exchange rate is $1.10 per euro, that computer costs 1,000 euros; if the exchange rate is $1.25 per euro, it costs only 880 euros. The number of Dell computers demanded in Euroland increases as the dollar-per-euro exchange rate increases, other things constant, so more euros will be supplied on the foreign exchange market to buy dollars.

More generally, the higher the dollar-per-euro exchange rate, other things constant, the greater the quantity of euros supplied to the foreign exchange market. The positive relationship between the dollar-per-euro exchange rate and the quantity of euros supplied on the foreign exchange market is expressed in Exhibit 3 by the upward-sloping supply curve for foreign exchange (again, euros in our example).[2] The supply curve is drawn holding other things constant, including Euroland incomes and preferences, expectations about the rates of inflation in Euroland and the United States, and interest rates in Euroland and the United States.

Determining the Exchange Rate

Exhibit 3 brings together the supply and demand for foreign exchange to determine the exchange rate. At an exchange rate of $1.10 per euro, the quantity of euros demanded equals the quantity of euros supplied—in our example, 800 million euros. Once achieved, this equilibrium exchange rate will remain constant until a change occurs in one of the factors that affect supply or demand. If the exchange rate is allowed to adjust freely, or to *float,* in response to market forces, the market will clear continually, as the quantities of foreign exchange demanded and supplied are equated.

What if the initial equilibrium is upset by a change in one of the underlying forces that affect supply or demand? For example, suppose an increase in U.S. income causes Americans to increase their demand for all normal goods, including Euroland goods and services. Such an increase in income will shift the U.S. demand curve for foreign exchange to the right, as Americans seek more euros to buy more Italian marble, Dutch chocolate, French couture, German machines, and euro securities.

This increased demand for euros is shown in Exhibit 4 by a shift to the right in the demand curve for foreign exchange. The supply curve does not change. The shift of the demand curve from D to D' leads to an increase in the exchange rate from $1.10 per euro to $1.15 per euro. Thus the euro increases in value, or appreciates, while the dollar falls in value, or depreciates. The higher exchange value of the euro prompts some Euroland residents to purchase more American products, which are now cheaper in terms of the euro. In our

2 As the exchange rate rises, Europeans have a greater incentive to buy more U.S. goods and services because their prices in terms of euros have decreased. As more is bought at lower prices, however, the total expenditure of euros rises only if the percentage increase in quantities of U.S. products demanded by the Europeans exceeds the percentage decrease in the prices in terms of euros. If the percentage increase in quantities demanded is less than the percentage decrease in the price in terms of euros, the supply curve of euros will slope downward.

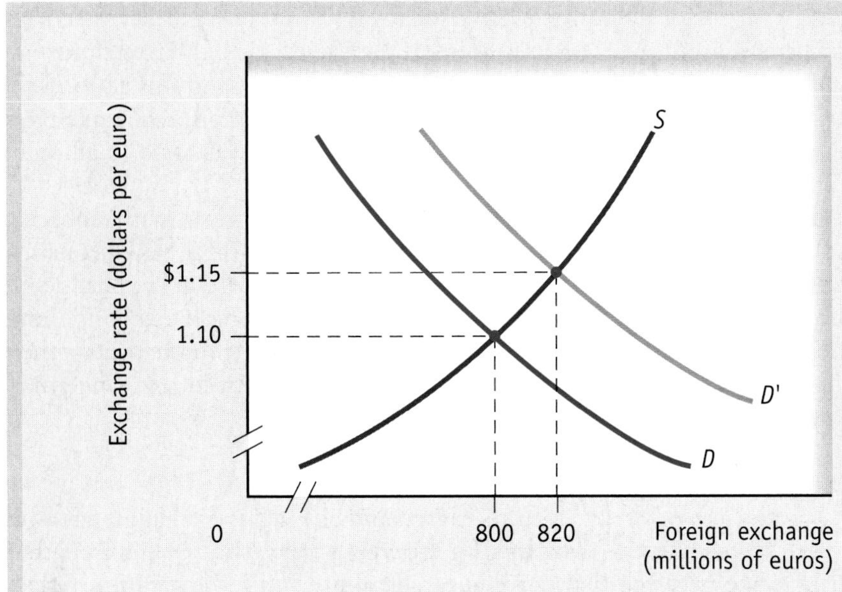

EXHIBIT 4

Effect on the Foreign Exchange Market of an Increase in Demand for Euros

The intersection of supply curve *S* and demand curve *D* determines the exchange rate. At an exchange rate of $1.10 per euro, the quantity of euros demanded equals the quantity supplied. An increase in the demand for euros from *D* to *D'* leads to an increase in the exchange rate from $1.10 to $1.15 per euro.

example, the equilibrium quantity of euros increases from 800 million to 820 million.

Any increase in the demand for foreign exchange or any decrease in its supply, other things constant, causes an increase in the number of dollars required to purchase one unit of foreign exchange, which is a depreciation of the dollar. On the other hand, any decrease in the demand for foreign exchange or any increase in its supply, other things constant, causes a reduction in the number of dollars required to purchase one unit of foreign exchange, which is an appreciation of the dollar.

Arbitrageurs and Speculators

Exchange rates between specific currencies are nearly identical at any given time in the different markets around the world. For example, the price of a dollar in terms of the euro is the same in New York, Frankfurt, Tokyo, London, Zurich, Istanbul, and other financial centers. This equality is ensured by **arbitrageurs**—dealers who take advantage of any temporary difference in exchange rates between markets by buying low and selling high. Their actions help to equalize exchange rates across markets. For example, if one euro costs $1.09 in New York and $1.10 in Frankfurt, an arbitrageur could buy, say, $10,000,000 worth of euros in New York and at the same time sell them in Frankfurt for $10,091,743, thereby earning $91,743 minus the transaction costs of executing the trades. Because exchange rate differences tend to be very small and because of transaction costs, an arbitrageur has to trade huge amounts to make enough profit to survive.

Arbitrageur A person who takes advantage of temporary geographic differences in the exchange rate by simultaneously purchasing a currency in one market and selling it in another market

Because an arbitrageur buys and sells simultaneously, relatively little risk is involved. In our example, the arbitrageur increased the demand for euros in

New York and increased the supply of euros in Frankfurt. Therefore, the actions of arbitrageurs increase the dollar price of euros in New York and decrease it in Frankfurt, thereby eliminating the differential. Even a tiny difference in exchange rates across markets will prompt arbitrageurs to act, and this action will quickly eliminate discrepancies in exchange rates across markets. Exchange rates may still change because of market forces, but they tend to change in all markets simultaneously.

Speculator A person who buys or sells foreign exchange in hopes of profiting from fluctuations in the exchange rate over time

The demand and supply of foreign exchange arises from many sources: from importers and exporters, investors in foreign assets, central banks, tourists, arbitrageurs, and speculators. **Speculators** buy or sell foreign exchange in hopes of profiting by trading the currency at a more favorable exchange rate later. By taking risks, speculators aim to profit from market fluctuations—they try to buy low and sell high. In contrast, arbitrageurs take little risk, since they *simultaneously* buy and sell a currency in different markets.

Purchasing Power Parity

Purchasing power parity (PPP) theory The theory that exchange rates between two countries will adjust in the long run to reflect price level differences between the countries

As long as trade across borders is unrestricted and as long as exchange rates are allowed to adjust freely, the **purchasing power parity theory** predicts that the exchange rate between two currencies will adjust in the long run to reflect price-level differences between the two currency regions. *A given basket of internationally traded goods should therefore sell for similar amounts around the world (except for differences reflecting transportation costs and the like).* Suppose a basket of internationally traded commodities that sells for $11,000 in the United States sells for 10,000 euro in Euroland. According to the purchasing power parity theory, the equilibrium exchange rate between the dollar and the euro should be $1.10. If this were not the case—if the exchange rate were, say, $1.00 per euro—then the basket of goods could be purchased in Euroland for 10,000 euro and sold in the United States for $11,000. The $11,000 could then be exchanged for 11,000 euro, yielding a profit of 1,000 euro (minus any transaction costs). Selling dollars and buying euros drives up the dollar price of euros.

The purchasing power parity theory is more of a long-run predictor than a day-to-day predictor of the relationship between changes in the price level and the exchange rate. For example, a country's currency generally appreciates when its inflation rate is lower than the rest of the world's and depreciates when its inflation rate is higher. Likewise, a country's currency generally appreciates when its real interest rates are higher than the rest of the world, since foreigners are more willing to buy and hold investments denominated in that currency. As a case in point, the dollar appreciated during the first half of the 1980s, when real U.S. interest rates were relatively high, and depreciated in the early 1990s, when real U.S. interest rates were relatively low.

Because of trade barriers, central bank intervention in exchange markets, and the fact that many products are not traded or are not comparable across countries, the purchasing power parity theory usually does not explain exchange rates at a particular point in time. For example, if you went shopping in Zurich, you would soon notice that one dollar's worth of Swiss francs buys less than that dollar will buy in the United States. The following case study considers the theory in light of the price of Big Macs around the globe.

The Big Mac Price Index

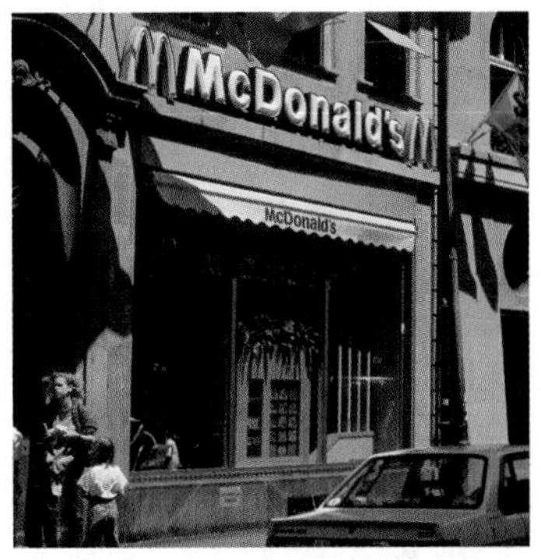

As you have already learned, the purchasing power parity (PPP) theory says that, in the long run, the exchange rate between two currencies should move toward the rate that equalizes the prices, in each country, of an identical basket of internationally traded goods. A lighthearted test of the theory has been developed by the *Economist* magazine, which each year compares prices across countries of a "market basket" consisting simply of one McDonald's Big Mac—a product that, although not internationally traded, is made using the same recipe in more than 100 countries. The *Economist* begins with the price of a Big Mac in the local currency, then converts that price into dollars based on the actual exchange rate prevailing at the time. A comparison of the dollar price of Big Macs across countries offers a crude test of the PPP theory, which predicts that these prices should move toward equality in the long run.

Exhibit 5 lists the dollar price of a Big Mac on March 30, 1999, in each of 31 countries plus an average for the 11 countries in Euroland. By comparing the price of a Big Mac in the United States with prices in other countries, we can derive a crude measure of whether particular currencies are undervalued or overvalued relative to the dollar. For example, because the price of a Big Mac in Switzerland, at \$3.97, was 51 percent higher than the U.S. price of \$2.43, the Swiss franc seemed overvalued by 63 percent compared to the dollar. The same approach suggests that the Danish krona was 47 percent overvalued, the Israeli shekel 42 percent overvalued, and the British pound 26 percent overvalued. The cheapest Big Mac was in Malaysia, where recent devaluations because of the "Asian contagion" cut the price to \$1.19, or 51 percent below the U.S. level.

Big Mac prices around the world have been converging in recent years. In 1995 the price of a Big Mac in Switzerland was tops in the world, 124 percent above the U.S. price. By 1999, the Swiss price was still tops but only 63 percent above the U.S. price. At the bottom end, the lowest price in 1995 was 55 percent below the U.S. price. By 1999 the lowest price was only 51 percent below the U.S. price. Finally, in 1995 the price of a Big Mac in Japan was double the U.S. price. In 1999, the Japanese price was about the same as the U.S. price. So prices around the world have converged since 1995 in a way consistent with the PPP theory.

Still, prices in 1999 ranged from 63 percent above to 51 percent below the U.S. price. Some may view this misalignment as a rejection of the PPP theory, but that theory relates only to traded goods. The Big Mac is not traded internationally. A large share of the total cost of a Big Mac is rent, which varies substantially across countries. Local prices may also be distorted by taxes and trade barriers, such as a tariff on beef. Furthermore, prices for similar goods vary across the United States even though we all use dollars here. For example, housing prices are higher in the Northeast and the West Coast than in the Midwest and the South. Still, the Big Mac index offers a crude test of the PPP theory.

CaseStudy

Other Times, Other Places

The *Economist* has published a focus article titled "Ten Years of the Big Mac Index." It is available at http://www.economist.com/editorial/freeforall/focus/bigmac_webonly.html. From there you can also access the latest edition of the index. Which currencies have had the largest changes in value? Which currencies went from being overvalued to undervalued between 1989 and 1998? Compare the index numbers among countries that are adopting the new euro as their currency. How close are they to one another?

EXHIBIT 5

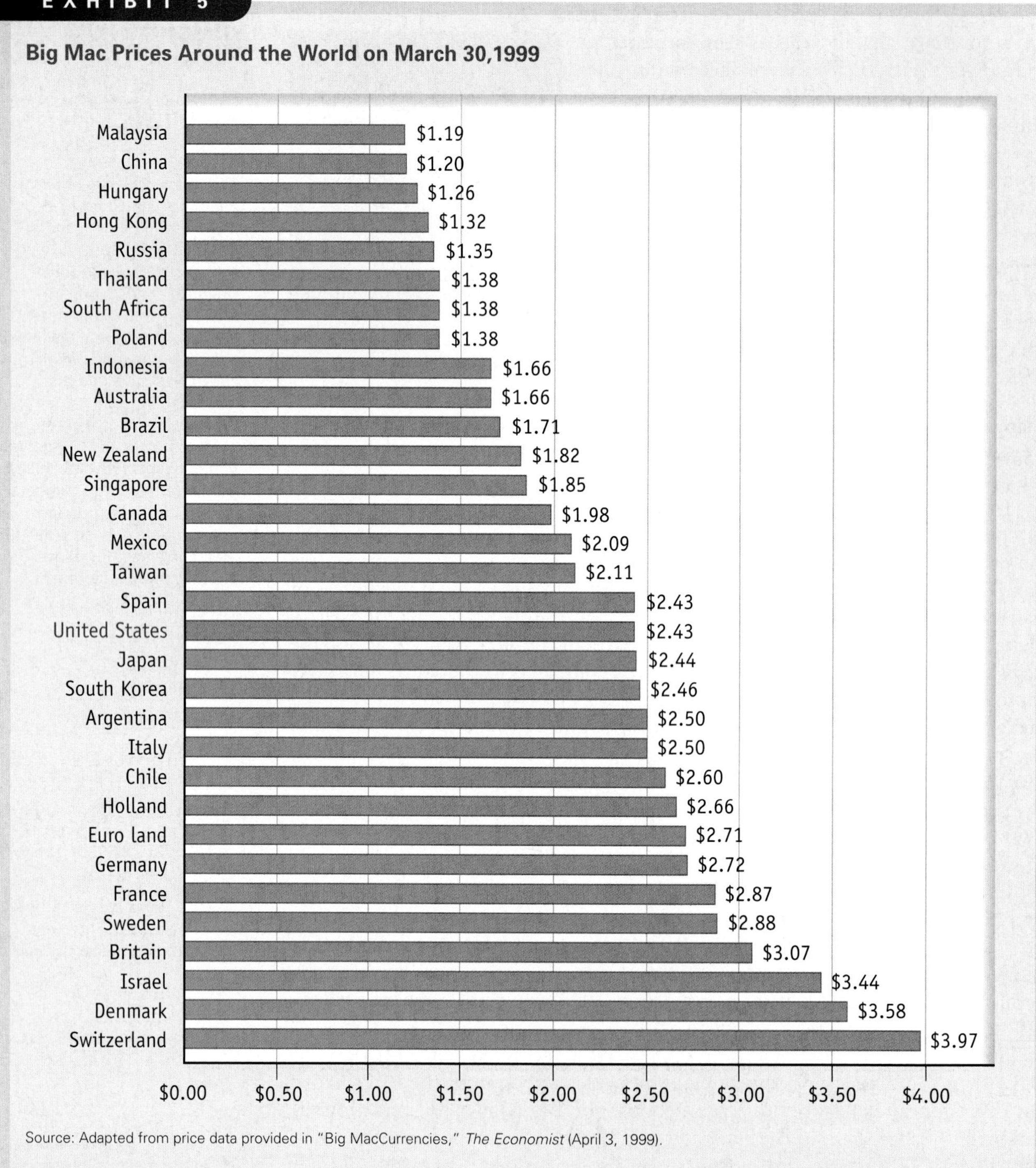

Source: Adapted from price data provided in "Big MacCurrencies," *The Economist* (April 3, 1999).

Sources: "Big MacCurrencies," *Economist* (3 April 1999); "Big MacCurrencies," *Economist* (15 April 1995); and Peter Liu and Paul Burkett, "Instability in Short-Run Adjustments to Purchasing Power Parity: Results for Selected Latin American Countries," *Applied Economics* (October 1995): 973–83.

Flexible Exchange Rates

For the most part, we have been discussing a system of **flexible exchange rates,** in which each exchange rate is determined by the forces of supply and demand. Flexible, or *floating,* exchange rates adjust continually to the myriad forces that buffet the foreign exchange market. Consider how the exchange rate is linked to the balance of payments accounts. Debit entries in the current and capital accounts increase the demand for foreign exchange, resulting in a depreciation of the dollar. Credit entries in these accounts increase the supply of foreign exchange, resulting in an appreciation of the dollar.

Flexible exchange rates Rates determined by the forces of supply and demand without government intervention

Fixed Exchange Rates

When exchange rates are flexible, government officials usually have little direct role in foreign exchange markets. But if government officials try to set exchange rates, active and ongoing central bank intervention is necessary to establish and maintain these **fixed exchange rates.** Suppose the European Central Bank selects what it thinks is an appropriate rate of exchange between the dollar and the euro. It attempts to *fix,* or to "peg," the exchange rate within a narrow band around the particular value selected. If the value of the euro threatens to drop below the minimum acceptable exchange rate, monetary authorities will sell dollars and buy euros in foreign exchange markets. This increased demand for the euro will keep its value up relative to the dollar. Conversely, if the value of the euro threatens to climb above the maximum acceptable exchange rate, monetary authorities will sell euros and buy dollars, thereby keeping the dollar price of the euro down. Through such intervention in the foreign exchange market, monetary authorities can stabilize the exchange rate, keeping it within the specified band.

Fixed exchange rates Rates pegged within a narrow range of values by central banks' ongoing purchases and sales of currencies

If monetary officials must keep selling foreign exchange to maintain the pegged rate, they risk running out of foreign exchange reserves. When this threat occurs, the government has several options for eliminating the exchange rate disequilibrium. First, the pegged exchange rate can be increased, which is a **devaluation** of the domestic currency. (A decrease in the pegged exchange rate is called a **revaluation.**) Second, the government can attempt to reduce the domestic demand for foreign exchange directly by imposing restrictions on imports or on capital outflows. China and many other developing countries do this. Third, the government can adopt contractionary fiscal or monetary policies to reduce the country's income level, increase interest rates, or reduce inflation relative to that of the country's trading partners, thereby indirectly decreasing the demand for foreign exchange. Several Asian economies, such as Korea and Indonesia, pursued such policies to stabilize their currencies in 1998. Finally, the government can allow the disequilibrium to persist and ration the available foreign currency through some form of foreign exchange control.

Currency devaluation An increase in the official pegged price of foreign exchange in terms of the domestic currency

Currency revaluation A reduction in the official pegged price of foreign exchange in terms of the domestic currency

We have now concluded our introduction to international finance in theory. Let's examine how international finance works in practice.

DEVELOPMENT OF THE INTERNATIONAL MONETARY SYSTEM

From 1879 to 1914, the international financial system operated under a **gold standard,** whereby the major currencies were convertible into gold at a fixed

Gold standard An arrangement whereby the currencies of most countries are convertible into gold at a fixed rate

rate. For example, the U.S. dollar could be redeemed at the U.S. Treasury for one-twentieth of an ounce of gold. The British pound could be redeemed at the British Exchequer, or treasury, for one-fourth of an ounce of gold. Since each pound could buy five times as much gold as each dollar, one pound exchanged for $5.

The gold standard provided a predictable exchange rate, one that did not vary as long as currencies could be redeemed for gold at the announced rate. But the money supply in each country was determined in part by the flow of gold between countries, so each country's monetary policy was influenced by the supply of gold. A balance-of-payments deficit resulted in a loss of gold, which theoretically caused a country's money supply to drop. A balance-of-payments surplus resulted in an increase in gold, which theoretically caused a country's money supply to rise. The supply of money throughout the world also depended to some extent on the vagaries of gold discoveries. When gold production was so slow that the money supply did not keep pace with the growth in economic activity, the result was a drop in the price level, or *deflation*. When gold production grew so much that the growth of the money supply exceeded the growth in economic activity, the result was a rise in the price level, or *inflation*. For example, gold discoveries in Alaska and South Africa in the late 1890s expanded the U.S. money supply, leading to inflation.

The Bretton Woods Agreement

During World War I, many countries could no longer convert their currencies into gold, and the gold standard eventually collapsed, disrupting international trade during the 1920s and 1930s. Once an Allied victory in World War II appeared certain, the Allies met in Bretton Woods, New Hampshire, in July of 1944, to formulate a new international monetary system. Because the United States was not ravaged by World War II and had a strong economy, the dollar was selected as the key reserve currency in the new international monetary system. All exchange rates were fixed in terms of the dollar, and the United States, which held most of the world's gold reserves, stood ready to convert foreign holdings of dollars into gold at a rate of $35 per ounce. Even though exchange rates were fixed by the Bretton Woods accord, *other* countries could adjust *their* exchange rates relative to the U.S. dollar if they found a fundamental disequilibrium in their balance of payments—that is, if a country faced a large and persistent deficit or surplus.

International Monetary Fund (IMF) An international organization that establishes rules for maintaining the international monetary system and makes loans to countries with temporary balance of payments problems

The Bretton Woods agreement also created the **International Monetary Fund (IMF)** to set rules for maintaining the international monetary system and to make loans to countries with temporary balance of payments problems. IMF loans to Russia, to Brazil, and to struggling Asian economies, such as Indonesia and South Korea, have been in the news lately. The IMF, which today has more than 150 member countries, also standardized financial reporting for international trade and finance.

Demise of the Bretton Woods System

During the latter part of the 1960s, inflation began heating up in the United States, and the higher U.S. prices meant that those exchanging foreign currencies for dollars at the official exchange rates found these dollars bought less in U.S. goods and services. Because of U.S. inflation, the dollar had become *over-*

valued at the official exchange rate, meaning that the gold value of the dollar exceeded the exchange value of the dollar. With the dollar overvalued, foreigners redeemed more dollars for gold. To stop this outflow of gold, something had to give. On August 15, 1971, President Richard Nixon closed the "gold window," refusing to exchange gold for dollars. In December 1971, the 10 richest countries of the world met in Washington and devalued the dollar by 8 percent. The hope at the time was that this devaluation would put the dollar on firmer footing and would save the "dollar standard." With prices rising at different rates around the world, however, an international monetary system based on fixed exchange rates was doomed.

In 1971, U.S. merchandise imports exceeded merchandise exports for the first time since World War II. When the trade deficit tripled in 1972, it became clear that the dollar was still overvalued. In early 1973, the dollar was devalued another 10 percent, but this did not quiet foreign exchange markets. The dollar, for three decades the anchor of the international monetary system, suddenly looked vulnerable, and speculators began betting the dollar would fall even more. Dollars were exchanged for German marks because the mark appeared to be the most stable currency. Monetary officials at the Bundesbank, Germany's central bank, exchanged marks for dollars in an attempt to defend the official exchange rate and to prevent an appreciation of the mark. Why didn't Germany want the mark to appreciate? Appreciation of the mark would make German goods more expensive abroad and foreign goods cheaper in Germany, thereby reducing German exports and increasing German imports. This would reduce German output and employment. But after selling $10 billion worth of marks, the German central bank gave up defending the dollar. As soon as the value of the dollar was allowed to float against the mark, the Bretton Woods system, already on shaky ground, collapsed.

The Current System: Managed Float

The Bretton Woods system has been replaced by a **managed float system,** which combines features of a freely floating exchange rate with sporadic intervention by central banks as a way of moderating exchange rate fluctuations among the world's major currencies. Most smaller countries, particularly developing countries, peg their currencies to one of the major currencies (such as the U.S. dollar) or to a "basket" of major currencies. What's more, in developing countries, private international borrowing and lending are severely restricted; governments may allow residents to purchase foreign exchange only for certain purposes. In some countries, different exchange rates apply to different categories of transactions.

Managed float system An exchange rate system that combines features of freely floating rates with intervention by central banks

The exchange rate between the Japanese yen and the U.S. dollar has been relatively unstable, particularly because of international speculation about official efforts to stabilize that exchange rate. Major criticisms of flexible exchange rates are that (1) they are inflationary, since they free monetary authorities to pursue expansionary policies, and (2) they have often been volatile, especially since the late 1970s. This volatility creates uncertainty and risk for importers and exporters, increasing the transaction costs of international trade and thus reducing its volume. Furthermore, exchange rate volatility can lead to wrenching changes in the competitiveness of a country's export sector and of those domestic producers who must compete with imports. These changes in competitiveness cause swings in employment, resulting in louder calls for import restrictions.

Policy makers are always on the lookout for an international monetary system that will perform better than the current managed float system, with its fluctuating currency values. *Their ideal is a system that will foster international trade, lower inflation, and promote a more stable world economy.* International finance ministers have acknowledged that the world must find an international standard and establish greater exchange rate stability.

The wild swings in exchange rates that sometimes occur with flexible exchange rates have caused policy makers to intervene to reduce undesirable fluctuations, as discussed in the following case study about financial troubles in Asia.

CaseStudy

Other Times, Other Places

The Institute for International Economics Policy Brief, "The Depressing News from Asia" at http://www.iie.com/NEWSLETR/news98-5.htm, predicts the impact of the Asian financial crisis on other countries. Notice how it uses various scenarios involving different potential changes in key variables. How is the crisis expected to affect industrialized economies, and the United States in particular? Other economists' views and analyses were published in the Summer 1998 edition of the Brookings Institution magazine accessible through http://www.brook.edu/pub/review/oldtoc.htm.

The Asian Contagion

It started in Thailand in early 1997, when a booming economy ran into trouble because of a decline in exports and over-lending in the property sector. Speculators began betting that the Thai currency, the baht, was in for a fall. The Thai central bank attempted to defend the baht's value, which at the time was tied to the U.S. dollar, by buying baht and selling foreign reserves. As the central bank's foreign reserves dwindled, the government decided in July 1997 to let the baht float. It immediately went into free-fall, losing 40 percent of its value against the dollar in a matter of weeks. With the baht worth so much less, Thai businesses and the government had difficulty paying foreign loans, most of which were denominated in dollars.

The crisis prompted a $17-billion bailout supervised by the International Monetary Fund (IMF) aimed at helping Thailand pay back some foreign debts. But problems in Thailand deepened, as outside credit agencies continued to downgrade Thai debt. Trouble soon spread to neighboring Indonesia, Malaysia, South Korea, Hong Kong, Singapore, and even mighty Japan, as the so-called Asian Contagion ripped through the region. South Korea and Indonesia were forced to seek IMF assistance; Indonesia was promised $40 billion in loans and South Korea, $58 billion, the most costly rescue package in history. In exchange for the aid, both countries agreed to cut government spending and open up their markets to foreign goods and foreign investors.

In Japan, where the economy had been struggling since 1990, matters worsened. In November 1997, four large financial institutions went bankrupt, the yen suffered its biggest drop against the dollar in years, and the stock market continued its eight-year slide. In June 1998, Japanese officials confirmed that national output had declined two quarters in a row and thus the country was officially in recession. For the full fiscal year, Japan's GDP declined, the first officially acknowledged annual drop since the oil shocks of the mid-1970s.

A big problem overhanging the Japanese economy was a trillion dollars worth of bad debts in the banking system. Banks had extended real estate loans during the booming 1980s. But when property values crashed, the loans could not be repaid, so the banks were in big trouble. Japan, the second-largest economy in the world (after the United States), is by far the largest economy in Asia. A weakened Japan threatened the fragile economies of Asia as they tried to recover from financial chaos. A weakened economy meant Japan would buy less from its Asian neighbors, and a weakened yen meant Japanese exports would be cheaper on world markets, thus competing with exports from elsewhere in Asia.

Faced with growing problems in Asia, the U.S. government joined forces with the Japanese government on June 17, 1998 to intervene in currency markets and spent $2 billion buying yen. In return for help from the United States, Japan agreed to allow more companies to fail by abandoning the system whereby the government forced stronger companies to bail out weaker ones.

By increasing the demand for yen, the U.S. intervention reversed the slide in the yen's value. In one day the yen-per-dollar exchange rate appreciated from 143.3 yen to 136.6, or by 4.7 percent. This was the first U.S. intervention in world currency markets in nearly three years. As the yen appreciated against the dollar, other currencies in Asia also stabilized. By the end of April 1999, the yen had appreciated to 118 yen to the dollar, and Asia was showing preliminary signs of recovery.

Sources: David Wessel, "Wealthy Nations Are Trying to Save Japan from Itself," *Wall Street Journal* (18 June 1998); "Stocks Stumble Across Asia as Yen Hits Lowest Since '90," *Wall Street Journal* (11 June 1998); "Asia's Symptoms," *Economist* (13 June 1998): 14; "Will Tokyo Finally Clean House?" *Economist* (27 June 1998): 71–72; and Fareed Zakaria, "Will Asia Turn Against the West?" *New York Times* (10 July 1998).

CONCLUSION

At one time the United States was largely self-sufficient. A technological lead over the rest of the world, an abundance of natural resources, a well-trained work force, a modern and extensive capital stock, and a currency as good as gold made the United States the envy of the world, with an economy that produced 40 percent of the world's output in the 1950s.

The situation has changed. The United States is now very much a part of the world economy, not only as the largest exporter but also as the largest importer. Although the dollar remains the unit of transaction in many international settlements—OPEC, for example, still states oil prices in dollars—the wild gyrations of exchange rates have made those involved in international finance wary of putting all their eggs in one basket. The euro could replace the dollar as the currency of choice on world markets.

The international monetary system is now going through a difficult adjustment period as it continues to grope for a new source of stability nearly three decades after the collapse of the Bretton Woods agreement.

SUMMARY

1. The balance of payments reflects all economic transactions across national borders. The current account measures the flows of (1) merchandise; (2) services, including investment income, military transactions, and tourism; and (3) unilateral transfers, or public and private transfer payments to foreign residents. The capital account measures international flows involving purchases or sales of financial and real assets.

2. Currencies support the flow of goods and services across international borders. The interaction of the supply and demand for foreign exchange determines the equilibrium exchange rate.

3. Under a system of floating exchange rates, the value of the dollar relative to foreign exchange varies over time. An increase in the demand for foreign exchange or a reduction in its supply, other things constant, will cause an increase in the value of foreign exchange relative to the dollar, which is a depreciation of the dollar. Conversely, a reduction in the demand for foreign exchange or an increase in its supply will cause a decrease in the value of foreign exchange relative to the dollar, which is an appreciation of the dollar.

4. Under a system of fixed exchange rates, monetary authorities usually try to stabilize the exchange rate, keeping it between a specified ceiling and floor.

5. For much of this century, the international monetary system was based on fixed exchange rates. A managed float system has been in effect for the major currencies since the demise of the Bretton Woods system in the early 1970s. Although central banks have often tried to stabilize exchange rates, recent swings in exchange rates have troubled policy maker.

QUESTIONS FOR REVIEW

1. *(Balance of Payments)* Suppose the United States ran a balance on goods and services surplus by exporting goods and services while importing nothing.
   a. How would such a surplus be offset elsewhere in the balance-of-payments accounts?
   b. If the level of U.S. production does not depend on the balance on goods and services, how would running this surplus affect our *current* standard of living?
   c. What is the relationship between total debits and total credits in the goods and services balance?
   d. When all international economic transactions are considered, what must be true about the sum of debits and credits?
   e. What is the role of the statistical discrepancy account?

2. *(Foreign Exchange)* What is the difference between a depreciation of the dollar and a devaluation of the dollar?

3. *(Purchasing Power Parity)* According to the theory of purchasing power parity, what will happen to the value of the dollar (against foreign currencies) if the U.S. price level doubles and price levels in other countries remain constant? Why is the theory more suitable to analyzing events in the long run?

4. *(Case**Study**: The Big Mac Index)* The Big Mac Index computed by the *Economist* has found the U.S. dollar to be undervalued against some other major currencies, which seems to call for a rejection of the purchasing power parity theory. Explain why this index may not be a valid test of the theory.

5. *(The Current System: Managed Float)* What is a managed float? What are the disadvantages of freely floating exchange rates that led countries to the managed float system?

6. *(Merchandise Trade Balance)* Explain why U.S. recessions (which are not at the same time world recessions) tend to reduce the U.S. trade deficit.

PROBLEMS AND EXERCISES

7. *(Balance of Payments)* The following are hypothetical data for the U.S. balance of payments. Use the data to calculate each of the following:
   a. Merchandise trade balance
   b. Balance on goods and services
   c. Balance on current account
   d. Capital account balance
   e. Official reserve transactions account balance
   f. Statistical discrepancy

	Billions of Dollars
Merchandise exports	350.0
Merchandise imports	-425.0
Service exports	170.0
Service imports	-145.0
Net unilateral transfers	-21.5
Outflow of U.S. capital	-45.0
Inflow of foreign capital	70.0

Decrease in U.S. official assets abroad	2.5
Increase in foreign official assets in U.S.	35.0

8. *(Balance of Payments)* Explain where in the U.S. balance of payments an entry would be made for each of the following:
   a. A Hong Kong financier buys some U.S. corporate stock
   b. A U.S. tourist in Paris buys some perfume to take home
   c. A Japanese company sells machinery to a pineapple company in Hawaii
   d. U.S. farmers make a gift of food to starving children in Ethiopia
   e. The U.S. Treasury sells a thirty-year bond to a Saudi Arabian prince
   f. A U.S. tourist flies to France on Air France
   g. A U.S. company sells insurance to a foreign firm

9. *(Determining the Exchange Rate)* Use these data to answer the following questions about the market for British pounds:

Price of pounds (in $)	Quantity Demanded (of pounds)	Quantity Supplied (of pounds)
$4.00	50	100
3.00	75	75
2.00	100	50

   a. Draw the supply and demand curves for pounds, and determine the equilibrium exchange rate (dollars per pound).
   b. Suppose that the supply of pounds doubles. Draw the new supply curve.
   c. What is the new equilibrium exchange rate?
   d. Has the dollar appreciated or depreciated?
   e. What happens to U.S. imports of British goods?

EXPERIENTIAL EXERCISES

10. *(Foreign Exchange Rates and Markets)* Trade among European nations will be bolstered by the introduction of a common European currency called the euro. Not surprisingly, there is a special Web page devoted to the introduction of the euro—EmuNet at http://www.euro-emu.co.uk/. Go to the EmuNet home page to review the latest developments in the introduction of the euro.

11. *(Case**Study:** The Asian Contagion)* Yahoo, an online search engine, maintains a page devoted to the Asian financial crisis. Visit this page at http://headlines.yahoo.com/Full_Coverage/World/Asian_Economic_Woes/ and determine whether the crisis seems to be easing or getting worse.

12. *(Wall Street Journal)* The latest data on exchange rates appear in the Currency Trading column in the daily *Wall Street Journal*. You can find it in the Money & Investing section. Try tracking a particular foreign currency over the course of several weeks. Has the dollar been appreciating or depreciating relative to that currency? Try to explain why it has been appreciating or depreciating.

CHAPTER

34 *Developing and Transitional Economies*

People around the world face the day under very different circumstances. Many Americans rise from a comfortable bed in a nice home, select the day's clothing from a wardrobe, choose from a variety of breakfast foods, and drive to school or to work in one of the family's personal automobiles. But most of the world's nearly six billion people have little housing, clothing, or food. They own no automobile, and many have no formal job. Their health is poor, as is their education. Many cannot read or write. An estimated one billion people need glasses but can't afford them. Why are some countries so poor while others are so rich? What determines the wealth of nations?

In this chapter, we sort out rich nations from poor ones and try to explain the difference. Although there is no widely accepted theory of economic

Visit the McEachern Interactive Study Center for this chapter at *http://mcisc.swcollege.com*

development, one approach that seems to be gaining favor lately is the introduction of market forces, especially in formerly socialist countries. Around the world, the demise of central planning has been stunning and pervasive. We close the chapter with a discussion of these rich experiments—these works in progress. Topics discussed in this chapter include:

- Developing countries
- Obstacles to development
- Import substitution
- Export promotion
- Foreign aid
- Transitional economies
- Big bang versus gradualism
- Privatization

WORLDS APART

Differences in economic activity among countries are profound. For example, the United States, with its 270 million people, has a gross domestic product that exceeds the *combined* output of 2.7 billion people living in poor countries. The United States, with only 5 percent of the world's population, produces more than does the poorer half of the world's population.

Countries are classified in a variety of ways based on their level of economic development. The yardstick most often used to compare living standards across nations is *output per capita*. The World Bank, an economic development institution affiliated with the United Nations, attempts to estimate comparable output per capita figures and then uses these figures to classify economies. The World Bank divides countries into three major groups based on their per capita output: low-income economies, middle-income economies, and high-income economies.

Developing and Industrial Economies

The low- and middle-income economies are usually referred to as **developing countries**, and the high-income economies are usually referred to as **industrial market countries** (though some of the high-income countries have incomes based primarily on oil and are viewed as still developing). A few primarily socialist countries, such as Cuba, North Korea, and Libya, do not report data on their economic status and consequently are classified by the World Bank as *nonreporting countries*.

Developing countries Nations typified by high rates of illiteracy, high unemployment, high fertility rates, and exports of primary products

Industrial market countries Economically advanced capitalist countries of Western Europe, North America, Australia, New Zealand, and Japan; also known as developed countries

Developing countries usually have a high rate of illiteracy, high unemployment, extensive underemployment, rapid population growth, and exports consisting primarily of agricultural products and raw materials. On average, about two-thirds of the labor force in developing countries is in agriculture. Because farming methods are relatively primitive, farm productivity is low and most people barely subsist. Industrial market countries or *developed countries* are the economically advanced capitalist countries of Western Europe, North America, Australia, New Zealand, and Japan. They were the first to experience long-term economic growth during the 19th century.

The measure of output used by the World Bank to classify countries is gross national product (GNP) per capita. GNP measures the market value of all goods and services produced by resources supplied by the countries' residents and firms, regardless of the location of the resource. For example, U.S. GNP includes profit earned by a Ford factory in Great Britain but excludes profits earned by a Toyota factory in the United States.

Data on total population, GNP per capita, and growth in private consumption per capita are summarized in Exhibit 1 for all reporting countries with a population of 1 million or more. GNP per capita figures have been adjusted to reflect the actual purchasing power of the native currency in its respective economy. The idea is to measure the actual GNP per capita for each country. Low-income countries made up about one-third of the 5.8 billion people on Earth in 1997, middle-income countries accounted for half, and high-income countries accounted for only one-sixth.

India and China are two population giants shown separately in Exhibit 1. Together they account for more than one-third of the world's population, but produce only about one-twentieth of the world's output. India's GNP per capita of $1,650 in 1997 was slightly above the average of $1,400 for all low-income economies. India's 1.6 percent average growth rate in private consumption per capita between 1980 and 1996 was above the 1.0 percent average for all low-income economies. China's GNP per capita of $3,570 was below the average of $4,550 for all middle-income economies, but its growth rate in private consumption exceeded that of all middle-income economies. High-income economies averaged $22,770 per capita in 1997, or about 16 times the average for low-income economies—quite a difference.

Exhibit 2 presents GNP per capita in 1997 for selected countries, arranged from top to bottom in descending order. Again, figures have been adjusted by the United Nations to reflect the actual purchasing power of the native currency in its respective economy. The United States, the top-ranked country, had a GNP per capita that was 7.5 times that of Paraguay. But GNP per capita in Paraguay, in turn, was 7.5 times that of Sierra Leone, the poorest country in the world. Residents of Paraguay likely feel poor relative to industrialized nations, but they appear well off compared to the poorest developing nations. Per capita GNP in the United States was 56 times greater than in Sierra Leone. Thus there is a tremendous range in productive performance around the world.

Health and Nutrition

Differences in stages of development among countries are reflected in a number of ways besides per capita income levels. For example, many people in

EXHIBIT 1

Population, GNP per Capita, and Annual Growth Rate in Private Consumption per Capita

Classification	Population, 1997 (millions)	GNP per Capita 1997 Dollars	Annual Growth Rate, in Private Consumption per Capita, 1980–1996 (percent)
1. Low-income economies	2,048	1,400	1.0
India	961	1,650	1.6
2. Middle-income economies	2,855	4,550	2.8
China	1,227	3,570	4.5
3. High-income economies	926	22,770	1.4

Source: Based on data presented by the World Bank in *World Development Report 1998/99* (New York: Oxford University Press, 1998), Tables 1 and 2. Data are for countries with populations of 1 million or more.

EXHIBIT 2

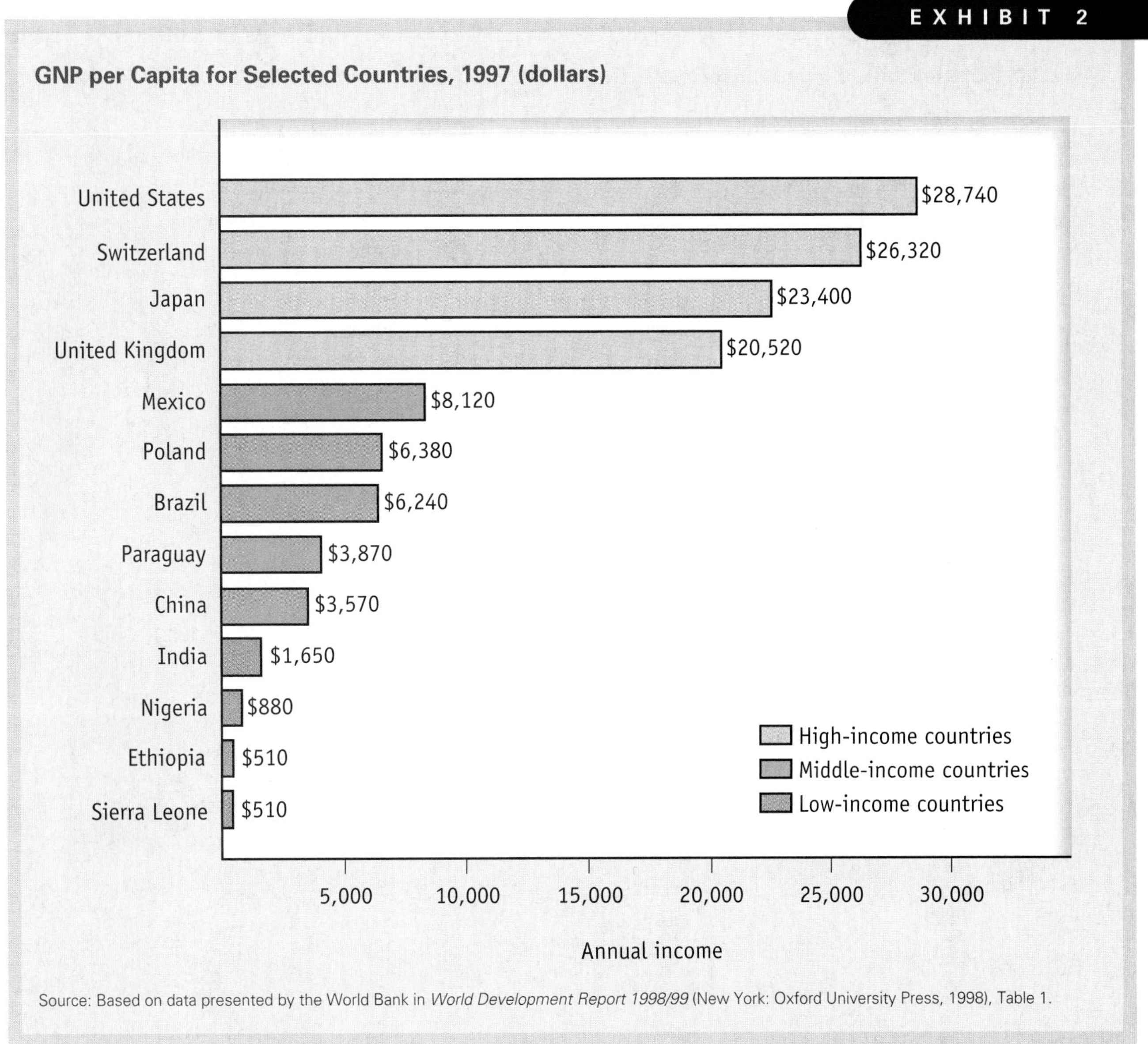

Source: Based on data presented by the World Bank in *World Development Report 1998/99* (New York: Oxford University Press, 1998), Table 1.

developing countries suffer from poor health as a result of malnutrition and disease. AIDS is devastating some developing countries, particularly those in central and east Africa. Life expectancy at birth in 1996 averaged 59 years in low-income economies, 68 years in middle-income economies, and 77 years in high-income economies. Average life expectancy ranged from 37 years in Sierra Leone to 80 years in Japan.

Infant Mortality. Health differences among countries are reflected in infant mortality rates. Mortality rates for selected countries are presented as Exhibit 3.

EXHIBIT 3

Mortality Rate up to Age 5 per 1,000 Live Births for Selected Countries: 1996

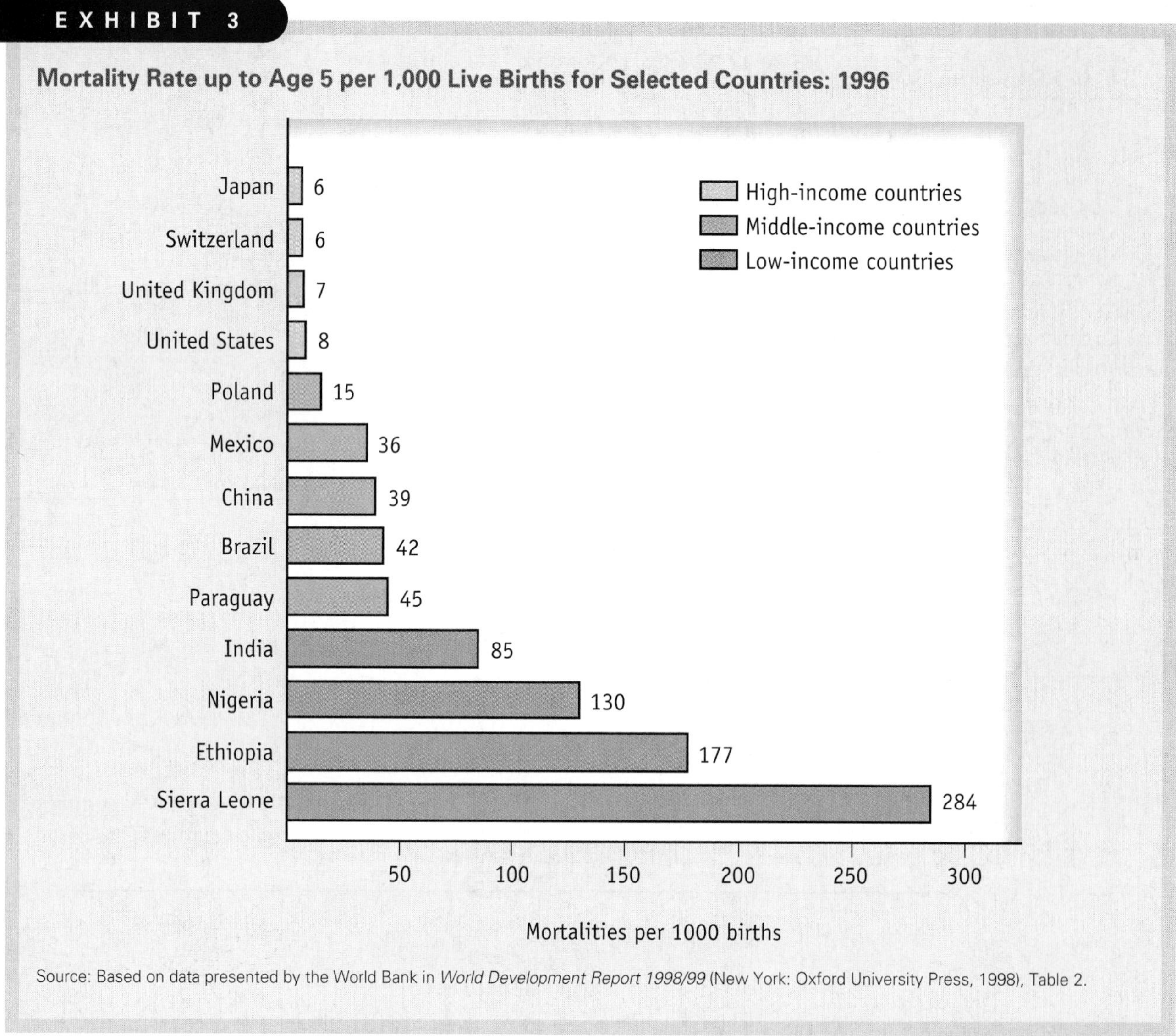

Source: Based on data presented by the World Bank in *World Development Report 1998/99* (New York: Oxford University Press, 1998), Table 2.

As might be expected, countries with the longest life expectancies also have the lowest infant mortality rates. Similarly, the countries with the shortest life expectancies have the highest infant mortality rates. The infant mortality rate in Sierra Leone is at least 35 times the rates in Japan, Switzerland, the United Kingdom, and the United States.

Malnutrition. Many people living in Africa, South Asia, and the Indian subcontinent often do not have enough food to maintain good nutrition. Those in the very poorest countries consume only half the calories of those in high-income countries. Even if an infant survives the first year, malnutrition can turn normal childhood diseases, such as measles, into life-threatening events. Malnutrition is a primary or contributing factor in more than half of all deaths among children under five in low-income countries. Diseases that are well controlled in the industrial countries—malaria, whooping cough, polio, dysentery, typhoid, and cholera—become epidemics in poor countries. Many of these diseases are water borne, because residents of urban areas in less-developed countries are often unable to obtain safe drinking water.

High Birth Rates

Developing countries are identified not only by their low incomes and high mortality rates but also by their high birth rates. This year, about 80 million of the 90 million people added to the world's population will be born in developing countries. In fact, the birth rate is one of the clearest ways of distinguishing between industrial and developing countries. Few developing countries have a total fertility rate per woman of less than 2.2 births, but no industrial country has a fertility rate above that level.

Exhibit 4 presents total fertility rates per woman for 1980 and 1996. Note that fertility rates for all groups declined between the two years. Note also that fertility rates are highest in the low-income economies and lowest in the high-income economies. The fertility rate dropped most in India, where it went from 5.0 in 1980 to 3.1 in 1996. Fertility rates dropped the least in high-income economies, where they were already relatively low in 1980.

Families tend to be larger in developing countries because children are viewed as a source of farm labor and as economic and social security as the parents age. Most developing countries have no pension or social security system for the aged. The higher infant mortality rates in poorer countries also engender higher birth rates, as parents strive to ensure a sufficiently large family.

Sub-Saharan African countries are the poorest in the world and have the fastest-growing populations. Because of high fertility rates in developing countries, children under 15 make up almost half their total population. In industrial countries, children make up only about a quarter of the population. Italy recently became the first country in history to have more people over the age of 60 than under the age of 20. Germany, Greece, and Spain will soon join Italy.[1]

EXHIBIT 4

Total Fertility Rates: Births per Woman

The total fertility rate is the number of children that would be born to a woman if she were to live to the end of her childbearing years and to bear children in accordance with current age-specific fertility rates.

Classification	1980	1996
1. Low-income economies	5.6	4.1
India	5.0	3.1
Sub-Saharan Africa	6.6	5.6
2. Middle-income economies	3.2	2.3
China	2.5	1.4
3. High-income economies	1.9	1.7

Source: Based on data presented by the World Bank in *World Development Report 1998/99* (New York: Oxford University Press, 1998), Table 7.

1 As reported in Michael Specter, "Population Implosion Worries a Graying Europe," *New York Times* (10 July 1998).

*Net***Bookmark**

Transition is a newsletter of the World Bank's Development Economic Research Group. You can find it online at http://www.worldbank.org/html/prddr/trans/WEB/trans.htm. The International Monetary Fund publishes "World Economic Outlook," an annual review of the world and national economies that gives special attention to economies in transition. The most recent report can be found at http://www.imf.org/external/pubind.htm.

In some developing countries, the population growth rate has exceeded the real GNP growth rate, so the standard of living as measured by per capita GNP has declined. Still, even in the poorest of countries, attitudes about family size are changing. According the United Nations, the birth rate during a typical woman's lifetime in a developing country has fallen since 1965 from six children to three children. Evidence from developing countries more generally indicates that when women have better employment opportunities outside the home, fertility rates decline. And as women become better educated, they tend to earn more and have fewer children.

Women in Developing Countries

Throughout the world, poverty is greater among women than men, particularly women who head households. The percentage of households headed by women varies from country to country, but exceeds 40 percent in some areas of the Caribbean and Africa. Because women often must work in the home as well as in the labor market, poverty can impose a special hardship on them. In many cultures, women's responsibilities include gathering firewood and carrying water, tasks that are especially burdensome if firewood is scarce and water is far from home.

Women in developing countries tend to be less educated than men. In the countries of sub-Saharan Africa and South Asia, for example, only half as many women as men complete high school. And in Indonesia, girls are six times more likely than boys to drop out of school before the fourth grade. Women have fewer employment opportunities and earn lower wages than men do. For example, Sudan's Muslim fundamentalist government bans women from working in public places after 5:00 P.M. In Algeria, Egypt, Jordan, Libya, and Saudi Arabia, women account for only about one-quarter of the labor force. Women are often on the fringes of the labor market, working long hours in agriculture. They also have less access to other resources, such as land, capital, and technology. Worse yet, according to social workers and press reports, during the recent economic crisis in Asia, some peasant girls were sold to traders who in turn sold them to brothels in places like Bangkok, Thailand.[2]

PRODUCTIVITY: KEY TO DEVELOPMENT

We have examined some symptoms of poverty in developing countries, but not why poor countries are poor. At the risk of appearing simplistic, we might say that poor countries are poor because they do not produce many goods and services. In this section, we will examine why some developing countries experience such low productivity.

Low Labor Productivity

Labor productivity, measured in terms of output per worker, is low in low-income countries. Why? Labor productivity depends on the quality of the labor and on the amount of capital, land, and other resources that combine with labor. For example, one certified public accountant with a computer and specialized

2 As reported in Nicholas D. Kristof, "Asian Crisis Deals Setbacks to Women," *New York Times* (11 June 1998). This story tells of a 15-year-old sold by her grandmother for $40.

software can sort out a company's finances more quickly and more accurately than can a thousand high-school–educated file clerks with pencils and paper.

One way a country raises its productivity is by investing more in human and physical capital. This investment must be financed by either domestic savings or foreign funds. Income per capita is often too low in developing countries to permit extensive investments to be financed with internal funds. In poor countries with unstable governments, the wealthy minority frequently invests in more stable foreign economies. Thus there are few domestic funds available for investment in either human or physical capital; without sufficient capital, workers are less productive.

Technology and Education

What exactly is the contribution of education to the process of economic development? Education makes people more receptive to new ideas and methods. Countries with the most advanced educational systems were also the first to develop. In this century, the leader in schooling and economic development has been the United States. In Latin America, Argentina was the most educationally advanced nation 100 years ago, and it is one of the most developed Latin American nations today. The growth of education in Japan during the 19th century contributed to a ready acceptance of technology and thus to Japan's remarkable economic growth in the 20th century.

If knowledge is insufficient, other resources may not be used efficiently. For example, a country may be endowed with fertile land, but farmers may lack knowledge of irrigation and fertilization techniques. Or farmers may not know how to rotate crops and avoid soil depletion. In low-income countries, about 60 percent of adults were illiterate in 1995, compared to less than 5 percent in high-income countries.

Child labor in developing countries reduces educational opportunities. In Pakistan, for example, the education system can accommodate only one-third of the country's school-age children. More than 10 million Pakistani children work full-time—half of whom are less than 10 years old.[3] Worldwide, more than 200 million children under 14 years of age work full-time.

Inefficient Use of Labor

Another feature of developing countries is that they use labor less efficiently than developed nations. Unemployment and underemployment reflect inefficient uses of labor. *Underemployment* occurs when skilled workers are employed in low-skill jobs or when people are working less than they would like—a worker seeking full-time employment may find only a part-time job. *Unemployment* occurs when those willing and able to work cannot find jobs.

Unemployment is measured primarily in urban areas, because in rural areas farm work is usually an outlet for labor even if many workers are underemployed there. The unemployment rate in developing nations on average is about 10 to 15 percent of the urban labor force. Unemployment among young workers—those aged 15 to 24—is typically twice that of older workers. In developing nations, about 30 percent of the combined urban and rural work forces is either unemployed or underemployed.

3 Pakistani children in the lowest castes become laborers almost as soon as they can walk. See Jonathan Silvers, "Child Labor in Pakistan," *Atlantic Monthly* (February 1996).

In some developing countries, the average farm is as small as two acres. Productivity is also low because few other inputs, such as capital and fertilizer, are used. Even where more land is available, the absence of capital limits the amount of land that can be farmed. *Although about two-thirds of the labor force in developing countries works in agriculture, only about one-third of GNP in these countries stems from agriculture.* In the United States, where farmers account for only 2.5 percent of the labor force, a farmer with modern equipment can farm hundreds of acres. In developing countries a farmer with a hand plow or an ox-drawn plow can farm maybe 10 to 20 acres. As you would expect, U.S. farmers, though one-fortieth of the workforce, grow enough to feed a nation and to lead the world in farm exports.

Low productivity obviously results in low income, but low income can, in turn, affect worker productivity. Low income means less saving and less saving means less investment in human and physical capital. Low income can also mean poor nutrition during the formative years, which can retard mental and physical development. These difficult beginnings may be aggravated by poor diet and insufficient health care in later life, making workers poorly suited for regular employment. Thus, *low income and low productivity may reinforce each other in a vicious cycle.* Poverty can result in less saving, less capital formation, an inadequate diet, and insufficient attention to health care—all of which can reduce a worker's productive ability.

Natural Resources

Some countries are richer than others because they are blessed with natural resources. The difference is most striking when we compare countries with oil reserves and those without. Some developing countries of the Middle East are classified as high-income economies because they are lucky enough to be sitting atop major oil reserves. But oil-rich countries are the exception. Many developing countries, such as Chad and Ethiopia, have little in the way of natural resources. Most developing countries without oil reserves were in trouble when oil prices rose. Oil had to be imported, and these imports drained the oil-poor countries of precious foreign exchange.

Financial Institutions

Another requirement for development is an adequate and trusted system of financial institutions. An important source of funds for investment is the savings of households and firms. People in developing countries often have little confidence in their currency because some governments finance a large fraction of public outlays by printing money. This practice results in high inflation and sometimes very high inflation, or hyperinflation, as occurred recently in Russia. High and unpredictable inflation discourages saving and hurts development.

Developing countries have special problems because banks are often not held in high regard. At the first sign of economic problems, many depositors withdraw their funds. Since banks cannot rely on a continuous supply of deposits, they cannot make loans for extended periods. Also governments often impose ceilings on the interest rates that lenders can charge, forcing lenders to ration credit among borrowers. If financial institutions fail to serve as intermediaries between borrowers and lenders, the resulting lack of funds for investment becomes an obstacle to growth.

Capital Infrastructure

Some development economists believe that the most important ingredient in economic development is the administrative competence of the government. Production and exchange rely on an infrastructure of communication and transportation networks provided by the public sector. Roads, bridges, airports, harbors, and other transportation facilities are vital to commercial activity. Reliable mail service, telephone communication, clean water, and electricity are also essential for advanced production techniques. Imagine how difficult it would be to run even a personal computer if the supply of electricity and phone service were continually interrupted, as is often the case in developing countries. Many developing countries have serious deficiencies in their infrastructures. And some of the poorest countries in Africa have been ravaged by internal strife. For example, Ethiopia, one of the poorest countries in the world, has been caught up in a war with the break-away province of Eritrea. Both sides have spent millions on jet fighters, even though neither has any qualified pilots to fly the new planes.

communication
transportation

Entrepreneurial Ability

An economy can have abundant supplies of land, labor, and capital, but without entrepreneurial ability, the other resources will not be combined efficiently to produce goods and services. Unless a country has a class of entrepreneurs who are able to bring together resources and take the risk of profit or loss, development may never begin. Many developing countries were once under colonial rule, a system of government that offered the local population little opportunity to develop entrepreneurial skills.

individual takes capital risk to sell goods or services for a profit.

Government Monopolies

Government officials often decide that local private-sector entrepreneurs are unable to generate the kind of economic growth the country needs. State enterprises are therefore created to do what government believes the free market cannot do. State-owned enterprises may have objectives other than producing goods efficiently—objectives that could include maximizing employment and providing jobs for friends and relatives of government officials, as discussed in the following case study.

CaseStudy

Other Times, Other Places

Is crony capitalism an example of market failure or government failure? "TRB From Washington: Super Markets," by Charles Lane in the *New Republic,* takes the latter view, citing Indonesia and Russia as examples. See http://www.thenewrepublic.com/magazines/tnr/archive/1198/110298/trb110298.html. What else does he blame for the financial crisis? What good does he think might follow from it?

Crony Capitalism in Indonesia—All in the Family

Indonesia is a country of more than 200 million people spread across some 13,000 islands in the Indian Ocean. The country is rich in natural resources, including oil, yet economic development has been hampered by bureaucratic red tape and corruption. At the center was President Suharto, who ruled the nation as a virtual dictator between 1965 and his forced resignation in 1998. Over the years, he conferred monopoly privileges on family and friends.

Based on the strength of government-granted monopolies, President Suharto and his six children were able to build an economic empire valued at more than $4 billion, spanning over 2,000 Indonesian companies. Because of government-imposed monopolies, the prices of products in Indonesia were higher than those prevailing on the world market. For example, friends and relatives held the exclusive rights to import steel, plastic, tin, cotton, industrial machinery, cement, and other key resources. In 1990 one of Suharto's sons and some business partners were awarded an exclusive license to import, buy, and sell cloves, a spice used in cooking and to flavor tobacco in Indonesian cigarettes. To finance the monopoly, the central Bank of Indonesia advanced the group $325 million in loans and credits, or half the Bank's annual budget for agricultural subsidies. At the time the son claimed, "We're doing it for the good of the farmers." The monopoly purchased cloves from farmers for less than the world price and sold the cloves to cigarette manufacturers for twice the world price. The monopoly was a hugely profitable.

These monopolies reduced competition, increased costs to consumers, and hindered the development of an export sector that could compete on the world market. In this environment, a combination of "crony capitalism" and nepotism, political connections become more important than ability or expertise; free enterprise was thereby discouraged. Businesses were better off developing political contacts than producing goods and services more efficiently.

By the time Suharto resigned in 1998, the Indonesian economy was in shambles. Economic output declined 12 percent in the first half of 1998. The government had taken over 70 percent of the nation's banks. The national currency, the rupiah, had fallen 80 percent against the dollar. And half the population was living below the poverty level. Some of this was caused, no doubt, by the economic malaise sweeping through Asia, but Indonesia was hit hardest because its economy had been distorted for so long.

Sources: Maggie Farley, "A Familiar Scent of Monopoly," *Los Angeles Times* (21 March 1998); Steven Erlanger, "Suharto's Cling to Power Undermines His Legacy," *New York Times* (22 May 1998); Peter Waldman, "Hand in Glove: How Suharto's Circle, Mining Firm Did So Well Together," *Wall Street Journal* (29 September 1998); and "The World's Working Rich," *Forbes* (6 July 1998): 198–199.

INTERNATIONAL TRADE AND DEVELOPMENT

Developing countries need to trade with developed countries in order to acquire the capital and technology that will increase labor productivity on the farm, in the factory, in the office, and in the home. To import capital and technology, developing countries must first acquire the funds, or foreign exchange, needed to pay for imports. Exports usually generate more than half of the annual flow of foreign exchange in developing countries. Foreign aid and private investment make up the rest.

Primary products, such as agricultural goods and other raw materials, make up the bulk of exports from developing countries, just as manufactured goods make up the bulk of exports from developed countries. Developing countries must export a large amount of raw materials in order to buy back the finished products made from these same materials. Another problem is that the prices of primary products, such as coffee, cocoa, sugar, and rubber, fluctuate more widely than do the prices of finished goods, because crop production fluctuates with the weather.

A third problem of developing countries has been their deteriorating trade position. In recent years, the prices of raw materials have fallen as demand has softened (in part because of the troubles in Asia) and as substitutes have been developed for products such as rubber. Since the prices of manufactured imported goods have not dropped as much, developing countries receive less money from exports than they spend on imports, resulting in trade deficits. To reduce these deficits, developing countries have tried to restrict imports. Because imported food often is critical to survival, developing countries are more likely to cut imports of capital goods—the very items needed to promote long-term growth and productivity. Thus many developing countries cannot afford the modern machinery that will help them become more productive. Developing countries must also confront industrial countries' trade restrictions, such as tariffs and quotas, which often discriminate against primary products. For example, the United States strictly limits sugar imports. *Developing countries' share of world trade has fallen since 1950.*

Import Substitution Versus Export Promotion

Economic development frequently involves a shift from the production of raw materials and agricultural products to manufacturing. If a country is fortunate, this transformation occurs gradually through natural market forces. Sometimes the shift is pushed along by government. Many developing countries, including Argentina and India, pursued a policy called **import substitution**, whereby the country manufactures products that until then had been imported. To insulate domestic producers from foreign competition, the government imposes tariffs and import quotas. This development strategy became popular for several reasons. First, demand already existed for these products, so the "what to produce" question was readily answered. Second, by reducing imports, the approach addressed the lack of foreign exchange so common among developing countries. Third, import substitution nurtured infant industries, providing them a protected market. Finally, import substitution was popular with those who supplied capital, labor, and other resources to the favored domestic industries.

Import substitution A development strategy that emphasizes domestic manufacturing of products that are currently imported

Like all protection measures, however, import substitution erases the gains from specialization and comparative advantage among countries. Often the developing country replaced relatively low-cost foreign goods with high-cost domestic goods. And domestic producers, insulated from foreign competition, usually fail to grow efficient. Even the balance-of-payments picture did not improve, because other countries often retaliated with their own trade restrictions.

Critics of the import-substitution approach claim that export promotion is a surer path to economic development. **Export promotion** is a development strategy that concentrates on producing for the export market. This approach begins with relatively simple products, such as textiles. As a developing country builds its technological and educational base—that is, as the developing economy learns by doing—producers can then export more complex products. Economists tend to favor export promotion over import substitution because the emphasis is on comparative advantage and trade expansion rather than trade restriction. Export promotion also forces producers to grow more efficient in order to compete

Export promotion A development strategy that concentrates on producing for the export market

on world markets. Recent research shows that global competition has a profound effect on domestic efficiency.[4] What's more, export promotion requires less government intervention in the market than does import substitution.

Export promotion has been the more successful development strategy, as reflected for example by the newly industrialized countries of East Asia, which in recent decades have grown much more quickly than import-substituting countries such as Argentina, India, and Peru. Since 1965 the four Asian newly industrialized economies raised their average real income from 20 percent of the high income countries' level to 70 percent. Most Latin American nations, which for decades had favored import substitution, are now pursuing free trade agreements with the United States. Even India is in the process of dismantling trade barriers, although the emphasis has been on importing high-technology capital goods. One slogan of Indian trade officials is "Microchips, yes! Potato chips, no!"

Migration and the Brain Drain

Migration plays an important role in the economies of developing countries. A major source of foreign exchange in some countries is the money sent home by migrants who find jobs in industrial countries. Thus migration provides a valuable safety valve for poor countries. But there is a downside. Often the best and the brightest professionals, such as doctors, nurses, and engineers, migrate to developed countries. Since human capital is such a key resource, this "brain drain" hurts the developing economy.

Trade Liberalization and Special Interests

Although most people would benefit from freer international trade, some would be worse off. Consequently, governments in some developing countries have difficulty pursuing policies conducive to development. Often the gains from economic development are widespread, but the beneficiaries, such as consumers, do not recognize their potential gains. On the other hand, the losers tend to be concentrated, such as producers in an industry that had been sheltered from foreign competition, and they know quite well the source of their losses. So the government often lacks the political backing to remove impediments to development, because the potential losers fight reforms that might harm their livelihood while the potential winners remain largely unaware of what's at stake. What's more, consumers have difficulty organizing even if they become aware of what's going on. A recent study by the World Bank suggests a strong link in Africa between governments that cater to special-interest groups and low rates of economic growth.

Nonetheless, many developing countries have been opening their borders to freer trade. People around the world have been exposed to information about the opportunities and goods available on world markets. So consumers want the goods and firms want the technology and capital that are available abroad. Both groups want government to ease trade restrictions. Studies by the World Bank and others have underscored the successes of countries that have adopted trade liberalization policies.

4 See Martin Baily and Hans Gersbach, "Efficiency in Manufacturing and the Need for Global Competition," in *Brookings Papers on Economic Activity: Microeconomics*, M. Baily, P. Reiss, and C. Winston, eds. (Washington D.C.: Brookings Institution, 1995): 307–347.

FOREIGN AID AND ECONOMIC DEVELOPMENT

We have already seen that because poor countries do not generate enough savings to fund an adequate level of investment, these countries often rely on foreign financing. Private international borrowing and lending are heavily restricted by the governments of developing countries. Governments may allow residents to purchase foreign exchange only for certain purposes. In some developing countries, different exchange rates apply to different categories of transactions. Thus the local currency is not easily convertible into other currencies. Some developing countries also require foreign investors to find a local partner who must be granted controlling interest. All these restrictions discourage foreign investment. In this section, we will look primarily at foreign aid and its link to economic development.

Foreign Aid

Foreign aid is any international transfer made on *concessional* (i.e., especially favorable) terms for the purposes of promoting economic development. Foreign aid includes grants, which need not be repaid, and loans extended on more favorable repayment terms than the recipient could normally secure. Concessional loans have lower interest rates, longer repayment periods, or grace periods during which repayments are reduced or waived (similar to some student loans). Foreign aid can take the form of money, capital goods, technical assistance, food, and so forth.

Foreign aid An international transfer made on especially favorable terms for the purpose of promoting economic development

Some foreign aid is granted by a specific country, such as the United States, to another specific country, such as the Philippines. Country-to-country aid is called *bilateral* assistance. Other foreign aid goes through international bodies such as the World Bank. Assistance provided by organizations that use funds from a number of countries is called *multilateral*. For example, the World Bank provides loans and grants to support activities that are viewed as prerequisites for development, such as health and education programs or basic development projects like dams, roads, and communications networks. And the International Monetary Fund extends loans to countries that have trouble with their balance of payments, with recent loans to Indonesia, Korea, and Brazil.

During the last four decades, the United States has provided the developing world with over $400 billion in aid. Since 1961, most U.S. aid has been coordinated by the U.S. Agency for International Development (AID), which is part of the U.S. Department of State. This agency concentrates primarily on health, education, and agriculture, providing both technical assistance and loans. AID emphasizes long-range plans to meet the basic needs of the poor and to promote self-sufficiency. Foreign aid is a controversial, though relatively small, part of the federal budget. Since 1993, official U.S. aid has been less than 0.2 percent of U.S. GDP, compared to an average of 0.3 percent from 21 other industrialized nations.

Does Foreign Aid Promote Economic Development?

In general, foreign aid provides additional purchasing power and thus the possibility of increased investment, capital imports, and consumption. But it remains unclear whether foreign aid *supplements* domestic saving, thus increasing investment, or simply *substitutes* for domestic saving, thereby increasing consumption rather than investment. What is clear is that foreign aid often becomes a source of discretionary funds that benefit not the poor but their leaders. More than 90 percent of the funds distributed by AID go to governments, whose leaders assume responsibility for distributing these funds.

Much bilateral funding is tied to purchases of goods and services from the donor nation, and such programs can sometimes be counterproductive. For example, in the 1950s, the United States began the Food for Peace program, which helped sell U.S. farm products abroad, but some governments sold that food to finance poorly conceived projects. Worse yet, the availability of low-priced food drove down farm prices in the developing countries, hurting farmers there.

Foreign aid may have raised the standard of living in some developing countries, but it has not necessarily increased their ability to become self-supporting at that higher standard of living. Many countries that receive aid are doing less of what they had done well. Their agricultural sectors have suffered. For example, though we should be careful when drawing conclusions about causality, per capita food production in Africa has fallen since 1960. Outside aid has often insulated government officials from the fundamental troubles of their own economies. No country receiving U.S. aid in the past 20 years has moved up in status from developing to industrial. And most countries today that have achieved industrial status did so without foreign aid.

Because of disappointment with the results of government aid, the trend is toward channeling funds through private nonprofit agencies such as CARE. More than half of the flow of aid now goes through private channels.

The privatization of foreign aid follows a larger trend toward privatization around the world. We discuss that important development in the balance of this chapter.

TRANSITIONAL ECONOMIES

As we have seen, there is no widely accepted theory of economic development, but around the world markets are replacing central plans in once-socialist countries. Economic developments in these emerging market economies have tremendous significance for those who study economics. Like geologists, economists must rely primarily on natural experiments to figure out how things work. *The attempt to replace central planning with markets is one of the greatest economic experiments in history*. In the study of geology, this would be comparable to a huge earthquake. In this section, we take a look at these so-called transitional economies.

Types of Economic Systems

First, let's briefly review economic systems. In Chapter 2, we considered the three questions that every economic system must answer: what to produce, how to produce it, and for whom to produce it. Laws regarding resource ownership and the role of government in resource allocation determine the "rules of the game"—the incentives and constraints that guide the behavior of individual decision makers. Economic systems can be classified based on the ownership of resources, the way resources are allocated to produce goods and services, and the incentives used to motivate people.

As we discussed in Chapter 2, resources in *capitalist* systems are owned mostly by individuals and are allocated through market coordination. In socialist economies, resources other than labor are owned by the state. For example, a country such as Cuba or North Korea carefully limits the private ownership of resources such as land and capital. Each country employs a slightly different system of resource ownership, resource allocation, and individual incentives to answer the three economic questions.

So under capitalism, the rules of the game include private ownership of most resources and the coordination of economic activity by price signals generated by market forces; market coordination answers the three questions. Under socialism, the rules of the game include government ownership of most resources and the allocation of resources through central plans.

Enterprises and Soft Budget Constraints

In the socialist system, enterprises that earn a "profit" see that profit appropriated by the state. Firms that end up with a loss find that loss covered by a state subsidy. Thus socialist enterprises face what has been called a **soft budget constraint**. This can lead to inefficiency, a lack of response to changes in supply or demand, and poor investment decisions. Quality has also been a problem under central planning, because plant managers would rather meet production quotas than satisfy consumer demand. For example, plant managers do not score extra bureaucratic points by producing garments that are in style and in popular sizes. Tales of shoddy products in socialist systems abound.

Soft budget constraint The budget condition faced by socialist enterprises that are subsidized if they lose money

Most prices in centrally planned economies are established not by market forces but by central planners. As a result, consumers have little to say about what to produce. Once set, prices tend to be inflexible. For example, in the former Soviet Union, the price of a cabbage slicer was stamped on the metal at the factory. In the spirit of equity, Soviet planners priced most consumer goods below the market-clearing level, so shortages (or "interruptions in supply," as they were called) were common. As of 1990, the price of bread had not changed since 1954, and that price in 1990 amounted to only 7 percent of bread's production cost. Meat prices had not changed since 1962. Some rents had not changed in 60 years.

Capitalist economies equate quantity supplied with quantity demanded through the *invisible hand* of market coordination; centrally planned economies use the *visible hand* of bureaucratic coordination assisted by taxes and subsidies. If quantity supplied and quantity demanded are not in balance, something has to give. In a capitalist system, what gives is the price. In a centrally planned economy, what usually gives is the central plan itself. A common problem in the Soviet system was that the amount produced often fell short of planned production. When the quantity supplied fell below the planned amount, central planners reduced the amount supplied to each sector, cutting critical sectors such as heavy industry and the military the least and cutting lower-priority sectors such as consumer products the most. Evidence of shortages of consumer goods included long waiting lines at retail stores; empty store shelves; the "tips," or bribes, shop operators expected for supplying scarce consumer goods; and higher prices for goods on the black market. Shoppers would sometimes wait in line all night and into the next day. Consumers often relied on "connections" through acquaintances to obtain most goods and services. Scarce goods were frequently diverted to the black market.

Another distinction between socialist economies and capitalist economies involves the ownership of resources. The following case study considers the effect of ownership on the efficient use of resources.

Other Times, Other Places

Médecins Sans Frontières is an international medical relief agency aiding victims of armed conflict, epidemics, and natural and man-made disasters. The ecological catastrophe that resulted from Soviet mismanagement of the Aral Sea has gained this group's attention. Their Web site contains a special section, at http://www.msf.org/aralsea/index.html, that gives you some feel for magnitude of the disaster. An .mpeg animation file showing the shrinking of the sea can be found at http://www.dfd.dlr.de/app/land/aralsee/index.html.

Ownership and Resource Use

Because most property is owned by the state in a socialist economy, nobody in particular owns it. Because there are no individual owners, resources are often wasted. For example, in the former Soviet Union, about one-third of the harvest reportedly deteriorated before it reached retailers. Likewise, to meet Soviet planning goals, oil producers often pumped large pools of oil reserves so quickly that the remaining oil became inaccessible. Soviet workers usually had little regard for equipment that belonged to the state. New trucks or tractors might be dismantled for parts, or working equipment might be sent to a scrap plant. Pilfering of state-owned property, though officially a serious crime, was a high art and a favorite sport. As an old Soviet saying goes, "If you don't steal from the State, you are stealing from your family."

A narrow focus on meeting the objectives of the central plan also imposed a heavy cost on the environment. The Aral Sea, which is about the size of Lake Michigan, has been called "a salinated cesspool." Thousands of barrels of nuclear waste were dumped into Soviet rivers and seas. The 1986 Chernobyl reactor meltdown still poses a threat of nuclear contamination; similar reactors continue to supply energy to Russia, Ukraine, and Lithuania. In a drive for military supremacy, the Soviet government set off 125 nuclear explosions *above* ground. The resulting bomb craters later filled with water, forming contaminated lakes.

In contrast to the treatment of state property, Soviet citizens took extremely good care of their personal property. For example, personal cars were so well maintained that they lasted 20 years or more on average—twice the official projected automobile life. The incentives of private ownership were also evident in agriculture, where farmers typically worked as a group on a *collective*. But each farmer on the collective was also allowed a small plot of land on which to cultivate crops for personal consumption or for sale at prices determined in unregulated markets. Despite the small size of the plots and high taxes on earnings from these plots, farmers produced a disproportionate share of output on private plots. Privately farmed plots constituted only 3 percent of the Soviet Union's farmland, but they supplied 30 percent of all meat, milk, and vegetables and 60 percent of all potatoes.

Perhaps the benefits of privately held resources are no better illustrated than where countries were divided by ideology: West and East Germany before unification, South and North Korea, and Taiwan and mainland China. In each case the economies began with similar human and physical resources, but income per capita diverged sharply, with the market economies outperforming the centrally planned markets. For example, despite recent turmoil in Asia, per capita income in South Korea was still at least five times greater than in North Korea, a communist country.

Recognizing the incentive power of private property, even the most die-hard socialist economies now allow some free-market activity. For example, Cuba allows foreigners to buy Cuban companies and repatriate profits earned in Cuba. On a more down-to-earth level, hundreds of farmers' markets have been established in Cuba to sell everything from live goats to tropical fruit. And for the first time in fifty years, in 1998 China announced plans to allow urban residents the ability to buy homes. But sale prices will still be dictated by the government. The point is that the personal incentives provided by private property usually promote a more efficient use of that property than does state, or common, ownership.

Sources: "Stuck in a Rut," *Wall Street Journal* (23 June 1998); Esther Dyson, *Release 2.0 : A Design for Living in the Digital Age* (New York: Broadway Books, 1997); Erik Eckholm, "China Spells Out Rules On New National Housing Policy," *New York Times* (19 June 1998); Vito Echevarria, "Capitalism Grows in Cuba," *New American News Service* (30 April 1998); and "Viewing Cuba's Market Culture," *Times-Picayune* (29 April 1998).

MARKETS AND INSTITUTIONS

A study of economic systems underscores the importance of institutions in the course of development. *Institutions*, or "rules of the game," are the incentives and constraints that structure political, economic, and social interaction. They consist of (1) formal rules of behavior, such as a constitution, laws, and property rights, and (2) informal constraints on behavior, such as sanctions, manners, customs, traditions, and codes of conduct. Throughout history, institutions have been devised by people to create order and reduce uncertainty in exchange. Thus underlying the surface of economic behavior is a grid of informal, often unconscious, habits, customs, and norms that make the functioning of markets possible. *A reliable system of property rights and enforceable contracts are prerequisites for creating incentives that support a healthy market economy.*

Together with the standard constraints of economics, such as income, resource availability, and prices, institutions shape the incentive structure of an economy. As the incentive structure evolves, it can direct economic change toward growth, stagnation, or decline. Economic history is largely a story of economies that have failed to produce a set of economic rules of the game that lead to sustained economic growth. After all, more than three-quarters of the world's economies are still trying to develop—still trying to get their act together.

Customs and conventions can sometimes be obstacles to development. In developed market economies, resource owners tend to supply their resources where they are most valued; but in developing countries, links to the family or clan may be the most important consideration. For example, in some cultures, children are expected to remain in their father's occupation even though some are better suited to other lines of work. Family businesses may resist growth because such growth would involve hiring people from outside the family.

Institutions and Economic Development

Institutions shape the incentive structure of an economy, but, as we have already noted, most countries in the world have failed to produce a set of economic rules of the game that lead to sustained economic growth. Although political and judicial decisions may change formal rules overnight, informal constraints embodied in customs, traditions, and codes of conduct are more immune to deliberate policies. For example, respect for the law cannot be legislated.

Prior to the market reforms in the former Soviet Union, widespread corruption and a lack of faith in formal institutions were woven into the social fabric. Workers bribed officials to get good jobs and consumers bribed clerks to get desired products. Bribery became a way of life, a way of dealing with the distortions that arise when prices are not allowed to allocate resources efficiently.

In centrally planned economies, the exchange relationship was typically personal, based as it was on bureaucratic ties on the production side and inside connections on the consumption side. But in the United States and other market economies, successful institutional evolution permits the *impersonal* exchange necessary to capture the potential economic benefits of specialization and modern technology. Impersonal exchange allows for a far greater division of labor, but it requires a richer and more stable institutional setting.

The Big Bang Versus Gradualism

The Hungarian economist Janos Kornai believes that a market order should be grown from the bottom up. First, small-scale capitalism in farming, trade, light manufacturing, and services thrives. These grass-roots markets can serve as a foundation for the privatization of larger industrial sectors. Large industrial enterprises should quickly find the market-clearing price so that input and output decisions are consistent with market preferences. In the meantime, state-owned enterprises should be run more like businesses in which state directors attempt to maximize profit. Money-losing enterprises should be phased out. This "bottom-up" approach proposed by Kornai could be termed **gradualism**, which can be contrasted with a **big-bang** approach, whereby the transition from central planning to a market economy would take place in a matter of months.

Gradualism A "bottom-up" approach to moving from a centrally planned to a market economy emphasizing established markets at the most decentralized level first, such as on small farms or in light industry

Big-bang theory The argument that the transition from a centrally planned to a market economy should be broad and swift, taking place in a matter of months

One example of gradualism is taking place in China. In 1978, the government began dismantling agricultural communes in favor of a "household-responsibility" system of small-farm agriculture. Land was assigned to individual families, which could keep any excess production after meeting specific state-imposed goals. Initially the system was to be applied only to the poorest 20 percent of rural areas. Once the positive effects became apparent, however, the system spread on its own. Eventually farmers established their own wholesale and retail marketing systems and were allowed to sell directly to urban areas at market-clearing prices. This gave rise to a market for truckers to buy, transport, and resell farm products. Over the next seven years, agricultural output increased by an impressive 8 to 10 percent per year.

In structuring the transition from central planning to a market system, economists are feeling their way. Nobel prize-winner Friedrich von Hayek argued that competitive markets provide instant information about the price and quantity resulting from the interaction of supply and demand. But central planning provides no way to discover what the equilibrium price and quantity should be. And the more rigid prices become, the less information they convey. According to Hayek, not only is finding equilibrium price and quantity a discovery process, but developing appropriate rules of the game to nurture market activity is also a discovery process. Both discovery processes are especially difficult for transitional economies, which usually have no history of market interaction and no established record of codified law or rules of conduct for market participants. For example, based on China's success with privately run farms, Russia's 1993 constitution guaranteed the right to buy and sell land. But that guarantee was never fleshed out with supporting legislation. Thus farm cooperatives in Russia today operate much as they did in the Soviet days. Hayek believed that *government's role should be to help establish competitive markets by identifying and codifying the conventions of trade and by protecting property rights.*

Privatization

Privatization is the process of turning public enterprises into private enterprises. It is the opposite of *nationalization.* For example, Russian privatization began in April 1992 with the sale of municipally owned shops. Although most property in countries of the former Soviet Union is nominally owned by the state, it often remains unclear who has the authority to sell the property and who should receive the proceeds. This ambiguity results in cases in which the same property has been purchased from different officials by different buyers. Yet *there is no clear legal process for resolving title disputes.* Worse still, some enterprises have been stripped of their assets by self-serving managers, a process that derisively came to be called "spontaneous" privatization. The necessarily complex process of privatization will be undermined if the general population perceives it to be unfair.

Privatization The process of turning public enterprises into private enterprises

Transparent Finances

Privatization requires modern accounting and other information systems, the training of competent managers, and the installation of adequate facilities for telecommunication, computing, travel, and transportation. This transformation cannot be accomplished overnight. Consider just the accounting problem. A market economy depends on financial accounting rules as well as on an independent system for auditing financial reports. The needed information must show up in a company's balance sheet and income statement. Prospective buyers of enterprises need such information, as do banks and other lenders. Thus, a firm's finances should be **transparent**, meaning someone should be able to look at the books and the balance sheet and tell exactly what's going on.

Transparent finances A firm's financial records that clearly indicate the economic health of the company

By all reports, the accounting systems of most formerly socialist firms are almost worthless. For decades, data had been aimed more at central planners, who wanted to know about *physical* flows, than at someone who wanted to know about the efficiency and financial promise of the firm. So there is much information, but little that is relevant. Incidentally, the major advantage of the market economy is that it minimizes the need for the kind of resource-flow data that had been reported under central planning. Prices convey most of the information necessary to coordinate economic activity among firms.

Institutional Requirements of Efficient Markets

Some may look at the initial instability that resulted from the dismantling of socialist states and argue that the move toward markets has been a failure. But in the former Soviet Union the state dismantled central controls before institutions such as property rights, customs, codes of conduct, and a legal system were in place. For example, more than half of the 17-year-olds surveyed in Russia saw nothing wrong with looking for a job that offered opportunities to collect bribes and nearly half believed it acceptable to take what they wanted by force.[5]

Tax laws are applied unevenly and the rates change frequently. For example, the personal income tax in Russia jumped from a graduated rate topping at 13 percent to a flat rate of 60 percent and then to a graduated rate topping at 40 percent. Most Russians evade taxes—only one million people filed income tax returns in 1997, a tiny fraction of the 147 million population.[6] Corporate taxes appear just as arbitrary in Russia, with politically connected companies paying little or no taxes. The head of Russia's Statistics Service was fired in 1998 after his arrest for helping big companies evade taxes.[7] Harvard economist and Russian expert Marshall Goldman argues that "tax evasion by both enterprises and individuals is a source of pride dating back to czarist times."[8] Millions of Russians carry out their business in the underground economy.

The shift from central planning to a market economy is easier said than done. Simply loosening constraints to create private property may not be enough for successful reform. The development of supporting institutions is essential, but *there is no unified economic theory of how to construct the institutions that are central to the success of capitalism*. Most so-called economists employed in Soviet-type systems did not understand even the basics of how markets work. They had been trained to regard the alleged "anarchy" of the market as a primary defect of capitalism.

A more fundamental problem is that, although Western economic theory focuses on the operation of efficient markets, *even market economists usually do not understand the institutional requirements of efficient markets*. Market economists often take the necessary institutions for granted. Those involved in the transition must develop a deeper appreciation for the institutions that nurture and support impersonal market activity.

So the jury is still out on the transition to markets. Exhibit 5 presents, for some key transitional economies, the GNP per capita in 1997 based on the purchasing power of the domestic currency. Notice the dramatic differences across these economies, with per capita GNP in the Czech Republic more than five times greater than that of the Ukraine. By way of comparison, U.S. GNP per capita in 1997 was $28,740, or about 150 percent above the Czech Republic, the most successful transitional economy.

Lessons about the nature of economic processes will likely emerge from the analysis of these transitional economies. The course of economic reform will provide insights into both the potential and the limits of economics itself.

5 As reported by James Meek, "For Youth, Bribery a Matter of 'Maybe' Rather than 'Nyet,'" *Sydney Morning Herald* (21 March 1998).

6 Michael R. Gordon, "Russia's New Enforcer of Taxes Is Taking On a Land of Evaders," *New York Times* (4 July 1998).

7 "Russia's Finance: Taxman in a Tank," *Economist* (13 June 1998): 72.

8 Marshall Goldman, "Russian Tax Evasion Is Source of Pride," letter to the editor, *New York Times* (9 August 1998).

EXHIBIT 5

GNP per Capita in Transitional Economies in 1997

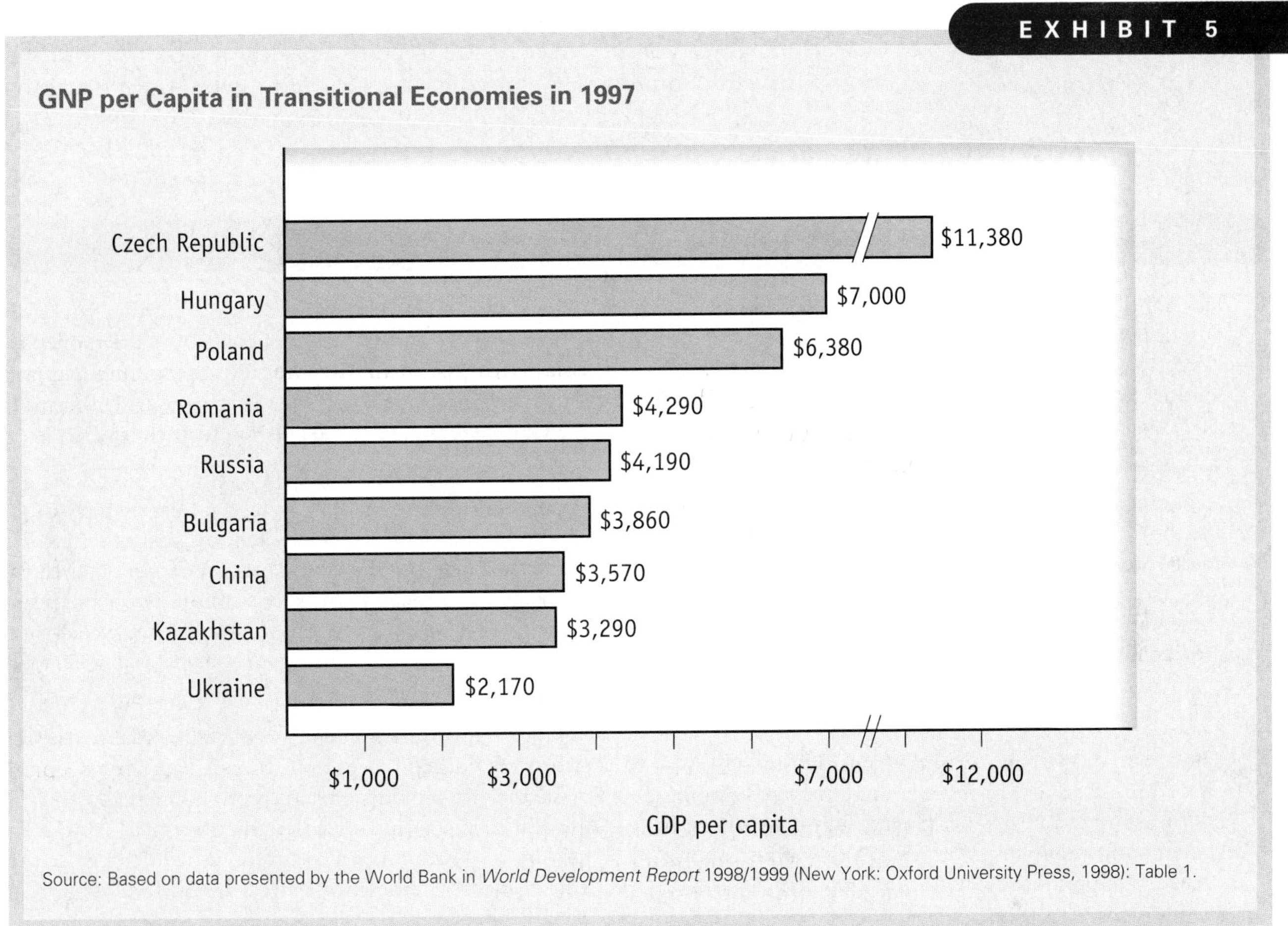

Source: Based on data presented by the World Bank in *World Development Report* 1998/1999 (New York: Oxford University Press, 1998): Table 1.

CONCLUSION

Because no single theory of economic development has become widely accepted, this chapter has been more descriptive than theoretical. We can readily define the features that distinguish developing from industrial economies, but we are less sure how to foster growth and development. Economic history is largely a story of economies that have failed to produce a set of economic rules of the game that lead to sustained economic growth.

Perhaps the most elusive ingredients for development are the formal and informal institutions that promote economic activity: the laws, customs, conventions, and other institutional elements that encourage people to undertake productive activity. A stable political environment with well-defined property rights is important. Little private sector investment will occur if potential investors believe their capital might be appropriated by government, destroyed by civil unrest, or stolen by thieves. Education is also key to development, both because of its direct effect on productivity and because those who are more educated tend to be more receptive to new ideas. A physical infrastructure of transportation and communication systems and utilities is needed to link economic participants. And trusted financial institutions help link savers and borrowers. Finally, a country needs entrepreneurs with the vision to move the economy forward. Some newly emerging industrial countries prove that economic development is achievable, though not necessarily easy.

SUMMARY

1. Developing countries are distinguished by low levels of output per capita, poor health and nutrition, high fertility rates, low levels of education, and saving rates that are too low to finance sufficient investment.
2. Worker productivity is low in developing countries because the stocks of physical and human capital are low, technological advances are not widely diffused throughout the economy, natural resources and entrepreneurial ability are scarce, financial markets are not well developed, some talented professionals migrate to high-income countries, formal and informal institutions do not provide sufficient incentives for market activity, and governments may serve the interests of the group in power rather than the public interest.
3. The key to growth and a rising standard of living is increased productivity. To foster productivity, developing nations must stimulate investment, support education and training programs, and provide the infrastructure necessary to promote economic development.
4. Increases in productivity do not occur without prior saving, but most people in developing countries have such low incomes that there is little opportunity to save. Even if some higher-income people have the money to save, financial institutions in developing countries are not well developed, and savings are often sent abroad, where there is a more stable investment climate.
5. Foreign aid has been a mixed blessing for most developing countries. In some cases, that aid has helped countries build the roads, bridges, schools, and other capital infrastructure necessary for development. In other cases, foreign aid has simply increased consumption and insulated government from painful but necessary reforms. Worse still, subsidized food from abroad has undermined domestic agriculture.
6. Major reforms have been introduced in recent years in formerly socialist economies to decentralize decision making, to provide greater production incentives to workers, and to introduce competitive markets. But in many cases, central controls were dismantled before the institutional framework had developed to support a market economy.

QUESTIONS FOR REVIEW

1. *(Worlds Apart)* Compare developing and industrial market economies on the basis of each of the following general economic characteristics, and relate the differences to the process of development:
   a. Diversity of the industrial base
   b. Distribution of resource ownership
   c. Educational level of the labor force
2. *(Developing Countries)* How would you explain why agricultural productivity in developing countries is usually low?
3. *(Classification of Economies)* What are the arguments for using real per capita GNP to compare living standards between countries? What weakness does this measure have?
4. *(Productivity and Development)* Among the problems that hinder growth in developing economies are poor infrastructure, lack of financial institutions and a sound money supply, a low saving rate, poor capital base, and lack of foreign exchange. Explain how these problems are interconnected.
5. *(**CaseStudy:** Crony Capitalism in Indonesia)* How did President Suharto and his family undermine the economy of Indonesia? Did the Indonesian economy have any special features that made it vulnerable to crony capitalism?
6. *(International Trade and Development)* From the perspective of citizens in a developing country, what are some of the benefits and drawbacks of international trade?

7. *(Foreign Aid and Economic Development)* Foreign aid, if it is to be successful in enhancing economic development, must lead to a more productive economy. Describe some of the problems in achieving such an objective through foreign aid.

8. *(Foreign Aid and Economic Development)* It is widely recognized that foreign aid that promotes productivity in developing economies is superior to merely shipping products like food to these countries. Yet the latter is the approach frequently taken. Why do you think this is the case?

9. *(Types of Economic Systems)* One of the questions every economic system must answer is for whom products are produced. How is the answer determined in a market system? How is it answered in a centrally planned system?

10. *(Transitional Economies)* What special problems are being faced by Eastern European economies as they make the transition from central planning to free markets?

11. *(Case**Study:** Ownership and Resource Use)* In what ways were the incentives of private ownership evident even in the Soviet Union?

12. *(Markets and Institutions)* Why is a system of well-defined and enforceable property rights crucial when a country is converting to a market-based system of resource allocation?

13. *(Big Bang Versus Gradualism)* Explain the difference between the big bang and gradualism approaches to moving from central planning to market coordination.

PROBLEMS AND EXERCISES

14. *(Worlds Apart)* Per capita GNP most recently is about 56 times greater in the richest country on Earth than in the poorest country. Suppose per capita GNP grows an average of 2 percent per year in the richest country and 4 percent per year in the poorest country. Assuming such growth rates continue indefinitely into the future, how many years would it take before the per capita GNP in the poorest country reaches that of the richest country?

15. *(Import Substitution versus Export Promotion)* Using supply and demand curves for a particular good, show why domestic producers who supply a good that competes with imports would prefer an import-substitution approach to trade policy rather than an export-promotion approach. Which policy would domestic consumers prefer and why?

EXPERIENTIAL EXERCISES

16. *(Foreign Aid)* Review the most recent *World Bank News,* a weekly publication of events, activities, and initiatives involving the World Bank at http://www.world.bank.org/html/extdr/extcs/news.html. Review one report specific to a developing country. What is the World Bank doing to help this country? In return for assistance, what has the developing country done, or what does it plan to do?

17. *(Transitional Economies)* The World Bank's *Transition Newsletter* at http://www.worldbank.org/html/prddr/trans/WEB/trans.htm is a good source for the latest information on economies in transition. Review the latest issue of the *Newsletter.* What are some of the special problems currently faced by transitional economies?

18. *(Wall Street Journal)* Go to the Money & Investing section of today's *Wall Street Journal* and find an article relating to a developing or transitional economy. What kinds of changes are described there? What are the implications of those changes for investors in the United States?

Glossary

Glossary

A

Ability-to-pay-tax principle Those with a greater ability to pay should pay more tax

Absolute advantage The ability to produce something using fewer resources than other producers use

Accounting profit A firm's total revenue minus its explicit cost

Actual investment The amount of investment actually undertaken during a year; equals planned investment plus unplanned changes in inventories

Adverse selection A situation in which those on the informed side of the market self-select in a way that harms the uninformed side of the market

Adverse supply shocks Unexpected events that reduce aggregate supply, sometimes only temporarily

Agent A person who performs work or provides a service on behalf of another person, the principal

Aggregate demand curve A curve representing the relationship between the economy's price level and the amount of aggregate output demanded per period, other things being held constant

Aggregate demand The relationship between the price level in the economy and the quantity of aggregate output demanded, other things held constant

Aggregate expenditure line A relationship showing, for a given price level, planned spending at each level of income; the total of C + I + G + (X – M) at each level of income

Aggregate expenditure Total spending on final goods and services during a given time period, usually a year

Aggregate income The sum of all income earned by resource suppliers in an economy during a given time period

Aggregate output A composite measure of all final goods and services produced in an economy during a given time period; real GDP

Aggregate supply curve A curve representing the relationship between the economy's price level and the amount of aggregate output supplied per period, other things held constant

Allocative efficiency The condition that exists when firms produce the output that is most preferred by consumers; the marginal cost of each good just equals the marginal benefit that consumers derive from that good.

Alternative goods Other goods that use some of the same resources as used to produce the good in question

Annually balanced budget Budget philosophy prior to the Great Depression; aimed at equating revenues with outlays, except during times of war

Annuity A given sum of money received each year for a specified number of years

Antitrust activity Government activity aimed at preventing monopoly and fostering competition in markets where competition is desirable

Applied research Research that seeks to answer particular questions or to apply scientific discoveries to the development of specific products

Arbitrageur A person who takes advantage of temporary geographic differences in the exchange rate by simultaneously purchasing a currency in one market and selling it in another market

Asset Anything of value that is owned

Association-is-causation fallacy The incorrect idea that if two variables are associated in time, one must necessarily cause the other

Asymmetric information Unequal information known by each party to a transaction; borrowers usually have more information about their credit worthiness than do lenders

Autarky A situation of national self-sufficiency in which there is no economic interaction with foreigners

Automatic stabilizers Structural features of government spending and taxation that smooth fluctuations in disposable income, and hence consumption, over the business cycle

Autonomous A term that means "independent"; autonomous investment is independent of the level of income

Average revenue Total revenue divided by output; in all market structures, average revenue equals the market price.

Average total cost Total cost divided by output

Average variable cost Variable cost divided by output

B

Backward-bending supply curve of labor Occurs if the income effect of a higher wage dominates the substitution effect of a higher wage

Balance of payments A record of all economic transactions between residents of one country and residents of the rest of the world during a given time period

Balance on current account The section of a country's balance-of-payments account that measures the sum of the country's net unilateral transfers and its balance on goods and services

Balance on goods and services The section of a country's balance-of-payments account that measures the difference in value between a country's exports of goods and services and its imports of goods and services

Balance sheet A financial statement that shows assets, liabilities, and net worth at a given point in time; since assets must equal liabilities plus net worth, the statement is in balance.

Bank holding company A corporation that owns banks

Bank notes Papers promising a specific amount of gold or silver to bearers who presented them to issuing banks for redemption; an early type of money

Barrier to entry Any impediment that prevents new firms from competing on an equal basis with existing firms in an industry

Barter The direct exchange of one good for another without the use of money

Base year The year with which other years are compared when constructing an index; the index equals 100 in the base year

Basic research The search for knowledge without regard to how that knowledge will be used

Behavioral assumption An assumption that describes the expected behavior of economic decision makers

Beneficial supply shocks Unexpected events that increase aggregate supply, sometimes only temporarily

Benefits-received tax principle Those who receive more benefits from the government program funded by a tax should pay more tax

Big-bang theory The argument that the transition from a centrally planned to a market economy should be broad and swift, taking place in a matter of months

Binding arbitration Negotiation in which both parties in a union-management dispute agree to accept an impartial observer's resolution of the dispute

Bond A certificate reflecting a firm's promise to pay the holder periodic interest until the date of maturity, then to pay a fixed sum of money on the designated maturity date

Bounded rationality The notion that there is a limit to the amount of information an economic agent, such as a manager, can comprehend

Budget line A line showing all combinations of two goods that can be purchased at given prices with a given amount of income

Budget resolution A congressional agreement about total outlays, spending by major category, and expected revenues, which guides spending and revenue decisions by the many congressional committees and subcommittees

Bureaus Government agencies charged with implementing legislation and financed by appropriations from legislative bodies

C

Capital All buildings, equipment, and human skill used to produce goods and services

Capital account The record of a country's international transactions involving purchases or sales of financial and real assets

Cartel A group of firms that agree to coordinate their production and pricing decisions to maximize cartel profits, thereby behaving as a monopolist

Change in demand A shift in a given demand curve caused by a change in any of the determinants of demand for the good other than its price

Change in quantity demanded A movement along the demand curve in response to a change in the price, other things constant

Change in quantity supplied A movement along the supply curve in response to a change in the price, other things constant

Change in supply A shift in a given supply curve caused by a change in one of the determinants of the supply of the good other than its price

Checkable deposits Deposits in financial institutions against which checks can be written

Circular flow model A diagram that outlines the flow of resources, products, income, and revenue among households, firms, governments, and the rest of the world

Classical economists A group of 18th- and 19th-century economists who believed that recessions were short-run phenomena that corrected themselves through natural market forces; thus they believed the economy was self-correcting

Coase theorem As long as bargaining costs are small, an efficient solution to the problem of externalities will be achieved by assigning property rights.

Cold turkey The announcement and execution of tough measures to reduce high inflation

Collective bargaining The process by which union and management negotiate a labor agreement

Collusion An agreement among firms to divide the market or to fix the market price to maximize economic profit.

Commercial banks Depository institutions that make short-term loans primarily to businesses

Commodity money Anything that serves both as money and as a commodity

Common-pool problem Unrestricted access to a resource that results in overuse until the marginal value of additional use drops to zero

Comparative advantage The ability to produce something at a lower opportunity cost than other producers face

Competing-interest legislation Legislation that imposes concentrated costs on one group and provides concentrated benefits to another group

Complements Goods that are related in such a way that an increase in the price of one leads to a decrease in the demand for the other

Conglomerate merger A merger involving the combination of firms in different industries

Consent decree A legal agreement through which the accused party, without admitting guilt, agrees to refrain in the future from certain illegal activity if the government drops the charges

Constant elasticity demand curve The type of demand that exists when price elasticity is the same everywhere along the curve; the elasticity value is constant

Constant-cost industry An industry that can expand or contract without affecting the long-run, per-unit cost of production; the long-run industry supply curve is horizontal.

Consumer equilibrium The condition in which an individual consumer's budget is completely spent and the last dollar spent on each good yields the same marginal utility; therefore, utility is maximized

Consumer price index (CPI) A measure of the cost of a fixed "market basket" of consumer goods and services

Consumer surplus The difference between the maximum amount that a consumer is willing to pay for a given quantity of a good and what the consumer actually pays

Consumption All household purchases of final goods and services

Consumption function The relationship between the level of income in an economy and the amount households plan to spend on consumption, other things constant

Continuing resolutions Budget agreements that allow agencies, in the absence of an approved budget, to spend at the rate of the previous year's budget

Contractionary gap The amount by which actual output in the short run falls below the economy's potential output

Convergence A theory that the standard of living in economies around the world will grow more similar over time, with poorer countries catching up with richer countries

Coordination failure A situation in which workers and employers fail to achieve an outcome that all would prefer; and are unable to jointly choose strategies that would result in a more preferred outcome

Corporate profits A component of national income measuring the net revenues received by incorporated businesses before corporate income taxes are subtracted

Corporation A legal entity owned by stockholders whose liability is limited to the value of their stock

Cost-push inflation A sustained rise in the price level caused by reductions in aggregate supply

Craft union A union whose members have a particular skill or work at a particular craft, such as plumbers or carpenters

Cross-price elasticity of demand The percent change in the demand of one good as a result of the percent change in the price of another good

Crowding in The potential for government spending to stimulate private investment in an otherwise sluggish economy

Crowding out The displacement of interest-sensitive private investment that occurs when increased government deficit spending drives up interest rates

Currency appreciation A decrease in the number of dollars needed to purchase 1 unit of foreign exchange

Currency depreciation An increase in the number of dollars needed to purchase 1 unit of foreign exchange

Currency devaluation An increase in the official pegged price of foreign exchange in terms of the domestic currency

Currency revaluation A reduction in the official pegged price of foreign exchange in terms of the domestic currency

Cyclical unemployment Unemployment that fluctuates with the business cycle, increasing during recessions and decreasing during expansions

Cyclically balanced budget A budget philosophy calling for budget deficits during recessions to be financed by budget surpluses during expansions

D

Deadweight loss A loss of consumer surplus and producer surplus that is not transferred to anyone else; it can result from monopolization of an industry

Decision-making lag The time needed to decide what to do once a macroeconomic problem is identified

Decreasing-cost industry The rare case in which an industry faces lower per-unit production costs as industry output expands in the long run; the long-run industry supply curve slopes downward.

Deflation A sustained decrease in the price level

Demand A relation showing the quantities of a good that consumers are willing and able to buy at various prices during a given period of time, other things constant

Demand curve A curve showing the quantities of a particular good demanded at various possible prices during a given time period, other things constant

Demand deposits Accounts at financial institutions that pay no interest and on which depositors can write checks to obtain their deposits at any time

Demand for loanable funds The relationship between the market interest rate and the quantity of loanable funds demanded, other things constant

Demand for money The relationship between how much money people want to hold and the interest rate

Demand-pull inflation A sustained rise in the price level caused by increases in aggregate demand

Demand-side economics Macroeconomic policy that focuses on changing aggregate demand as a way of promoting full employment and price stability

Depository institutions Commercial banks and thrift institutions that accept deposits from the public

Depreciation The value of capital stock used up during a year in producing GDP

Depression A severe reduction in an economy's total production accompanied by high unemployment lasting more than a year

Derived demand The demand for a resource derived from the demand for the product the resource produces

Developing countries Nations typified by high rates of illiteracy, high unemployment, high fertility rates, and exports of primary products

Discount rate The interest rate used to convert income to be received in the future into present value

Discounting Determining the present value of income to be received in the future

Discouraged worker A person who has dropped out of the labor force because of lack of success in finding a job

Discretionary fiscal policy The deliberate manipulation of government purchases, taxation, and transfers in order to promote macroeconomic goals such as full employment, price stability, and economic growth

Diseconomies of scale Forces that cause a firm's average cost to increase as the scale of operation increases in the long run

Disequilibrium A mismatch between quantity supplied and quantity demanded as the market seeks equilibrium

Disinflation A reduction in the rate of inflation

Disposable income (DI) The income households have available to spend or save after paying taxes and receiving transfer payments

Dividends After-tax corporate profits that are paid to stockholders rather than reinvested in the firm

Division of labor The organization of production of a product into separate tasks in which people specialize

Double coincidence of wants A situation in which two traders are willing to exchange their products directly

Double counting The mistake of including the value of intermediate goods plus the value of final goods in gross domestic product, counting the value of the same good more than once

Dumping Selling a commodity abroad at a price that is below its cost of production or below the price charged in the domestic market

Duopoly A market with only two producers, who compete with each other; a type of oligopoly market structure

E

Economic fluctuations The rise and fall of economic activity relative to the long-term growth trend of the economy; also called business cycles

Economic growth A shift outward in the production possibilities frontier; an increase in the economy's ability to produce goods and services

Economic profit A firm's total revenue minus its explicit and implicit costs

Economic regulation Government regulations aimed at controlling prices, output, market entry and exit, and product quality in situations in which, because of economies of scale, average production costs are lowest when the market is served by only one or a few firms

Economic rent The portion of a resource's total earnings above its opportunity cost; earnings above the amount necessary to keep the resource in its present use

Economic system The set of mechanisms and institutions that resolve the what, how, and for whom questions

Economic theory, economic model A simplification of reality used to make predictions about the real world

Economics The study of how people use their scarce resources in an attempt to satisfy their unlimited wants

Economies of scale Forces that cause a reduction in a firm's average cost as the scale of operation increases in the long run

Economies of scope Forces that make it cheaper for a firm to produce two or more different products rather than just one

Economy The structure of economic life or economic activity in a community, a region, a country, a group of countries, or the world

Effectiveness lag The time necessary for changes in monetary or fiscal policy to have an effect on the economy

Efficiency The condition that exists when there is no way resources can be reallocated to increase the production of one good without decreasing the production of another

Efficiency wage theory The idea that offering high wages attracts a more talented labor pool, making it easier for firms to hire more productive workers; also a higher wage that encourages those more productive workers to do a good job

Elastic demand The type of demand that exists when a change in price has a relatively large effect on quantity demanded; the percent change in quantity demanded exceeds the percent change in price

Employee compensation A component of national income made up of wages and salaries plus payments by employers to cover Social Security taxes, medical insurance, and other fringe benefits

Entitlement programs Guaranteed benefits for those who qualify under government transfer programs such as Social Security and Medicare

Entrepreneur A profit-seeking decision maker who organizes an enterprise and assumes the risk of its operation

Entrepreneurial ability Managerial and organizational skills combined with the willingness to take risks

Equation of exchange The quantity of money, M, multiplied by its velocity, V, equals nominal GDP, which is the product of the price level, P, and real GDP, Y.

Equilibrium The condition that exists in a market when the plans of the buyers match the plans of the sellers; the market clears

Excess capacity The difference between the rate of output at a firm's minimum average cost and the profit-maximizing rate of output

Excess reserves Bank reserves in excess of required reserves

Exchange rate The price of one country's currency measured in terms of another country's currency

Exclusive dealing The situation that occurs when a producer prohibits customers from purchasing from other sellers

Exhaustible resource A resource available in fixed supply, such as crude oil or copper ore

Expansion A phase of economic activity during which there is an increase in the economy's total production

Expansion path A line connecting points of tangency that identify the least-cost input combinations for producing alternative output rates; the expansion path need not be a straight line, though it will generally slope upward

Expansionary gap The amount by which actual output in the short run exceeds the economy's potential output

Expenditure approach to GDP A method of calculating GDP by adding up spending on all final goods and services produced during the year

Explicit cost Opportunity cost of a firm's resources that takes the form of cash payments

Export promotion A development strategy that concentrates on producing for the export market

Externality A cost or a benefit that falls on third parties and is therefore ignored by the two parties to the market transaction

F

Fallacy of composition The incorrect belief that what is true for the individual, or part, must necessarily be true for the group, or whole

Featherbedding Union efforts to force employers to hire more workers than demanded for the task

Federal budget A plan for federal government outlays and revenues for a specified period, usually a year

Federal funds market A market for overnight lending and borrowing of reserves among banks; the market for reserves on account with the Fed

Federal funds rate The interest rate prevailing in the federal funds market; the interest rate banks charge one another for overnight borrowing

Federal Reserve System The central bank and monetary authority of the United States; also known as "the Fed"

Fiat money Money not redeemable for any commodity; its status as money is conferred by the government

Final goods and services Goods and services sold to final, or ultimate, users

Financial intermediaries Institutions that serve as go-betweens, accepting funds from savers and lending them to borrowers

Financial markets Banks and other institutions that facilitate the flow of loanable funds from savers to borrowers

Firms Economic units formed by profit-seeking entrepreneurs who employ resources to produce goods and services for sale

Fiscal policy The use of government purchases, transfer payments, taxes, and borrowing to influence aggregate economic activity

Fixed cost Any production cost that is independent of the firm's rate of output

Fixed exchange rates Rates pegged within a narrow range of values by central banks' ongoing purchases and sales of currencies

Fixed resource Any resource that cannot be varied in the short run

Fixed production technology The relationship between output rate and the generation of an externality is a fixed one; the only way to the reduce the externality is to reduce the output rate

Flexible exchange rates Rates determined by the forces of supply and demand without government intervention

Flow A variable that measures the amount of something over an interval of time, such as the amount of money you spend on food per week

Food stamps An in-kind transfer program that offers low-income households vouchers redeemable for food; benefit levels vary inversely with household income

Foreign aid An international transfer made on especially favorable terms for the purpose of promoting economic development

Foreign exchange Foreign currency needed to carry out international transactions

Fractional reserve banking system A banking system in which only a portion of deposits is backed by reserves

Frictional unemployment Unemployment that arises because of the time needed to match qualified job seekers with available job openings

Full employment The level of employment when there is no cyclical unemployment

Functional finance A budget philosophy aiming fiscal policy at achieving potential GDP rather than balancing budgets either annually or over the business cycle

G

Game theory A model that analyzes oligopolistic behavior as a series of strategic moves and counter-moves by rival firms

GDP price index A comprehensive price index of all goods and services included in the gross domestic product

General Agreement on Tariffs and Trade (GATT) An international tariff-reduction treaty adopted in 1947 that resulted in a series of negotiated "rounds" aimed at freer trade; the Uruguay Round created GATT's successor, the World Trade Organization (WTO)

Gold standard An arrangement whereby the currencies of most countries are convertible into gold at a fixed rate

Golden rule of profit maximization To maximize profit or minimize loss, a firm should produce at the rate of output at which marginal cost equals marginal revenue; this rule holds for all market structures.

Good A tangible item that is used to satisfy wants

Government budget deficit A flow variable that measures the amount by which total government outlays exceed total government revenues in a particular period

Government debt A stock variable that measures the net accumulation of prior budget deficits

Government purchase function The relationship between government purchases and the level of income in the economy, other things constant

Government purchases Spending for goods and services by all levels of government; government outlays minus transfer payments

Government subsidies Government transfers to businesses

Gradualism A "bottom-up" approach to moving from a centrally planned to a market economy emphasizing established markets at the most decentralized level first, such as on small farms or in light industry

Gresham's Law People tend to trade away inferior money and hoard the best

Gross domestic product, or **GDP** The market value of all final goods and services produced by resources located in the United States, regardless of who owns those resources.

H

Herfindahl index The sum of the squared percentages of market share of all firms in an industry; a measure of the level of market concentration in that industry

Hidden actions A type of asymmetric information when one side of an economic relationship can take a relevant action that the other side cannot observe

Hidden characteristics A type of asymmetric information problem in which one side of the market knows more than the other side about product characteristics that are important to the other side of the market

Horizontal merger A merger in which one firm combines with another firm that produces the same product

Householder The key decision maker in the household

Hyperinflation A very high rate of inflation

Hypothesis A statement about relationships among key variables

I

Implementation lag The time needed to introduce a change in monetary or fiscal policy

Implicit cost A firm's opportunity cost of using its own resources or those provided by its owners without a corresponding cash payment

Import substitution A development strategy that emphasizes domestic manufacturing of products that are currently imported

Income approach to GDP A method of calculating GDP by adding up all payments to owners of resources used to produce output during the year

Income assistance programs Welfare programs that provide money and in-kind assistance to the poor; benefits do not depend on prior contributions

Income effect A fall in the price of a good increases consumers' real income, making the consumers more able to purchase all goods; for normal goods, the quantity demanded increases

Income effect of a wage increase A higher wage increases workers' real income, increasing their demand for all normal goods including leisure, so the quantity of labor supplied decreases

Income elasticity of demand The percent change in demand (at a given price) divided by the percent change in income

Income-expenditure model A relationship between aggregate income and aggregate spending that determines, for a given price level, where income equals planned spending

Increasing marginal returns Marginal product increases experienced by a firm when another unit of a particular resource is employed, all other resources constant

Increasing-cost industry An industry that faces higher per-unit production costs as industry output expands in the long run; the long-run industry supply curve slopes upward.

Indifference curve A curve showing all combinations of goods that provide the consumer with the same satisfaction, or the same utility

Indifference map A set of indifference curves representing each possible level of total utility that can be derived by a particular consumer from consumption of two goods

Indirect business taxes Federal, state, and local business taxes that are partially or entirely shifted to other taxpayers; taxes on sales and on property are examples.

Industrial market countries Economically advanced capitalist countries of Western Europe, North America, Australia, New Zealand, and Japan; also known as developed countries

Industrial policy The view that government—using taxes, subsidies, regulations, and coordination—should nurture the industries and technologies of the future, to give domestic industries an advantage over foreign competition

Industrial Revolution Development of large-scale factory production that began in Great Britain around 1750 and spread to the rest of Europe, North America, and Australia

Industrial union A union of both skilled and unskilled workers from a particular industry, such as auto workers or steelworkers

Inelastic demand The type of demand that exists when a change in price has relatively little effect on quantity demanded; the percent change in quantity demanded is smaller than the percent change in price

Inferior good A good for which demand decreases as consumer incomes rise

Inflation A sustained increase in the economy's average price level

Initial public offering (IPO) The initial sale of stock to the public

Injection Any payment of income other than by firms or any spending other than by domestic households; includes investment, government purchases, transfer payments, and exports

Innovation The process of turning an invention into a marketable product

Interest The dollar amount paid by borrowers to lenders to forgo present consumption; the payment resource owners receive for the use of their capital

Interest rate Interest per year as a percentage of the amount loaned, or as a percentage of the amount saved

Interlocking directorate An arrangement whereby one individual serves on the boards of directors of competing firms

Intermediate goods and services Goods and services purchased for further reprocessing and resale

International Monetary Fund (IMF) An international organization that establishes rules for maintaining the international monetary system and makes loans to countries with temporary balance of payments problem.

Inventories Producers' stocks of finished or in-process goods

Investment The purchase of new plants, new equipment, new buildings, new residences, and net additions to inventories

Investment function The relationship between the amount businesses plan to invest and the level of income in the economy, other things constant

Isocost line Line identifying all combinations of capital and labor the firm can hire for a given total cost

Isoquant A curve that shows all the technologically efficient combinations of two resources, such as labor and capital, that produce a certain amount of output

K

Kinked demand curve A demand curve that illustrates price stickiness; if one firm cuts its prices, other firms in the industry will cut theirs as well, but if the firm raises its prices, other firms will not change theirs.

L

Labor The physical and mental effort of humans used to produce goods and services

Labor force Individuals 16 years of age and older who are either working or actively looking for work

Labor force participation rate The ratio of the number in the labor force to the adult population

Labor productivity Output per unit of labor; measured as total output divided by the number of units of labor employed to produce that output

Labor union A group of employees who join together to improve their terms of employment

Land Plots of ground and other natural resources used to produce goods and services

Law of comparative advantage The individual, firm, region, or country with the lowest opportunity cost of producing a particular good should specialize in producing that good.

Law of demand The quantity of a good demanded during a given time period is inversely related to its price, other things constant

Law of diminishing marginal rate of substitution The amount of good A a consumer is willing to give up to get one more unit of good B declines as the consumption of B increases.

Law of diminishing marginal returns As more and more of a variable resource is added to a given amount of a fixed resource, the resulting change in output will eventually diminish and could become negative

Law of diminishing marginal utility The more of a good consumed per period, the smaller the increase in total utility from consuming one more unit, other things constant

Law of increasing opportunity cost To produce each additional increment of a particular good, a successively larger increment of an alternative good must be sacrificed if the economy's resources are already being used efficiently

Law of supply The quantity of a product supplied in a given time period is usually directly related to its price, other things constant

Leakage Any diversion of income from the domestic spending stream; includes saving, taxes, and imports

Legal tender Anything that creditors are required to accept as payment for debts

Leisure Time spent on nonwork activities

Liability Anything that is owed to another individual or institution

Linear demand curve A straight-line demand curve; such a demand curve has a constant slope.

Liquidity A measure of the ease with which an asset can be converted into money without significant loss in its value

Loanable funds market The market in which savers (suppliers of funds) and borrowers (demanders of funds) come together to determine the market rate of interest

Long run In macroeconomics, a period during which wage contracts and resource price agreements can be renegotiated. In microeconomics, a period during which all resources under the firm's control are variable

Long-run aggregate supply (LRAS) curve The vertical line drawn at the economy's potential output; aggregate supply when there are no price surprises

Long-run average cost curve A curve that indicates the lowest average cost of production at each rate of output when the firm's size is allowed to vary; also called the planning curve and the envelope curve

Long-run equilibrium Combination of price level and real GDP, where (1) the actual price level equals the expected price level, (2) quantity supplied equals potential output, and (3) quantity supplied equals quantity demanded

Long-run industry supply curve A curve that shows the relationship between price and quantity supplied by the industry once firms fully adjust to any change in market demand

Long-run Phillips curve A vertical line drawn at the economy's natural rate of unemployment that traces equilibrium points that can occur when employers and workers have the time to adjust fully to any unexpected change in aggregate demand

M

M1 A measure of the money supply consisting of currency and coins held by the nonbanking public, checkable deposits, and travelers checks

M2 A monetary aggregate consisting of M1 plus savings deposits, small time deposits, and money market mutual funds

M3 A monetary aggregate consisting of M2 plus large-denomination time deposits

Macroeconomics The study of the economic behavior of entire economies

Managed float system An exchange rate system that combines features of freely floating rates with intervention by central banks

Marginal A term meaning incremental, additional, or extra; used to describe the result of a change in an economic variable

Marginal cost The change in total cost resulting from a one-unit change in output; the change in total cost divided by the change in output

Marginal product The change in total product that occurs when the use of a particular resource increases by one unit, all other resources constant

Marginal propensity to consume (MPC) The fraction of a change in income that is spent on consumption; the change in consumption spending divided by the change in income that caused it

Marginal propensity to import (MPM) The fraction of a change in income that is spent on imports; the change in import spending divided by the change in income that caused it

Marginal propensity to save (MPS) The fraction of a change in income that is saved; the change in saving divided by the change in income that caused it

Marginal rate of return on investment The marginal revenue product of capital expressed as a percentage of its marginal cost

Marginal rate of substitution (MRS) A measure of how much of one good a consumer would give up to get one more unit of another good, while remaining equally satisfied

Marginal rate of technical substitution (MRTS) The rate at which one resource, such as labor, can be substituted for another, such as capital, without affecting total output

Marginal resource cost The change in total cost when an additional unit of a resource is hired, other things constant

Marginal revenue The change in total revenue resulting from a one-unit change in sales; in perfect competition, marginal revenue equals the market price.

Marginal revenue product The change in total revenue when an additional unit of a resource is hired, other things constant

Marginal social benefit The sum of the marginal private benefit and the marginal external benefit of production or consumption

Marginal social cost The sum of the marginal private cost and the marginal external cost of production or consumption

Marginal tax rate The percentage of each additional dollar of income that goes to taxes

Marginal utility The change in total utility derived from a one-unit change in consumption of a good

Marginal valuation The dollar value of the marginal utility derived from consuming each additional unit of a good

Market A set of arrangements through which buyers and sellers carry out exchange at mutually agreeable terms

Market failure A condition that arises when unrestrained operation of markets yields socially undesirable results

Market power The ability of one or a few firms to maintain a price above the competitive level

Market structure Important features of a market, such as the number of firms, uniformity of product among firms, ease of entry and exit, and forms of competition

Market work Time sold as labor in return for a money wage

Means-tested program To be eligible for such a program, an individual's income and/or assets must not exceed specified levels

Median income The middle income in a series of incomes ranked from smallest to largest

Median voter model Under certain conditions, the preference of the median, or middle, voter will dominate other public choices

Mediator An impartial observer who helps resolve differences between union and management

Medicaid In-kind transfer program that provides medical care for poor people; by far the most costly welfare program

Medicare Social insurance program providing health insurance for short-term medical care to older Americans regardless of income

Medium of exchange Anything that facilitates trade by being generally accepted by all parties in payment for goods or services

Merchandise trade balance The value of a country's exported goods minus the value of its imported goods during a given time period

Microeconomics The study of the economic behavior in particular markets, such as the market for computers or for unskilled labor

Minimum efficient scale The lowest rate of output at which a firm takes full advantage of economies of scale

Mixed system An economic system characterized by private ownership of some resources and public ownership of other resources; some markets are unregulated and others are regulated.

Monetary aggregates Measures of the economy's money supply

Monetary policy Regulation of the money supply in order to influence aggregate economic activity

Money Anything that is generally accepted in exchange for goods and services

Money market mutual fund A collection of short-term interest-earning assets purchased with funds collected from many shareholders

Money multiplier The multiple by which the money supply increases as a result of an increase in excess reserves in the banking system

Monopolistic competition A market structure characterized by a large number of firms selling products that are close substitutes, yet different enough that each firm's demand curve slopes downward

Monopoly A sole producer of a product for which there are no close substitutes

Moral hazard A situation in which one party to a contract has an incentive after the contract is made to alter behavior in a way that harms the other party to the contract

N

National debt The net accumulation of federal budget deficits

National income The amount of national income earned by suppliers of resources employed to produce gross national product; net domestic product plus net earnings of U.S. resources abroad minus indirect business taxes (net of subsidies)

Natural monopoly One firm that can serve the entire market at a lower per-unit cost than can two or more firms

Natural rate hypothesis The natural rate of unemployment is largely independent of the stimulus provided by monetary or fiscal policy

Natural rate of unemployment The unemployment rate that occurs when the economy is producing its potential level of output

Net domestic product Gross domestic product minus depreciation

Net export function The relationship between net exports and the level of income in the economy, other things constant

Net exports The value of a country's exports minus the value of its imports

Net interest A component of national income made up of interest received by households, excluding interest paid by consumers to businesses and interest paid by government

Net taxes (NT) Taxes minus transfer payments

Net unilateral transfers The unilateral transfers (gifts and grants) received from abroad by residents of a country minus the unilateral transfers residents send abroad

Net wealth The value of a household's assets minus its liabilities

Net worth Assets minus liabilities

Nominal GDP GDP based on prices prevailing at the time of the transaction; current-dollar GDP

Nominal rate of interest The interest rate expressed in current dollars as a percentage of the amount loaned; the interest rate on a loan agreement

Nominal wage The wage measured in terms of current dollars; the dollar amount on a paycheck

Nonmarket work Time spent producing goods and services in the home or acquiring an education

Normal good A good for which demand increases as consumer incomes rise

Normal profit The accounting profit required to persuade a firm's owners to employ their resources in the firm; the accounting profit earned when all resources used by the firm earn their opportunity cost

Normative economic statement A statement that represents an opinion, which cannot be proved or disproved

O

Official reserve transactions account The section of a country's balance-of-payments account that reflects the flow of gold, Special Drawing Rights, and currencies among central banks

Oligopoly A market structure characterized by a small number of firms whose behavior is interdependent

Open-access good A good that is rival but nonexclusive, such as fish in the sea

Open-market operations Purchases and sales of government securities by the Federal Reserve in an effort to influence the money supply

Open-market purchase The purchase of U.S. government bonds by the Federal Reserve, for the purpose of increasing the money supply

Open-market sale The sale of U.S. government bonds by the Federal Reserve for the purpose of reducing the money supply

Opportunity cost The value of the best alternative forgone when an item or activity is chosen

Other-things-constant assumption The assumption, when focusing on key economic variables, that other variables remain unchanged

Output per capita Total output in the economy divided by the population

Outsourcing A firm sticks to its core competency, while buying inputs such as auto parts from outside suppliers

P

Partnership A firm with multiple owners who share the firm's profits and each of whom bears unlimited liability for the firm's debts

Patent A legal barrier to entry that conveys to its holder the exclusive right to supply a product for a certain period of time

Payoff matrix In game theory, a table listing the payoffs that each player can expect based on the strategy that each player pursues

Per se illegal A category of illegality in antitrust law, applied to business practices that are deemed illegal regardless of their economic rationale or their consequences

Per-worker production function The relationship between the amount of capital per worker in the economy and the output per worker

Perfect competition A market structure in which there are large numbers of fully informed buyers and sellers of a homogeneous product, with no obstacles to entry or exit of firms in the long run

Perfectly discriminating monopolist A monopolist who charges a different price for each unit of a good

Perfectly elastic demand curve A horizontal line reflecting a situation in which any price increase reduces quantity demanded to zero; the elasticity value is minus infinity

Perfectly elastic supply curve A horizontal line reflecting a situation in which any price decrease reduces the quantity supplied to zero; the elasticity value is infinity

Perfectly inelastic demand curve A vertical line reflecting a situation in which a price change has no effect on the quantity demanded; the elasticity value is zero

Perfectly inelastic supply curve A vertical line reflecting a situation in which a price change has no effect on the quantity supplied; the elasticity value is zero

Permanent income Income that individuals expect to receive on average over the long term

Personal income The amount of before-tax income received by households; national income less income earned but not received plus income received but not earned

Phillips curve A curve showing possible combinations of the inflation rate and the unemployment rate

Physical capital Manufactured items used to produce goods and services

Planned investment The amount of investment firms plan to undertake during a year

Political business cycles Economic fluctuations that result when discretionary policy is manipulated for political gain

Portfolio An collection of stocks, bonds, and other financial assets.

Positive economic statement A statement that can be proved or disproved by reference to facts

Positive rate of time preference A characteristic of consumers, who value present consumption more highly than future consumption

Potential output The economy's maximum sustainable output level, given the supply of resources, technology, and production incentives; the output level when there are no surprises about the price level

Predatory pricing Pricing tactics employed by a dominant firm to drive competitors out of business, such as temporarily selling below cost or dropping the price only in certain markets

Present value The value today of income or an income stream to be received in the future

Price ceiling A maximum legal price above which a good or service cannot be sold; to be effective, a price ceiling must be set below the equilibrium price

Price discrimination Increasing profit by selling the same good for different prices to different consumers for reasons unrelated to cost

Price elasticity formula Percent change in quantity divided by the percent change in price; the average quantity and the average price are used as bases for computing percent changes in quantity and in price

Price elasticity of demand A measure of the responsiveness of quantity demanded to a price change; the percent change in quantity demanded divided by the percent change in price

Price elasticity of supply A measure of the responsiveness of quantity supplied to a price change; the percent change in quantity supplied divided by the percent change in price

Price floor A minimum legal price below which a good or service cannot be sold; to be effective, a price floor must be set above the equilibrium price

Price index A number that shows the average price of a market basket of goods; changes in a price index over time changes in the average price level

Price leader A firm whose price is adopted by the rest of the industry

Price level A composite measure reflecting the prices of all goods and services in the economy relative to prices in a base year

Price searcher A firm that has some control over the price it charges because its demand curve slopes downward

Price taker A firm that faces a given market price and whose actions have no effect on that market price

Principal A person who enters into a contractual agreement with an agent in the expectation that the agent will act on behalf of the principal

Principal-agent problem A situation in which the agent's objectives differ from the principal's objectives and the agent can pursue hidden actions

Private property rights The right of an owner to use, rent, or sell, property

Privatization The process of turning public enterprises into private enterprises

Producer surplus The amount by which total revenue from production exceeds total variable cost

Product market A market in which goods and services are bought and sold

Production possibilities frontier (PPF) A curve showing alternative combinations of goods that can be produced when available resources are used efficiently

Productive efficiency The condition that exists when output is produced with the least-cost combination of inputs, given the level of technology

Productivity The ratio of a specific measure of output to a specific measure of input, such as output per hour of labor

Profit The payment resource owners receive for their entrepreneurial ability; the total revenue from sales minus the total cost of resources employed by the entrepreneur

Progressive taxation The tax as a percentage of income increases as income increases.

Proportional income tax Taxes remain a constant percentage of income as income increases

Proportional taxation The tax as a percentage of income remains constant as income increases; also called a flat-rate tax

Proprietor's income A component of national income made up of earnings of farmers and other unincorporated businesses

Public good A good that, once produced, is available for all to consume, regardless of who pays and who does not

Purchasing power parity (PPP) theory The theory that exchange rates between two countries will adjust in the long run to reflect price level differences between the countries

Pure command system An economic system characterized by public ownership of resources and centralized economic planning

Pure market system An economic system characterized by private ownership of resources and the use of prices to coordinate economic activity in unregulated markets

Q

Quantity theory of money If the velocity of money is stable or at least predictable, then changes in the money supply have predictable effects on nominal GDP

Quasi-public good A good that is nonrival but exclusive, such as cable TV

Quota A legal limit on the quantity of a particular product that can be imported or exported

R

Rational expectations A school of thought that claims people form expectations based on all available information, including the probable future actions of government policy makers

Rational ignorance A stance adopted by voters when they find that the cost of understanding and voting on a particular issue exceeds the benefit expected from doing so

Real GDP GDP adjusted for changes in the price level

Real income Income measured in terms of the goods and services it can buy

Real rate of interest The interest rate expressed in dollars of constant purchasing power as a percentage of the amount loaned; the nominal rate of interest minus the inflation rate

Real wage The wage measured in terms of dollars of constant purchasing power; hence, the wage measured in terms of the quantity of goods and services it will purchase

Recession A period of decline in total output usually lasting at least six months and marked by contractions in many sectors of the economy

Recognition lag The time needed to identify a macroeconomic problem and assess its seriousness

Recycling The process of converting waste products into reusable material

Regressive taxation The tax as a percentage of income decreases as income increases

Relevant resources Resources used to produce the good in question

Renewable resource A resource that can regenerate itself and so can be used periodically for an indefinite period of time if used conservatively, such as a properly managed forest

Rent The payment resource owners receive for the use of their land

Rent seeking Activities undertaken by individuals or firms to influence public policy in a way that will directly or indirectly redistribute income to them

Rental income of persons A component of national income consisting mainly of the imputed rental value of owner-occupied housing

Required reserve ratio The ratio of reserves to deposits that banks are required, by regulation, to hold

Required reserves The dollar amount of reserves a bank is legally required to hold

Reserves Funds that banks use to satisfy the cash demands of their customers and the reserve requirements of the Fed; reserves consist of deposits at the Fed plus currency physically held by banks

Residential construction Building new permanent homes or dwelling places

Resource market A market in which resources are bought and sold

Resources The inputs, or factors of production, used to produce the goods and services that humans want; resources consist of labor, capital, land, and entrepreneurial ability

Retained earnings After-tax corporate profits that are reinvested in the firm rather than paid to stockholders as dividends

Rule of reason A principle used by a court to examine the reasons for certain business practices and their effects on competition before ruling on their legality

S

Saving function The relationship between saving and the level of income in the economy, other things constant

Savings deposits Deposits that earn interest but have no specific maturity date

Scarcity When the amount people desire exceeds the amount available at a zero price

Screening The process used by employers to select the most qualified workers based on readily observable characteristics, such as level of education and course grades

Seasonal unemployment Unemployment caused by seasonal shifts in labor supply and demand

Secondary effects Unintended consequences of economic actions that develop slowly over time as people react to events

Seigniorage The difference between the face value of money and the cost of supplying it; the "profit" from issuing money

Separation of ownership from control The situation that exists when no single stockholder or unified group of stockholders owns enough shares to control the management of a corporation

Service An activity that is used to satisfy wants

Short run In macroeconomics, a period during which at least some resource prices are fixed by agreement. In microeconomics, a period during which at least one of a firm's resources is fixed.

Short-run aggregate supply (SRAS) curve A curve that shows the direct relationship between the price level and the quantity of aggregate output supplied in the short run, other things constant

Short-run equilibrium Combination of price level and real GDP, where the aggregate demand curve intersects the short-run aggregate supply curve

Short-run firm supply curve A curve that indicates the quantity a firm supplies at each price in the short run; that portion of a firm's marginal cost curve that intersects and rises above the low point on its average variable cost curve

Short-run industry supply curve A curve that indicates the quantity supplied by the industry at each price in the short run; the horizontal sum of each firm's short-run supply curve

Short-run Phillips curve A curve, based on an expected inflation rate, that reflects an inverse relationship between the inflation rate and the level of unemployment

Shortage An excess of quantity demanded compared to quantity supplied at a given price; a shortage puts upward pressure on price

Signaling Using a proxy measure to communicate information about unobservable characteristics; the signal is more effective if more productive workers find it easier to send the signal than do less productive workers.

Simple money multiplier The reciprocal of the required reserve ratio, or $1/r$; the maximum multiple of excess reserves by which the money supply can increase

Simple spending multiplier The ratio of a change in real GDP demanded to the initial change in expenditure that brought it about; the numerical value of the simple spending multiplier is $1/(1 - \text{MPC})$; it is called "simple" because consumption is the only component that varies with income.

Simple tax multiplier The ratio of a change in real GDP demanded to the initial change in autonomous net taxes that brought it about; the numerical value of the simple tax multiplier is $-\text{MPC}/(1 - \text{MPC})$

Social insurance programs Programs that replace lost income of those who contributed to the programs while working but who are now retired, temporarily unemployed, or unable to work because of total disability or work-related injury

Social regulation Government regulations aimed at improving health and safety

Social Security By far the largest social insurance program; supplements retirement income to those with a record of contributing to the program during their working years

Soft budget constraint The budget condition faced by socialist enterprises that are subsidized if they lose money

Sole proprietorship A firm with a single owner who has the right to all profits and who bears unlimited liability for the firm's debts

Special-interest legislation Legislation that generates concentrated benefits but imposes widespread costs

Specialization of labor Focusing an individual's efforts on a particular product or a single task

Speculator A person who buys or sells foreign exchange in hopes of profiting from fluctuations in the exchange rate over time

Stagflation A contraction, or *stag*nation, of a nation's output accompanied by in*flation* in the price level

Stock A certificate reflecting part ownership of a corporation

Stock A variable that measures the amount of something at a particular point in time, such as the amount of food in your refrigerator or the amount of money you have with you right now

Store of value Anything that retains its purchasing power over time

Strategy In game theory, the operational plan pursued by a player; for example, one strategy is to avoid the worst outcome

Strike A union's attempt to withhold labor from a firm

Structural unemployment Unemployment that arises because (1) the skills demanded by employers do not match the skills of the unemployed, or (2) the unemployed do not live where the jobs are located

Substitutes Goods that are related in such a way that an increase in the price of one leads to an increase in the demand for the other

Substitution effect of a wage increase When the wage increases, workers substitute market work for other activities, which now have a higher opportunity cost

Substitution effect When the price of a good falls, consumers will substitute that good for other goods, which are now relatively more expensive

Sunk cost A cost that has already been incurred in the past and, hence, a cost that is irrelevant to present and future economic decisions

Supplemental Security Income (SSI) An income assistance program that provides cash transfer payments to the elderly poor and the disabled; a uniform federal payment is supplemented by transfers that vary across states

Supply A relation showing the quantities of a good producers are willing and able to sell at various prices during a given time period, other things constant

Supply curve A curve showing the quantities of a good supplied at various prices, other things constant

Supply of loanable funds The relationship between the market interest rate and the quantity of loanable funds supplied to the economy, other things constant

Supply shocks Unexpected events that affect aggregate supply, sometimes only temporarily

Supply-side economics Macroeconomic policy that focuses on increasing aggregate supply through tax cuts or other changes to increase production incentives

Surplus An excess of quantity supplied compared to quantity demanded at a given price; a surplus puts downward pressure on the price

T

Tariff A tax on imports or exports

Tastes A consumer's preferences for different goods and services

Tastes Consumer preferences; likes and dislikes in consumption

Tax incidence The distribution of tax burden among taxpayers

Technologically efficient Produces the maximum possible output given the combination of resources employed; that same output could not be produced with fewer resources.

Temporary Assistance for Needy Families (TANF) An income assistance program run by the states that provides cash transfer payments to poor families with dependent children

Term structure of interest rates The relationship between the duration of a loan and the interest rate charged

Terms of trade How much of one good exchanges for a unit of another good

Thrift institutions, or thrifts Savings and loan institutions, mutual savings banks, and credit unions; depository institutions that make long-term loans primarily to households

Time deposits Deposits that earn a fixed rate of interest if held for the specified period, which can range anywhere from several months to several years

Time-inconsistency problem The problem that arises when policy makers have an incentive to announce one policy to influence expectations but then to pursue a different policy once those expectations have been formed and acted upon

Token money The name given to money whose face value exceeds the cost of producing it

Total cost The sum of fixed cost and variable cost; the opportunity cost of all resources employed by the firm

Total product The total output produced by a firm

Total revenue Price multiplied by the quantity sold at that price

Total utility The total satisfaction a consumer derives from consumption; it could refer either to the total utility of consuming a particular good or the total utility from all consumption

Transaction costs The costs of time and information required to carry out market exchange

Transfer payments Cash or in-kind benefits given to individuals as outright grants from the government

Transparent finances A firm's financial records that clearly indicate the economic health of the company

Tying contract An arrangement in which a seller of one good requires buyers to purchase other goods as well

U

U.S. official poverty level Benchmark level of income computed by the federal government to track poverty over time; based on three times the cost of a nutritionally adequate diet

Underemployment A situation in which workers are overqualified for their jobs or work fewer hours than they would prefer

Underground economy An expression used to describe all market exchange that goes unreported either because it is illegal or because those involved want to evade taxes

Unemployment insurance Cash transfers provided to unemployed workers who actively seek employment and who meet other qualifications

Unemployment rate The number of unemployed individuals expressed as a percentage of the labor force

Unit of account A common unit for measuring the value of every good or service

Unit-elastic demand The type of demand that exists when a given percent change in price causes an equal (but of opposite sign) percent change in quantity demanded; the elasticity value is -1.0

Unit-elastic supply curve A percent change in price causes an identical percent change in quantity supplied; depicted by a supply curve that is a straight line through the origin; the elasticity value is 1.0

Utility The satisfaction received from consumption; satisfaction, sense of well-being

V

Value added The difference at each stage of production between the value of a product and cost of intermediate goods bought from other firms

Variable A measure, such as price or quantity, that can take on different possible values

Variable cost Any production cost that changes as output changes

Variable resource Any resource that can be varied in the short run to increase or decrease the rate of output

Variable technology The amount of externality generated at a given rate of output can be reduced by altering the production process rather than by simply reducing the rate of output.

Velocity of money The average number of times per year a dollar is used to purchase final goods and services

Vertical integration The expansion of a firm into stages of production earlier or later than those in which it has specialized, such as a steel producer that buys a coal mine

Vertical merger A merger in which one firm combines with another from which it purchases inputs or to which it sells output

W

Wages The payment resource owners receive for their labor

Winner's curse The plight of the winning bidder for an asset of uncertain value who has overestimated the asset's true value

World price The price at which a good is traded internationally; determined by the world supply and demand for the good

World Trade Organization (WTO) The legal and institutional foundation of the multilateral trading system that succeeded GATT in 1995

Index

Note: The letter *d* after an entry indicates marginal *definition; e* indicates *exhibit; i* indicates *Internet address.*

D

F

G

H

I

M

S

T

W

Z

Photo Credits

Page 1	© 1998 PhotoDisc, Inc
9	© Paul Chesley/Tony Stone Images
12	© Morton Beebe-S.F./Corbis
25	© Andrew Sacks/Tony Stone Images
26	© Gary Conner/PhotoEdit
33	© Courtesy of Cyberian Outpost/ Feldman & Associates
45	© Connie Coleman/Tony Stone Images
62	© Nathaniel Butler/AllSport USA
65	© Reuters/Joe Traver/Archive Photos
69	© David Hanover/Tony Stone Images
74	© Michael Newman/PhotoEdit
83	© Andy Sacks/Tony Stone Images
89	© Greg Pease/Tony Stone Images
96	© Vincent Oliver/Tony Stone Images
106	© Jim Pickerell/Tony Stone Images
111	© 1998 PhotoDisc, Inc.
122	Photo Courtesy of Intel Corporation
126	© 1998 PhotoDisc, Inc.
134	© Rick Rusing/Tony Stone Images
140	© 1998 PhotoDisc, Inc.
145	© Jeff Greenberg/Archive Photos
157	© 1998 PhotoDisc, Inc
167	© Susan Van Etten/PhotoEdit
175	© Spencer Grant/PhotoEdit
182	© Richard Morell/The Stock Market
191	© Dana White/PhotoEdit
196	© Robert Holmes/Corbis
206	© Jon Riley/Tony Stone Images
215	© Rudi Von Briel/PhotoEdit
220	© Ron McMillan/Gamma Liaison
228	© 1998 PhotoDisc, Inc.
240	© John Neubauer/PhotoEdit
246	© BUU/Turpin/Gamma Liaison International
250	© 1998 PhotoDisc, Inc.
264	© Rueters/Peter Morgan/Archive Photos
265	© Wally McNamee/Corbis
272	© Sahun Egan/Tony Stone Images
280	© George de Keerle/Gamma Liaison International
290	© Haruyoshi Yamaguchi/SYGMA
294	© John Lund/Tony Stone Images
297	© Mary M. Steinbacher/PhotoEdit
311	© David Young-Wolff/PhotoEdit
315	© 1998 PhotoDisc, Inc.
326	© Art Zamur/Gamma Liaison International
333	© Rick Maiman/SYGMA
339	© AP/Wide World Photos
346	© Ira Wyman/SYGMA
351	© 1998 PhotoDisc, Inc,
363	© Tony Hutchings/Tony Stone Images
375	© Bonnie Kamin/PhotoEdit
380	© PhotoDisc, Inc.
385	© Jamey Stillings/Tony Stone Images
396	© Paul S. Howell/Gamma Liaison International
403	© Richard Hamilton Smith/Corbis
409	© Chales Thatcher/Tony Stone Images
416	© Amy C. Etra/PhotoEdit
422	© Steven Peters/Tony Stone Images
436	© David Harry Stewart/Tony Stone Images
451	© Mark Richards/PhotoEdit
452	© Swersey/Gamma Liaison International
462	© Mark Joseph/Tony Stone Images

475 © Xavier Tasteliin/Gamma Liaison International
486 © Thomas Veneklasen/Univeristy of Arizona/Economics Science Lab
492 © Joseph Sohm/Tony Stone Images
495 © Pail Almasy/Corbis
507 © Bonnie Kamin/PhotoEdit
514 © Greg Pease/Tony Stone Images
520 © Porter Gifford/Gamma Liaison International
523 © Dirck Halstead/Gamma Liaison International
538 © Tom Dietrich/Tony Stone Images
553 © PhotoDisc Inc.
555 © Ed Lallo/Gamma Liaison International
561 © Charles Thatcher/Tony Stone Images
571 © Jim Graham/Gamma Liaison International
580 © Barry King/Gamma Liaison International
584 © Deborah Davis/PhotoEdit
592 © Jeff Topping/Gamma Liaison International
596 © Joseph Sohm; ChromoSohm Inc./ Corbis
604 © Ferguson/Katzman/HMS/Tony Stone Images
610 © Michael Rosenfeld/Tony Stone Images
620 © PhotoEdit
624 © Keith Wood/Tony Stone Images
630 © Jeff Christensen.Gamma Liaison International
642 © Tom McCarthy/PhotoEdit
647 © Roger Tully/Tony Stone Images
655 © Mark Richards/PhotoEdit
659 © Peter Dean/Tony Stone Images
667 © Keren Su/Tony Stone Images
675 © Stephanie Maze/Corbis
681 © Stephanie Maze/Corbis
691 © Charles Thatcher/Tony Stone Images
707 © Stephen Ferry/Gamma Liaison International
709 © 1998 PhotoDisc, Inc.
713 © Elie Bernager/Tony Stone Images
727 © Herbert W. Booth III/Gamma Liaison International
733 © Alain Morvan/Gamma Liaison International
737 © Matthias Kulka/The Stock Market
749 © Ron McMillan/Gamma Liaison International
754 © Wolfgang Kaehler/Corbis
758 © Paul Chesley/Tony Stone Images
767 © Nik Wheeler/Corbis
774 © SYGMA